WAY'S PACKET DIRECTORY

1848-1994

Presented by Capt. Clarke Hawley.

The **NATCHEZ** (#4113), built in 1975, captures the grace and charm of the larger passenger steamboats of yore. Based at New Orleans, she carries sight-seers and tourists on harbor cruises, and also is staffed to handle dinner parties. The owners, in preparing for her construction, bought an outmoded steam towboat in the Pittsburgh area for its machinery and paddlewheel appliances. These were transferred to a new steel hull, the dimensions conforming to those of the steamer VIRGINIA (#5593) which was powered with the same size engines, successful as to power and speed. The upper cabins were purposely designed old-style. Great ingenuity was displayed to carry out this effect and still meet the stringent modern U.S. Coast Guard regulations wherein the very word ''wood'' is an anathema. The end result is the steamboat you see in this picture, pleasing to the eye. The two smokestacks are functional, carrying away exhaust gases from the oil-fired steam boilers. The name NATCHEZ honors the many prior river steamers of that name which were home-based at New Orleans.

WAY'S PACKET DIRECTORY 1848–1994

Passenger Steamboats of the Mississippi River System Since the Advent of Photography in Mid-Continent America

Compiled by Frederick Way, Jr.

Ohio University Press
Athens

Library of Congress Cataloging in Publication Data
Way, Frederick, 1901–1992
Way's Packet directory 1848–1994.
Includes index.
1. Ship registers—United States I. Title
II. TITLE: Packet directory, 1848–1983.
HE565.U5W39 1983 387.2'436'0973 83–8210
ISBN 0–8214–1106–3 (pbk)

Revised paperback edition printed 1994
All Ohio University Press books are printed on acid-free paper ∞
11 10 09 08 07 06 05 04 03 10 9 8 7 6 5 4 3 2

To my younger friends of the river
who make my latter days so much fun

Preface

The title "Packet Directory" has been selected inasmuch as the majority of the inclusions are combination passenger and freight steamers called packets, the term having been brought from the Eastern seaboard, although in a broader sense these listings are designed to include all types of passenger carriers propelled by steam which plied the waters of the Mississippi System in the United States. The first Mississippi steamboat was a packet, the *NEW ORLEANS,* a side-wheeler built at Pittsburgh in 1811, designed for the New Orleans-Natchez trade. Packets dominated during the first forty years of steam providing the quickest passenger transportation throughout mid-continent America, by which time they had penetrated to the headwaters of most of the tributary streams. These early-birds were utilitarian in design, devoid of the exterior frills of their successors, those "brides of Babylon," "floating wedding cakes," etc., of Mark Twain's time, the peak of such ostentation along the lower Mississippi being about 1870–1880. Handsome specimens in some numbers were still turned out 1890–1900, so that packets remained fairly numerous into the first two decades of the twentieth century when old age or calamity overtook them. By the 1930s the flock had been depleted to the point of no return, and today the show is over; the packet is extinct. Today's river passenger carriers, those operated by steam are excursion boats (*BELLE OF LOUISVILLE, NATCHEZ* and *JULIA BELLE SWAIN*) and the two tourist steamers (*MISSISSIPPI QUEEN* and *DELTA QUEEN.*) None handles freight, and they cannot be classed as packets, but they are legitimate to the purposes of this book, being passenger carriers, and may be found in their proper alphabetical places.

When freight revenues diminished, some of the illustrious packets were converted into excursion boats, a transition accomplished by eliminating staterooms to make way for full length second-deck dance floors, a bandstand, and liberal application of red paint on forecastle and main deck. The raucous steam calliope so popular and necessary to the operation of old-time transient showboats took root on excursion steamers and continues to thrive on today's passenger carriers, the names of which we have just recited. To the uninitiated let me say that "showboat" connotes a theater ornately housed on little other than a raft which, contrary to some movie versions, is not and never has been self-propelled. A towboat shoves it from place to place. Showboats are not included in these listings, and, if they excite your interest, we recommend the book *Showboats* by Philip Graham, University of Texas Press, first published in 1951.

River towns during packet days could be depended upon to have a riverfront hotel at the top of the wharf grade, a floating warehouse called a wharfboat at which the packets transacted business at the foot of the grade, and nearby a steam ferry and its landing float. I would almost guarantee that more passengers, more horses and mules, and more wagons, carriages and the like, have been handled on these ferries than on all of the packets and excursion boats since time began. These ferries were remarkable in the diversity of design and propulsion, some of the earlier ones being hay-burners powered by horses or mules on treadmills, others with the animals hitched to a circulating turnstile. We have confined our inclusions to those propelled by steam. At the other end of the spectrum were the wealthy individuals who traveled the rivers in their private steam yachts, or aboard gorgeous houseboats which, like the showboats, depended on towboats for motive power. The yachts are among our inclusions.

After Sumter was fired upon in April 1861 a vast number of river packets, both in the North and in the South, were appropriated for the prosecution of the war, hastily altered into gunboats, tinclads, rams, hospitals and flagships, and still others (the majority) were pressed into the movement of troops and supplies. Much of such activity is traced in these listings, and I felt it advisable also to include the gunboats designed and commissioned by Rebs and Yanks with rivermen as engineers and pilots.

When the railroads speared east-west and later north-south across the continent, they augmented river traffic. On the Ohio River the building of the Baltimore & Ohio Railroad from Baltimore to Wheeling resulted immediately in the formation of a daily line of side-wheelers between Wheeling and Louisville. The Illinois Central for a number of years terminated at Cairo, Illinois and depended on the "Railroad Line" of side-wheel packets to serve the south to New Orleans and points between. The Pennsylvania Canal, a herculean undertaking which by rail and canalboat connected Philadelphia and Pittsburgh, brought into being a daily side-wheel line between Pittsburgh and Cincinnati which flourished even more so when the Pennsylvania Railroad replaced the outmoded ditch. When the Chesapeake & Ohio Railroad arrived at Huntington, West Virginia from the Eastern seaboard a line of elegant side-wheelers provided daily connection to Cincinnati. Such river-rail connections were often profitable ventures along the Upper Mississippi and along the Missouri. Rather than span the Mississippi with bridges, rail lines used side-wheel car ferries complete with tracks, to transfer passenger trains and freight cars from shore to shore, and such carriers also were employed on the lower Ohio, the Missouri, and elsewhere. I have included these ferries in the listings.

The Mississippi River Commission, and later on the U.S. Engineers, built and operated rather elaborate steamboats, much on the order of packets, which were used occasionally to carry high brass on inspection tours along the Mississippi and on occasion were outfitted to fly the presidential flag during noteworthy trips taken by Theodore Roosevelt and William Howard Taft. I have included these craft, and also the fleet of packet-like sternwheelers and side-wheelers of the U.S. Lighthouse Service which supplied lamp oil to the keepers, and maintained the navigation lights (called "government lights") for the benefit of pilots. One of the early tenders, the side-wheel *LILY,* on her wheelhouses had the wording *U.S. Lighthouse Tender Lily,* the lettering applied in such a way that many shore-dwellers reading it, thought her name was *TENDER LILY.*

What I did not include herein are the hundreds of steam towboats which handled the barge commerce. My fond hope is to place them in a companion volume to follow this one within the next year or so. The preparation will be relatively easy inasmuch as it requires only an updating and some revision and additions to *Way's Directory of Western Rivers Steam Towboats,* published in 1954 and long out of print.

Steamboating on the Mississippi System commenced in 1811 when the *NEW ORLEANS* was launched at Pittsburgh. The reasons I have not included the 1811–1847 packets in the present compilation are several-fold. From the time I was knee-high to a duck I have been keen on collecting photographs of all classes of Mississippi System steamboats and hence the bulk of my investigations and research over the years has been limited to those which existed since the advent of the camera. The earliest known daguerreotype depicting steamboats on the Ohio, or any other Western stream, dates 1848, the year when Charles Fontayne and W. S. Porter created a panorama of eight daguerreotypes of the Cincinnati waterfront, the original of which today reposes in the vaults of the Public Library of Cincinnati and Hamilton County at Vine and Eighth, Cincinnati. So that was my starting point, 1848, and my knowledge of earlier ones is sparse, in most cases no more than is available in that remarkable volume *Merchant Steam Vessels of the United States 1790–1868,* familiarly known as the *Lytle-Holdcamper List,* published by the Steamship Historical Society of America, Inc. I would estimate that some 900 Western steamboats are involved in that 1811–1848 period. Paintings, sketches, and drawings exist of some of these, leaving me with the impression that many of the early artists were poor marine architects.

For the names and statistics of the 1848–1868 steamboats I am heavily indebted to the *Lytle-Holdcamper List* and its authors, William M. Lytle and Forrest R. Holdcamper, both deceased, and to C. Bradford Mitchell who relentlessly pursues the quest for accuracy. Since 1867–1868 the government has issued an annual *List of Merchant Vessels of the United States* providing bare-bone dates, dimensions, tonnage and the like, which has been continued without interruption even until today. The type of rig is specified (whether side-wheel, sternwheel, etc.), also the place of build, and, of late years, the legal owner and address.

During my high school days I corresponded with Fielding L. Wooldridge, then stationed at Parsons, Kansas, who was compiling information of the type and scope most rivermen were interested in: engine size, boiler details, trades, accidents, adventures, crews—the biography of each steamboat. Following the death of Mr. Wooldridge in 1941, these records came into the possession of Capt. Donald T. Wright, owner-editor of *The Waterways Journal,* St. Louis, who often quoted Wooldridge when writing captions under old-time steamboat pictures, regarding him as a foremost expert on steamboat history.

Capt. Sam G. Smith, associated with *The Waterways Journal* in his latter days, also compiled, much on the order of Wooldridge, and his findings appeared serially, progressing through the alphabet in the *Journal*'s news columns. I do not presume that either Wooldridge or Sam Smith entertained serious ideas of presenting the fruits of his labors in book form.

Neither did I, for that matter.

Lytle-Holdcamper and *Lists of Merchant Vessels* do not attempt to classify a boat's occupation, as to whether she was a packet, a towboat, an excursion boat, etc. I don't suppose this lack is any great shakes; that is, until a person gets himself involved in sorting them out. Some of these boats, especially the smaller fry, were adaptable to serving both as short-trade packets or towboats. Raftboats on the Upper Mississippi, with no alteration other than hanging a swinging stage out ahead, ran excursions or did packet work. Some of the early-day side-wheel packets in old age chauffeured barges and flats of coal down the Ohio and the Mississippi. During the Civil War packets and towboats were converted into gunboats and rams; and some of the tinclads went back to being packets. Tracing the adventures of such boats is like watching them through a kaleidoscope, and let me be the first to admit that I may have made my share of bloopers in attempting to pin down whether some of the earlier ones actually were packets and whether they should or should not be included in the listings. Where there was doubt, I put them in anyhow.

The notion of preparing steamboat "biographies" struck me in 1914, at the age of 13. I bought a notebook with lined pages, completed the "A" listings (six listings, the sum-total of "A" boats I knew about) and did ten "B" boats, thirteen "C" boats, and wound up on three "E" ones. At this point it seemed like I'd be an old man before "Z" was visible in a telescope and the risk of getting writer's cramp was getting too great. Then, in 1938, Fred D. Morrison gave me a box of 3″x5″ file cards at Christmas-time which since has been expanded to occupy ten 14-inch-deep drawers of steamboat information, the "brains" of this compilation.

Most of the prominent newspapers from Pittsburgh to New Orleans carried extensive river news, roughly 1840–1920, written by a staff specialist personally acquainted with the owners, captains, pilots and all. In addition to reporting the happenings along their local wharves, these editors lifted choice paragraphs from one another, so by reading the *Cincinnati Enquirer,* for example, the reader was presented with paragraphs of fact and gossip from the headwaters of the Missouri via St. Louis "exchanges" to the latest from Memphis, New Orleans, and Pittsburgh. In addition to attracting readership it paid off well, too; the river news editors also solicited advertising notices from packets about to depart from their cities, and from twenty to thirty of these in an issue was not uncommon. Many of the tidbits included herein came from such catnip researched in valley libraries while I was piloting excursion steamers between Pittsburgh and Louisville, with special thanks to Russell M. Lintner, who methodically researched Pittsburgh newspapers over a great span of years and made his reams of typed pages available to me. Two others who pursued this pleasant avocation were Capt. Jesse P. Hughes and Capt. William H. Tippitt, both of whom shared the fruits with me.

In preparing a work of this type, the greatest hazard, perhaps, is that of becoming regional. It is all too easy to devote too much emphasis to home territory which, in my case, is bounded by the Ohio River from Pittsburgh to Louisville and the tributaries of the area, the Allegheny, Monongahela, Muskingum, Little Kanawha, Kanawha, Big Sandy, and the Kentucky. The Missouri River, remote as it is from my bailiwick, and which I have never navigated, did not present too great a problem; most of the "mountain boats" associated with its fur trade and gold rush were built in the Pittsburgh area and many of the hardy rivermen who owned and manned them came from hereabouts. This applies also to the many side-wheelers of the Upper Mississippi, built for the most part in Cincinnati, Wheeling, and in the Pittsburgh area. New Orleans had me bothered; that is, until Bert Fenn loaned me *Ship Registers and Enrollments of New Orleans, Louisiana,* prepared from the original documents as a WPA project and published by Louisiana State University in 1942. Here, laid out in detail, are the dimensions, owners and captains of these southern steamers from my starting point, 1848, up through 1870. Also a boon is the book *Advertisements of Lower Mississippi Steamboats 1812–1920,* compiled by the prolific Louisiana author, Leonard V. Huber, and published in 1959 by the Steamship Historical Society of America.

Speaking of bothersome things, many of the contemporary newspaper ads and notices listed the captain and clerk by name, the text reading, let's say, "Capt. Smith, master, with Byington in the office." What Smith? What Byington? The many entries in this book's index starting off with Smith, Capt. (   ), and so on, are for the most part traceable to such omissions. Family genealogists tracing rivermen pioneers via our index are requested to have mercy on our soul when they find great-grandpa Isaac Jones mixed up with another Isaac Jones, or listed I. Jones because we didn't know his name was Isaac, or, worse still, not listed at all. Straightening out these rivermen makes for interesting reading in the *S&D Reflector,* published quarterly since 1964 by the Sons and Daughters of Pioneer Rivermen, with genealogy as a priority objective. Letters float in from descendants, often freighted with lovely, and sometimes frightful, details getting first exposure to print. I have edited this magazine since its inception and the arrival of the morning mail is such an adventure that Sunday seems like a day lost.

In these listings are a number of steamboats which spent their careers on the Alabama, Tombigbee, and Warrior, or over in Florida and Georgia on the Chattahoochee and Apalachicola; some few in Mexico, and others pop up on the St. Johns in Florida. One of them which comes to mind, the *KATE FRISBEE,* was around Cape Horn and to San Francisco and back to New Orleans before her hull timbers were planked. They are included in these listings, as are ocean steamers built complete at Ohio River yards for Atlantic service. Not included are the dozens and dozens of steel hull packets built by one firm, James Rees & Sons Co., Pittsburgh, for river service all over the world, shipped knock-down to destination for assembly. Nor did I include the three largest packets in Yukon River service, *HANNAH, SUSIE,* and *SARAH,* contracted to the Howard Ship Yard, Jeffersonville, Indiana and framed at Unalaska in the Aleutian Islands. One would suppose that the most famous of all boats listed herein is the *ROB'T E. LEE,* the racer, built at New Albany, Indiana, although the modern generation knows better the *DELTA QUEEN* with origin in Scotland and Germany.

The longness or shortness of these descriptions has little or no bearing on the importance of the subject boat, but it helps. The larger ones, the aristocrats of the river, got more news coverage due to the attention they attracted, and more has been written about them. Their owners, captains, pilots, engineers, mates, and clerks were well known in the best cirlces, and attracted popular attention on a par with governors and senators, to and including the pompous Negro fireman who stunned the occupants of a Beale Street saloon by announcing he "fired de middle doah on d' *ALECK SCOTT.*" Less attention was given to the small-fry boats in the public print but each has its story if only we know where to look. Jean Henri Fabre said it well when he observed:

> If we had to wait until we knew every detail of the question studied, no one would venture to write the little that he knows. From time to time, a few new truths are revealed, tiny pieces of the vast mosaic of things. Better to divulge the discovery, however humble it be. Others will come who, also gathering a few fragments, will assemble the whole into a picture ever growing larger and ever notched by the unknown.

Our weekly river magazine, *The Waterways Journal,* brags on the masthead "Weekly Since 1887," a claim which has its doubters, but it does own a file dating back into the 1890s, as well as a file of Volumes 1 and 2 of *The River,* a progenitor, which commenced business August 29, 1891. My dad's business partner, Joseph C. McDonald, entered a subscription in my name as a Christmas present in 1914 and I still look forward to each issue. Much of the wisdom about boat persons, death dates, relationships, activities, and so on, presented herein, comes from this source. *The Waterways Journal* has never been indexed or microfilmed.

This *Packet Directory* you are reading is an extension of several previous books of similar nature. J. Woodason (Woody) Rutter, now my son-in-law, and I in 1939 entered into a joint venture we called Steamboat Photo Co., and sold steamboat pictures, the selections listed in a mimeographed leaflet. The response exceeded expectations and led to much correspondence with customers seeking historical information to go with the photographs they had bought. So in 1942 I prepared and issued a 102-page mimeo soft-bound book called *Western Rivers Steamboat Directory* containing brief sketches of each of the some 900 packets in our negative file, actually a catalogue of our wares. In seemingly no time flat the supply was exhausted, leading to the preparation of *Way's Steamboat Directory,* Packet Edition, 1944. This rather ambitious 292-page book also was mimeographed, and was professionally bound in green linen hard cover; again the inclusions were limited to boats in our photo file, but this time I expanded the historical treatment of each of them. These were war times and mimeo paper was impossible to procure, so from a Pittsburgh wholesaler I bought a supply of stock which looked like it would work, but it didn't, and my hand-cranked mimeo machine refused to cooperate with the dismaying result that the inked lettering came out anemic and pale. Some of these 200-plus copies went to libraries from whence I would hope they ultimately were discarded.

Way's Directory of Western River Packets, 1950 Edition, ran 366 pages, red clothbound hard cover, again a detailed descriptive compilation of Steamboat Photo Co. photographs, the pages in mimeo. This was followed in 1954 by *Way's Directory of Western Rivers' Towboats,* of similar format, green cover, 452 pages, in which I attempted (with fair success) to list and describe in detail all of the towboats built for river service from the beginnings in the late 1840s (towboats as such were not invented until then). These two volumes required a horrible amount of research made possible by a cash grant from the Martha Cooper Kinney Ohioana Library Association. In 1955 came an updated edition of the Packet Directory, 383 pages.

Seems to me no one of the editions exceeded 250 copies, a serious underestimate of the demand due to my stubborn refusal to believe that customers would pay $10 for a hand-cranked mimeo job, the price of the last three. But they did, and today it shocks me to see an occasional copy advertised on the market at some outrageous asking price. Steamboat Photo Co. has long been out of business, but the catalogues live on.

Steamboat Photo ground to a slow halt after I had furnished the Cincinnati Public Library with 8″x10″ enlargements from each of our some 8,000 negatives, complete with captions, a job which kept me in a darkroom during spare time for four and a half years. These pictures are available for inspection in the Inland Rivers Library section of the main library building at Eighth and Vine. In 1964 I became editor of a new magazine, *S&D Reflector,* issued quarterly by the Sons and Daughters of Pioneer Rivermen, in which the truthful reproduction of boat photographs by the offset method of printing is almost too good to be true, providing a constant outlet for new discoveries in the field of steamboat pictures, as well as liberal use of our older Steamboat Photo negatives. Some few years ago the University of Wisconsin launched forth upon a program dedicated to the proposition of assembling a negative file of Mississippi System steamboats, the project quartered in the Murphy Library, La Crosse, Wisconsin, where they maintain and operate a modern photo lab. Ralph DuPae was engaged to seek out collections lying dormant in other universities, libraries, and more often in private hands, and so Ralph prowls up and down the land in a station wagon, oftentimes bringing home catches almost beyond belief. Copy negatives using modern techniques are made at La Crosse, and the originals are returned to the owners. It's the old Steamboat Photo Co. approach magnified many-fold, adequately staffed and funded.

The proper identification of this Wisconsin University collection suggested the permanent numbering of each boat used in this volume. Private collectors (and there are many) also may use the sytem to advantage. As example there are eleven steamers herein named *COLUMBIA,* six of them sternwheelers and five side-wheelers. Cases of two or three boats bearing the same name are numerous; we have included herein twelve packets named *NATCHEZ.* The *SULTANA,* which blew up above Memphis in 1865 killing so many soldiers, was the fifth of that name and, almost needless to say, there never was another one. These permanent numbers may assist in sorting boats out.

The extinction of the packet was followed only several years back with the extinction of the steam towboat. Modern river towing (actually pushing) is today handled exclusively by diesel-powered propeller-driven craft ranging in horsepower from one to two hundred up to ten thousand five hundred laced securely to fleets of barges. More tonnage is transported today along the Mississippi and its tributaries than during the palmiest of the old-time palmy days, all of it bulk tonnage, grain, soy beans, sulphur, coal, chemicals, oil, gasoline, iron and steel products, ore, sand and gravel, to name the more important items. As late as 1945 steam and diesel towboats were about equally divided, and that was the year I commenced publication of the river directory called *Inland River Record,* an annual devoted to thumbnail sketches of these boats and information about the ownerships. Perhaps I'm telling you this to allay your impression that I've spent far too much time delving into the past, to the neglect of the present. Not so. Many a pilothouse argument right today about whether the *DIXIE QUEEN* still has in her her original diesels, etc., winds up with "Get the Book, get the Book," meaning of course the *Inland River Record.*

The remnants of my modesty will be fractured to splinters if the youth of the present time (many to become the river people of tomorrow) get to arguing about the size of the engines on the *ROB'T E. LEE,* and wind up with "Get the Book, get the Book," meaning this one.

Frederick Way, Jr.
Sewickley, Pennsylvania
February 17, 1983, my 82nd birthday.

Acknowledgments

A moment ago I looked back upon the persons to whom credit had been extended in the earlier editions of this work (recounted in the Preface) with the shocking realization that many of them have made their final crossings. The contributions they made those thirty or forty years ago in large measure have been carried forward into the present listings. Rather than repeat the names of those who have died I am honoring their memory by this notice. Also, many of them have been quoted and identified in the text.

My gratitude for assistance over the past eight or ten years while this volume was being prepared is extended to the many contributors to the *S&D Reflector* and in particular to the following friends:

Yeatman Anderson III, Alan L. Bates, Dr. Carl R. Bogardus, Capt. Thomas K. Booth, Clyde N. Bowden, Mrs. Rhoda Boyd, William E. Brandt, John A. Breslin, Jr., Herschel W. Burford, John B. Briley, R. Jerome Collins, Paul R. Coppock, Mrs. Helen Crayden, Jack E. Custer, Jerry B. Devol, Ralph DuPae, Bert R. Fenn, Ruth Ferris, Dr. Thomas H. Gandy, John W. Garden, Mrs. Letha C. Greene, Capt. Roddy Hammett, William S. Hanable, Mrs. Agnes S. Harralson, John Hartford, Capt. Clarke Hawley, Allen Hess, Ralph C. Hitchcock, S. Durward Hoag, George P. Hogg, Leonard V. Huber, Capt. Fontain M. Johnson, Dr. Leland R. Johnson, Capt. Thomas E. Kenny, Michelle Kingsley, J. W. Kisinger, Ben F. Klein, George Gunther Lee, Richard W. Lemen, John H. Leslie, Russell M. Lintner, Sandra Rae Miller, Mrs. Jane Morningstar, Fred D. Morrison, Edward A. Mueller, Ed Hill, Keith E. Norrington, Earl F. Olson, Lloyd Ostendorf, James R. Paisley, Capt. Lexie Palmore, Judy Patsch, Howard B. Peabody, Capt. William S. Pollock, Mrs. Helen Prater, H. Chase Putnam, William E. Reed, Mrs. Catherine Remley, Mrs. Delly Robertson, Capt. Ross Rogers, Jr., Capt. J. W. Rutter, Mrs. Bee Rutter, Ray Samuel, Paul W. Seabrook, Robert M. Smith, Mr. and Mrs. William R. Smith, Jeffrey L. Spear, Capt. C. W. Stoll, Charles Henry Stone, Mr. and Mrs. John J. Strader, Gerald W. Sutphin, Clyde K. Swift, James V. Swift, William L. Talbot, Col. Tom E. Tappan, Capt. William H. Tippitt, Lawrence E. Walker, James A. Wallen.

Foreword

This revised edition of Way's Packet Directory, 1848–1983 includes corrections of information for a number of the boat histories, largely typographical errors or mistakes in dates. (An instance is the great tornado in St. Louis that caused much damage to floating equipment occurred on May 27, 1896 rather than on May 26.) More lengthy revisions and forty-seven additional boat histories will be found in the "Addendum" at the back of this volume; the forty-eighth boat added is the ZOUAVE which conveniently comes at the end of the last page in the main body. The Compound Name Index has been expanded to include boat names with a number suffix and several of the woodcut or engraving illustrations have been replaced with photos.

Significant new information that has been brought to light about a boat since 1983 has been added for thirty entries. This will be found either in a rewriting of the main listing, where it could be fitted in without rearranging the entire page, or in the Addendum. An asterisk at the end of a particular boat history indicates that more information will be found in the Addendum and it may be worthwhile to have a look.

The forty-eight boats not mentioned in the original edition range from the 420 passenger AMERICAN QUEEN now under construction for The Delta Queen Steamboat Co. down to small boats which may have been glorified steam launches but operated in ferry or packet service. Included are the boats discovered and reported upon in the pages of the *S&D Reflector* and those found in U.S. Inspection Service reports, 1869 through 1882. Ralph DuPae of the Murphy Library has uncovered several photos of boats which later research disclosed should be included. A number of the steamboats added were early Missouri River ferry boats, large and small, turned up through the research of Clint Orr, Omaha, Nebraska whose assistance is much appreciated.

You might wonder why all of the new information wasn't incorporated into the main body of the Directory pages and the answer is, "Cost". Mixing in the forty-eight new listings plus expanded information would necessitate a wholesale rearranging of the book, an expensive proposition. Researchers should find only minor annoyance in going to the Addendum where indicated or checking it before deciding the boat just might be found in the companion reference, Way's Steam Towboat Directory.

The lifetime work of Frederick Way, Jr. is found n his Packet and Towboat Directories, indispensible resources for those interested in the Steamboat Age on the Western Rivers.

Joseph W. Rutter, Editor,
February 24, 1994.

Terms, Abbreviations and Discussion

Rig and class

SW p and ex wh	Side-wheel packet and excursion boat, wood hull
SW p wh	Side-wheel packet, wood hull
Stw p wh	Sternwheel packet, wood hull
Stw p ih	Sternwheel packet, iron hull
SW p sh	Side-wheel packet, steel hull
SW f wh	Side-wheel ferry, wood hull
Stw wh	Sternwheel, wood hull, class undetermined
P wh	Packet, wood hull, rig undetermined
SW f sh	Side-wheel ferry, steel hull
Stw	Sternwheel, rig and class undetermined
Prop f wh	Propeller ferry, wood hull
SW p and f wh	Side-wheel packet and ferry, wood hull
SW tr sh	Side-wheel railroad transfer, steel hull
Stw US wh	Sternwheeler in U.S. service, wood hull
Stw pl sh	Sternwheel pleasure boat, steel hull
SW ex wh	Side-wheel excursion boat, wood hull
Rig?	Absence of information

Absence of prefix initials means either lack of information or a renamed vessel previously identified.

Other abbreviations

b.	Built, usually the year of first documentation
Miss. R.	Mississippi River
N.O.	New Orleans
USQMD or USQMC	U.S. Quartermasters Department or Corps
Batwing	Side-wheelers with no covering over wheels
c.	Circa, approximately

Engines

Usually plural inasmuch as the usual steamboat had two main engines. On side-wheelers, unless otherwise noted, each wheel was driven by one engine, entirely independent of the other, requiring two engineers, one on the starboard and the other on the port engine, each answering separate signals from the pilot; one side could be in full reverse while the other side was coming ahead, etc. Such side-wheelers had great dexterity while turning about and in maneuvering. The sternwheel engines, one on each side, were set like those of a steam locomotive, the cranks on the extremities of the paddlewheel shaft at 90 degrees. Deviations from these two types are noted in the text. Accurate engine sizes were hard to come by, and I regret the frequent omissions.

Example: Engines 20's- 6½ ft. River shorthand for cylinders 20 inches inside diameter by 6½ feet length of piston stroke, denoting high pressure engines, the exhaust escaping into the atmosphere.

Example: Engines 16's- 32's- 8 ft. Cylinders of the tandem compound type, the small (or high pressure) cylinder 16 inches inside diameter, the large (or low pressure) cylinder 32 inches inside diameter, with common piston stroke of 8 feet. Such installations by option could be either condensing or non-condensing, specified in the descriptions when known.

Steamboat engines were most often linked to the paddlewheel crank by a long arm called the pitman. The engine's piston-rod terminated in the jaw of a cross-head mounted on parallel slides, and the pitman bridged the distance from cross-head to crank-pin. The surviving excursion and tourist steamboats employ this method.

Boilers

The Western-style return-flue boiler predominated; long cylindrical boilers with relatively small diameter. These were mounted horizontally, in fore and aft position, singly or in batteries of two, three, and on the larger boats up to eight or more, interconnected by a common thwartship steam drum overhead, and underneath by one or two sediment-catcher drums called mud drums. The furnace, at the forward end, carried heat and flames under the boilers, aft, and at the rear end upward and into the boiler flues through which the flames were returned forward into the breechings over the firebox, and thence to the smokestacks. Steamboat engines with long stroke and relatively small bore required high pressure steam, and the Western-style boiler set-up best solved the problem on these light-weight, flat-bottomed steamers so often confronted with shallow channels. Raw river water was used to steam these boilers, always a problem on the highly sedimented Mississippi (middle and lower), Missouri, Arkansas and Red, and frequently on other tributaries during times of freshet and flood, requiring constant vigilance and frequent cleaning. The water level within the boilers could not be measured with the usual glass-column gauge due to encrustation, so engineers relied on three petcocks screwed into the aft boiler-heads mounted in vertical positions, tested manually and frequently, judging water level to their practiced ears by the sound emitted, augmented later on by the Vanduzen gauge which operated quite like a toilet bowl set-up, employing a hollow float at the end of an arm mounted inside the boiler, levered to an exterior indicator, clock-like in appearance, with pointer and notches. Many early boiler failures, due to flue-collapse or bursting of the shell, can be attributed to the use of faulty materials by the manufacturer who, however honorable, knew very little about testing his wares. River engineers come in for their share of the blame by persuading boiler pressure beyond the prescribed allowance, accomplished usually by hanging additional weight on the safety valve-arms, a sin which may be extended to the captain and owners who hired engineers with the proviso they "could get the boat around." Boiler explosions on passenger-carrying steamboats came to a merciful halt before the river days of this scribe, and Western-style boilers persisted until the end of the packet era. One of today's excursion boats still uses a set of them as this is written.

Shipyards

Where possible I have used the site where the hull was built, followed by identification of the city the hull was taken to for superstructure, engines, boilers, and completion. Such procedure was particularly employed in the Pittsburgh area, the hulls and boiler deck framing put up at an outlying location, Belle Vernon, Shousetown, Freedom, and perhaps a half-dozen other places, then towed to Pittsburgh for the balance of the work. Many early boats were documented "built at Pittsburgh" without bothering to identify where the hulls came from, and it irks me that for this reason, even at this late date, I cannot supply the location of the yard where the hull of the famed *FAR WEST* was built and am forced to start off her description with "built at Pittsburgh, Pa." Wheeling presents a composite puzzle for the researcher; many of its steamboats were built there complete, hull and all; many hulls were towed to Wheeling for machinery and cabins, and many Wheeling hulls were sent to Pittsburgh for finishing. Marietta was more self-sufficient, and the boats listed as built at Harmar, Oh., are in reality Marietta products. By the same token boat-building at Cincinnati, Jeffersonville, and New Albany generally was everything from the hull up. Fortunately for the purposes of this book, all of the steamers built at the Howard Ship

Yard in Jeffersonville, and there were many, have been tracked down by Charles Preston Fishbaugh in his book *From Paddle Wheels to Propellers,* published by the Indiana Historical Society in 1970. Boats built at Jeff. not identified in these listings as "built by Howard" were from other local yards there, stated if known. I could have identified the Shousetown steamers as built by E. & N. Porter, an uncle and nephew team—most of them were—and today Shousetown is no longer on the map, now known as Glenwillard, Pa. Cincinnati has had an array of shipyards over the years and one of them still was in business when I first started boating, in the East End, where the *QUEEN CITY* was built. Other than the old Howard Yard, now part of Jeffboat, Inc., most of these old building sites have been obliterated save for an occasional rusty ring-bolt.

Dimensions

Most of the dimensions given in the text are the size of the hull expressed in linear dimensions. The length is the center line distance from the stem to the main stern transom. The width is the thwartship measure taken at the widest part of the hull. The depth is the vertical distance from the bottom timbers to the main deck floor timbers in the body of the hull about amidships. The over-all length of a sternwheeler is considerably more, due to the paddlewheel hung at the rear, and the over-all width of a side-wheeler is much greater due to the wide guards necessary to enclose and support the wheels. Government records express the hull size of commercial vessels in feet and decimals thereof, and records of vessels employed in various U.S. services are expressed in feet and lineal fractions thereof. Hull statistics for a number of the early-built steamers were not available for inclusion herein, so we compromised in most cases of such omission by quoting the registered gross tonnage, approximating about 100 cubic feet to the ton. Fractions were expressed in 95ths to about 1865. Model builders are cautioned to regard official dimensions as approximations and to dig, where possible, for contemporary details.

Architect's model photo by Delta Queen Steamboat Co.

The last word in steamboats is the new **AMERICAN QUEEN** (#0246A), a 420 passenger tourist boat owned by The Delta Queen Steamboat Co., New Orleans. Launched in 1994 and scheduled to go into service in 1995 the AMERICAN QUEEN is 425 feet overall and with all modern cruise boat amenities. She will operate an overnight cruise service from New Orleans with the company's other boats DELTA QUEEN and MISSISSIPPI QUEEN.

A

0001 A.B. CHAMBERS

SW p wh b. Cincinnati, Oh., 1855. 225 x 33. 417 tons. Engines 22's-6 ft. Five boilers, 151 psi. Named for the editor of the newspaper *Missouri Republican.* Capt. Jim Gormley built her for Missouri River. Grant Marsh was watchman on her at St. Louis winter 1855–1856 during the big ice. Snagged and sunk on her first trip up the Missouri, Capt. G.W. Bowman, master, above Atchison, Kans., March 1856. Raised and sold to Alexander Gillam, Thompson McDavid, John Lee, and Benjamin Courier. Sam Clemens stood pilot watches on her winter 1858–1859 in Mississippi River trades. Snagged in the Missouri River just above the mouth, Capt. Alex Gillam, Sept. 24, 1860, and was lost. Note: Joseph Mills Hanson calls her *A. B. CHAMBERS No. 2* in recounting in his book *The Conquest Of the Missouri* (1908) about Mark Twain being pilot on her with Capt. George W. Bowman, master, and Grant Marsh as mate (pages 26–29).

0002 A.B. SAFFORD

Stw p wh b. Mound City, Ill., 1882. 51 x 13.6 x 3.6. Registered at Memphis, 1886.

0003 A.B. SEGER

Advertised at New Orleans for forts Berwick and Chene, Capt. R.H. Kerr, 1861. She will leave Brashear City every Sunday on arrival of the noon cars from Algiers, accepting passengers and light freight.

0004 A.B. SHAW

SW p wh b. Louisville, Ky., 1847. 67 tons. Burned at Memphis, May 20, 1850.

0005 A.C. DONNALLY

SW p wh b. Cincinnati, Oh., by Cincinnati Marine Railway Co., 1876. 293 x 41.8 x 7.8. Overall width 65 ft. Engines 22's- 7 ft. Paddlewheels 26. dia., 12. buckets. Rated 1,045.66 tons. Built for Capt. Henry U. Hart, who commanded, and Ed A. Donnally was clerk. Named for son of Capt. Donnally who died a short while before boat was completed, the "flower of the flock." Ran Cincinnati-New Orleans. Burned at the Missouri shore a short distance below Cairo, February 1879. Replaced in the trade by the *R.R. SPRINGER* (see) which Captain Hart also commanded.

0006 A.C. GODDIN

SW p wh b. Madison, Ind., 1856, 351 tons. Ran on Missouri River, Capt. J. Ives, master, 1856. Snagged and lost at Lower Bonhomme Island, including cargo, Apr. 20, 1857, Capt. John LaBarge, master. Bonhomme Bend on the Missouri River is between Miles 41.3 and 37.6.

0007 A.C. JAYNES

Stw f sh b. Grafton, Ill., by Midwest Boat & Barge Co., 1925. 125 x 30 x 4.3. Compound engines, 12's, 48's- 4 ft. One boiler, coal burner. Carried 24 autos. Originally operated at Cape Girardeau, Mo., then Greenville, Miss., until bridges were built at those cities and then was taken to Helena, Ark., owned there by Capt. A.C. Johnson and operated by Charles Halbert. Burned May 1960.

0008 A.D. ALLEN

Stw p wh b. Jeffersonville, Ind., by Howard, 1901. 125 x 23 x 3.5. Engines 8- 3 ft. One boiler. Rebuilt 1907 and new engines placed, 10- 4 ft. Ran on Arkansas River, in 1909 ran Little Rock-Pine Bluff, Capt. Ed Botsford, and Frank A. Morgan, chief engineer. Sold in 1910 while at Little Rock to U.S. Engineers who used her on upper White River through 1929, possibly some later.

0009 A.G. BROWN

SW p wh b. Brownsville, Pa., 1858. 136 x 26 x 5. Two boilers. Built for Pearl River and New Orleans trade. Advertised 1861 to leave the lake-end of the Pontchartrain RR for Mandeville, Lewisburg, Madisonville, and Covington four days a week, Capt. W.V. Pointevant. In 1866 advertised from New Orleans to the forts (Berwick and Chene), Quarantine Station, Buras Settlement, Pointe-a-la-Hache and all landings on the Coast, Capt. Alex Queant, each Sunday and Wednesday. Sold October 1866 to John L. Baringer, New Orleans. Owned 1867 by A.H. Sieward, A.P. Kip, and others of New Orleans. Collided with German steamship *TEUTONIC* 45 miles below New Orleans and was lost, Dec. 30, 1868.

0010 A.G. HENRY

Stw p wh The *JOSH V. THROOP* (see) was sold at a U.S. marshal sale c. 1885, to the Chattanooga & North Alabama Packet Co., renamed *A. G. HENRY*, and ran upriver from Chattanooga on the Tennessee, Capt. A.G. Henry; later Capts. W.O. Jones and Wiley Fritz. Once struck a pier of the railroad bridge at Bridgeport and was badly damaged. Sank above Chattanooga, dismantled, and parts used 1886 building the *R. C. GUNTER* (see).

0011 A.G. MASON

Stw p wh b. West Brownsville, Pa., 1855. 156 x 27.5 x 4.5. Ran on the upper Mississippi out of St. Paul, Capt. Barry, with Pearman, clerk. Snagged and lost at Davenport, Iowa, Oct. 30, 1857.

A.G. ROSS

See *ALFRED G. ROSS,* full name.

0012 A.H. SEVIER

Stw p wh b. Cincinnati, Oh., 1860. 193 tons. Sank in the Grand Chain, Ohio River, on first trip, October 1860, raised. Sank on the Arkansas near Pine Bluff, Dec. 31, 1860, Capt. William Windsor, with J.L. Carter, clerk. The *CEDAR RAPIDS* was sent up to bring out the outfit of the wrecked boat, but sank at Douglas on the Arkansas. Then the *FRONTIER CITY* was sent up to recover goods from these two losses, loaded it aboard, and also sank (see).

0013 A.J. DORCHESTER

A small craft of 7.81 tons. b. Bellevue, Iowa, 1867. 51 x 10.2 x 2.2. Was rebuilt at Bellevue in 1875. Registered at Galena in 1886.

0014 A.J. SWEENEY

Stw p wh b. Wheeling, W. Va., 1863. 244 tons. Bound for Nashville loaded with 7,000 sacks of corn and 28 horses, she hit a pier of the bridge at Clarksville, sank and burned, Mar. 9, 1864. The wreck was raised, towed back to Wheeling, dismantled. The machinery went to the *BERTRAND* (see) then under construction at Wheeling.

0015 A.J. WHITE

SW p wh b. Jeffersonville, Ind., 1870. She was floated over the Falls on July 20 and completed at New Albany. Rated 394.88 tons. Ran out of Memphis to Friar's Point, Capt. Mark R. Cheek. Sold at U.S. marshal sale January 1877 to Capt. John N. Harbin. In latter November 1878 enroute Memphis to Helena, Capt. William Ashford, landed at Glendale, the railroad landing opposite Helena. She ran on a snag, tore a hole 75 ft. long in her bottom, and sank on the snag. Could not be raised. Her whistle was transferred to the *COAHOMA,* thence to *LADY LEE* and then to *CITY OF OSCEOLA, ROBERT E. LEE, HARRY LEE* (first) and *BOB LEE, JR.*

0016 A.L. DAVIS

Stw wh b. Nashville, Tenn., 1853. 102 tons. Snagged and lost at Shelbyville, Tenn., Mar. 23, 1857.

0017 A.L. GOLDBERG

Stw wh b. Nashville, Tenn., 1895. 129 x 20 x 3. Registered at Nashville 1896.

0018 A.L. GREGOIRE

SW f wh b. Cincinnati, Oh., 1854. 172 tons. Documented out of Galena, 1867. Ferried on the Upper Mississippi, probably Dubuque. Out of service 1872.

0019 A.L. MASON

Stw p wh b. Madison, Ind., 1890. 252 x 56.2 x 6. Owned by the Kansas City and Missouri River Transportation Co., A.L. Buxton of Kansas City, managing owner. Capt. Archie Bryan was her master on Missouri River, running Kansas City to St. Louis. Soon transferred to St. Louis-New Orleans trade, same owners, Capt. J.P. McKenney as master. Downbound with a heavy cargo near Sunflower Landing, she parted a hogchain and sank right now, this in June 1894. One of the stacks fell on Capt. George Keith, injuring his legs, and he never fully recovered. This boat primarily was a freight carrier, much on the order of the *STATE OF KANSAS* and *STATE OF MISSOURI,* all three built at Madison about the same time (see).

0020 A.L. NORTON

P wh b. Ironton, Oh., 1874. 130 x 20 x 3.7. Named for Dr. A.L. Norton, father of Frank A. and Joe Norton. Ran local trades on the upper Ohio. Was in Marietta-Gallipolis trade 1880, Capt. Alf Day, master, and with H.W. Ressener and John F. Cromley, clerks. Same trade 1882 with Capt. Edwin F. Maddy, master, and C.H. Welton, clerk. She was said to have been the slowest boat on the river, even the current beat her downstream. In mid-1880s bought by Capt. Jeff Bell and Capt. Bill Roberts who used the machinery on a boat they were building at Letart, W. Va.

0021 A.L. SHOTWELL

SW p wh b. New Albany, Ind., 1852. 310 x 36 x 8. Six boilers, each 32" by 42' Buckets 14'. Hull by John Evans. Largely owned and commanded by Capt. B.L. Elliott, New Albany, who had previously commanded *LUNA* and *EMPIRE* (see). Named for A.L. Shotwell, Louisville, president of the Louisville Chamber of Commerce (1854). Ran Louisville-New Orleans. She loaded out at Louisville on maiden trip Jan. 7, 1853. Celebrated for the much-disputed "fast-trip" from New Orleans to Portland, Ky., in May 1853 following the *ECLIPSE* by three days, and claiming faster time. Capt. William F. Fuller led the delegation who were convinced that the *SHOTWELL* was the faster, and presented her with the deer horns worn by the *J.M. WHITE* of 1844. James Holmes, chief engineer, later was chief on the *JACOB STRADER.* Lost both stacks overboard in a storm near Vicksburg night of Mar. 31-Apr. 1, 1854, and replaced them at New Albany. Ran aground in Sisters Islands above Smithland, Ky., Apr. 11, 1855, had to be unloaded there at the bar, and was repaired at Paducah. Snagged and lost at Paddy's Hen and Chickens Islands four miles above Memphis, Tuesday, Mar. 24, 1857. Went down in 13 ft. of water. A comprehensive article about the *ECLIPSE-SHOTWELL* contest appears in *S&D Reflector,* September 1975 issue.

0022 A.M. HALLIDAY

Centerwheel f sh b. Jeffersonville, Ind., by Howard, 1903. Catamaran (double) hulls. 121 x 59 x 7.7. Engines 16's- 6 ft. by Ainslee-Cochran. One boiler. Allowed 225 passengers, 30 cars. Built for Union Ferry Co., New Orleans, and later owned by Algiers Public Service Co. She was retired and dismantled 1954.

0023 A.N. JOHNSTON

SW p wh Hull built at Murraysville, Va. and completed at Wheeling, 1847. 199 tons. Upbound, Cincinnati to Wheeling, exploded boilers near Manchester, Oh., at 2:00 A.M., Dec. 29, 1847, with big life loss, probably 60. Capt. Jos. Nixon, Pittsburgh, was among those who survived, badly scalded.

0024 A.O. TYLER

SW p wh b. Cincinnati, Oh., 1857. 419 tons. Engines 22's-8 ft. Four boilers. Built for Capt. Daniel Collier for the Cincinnati-New Orleans trade. Machinery came from the *HUNGARIAN,* a former boat owned by Collier. Collier and A.O. Tyler were brothers-in-law; Collier married Tyler's sister; both were great uncles of Col. Harry D. Knox, Marietta, on his mother's side. Hit a wreck and sank 30 miles below Cincinnati, Jan. 27, 1860, raised. She was upbound on the Mississippi when Sumter was fired on, and was one of the first of inland steamboats to receive enemy attention; she was fired on, but not damaged. Capt. John Collier was in command at the time, brother of Capt. Dan Collier. Sold to the U.S. in early June 1861 and converted into a U.S. gunboat renamed *TYLER*. Admiral John Rodgers, who handled these affairs, wrote a request to the U.S. Secretary of the Navy to change the name to *TAYLOR*, "a name of better augury than TYLER." He was referring to former U.S. President John Tyler who had joined the Rebels. Officially the name was changed to *TYLER* nevertheless, but unofficially she was referred to as *TAYLOR* and much confusion resulted. See *TYLER* for news of her gunboat career.

0025 A.R. BRAGG

Stw p wh b. Newport, Ark., 1890. 115.6 x 26.8 x 4.7. Full cabin, no texas. Spent her career on White, Black, and Current rivers in Arkansas. Owned 1899 by Inman-Decker Packet Co. In April 1901 running Black Rock to Newport, Ark., Capt. Leslie Inman. Ran until c. 1904.

0026 A.S. RUTHVEN

SW p wh b. Cincinnati, Oh., 1860. 144 tons. Disappeared into the South during the Civil War as a Confederate steamer. Redocumented Aug. 16, 1867. Out of service 1869.

A.T. LACY

See *ALFRED T. LACY*, full name.

0027 A.W. BAKER

SW p wh b. Louisville, Ky., 1856. 95 x 25 x 4.5. Advertised at New Orleans for Attakapas, Capt. William Greig, 1859. Became a Confederate transport and supply boat on Red River. She was taken by U.S. steamer *QUEEN OF THE WEST* near the mouth of Red River, Feb. 8, 1863, run ashore and burned.

0028 A.W. QUARRIER

SW p wh b. Cincinnati, Oh., 1856. 185 x 33 x 3.5. The hull was built at mouth of the Big Sandy River. Ran Parkersburg-Cincinnati in 1858. In the Cincinnati-Kanawha River trade in 1859, Capt. James K. Johnson, master, with Mr. Stratton, clerk. During an ice run-out at Cincinnati on Feb. 7, 1857, the *QUARRIER* was squeezed into the *JAMES WATT* which proved a total loss. Was sold to New Orleans and in 1862 running to Jefferson and Shreveport, in charge of Capt. F. A. Biossat, pinch-hitting for the *W. BURTON*. Was used in Confederate service and lost on Red River. The U.S. snagboat *C.W. HOWELL* removed her wreck in 1894.

0029 A. BAKER

Stw p wh b. Louisville, Ky., 1864. 134 tons. Operated on the lower Ohio. Went to U.S. marshal sale at Cairo mid-May 1871, sold to Capts. Sam Orr, J.M. Phillips, and John B. Phillips for $1,810. In August 1871 with Capt. J.M. Phillips in charge (his first command) running low water Cairo-Cape Girardeau. Dismantled 1873.

0030 A. BALDWIN

Centerwheel f sh b. Jeffersonville, Ind., by Howard, 1905. 127 x 58.9 x 7.5. for Union Ferry Co., New Orleans. Engines 13's- 6 ft. Two boilers 44 x 20 ft. Catamaran hulls. Carried 231 passengers, 35 autos. Later owned by Bisso Ferry Co., New Orleans. Out of service c. 1971.

0031 A. BURTON

SW f wh b. Montrose, Iowa, at George Anderson yard, 1874. 92.5 x 20 x 3. Ferried Nauvoo-Montrose, 10 years operated by Andrew Burton. Replaced 1886 by *CITY OF NAUVOO* (see).

0032 A. CAREY

b. Grayville, Ill., 1885. 75 x 14.3 x 5. Registered at Evansville, 1886.

A. DE LAMARTINE

See *ALPHONSE de LAMARTINE*, full name. Also see *LAMARTINE*, contemporary.

0033 A. DURIO

Stw b. New Iberia, La., 1881, 66 x 18 x 3. Registered at Brashear, La., 1886-1896.

0034 A. FRANK

Stw b. Nashville, Tenn., 1891. 98 x 18 x 4. Off the list by 1895.

0035 A. FUSELIER

SW p wh b. Franklin, La., 1851. 357 tons. Operated between New Orleans and Mobile. Exploded her boilers during first season. Later ran Mobile-Montgomery on Alabama River. Carl Carmer mentions her in his book *Stars Fell on Alabama*. Owned by Cox, Brainard & Co. Out of service after 1859.

0036 A. GALLAGHER

Prop f wh b. Pittsburgh, Pa., 1916. 53.7 x 11.4 x 4.2. Ferried between Manchester and West End, Pittsburgh, owned by John Gallagher and named for his mother. Still registered in 1929.

0037 A. MAJORS

SW p and f wh b. St. Louis, Mo., 1857. 371 tons. Engines 20's- 6 ft. Two boilers, 100 psi. Named for Alex Majors, and was operated at St. Joseph, Mo., in connection with the Hannibal & St. Joseph RR to Omaha. A tornado on Mar. 15, 1862, blew her from her moorings at St. Joseph, damage slight, but destroyed the other railroad steamboat *DACOTAH* (see). On Apr. 7, 1866, took a sheer on the pilot at Brunswick, Mo., hit shore head-on, sank. Then owned by John L. Lathrop, with Capt. Samuel Bently, master. Burned in great steamboat fire at St. Louis, Apr. 7, 1866 (see *FANNY OGDEN*). She originally was built for the U.S., first named *MINK* (see).

A. McDowell

See *AUGUSTUS McDOWELL,* full name.

A. Wathen

See *ARTHUR WATHEN,* full name.

0038 Aaron Hart

SW p wh b. Elizabethtown, Pa., 1848. 261 tons. Built for Capts. William J. Kountz and John Birmingham, both of Pittsburgh. Named for a river pioneer, father of Capt. Jesse Hart who operated packets New Orleans-Bayou Sara (see *BRILLIANT*). Had "Clipper" engines built by Thomas K. Litch, Pittsburgh (see *CLIPPER*). Burned in wharf fire at New Orleans Oct. 8, 1849, which also destroyed *FALCON, NORTH AMERICA, ILLINOIS, MARSHALL NEY.* An enterprising mate dragged the office safe ashore with ropes, and a set of colors presented by Capt. Jesse Hart was safely removed, all else lost. Captain Kountz commanded at the time.

0039 Abeona

SW p wh b. Cincinnati, Oh., 1864. 157.5 x 31.5 x 4.5. Engines 14's- 5 ft. Sold to U.S. Navy, Dec. 31, 1864, retaining same name, and was tinclad #32. Sold at public sale while at Mound City, Ill., Oct. 17, 1865, to Capt. J.A. Williamson. Entered Cincinnati-St. Louis trade. Downbound at Cottonwood Bar, above Paducah, mid-September 1868, hit the tow of the *SAM BROWN* which was upbound with iron ore in model barges. The collision tore off cookhouse and guard, and disabled the engine on one side of *ABEONA.* A German couple and two children were sleeping on the guard, bound for Waterloo, Ill. Both children were drowned and the mother's skull was crushed fatally. Capt. Hiram J. Vinton, Cincinnati, was master of her several years in the St. Louis trade, and had with him H.D. Crane as clerk (1869) and then Charles Regnier (1870). Burned at Cincinnati on Mar. 7, 1872, along with *ST. CHARLES* and *MAJOR ANDERSON* (both see).

0040 Aberdeen

SW p wh b. New Albany, Ind., 1848. 209 tons. Snagged at Devil Shoals, Ala., Dec. 21, 1851.

0041 Abigail

Stw p wh The *LUCILLE NOWLAND* (see) burned at Evansville, Ind., 1912. Capt. Fred Hornbrook had her rebuilt at the Howard Yard, Jeffersonville, Ind., and renamed her *ABIGAIL* for his wife. Ran excursions at Nashville summer 1914 and started her to Pittsburgh early 1915. She burned at Cedar Farm Landing, Ind., enroute, Feb. 15, 1915.

0042 Abner O'Neal

Stw p wh b. Brownsville, Pa., 1875. 138 x 26.6 x 4. Built for Capt. Abner O'Neal, Steubenville, for the Steubenville-Wheeling trade and ran there until the PRR ran their branch line down from Weirton Junction. Then entered Pittsburgh-Wheeling trade, three trips a week, October 1877. Capt. O'Neal died at Steubenville Feb. 11, 1878, then Capt. Nate Wintringer took charge (he was engineer on the *SULTANA* [see] when she blew up). John A. Eddy was clerk near as long as she ran on the upper Ohio. Ran through herself at Wellsville late June 1878, hobbled to Rochester on one side, and was towed thence to Pittsburgh by *COAL BLUFF NO. 2.* Sold to Cumberland River and was renamed *CUMBERLAND* (see).

0043 Abner O'Neal

Stw p wh b. Freedom, Pa., 1884. 150 x 28 x 3.8. Engines 14's- 5 ft. Designed and built by John M. Sweeney of Wheeling for the Wheeling-Steubenville trade. Owned by Capt. Nate Wintringer and Capt. George O'Neal, both of Steubenville. W.L. Wilkins, clerk. Capt. Wintringer died at Steubenville, October 1886, then Capt. George O'Neal commanded until boat was sold to Missouri River Transportation Co. on Mar. 31, 1890. Capt. Sam V. Williamson went out along (see *HELEN E*) and got his pilot license extended to include Missouri River in North and South Dakota. Snagged at Painted Woods, N.D., on July 17, 1892, lost. Her name was changed on the Missouri to *CHASKE* but was not approved by Customs. A photograph exists showing her with *CHASKE* on the pilothouse, but original name was soon restored. Capt. R. A. Talbott commanded on the Missouri.

0044 Abraham

SW p wh Originally named *VICTORIA* b. Elizabeth, Pa., 1858 (see). The USQMC bought *VICTORIA,* transferred her to Navy, renamed *ABRAHAM* Sept. 30, 1862. Did transport service on the Mississippi. Sold at public sale Mar. 16, 1866, renamed *LEXINGTON* (see).

0045 Acacia Cottage

Stw p wh b. California, Pa., 1857. 145 x 28 x 3.5. Engines from the *FANNIE MALONE* (see). Two boilers. Built for James Williams, Nashville, Tenn. Capt. R. B. Baugh, Florence, Ala., first master. Two years later sold to T.C. Discumbees, Louisville, Ky. *Lytle-Holdcamper List* says she was lost by snagging 25 miles above Helena, Ark., on Aug. 21, 1862. The report of loss is incorrect; contemporary newspaper accounts attribute the sinking to the ACACIA (0044A).

0046 Acadia

Stw p wh b. Freedom, Pa., 1845. 118 tons. Ran on the Illinois River, Capt. John Russell. Burned at St. Louis in the wharf fire of May 17, 1849, when 23 steamboats were lost.

0047 Acadia

SW p wh b. Jeffersonville, Ind., at the Howard Yard, 1860. 188 x 35 x 7. Owned by the New Orleans & Bayou Sara Mail Co., Eugene Lanone, president. Capt. E. P. Grop, master. In U.S. service as a transport during the Civil War, and burned in Yalobusha River, Miss., July 17, 1863.

0048 Acme

On the Ouachita River running up Bayou Bartholomew in 1877, connecting with the *JOHN H. HANNA* (see).

0049 ACORN

Ferry wh b. Middleport, Oh., 1871. 65 x 18 x 3. Ran ferry service Middleport-Clifton operated by Pete Schott. Replaced by the *LITTLE BEN* (see) in 1895.

0050 ACORN

Stw p wh b. Davenport, Iowa, 1905. 80 x 20 x 4. Documented at Rock Island, Ill., 1908.

0051 ACTIVE

Stw p wh b. Brownsville, Pa., 1867. 95 tons. Engines 9"-30" stroke. Ran on the Kanawha River, Charleston-Cannelton, then Charleston-Gallipolis. Capt. William Hix was master 1872–1874, maybe longer. Clerks included J.B. Dudding, C.N. Coleman, and William Rock. Capt. Wm. Penn Wright was part owner. Went south and lost at Brashear, La., Jan. 29, 1877.

0052 AD HINE

Stw p wh b. Monongahela City, Pa., 1860. 129 x 24 x 3.5. Two boilers. Ran on the upper Mississippi. In latter February 1864 sank on the Arkansas River with cargo from St. Louis, much of it shipped by M.S. Mepham & Bro., this near Pine Bluff. Then owned by L.B. Hine ½, Adam Hine ¼ and R.H. Martin ¼. Sold to USQMC on June 1, 1864. Sold at public sale Mar. 19, 1866, renamed *NUGGET* (see).

0053 ADA

b. Grayville, Ill. on Wabash River, 1876. 81.34 tons. First registered at Evansville.

0053-A ADA B

Stw p wh b. Stillwater, Minn., 1874. 130 x 19.5 x 3.9. Operated on the St. Croix River. Later acquired by U.S. Engineers, Rock Island, Ill. and renamed ALERT, used as a towboat.

0054 ADA B

Stw p wh b. Klotzville, La., 1906. 60.8 x 12.6 x 2.5. Registered at New Orleans 1908.

0055 ADA HEILMAN

Regular Wabash River packet, Capt. Henry Scott is master and Lew. Morris, clerk, this in March 1871.

ADA JOHNSON

Appears in early *LMVs* this spelling. Customs has her as *ADDIE JOHNSTON* (see).

0056 ADA LYON

Stw p wh b. New Albany, Ind., 1864. 114 tons. Evansville and Green River. Carried provisions for U.S. Army on the Cumberland to Nashville. Capt. Jesse Berry, first master. Sold after the war to Capt. A.H. Edwards who took her back to Green River trade with Ewing Graham, Sr., and Penuel Jones, pilots. Sold later to Green and Barren Rivers Navigation Co. Dismantled 1869, parts used in building *EVANSVILLE* (see).

0057 ADA V

Stw p wh b. Little Hocking, Oh., 1888. 82 x 13.6 x 2.6. Engines 9"-28" stroke. One boiler. Machinery came from a mill in Belpre, Oh. Named for Ada Varian. Capt. Bill Horn told this scribe she was a packet on the upper Kentucky River when he was a boy, c. 1889. She changed hands many times. B.J. Riggs, New Haven, W. Va., owned her entire 1899. Capt. Jacob Riggs owned her 1903. Capt. John Donald of Ripley, Oh., owned her when she burned Feb. 23, 1912, at lower end of town, drifted across and lodged. Capt. Jesse Hughes recalled a clump of willows growing in the old hull.*

0058 ADAM JACOBS

SW p wh b. Brownsville, Pa., 1864. 231 x 36 x 6. Engines 26's- 7 ft. Four boilers. Was in Gen. Grant's fleet on Tennessee River. Named for Capt. Adam Jacobs, Brownsville, Pa. Machinery built by John Snowden & Son, Brownsville. Entered St. Louis-Memphis trade as an independent boat, September 1864. Became one of the early Anchor Line fleet. Dismantled in 1874 and machinery went to *STE. GENEVIEVE* of the Anchor Line (see).

0059 ADAM JACOBS

SW p wh b. Brownsville, Pa., 1885 at Axton yard. 162.2 x 28 x 4.6. Engines 17's- 6 ft. Three boilers. Machinery and boilers by J. Herbertson & Son, Brownsville; cabin by Leonard & Co., Brownsville. Built for the Pittsburgh, Brownsville & Geneva Packet Co. Had electric lights and an arc searchlight, one of the first seen in the region. Capt. M.A. Cox came out on her. Dismantled about 1900 and the hull used as a wharfboat at McKeesport, Pa. Machinery went to *COLUMBIA* (see).

0060 ADDIE

Stw b. Monroe, La., 1890. 84.1 x 18 x 2. Registered at New Orleans, 1892.

0061 ADDIE E. FAISON

Stw p wh b. Marietta, Oh., at Knox Yard, 1887. 135 x 30 x 4.5. The old steamer *HEADLIGHT* was brought to Marietta, dismantled, and parts used building this boat. She ran out of Vicksburg to Yazoo and Sunflower rivers. Sank and lost at Nelson Landing, Miss., Nov. 20, 1893.

0062 ADDIE JOHNSTON

Stw p wh b. Port Byron, Ill., opposite from Le Claire, Ia., 1865. 315 tons. Owned for some time by Keokuk Northern Line. Out of service in 1882.

0063 ADDIE T

Stw p wh b. Higginsport, Oh., 1904. 112.6 x 24.8 x 3.8. Built by Capt. Robert Taylor and first ran Cincinnati-Vanceburg. He commanded and Enos Taylor was clerk. Soon sold to Vicksburg where she was renamed *MARY H. MILLER* (see).

0064 ADELAIDE

SW f wh b. Louisville, Ky., 1853. 136 tons. Dismantled 1861.

0065 ADELAIDE

SW p wh b. Pittsburgh, Pa., 1863. 149 tons. Dismantled 1865.

0066 ADELIA

Stw p wh b. California, Pa., 1853. 127 tons. Built for Pittsburgh-Zanesville trade to replace *JULIA DEAN* (see). Capt. Joseph McVay, first master. Owners lived at Zanesville each having one-fourth interest; C. Galigher, N.W. Graham, G.W. Graham, and Daniel Hurd. When cut down by ice at Wheeling, Feb. 16, 1855, in command of Capt. N.W. Graham. Summer of 1855 ran five trips a day Wheeling-Bellaire, connecting with B&O, Capt. G.W. Graham. Sold that fall to St. Paul, Minn., Capt. Bates, master, Worsham, clerk. Rebuilt 1859. Last owned by St. Louis Tow Co., Capt. Henry Bollman, master. Dismantled 1871.

0067 ADELIA

Stw f wh b. Port Byron, Ill., 1864. 25 tons. Dismantled 1877.

0068 ADELINE

Stw p wh Originally named *GALLARDO* (see) and was running out of Peoria in 1908, and later out of Memphis. Was in the Cairo-Caruthersville trade when lost by sinking at Caruthersville in January 1913.

0069 ADMIRAL

SW p wh b. McKeesport, Pa., 1853. 169 x 26. Engines 20's- 5½ ft. Three boilers. First master, Capt. J.T. Stockdale, Pittsburgh. Was at St. Paul in 1854, and then ran principally on Missouri River. Ran St. Louis-Council Bluffs, 1856. Sank in shallow water at Weston Island, Mo., October 1858, raised. Phil E. Chappel, steamboat clerk of the time, later listed her as one of the finest packets during the banner years of Missouri boating (1858-1860). Burned at Columbus, Ky., Apr. 5, 1862.

0070 ADMIRAL

Memphis-White River trade, c. 1869-1870. Also reported in New Orleans-Shreveport trade 1870.

0071 ADMIRAL

SW ex sh Built on steel hull of former railroad transfer *ALBATROSS* (see) at St. Louis by Streckfus Steamers, Inc., 1938-1940. Overall 374 x 92. Engines 26's- 10 ft. Allowed 4,400 passengers. The foremost excursion boat on inland streams, entirely air-conditioned. In the winter of 1973-1974 was converted to diesel-props at St. Louis, given three Murray-Tregurtha units, each 900 hp., total 2700 hp. Based at St. Louis, and still operating 1979.

0072 ADMIRAL DEWEY

Stw p wh b. West Brownsville, Pa., at Axton yard, 1898. 125 x 24 x 4. Engines 12's- 4 ft. Two boilers. The engines came from a sand digger, *GEORGE R. FORD.* Boilers, etc., from *HARRY D. KNOX* (see). Came out in Monongahela River trade, Pittsburgh-Brownsville, then extended to Morgantown, Capt. John G. Britton. By 1906 she had been through a U.S. marshal sale and went to the Allegheny River owned by Thomas J. and William K. Hudson. They had her at Emlenton, Pa., on a contract job, c. 1910. Sold to John W. Hubbard, Pittsburgh, Oct. 21, 1912, and ran briefly Pittsburgh-Parkersburg. Principally noted for her "Flood Relief Trip" in spring 1913 when, loaded with donated supplies, she was sent from Pittsburgh to alleviate distress along the Muskingum with much fanfare and, as it turned out, poor results. Details of this are expanded in *S&D Reflector,* issue March 1970. Capt. Michael B. Davis commanded, Ed Sims, pilot. On this trip she was equipped with a wireless telegraphy set manned by three Carnegie Tech students, probably the first instance on inland rivers. Hubbard sold *DEWEY* Jan. 6, 1914 to Capt. Lewis Tanner who converted her to towing, and handled a railroad transfer barge at Ashland, Ky. Sold in June 1914 to Capt. John Donald, Ripley, Oh. The Spang-Chalfant Co., Pittsburgh, bought her December 1917 and sent Capt. John G. Britton down to bring her up. She was caught in ice at Apple Grove, Oh., just below old Lock and Dam 23, Ohio River and sank Feb. 12, 1918.

0073 ADMIRAL FARRAGUT

Stw p wh b. Beardstown, Ill., 1864. 158 x 29 x 4.5. Engines 14's- 4 ft. Two boilers. Machinery from *KEY WEST NO. 2* (see). Ran New Orleans-Red River in 1865. Then back to St. Louis. Dismantled 1871. Engines went to *MARY E. POE* (see).

0074 ADRIATIC

Stw p wh b. Shousetown, Pa., 1854. 200 x 45 x 6.5. This was the largest sternwheeler of her time. Actually she had two sternwheels, each handled by two engines. These singular four-engine sternwheelers were few; others were *ALMA, AUNT LETTY, J.S. PRINGLE,* and *CHALLENGE* (all see). Capt. Charles Stone made trips up Missouri River with her. In mid-April 1862 arrived at Pittsburgh from St. Louis with 700 tons of "pig metal" and miscellaneous freight. She was in Porter's Red River expedition 1864. Sank at the head of Palmyra Bend in Missouri River Mar. 28, 1865, raised. Dismantled and hull used as a freight barge.

0075 ADRIATIC

Prop p wh b. Akron, Oh., 1862. 65.90 tons. Apparently a canalboat with power, first registered at Wheeling. Ran on the Muskingum, Capt. David T. Pittman. Based at Cincinnati in 1867. Dismantled 1873.

0076 ADRIENNE

Stw p wh b. Amite River, La., 1866. 76 x 19.5 x 4.8. Owned by Jean LaSalle of New Orleans. First master, Capt. Peter L. Cornet. Indications are that she was rebuilt that summer by new owner Sheldon L. Wheeler, New Orleans who transferred her papers to Galveston, Tex., July 1865. Last documentation 1871. She may have been converted to sidewheel by Wheeler.

0077 ADVANCE

Stw p wh b. Shousetown, Pa., 1852. Three boiler boat. Ran Marietta-Cincinnati, and once sank at Haskellville, Oh. (lower end of Athalia). Freight removed by *SALEM* (see) and after raised she was returned to Cincinnati for docking. Sold to Mobile, there 1854. In July 1858 advertised Mobile-Demopolis, Capt. Samuel Ables; in 1859 same master, Mobile-Bladon-Cullem Springs. Snagged and lost at Peavey Landing, Ala., Nov. 14, 1859.

0078 ADVANCE

Stw p wh b. Franklin, Pa. on Allegheny River, 1862. 39 tons. Owned by D.T. Lane, John and Benjamin Kunkel, all of Franklin. Sold after one season. Snagged at Hutsonville, Ill., Feb. 6, 1863.

0079 ADVANCE NO. 2

Stw p wh b. Franklin, Pa. on Allegheny River, 1863. 122 x 18 x 3. Engines 9″- 3′3″. Two boilers. Owned by Capt. S.H. Marshall, Benjamin Williams, D.K. Stanford, and Harvey Crawford, all of Venango County, Pa. This boat was quite active between Pittsburgh and Oil City, Pa., during the "oil boom." Sold to Capt. James Dickey, December 1866, who planned to take her to White River, Ark. Was running on the Wabash River, Vincennes-Terre Haute, November 1869, Capt. A. Tindolph. Dismantled 1871.

0080 ADVENTURE

SW p wh b. Reeds Landing, Minn., 1865. 30.45 tons. Primarily a freight boat. Dismantled 1868.

0081 AERIEL

Stw p wh b. St. Louis, Mo., 1860. 62 tons. Also documented *ARIEL*. Dismantled 1868.

0082 AFTON

SW p wh b. Louisville, Ky., 1851. 287 tons. Advertised in 1854 at New Orleans to leave Carrollton and Lake RR every Thursday for Pass Manchac, Capt. T.H. Dunnica, master. Pleasure excursions Sundays to Pass Manchac via Lewisburg and Madisonville. Fare $3 including meals. Burned in the Yazoo River, Apr. 13, 1855.

0083 AFTON JR.

SW p wh b. Louisville, Ky., 1856. 155 tons. Advertised at New Orleans for Yazoo River, to Leflore, Greenwood, and Yazoo City, Capt. J.N. White. On Red River, 1857. Snagged and lost 19 miles above Baton Rouge, Dec. 8, 1858.

0084 AGGIE

Stw p wh b. Manchester, Oh., 1875. 92.4 x 20.4 x 3. Engines 9½″- 3 ft. Running Evansville-Owensboro daily in fall 1875, Capt. John H. Triplett. Capt. Tom Wilson and Messrs. O'Neil sold her April 1876 to Azro Powell, Uniontown, Ky., with no cash involved. This $5,000 swap was for a farm of 250 acres in Mississippi Bend. On Feb. 15, 1878, was at St. Louis just in from Chester, Ill. James Tetlow of Chester had sold her to Missouri River persons living at Washington, Mo., who planned to run her in connection with the railroad at Portland. Was on the Osage River 1880–1881. Registered at Kansas City in 1892.

0085 AGLIA

Stw f wh b. Cincinnati, Oh., 1878. 109 x 37.6 x 6. One-stack ferry operated at Vicksburg. Still documented 1896.

0086 AGNES

Stw p wh Originally *FLORENCE MILLER No. 3,* b. Cincinnati, 1864. In war service was known as tinclad *ORIOLE* (see). *ORIOLE* was sold at public sale, Oct. 14, 1865, to Thomas Scott. Made trips on Missouri River 1866. In the next several years made trips St. Louis to White River, Ark. Snagged and lost enroute from St. Louis to New Orleans 10 miles below Vicksburg, Mar. 3, 1869.

0087 AGNES

Stw p wh b. Barataria, La., 1867. 88 x 13.5 x 4. Owned 1868 by John Baird, Jefferson Parish, La. Capt. George Rolfe, master. Sold in August 1871. Lost in 1872.

0088 AID

Advertised from Pittsburgh to Wabash River, spring 1854, Capt. Davison. In 1855 a boat of this name was running Vicksburg-Yazoo River connecting with the *P.C. WALLIS* for New Orleans.

0089 AID

SW f wh b. Evansville, Ind., 1860. 60 tons. Snagged and lost in the St. Francis River, Ark., Jan. 28, 1861.

0090 AID

Stw p wh b. New Albany, Ind., 1864. 62.68 tons. 80 x 20, and draws 20″. Built by Gardner and Lloyd for low water work, and was chartered to the U.S. immediately upon completion. Went to Cumberland River. Dismantled in 1875.

0091 ALABAMA

SW p wh b. Cincinnati, Oh., 1851. 297 tons. Operated to New Orleans. Burned at Louisville, Ky., Aug. 12, 1855.

0092 ALABAMA

SW p wh b. Elizabeth, Pa., 1852. 213 tons. Exploded with loss of nine lives at Minden, La., Jan. 15, 1856.

0093 ALABAMA

Originally *DESOTO* b. Madison, Ind. (hull), and completed at New Albany, Ind., 1860. Saw war service both as *DESOTO and GENERAL LYON* (both see) and was renamed *ALABAMA* when sold at public sale Oct. 20, 1865. Was taken to New Orleans and operated there to Red River, Capt. William C. Harrison, master, teamed up with the *LOUIS D'OR* and *NATIONAL* in a "Line." In November

1866 bought by Capt. H.L. Lee and others including Capt. W.H. Thorwegan. Burned at Grand View Reach, above New Orleans, 3:00 A.M., Apr. 1, 1867. She was downbound with 100 passengers and 1,200 bales. No life loss.

0094 ALABAMA

Stw p wh b. Pittsburgh, Pa., 1883. 177.6 x 34.7 x 5. Engines 16's- 6 ft. Three boilers. Texas 68′ long with 6′ porch both fore and aft. Built for Alexander Pratt, Mobile, Ala., who gave mortgage, defaulted, and a lawsuit resulted. The Comeaux family, New Orleans, bought her 1887–1888, took her to New Orleans and renamed her *MARY Z. COMEAUX* (see).

0095 ALABAMA

Stw p wh b. Gadsden, Ala., 1904. 137.5 x 27.7 x 4.3. Ran on upper Coosa River, owned by LeFevre Bros., who had come from Wisconsin to Rome, Ga., and Gadsden, Ala. Dismantled 1917.

0096 ALABAMA

Stw p wh b. Pt. Pleasant, West Va., 1912. 170 x 32 x 6. Owned by St. Louis & Tennessee River Packet Co. Came out with no texas, but one was added later. She ran the Paducah-Shiloh trade in 1929, the last regular steam packet on the Tennessee. Was in the Cincinnati-Louisville trade under charter to the Louisville & Cincinnati Packet Co., in spring of 1931. Chartered to George Partin, Memphis, in 1932 for Memphis-Caruthersville trade. Was retired soon thereafter and made into a quarter boat.

0097 ALABAMA BELLE

Originally the *OHIO BELLE* b. Cincinnati 1855, (see). Sold by the USQMC on Jan. 4, 1866, and renamed. Owned by W.H. McAllister, New Orleans with Capt. W.C. Wagley, master. Resold to Charles Newman and others, and dismantled in March 1867.

0098 ALAMAKEE

SW f wh b. Cincinnati, Oh., 1858. 136.03 tons. Ferried between Prairie du Chien and McGregor. Was on hand, Capt. James Lawler, to pick up survivors when the rafter *D.A. McDONALD* exploded at North McGregor in 1872. Also picked up survivors of the *JAMES MALBON* explosion a month later. Dismantled 1872.

0099 ALAMO

SW p wh b. Paducah, Ky., 1850. 66 tons. Advertised Mobile-Bladon Springs every Wednesday, 1851, Capt. Stephens, master. Lost June 1, 1856, at Mobile, Ala.

0100 ALAMO

SW p wh b. Wheeling, Va., 1860. 123 tons. The Memphis *Bulletin* reports, Mar. 18, 1864, "The ALAMO arrived from Fort Smith on the 15th inst. General Kimball and staff came down on her." Dismantled in 1867.

0101 ALASKA

Stw p wh b. Cincinnati, Oh., 1867. 670 tons. Owned by Cincinnati & New Orleans Packet Co., Capt. W.G. Voris, master, often alternating with Capt. Frank J. Oakes. Made trips to St. Louis, as well as to New Orleans, and in mid-April 1869 ran a Pittsburgh-St. Louis trip. Capt. Voris announced that he was taking her to Pittsburgh "on a pleasure trip, the price of freight no object." The Cincinnati *Gazette* commented: "She will create a sensation in Pittsburgh—it is not often that the people who inhabit the Smoky City have an opportunity to look at a sternwheel boat that will carry 1,000 tons, and short enough and narrow enough to pass through the canal at Louisville." A dispatch from Memphis dated Nov. 22, 1873, said the *ALASKA* downbound from Cincinnati, heavily laden and with a barge in tow, struck an obstruction Friday evening [21st] ten miles below Point Pleasant. "She lies evenly with eight feet of water over the main deck, and the wreck boat *T.F. ECKERT* has gone to her." The accident proved fatal.

0102 ALBANY

Stw p wh b. Ottawa, Minn., 1860. 42 tons. Originally operated on the Minnesota River, then the Chippewa, and for several seasons on the Wisconsin. Then did some rafting, running half-rafts only. She "dropped out of view" for a year or so, and then appeared as a daily packet Clinton-Davenport, Capt. H.A. Barr, in 1882. Dismantled that year.

0103 ALBANY

Stw p wh b. Burnside, Ky., on the Cumberland River, 1901. 120 x 21 x 2.5. Engines 15½'s- 5 ft. Two boilers. Originally ran packet service on the upper Cumberland, owned by the Burnside Packet Co. In 1908 she had a new set of boilers (3) installed. Rebuilt at Madison, Ind., 1912. Spent most of her career as a towboat. Documented at St. Louis, 1918.

0104 ALBATROSS

SW tr sh b. Dubuque, Iowa, 1907. 308 x 53.8 x 7.6. Overall width 90 ft. Engines 26's- 10 ft. Four boilers (two on each side) 72″ by 18 ft. Owned by Louisiana & Mississippi Valley Transfer Co., and operated at Vicksburg. Built by Dubuque Boat & Boiler Co. Could load 16 railroad cars. When new she came down from Dubuque and had to moor at Montrose awaiting a rise in the Mississippi to descend the rapids at Keokuk. An unexpected summer rise materialized, and the fire bells in Keokuk were rung so the natives could flock to the river and see the big boat run the bridge. In winter of 1920–1921 she was taken out on the U.S. drydocks at Keokuk and the hull enlarged to become 365.0 long. The work was done by the Ripley Boat Co., Alton, Ill. She departed from Keokuk in February 1921, one of the few boats ever to make the run to St. Louis that time of year. About 1937 she was sold to Streckfus Steamers, Inc., St. Louis, and was brought up from the lower Mississippi on her own power. Over the next several years she was converted into an excursion boat named *ADMIRAL* (see).

0105 ALBEMARLE

Stw p wh b. Wheeling, Va., 1855. 186 tons. Ran local trades on Ohio River mostly. In 1855, Capt. J.C. Jelly, master; J.C. Battelle, clerk. Ran Wheeling-Parkersburg spring 1858. Dismantled 1862.

0106 ALBERT

Stw f wh b. Dravosburg, Pa., 1914. 104.3 x 38 x 3.7. First owned by Albert C. Polley, Wheeling. Ownership changed April 1915 to 43rd Street Ferry, Wheeling. Sold January 1916 to Wellsburg (W. Va.) Brilliant (Ohio) Bridge & Ferry Co. Operated Wellsburg-Brilliant until sold June 1923 to John F. Klein. He took her to Cairo, rebuilt her, and renamed her *FLORIDA* (see).

0107 ALBERT PEARCE

SW p wh b. Brownsville, Pa., 1863. 577.61 tons. Built for St. Louis-New Orleans trade. The St. Louis *Democrat* speculated in 1867 that the *PEARCE* was the first boat to take cargo through from St. Louis to New Orleans after the Civil War blockade was broken, this in July 1863, Capt. D.N. Greenleaf, master. Burned at Lake Providence, La., May 19, 1867.

0108 ALBERTA

Stw p wh b. Jeffersonville, Ind., by Howard, 1876. 116 x 25 x 3.5. 107 tons. Built for A.B. Smith and operated in White River.

0109 ALBERTA

Stw p wh b. Jeffersonville, Ind., by Howard, 1880. 150 x 18.5 x 3.5. Arkansas and White rivers. Inspected at Memphis in 1882.

0110 ALBERTA NO. 3

Stw p wh b. Jeffersonville, Ind., by Howard, 1884. 145 x 28 x 3.6. Built for A.B. Smith, and went to White River. Registered at Memphis in 1886.

0111 ALBERTINE

SW p wh b. Louisville, Ky., 1855. 160 tons. Lost in ice at Covington, Ky., Feb. 24, 1856.

0112 ALCEDO

Prop ex wh b. Pittsburgh, Pa., 1895. 40 x 7 x 1.5. Single prop. Pipe boiler. Owned by R.C. Price and brother, based in the Allegheny River at Sixth Street. Chartered out for all-day excursions at $20 a day. Ollie Shepler fired her. Later owned by Beck and Ganoe, Fayette County, Pa. Cut down by ice at New Geneva on Monongahela River 11:00 P.M., Jan. 22, 1904. Went off with the ice.

0113 ALCO

Stw f wh b. Athalia, Oh., 1924. 64.7 x 17 x 8. Parts from dismantled ferry *WHISPER* used in construction. Owned by Beckett Bros., and ferried at Athalia, Oh. Listed in 1929.

0114 ALDA

Stw p wh b. Boonville, Mo., 1891. 121 x 21.2 x 4. Engines 10"- 5 ft. One boiler. Used on Missouri River several years. Was in the Yazoo City and Sunflower River trade, May 1902, Capt. W.W. Pugh. Docked at Madison, Ind., fall 1904, then went Memphis-Fulton trade briefly.

0115 ALDEBARAN

Stw US wh b. Wabasha, Minn., 1924. 132 x 26 x 4. Engines 12's- 6 ft. Built by William J. Peters of Wabasha. She became a U.S. survey boat on the lower Mississippi in October 1925. Capt. Henry K. Whitehead, master, Olyn E. Phillips, chief engineer, Key Woods, survey-man. Sold at public sale, Memphis, December 1934, bought by Capt. Rush Burnside. Renamed *RUSH KRODELL* and used for towing.

0116 ALECK SCOTT

SW p wh b. Louisville, Ky., and completed at St. Louis, 1848. 296 x 44. Engines 25's- 10 ft. Six boilers. Ran St. Louis-New Orleans, Capt. John C. Swon. Later in the "Railroad Line," commanded by Capt. Switzer, and at the outbreak of the war by Capt. Robert A. Reilly. Capt. Horace Bixby was pilot on the *SCOTT* and had with him the embryo celebrity Mark Twain. When Maj. Gen. Henry W. Halleck, Western Dept., sent Brig. Gen. U.S. Grant with 17,000 troops on transports to Fort Henry in February 1862 the *ALECK SCOTT* was one of the fleet which ascended the Tennessee. A photograph of her at Cairo with troops aboard appeared in the December 1975 issue of *S&D Reflector,* discovered by Lloyd Ostendorf. The USQMC acquired her May 18, 1862, renamed her *FORT HENRY*. Later that year she was converted into a gunboat, renamed *LAFAYETTE* (see).

0117 ALEONIA

SW p wh b. West Elizabeth, Pa., 1851. Three boilers. 286 tons. Owned principally by Jackman T. Stockdale (5/16), shared by three other Pittsburgh men, and three from Georgetown, Pa. Dismantled in 1858.

0118 ALERT

Stw p wh b. Belle Vernon, Pa., 1846. 92 tons. Snagged on Arkansas River in 1847.

0119 ALERT

Stw p wh b. Paducah, Ky., 1866. 123.14 tons. Ran on the upper Tennessee. Dismantled in 1871. Parts used building *R.C. JACKSON* (see).

0120 ALERT NO. 2

Stw p wh b. Brownsville, Pa., 1848. 94 tons. Ran Cincinnati-Arkansas River, Capt. Gregg. Upbound at Golconda, Ill., Nov. 24, 1849, in collision with *JAMES MILLINGAR* and was sunk and lost.

0121 ALEX KENDALL

Stw p wh b. New Albany, Ind., 1874. Built for Cumberland River by Capt. Tim Armstrong and others. The Evansville *Courier* reported Sept. 30, 1876, that the *KENDALL* was being "elongated" at the local docks there, cut apart amidship, and her stern section set aft 30 feet. The Pittsburgh *Gazette* on June 14, 1878, reported her out on the Missouri Docks being lengthened 45 feet, to make her 185 ft. long. She was given a full cabin at the Keokuk Northern yard. The original builders sold her to Ohio River people, and later she wound up in the St. Louis-Calhoun County apple trade. Capt. Tim Armstrong and his partners later built the *H.K. BEDFORD* (see).

ALEX. MAJORS

See *A. MAJORS*.

0122 ALEX MCGREGOR

SW f wh b. Cincinnati, Oh., 1859. 142.80 tons. Upper Mississippi ferry. Dismantled in 1884.

0123 ALEX MITCHELL

SW p wh b. Paducah, Ky. (hull), and completed at La Crosse, Wis., 1870. 241 x 37.5 x 5.5. Engines, 20's- 7 ft. Four boilers. Belonged to the N.W. Union Line and in Keokuk Northern Line. Arrived at Pittsburgh Mar. 12, 1871, with a cargo of iron ore, Capt. Lon Bryson, and then loaded out direct for St. Paul. Her upper Ohio pilots were James Rowley (Sr.) and James Hughes. Named for the president of the Milwaukee & St. Paul RR, with which her owners had prorating arrangements at Prairie du Chien and at La Crosse. She is reported to have run New Orleans-Shreveport, Capt. Charles Boardman, on several occasions. Dismantled at La Crosse in 1881. Cabin and machinery went to the *GEM CITY* (second).

0124 ALEX PERRY

Stw p wh b. Jeffersonville, Ind., by Howard, 1891. 149.9 x 18.5 x 3.5. Engines, 10's- 3½ ft. Two boilers. Built for Capt. Tom C. Ryman for trades out of Nashville, and was named for a stock merchant of that city. Capt. James S. Tyner was master. She was in the Evansville-Nashville trade on Apr. 18, 1896, when lost. Moored at the Evansville wharfboat, a high wind was blowing. The wharfboat caught fire, also burned the *PERRY* and *W.L. NORTON*. The *JOE FOWLER* was just landing at the time but was backed away undamaged.

0125 ALEX. SCOTT

SW p wh b. Jeffersonville, Ind., 1842. 266 x 34 x 8. Overall width 69 ft. Engines 25's- 10 ft. Six boilers. Paddlewheels 30 ft. dia. with 15 ft. buckets, 28" dip. Capt. John C. Swon was principal owner and master. Ran in St. Louis-New Orleans trade. In 1847 sold to Capt. Edward T. Sturgeon and others who ran her Louisville-New Orleans. Clerks in 1849 were Orlando L. Smith and Thomas Shearer. Replaced by the *ECLIPSE* in 1852 (see). Also see *ALECK SCOTT*.

0126 ALEX YOST

Originally *J.C. HOPKINS NO. 2* b. Catlettsburg, Ky., 1895, for Big Sandy River (see). She sank and was lost in January 1899.

0127 ALEXANDER HAMILTON

SW p wh b. Cincinnati, Oh., 1847. 212 tons. Ran Galena-St. Paul, Capt. W.H. Hooper, 1848. Made trips up the Missouri. Burned at St. Louis in the wharf fire which consumed 23 steamboats, May 17, 1849.

0128 ALEXANDRIA

SW p wh b. Plaquemine, La., 1862. 89.6 x 15.2 x 5.1. Engines 10's- 3½ ft. Went to Confederate service when war broke out, renamed *SAINT MARY*. Captured in 1863 by U.S. forces and used on patrol duty. Sold at public sale in 1865 and again renamed *ALEXANDRIA* for Red River. Sank and lost on the Amite River, La., Oct. 5, 1867.

0129 ALEXANDRIA

Stw p wh b. Madison, Ind., 1877 for Capt. George W. Rea for Red River out of New Orleans. Her machinery later was used on the *HALLETTE* (see).

0130 ALEXIS DUMESTRE

Stw f wh b. New Orleans, La., 1881. 120.3 x 35.8 x 5.4. A recess-wheel ferry used at Canal Street, New Orleans, later at Jackson Avenue. One stack. Still documented 1896.

0131 ALF. STEVENS

Stw p wh b. Portsmouth, Oh., 1874. 156.5 x 26 x 7. Apparently a freight boat. There is an item in the Pittsburgh *Gazette* dated Jan. 7, 1876, saying that she has proved such a great success that Capt. J.W. Pharr of Dyersburg, Tenn., has concluded to build a new boat like her. Sank on the dam at the head of the Louisville Falls, April 19, 1877 and charges were made that the *DICK FULTON NO. 3* had caused the accident, but were not sustained. She was raised. Registered at Memphis 1886.

0132 ALFRED D. OWEN

Stw f wh b. Mount Vernon, Ind., 1896. 76 x 20 x 3. She was the regular ferry at Mount Vernon, still there in 1903.

0133 ALFRED G. ROSS

Stw p wh b. Fowl River, Ala., 1858. 126 tons. Advertised at Mobile in 1859 operating to Bladen and Cullum Springs, also Demopolis and Finche's Ferry, Capt. T.M. Tindel. She was snagged and lost at Demopolis on Sept. 27, 1860.

0134 ALFRED RIBEYRE

Stw f wh b. New Harmony, Ind., 1925. 64.2 x 18 x 3.2. Owned by Clarence B. Hale of New Harmony and ferried across the Wabash River. Still listed in 1929.

0135 ALFRED ROBB

Stw p wh b. Pittsburgh, Pa., 1860. 114 x 20 x 4. Engines 16's- 5 ft. Three boilers. She was in Confederate service when captured by U.S. forces on gunboat *TYLER* at Florence, Ala., Apr. 19, 1862. Used by the U.S. as a tinclad briefly renamed *LADY FOOTE*. Was with Porter on Red River, 1864. Sold at Mound City, Ill. to H.A. Smith, Aug. 16, 1865. Was renamed *ROBB* on Sept. 9, 1865. Removed from documentation in 1873.

0136 ALFRED T. LACY

SW p wh b. Cape Girardeau, Mo., 1857. 269 x 41.5 x 9. Engines 25's- 9 ft. Five boilers. She was one of the "Railroad Line" between St. Louis and New Orleans, Capt. George Taylor. When Sam Clemens decided to learn the river he first cubbed aboard this boat. She burned at Island 16, Mississippi River, Apr. 26, 1860, at 10:00 P.M. Captain Taylor was in charge, and Capt. A.T. Lacy's daughter was a victim of the blaze in which sixteen lives were lost. The *MAGNOLIA* came to the scene and assisted in rescue.

0137 ALGERINE

SW p wh b. Cincinnati, Oh., 1856. 173 tons. She was reported out of service in 1858. A boat of this name was in the New Orleans and Lower Coast trade, twice weekly, Capt. W. Scanlan, and with E. Maura and N. Barrios, clerks, in 1865.

0138 ALGIERS

Stw f sh b. Jeffersonville, Ind., by Howard, 1925. A catamaran ferry, 144 x 55 x 7.7 with overall width 67 ft. Engines 18's- 6 ft. Two boilers. Allowed 800 passengers and 40 cars. Machinery built by Iowa Machine Works. Sold to Florida in 1958. She was owned at New Orleans by the Algiers Public Service Co. and was teamed up with the *NEW ORLEANS* (see).

0139 ALGOMA

SW p wh b. Cincinnati, Oh., 1846. 209 tons. Ran on Missouri River. In fall of 1848 was in St. Louis-New Orleans trade. Burned at St. Louis, May 28, 1849.

0140 ALHAMBRA

SW p wh b. Cincinnati, Oh., 1845. 290 tons. Running Louisville-New Orleans, 1848. Snagged and lost at Commerce, Mo., January 1851.

0141 ALHAMBRA

Stw p wh b. McKeesport, Pa., 1854. 187 tons. Owned 1856 by Galena, Dunleith & Minnesota Packet Co., Capt. W.H. Gabbart. Ran to St. Paul. In 1860 described by a passenger as "old and bad at the best." Capt. William Faucette, last skipper. Burned and lost at Commerce, Mo., 1863.

0142 ALICE

SW p wh b. Elizabeth, Pa., 1848. 232 tons. Went to the Missouri River. Burned in the great steamboat fire at St. Louis, May 17, 1849.

0143 ALICE

SW p wh b. Cincinnati, Oh., 1852. 130 tons. Went to New Orleans. Off the record 1854.

0144 ALICE

Stw p wh b. California, Pa., 1853. 72 tons. 116 x 21 x 3.2. First master, Capt. W.E. Farris who owned 9/10. Had one boiler. Ran on the Muskingum briefly. At St. Paul in 1854 and off the record by 1858.

0145 ALICE

Stw p wh b. Wellsville, Oh., 1858. 76 tons. First home port was Galveston, Tex. Went to Confederate service 1861.

0146 ALICE

Stw p wh b. Brownsville, Pa., 1864. 234 tons. Built for Capt. S.B. French. "She is certainly a nice looking craft," said the Pittsburgh *Commercial,* on Aug. 4, 1864. She was sold to Capt. William B. Donaldson in 1866, who dismantled her, using parts in building the *QUICKSTEP* (see).

0147 ALICE

Ferry wh b. Waverly, Mo., 1874. 27.78 tons. Probably used at Waverly. Registered at St. Louis, 1876.

0148 ALICE

SW p wh Capt. Joseph Kinney owned *ALICE* on the Missouri River in early 1870s, named for his younger daughter. Sunk by a snag near Frankfort, Mo., Sept. 12, 1874, raised. A side-wheeler named *ALICE* established the first government lights on the Ohio and many on the Mississippi. The Ohio River lights were first placed by *ALICE* in 1875, and after that the work was done by *LILY* (see). The *ALICE* serviced lights on the Missouri to Kansas City in 1876, and was working the Mississippi as well. She departed St. Louis Feb. 25, 1878, Capt. William Crapster, servicing lights to New Orleans. In the spring of 1878 she broke 70 or 80 timbers on a snag up the Missouri and was returned to St. Louis for docking.

0149 ALICE

Stw p wh Originally named *MARK TWAIN* b. Covington, Ky., 1877 (see). Rebuilt 1886 and renamed *ALICE,* registered at Memphis. Still on the register at Memphis 1892.

0150 ALICE

Stw p wh b. Brownsville, Pa., at the H.B. Cook Bros., yard and completed at Pittsburgh, 1878. 250 x 38 x 5. Engines 17's- 5½ ft. Four boilers. Capacity 1,200 tons. Owned in part by Capt. Charles F. Adams, master. Alex Carlisle, clerk. Her first trip was Pittsburgh-New Orleans, departing Pittsburgh on Jan. 12, 1878. Second was Pittsburgh-St. Louis. On May 18, 1878, she was advertised at Pittsburgh to St. Paul. After that she ran usually Pittsburgh-St. Louis. Captain Adams had owned in and operated the towboat *WHALE* just prior and was something of a character. The *ALICE,* so goes the story, was named for his sweetheart. On Apr. 18, 1880, he went uptown in Louisville, met friends, and imbibed Kentucky bourbon. Conveyed back to the boat, he rang the roof bell, ordered lines cast off, and in another moment the boat was sunk on the Falls due to lack of sufficient steam to run her engines. Lee Patterson was the pilot on watch. She was successfully raised, sold to other owners, and renamed *BRIGHT LIGHT* (see).

0151 ALICE

Stw f wh b. Rodney, Miss., 1881. 24.30 tons. Apparently a ferry at Rodney. She was inspected there in 1882.

0152 ALICE B. MILLER

Stw p wh Originally *FRANK B. HAYNE* b. Jeffersonville, Ind., 1904. Renamed in 1908 when bought by C.J. Miller, Vicksburg, who ran her in Yazoo and Sunflower River trade. Burned on Mar. 26, 1915, at Vicksburg.

0153 ALICE BELL

Stw p wh b. Pittsburgh, Pa., 1878. 50 x 10.5 x 2.7. She may have been a towboat; no information available. Still registered at Pittsburgh in 1896.

0154 ALICE BLAIR

Stw p wh b. Osceola, Mo., 1890. 130 x 25 x 4. Engines 10's-4 ft. One boiler. Owned by R.D. Blair. Capt. Henry M. Dodds, master. Osceola, Mo., is on the upper Osage River. She was snagged at Earl Point, Mo. (about 100 miles above St. Louis), on Oct. 13, 1890. She was raised and sold to T.L. Smith, Sr., who took her to Texas and ran her on the Brazos River between East Columbia and Velasco, connecting with the Columbia Top RR at East Columbia for Houston. Freeport, Tex., today is across the Brazos from Velasco. Her competitor was the *HIAWATHA* (see). Registered out of Galveston 1892–1896, maybe longer. She sank at Columbia soon after her initial arrival on the Brazos, but was soon raised.

0155 ALICE DEAN

SW p wh b. Cincinnati, Oh., 1863. 411 tons. Ran Cincinnati-Memphis, Capt. James H. Pepper. When Gen. John Hunt Morgan and his cavalry, often referred to as Morgan's Raiders, crossed the Ohio River from Kentucky into Indiana on July 8, 1863, they appropriated a small packet named *JOHN T. McCOMBS* (see) and used her as a decoy to hail down and capture the *ALICE DEAN*. They used the *DEAN* as a ferry, and afterwards burned her. The machinery was salvaged in the fall of 1863 and auctioned off to the C.T. Dumont Co. for $4,500. The Morgan crossing was at Brandenburg, Ky., and the *DEAN* was burned along the Indiana shore between Morvin's Landing and Mauckport. Associated with this affair was "Sherman's Ride," in which a self-appointed Paul Revere, Jacob Sherman, mounted a horse and galloped upriver to head off the downbound *GRAY EAGLE* (see) to prevent her from falling into the hands of Morgan. He succeeded. The grateful owners of the *GRAY EAGLE* presented a bell to the citizens of Mauckport in appreciation, and it still is there. This story is detailed in the June 1976 issue of *S&D Reflector*, page 13, with photographs of the bell.

0156 ALICE DEAN

SW p wh b. Cincinnati, Oh., 1864. 394 tons. Replaced the first of the name (see). Ran Cincinnati-Memphis, and made her maiden trip from Cincinnati on Feb. 25, 1864, Capt. James H. Pepper. "Commodore" Thompson Dean was aboard for the occasion, as well as other noteworthy gentlemen. On Mar. 25, 1864, she hit the bank ten miles below Cincinnati on a downbound trip and sank with her stern in 12 feet of water. She was on her third trip. The *JENNIE HUBBS* and *LADY PIKE* took off her freight, and the *KATE CASSEL* her passengers. Was successfully raised. In March 1865 Capt. Charles A. Dravo went master. In late December 1865 she hit the suspension bridge at Cincinnati and tore down both stacks. In December 1869 about 40 miles above Memphis she hit a log and would have sunk save for a cargo of cotton which buoyed her up until the *THOMPSON DEAN* came along to assist. In 1866 Capt. C. Dan Conway, master, with William Dunlop, clerk. Rounding out from Cincinnati on Apr. 26, 1870, there was a mistake in signals between pilot and engineer. She hit the Covington pier of the suspension bridge and again knocked down both stacks. The *ROBERT BURNS* took her passengers to Memphis. She was retired in 1872. Machinery went to the *THOMAS SHERLOCK* (see) and the hull was used as a wharfboat at Lake Providence, La., with the upper works still intact until a gale blew off the cabin during August 1875.

0157 ALICE EDNA

Stw pl sh b. St. Louis, Mo., 1898. 120 x 18 x 4.2. Engines 10's- 4 ft. Two boilers. A very fine pleasure sternwheeler owned by August A. Busch of the brewery firm Anheuser-Busch. Sold in 1902 to Russell Gardner, who enlarged her and changed the name to *ANNIE RUSSELL* (see). Her photograph graced the cover of the March 1972 issue of *S&D Reflector*.

0158 ALICE GREY

SW p wh b. Louisville, Ky., 1841. 267 tons. Ran Louisville-New Orleans, Capt. Carter. Dismantled in 1847. Also spelled Alice Gray.

0159 ALICE LE BLANC

Stw p wh Originally named *LACKAWANNA*. b. at Donaldsonville, La., 1884 (see). Renamed when fairly new. Advertised between New Orleans and Bayou LaFourche, Capt. F. Le Blanc, three trips a week, 1890. Also same in May 1892, with *ST. JOHN* as partner. Registered at Brashear, La., 1896.

0160 ALICE M

SW p wh b. New Albany, Ind., 1865. 185 tons. Apparently was sent to Mobile. Stranded and lost at Galveston, Tex., Oct. 3, 1867.

0161 ALICE V

SW p wh Confliction as to the origin of this packet. The *Lytle-Holdcamper List* says she originally was the *WILLIAM M. MORRISON* b. Cincinnati, 1856. This seems unlikely inasmuch as the *MORRISON* was in Confederate service, and several sources report her destroyed by fire. E.W. Gould says she was at New Orleans when the city surrendered and the Confederates purposely burned her. So much for the *MORRISON*. A more likely story is that she descends from the *GREAT WESTERN* b. Cincinnati, 1857. She was in the Cincinnati-New Orleans trade after the war as *ALICE V*, and in March 1867 Capt. Henry U. Hart, Cincinnati, bought three-fourth interest and continued her there. She arrived at Pittsburgh on Apr. 16, 1868, with a big trip, mainly iron ore, at which time the Pittsburgh *Gazette* remarked that she was the former *GREAT WESTERN*, which ran Cincinnati-New Orleans before the war. She was sold at a U.S. marshal sale at Madison, Ind., February 1869. The machinery went to the *ROBT. MITCHELL* in 1871 (see). For particulars of build see *GREAT WESTERN*. The hull in all probability became an ice barge owned by Huse on the Illinois River. He lost his *ALICE V* barge with 1,100 tons of ice aboard in March 1875.

0162 ALICE VIVIAN

SW p wh b. New Albany, Ind., 1856. 215 x 42 x 7.5. Engines 26's- 9 ft. Six boilers. She was in the Memphis & New Orleans Packet Line in 1859, Capt. Ables, master. Her partners in the line were *CAPITOL, JOHN SIMONDS*, and *MESSENGER*. Was at Mobile, Ala., at the outbreak of the war. In the period 1861–1864 she made two trips to Charleston, S.C., and two trips to Havana, Cuba, a Confederate blockade runner carrying cotton. During this period her name was changed to *SOUTH*. She was captured at sea by the USS *DeSOTO*, taken to New Orleans and used as a U.S. transport on Red River. For her later history see *SOUTH*. Also see *JAMES BATTLE* for another sea-going steamboat story.

0163 ALICE W. GLAZE

Stw p wh b. Jeffersonville, Ind., by Howard, 1853. 140 x 32 x 7. Built for A. Johnson, Attakapas, La. Ran New Orleans-Red River; also New Orleans and Upper Bends. Burned Mar. 3, 1857, above Bayou Sara, La.

0164 ALIDA

Stw p wh b. Belle Vernon, Pa., 1853. 94 tons. Showed up on Red River on occasion. In collision at Smithland, Ky., with the *FASHION* and lost June 9, 1857.

0165 ALIDA

SW p wh b. New Albany, Ind., 1853. 99 tons. Out of documentation in 1859.

0166 ALINE

Stw p wh b. Jeffersonville, Ind., by Howard, 1858. 125 x 30 x 6. Built for Capt. O. Hinckley, Red River, La. In 1859 running between New Orleans and Opelousas, Capt. G.E. Louaillier, master, pinch-hitting for the *ANNA PERRET*. Owners lived at Franklin, La. Went to Confederate service in 1861.

0167 ALIQUIPPA

SW p wh b. Pittsburgh, Pa., 1844. 175 x 23.5 x 5.5. Advertised in the Wheeling *Daily News* as a regular Pittsburgh-Cincinnati packet commencing Feb. 27, 1845, Capt. Smith. She was owned by the Estate of John Freeman, deceased, Robert Hannah, and Alpheus Martin. She had run Pittsburgh-St. Louis in 1844 and her first trip collided south of St. Louis with the *WESTON* (see). Out of service in 1847 and her hull was acquired by William Bohlen for carrying ice to Memphis.

0168 ALL OAK

SW f wh b. Chrisler's Landing, Pa., 1851. 56 tons. No clue as to where she ferried. Out of service in 1859.

0169 ALLEGHANY NO. 3

SW f wh b. Pittsburgh, Pa., 1865. 74 tons. Operated Bellaire-Benwood in early 1870s with partner ferry *HERE I AM* (see). Out of service by 1880.

0170 ALLEGHANY

Ocean going steamer "propelled by a submerged horizontal wheel." b. Pittsburgh 1847 and taken to Memphis where she was fitted out by a Capt. Hunter. She sailed from Memphis June 4, 1847, under Lieut. Cmdr. Hunter for New Orleans. She was in the Indian Ocean later, built of iron, and carried 44 guns, a steam frigate. Then the largest iron vessel built in the U.S. Mentioned in Gould's *History of River Navigation*, page 356.

0171 ALLEGHENY

SW p wh b. Pittsburgh, Pa., 1841. 160 x 23 x 5.4. 188 49/95 tons. Owned by Capt. Thomas Carmac (master), Robert Beer, Wm. Holmes & Co., Lewis Hutchison & Co., Walingford & Taylor, and Forsythe & Co., all of Pittsburgh. Advertised Cincinnati-New Orleans, Capt. Carmac, January 1842. Capt. William Dean became part owner and master in 1942, Richard C. Gray as clerk. Entered Pittsburgh-Cincinnati trade 1842 along with *LEHIGH* (see). In later years Dean claimed her to be the pioneer in the P&C trade. Capt. R.C. Gray bought Dean out 1846. She was on the Illinois River May 1845 bound from St. Louis to Hennepin. Dismantled 1846.

0172 ALLEGHENY

SW p wh b. Shousetown, Pa., 1852. 278 x 30 x 6. Five boilers. 520 tons. Owned by R.S. Hayes 1/4, David Holmes 1/8, George Black 1/8, Wm. Bingham 1/8, Thomas S. Clarke 1/8, William Thaw 1/8, William Frampton 1/8, all of Pittsburgh (taken from Customs Mar. 15, 1853). Entered Pittsburgh-Cincinnati trade Mar. 16, 1852, Capt. C.W. Batchelor, master, and at that time, also heavy stockholder. Stephen C. Foster was a downbound passenger on this first trip. Capt. Batchelor took her to Louisville and ran a "speed trip" to Cincinnati on May 27, 1852; came to Madison in 3 hr. 20 min., and to Cincinnati in 10 hr. 5 min., taking the horns from the *TELEGRAPH NO. 2*. In the fall of 1852 Pittsburgh and Cincinnati were connected by railroad, at which time Capt. Batchelor sold his interest to Robert S. Hayes, Thomas S. Clarke, and William Thaw. Capt. Geo. B. McLean, who had been clerk, took command. Ran Cincinnati to Maysville 5 hr. 15 min. on Mar. 25, 1853, racing the *THOS. SWANN* (see). Capt. James O'Neil, later with the

Anchor Line and U.S. Supervising Inspector at St. Louis, was pilot on her. Also Capt. Evan Morgan. During her last P&C season, 1855, commanded by Capt. J.W. Cooke. On Dec. 28, 1855, a dispatch from Wheeling noted the *ALLEGHENY* had passed up "with $1,100,000 in coin and bullion in charge of W. Reynolds of Adams Express Co., destined to Philadelphia." Last ran in the St. Louis-New Orleans trade where, in May 1857 she was advertised "as a passenger carrier exclusively," Capt. Richard Phillips. Ice appeared in the Mississippi very early in 1857. In November the *ALLEGHENY* was sunk by ice below Jefferson Barracks at Carroll Island.

0173 ALLEGHENY BELLE

Stw p wh b. Elizabeth, Pa. by Samuel Walker, 1842. Machinery by Stackhouse & Nelson, Pittsburgh. Capt. John Hanna, master and owner. Her first trip was Pittsburgh to Cincinnati and return, after which she entered the Pittsburgh-Franklin-Oil City trade on the Allegheny River and stayed eight years. Collided with *IDA* at Tarentum on Nov. 24, 1843, causing loss of *IDA*. Capt. William Hanna was in command in 1848. Dismantled.

0174 ALLEGHENY BELLE NO. 2

Stw p wh b. Brownsville, Pa., 1850. Some larger than the first one, three boilers. She was commanded by Capt. William Hanna. Ran in the Pittsburgh-Franklin-Oil City trade. There was no railroad at the time. A "great railroad convention" was held Feb. 22, 1851, at Rimerton, and the delegates went up on the ALLEGHENY BELLE NO. 2 but could not get under the aqueduct at Freeport. Dismantled 1860.

0175 ALLEGHENY BELLE NO. 3

Stw p wh b. Brownsville, Pa., 1850. This was the largest of the flock, three boilers. Owned by the Hanna brothers, Capt. John Hanna, master. Two trips a week during the navigation season Pittsburgh-Franklin, and often went up to Warren, Pa. During off seasons she ran on the Ohio. The Marietta *Intelligencer* in 1851 reported: "Henry Clay passed up Tuesday A.M., Nov. 11 on the *ALLEGHENY BELLE.*" Sold in April 1859 to Capt. C.W. Batchelor acting as agent for the Louisiana Tehauntepec Co., and she was taken across the Gulf of Mexico and used on the Coatzacholas River. She arrived at Minatitlan on May 18, 1859, with Capt. Andrew W. McKee in charge. In the fall of 1859 Capt. McKee came back to Pittsburgh and had a similar boat built for the Brazos and Trinity rivers in Texas (see *LUCY GWIN*).

0176 ALLEGHENY BELLE NO. 4

Stw p wh b. Pittsburgh, Pa., 1859. 143 tons. Engines 16's-6 ft. Capt. William Hanna owned 3/8, and Capt. John Hanna owned the rest. This boat arrived on the scene in time for the Allegheny River oil excitement and transported much barreled oil. She could bring down 500 to 600 barrels. Capt. William Hanna ran her, and Capt. John erected and ran an oil warehouse at Oil City until his death on Mar. 20, 1863. At that time he was the dean of Allegheny boatmen, having started on the *PULASKI* (see) in 1837. The Hanna brothers carried U.S. Mail on these boats. On Apr. 16, 1863, the *NO. 4* was sold to Capt. William J. Kountz, D.S.H. Gilmore, and others for $21,000 and entered in the Pittsburgh-Wheeling trade, Capt. George D. Moore, master. She was taken over by the U.S. for war service but was returned from Cincinnati deemed too small. Sold to Capt. John K. Booth who converted her into a towboat and operated Parkersburg-Cincinnati, Capt. Nels Davis, master. Finally hit a barge and sank at Portland Bar, below Louisville, May 23, 1875. The machinery was recovered and used on the packet *CALUMET* (see).

0177 ALLEGHENY CLIPPER

Stw p wh b. Shousetown, Pa., 1848. 100 tons. Ran on the Allegheny River during the navigation seasons, Capt. William Watterson. Ran on the Ohio in off seasons, and made trips on the Muskingum, Capt. G.W. Graham. In September 1850 sold to Capt. John McLure, John Reed and J.H. Roberts of Wheeling, and was in the Wheeling-Parkersburg trade, Capt. William George. Snagged and lost Dec. 2, 1854, location undetermined.

0178 ALLEGHENY MAIL

Stw p wh b. Pittsburgh, Pa., 1844. 77 tons. Although primarily employed on the Allegheny River she made a special excursion from Pittsburgh to Wheeling on Sept. 13, 1844, taking 250 delegates to a Whig convention. A cannon on the forecastle misfired and two youths were injured. A landing was made at Wellsville, Oh. and the two injured were placed in the hands of Benjamin Way and his kind lady at the Union Hotel there. Dr. J.F. Patterson treated them with no charge. A testimonial of appreciation later appeared in the Wheeling *Daily Times,* sponsored by the delegates. Capt. John Goff was the boat's master and part owner. In August 1845 was at the Great Western Iron Works on the Allegheny at Brady's Bend loading iron for Cincinnati. Sold Feb. 9, 1846, to Cumberland River and ran Smithland-Nashville. Out of service in 1853.

0179 ALLEN COLLIER

Stw p. wh b. Cincinnati, Oh., 1860. Ran in the Cincinnati-Kanawha rivers trade, Capt. J.T. Johnson, with Charles Sonstag, clerk. On Sept. 27, 1862, she appeared along with the *BELFAST* at Augusta, Ky., when Morgan's Raiders invaded that town. The two impromptu gunboats retired from the fray when it was learned that Morgan had howitzers. Burned in December 1863.

0180 ALLEN COLLIER

Stw p wh b. Cincinnati, Oh., 1864. 176 tons. Replaced the first of the name. She was taken over by the U.S. at Cincinnati on Dec. 8, 1864, for war service, renamed *COLLIER* (see).

0181 ALLEN GLOVER

SW p wh b. Elizabethtown, Pa., 1847. 241 tons. She was

built for service on the Alabama and Tombigbee rivers. Is mentioned in Carl Carmer's *Stars Fell on Alabama* and identified as having been named for an Alabama plantation owner. Transferred to Red River and was lost in collision with the *P. DALMAU* at or near Alexandria, La., Mar. 20, 1854.

0182 ALLEN J. DUNCAN

Stw p wh b. Jeffersonville, Ind., 1881 as the *CITY OF NASHVILLE* (see). Renamed prior to 1889. Ran in Evansville and Tennessee river trade, Capt. McMechan. While enroute from Waterloo to Evansville in early September 1889, Capt. R.D. Morrow, she sank at Highland, Ky. on the Tennessee and was raised. While attempting a head-on landing near Perryville, Tenn., on the Tennessee, October 1894, she hit the rocky shore with headway. Later she was extricated from the rocks and settled in deep water. The wreck was abandoned.

0183 ALLENA MAY

Stw p wh b. Wheeling, W. Va., 1864. 115 x 20 x 3. 144 tons. She was taken over by the USQMC upon completion at Wheeling and first named *GENERAL MEIGS* (see). Sold to private owners Oct. 12, 1865, and renamed *ALLENA MAY* for daughter of Capt. Jonathan Hamilton, Gallipolis, Oh., part owner and master. Ran short trades on the upper Ohio. She exploded her boilers Sept. 15, 1866, backing out from a landing at the head of Raccoon Island, Ohio River, on the Virginia side. Captain Hamilton was badly injured, two of the crew killed, and others hurt. Was repaired, and in 1868 was in Pittsburgh-Parkersburg trade, Capt. Jacob Flicker. Went to New Orleans, owned there by Samuel Latta, Capt. William Maitland, master. Advertised for sale moored at Algiers, La., in August 1870. A daughter of Capt. Jonathan Hamilton later lived at Shreveport, La., and died there at an advanced age in the 1950s. Dr. Hamilton Harper, also of Shreveport, was grandson of Captain Hamilton.

0184 ALLENE

Prop yacht sh b. Pittsburgh, Pa., 1891. 59.2 x 8.4 x 3. This yacht was owned by the Hostetter family (Hostetter's Bitters) of Pittsburgh who had a two-story log summer home on the left bank below Raccoon Creek, Ohio River. The yacht was sold to Louisville and renamed *GREYHOUND* (see).

0185 ALLIANCE

Stw p wh b. Shousetown, Pa., 1852. 144 x 27.2 x 3.9. 136 tons. Two boilers. Capt. Samuel Dean was master and one-half owner. Ran in tramp trades, principally Pittsburgh-St. Louis and was lost by stranding at Devil Island near Cape Girardeau, Mo., Mar. 17, 1863.

0186 ALLIS GREY

Stw p wh b. Tuscumbia, Mo., 1871. 96 tons. Engines 10's- 3 ft. One boiler. Owned by A.A. Hibbard and others. Exploded at the head of Payne's Island, five miles below Rocheport, Mo., Dec. 16, 1875. One Negro fireman killed.

0187 ALMA

Stw p wh b. Belle Vernon, Pa., 1855. 154 x 40 x 6. This was a tandem high-pressure boat, with two cylinders on each side, same bore and stroke. Four boilers. Ran low water trades on the Ohio River, and also was up the Allegheny. Owned by Capt. George D. Cochran, long a resident of Sewickley, Pa. Dismantled 1861.

0188 ALMA

Stw p wh b. Belle Vernon, Pa., 1855. 311 tons. 220 x 36 x 5. Engines 21's- 7 ft. Three boilers. Built for Missouri River for Charles P. Chouteau, St. Louis. Out of service in 1861.

0189 ALMA

Stw p wh b. Jeffersonville, Ind., by Howard, 1900. 155 x 32 x 4. Engines 12's- 5 ft. Two boilers. The Red River Line acquired her 1901 and ran her New Orleans-Shreveport, Capt. Geo. L. White, master, H.C. Boazman, clerk. She was lost by striking a pier of the Grand Ecore bridge, c. 1904.

0190 ALMA

Stw p wh Originally the *MARY E. STAPLES* b. 1905 (see). Ran on the Alabama and Tombigbee rivers, owned by Atkins Brothers. Later renamed *HENRY BURKE* (see).

0191 ALMA

Stw p wh b. Pt. Pleasant, W. Va., 1907. 95.4 x 17.7 x 2.8. First owned by Albert Monteith three fourths, and M.A. Barrows of Gallipolis, Oh. Did low water packet work and also handled produce barges. Documented 1915 at Evansville, Ind.

0192 ALMA JANE

Stw p wh b. Poplar Bluff, Mo., 1901. 65.7 x 14 x 2.5. Operated out of Pocahontas, Ark., on White River, Capt. A.M. Stroud. Listed in the *Railway Guide* December 1905 owned by Black River Transportation Co., H.D. Williams, pres. and general manager. Running Poplar Bluff-Carola. Others in the Line: *ARRAC* and *HARWELL*.

0193 ALOE

SW p wh b. Gretna, La., 1866. 138.8 x 24. 5 x 5. Owned by Christian Nelson, Sr., with Capt. W.H. King, master, January 1867. Sold April 1867 to Vincent J. Wood of New Orleans, with Capt. M.N. Radovich, master. Snagged and lost at Battleground, La., Jan. 26, 1869.

0194 ALONE

Stw p wh b. Madison, Ind., 1863. 211 tons. Sold to USQMC upon completion, and used during the war. Sold to private owners, Oct. 21, 1865, renamed *GOVERNOR SHARKEY* (see).

0195 ALONE

Stw p wh b. Warrenton, Wis., 1864. 109.9 x 27 x 3.8. Owned at New Orleans, January 1866 by E.H. Skaggs. Sold April 1866 to Louis F. Generes, New Orleans. Sold July 1867 to a New Orleans stock company. Capt. William G.

Henry was master in April 1868. Snagged and lost in Bayou Lafourche, July 5, 1868.

0196 ALONZO C. CHURCH

Recess wheel ferry wh b. Jeffersonville, Ind., by Howard, 1893. 172.3 x 43.3 x 6.5. Arrived at St. Louis in tow of the *H. F. FRISBEE* in May 1893, and engine was placed there. Capt. George Hoffman, master, 1895. Owned by Wiggins Ferry Co. She was single-engine, 28"- 6 ft. stroke. Three boilers. Dismantled in 1914 and hull was used as a wharf-boat by the Belle of the Bends Co.

0197 ALONZO CHILD

SW p wh b. Jeffersonville, Ind., by Howard, 1857. 236 x 38 x 7. Engines 26¼'s- 7½ ft. Six boilers. Built for S.B. Holland. Ran St. Louis-Omaha on the Missouri, Capt. Joe Holland, 1857. On one trip it is said she left Kansas City at sunup, during high water, and was at St. Louis, 400 miles, at sundown, averaging 29 mph. In 1861 owned outright by Capt. David DeHaven, then running in the St. Louis-New Orleans trade. At the outbreak of the war she was taken up Yazoo River by the Confederates to prevent capture. Her engines were removed and hauled overland to the Alabama River for use on the Confederate ram *TENNESSEE*. Acquired by U.S. Navy Sept. 29, 1863, but was not recommissioned.

0198 ALPHA

Stw p wh b. Shousetown, Pa., 1863. 150 x 29.5 x 4.3. 165 tons. Engines 12's- 4 ft. One boiler. Departed Pittsburgh, Capt. James H. Porter, for Nashville, May 1864. Was sold to New Orleans and ran there to Shreveport in 1866, Ammon L. Davis, owner, and Capt. O.W. Davis, master. Capt. Thomas G. Ryman had seen her at Nashville in 1864, went to New Orleans and bought her. Brought her back for the Nashville-Evansville trade. He was master and W.R. Gracey, clerk. This was the first boat in the Ryman Line. Out of service in 1871.

0199 ALPHA

Stw p wh b. Covington, Ky., 1887. 82 x 14.5 x 3.5. Probably towed produce boats. Listed at Cincinnati 1892, and at Wheeling, 1896.

0200 ALPHA

Stw p wh b. Burnside, Ky., 1894. 73.3 x 12 x 2.3. A trading boat. She was up Kanawha River in 1894 to Malden, W. Va., owned by a Mr. Chapman. Listed at Louisville, Ky., 1896.

0201 ALPHONOSE DE ALMARTINE

SW p wh b. St. Louis, Mo., 1848. 536 tons. Ran St. Louis-New Orleans. Burned on the Illinois River opposite Bath, Mar. 23, 1849.

0202 ALPINE

Stw p wh b. Cookstown, Pa., 1842. 39 tons. Very small boat, and a small matter, but some question as to location of Cookstown. Might be Cook's Ferry, Pa. Dismantled 1846.

0203 ALPS

SW p wh b. Pittsburgh, Pa., 1842. 112 tons. Advertised Cincinnati-Pittsburgh, Capt. James Todd, July 15, 1842. Cincinnati-Nashville, Capt. J.M. Scantland, March 1845. Out of service 1845.

0204 ALTAMONT

Stw p wh b. McKeesport, Pa., 1954. 154.7 x 38.4 x 5.4. 248 tons. First home port was at Wheeling. Sank in the mouth of the Muskingum River, Dec. 23, 1856 and was raised in January 1857. Capt. M.L. Virden was connected with her then. Sold for war service to USQMC on Mar. 15, 1864. Sold Apr. 16, 1866, to Moses W. Wetmore, New Orleans. Lost at the mouth of Red River, April 1866.

0205 ALTO

Stw p wh b. Jeffersonville, Ind., 1879, originally named *WILLIAM FAGAN* (see). She was renamed *ALTO* after being rebuilt at Jeffersonville in 1883, Capt. James Hamilton. Operated out of Mobile to Alabama and Tombigbee rivers. Still documented at Mobile in 1896.

0206 ALTON

SW p wh b. Brownsville, Pa., 1847. 344 tons. Ran St. Louis-New Orleans, Capt. John Simons. Henry A. Ealer was pilot. Burned in the Yazoo River, May 7, 1855.

0207 ALTON

SW ex wh b. Jeffersonville, Ind., by Howard, 1906. 241.1 x 38 x 7.3. Engines 24's- 8 ft. made by St. Louis Iron & Machine Co. This boat was the pride of the Eagle Packet Co. of St. Louis and, until his death in 1914, always in command of Commodore Henry Leyhe, uncle of Capts. Henry W. and William H. (Buck) Leyhe. Fast time Eads Bridge to Alton, 1 hr. 44 min. She was designed for the daily trade St. Louis-Alton to replace *SPREAD EAGLE* (see), then slated for dismantling. Commodore Leyhe tried her as an all-time excursion boat, so successful that $20,000 was spent revamping *SPREAD EAGLE*. The *ALTON* ran, except Mondays, to Six-Mile Island on the Illinois River stopping both ways at Alton and Chautauqua. Mondays she ran to Kampsville. Daily evening trips were run at St. Louis. She took part in the "Roosevelt Parade" in October 1907, sponsored by the Lakes to the Gulf Deep Waterways Association. The St. Louis Business Men's Association picked up the tab for entertaining Theodore Roosevelt. He rode the *MISSISSIPPI* (see) and fourteen governors rode the *ALTON*. The Inland Waterways Commission rode the *COL. A. MACKENZIE* (see). The cry was "Fourteen Feet Through the Valley." The affair started at Keokuk on Oct. 1, 1907, and ended at Memphis on the 4th. Joe McCulloch was pilot on the *ALTON*, and was extensively written up in *Everybody's Magazine*, issue of April 1908, the lead article authored by John L. Mathews. The *ALTON* collided with the Alton, Ill., bridge with extensive damage to her port wheelhouse and cabin, July 12, 1909. She was moored at the Duck's Nest, Paducah, Ky., winter of 1917-1918, and was lost in ice there on Jan. 29, 1918.

0208 ALTON

Stw p wh Originally the *GEORGE COWLING* b. 1904 (see). Renamed in 1923 when bought by the Williams brothers of Evansville, Ind. They ran her Louisville-Stephensport, and when the *BAY QUEEN* was crossed out, Paducah-Evansville. She was being taken to Green River in the winter of 1927-1928 when ice cut her seams and she sank in the mouth of Green River. She was replaced in the trade by the *H. N. SHERBURNE,* operated by the McCandless brothers.

0209 ALTONA

SW p wh b. St. Louis, Mo., 1852. 255 x 31 x 6. (27 ft. floor.) Engines 26's- 8 ft. Five boilers. Her paddlewheels were unique, 32 ft. dia. (extreme), 13 ft. buckets, and these buckets were 22", 18", 14" and 10" width, called by rivermen "oral" wheels. Some accounts say she was built at Memphis. The model was designed by Sam Gaty, for whom a steamboat once was named (see). Primus Emerson was master ship carpenter. She was built for Capt. Joseph Brown, St. Louis. She made the fastest upstream run St. Louis to Alton of record, one hour 37 minutes. The *PEORIA* in 1915 did it in 1 hour 59 minutes (see). The St. Louis *Republican* reported her sunk between St. Louis and Alton on Dec. 31, 1853; raised. She made trips to Peoria and one, at least, to Cincinnati. The *Lytle-Holdcamper List* reports her loss in ice at St. Louis, Feb. 26, 1856. A contemporary account states that when the *BADGER STATE* (see) was lost in Chain of Rocks above St. Louis, the accident was caused by her striking the wreck of the old *ALTONA*.

0210 ALTONIAN

Center wheel f wh b. Cincinnati, Oh., 1881. 102 x 28 x 4. Documented at St. Louis 1886-1896, maybe longer.

0211 ALTOONA

Stw p wh b. West Brownsville, Pa., 1853. 140 x 27.5 x 4.7. Three boilers. Owned by David Holmes 3/4 and Capt. Richard C. Gray 1/4. Operated principally Pittsburgh-St. Louis, and made trips up Wabash River to Terre Haute, Capt. Gray. Lost at Montgomery Towhead (presumably at old mouth of White River, Ark.) in 1859.

0212 ALVARADO

SW p wh b. St. Louis, Mo., 1846. 134 tons. Lost in ice at Columbia, Ill., Dec. 10, 1850.

0213 ALVIN

Stw p wh b. Jeffersonville, Ind., 1877. 143 x 29.1 x 7.1. In the New Orleans & Gulf Transportation Co., 1879-1880, Capt. W.T. Scovell, master, John Taylor, clerk. Ran from New Orleans to Port Eads and Pilot Town, along with *ISABEL, MARTHA* and *KITTIE NYE* (all see). Advertised at New Orleans in 1885 "Ho for the Orange Groves and Sugar Plantations" twice weekly to the forts, Capt. J.T. O'Pry, master and Frank E. Scovell, clerk. Still documented at New Orleans in 1896.

0214 ALVIN ADAMS

SW p wh b. McKeesport, Pa. (hull), and completed at Pittsburgh, 1853. 266.5 x 35 x 6.6. Engines 29 ½'s- 9 ft. by John Snowden. Six boilers 42" by 28 ½ ft. by Blair & Co., Pittsburgh. Paddlewheels 11 ½ ft. buckets, 24 arms to the wheel, 30" dip. Cabin by James Milligan, Pittsburgh. Stacks 71" dia. reaching 54 ft. above the roof. 81 ft. from water line. Light load draft 3'8" forward, 3'9" aft. Named for the president of Adams Express Co., who lived in Boston and owned ⅛ interest. Other original stockholders were George W. Cass, Pittsburgh, ¼; E.S. Sandford, Philadelphia, ⅛; S.M. Shoemaker, Baltimore, ⅛; James P. Jack, Cincinnati, 1/40; White Cunningham, Madison, Ind., 1/16; also two stockholders of Wheeling, J.C. Acheson & Co., ¼; and G.W. Norton, 3/40. Her first master was Capt. George W. Norton. She was entered in the Wheeling-Louisville Union Line which, with a fleet of seven boats, offered daily service between terminals, in effect an extension of the B&O Railroad which had lately arrived at Wheeling from the East. She entered service in March 1853, suffered heavy financial loss, and was sold early 1854 to the "Lightning Line," largely owned by the Madison & Indianapolis RR, who entered her in the Cincinnati-Louisville trade along with the *DAVID WHITE* (see). Soon sold to the U.S. Mail Line Co., who ran her Louisville-St. Louis, Capt. Boies. Finally ran St. Louis-New Orleans and was noted for speed. On one occasion she is recorded having been five miles above the *J. M. WHITE* "24 Hour Mark" out of New Orleans in one-day run. Dismantled 1860. Her engines went to the *MAGENTA* (see) 1864. Her first skipper, Capt. George W. Norton, was killed when the *HARRY DEAN* exploded 1868 (see). She is reputed to have made a trip to Nashville on the Cumberland, the largest boat to arrive at the time.

0215 AMANDA

SW p wh b. Louisville, Ky., 1852. 130 x 26 x 5. Ran in Memphis-Hatchie river trade, Lenter, master. In June 1854 was running New Orleans-Mobile, later New Orleans-Aberdeen (Miss.). Wound up in New Orleans-Red River trade. Dismantled 1860.

0216 AMANDA

SW p wh b. Metropolis, Ill. (hull), and completed at St. Louis, 1865. Engines 16's- 5 ft. Three boilers allowed 132 psi. Capt. Edward Dix ran her out of St. Louis. Sold February 1867 to St. Joseph-Omaha trade, Missouri River. Running light from Omaha bound for Sioux City she burned at Peters Landing, Iowa, Nov. 3, 1867, Capt. James Lockhart in charge.

0217 AMARANTH

SW p wh b. Sharpsburg, Pa., on the Allegheny River, 1841. 147 x 25 x 5.5. Two model barges were also built at Sharpsburg at the same time by the boat's owners. They were 140 x 20 x 4, open hold and cargo boxes, said to be the first of the type, designed to be towed alongside the *AMARANTH.*

Capt. George W. Atchison commanded her in the St. Louis-Galena trade. Stranded and lost at Amaranth Island, Mississippi River, September 1842.

0218 AMARANTH

SW p wh b. New Albany, Ind., 1845. 185 tons. First home port was Mobile, Ala. Snagged July 14, 1848, at location undetermined.

0219 AMARANTH

SW p wh b. St. Louis, Mo., 1846. 165 x 25 x 5.5. Operated St. Louis-New Orleans Capt. John Malloy, later on the *EMPRESS* as master, was clerk on her two seasons. She collided with the *DR. FRANKLIN* a few miles below Clarksville, Mo., on Mar. 23, 1849, and was sunk. There still is an Amaranth Island about five miles below Clarksville (1977) where this accident happened. The *Lytle-Holdcamper List* reports her loss at Island 76, Mississippi River, June 21, 1852.

0220 AMARANTH

Stw p wh b. Warsaw, Ill., 1864. 156 x 29 x 4.5. Engines 12's-3½ ft. Two boilers. Ran St. Louis-Illinois River, the first boat of the Eagle Packet Co. Owners included Capt. R.E. Hill, G.W. Hill, Henry Leyhe, and William Leyhe. In cotton season 1866 she ran New Orleans-Red River. On a Missouri River trip she was lost by sinking at Smith's Bar above Doniphan, Mo., Nov. 17, 1867. Capt. William Bell was pilot on watch. Cargo was mostly saved.

0221 AMAZON

SW p wh b. Murraysville, Va. (hull), and completed at Wheeling, 1839. 231 tons. She had a roof bell brought from Spain and bought in New York by Mr. McKee of McKee, Harding & Co., Wheeling, and shipped west. It bore the date 1690, weighed 120 pounds, and impressed on it was the symbol J.H.S. (Jehu Hominis Salvador); originally hung in a Spanish convent. The original stockholders were Wheeling men, one of whom was John McLure, who had previously run as engineer on other boats. Capt. James H. Louderback was master, grandfather of Capt. Jesse P. Hughes. The boat's clerk was James Maxwell. Louderback endorsed a note for clerk Maxwell—it went to default and Louderback was forced to sell his interest in the boat to pay it. Buyers were Capt. John Fink, Hiram Martin, and John McLure. The latter succeeded Louderback as master, McLure's first command. This was the first steamboat built at the Murraysville yard. With other owners she later ran Cincinnati-New Orleans, Capt. Wylie. Matt L. Virden clerked her for a time, and later was in charge of the *THOMAS SHERLOCK* (see). She was snagged and lost at Birds Point, Mo., Feb. 21, 1843.

0222 AMAZON

SW p wh b. Jeffersonville, Ind., 1847 and possibly rebuilt at Pittsburgh 1849. 250 x 32. Engines 20's-6 ft. Three boilers allowed 115 psi. She had St. Louis owners. Snagged at Rattlesnake Springs, three miles above the mouth of Missouri River, Feb. 15, 1856, having shortly before been sold to Menard Chouteau.

0223 AMAZON

SW p wh b. Belle Vernon, Pa., 1855. 234 x 36 x 6. Owned in Pittsburgh, rated 410 tons. Dismantled in 1857.

0224 AMAZON

SW p wh b. Cincinnati, Oh., 1857. She was first named *JUDGE TORRENCE* (see), renamed Jan. 2, 1866. Capt. Hiram Vinton commanded. On a downbound trip from Cincinnati to New Orleans at Ozark Island, Napoleon, Ark., she was lost by snagging, Feb. 19, 1868. The bow was on shore and the stern sunk fifteen feet. The *STARLIGHT* took off crew and passengers.

0225 AMAZONIA

SW p wh b. Elizabeth, Pa., 1849. 257 tons. Three boilers. Snagged at Hat Island, Mississippi River, Nov. 5, 1853. Repaired. The *DELAWARE* also was snagged there about same time. Lost by stranding at St. Louis, Feb. 16, 1854.

0226 AMBASSADOR

SW p wh b. Cincinnati, Oh., 1840. 215 x 35. Engines 25's-8 ft. Allowed 90 psi. Capt. Junius J. James, master, Louisville-New Orleans. Shows up in the New Orleans-Vicksburg trade 1844, Capt. Charles J. Brenhem, a "bon vivant" and quite popular with the better class in Vicksburg and along the river. He quit the river in a few years and moved to California where he became a successful banker and died there. Burned at Luxemburg, Mo., Apr. 25, 1847.

0227 AMBASSADOR

SW p wh b. New Albany, Ind., 1851. 324 tons. Built for owners in Mobile, Ala., and burned there on Feb. 24, 1854.

0228 AMBASSADOR

SW p wh b. Monongahela City, Pa., 1851. 367 tons. Three boilers. Louisville-New Orleans trade, Capt. Lynn. Dismantled 1857.

0229 AMELIA

SW p wh b. St. Louis, Mo., 1846. 151 tons. Snagged at Fayette, Mo., Dec. 11, 1849.

0230 AMELIA

SW p wh b. Louisville, Ky., 1847. 92 tons. Snagged Dec. 11, 1849, at Glasgow, Mo.

0231 AMELIA

Ferry Sank in ice while operating between Bellaire and Benwood, Ohio River, Dec. 12, 1904. Had a trip of people on her when she went down in the middle of the river.

0232 AMELIA HARVEY

Stw p wh b. New Orleans, La., 1890. 55.4 x 12 x 2.5. Advertised to leave Harvey's Canal for Peach Orchard every Sunday on arrival of the 6:40 A.M. Louisiana Avenue ferry, R. Gardere, master; fishing excursions.

0233 AMELIA POE

Stw p wh b. Georgetown, Pa. (hull), and completed at Pittsburgh, 1865. 165 x 27 x 4.5. Engines 13's- 3½ ft. Two boilers. Made a trip to Nashville, spring 1865, and brought back a cargo of pig iron for John Kyle, Cincinnati. Owned largely by Capt. Thomas Poe, Georgetown, Pa., and named for his wife. She made trips to Fort Benton, Mont., in 1866 and in 1867, both successful. Thomas S. Calhoon was clerk on the first "mountain" trip. J.Q.A. Parr also clerked her. She was one of the relatively few steamboats wrecked in present-day Montana. On May 20, 1868, she passed Fort Buford without stopping, loaded down with a quartz mill for the Montana mines. Three days later she speared a snag at Little Porcupine Creek near Oswego, Mont. Part of the cargo was saved and taken to Helena by the underwriters. The quartz mill was stowed on shore, and late as 1927 was still there. At the time of loss Capt. Thomas Townsend was master, and the pilots were Joe Fecto and George Hughes. Several St. Louis speculators bought rights to the *AMELIA POE* wreck, went there to salvage it, were driven off by Indians, and returned home empty-handed. Later the *HIRAM WOOD* went to the scene, got out the engines and the remaining freight.

0234 AMERICA

SW p wh b. Freedom, Pa., 1846. 142 tons. Ran Pittsburgh-Wheeling, 1847, Capt. Calhoon, later Capt. W. DeCamp. A steam explosion fifteen miles below Madison, Ind., killed four, with ten injured, Dec. 19, 1848. Sank and lost at Niota, Ill., opposite Fort Madison, Iowa in 1852.

0235 AMERICA

SW p wh b. New Albany, Ind., 1849. 740 tons. Designed for the New Orleans-Nashville trade. 260 ft. long on deck, 40 ft. wide, 9½ ft. deep. Engines 25's- 10 ft. Five boilers, each 42" by 32 ft. Wheels 33' dia., 14' buckets. Capt. Jesse Johnson first master. Snagged and lost on the St. Francis River, Ark., Jan. 20, 1857.

0236 AMERICA

Stw p wh b. Brownsville, Pa., and enrolled at Pittsburgh on Jan. 2, 1852, for the Apalachicola River in Florida. Had two masts. Four boilers. 172 x 26.5 x 8.5. Renamed *ENTERPRISE* under Confederate registry on Feb. 6, 1862, owned by Stephen K. Fawler, New Orleans, and commanded by Capt. O.A. Pitfield.

0237 AMERICA

Stw ferry wh b. St. Louis, Mo., 1854. 221 tons. Apparently served in the St. Louis vicinity for many years, inspected there in 1867. The Memphis & Arkansas Packet Line operated her last, and lost her on the Arkansas River near Little Rock, Jan. 28, 1870. Four persons drowned.

0238 AMERICA

Stw p wh b. Brownsville, Pa., and completed at Pittsburgh, 1863. 165 x 32 x 4.5. Three boilers. Built by Capt. William Dean for the Pittsburgh-St. Louis trade. Usually in command of Capt. Thomas H. Golding. In September 1865, due to illness of Capt. Golding, Capt. Sam Dean, "one of the oldest and most popular steamboatmen on the Western Waters," took her out of Pittsburgh on a St. Louis trip. William F. Blackstock, Allegheny City, was first clerk. She was sold to the Big Sandy Packet Co., in October 1868, and then ran Cincinnati-Pomeroy, Capt. Charles M. Holloway, master, with John Thornburg, clerk. Was in a near tornado at Portsmouth, Oh., in November 1869, but was safely landed after the sash departed from the pilothouse. About 1870 sold to Nashville & Cincinnati Packet Co., Capt. E. Pierce, master, with C.W. Bradley, clerk. Downbound for Memphis on Dec. 23, 1871, she was cut down by ice opposite Madison, Ind., with water over the cabin floor. "The *AMERICA* has always been considered a poor investment," remarked the Cincinnati *Commercial* on Dec. 26, 1871.

0239 AMERICA

SW p wh b. Cincinnati, Oh., at the Morton and Startzman yard, 1867. Actual dimensions not available but noticed in an account as 315 x 44 x 7. Engines 26's- 10 ft. by Robert Moore & Son, Cincinnati. Eight boilers. Wheels 38 ft. dia. working 13½ ft. buckets. Cabin and joiner work by Johnson, Morton & Co., Cincinnati. She had a "double cabin," two tiers of stateroom decks, same as *UNITED STATES* (see). Owned by the U. S. Mail Line Co., and built expressly for the Cincinnati-Louisville trade. Launched Nov. 21, 1866, at 3:00 P.M. Made her trial trip Apr. 27, 1867, Capt. David Whitten in charge. The regular crew of *UNITED STATES* took her out on this occasion. She departed from the foot of Race Street with several hundred invited guests and went down to the head of Medoc Bar, rounded to, and returned. On the night of Dec. 4, 1868, she was upbound on a regular trip, landed at Ghent, Ky., where one of her regular pilots, Capt. Charles Dufour, got off to visit at his home. In his place, and on watch above Warsaw, Ky., was Capt. Napoleon B. Jenkins, elderly, an "extra." Not far above Warsaw, at Rayl's Landing, Ind., above the mouth of Bryants Creek, the *AMERICA* and her partner *UNITED STATES* collided. Both sank and burned (see *UNITED STATES* for details). The crew of *AMERICA* the night of her loss was made up of: Capt. David Whitten, master; Will Taylor, first clerk; John Mullen, second clerk; Lloyd B. Gaff, mate; Charles Steele, second mate; Henry Steele, watchman; Joseph Holmes, chief engineer; Alex Ewell, second engineer; J.J. Kelley, barkeeper; Napoleon Jenkins, pilot; L.J. Light, steward, and Mrs. S. Jones, chambermaid. Capt. David Whitten was 66. He had commanded the *BELLE OF THE WEST* (see) and had been captain on the *ITASCA* on the Upper Mississippi (also see). Three days prior to the collision a letter written to the Louisville *Democrat* had been published describing the *AMERICA*: "So slight is her frame that she might be said to amble under headway. Every distinct motion of the propulsive power is vibrated through her entire frame; not unpleasantly, but distinguishably, to the remote parts of her structure." The wreck of the *AMERICA* lay in close to Bryants Creek and as late as 1895 it showed in extreme low water. Relic hunters often were rewarded by finding souvenirs.

0240 AMERICA

Stw p wh b. Jeffersonville, Ind., by Howard, 1898. 200 x 38 x 6.5. Engines 18's- 8 ft. Three boilers each 44" by 32 ft. An impressive cotton-style packet built for Capt. L.V. Cooley, New Orleans, designed for the Ouachita River trade, Monroe to New Orleans. Along about 1904 she commenced running New Orleans to Vicksburg and Greenville. W.B. Foulke was head clerk for many years. She was chartered for making a movie in January 1924 and was temporarily renamed *WINFIELD SCOTT*: the flick was called "Magnolia." In April that year she made a trip to Monroe after an absence of about 20 years. Her one geographical adventure was a trip in April 1923 to East Alton, Ill., and return, taking up a cargo of smokeless powder. At St. Louis on the return she took aboard five carloads of Anheuser-Busch beer, four carloads of soap, some autos and a camping outfit for delivery south. She was laid up near the foot of Walnut Street, New Orleans, and foundered there on Aug. 13, 1926. Capt. LaVerrier Cooley, native of Savanna, Ill., died on Dec. 19, 1931, and is buried in New Orleans. Over his grave is the roof bell of the *AMERICA*, his best loved boat.

0241 AMERICA

SW p and ex wh b. Jeffersonville, Ind., by Howard, 1917. 285 x 45 x 6. Engines 25's- 8 ft. Five boilers, each 42" by 26 ft. The hull and machinery came from *INDIANA* which had burned off her upper works at Cincinnati on May 1, 1916. She came away from Howards as a packet complete with staterooms, and was entered in the Louisville-Cincinnati trade by the Louisville & Cincinnati Packet Co. The engines originated on the *BOSTONA* b. 1879 (see), classic examples of the "broadhorn" type, although Jack Shields of the Frisbie Engine & Machine Co., Cincinnati, had installed Frisbie valve gear. After several years she was remodeled to become a full-fledged excursion boat, all staterooms removed, etc., and operated principally at Louisville. She made a trip to Pittsburgh in September 1923, tramping, and at least one to New Orleans. She and the *CINCINNATI* ran a staged race at Louisville in 1928, a spectacular affair in which the *AMERICA* showed ability to win, but was prevented by management, a hotly debated topic for many years after. Her crew those days included: Capt. James O'Brien, master; Roy McBride and Wymond Brasher, pilots; Frank Buening, purser; Floyd Goffenett, clerk; Henry McClanahan, chief engineer; Floyd "Skyjack" Turner, second engineer, and Billy Sampson, steward. While laid up for the winter above Jeffersonville, Ind., she burned Sept. 8, 1930. Arson was suspected but nothing proven.

0242 AMERICAN

Stw p wh b. Smiths Ferry, Pa. (hull), and completed at Pittsburgh, 1845. 118 tons. Her first master was Capt. Richard Calhoon, and Jackman T. Stockdale was clerk—his first job afloat. She operated in various tramp trades, often up Wabash River. The Louisville *Times* reported she had exploded her fore and aft cross pipes (mud drums) at Garrett's Landing downbound between Louisville and Madison, Dec. 19, 1848; eight scalded, three seriously. This same accident also was ascribed to the *AMERICA* b. 1846 (see), and is reported in our account of her. Dismantled 1850.

0243 AMERICAN

Originally the *DAVID C. HORTON* b. Cincinnati, 1864 (see). Following U.S. war service she was sold to private hands Sept. 8, 1865, and renamed. Lost in 1871.

0244 AMERICAN

Stw p wh b. New Decatur, Ala., 1902. 158 x 27.6 x 4.2. Engines 12's- 4½ ft. Two boilers 38" by 30 ft. Built for Lee Richardson and others and operated at Vicksburg. In May 1903 running up Yazoo River in charge of the veteran Capt. S.H. Parisot. She was sold to Mobile and went there under her own steam in November 1906. Owned there by Stewart H. Lindsay and others. Burned in the Mobile River, Apr. 4, 1915.

0245 AMERICAN EAGLE

SW p wh b. Louisville, Ky., 1842. 295 tons. Advertised at Cincinnati for New Orleans, January 1842, Capt. Montgomery. Off the list in 1845.

0246 AMERICAN EAGLE

SW p wh b. Freedom, Pa., 1847. 216 tons. Capt. James Atkinson took command, formerly on the Allegheny River packet *ARROW*. Ran in the Keokuk and Upper Mississippi trade, Capt. Cossen. Burned in the great fire at St. Louis, May 17, 1849, when 23 boats burned.

0247 AMERICAN STAR

Stw p wh b. Pittsburgh, Pa., 1846. 133 tons. Two boilers. Capt. William Hanna commanded first season. The cables for the Nashville suspension bridge were made on Wheeling Island, Ohio River, from wire made in Wheeling by J. Bodley & Co. and were shipped aboard this boat to Nashville April 1850. Citizens of Steubenville came aboard this boat to Wheeling Jan. 11, 1853, to see the first B&O train arrive from Baltimore. The Steubenville Grays, numbering 40, uniformed, with fire and side arms (flintlocks) accompanied. The train was late arriving, got to Wheeling at 1:55 A.M., Jan. 12. The Wheeling suspension bridge was illuminated with 1,010 oil lanterns for the occasion. Dismantled 1854.

0248 AMERICUS

Stw p wh b. Brownsville, Pa., 1853. 205 tons, 137 x 36 x 4.5. Built under supervision of Capt. C.W. Batchelor for the Pittsburgh-Nashville trade. Was at St. Paul in 1856. Running St. Louis-Peoria January 1861 with *SAM GATY* and *LA SALLE*. Was in Grant's fleet up Tennessee River. Burned on the Illinois River. Capt. E.W. Gould ascribed this misfortune to the fact she was launched on a Friday, and had landed on the Illinois to pick up a preacher and a white horse.

0249 AMOS HAYS

Stw p wh b. Jeffersonville, Ind., 1883. 130 x 26 x 4.5. Ran on the Chattahoochee River to Columbus, Ga. Was active there until dismantled at Columbus 1891. The *QUEEN CITY* was built there same year and much equipment from the *HAYS* was used.

0250 AMULET

Stw p wh b. West Wheeling, Oh., 1844. 62 tons. An odd-looking lot built for low water work around Wheeling. Was on the Illinois in fall of 1845, and at Galena from St. Louis in April 1846. Snagged in 1848.

0251 ANDES

Stw p wh b. Cincinnati, Oh., 1871. 576.26 tons. Ran Cincinnati-New Orleans, Capt. G.W. Cullen, master. Charles Muhleman was clerk on her and in a few years bought control. He entered her in Wheeling-Cincinnati trade with great success. In the winter 1876-1877 he was ringing the roof bell for departure from Cincinnati when a snowstorm set in. The weather got so cold he turned her back from Moscow, Oh., and laid her up at Cincinnati. The river gorged and in the break-up, Jan. 11, 1877, she sank. High water later destroyed her. He immediately contracted for a new boat (see next listing) and chartered the *COURIER* meanwhile to care for the trade.

0252 ANDES

Stw p wh b. Cincinnati, Oh., 1877. 220 x 39 x 5.5. Engines 20's- 6 ft. Three boilers. The contract for this boat was let Feb. 16 and on June 15, four months later, she was at the Cincinnati wharf ready to go. She was owned by the Wheeling & Cincinnati Packet Co., David Gibson, pres., Martin F. Noll, sec., and Capt. Charles Muhleman, supt. She left Wheeling Tuesdays 3:00 P.M., Bellaire at 6:00 P.M., until 1889 with Capt. Muhleman, master, and Martin F. Noll, clerk. Capt. Muhleman was raised below Clarington, Oh., all his life a bachelor, and died at Hannibal, Oh., at home, September 1912. He sold out of *ANDES* to Capt. Ed Cooper, Al Slavin, and Ben D. Stout who continued her in the trade, sometimes coming through to Pittsburgh. In early 1893 she was acquired by Capt. Lee Anshutz and Charles Ollum, backed financially by Harry Davis, Pittsburgh theater man. They ran excursions terminating in one whoop-la trip with a mob of tough characters aboard who nearly wrecked the boat. In May 1895 John A. Wood & Son of Pittsburgh bought the boat, dismantled her, using the engines on the towboat *DAVE WOOD*. The old hull, loaded with 31,000 bundles of cotton ties was shipped south in tow of the *JOHN A. WOOD* in May 1897. In one season, when Capt. Muhleman ran her, she made 51 round trips out of a possible 52, a record. She carried a bar, one of the last of the Upper Ohio packets to do so. George D. Harvey, clerk, died at New Matamoras, Oh., on Jan. 2, 1949, last surviving crew member.

0253 ANDES

Stw p wh Built from the wreck of the packet *LOUCINDA* which had been cut down by ice at Cincinnati, 1918. Owned by Louisville & Cincinnati Packet Co., and so named inasmuch as Capt. Martin F. Noll, identified with the last *ANDES*, was treasurer of L&C. She was cheaply built, no skylight, etc., and ran Cincinnati-Madison until the big Cincinnati fire, November 1922. Greene Line Steamers ran her under charter in upriver trades for some time. Was sold in March 1927 to Capt. Oliver F. Bradford in New Orleans. Sank and was lost while approaching Plaquemine Lock, July 1, 1931.

0254 ANDREW ACKLEY

Stw p wh b. Pittsburgh, Pa., 1868. 162 x 25 x 3.5. Engines 12's- 5 ft. Two boilers. Was built by Capt. William J. Kountz and was named for a Pittsburgher who ran a boat store and dabbled in packets. She departed Pittsburgh latter March 1868 advertised for upper Missouri River, Capt. Boise, with Sharp Hemphill in the office. Ran on Red River on occasions. In all she made seven trips to Montana points, coming to Fort Benton six times and once to Cow Island. She made her first appearance at Fort Benton June 17, 1868, and that year made two more arrivals there bringing up goods from boats too heavy to get there. In 1869 she was at Fort Benton on July 8, and made two more trips from Dauphin's Rapids to bring up cargo left behind because of low water. Sold at U.S. marshal sale in New Orleans, July 1873 and fetched but $2,000. Not much more was heard of her after that.

NB: Worthy of note is that historian F.L. Wooldridge insists there was an ANDREW ACKLEY running New Orleans-Ouachita River 1858-1860. He reports her scuttled in the Ouachita 1864, raised and rebuilt.

0255 ANDREW CHRISTY

Recesswheel f wh b. Louisville, Ky., 1880. 174.6 x 48.9 x 6. Owned by the Wiggins Ferry Co., St. Louis. Lost in tornado at St. Louis. May 27, 1896.

0256 ANDREW CHRISTY

SW ferry sh b. Jeffersonville, Ind. by Howard, 1897. 170 x 48 x 7.4. Owned by Wiggins Ferry Co., St. Louis. Had two pilothouses, and was painted dark red when new. The engines were built in Detroit and placed in the hold. Cabin of hardwood. Had three boilers, each 48″ by 28 ft. Engines were compound, 16″ and 32″, stroke not known. In latter days came to Louisville, renamed *HENRY WATTERSON* (see).

0257 ANDREW FULTON

SW p wh b. Elizabeth, Pa., 1848. 180 x 35 x 8. Engines 22½'s- 8 ft. Boilers 42″ by 30 ft. Machinery by Robinson & Minnis, Pittsburgh. James Millinger built the cabin. Hull by Samuel Walker. Capt. William H. Fulton was first master. Upbound from New Orleans to St. Louis she stranded on Plateau Rocks, Crystal City, Mo., Feb. 21, 1849, during a fog. Sank slowly. The *JOHN QUINCY ADAMS* happened along and removed passengers, many of them emigrants bound to Upper Mississippi. Three were drowned. It was reported at the time she was largely owned in Steubenville, Oh., and insured at Pittsburgh.

0258 ANDREW JACKSON

SW p wh b. Cincinnati, Oh., 1845. 176 x 31 x 7. Engines 26's- 8 ft. Three boilers, 42" by 26 ft. Hull by Burton Hazen, engines by David Griffin, cabin by Swain & Green. Capt. Thomas F. Eckert, first master, with G.R. Dudley in the office. Ran Cincinnati-New Orleans, later in charge of Capt. Charles Ross. She was laid up at East St. Louis when she burned Aug. 7, 1850.

0259 ANDREW . BENNETT

Stw ferry wh b. Sioux City, Iowa, 1880. 115 x 30 x 3.5. Machinery from former ferry *DR. BURLEIGH* (see). Capt. Grant Marsh built her for ferry service at Sioux City, and hired a captain to manage it. Still listed 1896.

0260 ANDREW S. HERRON

SW p wh b. Algiers, La., 1859. 102 tons. Documented at New Orleans, and went to Confederate service 1861.

0261 ANDY BAUM

SW p wh b. Cincinnati, Oh., 1872. A sprightly looking boat, dimensions unavailable, rated 735.76 tons. Owned by the Memphis & Ohio River Packet Co., James M. Wise, supt., and James D. Parker, secy. Capt. Hiram Vinton was her master, with M.M. Deem, clerk. Ran in the Cincinnati-Memphis trade. Went to U.S. marshal sale at Cincinnati on Aug. 6, 1873, bid in at $27,500 by two local attorneys. Collided with the *UNITED STATES* two miles below Aurora, Ind., on Dec. 19, 1877, and knocked starboard wheelhouse from US. During high water, Feb. 25, 1884, she was transferring railroad passengers between Storr's Landing and Aurora, Ind., and got caught on the bank at Storr's. She was caught in a pocket and looked like she was doomed to being dismantled right there. Another flood came along in March 1884 and released her. She ran no more.

0262 ANDY FULTON

Stw p wh b. Freedom, Pa., 1859. 125 x 27 x 4.9. Two boilers. Designed for Red River. Burned at Carrollton, Ky., July 29, 1861.

0263 ANDY HATCHER

Stw p wh b. Charleston, W. Va., 1889. 116 x 20 x 3.6. Engines 10's- 3 ft. Built by Capt. John Hopkins and others. Ran opposition to the *FRANK PRESTON* on Big Sandy River. In her latter days she was owned by Capt. Green Meek, and burned while tied up on the Big Sandy at the mouth of Paint Creek. The roof bell went to the Paintsville City School, and when that structure was torn down it was placed on a pedestal on the City School lawn and remains there today. The whistle went to the *THEALKA*, Machinery went to the sawmill boat *RAY*, thence to the *W. F. SMITH, COP-R-LOY, DETROITER,* and in 1980 is on the Sacramento River steamboat *ELIZABETH LOUISE*.

0264 ANDY JOHNSON

SW p wh b. Madison, Ind., and completed at St. Louis, 1866. Engines 28½'s- 7 ft. Five boilers. Belonged to the Keokuk Northern Line; their fleet in 1876: *ANDY JOHNSON, ROB ROY, MINNEAPOLIS, LAKE SUPERIOR, ALEX MITCHELL CLINTON, NORTH WESTERN, DUBUQUE, RED WING, BELLE OF LA CROSSE, J. M. JOHNSON* and *MINNESOTA* (all see). Capt. William F. Davidson was president of the line; P.S. "Fuce" Davidson was superintendent; Capt. Isaac M. Mason was freight agent, assisted by James A. Lyon. Capt. D.R. Asbury long commanded the *ANDY JOHNSON*. The boat was named for U.S. President Andrew Johnson, who, together with Gen. U.S. Grant and others, rode aboard during the course of an elaborately staged parade, Alton to St. Louis, on Sept. 8, 1866. Thirty-seven steamers participated, each carrying a banner proclaiming the name of the state it represented. They were:

Andy Johnson	District of Columbia
Ruth	New York
Olive Branch	Pennsylvania
Belle St. Louis	New Hampshire
Belle of Pike	Connecticut
Yellowstone	Rhode Island
Southwester	Massachusetts
Albert Pearce	Maryland
M. S. Mepham	Virginia
Bart Able	North Carolina
Magenta	South Carolina
W. T. Lewis	Georgia
Sucker State	New Jersey
Hawkeye State	Vermont
Gold Finch	Arkansas
Rob Roy	Alabama
Lilly	Colorado
Bridgeport	California
R. L. Woodward	Delaware
Miner (sw)	Florida
Comet	Iowa
Lillie Martin	Indiana
Francis Fisher	Illinois
Isabella	Kansas
Platte Valley	Kentucky
Montana	Louisiana
Dora	Mississippi
J. G. Blackford	Minnesota
Michigan	Michigan
New Bon Accord	Maine
Jennie Lewis	Missouri
War Eagle	Nebraska
W. H. Osburn	Ohio

Mohawk . . . . Oregon
Iron City . . . . Texas
G. W. Graham . . . . Tennessee
Joseph Gartside . . . . Wisconsin

The St. Louis *Daily Missouri Republican* reported in its issue Sept. 9, 1866;

"The *ANDY JOHNSON,* leading the fleet, and bearing the martial-looking St. Louis Commandery of Knights Templar, was the first steamer to reach Alton. Then came the *RUTH* and the *OLIVE BRANCH,* followed in a few minutes by the *BART ABLE,* with its conspicuous motto 'We are able and willing to support my policy.' Then came the *M. S. MEPHAM* bearing a picturesque company of Scottish Highlanders in full Highland costume together with various members of the Army and Navy of the U.S. Along down the river came into view—graceful and beautiful as swans, gay with the stars and stripes, crowded with joyous people, puffing wreaths of snowwhite steam and overtopped by black clouds of smoke—the balance of the steamboats, as picturesque and exhilerating a scene as painter or poet could desire to see."

The President's train arrived on time at noon at Alton and the Commandery of Knights Templar marched to the station to form an honor guard. They were led by Capt. Bart Able who had been appointed chairman of a welcoming committee by the steamboat fraternity. When the presidential group arrived they were escorted to the forecastle of the lower deck of the *ANDY JOHNSON,* where Capt. Able made his address of welcome. The party then went upstairs and entered the main cabin. The *ANDY JOHNSON* immediately backed out into the stream where the *RUTH* was lashed to her port side and the *OLIVE BRANCH* then lashed onto the port side of the *RUTH.* The three steamers, abreast, then led the parade into St. Louis.

While the President and his retinue did start out from Alton aboard his namesake, the presidential party soon passed over to the steamer *RUTH* where a collation was served; and he arrived in St. Louis on that vessel.

In November 1871, Capt. Lee, she sank thirteen miles below Quincy, Ill. There was no time to beach her and she went down in six feet. She made at least one trip to New Orleans, Capt. D.R. Asbury, in 1873. Finally was cut down by ice at St. Louis, Dec. 13, 1876, at the same time the *JENNIE BALDWIN, BAYARD, ROCK ISLAND,* and *DAVENPORT* were sunk.

0265 ANDY MACK

Built as a barge, but rebuilt 1866 into a steamboat at New Orleans named *MOLLIE FELLOWS* (see).

0266 ANGLER

Stw wh b. Peoria, Ill., 1892. 40 x 10 x 3. No information but the name suggests piscatorial proclivities. Still registered at Peoria in 1896.

0267 ANGLO-NORMAN

SW p wh b. Algiers, La., 1850. 558 tons. There is an account in Gould of a disastrous explosion aboard this boat at New Orleans in 1850. She was entered in Confederate service 1862, and burned at New Orleans April 7 that year.

0268 ANGLO-SAXON

SW p wh b. Brownsville, Pa., 1846. 214 tons. Ran Pittsburgh-St. Louis. Snagged and lost at Chester, Ill., Feb. 16, 1848.

0269 ANGLO-SAXON

SW p wh b. Beaver County, Pa., 1857. 157 x 33 x 4.5. Advertised Cincinnati-New Orleans in October 1859, Capt. Hiram K. Hazlett. Was one of Grant's fleet in the Tennessee River campaign. Cincinnati-Memphis, Capt. Patterson, summer 1864. Dismantled in 1868. Her hull served as a wharfboat at Ashland, Ky., until 1875. That winter it was transferred to Huntington but sank there March 1876. Machinery went to *CHEYENNE.*

0270 ANN BAILEY

SW ferry wh b. Pt. Pleasant, W. Va., 1909. 70.3 x 22.4 x 3.4. Operated across the Ohio River to Kanauga, Oh. Originally owned by T.S. and U.G. Hanes, Gallipolis, Oh. Named for the heroine of the Battle of Point Pleasant. Later owned by Capt. W.E. McDade who ran her until the "Silver Bridge" opened, May 1928. Sold to Clate Pickens, Racine, Oh., October 1929. Caught in heavy ice at New Haven, W. Va., in February 1936 and extricated by towboat *VESTA.* Dismantled.

0271 ANN CHASE

SW wh b. Cincinnati, Oh., 1847. 120 x 30 x 9. An ocean-going transport built for the U.S., 341 tons. Wheels 24′ dia. with 8 ft. buckets. She was locked through the Louisville-Portland Canal, and a 60 ft. mast was set at New Orleans. Built to aid the prosecution of the Mexican War. Stephen H. Long had a part in her construction.

0272 ANN LANCASTER

SW p wh b. New Albany, Ind., 1848. 62 tons. Went to New Orleans. Dismantled in 1855.

0273 ANNA

SW p wh b. New Albany, Ind., 1849. 83 tons Went to New Orleans and ran on Red River. Dismantled 1859.

0274 ANNA

SW p wh b. Elizabeth, Pa., 1849. 156 tons. First home port, St. Louis. Advertised from New Orleans to Opelousas via Atchafalaya, Capt. J. Johnston, master. Snagged and lost in Atchafalaya Bayou, La., Sept. 3, 1852.

0275 ANNA

SW p wh b. Cincinnati, Oh., 1860. 110 tons. Burned at Johnsonville, Tenn., Oct. 30, 1864.

0276 ANNA

Stw p wh b. Freedom, Pa., 1864. 156 x 31.5 x 4. Engines 15's- 5 ft. Two boilers. Came out in Pittsburgh-Cincinnati trade, Capt. J.H. Maratta, master, with William Maratta as clerk. Attacked by Rebel batteries on Tennessee River Oct. 28, 1864, at Paris Landing. Boat was fairly riddled with shot, the steam line was disabled, and she was 1½ hours under fire. Many narrow escapes; clerk William Maratta had a nicked shoulder, and pilot James O. Mortimer had a bullet pass through his hat and he also got a splinter from the pilotwheel when it was hit. She came to Pittsburgh drawing vast crowds at all landings enroute to see the victorious boat and crew. By actual count the pilothouse had 30 bullet holes and one cannon shot. The port smokestack was ripped off. Sold 1865 to run Cincinnati-St. Louis-Memphis under Capt. Oliver P. Shinkle, and later Capt. E.J. Smith (who was great grandfather of Virginia Bennett, long with Greene Line Steamers at Cincinnati.) Also made trips to New Orleans. Dismantled 1874.

0277 ANNA

Ferry b. Grafton, Ill., 1872. 101.2 x 28.2 x 4.4. Inspected at Louisiana, Mo., in 1881. Still listed in 1886.

0278 ANNA B. ADAMS

Stw p wh b. Little Rock, Ark., 1889. 157 x 31.6 x 3.1. Engines 15's- 5½ ft. stroke. Two boilers. Owned by Arkansas Packet Co., until May 1891 when sold to the Red River Line for the Shreveport-Jefferson, Tex., trade. Was still in Red River, Capt. Frank M. Sadler, in 1893.

0279 ANNA E

SW p wh b. New Albany, Ind., 1864. 114.8 x 22.2 x 3.4. Went to New Orleans, owned by A. Bruhn, Capt. J.C. Wingard, master. Sold June 1866 to a New Orleans stock company, Capt. John J. Atkinson, master. Sold November 1866 to Capt. E.P. Trinidad. In July 1867 owned by Atakapas Mail Transportation Co., Capt. A.P. Rooker, master. Owned in 1870 at Franklin, La., same master. Snagged and lost at Bayou Teche, La., Nov. 15, 1871.

0280 ANNA PERRETT

Stw p wh b. Jeffersonville, Ind., 1857. 133 x 32 x 4.5. In 1859 New Orleans-Opelousas, Capt. G.E. Louaillier, master. Same trade in 1861, Capt. James Capps, master, teamed up with the *NINA SIMMES.* Went to Confederate service 1863-1865. Sold to private hands and rebuilt with a somewhat larger hull in 1866, Capt. Isaac Wright. In August 1866 sold to Capt. Joseph J. Alston, New Orleans. Enrolled at Mobile on Mar. 29, 1867. Back at New Orleans August 1867. Dismantled 1869.

0281 ANNA TARDY

Built and owned by Capt. Frank Tardy of Evansville, Ind., who owned a boat store there. She went to Pine Bluff, Ark., and was transferred to Red River in October 1901.

0282 ANNA WHITE

Stw p wh b. Pittsburgh, Pa., 1863, originally named *FOREST ROSE* (see). Renamed in 1865 then owned by David White ½, and T. Taylor ½. In 1867 was loading ordnance at the St. Louis Arsenal for delivery to Parkersburg, W. Va. She was cut down by ice and lost Feb. 4, 1868 at the foot of Anna Street, St. Louis. She was tied outside the *LIZZIE GILL* when the gorge moved, although the *GILL* was unharmed.

0283 ANNABELL KING

Stw ex wh b. 1903, owned by Oliver King, Knoxville, Tenn. A right nice excursion boat, 86 tons, lost Dec. 31, 1911, at Knoxville when she struck a bridge pier.

0284 ANNAWAN

SW p wh b. Ravenswood, W. Va., 1855. 163 tons. First home port, Cincinnati. Burned June 28, 1856 at Wheeling, W. Va.

0285 ANNE EVERSON

SW p wh Memphis-White River, 1865. Ran from Alexandria to Shreveport in 52 hours, a record in August 1866, Capt. Charles Lester. Regular in Shreveport-New Orleans trade until 1874, Capt. J.C. Wingard.

0286 ANNE LIVINGSTON

SW p wh b. New Albany, Ind., 1849. 156 tons. Snagged and lost at Atlas Island below Cincinnati, Oct. 27, 1852, so says *Lytle-Holdcamper List.*

0287 ANNIE

Stw p wh b. La Crosse, Wis., 1877. 238 x 29 x 3.8. Keokuk Northern Line. Was renamed *WHITE EAGLE* (see).

0288 ANNIE BARNES

Recess wheel wh b. Prescott, Wis., 1880. 53 x 10.7 x 3. A little one-stack boat with recess wheel and a single boiler which carried the U.S. Mail before the Burlington RR was built, and owned by Frank Havens, a Prescott merchant. After the railroad came through, she towed lumber from the John Dudley sawmill to Point Douglas, Minn., to Hastings, and ran small excursion party trips. Registered at Paducah, Ky., 1892.

0289 ANNIE CADE

Prop ferry wh b. Leavenworth, Kans., 1879. 127.5 x 32 x 4.5. Apparently served at Kansas City some years. In June 1903 she was high and dry on a sandbar there, along with the tug *JOHN RENZ.*

0290 ANNIE JACOBS

Stw p wh b. Mound City, Ill., 1863. 148 tons. Original home port, St. Louis. Sold to the USQMC on Oct. 15, 1864. Sold to private owners Oct. 2, 1865, and renamed *MILBREY* (see).

0291 ANNIE JOHNSTON

Stw p wh b. La Crosse, Wis., 1863. 202.87 tons. Noted for speed, and once a rumor got abroad she had licked the *PHIL SHERIDAN* causing an uproar amongst local natives, but the story was untrue. Documented until 1877.

0292 ANNIE LAURIE

Stw p wh b. Cincinnati, Oh., 1864. Owned by Capt. Job Thayer for Charleston-Cincinnati trade. In October 1864, Capt. Fred A. Laidley took charge, his first command. She made a trip to Nashville for the U.S. under his command. Laidley (who later formed the Louisville & Cincinnati Packet Co.) sold his interest in 1867. Capt. J.D. Hegler took command, with W.G. Norvell, clerk, and continued her in the trade. She sank in Kanawha River in June 1869, was raised, and was taken to Malden, W. Va., while stockholders pondered whether to make needed repairs. Not much was heard of her after that. See *S&D Reflector,* issue June 1977, for article and pictures.

0293 ANNIE LAURIE

Stw p wh b. Harmar, Oh., at Knox Yard, 1892. 138 x 27 x 4.8. Engines 16's- 5 ft. Two boilers. Original crew in Zanesville-Parkersburg trade: Capt. George Wallace, master; Dana Scott and Lou Myrick, clerks; W.W. Richardson, pilot. In a few years she was sold to the Vicksburg & Greenville Packet Co., and ran that trade with success. Finally was beached above Glass Bayou in Lake Centennial at Vicksburg. The cabin and engines were removed and the hull became a barge. The June 27, 1903 issue of *The Waterways Journal* offered her engines for sale, care of P. J. Foley & Son, Vicksburg.

0294 ANNIE LEE

Stw p wh b. Boonville, Mo., 1876. Quite small. 8"- 2 ft. stroke. One boiler. Owned by Horace Kingsley. Snagged and lost at Euphrasie Bend, Griffith's Landing, Mo., Nov. 11, 1881, Capt. John L. Farris, pilot.

0295 ANNIE P

Stw p wh b. Campti, La., 1904. 98.4 x 22.9 x 3.1. Made a special trip from New Orleans to Denison, Tex. on Red River, arriving at destination Apr. 22, 1905. She was the only steamboat in the 20th century to go there. Sold to Trinity River, Tex., 1905. Back in the Red River, 1906. Rebuilt by the Pugh Line at Vicksburg in 1909, renamed *LUCILE* (see).

0296 ANNIE P. SILVER

SW p wh b. Cincinnati, Oh., 1878. 300 x 40 x 9. Engines 22's- 8 ft. Four boilers. Ran Cincinnati-New Orleans, also St. Louis-New Orleans, Capt. David H. Silver. Green Shields, clerk. She came near burning at Cairo when quite new, when hay stowed in the hull caught fire, Sept. 12, 1879. She went under her own steam to the Kentucky shore where the crew scuttled her with water over the main deck. The *T. F. ECKERT* pumped her out. Advertised New Orleans-St. Louis in 1886, Capt. William Thompson, master; John S. Lehmer, clerk. Sank and was lost Nov. 8, 1889, at Paw Paw Island, fifteen miles above Vicksburg, Miss. Parts of *SUSIE SILVER* were used in building her (see).

0297 ANNIE RUSSELL

Stw pl sh b. Dubuque, Iowa, 1902. 125 x 25 x 4.5. Engines 10"- 4 ft. Two boilers 40" by 14 ft. A trim steel hull pleasure craft owned by Russell Gardner, St. Louis. Much equipment from former *ALICE EDNA* (see). The Kansas City-Missouri River Navigation Co., bought her May 1911, converted her into a single-stack towboat named *ADVANCE.* Federal Barge took her over, transferred her to Mobile, where she sank. The wreck was raised in May 1928 and junked.

0298 ANNIE WAGLEY

SW p wh b. Louisville, Ky., 1863. 202 tons. Originally named *CARABASSET.* Was in U.S. service under original name. Sold to private owners, Aug. 17, 1865, and renamed. Advertised New Orleans-Minden-Lake Bistereau, Capt. J.J. Compere, aster, with J.C. Jeffrion, clerk, c. 1866. New Orleans-Opelousas, 1869, Capt. M. Kenison, master; T. Jobin, clerk. Snagged and lost at Labadieville, La., May 1, 1870.

0299 ANNIS CROCKER

SW p wh b. Louisville,Ky., 1848. 118 tons. Went to New Orleans. Sank in Red Bayou on Apr. 27, 1849 with 800 bales of cotton on board, "supposed to be a total loss." Removed from documentation 1851.

0300 ANSON NORTHUP

Rig? b. Lafayette, Minn., 1859. 100 tons. Built for Minnesota River, but was knocked apart and transported to Moorhead, Minn., reassembled, and operated on the Red River of the North, Capt. Edwin Bell. Owned there by J. C. Burbank & Co., proprietors of the Great Northwestern Stage Lines. Renamed *PIONEER* in 1860, the first steamer on that waterway. Was lost by sinking at Lower Fort Garry, Manitoba, 1861.

0301 ANTELOPE

SW p wh b. New Albany, Ind., 1853. 587 tons. Ran Louisville-New Orleans, Capt. E. Brown, master. Snagged and lost at New Orleans, La., Sept. 27, 1864.

0302 ANTELOPE

SW p wh b. Kasota, Minn., 1856. 45 tons. Operated up Minnesota River. Off the record in 1862.

0303 ANTELOPE

SW p wh b. Metropolis, Ill. (hull) and completed at St. Louis, 1866. 180 x 32. Engines 18's- 6 ft. Two boilers. Operated St. Louis and Missouri River. Burned five miles below Upper Bonhomme Island, Apr. 12, 1869. Two passengers lost, and a Dr. Page of Boston was badly burned. Bonhomme Bend, where this accident took place, is the stretch between Miles 37.6 and 41.3, Missouri River.

0304 ANTHONY WAYNE

SW p wh b. Wheeling, Va., 1846. 164 tons. Hull by Dunlevy & McNaughton. Engines by Hobbs & Taylor. Made her trials in September 1846, Capt. A. Bennett. Went to the Galena-St. Louis trade, Capt. Morrison; later Capt. Dan Able. A purse of $250 was offered for the first boat to the

Falls of St. Anthony, and Capt. Dan Able took her there and collected in 1850. That same year he had her up Minnesota River into Indian country, far as Traverse des Sioux, with an excursion party aboard. The *EXCELSIOR,* Capt. James Ward, was up the Minnesota in 1851. This boat briefly ran in the St. Louis-Naples trade, Illinois River, sponsored by Capt. E.W. Gould and C.S. Rodgers, this in 1848. In Gould, page 351, is mentioned that *ANTHONY WAYNE* carried a steam whistle. Snagged and lost above Liberty Landing, Mo., near Independence, Missouri River, Mar. 25, 1851.

0305 ANTOINETTE

Prop p wh b. Memphis, Tenn., 1908. 41.7 x 12.7 x 5.2. Name changed in 1912 to *ONWARD* (see).

0306 ANTOINETTE DOUGLASS

SW p wh b. Cincinnati, Oh., 1850. 242 tons. Went to Mobile, Ala. Exploded on the Alabama River, Nov. 25, 1850, with loss of nine lives.

0307 ANY ONE

SW p wh b. Jefferson City (New Orleans), La., in 1863. 79.5 x 17.5 x 3. Owned when new by William Taylor, New Orleans. Was with the Porter expedition up Red River. Sold January 1867 to Emile Duhon, Vermilion Parish. Had several other owners, the last being Alfred Millott, St. Mary Parish. Snagged in Bayou Teche, Aug. 20, 1869.

0308 APALACHEE

Stw p wh b. Wheeling, W. Va., 1890. 135 x 28 (26′ floor) x 4.5. Capacity 700 bales of cotton. Had a "composite" hull, iron framing and wood sides and bottom. Was operated by the Plant System (later Atlantic Coast Line) on the Flint and Chattahoochee. She was built by the Wheeling firm A. J. Sweeney& Son. Snagged and lost in the Chipola River Cut Off, near Iola, Fla., June 23, 1899. One person was killed when the roof bell fell on him.

0309 APPLETON BELLE

Stw p wh b. West Newton, Pa., 1856. 103 tons. This building site is on the Youghiogheny River, tributary of the Monongahela. Two locks and dams carried slackwater there at the time this craft was built. She was in Confederate hands at Fort Henry, Tenn., and they burned her to prevent capture, Feb. 7, 1862.

0310 AQUILA

Stw p wh b. West Newton, Pa., 1854. 59 tons. Capt. Joseph Nixon and Dan McAlier, Pittsburgh, owned her. They used her on the Monongahela River. In 1855 she carried passengers to a Camp Meeting held two miles above Tarentum on the Allegheny. In 1856 she went through the Fox River improvement connecting the Mississippi with Lake Michigan. Three steamboats were built at West Newton in these early days, the *APPLETON BELLE, AQUILA,* and *JUSTICE.* Dismantled 1860.

0311 ARABIA

SW p wh b. Brownsville, Pa., 1853. 181 x 31 x 5.5. Three boilers. Capt. John Shaw had her on the Missouri, and sold her to Capt. Wm. Terrill. He owned her when she was snagged and lost on the Missouri 1½ miles below Parkville, Mo., Aug. 10, 1856. She was reported to have been carrying a large cargo of whiskey and numerous attempts were made to salvage it. The team who located the wreck of the *BERTRAND* (see) thought they had located it in early spring of 1974.*

0312 ARABIAN

Stw p wh b. Brownsville, Pa., 1866. 145 x 30 x 4.5. Engines 13's- 3 ft. Two boilers. Capt. J.H. Bishop was first master. Ran Pittsburgh-Cincinnati in summer 1866, Capt. Bishop, with J.H. Beazell in the office. Capt. M.A. Cox left Pittsburgh with her the last week of December 1866 for Cincinnati. Heavy ice and nearly all boats laid up. He got to Cincinnati by floating most of the way; had 1,000 plows aboard to reship south. She was sold to St. Louis parties first week January 1867 while at Cincinnati. Capt. Ben Johnson was the new owner, but Bishop retained interest. They ran her St. Louis-Tennessee River in 1867, Capt. Tim Packard. Capt. Lloyd Belt was in charge 1868 on Missouri River. Capt. Packard was again master when she was snagged and lost at Atchison, Kans., on May 4, 1868. She was upbound with a duplicated cargo to replace the one lost on *CARRIE* (see) just prior, consigned to the U.S. It also was lost.

0313 ARAGO

SW p wh b. Brownsville, Pa., 1860. 176 x 33 x 6. Engines 20's- 5 ft. Three boilers. Ran Pittsburgh-St. Louis, Capt. Thomas H. Golding. John Lamont, lately of the *DIADEM,* was clerk in 1862. Was owned by parties from St. Louis and Memphis when she burned in Dog Tooth Bend, near Commerce, Mo., Feb. 6, 1865. Her engines were said to have come from the *F.X. AUBREY* (see). She had been sunk by ice and a cargo of lime in the hold caught fire.

ARCADIA

Civil War records use this spelling, but her proper name was *ACADIA* (see).

0314 ARCHER

SW p wh b. Pittsburgh, Pa., 1844. 145 x 22 x 4.10. Galena-St. Louis, 1845. Shreveport-New Orleans, December 1845, Capt. Ankrim. Sunk in collision with *DIE VERNON* in the chute between two islands five miles below mouth of the Illinois, Mississippi River, Nov. 27, 1851, with large life loss. She was cut in two. Life loss given between 34 and 41.

0315 ARCHIE P. GREEN

Stw p wh b. Jeffersonville, Ind., by Howard, 1873. 110 x 22 x 3. Built for J.W. Lovell, Nashville, Tenn. Advertised at Cincinnati for White River and Batesville, Ark., September 1877, Capt. Charles B. Woodbury who lived at Dayton, Ky. Sank three miles below Batesville with cotton cargo on Feb. 10, 1880, Capt. Woodbury.

0316 ARCOLA

Stw p wh b. Brownsville, Pa., 1856. 170 tons. Lost in ice at Reeds Landing, Minn., Apr. 2, 1857.

0317 ARCOLA

Stw p wh b. Belle Vernon, Pa. (hull), and completed at Pittsburgh, 1863. 156 x 32 x 4½. Engines 15's- 4½ ft. from old *AUNT LETTY*. Three boilers. Built by Capt. John L. Rhoads for Capt. A.C. McCallum, Jr., and others. Departed Pittsburgh first trip Nov. 7, 1863, for Cincinnati and Louisville, S. Spear, clerk. Was impressed to U.S. service and didn't get back to Pittsburgh until April 1864. Sold a month later to Capts. Sherley, Woolfolk, Pink Varble, and W. May for Louisville-Nashville trade. Upbound on the Cumberland night of July 18, 1864, sighted the burning *ST. LOUIS* which had been captured by the Rebels. She was turned about in an attempt to escape, but was ordered to land by the Rebels. Did so, but on the opposite shore, and a barge she had in tow was cut adrift. The engines were working ahead slow. The *ARCOLA* got free from shore, rounded to headed downriver unexpectedly, so pilot Meek went back on watch and returned her to Fort Donelson. The Rebels seized the loaded barge and burned it. However she became victim of the war—burned at Johnsonville, Tenn. on Nov. 4, 1864. A number of other boats were lost at the same time (see *J. B. FORD*).

0318 ARCTIC

SW p wh b. Shousetown, Pa., 1852. 175 x 31 x 6.9. 351 tons. Three boilers. Ran in the Pittsburgh-St. Louis trade, Capt. John S. Devinney. Burned at the Manchester docks, Pittsburgh, July 15, 1858, along with the *GREAT WEST*.

0319 ARCTIC

Stw p wh b. Moline, Ill., 1890. 47.3 x 10.2 x 3.4. Still listed, at Rock Island, 1896.

0320 ARCTIC

Stw p wh b. Muscatine, Iowa, 1901. 60 x 10.4 x 3. Listed at Rock Island 1908, and at Des Moines, Iowa, 1918.

0321 ARENA

Stw p wh b. Elizabeth, Pa., 1846. 53 tons. Capt. Joel C. Peebles ran her on Monongahela River. Then she changed ownership and made trips up the Allegheny thru 1849. Was in the Pittsburgh-Wheeling trade, Capt. Hazlett, in 1847. Ran regularly Pittsburgh-Wellsville, Capt. D.P. Kenney, 1850 thru 1851. Off the lists in 1854.

0322 ARGAND

Stw p wh b. Levanna, Oh., 1896. 132.6 x 24 x 5. Engines 10's- 3½ ft. from ferry *H. A. MEAD* (see). One boiler 42" by 20 ft. Built for Capts. Newt Flesher and Gordon C. Greene, and named for an oil refinery below Marietta. Capt. J. Mack Gamble gave them the original whistle from the *WILL J. CUMMINS* to blow. Came out in Pittsburgh-Parkersburg trade with Capt. Flesher, master. After ten weeks Flesher sold his interest to Capt. Greene. Then entered Wheeling-Parkersburg trade, Capt. Mary B. Greene, master, Jesse P. Hughes and Henry Brookhart, pilots. George Mitchell and Harold Wolfe were the clerks; Alex Shaw and Manuel Landis, mates; Charles Hardy and George Price, engineers. This lasted several years (until October 1898) at which time she was sold to the Big Sandy Navigation Co., which ran her up Big Sandy River. She was sold, April 1901, to Capt. Edwin A. Price, New Martinsville, W. Va., who used her to tow his showboat *WATER QUEEN*. He usually wintered in the Muskingum River at the Lowell, Oh., lock, and *ARGAND* burned there in December 1927. The boiler was still there in the mud late as 1949.

0323 ARGO

Stw p wh b. Louisville, Ky., 1845. 41 tons. Ran Galena-St. Peters, Capt. Kennedy Lodwick, 1846. Galena-St. Paul-Stillwater in 1847, Capts. M.W. Lodwick and Russell Blakeley. Sank and lost fall of 1847 above Winona, Minn.

0324 ARGO

Stw p wh b. Freedom, Pa., 1856. 136 x 21 x 4. One boiler. Ran Vicksburg-Yazoo River connecting with New Orleans packets. She was burned by the Confederates to prevent her capture about 75 miles up Sunflower River in a small bayou, May 25, 1863.

0325 ARGO

Stw p wh b. Parkersburg, W. Va., 1864. 48 tons. Off the lists, 1867.

0326 ARGONAUT

Stw p wh b. Brownsville, Pa., 1855. 154 x 33 x 5. Three boilers. Owned in 1858 by R.D. Cochran, Jane and Mary A. Nimick, Dan McAleer, J. and W. Rea, and George W. Cochran, all of Pittsburgh, and H. Williams, Cincinnati. Capt. George C. McLean, master. Ran to Cincinnati and St. Louis principally. Impressed into U.S. service 1862 with Capt. J.W. Porter as master. In latter February 1862 took Col. Sullivan and part of 48th Ohio Volunteers from Cincinnati to Paducah, and then returned to Jeffersonville, Ind., with Rebel General Buckner on board, and his staff, and a cargo of prisoners bound for Indianapolis. Among the staff was Col. J.B. Clay, grandson of Henry Clay. Dismantled later that year.

0327 ARGONAUT NO. 2

Stw p wh b. Elizabeth, Pa., 1862. 157.5 x 35 x 6. Engines 17's- 6 ft. from prior boat of the name. Three boilers. Came out in charge of Capt. John W. Porter, Pittsburgh-St. Louis trade. In June 1864 impressed into war service at Cairo and loaded for White River "to the land where Rebels are as thick as blackberries." Got to Duvalls Bluff to find ten other packets awaiting turn to unload cargo there. One of the crew wrote home to say that the country below the Bluff "abounds with frogs, snakes, wolves, bears, etc., and the river is full of fish." Capt. George W. Reed had her in Pittsburgh-Louisville trade, early 1865. In November 1865 arrived at Pittsburgh with "a brand new gilt ball on top of her pilot-house." Capt. H.C. Richmond had her in the Pittsburgh-St. Louis trade, 1866. Upbound at New Albany, Ind., on Dec. 19, 1866, she got lost in a fog, hit the Indiana shore, and sank. Raised, and then Capt. E. Lockhart bought her at U.S. marshal sale at Portland, Ky. She was dismantled and by Feb. 17, 1867, Capt. H. Clay Richmond had bought three-fourths interest in the *NEW YORK* (see).

0328 ARGOS

Stw p wh b. Brownsville, Pa., 1864. 115 x 24 x 3. Engines 9½'s- 2½ ft. Two boilers. Open hold. Said the Pittsburgh *Commercial* on Mar. 26, 1864: "The lightest draught boat of the season is now at the landing. She is named *ARGOS* and was built by Capt. E.D. Abrahams and was constructed at Brownsville. She draws 8½ inches and is intended to run between this port and Morgantown, W. Va. She will be able to navigate when the gravel is a little damp." Sank and was lost at Batesville, Ark., July 27, 1871.

0329 ARGOSY

Stw p wh b. Monongahela, Pa., 1862. 157 x 33 x 4.5. Engines 15's- 5 ft. Three boilers. Built for Capt. George W. Reed. "This is a queer name but very appropriate," mused the Pittsburgh *Gazette,* on Dec. 25, 1862. "*ARGOSY* means a large vessel for the transportation of merchandise." She was taken over by the U.S. at Cairo in March 1863 and converted into a tinclad #27. Sold to U.P. Schenck, Vevay, Ind., Aug. 17, 1865. Burned at Cincinnati, Mar. 7, 1872.

0330 ARGOSY NO. 2

Stw p wh b. Monongahela, Pa., 1863. 154 x 31 x 4.5. Engines 15's- 4 ft. from side-wheel *MINNETONKA*. Two boilers. Capt. George W. Reed built her when first of the name was taken over by the U.S. Bought by the U.S. at Cincinnati Nov. 14, 1863. Renamed *WAVE* on Nov. 14, 1863, a six-gun tinclad. Captured by the Confederates May 6, 1864, at Calcasieu Pass, Tex.

0331 ARGOSY NO. 3

Stw p wh b. Monongahela, Pa., 1864. 155 x 33 x 5. Engines 15½'s- 5 ft. Three boilers, each 38" by 24 ft. Hull by Latta. Engines from Foster & Co., and boilers built by the Herron Works. Buntling, Miller & Co., built the cabin. Capt. Lew Vandergrift bought control, and took charge. She became a fairly regular Pittsburgh-Cincinnati packet. Captain Vandergrift had her rebuilt at the James Rees shop, Pittsburgh, summer 1866, and put in larger engines, 16's- 5 ft. There is a full account in *S&D Reflector,* issue Sept. 1976, pages 24–25, of a mud drum explosion near Rono, Ind., some 80 miles below Louisville on Aug. 21, 1865, in which ten Union soldiers were lost, drowned or scalded, upbound for Cincinnati. The story includes photograph of the boat, and also the mass grave still in the locality. In November 1866, after getting the new engines, she again entered Pittsburgh-Cincinnati trade, Capt. Lew Vandergrift in charge, W.H. Scott, clerk, and James Rowley and William Hall, pilots. In September 1868 Capt. Vandergrift loaded aboard 600 tons of iron ore at LaGrange Landing, Tennessee River, and brought it to the upper Ohio. Summer 1869 in Pittsburgh-Cincinnati trade, Capt. George D. Moore, master, A.R. Bunting, clerk. Sold December 1869 to Capt. William J. List and W.J. Anderson of Wheeling who ran her Pittsburgh-Portsmouth. She was chartered in 1873 to carry Dan Rice's Circus, and after touring the Ohio River went below New Orleans 50 miles to Myrtle Grove Plantation. She was in charge of Capt. D.K. Barrett, Murraysville, W. Va., father-in-law of A.J. Flesher who ran the boatyard there. Finally *ARGOSY NO. 3* was degraded to towing salt from Pomeroy Bend to Louisville, and was dismantled soon thereafter.

0332 ARGUS

Rig? b. Cincinnati, Oh., 1878. 71 x 17.3 x 3.2. Was regularly inspected at Cincinnati thru 1886.

0333 ARGYLE

SW p wh b. Freedom, Pa., 1853. 319 tons. Three boilers. Built for Capt. Jacob Poe and others. Ran tramp trips to New Orleans and St. Louis. Was in Cincinnati-New Orleans trade, January 1861, Capt. George W. Ebert, master, and clerks Standish Peppard and Andy Wilson, Jr. Was with Grant's fleet up the Tennessee River. Bought April 1862 by Capt. John Kyle and others, Cincinnati. She was lost in ice at Cincinnati, Jan. 17, 1867, sinking at Taylorsport, Ky., in deep water. On Jan. 22, only a bit of her was visible. The cabin and pilothouse floated to Louisville and lodged at the foot of Sixth Street in early February 1867.

0334 ARIADNE

Stw p wh b. Brownsville, Pa., 1848. 26 tons. Custom records carry her until 1860.

0335 ARIADNE

Prop yacht wh b. Buffalo, N.Y., 1868. 34.27 tons. Sank in the fall of 1876 above Cairo, was raised and put back in order.

0336 ARIADNE

Stw p wh b. Cincinnati, Oh., 1879. 200.6 x 35 x 5.5. Ran in the "peanut trade" between Tennessee River and Cincinnati. When about two years old was sold to the T. J. Moss Tie Co., Paducah, and was renamed *IDLEWILD* (see).

0337 ARIEL

SW p wh b. Cincinnati, Oh., 1854. Operated on the Minnesota River, 1861. Went to Confederate service that year.

0338 ARIEL

Stw p wh b. Wheeling, Va., 1855. 30 tons. Dismantled 1860.

0339 ARIEL

Stw p wh b. St. Louis, Mo., 1860. 120.44 tons. 117 x 23 x 2.5. In 1868 owned by the Holton Bros., of La Crosse, Wis., who ran her in the La Crosse and Chippewa River trade, Capt. Lafayette Holmes. Bought 1872 by Capt. George Houghton and James Houghton (brothers) and Capt. W.F. Davidson. That year carried Grant's Sixth Minnesota Infantry from Fort Snelling to Carver on the Minnesota River, enroute to New Ulm. Still operating out of St. Paul in 1873. Finally snagged and lost near Clinton, Iowa.

0340 ARION

Stw ferry wh b. Jeffersonville, Ind., 1891. 85 x 26 x 3.5. Engines 9″- 3 ft. One boiler, 38″ by 20 ft. Owned by E.B. Smith, who ran her Proctorville-Guyandotte. Extensively repaired at Pt. Pleasant and registered as a new boat in 1902. George Smith, also of Proctorville, also ran her. Boat was named for a racehorse. Sold in 1929 and renamed *DAVID F. THOMAS* (see).

0341 ARIZONA

Stw p wh b. Belle Vernon, Pa., 1857. 155 x 35 x 5.5. Engines 18's- 4½ ft. Three boilers. Capt. Robert Herdinan, Birmingham, Pa., was first master. He held stock along with F.F. Plunkett and John A. Wolf, also of Birmingham; Wash Mason, John B. Conway and James Park, Pittsburgh; and James H. Robb, St. Clair County, Pa. Ran Pittsburgh-St. Louis, and was at St. Paul her first season. Got caught in a "jimmycane" at Louisville, having just ascended the Falls, and crashed into an abutment at the Louisville landing and was sunk. An elderly pilot, Alf Williamson, was on watch at the time, his first trouble in 25 years. This happened in mid-January 1862. A flood covered her to the roof, but was raised a month later. In Cincinnati-Tennessee River trade, July 1864 in charge of Capt. Shaw. In March 1865 in New Orleans and Lower Coast trade, two trips a week, Capt. W.S. Bassett, master, James Moulton and N. Barrios, clerks, going down to Pointe-a-la-Hache and Jesuits Bend. Owned at New Orleans 1867 by A.S. Mansfield, that city, and commanded by Capt. William H. Holland. Dismantled that year.

0342 ARK

SW p wh b. Red House, Va., on the Kanawha River, 1845. 122 tons. Owned by Capt. James A. Payne. Had machinery from the *JULIA GRATIOT* (see). When launched, Capt. I.B. Parker commanded, formerly engineer on Payne boats. She is described as heavily-built and consequently slow, and "slow as the Ark" was a household term along the Kanawha. She is said, nevertheless, to have taken out one of the largest salt cargoes in her time. Dismantled 1850.

0343 ARKADELPHIA CITY

Stw p wh b. New Albany, Ind., 1859. 53 tons. A Ouachita River packet which exploded a short time before the Civil War at DeCeipher Shoals, twelve miles south of Little Rock, Ark. Capt. W.A. Britton, master. His wife and baby were aboard and were blown ashore unhurt. Owned by Capt. T.R. Tennyson and Capt. M.S. Carpenter. Five black deckhands were killed. The engines on her came from the *JOE JAKES*.

0344 ARKANSAS

Stw p wh b. California, Pa., 1852. 158 x 31.2 x 5.4. Capt J.A. Stevenson, part owner and first master; principal owner Marcus J. Dents, New Orleans ¾, and Atkinson & Oakley, Pittsburgh ¼. She was taken to Mobile and owned there by J.S. Harris ½ and J.A. Stevenson ½, both of New Orleans. Snagged and lost near 27-Mile Bluff on Mobile River, Jan. 26, 1856.

0345 ARKANSAS

Stw p wh b. Shousetown, Pa., 1856. 154 tons. Snagged and lost at Bayou Sara, La., Feb. 19, 1859.

0346 ARKANSAS

Stw p wh b. Belle Vernon, Pa., 1860. 154 x 33 x 5. Three boilers. Built for the Arkansas River and New Orleans trade. On Nov. 11, 1860, collided with *ELLEN GRAY* at Walker's Bar, 90 miles below Evansville, Ind., resulting in loss of the latter. Burned and lost at Little Rock, Ark., Sept. 10, 1863.

0347 ARKANSAS

Confederate gunboat b. on Yazoo River 60 miles above Vicksburg during the Civil War under the supervision of Capt. Isaac N. Brown, formerly of U.S. Navy. On July 15, 1862, she came out of the Yazoo and engaged U.S. gunboats *CARONDELET* and *TYLER* and ram *QUEEN OF THE WEST*. She made her escape down the Mississippi. On July 22, 1862, an unsuccessful attempt was made to sink her by U.S. gunboat *ESSEX* and *QUEEN OF THE WEST*. On Aug. 6, 1862, she was destroyed by her commander at Baton Rouge to prevent her capture. The Chicago *Daily News* in issue of Oct. 14, 1911 ran a story of this affair by Capt. Brown himself. A book titled *By Valour and Arms* authored by James Street (Dial Press; N.Y., 1944) recounts the *ARKANSAS* story. Capt. John T. Sherley's obit when he died at Memphis September 1873 notes him as the builder of this gunboat.

0348 ARKANSAS

Stw p wh b. Elizabeth, Pa. and completed at Pittsburgh, 1868. 185 x 36 x 5. Engines 16's- 5½ ft. Three boilers 38″ by 26 ft. Hull by Latta and Osborne. Engines by Robert Lea. Construction superintended by D.S.H. Gilmore for principal owner Capt. A.H. Shaw. Built for Arkansas River-New Orleans trade. Arrived at New Orleans Dec. 29, 1870, with 2,301 bales, biggest cotton load out of the Arkansas River to that date. In spring 1871 she bettered that record, bringing out 2,322 bales. These cotton trips extended up to Fort Smith, Ark. On a trip to St. Louis, August 1871, she was sold to Capt. "Diamond Jo" Reynolds for handling Upper Mississippi grain and packet cargoes. She was sunk near Dubuque in mid-March 1876 and raised. In 1878 sold to Capt. Pate Davidson of La Crosse who used her several seasons in the Missouri and then on the Upper Mississippi. Sunk by ice, c. 1884, either at Louisiana, Mo., or St. Louis.

0349 ARKANSAS BELLE

SW p wh b. Cincinnati, Oh., 1870. 203.5 x 32.5 x 5.1. Engines 17½'s- 5½ ft. Three boilers, 37½" by 24 ft. Built for the Memphis and Arkansas River trade, Capt. Woodburn. She had two bridal chambers opposite one another named "Tennessee" and "Arkansas" with beds a trifle high equipped with short ladders for the bride to climb up. Built in the autumn of 1870, she got first inspection Nov. 3 that year, and was sold to the Evansville & Cairo Line, entering that trade Dec. 20, 1870, with Capt. G.J. Grammer, master, and Nick S. Pennington in the office. Capt. Ben Howard became master, and last of all Capt. John Weed. She left Evansville at 4:00 P.M., three days a week. Laid up at Evansville August 1880. Her machinery was taken out, rebored, and placed over on the new *H. T. DEXTER*.

0350 ARKANSAS CITY

Stw p wh b. Arkansas City, Ark., 1875. 70 tons. 99 x 18 x 4. Originally based at Memphis, later at Vicksburg. Still listed 1886.

0351 ARKANSAS CITY

SW p wh b. Jeffersonville, Ind., by Howard, 1882. 273 x 44 x 7. 1,236 tons. Capt. C. B. Zeigler, master. Owned by the Anchor Line of St. Louis-New Orleans fame. Captain Zeigler was a great story teller and famed as an entertainer. Demolished in the St. Louis tornado, May 27, 1896.

0352 ARKANSAS MAIL

SW p wh b. Cincinnati, Oh., 1843. 107 tons. Burned at Louisville, Ky., foot of Fifth Street, along with steamer *TRIBUTARY*, on Dec. 29, 1848, with Capt. Diller in command.

0353 ARKANSAS NO. 4

SW p wh b. Cincinnati, Oh., 1844. 281 tons. Went to New Orleans. Lost in collision with the *DIE VERNON* at Rigolets, La., June 21, 1849.

0354 ARKANSAS NO. 5

SW p wh b. Louisville, Ky., 1845. 162 tons. Snagged and lost at Mobile, Ala., June 5, 1856.

0355 ARKANSAS TRAVELER

Stw p wh b. New Albany, Ind., 1856. 170 tons. Advertised at New Orleans for Fort Smith, Ark., Capt. Thomas, 1860. Snagged and lost at Pine Bluff, Ark., Mar. 21, 1860, with loss of one life.

0356 ARKANSAW

Stw p wh b. Louisville, Ky., 1857. 132 x 29 x 3.9. Owned 1861 at New Orleans by Phelps & Jones and others, Capt. J.M. Bennett in command. Went to Confederate registry 1861.

0357 ARLINGTON

SW p wh b. Elizabeth, Pa., and completed at Pittsburgh, 1869. 228 x 36 x 6. Rees engines 22's- 7 ft. from *J. N. McCULLOUGH* (see). Five boilers, each 38" by 24 ft., two flues. Wheels 30 ft. dia., with 11 ft. buckets. Hull by Latta, Ausburn & Co., cabin by M.F. Cassidy. Construction superintended by Andrew Ackley. Original crew: Capt. Daniel Moore, master; A.S. Shepard, first clerk; Wm. J. Abrams and W.E. Dever, pilots; John Kennedy, chief engineer; George Thompson, 2nd engineer; W.R. Romick, mate; James P. Given, steward. Designed for Pittsburgh-Cincinnati trade. In summer 1870 ran Cairo-Columbus making railroad connections, terminated March 1871. In summer 1873 was hauled out on marine ways at Cincinnati and lengthened 35'3" forward of the boilers. She then drew light 28" aft and 20" forward, lightest of her size. She then ran principally Cincinnati-Memphis-New Orleans, Capt. Dan Moore, master, with Charles and Wes Owens, pilots, A.J. McConnell, clerk. In January 1876 loaded out flat at Pittsburgh to New Orleans. Sank and was lost downbound for New Orleans at Cumberland Island, near Smithland, Ky., Ohio River, late fall 1876. The *JOHN H. HANNA*, Capt. Blanks, was the first boat along after the accident and took aboard the passengers. She had six feet of water in the cabin. Capt. R.W. Dugan of Cairo dismantled her with his *SALVOR No. 1*. Her machinery went later to the *BELLE OF SHREVEPORT*. A hogshead of queensware found partly buried in sand on the foot of Cumberland Island in October 1895 was thought to have come from the wreck.

0358 ARMADA

SW p wh b. California, Pa. (hull), and completed at Pittsburgh, 1863. 174 x 32 x 5. Engines 20's- 6 ft. Three boilers. Designed for Pittsburgh-Wheeling trade, and started running there late January 1863, Capt. G.W. Johnston, master. Half-owner was Adam Jacobs, Jr., Brownsville, Pa., and the minority included John O. Russell, Steubenville, and John List, Wheeling. Was soon sold to the Evansville-Cairo trade owned by Capt. Joseph H. Fowler and others. Sank at Caledonia above Mound City in March 1867, raised by Capt. R.W. Dugan with the *UNDERWRITER*. In mid-November 1869 a tornado at Evansville tore off the cabin from the wheelhouses forward, took off both stacks, and blew wreckage 400 feet up the levee. The *CAMDEN*, nearby was unharmed. Capt. Gus Dusouchet was master of her quite some time, later Capt. R.Y. Norther. Ran Paducah-Cairo in 1870 and was retired January 1871 when the *JAMES FISK, JR.*, took her place (see). Went to U.S. marshal sale August 1871 and dismantled soon thereafter. Her engines went to the towboat *JOHN MEANS* in 1873.

0359 ARMADILLO

Stw p wh b. Pittsburgh, Pa., 1865. 157 x 33 x 5.7. Capt. D.H. Swaney, principal owner and master. First trip Pittsburgh to Nashville, February 1865, Thomas S. Calhoon, clerk. Then went to St. Louis, same crew. Left Pittsburgh mid-March 1866 for Council Bluffs and Omaha with 200, mostly farmers, emigrating, with Capt. D.L. Hendrickson in charge. That summer ran New Orleans-Shreveport, Capt. Isaac Kouns, in place of the *NAVIGATOR*. Was towed from Grandview, Oh., to Pittsburgh early February 1869 with a broken shaft. Finally was dismantled at Cincinnati 1873, owned by Messrs. Byers and Wolfe, and much equipment used in their new boat *CHEROKEE*.

0360 ARMENIA

Stw p wh b. Brownsville, Pa., 1862. 152 x 38 x 6. Engines 18's- 5 ft. Three boilers. Engines came from *MARENGO*. Ran principally in Pittsburgh-St. Louis trade, Capt. A.C. McCallum, Sr. Also made trips Pittsburgh-New Orleans. Capt. McCallum died at Pittsburgh in the spring of 1869, whereupon Capt. A.S. Shepard, late of the *BAYARD*, took charge. He took her to St. Louis where she burned Mar. 29, 1869. The Cincinnati *Gazette* commented that Capt. Shepard was somewhat of a hoodoo; he had been associated with twelve boats, all of which met misfortune, and never had owned in a lucky one.

0361 ARROW

Stw p wh b. Pittsburgh, Pa., 1844. 118 x 19 x 3. Capt. Andrew Miller, first master. He owned in part along with William B. Scaife and James Bryden, all of Pittsburgh. Made frequent trips up to the Allegheny oil region under Capt. Miller, and later Capt. James Atkinson and Capt. William H. Gordon, this through 1848. Ran on the Muskingum when the Allegheny was low. She hitched to three loaded coalboats at Pittsburgh and took them to Cincinnati in the fall of 1845, Capt. Atkinson, one of the pioneer towing attempts. The coalboats were 120 x 20 x 3½, totaling about 20,000 bushels. James Patterson and Abe Haines were the pilots, and S.W. Sylvus, engineer. The *WALTER FORWARD* had taken a similar tow just prior. She had a steam whistle, certainly the first one heard up the Allegheny. Dismantled in 1849.

0362 ARROWLINE

Stw p wh b. Elizabeth, Pa., 1847. 90 tons. Built for William B. Scaife and commanded by Capt. Andrew J. Miller. Ran Pittsburgh to Franklin, Pa., on the Allegheny, 1848. Sold to Monongahela River summer 1848 and ran as an independent Pittsburgh-Brownsville. Entered Wheeling-Parkersburg trade, Capt. J.H. Reed, January 1849. In same trade, Capt. N. Harris, was snagged and lost at Peytons Island, Sept. 8, 1852. She carried U.S. Mail in this trade.

0363 ARROW LINE

Stw p wh b. Marietta, Oh., 1868. 80 tons. Left Memphis Nov. 10, 1870, with settlers migrating to Jefferson, Tex., on Red River. Sank Mar. 31, 1874 (where?).

0364 ART

Stw p wh b. Moscow, Oh., 1845. 68 tons. Was off the lists by 1847.

0365 ARTHUR

SW p wh b. Abbeville, La., 1852. 230 tons. Lost in 1853.

0366 ARTHUR

Stw p wh b. Poplar Bluff, Mo., 1889. 76.7 tons. An ad appears in the October 1899 *Railroad Guide* for Black River Transportation Co., operating *LOUISA* and *ARTHUR* on lower Black River out of Poplar Bluff, and going to Carola, H.D. Williams, pres. and gen. mgr.; W.R. Foley, secy.-treas.; T.P. Rily, eastern agent in New York.

0367 ARTHUR WATHEN

Recess wheel ferry wh b. Jeffersonville, Ind., 1852 by Howard. 150 x 40 x 5.5. Ran Louisville-Jeffersonville. Dismantled 1866.

0368 ASA WILGUS

SW p wh b. Louisville, Ky., 1857. 210 x 36 x 6. Engines 22's- 6½ ft. Three boilers, 46" by 26'. Sank at the mouth of Lost Creek, near Weston, Mo., 114 miles up Missouri River, Sept. 3, 1860. Owned at the time by R.R. Hopkins, A.C. Hopkins and Henry Thornbrough. Capt. R.R. Hopkins was master, William R. Massie, pilot, and George G. Keith, steersman. Until 1903 the rudder post of this old boat stuck straight up in the air in low water. A diving bell used in salvage work also showed up in 1903. "Steamboat Bill" Heckman bought it, took it to St. Louis to sell for junk, and lost money on the deal. Asa Wilgus Farney, Missouri River contractor, was named for this boat.

0369 ASCENSION

Catamaran steel hull ferry b. Donaldsonville, La., 1896. 84.9 x 30 x 5.5. Engines 8½"- 3½ ft. One boiler, 58" by 13 ft. Owned by C. Bragand & Co. Operated at Donaldsonville, Capt. Joseph Constantine. Later was transferred to Napoleon Ave., New Orleans, and was lost there in the storm of September 1912.

0370 ASHLAND

SW p wh b. Cincinnati, O., 1842. 155 tons. The Cincinnati *Gazette* on July 14, 1843, noticed her thusly: "The brandy bottle finds no place, and there is no bar; the cabin is not perfumed with tobacco smoke; nor the Bible thrust off its table to make way for cards; profanity and ribaldry do not offend the ear of religion and decency; and passion, violence and uproar never raise their voices." She was loading at Pittsburgh for Illinois River, Captain Tucker, spring 1846. Dismantled 1847.

0371 ASHLAND

Stw p wh b. Paducah, Ky., 1859. 274 tons. Owned locally. Burned and lost Feb. 15, 1861.

0372 ASHLAND

Stw p wh b. Cincinnati, Oh., 1872. 175 x 36 x 6. Engines 20's- 7 ft. Three boilers. Built for Capt. Will H. Kyle who was master, with James Alexander, clerk. In summer 1873 running Wheeling-Cincinnati in place of the *ANDES*, chartered by Capt. Charles Muhleman. Came from Cincinnati that fall to Pittsburgh several trips with W.H. Hall and James Witten as pilots. Up through 1875 had run various trips to Little Rock on the Arkansas, some of them from Pittsburgh. Also ran Little Rock-New Orleans, and on one such trip, March 1878 hit the bank downbound below Vicksburg, 30 miles above mouth of Red River. The *SUSIE SILVER* assisted twelve hours pumping, etc., entered claim for salvage, and collected $5,000. In 1880 was running New Orleans-Shreveport, Capt. C.S. Kouns. In 1881 she brought the first locomotive to Alexandria, La. Burned at New Orleans, July 14, 1882.

0373 ASHLAND CITY

Stw p wh b. Jeffersonville, Ind., by Howard, 1892. 120 x 20 x 3.9 Engines 10's- 3½ ft. Bult for Capt. Tom G. Ryman for Nashville-Clarksville trade to discourage competition in that area. Later ran in Paducah-Danville trade, connecting with the *EDGAR CHERRY* for Clifton and Savannah, this c. 1896-1897. Sold to Capt. W.D. Pugh, Vicksburg, November 1897. Was reported to have made a trip Garland, Ark., to Shreveport in 1900.

0374 ASIA

SW p wh b. Monongahela City, Pa., 1850. 199 tons. She made twelve round trips St. Louis-St. Paul in 1853. Lost in ice at St. Louis, Feb. 2, 1854.

0375 ASSUMPTION

Stw p wh b. Jeffersonville, Ind., by Howard, 1875. 151 x 35.8 x 6.5. Advertised 1878 New Orleans-Thibodaux, Capt. P.A. Charlet, master with N.Z. Dupuis and Joe Lagroue, clerks. In New Orleans-Bayou Lafourche trade, 1880, Capt. Charlet, master; Edw. Nicolle and J.W. Lagroue, clerks. Same 1883, M.H. Landry as clerk. Running New Orleans-Bayou Vermilion in July 1895 she hit a bluff bar and had to be beached while *DANUBE* and *STELLA WILDS* unloaded her. One scribe disposed of her saying "She laid up for repairs until she rotted away."

0376 ATALANTA

Stw p wh b. Wheeling, Va., 1853. 141 tons. She wintered in the mouth of the Muskingum 1854–1855, was sunk by ice, raised. Capt. M.L. Virden ran her out of Cincinnati 1855. She hit the bridge on the Cumberland at Clarksville, Tenn., on Mar. 2, 1863, downbound from Nashville. The cabin parted company from the hull. The pilot, W.H. Carroll, Sr., had contracted to round trip her from Smithland, Ky., so he stuck to the wreck, refusing to be removed, saying he was sticking to his contract. At Smithland he tapped the roof bell as he approached the wharfboat. She didn't land, and finally caught in a tree above Paducah. Capt. Carroll was removed in a skiff; he failed to get paid.

0377 ATALANTA

Stw p wh b. Cincinnati, Oh., 1855. 180 x 40½ x 5½. Three boilers. Went to New Orleans. At St. Paul from St. Louis, Capt. Woodruff, 1857–1858. Snagged and lost at Platin Rock below St. Louis, Dec. 20, 1860. Capt. Baldwin, part owner, was in charge, and his clerk was a Mr. Lowrie. Almost a century after she was built, in 1954, the U.S. dredge *STE. GENEVIEVE* was working at Calico Island, between Herculaneum and Crystal City. They ran upon the wreckage of this boat. White oak planks were recovered, still in good condition. Fire brick, copper piping (about #14 gauge), hogchains and bolts were found. Also a hand-operated water pump.

0378 ATCHAFALAYA

Stw p wh b. Franklin, La., 1848. 60 tons. Off the lists in 1850.

0379 ATLANTA

SW p wh b. Pittsburgh, Pa., 1866. 330 tons. First documented at Apalachicola, Fla. Snagged and lost on Tombigbee River, Ala., Jan. 12, 1877.

0380 ATLANTA

Stw p wh b. Stillwater, Minn., 1891. 93 x 16.4 x 3.7. Registered at St. Paul, 1892, and at Vicksburg, 1896.

0381 ATLANTIC

SW p wh b. Cincinnati, Oh., 1848. 275 x 36 x 6.5. 666 tons. Ran Cincinnati-St. Louis, Capt. James M. Broadwell, master, with John N. Bofinger, clerk. Capt. J.H. Oglesbay, in St. Louis—New Orleans trade, 1849. Capt. John N. Bofinger thru 1854. Collided with *PAUL ANDERSON* at Cairo, May 1853 (see). Dismantled 1857.

0382 ATLANTIC

SW p wh b. Brownsville, Pa., 1848. 166 x 25 x 4.9. 188 tons. Isaac M. Mason was clerk on her, later master. Made frequent trips on Monongahela River. Carried Jenny Lind from Pittsburgh to Brownsville after her Pittsburgh concerts, 1851. Carried a Pittsburgh delegation to the opening ceremonies of the Youghiogheny River locks held Nov. 5, 1850. Her master in 1853 was Capt. J.R. Hendrickson, and then owned by David White of Madison, Ind. Was at St. Paul, Capt. Isaac M. Mason, 1856. Dismantled later that year.

0383 ATLANTIC

SW p wh b. Jeffersonville, Ind., 1859. 275 x 39 x 6.8. Engines, 26's- 10 ft. Five boilers. Built for J.B. Ford, New Albany, Ind. and ran Louisville-New Orleans, Capt. Anson McGill. She set the pace to Hard Times Landing, 35 miles below Vicksburg, 24 hours out of New Orleans. She was at New Orleans during the storm of Feb. 21, 1860, when *ECLIPSE* was wrecked, and lost her stacks. Operated as a U.S. troop carrier during the War. Sold to Dan Able & Co., St. Louis spring 1864 and was rebuilt to become 45 ft. wide, and got engines 32's- 8 ft. Ran St. Louis-New Orleans. Dismantled at St. Louis, 1867. Her engines, cabin, etc. were used in building *DEXTER* at New Albany in 1868. The hull was used as a wharfboat at New Albany, operated by Hiram J. Reamer.

0384 ATLANTIC NO. 2

Stw p wh b. New Albany, Ind., 1874. 101.5 x 22.2 x 3. Went

to New Orleans, owned 1865 by John P. Rodney and Charles H. Bland. Sold to Mobile, Ala., that fall and was soon lost.

0385 ATLANTIS

SW p wh b. Louisville, Ky. (hull), and completed at New Albany, Ind., 1846. 233 tons. Ran Louisville-St. Louis principally, Capt. George W. Wicks. James Holmes, chief engineer. Once ran a celebrated race New Orleans to Louisville with *JAMES MADISON,* both in sight much of the time, evenly matched. Ended up in the Louisville-Evansville-Henderson trade, Capt. Stephen Paxton. Off the list in 1852.

0386 AUDUBON

Stw p wh b. Murraysville, W. Va. (hull) and completed at Cincinnati, 1853. 191 tons. Owned by Martin and Anshutz. Three boilers. Was at St. Paul, 1855. Burned and lost at Galena, Ill., Dec. 7, 1858.

0387 AUGUST WOHLT

Stw p wh b. Hermann, Mo., 1909. 91.1 x 18.1 x 3.3. Owned in 1925 by Capt. Edward C. Roehrig, Rocheport, Mo. Later sold to Wesley Cox on the Missouri River.

0388 AUGUSTA

b. Elizabeth, Pa., 1853. 27 tons. Went to New Orleans, and was operating on Red River to Jefferson in 1855. Off the list that year.

0389 AUGUSTA

SW ferry wh b. Clinton, Iowa, 1875. 100 x 29 x 5. Ran between Clinton and Garden Plain, owned by C. Lamb & Sons, sawmill proprietors at Clinton. After the Clinton bridge was built sold to a man named Cutler for Albany-Comanche trade, but he sold her to Rock Island-Davenport trade. In a rebuilding was renamed *T. J. ROBINSON* (see).

0390 AUGUSTA

Stw ferry wh b. Augusta, Ky., 1923. 64.7 x 32 x 4.1. Engines 9″- 3 ft. stroke from ferry *CENTRAL CITY.* One boiler. Ferried at Augusta owned by Kline O'Neill. She was finally beached out at Augusta and was being dismantled in summer 1950.

0391 AUGUSTUS McDOWELL

SW p wh b. St. Louis, Mo., 1860. 451 tons. Was with Grant's fleet on Tennessee River. Burned and lost at St. Louis, Oct. 27, 1862.

0392 AUNT LETTY

Stw p wh b. Elizabeth, Pa., 1855. 187 x 36 x 5. Three boilers. She was a four-engine boat similar to *CHALLENGE* (see). Capt. Thomas Baldwin came out on her. Operated in the Northern Line, St. Louis-St. Paul, Capt. C.G. Morrison 1857-1859. Snagged and lost at Beram Island, Feb. 11, 1861.

0393 AUNT SALLY

Rig? She made a noteworthy trip to the upper Arkansas River, going from Little Rock to Arkansas City, Kan., with arrival there on June 30, 1878, owned by residents of Cowley County, Kan. Capt. Harvey Lewis was in command. The round trip from Little Rock required 31 days. This audacious voyage led to the building of the *CHEROKEE* (see) later that year.

0394 AURORA

Rig? b. Evansville, Ind., 1873. 16 tons. At Evansville in 1876. Inspected at Commerce, Mo., June 1, 1881, in use as a ferry.

0395 AURILLA WOOD

Stw p wh b. Wheeling, Va., 1852. 91 tons. Built for low water work. Ran Wheeling-Clarington, Capt. Steve Thompson. Capt. William F. Gregory had a one-fourth interest which he sold to William H. Cox for $750 in May 1857. Was dismantled at Wheeling 1858 and engines went to *INGOMAR* (see).

0396 AURORA

Stw p wh b. Brownsville, Pa., 1857. 151 x 43 x 6. Four boilers. Built by Capt. John L. Rhoads. Owned by David Gibson & Co., Aurora, Ind. At Pittsburgh loading for St. Louis on Mar. 10, 1864, Capt. John Dale. Dispatch from Cairo, Ill. dated Oct. 18, 1864: "On account of the death of Capt. Patterson Marshall of the *AURORA* and 20 soldiers killed at Eastport during the fight with Forrest, that steamer has her flag flying at half mast." She was burned and lost at Johnsonville, Tenn. on Nov. 4, 1864, one of many. (See *J. B. FORD*).

0397 AUSTRALIA

SW p wh b. Brownsville, Pa., 1853. 182 x 31 x 7.5. Engines 20's- 6½ ft. 26′ dia. wheels, 8′ buckets. Built at John S. Pringle yard, West Brownsville. Cabin by Hopkins & Co. Capt. A.G. Mason, first master. Ran Pittsburgh-St. Louis-New Orleans. Snagged and sunk at Hat Island, Mississippi River first season, raised. Was in the Pacific Railroad Packet Line on the Missouri River, Capt. Bart Able, 1856. Burned and lost at St. Louis, Apr. 1, 1859.

0398 AUSTRALIA

Stw p wh b. California, Pa., 1869. 163.3 x 32 x 6.2. Engines 20's- 5½ ft. Three boilers 36″ by 24′. Capt. Jackman T. Stockdale of Allegheny City, Pa., contracted with William H. Chapman of New York City, agent for a South American company, to build her. Eberman & Co., built the hull, and W.F. Richardson put up the cabin. Machinery by J.N. Snowden, Brownsville. Departed Pittsburgh Apr. 22, 1869, Capt. Dan Moore, master, James Hamilton, pilot. Left New Orleans May 15, got to Key West May 20, stranded, and was six days getting free. She island-hopped via Jamaica and got to destination, the Magdalena River, badly battered but operative. She proved successful there. Name was changed to *BISMARK* in December 1869. Lost in 1877.

Eberman & Co., built a half-section hull model of her scaled 1:48 and sent it to Germany where the owning company was headquartered, this in 1877. Capt. Stockdale in 1869 also built and delivered the BARRANQUILLA to South America.

0399 AUTOCRAT

SW p wh b. St. Louis, Mo., 1847. 846 tons. Machinery from the *J. M. WHITE* (2nd), 30's- 10 ft. Ran St. Louis-New Orleans, Capt. James W. Goslee. She took 4,407 bales Memphis to New Orleans in 1848, a record load. An oil painting of her by St. Louis artist Leon Pomrede was widely admired in that city. She was sunk in collision at night with the *MAGNOLIA* at Bayou Goula, La., Feb. 10, 1851. Ten lives were lost. Captain Goslee, former master of the *J. M. WHITE* (2nd) and owner in *BELFAST, AUTOCRAT, GEO. COLLIER, JOHN SIMONDS,* and *INGOMAR* was run over by a train and killed at Anchorage, Ky., Apr. 1, 1875.

0400 AUTOCRAT

SW p wh b. Paducah, Ky., 1860. 255 x 40 x 7½. Engines from *SOUTHERN BELLE,* 26½'s- 9 ft. Ran Louisville-New Orleans, Capt. Hy Scott. There is an account that the hull was built on the grade at Evansville for Capt. J.A. Lemcke who ran out of cash, and was completed at Paducah by the purchasers. In 1862 was taken over by USQMC and converted into a hospital boat. At war's conclusion was sold to private owners and renamed *SOUTHERNER* (see) on Feb. 8, 1866.

0401 AVALANCHE

SW p wh b. Belle Vernon, Pa., 1847. 198 tons. Burned and lost at Peoria, Ill., Feb. 5, 1853.

0402 AVALON

Stw p wh b. Clarington, Oh., 1898. 167.1 x 33.4 x 4. Engines 12's- 4½ ft. Two boilers, 38″ by 24 ft. Built and operated by the Cramer family of Clarington, Oh., headed by Capt. Lanford Cramer. Engines came from *ELAINE.* Came out new in Pittsburgh-Parkersburg trade in early August 1898 and ran there through 1900. In January 1901 was taken to Tennessee River for trade out of Chattanooga. This proved so successful she was returned to the docks at Parkersburg, W. Va., and lengthened 35 feet that summer. She returned in November to the Cairo-Chattanooga trade. In January 1902 she brought down a number of the gun carriages for Shiloh battlefield. A reduction in local railroad rates caused her withdrawal from the trade. Then she ran Cincinnati-Memphis with not much success. Ran as an excursion boat between Wheeling and Sisters Island park one summer. Sold to Capts. Ben S. Pope, William E. Roe, and Martin F. Noll for the Pittsburgh-Charleston trade. They compounded her engines at Marietta Mfg. Co., renamed her *OHIO* (see). Capt. Lanford Cramer died aboard the *AVALON* near Ambridge, Pa., September 1906. On Nov. 30, 1906, she sank at Scull Run, Ohio River, and was raised a week later.

0403 AVALON

Stw ex sh The *IDLEWILD* b. 1915 was renamed in February 1948 by J. Herod Gorsage, Peoria, Ill. to grant the death-bed wish of Capt. Ben Winters, who had first worked on the former *AVALON.* Sold in 1950 to Steamer Avalon, Inc., based at Cincinnati. Operated excursions on the Mississippi, Ohio, Missouri, Kanawha, etc., until sold at Cincinnati in 1962 to Jefferson County Fiscal Court, Louisville, Ky. They renamed her *BELLE OF LOUISVILLE* (see). As *AVALON* she had several minor accidents, worst of which happened entering the Emsworth Lock, Ohio River, May 24, 1958. Engine failure caused her to hit the lower gate, and 23 were injured. She hit a low overhead wire at Nitro, W. Va. on the Kanawha in May 1961 and damaged her stacks. In 1961 she became celebrated taking a boatload of Girl Scouts Memphis to New Orleans and another delegation back to Memphis, during which Capt. Ernest E. Wagner and first mate Clarke (Doc) Hawley were joined up as official Girl Scouts (see *S&D Reflector,* December 1968, pages 6-7).

0404 AVENGER

SW ram wh b. New Albany, Ind., 1864. 181 x 41.5 x 9.5. Engines 28's- 6 ft. Built for the USQMC but completed as a U.S. ram for war service. She was sold at war's end to private owners and became the packet *BALIZE* (see).

0405 AVONDALE

There is a letter in the Missouri Historical Society written by Capt. Matthew L. Virden mentioning the sinking of this boat in 1854 and another sinking on Sept. 10, 1856. The first incident happened at Island 66, Mississippi River while she ran Cincinnati-New Orleans. Virden owned in her jointly with Capt. George D. Hoople, Cincinnati.

0406 AYER

Stw p wh b. Brownsville, Pa., 1868. 115 tons. 118 x 26 x 5.5. Engines 15's- 5 ft. Three boilers.

0407 AZILE

SW p wh b. New Albany, Ind., 1852. 132 tons. Delivered to Mobile, Ala. Advertised 1852 Mobile-Dempolis-Gainesville, Capt. McCartney.

B

0408 B.B.

Stw ferry wh b. Jeffersonville, Ind., by Howard, 1899. Originally named *MARY HILL* (see). Under both names she brought barrel staves from Arkansas to Keokuk and Warsaw for her owners, Bott Bros. (and hence the name). Did ferry service at Warsaw and also at Quincy.

0409 B. PARSONS

Mentioned in Cincinnati-Wabash River trade in 1878, Capt. P. Eichols, master.

0410 B.B. BARKER

Stw p wh b. McKeesport, Pa., 1852. 83 tons. Registered at Louisville, Ky. Lost on Nov. 18, 1857.

0411 B. C. LEVI

Stw p wh b. Belle Vernon, Pa., 1862. 110 tons. Named for the well-known steamboat agent at Louisville, Ky. Capt. R. Gracey turned her over to USQMC in December 1862. She loaded military stores at Pt. Pleasant, Va., for delivery to the upper Kanawha, Capt. Charles Regnier, master, and laid up for the night at the foot of Red House Chute. There she was captured by the Confederates who returned her five miles downriver to Vintroux's Landing and unloaded and burned her. Capt. C.C. Bowyer, who was raised at Winfield, just below Red House Chute, says he saw her downbound to Vintroux's with the crew under guard, this on Feb. 3, 1864. Later he visited the wreck many times. This account collides with U.S. records which say the USQMD renamed her *GENERAL CROOK* in 1863, and at war's end she was sold to private hands, again renamed *CUBA NO. 2.*

0412 B.E. CLARK

SW p wh b. Fulton (Cincinnati), Ohio, 1853. 199 tons. Operated New Orleans-Red River. Burned and lost at New Orleans, May 30, 1860.

0413 B.F. BENNETT

Stw ferry wh b. Fullerton, Ky., 1895. 100 x 26 x 3.6. Ran from Fullerton down to about where the bridge approach now is at Portsmouth, Oh.

0414 B.F. JOHNSON

An open hull "bat wing" side-wheeler single deck, which operated up the Big Sandy River from Catlettsburg, Ky., in 1903.

0415 B.F. WEAVER

Stw p wh b. Galena, Ill., 1872. 89 x 21.8 x 4. A small boat which went up with the Yellowstone Expedition in 1878. Was used to scout ahead, get fuel and supplies, etc. She was in continual trouble and finally was left moored at Fort Pierre. On the return she was tied alongside the *TIDAL WAVE* and towed back. Ended up as a rafter on the Upper Mississippi and popularly known as the "B.F. Loser."

0416 B.F. YOAKUM

SW railroad tr sh b. Dubuque, Iowa, 1910. 308 x 53.8 x 7.6. Engines 26's- 10 ft. Four boilers, each 72 by 18 ft. Owned by the Frisco Railroad and operated at Baton Rouge. Name changed to *WILLARD V. KING* (see).

0417 B.H. CROOKE

Stw p wh b. Jeffersonville, Ind., by Howard, 1873. 151 x 30 x 4.5. Built for Capt. J.W. Lovell and others for Evansville-Nashville trade. Some accounts call her *BOLIVAR H. COOKE.* She was in the People's Line at Nashville, spring of 1878. Sold at U.S. marshal sale June 1878 to Josh V. Throop, Evansville. The *E. B. STAHLMAN* and *JOHN S. BRANSFORD* were sold at the same sale. Dismantled c. 1880 and equipment used in building *J. P. DROUILLARD.* The *JOSH V. THROOP* took her place.

0418 B.H. HURT

Evansville, Owensboro, Rockport, and Cannelton daily packet in 1872, Capt. Lafe Elder, master; Robert Adams, clerk.

B.J. ADAMS

See *BEN J. ADAMS.*

0419 B.L. HODGE

SW p wh b. New Albany, Ind., 1857. 176 x 33 x 5.5. 289 tons. Named for B. L. Hodge, Esq., prominent Shreveport attorney. New Orleans and Red River, 1858, Capt. John Smoker, master, with C.E. Marshall, clerk. Also ran New Orleans-Vicksburg. Capt. Charles E. Marshall became master 1859, brother of Humphrey Marshall of Kentucky. Sold February 1862 to W. Adams, New Orleans, Capt. Richard Sinnott, master. Served the duration of the war as a Confederate troop and supply boat, and was kept in upper Red River. In April 1865 Gen. E. Kirby-Smith commanding the Confederate Trans-Mississippi Dept. chartered the HODGE for a trip Shreveport to mouth of Red River to bring up U.S. Commissioners to whom he surrendered, the last Confederate general to capitulate (May 26, 1865). Capt. Sinnott commanded on this trip, and was to be paid 37 bales of "good middling cotton" for services rendered, which he never got. After the war the *HODGE* reentered the N.O. and Red River trade, soon dismantled.

0420 B.L. HODGE No. 2

SW p wh b. Louisville, Ky., 1867. 210 x 38 x 7. 699 tons. New Orleans-Shreveport in 1868, Capt. P.C. Montgomery, master, with Fred G. Cellos, clerk. In 1869 same trade, Capt. W.T. Boardman, master, with Jos. Aiken, clerk. Ran New Orleans-Donaldsonville fall 1869, also spring 1870, Capt. Jos. Dalferes, master, with H.M. Landry, clerk. January-May 1871, New Orleans-Grand Encore, Capt. John Hein, master, with William Culbertson, clerk. May-December 1871, New Orleans-Red River, Capt. John Hein, master, with B.B. Hotchkiss, clerk. December 1871 thru spring 1873, same master, John C. Mitchell, clerk. Later John C. Libano, clerk. Sold at U.S. marshal sale at New Orleans latter June 1873 to William Fagan. Capt. W.R. Greathouse bought her that fall. Was taken to the Barmore yard, Jeffersonville, for a new hull in 1876. When completed she emerged as *SOUTHERN BELLE* (see).

0421 B.M. RUNYAN

SW p wh b. Cincinnati, Oh., 1858. 230 x 34 x 6.5. Engines 20's- 7 ft. Four boilers, 38 by 26 ft. Built by Capt. James Miller and others for Nashville-New Orleans trade, and also ran Nashville-St. Louis. Sold to a Mr. Mitchell of Alton, Ill., in June 1862 for St. Louis-Alton trade. Sank below Alton in shallow water that December, Capt. Bellas, raised. Extensively repaired at St. Louis in spring of 1864 and was fatally snagged on July 21, 1864, at Island 84, Gaines Landing, Miss. She was in U.S. service. The *FOREST ROSE* rendered aid. Many of the passengers were soldiers whose enlistments had expired bound for Cairo, Ill., to be mustered out. Estimates of life loss ran from "more than 70" to "more than 150." The cabin separated from the hull and lodged on a sandbar in American Cut Off. This Cut Off was formed in 1858 and the old course of the river today is Lake Lee in Arkansas on the east bank not far below Greenville, Miss. Today (1980) the river channel is west of American Cut Off near Lakeport, Ark. Mark Twain was aboard the first steamboat to ascend American Cut Off and tells of this.

0422 B.P. CHENEY

SW p wh b. Pomeroy, Oh., 1859. 247 tons. Capt. Daniel V. Stewart, first master. Ran out of Memphis. Became a Confederate boat 1861 and was burned on Yazoo River, Miss., July 14, 1863, said to have been renamed *MILTON BROWN* at the time.

0423 B.S. RHEA

Stw p wh b. Louisville, Ky., 1878. 162.3 x 31.9 x 4.5. Built for T.G. Ryman. Operated out of Nashville, Tennessee, and appears to have been dismantled at the time her successor (see) was built. The hull was used as a wharfboat at Ghent, Ky., and it was still there in 1894.

0424 B.S. RHEA

Stw p wh b. Jeffersonville, Ind., by Howard, 1886. 165 x 27.1 x 4.6. Engines 14's-4½ ft. Named for B.S. Rhea, Esq., the "Corn King of Tennessee." Built for the Ryman Line and ran Nashville-Paducah connecting with the *C. W. ANDERSON* for upper Cumberland. Capt. J.S. Tyner was master, of Ryman Line. Capt. John Barrett, Cincinnati, bought her for the Louisville-Cincinnati trade in 1894, painted her stacks red, and ran her in opposition to the U.S. Mail Line. Burned at Cincinnati laid up for low water along with the *SCOTIA* and towboat *SIDNEY DILLON,* Nov. 5, 1895.

0425 B.T. ENOS

Stw p wh b. Ironton, Oh., 1881. 150 x 23 x 4. Built by the Brown brothers for the Gallipolis-Huntington trade but was sold upon completion to the Bay Line which entered her in the same trade. Sank and lost at Limeville, Ky. above present-day location of the C&O bridge at Sciotoville in November 1892.

0426 B.W. LEWIS

SW p wh b. Mound City, Ill., and completed at St. Louis, 1858. 237.5 x 33 x 6.2. Owned by Capt. Thomas H. Brierly ¼ and Abram Wolfe ⅛, both of St. Louis; M.B. Witherow ⅛, St. Joseph, Mo.; James Lewis ¼ of Glasgow, Mo.; and W.G. Barclay ¼ of Kansas City, Mo. She ran in the St. Louis & St. Joseph Union Line, Captain Brierly, 1858. Exploded her boilers and burned at Cairo, Ill., June 24, 1860. Capt. Nanson, in charge, was killed and his body later was recovered at New Madrid by the crew of the *PLATTE VALLEY*. Fire broke out in the ladies' cabin moments after the blast. Life loss was set at 40 persons. The crew of the *BAY CITY* was bitterly censured for not rendering aid.

0427 BABY ROSE

Stw p wh b. Fort Benton, Mont., 1909. 71 x 18. Owned by Charles Crepeau. The intention was to supply homesteaders of that area with lumber, hardware, groceries, etc. She made her first trip on July 4, 1909, but lacked the power to shove her barge. The venture was not a success. Cut down at Fort Benton that winter by ice.

0428 BABY ST. JACOBS OIL

Stw p wh b. Fountain City, Wis., 1882. 2.44 tons. (Also see *ST. JACOBS OIL*).

0429 BADGER STATE

Stw p wh b. California, Pa., 1852. 140 x 28 x 3.5. Owned originally by Ephriam Herriott 1⁄16 of Allegheny City, Pa., Hemstead & McMaster ¼ and Thomas Gordon ¼ both of Galena, Ill. and David Fletcher & Co., 7⁄16 of Ogle County, Ill. Capt. Samuel Humbstone, first master. Ran on the Upper Mississippi. Was snagged and sunk in the Des Moines River, May 15, 1853, raised. Was sold to Capt. Lewis Swarmes, Hamburg, Ill., who owned her when she was lost at Chain of Rocks, twelve miles above St. Louis, Dec. 4, 1862.

0430 BAGASSE

Stw wh b. Bayou Ramos, La., 1895. 101.8 x 21 x 2.8. Registered at New Orleans, 1896.

0431 BALD EAGLE

Stw p wh b. Madison, Ind., 1879. 202.3 x 30 x 5.4. Owned by the Schwartz Bros. Commission Co., and ran in the St. Louis and Clarksville trade until 1895 when the *BELLE OF CALHOUN* (see) was built to take her place Capt. Alex Lamont was master many years. She made several trips St. Louis-Red River and St. Louis-Ouachita River during winter months with large grocery trips. Charles Henry, Esq., superintended building this boat, great-grandfather of actress Irene Dunne, and Capt. Henry Leyhe had charge of construction from start to finish. Was caught at St. Louis in the cyclone of May 27, 1896, broke her moorings, struck the middle pier of Eads Bridge, and members of the crew climbed on a projection of the pier and were rescued with ropes lowered from the bridge to them. The watchman was lost. The boat floated on down the river and sank. The machinery was salvaged and later was installed on the *J.M. HANNAFORD* built at Potlach, Wash., for Snake River service, and last was on the *SHAVER* which was converted to diesel in 1950.

0432 BALD EAGLE

Stw p wh b. Madison, Ind., 1898. 206.5 x 34.2 x 5.5. Engines, 15's- 5 ft. Two boilers 44" by 24 ft. Much equipment from the *D. H. PIKE* (see). Owned by the Eagle Packet

Co., and ran principally St. Louis-Illinois River, although in latter years St. Louis-Cape Girardeau-Commerce. Last trade was St. Louis-Fort Madison, this in 1929. Was last used as a quarterboat, broke in two and sank in 1934.

0433 BALIZE

Originally *AVENGER* b. New Albany, Ind., 1864 (see). Sold to private owners Apr. 16, 1867. Dismantled in 1871.

0434 BALLOON

SW p wh b. New Albany, Ind., 1843. 154 tons Said to have had the pilothouse from the old *MISSOURIAN*, first—or one of the first—to have glass windows. Snagged below Augusta, Mo., on the Missouri River, Capt. John McCloy, 1848. The same pilothouse is said to have been used building *WARDEN POPE*.

0435 BALTIC

SW p wh b. Brownsville, Pa., 1848. 188 tons. Said the Pittsburgh *Gazette* on Jan. 8, 1848: "The fine steamers *ATLANTIC* and *BALTIC* built expressly for the packet service between this place and Brownsville are nearly finished and will probably be running by the first of February. Capt. James Parkinson is to take charge of the *ATLANTIC*, and Capt. Adam Jacobs, formerly of the *NIAGARA*, that of the *BALTIC*. They are large and handsomely decorated four boiler boats, and are built so near alike, in every particular, from the cabin to the engineroom, that but for the names would be hard to draw distinction between them." Dismantled in 1854.

0436 BALTIC

SW p wh b. New Albany, Ind., 1856. 399 tons. Went to Mobile, Ala. Exploded and lost at that place, Nov. 3, 1860, with loss of 20 lives.

0437 BALTIC

SW p wh b. New Albany, Ind., 1857. 250 x 37 x 7. Engines, 26's- 9 ft. Five boilers. Principally owned by Capt. C.H. Meekin, New Albany, who was master. Head clerk was George P. Jouett, late of the *A.L. SHOTWELL*. Ran Louisville-New Orleans. Ran a race with the *DIANA* (see) all the way from New Orleans to Louisville in March 1858, a classic of the rivers. On Sunday, Mar. 21, 1858, these two boats left New Orleans within two minutes of one another. At Point Worthington they locked horns and ran together some fifteen miles. The first three nights were cloudy and very dark after the moon went down and shifting fogs before daylight. There was a strong rise out of the Arkansas River to fight, and then a rise in the Mississippi with heavy drift running, and the Ohio River was rising all the way to Louisville. The *BALTIC* arrived at the foot of Third St., Louisville, at 11:12 P.M. Thursday, March 25. Time: five days six hours twenty-two minutes. She was declared the winner. The *DIANA* came up in five days eight hours seven minutes. Neither of these times stood up to the *ECLIPSE* (see). The race was widely watched inasmuch as the contestants were in sight of one another a great part of the way, in this respect undoubtedly the longest and most animated race ever run on the Mississippi System. An oil painting of the event gained wide acclaim. Said the Louisville *Journal* on Feb. 9, 1860: "A fine painting by Mr. George F. Fuller, descriptive of the trial of speed between the *BALTIC* and *DIANA* has been lithographed by Weingartner, one of the best artists in the country, for M. Knoedler of New York and the London and Parisian publishing houses of Goupel & Co. Our citizens had an opportunity of inspecting this picture last year when it elicited much praise for the spirit of its delineation, the truth of its coloring and the admirable disposition of its details. It is a moonlight scene, the rival boats under full head of steam, and the waters lurid with the glare of fires, while busy hands are engaged in cramming the furnaces with combustibles. Each of the steamers takes a sheer to avoid a flatboat, which is lazily drifting down with the current, while the boatmen are all excited at the race. There is fine repose in the scenery which contrasts forcibly with the action portrayed, and the whole forms one of the most characteristic Western pictures we have ever seen. Mr. Fuller has achieved several successes and we are glad to see his picture reproduced by lithograph and so handsomely colored. The Gouples will introduce it to the European connoisours, and we have no doubt it will bring forth fame and profit to the artist." She was acquired by the USQMD during the War and served with Porter on the Red River in 1864. Was said to have made a trip to Mobile as a transport later. Sold back to private hands in 1866. Last owner was William M. McPherson, St. Louis. Capt. Patrick Yore took her there, and she was dismantled. Engines went to *BISMARCK* (see) in 1867.

0438 BALTIC

SW p wh b. Algiers, La., 1860. 604 tons. Burned and lost at Algiers, La., May 6, 1861.

0439 BALTIMORE

SW p wh b. New Martinsville, W. Va. (hull) and completed at Wheeling, 1853. 275 x 38 x 7. Engines, 30's- 9 ft. Four boilers, each 46" by 30 ft. with five 10" flues. Wheels 36 ft. dia., 10 ft. buckets. Cabin by Hanes & Beam, engines by H.W. Phillips. Launched Dec. 19, 1852. Built for the Wheeling-Louisville Union Line, and started running in March 1853. Soon transferred to run Louisville-St. Louis, and St. Louis-New Orleans. Sold at public auction at Portland, Ky., June 12, 1856. The Alton & St. Louis Packet Co., acquired her. She was snagged and lost at Chain of Rocks, above St. Louis on Dec. 13, 1859. The *SPREAD EAGLE* arrived at St. Louis one May day in 1900 with the *BALTIMORE*'s roof bell aboard. It had been serving in the belfry of a church at Shipman, Ill., and went to the *FRED A. BLANKS*.*

0440 BANJO

SW showboat wh b. Cincinnati, Oh., 1855. 105 tons. Fitted up as a showboat, fully equipped stage at the rear, seated 200. Operated by G.R. Spaulding, a circus man. Played mostly on the Upper Miss., Cairo to St. Paul. In September 1860 brought a minstrel show up Red River for the Gaiety Theater in Shreveport. Went to Confederate registry 1861.

0441 BANNER

Stw p wh b. Jeffersonville, Ind., 1850. 38 tons. Off the lists in 1855.

0442 BANNER

SW p wh b. Maysville, Ky., 1862. 27 tons. Apparently enlarged at Catlettsburg, Ky., 1865 and increased to 44 tons. Ran low water in the upper Ohio in Oct. 1867, Capt. George Hamilton. Dismantled 1868.

0443 BANNER OF ATTAKAPAS

SW p wh b. Lake Chicot Pass, La., 1848. 208 tons. First home port, Franklin, La. Ran on Red River. Lost at President Island, Mississippi River on June 10, 1852.

0444 BANNER STATE

SW p wh b. Brownsville, Pa., 1851. 254 tons Engines 20's- 6 ft. Three boilers. First owned in Pittsburgh. Coming up the Mississippi River in 1852 struck a snag which went up through the starboard guard, turned eight passengers out of their beds, at the same time bursting the staterooms to splinters, and then continued its course upward through the hurricane roof, cut the texas in two, and disappeared over the other side of the boat. In spite of this rough treatment none of the passengers was hurt. In 1855 sold to Capt. Josh B. Holland, Capt. Joseph S. Nanson and others for Missouri River. On the third trip she was snagged and lost at Brickhouse Bend, Apr. 11, 1855.

0445 BANNOCK CITY

Stw p wh b. Le Claire, Iowa, 1866. 150 x 28 x 5. Engines 13's- 4 ft. Two boilers. First home port was Keokuk. Gravitated to New Orleans and by 1873 had been through three U.S. marshal sales. Finally was bought by W.H. Kirby and others of Warsaw, Ky., who ran her Cincinnati-Vevay in 1876 in opposition to the U.S. Mail Line. It is said the mail line built the *LOUIS A. SHERLEY* to "run her out." She was laid up in the mouth of the Kentucky River for ice, January 1877. Broke away and ice demolished her.

0446 BARATARIA

Stw p wh b. Barataria, La., 1857. 96 x 17.4 x 4.8. In November 1861 enrolled at New Orleans owned by R.R. Barrow of Terrebonne Parish. Went to Confederate registry.

0447 BARNARD

Stw p wh b. Parkersburg, W. Va., 1871. 125 x 25 x 4.1. Built for a Mr. Barnard who had coal properties in the area of Bellaire, Oh. Occasionally she ran low water packet trades and was noticed 1879 in the Zanesville-Pittsburgh trade, Capt. James Martin. Capt. Jake Cramer, Clarington, Oh., towed railroad crossties from Parkersburg to Pittsburgh with her for quite a while.

0448 BARNETT

Stw p wh b. Pittsburgh, Pa., 1865. 311 tons. First home port was Apalachicola, Fla. Owned by the Barnett Line on Chattahoochee River. On Dec. 1, 1871, collided with a survey steamer at night, tore out eight staterooms and part of the roof, and was dismantled.

0449 BARON DEKALB

U.S. gunboat, recess wheel wh Originally the *ST. LOUIS* built by James B. Eads (see) for Civil War service, renamed 1863.

0450 BARRANQUILLA

Stw p wh b. Pittsburgh, Pa., 1869. She was built under the supervision of Capt. Jackman T. Stockdale for use on the Magdalena River in South America. Left Pittsburgh on Aug. 23, 1869, on low water, Capt. Thomas S. Calhoon, master, with Jake Poe and Andrew Parr, pilots. This was the second packet within the year built at Pittsburgh for South American delivery (see *AUSTRALIA*).

0451 BART ABLE

SW p wh b. Louisville, Ky., 1864. 206 x 40 x 6½. Engines, 22's- 8 ft. Three boilers, each 46" by 26 ft. When new she was taken down over the Falls to Portland, Ky., before her stacks were placed, smoke pouring from the breechings, with Pinkey Varble piloting. She was built for the St. Louis-New Orleans trade, and ran in the Merchants & Peoples' Line, Capt. H.H. Symmes. Capt. Bart Able of St. Louis was an accomplished riverman and was selected chairman of the welcoming committee when U.S. President Andrew Johnson visited St. Louis in 1866 (see *ANDY JOHNSON*). The *BART ABLE* was in the river parade from Alton to St. Louis on that occasion. She was sold to New Orleans and in 1867 Capt. W.C. Harrison had her running New Orleans-Shreveport. He was part owner along with John G. Prather, W.H. Thorwegan and J.N. Terrel of St. Louis. Capt. Richard Sinnott and others later ran her New Orleans-Grand Encore on Red River. They rebuilt her in 1872 and advertised her as the *NEW BART ABLE,* same trade. Dismantled in 1879. Her engines went to the *JESSE K. BELL* (see).

0452 BASTROP

Stw p wh b. Madison, Ind., 1873. 285 tons. In 1877 owned by New Orleans & Ouachita River Transportation Co., Capt. F.A. Blanks, master, with Ben G. Cornwell, clerk. Ran from New Orleans to Monroe, La., in place of the *JOHN H. HANNAH* (see). Sank in Bayou Bartholomew, La., Apr. 24, 1879.

0453 BATESVILLE

SW p wh b. Cincinnati, Oh., 1844. 178 tons. She passed Wheeling in May 1845 loaded down with 60 tons of cannonballs (presumably from Pittsburgh) destined for a Gulf port. She ran on Arkansas and White Rivers and occasionally in off seasons ran New Orleans-Alexandria up the Red, Capt. S.T. Smith, master. Dismantled 1849.

0454 BATESVILLE

Rig? A dispatch to the Pittsburgh *Commercial* dated Mar. 29, 1871, reports *BATESVILLE* having gone up White River to Buffalo Shoals, 150 miles above Jacksonport, and having brought out 475 bales of cotton at $4.50 to $5 a bale. She reshipped this cargo at Jacksonport and then went up Black River to Pocahontas. This was away up there on both streams; Buffalo Shoals was in Baxter County, and Pocahontas in Randolph County. In March 1873 was running Memphis-White River, Capt. Albert Smith, master.

0455 BATESVILLE

Stw p wh b. Brownsville, Pa., 1875. 172.80 tons. In May 1876 she and the *ARCHIE P. GREEN* raced from Batesville to Newport, and the *BATESVILLE* was said to have won by a length or two. Was advertised at Cincinnati for Helena, Ark., and St. Francis River, Capt. J.D. Randall, this in October 1878.

0456 BAXTER

Stw p wh b. Pt. Pleasant, W. Va., 1901. 121 x 22.4 x 3.6. Engines 9″ - 30″. One boiler, 40″ by 16 ft. Built for the Carr Line for use on Kanawha River. Sold January 1901 to Capt. Lon Ritchie for Parkersburg-Waverly trade. Capt. Ritchie owned the wharfboat at Parkersburg and occasionally dabbled in packets. She ran Marrietta-Middleport on opposite days to the *VALLEY BELLE* in the fall of 1901, and previously had been running Marietta-Parkersburg, Capt. William Hall. Sold in February 1902 to Capt. E.A. Calvert, Charleston, W. Va., and from then on ran in Kanawha River. Later sold and renamed *ORIOLE* (see). When originally built she got much equipment and engines from *LEXINGTON* (see).

0457 BAY CITY

Stw p wh b. Brownsville, Pa., 1854. 150 x 35 x 5. Three boilers. She was at Cairo when the *BEN LEWIS* exploded and burned in the summer of 1860, Capt. A.D. Miller. Miller was criticized for not rendering aid. Ran in the Pittsburgh-Cincinnati trade, Capt. Anawalt in charge, winter 1861-1862. Was with Gen. Grant's fleet on Tennessee River. Capt. William Dean bought her 1862 and used equipment in building the *NAVIGATOR* (see).

0458 BAY QUEEN

Stw p wh b. Ironton, Oh., 1912. 147.1 x 28 x 4. Built by the Bay Line to replace the *GREYHOUND* in the Huntington-Portsmouth trade. Was sold to H.C. Myers, Pine Bluff, Ark., in December 1915 to replace the *LIGHTWOOD*. She was a single decker at the time. Ran out of Pine Bluff to Rosedale connecting with the *KATE ADAMS* for Memphis, and at Pine Bluff with *LIGHTWOOD* for upper Arkansas. In the early 1920s came to Evansville, owned by the Williams family, and ran Evansville-Paducah, now grown up with a texas. Eventually was dismantled and the hull converted into a freight barge named *JEANIE*. Machinery went to towboat *DICK WILLIAMS*. Both burned, along with others, at Spottsville, Ky., on Dec. 16, 1932. The packet *SOUTHLAND* (see) and towboat *RIVAL* also were lost in the blaze.

0459 BAY STATE

SW p wh b. Cincinnati, Oh., 1848. 210 tons. Designed for Cincinnati-New Orleans trade, Capt. Collier. The Cairo *Delta* reported on Mar. 15, 1849, the arrival of the *BAY STATE* from Cincinnati, having on board 50 young men and 10 wagons composing the California Mining Co. Each member had put in $500. Off the lists 1854.

0460 BAYARD

SW p wh b. Monongahela City, Pa., 1864. 354 tons. Ran Pittsburgh-Elizabeth on the Monongahela River, Capt. Joel C. Peebles, master, with Samuel W. Vankirk, clerk. In mid-December 1864 was sold to Capts. William J. Kountz and J.C. Saint for the Pittsburgh-Parkersburg trade. Capt. Saint was master, with George D. Moore, clerk. Moore bought control in March 1865, assumed command, with Dan Moore, clerk. In 1867 same trade, Capt. Moore, with J. Hays Moore and J.B. Dayles, clerks. Was rebuilt early 1868 and came out again in mid-April "looking splendid" in same trade. That September made a special trip Pittsburgh to Buffington Island taking down 205 towboatmen to crew towboats laid up for low water and bring them to Pittsburgh on a rise. Capt. George D. Moore commanded on that trip. Sold to the St. Louis & Keokuk Packet Co., in latter April 1869 "and will depart forthwith." By 1874 was in the Keokuk Northern Line until cut down by ice at St. Louis on Dec. 13, 1876.

0461 BAYLISS LEE

Stw p wh b. Jeffersonville, Ind., by Howard, 1899. 190 x 38 x 5.8. Built for the Lee Line of Memphis, which ran her to Friars Point. When still very new she was bought by Capt. E.W.B. Nowland, Memphis, who promptly renamed her *DELTA* (see) for the Memphis-Vicksburg trade. At the time of this sale she had roof signboards reading LEE LINE—PADUCAH AND WATERLOO. She had been built to "buck" the St. Louis & Tennessee River Packet Co., but differences had been settled. The Nowland Line relettered the signboards to read REGULAR MEMPHIS and VICKSBURG PACKET.

0462 BAYOU BELLE

Stw p wh b. Murraysville, Va. and completed at Wheeling, 1855. 168 tons. Built for a Capt. Walker and went to New Orleans. In 1858 running New Orleans-Opelousas, Capt. John Lyons. Snagged and lost on Cahaba River, Ala., Oct. 1860.

0463 BAYOU BOEUF

Stw p wh b. Bayou Boeuf, La., 1847. 104 tons. First home port, Franklin, La. Sank at Clear Lake, Ark., Mar. 25, 1848.

0464 Bayou City

SW p wh b. Jeffersonville, Ind., by Howard, 1859. 165 x 28 x 5. Launched in August 1859 for J.H. Starrett, and ran Galveston-Houston. She was bulkheaded at Howards for the Gulf trip.

0465 Beacon

SW p wh b. Murraysville, Va. (hull) and completed at Cincinnati, 1848. 175 tons. Owned and commanded by Capt. D. H. Shaw. In 1851 advertised at New Orleans for Cincinnati, and "no fear of low water" inasmuch as she was to pick up a lighter barge at Cairo. That fall Capt. Shaw had her in the Mobile-Montgomery trade. Lost on Lake Pontchartrain, 1852.

0466 Beardstown

SW p wh b. St. Louis, Mo., 1847. 77 tons. Exploded and lost at Bath, Ill., June 8, 1854, with loss of one life.

0467 Beardstown

Stw p wh b. Wheeling, W. Va., 1865. 339 tons. Operated out of St. Louis to Illinois River. She passed Cairo, Ill., in July 1871 bound to Galveston, Tex., going by way of the Atchafalaya River, thence to Vermillion Bay.

0468 Beauty

SW p wh b. Newport, Ky., 1848. 169 tons. She was caught on Richmond Bar above New Richmond, Oh., in 1848 and spent the whole summer there high and dry. This humiliation was amply recompensed on Jan. 28, 1850, when on a high river she explored up Licking River to 86 miles above Falmouth, Ky., and brought out freight. Off the lists in 1857.

0469 Beaver

Stw p wh b. Shousetown, Pa., 1847. 100 tons. Three boilers. Ran Pittsburgh-St. Louis, 1852 with Capt. Sharp Hemphill, master. Grant Marsh went around on her as a deckhand that year. Ran on the upper Illinois that summer and fall, and returned to Beaver, Pa., with a large wharfboat for the use of the Pittsburgh-Beaver packets. In the spring of 1854 was noticed leaving Pittsburgh with 22,000 bushels of coal in tow, plus two boats of lumber for lower ports, and a cabin filled with Pittsburgh furniture. Burned at the foot of West Street, Pittsburgh, hitched to a tow ready to depart. Machinery went to the packet *J. W. HAILMAN* built 1855. *Lytle-Holdcamper* disposes of her in collision with the *L.M. KENNETT* at Ste. Genevieve, Mo., Apr. 28, 1854. A daguerreotype of this *BEAVER* appeared in the March 1975 edition of *S&D Reflector,* page 14.

0470 Beaver

Prop p wh b. La Crosse, Wis., 1897. 65 x 11 x 3.6. Ran Brownsville-La Crosse, operated by George L. Winslow and son Edward M. Winslow, Brownsville, Minn. Still listed 1904, maybe later.

0471 Bedford

Stw p wh b. Christler's Landing, Pa., 1852. 180 tons. Three boilers. Burned and lost at Harpeth Shoals, Tenn., June 1, 1854. Location probably about 40 miles below Nashville on the Cumberland.

0472 Bedford

Stw p wh b. Portsmouth, Oh., 1878. 183 x 37 x 6.5. Engines 17's- 5 ft. Three boilers. Owned by Capt. A.W. Williamson, Portsmouth, Oh. On her first trip she came to Parkersburg, W. Va., and loaded 4,000 brl. potatoes, 200 brl. apples, 865 plows, 50 brl. cider, 40 jars apple butter, 219 oil barrels, 85 pkg. wheels, 16 horses, and about 100 passengers for southern delivery. Ran Pittsburgh-St. Louis for a time.

0473 Bee

Stw p wh b. New Albany, Ind., 1851. 153 tons. Off the lists in 1856.

0474 Bee

SW p wh b. Cincinnati, Oh., 1852. 88 tons. Off the lists in 1860. NOTE: One of these two boats exploded boilers at the head of Diamond Island, Ohio River, Mar. 16, 1853, with loss of two lives and several injured.

0475 Bee

Stw p wh b. Portsmouth, Oh., 1859. 59 tons. Went to New Orleans and Confederate registry in 1861.

0476 Bee

Ferry b. Decatur, Neb., 1875. 10 tons.

0477 Bees Wing

SW p wh b. New Albany, Ind., 1844. 133 tons. Ran New Orleans-Minden, Capt. Hiram Wilson. Burned and lost at Port Hudson, La., on Mar. 17, 1845, with loss of one life.

0478 Belfast

SW p wh b. St. Louis, Mo., 1854. 280 x 36 x 8½. Engines 24's- 8 ft. Five boilers. Ran principally Memphis-New Orleans. Created much comment when new, as her 80 ft. high stacks (from the roof) had square-cut tops with her name cut in each side, 15 ft. square. Collided with and sank the *HUMBOLDT* at Island 75 on Feb. 21, 1857. Grounded at Island 66 on Mar. 20, 1857, and came near breaking in two as the river fell, Capt. Charles B. Church. Was downbound with 3,000 bales and 50 passengers when she sank and was lost near Morgan's Plantation, East Carroll Parish, La., in the vicinity of Lake Providence, this on Nov. 19, 1860. No life loss, but cotton was lost.

0479 Belfast

Stw p wh b. Freedom, Pa., 1857. 158 x 30. Engines, 13's- 3 ft. Built for Capt. Hy A. Forn. Capt. Adam Poe, Georgetown, Pa., took her to Wabash River, new, and sold her. Capt. Carleton was in charge on May 6, 1862, when she loaded at Pittsburgh for St. Louis. Capt. W.C. Mann probably owned her Sept. 27, 1862, when she was at Augusta,

Ky., as Morgan's Raiders descended upon that town. Capt. Sedam had her protected with hay bales but when he learned Morgan had howitzers the *BELFAST* departed in unseemly haste. She had various owners, including Capt. Lon Bryson. In 1867 running Cincinnati-New Orleans, Capt. J.P. Sedam, with R.H. Kerr, clerk. Went to Mobile later that year. Burned on the Tombigbee River, Mar. 7, 1868.

0480 BELFAST

Stw p wh Memphis, Nov. 2, 1872: Passengers on the *E.H. DURFEE* which passed down this p.m. report that the steamer *BELFAST*, Capt. Sedam, from St. Louis to New Orleans, struck a snag yesterday at the head of Island 26, some 100 miles above here, and is sunk in five feet. Cairo, Nov. 5, 1872: The *T.F. ECKERT* has gone to raise the *BELFAST* which has some 1300 tons of freight on herself. Later: She was raised and docked at Mound City. Owned by Belfast Transportation Co. On Feb. 26, 1874, she was ascending the Falls at Louisville. Drift in her rudders caused her to sheer, and she stove on a rock. She lay in 40 feet at the stern and in 25 feet at the bow. Her load comprised 500 tons of pig iron, 200 tons of ship stuff and 100 tons of freight. She was bound from St. Louis to Pittsburgh.

0481 BELGRADE

Stw p wh b. Vincennes, Ind., 1877. 96 x 18 x 2.5. Owned and operated on the Wabash River, by Theodore P. Egnew, who also ran the *VIGO* (see). Listed in 1886.

0482 BELINDA H. BISSELL

SW p wh b. LaGrange, Ill., 1860. 93 tons. Off the lists, 1862.

0483 BELL

Stw p wh b. Dubuque, Iowa, 1895. 41 x 11 x 7. Documented at Memphis, 1896.

0484 BELLA DONNA

SW p wh b. Louisville, Ky., 1852. 285 x 35½ x 6. New Orleans-Upper Bends, Capt. I.H. Morrison, 1853. New Orleans-Bayou Sara, Capt. J.H. Donaldson, 1855. Captain John W. Cannon was a major stockholder. Converted into a wharfboat in the fall of 1858.

0485 BELLA DONNA

SW p wh b. New Orleans, La., 1864. 142 x 32.2 x 4.8. Owned in part by J.O. Noyes, New Orleans. Capt. Abe Smith. Snagged and lost on Red River 50 miles below Alexandria, La., July 1865. She ran Natchez-New Orleans. Was with Porter on Red River, and was at Shreveport.

0486 BELLA ISREAL

Stw p wh b. Berwick City, La., 1883. 71.3 x 27.3 x 4.6. Still documented at New Orleans in 1892.

0487 BELLAIRE

Stw p wh b. Harmar, Oh., at Knox Yard, 1887. 127.3 x 24.2 x 3.6. Engines 11's- 5 ft. The machinery was built by W.F. Robertson & Co., Marietta, with J.H. McConnell as foreman. Originally owned by Capt. James S. McDonald and others, and ran Wheeling-Bellaire in opposition to the Prince boats. Apparently did no good, and 1890 was running Middleport-Marietta with Capt. M.M. Brown in charge. She burned in 1892 and was rebuilt to become the *KANAWHA BELLE* (see).

0488 BELLE

Stw p wh b. Monongahela City, Pa. (hull), and completed at Pittsburgh, 1865. 155 x 29 x 4½. Engines 10's- 5½ ft. Three boilers. Hull was built at the Latta yard. Machinery by A. Hartupee, Pittsburgh. Came out new in March 1865 and entered Pittsburgh-Oil City trade, Capt. T.W. Laughrey, who owned half interest along with James Kennedy. Frank Whiting was clerk. This was the largest boat on the Allegheny River, 262 tons. When water was low she ran Ohio River trades; Pittsburgh-Cincinnati in summer 1867 with A.D. Reno and Jerry Witten, pilots. Ran Parkersburg-Gallipolis summer of 1868 in place of the *EMMA GRAHAM*. That winter with Capt. Laughrey in charge, towed a circus to southern waters. Ran Pittsburgh-Parkersburg spring 1870, Capt. John Ritchey, and in June tried the Pittsburgh-Geneva trade on Monon River, Capt. J.P. Smith with J.W. Scott, clerk. Sold in 1871 to Capt. Marsh McDonald and others who used her in bringing iron ore from the St. Louis area to Pittsburgh, Capt. William McClintock. That fall she broke cylinder timber and had to be towed to Pittsburgh by the *FEARLESS* and was to be dismantled.

0489 BELLE

Stw p wh b. Madison, Ind., 1875. 169.10 tons. Ran in New Orleans-Upper Coast trade in 1878, J.E. Brou, clerk. New Orleans-Bayou Lafourche in 1880, Capt. Max Blanchard, with J.C. Bergeron and C.J. Blanchard, clerks. Still documented in 1882.

0490 BELLE AIRE

SW p wh b. Jeffersonville, Ind., 1842. 166 tons. Advertised at Pittsburgh for Illinois River, Capt. Barclay, early spring 1844. In New Orleans-Bends trade 1844, Capt. F. M. Streck. Off the lists in 1848.

0491 BELLE CREOLE

SW p wh b. Cincinnati, Oh., 1845. 447 tons. Ran New Orleans-Bends 1846, Capt. Champromere. Burst a steam line Nov. 16, 1849, near New Orleans, five killed. In New Orleans-Vicksburg trade, 1850, Capt. J.M. White. Off the lists 1852.

0492 BELLE CREOLE

Stw p wh b. Moundsville, Va., 1856. 190 x 33 x 7½. Operated New Orleans-Red River 1856-1861. Advertised Memphis-Cincinnati, Capt. W.J. Lusk, March 1861. Snagged and lost at Plum Point, Tenn., Feb. 1, 1864, with loss of one life, then running Cairo-Little Rock.

0493 BELLE CREOLE

SW p wh The Missouri *Republican* on Feb. 20, 1864, noticed

this boat, 250 x 36 x 7. Was with Porter on Red River. Reported burned in the wharf fire at New Orleans which destroyed nine boats, May 28, 1864.

0494 BELLE CREOLE

SW p wh b. New Albany, Ind., 1862. Built for Louisville-Pittsburgh Landing trade, Capt. H. McDougal. Capt. J.B. Ford of New Albany had a hand in her. She was sunk and lost at or near West Columbia, W. Va., winter of 1863-1864. In May 1864 C.T. Dumont recovered the machinery and took it to Cincinnati. The *CAPT. JOHN BRICKELL* was sunk nearby at the time (see).

0495 BELLE CROOKS

Stw p wh b. Jeffersonville, Ind., 1881. 91 x 22 x 3. Documented at New Orleans, 1886. Sank near Texarkana, Ark., Apr. 16, 1892.

0496 BELLE D'ARBONNE

Stw p wh b. Monroe, La., 1893. 111 x 22 x 3.7. Documented at New Orleans, 1896.

0497 BELLE GATES

SW p wh b. New Albany, Ind., 1851. 278 tons. New Orleans-Red River 1851. Went to Mobile, Capt. Dyche, December 1851, and returned to New Orleans in the fall of 1852. In 1856 New Orlean-Shreveport-Lake Bistineau, Capt. L. Bryan. In 1859 in New Orleans-Lower Coast trade to Balize and South West Pass, Capt. M.N. Radovich. Went to Confederate registry 1861.

0498 BELLE GOLDING

Stw p wh b. Brownsville, Pa., 1854. 150 x 30 x 4½. Three boilers. Was at St. Paul 1855 with Capt. Isaac M. Mason in charge. Snagged and lost on the Missouri River, June 14, 1855.

0499 BELLE GOULD

SW p wh b. New Albany, Ind., 1852. 200 x 36 x 6½. 207 tons. Built for St. Louis-Keokuk trade, Capt. E.W. Gould. Ran regularly on the Illinois River in 1853 and was the first spring arrival at Peoria that year. Snagged and lost at Island 25 below Cairo, Mar. 3, 1854.

0500 BELLE IDA

SW p wh b. St. Louis, Mo., 1861. 133 tons. 122 x 20 x 4. Built for Red River trade and ran there until returned to St. Louis for rebuilding in 1865 (see next listing).

0501 BELLE IDA NO. 2

SW p wh b. St. Louis, Mo., 1865. 133.94 tons. This was a rebuilding job. Operated on Red River until burned, laid up at Algiers, La., on Jan. 9, 1873.

0502 BELLE ISLE

SW p wh b. Cincinnati, Oh., 1846. 219 tons. Ran St. Louis-New Orleans, Capt. Smith. Burned in the St. Louis fire, May 17, 1849, along with 22 more.

0503 BELLE KEY

SW p wh b. New Albany, Ind., 1849. 267 x 34 x 8. Engines 24's- 8 ft. Six boilers, each 40′ by 30 ft. Cabin 230 feet long. Hull by Humphrey. Capt. Peyton A. Key commanded, with Mr. Sinton and Aleck Adams, clerks. She came up from New Orleans to Louisville, arriving at the destination Apr. 23, 1849, in 4 days 23 hours 7 minutes, having wooded 11 times, and made six landings on the Ohio River. She owns claim of having come up the Ohio from Diamond Island to Portland, Ky., in daylight (16 hours) reckoned at 224 miles. Dismantled 1854.

0504 BELLE LEE

Stw p wh b. New Albany, Ind., 1863. 101.6 x 21.8 x 4.6. 93 tons. Louisville-Nashville trade, March 1864. Partially burned 1864 and rebuilt 1865. Enrolled at New Orleans July 1866 owned by Phillip Drumm, that city. Inspected as a ferry in the New Orleans District in 1873. Off the lists 1877.

0505 BELLE LEE

SW p wh b. Jeffersonville, Ind., 1868. 1284 tons. 291 x 42.4 x 8.4. Engines 34½'s- 9 ft. Eight boilers. Built at the Barmore yard. Engines were cast at the Washington Foundry of John B. Davis & Co., Louisville. Named for daughter of James Bridgeford, Esq., Louisville, who married Col. Phil Lee of the Confederate Army. She came out under charter to Capt. T.P. Leathers who ran her that winter New Orleans-Vicksburg wherein he incurred the displeasure of Capt. John W. Cannon, a circumstance brought on by reason of the terms of the charter and cutting of rates. Cannon confronted Leathers about this violation, and soon a story commenced to trickle into newspapers all the way to Cincinnati. From the New Albany *Commercial* of Nov. 14, 1868: "Capt. John W. Cannon and Capt. Tom Leathers, we are informed, indulged in a knock-down at New Orleans Saturday. The difficulty arose out of the charter of the *BELLE LEE* by Leathers and his subsequent violation of the charter. Capt. Cannon had the best of the fight, so our informant states." A few days later in a Cincinnati paper: "In the recent fight, we understand very little claret was drawn." This altercation in many ways set the stage for the *ROBT. E. LEE-NATCHEZ* contest. Capt. Anson McGill assumed command of the *BELLE LEE* in 1869, attempted the Louisville-New Orleans trade with the following officers: James Ostrander and William Underwood, pilots; Adolph Martin, first clerk; John Lenz and Ed Neff, engineers; William Whitlow, mate; assistant clerks J.A. Dinwiddle and Ed Broughton. In June 1869 she was foreclosed in behalf of the Barmore Shipyard, with a debt of $113,000 hanging over, and was auctioned at the Louisville Court House steps. She brought $60,000 and was reenrolled owned by Capt. John Smoker of New Orleans. Capt. J.M. White went master. On Nov. 12, 1869, the ownership again changed with Capt. John C. Sinnott ½, Capt. John W. Tobin ¼, and Capt. John W. Cannon ¼. She arrived at New Orleans Dec. 31, 1874, with 5,908 bales on board, plus two bargeloads in tow, one with 762 and the other with 7,600 sacks of seed. This was the biggest trip since *MAGNOLIA* times before the War. The crew of the *ROBT. E. LEE* yielded a set of deer horns to the *BELLE LEE* on this occasion. Attached to the antlers was a sign reading: "Champion *ROBT. E. LEE* 5,741; P. Peppard, mate, Beat 'Em and Take 'Em." To this was added "*BELLE LEE,* Champion, Moses Gibbs, Mate, 5,908." This was hung in the cabin, port side. Across the way in the cabin was a similar set of antlers inscribed to the second mates: "C. Stokes, *ROBT. E. LEE.* William Larkins, *BELLE LEE.*" Moses Gibbs was an old Leathers mate and brought down the banner trip of the *NATCHEZ* (see). The cabin of the *BELLE LEE* was a sight to behold: "a dozen chandeliers in her gold and white cabin, 36 oil lamps in each with glass pendants, plus draperies in front of every stateroom door. . ."

Belle Lee, Belle Lee,
Tell me, ole gal,
Is you thinkin' o' me
When steamin' along?

Belle Lee, Belle Lee,
Lis'n to mah song.
Kaze you's all mine—
Belle Lee, Belle Lee

So penned songwriter Will S. Hays when his friend Anson McGill lost the boat to creditors on the Louisville Court House steps. By the time she brought down her banner cotton trip just described she was owned by the group from New Orleans plus Capt. J. Frank Hicks and Martin Walt of Memphis. In the summer of 1876 the *BELLE LEE* was taken to Metropolis, Ill., the hull greatly enlarged, and she emerged as the *MARY BELL* (see).

0506 BELLE M.

Stw p wh b. Plaquemine, La., 1900. 80 x 17.8 x 3. Later renamed *MARJORIE,* so registered at Memphis 1908.

BELLE MEMPHIS

Often referred to as such, but documented as simply *MEMPHIS,* built at Jeffersonville, Ind., 1860 (see).

0507 BELLE MEMPHIS

SW p wh b. Jeffersonville, Ind., by Howard, 1866. 260 x 40 x 7. Ran in the Memphis & St. Louis Packet Co., St. Louis-Memphis. Dismantled in 1880.

0508 BELLE MEMPHIS

SW p wh b. Jeffersonville, Ind., by Howard, 1880. 267 x 42 (68 ft. over all) x 7.5. Engines 26's- 8 ft. Five boilers, each 44' by 28 ft., four flues. Allowed 175 psi. Wheels 35½ ft. dia., buckets 14½ ft. The engines were not new, probably from the predecessor. She came out in the early spring of 1881, St. Louis–Memphis. The citizens of Memphis presented her with a piano and a full set of colors. Capt. Ike McKee was her master, 64, the oldest skipper in the Anchor Line. Henry E. Corbyn was first clerk. Later on Capt. R.W. McCoy was master. Made trips through to New Orleans. In 1891 Capt. Thomas W. Shields was master. About 1895 Capt. Milt Harry took charge and his pilots were Capts. Horace Bixby and Mike Kelly. She was snagged and lost at Crane's Island below Chester, Ill., early September 1897. Good picture of the cabin, and of the boat, in an article in *S&D Reflector,* September 1971 issue, pages 40-41.

0509 BELLE MORGAN

Ferry wh b. Plattsmouth, Neb., 1880. Inspected there in 1881.

0510 BELLE NIOTA

Ferry wh b. Brownsville, Pa., 1858. 74.70 tons. Documented at Keokuk, Iowa, 1867. Also registered as *NIOTA BELLE* (see).

0511 BELLE OF ALTON

SW p wh b. Jeffersonville, Ind., by Howard, 1868. 229 x 34.5 x 6. Engines 24½'s- 7 ft. Six boilers, each 44' by 26 ft. Machinery came from *SOUTHWESTER* (see). Owned by Alton & St. Louis Packet Co., Capt. John A. Bruner. Soon gravitated to New Orleans. In 1870 New Orleans-Grand Encore, Capt. J.P. McKinley, master, with William A. Hurd, clerk. She burned at Algiers, La., laid up, Mar. 28, 1871. Her engineer, William W. Marsh, was jailed in New Orleans charged with arson, later released on $6,000 bond. At the trial he was honorably acquitted. Machinery went to the *CARONDELET* (see). The hull was used as a barge which burned at Vicksburg, Nov. 18, 1873.

0512 BELLE OF ASHLAND

Ferry wh b. Cincinnati, Oh., 1873. 80.3 x 24.2 x 3. A wooden covered bridge over the Little Kanawha at Parkersburg drifted off in high water 1875. The *BELLE OF ASHLAND* shoved it ashore at Ice Creek where it supplied kindling for the natives several years. Then a $20 goldpiece was found in it, resulting in a search which netted several more. This ferry was still listed in 1892.

0513 BELLE OF AUGUSTA

SW ferry wh b. Augusta, Ky., 1866. 40 tons. Dismantled in 1876.

0514 BELLE OF BELLEVUE

Ferry wh b. Bellevue, Iowa, 1870. 88.7 x 13.5 x 3.9. Still listed 1892.

0515 BELLE OF BROWNSVILLE

Stw ferry wh b. Grafton, Ill., 1880. 110 x 30.1 x 4. Operated on Missouri River at Brownsville, Neb. Listed at St. Joseph, Mo., in 1892, and at Cairo, Ill., 1896.

0516 BELLE OF CALHOUN

Stw p wh b. St. Louis, Mo., 1895. 180.9 x 36.4 x 4.7. Engines 15's- 6 ft. Two boilers, 44" by 26 ft. Built at the Carondelet marine ways and completed at the St. Louis wharf for the St. Louis & Clarksville Packet Co., Frederick W. Schwartz, pres. Crew on maiden trip included Capt.

Aaron Hall, master; Joe Chatterton and Harry H. Monaghan, pilots; Edward Young, first clerk; Zollie Block, second clerk; Oliver Cotrell, chief engineer, and William Tracy, mate. The boat was named for Miss Anna Wood, chosen as the "belle of Calhoun County, Ill." in a contest run by the Hardin *Herald*. She afterward married Zollie Block. The *Waterways Journal* in 1895 ran a contest for the most popular packet crew members out of St. Louis. The *BELLE OF CALHOUN* hauled off all honors. Badly damaged May 27, 1896 by the tornado at St. Louis and she sank up to the cabin; raised and repaired. Sold to the Memphis & Vicksburg Packet Co., in May 1899 and her name changed to *JULIA* (see). By 1905 she got back her original name, then owned by the St. Louis & Calhoun Packet Corp. Sank four miles above Alton with 4,700 barrels of apples in October 1914. Her head was on shore and the stern in 20 ft. About 800 barrels were lost. Raised and repaired. In October 1929 she again sank about three miles above Hannibal, Mo., and was raised. Burned in Alton Slough, winter 1930–1931.

0517 BELLE OF CHESTER

Stw ferry wh b. Grafton, Ill., 1878. 112 x 26.3 x 3.8. Operated at Chester, Ill., owned by Capt. Harvey Neville. Still listed 1903.

0518 BELLE OF CINCINNATI

SW ferry wh b. Newport, Ky., 1853. 110 tons. Following a rebuilding in 1865 she was renamed *CINCINNATI BELLE* (see).

0519 BELLE OF FOUNTAIN

Rig? b. Hannibal, Mo., 1882. 165 x 18.3 x 2.8. Still documented 1886.

0520 BELLE OF JEFFERSON

Rig? Apparently a ferry at Jefferson City, Mo. Got in the news when a steam drum exploded on July 3, 1874, the fireman drowned. Sank at the head of Osage Chute, Missouri River, July 13, 1875, lost.

0521 BELLE OF JEFFERSON

Stw wh b. Morgan City, La., 1889. 87.5 x 21.2 x 6.3. Still listed in 1896.

0522 BELLE OF KASKASKIA

Stw ferry wh b. Chester, Ill., 1897. 59.8 x 22.3 x 4.4. Later sold to the Missouri River and renamed *MEEKER* (see).

0523 BELLE OF LA CROSSE

SW p wh b. Paducah, Ky., and completed at St. Louis, 1870. 232 x 37.8 x 5½. Engines 22's- 7 ft. Three boilers, 41" by 26 ft., 5 flues. Wheels 28 ft. dia., with 20 ft. buckets. Engines from *ITASCA* (see), later got engines from *KEY CITY* said to have been identical in size but improved her speed. Belonged to the Keokuk Northern Line. Burned at St. Louis on July 12, 1882, at 4:00 P.M., foot of Alma Street, setting fire to the *NORTH WESTERN* which also burned.

0524 BELLE OF LEXINGTON

Ferry wh Apparently ran at Lexington, Mo., on the Missouri River. Inspected in 1867, and in 1874 noticed as owned by Lexington Ferry, Coal & Railroad Transportation Co. 124.85 tons.

0524-A BELLE OF LOUISVILLE

Stw ex sh The *AVALON* (#0403) after purchase by the Jefferson County (Ky.) Fiscal Court in 1962 was renamed *BELLE OF LOUISVILLE*, with Louisville, Ky. as her home port. On April 31, 1963 she ran a staged race at Louisville with the *DELTA QUEEN* in which the DQ won handily. Since that time the contest has become an annual event, scheduled a few days prior to the Kentucky Derby, and easily the river's most popular sporting classic. In early 1968 the *BELLE* was extensively rebuilt at Jeffboat, Inc., acquiring a longer bow, and increasing her overall length to become 191'2". Also during this renovation she was given three Western-style boilers, each 56" dia. by 28 ft. long, 13 flues. The paddlewheel continues to be driven by her original Rees high pressure engines installed at Pittsburgh when she came out new in 1915 as the *IDLEWILD*. The Operating Board feels obliged to keep her activities restricted to the Louisville area, although she has been making fall trips to Madison, Ind. and into the Kentucky River, and has wandered up the Ohio to Cincinnati, and has been "south" to Green River. The continuing success of this rather novel municipal adventure is due, in no small part, to Capt. C. W. Stoll, Clyde Glass, and a few other dedicated residents of the Falls City. The *BELLE* has been the "training ship" for many of the personnel presently operating the *NATCHEZ* at New Orleans, and, in lesser degree, for crews on the *DELTA QUEEN* and *MISSISSIPPI QUEEN*. She continues in service as this is typed in February 1983.

0525 BELLE OF MILTON

SW ferry wh b. New Albany, Ind., 1865. 220 tons. Apparently ferried Madison, Ind., and Milton, Ky. Lost in ice at Madison on Dec. 24, 1872.

0526 BELLE OF PEPIN

SW ferry wh b. Pepin, Wis., 1877. 66 x 17 x 3. Inspected at Lansing, Iowa, 1881. Listed at Memphis, 1892.

0527 BELLE OF PIKE

SW p wh b. Cincinnati, Oh., 1866. 235 x 35 x 5. Engines 21's- 6½ ft. Owned by the St. Louis and Naples Packet Co., Capt. James Abrams, master. On Oct. 16, 1872, in collision with *HENRY AMES* near Cairo. E.P. King, pilot on the *BELLE OF PIKE* got six month suspension at the trial. Sunk in ice at Memphis, Dec. 24, 1872. Several weeks later the cabin departed for the south. The hull with machinery intact landed on Presidents Island. She had considerable cotton aboard when she sank, much of it removed by the *T.F. ECKERT*. The *R.P. WALT* was also sunk (see).

0528 BELLE OF PIKE

Ferry wh b. Carondelet, Mo., 1868. 105 tons. Operated at Clarksville, Pike County, Mo. Rebuilt at Madison, Ind., 1872. Out of service in 1886.

0529 Belle of Shreveport

Stw p wh b. Metropolis, Ill. (hull), and completed at St. Louis, 1872. 200 x 44 x 7. Engines 19½'s- 6 ft. Four boilers. Capt. Tom Rea ran her St. Louis-Shreveport. She was stranded on Horsetail Bar, below St. Louis, high and dry, January-February 1876. Captain Rea took down 1,000 "gunny" sacks to fill with sand and place under the stem to keep her from twisting her hull. She was given a new shaft and engines at St. Louis, fall of 1878, the engines coming from *ARLINGTON*, 22's- 7 ft. In January 1886 enroute Cincinnati to the Cotton Exposition in New Orleans she sank three miles above Sunflower Landing. She got in an eddy and hit the bank head on. Took an hour to sink and everybody off safely. Capt. Wash Thompson was in command. Charles Owens was pilot on watch, and his partner pilot was Frank Carrel. George Carrel, his brother, was third clerk—later mayor of Cincinnati. The *KATE ADAMS* came along and took the marooned passengers and crew to Vicksburg.

0530 Belle of Texas

SW p wh b. Brownsville, Pa. (hull), and completed at Pittsburgh, 1871. 134 x 33 x 5. Engines 16's- 5½ ft. Three boilers. Built by James Rees & Sons for the Trinity River in Texas. Capt. Frank Maratta took her down the rivers. Soon was bought by the Memphis & Arkansas River Packet Co. for the Little Rock-Memphis trade. Capt. John J. Darragh and others bought her with the idea of taking her to Jacksonville, Fla., to run on St. Johns River. She left New Orleans Jan. 15, 1879. Got to Jupiter Inlet February 11 and lay there until February 13 and again put out to sea at 7:00 A.M. At 8:10 that night due to a wind shift she was in trouble. At 2:00 A.M. next morning the stacks had gone overboard, steam line to the doctor was broken, and she was run ashore and beached eight miles south of Mosquito Inlet. The captain, Si O. Hemenway, sloshed 35 miles in water ankle to waist deep to get aid. The boat was wrecked.

0531 Belle of the Bends

SW p wh b. Jeffersonville, Ind., by Howard, 1898. 210 x 32.6 x 7.4. Engines 18's- 8 ft. Three boilers, each 44" by 28 ft. Built for Vicksburg & Greenville Packet Co., J.J. Powers, pres., and D.C.B. Robinson supervised construction, both of Vicksburg. This was one of the more notably handsome of medium-sized side-wheelers. She had all the Anchor Line grace, double stages and all. Ran Greenville-Vicksburg many years. Her captain in 1900 was Capt. A.F. Nimtz, and the following year his crew composed Charlie Kain, Harry Bumgartner and Henry McFarland, clerks; Billy Newbill and Joe Delahunt, pilots; Mike O'Keefe and George Meir, engineers; and James McGowan, steward. She was flagship of the parade celebrating the opening of the canal at Vicksburg when the Yazoo River mouth was diverted on Jan. 27, 1903; quite an occasion inasmuch as Vicksburg had virtually been cut off the river since Centennial Cut Off which happened Apr. 26, 1876. She sank at Peeler's Landing, 40 miles above Vicksburg, September 1909, was raised. Sank at Fitler's Landing, 20 miles below Lake Providence during a snowstorm in February 1910. Was again raised. By then operated by Capt. Morrissy. Ran excursions at New Orleans in the winter 1910–1911. Was converted into an excursion boat and renamed *LIBERTY* (see). In 1940 her roof bell was at the Altheimer Plantation near Pine Bluff, Ark.

0532 Belle of the Coast

SW p wh b. Cincinnati, Oh., 1880. 187.4 x 37 x 6.9. Engines, 21's- 7 ft. Four boilers, each 42" by 28 ft., two flues. Built at the Cincinnati Marine Ways Co., cabin by Elias Ealer, machinery by C.T. Dumont. Built for Capts. J.F. Aucoin and P.A. Charlet to run New Orleans-Bayou Lafourche. In the fall of 1885 was taken around Florida to the St. Johns River and ran that winter with the *CHESAPEAKE* and *QUEEN OF ST. JOHNS* in the Tourists and Shippers Fast Line, Jacksonville-Enterprise. Was returned to New Orleans and became a fixture in the Upper Coast trade. Burned at Carrollton, La., in January 1897.

0533 Belle of the West

SW p wh b. Cincinnati, Oh., 1841. 249 tons. Ran Cincinnati-New Orleans, Capt. David Whitten. Burned on the Ohio River near Florence, Ind., Capt. D.S. James, Apr. 22, 1850, with loss of 35 lives.

0534 Belle Peoria

SW p wh b. Monongahela, Pa., 1859. 180 x 32. Engines, 15's- 6 ft. Two boilers. Ran St. Louis-Peoria as an independent. Burned at Sharp's Landing, Illinois River, Mar. 11, 1860, rebuilt. In 1862 in U.S. service taking supplies to Cumberland River. In November 1863 again on the Illinois, up to Havana. Spring of 1864 making trips to Fort Benton. She came along after the *ISABELLA* (see) was wrecked at Fort Buford and took off the machinery. Ran on a bar near Acrow's Trading Post, five miles above Cheyenne River, October 1864, lay there all winter, and was wrecked by ice in the spring of 1865. Settlers found the pilothouse on the prairie near the river and named the locality Peoria Bottoms.

0535 Belle Quigley

SW p wh b. Brownsville, Pa., 1852. 145 x 24 x 4.5. Engines, 14's- 5 ft. Two boilers. Built at the John S. Pringle yard. Cabin by James Lanning. Machinery by Haigh, Hartupee of Pittsburgh. Left Pittsburgh December 18, 1852, Capt. A. Baird, for Green River, Ky. Burned at Carrollton, Ky., Feb. 5, 1856.

0536 Belle Rowland

Stw p wh b. Brownsville, Pa., and completed at Pittsburgh, 1871. 160 x 35 x 4. Engines, 12's- 4 ft. Two boilers, each 38" by 24 ft. Machinery by James Rees. Owned by A.A. Rowland and Capt. George W. Rea. Made trips St. Louis-Shreveport, and was well known during cotton season on the Ouachita, Old, and Black rivers. Sank in Swan Lake, Tex., on Red River, Feb. 23, 1877.

0537 BELLE ST. LOUIS

SW p wh b. Metropolis, Ill. (hull), and completed at St. Louis, 1864. 277 x 38.5 x 7.5. Engines, 26's- 8 ft. Four boilers, each 46" by 18 ft. Operated in the early Anchor Line, rated 902.25 tons. Dismantled in 1881 and the hull was used as a barge.

0538 BELLE ST. LOUIS

SW p wh b. Jeffersonville, Ind., at the Barmore yard, 1875. 225 x 37 x 4.5. Engines, 20's- 7 ft. Three boilers. An early Anchor Line boat, Capt. William Blake. Capt. Jud Cartwright, master, with J.B. White, clerk, in 1877. Cut down by ice at Ste. Genevieve, Mo., on Jan. 31, 1877, raised within two weeks. She was downbound St. Louis to Vicksburg, Capt. McKee, when she was snagged and lost near Island 40, Nov. 12, 1879. The *FANNIE TATUM* went to the wreck with a barge to salvage deck cargo.

0539 BELLE SHERIDAN

SW p wh b. New Albany, Ind., 1853. 285 x 34 x 7.5. Engines, 34's- 9 ft. Four boilers, each 42" by 26 ft. Hull by Wihl, machinery by Lent, South & Shipman. Ran Louisville-New Orleans, Capt. Ed Montgomery. Capt. M.F. Webb commanded in 1855. Dismantled in 1856.

0540 BELLE SULPHUR

SW p wh b. Louisville, Ky., 1856. 126 tons. Ran principally New Orleans-Shreveport. Went to Confederate registry in 1861.

0541 BELLE VERNON

Stw p wh b. Belle Vernon, Pa., and completed at Pittsburgh, 1867. 155 x 36 x 5.5. Engines 18's- 5 ft. Three boilers, each 38" by 26 ft. Hull by L.M. and W.F. Speer. Engines by James Rees, boilers by James Thorn. Entered Pittsburgh-St. Louis trade, Capt. John J. Darragh, Jr., with William Blackstock, clerk. She replaced the *FINANCIER* lost the year before (see). In January 1868 delivered at Marietta, Oh., six hogsheads of New Orleans sugar consigned to McConnell & Edwards, McConnelsville, Oh., first in seven years since the war started. First boat through the enlarged Louisville and Portland Canal when it was opened in late fall 1870. Brought New Orleans sugar and molasses to Pittsburgh February 1871 and that April loaded at Pittsburgh for St. Paul and return to St. Louis. Sunk in ice at Cincinnati, February 1872, raised and rebuilt. Struck wreck of the *JENNIE HOWELL* (see) near Shawneetown, Ill., late August 1873 and was lost with four deaths, then in command of Capt. Kenniston. She was downbound Cincinnati to Memphis. The machinery was salvaged and returned to Cincinnati aboard the *JAMES D. PARKER*. Billy Shaw, second clerk, had also been second clerk on the *JENNIE HOWELL* when she sank.

0542 BELLE YAZOO

SW p wh Owned by the Parisot Line and ran Vicksburg-Yazoo River. First mention we notice is in mid-April 1871 when she lost her stacks eight miles above Yazoo City during a storm and was otherwise damaged. On Jan. 7, 1876 downbound from Yazoo River to New Orleans she was snagged and sunk about 12 miles above Bayou Sara with no life loss.

0543 BELLE ZANE

Stw p wh b. Zanesville, Oh., 1844. 128 tons. Ran Zanesville-Marietta-Cincinnati in 1845, Capt. Cogswell. That December she loaded out for New Orleans and 12 miles below White River was snagged. Turned bottom-side up, night of December 19, 1845. The death toll was placed at 40 lives. Many of the bodies were buried along the river bank.

0544 BELLEMONT

SW p wh b. Monongahela, Pa., 1857. 119 ton. Probably went foreign; first home port of owners listed New York, N.Y. Out of documention 1860.

0545 BELLEVILLE

Centerwheel ferry wh b. New Albany, Ind., 1864. 234 tons. Operated at St. Louis. Dismantled in 1878. Owned by Wiggins Ferry Co.

0546 BELLEVUE

Stw p wh b. Levanna, Oh., 1890. 120 x 24 x 3.6. Engines, 13's- 4½. Two boilers, each 44" by 16 ft. Built to run between Cincinnati and Bellevue, Ky., replacing the *FLORENCE SHANKS* (see) which had proved too small. An electric car line ran her out. Capt. Joe Webb bought her, and towed stone from Moscow, Oh. to Cincinnati. The Louisville & Evansville Packet Co. bought her for the Owensboro-Evansville trade. Retired about 1912 and equipment used building towboat *RED SPOT*.

0547 BELLMAN

Steam yacht b. Pittsburgh, Pa., 1894. 50 x 11 x 1.7. Still documented at Pittsburgh in 1896.

0548 BELMONT

Stw p wh b. California, Pa. and completed at Pittsburgh, 1856. 153 x 31 x 4.5. Ran tramp trades Pittsburgh-Cincinnati-St. Louis, etc. Capt. George W. Ebert, first master, also part owner along with others principally from Georgetown, Pa. In spring of 1859 Capt. S.C. Trimble, Hookstown, Pa. bought control. She was moored at Pittsburgh May 7, 1859 when a number of boats burned (see *COUNCIL BLUFFS*) but was dragged out safely to mid-river and floated by the conflagration unscathed. Wind blew her in alongside the *J.H. CONN* and these two burned together.

0549 BELVIDERE

SW p wh b. Cincinnati, Oh., 1848. 197 tons. Operated out of New Orleans. Went to Mobile fall 1850 and ran to Montgomery in the "Thru Line" direct to New Orleans. Was on Red River early 1850s. Dismantled 1854.

0550 BELVIDERE

Stw p wh b. Covington, Ky., 1859. 46 tons. Possibly handled produce boats, etc., south. Reported to have been in Porter's fleet on the Red River in 1864.

0551 BEN ADAMS

SW p wh b. Louisville, Ky., 1846. 158 tons. Removed from documentation in 1855. Also see *BEN J. ADAMS.*

0552 BEN BOLT

SW p wh b. California, Pa., and completed at Pittsburgh, 1853. 167 x 29 x 5. 228 tons. Ran Pittsburgh-St. Louis-St. Paul, Capt. James T. Boyd. Original owners included Charles F. Frisbee 7/16; Andrew Miller 3/16, both of Pittsburgh; D.S.H. Gilmore, Pomeroy, Oh., and A.B. Fisher, Gallipolis, Oh. Later sold to Capt. Thomas W. Scott, St. Louis, and other owners of Omaha, Neb. Inspection ceased in 1858.

0553 BEN CAMPBELL

SW p wh b. Shousetown, Pa., and completed at Pittsburgh, 1852. 287 tons. Built for the Galena, Dubuque & Minnesota Packet Co., under supervision of Capt. M.W. Lodwick. Later was in Davenport-Keokuk trade on opposite days to the *J. McKEE* (see), Capt. R.F. Bartlett. Owned then (1855) by Capt. L.W. Clark, Buffalo, Iowa. She burned while laid up in front of Clark's home there at Buffalo. Equipment went to the sternwheeler of the same name. Date of the fire was Aug. 23, 1860.

0554 BEN CAMPBELL

Stw p wh b. Buffalo, Iowa, 1865. 130 x 24 x 3.5. Engines 10's- 3½. Two boilers, each 44" by 16 ft. Ran on Red River during cotton seasons. Dismantled in 1870.

0555 BEN COURSIN

Stw p wh b. McKeesport, Pa., 1851. 149 tons. Ran tramp trades. Was rebuilt at Cincinnati in 1854, tonnage increased to 161. Was on the Upper Mississippi 1856-1857. Came in collision with the *KEY CITY* at the mouth of Black River above La Crosse, Wis., on Aug. 24, 1857 and sank with loss of seven lives. She had been in at least two prior collisions; first at Louisville, Ky., on Sept. 12, 1853 when she rammed and sank the *U.S. MAIL*; second in Agust 1854 while running Cincinnati-Madison, in collision with the *JANE FRANKLIN* at Rising Sun Bar. She was named for the noted boat builder Ben Coursin of McKeesport, Pa., whose yard was in the mouth of the Youghiogheny River on the McKeesport side.

BEN FRANKLIN

Ed. Note: Due to the prominence of boats of this name in the Louisville-Cincinnati trade we are tabulating the complete list dating back to 1826.

0556 BEN FRANKLIN

SW p wh b. Cincinnati, Oh., winter 1826-1827. 163 tons. This was a low pressure boat, her single engine built by William Tift. Owned by Jacob Strader, James Gorman, Philip Grandon, James Kelly (engineer on the boat) and a few others. She was an "extra boat" in the Louisville-Cincinnati trade and ran only when business warranted. John Blair Summons was mate and pilot, and John Wesley Brown was his pilot partner. Capts. Strader and Gorman were on her 4½ years and then sold out to Robert G. Ormsby, Louisville. Capt. Edward Carroll went master, with James M. Noble, clerk. This combination continued until after the flood of 1832. Dismantled in 1833.

0557 BEN FRANKLIN

SW p wh b. Cincinnati, Oh., 1834. 98 tons. Smaller than the original of the name, with a single stiff-shaft engine 27"- 5½ ft. Four boilers, each 39" by 18 ft. Owned by the U.S. Mail Line Co., which commenced running daily boats same year she was built, 1834, her partner being the *PORTSMOUTH.* Capt. John Blair Summons was master, and owned in the boat with Jacob Strader. Considered very fast, and her record upstream time Louisville-Cincinnati was 14 hours 12 minutes. In the fall of 1835 was sold to a Capt. Slade and others of Mobile after having made 200 round trips in the L&C trade. She exploded boilers at Mobile on Mar. 13, 1836 with great life loss. Thirty-five years later, in June 1873, divers recovered the machinery, boilers, anchor, etc.

0558 BEN FRANKLIN

SW p wh b. Cincinnati, Oh., 1836. 194 tons. 183 x 25 x 6.5. Engines, 25½'s- 7 ft. Six boilers, each 60" by 23 ft., two 15" flues. Paddlewheels 22 ft. dia., 11 ft. buckets, 22" dip. Owned by U.S. Mail Line Co. Her record upstream time Louisville-Cincinnati was 12 hours eight minutes. In March 1838 she made a special round trip Cincinnati-Pittsburgh and was noticed in the press at Wheeling and elsewhere as "very fast." Capt. John Blair Summons came out master on her. Sank and lost at Cincinnati, Mar. 13, 1841.

0559 BEN FRANKLIN

SW p wh b. Cincinnati, Oh., 1841. 311 tons. 200 x 30. Six boilers, each 38" by 24 ft., two flues. She made a trip to New Orleans and upon return loaded aboard U.S. President-elect Benjamin Harrison and brought him and entourage from Cincinnati to Pittsburgh enroute to the inauguration. She could sleep 100 cabin passengers and was considered too large for the regular Louisville-Cincinnati trade. She was placed in the St. Louis-New Orleans trade, Capt. Casey. Dismantled in 1846.

0560 BEN FRANKLIN

SW p wh b. Brownsville, Pa., 1854. 145 x 24 x 5.5. Three boilers. This was a cotton carrier operated out of New Orleans. Went to Confederate registry in 1861. Captured by the U.S. tinclad *ARGOSY* in Red River, Dec. 14, 1863.

0561 BEN FRANKLIN

SW p wh b. Jeffersonville, Ind., by Howard, 1856. 300 x 40 x 7.5. 732 tons. Ran Louisville-New Orleans, and in cotton season Memphis-New Orleans. Capt. Anson McGill was the first master; later Capt. Dollis. In 1857 Capt. Anders, master; in 1858 Capt. J.D. Clarke. Burned and lost at Ashton, Miss., Oct. 21, 1858.

0562 BEN FRANKLIN

SW p wh b. Parkersburg, W. Va., 1861. 260 tons. Built from the *CARRIE CAMPBELL*. Was in Wheeling-Cincinnati trade, Capt. James P. Jack, May 1861. Continued to run there for several years. Dismantled in 1867.

0563 BEN FRANKLIN

SW p wh b. Jeffersonville, Ind., by Howard, 1869. 261 x 37.5 x 6.1. Engines, 21's- 8 ft. Four boilers, each 38" by 30 ft. Owned by the U.S. Mail Line Co. Capt. David Whitten came out master, William Taylor, first clerk, and James Holmes, chief engineer. Ran Louisville-Cincinnati teamed up with *UNITED STATES* (2nd) and *GENERAL LYTLE*. Still there in 1878, Capt. Charles David, master. For a time she ran Cincinnati-Madison until replaced in June 1877 by the *GENERAL PIKE* (see). In early October 1878 she collided with the Lawrenceburg, Ind., wharfboat and sank it. Pilot Charles Williams had been unable to ring the stopping bell, and investigation disclosed a rat wedged in the angle box. It popped out when the angle box was opened and was caught by Capt. Reilley's terrier named Fannie. On Oct. 30, 1878 she sank in the foot of Laughrey Island, was pumped out and docked. On several occasions she ran Cincinnati-Memphis, auspices of the Cincinnati & Memphis Packet Co.; was there spring 1874 with Capt. William B. Miller, master, with A.J. Harrigan and T.H. Clinton, clerks. Probably her last running was in that trade in 1881, Capt. Tichenor.

0564 BEN FRANKLIN NO. 6

SW p wh b. Cincinnati, Oh., 1843. 289 tons. Owned by the U.S. Mail Line Co. Ran Cincinnati-Louisville, Capt. John Blair Summons. She made a special trip, Cincinnati to Pittsburgh, arriving in Pittsburgh Nov. 16, 1843 with John Quincy Adams on board. Her partner in the L&C trade was *PIKE NO. 7* (see). Made trips to St. Louis on occasion. Dismantled in 1849.

0565 BEN FRANKLIN NO. 7

SW p wh b. Cincinnati, Oh., 1844. 238 tons. Owned by U.S. Mail Line Co., and was used for low water work Louisville-Cincinnati. The *Wheeling Daily News* noted, April 1845, that this boat was illuminated with 20 gas lights, the gas generated on board the boat. "This is the first boat so lighted in the world," concluded the story. Running trips Cincinnati to New Orleans, Capt. McFall, Jan. 1848. Dismantled and machinery went to *HIRAM POWERS* (see).

0566 BEN FRANKLIN NO. 8

SW p wh b. Cincinnati, Oh., 1848. 473 tons. Owned by U.S. Mail Line Co., and replaced the *BEN FRANKLIN NO. 7*. 265 x 34 x 6.5. Wheels 32 ft. dia., 15 ft. buckets, 28" dip. Ran in Louisville-Cincinnati trade until replaced by *JACOB STRADER* (see). Hull by John Leatherburg, a noted shipwright. Brought U.S. President-elect Zachary Taylor from Carrollton, Ky., to Cincinnati, February 1849, on his way to the inauguration. Ran Louisville-St. Louis in 1853, Capt. Pat Rogers. Lost in collision with the *GALENA* at North Buena Vista, Iowa, May 1, 1854.

0567 BEN GAYLORD

Stw p wh b. Cincinnati, Oh., 1863. 179 tons. Built by Capt. Uriah B. Scott for the Portsmouth-Parkersburg trade, Ohio River. Sold to the U.S. in spring 1864, became a tinclad named *UNDINE* captured by the Confederates in October that year. Burned at Johnsonville, Tenn., on Nov. 3, 1864.

0568 BEN HUR

Stw p wh b. Harmar, Oh., at the Knox Boat Yard, 1887. 165 x 30.5 x 4.8. Engines, 16's- 5½ ft. Three boilers, 42" by 24 ft. Machinery came from towboat *ED HOBBS*. Came out in Pittsburgh-Parkersburg trade, Capt. Fred Kimpel, Jr., master, with Ed Dunn, clerk. During her first year she carried John Robinson's famous circus on tour. Monroe (Doggy) Cross and Bert Cramer were her pilots. By 1904 her master was Capt. Ed Sims. Capt. Harry Donnelly had her briefly. In June 1904 sold to the Mississippi River Amusement Co., St. Paul and went there to run excursions. Capt. Tom Morrissey bought her for trades out of Vicksburg, and she soon was transferred to Prince & Wild. In 1912 was running New Orleans-Bayou Teche twice weekly, Capt. Wallace M. Ditch, master, with W. A. Roberts and Warren Kouns, pilots, managed by Capt. L.M. Gray. While owned by Capt. George Prince she sank and was lost at Duckport, La., March 1916. Her three-chime whistle came from the *GEORGE STRECKER* (1880–1887) made by a mechanically-minded farmer who lived above Waverly, W. Va. When *BEN HUR* was sold to the Upper Miss., it went to the *BESSIE SMITH*, then to *LIBERTY* (b. 1912), thence to towboat *MILDRED*. Today it is in the collection of the Missouri Historical Society, but alterations have ruined the tone. A duplicate went to Vicksburg on her.

0569 BEN J. ADAMS

SW p wh b. New Albany, Ind., 1860. 497 tons. Capt. J.B. Ford was said have a hand in financing her. Was in Louisville-New Orleans trade, Capt. Ritchie, spring 1861. Sold to USQMD on Dec. 27, 1862. After the war sold to Capt. Jacob Barker, New Orleans, Jan. 11, 1866. In July 1866 sold to Alfred Bradley, New Orleans. Burned at New Orleans, Aug. 9, 1866.

0570 BEN JOHNSON

SW p wh b. Metropolis, Ill. (hull), and completed at St. Louis, 1866. 525 tons. Engines 22's- 8 ft. Three boilers. Owned by Capt. Ben Johnson and ran Missouri River. Capt. Joe LaBarge chartered her 1866 and took a U.S. peace commission to Fort Sully to treat with the Sioux. Made a Fort Benton trip in 1867. Snagged several miles below Brownville, Neb., in 1868, raised. Burned in the steamboat fire at St. Louis, Mar. 29, 1869. A watchman on the *BEN JOHNSON* discovered the boat afire at 8:00 P.M.

The *HENRY ADKINS* was just above, and the *CARRIE V. KOUNTZ* below. All three caught fire and the *KOUNTZ* floated away, burning. The *BEN JOHNSON* also floated away and came alongside the *G.B. ALLEN*, setting her afire. The *ONLY CHANCE* and *FANNIE SCOTT* were set adrift by their crews to save them. Meanwhile the *CARRIE V. KOUNTZ* lodged on a bar, ablaze. As fate would have it, the *ONLY CHANCE* and *FANNIE SCOTT* lodged against the burning *KOUNTZ*, and also burned. The *JENNIE LEWIS* went to the rescue of some passengers aboard the *FANNIE SCOTT*, also grounded on the bar, and burned with the others. No lives were lost.

0571 Ben Lee

Stw p wh b. Cincinnati, Oh., 1852. 122 tons. Carl Carmer mentions her in *Stars Fell on Alabama*. She ran Mobile-Alabama River, and was snagged and lost at Mobile, Dec. 13, 1856.

Ben Lewis

See *B. W. Lewis*.

0572 Ben McCulloch

Stw p wh b. Cincinnati, Oh., 1860. 100 x 22 x 3.9. Engines, 12's- 3½ ft. Two boilers, each 36″ by 14 ft. Ran Memphis-Dyersburg. Captured as a Confederate steamer and sold after the war to private owners. Burned at Monroe, La., May 26, 1868 with loss of three lives.

0573 Ben Rush

SW p wh b. Freedom, Pa., 1847. 147 tons. Burned at Pittsburgh, Pa., on June 2, 1848.

0574 Ben South

SW ferry wh b. New Albany, Ind., 1860. 176 tons. Ran between New Albany, Ind., and Portland, Ky., with the *THOMAS CONNER* and *EXCELSIOR* (both see). She was in U.S. service during the war and was captured by Confederate forces at Cumberland City, Tenn., Dec. 9, 1864. She and the *THOMAS E. TUTT* both were taken, and both were burned.

0575 Ben Stickney

SW p wh b. Cannelton, Ind., (hull), and completed at New Albany, Ind., 1864. 285 x 40 x 8. Engines, 26's- 9 ft. Five boilers. The machinery originated on *BOSTONA* (b. 1849) and then was on *JAMES GUTHRIE*, side-wheel towboat b. 1853. Departed Louisville for New Orleans on maiden trip, August 1864, Capt. E.A. Sheble, master; A.D. Armstrong and E.A. Sheble, Jr., clerks; Charles Sebastian and James Ostrander, pilots; H. Richardson and T. Cook, engineers. Principal owner was said to be Commodore David Gibson, Cincinnati. Capt. Charles Dravo was in command October 1865 in St. Louis-New Orleans trade. Snagged and sunk at Island 18, Mississippi River, Nov. 16, 1865.

0576 Ben West

SW p wh b. Brownsville, Pa., 1849. 241 tons. Engines, 17½'s- 6 ft. Three boilers. Ran in Pittsburgh-St. Louis trade usually. Was in St. Louis-St. Paul trade, spring 1855. En route up Missouri River with lumber consigned to Lexington, Mo., she was fatally snagged near Washington, Mo., on Aug. 10, 1855.

0577 Benefit

SW p wh b. Metropolis, Ill. (hull), and completed at St. Louis, 1863. 213 tons. Was up Red River with the Porter expedition in 1864. Operated under charter to the U.S. in the Mississippi Squadron in 1865. Burned and lost at Starke Landing, Ala., Apr. 6, 1867.

0578 Benjamin

Stw p wh b. Moline, Ill., 1904. 60 x 14 x 3.2. Documented at Rock Island in 1908, and had Chicago registry in 1915.

0579 Benj. Lee

Stw p wh b. Cincinnati, Oh., 1852. 122 tons. Snagged and lost at Mobile, Ala., Dec. 13, 1856.

0580 Benton

SW gunboat wh Originally a wrecking boat built and owned by James B. Eads, St. Louis, called *SUBMARINE NO. 7*. 184 x 75 x 8. Engines, 20's- 7 ft. Converted to a U.S. gunboat in 1861. The forward plating was 3″ of iron backed by 30″ of oak, and the rest of her was plated with 5/8″ iron. She mounted 16 guns, drew nine feet, and was the most powerful weapon on the Mississippi. Very slow, and known as the "Old War Horse." Capt. Horace Bixby was pilot on her in 1862. She saw plenty of action. Sold at a sale, Mound City, Ill., Nov. 29, 1865, to D. Jacobs for $3,000 and scrapped.

0581 Benton

Stw p wh b. McKeesport, Pa., 1864. Engines 15's- 5 ft. Three boilers. Advertised at St. Louis for Fort Benton, Mar. 15, 1864, Capt. T.W. Rea, master, with Henry A. Dohrman, clerk. She arrived at Fort Benton on June 10, a record "early arrival." Most of her career was run by fur traders Durfee & Peck. In 1865 Chief Red Cloud's Sioux had blocked the Bozeman Trail and Montana miners were begging for supplies at any price. The *BENTON* left St. Louis on Mar. 11, 1865, sheathed about her pilothouse by boiler iron. She was fired on at wooding places and had an awful trip through low water in the Dakotah Territory. Working as part of a chain with the *DEER LODGE* above her, and the *GENERAL GRANT* below, she transshipped cargo from Milk River to Round Butte. The *DEER LODGE* shuttled the cargo on to Fort Benton. On this trip she was out from St. Louis 169 days, until August 26. In that period she had logged 10,000 miles commanded by Capt. William Howard. The pilots were C.J. Atkins and John Gunsollis. Altogether she made nine trips to Montana points, the last one in 1868. Upbound on May 9, 1869 she was snagged and lost a few miles above DeSoto, Neb., thereafter called Benton Bend. This rather famed boat was originally built for Capt. Charles Stevens who christened her *INTREPID*, but who sold her to Thomas W. Rea at Pittsburgh, brand new and Rea changed the name and loaded her out direct for Fort

Benton, mid-February 1864. Her engines later went to the *CHARLES H. DURFEE* (see).

0582 BENTON

SW ferry wh b. Pittsburgh, Pa., 1865. 88 tons. Dismantled in 1870.

0583 BENTON

Stw p wh b. Pittsburgh, Pa., 1875. 197 x 33 x 5. Engines by James Rees, 15's- 5 ft. Three boilers, each 38" by 24 ft., two flues. When new she drew 18", light. Built for T.C. Power & Bros., and I.G. Baker & Co., for Missouri River service. Departed Pittsburgh on maiden trip early 1875 with Capt. James McGarry, master, and Joseph S. Hill, clerk. Got to Fort Benton on May 27 and so commenced a long career in which she made 44 trips to Fort Benton, plus 15 others to Montana points. The *BENTON* went off to the wars on the Yellowstone in late summer of 1876, when virtually every boat on the upper Missouri was impressed into service of the soldiers trailing Sitting Bull and his Sioux. The boat set a record of 11 days one hour from Bismarck to Fort Benton May 31, 1877, and bettered this June 27 with a time of 10 days and 18 hours. The record stood for only a few days, until the *RED CLOUD* (see) did better. She served in the windup of the Nez Perce campaign of 1877 around Cow Island. Altogether, the *BENTON* made more trips, almost certainly carried more freight than any other boat serving Fort Benton. In 1884 she took down 250 tons, the largest cargo ever shipped from Fort Benton. By 1886 she was the "old reliable" in the Bismarck-Benton trade. In July of 1887 she left Fort Benton with 1,004 bags of wool, 350 bales of pelts, looking for all the world like a southern cotton boat with wood stacked all around. The departure of July 24, 1887, was her last time out of Fort Benton. Sold in 1889 to James P. Boland and T.B. Sims. She was snagged five miles above Washington, Mo., on Sept. 15, 1889, Capt. Asa P. Boland, master, and George Keith, pilot. Raised. Downbound opposite Arrow Rock, Mo., on July 31, 1895, a tiller line parted, she swerved onto a snag, and sank a cargo of 600 sacks of wheat. Raised. In August 1896 she came to St. Louis with 2,500 sacks of Missouri River wheat, Capt. Jim Boland. Downbound July 18, 1897, she came to the drawbridge at Sioux City and had to wait, got out of shape, backed into submerged piling, knocked a hole in her hull. In sinking condition she floated down under the still unopened draw, tore off her upper works, and was wrecked.

0584 BENTON MCMILLIN

Stw p wh b. Jeffersonville, Ind., by Howard, 1883. 155 x 33 x 5.5. Engines 14½'s- 5 ft. Three boilers, each 40" by 18 ft., six flues each. She was named for the Tennessee congressman Benton McMillin, an old-line Democrat, a low tariff man, an advocate of high income tax law on "those millionaires back East." Ran on Cumberland River for several years. Then was entered in Pittsburgh-Cincinnati trade in summer of 1886 owned by Capt. Hod Knowles, Ira B. Huntington, and others. Capt. Hod Knowles was master; Ira Huntington, first clerk; Wm. F. Brookhart and Aaron McLaughlin, pilots; James Chamberlain, chief engineer; Bub Baer, second; W.H. Baker, mate; and James Daniels, steward. Operated until latter February 1888, and March 1 that year was sold to Illinois River parties who lengthened her at Cincinnati and renamed her *D.H. PIKE* (see). She is remembered on Cumberland River for her "wild cat" whistle, which may still exist. In 1942 it was owned by Capt. John L. Belk, Cottontown, Tenn. Capt. Ira B. Huntington recalled her as the first steamboat lighted throughout by electricity.

0585 BENWOOD

Stw ferry wh b. Wheeling, W. Va., 1866. 64 x 12 x 2.2. In May 1873 owned by William H. Brooks, Parkersburg, W. Va. Dismantled 1876 and engines went to *R.S. TRIPLETT.*

0586 BERLIN

Stw p wh b. Oshkosh, Wis., 1851. 54 tons. She was a regular at St. Paul 1855-1856. Dismantled 1857.

0587 BERMUDA

Stw p wh b. Wheeling, W. Va., 1864. Built by the Sweeneys of Wheeling who were reported selling her to Capt. Pink Varble, Louisville, that November. In the latter 1860s, ran in the Louisville-Florence, Ala., trade, Capt. Milt Aiken, master, J. Morgan Smith, clerk. Capt. Sam T. Jones, Rockport, Ind., and others ran her Cincinnati-Evansville, and she was last owned by Capt. Tom Ryman, Nashville. She was dismantled in 1876 and the hull used as a wharfboat at Brandenburg, Ky.

0588 BERTHA

Stw p wh b. Belle Vernon, Pa., 1863. 180 x 28. Engines, 15's- 5 ft. Three boilers. Her first master was Capt. J.S. Vanhook. She was primarily a freight boat and ran trips on the Missouri River. In 1868 Capt. R.S. Yerkes, master, with John C. Enyart, clerk. She hit a pier of the St. Joseph, Mo., bridge on June 24, 1872, then owned by C.S. Ebaugh, and was lost.

0589 BERTHA

Stw p wh b. Louisville, Ky., 1870. 135.6 x 32 x 4.9. Went to New Orleans owned by Capt. Gus Hodge ½, and Cornelius Dewees ½. She was a regular on Ouachita and Old rivers, handling cotton. In New Orleans-Opelousas trade, 1879, Capt. M. Kenison, with T. Jobin, clerk. Burned on the Sabine River, Feb. 8, 1881, Capt. Mark Smith. She had been running between Orange, Tex., and upper Sabine River points.

0590 BERTHA BRUNNER

Stw p wh b. Cincinnati, Oh., 1873. 174 tons. She was taken over the Louisville Falls on delivery trip south. Burned at Bayou D'Arbonne, La., Apr. 10, 1879.

0591 BERTHA LEE

Stw p wh b. Portsmouth, Oh., 1879. 120 x 21 x 3.8.

Originally owned by W.H. Stricklett, Vanceburg, Ky., and others. Sold July 9, 1880 to E. Porter, Helena, Ark. Then to James E. Yost, A. Bigelow, and Eli Conners, Metropolis, Ill. Bought by the Louisville & Evansville Mail Co., in May 1882. She ran an excursion at Louisville on Sunday, Aug. 6, 1882, Capt. R.H. Ballard, with 425 passengers. Sold Aug. 3, 1883 to Kissimmee, Okechobee and Gulf Stream Navigation Co., and her home port was changed to Cedar Keys, Fla., on Sept. 12, 1884. They sold her Apr. 30, 1885 to Benj. F. Hall, Cedar Keys, Fla., who owned her until the end. Documentation was surrendered at Cedar Keys on June 30, 1892 with the notation "sunk in Apalachicola River."

0592 BERTRAND

SW p wh b. Pittsburgh, Pa., 1844. 145 tons. Went to the Upper Mississippi. Ran St. Louis-Galena, 1846, Rogers, master. Advertised for an excursion to St. Peters, June 19, 1846. Bought 1847 by Capt. John W. Keiser, associated with American Fur Co., 1847 for Missouri River. She may have returned to the Wheeling area, as Capts. Sam Mason and William Cecil ran a boat of this name briefly about 1848 and sold her a year later to run on Bayou Teche. She was snagged and lost Jan. 11, 1850 at Bayou Sorrel, La.

0593 BERTRAND

Stw p wh b. Wheeling, W. Va., 1864. 251 tons. 161 x 32.9. x 5.2. Machinery from the *A.J. SWEENEY* (see). Hull by Dunlevy & Co., engines by A.J. Sweeney. First owned by George Feller and Thomas H. Reed, Wheeling, and George Laing, Lewis W. Cochran and Jeremiah Cochran, Monroe County, Oh. Came out with Capt. Ben Goodwin, master, with Jerry Cochran, clerk. Was sold at St. Louis to Montana & Idaho Transportation Co., owned largely by John J. Roe and John G. Copelin. In spring of 1865 she was loaded at St. Louis for a Missouri River trip, Capt. John Jacobs, master; Horace E. Bixby, pilot; John Owens, first clerk, and William Pim, second clerk. Capt. J.E. Yore accompanied to Omaha to help pilot to that place, then returned to St. Louis. On Apr. 1, 1865, she was snagged and sunk above Omaha at Portage La Force, no life loss. Part of the deck cargo was recovered. A large quantity of quicksilver (mercury) consigned to Virginia City was aboard, and several attempts were made over the years to locate the wreck and recover it. The Missouri River changed course and the site of the wreck was located in February 1968 by two Omaha salvagers, Jesse Pursell and Sam Corbino, in the old ox-bow loop 25 miles above Omaha on the DeSoto National Wildlife Refuge. Salvage was hampered by water seepage into the excavation site, but in 1969 equipment was brought in and much general cargo was removed which had been stowed in the hull. Some mercury turned up. The scope and diversity of the salvaged freight surprised everybody, much of it well preserved, and removal was made by experienced delvers. A very exciting book on the subject was released in 1974 authored by Jerome E. Petsche, under the auspices of the National Park Service.

0594 BERWICK BAY

SW p wh b. Plaquemine, La., 1857. 64 tons. Went to Franklin, La., and to Confederate registry in 1861. She was used by the Confederates on Red River 1862-1863 until captured and burned by crew of *QUEEN OF THE WEST* on Feb. 2, 1863.

0595 BESSIE

SW p wh b. Lecompte, La., 1858. 86 tons. Went to Confederate registry, 1861.

0596 BESSIE

Ferry wh b. Racine, Oh., 1877. 60 x 15 x 3.3. Inspected in Cincinnati District 1881, 1882. Documented at Louisville, 1886.

0597 BESSIE

SW p sh b. St. Louis, Mo., 1881. 122.7 x 24.4 x 3.6. This steel hull steamboat was documented at Brownsville, Tex., 1886-1896.

0598 BESSIE F.

Ferry wh b. Cincinnati, Oh., 1881. 100 x 26 x 3.6. One boiler. In Memphis District, 1886.

0599 BESSIE M. STONE

SW ferry wh b. Pt. Pleasant, W. Va., 1925. 54.8 x 28 x 3.9. Ran Pt. Pleasant-Henderson until the bridge was built, then sold to the Proctorville, Oh., ferry trade, and after running there a while was sold to James E. Hannah of Portsmouth, Oh. (1929). Later was converted to diesel, renamed *HAZEL S* and operated at Dover, Ky. In 1944 was at Fullerton, Ky.

0600 BESSIE PEARL

Rig? wh b. Cincinnati, Oh., 1874. 87.16 tons. Listed at Cincinnati in 1876.

0601 BESSIE RONE

Originally *CARUTHERSVILLE* (see) b. Dyersburg, Tenn., 1903. Name changed Mar. 11, 1911.

0602 BESSIE SILER

Stw p wh b. Marietta, Oh. at Knox Yard, 1884. 93 x 16 x 3. Engines, 9″ - 3 ft. stroke. Her machinery came from *WASH OBENCHAIN* (see). Owned by Capt. Cris F. Siler, and did towing first several years, then ran McConnelsville-Zanesville 1887-1892, owned after May 1889 by Capt. Newton Price. Was sold to Bayou Teche in 1892 and sank there June 9, 1894. The engines later went to the *U & I* (see).

0603 BESSIE SMITH

Stw p wh b. Smithsonia, Ala. (hull), and completed at Florence, Ala., 1897. 140 x 26.4 x 3.5. Engines, 10's - 3½ ft. Two boilers, each 36″ by 18 ft. She originally was scow bow. Capt. Fred Hornbrook and Harry Donnally got her for the Upper Ohio, and sold her to Capts. Fred Kimpel and Sam Williamson. She was rebuilt with a model bow at Parkersburg, W. Va., in December 1901. Ran Wheeling-

Parkersburg, Capt. Henry Kraft. Capt. Martin F. Noll bought her entire, May 31, 1910, and ran her Pittsburgh-Morgantown, W. Va. She was returned to Parkersburg for repairs that winter, and burned there on Mar. 20, 1911. Capt. Harry B. Hulings bought the wreck, towed it to Pt. Pleasant in early 1914, and used the machinery, etc., building a towboat he named *UNCLE SAM.*

0604 BETSY ANN

Stw p ih b. Dubuque, Iowa, 1899. 165 x 33 x 5.5. Cross compound condensing engines, 16″ and 32″- 6 ft. Originally had one boiler 72″ by 12 ft. Built by Iowa Iron Works, and the engines by Clinton Novelty Iron Works. Owner was R.F. Learned, Natchez, Miss., and named for his wife Elizabeth. Ran principally in the Natchez-Bayou Sara trade and carried U.S. Mail. Whistle from the *STELLA WILDS.* Sold in fall of 1921 to D. Grover Gill, Gallipolis, Oh., and others who ran her Pittsburgh-Portsmouth, then Pittsburgh-Cincinnati, incorporated as Independent Packet Co. Frederick Way Sr., and Jr., bought stock late 1925 and continued her Pittsburgh-Cincinnati into 1929. Ran Pittsburgh-Louisville summer 1930, then Pittsburgh-Charleston, and finally back again Pittsburgh-Cincinnati Nov. 3, 1930, through Apr. 25, 1931. Left Pittsburgh Nov. 2, 1931, and went to Memphis under charter to tow cotton. Made one trip to Caruthersville and another to Vicksburg, returning to Memphis Dec. 6, 1931. Sold to John I. Hay Co., spring of 1932 and was put to towing barges. Was dismantled at the St. Louis wharf in the fall of 1940. The hull was used by the Wood River Refining Co., at Wood River, who sold it August 1946 to the Meramec Power Boat Club. In towing it to Meramec River struck the Merchants Bridge, St. Louis, head-on and damaged the stem, but proceeded to destination. Boat club facilities were built on the hull and it was used until winter of 1952–1953 when it beached on a falling river and was sunk. The original tubular boiler was replaced 1925 by two Western-style boilers from *JOE FOWLER.* The pilotwheel is exhibited in the Old Court House, St. Louis, presented by Capt. Robert Roehrig. The roof bell is owned by a Garden Club at Natchez, Miss. A book published by Robert M. McBride Co., N.Y., in 1933, *The Log of the Betsy Ann,* went through seven editions and was a Junior Literary Guild selection, authored by F. Way, Jr. The boat is best remembered for having run three staged races at Cincinnati, July 24, 1928 with *CHRIS GREENE,* and July 16, 1929 with *TOM GREENE,* and again in 1930 with *TOM GREENE.* These events led to the "rebirth" of steamboat racing as a popular sport.

0605 BETTIE GILBERT

Stw p wh b. Parkersburg, W. Va., 1869. 54 tons. Ran Gallipolis-Charleston, and Capt. C.C. Bowyer recalled making a trip on her 1872 or 1873 with W.F. Gregory and Phil Dodridge as pilots. Capt. Mike H. Campbell bought her for the Evansville-Newburgh-Scuffletown trade, and in fall of 1876 she was sold to Capt. Henry Campbell and ran Wheeling-Powhatan Point and sank at the latter place in ice, January 1877. Raised. Sold to Messrs. Spencer and Leavitt for Parkersburg-Belleville trade in the spring of 1878. Inspected at Nashville in 1881, Evansville in 1882. Dismantled at Metropolis, Ill., in August 1884, and the machinery went to a hub factory there.

0606 BETTIE LEE

Stw p wh b. Guntersville, Ala., 1895. 56 x 12 x 1.5. Documented at Chattanooga, 1896.

0607 BETTIE OWEN

Recess wheel ferry wh b. Paducah, Ky., 1891. 137 x 39.9 x 4. Engines, 13's- 4½ ft. Two boilers, each 47″ by 23 ft. Owned by Owen Bros., and ferried at Paducah replacing the old *V. OWEN* (see). Last owned by the Paducah & Illinois Ferry Co., and served 19 years. Burned at Paducah in February 1910. Was succeeded by the *G. W. ROBERTSON* (see).

0608 BETTY SUE

Stw p wh b. Little Rock, Ark., 1914. 64.7 x 16 x 3. Documented at St. Louis, 1918.

0609 BEULAH

SW p wh b. Mobile, Ala., 1860. 261 tons. Ran between Mobile and Montgomery. Went to Confederate registry, 1861.

0610 BEULAH

Stw p wh b. New Martinsville, W. Va., 1865. 127.9 x 24.2 x 3.5. In December 1865 owned by C.W. Wills and F.J. Herron, New Orleans, Capt. E. Doming, master. Lost Sept. 22, 1866. She made trips on Red River.

0611 BEULAH BROWN

SW p wh b. Paintsville, Ky., 1891. 113.6 x 15 x 2.8. A batwing, owned by Capt. Green Meek, Paintsville. When she wore out the engines, etc., went to the *THEALKA* (see).

0612 BEVERLY

Ferry wh b. Beverly, Oh., 1873. 22.27 tons. Still documented 1876.

0613 BEVERLY

SW ferry wh b. Clarington, Oh., 1925. 64.9 x 22 x 3.5. Owned by Clifton, New Castle & Ohio River Ferry Co., Clifton, W. Va. President of the company was F.B. Williamson, Clifton. Sank and lost at Mason City, W. Va., January 1929.

0614 BIG-A-PLENTY

Running in Sunflower River, La., owned by Capts. Miller and Banks, April 1901. Rebuilt at New Orleans in November 1901 and renamed *LUNA* (see).

0615 BIG FOOT

Stw p wh b. 1875 in Pittsburgh area. Owned by Capt. Adam Poe and others, Georgetown, Pa. Sold soon after completion to Central RR of Georgia and Capt. Poe delivered her across the Gulf. From the Memphis *Daily Appeal* in 1876:

The *BIG FOOT* sank 10 miles above Eufaula, Ala., Saturday night, Dec. 9th. She sank to her boiler deck and her cargo of cotton floated off a total loss." A photo survives, showing a large Indian on top of the pilothouse, representing the Wyandot chief Big Foot, famed for a battle at Yellow Creek, Oh.

BIG GREY EAGLE

See *GREY EAGLE* b. Jeffersonville, Ind., 1860.

0616 BIG HATCHIE

SW p wh b. Pittsburgh, Pa., 1844. 195 tons. Today (1977) in the Protestant Cemetery, Hermann, Mo., is a three foot column surmounted by a sundial. Inscribed thereon: "In memory of the early pioneers who perished in the explosion of the steamboat *BIG HATCHIE* at the wharf at Hermann in 1842, the thirty-five dead that lie buried here in unidentified graves and the many whose bodies were never recovered from the waters of the Missouri River." The explosion happened on July 25, 1845 (not 1842), and apparently the boat survived, inasmuch as Customs records show she was turned over to the U.S. War Department in 1846.

0617 BIG HORN

Stw p wh b. New Albany, Ind., 1865. 312 tons. 154 x 33.5 x 4.5. Engines, 16's- 4 ft. Three boilers, each 36" by 20 ft. In the St. Louis and Missouri River trade 1865–1869. In fall of 1869 was running in the New Orleans, Coast and Lafourche "Crescent Line." In 1870 owned at New Orleans by W.T. and John Gilham, then running New Orleans-Minden. Sank and lost in Bayou Bartholomew, La., Apr. 10, 1873. A cargo of lime in the hold caught fire and the boat was destroyed.

0618 BIG HORN

Stw p wh b. California, Pa., 1879. 178 x 31. Engines, 13's- 5 ft. Three boilers. On her maiden trip Pittsburgh to Missouri River commanded by Capt. W.S. Evans, accompanied by his family. Capt. David S.H. Gilmore and family also were aboard. Stockholders included D.W. Maratta, Josephus Todd, and Nicholas Buison, all of Columbiana County, Oh.,; W.S. Evans and Sanford B. Coulson. The material used in building Fort Custer went up on this boat. She was snagged and lost about five miles below the mouth of Poplar River, on the Missouri, morning of May 8, 1883. Officer at the time was Capt. John A. Williams, master; Ben Jewell and James Clarke, pilots; J.Q.A. Parr, clerk, and Milt Pickering, chief engineer.

0619 BIG KANAWHA

Stw p wh b. Madison, Ind., 1887. 152 x 30 x 4.5. Built for Capt. Marlin Brown, Gallipolis, Oh. Ran Pomeroy-Gallipolis-Charleston-Coal Valley, Capt. M.E. Brown, master, with A.H. Brown, clerk. Sold to the White Collar Line which ran her Louisville-Madison. Capt. Sam Parsons ran opposition to her with his *HELEN M. GOULD*. Finally a swap was made in which Parsons acquired the *BIG KANAWHA* and White Collar bought the *GOULD* with the proviso that Parsons would vamoose. Parsons took the *BIG KANAWHA* to Pt. Pleasant, had her docked and repaired, and then entered her in the Cincinnati-Huntington trade in opposition to the Greene Line, early 1906. On the first trip upriver heavy ice was encountered at Maysville and the *BIG KANAWHA* was sunk and lost. She ran briefly Pittsburgh-Parkersburg spring 1904 in place of the *AVALON* which was under charter to Coney Island Co., to augment the *ISLAND QUEEN* in the park trade. Her roof bell wound up in the belfry of the Trinity Church, Point Pleasant, W. Va.

BIG MISSOURI

Often so-called, but properly *MISSOURI*, b. Cincinnati, 1845 (see).

0620 BIG SANDY

SW p wh b. Cincinnati, Oh., 1884. 292 x 47 x 7. Built for an offshoot of the White Collar Line, the Cincinnati, Portsmouth, Big Sandy & Pomeroy Packet Co. Capt. Charles M. Holloway was manager when she was built. Ran Cincinnati-Pomeroy, also Cincinnati-Louisville. Made a Mardi Gras trip 1885 from Cincinnati including a special trip to the Jetties. Went a bit too far and high Gulf waves rocked her violently in turning. A tug was sent to assist. Capt. Will Kirker commanded in the Pomeroy trade, one of four steamboating brothers from Kirker's Landing, Ky. She burned at Cincinnati along with the *CARROLLTON* (see) on Aug. 5, 1895.

0621 BIG SANDY

SW batwing p wh b. Guyandotte, W. Va., 1899. 111.6 x 15.6 x 2.6. Engines, 6"- 12". One boiler 36" by 10 ft. Built for Big Sandy River service. Sold fall of 1901 to Steven Thompson and C.C. Thomas, Clarington, Oh., who operated her in low water trades. Later back to Big Sandy owned by W.C. Vaughan. Still documented 1908.

0622 BIG SUNFLOWER

Stw p wh b. Jeffersonville, Ind., by Howard, 1869. 125 x 28 x 4. Ran Vicksburg to Yazoo and Tallahatchie rivers, Capt. T.G. Ledbetter in command, connecting with *NATCHEZ* for New Orleans. There is some evidence she was extensively altered to become 147.8 x 28.9 x 4.5 with props, renamed *JENNIE LANE*, and is so registered in 1886 with home port at New Haven, Conn.

0623 BILL HENDERSON

Stw p wh b. Brownsville, Pa., 1861. 130 x 24.5 x 3.5. Engines, 14's- 4 ft. Built for the Northern Line who ran her Rock Island-Galena-Dubuque along with *JAMES MEANS*. Later ran Savanna-Dubuque connecting with Western Union RR (later Milwaukee System). Rebuilt 1870 at Bellevue, Iowa, to become a towboat. Sold south. On Feb. 18, 1876, downbound near Port Hudson she came in collision with *JOHN F. TOLLE* and was lost. Capt. W.W. Cooley was in command, and T.C. Curry, pilot. The cotton cargo was largely lost, some bales floating down by Donaldsonville.

0624 BILL PATANN

SW p wh b. Roseville, Ark., 1925. 64.8 x 16 x 3.9. In 1929 owned by W.M. Quaile, Fort Smith, Ark.

0625 BILL TATE

Stw p wh b. Knoxville, Tenn., 1897. 93 x 15 x 3. Built by Holston River Transportation Co., for Knoxville-Kingsport trade. Still documented in 1903.

0626 BILLY COLLINS

SW p wh b. Ironton, Oh., 1872. 114 x 21.5 x 3.5. Engines, 8"- 2 ft. Owned by A. Wise & Co., Ironton. Did low water work. She gravitated to the Pittsburgh area and in late 1878 was at McKeesport, Pa., being readied for a trip south by Capt. W.S. Packer. Sold at New Orleans to a Capt. Cole of Selma, Ala. Rebuilt at Mobile in 1880 and was still documented at Mobile in 1896.

0627 BILLY PARSONS

Stw p wh b. Parkersburg, W. Va., 1871. 34 tons. Ran low water, July 1871, Pittsburgh-Parkersburg. Owned for some time by Capt. Charles Clendennin, Gallipolis, Oh., who also and later, owned towboat *JOHN R.* and *NEW ERA*. Documented at Wheeling, 1876.

0628 BIRDIE BAILEY

Stw p wh b. Little Rock, Ark., 1885. 109.79 tons. 111 x 22 x 3.5. Ran Memphis-Arkansas River several years, and later operated out of Vicksburg. Still documented in 1896. She was snagged and lost below Belzoni, Miss., on the Yazoo River, no date.

0629 BIRDIE BRENT

Recess wheel ferry wh b. Jeffersonville, Ind., by Howard, 1866. 112 x 35 x 4.8. Owned by John Porter and operated at Boonville, Mo., until sunk there Nov. 24, 1887.

0630 BISMARCK

SW p wh b. Carondolet, Mo., 1867. 287 x 45.5 x 9. Engines, 26's- 9 ft. Five boilers each 40" by 26 ft. Machinery from the *BALTIC* (see). Ran St. Louis-New Orleans, Capt. Sam S. Entriken, master. Later Capt. Pat Yore was in charge, with John Spane, clerk. Operated by Bismarck Transportation Co. Burned and lost at St. Louis, Nov. 2, 1877.

0631 BISMARCK

Stw p wh b. Pittsburgh, Pa., 1878. 194 x 33 x 4.5. Was bought by Isaac P. Baker who used her on the upper Missouri River. Sold later to A.S. Bryan and others for use on the lower Missouri. Snagged at Lower Bonhomme Island in 1887, raised. On Oct. 23, 1891, at the same location, was again snagged, this time fatally. Ed Anderson was the pilot on watch. The roof bell went to the belfry of a church in Washington, Mo.

0632 BLACKHAWK

SW p wh b. Rock Island, Ill., 1852. 83 tons. Built for Capt. M.W. Lodwick and others, who soon sold her to Galena Packet Co., for a low water boat. She made trips to St. Paul in 1853. Capt. R.M. Spender commanded briefly in 1854, then Capt. O.H. Maxwell who still was in charge 1855 running her in Minnesota River. Last recorded appearance at St. Paul in 1859.

0633 BLACK HAWK

SW p wh b. New Albany, Ind., 1859. 211 tons. Engines, 21's- 6 ft. Three boilers. Built for Capt. Silas Haight for Fort Madison-Rock Island trade, round trip a day, "and it took a smart boat to do this," said Capt. Walter Blair later. Ran St. Louis-Memphis 1860–1861, then went to Missouri River where she was snagged at mouth of Bee Creek, two miles below Weston, Mo., raised. The U.S. took her over at Port Hudson, Miss., Nov. 3, 1863, confiscation procedure. In 1864 ran New Orleans-Bayou Sara twice weekly, Capt. Sam Ayles, master with R.M. McMahon, clerk. Later ran to Baton Rouge. She caught fire at New Orleans May 28, 1864, and set fire to other packets, burning also *IBERVILLE, FAWN, TIME AND TIDE, NEW ORLEANS, LOUISIANA BELLE, EMPIRE PARISH, BELLE CREOLE,* and *METEOR.*

0634 BLACK HAWK

SW gunboat wh Originally *NEW UNCLE SAM* b. New Albany, Ind., 1857 (see). She was sold to U.S. Navy in November 1862, refitted and renamed *BLACK HAWK,* and was Porter's flagship during the war. She visited Cincinnati Mar. 8–11, 1865, anchored near the waterworks, with Admiral Lee aboard. Caught fire in her oil locker moored opposite Mound City, Ill. on Apr. 22, 1865. She floated down a short distance, the magazine exploded, and then she sank. The *PEERLESS* later hit the wreck and was lost. The *HUNTSVILLE* also hit it but was salvaged. The snagboat *ALBERT* got the wreck out in October 1872, a month's work.

0635 BLACK HAWK

Stw p wh b. Wabasha, Minn., 1909. 135 x 27.5 x 4.5. Engines, 14's- 4½ ft. Two boilers, each 42" by 21 ft. Built for Capt. Walter Blair, using machinery and cabin of the *SILVER CRESCENT* (see). Ran Davenport-Burlington, later Burlington-Quincy. Capt. Blair sold her to Cairo-New Madrid trade, three trips a week. She was moored at Paducah in ice harbor early 1918, and was cut down and lost. Later a fisherman at the mouth of Red River found one of her life preservers, and that is all that ever was found of her.

0636 BLACK HILLS

Stw p wh b. California, Pa. (hull), and completed at Pittsburgh, 1877. 190 x 32 x 4. Engines, 13's- 5 ft. Two boilers. First master, Capt. Timothy B. Burleigh, Yankton, Dakota Territory. He also was half owner, along with Thomas M. Rees ¼, and J.C. McVay ¼. She left Pittsburgh for Missouri River piloted by William Gordon and Jim Witten. She operated in the Block P Line, and her first arrival at Fort Benton was in 1882. On June 27, 1883, in charge of Capt. Josephus Todd, she again was at Fort Benton, unloaded freight in 14 hours, and lit out for Bismarck where she arrived 2 days 22 hours later, a record. Her round trip time Bismarck to Fort Benton and back to Bismarck was 13 days 23 hours, another record. On this trip she was electrically lighted, the first at Fort Benton. The *ROSEBUD* had a light plant placed in 1882 but it wasn't working at the fort. She wintered at Bismarck and was cut down by ice there, Mar. 28, 1884. The *W.J. BEHAN,* also moored there, was lost.

0637 BLACK LOCUST

Recess wheel ferry wh b. Jeffersonville, Ind., 1847. 106 tons. Operated Louisville-Jeffersonville along with *A. WATHEN* and others. Owners were John Shallcross, James J. Thompson, Charles Strader, and A. (for Athanasius) Wathen. This service continued until the severe winter of 1866-1867 when, due to lack of fuel, and ice, the ferries quit. The *BLACK LOCUST* was lost, and Capt. R.W. Dugan with his wrecking boat *UNDERWRITER* took out her wreck. Interesting, perhaps, is that one of the two first Howard-built boats at Jeffersonville was a ferry with this same name, *BLACK LOCUST.* They built her 1834, 110 x 25 x 4.5, for Wathen & Gilmore, and she ran Louisville-Jeff. The subject of the above sketch succeeded her.

0638 BLANCH EDNA

Stw p wh b. Pittsburgh, Pa., 1898. 65 x 11 x 1.5. Originally built to carry passengers, but later towed for McClain Bros., Point Marion, Pa., on Monongahela River. Still there in 1908.

0639 BLANCHE EDMUNDSON

Stw p wh b. Pittsburgh, Pa., 1891. A small private steamer built by Charles Rogers, Jr., first named *GULNARE,* renamed when sold to Howard Jones, Pittsburgh. Engines 3"- 12". One boiler. Named for Mrs. George Lyon Herron of Aspinwall, Pa. Once with a houseboat in tow went to Cincinnati, thence via Miami Canal to Lima, Oh., and return to Pittsburgh. The idea was to go to Toledo but grass and weeds in the canal prevented. Herman B. Mertz, of Pittsburgh, was engineer on her that trip, then 17.

0640 BLANCHE LEWIS

Stw p wh b. Dycusburg, Ky., 1855. 155 tons. When completed at Louisville she ran Nashville-Paducah. Sank at Nashville, Nov. 5, 1860. Machinery went to *LAWRENCE* b. Cincinnati, 1863.

0641 BLANKS CORNWALL

Stw p wh b. Jeffersonville, Ind., by Howard, 1887. 140 x 29 x 4.6. Engines, 10's- 4 ft. stroke. Two boilers. Built for Capt. Jack Blanks to run on Ouachita River but was bought new by S.H. Parisot, Vicksburg, for Yazoo and Tallahatchie service. She was snagged and lost on the Tallahatchie, under full headway, Jan. 24, 1896.

0642 BLOOMER

SW p wh b. Louisville, Ky., 1851. 79 tons. Served on Red River 1851-1855. Arrived at Mobile on Apr. 26, 1855, Capt. Boyd, in the "Thru Line" trade to Fulton, Miss., on Big Bee River.

0643 BLOOMER

Stw p wh b. New Albany, Ind., 1856. 95 tons. Ran on Red River. Mrs. Dewey Somdal in 1974 presented a large poster advertising a sheriff's sale of this boat to the Louisiana State University at Shreveport. The sale was held at City Hotel, New Orleans, Aug. 28, 1858, W.M. Knox vs. Wm. H. Marshall. The boat went to Confederate registry 1861, became U.S. property Jan. 1, 1863. After the war she was sold to private hands Apr. 5, 1866, and renamed *EMMA*—sold foreign in 1868.

0644 BLUE BIRD

SW p wh b. Louisville, Ky., 1859. 49 tons, delivered to New Orleans, and went to Confederate registry 1861.

0645 BLUE HAMMOCK

SW p wh b. Plaquemine, La., 1855. 74 tons. Went to Franklin, La. Out of documentation in 1857.

0646 BLUE RIDGE

SW p wh b. Cincinnati, Oh., 1844. 138 tons. Advertised in Cincinnati *Daily Atlas* in March 1845, Cincinnati, Louisville and Kanawha River, Capt. Robertson. Built by Warth and English, Cincinnati, and soon sold to Capt. Payne and others for the above trade. Capt. William Summers commanded. Exploded boilers downbound at Raccoon Island, soon after leaving Gallipolis, 1:00 A.M. on Jan. 9, 1848, with life loss of 15. A snowstorm was going on at the time. Many persons clung to the after part of the cabin and were taken off in skiffs eight miles below. U.S. Major Jubal Early had been visiting with his parents whose farm was near Winfield on Kanawha River, and was aboard. He drifted with the cabin and was safely set ashore four miles down. This was the same Gen. Jubal Early prominent in the Confederate Army later. Capt. William Penn Wright got ashore and walked in the snow 40 miles home to Red House, Va. An account appears in *S&D Reflector,* Dec. 1975 issue, page 45.

0647 BLUE WING

SW p wh b. Louisville, Ky., 1845. 158 tons. 152 x 27 x 5. Hull by William French. Engines by Curry & Miller. Ran regularly in the Louisville-Frankfort trade, up Kentucky River. Capt. Harry I. Todd, grandson of Judge Harry Innes, was master. Quite swanky; had bedsteads in ladies' cabin rooms with trundle beds underneath. She went up Kentucky River to within a couple of miles of Irvine, in Estelle County, on high water, being the first steamboat that far up. Brought down her share of '49ers, one party of 70, bound for California. Dismantled.

0648 BLUE WING NO. 2

SW p wh b. Jeffersonville, Ind., by Howard, 1850. 150 x 30 x 6.5. 170 tons. Three boilers, each 42" by 22 ft. Capt. Samuel Saunders, who had been mate and pilot on the predecessor, was master. On Dec. 10, 1862, she was seized by the U.S. gunboat *PATROL* charged with trading with the enemy and was taken to Helena, Ark., and was placed in the USQMD. She was captured by the Confederates at Napoleon, Ark., and burned, Dec. 28, 1862. Prior to the war she long served Louisville-Kentucky River.

0649 BLUE WING NO. 3

SW p wh b. Jeffersonville, Ind., by Howard, 1863. 150 x 31 x 5.7. 158 tons. Owned by John Watson & Co. and was launched Nov. 10, 1863, designed for Louisville-Kentucky River. She often went above Frankfort; once while loading wheat at Shaker's Ferry, 56 miles above, the Kentucky River rose 10 feet in something like an hour and a half. The notorious Capt. Jesse with 14 of his guerrillas once boarded this boat about seven miles up from Carrollton, at Chauncey Dean's hay shed, demanded supper, cigars and bourbon, then departed in peace. She was taken on a somewhat astonishing foray in 1866, operating New Orleans-Mobile, Capt. Isaiah Little, master, William Milliken, clerk. She connected with the *MIST* for Montgomery. At that time she was owned by Henry E. Harper, D. Harper, and D. Harper Jr., all of Cincinnati; A.W. Darlington, Carrollton, Ky., and Captain Little of New Orleans. At various times thereafter she ran on Red River in cotton seasons. In 1876 she was back at Louisville, and on a July 16 excursion her captain, Capt. Pemberton died aboard of sun stroke. In April 1878 the towboat *CHARLEY McDONALD* was bringing her up from New Orleans in tow, and her machinery was to go on the packet *WHISPER,* then being built at Jeffersonville.

0650 BLUE WING

Stw p wh Originally the *FANNIE FREESE* b. Ashland, Ky., 1882 (see). Capt. George W. Anderson, Carrollton, Ky., bought the *FREESE* and *GENERAL LYTLE* (see). He commanded her in the Louisville-Kentucky River trade, then sold her after a couple of years to the Williams Bros., of Evansville who ran her in Green River. Then she went to St. Louis as one of the Carter Line operating to Shreveport, and was making Red River trips 1890–1892. She finally sank at Craighead Point, 16 miles below Osceola, Ark., September 1894, in charge of Capt. Milt Harry. Capt. George Anderson, noted for a fine crop of red whiskers, died, 89, at home in Carrollton, Ky., Jan. 24, 1935.

0651 BLUELLA

Stw p wh b. Arkadelphia, Ark., 1868. 86.2 x 21.2 x 3.4. Arkadelphia-Camden, Ark., trade, Capt. M.B. Carpenter, owner and master, in 1868 and early 1869. Enrolled at New Orleans in 1869, same owner and master.

0652 BLUFF CITY

SW p wh b. Paducah, Ky. (hull) and completed at St. Louis, 1853. 186 x 33 x 7. Engines, 22's- 8½ ft. Four boilers, 44″ x 28′. Built for St. Louis-Council Bluffs trade. Burned at St. Louis, July 27, 1853, Capt. McCloy. This skipper also was master of the *ROBERT CAMPBELL* (see) when she burned at St. Louis.

0653 BLUFF CITY

SW p wh b. Louisville, Ky., 1854. 252 tons. Owned originally at Memphis. Lost at Sayder Landing, Yazoo River, Miss., Oct. 20, 1859.

0654 BLUFF CITY

Rig? From the Pittsburgh *Gazette,* Jan. 25, 1876: "The *BLUFF CITY,* a small steamer, and commanded by Paine, hit a snag near Lauratown, 100 miles above Jackport on Black River last Monday and will likely prove a total loss, she was not insured."

0655 BLUFF CITY

Stw p wh b. Jeffersonville, Ind., by Howard, 1896. 225 x 42 x 6. Built for the St. Louis Anchor Line, and was the only sternwheeler they built, and the last of any sort. The intention at the start was to name her *AUSTIN CORBIN* but along toward launch date this idea was scrubbed. Capt. D.M. Connors commanded. Ran St. Louis-New Orleans. Engines, 20's- 8 ft. Four boilers. She departed St. Louis on the morning of Nov. 18, 1897, loaded for New Orleans, with two loaded barges in tow. Fire broke out and she was landed at Chester, Ill., and burned. All 40 passengers and crew got to safety. During exceptionally low stages in the Mississippi in 1976 the wreck was exposed, an attraction which drew many souvenir hunters. See *S&D Reflector,* December 1976, pages 28–29.

0656 BOB BALLARD

Stw p wh b. Murraysville, W. Va. (hull), and completed at Mason City, W. Va., 1890. 130 x 26.2 x 4. Engines, 13's- 5 ft. Three boilers, each 38″ x 20 ft. Machinery, whistle, and equipment came from packet *BOONE* (see). Frank L. Sibley said she was the only packet he knew of with a tin roof. Ran Gallipolis-Marietta, Capt. E.E. Varian, master, with W.E. Hayman, clerk. During her early years she also ran in the Louisville-Kentucky River trade, going high as Tyrone, Capt. C.H. Varian, master, with H.L. Ritchie, clerk. Later was converted into a towboat owned by Capt. Frank Morgan, Ironton, Oh., and others. Sank and lost at Coal Haven, above Ironton, Dec. 10, 1909.

0657 BOB BLANKS

Stw p wh b. Jeffersonville, Ind., by Howard, 1903. 175 x 35 x 5. Engines, 16's- 7 ft. Three boilers. Owned by J.P. Parker, then the Carter Bros., and ran out of New Orleans to Red River and elsewhere. She was cotton style with double stages, quite handsome. Burned at Raccourci Landing, La., Mar. 2, 1912.

0658 BOB DUDLEY

Stw p wh b. Jeffersonville, Ind., by Howard, 1897. 160 x 29 x 3.8. Engines, 10½'s- 3 ft. Two boilers, each 40″ x 16 ft. Named for the founder of the Gray-Dudley Hardware & Foundry Co., Nashville. Owned by the Ryman Line of

Nashville and ran principally on the upper Cumberland, Nashville-Burnside. Often chartered out for low water work on the Ohio River. One of the first of such jobs was running Paducah-Evansville, October 1897, chartered to Capt. Joe Fowler—water too low for even the *R. DUNBAR* (see). Crew on the upper Cumberland in June 1901: Capt. William T. Hunter, master; Huston Robison and Will Lovell, pilots; Mike Martin, mate; Dave and Will Leek, engineers; John Freedle and Bob Turner, clerks. While in Paducah-Evansville trade Oct. 11, 1904, sank at the foot of Cumberland Island, raised. Sank at Nashville on Apr. 29, 1910, and when raised was extensively rebuilt. Hit lock wall at Dam 2, Cumberland River and sank, March 1914, raised. On Dec. 20, 1916, she was laid up at Nashville outside the *HENRY HARLEY,* broke loose, and sank at the head of Gowers Island. She was dismantled there. Her boilers went to the towboat *WENONAH.*

0659 BOB LEE

Ferry wh b. Evansville, Ind., 1876. 24.60 tons. She was a ferry at Memphis, and was returned to Paducah in 1880 for a complete rebuilding, and came away documented as a new boat.

0660 BOB LEE

Ferry wh b. Paducah, Ky., 1881. 102 x 20 x 3.5. Documented at Memphis 1886, perhaps longer.

0661 BOB LEE

Steam prop tug b. Burlington, Iowa, 1915. 37.5 x 9.2 x 3.8. Listed as a passenger boat.

0662 BOB LEE JR.

Stw p sh b. Memphis, Tenn., 1912. 145 x 32. She was built on the levee by the Southern Tank & Boiler Works for the Lee Line. Originally had cross compound engines, 15's, 30's- 6 ft. stroke, and a firebox boiler. Burned at the Memphis wharf, destroying upper works, in August 1913. Sold to Standard Oil, which made a towboat of her and renamed her *CORONA.* They sold her to Transcontinental Oil (Standard subsidiary) and she was taken to the Panuco River, Mexico, where she was renamed *ROBALO.* Ultimately Standard brought her back, again called her *CORONA,* and she flopped over at Island 35, c. 1932.

BOLIVER H. COOKE

See *B.H. COOKE*

0663 BON ACCORD

SW p wh b. St. Louis, Mo., 1846. 147 tons. Ran on the Upper Mississippi, Capt. Hiram Bersie, out of Galena for St. Louis and St. Paul. Lost in ice at St. Louis, Feb. 26, 1856. Also see *NEW BON ACCORD.*

0664 BONANZA

SW p wh b. Madison, Ind., and received machinery and boilers at Portsmouth, Oh., 1876. Hull and engine sizes not determined. She was a fairly large steamboat and came out in the Cincinnati-Portsmouth trade, Capt. E.B. Moore, master, with Duvall Young, clerk. The engines and boilers came from Moore's shop at Portsmouth. Made her trial trip June 19, 1876, and replaced the *ST. JAMES* (see). On a trip to Pomeroy in place of the *FLEETWOOD* she grounded above Portsmouth Aug. 8, 1877, and stayed there until October 11. This bar was then known as Funk's Gut, but ever after has been, and still is, Bonanza Bar. There was a long low water spell in the summer of 1884 and the *BONANZA* had been laid up 3½ months when she burned at Cincinnati along with the *MORNING MAIL* and *LILY,* this on September 20. When the river rose her crew went on the *ANDY BAUM* until a new *BONANZA* was built (see next listing).

0665 BONANZA

SW p wh b. Cincinnati, Oh., 1885. 267.5 x 42.8 x 6.7. Engines, 22's- 7½ ft. Three boilers, each 48″ x 30 ft. Launched at Mack's Yard, Jan. 17, 1885. She received new engines and boilers, but used cranks, pitmans, etc., from the first *BONANZA.* Ran her trial trip on Apr. 28, 1885. On the forward cabin bulkhead was a painting of Portsmouth, Oh., done by artist Scott Hummel. She carried the whistle formerly on the old *BONANZA,* which had started on the *ST. JAMES.* The White Collar Line ran her Cincinnati-Portsmouth, and later through to Pomeroy. On one occasion she came up to East Liverpool, Oh., with a special excursion, this in April 1889. Also she made Cincinnati-Memphis trips, bringing up baled cotton, cottonseed meal and stock. Capt. J.T. Campbell was master in 1891. Capt. Julian F. Davey had been clerk and purser on the first *BONANZA* and was purser and master of this one. He was grandfather of James A. Wallen, Huntington. White Collar Line sold rights to upriver trade out of Cincinnati to the Greene Line in 1904, after which *BONANZA* was used below as a spare, and on Memphis trips. She was dismantled at the Cincinnati wharf in May 1909. Her whistle later was on *CITY OF CINCINNATI, KENTUCKY,* and last on *CINCINNATI.*

0666 BONITA

SW p wh b. New Albany, Ind., 1857. 211 tons. Before completion she went to U.S. Marshal sale and was bought in by W.H. Daniel and Capt. Dennis Long, Louisville. They took her south and ran New Orleans-Minden up Red River. She burned two miles below Bayou Sara, La., on May 7, 1860. Capt. W.H. Daniel left her in 1859 to command the *GREY EAGLE,* Louisville-Henderson (see).

0667 BONNE

Recess wheel ferry wh b. South Point, Oh., 1897. 81.2 x 22.4 x 3. Engines, 7½″- 28″. One boiler, 40″ x 14 ft. Owned by Catlettsburg Ferry Co. Ran Catlettsburg-South Point. Lost in ice at New Boston, Oh., Dec. 12, 1917.

0668 BONNETS O' BLUE

SW ferry wh b. Manchester, Pa., 1860. 129 tons. Operated at Pittsburgh. Removed from documentation in 1865.

0669 BONNIE LEE

Stw p wh b. Jeffersonville, Ind., by Howard, 1875. 165 x 30 x 3.5. Owned by New Orleans & Red River Transportation Co., Capt. Noah Scovell. Exploded boilers and sank at Lone Wall Landing, lower Mississippi, Aug. 9, 1880.

0670 BOONE

SW p wh b. Cincinnati, Oh., 1848. 196 tons. Removed from documentation in 1856. See *DANIEL BOONE.*

0671 BOONE

SW ferry wh b. Constance, Ky., and completed at Cincinnati, 1867. 22.24 tons. Ran between Constance and Andersons Ferry until worn out in 1874.

0672 BOONE NO. 2

SW ferry wh b. Constance, Ky., 1874. 21.25 tons. Apparently operated until the third one was built (see).

0673 BOONE

Stw p wh b. Harmar, Oh., 1877. 135 x 25 x 4. Engines 12½'s- 5 ft. Two boilers, each 40" x 22 ft. Built at the Knox Boat Yard, and the machinery by J.H. McConnell. Owned by Capt. R.L. Hamilton, J.A. McClurg, and J.J. Bright of Gallipolis and Pt. Pleasant. Ran Gallipolis-Kanawha River. Capt. R.L. Hamilton was master; J.A. McClurg and Howard Donnally were the clerks. Ran low water in Wheeling-Parkersburg trade occasionally. Capt. Zenus Baxter commanded when she was lost at Pine Creek, above Sciotoville, Oh. Baxter lived along there, ran the boat close in to throw ashore a newspaper, and she hit a snag. She was enroute to Charleston at the time. Freight and passengers were taken off by Bay Line's packet *LOUISE* (see). Engines went to the *BOB BALLARD* in 1890 (see), also the whistle. The same whistle showed up later on *MATT F. ALLEN.*

0674 BOONE NO. 3

SW ferry wh b. Constance, Ky., 1881. 64 x 19 x 3. This was a continuation of the series starting with *BOONE* of 1867 (see).

0675 BOONE NO. 4

SW ferry wh b. Constance, Ky., 1891. 64 x 19.5 x 3.5. Also ran Constance-Andersons Ferry owned by the Kottmyer family who started this service in 1865. *BOONE NO. 4* was sold Jan. 14, 1903 to George M. Wartenburg, Pt. Pleasant, W. Va., entire. She was run Pt. Pleasant-Kanauga. Sold July 24, 1905 to J.F. Doss, Redmund, W. Va., and continued until the *ANN BAILEY* (see) was built.

0676 BOONE NO. 5

SW ferry wh b. Constance, Ky., 1900. 65.2 x 34.5 x 4.2. Engines 8"- 10½". One boiler, 42" x 18 ft. Owned by the Kottmyer family in Constance-Andersons Ferry service.

0677 BOONE NO. 6

SW ferry wh b. Constance, Ky., 1920. 64.7 x 22.6 x 4.2. Owned by Henry Kottmyer.

0678 BOONE NO. 7

SW ferry sh b. Covington, Ky., 1937. 64.8 x 23.1 x 4.3. She was originally steam, but was converted to diesel in 1947. Continues in operation as this is written in 1977. Owned by Henry Kottmyer, and in Constance-Andersons Ferry service.

0679 BORDER CITY

Stw p wh b. Fort Smith, Ark., 1885. 108 x 21 x 2.5. Was still documented in 1892, possibly longer.

0680 BOREALIS REX

Stw p wh b. Stillwater, Minn., 1888. 121.5 x 22 x 4.3. Cross compound engines, 12" and 24"- 6 ft. Two boilers, 40" x 16 ft. Built for Capt. David Swain. Operated around Stillwater until 1890 when she was brought to the Peoria-La Salle trade on the Illinois. Capt. Charles Ebaugh commanded. On June 4, 1903, she was sold to Capt. George Prince who ran her out of Natchez twice weekly, one trip to Atchafalaya, the other to Black, Ouachita, Tensas and Little rivers. Several years later she went to the Lake Charles & Cameron Transportation Co., Lake Charles, La. A modern highway ended that. She then was moored at the foot of Pugo Street, Lake Charles where she idled until sold for junk in 1938, bringing $110. The resemblance of the lines, shape and size of paddlewheel of *JULIA BELLE SWAIN* shows much *BOREALIS REX* influence.

0681 BOREAS

SW p wh b. Pittsburgh, Pa., 1841. 157 tons. Built for Capt. Thomas M. Fithian and George Barnard. Ran in the St. Louis-Keokuk trade, and later in Missouri River. Lost in the big wharf fire at St. Louis when 23 boats burned, May 17, 1849.

0682 BOREAS NO. 2

SW p wh b. Pittsburgh, Pa., 1845. 222 tons. Removed from documentation in 1847.

0683 BOREAS NO. 3

SW p wh b. Elizabeth, Pa., 1847 by Capt. Thomas J. Fithian and George Barnard. 264 tons. She burned at Gonsole's Landing, one-half mile below Hermann, Mo., on May 17, 1849. On board was a large shipment of silver bullion and Mexican money which apparently did not show up in the wreckage. Evidence pointed that it had been removed prior to the blaze.

0684 BOROUGH BEE

SW ferry wh b. Pittsburgh, Pa., 1865. 51 tons. Removed from documentation in 1869. Ran somewhere in the Pittsburgh area.

0685 BOSSIER

Stw p wh b. 1869. Ran on Red River. Burned and lost at Algiers, La., Nov. 16, 1870.

0686 BOSSIER

Stw p wh b. Jeffersonville, Ind., 1871, 115 tons. Said the

New Orleans *Times*, Oct. 12, 1873: "Yesterday morning between the hours of 8 and 9 as the steamer *GEORGE CROMWELL* rounded out from her wharf at the foot of Toulouse Street, she darted across the river and struck the Red River packet *BOSSIER* a little forward of the cylinder timbers and sunk her. She was owned by Capt. C.J. Boardman and valued at $8,000. When we left the wreck last evening her stacks were still standing but in a slant position. She lies a short distance above the Canal Street ferry wharf. At the time she was sunk she was alongside the Red River packet *MARIA LOUISE*."
Note: The *GEORGE CROMWELL* was an ocean liner built New York City 1862, propeller.

0687 BOSTON

SW p wh b. Brownsville, Pa., 1849. 163 tons. Lost in ice below Cairo, Ill., Jan. 9, 1850.

0688 BOSTON

SW p wh b. Cincinnati, Oh., 1856. 395 tons. She was frequently used by the U.S. Mail Line Co., during low water seasons between Cincinnati and Louisville, taking the place of the larger regulars *TELEGRAPH NO. 3* and *JACOB STRADER*. Capt. Wash Honshell ran her in the Cincinnati-Big Sandy trade. Sank and burned at Moore's Bar near Portsmouth, Oh., July 25, 1863.

0689 BOSTON

Stw p wh b. Pittsburgh, Pa., 1876. 65 x 16 x 2.5. 20 tons. Ran between Elizabeth and McKeesport on the Monongahela River along with *MARKET BOY* and *TILLIE*. Still documented at Pittsburgh in 1892.

0690 BOSTONA

SW p wh b. Louisville, Ky., 1849. 468 tons. 266 x 34 x 7.5. Engines, 26½'s- 9 ft. Five boilers, each 42" by 34½ ft. Wheels 31½ ft. with 14 ft. buckets. Hull by James Murray. Engines by Inman, Gault & Co., Capt. E.T. Dustin, Louisville, master and part owner. Ran Louisville-New Orleans. Quite ornate; each of 50 staterooms had columns at doors upon which rested porticos richly gilded. Had bedsteads and spring mattresses. Doors glassed with many colors divided ladies' and men's sections; tub baths connect with men's and ladies' rooms. She was at New Orleans when the *LOUISIANA* exploded alongside, Nov. 15, 1849, and was badly damaged. Captain Dustin died several days after the blast. On an upbound trip she stranded at or near Ford's Ferry, Ky., above Cave-In-Rock, sank, and was cut down by ice. Sinking happened Nov. 25, 1852.

0691 BOSTONA

SW p wh b. Cincinnati, Oh., 1854. 355 tons. Owned by the Cincinnati, Maysville & Portsmouth Packet Co., running Cincinnati-Portsmouth three days weekly, Capt. William McClain in charge. This same company ran *BOONE* and *KENTON* in Cincinnati-Maysville trade, and the *SCIOTO* in the Cincinnati-Big Sandy trade. In off seasons ran Cincinnati-St. Louis. On one such trip Captain McClain talked with a 10-year-old boy on the levee at St. Louis, learned he was an orphan, and took him home to his farm at Utopia, Oh., and raised him. His name was George Hughes; he became a proficient pilot Pittsburgh-Cincinnati. The aforementioned company did not long endure, after which time Admiral David Gibson and Capt. Wm. McClain became the boat's sole owners. She was continued in the trade until 1863 when she was placed in the Cincinnati-Madison trade briefly, and then sold to Capt. John H. Watson and others. She was taken to Memphis and ran from there to Vicksburg. Sold for debt by a U.S. marshal and was taken to St. Louis for dismantling. She burned there, June 2, 1866, along with the *IDA HANDY* and *JAMES RAYMOND* (see).

0692 BOSTONA

SW p wh b. Cincinnati, Oh., 1867. 816 tons. 260 x 40 x 6.7. Engines, 25's- 8 ft. Six boilers, each 38" x 28 ft., five flues. Paddlewheels, 30 ft. dia., with 14 ft. buckets. She was a replacement built following the loss of the prior *BOSTONA*. Came out new in the Cincinnati-Portsmouth trade, Capt. Pres. Lodwick, mid-January 1867. Hull by Litherbury and machinery by Robert Moore & Sons, Portsmouth. On Thursday, July 6, 1868, Gen. U.S. Grant rode the boat Cincinnati to Maysville to visit his uncle. The White Collar Line bought this boat to replace the slow *POTOMAC* (see) in the Cincinnati-Huntington trade. Capt. Ike Bryson, South Point, Oh., was master; Owen Jolly was mate; Gus Honshell, clerk, William Handley, chief engineer, and Jim Kirker, mate. Her best time, Cincinnati to Huntington, was 13 hours 30 minutes with seven landings. She once came Cincinnati to Rock Springs (Tietzville) in three hours flat. On Feb. 8, 1877, she was coming up around the point at Sciotoville in high water and collided with the towboat *SAM MILLER*. The *BOSTONA* was sunk and when raised an entire new head was put on her. Jim Mace was the pilot on watch at the time. Dismantled 1879.

0693 BOSTONA

SW p wh b. Cincinnati, Oh., 1879. 302.5 x 43.5 (42 ft. floor) x 6. 79½ ft. overall width. 759 tons. Engines, 25's- 8 ft. Four boilers, each 47" x 30 ft., with six flues 10" dia. Wheels 27 ft. dia., with 16 ft. buckets; 18 arms and four flanges on each wheel shaft. Carried her fuel (coal) in the hold and had double railroad tracks with 24 cars, each 50 bu. capacity in the hold. Owned by the Cincinnati, Portsmouth, Big Sandy & Pomeroy Packet Co. First crew: Capt. Isaac Bryson, master; Gus Honshell and Samuel Hawke, clerks; Peter Boughner and Jim Mace, pilots; John Perry, steward; Owen Jolly, mate, and Mrs. Mary Nelson, stewardess. Admiral David Gibson rode the trial trip, along with Commodore Wash Honshell, Capt. E.B. Moore (of the *BONANZA*), and C.T. Dumont. Capt. John Holloway took command about 1882 and was still there in 1891. She ran the "railroad trade" Cincinnati-Huntington until 1883 when the C&O arrived at Cincinnati; then ran Cincinnati-Pomeroy. In latter years made frequent trips Cincinnati-

Memphis, Capt. Charles B. Church. She was dismantled about 1899, and her machinery went to the *INDIANA*. The hull was remodeled into a wharfboat for Vevay, Ind.

0694 BOSTONA NO. 2

SW p wh b. Cincinnati, Oh., 1860. 304 tons. Built in partnership by Commodore David Gibson, Cincinnati, and Capt. William McClain as a low water boat Portsmouth-Cincinnati. She was about 240 ft. long. Ran Wheeling-Cincinnati at various times; in 1861 with Capt. Evan H. Morgan, master, and S.P. Simpson and Wm. G. Battelle, clerks. Ran Cincinnati-Marietta in 1864 with Capt. H.H. Drown, master, and Chris Best, clerk. In November 1864 while in the Cincinnati-Madison trade, Capt. Charles David, she was attacked at Carrollton, Ky., by the notorious raider Jesse and his guerrillas, but escaped with but a few bullet holes in the pilothouse sash where John David was on watch. Several weeks later the raiders again attempted boarding the boat at Carrollton, but the crew had a cannon on the forecastle this time, and fired it. She was snagged at Craig's Bar, above Carrollton, on Oct. 17, 1865. Later the wreck was raised and brought to Cincinnati.

0695 BOSTONA NO. 3

SW p wh b. Jeffersonville, Ind., by Howard, 1863. 375 tons. 245 x 35 x 5.5. Engines, 22's- 8 ft. Built under the personal supervision of Capt. William McClain. This boat was the successor to *BOSTONA* b. 1854 which McClain et. al., sold in 1863 (see). He ran her the first year Cincinnati-Portsmouth under his personal command. Then, his health failing, McClain sold one-half interest to Capt. Pres Lodwick who took charge and continued her in the run. This boat was at Maysville doing business at the wharfboat on the evening of Oct. 8, 1866, when she took fire. She was run across the river and nosed to shore just below the mouth of Fishgut Creek. Pete Boughner was the pilot who did it—he lived in Maysville and later he planted the jackstaff from the wreck in his front yard where it stood for years. The only casualty was Mrs. Spillman, wife of the Rev. J.K. Spillman of Maysville. The wreck used to show plainly in times of extreme low water before Dam 34 created a pool stage.

0696 BOWLING GREEN

SW p wh b. Cincinnati, Oh., 1839. 148 tons. 125 x 33. Owned at time of loss by John J. Roe and others, St. Louis. She hit a rock at the head of Osage Chute, Mo., on the Missouri River, Dec. 12, 1842, and was lost. The wreck still showed plainly as late as 1927.

0697 BOWLING GREEN

Stw p wh b. Cincinnati, Oh., 1855. 125 tons. Capt. William McLean sold his farm to acquire this boat and was not successful with her. He ran her 1856 Evansville-Bowling Green on Green River. Pres Austin, Louisville, was pilot. Graf (brother) Austin was engineer. Later ran Louisville-Owensboro. Removed from documentation in 1861.

0698 BOWLING GREEN

Stw p wh b. Louisville, Ky., 1870. 121.7 x 28.8 x 5.9. Engines, 16's- 5 ft. Two boilers. Owned by Green and Barren River Navigation Co., Capt. S.W. Coombs, master, with T.L. Burnham, clerk. Ran Evansville-Bowling Green. Rolled over a log coming through Lock 2 on May 23, 1887, wet much freight, and had to be docked. She burned at Enola, Ky., three miles above Lock 3, Feb. 1, 1889. The outside lock wall at No. 3 had failed, or crumbled, and *BOWLING GREEN* was reshipping with a boat moored below when this happened.

0699 BOWLING GREEN

Stw p wh b. Jeffersonville, Ind., by Howard, 1904. 122 x 32 x 5. Engines, 14's- 6 ft. Two boilers, each 42" x 26 ft. Owned by the Evansville & Bowling Green Packet Co. One of her masters was Capt. Sam G. Smith, later an editor with *The Waterways Journal.* Mike Keplinger and Jim Burnett were the pilots, and Courtney Ellis was striker engineer. She was lost at South Carrollton, Ky., on Green River, night of Mar. 31, 1920. Capt. C.W. Sturgeon was master, and Owen Jones, 25, was pilot. A storm was going on, and Jones was all for letting her lay at the landing for a while. Sturgeon hoisted the stage and tapped her out. She hit rock just below the landing and opened the hull. Jones drove her across the river and beached her—all this about 10:30 P.M.

0700 BRACELET

SW p wh b. Louisville, Ky., 1857. 169 tons. She was running Louisville-Memphis, spring of 1861, Capt. Ben Duncan, master, with Richard Cox, clerk. She was moored at J.W. Jones' Landing near Little Rock on the Arkansas River when the war broke out, then owned by a Capt. Miller. She was burned there as a Confederate cottonclad transport, Sept. 10, 1863. The wreck was not removed until 1906 when the snagboat *C. B. REESE* was sent up to remove it.

0701 BRADDOCK BELLE

SW ferry wh b. Elizabeth, Pa., 1894. 82 x 17 x 4. Still documented 1896.

0702 BRADISH JOHNSON

SW p wh b. Jeffersonville, Ind., 1869. 121.6 x 33.6 x 6. Engines, 20's- 5 ft. Three boilers, each 40" by 28 ft. Ran New Orleans-Red River, Capt. W.S. Bassett. Was taken to Mobile in May 1876. Still documented at Mobile in 1886.

0703 BRAZIL

Stw p wh b. McKeesport, Pa., 1854. 211 tons. 150 x 31 x 4. Three boilers. Built for Capt. Redmund J. Grace. Went to the Upper Mississippi and was fairly regular in and out of St. Paul 1856–1858. Ran in the upper Illinois 1861 above Peoria. After the war she was sold to New Orleans and was sunk in collision with the *MAGENTA* on Nov. 11, 1865, Capt. A. Hensinger in command. The *GOSSAMER* was coming along behind and picked up Capt. H. and six of his crew who had overturned in a yawl.

0704 BRAZOS

Stw p wh b. West Elizabeth, Pa., 1848. 101 tons. Was taken to Galveston, Tex., and was removed from documentation in 1856.

0705 BRIDE

SW p wh b. Louisville, Ky., 1848. 295 tons. Operated on Red River, and exploded boilers at Cloutierville, La., in 1851. In 1853 she was on the Wabash River having her troubles. Got aground February 8 and while sparring the capstan broke and killed three men. Snagged and lost on the Wabash at Vincennes, Ind., Apr. 18, 1853.

0706 BRIDGE CITY

Stw p wh b. Wheeling, Va., 1854. 199 tons. Three boilers. Was renamed *KATE FRENCH* on Nov. 19, 1856 and burned at Napoleon, Ark., Nov. 29, 1860 (see).

0707 BRIDGEPORT

Stw p wh b. Bridgeport, Ala., 1865. 184 tons. Built by US-QMD for Tennessee River service. Sold to private owners, Apr. 24, 1866. Engines, 16's- 4½ ft. Three boilers. She was on the Missouri River with a load of government supplies when snagged and lost one and one-half miles below Decatur City, Neb., June 1, 1868, Capt. T.L. Chappelle, master.

0708 BRIDGEWATER

Stw p wh b. Pittsburgh, Pa., 1842. 58 tons. Ran Pittsburgh-Wheeling, August 1843, Capt. C.E. Clark. Capt. G. Wash Ebbert ran her for some time. This was said to be the first, or about the first, packet to have her roof extended clear forward with the stacks cased in. Capt. Jacob Jay Vandergrift had his first river job on her as cabin boy when Capt. Ebbert commanded. She was at Galena, Ill., in 1846. Removed from documentation in 1849.

0709 BRIG. GEN. R.H. STOKES

SW p wh b. Cincinnati, Oh., 1852. 140 tons. Owned and operated by Capt. Clitus A. Brown, Yazoo City, Miss. Sold March 1854 to Apalachicola, Fla., Capt. William L. Staples, Columbus, Ga. Off the lists in 1857.

0710 BRIGHT LIGHT

Stw p wh Originally b. Pittsburgh, Pa., 1878 as *ALICE* (see). After having sunk on the Falls at Louisville she was raised, sold and renamed *BRIGHT LIGHT* because of the new electric arc lights then coming into use. In 1883 Capt. David H. Silver and Capt. William Thompson owned her on Missouri River. On June 30, that year, she hit the railroad bridge at Boonville, Mo., became disabled, floated down and lodged on Boone Island. That fall and winter she was high and dry. Later the machinery was removed and the hull refloated. Capt. Henry Leyhe used the hull as a barge at St. Louis.

0711 BRIGHT STAR

Centerwheel ferry wh b. New Albany, Ind., 1864. 85 tons. One engine, 16″- 5 ft. She operated at Washington, Mo., on the Missouri River. Joseph Kettler was an early owner, and Capt. A.S. Bryan, master. Later skippered by Capt. Frank Hoelscher, Robert Roehrig, Sr., and Harry Kettel. The ferry *MAY BRIAN* took her place (see) in April 1875. Dismantled and hull used as a barge.

0712 BRILL

Stw p wh b. Brownsville, Pa., 1870. 156 x 33 x 4.5. Three boilers. Built at the Pringle yard for Capt. Adam Jacobs. Her first work September 1870 was Pittsburgh-Brownsville, Capt. Auld, running with *PETROLIA* during low water. She ran Pittsburgh-Nashville, Capt. Sam Shuman, 1872, with J.M. Vandergrift in the office. In early March 1873 she sank at the head of the new Canal locks, Louisville. A rising river carried off the cabin and she was lost. Capt. M.A. Cox was on her at the time. The wreck was removed in mid-April 1873.

0713 BRILLIANT

SW p wh b. Pittsburgh, Pa., 1842. 200 x 32 x 6.7. Engines, 25's- 10 ft. Five boilers, each 40″ x 26 ft., two flues. Built for the New Orleans-Bayou Sara trade, Capt. Jesse Hart. Owned by Charles Stetson and William Avery, of the New Orleans firm Stetson & Avery. "She died in 1847," said Capt. Hart in 1850, then 62, living in West Baton Rouge.

0714 BRILLIANT

SW p wh b. Shousetown, Pa. (hull), and completed at Pittsburgh, 1848. 217 x 31.5 x 5.5. Engines, 26's- 8 ft. Five boilers, each 40″ by 26 ft. Wheels 30½ ft. dia. with 12 ft. buckets. Hull by E. and N. Porter. Machinery by Robinson & Minis. Tudor-Gothic cabin 192 ft. long, 15½ ft. wide, designed by J.W. Kerr and built by James Millinger. Construction superintended by Capt. Redmund J. Grace. Furniture in black walnut, crimson cushions on the chairs. Ran Pittsburgh-Cincinnati, Capt. Grace commanding. Stockholders included Capt. M.W. Beltzhoover, Clarke & Thaw, William Bingham, Robert S. Hays and William Frampton. Dismantled in 1853 and machinery, etc., went to building the *PHILADELPHIA* (see).

0715 BRILLIANT

SW p wh b. New Albany, Ind., 1850. 395 tons. She was 225 ft. long. Engines, 30's- 8 ft. Five boilers, each 40″ by 30 ft. Wheels 34 ft. dia. Ran New Orleans-Bayou Sara, Capt. Jesse Hart. On Jan. 20, 1851 she collapsed a boiler flue at Bayou Sara, killing three. She then received new boilers. On Sept. 31, 1851 the second starboard boiler exploded at Dr. Stone's plantation, above Bayou Goula and six miles below Plaquemine. It went forward and overboard with fragments thrown upward into the cabin. Forty-seven persons were killed or wounded, 27 of whom died. Of the four engineers, three died. There was extensive destruction of cabins, engines, and furniture. The *NATCHEZ* and *MOHICAN* came to aid.

0716 BRILLIANT

SW p wh b. Cincinnati, Oh., 1863. 241 x 35 x 5.6. Built for

the Cincinnati & Madison Packet Co., Capt. Charles David, master. She was chartered to the U.S. on several occasions to transport troops Cincinnati to Louisville and elsewhere. Soon sold to M.S. Mepham and others, St. Louis, and ran south. She burned at New Madrid, Mo., Oct. 16, 1865. Had landed there to deliver a lady passenger at 6:00 A.M. in a dense fog. Backed out and hardly had headway when fire was discovered. The watchman had been putting oil lamps away in the locker, blew one out, and it exploded. Pilot Ben Shively landed the boat and some 65 passengers got ashore, many in nightdress.

0717 BROOKLYN

SW p wh b. Shousetown, Pa. (hull), and completed at Pittsburgh, 1847. 245 tons. Ran Pittsburgh-St. Louis, Capt. Bryce Boies. Her picture shows up handsomely in the famed daguerreotype taken at Cincinnati, 1848. In the Cincinnati-Nashville trade, Capt. S.J. Fowler in 1849. Collided with and sank *CONFIDENCE* at Big Bone Island, Ohio River, Nov. 6, 1849. Removed from documentation 1854.

0718 BROOKLYN

SW p wh b. Oshkosh, Wis., 1866. 257 tons. From the St. Paul *Pioneer,* June 15, 1867: "Yesterday marked an era in the history of steamboating, by bringing to our levee the steamer *BROOKLYN* from Green Bay, Wis. She left Green Bay one week ago last Wednesday (June 5) with about 90 tons of freight for St. Paul. She came up the lower Fox River to Winnebago Lake and through the Upper Fox to Portage; from thence through the canal which connects the Upper Fox with the Wisconsin River, and thence down the Wisconsin into the Mississippi River and to St. Paul. This trip is the first of the kind ever made, we believe."

0719 BROWN DICK

Stw p wh b. McKeesport, Pa., 1855. 95 x 19 x 3.5. 55 tons. Built for the Zanesville-Dresden trade, Muskingum River, Capt. James Darlington. Extended to McConnelsville-Dresden same year, Capt. C.C. Morgan. Named for a noted racehorse of Alabama owned by a Colonel Goldsby, mentioned in Carl Carmer's *Stars Fell on Alabama.* This was the first boat used by the B&O Railroad to transfer Wheeling, Benwood, and Bellaire. Made a trip or so to Red River. She was being dismantled at Wheeling when she caught fire on Nov. 23, 1862, and she burned in midstream. The machinery had been transferred to the new *W.H. HARRISON.*

0720 BROWNSVILLE

SW p wh b. Louisville, Ky., 1845. 99 tons. Sold to USQMD on Jan. 2, 1847. Snagged and sunk in Brownsville Chute, Upper Mississippi, June 11, 1849. This location probably is near Brownsville, Minn., below La Crosse.

0721 BRUNETTE

SW p wh b. Pittsburgh, Pa., 1842. 172 x 22.8 x 5.6. 207 tons. First master, Capt. Joseph Nevin, who owned stock along with Joseph Irwin, Joseph Love, and John C. Crampton. Ran Pittsburgh-St. Louis. Joe Hall, who became noted as a safe and lock manufacturer at Cincinnati was steward on this boat while Capt. J. Irwin was master. Snagged and lost in Tunica Bend, Mississippi River, Jan. 23, 1847.

0722 BRUNETTE

SW p wh b. Jeffersonville, Ind., by Howard, 1852. 180 x 29 x 6. Built for Charles Barger, designed for Missouri River. Burned at Bloody Island, St. Louis, Oct. 15, 1859.

0723 BRUNSWICK

SW p wh b. Pittsburgh, Pa., 1844. 293 tons. Hit the bank in a fog five miles above Vicksburg in November 1848. Sank with her bow on shore and the stern went down to the hurricane roof. She was deeply loaded with freight.

0724 BUCK ELK

Stw p wh b. Hermann, Mo., 1900. 100.7 x 18.3 x 3. A light draft carrier. Had gravitated to the Yazoo River by 1908.

0725 BUCKEYE

SW p wh b. Wellsville, Oh., 1854. 48 tons. Out of documentation in 1859.

0726 BUCKEYE

Stw ferry wh b. West Wheeling, Oh., 1896. 103.1 x 25.4 x 3.3. Engines, 10"- 4 ft. One boiler, 42" x 20 ft. Owned by Ira D. Wolfe and George F. Wolfe, equal shares. Long ferried at Wellsburg, W. Va., operated by the Waddle family who had been in the ferry business there since 1870. Capt. W. Scott Heatherington was master in 1916 when *BUCKEYE* was swapped for the *ALBERT.* The Wilson Sand & Supply Co., Huntington, converted her into a towboat, and sold her to Capt. Lewis Tanner in October 1920.

0727 BUCKEYE BELLE

SW p wh b. Marietta, Oh., 1852. 151 x 22 x 5. Engines, 17's- 6 ft. Two boilers, each 42" x 28 ft., two flues. The *DAN CONVERS* and *BUCKEYE BELLE* handled U.S. Mail between St. Marys, Va. (Middle Island), Newport, Oh., and Zanesville, although they did it by connecting with a third boat, Marietta-St. Marys. Capt. James T. Hahn was first skipper. She was upbound on the Muskingum, having just locked at Beverly, and was about abreast of the upper guard lock at the head of the canal when the boilers exploded. Twenty were killed, and fourteen injured. Thirteen victims were buried in the Beverly Cemetery, and later on a monument was supplied there by Edward M. Ayres who was grandson of pilot Calvin R. Stull. The boat's safe was not located until latter October 1871 when a man in a skiff saw it 300 yards from the site of the explosion. He grappled it ashore. The news account telling of this fails to mention what was found in it. Nothing, apparently. If so, it spoiled a good local tradition that it contained $1,500 in specie and $1,200 in bank notes. But this does not end the story of the *BUCKEYE BELLE*—she was rebuilt after this catastrophe of Nov. 12, 1852, and we find her running Pittsburgh-

Portsmouth, Capt. Smith, spring 1854, and then Mound City-Cairo-Hickman, daily, Capt. J.W. Brown, fall of 1857. Again exploded boilers at Columbus, Ky., Nov. 26, 1857, no life loss.

0728 BUCKEYE STATE

SW p wh b. Shousetown, Pa. (hull), and completed at Pittsburgh, 1850. 260 x 29.4 x 6.6. Engines, 29½'s- 8 ft. Five boilers. Paddlewheels 31'8" dia., 12 ft. buckets and 36" dip, with 20 arms. Hull and framing by E. & N. Porter. James Nelson built engines. Cabin and joiner work by James Milligan. David Holmes, Pittsburgh, superintended construction. Original stockholders: David Holmes, Thomas S. Clarke, William Bingham, Robert S. Hays, and Samuel J. Reno. Operated in the Pittsburgh & Cincinnati Packet Line. Left Pittsburgh on maiden trip Feb. 17, 1850, Capt. Samuel J. Reno. She ran hot competition with the *CINCINNATI*, Capt. Wm. J. Kountz, an independent. After several weeks of this one of the "Line" boats, *NEW ENGLAND NO. 2*, sank opposite Greenup, Ky., and the *CINCINNATI* was adopted into the Line and given another day. The wear and strain of the fray proved too much for Captain Reno's health, and he died at Cincinnati Mar. 28, 1850. Command went to Capt. Samuel Dean, Martins Ferry, Oh., uncle of William Dean Howells. Reno's body was brought to Pittsburgh on the *BUCKEYE STATE*. He was survived by his wife and by a six-year-old son Sam Jr., who also became a river captain and pilot. Under Dean's command a special "speed trial" was run Cincinnati to Pittsburgh. She left Cincinnati at 5:11 A.M., May 1, 1850, and 43 hours later she was at Pittsburgh. No boat had done as well, and no steamboat ever since has equalled this. She fired a cannon at the upper end of Belpre, Oh., at the end of her first 24 hours, was at Brown's Island in 36. Crew on this fast trip: Capt. Samuel Dean, master; Standish Peppard, first clerk; John D. Williams, second clerk; William Clark and Thomas Witten, pilots; Thomas Kennedy, chief engineer; C.B. Matthews, second engineer; Thomas Davis, mate. A carved wooden full-size buck deer was carried on top of the pilothouse and pilot Tom Witten mounted it while passing under the Wheeling suspension bridge and waved his silk hat to the spectators. One year later P.T. Barnum chartered the *MESSENGER NO. 2* to convey Jenny Lind Cincinnati-Pittsburgh and rigged a race with the *BUCKEYE STATE* to attract attention. The B.S. won handily. Capt. M.W. Beltzhoover commanded the last several years. James Nelson, engineer, later was the superintendent of the Pittsburgh City Water Works. Standish Peppard, Georgetown, Pa., her head clerk, died 1874. Thomas Kennedy, engineer, died at St. Louis in 1866. This boat had several minor accidents; she rammed and sank the *SCHUYLKILL* at Pittsburgh, Apr. 5, 1850 (see). She burst a starboard steam line in Merriman's Riffle on May 25, 1853, and first cook William Rainbow died. Finally dismantled in 1857. Detailed drawings of *BUCKEYE STATE* by Thomas Tredgold were published in London, 1851, and since have been reproduced.

0729 BUCKEYE STATE

Stw p wh b. Freedom, Pa. (hull and framing), and completed at Pittsburgh, 1878. 235 x 36 x 5. Engines, 18's- 7 ft. Four boilers, each 41" by 26 ft., two flues. Came out drawing 28" light. Landscape paintings in the cabin by artist Emil Bott; cabin had 41 staterooms, and 14 more in the texas. Came out in the Pittsburgh-Cincinnati trade with Capt. Wash Kerr, master; Charles Regnier and John Neal, clerks; Davis Alexander and Thomas Morris, pilots; Hiram Tyler, chief engineer; William Cupps, second engineer; William McClain, mate; Joseph Daniels, second mate; Sam White, steward, and Thomas Morrison, cook. The original stockholders were William M. Rees, W.H. Kerr, Wash Honshell, Shadrick Ward, T.T. Johnston, and Jacob Ensinger. Capt. George H. Rowley was in command in 1881. She was part of the Pittsburgh & Cincinnati Packet Line, running along with the *EMMA GRAHAM, KATIE STOCKDALE*, and the *SCOTIA*. Later she entered the "Big Eight," in the trade to St. Louis, in charge of Capt. Kirker. Hit a pier at the Louisville Canal and was wrecked. The pilot on watch was Capt. Henry Nye.

0730 BUCKEYE STATE

Stw p wh b. Cincinnati, Oh., 1883. 252.3 x 39.8 x 6.8. Much equipment from the former *BUCKEYE STATE* salvaged from the wreck at the Louisville Falls (see). Owned largely by the Rees family, Pittsburgh, Capt. John Thornburg, and Capt. Wash Honshell. Operated in the Memphis & Cincinnati Packet Co. In 1892 in charge of Capt. M.M. Deem, with R.F. Hendrickson in the office. Burned at Barfield Point, Ark., on Jan. 19, 1901. The pilot, William Stricker, stuck to his post, as did chief engineer Jack Robinson, and got her landed. There was but one casualty.

0731 BUENA VISTA

SW p wh b. Elizabeth, Pa., 1847. 266 tons. Went to St. Louis. In March 1849 she caught fire under the boilers passing Kaskaskia Landing, Mississippi River. She was run ashore and "after great exertions the fire was extinguished." Off the lists in 1853.

0732 BUFFALO

Prop p wh b. Huntington, Ind., 1863. 52 tons. Ran Henderson-Evansville along with the *WAMADEE* (see). Sold summer 1864 to Memphis parties. Off the lists in 1866.

0733 BULL OF THE WOODS

Freight boat. b. Poplar Bluff, Mo., 1878. 65 x 16 x 3. Documented at Memphis through 1886. 28.50 tons.

0734 BULLETIN

SW p wh b. Cincinnati, Oh., 1845. 498 tons. Apparently operated Memphis-New Orleans. Off the lists in 1851.

0735 BULLETIN NO. 2

SW p wh b. New Albany, Ind., 1850. 692 tons. Ran Memphis-New Orleans, Capt. C.B. Church. Burned downbound at Island 96, Mississippi River, with loss of large cotton cargo and 23 lives. One account says the Negro crew was insured at Memphis. W.J. Miller, pilot on watch, was warmly complimented on getting the boat safely landed. This disaster happened on Mar. 27, 1855.

0736 BUNKER HILL NO. 3

SW p wh b. New Albany, Ind., 1849. 398 tons. Louisville-New Orleans, January 1851, Capt. Silas F. Miller, master, with Henry W. Smith, clerk. The Cairo *Delta* reported Capt. Job. Whipple of this boat died aboard between Natchez and Memphis, Mar. 25, 1849. Several of the crew died of cholera. Off the lists in 1857.

0737 BUNKER HILL

Centerwheel ferry wh b. St. Louis, Mo., 1868. 272 tons. Continued as a ferry at St. Louis until dismantled in 1883.

0738 BURD LEVI

Stw p wh b. New Albany, Ind., 1864. 206 tons. Exploded and lost at West Franklin, Ind., on May 19, 1865, with loss of five lives. Also see *B.C. LEVI,* probably named for the same person.

0739 BURKESVILLE

Stw p wh b. Cincinnati, Oh., 1898. 116.5 x 17.1 x 3.8. Engines, 8"- 3½ ft. One boiler, 54" by 7 ft. Owned by Burkesville & Burnside Transportation Co., operating on upper Cumberland River. Sold in 1904 to Capt. Oscar Knapp, Dubuque, Iowa, who renamed her *O.K.* (for himself). This boat under both names is written up in *S&D Reflector,* Sept. 1969, pages 34-36. See *O.K.*

0740 BURLINGTON

SW ferry wh b. Wellsville, Oh., 1852. 61 tons. Ferried at Burlington, Iowa. Off the lists in 1854.

0741 BURLINGTON

SW p wh b. Wheeling, W. Va. (hull), and completed at Cincinnati, 1864. 210 x 35 x 5.5. Capt. Richard C. Gray superintended construction. Made trial trip at Cincinnati on July 5, 1864, Capt. J.J. Robinson. Taken to the Upper Mississippi and ran in the Northern Line Packet Co. In 1866, Capt. J.B. Rhodes, master, with Sam Barr, Jr., clerk. Snagged and lost one mile above Wabasha, Minn., Sept. 7, 1867.

0742 BURNSIDE

Stw p wh b. Harmar, Oh., 1882. 114 x 20 x 3. Originally named *G. W. THOMPSON* (see) and renamed when sold to Cumberland River, c. 1885. Capt. O.J. Stowe brought her to the Muskingum River in 1886 for various short trades, principally Beverly-Parkersburg. Sank below the lock at Lowell, Oh., May 6, 1888. Dismantled at Wheeling later.

0743 BURNSIDE

Stw p wh b. Cincinnati, Oh., 1896. 136 x 21 x 4.6. Owned by Burnside & Burkesville Transportation Co., C.W. Cole, pres., A.B. Massey, secy. Capt. D.C. Heath, master, H.H. Beaty, clerk. During low water on the upper Cumberland she often ran elsewhere. Was running on Kentucky River in summer 1897. In 1899 was up the Ohio as far as Marietta. In summer 1901 chartered to the Bay Line.

0744 BURNSIDE

Stw p wh Built for Cumberland River and burned at McMillin's Landing, Mile 122.8 on the Cumberland, on her maiden trip, Dec. 31, 1904. A can of oil used in painting the boat overturned and became ignited. She was a total loss.

0745 BURNSIDE

SW p wh b. Bridgeport, Ala., 1864, 248 tons. Built by USQMD. Sold to private owners on June 7, 1866, who renamed her *MINER* (see).

0746 BUSINESS

Stw p wh b. Jeffersonville, Ind., 1872. 70 tons. Operated around Evansville. She was hauled out on the Covington, Ky., docks in November 1876, lengthened, and renamed *MARK TWAIN* (see).

0747 BUSY

SW ferry wh b. Newport, Ky., 1852. 97 tons. Off the lists in 1854.

0748 BUTTE

Stw p wh b. Sewickley, Pa. (hull), and completed at Pittsburgh, 1879. She was the first boat built by the Sewickley yard, launched in April 1879. She was the third boat of the Block P Line (*BENTON* and *HELENA* preceded) for upper Missouri service. She made 25 trips to Montana. Burned and lost 12 miles above Old Fort Peck, Mont., Aug. 1, 1883, Capt. Johnson, master.

C

0749 C.A. HILL

Stw p wh b. Pt. Pleasant, W. Va., 1884. 119.5 x 21.3 x 3.6. Originally ran Gallipolis-Charleston, Capt. M.E. Brown, master, with Hutchinson, clerk. Became a regular in the Gallipolis-Pomeroy-Syracuse trade, Capt. M.M. Brown, master and clerk. Same trade 1891 with Capt. Will H. Newton, master. A report from Gallipolis, Oh., dated Feb. 18, 1896: "The *C.A. HILL* passed down today for Red River having been sold there for packet work."

0750 C.B. BRYAN

Stw wh b. Memphis, Tenn., 1888. 114.2 x 29 x 4.5. Still documented at Memphis, 1896.

0751 C. BEALER

Stw p wh b. Cincinnati, Oh., 1854. 262 tons. In 1856 advertised at New Orleans for Selma, Montgomery, and Alabama River points, Capt. William S. Walker, master. Snagged and lost at Carroll Island, Cairo, Ill., on Mar. 7, 1858.

0752 C.C. BOWYER

Stw p wh b. Pt. Pleasant, W. Va., 1909. 117.8 x 22.3 x 3.6. Engines, 10½'s- 3½ ft. Two boilers, each 36" x 16 ft. Built at the Gardner Docks using hull of the *NEVA* (see), also engines and boilers. Owned by George P. Gardner and ran Gallipolis-Huntington, Capt. Sil Gardner, with W.L. Guthrie, clerk. Named for the popular Pt. Pleasant banker. In the spring of 1910 there were three packets in this trade, the others being *ORIOLE* and *CARRIE BROWN*. She was sold and left Gallipolis Apr. 14, 1919, for Dycusburg, Ky., on Cumberland River, owned by Capt. F.O. Devers of that place. She was snagged at Rampey's Landing, Ky., that December. Raised, rebuilt, and renamed *GRACE DEVERS* (see).

0753 C.C.K.

Stw ferry wh b. Jeffersonville, Ind., by Howard, 1913. 90 x 24 x 4. Engines, 8"- 44". One boiler. Left Jeff for delivery Aug. 19, 1913. Went to Chester, Ill.

0754 C.C. MARTIN

Stw p wh b. Harmar, Oh., at Knox Yard, 1882. 103.2 x 18.3 x 2.9. Engines, 9½"- 3 ft. One boiler. Built for Capt. F.A. Athey. Later ran on Little Kanawha River, Capt. John A. Somers. In 1894 tried a whirl in the Steubenville-East Liverpool trade, Capt. George O'Neal, with Horace Simmons, clerk, A. Shouse, mate, and William Hunt, engineer. Dismantled at Wheeling, March 1897, and engines, etc., went to *CANDO* (see).

0755 C.D. FRY

Stw p wh b. Pittsburgh, Pa., 1865. 332 tons. Built for Chattahoochee River. Snagged and lost at Wright's Landing, 32 miles below Columbus, Ga. The pilot on watch, Juan Jenkins, had his license lifted as a result.

0756 C.D. JR.

SW p wh b. Jeffersonville, Ind., by Howard, 1853. 347 tons. 200 x 30 x 7.5. Engines, 26's- 8 ft. stroke. First owner was Celestine Dalferes. Ran New Orleans-Vicksburg in "off" seasons, Capt. Truman C. Holmes, in place of the *PRINCESS* (see). Was running New Orleans-Grand Gulf in fall 1855, Capt. Richard Holmes in command. Ran New Orleans-Bayou Sara, Capt. J.A. Cotton, 1856, teamed up with *LAUREL HILL* (see). Was running New Orleans-Lower Coast and Quarantine Station, summer 1859, Capt. J.A. Cotton. Said to be the first with a steam hoisting rig for moving freight out of the hold. Dismantled 1861.

0757 C.E. HILLMAN

SW p wh b. Shousetown, Pa., and completed at Pittsburgh, 1860. 230 x 35 x 6. Engines 22's- 7 ft. stroke. Four boilers, each 40" dia. by 28 ft. long. 420 tons. Built for Cincinnati-Nashville trade, Capt. J.N. Corbett, teamed up with the *B.M. RUNYAN* (see). She was captured by the Rebels at Paducah who took her to Nashville with the idea of making a gunboat of her, but soon recaptured by the U.S. During the war she did much U.S. transport service. In December 1865 bought by Capt. Theo. Fink and others to run Wheeling-Cincinnati in place of the *WILD WAGONER* just sold. Capt. Sam Mason, master; Theo. Fink, clerk. Collided with and sank the *NANNIE BYERS* at Eagle Hollow, above Madison, Ind., Mar. 4, 1866. Sold at public sale early March 1867 at Cincinnati to Capt. D.H. Morton for $13,000. A lawsuit over the *NANNIE BYERS* was settled by compromise for $18,500, April 1867. Dismantled later that year. Machinery went in 1871 to the *PHIL ALLIN* (see).

0758 C.E. SATTERLEE

Stw p wh b. Jeffersonville, Ind., by Howard, 1889. 162 x 30 x 4.5. Two boilers. Owned by the Texas & Pacific RR along with the *E.B. WHEELOCK* to compete with the Red River Line. Later in the Red River Line, Capt. Charles B. Truslow, pres., Chas. W. Drown, traffic mgr., Geo. C. Hamilton, secy., 110 Gravier Street, New Orleans. Ran New Orleans-Shreveport, Capt. H.J. Brinker. Sank in Rock River Bend, Red River, Oct. 29, 1893.

0758-A C.E. TAYLOR

Stw p wh b. Lewisburg, Ark., 1899. 78 x 13.6 x 3.7. Sank July 23, 1907, in Black River, Ark.

0759 C.E. WATKINS

SW p wh b. New Albany, Ind., 1847. 448 tons. Originally documented at New Orleans. In New Orleans-Memphis trade 1851, Capt. S.B. Frost. Also ran Nashville-St. Louis. Ex-U.S. President James K. Polk rode to Nashville on her shortly before he died. Later was bought by King & Co., Cincinnati, coal merchants. In April 1853 upbound at Wheeling with 13 empty coal barges, largest upbound tow seen at that place and several days later returned back down with 10 loads of coal and railroad iron, and with lumber loaded on the steamboat, in command of Capt. James Baugher, Steubenville. Off the lists in 1855.

0760 C.F. SHEPARD

Prop p wh b. Peninsula, Oh., as a canalboat and outfitted with machinery at Marietta, 1874. 59.6 tons. Capt. William Davis ran her on the Muskingum 1874–1875. Inspected at Memphis 1881 and in the Pittsburgh district 1882.

0761 C. HAYS

SW p wh b. Elizabeth, Pa., 1851. 240 tons. First home port, St. Louis. Reported lost on Jan. 7, 1857.

0762 C.H. DURFEE

Rig and place of build? Ran New Orleans and Ouachita River, Capt. Frank Dozier, early 1870s. Sank on the falls in Red River October 1876 with 651 bales, raised. New Orleans-Red River 1876–1877–1878. Capt. Richard Sinnott was master at times.

0763 C.H. HUGO

Stw ferry wh b. New Haven, W. Va., 1897. 38 tons. 79 x 20 x 4. Engines, 7"- 3 ft. One boiler, 50" by 13.1. Owned 1906 by West Memphis Ferry Co. Rebuilt in 1907 after having been caught on a ringbolt during a flood. Capt. Miles

Bridgewater was master at Memphis in 1902. Off the lists 1910.

0764 C.H. MOOAR

SW p wh b. Cincinnati, Oh., 1860. 26 tons. Registered at Wheeling. Went to Confederate registry 1861.

0765 C.H. WOODS

Stw p wh b. Friendly, W. Va., 1892. 110 x 22 x 3.2. This was a combination sawmill and low water packet, owned by William Baker, New Matamoras, Oh. Had geared power, gunnel hull, scow bow. Ran Wheeling-New Matamoras October 1893, Capt. S. Walker Litten, master, with Will Goodwin, clerk. Jesse Hughes says she had a tin roof. Still running 1896.

0766 C.J. CAFFREY

SW p wh b. Louisville, Ky., 1861 as the *J.H. BALDWIN* (see). The USQMD acquired her Mar. 21, 1864 under original name, renamed her Oct. 4, 1865. C.J. Caffrey, Esq., operating as Johnsonville Packet Co., ran her St. Louis-Johnsonville until July 1866 when the sheriff stepped in. Sold to the U.S. in August 1867 for improvement work on the Upper Mississippi. In 1874 the lumber firm Weyerhaeuser and Denkmann converted her to sternwheel and used her as a raftboat until 1892.

0767 C.K. PECK

Stw p wh b. Mound City, Ill. (hull), and completed at St. Louis 1875–1876. 210 x 36 x 5. Engines 16's- 6 ft. Three boilers, 38" x 24 ft. 357 tons. Made six trips to Fort Benton, Mont. Her most spectacular cargo was carried in 1881 when she brought 10,000 buffalo robes from the mouth of the Yellowstone to Bismarck. These had been brought out of the Yellowstone by the *GENERAL TERRY* (see). Renamed *KEOKUK* on Sept. 23, 1882 (see).

0768 C.M. FOUCHE

Stw p wh b. Lenoirs, Tenn., 1889. 93 x 14 x 2. Documented at Chattanooga 1896.

0769 C.N. DAVIS

Stw p wh b. Jeffersonville, Ind., by Howard, 1879. 150 x 27.3 x 4.5. Built for Cumberland River. In 1880, owned by J.W. Lovell and W.S. Bowman, ran on Cumberland and Wabash rivers. Sold September 1880 to Evansville, Cairo & Memphis Steam Packet Co., for low water work. Sank opposite Mt. Vernon, Ind., raised, renamed *CARRIE CALDWELL* (see).

0770 C.N. KRAFT

Stw p wh b. Pittsburgh, Pa., 1882. 102 x 20 x 3. Sank eight miles above Little Rock, Ark., on Oct. 12, 1886, raised. Later in upper Red River.

0771 C.O.

Stw pl wh b. Cincinnati, Oh., 1885. 81.6 x 15.7 x 2.7. Engines, 9"- 1½ ft. One boiler. Owned by the Longworth family at Cincinnati who took lengthy hunting excursions on board. Named for Sue Walker Longworth. The name was painted on the boat simply *CO*. Young Longworth once as a child professed his love for Sue by scratching on glass the words "I LOVE CO" figuring "Sue" and "do" must be spelled alike. Capt. Callie French of showboat fame bought *C.O.* and towed the showboat with it. Jesse Hughes recalled that *C.O.* was high and dry on Little Grave Creek bar, summer 1897 for some time. While in tow of the *OAKLAND* upbound near Hickman, Ky., the *C.O.* capsized, a total loss.

0772 C.P. HUNTINGTON

Stw p wh b. Cincinnati, Oh., 1870. 147 tons. Ran Pomeroy-Portsmouth, November 1871, Capt. James Newton, master with C.P. Sheplar, clerk. In Kanawha River-Gallipolis trade 1872, Capt. J.W. Oakes, master, Wm. B. Donnally, clerk. In 1874 Cincinnati-New Richmond, Capt. Wm. Riggs, master. That year was acquired by the Cincinnati, Portsmouth, Big Sandy & Pomeroy Packet Co. They leased her spring 1876 to tow a circus between Cincinnati and Pittsburgh, and ownership was changed to Mary Stone of Michigan. Capt. C.A. Bocaletti, Pittsburgh, bought the boat, insured it against sinking, and it burned.

0773 C.R. CUMMINGS

Stw p wh b. Arthur City, Tex., 1893. 62 x 14.6 x 3. Was operating between Shreveport and Fulton, Ark., in 1894.

0774 C.R. SUTER

SW snagboat ih b. Pittsburgh, Pa., 1888. 187 x 52 x 7. Had compound oscillating engines, the piston rods connected direct to the cranks, the cylinders oscillating on trunions. Owned by the Missouri River Commission and used on the Missouri River. Rebuilt and renamed *MISSOURI* (see).

0775 C. SMITH

Stw p wh b. Mound City, Ill., 1888. 132 x 29 x 3.5. A low water packet owned by the Evansville & Tennessee River Packet Co. Burned at Riverton, Ala., August 1894.

0776 C.T. DUMONT

SW p wh b. Cincinnati, Oh., 1864. 250 x 35 x 5.5. Engines, 21's- 7 ft. Four boilers, each 40" by 26 ft. Built for the Cincinnati-Pomeroy trade, Capt. William Knight, master, Ed Knight, clerk, and Barlow Knight, pilot. Competed with the *WILD WAGONER*. Sold to the U.S. Mail Line Co., Dec. 6, 1864, for Cincinnati-Madison trade, Capt. Charles David. Collided with towboat *TOM REES* at Big Bone Island, Dec. 14, 1865, wherein one paddlewheel was ripped off the *DUMONT* and landed in an empty barge in tow of the *REES*. Several of the cookhouse crew on the *DUMONT* were killed. She was at the wharfboat, Warsaw, Ky., at 5:00 P.M., Aug. 19, 1867, when a tornado struck, literally demolishing the upper works and driving her across to Florence, Ind. Capt. David sustained some injuries but nobody was killed. After the *UNITED STATES-AMERICA* disaster November 1868, she ran Louisville-Cincinnati. While in the Madison trade in 1865 she was selected to convey Gen. U.S. Grant, Mrs. Grant, the four Grant children—Fred,

Ulysses Jr., Nellie, and Jesse—from North Bend to Cincinnati. They had come from St. Louis on the Ohio & Mississippi RR in a special car. This was on Sat., Sept. 3, 1865, and also along were Gen. Kirby Smith, Col. Adam Badeau, and other notables. The *DUMONT* was named for a noted engine and machine manufacturer of Cincinnati. Dismantled 1872.

0777 C.W. ANDERSON

Stw p wh b. Jeffersonville, Ind., by Howard, 1876. 161 x 31.8 x 4.8. Much equipment from the *BERMUDA* (see) used in building. Named for an old Cincinnati merchant who was Chief of Staff under Gen. N.B. Forrest and a former river skipper. Capt. Tom Ryman ran her on the Cumberland River. Sold 1882 to Capt. Jack Harrison, Belpre, Oh., who, with A.W. Voegtly, clerk, ran her Pittsburgh-Portsmouth, culminating in hitting the K&M bridge, Pt. Pleasant, W. Va., and sinking her. Capt. Sol York took her to the Illinois River 1884 and sold her in 1885 to Capt. Peter Burke of Mobile. Burned laid up opposite Mobile, Ala., Aug. 6, 1892.

0778 C.W. BATCHELOR

Stw p wh b. Brownsville, Pa., at Axton yard, 1879. 175 x 34. Engines, 15's- 5 ft. Three boilers, each 38" by 24 ft., two flues. Built for the Pittsburgh-Wheeling trade, Capt. Abner O'Neal. Interested with him was Capt. Nate Wintringer. Named to honor Capt. C.W. Batchelor (1823–1896), native of Steubenville, Oh., who boated earlier (see *ALLEGHENY*). Clerk was Capt. John A. Edie (1836–1890), and when he died Theodore C. Poe was clerk. The boat was sold to the Pittsburgh & Cincinnati Packet Line and ran Pittsburgh-Cincinnati several years, Capt. George O'Neal. Sold in 1895 to Capt. T.B. Simms of St. Louis who took her to the Missouri River. This boat carried dignitaries to the ceremonies at the opening of the first lock on the Ohio River at Davis Island, West Bellevue, Pa., Oct. 7, 1885. Her roof bell was later on the *ROBERT DODDS, J.H. DONALD, JR.*, ferryboat *LAURANCE,* ferry *COL. W.S. TAYLOR,* and thence to the Suiter family at Manchester, Oh., who gave it to S&D.

0779 C.W. DORRANCE

SW p wh b. New Albany, Ind., 1857. 340 tons. First home port, Mobile, Ala. Snagged and lost on the Alabama River, Jan. 15, 1870.

C.W. MEADE

See *GENERAL MEADE,* correct name.

0780 C.W. SOMBART

SW p wh b. Jeffersonville, Ind., 1858. 411 tons. Engines, 22's- 7 ft. Three boilers. Owned by A.L. Shortridge & Co., and Capt. Henry McPherson, master. Burned above St. Louis on June 27, 1859.

0781 C.Y. LUCAS

Stw p wh b. Harmar, Oh., at the Knox Boat Yard, 1881. 120 x 21 x 2. Named for a Wheeling man who ran a music store. Renamed *PRINCE,* Feb. 21, 1883 (see).

0782 CABINET

SW p wh b. Wheeling, Va., 1849. 190 tons. 172 x 27 x 5.6. Engines, 16's- 5½ ft. Two boilers, each 42" by 26 ft. Ran Steubenville-Wheeling. In 1853 ran Ironton-Wheeling, Capt. Shin Smith, master, and Mart Smith (brother-in-law) as pilot. Took pig iron up, and general merchandise down. Last enrollment 1858.

0783 CACHE

Prop p wh b. Cairo, Ill., 1871. 50 x 13.4 x 5. In 1872 making three round trips daily in Cairo-Mound City trade. Registered 1892, maybe longer.

0784 CADDO

SW p wh b. Louisville, Ky., 1848. 188 tons. Ran Shreveport-New Orleans. Sank and lost near New Orleans, Feb. 14, 1852, with loss of five lives.

0785 CADDO

Stw p wh Originally *J.T. STOCKDALE* b. West Brownsville, Pa., 1863 (see). Sold by the U.S. Navy to Capt. John Smoker and Capt. Richard Sinnott, Aug. 24, 1865, who renamed her *CADDO.* In February 1866 owned by Thornton E. Jacobs and others of Shreveport, La., Jacobs master. In November 1866 owned by Thomas E. Pitts and others of Shreveport. In January 1867, Capt. William Greig and new owners. In May 1869 owned by Good Intent Dry Dock Co., New Orleans. Went to Galveston, Tex., November 1869.

0786 CADDO

Stw p wh b. Arkadelphia, Ark., 1890. 65 x 16.2 x 2.3. Documented at Memphis, 1896.

0787 CADDO BELLE

SW p wh b. New Albany, Ind., 1857. 134 tons. Ran New Orleans-Shreveport. Sank on Red River in September 1858. Off the records, 1860.

0788 CADDO BELLE

P wh b. Portsmouth, Oh., and completed at Cincinnati, 1880. 125 x 25 x 3.5. Owned by A.R. and Jacob Ketchum, Cincinnati. Burned at Cross Bayou near Shreveport, La., March 1881, tied up for debt. Was rebuilt and taken to the Chattahoochee River. Still registered at Apalachicola, Fla., 1886.

0789 CADDO NO. 2

SW p wh b. Louisville, Ky., 1851. 273 tons. Owned at Nashville, Tenn. Her master was Capt. Charles E. Marshall, brother of Hon. Humphrey Marshall of Kentucky (see *B.L. HODGE NO. 2*). Ran on Red River 1851–1860 when Capt. Marshall delivered her to Mobile. Ran Mobile-Tuscaloosa, Capt. George Kirk, 1861–1862. Was returned to the Mississippi River and May 23, 1866 was advertising a special trip from Shreveport to St. Louis.

0790 CADMUS

Stw p wh b. Moscow, Oh., 1845. 70 tons. Off the lists in 1847.

0791 CAHOKIA

Centerwheel ferry wh b. Madison, Ind., 1864. 167.5 x 46.2 x 5.5. Owned by the Wiggins Ferry Co., St. Louis. Dismantled in 1891.

0792 CAIRO

SW p wh b. New Castle, Pa., 1864. 40 tons. Capt. Steen, first master. Probably some relation to a canalboat. Exempt from documentation in 1881.

0793 CAIRO

U.S. recess wheel gunboat wh b. Mound City, Ill., 1861. 175 x 50 x 7. Seven such gunboats, of which the *CAIRO* was one, were built by James B. Eads. Three were built at Mound City, Ill., the *CAIRO, MOUND CITY, and CINCINNATI*; four at Carondelet, Mo., the *CARONDELET, LOUISVILLE, ST. LOUIS,* and *PITTSBURG* (all see). Samuel M. Pook was the designer, and these became known as the "Pook gunboats." The machinery and boiler details were worked out by A. Thomas Merritt. Eads signed the contract with the government on Aug. 7, 1861, agreeing to deliver all seven at Cairo, Ill., on Oct. 10, 1861, a "crash" program. The first to be launched was the *ST. LOUIS* on Oct. 12, 1861, boilers and machinery in place. Each of the Pook gunboats carried 13 guns; six of them mounted six 32-pounder smoothbores, three 8-inch Dahlgren smoothbore shell guns, and 4 rifled 42-pounders. Armament on the seventh, the *ST. LOUIS,* varied only to the extent that another 32-pounder was mounted in lieu of one 8-inch gun. The *CAIRO* was the first of the "Pook turtles" to be actually lost. While ascending the Yazoo River, Dec. 12, 1862, she fell victim to two Confederate mines, or torpedoes, planted in the channel and joined by a triggering wire. When she ran upon this wire the mines were drawn against the hull, setting off the charges. She sank up to her stacks. All personnel got ashore safely. The wreck was abandoned. In 1961 the remains of the *CAIRO* were "rediscovered" about 14 miles up the Yazoo from Vicksburg by several skin divers. In 1964 the wreck was raised in badly damaged condition. Many artifacts were recovered and preserved. At the present time (1980) a program is under way to preserve the old gunboat and its souvenirs at Vicksburg.

0794 CAIRO

Ferry b. Metropolis, Ill., 1869. 73 tons. Probably operated at Cairo, Ill. Still documented 1876.

0795 CAIRO BELLE

Stw p wh b. Hartford City, W. Va., 1865. 365 tons. First home port, Louisville, Ky. Off the list 1867.

0796 CALEB COPE

Stw p wh b. Glasgow, Pa., 1847. 79 tons. In January 1848 running Pittsburgh-Beaver-Wellsville, leaving from a wharfboat between Wood Street and the bridge. Three trips a week, departing Pittsburgh 9:00 A.M. The *BEAVER* was in the same trade, same time. In St. Paul 1852, owned by Galena & St. Paul Packet Co. Off the records 1856. Place of build just below Smith's Ferry and opposite Georgetown, Pa.

0797 CALEDONIA

Stw p wh b. Industry, Pa., 1848. 124 tons. Ran Pittsburgh-St. Louis, Capt. Richard Calhoon. She was at Evansville, Ind., on Aug. 9, 1851, when a great storm struck. She and the *DOVER* (see) both were capsized and lost.

0798 CALEDONIA

SW p wh b. McKeesport, Pa., 1853. 239 tons. Ran Pittsburgh-St. Louis, Capt. Richard Calhoon. She came in collision with *ENDEAVOR* at Letart Islands Feb. 22, 1855, and was sunk. Her passengers were transferred to the *ALLEGHENY* (which had to lay up for low water) and thence to *WM. KNOX* to Wheeling. Raised. In December 1855 she laid up for ice in the mouth of the Muskingum River, and stayed 80 days. Capt. Calhoon, in an itch to get away, jumped the gun and took off for Pittsburgh. No more had the boat entered the Ohio River when a huge ice pack cut her down, Mar. 17, 1856. Off the lists in 1860.

0799 CALHOUN

SW gunboat wh This Rebel gunboat was at Island 10 along with *McRAE, POLK, JACKSON, IVY, PONTCHARTRAIN, MAUREPAS,* and *LIVINGSTON.* She fell into Union hands and was used in various expeditions throughout the war. Burned after the fall of New Orleans.

0800 CALHOUN

SW p wh b. Jeffersonville, Ind., 1876. 230 x 36 x 5. Engines, 20's- 7½ ft. Three boilers. Wheels 27 ft. dia., 10½ ft. buckets. First owned by Naples Packet Co., and later by St. Louis, Naples & Peoria Packet Co., Capt. C.C. Keener. Crew in 1886: Capt. James Abrams, master; Oliver Watt, purser; Edward S. Hoyt and James Spencer, clerks; John Martineau and Charles E. Abrams, pilots; Wash J. McCann and George Pierson, engineers; James H. Powers and Charles Wilson, mates. In June 1889 had aboard a "lady" band led by Prof. Gilliland, seven in all, from Ashtabula, Oh. Dismantled at Madison, Ind., 1892. Cabin and machinery went to *GREY EAGLE* (see). The Eagle Packet Co. used her whistle on various of their packets, lastly on *CAPE GIRARDEAU* (stw.), which became *GORDON C. GREENE.*

0801 CALIFORNIA

SW p wh b. Elizabethtown, Pa., 1846. 126 tons. Collided with *ISAAC NEWTON* (see) Feb. 13, 1847, with loss of six lives. The *NEWTON* took passengers and crew to Guyandotte. This may have happened opposite Huntington, W. Va., where a jutting rock outcrop long has been known as "California Rock." This rock was blasted out by the U.S.

Engineers in 1961, above and opposite 25th Street, Huntington.

0802 CALIFORNIA

SW p wh b. New Albany, Ind., 1850. 269 tons. Snagged and lost Mar. 25, 1853, in Shirt-tail Bend, 16 miles below Greenville, Miss.

0803 CALM

SW p wh b. McKeesport, Pa., 1852. 26 tons. Off the lists in 1854.

0804 CALUMET

Stw p wh b. Madison, Ind., 1865. 151.7 x 26.2 x 5. In March 1866 owned by S.H. Parisot of Vicksburg, and G.M. Hunter and R.E. Champion of Columbus, Oh. Ran in Yazoo River trade out of Vicksburg 1866–1870. In latter July 1871 her head caught on shore at Vicksburg, and she filled and sank.

0805 CALUMET

Stw p wh b. Madison, Ind., 1876. 245 x 38 x 6. Engines, 16's- 6 ft. Three boilers, each 42" by 26 ft., five flues. Machinery from the *ALLEGHENY BELLE* (see). Built for Capt. Phil Anshutz, J.A. Voegtly, and Capt. Dan Moore. Was loading out at Cincinnati for New Orleans on her maiden trip when ice gorges cut her down. The wreck floated back to Madison and lodged below the marine ways where she was built. Loss occurred Jan. 27, 1877. She never made a trip.

0806 CALUMET

A freight bill in the collection at the Inland Rivers Library, Cincinnati, dated October 1879 at Sunfish, Oh., carries the name *CALUMET,* Capt. Phil Anshutz, master, and E.J. Anshutz, clerk with no trade indicated. This may be a hangover from the loss of the prior *CALUMET.*

0807 CALVERT

Stw p wh Originally named *ESTOLA.* b. Charleston, W. Va., 1899 (see). Renamed May 10, 1901, owned by J.F. Calvert, Charleston, and M.A. and M.W. Calvert, same address. Ran in Charleston-Montgomery trade and others. Sold to Gardner Dock Co., Pt. Pleasant, W. Va., and soon turned over to Ralph Emerson Gaches, Feb. 7, 1911. Patent Kidney boiler was put on her, and she towed *COTTON BLOSSOM* showboat into the Teche country that fall. Gaches renamed her *SOPHIA M. GARDNER* (see).

0808 CALYPSO

SW p wh b. Wellsville, Oh., 1863. 193 x 30 x 5. Engines, 18's- 5 ft. Two boilers. Operated on the Missouri River, Capt. Burton. Lost in ice break-up at St. Louis on Dec. 16, 1865 along with many others.

0809 CAMBRIA

SW p wh b. Pittsburgh, Pa., 1845. 172 x 24.5 x 5. Originally owned by Capt. William Forsythe, Pittsburgh, and Thomas Arbuckle of Allegheny City, Pa. Ran Pittsburgh-Cincinnati in a "Line," 1846. News of the initial skirmishes leading to the Mexican War came from New Orleans to Louisville in April 1846 aboard the *PEYTONA,* thence to Cincinnati on *YORKTOWN,* and on up the Ohio to Wheeling and Pittsburgh on *CAMBRIA.* The *J.M. WHITE* carried the news to St. Louis. Later ran Pittsburgh-St. Louis, Capt. Kindrick. Sank and lost upbound near Ste. Genevieve, Mo., Feb. 3, 1851, owned by a Capt. Ludlow who was in command.

0810 CAMBRIDGE

Stw p wh b. Brownsville, Pa., 1856. 242 tons. Capt. William Dean superintended construction and commanded. Ran Pittsburgh-Cincinnati-St. Louis. He was still on her in 1861. Snagged and lost at Grand Glaise, Ark., Feb. 23, 1862.

0811 CAMDEN

Stw p wh b. Elizabethtown, Pa., 1847. 80 tons. Off the lists 1853.

0812 CAMDEN

Stw p wh b. Louisville, Ky., 1855. 122 tons. First registry at New Orleans. Snagged and lost at Fulton, Ark., April 1857.

0813 CAMDEN

Stw p wh b. Parkersburg, Va., 1858. 92 tons. Trip to Shreveport 1859. Went to Confederate registry 1861.

0814 CAMDEN

SW p wh b. Paducah, Ky., 1866. 112 x 28 x 3.3. 103 tons. In April 1869 sold to Thomas S. Flourney and others, mostly Kentucky men, and based at Evansville. She had been at New Orleans prior. The loss of the boat was due to a tornado at Evansville on Nov. 16, 1869. The cabin was blown completely off the *CAMDEN,* also from the *ARMADA,* and the *LOUISA* lost her hurricane roof.

0815 CAMELIA

Stw p wh b. Brownsville, Pa., 1863. 204 tons. Running Pittsburgh-St. Louis 1864 with Capt. J.L. Lytle, master, and F.B. Holmes in the office. Capt. Jesse Dean became master with Lytle in the office, June 1864. Upon arrival at Pittsburgh mid-Nov. 1865, from St. Louis a buffalo being unloaded got away and a lively time was had by all, Capt. Dean commanding. In July 1867 in Cincinnati-Maysville trade, low water, Capt. E.S. Morgan, with Chris Young, clerk. Left Pittsburgh in July 1868 with 27 inches on the marks, loaded with 340 tons and towing a barge with 1,400 kegs of nails for St. Louis. Capt. Jesse Dean in command with pilots William Burt and Levi Dix. On this occasion she spent several weeks on Carpenter Bar above Marietta. Still in the Pittsburgh-St. Louis trade September 1873, both *CAMELIA* and *R.R. HUDSON* aground in Four Mile, above Cincinnati with 22 inches in the channel. She struck a log and turned bottom side up at Raleigh, Ky., below Wabash Island, Apr. 20, 1874.

0816 Campbell

SW tr wh b. St. Louis, Mo., 1875. 167 x 34.6 x 5.6. 267.28 tons. She was long used on the Missouri River at Blair Crossing, Iowa. In February 1892 sold to the Ohio Valley RR, John Echols, Louisville, Ky., as representative, and documented at Evansville.

0817 Canada

SW p wh b. Brownsville, Pa., 1858. 197 x 32 x 5. 299 tons. Owned when new by James Ward, St. Louis 3/8; Willaim Anderson, St. Louis 1/4; and Adam Jacobs 3/8. She was one of the pioneers of the Northern Line Packet Co., organized by James Ward, R.C. Gray, Thomas Griffith and others for Upper Mississippi trades. Dismantled at Madison, Ind., in 1870 and machinery went on the *ROCK ISLAND* (see).

0818 Canary

Ferry b. Vevay, Ind., 1873. 20 tons. Still documented in 1876, maybe longer.

0819 Canary No. 2

Ferry? b. Cincinnati, Oh., 1878. 102 x 20.7 x 3.1. Documented at Mobile 1886.

0820 Candianmarea

Rig? b. Cincinnati, Oh., 1873. Built by C.T. Dumont for South American parties. The Pittsburgh *Gazette* said on Dec. 17: "A rumor is in circulation that the *CANDIAMAREA* which left New Orleans a month ago for the Magdalena River was lost in a gale and all on board save one man were lost." This report needs confirmation.

0821 Cando

Stw p wh b. Ashland, Ky., 1899. 127.6 x 23.8 x 3.5. Engines 9 3/4's- 3 ft. One boiler, 42" x 26 ft. Owned by Catlettsburg & Paintsville Navigation Co. Equipment from the *C. C. MARTIN* used in construction. Named for the C&O Railroad, and used on Big Sandy River during completion of the C&O to Pikeville in 1904, principally between White House and Pikeville, along with *DONCA* (see). Broke away in a wind squall at the mouth of Big Sandy on June 19, 1907, capsized. Machinery used on the *GERALDINE* (see).

0822 Caney Fork

Stw p wh b. Nashville, Tenn., 1845. 37 tons. Ran on upper Cumberland River. Off the lists, 1847.

0823 Caney Fork

Rig? b. Paducah, Ky., 1880. 126 x 19 x 2. Built to take the place of the *CELINA* (b. 1876 see) in upper Cumberland River. Documented at New Orleans in 1886.

0824 Canton

Ferry wh b. Quincy, Ill., 1866. 47.62 tons. Off the lists, 1869.

0825 Cantonia

Stw ferry wh b. Rock Island, Ill., 1891. 92 x 20 x 4.6. Engines 8"- 4 ft. One boiler, 42" x 18 ft. Operated at Canton, Mo., owned by C.M. Bradshaw. Later renamed *ILLINO*.

0826 Cape City

Stw p wh b. Grafton, Ill., 1882. 98.4 x 29.7 x 4. 72.64 tons. Documented at St. Louis in 1896.

0827 Cape Girardeau

SW p wh Originally *WAR EAGLE* b. 1899, Madison, Ind. Was rebuilt at the Carondelet ways, St. Louis, 1901, and renamed *CAPE GIRARDEAU*. 255 x 38 x 6. Engines, 22's- 6'8". Four boilers, each 42" by 20 ft. Owned by Eagle Packet Co., and ran regularly in the St. Louis-Cape-Commerce trade, Capt. Buck Leyhe. Sank and lost at Turkey Island, about 50 miles below St. Louis, mid-July 1910.

0828 Cape Girardeau

SW p wh Originally *CITY OF NEW ALBANY* b. 1892, then *NEW IDLEWILD, SPREAD EAGLE* (all see) and renamed *CAPE GIRARDEAU* to replace the sunken boat of same name 1910 (see last listing). Ran St. Louis-Cape-Commerce trade, Capt. Buck Leyhe. Sank during a storm at Fort Gage, below St. Louis, Oct. 21, 1916. Capt. Wm. H. (Buck) Leyhe was in command, and sent all passengers ashore in yawls. Within two hours only the pilothouse remained visible. The *STACKER LEE* (see) sank the same day.

0829 Cape Girardeau

Stw p sh b. Jeffersonville, Ind., at Howard yard, 1923. 210 x 38 x 6.5. Engines 18's- 8 ft. stroke from *FERD HEROLD*. Three boilers, each 44" x 28 ft., 5 flues 10" dia. Paddlewheel 22' dia., with 28 ft. buckets. Designed by Tom Dunbar for Eagle Packet Co. She went from Louisville to St. Louis in November 1923. Came out in St. Louis-Cape-Commerce trade in April 1924. Christened at Cape Girardeau on Apr. 24, 1924, by Miss Christine Rowling. Made St. Louis-New Orleans Mardi Gras trips 1925–1930 inclusive. Took a MVBL tow St. Louis to Cairo in October 1934. Sold spring 1935 to Greene Line Steamers, Cincinnati, who renamed her *GORDON C. GREENE* (see).

0830 Cape May

SW p wh b. Brownsville, Pa., 1850. 124 tons. Snagged and lost at Mount Vernon, Ind., on Aug. 2, 1854, with loss of 18 lives.

0831 Capital City

SW p wh b. Jeffersonville, Ind., at Barmore yard, 1871. 225 x 38 x 6.5. Engines, 22's- 7 ft. Built for Capt. E.W. Gould for Missouri River service. Sold about 1876 to the Anchor Line. Capt. James O'Neal, master, left her to go to Washington, D.C., to qualify as a U.S. Supervising Inspector, and was succeeded by Capt. John Crane. Later Capt. Sam McPheeters, master. Burned at the grain elevator, Memphis on July 2, 1878. The *CITY OF CHESTER* had burned at same location some months before (see).

0832 CAPITOL

SW p wh b. Pittsburgh, Pa., 1844. 133 tons. Capt. Birmingham, master. Burned and lost at Seventy Six Landing, Mo., above Grand Tower, Dec. 27, 1844, with loss of three lives.

0833 CAPITOL

SW p wh b. Jeffersonville, Ind., at Howard yard, 1854. 224 x 32 x 6. Engines 30's- 9 ft. Six boilers. Built for Capt. James H. Ure. "Had the name in her day of being the fastest boat in the world." Built for the New Orleans-Bayou Sara trade, and later ran New Orleans-Memphis, Capt. J.D. Clarke in a "line" along with the *MESSENGER, JOHN SIMONDS, ALICE VIVIAN.* She was bought by William Bohlen and others to bring ice south in summer from the Upper Mississippi. Went to Confederate registry in 1861 and towed the uncompleted Confederate ram *ARKANSAS* from Memphis to Yazoo City for completion a few days before the Battle of Memphis. Her machinery was said to have been used in completing the ram, and her hoisting engines were made over into drilling machines, etc. Burned to prevent capture at Liverpool, Miss., June 28, 1862.

0834 CAPITOL

Stw ex wh Built from the packet *DUBUQUE* in 1920 by Streckfus Steamers, Inc. 256.6 x 50.7 x 6.2. Engines, 22's- 7 ft. from the *PITTSBURGH* (see). Four boilers, 250 psi. She had four main rudders and two monkey rudders. Paddlewheel 25′ dia., with 30 ft. buckets, 24″ dip. Pitmans 24 ft. long. Operated variously at St. Louis and New Orleans with many tramp trips. She carried notables at the opening of the Industrial Canal, New Orleans, May 5, 1923. Dismantled at St. Louis, summer of 1945.

0835 CAPITOL CITY

Stw p wh b. Harmar, Oh., at the Knox Yard, 1888. 132.2 x 25.7 x 4. Engines, 12's- 4½ ft. Two boilers, each 36″ by 22 ft. Ran in Gallipolis-Charleston trade, Kanawha River, Capt. Howard Donnally, with Wirt Donnally, clerk. Rebuilt 1893 and became *COLUMBIA* (see).

0836 CAPITOLA

SW p wh b. Wheeling, Va., 1860. 137 tons. Ran local trades out of Wheeling, Capt. Steve Thompson (who later ran *JAMES REES* and *TELEGRAM,* see). Was chartered to U.S. service during most of the war, then ran Louisville-Nashville. Capt. James B. Thompson who later ran *JEWEL* and *ROYAL* at Evansville was on her during the war, and made one trip up Big Sandy River with her. Snagged and lost at Shreveport, La., Nov. 15, 1865.

0837 CAPITOLA BUTT

Stw ferry wh b. Montrose, Iowa, 1885. 83.7 x 23.3 x 3.3. Engines, 11's- 2½ ft. One boiler. Operated on Missouri River. Burned opposite Sioux City, Iowa, May 11, 1895.

0838 CAPT. A.O. BEHM

Stw p wh b. Lafayette, Ind., 1892. 60 x 16 x 2.4. Probably towed produce boats, etc. Registered at Evansville, 1896.

0839 CAPT. E. HARDING

SW p wh b. Freedom, Pa., 1852. 73 tons. Not listed in 1854.

0840 CAPT. HARRISON

A four-horse powered ferry operated at Waverly, Mo., on the Missouri River by William S. Thomas in 1880s. The horses were Tom, Charley, Judy, and Kate. At departure time the horses would come to their stalls when the roof bell was rung. Meanwhile between trips they grazed on shore. Capt. Henry K. Thomas, Waverly, Mo., in 1962, was living, grandson of Capt. William S. Thomas.

0841 CAPTAIN JOHN

Stw ferry wh Originally *NINA PADEN* b. 1896, then *CITY OF ASHLAND* (both see). 103 x 26.8 x 4.5. When the bridge was built at Ashland, Ky., she was sold to Capt. John F. Davis, Fullerton, Ky., renamed. Ran ferry service to Portsmouth, Oh. When the 1937 flood came along she was ferrying passengers Portsmouth-West Portsmouth across the flooded Scioto River bottoms. On Jan. 21, 1937, she struck a log and sank. Captain Davis was doing the piloting at the time.

0842 CAPT. JOHN BRICKELL

Stw p wh b. Freedom, Pa., 1863. 188 tons. When new and just outfitted at Pittsburgh she was sold by Capts. Martin and Brickell to Capts. J.H. Maratta and J.H. Dunlap, this on Nov. 4, 1863. They loaded her for the south, and at West Columbia, Va., she collided with a flatboat, and was run ashore on the Ohio side, sinking to her boiler deck on a rising river. Passengers were forwarded on the *MIAMI.* The towboat *CRESCENT CITY,* Capt. A. Q. Ross, did salvage work. This happened Nov. 11, 1863, on her second trip. The salvaged wreck was taken to Cincinnati and dismantled.

0843. CAPT. W.C. DENNY

SW ferry wh b. Pittsburgh, Pa., 1865. 99 tons. When the 1877 ice went out, she broke loose from the Chartiers Street ferry wharf, Pittsburgh, and was never found.

0844 CAR OF COMMERCE

SW p wh b. Murraysville, Va., 1848, 294 tons. Owned by Davis and Smith (see *OHIO VALLEY*) and was the fourth boat of the name. She was wrecked on the Louisville Falls, Dec. 17, 1848, after hitting the rocks opposite the lime kiln. A large hole was knocked in the hull. The *HOMER,* following behind, towed her to Sand Island opposite Shippingport where she sank over the cabin floor. The passengers and crew transferred over to a new hull she had in tow, which drifted down until *HOMER* caught it, and nobody hurt. Her picture appears in the famed Cincinnati 1848 daguerreotype.

0845 CARDENAS

Stw p b. Pittsburgh, Pa., by James Rees & Sons Co., for export. Double deck, one stack. Went under her own steam from Pittsburgh. Date?

0846 CARL

SW p wh b. Madison, Ind., 1860. 52 tons. First home port, Memphis. Went to Confederate registry 1861.

0847 CARL SCHURTZ

Stw p wh b. Memphis, Tenn., 1875. 83.85 tons. Towed produce boats, etc. In November 1878 she was on the docks at Wheeling, preparing to take south 2,500 brl. potatoes, 3,500 brl. apples, 10,000 gal. stoneware, and a barge loaded with 5,000 bu. coal.

0848 CARL SCHURZ

Stw p wh b. Memphis, Tenn., 1885. 90 x 19 x 4. Renamed *MAY FISHER* a year later (see).

0849 CARLOS S. GREELEY

Recess wheel ferry wh b. Jeffersonville, Ind., by Howard, 1883. 160.7 x 48.5 x 6.4. Operated across Mississippi River above St. Louis to Madison County, Ill. Still listed 1908.

0850 CARMANIA

SW ex sh b. Newport News, Va., 1896. 175 x 26 x 7.5. Originally Mexican registry then named *TLACOTALPAM*. Sold to Mobile, Ala., where she rammed a dock and killed some 50 persons, then named *MARGARET*. Harry Means brought her to Louisville, Ky., in 1914 and ran excursions with her. This was an ocean vessel, quite a novelty on the Ohio. Sold that fall to Philadelphia, Pa., parties. Registered at Philadelphia in 1918, and at New York in 1923. Foundered at Fall River, Mar. 12, 1924. She got the name *CARMANIA* at Louisville, operated there by Louisville & Jeffersonville Ferry Co.

0851 CARMI BELLE

Rig? b. Carmi, Ill., 1876. 11.16 tons.

0852 CARNEAL GOLDMAN

Stw p wh b. Jeffersonville, Ind., 1885. 143 x 25.1 x 6.1. Built for the Natchez-Vicksburg trade and named for a Louisiana cotton planter with extensive acres in Tensas Parish on the west shore of the Mississippi River. Made three trips weekly. Was taken to Madison, Ind., and parts used building *ST. JOSEPH* in 1893 (see).

0853 CAROLINE

Stw p wh b. Elizabeth, Pa., 1847. 77 tons. Ran Pittsburgh-Zanesville, Capt. Nixon, 1847-1848. Same, Capt. Binning, 1849. Lost in collision with *CONSIGNEE* at Wellsville, Oh., on Mar. 16, 1849, with loss of three lives.

0854 CAROLINE

Stw p wh b. Pittsburgh, Pa., 1853. 103 tons. 134 x 24 x 3.5. Ran Memphis-White River. Burned Mar. 5, 1854, 20 miles above mouth of White River with loss of 45 lives.

0855 CAROLINE

Stw p wh b. Parkersburg, Va., 1858. 122 tons. First home port, Louisville, Ky. Lost Jan. 11, 1861, at Terre Haute, Ind., in ice.

0856 CAROLINE

Stw p wh b. Madison, Ind., 1863. 198 tons. 155.1 x 31.7 x 5.2. Was at New Orleans in December 1866 through October 1868, Capt. William D. Bateman, running New Orleans-Arkansas River. Ran to Shreveport, La., in 1869. Lost on Red River, May 15, 1870.

0857 CAROLINE

SW ferry wh b. Van Buren, Ark., 1901. 76 x 18 x 5. Still listed in 1908.

0858 CAROLINE

Steam prop yacht wh b. St. Louis, Mo., 1916. 61.3 x 10.5 x 3. Ran for a time on Green River, Ky., Bowling Green-Morgantown, Capt. J. Porter Hines.

0859 CAROLYN

Stw ferry wh b. Memphis, Tenn., 1922. 64 x 29.9 x 4.3. Owned in 1929 by Capt. A.C. Johnson, Helena, Ark.

0860 CARONDELET

U.S. gunboat wh b. Carondelet, Mo., 1861. 176.5 x 52 x 6.5. Engines, 22's- 6 ft. Built by James B. Eads. Capt. Richard M. Wade, Capt. William R. Hoel, Capt. Dan Weaver, and others played prominent parts in her exploits. Sold at Mound City, Ill., Nov. 29, 1865, for scrap. Her hull became the wharfboat at Gallipolis, Oh., and engines went to towboat *QUAKER* in 1867.

0861 CARONDELET

Stw p ih b. Carondelet, Mo., 1875. Primarily a freight boat, one stack aft, engines from *BELLE OF ALTON*. Entered St. Louis-New Orleans trade January 1875, Capt. W. Dick Love, master, George W. Purdy, clerk. Sank below St. Louis, Jan. 26, 1876, thought to have hit a wheel shaft of the *ALLEGHENY* sunk there in 1857 (see). Cargo of sugar and salt badly damaged. Raised. Was caught in a storm 30 miles above New Orleans at night, March 1876, and lost much of her superstructure, furniture, and outfit. Sold at U.S. marshal sale at St. Louis, April 1876 to David Powell. In mid-May 1876 again sold at U.S. sale at St. Louis, and Henry A. Haarstick bid her in at $13,000 for Brown & Jones, Memphis. This firm sold her to Capts. J. Frank Hicks and Alf Grissom who put her in Memphis-New Orleans trade. She was at St. Louis for repairs, moored alongside the *GRAND REPUBLIC*, when both burned night of Sept. 19, 1877 (see *CHARLES P. CHOUTEAU*).

0862 CAROZAL

Rig? b. Cincinnati, Oh., 1883. Passed down at Cairo, Ill., Dec. 8, 1883, bound for Balize, owned by Balize Transportation Co.

0863 CARRABASSET

SW p wh b. Louisville, Ky., 1863. 202 tons. Went to U.S. service, Nov. 16, 1863, and after the war was sold to private hands and renamed *ANNIE WAGLEY* on Aug. 17, 1865 (see).

0864 CARRIE

Stw p wh b. Vanport, Pa., 1863. 159 x 30 x 4. Engines, 14's- 4 ft. Two boilers. Owned by Capt. William J. Kountz and others, Capt. D. M. Brady, master. Ran St. Louis-New Orleans, also on Missouri River. During the war she was running Evansville-Nashville, and Capt. Brady was known in the region as "Lone Tree." Upbound with government supplies from St. Louis to Fort Benton she was snagged two miles from Indian Mission, Neb., Apr. 14, 1868.

0865 CARRIE

Ferry wh b. Wheeling, W. Va., 1870. 76.14 tons. Still registered at Wheeling 1876.

0866 CARRIE

Stw p wh b. Ironton, Oh., 1874. 95 x 16 x 3. Original owners were John P. Coulter, John Charlston Jr., and Felix Bramer, all of Ironton, Oh. Sold September 1877 to Capt. Edwin F. Maddy and others, Gallipolis, Oh. Sold a month later to Capt. William Hardy and others of Chambersburg, Oh. First ran Gallipolis-Middleport, then Portsmouth-Vanceburg, Ironton-Proctorville, then settled down Ravenswood-Middleport. Exploded her boiler three miles below Ravenswood, Jan. 20, 1881. Capt. Hardy was blown overboard but rescued; nobody hurt.

0867 CARRIE

Rig? b. LaCrosse, Wis., 1880. 70 x 24 x 3.4. Still listed there in 1892.

0868 CARRIE

Stw p wh b. St. Louis, Mo., 1881. 75 x 13 x 2. Listed out of Kansas City 1886-1892.

0869 CARRIE

Stw p wh b. Slidell, La., 1906. 94 x 21 x 4.6. Listed out of New Orleans 1908.

0870 CARRIE A. THORN

Rig? b. Jeffersonville, Ind., 1871. 247 tons. Ran on Ouachita and Red rivers. Still running 1877.

0871 CARRIE B. SCHWING

Stw p wh b. Plaquemine, La., 1904. 110.2 x 22.8 x 5.4. Engines, 11's- 6 ft. Two boilers each 44" x 4 ft. Owned by Schwing Lumber Co. Primarily a towboat, but carried excursions, etc. Burned at Bayou Natchez, La., on Feb. 28, 1912.

0872 CARRIE B. SCHWING

Stw p-tb wh b. Plaquemine, La., 1912. 100.7 x 24 x 3.8. Owned by Schwing Lumber Co., and primarily a towboat, but carried excursions also. Sank at the Standard Oil docks, Baton Rouge, La., Jan. 17, 1946.

0873 CARRIE BROOKS

Stw p wh b. Pittsburgh, Pa., 1866. 140 x 29 x 5. Engines, 14's- 4'7". Three boilers. First ran Zanesville-Parkersburg, Capt. James Darlington. In 1870 she departed Zanesville with emigrants and possessions bound for Kansas, and reshipped them at St. Louis to destination. Returned to run Pittsburgh-Zanesville and briefly Pittsburgh-Wheeling, Capt. Harvey Darlington. Capt. John A. Trimble bought control in 1878, ran her Pittsburgh-Gallipolis, then Pittsburgh-Zanesville with not much success. In May 1878 sold to Capt. Wm. J. Kountz who stripped her of machinery and sold the hull to Sistersville, W. Va., for a wharfboat.

0874 CARRIE BROWN

Stw p wh b. Harmar, Oh., 1890. 122 x 24.4. Engines, 12's- 4 ft. Two boilers, 40" by 18 ft. Owned by Capt. M.H. Brown and others, Gallipolis, Oh. She ran Gallipolis-Huntington for 23 years, and Charles Warner was pilot on her the whole time. Burned at Gallipolis, Nov. 17, 1913, at 11:30 P.M. The hull became a wharfboat at Catlettsburg, Ky. Engines went to ferry *OWEVA,* later on *PAUL F. THOMAS.*

0875 CARRIE CALDWELL

Stw p wh b. Jeffersonville, Ind., by Howard, 1879, originally named *C.N. DAVIS* (see). Later renamed *CARRIE HOPE* (also see).

0876 CARRIE CONVERSE

Stw p wh b. Belle Vernon, Pa., 1870. 160 x 33 x 4. Engines, 13½'s- 5 ft. Built at the Speer yard for Capt. George W. Rea, and ran New Orleans-Red River. Sank at Bayou Sara, La., Jan. 11, 1872.

0877 CARRIE HOPE

Stw p wh b. Jeffersonville, Ind., 1879. 150 x 27.3 x 4.5. Originally named *C.N. DAVIS,* then *CARRIE CALDWELL.* As the *CARRIE HOPE* ran Louisville-Evansville in low water, otherwise Evansville-Owensboro, except Sunday, Capt. Cox, this c. 1890-1894. Shoved out on the bank by ice at Louisville and wrecked in February 1895.

0878 CARRIE JACOBS

SW p wh b. Brownsville, Pa., 1863. 156 tons. Sold to US-QMD on Oct. 10, 1864. Sold back to private owners, Sept. 28, 1865, who renamed her *LOUISA* (see).

0879 CARRIE M. KRAFT

Stw p wh b. Parkersburg, W. Va., 1882. 102 x 20 x 3. Operated on the Little Kanawha River under management of Capt. Samuel B. Rathbone who also ran the *ONEIDA* (see). Documented at Memphis 1886.

0880 CARRIE POOLE

Stw p wh b. Evansville, Ind., 1865. 118.7 x 21 x 3.7. Advertised August 1866 running New Orleans-Red River, Capt. J.F. Muse, "draws only 12 inches light." Had four or five owners including Red River Packeet Co., and Capt. Noah Scovell. When she burned at Algiers, La., was owned by

James M. Kane, New Orleans, with Capt. W.H. King, master. This on July 27, 1870.

0881 CARRIE S

Stw p wh b. Evansville, Ind., 1869. 131.8 x 28.5 x 4. Ran New Orleans-Bayou Bartholomew, Capt. Robert D. Montgomery, master, with William Miller, clerk. Lost by snagging at Grand Bayou Island in Red River, 1870.

0882 CARRIE S. DOUGLAS

Rig? b. Morrilton, Ark., 1883. 91 x 25 x 3.5. Possibly a ferry. Still listed 1886.

0883 CARRIE V. KOUNTZ

Stw p wh b. Pittsburgh, Pa., 1869. 187 x 40 x 4.5. Hartupee compound engines, 12's, 26's- 5 ft. Three boilers, each 36" by 26 ft. She was primarily a freight boat, said to have had one stack. Capt. Dan Brady took her to St. Louis where she burned in a levee fire, Mar. 29, 1869. Promptly rebuilt, see next listing.

0884 CARRIE V. KOUNTZ

Stw p wh b. St. Louis, Mo., 1869 using hull and equipment from the former boat (see above) of the name. Had two smokestacks. Both boats were owned by Commodore William J. Kountz and others. Sank near Cairo, Ill., August 1871 after being snagged near Wolf Island. Water was extremely low, and Dave Hiner was the pilot on watch. Rebuilt at St. Louis that fall and was equipped to carry cotton. Ran in Ouachita and Red rivers out of New Orleans, Capt. I.N. Van Hook. Machinery went to the *E.O. STANARD* in 1873 (see).

0885 CARRIE WILLIAMS

Prop p wh b. Cincinnati, Oh., 1867. 59 tons. En route up from Louisville, she burst a steam supply line at Petersburg, Ky., on May 26, 1868 and her engineer died several days later at Florence, Ind. Capt. Louis Krutz's four children were aboard and one of them, a girl of 12, was badly scalded. Foundered Mar. 31, 1874.

0886 CARRIER

Stw p wh b. Harmar, Ohio, 1851 at Knox Yard. 164 x 32 x 6. Built for Messrs. Franks and Ankrin, both of Marietta. Ran upper Ohio; her original crew: Capt. Horatio Booth, master; J.L. Stephens, clerk; G.H. Richards, engineer, and Stephen Davis, pilot. Ran in the New Orleans-Bayou Lafourche trade, 1859, Capt. J.J. Brown, master. Also that year ran in Bayou Boeuf-Attakapas trade twice weekly, Capt. Alcide Meynier. Dismantled 1859.

0887 CARRIER

SW p wh b. Jeffersonville, Ind., by Howard, 1855. 215 x 33. Had a double stern with sternposts 10′ apart. John Howard, of the Howard yard, said the boat was built for Capt. Draffin, a particular friend of his. John went on the maiden trip to St. Louis, stayed aboard and went to Council Bluffs that October. He says the boat cost $34,000 and on that one trip of 32 days netted $5,200. Draffin made two trips to New Orleans with her, then sold the boat for $5,000 more than he paid for it. Running St. Louis-Glasgow, Mo., April 1856, Capt. William C. Postal. Snagged in head of Penn's Bend, Missouri River, Oct. 12, 1858, running in St. Louis-Cambridge trade, Capt. McPherson. Sank at Island 25, Mississippi River, upbound from New Orleans on Feb. 21, 1861. Lost at St. Charles, Mo., Sept. 12, 1861.

0888 CARRIER

Stw p wh b. Freedom, Pa., and completed at Pittsburgh, 1879. 815.16 tons. Owned largely by the Rees family, Pittsburgh. A large boat, and ran Pittsburgh-St. Louis-New Orleans. She was under charter to Southern Transportation Co., downbound Cincinnati to New Orleans when she sank at Little Hurricane Island, Ohio River, Dec. 29, 1883, Capt. W.C. Tichenor. There was a big river and she ran on to the island in a fog. Stage at Evansville was 38 feet. John Emrie and W.C. Underwood were pilots on her at the time.

0889 CARRIER

Stw p wh b. Jeffersonville, Ind., 1884. 165.4 x 26.4 x 4. Ran on Missouri River a season or so, then went to Mobile, Capt. John Quill, master, H. Clay King, clerk, September 1885. Came to Mobile, October 1895 with 1,873 bales out of Alabama River. Contemporary with *TINSIE MOORE* in Alabama River (see).

0890 CARRIER

SW sh b. Newburgh, N.Y., 1892. 280.3 x 44 x 10. Operated in the bend below Canal Street, New Orleans, for many years owned by the M.L. & T. Railroad SS. Co., subsidiary of Southern Pacific RR. Became surplus when Huey Long bridge was completed and sold to Mexico in November 1936.

0891 CARRIER

Stw p wh Originally the packet *MATT F. ALLEN* (see). Owned by Capt. Walter Blair, and he ran her 1897 out of Davenport, Iowa, along with the *WM. J. YOUNG, JR.* In March 1900 in the St. Louis-Calhoun County trade, Capt. Ed D. Young, master, with Gus Block, head clerk. Burned at St. Louis on Sept. 20, 1900, with loss of one life. The *WAR EAGLE* was damaged in the same blaze.

0892 CARROLL

Stw p wh b. Pittsburgh, Pa., 1875. 185.7 x 31 x 6. Engines, 13's- 4 ft. Departed from Pittsburgh direct to Fort Benton, Mont., in March 1875, Capt. T.B. Burleigh, master, with J.Q.A. Parr, clerk. Named for Matthew Carroll of the pioneer Fort Benton firm of Carroll & Steel. Made nine trips to Montana points and in 1876 was the first arrival at Fort Benton on May 14, Capt. Tim Burleigh. She burned Apr. 16, 1877, at Aubuchon's woodyard, 50 miles above Fort Randall, S.D., with no insurance.

0893 CARROLLTON

Stw p wh b. Harmar, Oh., at Knox Yard, 1891. 228 x 37 x 6. Engines, 18's- 7 ft. Inspected and left Marietta, new, Jan.

28, 1891. Capt. Ben Hall piloted her to Cincinnati, with Capt. Ed Maddy, master. Owned by White Collar Line, and sister to *CONGO* (see). Capt. Sam Bryant was later master. In 1895 made several round trips Pittsburgh-Cincinnati when the *IRON QUEEN* burned. Burned at Cincinnati on Aug. 5, 1895, along with side-wheel *BIG SANDY* (see).

0894 CARUTHERSVILLE

Stw p wh b. Dyersburg, Tenn., 1903. 71 x 18 x 2.5. A short-trader which wound up in the Morgantown-Bowling Green trade on Green River, owned by Bowling Green & Morgantown Packet Co., Capt. J.L. Wilson was master, and in 1910 Capt. I.R. Moats succeeded him. This was the last steam packet in that trade, and was replaced by a gasboat named *CAROLINE*. Name was changed Mar. 11, 1911, to *BESSIE RONE* (see).

0895 CARY-BIRD

Stw ferry-p sh b. Pt. Pleasant, W. Va., by Marietta Mfg. Co., 1925. 139 x 30 x 5.2. Ran as a ferry Cairo-Bird's Point starting in May 1925. When the bridge was built there she was sold to the Ohio River Transit Co., and ran in Cincinnati-Louisville trade until sold in November 1936 to Greene Line Steamers, Inc. Hull was used for a Cincinnati boat club in 1946.

0896 CASHIER

Stw p wh b. Industry, Pa., 1847. 126 tons. Entered Pittsburgh-Wheeling trade in June 1848 in charge of Capt. Dawson. Ran there 1850. Off the lists in 1853.

0897 CASPIAN

SW p wh b. West Elizabeth, Pa., 1851. 248 tons. New Orleans-Alexandria, Capt. Dunn. Snagged and lost on Red River, Mar. 3, 1854.

0898 CASTLE GARDEN

Stw p wh b. McKeesport, Pa., 1853. 162 tons. Tramp trades from Pittsburgh. Pittsburgh-Louisville, 1855, Capt. Devinney. Ran Evansville-Cincinnati, Capt. Thad L. Conant, early 1860s. Made at least one trip to St. Paul, 1858. Broke loose from the wharf at Pittsburgh during January flood 1862 and floated free-astray to Baden, Pa. Caught out and sunk at Mound City, Ill., July 25, 1862.

0899 CATAHOULA

SW p wh b. Murraysville, Va., 1858. 137 x 33 x 5. Built for Capt. J.D. Walker, who ran her New Orleans—Ouachita River into 1860. Owned at New Orleans by S.H. Rognest & Co., 1862. Burned at St. Louis along with *FOREST QUEEN* and *CHANCELLOR*, Oct. 4, 1863, Capt. J.D. Walker was charged with being a Yankee spy when the war broke out and spent four months in a New Orleans prison. When released he joined Gen. Butler's forces and became a pilot with Admiral Porter. The *CATAHOULA* was taken by the Rebels at the war's start, but was captured during the Battle of Memphis and sent north. Capt. Walker came to Cincinnati in March 1866 from New Orleans on the *JOHN H. GROESBECK*, looking for employment.

0900 CATARACT

SW p wh b. Brownsville, Pa., 1851. 283 tons. Engines, 21's-7 ft. Three boilers. Built for Capt. E.W. Gould and C.S. Rodgers, both of St. Louis, for Illinois River. She ran in the Pacific Railroad Packet Line ("Lightning Line") St. Louis-Jefferson City-Kansas City in 1856 along with *F.X. AUBRY* and *AUSTRALIA*. Capt. John P. Keiser was pilot on her 1856 at salary of $1,000 a month; as master-pilot in 1857 received $1,250. Exploded a mud drum in 1857, killing five passengers and ten in the crew, injuring 25 others. Dismantled in 1859.

0901 CATAWBA

Stw p wh b. Burlington, Iowa, 1862. 60 tons. Snagged and lost at Jacksonport, Ark., Feb. 7, 1866.

0902 CATHERINE

Stw p wh b. Bayou Boeuf, La., 1851. 67 tons. Documented at New Orleans. Out of service, 1857.

0903 CATHERINE

Steam prop p b. Zanesville, Oh., 1922. 40.7 x 8.8 x 4.7. Owned 1929 by Barnard R. LeRoy, Zanesville.

0904 CECELIA

Stw p wh b. Hinton, W. Va. on New River, 1879. 110 x 20.4 x 3.3. Built by the New River Steamboat Co., to run from Hinton to the Tazewell Road, above. She was too much boat for the narrow chutes. Later used as an excursion boat at Hinton, and ultimately lost in a flood. Standard Oil Co., also built a boat on New River about this same time, 75 x 10, and with her brought barrel staves down to Hinton.

0905 CECIL N. BEAN

Stw ferry wh Originally packet *MARY E. STAPLES*, then *ALMA*, then *HENRY BURKE* (all see), and was reduced in length when converted to a ferry, now 130 x 37.8 x 3.9. Capt. John R. Drackett, Morgan City, La., commenced running her at Nine Mile Point, above New Orleans, in April 1928. Prior to that time she had been operating at Pass Christian, La., until a bridge was opened.

0906 CEDAR RAPIDS

Stw p wh b. Freedom, Pa., 1858. 153 x 25. Engines, 12's-3 ft. Two boilers. 131 tons. Built for the Cedar Rapids Transportation Co., Capt. John M. Andress. Actually went to Cedar Rapids, Iowa. She ran into the *LUCIE MAY* night of May 14, 1859, near La Grange, Mo., sank the latter and drowned three deckhands. Pilot A.M. Root proved to the inspectors that his boat was a poor handler and apt to sheer. She was taken up the Arkansas River to bring out salvage from the sunken *A.H. SEVIER* at Jenkins Landing below Pine Bluff. Loaded up, and sank at Douglas on the way out, this on Feb. 12, 1861. The *FRONTIER CITY* was sent up to bring out salvage from these two, and also was lost.

0907 CELESTE

Stw p wh b. Cannelton, Ind., 1863. 79 tons. Snagged and lost at Duvall's Bluff, Ark., March 1865.

0908 CELESTE

Stw p wh b. Cincinnati, Oh., 1864. 140 x 33.4 x 4. Ran New Orleans-Red River in place of the *ST. NICHOLAS* during low water, Capt. J.C. Dowty, master, with A.P. Rodney, clerk, November 1868. Regular in Red River 1870, owned by Rees Pritchard, Little Rock, Ark., and J.H. Lane, Memphis; Capt. Phillip Crooks, master. New Orleans-White River, November 1870, Capt. Pat H. Wheat. Memphis-Arkansas River, Capt. Tom Berry in 1871. Cut down by ice at Randolph Landing, Tenn., on Mississippi River above Island 35, Dec. 24, 1872.

0909 CELINA

Stw p wh b. Jeffersonville, Ind., at Howard Yard, 1876. 140 x 25 x 3. Built for Capt. J.W. Lovell and operated on upper Cumberland River. Still listed 1882.

0910 CELINA

Stw p wh b. Burnside, Ky., 1913. 145.5 x 24.5 x 4.4. Engines, 10's- 6½ ft. Owned by Cumberland Transportation Co. She had a gunnel hull with scow bow. Machinery came from *FOUNTAIN CITY,* originally on *CHANCY LAMB.* Ran on upper Cumberland along with *ROWENA* and *CITY OF BURNSIDE.* The trade played out. Boat broker John F. Klein bought *CELINA* and *ROWENA* and hired a motorboat to tow them down the river from Burnside. Both were lost en route, the *CELINA* at Indian Creek Shoals.

0911 CENTENNIAL

Rig? In mid-September 1871 caught fire at St. Louis. Pilothouse, all of the texas, and parts of nine staterooms were destroyed, as well as part of the ladies' cabin. A nearby ferryboat, by use of her hoses, prevented total destruction. Owned by Capt. Sedam and others.

0912 CENTENNIAL

Rig? b. Terre Haute, Ind., 1873. 28.25 tons. Primarily a freight boat. A dispatch dated Jan. 19, 1878, reported that Capt. William Barrick, Terre Haute, had just sold her to Capt. David Modesett, Vego County, Ill., for $1,200 cash.

0913 CENTENNIAL

SW p wh b. St. Louis, Mo., 1876. 295.1 x 41.6 x 7.5. This was a rebuilding job, using the *TOM JASPER* (see). Operated by the St. Louis & St. Paul Packet Co. Her last active year was 1878 running excursions out of Davenport and Burlington. She was laid up winter of 1878–1879 at Dallas City, Ill. When the ice ran out in the spring of 1879 she was carried opposite Fort Madison just above the present Santa Fe bridge. The *SAINT PAUL* went alongside, pumped out the hull, and she was dismantled. The hull was used to carry sugar to the lower Mississippi and eventually sank at Island 21, Sept. 23, 1883.

0914 CENTRAL CITY

A small boat which was run down by the sidewheeler *CHARLES MORGAN* at Twin Hollows, below St. Louis, during a thunderstorm on the night of July 12, 1884. The *MORGAN* was out with an excursion, the Germania Club, and had just overtaken the *CHAS. P. CHOUTEAU* which also was out on an excursion. The *CENTRAL CITY* was rammed, then brought alongside the *MORGAN,* and all the crew saved. The river later was covered with her freight as far down as Ste. Genevieve.

0915 CENTRAL CITY

Stw ferry wh Originally ferry *PIONEER CITY* b. Harmar, Oh., 1891 (see). Ellis C. Mace, Dr. Vickers, and George M. Biggs rebuilt her 1906 and name was changed to *CENTRAL CITY* in April 1907. They operated her at Central City, W. Va. (lower end of Huntington), for two years. Then she ran at 26th Street, Huntington, quite successfully run by Paul Thomas and his brother-in-law Ed Smith. They sold her to Kline O'Neill, Augusta, Ky., who used parts building ferry *AUGUSTA* in 1923.

0916 CENTRALIA

Stw p wh b. Wheeling, W. Va., 1864. 423.65 tons. Built for Capt. William Reno and others designed for Pittsburgh-St. Louis trade. In August 1865 sold at Pittsburgh to Capts. Green and Able, St. Louis, who loaded her out for New Orleans, the first freight so solicited since before the war. Sold to Capt. William B. Nowland and others, Memphis, and ran from there to Arkansas River. She hit the bank at Auburn Landing, Arkansas River, May 27, 1868, lost.

0917 CERES

SW p wh b. Jeffersonville, Ind., by Howard, 1853. 166 x 37.6 x 5. In 1854 running New Orleans-Bayou Sara, Capt. William McCombs, in place of the *BELLA DONNA.* In 1960, New Orleans-Red River, Capt. J.J. Labarthe. In 1861 owned at New Orleans by New Orleans, Opelousas & Great Western RR, Capt. T.K. Porter. Exploded and lost at St. Joseph Island, La., Oct. 9, 1862, with loss of 12 lives.

0918 CHALLENGE

Stw p wh b. Shousetown, Pa., 1854. 147 x 39 x 4.5. 229 tons. Owned by Capt. Samuel C. Young and others. Primarily a freight boat, and had double sternwheels. Ran Pittsburgh-St. Louis, and was at St. Paul in 1858. In 1860 loaded out for below at Muscatine with 2,000 bales of hay, 97,000 bundles of lath, etc. She was snagged and lost above St. Louis apparently on that trip, Feb. 25, 1860.

0919 CHALMETTE

SW p wh b. Mound City, Ill. (hull), and completed at Cairo, Ill., winter of 1898–1899, using hull of *CITY OF VICKSBURG* (see). John T. Hardy Sons & Co., New Orleans, operated her. Capt. Mike Corbine, first master. Ran in the cotton trade New Orleans-Vicksburg-Grand Lake in 1902 with Capt. B.C. Rea, master, V.G. Entriken, clerk. Ran St. Louis-New Orleans in 1904, Capt. Jack

Brinker. Sank at Legon's Landing, Miss., in summer of 1904.

0920 CHAMP CLARK

Stw p-tb wh b. Mudd's Landing, Ill., 1912. Originally a towboat used by Rust & Swift, contractors. They sold her to Rocheport Ferry & Transportation Co., Capt. Thomas P. Craig, pres. Then Hermann Ferry Packet Co., got her, lengthened her, and used her for a packet on Missouri River. Finally dismantled her on the bank at Hermann, Mo.

0921 CHAMPION

SW p wh b. Cincinnati, Oh., 1853. 257 tons. Operated out of Mobile, Ala. Off the lists in 1858.

0922 CHAMPION

SW p wh b. Cincinnati, Oh., 1858. 676 tons. Ran principally St. Louis-New Orleans, Capt. E.B. Moore. Burned and lost at Memphis, Aug. 21, 1863, with loss of one life.

0923 CHAMPION

Stw p wh b. Freedom, Pa., 1864. 292 tons. 145.8 x 26.5 x 3.8½. Engines, 15's- 6 ft. Built for Capt. Frank Maratta and left Pittsburgh on first trip latter November 1864 for Cincinnati and Louisville. Maratta sold her in February 1865 at Cincinnati to Capt. Wm. Gregg and she was acquired by the U.S. Sold at Mound City, Ill., Aug. 17, 1865, to W.H. Harrison. In 1869 in Cincinnati-St. Louis trade, Capt. W.C. Grubb, master, with Thad Wirthlin, clerk. Burned and lost at Cincinnati, Mar. 7, 1872.

0924 CHAMPION

Recess wheel ferry wh b. Mason City, W. Va., 1874. 84 x 22.8 x 3.5. Originally operated at Pomeroy, Oh. Later, at Gallipolis, Oh., run by widow of Capt. Rafe Hamilton. Burned at Gallipolis, Oct. 13, 1902, Capt. Burt Faudree.

0925 CHAMPION NO. 2

SW wh b. Newport, Ky., 1854. 145 tons. 145.8 x 26.5 x 3.8. Engines, 15's- 6 ft. Built for the Shinkle family, Covington, Ky., for use as a harbor boat. Was acquired by the U.S. in 1861 and sold at public sale, Mound City, Ill., Nov. 29, 1865, to T. Wilson.

0926 CHAMPION NO. 2

Stw ferry wh b. Mason City, W. Va., 1882. 76 x 22.8 x 3.4. Engines, 10's- 3 ft. Two boilers, each 40" by 14 ft. Ran between Pomeroy and Mason City until sold January 1902 to Burt Faudree, Gallipolis, Oh. She operated at Gallipolis for a time. In summer of 1903 Capt. Miles Brown bought the ferry *LITTLE LAFIE,* changed her name to *FRANCIS,* and took over the Gallipolis ferry business. B.F. Flesher, Middleport, bought *CHAMPION NO. 2* in October 1904. She was completely rebuilt at the Gardner Docks, Pt. Pleasant, W. Va., in 1910 and renamed *RELIEF* (see).

0927 CHAMPION NO. 2

Stw sawmill boat wh b. Mason City, W. Va., 1892. 76 x 22.8 x 3.4. In 1906 owned by B.F. Flesher, Middleport, Oh. She lay at the Enterprise Docks, Pt. Pleasant winter 1905–1906, and on Jan. 11, 1906, sank there. Was raised and docked.

0928 CHAMPION NO. 3

SW wh b. Cincinnati, Oh., 1856. 160.6 x 29.5 x 4.7. Owned by the Shinkle family, Covington, Ky., and used for harbor work, etc. She was acquired by the U.S., was with Porter on Red River, sank, raised, and listed in 1865 as a USQMD wharfboat. Sold by the U.S. Jan. 26, 1866, to Capt. Thomas Janney, New Orleans. Had several ownership changes, finally taken to St. Louis in 1870, bought by Capt. David Campbell and dismantled.

0929 CHAMPION NO. 3

Stw ferry wh b. Mason City, W. Va. (hull), and completed at Middleport, Oh. 1901. 98.9 x 25.7 x 3.5. Engines, 3 ¾'s- 3½ ft. One boiler, 44" x 18 ft. Owned by J.F. Jividen, and his brother Charles operated it. Ran Pomeroy-Mason City until the bridge was built, then ran at Proctorville, Oh., where she was dismantled in spring of 1935.

0930 CHAMPION NO. 4

SW wh b. Cincinnati, Oh., 1860. 115 tons. Owned by Amos and Vincent Shinkle, Covington, Ky. Sold to the U.S., Mar. 14, 1863, and was turned back to private ownership Apr. 14, 1866. Dismantled.

0931 CHAMPION NO. 5

SW wh b. Cincinnati, Oh., 1863. 184 tons. She was in U.S. service on Red River when she was shelled and sunk above Colfax, La., where she burned, Apr. 26, 1864. A dispatch date-marked Louisville, Ky., May 16, 1864, recounts that her engineer had arrived there the day previous. He had jumped off the stern of the boat, swam ashore, and hid in ravines by day, traveling at night, until he hailed a gunboat and got to Alexandria. He took passage on the *W.L. EWING* to the mouth of Red River. He reported pilot David Dunseth and the balance of the crew captured.

0932 CHAMPION NO. 6

SW wh b. Cincinnati, Oh., 1864. 249 tons. Owned by the Shinkle family, Covington, Ky. Used as a harbor boat, and sometimes ran excursions. Dismantled in 1875.

0933 CHAMPION NO. 9

SW ex wh b. Cincinnati, Oh., 1875. 462.79 tons. 202.4 x 36.4 x 5.2. Owned by the Shinkle family. NOTE: *CHAMPION NOS. 7* and *8* were towboats. She frequently carried baseball crowds from the foot of Walnut Street in Cincinnati to the East End where the field was located near what later was the Cincinnati Gym property. In the latter 1870s she ran competition for a time with the *JAMES FISKE JR.,* in the Paducah-Cairo trade and lost out. Her owner at the time was a Mr. Byrd who joined forces with circusman Dan Rice. They transformed this side-wheeler into a showboat and toured the south. Still listed 1886.

0934 CHANCELLOR

SW p wh b. New Albany, Ind., 1846. 380 tons. Took *EMBASSY* (see) in tow after the latter had exploded boilers at Three Mile Bar, near the mouth of Green River, and delivered her to Evansville, Ind., this in June 1849. Off the lists in 1850.

0935 CHANCELLOR

SW p wh b. Louisville, Ky., 1850. 372 tons. In July 1850 advertised at Natchez for Louisville, Capt. Bacon. Snagged and lost at Cairo, Ill., Dec. 7, 1854.

0936 CHANCELLOR

SW p wh b. New Albany, Ind., 1856. 392 tons. Collided at the Louisville Falls, July 26, 1860, with *SAMUEL P. HIBBARD,* resulting in the loss of the latter (see). Louisville-New Orleans trade, spring 1861, Capt. Sol Marbon. Burned at St. Louis, Oct. 4, 1863, along with *FOREST QUEEN* and *CATAHOULA.*

0937 CHAPERON

Stw p wh Originally *J. C. KERR* b. 1884 (see), and renamed by Evansville & Bowling Green Packet Co., in 1904 after a rebuilding. Ran in the Bowling Green-Mammoth Cave trade, Capt. Jeff H. Williams, master. Also ran out to Evansville and up to Bowling Green filling in for other packets. Sold to Capt. Gid Montjoy, Greenwood, Miss., in 1917, who changed her name to *CHOCTAW* (see).

0938 CHAPERON

Stw pl wh b. Clinton, Iowa, 1904. 110 x 24 x 4.5. One Bronson-type boiler, 60" dia. by 18 ft. long. Owned by Garrett Lamb of C. Lamb Sons. Often was hitched to the family houseboat *SUMMER GIRL* for river excursions and tours, several times through to New Orleans. Capt. J.W. Menke bought her c. 1927 for towing his showboat. She hit an obstruction at the Paducah-Brookport bridge Oct. 23, 1929, and sank. Was raised, lay around Paducah for a year or more, then was sold to the Indiana Tie Co., and then, in November 1934, to the Tri-State Dredging Co., Keokuk, Clarence Miller, president. They converted her into a sand dredge. NOTE: Capt. Menke later had another *CHAPERON*, originally towboat *SUTER* b. Gasconade, Mo., 1928. He bought her in February 1952.

0939 CHARLES AVERY

Stw p wh b. Allegheny, Pa., 1856. 125 tons. Lost in ice at Hockingport, Oh., Feb. 10, 1857.

0940 CHARLES B. CHURCH

Stw p wh b. Jeffersonville, Ind., 1870. 818 tons. Engines, 24's- 8 ft. Named for Capt. Chas. B. Church, Aberdeen, Oh. The rousters called her the "Colored Baptist Church." Ran Cincinnati-New Orleans, Capt. John S. Patterson, master. Among her clerks were W.G. Voris and Wm. F. McIntyre. Sometimes came to Pittsburgh. She was sunk by ice at Alton, Ind., 40 miles below Louisville, Jan. 19, 1879. Was upbound with a cargo of sugar and molasses from New Orleans. The wreck boat *T.F. ECKERT* went to the scene and found a hole 30 feet long. Work of bulkheading was started but a fast rise on February 23 caused the work to be abandoned. Later on the machinery was removed and placed on the *R.R. SPRINGER* (see).

0941 CHARLES B. PEARCE

Stw p wh b. Augusta, Ky., 1900. 145 x 33.3 x 5.4. Engines 12's- 4'2". Two boilers, each 38" by 18 ft. Owned by Capt. George B. Edgington, Augusta. He bought the old *FALLS CITY* (first, see) and used much equipment in building the *PEARCE.* Ran Cincinnati-Portsmouth briefly. Sold to Capt. John Carnes in June 1903 and ran Paducah-Golconda. Carnes died that same month, and his partner in the boat was Capt. Otto Bauer. Towed showboats for some years. Was moored at the Enterprise Docks, Pt. Pleasant, February 1918 in use as a storage boat. Turned over on her side and was lost.

0942 CHARLES BELCHER

SW p wh b. St. Louis, Mo., 1852. 823 tons. 280 x 46.5 x 8. Engines, 26's- 9 ft. Six boilers. Ran St. Louis-New Orleans, Capt. Carlisle. She was at New Orleans Feb. 6, 1854, just in from Nashville with 2000 bales when she burned, taking with her six or seven other packets, among them the *NATCHEZ* (No. 3), *GRAND TURK.* Owned at the time by Cutter and Valentine.

0943 CHARLES BODMAN

SW p wh b. Cincinnati, Oh., 1870. A large Cincinnati-New Orleans packet commanded by Capt. O.P. Shinkle. She came out in November 1870 and on the return from her second round trip she grounded on the Louisville Falls, heavily loaded, Mar. 19, 1871 at Wave Rock. The river was falling and she was not released until May 4 that year. She was docked at Cincinnati, got 50 new floor timbers, and when the work was done the river had become low. She lay at the East End, Cincinnati, all that summer. A photograph showing her grounded at Wave Rock exists, featuring *LE CLAIRE NO. 2.* Charles Bodman, Esq.., was a tobacco dealer of consequence, long a resident of Cincinnati. She burned in a steamboat fire at New Orleans in April 1875 along with *JOHN KYLE* and *EXPORTER* (both see).

0944 CHARLES CARROLL

SW p wh b. Cincinnati, Oh., 1846. 349 tons. Was noticed at Cairo, upbound, in March 1849 with 748 tons of freight procured at Field's Mills, Bayou Lafourche—said to be the largest single cargo ever brought up the Ohio by a Cincinnati boat. She was snagged and lost at Eddyville, Ky., on Cumberland River, Jan. 13, 1850.

0945 CHAS. C. CARROLL

Stw p wh b. Pittsburgh, Pa., 1875. 222 x 36 x 5.5. Engines, 16's- 5 ft. Three boilers. Originally the *JOHN L. RHOADS* b. 1875 (see). Owned by the Missouri River Transportation Co., and sank on a snag at Chapman's Landing, Mo., on the Missouri River, Sept. 15, 1886, Capt. David Silver in command. She was lost.

0946 CHARLES CHEEVER

Stw p wh b. Brownsville, Pa., 1864. 116.60 tons. In 1872 her home port was Savanna, Ill. Lengthened in 1887 at La Crosse to 230 ft. Often called *CHARLIE CHEEVER* in news accounts. Off the lists in 1882.

0947 CHARLES D. SHAW

Stw p wh b. Jeffersonville, Ind., 1883. 132 x 25 x 4. Ran in the Natchez-Vicksburg trade, Capt. John C. Fowler. The *ST. JOSEPH* was built for that trade in 1893 and shortly after that the *SHAW* was sold to Apalachicola, Fla.

0948 CHARLES E. CESSNA

SW p wh b. Santa Rosa, Fla., 1913. 169.1 x 34.4 x 5.5. Built by the Swains and had their compound oscillating engines, 12's, 24's- 7 ft. Dr. Charles E. Cessna in 1909, living in Chicago, bought 65,000 acres of Florida land for a colonization project. By 1913 there were about 1,000 persons there and Pensacola was the nearest town of consequence. The boat ran Santa Rosa-Pensacola to convey them, as there were no roads. She ran twice-weekly in this trade until September 1914. The outbreak of World War I changed the picture —many of the people were Canadians who headed for home, and there were freezes and discouraging salt-spray storms. Thenceforth the boat ran excursions out of Mobile for about a year and then was laid up. In the hurricane of July 5, 1916, she was carried up onto a wharf at the foot of Theatre Street in Mobile. In the fall of 1916 the Swains bought the boat at New Orleans and took her to La Salle, Ill., for the 1917 Illinois River excursion season. They changed her name to *JULIA BELLE SWAIN* (see).

0949 CHARLES E. ECKER

SW p wh b. North McGregor, Iowa, 1888. 40 x 7 x 6.5. Still documented at Dubuque 1892.

0950 CHARLES FOWLER

Rig? b. New Albany, Ind., fall of 1871 for the Galveston-Houston trade.

0951 CHAS. H. BACON

Stw p wh A small packet on the upper Tennessee River built from the *E.P. DAWSON*. Ran between Loudon and Kingston carrying U.S. mail. Exploded her boiler at Huff's Ferry, six miles below Loudon. Built about 1900.

0952 CHAS. H. DURFEE

Stw p wh b. Pittsburgh, Pa., 1869. 178 x 35 x 5. Engines, 15's- 5 ft. Three boilers, each 36'' by 24 ft. Machinery came from the *BENTON*. New Orleans-Red River, Capt. Jos. H. Aiken, master, with Nat Puckette, clerk, September 1870. Burned at New Orleans at the levee, Mar. 21, 1870; rebuilt. Sank on Dec. 18, 1878, on Atchafalaya River.

0953 CHARLES H. ORGAN

Stw ferry sh b. Dubuque, Iowa, 1897. 135.3 x 30 x 5. Engines, 13's- 6 ft. Two boilers, 42'' by 20 ft. Owned by the West Memphis Ferry Co. Capt. John C. Wykoff, master. She was bought by the Patton-Tully Transportation Co., Memphis, in June 1918. They converted her into a towboat named *DAN QUINN*.

0954 CHARLES H. WEST

Stw snagboat sh b. Nashville, Tenn., by Nashville Bridge Co., 1934. 195 x 38 x 7.6. Compound engines, 14's, 28's- 6 ft. stroke by Iowa Machine Works. Foster Wheeler boilers (two) allowed 250 psi. The low pressure cylinders were set aft. Named for a gentleman of Greenville, Miss., long a member of the Mississippi River Commission. Owned by U.S. Engineers, Vicksburg. Decommissioned in 1958. The Eagle Boat Store, St. Louis, used her until 1970 when she was transferred to the James B. Eads Corp., headed by Fred H. Leyhe. The United American Construction Co., Greenville, Miss., converted her into a floating restaurant placed at St. Louis. Name was changed to *LIEUT. ROBERT E. LEE*. Still in service there, 1978.

0955 CHARLES HAMMOND

SW p wh b. Cincinnati, Oh., 1847. 296 tons. Machinery from the *METAMORA* b. 1844. Built by Capt. Henry A. Jones, Cincinnati, and others for Cincinnati-New Orleans trade. Capt. Charles Davis commanded. Came to the rescue of the *MARTHA WASHINGTON* at Island 65, Jan. 14, 1852 (see). Dismantled 1853 and machinery went to *MADISON* (see).

0956 CHARLES HENRY STONE

SW ferry wh b. Pt. Pleasant, W. Va., 1917. 64.8 x 19 x 3.2. Owned by Capt. Charles C. Stone, Pt. Pleasant, who ran her Pt. Pleasant-Henderson. Ceased operations when the bridge was built August 1931. Bob Hamilton, Huntington, W. Va., bought her November 1932 and ran her Huntington-Chesapeake, replacing *CITY OF HUNTINGTON*. Cut down by ice at Symmes Creek, Oh., in 1935.

0957 CHARLES J. MILLER

Stw ferry sh b. Jeffersonville, Ind., at Howard yard, 1925. 130 x 32 x 5. Owned by the Mississippi River Ferry Co., and operated at Vicksburg, Miss., along with *GEORGE W. MILLER* (see) until the bridge was built. Both boats were given hardwood dancefloors and operated at Vicksburg for a time. Then the *CHARLES J. MILLER* was sold to Capt. A.C. Johnson, Helena, Ark., who renamed her *GENERAL* (see).

0958 CHARLES MERRIAM

SW ferry wh b. Jeffersonville, Ind., 1883. 206 x 45 x 6.5. Engines, 20's- 8 ft. Four boilers, two on a side, 42'' by 28 ft. This was a railroad transfer boat owned by the St. Louis & Iron Mountain RR. In 1911 she was at Columbus, Ky. Dismantled 1913 and used as a landing dock.

0959 CHARLES MILLER

Stw p wh b. Elizabeth, Pa., 1860. 93 tons. Ran Louisville-Cumberland River. Carried supplies for the U.S. during the war. Downbound from Nashville on Mar. 23, 1865, she got in a storm about 12 miles below Nashville, capsized and sank with loss of two lives. She was owned at the time by Capt. Pink Varble and his brother W. Varble, both of Louisville.

0960 CHARLES MORGAN

SW p wh b. Cincinnati, Oh., 1873. 302.2 x 43.4 x 7.6. Engines, 28's- 8 ft. Six boilers. Built at the Cincinnati Marine Railway & Dock Co., and originally had the machinery from the *JOHN KILGOUR* (see) and about 1877 these were taken off and new engines placed, size given above. Built for Cincinnati-New Orleans trade and commanded by Capt. Albert Stein. Captain Stein had graduated from the *JOHN KILGOUR*, was far-famed as a captain and he seldom if ever went to bed on a downbound trip, often sleeping in the barber's chair with his clothes on. The boat was named for Charles Morgan, Esq., the steamship and railroad magnate. On the wheelhouses were the Morgan Line emblems, a star with the initials CM woven in. In 1875 Mr. Morgan visited the boat at New Orleans; he then was at an advanced age, around 80. When the racer *NATCHEZ* was dismantled at Cincinnati in 1879 some of her equipment was transferred to the *CHARLES MORGAN* including chandeliers, stained glass doors and the forecastle sign-boards. In June 1877 she made the run from New Orleans to Cincinnati in 6 days 11 hours, racing the *ROBERT MITCHELL* and making 42 landings, and lost 34 hours in the Louisville Canal. Was in the "O" Line for a while but usually was operated as an independent, sometimes whacking rates to 15 cents cwt. Up to Jan. 31, 1878, she had made 38 round trips with total passenger and freight receipts of $100,874.49. Her largest trip receipts in that period, for a single trip, amounted to $6,248.40; smallest was $1,443.50. The Anchor Line chartered her in 1885 for a round trip St. Louis-New Orleans for the Cotton Exposition, and on this voyage she was commanded by Capt. James O'Neal with Archie Woods, purser. According to E. Cattoll Taber the boat was then owned by C.C. Carroll of the marine insurance firm Carroll & Powell. In the season 1874–1875 while in her regular trade she carried 2,763 cabin and 3,164 deck passengers in the course of 11 round trips. On Apr. 24, 1880, the *MORGAN* and *JOHN W. CANNON* left New Orleans together. When at the foot of St. Marys Street, running almost abreast, the *MORGAN* sheered into the *CANNON* taking away the *CANNON's* starboard wheel, wheelhouse and shaft. The shaft dropped into the river. The *MORGAN* towed the damaged *CANNON* to Gretna for repairs. The *MORGAN* hit and sank the small steamer *CENTRAL CITY* (see) at Twin Hollows below St. Louis during a thunderstorm on July 12, 1884, at night.

The Morgan Charles, at 5 today
Leaves here for Cincinnater,
She lives so well one trip alone
Will make you 10 pounds fatter.

—Jackstaff in *New Orleans Picayune*.

The *MORGAN* burned, laid up at the foot of Niagara Street, Cincinnati, Dec. 4, 1886.

0961 CHARLES MULLIKEN

Stw ferry wh b. New Albany, Ind., 1863. 268.16 tons. Owned by the Wiggins Ferry Co., St. Louis. Off the lists in 1879.

0962 CHARLES P. CHOUTEAU

Stw p ih Capt. W. H. Thorwegan, St. Louis, bought the burned *CARONDOLET* (see) in 1877, rebuilt her and entered her in the St. Louis-New Orleans trade. In the summer of 1878 she was hauled out on the Carondelet marine ways and lengthened 50 feet, and was given four new boilers. The cabin was altered to accommodate 50 passengers. She now measured 296.7 x 54 x 7.6. Engines, 22's-8 ft. This made her the longest sternwheel packet on the rivers, a distinction she retained until the building of the *MISSISSIPPI QUEEN* (see). She was built to carry cotton, and during the cotton season ran Memphis-New Orleans. Her banner trip came in 1878 when on one trip she took to New Orleans 8,841 bales, second to the record of the *HENRY FRANK* (see). In the season of 1881 she delivered a total of 76,950 bales, the all-time record for one boat in a single season. Capt. W.H. Thorwegan commanded, and G. Miltenberger was clerk. She was one of the first boats seen at St. Louis with electric lights. She burned at Sunflower Landing, below Memphis, on Nov. 22, 1887..

0963 CHARLES REBSTOCK

Stw p wh b. St. Louis, Mo., 1880. She was built for a wholesale liquor dealer to carry his goods and salesmen to the lower Mississippi and tributaries. Some error in his plans (possibly the crew and their friends got away with the stock!); anyhow two or three years put an end to this plan and she went up in the Davenport-Clinton trade in charge of Capt. Wm. Lumbeck, who was later U.S. Boiler Inspector. Al Congar was clerk and H.A. Barr, pilot (I think). Burned at Cordova, Ill., on Oct. 2, 1885. Capt. Sam Van Sant bought the wreck and the machinery went into a ferry built at Cape Girardeau. This account was written by Capt. Walter Blair.

0964 CHARLES ROGERS

Freight boat wh b. Manchester, Pa., 1858. A small sternwheeler, 27 tons. She is distinguished having made a trip in May 1859 from Keokuk to Fort Dodge, Iowa, up the Des Moines River. She was loaded with groceries and hardware, trading the cargo for gold en route. In 1888 this voyage was described as "the first and only trip to Fort Dodge."

0965 CHARLESTON

SW p wh b. Cincinnati, Oh., 1852. 345 tons. Built for Capt. Clifford B. Wayne and others for the Cincinnati-New Orleans trade, using engines from former *CHICKASAW*.

The name of the boat was selected, apparently, inasmuch as Wayne originally came from the upper Kanawha. Sank at Rising Sun, Ind., Apr. 2, 1853, raised. Burned and lost at Golconda, Ill., Dec. 21, 1855, with loss of one life.

0966 CHARLESTON

Stw p wh b. Bridgeport, Ala., 1864. 272 tons. Rebuilt at Cincinnati 1866. Ran St. Louis to Cincinnati and Pittsburgh. Spent the summer of 1868 perched on the bar at Captina Island, Ohio River, high and dry. A barge loaded with nails was stranded alongside of her. She was later used to tow coal out of Kanawha River where she sank May 8, 1869, at Cabin Creek but was recovered and taken to Pomeroy for repairs where she sank again. Capt. James H. Morris, Louisville, owned her then. She was raised but did very little thereafter.

0967 CHARLESTON

Stw ferry wh b. Charleston, W. Va., 1887. 94.9 x 25.6 x 4. Built at the mouth of Elk River by Charleston Dock Co., owned and run by Job E. Thayer. The machinery was built and placed by O.A. and W.T. Thayer who ran the South Side Foundry & Machine Shop. Owned by the Thayers and the Ruffner brothers. After the bridge was built at Charleston she continued to run for a time, Capt. John O'Keefe, offering reduced fare. Then she came to Wheeling and ran across to Wheeling Island, this about 1893-1894, and for a time was charging one cent, loaded all the time, fighting the bridge tolls there, Capt. A.A. Everett. Then she went to Hannibal, Oh., briefly, Capt. J.J. Noll. Sold in March 1899 to J.A. Crouch, Dycusburg, Ky., and S.D. Lewis, Blodgett, Mo. Capt. Frank Wagner, Paducah, bought her in 1905 and ran her at Hickman, Ky. She went aground there in February 1906 and was reported lost. Wagner gave the roof bell to the McKinley School, Paducah.

0968 CHARLEY BOWEN

Stw p wh b. California, Pa., 1856. 138 x 25 x 4'8''. Engines, 16's- 4½ ft. Three boilers. Built at the Ben Coursin yard and named for a gentleman from Waterford, Pa. Principal owner was Capt. Henry T. Dexter, Parkersburg, W. Va. Ran Parkersburg-Zanesville through November 1858, when Captain Dexter put her Evansville-Paducah and did quite well. During the war she flew the U.S. flag and had a four-pounder aboard to protect it. The story of the flag is recounted in Archer Butler Hulbert's *The Ohio River*, pages 323-327. A monument honoring the boat and her skipper long stood on the wharf grade at Evansville, Ind. After the war she was sold to W.C. Graham in New Orleans, who sold her January 1866 to Capt. James L. Thayer and others. On May 6, 1866, she was at Pittsburgh with the Thayer & Noyes circus aboard, and a newspaper reported that "her entire business is to carry the circus around from place to place." In 1867 was owned by Capt. Frederick Ford, Pt. Pleasant, W. Va., and others, towing coal out of Kanawha River. On one trip in 1868 she brought seven flats of cannel coal to Pittsburgh. Off the lists in 1869. She was replaced by the *CHARLEY BOWEN NO. 2*, a towboat built at Cincinnati in 1870.

0969 CHARLEY CURLIN

Stw p wh b. Jeffersonville, Ind., by Howard, 1895. 88 x 18 x 3. Engines, 7''- 30'' stroke. One boiler, 30'' by 14 ft. Built as a pleasure boat for a naturalist and taxidermist of Louisville, Seth Curlin, who invented a canvas folding decoy duck, manufactured them, and the sales paid for the steamboat. The boat was named for his son. Mr. Curlin Sr., had a pilot's license, hired an engineer, and otherwise the crew was composed of the family. Later was sold to Green River, owned by Walter G. Hougland, and in March 1903 sank and her passengers were taken ashore from treetops. Frank & Price owned her 1905-1906, and she burned at Caruthersville, Mo., in late October 1906.

CHARLIE CHEEVER

Proper name was *CHARLES CHEEVER* (see).

0970 CHARLIE POTWIN

Stw p wh b. Zanesville, Oh., 1860. 52 tons. Ran Zanesville-Marietta-Parkersburg, Capt. T. Wiles into 1862. She was downbound from Coalport (opposite Middleport, Oh.) to Ashland with a cargo of slack coal when she got in the swells of the *DIAMOND* and *COAL HILL* at 8-Mile Island above Pt. Pleasant, Ohio River, filled and turned turtle. The cabin separated from the hull and floated off, this on Nov. 28, 1864. The *LIZZIE HAMILTON* took off the crew. Owned at the time by Capt. Aaron Steed and by James H. Poage, the clerk. No life loss.

0971 CHARLIE STONE

Stw ferry wh b. Brownsville, Pa., at Axton yard, 1888. 102 x 26.5 x 3.5. Engines, 10's- 4 ft. by Sweeney. Ran Pt. Pleasant-Kanauga for a decade or more. Owned by J.H. and C.D. Stone. On Wednesday, Dec. 18, 1901, at 7:30 A.M., she sprung a leak. Charlie Stone was her master, and Clark DeWolf, pilot. Attempt was made to drop her in under the ferry flat on the Pt. Pleasant side. The line broke and she drifted off. The towboat *NELLIE ENGLAND* landed her bottom-side-up two miles down the Ohio. The wreck was bought by Sandy Suiter, Manchester, Oh., who used parts building the towboat *KATIE MAC* in 1903.

0972 CHARM

SW p wh b. Cincinnati, Oh., 1860. 223 tons. Ran Vicksburg-Yazoo River along with *DEW DROP, HOME, HOPE, PRINCE, ARGO,* and others, connecting with New Orleans packets. In official Navy records *CHARM* is noted at Battle of Belmont, Nov. 7, 1861, ferrying Confederate troops Belmont-Columbus, also conveying wounded and bodies of the slain. She and *PAUL JONES* (see) conveyed Col. Francis M. Cockrell's troops across the Mississippi from Vicksburg to meet Grant's forces coming down the Louisiana side. These two steamers went up Black River to the railroad bridge at Bovina, loaded large guns which had come in on the railroad and delivered these to Grand Gulf for the fortifications there. After Porter ran the Vicksburg batteries, both boats were taken up Big Black for safety. The railroad bridge was the head of navigation and they were moored near there. Grant went inland, captured Jackson, Miss., won at Champion Hill, and was flanking across the rear of Vicksburg. The Confederate troops were trying to hold open the Big Black crossing for General Loring's troops and fought the Battle of Big Black, May 17, 1863. Meeting reverses, they burned both boats to prevent their capture. The steamer *DOT* had been sunk previously nearer the bridge. The wrecks of *CHARM* and *PAUL JONES* were found side by side by skin-divers in August 1962 and many souvenirs were brought up.

0973 CHARMER

SW p wh b. Cincinnati, Oh., 1859. 278 x 40 x 9. 667 tons. Built for Capt. Richard Holmes, for New Orleans-Vicksburg trade to replace the *PRINCESS*, which had exploded shortly prior. In 1860 Capt. W.C. Wilson, master. Was downbound with a big load of cotton at Lauderdale, La., about 10 miles below Donaldsonville, when she burned with loss of five lives. Capt. Dick Holmes was aboard, and carried ashore to safety a young girl named Betsey who in later life became Mrs. R.F. Learned, for whom the packet *BETSY ANN* was named. Captain Holmes procured the *MARY T* to replace (see).

0974 CHARMER

Stw p wh b. Elizabeth, Pa., 1863. 249 tons. Built for Capt. George D. Moore and others and ran Pittsburgh-Cincinnati-Louisville. Brought nine blooded colts to Wheeling for Thomas Sweeney, Esq., bought at Lexington, Ky., in March 1864. Sold a few days later to Capt. Vincent Shinkle, Covington, Ky. In June 1868 Capt. Lew Vandergrift, Pittsburgh, bought interest and took command, running Pittsburgh-St. Louis, with Isaac Whittaker in the office. An Evansville dispatch dated July 14, 1868, says "Captain Vandergrift and clerk Whittaker have been doing nicely with the *CHARMER*, have paid off her debts, and redeemed her reputation." In June 1869 in Evansville-Cincinnati trade, Capt. P.K. Barclay, master, with S.T. James, clerk. That fall ran Cincinnati-Marietta, Capt. G.W. Thompson, master. Capt. W.F. Gregory recalled her briefly in the Gallipolis-Charleston trade at one time. In 1874 in the Louisville-Evansville trade, Capt. W.C. Tichenor, master, with S.T. and S. James, clerks. Burned at Evansville, laid up at the time, on June 23, 1874.

0975 CHARMER

Stw p wh b. Jeffersonville, Ind., 1879 at the Howard Yard. 185 x 34 x 5.8. Engines, 15's- 6 ft. Two boilers, each 47" by 26 ft., six flues. Built for the New Orleans-Red River trade, owned by Noah Scovell, Charles H. Truslow and Charles W. Drown. She was on her fourth trip when she burned 15 miles above Bayou Sara with loss of eight lives. Pilot on watch was W.H. Atkinson. The wreck went down in 30 feet, January 1880.

0976 CHARMER

Dispatch dated at Cairo, Ill., Feb. 17, 1880: Last week the *CHARMER* struck the Danville bridge and was smashed to pieces. No lives lost. She was loaded with cotton.

0977 CHARON

Stw ferry wh b. Brownsville, Pa., at Axton yard, 1889. 110 x 30 x 3.4. Owned by the Bellaire, Benwood & Wheeling Ferry Co., R.M. Gilleland, pres. Ran Bellaire-Benwood. Once in 1902 she was sent downriver to the docks for repairs, and on the return trip hit the foot of Grape Island (Dec. 18) head-on and sank. Had to go back to the docks. In the 1920s, en route downriver from Bellaire in tow of the ferry *RUTH ANN* (see), she hooked a mooring pin on the outside wall at Dam 23, Ohio River, and was wrecked.

0978 CHARTER

Stw p wh b. Paducah, Ky., 1856. 114 tons. She was owned by the U.S. when she burned at Dozier, Tenn., on the Cumberland River, about five miles above Harpeth Shoals, this on Jan. 15, 1863.

0979 CHARTER OAK

Built and owned by Capt. Hercules Carrel, Cincinnati, probably side-wheel. Burned at Bailey's Landing, Mississippi River, Apr. 12, 1848, with loss of life. The *Lytle-Holdcamper List* has her built at Buffalo, N.Y., as a 184-ton schooner, converted to steam in 1848.

0980 CHARTIERS VALLEY

SW ferry wh b. Pittsburgh, Pa., 1865. 152 tons. Probably ran between Pittsburgh and McKees Rocks. She is listed through 1876 and perhaps a little later.

0981 CHAUTAUQUA BELLE

Stw ex wh b. Mayville, N.Y., by Jim Webster for Chautauqua Lake Steam Navigation Co., 1976. 64.5 x 16 (hull later was widened). Engines, 6"- 2 ft. by Harry McBride, Fulton, Ill. One Johnston scotch marine boiler. Operated on Lake Chautauqua based at Mayville, N.Y. Picture and description of the launching ceremonies and principals involved, see *S&D Reflector*, June 1976, pages 42-43.

0982 CHATTAHOOCHEE

Stw p sh b. Pittsburgh, Pa., by James Rees & Sons Co., 1881. 155 x 31 x 5. Engines, 15's- 5 ft. Three boilers, each 42" by 20 ft., six flues. This was the first all-steel hull packet built for U.S. service, although the Rees firm had built in 1878 a steel hull packet, the *FRANCESCO MONTOYA*, for Magdalena River in South America, shipped knock-down and assembled at destination. Iron hull packets had their beginnings when the *VALLEY FORGE* was built at Pittsburgh (see). The *CHATTAHOOCHEE* was built for service on the Chattahoochee River. In the summer of 1884 she was on the St. John's River, Fla., plying between Jacksonville and Sanford, Capt. John W. Fitzgerald. She then belonged to the Peoples Line operated by Henry Bailey Plant. She was still operating there in June 1885. Later she was returned to the Mississippi River and ran Vicksburg-Greenville owned by Mulholland Bros., with Capt. Nimptz in charge. Burned at Vicksburg on Dec. 7, 1893. The Rees firm also claimed she was the first Western steamer with longitudinal and transverse bulkheads in the hull. The September 1972 issue of *S&D Reflector* features pictures of her, and more details.

0983 CHATTANOOGA

SW p wh b. Elizabeth, Pa., 1850. 104 tons. Off the lists in 1852.

0984 CHATTANOOGA

Stw p wh b. Kingston, Tenn., 1857. 182 tons. Operated on the upper Tennessee owned by James and William Williams, a team which also ran the *MOLLIE GARTH, FANNY MALONE, JEFFERSON*, and *JIM WILLIAMS*. Off the lists 1860.

0985 CHATTANOOGA

Stw p wh b. Bridgeport, Ala., 1863, 159 tons. Built for US-QMD, and sold to private owners May 12, 1866. She ran Evansville-Clarksville in 1867, Capt. Henry Scott, master, with C.T. Rudd, clerk. Off the lists in 1868.

0986 CHATTANOOGA

Stw p wh b. Henry's Mills, Tenn., 1878. 162.17 tons. Parts of the *LUCY COKER* used in building her. Ran below Chattanooga on the Tennessee. A novice pilot was at the wheel when she hit the bank full-head and sank. She was raised, completely rebuilt, and came out as the *WYETH CITY* (see), this in 1888.

0987 CHATTANOOGA

Stw p wh Originally the gospel boat *MEGIDDO*, renamed. In May 1904 she sank on rocks in the Big Chain, about Mile 20 Tennessee River, and was badly warped. She was pulled out on the marine ways at Paducah. Capt. Walter Blair superintended repairs and she emerged looking very little like her former self, now a fullfledged packet. She ran out of Chattanooga and once sank there with a large cargo of corn aboard. She became the last packet to make trips to Kingston, Tenn., this in 1919–1920. Crew on her last trip in that trade: Capt. Paul Underwood, master; Joe Farrell, mate; Harris Underwood, pilot; Bob Ellison, chief engineer; Bob Dodds, clerk. Running Chattanooga-Decatur in January 1921, Capt. Thomas D. Galy. Finally sank at Chattanooga.

0988 CHEROKEE

SW p wh b. New Albany, Ind., 1850. 417 tons. Original home port was Paducah, Ky. In 1856 advertised at New Orleans for Tennessee River, taking cargo and passengers for Eastport, Florence, and Tuscumbia, Capt. James Irwin. Collided with the side-wheel *J. McKEE* at Island 92, Mississippi River, wrecking the latter, Feb. 7, 1859. Rebuilt c. 1862, renamed *J. H. RUSSELL*, and burned the night of Mar. 28, 1864, near Plaquemine, La. (see).

0989 CHEROKEE

SW p wh b. New Albany, Ind., 1859. 337 tons. Went to Mobile, Ala. Off the lists in 1874.

0990 CHEROKEE

Prop wh b. Terre Haute, Ind., 1863. 59 tons. Probably handled produce boats, etc. Snagged and lost in White River, Ark., 1869.

0991 CHEROKEE

Stw p wh b. Monongahela, Pa., 1864. 261 tons. Built for Pittsburgh-St. Louis trade, Capt. William B. Dravo. Capt. George W. Neare was pinch-hitting as master in June 1864. Burned in the big steamboat fire at St. Louis, July 13, 1864. Her wreck, on the Illinois shore, was auctioned in August 1864 to Capt. Alexander Kelsy on high bid of $2,750. He had recently bought and rebuilt the *COURIER* (see).

0992 CHEROKEE

Stw p wh b. Smith's Crossroads, Tenn. (now Dayton), and machinery placed at Chattanooga, 1866. Capt. W.C. Henegar, master, with J.W.C. Wilson, clerk. In the "high tide" of 1867, a great flood, she went to Washington, Tenn., county seat of Rhea County. The bridge the Federals put across at Chattanooga was swept out on this high water; also the railroad at Bridgeport. *CHEROKEE* ferried at the latter place until the bridge was put back. This boat did not run very long; was sold to Hugh Martin, who rebuilt her into a packet bearing his own name *HUGH MARTIN* (see). Interesting is the fact that *CHEROKEE's* lifeboat was named *PAPOOSE*.

0993 CHEROKEE

Stw p wh b. Jeffersonville, Ind. by Howard, 1870. 130.9 x 32.5 x 4.4. Enrolled at New Orleans in July 1870 owned by Elizah R. Perry and J.D. Clark, both of New Orleans; Capt. A.M. Osgood, master. She was lengthened at Madison, Ind. in 1872. Sank on Arkansas River with 600 bales of cotton, January 1873. Capt. Kyle ordered the *T.F. ECKERT* to the scene. Later in January the *UTAH* left Pine Bluff with 500 bales of salvaged cotton, and on January 30 the owner of the *T.F. ECKERT*, W. Dugan, telegraphed that he failed to raise the boat and was wrecking her.

0994 CHEROKEE

Stw p wh b. Cincinnati, Oh., 1873. 656 tons. 215 x 39.5 x 6. Engines, 18½'s- 5 ft. Three boilers. Built for the Cincinnati-New Orleans trade, Capt. George Wolf, master, with A. Byers, clerk. This team had run the *ARMADILLO* just prior and much equipment was used in building *CHEROKEE*.. She came out new in November 1873 and grounded at Portland (Ky.) Bar, remaining some time. Her machinery was said to have come from *EMMA NO. 3* (see). Wolf and Byers still were on her January 1878 in the Cincinnati-New Orleans trade. She ran as an independent in the Pittsburgh-Cincinnati trade in May 1878, James Henderson and Marsh Hays, pilots. Collided with the *ST. LAWRENCE* about 14 miles above Marietta, Oh., early March 1880, "causing considerable injury to woodwork of both and frightening passengers." On Decoration Day 1878 she ran an excursion from Pittsburgh to Rochester, Pa., 11:00 A.M. to 10:00 P.M., quite a success, and no liquor was sold aboard. She is said to have brought to Alexandria, La., the first railroad rails of steel. Ultimately dismantled.

0995 CHEROKEE

Rig? b. Arkansas City, Kans., 1878. Built by the citizens of Cowley County, Kans. with great aspirations, stirred by the trip of the *AUNT SALLY* (see) earlier that year.

0996 CHEROKEE

Stw p sh b. Dubuque, Iowa, 1888. 216.4 x 33.9 x 6. Engines, 17's-7 ft. Four boilers, each 40" by 24 ft. The Iowa Machine Works built this long, slim steel hull packet for the St. Louis-Memphis trade. In 1894 she made a special trip St. Louis to Shreveport with groceries and hardware, Capt. Henry Keith. In 1897 she ran St. Louis-Illinois River in place of the *D.H. PIKE*. About 1906 she was sold to the St. Louis & Chester Packet Co. and renamed *CHESTER* (see).

0997 CHESAPEAKE

SW p wh b. Ironton, Oh., at the M. Wise & Co. yard, 1871. Machinery placed at Portsmouth, Oh. 151.8 x 26 x 4.4. Engines, 14's- 4 ft. Two boilers, each 38" by 24 ft., two flues. She turned 28 rpm., and made 9 mph. upstream. Made her trial run May 18, 1871. Construction was superintended by Capt. Uriah Scott. Came out in the Portsmouth-Guyandotte trade, Capt. Uriah B. Scott, master, with Ben Butterfield, clerk. In April 1873 sold to the Parkersburg & Ohio River Transportation Co., Capt. E.B. Cooper, master, with Thos. J. Wetherell, clerk, in Parkersburg-Huntington trade, soon shortened to Parkersburg-Gallipolis. In the fall of 1876 she was stranded high and dry at Sand Creek below Ravenswood, and alongside was the towboat *ENTERPRISE* and tow also stranded. Same trade in 1880 with Capt. Edwin F. Maddy, master, and W.A. and L.L. Maddy, clerks. Nearly everyone worked on her sooner or later, Capt. Sam Hamilton, Ira B. Huntington, John Brookhart, George Hamilton, George Knox, Ash Ruth, Charley Day, Park Allen, to name a few. Later on Steve Ball, who ran a shoe store in Wheeling, bought her for the Wheeling-Marietta trade with Capt. Steve Thompson, master, with Charles Cochran, clerk. She came to Pittsburgh to run excursions. In April 1887 some boys started a wagon down the wharf at the foot of Market Street, Pittsburgh, and the tongue stabbed the *CHESAPEAKE's* hull, sinking her.

0998 CHESAPEAKE

SW p wh b. Harmar, Oh., at the Knox Yard, 1883. 188 x 26 x 5. Engines, 16's- 5 ft. Three boilers, each 40" dia. by 24 ft., two flues. Wheels 20' dia., 15 arms, 10 ft. buckets. Had 36 staterooms, 40 electric lights. Carried her coal in the hull in ten coal cars; had no coal box. Had swinging stages both fore and aft, a distinct novelty. Made her trials in July 1883. Built for Capt. Edwin F. Maddy and others for Gallipolis-Parkersburg trade. She ran briefly Pittsburgh-Cincinnati, and shortly after the disastrous 1884 Flood Capt. Maddy took her to New Orleans and on May 1st that year proceeded with her to Jacksonville, Fla., where she ran on the St. Johns River to Palatka and Sanford, Capt. Maddy in command. She got in financial troubles and was sold at public sale in 1886 to Capt. W.P. Hall who returned her to the Mississippi River. She burned at New Madrid, Mo., on Mar. 26, 1887.

0999 CHESAPEAKE

Stw ferry wh b. Pt. Pleasant, W. Va., at the Smith Docks, 1904. 116.4 x 41.8 x 5.7. Engines, 13's- 5 ft. One boiler, 36" by 20 ft. Paddlewheel was set recess style. Owned by the C & O Railroad and operated at Portsmouth, Oh., Capt. Ed Williamson, and Capt. Harvey L. Redden. When the bridge was built there, she was sold to the Manchester (Ohio) Ferry Co., and burned at Manchester in October 1931.

1000 CHESTER

Stw ferry wh b. East Liverpool, Oh., 1880. 81 x 18 x 4. She ferried at East Liverpool until replaced by the *OLLIE NEVILLE* (see).

1001 CHESTER

Stw p sh Originally the *CHEROKEE* (see) b. 1888. Was renamed *CHESTER* when sold c. 1906 to St. Louis & Chester Packet Co. Was bought by the Kansas City Missouri River Navigation Co., Walter S. Dickey, pres., and entered the St. Louis-Kansas City trade in June 1907, Capt. William L. Thompson (father of Capt. Leonard W. Thompson). She was taken to New Orleans in winter 1910–1911 and converted to propeller drive, vastly altered; had three props in tunnel stern, reduced in length to 150 ft. This did not work, so she was returned to New Orleans in the fall of 1911 and made twin props. Capt. W.L. (Steamboat Bill) Heckmann was master in 1912 on Missouri River. She was not a howling success, often laid up, and several times caught out on shore. Finally sold to Sugar Products Co., New Orleans, who in 1920 converted her into a barge and sent it to Cuba.

1002 CHESTER ASHLEY

Stw p wh b. Cincinnati, Oh., 1860. 192 tons. Built for Capt. Rees Pritchard, Vicksburg, and during the war was kept by the Confederates on the Arkansas River above Little Rock. She was taken by the Union forces and was burned there on Sept. 10, 1863.

1003 CHEVALIER

Stw p wh b. Mason City, W. Va., 1888. 131.2 x 22 x 3.3. Engines, 13½'s-3½ ft. Two boilers, each 42" by 18 ft. Built for the Bay Line and long ran Huntington-Gallipolis under ownership of Capt. M.E. Brown, Gallipolis, with Capt. A.H. Brown, Guyandotte, master. Capt. Dick Brown also was master-pilot. On May 22, 1907, at 1:00 A.M., she burned at the C&O wharfboat, Huntington. The fire department could not reach her due to the road being blocked by C&O freight cars.

1004 CHEVOIT

Stw p wh b. California, Pa., 1853. 140 x 28 x 5.5. Engines, 18's- 4½ ft. Three boilers. Owned by Capt. William McIntosh, Zanesville, Oh., and ran Pittsburgh-Zanesville. When first seen by an editor of the Pittsburgh *Gazette*, he commented in his river column that the name had been misspelled, as indeed it was, the intention being *CHEVIOT* but never was it righted. After four years in the Muskingum River trade she was sold to Capt. Josiah Murray of Beaver County, Pa., who ran her Pittsburgh-Wheeling alternating with *MINERVA* (see). She was retired and dismantled in 1860.

1005 CHEWALA

Stw p wh b. West Brownsville, Pa., 1856. 162 tons. Went to Confederate registry in 1861.

1006 CHEYENNE

Stw p wh b. Cincinnati, Oh., 1868. Machinery came from *ANGLO-SAXON* b. 1857 (see). She ran Cincinnati-Pomeroy-Parkersburg, Capt. Charles M. Holloway, master, with William H. Kyle, clerk. Burned in the Cincinnati steamboat fire on May 12, 1869.

1007 CHICAGO

Stw p wh b. California, Pa., 1854. 150 x 31.5 x 5. 218 tons. Capt. Martin Mellinger was her first master. Soon sold, and Capt. Thomas Laverne was master in 1856. Lost on Feb. 7, 1857.

1008 CHICKASAW

SW p wh b. Cincinnati, Oh., 1851. 309 tons. Built for Cincinnati-Memphis trade owned by Clifford B. Wayne and Thompson Dean. She came in collision with the *W.B. CLIFTON* on Apr. 26, 1852, at French Islands, Ohio River, below Owensboro, Ky., went down in 40 feet, and the cabin parted from the hull. Twenty persons were drowned, among them Thomas Todd, whose wife was Sarah Ann Bugher Todd, sister to Capt. John W. Bugher of the *SILVER MOON, GLENDALE, and JEWESS* (all see). Todd's son Huston was engineer.

1009 CHICKASAW

Prop monitor ih b. St. Louis, Mo., 1863, for the U.S. 469 tons. Had four propellers. She saw active service in the war, attached to Farragut's fleet. Was renamed *SAMSON* on June 15, 1869. Sold at public auction at New Orleans in 1874 for $8,350 (original cost was placed at $389,597.55). Name *CHICKASAW* was restored to her. The New Orleans Pacific Railway acquired her, and she became part of the Texas & Pacific RR in 1881. She was converted into a railroad transfer ferry, renamed *GOULDSBORO* (see). This conversion happened after 1880. The old hull had been used as a coal barge below New Orleans, and was towed to St. Louis in April 1878 by the *SIMPSON HORNER*. The towboat *BEAVER* was downbound with it from St. Louis in December 1880, the hull then loaded with 1,200 tons of freight consigned to New Orleans—and at that time the boilers, pumps, etc., were still in place, and there was talk of making it over into a floating elevator.

1010 CHICKASAW

Stw p wh b. Pittsburgh, Pa., 1883. 185 x 38 x 6. Engines, 16's- 7 ft. Three boilers, each 48" by 26 ft., seven flues. Designed to carry 1,650 bales of cotton. Owned by the Memphis & White River Packet Co., and later by the Lee Line, Memphis. The Lee Line sold her to New Orleans in November 1897 where she ran to Bayou Lafourche, Capt. J.J. Dodd, master, with Leonard Noyes, clerk, teamed up with the *LAFOURCHE* (see). This machinery in 1904 was placed on the towboat *CHARLEY JUTTE* at Jeffersonville, Ind.

1011 CHICOT

Prop p wh b. Sistersville, W. Va., 1889. 97 x 14 x 2.9. The *U.S. Lists of Merchant Vessels* record place of build as "Sissonville, W. Va." and we are surmising Sistersville is intended. Capt. Charles Chambers built her and for years handled U.S. Mail and passengers between Greenville and Arkansas City with her. Frank L. Sibley is authority for the information that Chambers bought the *HUMMING BIRD NO. 2* from Capt. M. Brown (see) and built the *CHICOT* out of her. The *CHICOT* was still documented in 1896, perhaps later.

1012 CHIEF JUSTICE MARSHALL

SW p wh b. Wheeling, Va., 1832. 146 x 22 x 6'8". Single engine, 24"- 6 ft. built by Martin Phillips, Steubenville, Oh. Five boilers, single flue. Had a tin roof. Owned by Knox, McKee, and Clarke and commanded by the latter, who was Robert Pichens Clarke, brother of Thomas Shields Clarke of Clarke & Thaw, Pittsburgh. This Capt. R.P. Clarke was harbormaster at St. Louis in 1870 and was a speaker at the banquet given when the *LEE-NATCHEZ* race was concluded there. The striker engineer on this boat was John McLure, Wheeling, his first job afloat, later owner of *CITY OF WHEELING* (see). She ran Pittsburgh-Cincinnati-Louisville, proved too large, and Clarke built the *JUNIATA* to replace her in the trade, and ran her to New Orleans, Capt. John Russell, master John Lamb, clerk (brother of Hon. Daniel Lamb, Wheeling). Her engines were replaced in 1835. Dismantled in 1838.

1013 CHIEF JUSTICE MARSHALL

SW p wh b. Elizabeth, Pa., 1848. 182 x 32 x 7'10". Engines, 24's- 7 ft. Four boilers. Came out new in November 1848 owned by Charles D. Knox and others, Pittsburgh-New Orleans. She was intentionally built to fit the Louisville-Portland locks. Off the lists in 1852.

1014 CHIEFTAIN

SW p wh b. California, Pa., at McFall & Eberman yard, 1866. 164 x 26 x 5.7. Built for the Pittsburgh-Brownsville trade, Monongahela River, and came out new in May 1866, Capt. Robert R. Abrams, master, with R.C. Mason, clerk. Owned by the Peoples Line, teamed up with *ELECTOR* (see). They ran hot competition with the older established line. A merger was effected Feb. 21, 1868, called Pittsburgh, Brownsville & Geneva Packet Co. Her skippers over the years were Capt. Robert Phillips 1869–1872, Capt. Joseph L. Hendrickson 1872, Capt. Washington Stewart 1873, Capt. Doyle Bugher 1874, and Capt. Hendrickson 1875–1876. She ran excursions on the upper Monon in 1875. Was laid up at Brownsville winter 1876–1877, and was carried off by ice Jan. 13, 1877. She lodged at the lower end of Lock 4 where the cabin was sheered off by ice. The *ELISHA BENNETT* was lost in the same winter (see).

1015 CHILDE HAROLD

SW p wh b. Cincinnati, Oh., 1848. 182 x 34 x 8. Engines, 24's- 8 ft. Four boilers. Ran Cincinnati-St. Louis-New Orleans. Off the lists in 1854.

1016 CHILLICOTHE

SW gunboat wh b. Cincinnati, Oh., 1862. 159 x 46.5 x 6'10''. Engines, 23's- 4 ft. She was armor plated at New Albany, Ind. Went to U.S. service commanded by Capt. Harry Eytinge, Newport, Ky., later noted for amateur theatrical performances. Dispatch from Cairo, Ill. dated Sept. 17, 1872: "The old gunboat *CHILLICOTHE* which has been at and on the bank in the bends since the close of the war was set on fire Sunday afternoon and burned up. It was in the way of the Cairo & Vincennes RR and had to be destroyed."

1017 CHILO

Stw p wh b. Pt. Pleasant, W. Va., 1905. 135 x 24.7 x 4.6. Engines, 10's- 4 ft. One boiler, 42'' by 26 ft. Built from the *M.P. WELLS* (see). Owned by the Greene Line, Cincinnati, and long ran Cincinnati-Chilo, later extended to longer runs. On the night of Nov. 18, 1921, she was delivering freight at Lock 35 near New Richmond, Oh., and caught on a guidewall pin, tore a hole in the hull, and sank.

1018 CHIPPEWA

Stw p wh b. Belle Vernon, Pa., 1857. 173 tons. 160 x 30. Engines, 16's- 4 ft. Three boilers. In charge of Capt. Greenlee made a trip to St. Paul in 1857, and operated in the Northwestern Line, Upper Mississippi, 1858–1859. No steamboats had ever gone up the Missouri River to Fort Benton, Mont., until *CHIPPEWA* and the *KEY WEST* both arrived July 2, 1860. The *CHIPPEWA* was commanded on that trip by Capt. W.H. Humphreys, the boat owned by American Fur Co. She burned 15 miles below Poplar River, Mont., on the Missouri in May 1861. Passengers and crew came ashore safely, after which she was set adrift because of powder in the hold. She drifted across the river and exploded.

1019 CHIPPEWA

Stw p wh b. La Crosse, Wis., 1866. 74 tons. Ran five seasons tri-weekly La Crosse-Eau Claire. In July 1870 the arrival of the railroad ended that, and she did some rafting. She was moored winter 1870–1871 at Rumsey's Landing on the Chippewa River. Burned there on Jan. 21, 1871, along with the *JOHNNY SMOKER*, both owned by H.S. Rumsey, La Crosse.

1020 CHIPPEWA FALLS

Stw p wh b. Monongahela, Pa., 1857. 120 x 24 x 3.5. Engines, 10's- 3½ ft. One boiler. Built for Capt. Wm. R. Van Pelt. Appeared in Chippewa River in 1858, running Reads Landing to Eau Claire and continued several seasons. In 1864 she was one of eight boats transporting Gen. Alfred Sully's expedition up the Missouri River.

1021 CHIPPEWA VALLEY

Stw p wh b. Eau Claire, Wis., 1860. 101 tons. Ran on Chippewa River. When war broke out she went south in U.S. service and was captured by the Confederates at Vicksburg but soon was back in U.S. hands. She was snagged and sunk on the Cumberland River five miles below Gallatin Landing on Apr. 30, 1864, then in U.S. service. On August 15 that year she was auctioned off by the U.S. to the highest bidder, but ran no more.

1022 CHOCTAW

SW p wh b. Louisville, Ky., 1851. 133 tons. Went to New Orleans and was snagged and lost on Red River, Jan. 24, 1854.

1023 CHOCTAW

SW p wh b. New Albany, Ind., 1855. 245 x 38 x 7. Engines, 23's- 8 ft. Four boilers. Built for Capt. David H. Silver who ran her four or five round trips St. Louis-New Orleans in 1861 when she was taken over by the USQMD, and then converted into an ironclad U.S. ram.

1024 CHOCTAW

Stw p wh b. Dardanelle, Ark., 1899. 124 x 24 x 2.3. Engines, 10's- 4 ft. Two boilers, each 38'' by 16 ft. Originally used on the Arkansas River, and acquired c. 1905 by Capt. Gid Montjoy who used her out of Vicksburg to Yazoo River. Still listed 1915.

1025 CHOCTAW

Stw p wh Originally the *J.C. KERR*, then the *CHAPERON* b. 1884 (both see). Capt. Gid Montjoy bought *CHAPERON* in 1917, took her to Vicksburg, and ran her in trades up Yazoo and tributaries. She burned at Melrose Landing, Miss., on Tallahatchie River on Mar. 8, 1922.

1026 CHRIS GREENE

Stw p wh b. Pt. Pleasant, W. Va., 1915. 132.4 x 26.4 x 4. Built at the Gardner Docks for Capt. Gordon C. Greene, and named jointly for his father Chris and for his elder son Chris. Came out new in the fall of 1915 running Gallipolis-Charleston. Entered the Cincinnati-Huntington trade,

February 1919, and did well, Capt. Chris Greene. She burned in the steamboat fire at Cincinnati, Nov. 4, 1922. The wreck was raised and rebuilt into a towboat named *BEN FRANKLIN NO. 2,* later *JAYHAWKER*. Her whistle, from *GREENLAND,* was destroyed in the fire.

1027 CHRIS GREENE

Stw p sh b. Charleston, W. Va., at the Ward plant (hull) and completed at Gardner Docks, Pt. Pleasant, W. Va., 1925. 189.2 x 42 x 6.2. Engines, 16's- 6 ft. from *TACOMA*. Four boilers. Built for the Greene Line under supervision of Capt. Jesse P. Hughes. Ran Cincinnati-Pomeroy-Charleston, Capt. Chris Greene, and later Capt. Volney E. White until 1934. Then ran Cincinnati-Louisville. Her staterooms were removed fall of 1936 to allow her to carry automobiles. She had bad luck with shafts, in all broke seven of them, and ran through herself about a dozen times. She was withdrawn from service in February 1947. Was sold to George Harrison of the Dayton Boat Harbor, Dayton, Ky., Oct. 22, 1950, and converted into a yacht harbor club boat. Most of her career she used the whistle from the *HOMER SMITH* (see).

1028 CINCINNATI

SW p wh b. Cincinnati, Oh., 1845. 250 (on deck) x 27 x 7. Engines, 26's- 9 ft. Four boilers, each 42" by 35 ft., two 16" flues. She was built at the Burton Hazen yard, and is credited with having the first texas deck on a Western steamboat. She came out new in the Pittsburgh-Cincinnati trade. After three months sold south, and ran Vicksburg-New Orleans. She was too narrow, rolled badly, and was broken up in 1849.

1029 CINCINNATI

SW p wh b. Freedom, Pa., at the Charles Graham Jr., & Co. yard, 1850. 220 (249 on deck) x 30 (floor 28) x 6. Overall width 58 ft. Engines, 24's- 7 ft. Four boilers, each 40" dia. by 28 ft. Wheels 32'8" dia., buckets 11'4". Had 52 rooms, 106 berths. Her stacks were the highest on any Pittsburgh-Cincinnati packet, 84.7 ft. from water to tops. Machinery by Robinson & Minis. Made a trial trip from Pittsburgh to Beaver, Pa., and return, Feb. 21, 1850. The boatyard folks shot off a cannon as she passed there. Came out in the Pittsburgh-Cincinnati trade, Capt. William J. Kountz, as an opposition boat to the regular P&C Line, on same schedule as *BUCKEYE STATE* (see). When the line packet *NEW ENGLAND NO. 2* sank at Haverhill, opposite Greenup, Ky., the *CINCINNATI* was "adopted" into the line on a regular day. Capt. John Birmingham later was master, also Capt. Hiram Kountz. Both this *CINCINNATI* and the former one (see) were very narrow and carried a "chain wagon" aft of the boilers on the main deck. This was rolled thwartship to compensate listing. She remained in the Pittsburgh trade into fall of 1855, having made occasional trips Louisville-St. Louis. Dismantled in 1856.

1030 CINCINNATI

SW p wh b. Cincinnati, Oh., 1851. 276 tons. Wandered afar, and was lost by stranding at Brazos, Tex., May 23, 1853.

1031 CINCINNATI

U.S. gunboat wh b. Mound City Ill., 1861 by James B. Eads. She was sunk in an engagement above Fort Pillow on May 10, 1862, in charge of Commander Stembel who got a minie ball through his mouth, and first-master Hoel took over. Stembel recovered. After the war she was moored near the mouth of Cache River below Mound City, Ill., and sank there in 1866.

1032 CINCINNATI

SW ferry wh b. Cincinnati, Oh., 1876. 120.4 x 40 x 5.2. Originally named *FAVORITE* (see) and name was changed in late 1883 or early 1884. She and her floats were carried away from Cincinnati on Jan. 30, 1892, and were wrecked at Fleming's Landing. She operated Cincinnati-Newport.

1033 CINCINNATI

SW p sh b. Midland, Pa., by Midland Barge Co. (hull) and completed at Cincinnati, 1924. 285 x 45.6 x 7.3. Compound non-condensing engines by Barnes, 22's, 40's- 9 ft. Double cabin, parlor rooms, baths, separate dining room, steam heat and all the trimmings. She was designed by marine architect Tom Dunbar as a single-cabin packet for the Cincinnati-Louisville trade. She was to have a partner, same size and design to be named *LOUISVILLE.* Both hulls were built by Midland Barge. Plans were changed. The to-be *LOUISVILLE* hull was sold to the Coney Island Co., Cincinnati, and completed by them to become the *ISLAND QUEEN.* The stateroom capacity for *CINCINNATI* was vastly enlarged by the building of a second passenger cabin, not unlike the scheme used on *UNITED STATES* and *AMERICA* described herein. The *CINCINNATI* was owned by John W. Hubbard, Pittsburgh, and operated by the Louisville & Cincinnati Packet Co. She made Cincinnati-New Orleans Mardi Gras trips without a break 1924–1930. Was in Pittsburgh on several occasions, brought the 31st annual convention of the Ohio Valley Improvement Association there in October 1925, and again appeared for the 1929 celebration of the completion of the Ohio River locks and dams. The principal business of the boat was regular summer operation in the Louisville-Cincinnati packet trade, teamed up with *QUEEN CITY,* sometimes *JOHN W. HUBBARD* or *KENTUCKY.* She came in collision with the mv. *BELFONT* between Carrollton and Madison on the night of May 24, 1928, and engineer Homer Johnston of the *CINCINNATI* was killed. The original cost of this boat was about $417,000, of which she made back about $200,000 in the first eight years of operation. She was said to have cleared $40,000 on her first Mardi Gras trip. Hard times came along, the L. & C. Line had financial troubles, and *CINCINNATI* was sold to Streckfus Steamers, Inc., St. Louis. They tore her down to the hull and built a superstructure for an excursion boat which they named *PRESIDENT* (see). She carried the whistle of the *BONANZA.* Her roof bell was cast from metal recovered from the bells of the *CITY OF*

LOUISVILLE and *CITY OF CINCINNATI*. Further details are available by consulting the December 1973 issue of *S&D Reflector* where an article tells more, and also presented are deck plans of the cabin arrangements, photographs of the interior, exterior, etc.

1034 CINCINNATI BELLE

SW ferry wh Originally named *BELLE OF CINCINNATI*, and name was changed Sept. 19, 1865. She ran Cincinnati-Newport until the ferry business there was overwhelmed with bridges and street car lines c. 1889–1890.

1035 CINCINNATUS

SW p wh b. Cincinnati, Oh., 1845. 182 x 36 x 8. Engines, 22's- 8 ft. Three boilers. She was first run by Capt. William Hamilton in the Cincinnati-New Orleans trade. Then was bought by Henry A. Jones who placed Capt. Richard M. Wade aboard as master, where he stayed until the *QUEEN OF THE WEST* (see) came out. She later ran Cincinnati-Memphis, owned by Clifford B. Wayne and Thompson Dean. Off the list in 1856. Her photo appears in the famed 1848 daguerreotype of Cincinnati.

1036 CINCINNATUS

SW ferry wh b. Fulton, Oh., 1853. 90 tons. Off the lists in 1857.

1037 CINDERELLA

Stw p wh b. Elizabethtown, Pa., 1847. 98 tons. In the summer of 1847 ran on the Allegheny River Freeport-Pittsburgh handling passengers and freight after the Freeport aqueduct of the Pennsylvania Canal burned, Capt. A.D. Reno. Usually ran Pittsburgh-Wheeling, Capt. George C. Calhoon. Capt. Adam Poe, Sr., relates that he ran her four months during low water in the Pittsburgh-Cincinnati trade and cleared $8,000. "I then sold my half interest in the boat, quit the river, tried farming, and found it to be an uphill business, so I built the *FINANCIER* (second)." Off the lists in 1852.

1038 CIRCASSIAN

SW p wh b. Elizabethtown, Pa., 1845. 178 tons. Ran Pittsburgh-Cincinnati, Capt. Bennett, also Pittsburgh-St. Louis, Capt. M.A. Cox. Burned at Maysville, Ky., Feb. 27, 1848.

1039 CIRCUS FLEET

SW p wh Originally *NORTH RIVER* (see) renamed c. 1852 when towing Spaulding & Rogers "Floating Palace." Off the lists in 1855.

1040 CITIZEN

SW p wh b. Brownsville, Pa., 1849. 170 tons. Snagged and lost below Little Rock, Ark., on the Arkansas River, December 1850.

1041 CITIZEN

Stw p wh b. Elizabeth, Pa., 1860. 233 tons. Capt. Richard Calhoon ran her Pittsburgh-Cincinnati, sometimes to Evansville. Capt. John Shouse sometimes commanded, and had her to Memphis one trip. Capt. Wash Kerr bought her for the Pittsburgh-Portsmouth trade 1863–1864. Sold to Capt. James Gallagher, Pittsburgh, in March 1864 and commenced towing barges south. In latter September 1865 the Panhandle railroad bridge at Steubenville was under construction with falsework in the river, and *CITIZEN* tried running the span, tore down chimneys, pilothouse and did other damage to herself. Left Pittsburgh Apr. 5, 1866, with two barges containing 2,000 brls. of crude oil for a St. Louis refinery shipped by W.P. Logan, Pittsburgh. Off the lists in 1867.

1042 CITY BELLE

SW p wh b. Murraysville, W. Va., 1854. 215 tons. First home port, Wheeling. She was in Galena-St. Paul trade 1856, Capt. Kennedy Lodwick, and same trade in charge of Capt. A.T. Champlin part of 1858. Apparently migrated to the Missouri River. A photograph of her exists taken with *CALYPSO* necessarily 1863–1865 at a Missouri River landing.

1043 CITY BELLE

SW p wh b. Paducah, Ky., 1855. 153 tons. 179 x 35 x 5. First home port, Memphis. She was in USQMC service 1861, and served as a hospital boat. Arrived at Memphis Jan. 24, 1864, with 500 sick and wounded soldiers from Vicksburg, Major C.R. Kemball in charge. In March 1864 made Louisville-Memphis trips in charge of Capt. Tally, and one of his clerks was Will S. Hays, the noted songwriter and Louisville river reporter. She was assigned to Porter on the Red River expedition and a dispatch from Louisville dated May 22, 1864 says: "We learn from a gentleman just returned from New Orleans that the *CITY BELLE* was destroyed on Red River near Snaggy Point. Capt. Tally was thrown into the river by the force of the explosion of the boilers occasioned by the bursting of a shell from Rebel guns. Capt. Tally got ashore and was seen going up the bank. Nearly all the hands on the boat were killed as well as a number of soldiers. The boat was drawn to shore and burned by the Rebels." This happened May 4, 1864, while the boat was en route to Alexandria with an Ohio regiment about 40 miles above Fort Derussy.

1044 CITY OF ALMA

Prop p ih b. Philadelphia, Pa., at Cramp's yard, 1882. 110 x 20 x 4. Twin props, single deck. Built for the La Crosse-Alma, Wis., trade. She was brought around the coast and up the Mississippi River. After safe arrival a second, or cabin, deck was added. She was too deep draft for the venture. In winter 1883–1884 she was started south with three scows of produce loaded at Alma, and ice stopped her at St. Louis, where ice sank her, raised. Later the props were removed and she was converted to sternwheel and towed lumber barges at Cairo and elsewhere. Listed 1892 in *LMV* as sternwheel.

1045 CITY OF ALTON

SW p wh b. Madison, Ind., 1860. 283 x 40 x 7. Engines, 36's- 9 ft. Ran St. Louis-Alton, Capt. Mitchell. One of the first acts of derring-do in the Civil War was when 10,000 muskets were removed from the St. Louis Arsenal under cover of night and taken to Alton aboard this boat, this in April 1861 while sympathy for the South was running high in St. Louis. She was with Grant's fleet during the Tennessee campaign, and was running St. Louis-Memphis after the war.

1046 CITY OF ALTON

SW p wh b. St. Louis, Mo., 1868. 283 x 50 x 9. Engines, 30's- 9 ft. from *BALTIMORE.* Five boilers. This was a rebuilding job, using upper works of earlier *CITY OF ALTON.* She was sold in January 1871 to Capt. E.A. Sheble and others, St. Louis, for the St. Louis-New Orleans trade. She was again enlarged at St. Louis in 1873. Owners in 1874 were Capt. Horace E. Bixby ¼, E.A. Sheble ⅜, E.A. Sheble Jr. ¼, and W. Mason ⅛. Later was entered into the Anchor Line, Bixby, master, and P.W. Sheckley, clerk. Burned at the foot of Dorcas Street, St. Louis, Jan. 2, 1884, along with the side-wheel *COLORADO* (see).

1047 CITY OF ASHLAND

Recesswheel ferry wh b. Harmar, Oh. 1896 as the *NINA PADEN* (see), renamed when sold to the Ashland & Ironton Transfer & Ferry Co., Ashland, Ky. Ferried many years at Ashland and when the bridge was built there she was sold to Fullerton-Portsmouth Ferry Co., which renamed her *CAPTAIN JOHN* (see).

1048 CITY OF AUGUSTA

SWp wh Was in the New Orleans-White River trade 1878. Capt. Milt Harry ran her. In 1880 running New Orleans-Red River, Capt. W.C. Harrison, master, with J.E. Brous, clerk.

1049 CITY OF BATON ROUGE

SW p wh b. Jeffersonville, Ind., by Howard, 1881. 294 x 49 x 9'5". Engines, 26's- 10 ft. Five boilers, 44" by 30 ft., four flues. When new and on delivery trip, she stuck on rocks at the Louisville Falls and remained three weeks. Owned by the Anchor Line and ran St. Louis-New Orleans, long by Capt. Horace E. Bixby. His head clerk in 1890 was John W. Langlois. She sank and was lost at Hermitage, La., at 3:00 P.M. on Dec. 12, 1890, with loss of two deck passengers. This was at same location where the *PARIS C. BROWN* had been lost in 1889 (see).

1050 CITY OF BATON ROUGE

Stw ferry sh b. Jeffersonville, Ind., by Howard, 1916. 115.2 x 28 x 7.2. Engines, 12's- 5 ft. One boiler. Owned by Baton Rouge Transportation Co., and was used there. She had capacity for 500 persons and 21 cars. In 1971 these engines, built by Gillett & Eaton, Lake City, Minn., were placed on the *JULIA BELLE SWAIN* (see) and the ferry was converted into a landing boat for the *SWAIN's* operations at Peoria, Ill.

1051 CITY OF BAYOU SARA

SW p wh b. Jeffersonville, Ind., by Howard, 1884. 300 x 48 x 9'10". Engines, 26's- 10 ft. Five boilers. Wheels 36' dia., with 15 ft. buckets. Capt. Isaac Baker, master; John E. Massengale, purser (father of Capt. Rhea M.); Collin (Col) Baker, 2nd clerk; George Murray and Theodore Hall, pilots; Tobe Royal, mate. Purser Massengale later became president of the St. Louis & Tennessee River Packet Co. Burned at New Madrid, Mo., Dec. 5, 1885, with loss of eight lives.

1052 CITY OF BRUNSWICK

Stw ferry wh b. Brunswick, Mo., 1890. 88 x 20 x 4. 77 tons. Ferried at Brunswick. Sold south and ran Alexandria-Jonesville for a time operated by a Capt. Ward. She was pulled out on the ways at Baton Rouge and not repaired; was let back in the river and went to pieces on shore nearby. Machinery went to a boat being built on Bayou Teche. Capt. Orrie D. Stalions recalled most of above.

1053 CITY OF BURNSIDE

Stw p wh b. Burnside, Ky., 1916. 145.5 x 24.1 x 4.4. Owned by Bunside & Burksville Transportation Co., and later by Cumberland Transportation Co. Operated on Cumberland River out of Burnside. Dismantled at Burnside about 1930.

1054 CITY OF CAIRO

Stw p wh b. Dyersburg, Ky., 1856. 199 tons. Ran New Orleans-Ouachita River to Camden in 1856, Capt. I.D. Yocum, master, advertising "she draws only 18 inches light." Also ran Vicksburg-Yazoo River. Snagged and lost at Grand Chain, Ill., on the Wabash River, Apr. 12, 1858.

1055 CITY OF CAIRO

SW p wh b. Metropolis, Ill., at Alf Cutting yard, 1864. Completed at St. Louis. 272 (on deck) x 41 (39 ft. floor). Engines, 28's- 8 ft. Five boilers. Paddlewheels 32 ft. dia., with 14 ft. buckets. Ran St. Louis-Memphis, Capt. Robert K. Riley, owned by Memphis Packet Co. Walter E. Dill, clerk.

"Her captain is Bob Riley
And her clerk is Walter Dill
Who do their best to please you
—And do it with a will!"

Capt. Bob Riley was 34 in 1864, native of Bridgeport (Monongahela), Pa., born there Oct. 11, 1830. He started as mud clerk on the Ohio and was first clerk on *NEW LUCY* on the Missouri. During the war he was on the gunboat *LOUISVILLE.* Then commanded *SKYLARK* and *PLATTE VALLEY* in St. Louis-Memphis run. Went from there to the *CITY OF CAIRO.* Later was on both boats named *CITY OF VICKSBURG.* He died, 53, in New York City August 1883 leaving a wife and four daughters. Capt. Charles S. Schultz bought *CITY OF CAIRO* in October 1871 and ran her St. Louis-New Orleans, and also to Louisville. In April 1873 the boat was attached by creditors at New

Orleans and was sold at U.S. marshal sale on June 23, 1873 to W. Fagan for $2,100. Burned July 7, 1873 at New Orleans.

1056 CITY OF CAIRO

SW p wh b. Jeffersonville, Ind., by Howard, 1882. 271 x 44 (41 ft. floor) x 8.5. Engines 26's- 9 ft. Five boilers. Paddlewheels 34 ft. dia. with 15 ft. buckets. Hegewald & Co. built the engines. Owned by the Anchor Line, which usually ran her St. Louis-Vicksburg. Captain A.S. Lightner, master. Had the roof bell from *EMMA C. ELLIOTT*, awarded by the line to the boat making the fastest run. She gave it up to the *CITY OF MONROE* shortly before she was wrecked in a severe tornado at St. Louis, May 27, 1896.

1057 CITY OF CAIRO

Stw ferry wh b. Jeffersonville, Ind., by Howard, 1912. 117 x 27.4 x 3.4. Engines, 10''- 42''. One boiler, 66'' by 9 ft. Served at Cairo, Ill., and also at Paducah. Sold in 1929 to the Mississippi River Ferry Co., Vicksburg, Miss., and renamed *VICKSBURG* (see).

1058 CITY OF CAIRO

SW ex wh Long was the snagboat *DAVID TIPTON* b. 1900, see; then was *URSIE BOYCE* (also see). About 1923 John F. Klein made an excursion boat of her, capacity 800, and renamed her *CITY OF CAIRO*. She operated at Cairo one season, then went to St. Louis where Andrew J. Franz chartered her for a tramping trip up Missouri River. She got up to Jefferson City and was one of the few sidewheel excursion boats ever on the Missouri. The crew on the trip: Capt. Oakley Doolan, master; Capt. Gerald H. Friemonth, pilot; Everett Hicks, chief; and Dave Mangum, purser. That winter she was laid up in Alton Slough and sank. F.X. Ralphe, Hastings, Minn., took her to Mound City for repairs where she again sank and was lost.

1059 CITY OF CAMDEN

Stw p wh b. Jeffersonville, Ind., by Howard, 1893. 175 x 35 x 5. Engines 14's- 6 ft. Three boilers, each 40'' by 20', six flues. Ran New Orleans-Camden, on Ouachita River, Capt. L.V. Cooley, master, with M.E. Fahy, clerk. Also made trips up Red River. Capt. Cooley sold her in November 1904 to Capt. Frank Lumsden, Mobile, Ala. She got in a hurricane at Mobile and was blown out on mud flats and dismantled in 1910.

1060 CITY OF CHARLESTON

Stw ferry wh b. Cincinnati, Oh., 1875. 85 x 25 x 3.7. Ferried between Charleston and South Side until replaced by *CHARLESTON* (see).

1061 CITY OF CHARLESTON

Stw p wh b. Charleston, Tenn., 1900. 107.9 x 23.3 x 3. When new she ran Chattanooga-Kingston trade on Tennessee River, Capt. Ben H. Ferguson. Also operated up Hiwasee River where Charleston, Tenn., is located. The *OCOEE NO. 2* (see) was regularly in the Hiwasee. Was still going in 1908, maybe longer.

1062 CITY OF CHARLESTON

SW p wh Originally *I. C. WOODWARD*, then *VIRGINIA* (both see). Was renamed *CITY OF CHARLESTON* c. 1919 when she was briefly operated on the Kanawha as an excursion boat. Came to Pittsburgh in June 1920 with idea of operating up Monongahela River but could not pass under the Port Perry bridge. During the railroad strike at that time Jones & Laughlin Steel Co., chartered her to haul pipe, etc., from their Aliquippa Works to the Pittsburgh wharf. Capt. Silas A. Condict was the gentleman who brought her to Pittsburgh. Returned to Gallipolis and burned there, May 8, 1921.

1063 CITY OF CHARTIERS

Stw p wh b. Pittsburgh, Pa., 1886. 120.7 x 20.1 x 2.9. Ran between Pittsburgh and McKees Rocks, a trip an hour, 6:00 A.M. to 7:00 P.M. daily. Capt. Willis Stockdale was master in the early days, Jim Rowley, Jr., pilot, and John Lankard, engineer. Ran opposition to the regulars, *VENUS* and *VENICE* (both see). She was owned by Capt. J.T. Stockdale, who soon died, whereupon Capt. James A. Henderson acquired interest and placed Capt. John Ritchey in command. Sold April 1889 to Capt. Inglebright, Martins Ferry, Oh., who planned running her in Wheeling-Martins Ferry trade. Last owned by Evansville Contracting Co., Evansville, Ind., and burned May 12, 1895, at Ironton, Oh.

1064 CITY OF CHATTANOOGA

Stw p wh b. Chattanooga, Tenn., 1892. 144 x 30. Parts from towboat *HERBERT* b. 1883 used in construction. Ran Chattanooga-St. Louis, a long and ambitious trade and one not so profitable. There were many delays and troubles in the vicinity of Muscle Shoals. Capt. J.P. Kindrick was master, with J.B. Allison, pilot. In January 1895 was released from Tuscumbia Bar where she had been high and dry four months, at one time 300 feet from the river. Finally sold to Paducah and converted to towing, renamed *WOOLFOLK*.

1065 CITY OF CHESTER

SW p wh b. Louisville, Ky., 1870. 789.33 tons. 241 x 38 x 7. Belonged to the Memphis & St. Louis Packet Co., Capt. Alex Zeigler. On Mar. 7, 1878 at 2:30 A.M. she was at the elevator at Memphis when she took fire and burned, a complete loss, with two killed. There was an explosion about 4:00 A.M. jarring the whole city of Memphis.

1066 CITY OF CINCINNATI

SW p wh b. Jeffersonville, Ind., by Howard, 1899. 300 x 38 x 6. Engines, 26's- 10 ft. from Anchor Line's *CITY OF HICKMAN* (see). Six boilers, each 44" by 28 ft. Owned by Louisville & Cincinnati Packet Co., and teamed up with *CITY OF LOUISVILLE* (see) in that trade. Capt. Jack Lindenburn (d. 1936) long was master. William C. Lepper, Sr., came out on her as purser. Baylor Spratt was chief engineer on her for ten years. This was a well proportioned sidewheeler. She came out carrying the whistle from the last

TELEGRAPH (see) but it sounded so much like the *TELL CITY* (see) it was exchanged and after 1907 she had the old *BONANZA* whistle which last did service on the double-cabin *CINCINNATI.* Lost in ice at Cincinnati in January 1918.

1067 City of Clarksville

Stw p wh b. Paducah, Ky., 1886. 125 x 24.5 x 3.5. Originally owned at Clarksville, Tenn., on Cumberland River and ran Nashville-Paducah for about five years. In 1892 was on Kentucky River and sank May 1 that year, raised. Capt. S. J. Preston was master at the time. Ran Evansville-Bowling Green in 1894, Capt. A.J. Wolverton. Ran tri-weekly Paducah-Golconda in fall 1897. Sold to Capt. H.M. Williams, taken to the Ouachita River, rebuilt, and came out as *STELLA* (see) in 1900.

1068 City of Clifton

Stw p wh b. Jeffersonville, Ind., by Howard, 1900. 190 x 36 x 5. Engines, 16's- 7 ft. Three boilers. She was built for the Lee Line of Memphis, christened *ROWENA LEE,* but was bought by the St. Louis & Tennessee River Packet Co., before she left the builders. They renamed her *CITY OF CLIFTON.* Capt. R.W. McCoy, master. Sank at Seventy-Six Landing, a short distance above Grand Tower, Ill., in August 1901, raised. Burned at Clifton, Tenn. in February 1903.

1069 City of Evansville

SW p wh b. Elizabeth, Pa., at Latta yard, 1870. 225 x 35 (33 floor) x 5.5. Hartupee compound engines, 15's-33's- 6 ft. Three boilers, each 38″ by 26 ft., 2 flues. Paddlewheels 26 ft. dia., 12 ft. buckets. Capt. Henry T. Dexter superintended construction and R.E. Rodgers fitted up the machinery. Artist Emil Bott painted scenes in the cabin, one of the Evansville wharf, another of a steamboat race. The staterooms in the ladies' cabin were named for towns in the Evansville-Cairo area instead of being numbered. Came out in Evansville-Cairo trade in charge of Captain Dexter, with first clerk N.S. Pennington. Burned at Evansville on Nov. 21, 1870, in a blaze which also took the *NORMAN, PINE BLUFF,* and the Evansville wharfboat, with great loss of cargo. In 1876 her wheel shafts were taken to Metropolis and placed on *COAHOMA* (see).

1070 City of Florence

Stw p wh b. Jeffersonville, Ind., by Howard, 1882. 160 x 32 x 5.3. Originally named *SAM J. KEITH* (see) and renamed following a rebuilding at Howards in 1886. Owned by St. Louis & Tennessee River Packet Co. Burned at the foot of Meramec Street, St. Louis, just overhauled, in June 1893.

1071 City of Florence

Stw p wh b. Jeffersonville, Ind., by Howard, 1909. 130 x 26 x 3. Owned by St. Louis & Tennessee River Packet Co. She came in collision with towboat *TOMAHAWK* on the morning of Feb. 11, 1913, at Coffee Landing, Tennessee River, drifted about four miles down, sank and was lost. Several lives were lost. Scuba divers led by Dave Wilson, Jackson, Tenn., in 1976 found many relics.

1072 City of Frankfort

Stw p wh b. Madison, Ind., 1881. Operated on the Kentucky River to Madison and Louisville. Owned in part and commanded by Capt. Henry O. Brashear (1833–1924), native of Madison, Ind., and cousin of Dr. John Brashear, the eminent Pittsburgh astronomer. In 1884 she was sold to the Louisville & Cincinnati Packet Co., lengthened, and renamed *CITY OF VEVAY* (see).

1073 City of Golconda

Stw p wh b. Golconda, Ill., 1899. 102 x 17 x 3.5. Ran Paducah-Elizabethtown. She was not regarded as safe because of the narrow hull. Got in a windstorm at Cottonwood Bar above Paducah on Aug. 19, 1901, capsized, and renamed *JEWEL* (see).

1074 City of Greenville

SW p wh b. Jeffersonville, Ind., by Howard, 1879. 285 x 45 x 9. Engines, 26's- 10 ft. Five boilers, Paddlewheels 34 ft. dia., with 15 ft. buckets. Owned by Memphis & St. Louis Packet Co. Pilot Ben Berry took her away from the Howard Yard new, ran her aground, and she lay stranded seven months, had to be shored up, etc., until a rise came. No blame was attached to Berry. Capt. Jos. W. Bryant was long her master. Collided with the *LAURA LEE* at Bayou Goula, La., on Jan. 12, 1882, and was sunk and lost.

1075 City of Greenwood

Stw p wh b. Jeffersonville, Ind., by Howard, 1899. 130 x 28 x 3.5. Engines, 12's- 5 ft. Two boilers, each 38″ by 22 ft. Built for Capt. Gid Montjoy and others, and ran from Vicksburg up Yazoo River to Greenwood, Miss. Her crew in 1901: Capt. W.D. Pugh, master; John Young and Bob Portwood, pilots; John Jenkins and Lawrence Miller, engineers; James Thompson and Tom Briley, clerks; Jim Dye and Jim Lusk, mates. Didn't last long.

1076 City of Hartford

In 1904, in New Orleans and Bayou Lafourche trade via Harvey's Canal. Leaving the Canal every Tuesday at 11:00 A.M. Capt. H.A. Harvey, master.

1077 City of Havana

Stw p wh b. Havana, Ill., 1884. 76.5 x 12.1 x 2.9. Sold to Illinois Fish Commission c. 1895 and renamed *LOTUS.* Eventually became a small pleasure steamboat in the Louisville area, and was there 1903 but removed from the lists 1905.

1078 City of Helena

SW p wh b. Jeffersonville, Ind., by Howard, 1871. 268 x 42 x 7.5. Engines, 26's- 8 ft. Paddlewheels, 38 ft. dia., by 14½ ft. buckets. Belonged to the Anchor Line, Capt. John McCord was master. Burned Feb. 18, 1885, at the Memphis wharf at 4:00 P.M. in a fire which also destroyed the Arkansas River packet *IDA DARRAGH* (see).

1079 CITY OF HICKMAN

SW p wh b. Jeffersonville, Ind., by Howard, 1890. 285 x 44.5 x 9.5. Engines, 26's- 10 ft. Five boilers. Paddlewheels 34 ft. dia. Capt. R.W. McCoy, master. Sank and was lost in the chute of Island 40, 12 miles above Memphis, Aug. 23, 1896. Had 40 passengers and 1,500 tons of freight at the time. Machinery was salvaged and went on the *CITY OF CINCINNATI* (see).

1080 CITY OF HUDSON

Stw p wh b. Stillwater, Minn., 1899. 61.6 x 12.7 x 2.9. Named for Hudson, Wis., on the St. Croix River. Ran La Crosse-Brownsville, Minn. in charge of Capt. George Winslow. Hull was lengthened 1901 to 71.6 ft. Ran excursions up Minnesota River from St. Paul for the Minnesota River Packet Co. Burned at Brownsville, Minn., Aug. 29, 1906.

1081 CITY OF HUNTINGTON

Stw ferry wh b. Middleport, Oh., 1900. 84.3 x 26.8 x 3.6. Engines, 10"- 3½ ft. One boiler, 40" by 16 ft. Operated by Ben Flesher between Huntington and Chesapeake, Oh. She was replaced in 1918 by the ferry in the next listing., and was sold to the Manchester (Ohio) Ferry Co. Burned at Manchester in July, 1926.

1082 CITY OF HUNTINGTON

Stw ferry wh Originally *NEW PIKE* b. 1887 (see) brought to Huntington in November 1918 by Capt. Ben T. Flesher and renamed. When the bridge was built at Huntington the ferry continued to run. Ben Flesher died, and his son-in-law Robert Hamilton continued operations. To economize he bought the *CHARLES HENRY STONE* (see) and ran her until 1935.

1083 CITY OF HUNTSVILLE

SW p wh b. Elizabeth, Pa., 1852. 238 tons. Was running Nashville-Memphis summer 1856 with *JOHN G. CLINE, JOHN SIMPSON,* and *EMBASSY.* Was snagged and lost at Palmyra Island, Mississippi River, May 12, 1858, with loss of eight lives.

1084 CITY OF IDAHO

Stw p wh b. Memphis, Tenn., 1898. 88 x 21.7 x 3.5. Engines, 8"- 3½ ft. One boiler, 46" by 16 ft. A short trader out of Memphis to Fulton, Ark., and to Peters Landing. In 1903 she was on White River in Newport-Clarendon trade. In 1904 running out of Evansville owned by Capt. Frank L. Kennedy. In May 1907 in New Orleans-Bayou Lafourche trade along with *ARCHON.*

1085 CITY OF IRONTON

SW p wh b. Ironton, Oh., 1879. Engines, 16's- 5 ft. from towboat *KANAWHA.* Owned by the Bay Line and ran Portsmouth-Huntington. Had no texas and was quite speedy. The Bays sold her to Capts. Frank Morgan and Watt Shedd who ran her Cincinnati-Maysville competing with the *MORNING MAIL.* Then ran Cincinnati-Vanceburg, Capt. Sam Bryant. In June 1882 sold to Vicksburg & Greenville Packet Co., who remodeled her and added a texas at Cincinnati, renamed her *ISSAQUENA* (see).

1086 CITY OF JEFFERSONVILLE

SW ferry wh b. Jeffersonville, Ind., by Howard, 1891. 150 x 34 x 6.3. Engines, 20½'s- 6 ft. from *Z. M. SHERLEY* (see). Two boilers, each 44" by 26 ft. Owned by Louisville & Jeffersonville Ferry Co. Crew in 1901, Capt. Nick Durand, with George Stuart and Matt Dugan, engineers. Off the lists about 1914.

1087 CITY OF KEITHSBURG

Stw p wh b. Port Byron, Ill., 1864. She was built by the Kahlke brothers and John Theissen designed for the Fort Madison-Rock Island trade. Owned by B.H. Campbell, Galena, and B.W. Davis, Rock Island. Davis was master. Her partner boat was *NEW BOSTON* (see). The Northern Line bought both boats at the close of the 1864 season and kept them in the same trade. Snagged and lost above St. Louis, Nov. 25, 1872.

1088 CITY OF KNOXVILLE

Stw p wh b. California, Pa., 1854. 122 x 22 x 3. Built for the East Tennessee & Georgia Rail Boat Co., first master, Capt. Joseph Jaques. Later sold to New Orleans where Capt. W.D. Terrebonne was master, owned by Jean Webre, Ogene Dugas, and A. Dugas. Off the list in 1858.

1089 CITY OF KNOXVILLE

Stw p wh b. Kingston, Tenn., 1875. 140 x 25 x 4. Built under supervision of Capt. George Nicholason and his brothers. Ran Kingston-Knoxville, a profitable venture during the construction of the Cincinnati Southern RR. Later sold to Capt. Tom Fritts, Chattanooga, who ran her a while, then sold her to the Kindrick interests. Dismantled in 1883. The machinery went to the *J. C. WARNER.*

1090 CITY OF KNOXVILLE

Stw p wh b. Knoxville, Tenn., 1896. 130 x 18 x 3. Built by Capt. O.H. Love, Louisville, Tenn., for the Knoxville-Chattanooga trade. Not successful there. In September 1901, was running Paducah-E-Town and Golconda, Capt. Theo Clark, master, with G. Bauer, clerk.

1091 CITY OF LITTLE ROCK

Stw p wh b. Jeffersonville, Ind., at Howard yard, 1893. 145 x 29 x 5. Engines, 14's- 5½ ft. Two boilers. Ran on the Arkansas River Sold in 1897 to the Kouns family and they ran her New Orleans-Red River, Capt. Curt S. Kouns, master. She is said to have been lost by sinking at Moulrie Landing above Hurricane Bluff, La., on Red River.

1092 CITY OF LOUDON

Stw p wh b. Kingston, Tenn., 1902. 75 x 12 x 2. Ran U.S. Mail, Loudon- Kingston.

1093 CITY OF LOUISIANA

SW p wh b. Madison, Ind., and completed at St. Louis, 1857. 250 x 40. Owned by Keokuk Packet Co., and ran St. Louis-Keokuk. Chartered to U.S. in March 1862 and remodeled into a hospital ship by the Sanitary Commission. All of her staterooms were removed, turning the boiler deck into a large wardroom. She was on the scene at Island 10 and Pittsburg Landing. After the Battle of Shiloh she took 3,389 wounded to northern hospitals. Bought by the U.S. in spring of 1863 and renamed *R. C. WOOD* for the assistant surgeon-general of the U.S. Army who pioneered the Sanitary Commission.

1094 CITY OF LOUISIANA

Ferry wh b. Metropolis, Ill., 1869. 136.47 tons. Probably ferried at Louisiana, Mo. Was still documented 1876.

1095 CITY OF LOUISVILLE

SW p wh b. Jeffersonville, Ind., by Howard, 1894. 301 x 42.7 x 7. Engines, 30's- 10 ft. by Frisbie Engine & Machine Co., Cincinnati. Eight boilers, each 42" by 26 ft. Later on she had but seven boilers. Owned by the Louisville & Cincinnati Packet Co., and built expressly for the Louisville-Cincinnati trade. Had 72 staterooms and slept 160. Carried an excursion permit for 1,500. She had a side launching at Howards and ran her trial trip on Apr. 2, 1894, and left Cincinnati next day on her inaugural trip. On Wednesday, Apr. 18, 1894, she departed Louisville at 3:00 P.M. and made the record run to Cincinnati, never since equaled.

Time To	h.	m.
Utica		35
Charlestown		57
Westport	1	40
Bethlehem	2	4
Hanover	3	0
Madison	3	16
Carrollton	4	12
Vevay	4	48
Warsaw	5	30
Patriot	6	7
Rising Sun	7	4
Aurora	7	45
Lawrenceburg	8	2
Taylorsport	8	56
Cincinnati at Main Street.	9	42

Crew on this occasion: Capt. John Brennan, master; Charles C. Langhart, purser; George Bumgardner and William C. Lepper, Jr., clerks; Charles J. Dufour and C. Henry Thomas, pilots; Andy Hazlett, mate; William Turner, second mate; Henry R. McClannahan, chief engineer; George Kinney, 2nd engineer; Levi McCain and Charles Baglin, strikers; Henry Culver, carpenter; Charles Clark, watchman; George L. Wick, steward. Cincinnati gauge was 22′10″. Two years later on Apr. 5, 1896, she made the record downstream run in this trade, 5 hours 58 minutes. She departed Cincinnati at 7:13 A.M. and was landed in Louisville at 1:10 P.M. She then left Louisville at 2:15 P.M. and was back at Cincinnati at 11:55 P.M., a round trip in one day. This boat had but three captains in her career, Capt. John Brennan, then Capt. James Martin (who was on her for 20 years) and Capt. Clarence McElfresh. Her purser, Charles C. Langhart, stayed with the boat until stricken with apoplexy in June 1915 when he was taken ashore at Louisville and died several days later. Chief engineer Henry McClannahan lived most of his life on her. The big roof bell came from a set of chimes at the Chicago Fair of 1893 and was adorned with a massive set of antlers. For many years a sign was carried on the pilothouse sides exhibiting the numbers 9-42 which, as everyone knew, was her upstream record time. James Hafer, Jr., Newport, Ky., made a cannon which was carried on the main deck and fired on special occasions; it later was on the *GORDON C. GREENE* and today is in the River Museum, Marietta, Oh. She made one Mardi Gras trip, February 1903, and went down from Cincinnati to New Orleans in 4 days 9 hours, including all stops. Her whistle was inherited from the *FLEETWOOD* (see), a deep, hoarse, three-toned one, later used on the side-wheel *AMERICA* (see). The *CITY OF LOUISVILLE* was as fabled on the Ohio as the *ROBT. E. LEE* was on the Mississippi. Her great size and tremendous power called for the supreme pilots of her day and, as Capt. Ed Maurer once said, "When you had her hard down rattling down around Sugar Creek Bend, she was a lot of lumber." She left Louisville on May 16, 1917, on her last trip to Cincinnati. The next day she was laid up across the river at Covington, and remained there until early 1918 when she was returned to Cincinnati because of heavy ice. Ed Maurer and Wymond Brasher were her last pilots, and Henry McClannahan was at the throttle. The ice got her on Jan. 30, 1918, after a valiant fight; she had steam up and her wheels were working ahead when she went down—drafted back and settled at the doorway of the L&C wharfboat. Dismantled later that spring. Three of her boilers went to the towboat *H. B. HULINGS* and the other four went to the *J. T. HATFIELD*. The roof bell was placed on the *ISLAND QUEEN* (first).

1096 CITY OF LYONS

Steam ferry wh b. Lyons, Iowa, 1864. 142.76 tons. Still listed 1867.

1097 CITY OF MADISON

SW p wh b. Madison, Ind., 1860. 419 tons. Ran Cincinnati-New Orleans, Capt. J. Stut Neal as master, W.W. Collins, clerk. She was on the Tennessee in Grant's campaign, and was at Vicksburg during the seige. W.C. Lepper, Sr., was on her at Vicksburg. A cargo of gunpowder exploded aboard at Vicksburg on Aug. 18, 1863. W.W. Collins was captain at the time, and dove off the roof to safety. The life loss is reported officially as 156 persons, although contemporary accounts give much less, one stating 63. J. Stut Neal went to Washington, D.C., with his case and was awarded

$45,000 in March 1864. The *S&D Reflector,* issue of December 1964 contains an account of this explosion, etc., on page 14.

1098 CITY OF MADISON

SW p wh b. Madison, Ind., 1882. 265 x 42.1 x 6.3. Engines, 24½'s- 7 ft. Four boilers, each 42" by 28 ft. Paddlewheels 28 ft. dia., with 14 ft. buckets. Owned by the U.S. Mail Line Co. Dan H. Morton and D.C. Robinson were running the Madison yard at the time. The engines came from the shop of Stribling & Walsh, Madison. Boilers built at Portsmouth, Oh. Ran Cincinnati-Madison, and replaced the *UNITED STATES* in the L&C trade, 1884. Her ending was singular; she was returning from Memphis with a special club of bicyclists on board, headed straight through to Cincinnati. Pilot watches were changed just below the shipyard at Madison and a few moments later, at 4:15 A.M., June 18, 1894, she hit the dike and was wrecked. The pilot on watch, Wheeler Collier, was a Madison resident. All of which bears out a pilot's tradition that the spot most dangerous for a pilot is right in front of his own home town. Nobody was hurt, and the cyclists were forwarded on the next boat. The snagboat *E. A. WOODRUFF* removed the wreck. The dike she hit was a large one, jutting out from the Kentucky shore almost to mid-river, and perhaps a quarter-mile long.

1099 CITY OF MAYSVILLE

Rig? In 1873 this steamer, perhaps the ferry at Maysville, was attached by the U.S. Marshal for debt. Capt. William Cummins owned her and said if she could be released he knew fairer fields in the south where he could recoup. Capt. Logan Cook, Maysville, undertook to make the move. He got the engineer drunk, stole the boat, and was overtaken by the law at Louisville, Ky.

1100 CITY OF MCGREGOR

Recess wheel ferry wh b. Pittsburgh, Pa., 1867. 100 x 36 x 3.6. Engines, 8"- 30" stroke. One boiler, 40" by 24 ft. Rebuilt in 1898. Operated at McGregor, Iowa, owned in latter days by G.W. Hendricks. Burned at Cairo, Ill., in January 1911.

1101 CITY OF MEMPHIS

SW p wh b. Monongahela, Pa., 1857. 301 x 36 x 8. Engines, 32½'s- 8 ft. Six boilers, each 46" by 30 ft. The cabins, etc., were largely from the *CRYSTAL PALACE* (see), dismantled at the time. George Cunningham built the hull. Owned by Capt. William J. Kountz and entered the St. Louis-New Orleans trade with James Kerr, Jr., in the office. A daily newspaper was published aboard, *The Reporter,* edited by Kerr. Capt. J. Ed Montgomery was master in 1860. The day Sumter was fired on she was leaving New Orleans, and paid off the crew at Cairo. Laid up at Mound City, Ill. Converted into a hospital boat in April 1862. Took sick and wounded from Fort Donelson to St. Louis, made three trips to Keokuk with wounded, total of 928 soldiers; brought 350 from Tennessee River to Cincinnati early May 1862. Sold to Capt. John Bofinger and others at St. Louis in November 1862 and ran St. Louis-New Orleans. In spring of 1864 had been renamed *CONSTITUTION,* spring of 1864 and made several trips with that name. The change was disallowed by U.S. Customs and she got back her old name. Exploded boilers 30 miles below Memphis on May 31, 1866, with loss of eleven lives. The wreck was towed to St. Louis and torn up. It is said that her original engines were removed, probably after the sale to Capt. Bofinger, and she was given those formerly on *MOLLIE ABLE,* smaller.

1102 CITY OF MEMPHIS

Stw p wh b. Jeffersonville, Ind., by Howard, 1898. 200 x 36 x 6. Engines, 16's- 7 ft. Three boilers, each 44" by 24 ft. Owned by St. Louis & Tennessee River Packet Co. She was placed in St. Louis-Memphis trade in opposition to the Lee Line which had the *GEORGIA LEE* in the same run. A compromise was reached and she was taken to the Tennessee River trade where she remained until 1910. Bought by Capt. Tom Morrissey, Vicksburg, and was renamed *S. B. DUNCAN* (see).

1103 CITY OF MEMPHIS

SW ex wh Originally *VERNE SWAIN* b. 1913 (see), then *ROOSEVELT.* Owned in 1932 by the Rose Island Co., Louisville. Sank below the locks at the Louisville Canal Aug. 17, 1932. Had aboard 781 passengers, Capt. Nick DuRand in charge. Everybody was safely landed. The boat was torn up.

1104 CITY OF METROPOLIS

Prop p wh b. Metropolis, Ill., 1888. 70 x 13 x 3.5. Burned at Quincy, Ill., July, 1901.

1105 CITY OF MOBILE

Stw p wh b. Mobile, Ala., 1898. 176 x 34 x 4.2. Engines, 13's- 5½ ft. Two boilers, each 44" by 26 ft. Operated in the Peoples Line, Capt. G.W. Quaries. Wrecked in a hurricane at Mobile, July 1916, and was dismantled.

1106 CITY OF MONROE

SW p wh b. Jeffersonville, Ind., by Howard, 1887. 275 x 45 x 8. Engines, 26's- 9 ft. Five boilers. Paddlewheels 33 ft. dia. Belonged to the Anchor Line. Capt. Ben Howard came out master. George Foulks and John Lowrie were engineers, and Jimmy Manning and Ike Betts were strikers. Badly damaged in a tornado at St. Louis, May 27, 1896. Rebuilt, lengthened and came out as *HILL CITY* (see).

1107 CITY OF MUSKOGEE

Stw p wh b. Jeffersonville, Ind., by Howard, 1908. 127.6 x 28.5 x 4.7. Engines 10's- 4 ft. Two boilers, each 38" by 20 ft. Built for merchants of Muskogee, Okla. On first trip went up the Arkansas "on a grand tour with freight and tourists aboard." The Muskogee persons who built her included C.N. Haskell, who became governor of Oklahoma. Ran between Webbers Falls, Okla. (the river landing for Muskogee), and Fort Smith, Ark. Low water and lack of freight defeated the project. She lay near Muskogee several years, then was bought by Inman Packet Co., which ran her

Newport, Ark., to Black Rock, Ark., on White and Black rivers. Later ran Newport-Colver Bend, to the F.W. Tucker plantation 25 miles below Black Rock. Then ran Crocketts Bluff to Rosedale, Miss., handling rice for reshipment on Yazoo & Miss. Valley RR. Inman ran her into 1918 when she was sold to New Orleans, and renamed *LORAINE K* in 1922 (see).

1108 City of Nashville

Stw p wh b. Jeffersonville, Ind., by Howard, 1881. 149 x 31 x 4. Engines, 13's- 4½ ft. Two boilers, each 40" by 20 ft., nine flues. Operated by Capt. James Lovell out of Nashville. Was sold after about eight years, renamed *ALLEN J. DUNCAN* (see).

1109 City of Natchez

SW p wh b. Jeffersonville, Ind., by Howard, 1885. 300 x 48 (83 ft. over all) x 10. Engines, 26's- 10 ft. Five boilers. Paddlewheels 34 ft. dia., with 15 ft. buckets. Owned by the Anchor Line. Capt. Horace E. Bixby was her master with H.E. Corbyn, clerk. We pause here to say more about Captain Bixby, of more than usual fame because of his associations with Mark Twain and his inclusion in *Life On the Mississippi.* Bixby was born May 8, 1826, at Genesco, N.Y., and ran away from home at an early age to Cincinnati, where he worked in a tailor's shop. At 18 he was clerk on the Cincinnati-Kanawha River packet *OLIVIA,* and two years later was pilot on her. Then he went to the Cincinnati-New Orleans trade, later St. Louis-New Orleans, and had pilot's license on the Missouri. He and Susan Weibling were married 1860. She was from New Orleans, and died 1867. His second marriage came Jan. 2, 1868, to Mary, daughter of Capt. and Mrs. Edwin A. Sheble, St. Louis. She outlived him. In the Civil war he commanded the gunboat *BENTON.* After his Anchor Line days he last piloted on the snagboat *HORATIO G. WRIGHT*, which he left at the age of 86 and died two days later, Aug. 1, 1912, in Maplewood, Mo. He was of small physique, wiry, tremendously energetic. He visited with Mark Twain twice after the author became celebrated, in 1882 and 1902. The *CITY OF NATCHEZ,* brag boat of the Anchor Line, burned Dec. 28, 1886, at Cairo, Ill. The towboat *R.S. HAYES* was alongside, first took fire, and the flames spread to consume the *CITY OF NATCHEZ.*

1110 City of Nauvoo

Stw ferry wh b. Rock Island, Ill., 1885. 89 x 21 x 3.6. She ferried between Nauvoo and Montrose for 56 years, a record. L.E. Reimbold ran her last. She was laid up in 1943. The *A. BURTIN* (see) had preceded her.

1111 City of New Albany

SW p wh b. Jeffersonville, Ind., by Howard, 1892. 225 x 35 x 6. Engines, 20's- 7 ft. Three boilers, each 42" by 28 ft. Owned by Louisville & Evansville Packet Co. and operated in that trade. Equipment from the former *JAMES GUTHRIE* used in building her. She was too much boat, and was sold February 1893 to the T.J. Moss Tie Co., for the St. Louis-Cape Girardeau trade, and renamed *NEW IDLEWILD* (see).

1112 City of New Orleans

SW p wh b. Jeffersonville, Ind., by Howard, 1881. 290 x 48 x 8.5. Engines, 26's- 10 ft. Five boilers, each 44" by 30 ft., four flues. Paddlewheels 38 ft. dia., with 15 ft. buckets. Owned by the Anchor Line. Capt. A.J. Carter, master, in 1885, with Archie Woods, clerk. Same team, 1891. In 1896, Capt. A.S. Lightner, master, with J.W. Langlois, clerk. She was brought under her own steam in May 1898 to Harmar, Oh., where much equipment went into the *CITY OF PITTSBURG* (see) at the Knox Boat Yard.

1113 City of Newport

SW ferry wh b. Cincinnati, Oh., 1882. 123.7 x 38 x 5.5. Ran Cincinnati-Newport and ultimately dismantled. Hull went to Vevay, Ind., for wharfboat purposes, and was there in 1894.

1114 City of Osceola

SW p wh Originally *CITY OF OWENSBORO* (see). After ten years of operation the *CITY OF OWENSBORO* was sold to the Lee Line, Memphis, which in 1895 renamed her. It is said that the new name was selected inasmuch as the silverware, furniture, etc., was marked "City of O." The Lee Line ran her Memphis-Cairo. She sank with a big trip about 70 miles above Memphis in November 1896, raised. Finally sank one winter below Tiptonville, Tenn. Was replaced by the *ROBERT E. LEE* (see).

1115 City of Owensboro

SW p wh b. Jeffersonville, Ind., by Howard, 1885. 245 x 37.6 x 6.3. Much equipment came from the *GREY EAGLE* b. 1871 (see). Owned by Louisville & Evansville Packet Co. Capt. David L. Penny was master many years, then Capt. Marion Ryan. Capt. Jess Singleton told this scribe she once went high and dry in a cornfield at Scuffletown in Canadian Reach on the Kentucky shore. She was sold to the Lee Line in 1895, renamed *CITY OF OSCEOLA* (see above).

1116 City of Paducah

Stw p wh b. Jeffersonville, Ind., by Howard, 1891. 190 x 34 x 555. Owned by St. Louis & Tennessee River Packet Co. She sank near Crane's Island, five miles below Chester, Ill., December 1894, raised. Engines, 16's- 6 ft. Three boilers, each 40" by 24 ft., six flues. Owned by St. Louis & Tennessee River Packet Co. She sank near Crane's Island, five miles below Chester, Ill., December 1894, raised. Capt. D.W. Kirkpatrick long was her master, and was on her at the final sinking. She was downbound from St. Louis to Tennessee River, and had landed in at Brunkhorst Landing, Ill., to load corn. She caught a snag and went down in 30 feet, this about 10:00 P.M., May 12, 1901. Twenty of the deck crew and two passengers were lost. Capt. Kirkpatrick died at his home near Carrollton, Ky., January 1921.

1117 City of Parkersburg

Stw p wh Originally *LIBERTY* b. 1899 (see). In 1912 John

W. Hubbard, Pittsburgh, bought the *LIBERTY* at Mobile, Ala., and Capt. Henry Kraft and son Harry brought her through the Gulf and to Pittsburgh. She was docked at Dravosburg, Pa., considerably altered, and renamed *CITY OF PARKERSBURG.* Came out spring of 1913 and ran Pittsburgh-Cincinnati in Hubbard inspired Ohio & Mississippi Navigation Co. Upbound on second trip she hit a cofferdam at Ohio River Dam 26, February 4, and sank. Raised. Crew, P&C trade, October 1913: Capt. William English, master; John L. Kerr and Ed McLaughlin, pilots; George Knox, chief; Ed Dunaway, purser; Jeff Frame, mate. Same trade 1915 although low water June-November kept her laid up. Hit an obstruction at Raccoon Island on Mar. 25, 1915, and was towed to Pt. Pleasant for repairs by *SALLIE MARMET.* That summer towed a floating water circus owned by Rice & Dore to the Upper Mississippi with many tribulations. In 1916 was laid up at Pt. Pleasant in the Kanawha River all summer. Ran excursions at Pittsburgh summer 1917, Capt. Robert Hasley. Capt. J. Orville Noll entered her in Pittsburgh-Cincinnati trade, early 1918. She hit a half-sunken barge on a flooded river at Russell, Ky., and sank for keeps. Her boilers went to the packet *KENTUCKY* in November 1919.

1118 City of Pekin

Stw p wh b. Elizabeth, Pa., 1863. 415.57 tons. Ran Illinois River-St. Louis. Dismantled in March 1872. Machinery went to the *GEORGE C. WOLFF* (see).

1119 City of Peoria

Rig? b. Peoria, Ill., 1872. 4.33 tons. In 1874 owned by Jacob Schafer, registered at St. Louis. Still documented 1876.

1120 City of Peoria

Stw p wh b. Jeffersonville, Ind., by Howard, 1892. 130 x 26 x 4.5. Engines, 13's- 6 ft. Three boilers, 34" by 20 ft. Owned by Capt. Sol York, in Peoria-Henry trade. Later owned by G.M. Sivley and others. Ran New Orleans-Bayou Teche November 1910, Capt. Warren Kounz, pilot. Capt. W.L. Berry, Paducah, bought her at a U.S. marshal sale fall 1913. Burned at Cairo, Ill., Sept. 7, 1914. The machinery was taken to Paducah and put on towboat *WHITE SPOT* built there that fall.

1121 City of Pine Bluff

Capt. Rube Haynes, sank at the head of Evan's Bar, Powell's Landing, in the upper Arkansas River.

1122 City of Pittsburg

SW p wh b. Harmar, Oh. at Knox Yard, 1899. 292.7 x 48.8. Engines, 26's- 10 ft. Three Scotch marine boilers, each 166" dia. by 14½ ft. long, with two flues each 46" dia., plus ninety 3½" return flues. These were replaced, 1900, by six Western type boilers, each 44" dia. by 22 ft. long. Her overall width was 79'5". The paddlewheels were 32 ft. dia. with 14½ ft. buckets. Much equipment used from former *CITY OF NEW ORLEANS* (see). Owned by Capt. John M. Phillips, Pittsburgh; Dana Scott, Zanesville; George Wallace, McConnelsville; Charles Beckwith, Malta; and A.L. Brahm, Pittsburgh. Her first trip was a round trip Pittsburgh-New Orleans, after which she was entered in the Pittsburgh-Louisville trade 1899 and spring of 1900. Ran Cincinnati-Louisville briefly, then was entered Cincinnati-Memphis trade. After several haps and mishaps she burned at 4:00 A.M. Sunday, Apr. 20, 1902, along the Kentucky shore of the Ohio River in the Grand Chain, not far above Dam 53. Over 60 lives were lost including Capt. Sylvester Doss, pilot, and Tom Smith, cub pilot. An in-depth article with many photographs describes the boat and the tragedy, appearing in the March 1968 issue of *S&D Reflector.*

1123 City of Plattsmouth

Stw p wh b. Hermann, Mo., 1883. 92.6 x 24 x 3.2. Ran on the Missouri River After a year or so was renamed *VIENNA* (see).

1124 City of Portsmouth

The *Missouri Historical Review* (1927) reports loss of a boat of this name below Weston, Mo. in 1861. She was documented simply *PORTSMOUTH* (see).

1125 City of Portsmouth

SW p wh b. Cincinnati, Oh., 1873. Built for Capt. William Stricklett and raised steam for the first time Dec. 15, 1873. She tried running opposition to *FANNIE DUGAN* out of Portsmouth, Oh., but on Mar. 25, 1874 was sold to the White Collar Line, Cincinnati. They ran her Cincinnati-Augusta-Higginsport, Capt. S.W. Morgan. She was forced ashore at California, Oh., January 1877, by ice, and drifted to Cincinnati, Oh., when the gorge broke, unhurt. Ultimately dismantled.

1126 City of Providence

SW p wh b. Jeffersonville, Ind., by Howard, 1880. 273.7 x 44.5 x 7.8. Engines, 26's- 9 ft. Five boilers, each 44" by 30 ft., four flues. Paddlewheels, 34 ft. dia. with 15 ft. buckets. Capt. George Lennox, master, with Frank Perkins and James McMeen, clerks, 1882. Owned by the Anchor Line. She blew out a cylinder head on the port engine 30 miles above Memphis June 15, 1888, killing the striker engineer, George Betts. When the Anchor Line quit business she was sold to the Columbia Excursion Co., St. Louis, and converted into an excursion boat and operated there. Was pushed out ashore by ice, Jan. 20, 1910, and lost. Her whistle later was used on the Streckfus excursion steamer *WASHINGTON,* then on *SAINT PAUL* and *SENATOR.*

1127 City of Quincy

SW p wh b. Madison, Ind., and completed at New Albany, Ind., 1871. 275 x 47 x 7. In June 1871 made a through trip New Orleans to St. Paul, Capt. Judson T. West. Ran St. Louis-New Orleans and occasionally St. Louis-Keokuk. In April-May 1875 was loaded with ore near St. Louis and, towing two barges also loaded with ore, came to Steubenville, Oh. She proceeded to Pittsburgh and at Painter's Mill took on 300 tons of cotton ties, got a trip at the wharf, and returned. The *TOM JASPER* also was up the Ohio with iron ore at this time (see). She sank at Island 98, Mississippi River, Jan. 21, 1875, raised. Finally lost at Hardin's Point, Ark., 75 miles below Memphis, then owned by the City of Quincy Transportation Co., Capt. William F. Davidson and others. The *BELLE OF TEXAS* removed furnishings and brought the piano, etc., to Memphis. This happened on Feb. 13, 1876, at 8:00 P.M. during a tornado which blew her to the Mississippi shores. The IDLEWILD was in the vicinity and took off passengers and crew.

1128 City of Quincy

Stw p wh b. Quincy, Ill., 1891. 130.7 x 25.8 x 8. Engines 11's- 6 ft. Two boilers, each 34" by 20 ft. Ran Quincy-Keokuk. In March 1896 was sold to the Parmalees of St. Louis for a pleasure boat. Was wrecked in the May 27, 1896 tornado at St. Louis and lost. The boats damaged or lost in that storm included the *CITY OF CAIRO, ARKANSAS CITY, BALD EAGLE, LIBBIE CONGER, PITTSBURGH, J. J. ODIL, DOLPHIN NO. 2, HARVESTER, S. B. WIGGINS, NAPOLEON MILLIKEN, WILLIAM CHRISTY, GEORGE A. MADILL, H. L. CLARK,* and *HENRY SACKMAN.*

City of St. Joseph

Appears occasionally in lists of early Anchor Line steamers. Her name was simply *ST. JOSEPH* (see).

1129 City St. Joseph

Stw p wh b. St. Joseph, Mo., 1901. 162 x 36 x 5. Engines, 16's- 6 ft. Two boilers, each 40" by 26 ft. Built by Capt. A. Stewart of St. Joseph for Missouri River service, and came out with Capt. Stewart in command, with F.W. Turner, clerk; R.J. Stewart, pilot, and Perrin Kay, chief engineer. Made trips to the World's Fair at St. Louis in 1904. She was sold to Planters Packet Co., Memphis, and was last owned by the Lee Line, Memphis. Collapsed a flue in June 1911 killing 18 deck crew and injuring engineer Floyd Morgan. She was caught out high and dry at Luna Landing, Ark. in March 1916 and remained there some time. That November the Lee Line changed her name to *ECLIPSE* (see).

1130 City of St. Louis

SW p wh b. Jeffersonville, Ind. by Howard, 1883. 300 x 49 x 8.6. Engines, 26½'s- 10 ft. Five boilers, each 44" by 30 ft., four flues. Paddlewheels, 34½ ft. dia., with 15 ft. buckets. Owned by the Anchor Line. Capt. James O'Neal was master, and in 1894 his pilots were Joe Bryan and Charlie O'Neal. Capt. W.H. Thorgewan bought her at a U.S. marshal sale at St. Louis, March 1898, for his bid of $19,050. He went master, with C.M. Berkley, clerk. Columbia Excursion Co. had her briefly, and sold her July 1899 to James M. Grasty. She was running harbor excursions at New Orleans 1901, and President McKinley rode her that May. Grasty sold her early in 1903 to the Greater New York Home Oil Co. but a U.S. marshal stepped in and sold her to attorney T. Marshall Miller for $3,125. She was laid up at Carondelet, Mo., and burned there Oct. 29, 1903. The Anchor Line sold her original roof bell to Capt. J. Frank Ellison and it went to the *QUEEN CITY* (see).

1131 City of Saint Louis

SW harbor boat wh Originally *ELON G. SMITH* b. Madison, Ind. 1873 (see). Operated at St. Louis by the City Harbormaster. Her name was changed to *MARK TWAIN* on the occasion of a visit to the city by Sam Clemens (see).

1132 City of St. Louis

SW harbor boat sh Originally *ERASTUS WELLS* b. Grafton, Ill. 1907 (see). Was bought by Edwin C. Koenig, St. Louis, about 1932 and he ran her through 1935. Sold in August 1942 to Geo C. Bolz Dredging Co., and they sold her February 1944 to Allied Oil Co. Dismantled.

1133 City of St. Paul

SW p wh b. La Crosse, Wis., 1866. 220 x 36 x 6. Engines, 21's- 7 ft. Three boilers, each 42" by 26 ft. This was a rebuilding job, using much from former *MOSES McLELLAN* (see). Operated on Upper Mississippi and was inspected at St. Paul 1867.

1134 City of Saltillo

Stw p wh b. Jeffersonville, Ind. by Howard, 1905. 200 x 37 x 6.6. Engines, 16's- 7 ft. Three boilers, each 40" dia. by 32 ft. Owned by St. Louis & Tennessee River Packet Co. She was lost by sinking not far below St. Louis, after hitting a rock shore during a fog, this on May 11, 1910. Ed Pell was the pilot on watch.

1135 City of Savannah

Stw p wh b. Jeffersonville, Ind., by Howard, 1889. 186 x 31 x 5. Engines, 16's- 6 ft. Three boilers, each 42" by 22 ft. Paddlewheel 20 ft. square. Owned by St. Louis & Tennessee River Packet Co. They chartered her to the Lee Line to run out of Memphis in September 1895. Acquired by Capts. A.E. and L.P. Cummins to run Memphis-Vicksburg. Sank at Shiloh Landing, 60 miles above Vicksburg, Sept. 18, 1897, raised. Burned at the Memphis wharf, Mar. 9, 1898. The *WARREN* was chartered to replace her, and then the Cummins boys got the *OUACHITA* for the trade.

1136 City of Savannah

Stw p wh b. Jeffersonville, Ind., by Howard, 1902. 200 x 36 x 6. Engines, 17's- 7 ft. Three boilers, each 44" dia. by 22 ft., with ten 6" flues. Owned by St. Louis & Tennessee River Packet Co. She sank and was lost in Dog Tooth Bend, Miss. River, about 22 miles above Cairo, Ill., Dec. 5, 1911. The *STACKER LEE* took off the passengers and much of the freight.

1137 City of Sheffield

Stw p wh b. Jeffersonville, Ind., by Howard, 1890. 183 x 35. Owned by St. Louis & Tennessee River Packet Co. In July 1984 sank in the Little Chain, near Metropolis, Ill., then in command of Capt. Joe Todd (who had come from

Wellsville, Oh.). Raised. Sank on Mississippi River not far above Cairo, Ill., Aug. 18, 1895, raised. Burned at Grand Tower, Ill., enroute to Mound City marine ways for repairs, Oct. 22, 1902.

1138 CITY OF SHREVEPORT

Stw p wh b. Mobile, Ala., as *LUCILLE* (see). Renamed in 1909 when acquired by Capt. George L. White and others for New Orleans-Ouachita and Black rivers. H.A. Burley was clerk. Ran to Harrisonburg, La. Burned on Ouachita River near Monroe 1920-1921.

1139 CITY OF TAMPA

Prop p wh Originally *VOLUNTEER* b. Mason City, W. Va., 1887 (see). Operated in Florida waters through 1918, perhaps longer.

1140 CITY OF VEVAY

Stw p wh Originally *CITY OF FRANKFORT* (see) enlarged to measure 190.8 x 36.4 x 5.1 owned by White Collar Line which ran her Cincinnati-Madison, Capt. E.S. Morgan. Ran there at least 1888–1895. Dismantled.

1141 CITY OF VICKSBURG

SW p wh b. Jeffersonville, Ind. by Howard, 1870. 265 x 42 x 8. Belonged to the Anchor Line. Capt. Robert Riley commanded. Sank on a snag and was lost at Ashport, Tenn. Aug. 11, 1880. Had aboard a large freight cargo.

1142 CITY OF VICKSBURG

SW p wh b. Jeffersonville, Ind., by Howard, 1881. 272 x 44.5 x 8.2. Engines, 26's- 9 ft. Five boilers, each 44″ by 30 ft., four flues. Paddlewheels, 33 ft. dia., with 14 ft. buckets. Owned by the Anchor Line. Sold Apr. 29, 1894 to Columbia Excursion Co., St. Louis. Damaged in the tornado at St. Louis May 27, 1896. Sold 1898 to John T. Hardy Sons & Co., New Orleans, which rebuilt her into the *CHALMETTE* (see).

1143 CITY OF WABASHA

Stw ferry wh b. Wabasha, Minn., 1879. 80.4 x 26 x 2.9. Still listed 1892, gone by 1895.

1144 CITY OF WARSAW

Stw ferry wh b. Jeffersonville, Ind., by Howard, 1895. 100 x 35.4 x 3.1. Originally owned by Frank Myers, later by Juden and Craig. In her latter days, c. 1905–1908, operated in the vicinity of Cairo, Ill.

1145 CITY OF WHEELING

SW p wh b. Wheeling, Va., 1853. 250 x 34 x 6. Four boilers, each 45″ dia., by 22 ft. Built for Capt. John McLure, Jr., and others. Came out Wheeling-Louisville, but most of her days Wheeling-Cincinnati, Capt. McLure. She was abreast of Pomeroy, Oh., upbound, and was crowded into the Virginia shore by a passing raft. Hit rocks and sank. McLure was the pilot on watch but his steersman was at the wheel, George Conant. She broke in two and was lost. This happened just abreast of the Pomeroy Court House. Her roof bell went to the old uptown Methodist Church, and when the new church was built in 1892 it went along. The pastor was Rev. W.H. Arthur, father of Charles Arthur who long ran the Acme Boiler Works, Gallipolis, Oh.

1146 CITY OF WHEELING

Stw p wh b. Clarington, Oh., at the Mozena yard, and completed at Wheeling, 1899. 169.3 x 34.4 x 4.8. Engines, 16's- 6 ft. Boilers, each 42″ dia., by 22 ft., three. Engines and boilers came from *CITY OF SAVANNAH* (first; see). Capt. Thaddeus S. Thomas and Cy Higgs were instrumental in building her for short trades out of Wheeling. Soon sold to the Lee Line, Memphis, which renamed her *HARRY LEE* (see).

1147 CITY OF WINONA

Stw p wh b. Dubuque, Iowa, 1882. 137 x 29.1 x 4. Engines, 13's- 5 ft. Built as a rafter by Youmans Bros., and Hodgins of Winona, Minn. Later bought by Capt. John Streckfus to fight the *JO LONG* (see) in the Davenport-Clinton trade. Rebuilt at Kahlke yard, renamed *WINONA* (see).

1148 CITY OF YAZOO

Stw p wh b. Jeffersonville, Ind., by Howard, 1879. 630 tons. 200 x 38 x 6.8. Engines, 20's- 6 ft. Three boilers, each 45″ by 28 ft. with six flues. Built for S.H. Parisot, and operated out of Vicksburg, Miss. Inspected there Oct. 27, 1882.

1149 CLARA

SW p wh b. New Albany, Ind., 1848. 160 ft. long. Designed for Mobile-Montgomery trade, Capt. Bragdon. Apparently she had been returned to Cincinnati for rebuilding or dismantling. She burned laid up at Fulton, a section of Cincinnati, Sept. 8, 1853, along with the *NORTH AMERICA* (see).

1150 CLARA

SW p wh b. Elizabeth, Pa., 1851. 248 tons. Ran St. Louis-Missouri River. In 1854 ran St. Louis-St. Joseph, Capt. J. Cheever, with J.B. Weaver, clerk. Capt. John P. Keiser was pilot on her. In 1856, St. Louis-Cambridge, Capt. Isaac H. McKee, master. At St. Paul in 1858. Lost in ice at St. Louis.

1151 CLARA

SW p wh b. Cincinnati, Oh., 1864. 225 x 34. Engines, 20's- 6½ ft. Three boilers. Ran St. Louis-Missouri River. Was in the Star Line Packet Co., Capt. Ryder, when snagged and lost ½ mile above Ousley's Landing, Mo., on the Missouri River, May 24, 1870. Had aboard a large cargo. Capt. Wm. L. Heckman bought the cabin from the wreck, and built from it a two-story house at Bluffton, Mo. In 1927 a rebuilt home at that site still had gingerbread work, etc., from the original.

1152 CLARA

Rig? b. Madison, Ind., 1864. 305 tons. She was taken to Mobile, Ala. Registered there in 1867, maybe later.

1153 CLARA

Stw p wh b. Leon, W. Va., 1876. 60.95 tons. Single deck,

model hull. Built by James McKay, Racine, Oh., who had a flour mill at Leon. He took her to Vicksburg, ran her up the Yazoo, and sold her. On June 18, 1878, she sank after hitting a log in the Kanawha River eight miles above Pt. Pleasant. Raised. Eventually sank in Oldtown Island, Ohio River. The machinery went to the towboat *HOMER B* in 1889, b. Racine, Oh.

1154 CLARA DEAN

Stw p wh b. Brownsville, Pa., 1853. 190 tons. Built for Capt. William Dean. Capt. Sampson Cadman took interest in 1855. In the big winter 1856–1857 she laid up at Pt. Pleasant, W. Va., for ice on Christmas Day 1856 and didn't get away until Apr. 1, 1857, Capt. George W. Reed. Capt. Cadman had her in the Pittsburgh-Cincinnati trade 1861, and was in Pittsburgh-Portsmouth trade, Capt. Marsilliott in January 1862. Dismantled that year.

1155 CLARA DOLSEN

SW p wh b. Cincinnati, Oh., 1861. 273 x 42 (38 ft. floor) x 9. Engines, 28's- 9 ft. Five boilers, each 44" dia. by 28 ft., five flues. Paddlewheels, 36 ft. dia. by 14 ft. buckets. Hull built at the Leatherbury yard; machinery by C.T. Dumont. Built for Capt. William T. Dunning, master, A.P. Stewart, first clerk, and S.B. Edwards, second clerk, all of New Orleans. Ran St. Louis-New Orleans. In February 1862 Capt. George W. Cable took stock and went master. Captured as a Confederate steamer June 14, 1862, and was used in U.S. service until May 1864 when returned to owners. She was noted in her day as being the second largest packet afloat (939 tons) surpassed only by *RUTH.* To settle estate of Edward Walsh she was put up at auction at St. Louis, June 28, 1866, and was bid in by Capt. M.L. Henry. Burned at St. Louis, Feb. 4, 1868.

1156 CLARA DUNNING

Stw p wh b. Madison, Ind., 1864. 155 x 28 x 4.5. Engines, 15's- 5 ft. Built for the Louisville-Madison trade, Capt. H. Thompson. Sold to the U.S. War Dept. in 1874.

1157 CLARA EAMES

Stw p wh b. Wacouta, Minn., 1862. 105 tons. First documented at St. Paul Sold to the U.S. War Dept., 1864.

1158 CLARA FISHER

Stw p wh b. Brownsville, Pa., 1850. 108 tons. Came out new in February 1850 owned by Capt. William H. Gordon, G.E. Warner, and Amos Frisbee, all of Allegheny, Pa., and Charles Fisher and E.G. Owens, Warren County, Pa. Capt. W.H. Gordon, master. She ran on the Allegheny River to Franklin, Oil City, and Warren. By 1856 there was a considerable shuffle of stockholders but she still plied the Allegheny. By February 1857 she had been sold to Capt. Samuel Lewis, Mt. Washington (Pittsburgh), and William Dilworth, Allegheny City. She continued up the Allegheny spring of 1857, and then was sold to Council Bluffs, Iowa, although she now was redocumented as a barge.

1159 CLARA HINE

Stw p wh b. Brownsville, Pa., 1856. 79 tons. Was taken to Keokuk, Iowa. Sank and lost at Lake City, Minn., June 7, 1866.

1160 CLARA HOPKINS

Ferry wh b. Pomeroy, Oh., 1871. 26.08 tons. Still registered 1876, maybe longer.

1161 CLARA I NO. 2

Rig? b. Poplar Bluff, Mo., 1879. 72.4 x 15.5 x 2.8. Still registered at Poplar Bluff in 1886, maybe longer.

1162 CLARA L

Rig? b. Pocahontas, Ark., 1872. 43.02 tons. Registered at Memphis, 1876, maybe longer.

1163 CLARA POE

Stw p wh b. California, Pa., 1859. 149 x 32 x 4'9". First master, Capt. Thomas Poe, who also held stock along with Jacob Poe, Martin L. Poe, George Poe, Jonathan Kinsey, and George W. Ebert, all of Georgetown, Pa. Named for Capt. Thomas Poe's daughter. Ran Pittsburgh-Cincinnati until the war. She was impressed into U.S. service 1862. Was with Grant's fleet on the Tennessee River and was still in U.S. service when she burned near Eddyville on Cumberland River with a cargo of hay upbound for Nashville, Apr. 17, 1865.

1164 CLARA RAMOS

Stw p sh b. Pittsburgh, Pa., by James Rees & Sons Co., complete, and left under her own steam in May 1907 bound for Central America. Had a full length cabin, texas, and one stack. Designed to carry coffee and fruits.

1165 CLARA S

Rig? b. Cincinnati, Oh., 1877. Was completed in October 1877 and was ready to depart for Vicksburg, Capt. William Wenzel, master. In 1878 New Orleans-Ouachita River. In May 1883 in charge of Capt. Louis Ranson with E.G. Phelps, clerk. Snagged and sunk in Tehula Lake, Dec. 27, 1883, with 1,000 bales and 350 sacks of seed.

1166 CLARA SCOTT

Stw p wh b. 1869. Capt. Henry Scott owned her. In spring of 1869 he had her running Evansville-Wabash River. He commanded and had Cash Thomas and Charlie Chadwick, clerks. Ran a low water Evansville-Cairo that summer. In September 1869 running Evansville-Paducah in opposition to the *PHANTOM.* The two got in a race, the *PHANTOM* exploded with great loss of life. Capt. Allen Duncan was on the *SCOTT* at the time. Capt. Sam Christy, master, and W.H. Truslow, clerk, had her in the Parkersburg-Charleston trade 1871–1875. A board of engineers, led by Chief of Engineers Andrew A. Humphreys, inspected the Kanawha River on her, May 19, 1875, culminating in a banquet at the Hale House. This event led to the approval by Congress for Kanawha River locks and dams. On the way down the *SCOTT* sank in seven feet, but her distinguished guests were not aboard.

1167 CLARABELL

SW p wh b. Louisville, Ky., 1860. 139 x 28 x 5.5. Operated St. Louis-Cambridge, Mo., up Missouri River. Was with Porter on Red River in May 1864 doing U.S. transport service. Was upbound on the Mississippi River when Confederates opened fire from the west shore. Aboard were 400 men of the 6th Michigan Regiment. She was hit 30 times and 13 men were wounded. Landed above Caroline Landing, Miss., to make repairs to the hull where shot had caused injuries. The Rebels pursued her to the head of Louisiana Bend and shelled her. An exploding shell set her afire. The U.S. forces escaped on foot. Date of the above, July 24, 1864.

1168 CLARENCE

Centerwheel ferry wh b. Carondelet, Mo., 1867. 57.62 tons. Owned in 1874 by C.C. Williams, St. Louis. Out of service 1878.

1169 CLARENCE THORN

Stw ferry wh b. Mount Carmel, Ill., 1905. 63.2 x 18 x 2.6. In January 1911 the Fowler-Wolfe Co., Paducah, was delivering a new boiler for this Wabash River ferry.

1170 CLARIBELL

Stw p wh b. Pt. Pleasant, W. Va., 1880. 100 x 18.8 x 2. There is evidence that the hull was built at Buffalo, W. Va. Ran Buffalo-Pt. Pleasant-Gallipolis. In 1882 her crew was in the charge of Capt. F.A. Barrows, with Austin Barrows, clerk. In spring of 1898 was running Parkersburg-Gallipolis, Capt. Charles F. Stalder, master, with F.L. Barrows, engineer. She was dismantled that year, and the *NEVA* (see) built to replace her.

1171 CLARION

Stw p wh b. Monongahela, Pa., 1851. 73 tons. Built for Capt. Martin Millinger. Came out in the spring 1851, Pittsburgh-Zanesville, Capt. Jesse White. Then ran Pittsburgh-West Newton, up Youghiogheny River. The first locomotive ever seen at Wheeling was brought there on a barge towed by *CLARION* Nov. 8, 1852. It was an old engine named *GEORGE WASHINGTON,* for the B&O, and was drawn up the shore near the Belmont Mills by block and tackle. Two cars and a tender accompanied on another barge. The barges had been loaded at Pittsburgh. The *CLARION* ran on the Allegheny, Pittsburgh-Kittanning-Catfish, three trips a week. She was sold to the Upper Mississippi for St. Paul-Minnesota River trade, Capt. Hoffman (1853-1857). She was reported to have a "very big whistle in keeping with her name, so large that it made her topheavy." Off the lists 1857.

1172 CLARKSVILLE

SW p wh b. Louisville, Ky., 1845. 484 tons. Burned at Ozark Island near Napoleon, Ark., with loss of 21 lives, May 27, 1848, Capt. Holmes.

1173 CLARKSVILLE

Stw p wh b. Madison, Ind., 1869. 168 x 34 x 5. In November 1870 enrolled at New Orleans owned by Capt. Jesse K. Bell. In 1877 running New Orleans-St. Martinsville on Bayou Teche, Capt. Abe Smith. Also in that trade was the *GEORGE SPANGLER,* Capt. W.C. Smith. Called "Abe Smith's Line."

1174 CLAYTON H. WEBB

SW p wh b. Cincinnati, Oh., 1888. 112.5 x 24.7 x 3. Operated on the Cumberland above Nashville. Still listed in 1896, maybe longer.

1175 CLEON

Stw p wh b. Osceola, Wis., 1884. 129 x 21 x 3.7. Built by Capt. Oscar Knapp (see *G. B. KNAPP*). His son, Capt. Ben Knapp, ran the boat on Upper Mississippi three seasons, then died. The boat was sold south and ran Baton Rouge-Bayou Sara, daily. Burned at Bayou Macon, Rockdale, La., Apr. 2, 1900.

1176 CLEONA

SW p wh b. West Elizabeth, Pa., 1850. 201 tons. Operated on Red River 1853-1854. Burned at Alexandria, La., Sept. 20, 1854.

1177 CLEONA

Stw p wh b. Cincinnati, Oh., 1864. 123.6 x 26.1 x 4.3. Owned by Capt. Charles C. Pickett of New Orleans. Ran New Orleans-Opelousas trade to Washington, Pickett, master, with J.B. Schmit as clerk, this in 1866. Evidence is she was built for A.D. Bullock & Co., Cincinnati, which sold her south 1865. She had four other owners in the New Orleans area 1866-1869, then was sold to Galveston, Tex. Sank and was lost at Liberty, Tex., Oct. 3, 1869.

1178 CLEOPATRA

SW p wh b. Monongahela, Pa., 1852. 152 tons. Burned and lost Dec. 6, 1852, below Catahoula, La.

1179 CLERMONT

SW p wh b. Cincinnati, Oh., 1845. 121 tons. Lost on White River, Ark., Dec. 9, 1851, with loss of 20 lives.

1180 CLERMONT

Stw p wh b. New Richmond, Oh., 1863. 79 tons. Wire from Cincinnati, Mar. 15, 1864; "Capt. Irwin on Sunday sold the *CLERMONT* to Capt. Uriah B. Scott, late of the *BEN GAYLORD,* price $20,000." Next we hear of her, the *LUMINARY* (see) was upbound on the Mississippi and saw on shore a bonfire of driftwood with people huddled around it, this on Mar. 8, 1867. The *CLERMONT,* bound to Memphis from White River, Capt. Walbourne, had gone up into Zurdette Chute on a high river, near Helena, and had hit a snag. The boat turned turtle, losing the cabin and boilers. Amazingly only one life was reported lost.

1181 CLEVELAND

Stw p wh b. Freedom, Pa., 1840. 76 tons. Built for Capt. Sharp Hemphill, and ran Pittsburgh-Beaver, Pa. Collapsed two flues while coming up through Deadman's Island at the Sewickley Bottom, June 14, 1844. Killed the cook and a helper, five others wounded. The *BRIDGEWATER* took bodies and survivors to Pittsburgh. Dismantled 1846.

1182 CLIFFORD

Rig? b. Madison, Ind., 1871. 121 tons. Was in New Orleans-Shreveport trade 1872.

1183 CLIFTON

Stw p wh b. Glasgow, Pa., 1855. 183 tons. Off the lists in 1860.

1184 CLIFTON

SW p wh b. Cincinnati, Oh., 1864. 182 x 36 x 6. Engines, 21's- 7 ft. boilers, tubular, with 23 five inch flues in each. Capt. George D. Hoople and others built her, and she was entered in Memphis & Cincinnati Packet Co., Capt. Frank Stein. Came in collision with the *ROSE HITE* (see) at Troy, Ind., June 30, 1866, resulting in paddlewheel of *HITE* being badly damaged, and *TARASCON* towed her to Louisville. Burst starboard steam line a few miles below Henderson, Ky., May 2, 1868, tearing up the cabin floor. No serious injuries. She burned at Cincinnati on May 12, 1869, and the flames spread to consume many other steamboats. Gunpowder in the magazine exploded.

1185 CLIFTON

Ferry wh b. Middleport, Oh., 1869. 59.04 tons. Operated at Clifton, W. Va., along with the *EMPIRE* (see). Documented at Evansville in 1876.

1186 CLIFTON

Stw p wh b. Cincinnati, Oh., 1879. 252 x 39 x 6. Engines, 20's- 7 ft. Three boilers, each 47" dia. by 28 ft., six 10" flues in each. Built at Cincinnati Marine Ways Co. Owned by David Gibson, Wash Honshell, J.N. Williamson, T.N. Johnson, and others. Operated in the Pittsburgh & St. Louis Packet Co., Capt. J.M. Vandergrift, master, with Frank J. Oakes, clerk. She was southbound with 350 tons of iron and nails, etc., loaded at Pomeroy and Ironton and was forced to seek ice harbor in the Kentucky River Dec. 29, 1880. She sank there when the ice moved, Jan. 20, 1881. Was raised, rebuilt, and became the *OHIO* (see).

1187 CLIMAX

Stw ferry wh b. Freedom, Pa., 1880. 107 x 30.7 x 3.8. Ran between the Top Mill and Martins Ferry, Oh. Still registered in 1896.

1188 CLINCH

Stw p wh b. Kingston, Tenn., 1864. 131 tons. Built by the USQMD for war use on the upper Tennessee. Sold to private owners Apr. 10, 1866, renamed *GALLATIN* (see).

1189 CLINTON

SW p wh b. Pittsburgh, Pa., 1844. 267 tons. Ran New Orleans-Upper Bends, Capt. William Baird. Burned Mar. 23, 1847 five miles above Bonnet Carre, La., with loss of six lives.

1190 CLINTON

Stw p wh b. Elizabeth, Pa., 1851. 33 tons. First registered at Wheeling. Out of service in 1854.

1191 CLINTON

SW p wh b. St. Louis, Mo., 1872. 246.9 x 38.4 x 5.7. Built for Upper Mississippi trades, and was in Keokuk Northern Line Packet Co., Capt. Ben A. Conger, master, with A. Havlin, clerk. Ran St. Louis-Cincinnati, Capt. John N. Shunk, his last command. Was sold to New Orleans, and in 1884 was running New Orleans-Bayou Sara, Capt. J.J. Brown, master, with Theo. Jobin clerk, run by Merchants' & Planters Packet Co.

1192 CLINTON B. FISK

Stw p wh b. Kingston, Tenn., 1891. 100 x 18 x 3.1. Ran on Tennessee River, Louden-Kingston. Capt. G.W. Swartz, Sr. bought her, 1895. and ran her above and below Muscle Shoals. He sold her back to the upper Tennessee, and she finally sank at the Kingston, Tenn., landing.

1193 CLIPPER

SW p wh b. New Albany, Ind., 1840. 299 tons. Ran Louisville-New Orleans. Exploded boilers at Bayou Sara, La., Sept. 19, 1843. One of the more graphic descriptions of calamity in *Lloyd's Steamboat Directory* is an eye-witness account of this. Great life loss.

1194 CLIPPER

SW p wh b. Pittsburgh, Pa., 1843. 173 x 22'4" x 4'8". She had a single compound engine, 16", 32"- 6 ft. Came out with two boilers, later three. Owned by Capt. Nelson Crooks, Thomas K. Litch, and Ezra Porter. Capt. Crooks commanded. Litch was the builder of the engine. Ezra Porter ran the boatyard at Shousetown, Pa. This was the first installation of a compound engine on a Western steamboat. Sam Young was her engineer. She ran Pittsburgh-Cincinnati until outclassed by better boats, then tramped. Out of service in 1850. See *CLIPPER NO. 2.*

1195 CLIPPER

Stw p wh b. Ironton, Oh., 1859. 216 tons. Running Cincinnati-Nashville, 1861, Capt. Thomas J. Bruce. Snagged and lost at Station Bar, above Brush Creek Island, Ohio River, on July 23, 1866. She went down on a rising river and went to pieces.

1196 CLIPPER

SW p wh b. Cincinnati, Oh., 1865. 242 tons. Went to Mobile, Ala. Burned 70 miles above Mobile on Oct. 5, 1865, with loss of eight lives.

1197 CLIPPER

Stw p wh b. Brownsville, Pa., 1867. 84 tons. Owned by Samuel Clarke & Sons. Engines 16's- 4½ ft. Three boilers, each 36" dia. by 24 ft. Ran regularly, 1877, as a daylight packet in short trades out of Brownsville, Pa., Capt. G.W. Clarke, going to Lock 4 and to Monongahela City, Pa. This continued in 1878. She was primarily a towboat, and was lost in Glasshouse Riffle, Pittsburgh, Apr. 1882 while helping the *SAMUEL CLARKE* out with a tow.

1198 CLIPPER

Stw p wh b. Mason City, W. Va., and completed at Wheeling, 1880. 83 x 12 x 5.5. Inspected in the Cincinnati District for several years, and at New Orleans in 1886.

1199 CLIPPER

Stw p wh b. Slidell, La., 1916. 135 x 23 x 5. Engines 8's- 42" stroke. One boiler, 48" by 18 ft. Owned by Carter Bros., New Orleans. They operated her up Black and Ouachita rivers. This boat had origin as a sawmill boat built 1888 at Haynes Landing, W. Va., named *CLIPPER* which was variously owned, for some time by Doss Baker, Clifton, Tenn., on Tennessee River. It would appear that the 1916 *CLIPPER* got a new hull at Slidell, but may have inherited the machinery, etc., from the sawmill *CLIPPER*. She burned in a rather spectacular fire at the foot of Bienville Street, New Orleans in March 1928. Also see *SAWMILL CLIPPER*.

1200 CLIPPER NO. 2

SW p wh b. Shousetown, Pa., 1846. 210 x 28.9 x 6. Compound engines, 16's, 32's- 7 ft. Owned by Nelson Crooks, George Black, Robert S. Hays, Thomas S. Clarke, William Thaw, William Bingham, Edwin R. Wells, Thomas K. Litch, Alex Miller, and David Holmes. This was the first double engine compound steamboat on the Western streams. The first single compound boat was the *CLIPPER* b. 1843 (see). Sam Young of Shousetown, Pa., was engineer on both. He reported that she was a hard one to keep steam on, and both fan and steam blowers were tried. Young learned his trade on Chattahoochee River boats. Compound engines for years were called "Clipper engines" because of the pioneering on these two steamers. The *CLIPPER NO. 2* ran in Pittsburgh-Cincinnati trade. Capt. C.W. Batchelor was pilot on her three seasons and said she was hard to steer, and he finally got off to go home and die, which he didn't. John Shouse also piloted on her and recalled she had the first coal stove in a pilothouse that he knew of. J.H. Dunlap and James O'Neal were on her in 1845—Dunlap later was agent for Gray's Iron Line, and O'Neal was prominent in the Anchor Line at St. Louis. Jim Witten was pilot on watch at Pittsburgh when the Great Fire broke out in 1845 which destroyed much of that city. Rather curious is the fact that Litch took out no patent on his compound engines. Capt. Pres Devol later was master; then John Shouse. Dismantled 1854.

1201 CLYDE

Stw p wh b. Jeffersonville, Ind., by Howard, 1880. 181 x 32.5 x 5.6. Engines 15's- 6 ft. Two boilers, each 47" by 28 ft., six flues. Owned by the Evansville & Tennessee River Packet Co., Capt. Allen J. Duncan, master, with E.M. Lewis, clerk. She was acquired by St. Louis & Tennessee River Packet Co., and was lost by sinking spring of 1893 or 1894.

1202 CLYDE

Stw p wh b. Jeffersonville, Ind., by Howard, 1894. 175 x 33 x 5.5. Engines, 14's- 6 ft. Two boilers, each 44" dia. by 26 ft. Owned by St. Louis & Tennessee River Packet Co. When first built she had Scotch marine boilers which gave so much trouble they were removed in 1895 and the above mentioned Western boilers placed. She was sunk abreast of Buffalo Island, about 30 miles above Cairo on the Mississippi River, fall of 1899, raised. She last ran in the Calhoun County, Ill., apple trade, then was sold Oct. 9, 1914, to Henry Murnane and "Doc" Hottum, Memphis, for the Cairo-Memphis trade. Dismantled at Paducah, 1918.

1203 COAHOMA

SW p wh b. Metropolis, Ill., 1876. 205.2 x 32.5 x 7. Compound engines, 17's, 31's- 7 ft. Three boilers, five flues. Built for the Lee Line of Memphis. A widely circulated report while she was under construction was that Capt. James Lee intended naming her *KATE FRISBEE* to honor that old packet and her builder (see). The Ohio River was very low when she was launched. The new hull plowed in the mud and stuck. The *IDLEWILD* took a pull at it but had no luck. Her wheel shafts came from the burned *CITY OF EVANSVILLE* (see) and her cabin was from the *QUICKSTEP* (see). The job of moving the cabin to the new hull took only an hour and 30 minutes, and was done so easily that the night watchman, asleep in the texas, did not know he was on a new boat until he was called. Paddlewheels were 26 ft. dia., with 15 ft. buckets. She ran Memphis-Friars Point where the Lee Line had a U.S. Mail contract at $18,400 annually. Capt. Harry Cooper was master in 1882 with John Haley, clerk. In 1892 she was in Pittsburgh, having been bought by Capt. Lee Anshutz and theater owner Harry Davis. They had plans to make an excursion boat of her which died aborning. Dismantled.

1204 COBWEB

Stw p wh b. Dycusburg, Ky., 1867. 107 tons. 110 x 21 x 2.3. Operated on Cumberland River, and by 1870 was at New Orleans owned by Capt. Isadore Johnson of that city. Off the lists in 1874.

1205 COHASSET

Rig? b. Terre Haute, Ind., 1883. 82 x 17 x 3. Still listed 1886, maybe later.

1206 COLBERT

Stw p wh b. West Elizabeth, Pa., 1851. 164 tons. Operated

on Tennessee River, and was lost by fire at Bayne, Tenn., June 26, 1855.

1207 COLLIER

Stw p wh Originally *ALLEN COLLIER* b. Cincinnati, Oh., 1864 (see). When taken over for war service by the U.S. she was renamed *COLLIER* and assigned #29. Described as 161.5 long and equipped with engines 15's- 4½ ft. Capt. David White bought her at Mound City, Ill., on Aug. 17, 1865, for $12,000. One month later she was renamed *IMPERIAL* (see).

1208 COLONA

SW p wh b. Parkersburg, Va., 1859. 54 tons. In 1861 she was marooned up Red River when the Civil War started. No further news.

1209 COL. A. MACKENZIE

SW snagboat wh b. Jeffersonville, Ind., by Howard, 1900. 160 x 33 x 5. Operated on the Upper Mississippi by U.S. Engineers, Capt. David Tipton. Later was renamed *DAVID TIPTON* (see).

1210 COL. A. P. KOUNS

Stw p wh b. Cincinnati, Oh., 1874. 309 tons. Owned by the Kouns family, and ran New Orleans-Red River. She left New Orleans on Wednesday, Apr. 3, 1878. On the night of Friday the 5th at 11:00 P.M. she speared a snag at Negro Point, 70 miles up Red River. It came through the forecastle, up through the boiler deck, and then took away the hurricane roof forward. The hull was torn wide open and the boat sank in 12 minutes. When Capt. Mart Kouns left her she was lying on her starboard side with her skylights in the water, and the hull on the larboard side visible all along the bottom. Her boilers rolled overboard, as did her deck freight.

1211 COL. BAYARD

SW p wh b. McKeesport, Pa., 1852. 177 tons. Long ran in Pittsburgh-Elizabeth trade on the Monongahela River, Capt. Peebles. Out of service 1862.

1212 COL. BENEDICT

Stw p wh b. Algiers, La., 1864. 324 tons. Built by the USQMD and seems to have been taken to Brownsville, Texas. Sold to private owners, June 21, 1866. Lost in 1868.

1213 COL. CHANDLER

SW p wh Originally *ELLA* b. Cincinnati, 1860. The ELLA was taken over by USQMD and given this name June 4, 1862. Sold to private owners on Dec. 25, 1865, retaining the name. Sank and lost at Sabine Pass, Tex., Jan. 31, 1866, with loss of two lives.

1214 COL. CLAY

SW steamship wh b. Louisville, Ky., 1847. 257 tons. Built for USQMD to aid the prosecution of the Mexican War. Plans were stipulated by U.S. Stephen H. Long had a hand in building her. Her trial trip was run up river from Louisville. Sold to private hands, June 1851. Out of service 1861. Her engines were built by John Curry, Louisville. She had two stacks, and was designed to run between New Orleans and the mouth of the Rio Grande. When sold to private hands 1851 she was advertised as "the fine coppered steamer" in the Mobile-Pensacola trade, leaving Mobile every Saturday.

1215 COL. COLBURN

Recess wheel wh b. New Orleans, La., 1863. 125 tons. Built for USQMD. Sold privately on May 2, 1867. Last known document, Feb. 8, 1868.

1216 COL. CROSS

SW steamship wh b. Shousetown, Pa., 1846. 160 tons. Built for USQMD to aid in the prosecution of the Mexican War. Capt. John Birmingham took her to Mexico for the government. Went from New Orleans to Point Isabel, then into the Rio Grande where she was operated to Carmage, the head of navigation. Snagged and lost at San Francisco, Cal., Jan. 29, 1850. She had been turned over to private owners on Aug. 10, 1849.

1217 COLONEL CROSSMAN

SW p wh b. Cincinnati, Oh., 1857. 200 x 38 x 6. Engines, 24's- 7 ft. Three boilers, each 46" by 26 ft. Ran Louisville-New Orleans, Capt. Yore, first trip. Made a trip up the Missouri to St. Joseph that year. Exploded boilers and was lost at New Madrid, Mo., Feb. 2, 1858, with loss of 14 lives.

1218 COL. D. S. GAGE

Rig? b. Terrebonne Parish, La., 1870. 95.8 x 19.2 x 3.9. Owned by Samuel Wolf, Terrebonne Parish. In 1870 ran New Orleans-Grand Isle, leaving Harvey's Canal twice weekly, Capt. Louis Flatau, master, with Dell Roper, clerk. Sold to Galveston, Tex., April 1871.

1219 COL. DICKINSON

SW p wh b. Cincinnati, Oh., 1850. 222 tons. Snagged and lost at Island 18, Mississippi River, Sept. 13, 1853. Ten days later the *FARMER* was lost at the same location.

1220 COL. DRENNEN

SW p wh b. Cincinnati, Oh., 1852. 126 tons. Apparently owned at Memphis. Off the lists in 1859.

1221 COL. EDWARDS

SW p wh b. Louisville, Ky., 1856. 216 tons. 155 x 31 x 6.5. Built for Erastus Smith. Ran New Orleans-Red River. Burned at Shreveport, La., Dec. 12, 1857, with loss of nine lives.

1222 COLONEL FREMONT

Stw p wh b. Elizabeth, Pa., 1850. 74 tons Left Pittsburgh Oct. 28, 1850, on first trip, Capt. James A. Grant, having on board a complete steamer (knocked down) destined to the Sacramento River in California. Capt. Grant lived at El Dorado, Cal., and expected to go via the isthmus. Whether his Sacramento boat got to destination or not we have not ascertained. The *COL. FREMONT* was snagged and lost on Tombigbee River, Ala., Oct. 24, 1854. See *KATE FRISBEE* for another venture of this sort.

1223 COL. GUS LYNN

Stw p wh b. California, Pa., 1859. 132 x 25.7 x 2.8. 83 tons. First owned by C.P. Budd, St. Louis, and commanded by Capt. B.F. Beasley. She was downbound for St. Louis in April 1860, Capt. Beasley, when she was snagged and lost several miles below Sioux City, Iowa, on Missouri River in Henry Chattillion Bend.

1224 COL. HARNEY

SW p wh b. Port Fulton, Ind., 1844. 132 tons. Lost by stranding at Brozos, Tex., on Oct. 12, 1846, with loss of 15 lives.

1225 COL. HUNT

SW steamship wh b. Louisville, Ky., 1847. Built for US-QMD to aid in the prosecution of the Mexican War. Machinery, etc., apparently furnished by John Curry, Louisville. Stephen H. Long worked building her. Went to Point Isabel, Tex., where she was sold to private owners Aug. 28, 1849. Last known document June 29, 1850.

1226 COL. KING

Stw p wh b. Jeffersonville, Ind., 1849. 67 tons. First home port, Mobile, Ala. Exploded and lost on Tennessee River, 1852.

1227 COL. MCLEOD

Stw p wh b. Cincinnati, Oh., 1878. A small boat designed for the Fort Benton trade on the Missouri River. Built by C.T. Dumont and had an iron paddlewheel with wood buckets, and iron pitmans. Built for the I.G. Baker & Co., and named for a Canadian officer. Capt. William Massie took one-half interest before completion. In all she made 11 trips to Fort Benton and two to Cow Island in the two seasons she ran in the upper Missouri. In 1878 she arrived at the fort on October 10, the latest arrival of record. In 1883 she was smashed when the *BUTTE* slipped off the ways at Bismarck.

1228 COL. MORGAN

Stw p wh b. Brownsville, Pa., 1853. 83 tons. Ran on the Upper Mississippi, and was a regular at St. Paul 1855–1858.

1229 COLONEL SELLERS

Ferry wh b. Covington, Ky., 1878. 73.72 tons. Operated at Warsaw, Ky. Rebuilt 1882.

1230 COL. STELLE

SW p wh b. Pittsburgh, Pa., 1860. 198 tons. She went south and was captured as a Confederate steamboat. Sold to private owners, Feb. 26, 1867. Lost at sea, Dec. 31, 1867.

1231 COL. T. G. SPARKS

Stw p wh b. Paducah, Ky., 1893, 169 x 32 x 5.5. Built from the *W. H. CHERRY* (see) and had machinery from the *G. W. SENTELL*. She was built for Capt. S.L. James, lessee of the Louisiana pententiary, Baton Rouge, La. Her master was Capt. S.J. Dudley. All of the crew save officers were convicts. The cabin deck was enclosed with iron bars. Convicts were transported enroute to prison, and goods for the prison were brought in. Sank at St. Gabriel, La., on Mar. 19, 1898.

1232 COL. T. H. JUDSON

SW p wh b. Freedom, Pa., 1857. 191 tons. 140 x 28 x 5.2. Ran New Orleans-Yazoo River. Last U.S. registry was at New Orleans on Nov. 7, 1861, then owned by Mrs. Mary Hierm, New Orleans with Capt. Frederick Probst, master. Went to Confederate service in 1861.

1233 COL. W. S. TAYLOR

Stw ferry wh Originally ferry *LAURANCE* b. Madison Ind., 1891 (see). Owned by Manchester (Ohio) Ferry Co., and operated at Ripley, Oh. Austin D. Butler, in his 80's, was engineer. Condemned in November 1942 and was taken to Manchester where she sank up to the roof, May 29, 1943. Burned late that fall. Her replacement at Ripley was the H&C, formerly operated between Hawesville and Cannelton.

1234 COL. YELL

SW p wh b. Brownsville, Pa., 1847. 233 tons. Stranded and lost at Aransas Pass, Tex., July 13, 1847.

1235 COLONNA

Stw p wh b. Brownsville, Pa., 1859. 102 tons. Burned at Newburgh, Ind., Dec. 1, 1863.

1236 COLORADO

SW p wh b. Brownsville, Pa., 1846. 172 tons. A side-wheeler, same name and tonnage, is noted built at New Albany, Ind., 1848, which may have been a rebuilding job. She ran Pittsburgh-St. Louis. In summer 1848 during low water ran Cincinnati-Madison along with *MARYANN*. She appears in the famed daguerreotype of the Cincinnati waterfront 1848. Stranded and lost at Memphis, Tenn., June 18, 1850.

1237 COLORADO

SW p wh b. Monongahela, Pa., 1850. 97 tons. First home port, Wheeling, Va. Stranded and lost below La Grange, Tex., Mar. 1, 1853.

1238 COLORADO

SW p wh b. Madison, Ind., 1864. 225 x 35 (floor 34) x 6.10. Engines, 23's- 6½ ft. Three boilers, each 40″ by 26 ft. Sidewheels, 26 ft. dia. with 10½ buckets. Drew 36″ light and carried 650 tons. Built for the Hannibal & St. Joseph Railway. Her partner boat was the *DENVER* (see). A photograph exists showing both of these boats at Omaha, Neb., taken Oct. 22, 1866. The "Hundredth Meridian Party" rode the Hannibal & St Joseph RR to St. Joseph and were taken aboard for the trip to Omaha, auspices of the Union Pacific, which took the party to Denver, Colo., with stops to shoot and hunt en route. Sold to the Memphis & St. Louis Packet Co. (Anchor Line) in 1871. Sank at the foot of Island 10, Mississippi River in October 1879, raised. In 1881 Anchor Line sold her to Capt. Peter Manion, St. Louis, who ran excursions with her there. Burned at the foot of Dorcas Street, St. Louis, Jan. 2, 1884, along with the *CITY OF ALTON* (see).

1239 COLOSSAL

Stw p wh b. Pittsburgh, Pa., 1869. 185 x 36 x 8. Owned by M.A. Cox, Adam Jacobs, and others. Primarily a heavy freight carrier, and came out now with no passenger cabin. Sold May 1870 by Capt. Cox to Little Rock RR for transporting iron and other railroad material. Went to U.S. marshal sale at New Orleans in spring 1871, sold to Memphis & El Paso RR. Later was bought by A.B. Hall, Willard Blakeslee, and others, St. Louis. She was at Cincinnati from St. Louis, August 1873 with iron ore, and thence to Pittsburgh to load railroad iron for the Iron Mountain RR., in barges. Burned at St. Louis, Mar. 8, 1876.

1240 COLOSSUS

Stw p wh b. Brownsville, Pa., 1863. 183 tons. 155.2 x 31.9 x 4.2. Sold to the U.S. Navy Dec. 6, 1864, and became Tinclad #25 on Feb. 24, 1865. Sold at Mound City, Ill., Aug. 17, 1865, to R.B. Ward. Was renamed *MEMPHIS* on Sept. 27, 1865. Original owner not known to us, but probably owned by Capt. Vint Shinkle, Cincinnati, when acquired by Navy.

1241 COLUMBIA

SW p wh b. Pittsburgh, Pa., 1845. 149 tons. Off the lists in 1847.

1242 COLUMBIA

SW p wh b. Augusta, Ky., 1856. 164 tons. First home port, Savannah, Ga. Sold foreign in 1857.

1243 COLUMBIA

Stw p wh b. Monongahela, Pa., 1864. 350.20 tons. Capt. William Dean superintended construction. Came out August 1864 to run Pittsburgh-St. Louis, Capt. R.J. Porter, with Fred B. Holmes, clerk. Chartered to Keokuk Packet Co., mid-October 1864, Capt. Porter commanding and crew of *DIE VERNON* (see) running her. She was impressed to U.S. service that winter, and on Aug. 9, 1865, Capt. Porter showed up in Pittsburgh, coming by the cars, saying the *COLUMBIA* was at Cincinnati undergoing repairs. She went to Cumberland River and got caught above Harpeth Shoals by low water for a protracted period. Back in Pittsburgh, Capt. Porter, Jan. 6, 1866. Loading at Pittsburgh Apr. 3, 1866, for St. Paul direct. The Upper Mississippi packets *MINNESOTA* and *PHIL SHERIDAN* had just done likewise (see). Capt. Porter chartered the boat July 1866 to run between St. Joseph and Omaha. He came home to Pittsburgh, fell ill, and within a day he died. The boat was sold in 1868 to Capt. Jos. Throckmorton who ran her a trip to Fort Benton and several trips to the Illinois River. Lost in ice at St. Louis, Feb. 24, 1872.

1244 COLUMBIA

Stw p wh b. Pt. Pleasant, W. Va., 1893. 156 x 24.2 x 4. Engines, 12's- 4½ ft. Two boilers, each 36" by 22 ft. She was built from the *CAPITOL CITY* b. 1888 (see). She ran Charleston-Gallipolis-Racine, Capt. Miller Burdette, master with Wm. Berthisel, clerk. Birthisel later was master. The Kanawha Navigation Co. was formed May 18, 1899, John A. Carr, Charleston, pres. They took over the *COLUMBIA, MOUNTAINEER, T. D. DALE,* and later acquired *LEXINGTON* and *ESTOLA*. This lasted until spring of 1901. On June 12, 1901, the *COLUMBIA* went to Charleston & Gallipolis Packet Co., G.H. Honshell, pres., Huntington, W. Va. Sold to H.W. Senz, Malden, W. Va., entire, June 28, 1902. Two days later sold to Montgomery & Gallipolis Packet Co., Howard Donnally, Charleston, pres. On Mar. 25, 1904, she was backing out from Glenwood Landing, a mile below Charleston, when wind blew her into a rock and she sank. Capt. A.S. Leash, Red House, W. Va., was master at the time. Raised. Sold to Capt. E.E. Eisenbarth, entire, Feb. 1, 1905. He used her to tow his showboat. Downbound with the showboat from Marietta to Pt. Pleasant she hit the outside lock wall at Dam 18, Ohio River at 5:00 A.M. Mar. 25, 1908. The towboat *HENRY LOUREY* took off the people. The whistle went to the *HELEN LANE*.

1245 COLUMBIA

SW ex and ferry wh b. Jeffersonville, Ind., by Howard, 1892. 170 x 35 x 6. Engines, 20's- 6 ft. Three boilers, each 44" by 26 ft. Owned by Louisville & Jeffersonville Ferry Co., E.L. Dorsey, supt. Engines and doctor came from *NEW SHALLCROSS* (see). Burned at the foot of Watt Street, Jeffersonville in winter quarters, Jan. 20, 1913.

1246 COLUMBIA

Stw p wh b. Clinton, Iowa, 1897. 166.5 x 33.6 x 5. Engines, 14's- 6 ft. Two boilers. Built by W.J. Young & Co., Clinton, and was operated as a packet out of St. Louis. In March 1905 Capt. Walter Blair and others bought her from C.H. Young, in her winter quarters at Paducah. Blair removed ten foreward staterooms, made of her an excursion boat and placed Capt. S.R. Dodds as master. In September 1907 John Sagle, Keokuk, chartered her to participate in the Roosevelt parade from Keokuk to Memphis. Aboard were Governor Van Sant of Minnesota, his wife, and Capt. and Mrs. Blair. Capt. Blair was presented to the President on this occasion. Sold in January 1912 to Capt. H.F. Mehl, Peoria, Ill., for $14,500. Excursions were run on the Illinois River terminating in her disastrous sinking on July 5, 1918, with life-loss placed at 89. This happened near Pekin, Ill., during a fog; the boat was snagged.

1247 COLUMBIA

Stw p and ferry wh b. Osage City, Mo., 1898. Built for St. Louis & Hermann Packet Co. Sold to the Burress family, Miami, Mo., Aug. 5, 1903, and operated by Capt. John F.

Burress, as a packet and ferry. Sold and ran out of St. Louis (1907) owned by Capt. E.A. Nixon. Was at Memphis in 1913, and back at St. Louis in 1914. Taken out of service, Sept. 13, 1915.

1248 COLUMBIA

Stw p wh b. Stillwater, Minn., 1900. 117.3 x 24 x 4.6. Constructed from former rafter *PAULINE.* Owned by Capts. William Henning and Frank J. Fugina. Sold January 1906 to Florida interest, Capt. Comber. This and other boats, including *WANDERER, VIRGINIA, PHIL SCHECKEL,* were used in the lower Keys during the building of the FEC Railroad to Key West. She burned at Milton, Fla., Mar. 13, 1911.

1249 COLUMBIA

SW p wh b. West Brownsville, Pa., at Axton yard, 1902. 172 x 34 x 6. Engines, 16's- 5½ ft. Three boilers, each 42″ by 24 ft. Overall width, 48 ft. Owned by Pittsburgh, Brownsville & Morgantown Packet Co. A pot of roofing tar was being heated aboard, boiled over, and set her afire on Friday, Jan. 16, 1903, at Pittsburgh, 3:00 P.M. The Pittsburgh fire department responded and saved the hull. Capt. John L. Reno was master at the time.

1250 COLUMBIA

SW p wh b. Elizabeth, Pa., 1903 using hull from boat in last listing. 172 x 34 x 6. Engines, 17's- 5½ ft. from *JAMES G. BLAINE* (see). Same boilers as before. She was the largest Monongahela River packet ever built, had 75 staterooms. Capt. Robert Demaine was her first master. She left Pittsburgh on May 15, 1904, and went within one-and-one-half miles of Fairmont, W. Va., where a low bridge owned by B&O RR prevented passage above. The *ROSE HITE* had made the same voyage several weeks prior. She later made Fairmont trips. A U.S. marshal attached all holdings of the owning company in February 1906. A new company was formed May 1906 called Monongahela & Ohio Packet Co., headed by Capt. Martin F. Noll, and William E. Roe as secretary and general manager. Capt. William H. Loyd was appointed master of *COLUMBIA,* and it was on May 1, 1907, that she made the first through trip from Pittsburgh to Fairmont, made possible by the removal of the offending bridge. Pilots on that trip were R.L. Demain and George B. Hendrickson. Burned laid up at Moss Side Landing, Camden Station, opposite Glassport, Pa., Feb. 17, 1910 at 6:15 P.M.

1251 COLUMBIA

Stw p wh b. Jeffersonville, Ind., by Howard, 1903. 170 x 29 x 4. Compound engines, 10's, 20's- 6 ft. Two boilers, each 36″ by 24 ft. Owned by Carter Packet Co., New Orleans. She was a cotton-type packet designed for Red River, and also ran New Orleans-Upper Bends. Sank on Feb. 26, 1901, at Grand Levee, nine miles above Bayou Sara, La., having hit an obstruction. She listed, caught fire, and cabin burned off. Dismantled.

1252 COLUMBIAN

Stw p wh b. Brownsville, Pa., 1848. 138 tons. Built by Capt. William Dean. Had no passenger cabin, built for freight. The *UNCLE SAM* built same year was similar (see). Sold 1850 to Capt. Thomas Greenlee. Off the lists in 1855.

1253 COLUMBIAN

SW p wh b. New Haven, Mo. (hull), and completed at St. Louis, 1865. 237 x 36 x 6. Engines, 22's- 7 ft. Three boilers, each 44″ by 26 ft. Owned by St. Louis & Omaha Packet Co. This was the largest hull built at New Haven, put up at Miller's Landing, Mile 80, Missouri River. Hull was made of burr oak procured locally, in short lengths, and she leaked badly. Capt. A. Barnes commanded. Later ran St. Louis-Atchison, Kans., Capt. J.H. Willoughby. She rescued passengers from the sunken *EMMA NO. 3* (see) and took them to Cairo. Snagged and lost June 23, 1870, at head of Brunswick Island, en route Omaha to St. Louis.

1254 COLUMBIANA

Stw p wh b. Wellsville, Oh., 1843. 124 tons. Made trips Pittsburgh-Zanesville, 1843, Capt. Jesse Smith. She was reported sunk at Lexington Bar, Missouri River, Sept. 25, 1845. Sold to the U.S. in 1847.

1255 COLUMBUS

SW p wh b. Jeffersonville, Ind., 1850. 542 tons. Ran St. Louis-New Orleans, Capt. Post. Collapsed a flue near Island 4, Mississippi River, May 7, 1850. Eight passengers and two firemen killed, and five others drowned. The *MAGNOLIA* towed her to Cairo for repairs. Off the lists in 1856.

1256 COMANCHE

SW p wh b. Freedom, Pa., 1850. 164 tons. She went to Point Isabel, Tex. Sold foreign in 1852.

1257 COME AND SEE ME

Prop p wh b. Peninsula, Oh., 1867. 63 tons. Built from a canal boat by T.B. Townsend, Zanesville, Oh. Crockery was loaded aboard at Zanesville, produce boats taken in tow, and she made trips down the Mississippi peddling her wares. Capt. Steve Sprague commanded. Ran until 1882 when the *HATTIE BLISS* (see) was built to replace her. *COME AND SEE ME* was the first "cover girl" on the front page of the *S&D Reflector,* issue March 1964.

1258 COMET

Stw p wh b. Elizabeth, Pa., 1846. 116 tons. Ran Pittsburgh-Zanesville, Capt. James Boyd, with some regularity 1847–1849. Capt. Charles F. Boyd also was on her. Snagged and lost at Grafton, Ill., Sept. 18, 1850.

1259 COMET

SW p wh b. Louisville, Ky., 1857. 183 tons. Ran New Orleans-Jefferson, 1858, Capt. Reuben Sleade, master, with W.S. Sleade, clerk. In 1859 running New Orleans-Monroe, Capt. Len Moore, master, In 1860, New Orleans-

Red River, Capt. Reuben Sleade. In 1861, New Orleans-Lake Bisteneau, Capt. W.V. Harrell, master, with J.T. Reeder, clerk. Went to Confederate registry.

1260 COMET

SW p wh b. Red Wing, Minn., 1857. 100 tons. Ran St. Louis-Alton. Made a trip to Shreveport, La., arriving there Aug. 2, 1858. Sank and lost during a windstorm 18 miles below Memphis, Feb. 19, 1859.

1261 COMET

Steam prop p b. De Soto, Wis., 1873. 20 tons. Ran Alma, Wis.,-Wabasha, Minn., trade, Capt. H.C. Wilcox. He swapped her off for the *LION* (see).

1262 COMFORT

Rig? b. Wheeling, W. Va., 1875. 78.04 tons. Ran local trades out of Wheeling. Exploded boiler near Pipe Creek, Ohio River, Oct. 3, 1877, killing six of the crew and four passengers. Capt. Kirkbride and pilot Ummiseller were among those lost.

1263 COMMERCE

SW p wh b. Brownsville, Pa., 1845. 101 tons. Off the lists in 1850.

1264 COMMERCE

Stw p wh b. Paducah, Ky., 1856. 111 tons. First home port, Nashville, Tenn. Went to Confederate registry 1861.

1265 COMMERCE

Stw p wh b. Freedom, Pa., 1856. 198 tons. Lost in a big steamboat fire at Pittsburgh on May 7, 1859, at the time by Capt. J.R. Hendrickson, David Hendrickson, G.W. Rowley and others. There is record that Capt. Rowley had her to St. Paul, Minn. in 1857.

1266 COMMERCIAL

SW p wh b. Brownsville, Pa., 1860. 266 tons. First ran Cincinnati-St. Louis, Capt. R.C. Mason, with Mason and Fisher, clerks. Was quite active during the war carrying troops and U.S. supplies. After the battle at Pittsburg Landing, Tenn., she was loaded at Cincinnati with medical supplies, nurses, etc., and sent there along with the *DILIGENT* (see). Reported sold latter May 1862 to W. Wyatt, Louisville, Ky., and L.M. Flourney, Paducah. Sold soon thereafter to Capt. Samuel B. Archer and others, Cannelton, Ind. Archer was a Johnny Reb and once flew the Republican flag on this boat Memphis to Louisville. He and his wife Burnette Mason Archer smuggled quinine in a rag doll carried by daughter Mollie and sewed into Mrs. Archer's skirts. Ran Memphis-White River spring 1864 in the "Archer Line" along with *DES ARC* and *EMMA NO. 2* (both see). Archer, Hart & Co. dissolved partnership July 1866 and Capt. Ed Hart, New Albany, Ind., took the *COMMERCIAL, LIBERTY NO. 2*, and another boat under construction. She was first to the scene of the wrecked *MATTIE HAYS* after that boat exploded at Island 66, Mississippi River, Feb. 10, 1870, then commanded by Capt. Matt A. Glass. Sank and lost at Evansville, Ind., Jan. 1, 1872.

1267 COMMODORE

SW p wh b. Fulton, Ohio, 1853. 129 tons. Off the lists, 1856.

1268 COMMODORE

SW p wh Originally *FORT GAINES* b. New Orleans, 1863 (see). She was operated by the Confederates renamed *COMMODORE.* Captured by U.S. and original name restored, Feb. 5, 1864. (See *FORT GAINES.*)

1269 COMMODORE

SW p wh b. Cincinnati, Oh., 1866. 348 tons. Sold, new, to U.S. Engineers. Col. John N. McComb, in charge of the Cincinnati office, used her for clearing channels by gunpowder blasting. McComb then built the twin-hull toothpullers *S.H. LONG, J. J. ABERT, R. E. DERUSSY,* and *S. THAYER*. The Engineers renamed *COMMODORE* to become *GEN. G. G. TOTTEN* as of Apr. 13, 1867.

1270 COMMODORE

Stw b. New Haven, Mo., 1890. 97 x 23.2 x 3.2. Engines, 10"-4½ ft. One boiler. Owned by D.N. Burress and ferried at Miami, Mo. Sunk by ice in winter quarters one-half mile above Miami, Missouri River, Feb. 24, 1903.

1271 COMMODORE

SW ferry wh b. Lake City, Minn., 1898. 70 x 18 x 3. Still documented in 1908, maybe longer.

1272 COMMODORE PERRY

SW p wh b. Cincinnati, Oh., 1846. 293 tons. Ran Cincinnati-New Orleans, Capt. Henry A. Jones, with M.L. Virden, clerk. Stranded and lost at Island 8, Mississippi River, April 1850.

1273 COMMODORE PERRY

Stw p wh b. Freedom, Pa., 1857. Running Cincinnati-Nashville 1861, Capt. Brown. In February 1862 at Pittsburgh, taking heavy guns, shot, etc., to the lower Ohio. Capt. J.M. Andrews bought her at Pittsburgh Feb. 25, 1862, for Pittsburgh-Louisville trade. Upbound near Ashland, Ky., April 1862 sank the *EUNICE* (see) and was attached by a U.S. marshal at Wheeling as a result. She lay there six weeks while claims were settled. Collapsed a flue at the Louisville, Ky., wharf Aug. 2, 1862, bound from Nashville to Cincinnati. This happened at supper time at foot of Fifth Street, with 30 passengers aboard. She burned, with loss of three deckhands.

1274 COMMODORE ROLLINGPIN

Ferry wh b. Enterprise, Ind., 1871. 24.81 tons. Still listed 1876, maybe longer.

1275 COMMONWEALTH

SW p wh b. Shousetown, Pa., 1864. 261 x 43 x 8.6. Engines, 22's- 9 ft. Three boilers. Ran New Orleans-St. Louis 1866 with James Lloyd, master, and James K. Boyles, clerk. Owned 1868 by Benjamin F. Hutchinson ¾, St. Louis, and

M.W. Beltzhoover ¼, Allegheny City, Pa., with Capt. William Conley, master. In May 1873 sold to Capt. J.P. Sedam and others who extensively rebuilt her, and could not pay the bills. A U.S. marshal libeled her at St. Louis in Nov. 1873. She was bought in by Capt. Thomas W. Shields and others and ran New Orleans-St. Louis and also made Cincinnati-New Orleans trips. Her clerk Owen G. Cates also was a stockholder. It is said she once went up the Wabash River to New Harmony, Ind., and brought out a large cargo of corn. She was incorporated into the Anchor Line. In her old age she was sold to a gentleman of Dover, Ky., who ran several Cincinnati-New Orleans trips with her and then pinch-hit in the excursion trade between Cincinnati and Coney Island. One night she ran over the *LAME DUCK* and sank it. She burned at the foot of Whittaker Street, Cincinnati at 11:00 P.M., Aug. 25, 1889. Capt. Harry Doss once told this scribe that he saw the fire. Frank L. Sibley recalled that she had a mockingbird whistle, and had to lower her stacks to clear the Cincinnati suspension bridge even on ordinary stages.

1276 COMO

SW p wh b. Wheeling, W. Va., 1866. 367 tons. Burned and lost on the Trinity River, Tex., Apr. 28, 1867, with loss of one life.

1277 COMPANION

Stw p wh b. Wheeling, Va., 1847. 165 tons. Ran locally out of Wheeling. Collapsed a flue at Line Island, Ohio River, 11:00 P.M., Oct. 16, 1850. Off the lists in 1853.

1278 COMPROMISE

SW p wh b. Monongahela, Pa., 1850. 270 tons. Ran New Orleans-Natchitoches. Off the list in 1860.

1279 CONCERT

Stw ferry wh b. Brownsville, Pa., 1865. 8.59 tons. Operated in the Pittsburgh area. Sold to H. Davis who ferried at Ashland, Ky., with her until he dismantled her 1873. The original boiler went on the *SANDY FASHION* (see) and exploded, wrecking the boat April 1878.

1280 CONCORDIA

SW p wh b. Cincinnati, Oh., 1843. 469 tons. Ran New Orleans-Vicksburg, Capt. St. Clair Thomasson, later Capt. John Raine. It is said of Capt. Thomasson that he introduced "high living style on these packets, and made red fish and oysters a legal tender for the shipment of cotton." She exploded all boilers at Plaquemine, La., Sept. 16, 1846, Capt. Horace Pease in command. Twenty-eight were killed, many wounded.

1281 CONCORDIA

SW p wh b. Cincinnati, Oh., 1847. 499 tons. Replaced the former boat of the name listed above. In February 1847 running New Orleans-Milliken's Bend, Capt. John Raine. Running New Orleans-Lake Providence, September 1851, Capt. W.H. Cable in command. Off the lists 1854.

1282 CONCORDIA

SW ferry wh b. Jeffersonville, Ind., by Howard, 1872. 86 x 25.4 x 3.9. Owned by Natchez Ferry Co. Operated Natchez-Vidalia.

1283 CONCORDIA

SW ferry wh b. Jeffersonville, Ind., by Howard, 1880. 92 x 25.6 x 4.6. Owned by Natchez & Vidalia Ferry Co.

1284 CONCORDIA

Stw p wh b. Jeffersonville, Ind., by Howard, 1906. 152 x 36.6 x 6. Engines (compound), 10's, 20's- 6 ft. by Swain. Two boilers, each 40" by 20 ft. Built for Capt. George Prince and arrived at Natchez on Christmas Day, 1906. Engines were tandem compound, condensing, says Neare, Gibbs & Co.'s *Report Book,* same as Swain put on *VERNE SWAIN* b. 1904 (see). Ran Natchez-Atchafalaya and Black rivers, Capt. George Prince, master, with O.K. Wilds, clerk. She was rebuilt at Paducah in 1912. On June 7, 1913, doing flood relief work near Clayton, La., she sank drowning head clerk A.D. Primm and 12 workers. She was raised that July, ran up Red River 1913-1914. Renamed *UNCLE OLIVER* (see).

1285 CONDUCTOR

Stw p wh b. Smithland, Ky., 1849. 75 tons. Apparently ran on the Cumberland River. Off the lists 1851.

1286 CONESTOGA

SW U.S. gunboat wh b. Brownsville, Pa., 1859. 279 tons. Her engines, 24's- 7 ft., were from the packet *J. M. CONVERS* (see). Built as a side-wheel towboat by Daniel Bushnell and Jacob Jay Vandergrift, Pittsburgh. They sold her to USQMD on May 7, 1861. Capt. Vandergrift took her to Cincinnati and worked on her conversion into a gunboat, and then she was taken to New Albany, Ind., for armor-plating, and upon completion was turned over to Commodore Foote, USN, Oct. 1, 1862. Capt. John A. Duble was her first skipper and took her out to Cairo, Ill. After a series of engagements she was lost in collision with the *GEN. PRICE* below Grand Gulf, Miss., Mar. 8, 1864. An office building at the corner of Wood and Water, Pittsburgh, built in 1890, was named Conestoga Building in this boat's honor. See *S&D Reflector,* June 1975, page 3.

1287 CONEWAGO

Stw p wh b. Brownsville, Pa., 1854. 186 tons. In the St. Louis & St. Paul Packet Co., 1855-1857; same, Capt. James Ward, 1858-1859. Cincinnati-Arkansas River, Capt. D.S. James, master, with Chandler, clerk, January 1861. The Pittsburgh *Gazette,* Feb. 15, 1862: "*CONEWAGO* left suddenly Thursday night for Cincinnati where she will enter the government service. But for this she would have been taken to Brownsville yesterday and her machinery transferred to a new boat building at that place." Dismantled in 1864.

1288 CONFIDENCE

SW p wh b. West Wheeling, Oh., at the Garden yard (hull) and completed at Wheeling, 1845. 139 tons. Ran Galena-St. Louis 1845-1847. Sank following collision with *EDWARD BATES* two miles below Hamburg on Mississippi River, Sept. 13, 1847, with a cargo of groceries. Owned at the time by Miller & Bower, Hannibal, Mo. Raised. Collided with *BROOKLYN* at Big Bone Island, Ohio River, Nov. 16, 1849, downbound, and sank along the Kentucky shore. She was a big low-water packet running Louisville-St. Louis, Capt. McGuire.

1289 CONGO

Stw p wh b. Harmar, Oh., by Knox, 1890. 228 x 36.5 x 6.2. Engines, 18's- 7 ft. Owned by the White Collar Line, Cincinnati. Built under supervision of Capt. Edwin F. Maddy who came out master of her. After the *RAINBOW* burned (see) she was entered in the Pittsburgh-Cincinnati trade, November 1890; her crew: Capt. Maddy, master; Jules Wehrman, purser; William F. Brookhart and Aaron McLaughlin, pilots; Clay Dale, mate; and Irwin Johnson, steward. Later ran Cincinnati-Memphis, Capt. Charles B. Church. On Jan. 12, 1896, she was leaving Caruthersville, Mo. A stiff wind caused her to collide with a barge of lumber, and she sank and was lost. Four lives were lost.

1290 CONNECTICUT

SW p wh b. Shousetown, Pa., 1848. 248 tons. Stranded and lost at President's Island, Mississippi River, Oct. 29, 1852.

1291 CONQUEROR

SW p wh b. New Albany, Ind., 1847. 398 tons. First home port, New Orleans. Burned and lost at New Orleans, May 16, 1863.

1292 CONS MILLAR

Stw p wh b. Cincinnati, Oh., 1875. 209.5 x 34.5 x 5. Engines, 15's- 5 ft. Two boilers, each 40" dia. by 24 ft., six flues. Owned by Parker, Wise & Co., Cincinnati, and Capt. W.C. Tichenor and others. Named for the popular river news reporter for the Cincinnati *Commercial*. James Wilson, clerk. Was still there 1879.

1293 CONSIGNEE

SW p wh b. Wheeling, Va., 1848. 210 ft. long on deck. Engines, 17's- 5½ ft. Three boilers, each 36" dia. by 22 ft. Machinery by Phillips & Co., Wheeling. Ran Cincinnati-St. Louis. The Cairo, Ill., *Delta* reported on Mar. 22, 1849, that *CONSIGNEE* was there yesterday with 240 emigrants bound Pittsburgh to St. Joseph, Mo., bound for California, calling themselves Pittsburgh and California Enterprise Co. The *CONSIGNEE* had collided with the *CAROLINE* Mar. 19, 1849, and three were drowned. Lost by stranding at Cape Girardeau, Mo., Jan. 10, 1852.

1294 CONSTITUTION

SW p wh The *CITY OF MEMPHIS* (see) was renamed *CONSTITUTION* early 1864, and carried the name into May 1864. On May 10, 1864, notice was printed in many Valley newspapers: "The name of the *CONSTITUTION* has been changed to *CITY OF MEMPHIS,* her original name, by order of the Custom House, and in accordance with the late law of Congress, which forbids any boat changing her name under any pretense whatever. We understand that the *HOPE* will also be compelled to restore her original name which was *T. L. McGILL.*"

1295 CONSUL

SW p wh b. Brownsville, Pa., 1844. 127 tons. She was the first of the regular "line" boats in the Pittsburgh-Brownsville trade on Monongahela River, Capt. Samuel Clark. When Lock 4 was completed in 1844 the *CONSUL,* under the auspices of Gen. J.K. Moorhead, took aboard a party of Pittsburgh citizens and they went to Brownsville, Pa., then head of slackwater. The *CONSUL* more often ran down the Ohio, to Cincinnati or Wheeling. Capt. Morgan Mason was master, and in 1848, owned by Capt. Dorsey P. Kinney, ran Pittsburgh-Wheeling. In March, 1849 ran Cincinnati-Ripley, Oh., Capt. Metcalf. Capt. Isaac M. Mason recalled that his first job on the river was as clerk on *CONSUL,* 1846. Off the lists 1851.

1296 CONTINENTAL

SW p wh b. Shousetown, Pa., and completed at Pittsburgh, 1860. 282 x 41 x 8.5. Engines, 26's- 9 ft. Four boilers, each 44" by 30 ft. Paddlewheels 34 ft. dia. with 14 ft. buckets. Built for Capt. Ben F. Hutchinson and others, St. Louis. Ran St. Louis-New Orleans. She was impressed into U.S. service as a troop carrier early 1862, was in Grant's Tennessee River campaign, and in 1864 served as a hospital boat at St. Louis. Became one of the fleet of the Atlantic & Mississippi Steamship Co. in the St. Louis-New Orleans trade. Sank at Devil's Island below St. Louis after hitting the wreck of the *JAMES MONTGOMERY,* early December 1864, and was raised. In 1865 Capt. H.G. Carson, master, with J.P. Hamilton, clerk. Later was in John N. Bofinger's St. Louis & New Orleans Packet Co., Capt. McCloy. Sold by U.S. marshal at St. Louis Dec. 26, 1873, to a local wrecker who dismantled her.

1297 CONVEYOR

Stw ferry wh b. Middleport, Oh., 1898. 110.2 x 30.3 x 4.4. Originally owned by Capt. Levi W. Inglebright, Martins Ferry, Oh., and operated to Wheeling. Sold in July 1904 to Capt. S. Semonin, Evansville, Ind., and was taken there. Sank at Evansville late 1904 and was not raised until October 1905.

1298 CONVOY

SW p wh b. St. Louis, Mo., 1846. 749 tons. A large sidewheeler in the Memphis-New Orleans trade operated by Cornelius K. Garrison, and clerked by William Ralston. There are references in Gould about these two gentlemen, who sailed high later on in railroading and finance. Also a story about the boat (page 677). Burned Mar. 8, 1849, above Natchez with loss of two lives.

1299 CONVOY

Stw p wh b. Freedom, Pa., 1854. 123 tons. Ran Pittsburgh-Wheeling in 1855, Capt. Wolff. Noticed arriving at St. Paul in 1857. In U.S. service on the upper Tennessee during the war. In 1861 owned by her skipper Capt. Erwin Creel and J.S. McDonald, both of Beaver County, Pa. and ran on the Allegheny. In the early 60's was in Wheeling-Steubenville trade along with the *JAMES MEANS* and *S.C. BAKER*. Dismantled in 1864.

1300 CONVOY

Ferry wh b. Meredosia, Ill., 1874. 24.64 tons. Was inspected in St. Louis District, Aug. 27, 1881.

1301 CONVOY NO. 2

Stw p wh b. Cincinnati, Oh., 1863. 143 tons. Was acquired by USQMD on Jan. 12, 1864. Just prior to that she had been running Louisville-Nashville. Struck a monitor at Cairo, Ill., in 1865 while in war service and capsized. Was righted and repaired. Sold to private hands, Jan. 29, 1867, and renamed *IDA FULTON* (see).

1302 CONWAY

Stw p wh b. Lewisburg, Ark., 1859. 103 tons. Engines 12's-3½ ft. from the *VIRGINIA BELLE* (see). Operated by Capt. David Thomas. Sank at Badgett Landing, Ark., Dec. 15, 1860; raised, she is reported as assisting in the rescue of passengers from the *ACACIA* (0044A) on Aug. 21, 1862.

1303 COOSA

Stw p wh Originally *CRICKET NO. 4* b. Cincinnati, Oh., 1863 (see). In U.S. service she was the *TALLAHATCHIE*, and when sold to private hands Aug. 25, 1865, was renamed *COOSA* by T.A. Roberts of New Orleans, Capt. W.T. Boardman. Sold on Feb. 23, 1867, to Andren Knight, New Orleans, Capt. David H. Kenney. In January 1868 sold to John Robinson, the circus man, who organized a water carnival and towed it with *COOSA* in 1868; she was up the Ohio to Rochester, Pa., then to Charleston on the Kanawha, and back to Cincinnati. On May 22 she left there and went up the Tennessee to Johnsonville; thence up the Mississippi to St. Paul and St. Croix River. Wound up that fall back at Cincinnati. John Robinson sold her to some Cincinnati individuals and she quickly won a debatable reputation for running disreputable moonlight excursions. Several Sunday schools cancelled contracts for picnic parties. One trip she went to the Kentucky shore opposite the mouth of the Little Miami River and staged a prizefight on shore, Payton vs. Lafferty, 17 rounds in 29 minutes, Lafferty the winner when he closed both eyes of his opponent. Frederick Shoemaker was indicted by a grand jury of Kenton County, Ky., for arson when the boat burned at the mouth of the Licking River, on Sept. 7, 1869.

1304 COOSA BELLE

Stw p wh b. Louisville, Ky., 1855. 229 tons. 194 x 33 x 6. Went to Mobile for Alabama River trade, Capt. George H. Cloudes, master and owner. In 1858 was running New Orleans-Red River. In 1860 back on the Alabama, and sank and lost at Bridgeport, Ala., Apr. 25, 1860, going down with 667 barrels of lime and 36 bales of cotton.

1305 COQUETTE

Prop freighter wh b. Peninsula, Oh., 1864. 39.64 tons. Ran trips on the Muskingum River, converted from a canalboat, Capt. J.C. Bryant.

1306 CORA

SW p wh b. New Albany, Ind., 1845. 179 tons. Ran New Orleans-Shreveport, Capt. F.B. Kimball, 1846. New Orleans-Ouachita River, 1849. Off the lists 1850.

1307 CORA

SW p wh b. Rock Island, Ill., 1846. 144 tons. 140 x 24 x 5. She was single engine, stiff shaft, with cylinder 18"-5 ft. The hull was built by Capt. Jos. Throckmorton. Engines made in St. Louis. Two boilers. Capt. Throckmorton ran her on the Upper Mississippi; she was the first arrival at Fort Snelling, 1847. Ran Galena-St. Peters, 1848, and also made trips to St. Croix Falls. Capt. Frank Dozier and others bought her fall 1848 for Missouri River. Snagged and sunk below Council Bluffs, Iowa with loss of 15 lives, May 5, 1851.

1308 CORA

Stw p wh b. Elizabeth, Pa., 1856. 127 tons. First registered at New Orleans. Went to Confederate registry in 1861.

1309 CORA

SW p wh b. Franklin, La., 1860. 52 tons. First documented Jan. 11, 1863. Off the lists in 1866.

1310 CORA

Stw p wh b. Cincinnati, Oh., 1864. 215 tons. From a Cairo newspaper: "The steamer *CORA* sank in the Missouri River, May 1, 1865, at 9 A.M., near De Soto, about 50 miles above Omaha. The accident occurred near the wreck of the *BERTRAND* (see). She went down in six feet. She is a new sternwheeler built expressly for the Missouri trade, probably worth $40,000, and boat and cargo are fully insured." She had engines 15's- 5 ft. and two boilers. The *Missouri Historical Review* reported the accident near Calhoun, Nebraska, 30 miles above Omaha, and notes that the boilers and engines were salvaged.

1311 CORA NO. 2

SW p wh b. New Albany, Ind., 1849. 375 tons. Went to New Orleans, and in 1851 was running to Ouachita River. Running 1855 New Orleans-Vicksburg, Capt. D.B. Mosby. Off the lists 1855.

1312 CORA NO. 3

SW p wh b. St. Louis, Mo., 1865. 395 tons. Machinery from prior *CORA* (of 1864, see). Ran on the Missouri River, owned in part by Capt. Joe Kinney. She was snagged and lost at the island in the Missouri now known as Cora Island, the first one after entering the river from the Mississippi. This happened on Aug. 13, 1869, and the wreck caused the island to form. Capt. E.M. Baldwin was on watch, then a young man. His father had instructed him to go around an existing island because of a bad snag in the chute. Ed, anxious to save time, took the short cut and lost. This was his only sinking in a long career of piloting.

1313 CORA ANDERSON

SW p wh b. New Albany, Ind., 1856. 658 tons. 256 x 39 x 8. Engines, 24's- 10 ft. Three boilers, each 46″ dia. by 26 ft. This was primarily a freight boat, had a small passenger cabin and no rail around the boiler deck. Originally owned by Capt. John W. Carroll and others, and ran St. Louis-New Orleans in the "Railroad Line." Capt. John Bofinger bought stock in her, 1859. She sank and was lost 40 miles above Vicksburg in Eagle Bend, Jan. 22, 1861.

1314 CORA BELL

Rig? b. Pittsburgh, Pa., 1871. She ran a trial trip in the Allegheny River at Pittsburgh on Aug. 2, 1871, hit a bridge pier and knocked down her stacks. Next day took an excursion to Rochester, Pa., and broke down in Deadman's Island and returned her picnic party to Pittsburgh by rail. On August 5 slated to take an excursion from McKees Rocks, Pa.

1315 CORA BELL

SW ferry wh b. North McGregor, Iowa, 1888. 41 x 11 x 4. Inspected in the Cairo, Ill. area in 1896.

1316 CORA EMILY

Rig? b. Lyons, Iowa, 1879. 5.75 tons. She was documented at Davenport in 1886.

1317 CORA L. ROBERTS

Stw freight boat wh b. Helena, Ark., 1910. 133 x 30.7 x 5.6. Sank at Big Rock, Arkansas River, Oct. 15, 1914.

1318 CORA S.

Stw p wh b. New Albany, Ind., 1864. 201 tons. 155 x 31 x 4.5. Two boilers, each 42″ by 20 ft. Had a remarkable career for sinkings; once on the Alabama River, twice on the Arkansas, once on the Ohio, and once on the Mississippi. One of her Arkansas sinkings was in Oakley's Bend, Oct. 20, 1868. The *W. A. CALDWELL* brought her passengers to Memphis. Final loss was opposite Shawneetown, Ill., on the Ohio, Oct. 25, 1869, then owned by Capts. Hicks King and Al Croxal. She was thought to have struck the boilers from the recently demolished *CUMBERLAND* (see).

1319 CORDELIA

Ferry wh b. Cincinnati, Oh. 1873. 33.13 tons. Was in the Wheeling area, 1876.

1320 CORDELIA ANN

Stw p wh b. Paducah, Ky, 1862. 110 x 24.1 x 3. Built by Capt. William Thompson and named for his wife. Ran Louisville-Cairo in low water summer 1864, and was snagged below Grandview, Ind. Raised. Went to Memphis in October 1865, owned by John Erskine. In July 1866 owned by Rufus S. Rickey and Eugene E. Shelton, Natchez, Miss. In May 1867 owned by James Upshaw, Natchitoches Parish, La., running Trinity to points on Bayou Macon and Tensas. Snagged in Red River 1868.

1321 CORRINE

SW p wh b. Cincinnati, Oh., 1844. 183 tons. Went to New Orleans. Exploded and lost at McDonoughville, La., February 28, 1861, with loss of 15 lives.

1322 CORRINE

SW p wh b. Cincinnati, Oh., 1849. 121 tons. Off the lists in 1856.

1323 CORKER

Stw p wh b. Jeffersonville, Ind., by Howard, 1912. 130 x 30 x 3.7. Engines, 14's- 5 ft. Two boilers, each 42″ by 20 ft. Machinery and cabin from the *LIZZIE BAY* (see). Owned by the Louisville & Cincinnati Packet Co., for the Louisville-Madison trade. G.F. Bauersmith brought her to Pittsburgh, October 1919, to run Pittsburgh-Fairmont, and made one trip, then was returned to Cincinnati. Liberty Transit Co., Wheeling, bought her for Pittsburgh-Wheeling trade in 1920, and soon renamed her *GENERAL BEACH* (see).

1324 CORN SHELLER

SW p wh b. Cincinnati, Oh., 1847. 185 tons. Off the lists in 1849.

1325 CORNELIA

SW p wh b. McKeesport, Pa., 1851. 255 tons. Sank on Chain of Rocks, lower rapids, above St. Louis, Dec. 18, 1853, and "in all probability will be a total loss," said the St. Louis *Republican*.

1326 CORNELIA

SW p wh b. St. Louis, Mo., 1865. 647 tons. 224.8 x 37 x 5.6. Machinery from *DES MOINES* b. 1857. Three boilers, each 44″ dia. by 26 ft. Owned by Capt. Charles K. Baker and Jacob Conrad, both of St. Louis. Ran to New Orleans and in 1869 was running New Orleans-Camden, Capt. J.W. Blanks. Burned and lost at Algiers, La., Nov. 16, 1870.

1327 CORNELIA

Rig? b. Evansville, Ind., 1882. 74 x 15 x 3. Registered at Terre Haute, Ind., 1886.

1328 CORNIE

Stw p wh b. Freedom, Pa., 1860. 69 tons. 100.2 x 23.4 x 3.5. Sold to USQMD on May 10, 1864, and returned to private hands Feb. 2, 1866. Last owned in New Orleans by four local stockholders, Capt. O.S. Burdett, master. Removed from documentation in 1867.

1329 CORNIE BRANDON

Rig? Ran on upper Red River, La., Capt. Lewis E. Kouns, 1881–1882, maybe longer. Capt. Kouns lost his wife and three children in the burning of the *GOLDEN CITY* (see).

1330 CORNPLANTER

Stw p wh b. McKeesport, Pa., 1851. 117 tons. Engines, 16's- 6 ft. Four boilers. Built for Allegheny River service, Capt. William H. Gordon, and owned by Gordon and a group of men from Pittsburgh and Kittanning. When Gordon died he was replaced by Capt. Ezekiel Gordon. Made trips to Franklin, Pa., but usually ran Pittsburgh-Catfish Eddy. She was the hottest number on the Allegheny with big power. When the water was low she ran Pittsburgh-Wheeling in opposition to *DIURNAL* and *FOREST CITY*. Capt. Thomas H. Reynolds was master later. There were warehouses for handling packet freight at Red Bank, Catfish, Parker's Landing, and elsewhere, all of this before the oil excitement. She was moored at West Monterey for ice, and was lost there Feb. 12, 1857.

1331 CORONA

Stw p wh b. Brownsville, Pa., 1878. 173 x 36 x 6. She was built for Capt. T.C. Sweeney of Wheeling, a large cotton carrier, and her construction was completed at Wheeling where A.J. Sweeney & Son built and installed her engines, etc. Ran out of New Orleans. Capt. Jack DeHart was master in 1880, son of Capt. DeHart of the 1814 *NEW ORLEANS*. Later owned by Capt. Jack Blanks and others. They rebuilt her summer 1889 and she came out looking like a new boat. She started up the Mississippi and at the foot of Prophets Island met the Anchor Liner *CITY OF ST. LOUIS*. While the pilot on *CORONA* was blowing a whistle salute, *CORONA*'s boilers let go. Capt. H.W. Blanks was blown an estimated 150 feet in the air and was the only person who went up and came down alive. There was large life loss. The *CITY OF ST. LOUIS* gathered up survivors and took them to New Orleans. The *CORONA* had a duplicate of the famed *ST. LAWRENCE* (see) whistle which had been made for the *CALUMET* lost in ice at Cincinnati 1877. Much of her cabin furnishings, etc., also were from *CALUMET* (see).

1332 CORONA

SW ex wh The *W. C. HITE* (see) was rebuilt for excursions at Louisville and renamed. Operated until dismantled at Jeffersonville, Ind., in 1916 when the *PILGRIM* (see) was built.

1333 COROZAL

Stw p wh b. Cincinnati, Oh., 1883. 142.8 x 30.9 x 5.9. Documented at New Orleans through her career, and classed in 1910 as a freight boat. Burned at New Orleans, Jan. 18, 1912.

1334 CORRERO

Stw p wh b. New Albany, Ind., 1847. 89 tons. First home port, New Orleans. Snagged and lost at Mobile, Ala., May 20, 1856.

1335 CORVETTE

SW ship wh b. Brownsville, Pa., 1846. 159 tons. Built for the U.S. to aid in the prosecution of the Mexican War.

1336 CORWIN H. SPENCER

SW ex wh This was the *HILL CITY* (see) renamed at St. Louis in 1904 when she ran excursions there operated by the World's Fair Navigation Co., Capt. Harry Brolaski. A story of this operation, with pictures, appears in *S&D Reflector*, June 1975 issue. She burned above Jefferson Barracks, Mo., at 4:35 P.M., Thursday, Oct. 12, 1905. This fire ended all Anchor Line steamers except the *CITY OF PROVIDENCE* (see).

1337 COTILE

SW p wh b. New Albany, Ind., 1859. 162 tons. 138.8 x 27 x 4.9. First operated out of Vicksburg. Was captured as a Confederate steamer by the U.S. Aug. 18, 1862. Was assigned to USQMD called *FAIR PLAY*, then to Navy under same name. Redocumented *COTILE* Oct. 6, 1865. In 1866, running New Orleans-Bayou Macon and Tensas, Capt. R.G. Rawlings, master. The Good Intent Dry Dock Co., New Orleans, acquired her in August 1867 and sold her to A.H. Gieword and A.P. Kip of New Orleans. In April 1869 sold to Louis A. Highly, New Orleans, and thence a month later to David Campbell, St. Louis. Dismantled.

1338 COTTAGE

Stw p wh b. California, Pa., 1861. 73 tons. 128 x 33 x 2.9. Came out single deck for Allegheny River service, Capt. John G. Saint. Collided with towboat *J. S. COSGRAVE* at the Freeport (Pa.) aqueduct early 1862, rebuilt and a full cabin added. Sold to Barker, Hart & Cook, Cincinnati, that summer. She was used in U.S. service on the upper Tennessee, then went to Evansville owned by Capt. H.T. Dexter and others. Dismantled 1866.

1339 COTTAGE NO. 2

Stw p wh b. California, Pa., 1862. 136 x 27 x 3.10. Came out single deck for Allegheny River service, Capt. James G. Saint. Ran there until May 1864 when a full cabin was added. Soon sold to Capt. James Newton and others for Kanawha River. En route Charleston to Malden she exploded boilers in December 1865 and injured eight. John Luther Vance, later president of the Ohio Valley Improvement Association was clerk on her at the time and was badly injured. W.F. Gregory was pilot on watch. She was rebuilt and continued to run on the Kanawha. Capt. Newton took her to Brownsville, Pa., in March 1869, and engines, etc., were used in building the *MOUNTAIN BELLE* (see).

1340 COTTON

SW gunboat wh Originally *MARY T.* b. Jeffersonville, Ind., 1861 (see). She was converted to become a Confederate gunboat, surrendered to Union forces at Alexandria, La., June 3, 1865. In April 1866 was taken under her own steam, original name restored, for dismantling at Pittsburgh.

1341 COTTON PLANT

SW p wh b. Cincinnati, Oh., 1843. 122 tons. In the spring of 1845 she took a load of government supplies from New

Orleans to Fort Towson, Upper Red River, unloaded them, and in returning hit the bank in narrow 12-Mile Bayou with disastrous consequences. Her head stuck in the mud, she rounded broadside, and the stern caught on the opposite shore. She listed and filled and the cabin floated off. Five were drowned. A search was made later, after the river fell, for the hull, boilers and machinery, to no avail. Several years later the *NEW LATONIA* was upbound in the Bayou and the pilot was confronted with a steamboat hull coming toward him, boilers and engines intact, rolling over and over. He prudently landed under a false point, sucked in his breath, and the wreckage passed by without hitting him. It was the missing remains of the *COTTON PLANT*.

1342 COTTON PLANT

SW p wh b. Cincinnati, Oh., 1846. 295 tons. Burned and lost at Napoleon, Ark., May 22, 1852.

1343 COTTON PLANT

SW p wh b. Rochester, Pa., 1859. 59 tons. Went to Vicksburg for Yazoo River service. Went to Confederate registry in 1862. The Confederates purposely burned her to prevent U.S. capture, on the Tallahatchie River, July 23, 1863.

1344 COTTON PLANT

SW p wh Originally the *FLORA TEMPLE* b. Monongahela, Pa., 1858 (see). Went to Confederate registry renamed *COTTON PLANT* and exploded at Locopolis, Miss., July 24, 1863. The Federals found her in Lake George, 17.7 miles up the Sunflower River, with only the tops of her stacks showing.

1345 COTTON VALLEY

Stw p wh b. Ironton, Oh., and completed at Portsmouth, Oh., 1876. 401.70 tons. Capt. Wash Williamson looked after construction. She got wheel shaft from *R. W. SKILLINGER* (see). Ran New Orleans-Red River and Ouachita River, owned largely by Mark H. Kouns and W.T. Scovell. Sunk and lost in collision with the *CHARLES MORGAN* at Brunner's Point opposite Donaldsonville, La., Dec. 1, 1878, Capt. Mark Kouns, master.

1346 COUNCIL BLUFFS

Stw p wh b. California, Pa., 1857. 153 x 33.5 x 4.3. Original owners, Capt. Samuel Lewis, Mt. Washington, Pa., and William Dilworth, Allegheny City, Pa. There was a fire at the Monongahela wharf, Pittsburgh, May 7, 1859, which burned or damaged ten boats, all sternwheelers. The *COUNCIL BLUFFS* was lost.

1347 COUNTESS

SW p wh b. Smithland, Ky., 1847. 98 tons. This may have been the boat operated by Capt. G.D. Williamson Nashville-Smithland on the Cumberland. He died at Memphis in December 1915. Snagged and lost at Island 66, Mississippi River, June 22, 1851.

1348 COUNTESS

SW p wh b. Cincinnati, Oh., 1860. 150 x 30 x 4.8. Owned in December 1861 by Capt. William C. Harrison, New Orleans. In fleeing from Porter's invasion of Red River she sank on the falls above Alexandria, La., Capt. Wilson. The Rebels burned her to prevent capture, Mar. 15, 1864.

1349 COUNTESS

SW p wh b. Cincinnati, Oh., 1863. 192 tons. 155.6 x 30.2 x 4.4. She was taken over by the U.S. while new, was renamed *ELK,* and went through the war bearing that name. Sold to private hands Sept. 6, 1865, and got her original name back. In December 1865 owned by Capt. Chris Green, New Orleans. In February 1867 sold to Capt. Robert M. Cain of New Orleans, who turned her over to Charles H. Mumford, New Orleans. She was taken to Mobile, Ala., in April 1867, Capt. Burton Goode, owner. Sank in 1868.

1350 COUNTESS

SW p wh b. Paducah, Ky., 1864. 266 tons. 170 x 36 x 5. Two boilers. She may have been a ferry, and operated Rock Island-Davenport. Off the lists in 1870.

1351 COURIER

SW p wh b. Shippingport, Ky., 1846. 140 tons. First home port, Louisville, Ky. Snagged and lost at Davant, La., Mar. 9, 1849.

1352 COURIER

Stw p wh b. Parkersburg, Va., 1852. 165 tons. Built for the Wheeling-Parkersburg trade, Capt. James H. Roberts. John Mulrine, William Anderson and Wm. G. Battelle were in the office from time to time. Owned by W.E. Hunt in 1857, operating out of St. Paul.

1353 COURIER

Stw p wh b. Wheeling, Va., 1857. 258 tons. 168 x 30 x 5.5. Engines, 12½'s- 6½ ft. A poster advertising her in the Wheeling-Cincinnati trade exists, possibly 1861, Capt. Sam'l Mason, master; W.J.C. Anderson, clerk. The poster in January 1950 was advertised for sale by The Old Print Shop, N.Y., and $85 was asked for it. In 1858 Capt. J. McLure Jr., was master, with Wm. G. Battelle, clerk. A.J. Sweeney built her engines at Wheeling, the fourth set he constructed. About 1861 sold to the Evansville-Cairo trade, Capt. Josh V. Throop, and later Capt. Henry Dexter. She burned above the mouth of the Cache River, between Cairo and Mound City, Aug. 22, 1864. The *JAMES R. GILMORE* ran afoul of the wreck later on, sank on it, and was lost also.

1354 COURIER

SW p wh b. Harmar, Oh., 1870. 193.5 x 33 x 5.6. Engines from *REBECCA* (see), 18's- 5 ft. Owned by the Wheeling & Parkersburg Packet Co. In 1874, Wheeling-Parkersburg, Capt. Jack Harrison, master, with Martin F. Noll, clerk. They were together 1872–1876. From 1882 to the end, Capt. John K. Booth, master, with J. Mack Gamble, clerk.

The Ohio River Railroad was opened June 4, 1884, and the *COURIER* never made another trip in the trade after that happened. She carried a circus along the Ohio River in 1885 and that fall was laid up along the Kentucky shore at the lower end of Covington. That winter she stranded out, all furniture and machinery were removed, and the hulk was burned.

1355 COURIER

Stw p wh b. Belle Vernon, Pa., and completed at Wheeling, 1885. 153.8 x 32.2 x 4.6. Engines, 14's- 5 ft. from side-wheel *SCIOTO* b. 1875 (see). Two boilers, 42" by 20 ft. Entered Wheeling-Parkersburg trade, Capt. Tom J. Prince, master, with T.J. Martin, clerk. In winter 1885–1886 Capt. Prince took her to the Vicksburg-Bayou Sara trade. Then back to the Wheeling-Parkersburg trade, Capt. J. Mack Gamble, master, with Tim Penwell and William Wayman, clerks. She was sunk once at West Wheeling when new, and again in November 1893 at the Little Muskingum River while discharging a passenger who had paid 25¢ fare. Capt. Gamble sold her to the White Collar Line, Cincinnati on Aug. 5, 1895. They ran her Cincinnati-Maysville. Hit the Central Bridge, Cincinnati, and sank in November 1896, raised. White Collar sold her to Capt. Gordon C. Greene and others in 1904, and she was kept in the Cincinnati-Maysville trade, running there a total of 22 years. In the spring of 1917 she made two round trips Pittsburgh-Charleston in place of the *RUTH,* the last running she did. Dismantled at Ashland, Ky., spring of 1918. Her roof bell went to a church at Pliny, W. Va., and her whistle, from the *ST. LAWRENCE* (see) went to the *TACOMA*.

1356 COURTLAND

SW p wh b. Louisville, Ky., 1848. 230 tons. She was about 180 ft. long, built for the Louisville-Florence, Ala., trade, Capt. Dunning. Chartered by Louisville dignitaries who went down the Ohio to the mouth of the Cumberland to escort U.S. President-elect Zachary Taylor to Louisville, February 1849. She was at Shippingport, Ky., loading railroad iron en route to Madison, Ind., on May 6, 1851, when she burned there. Then was owned by a Capt. Hamilton and others of Madison, and had been in the Louisville-Henderson trade. Was on her way to be docked for repairs there.

1357 COVINGTON

SW ferry wh b. Cincinnati, Oh., 1854. 147 tons. Ran from foot of Vine Street, Cincinnati, to foot of Scott Street, Covington. In summer of 1869 was ferrying between South Wheeling and Lagrange. Off the lists in 1877.

1358 COVINGTON NO. 2

SW ferry wh b. Cincinnati, Oh., 1862. 224 tons. Taken over by U.S. Feb. 13, 1863, and made into a tinclad called *COVINGTON.* Burned by U.S. forces to prevent her capture by the Rebels at Dunn's Bayou, Red River, May 5, 1864. She had been badly damaged by shore batteries.

1359 COVINGTON NO. 2

SW ferry wh b. Cincinnati, Oh., 1866. 281 tons. Off the lists in 1880.

1360 CREMONA

Stw p wh b. New Albany, Ind., 1852. 266 tons. First home port, Mobile, Ala. Went to Confederate service 1861.

1361 CREMONA

Stw p wh b. Belle Vernon, Pa., 1856. 176 tons. Ran tramp trades. Reported on the Minnesota River, Capt. Martin, 1857. She was victim of a Monongahela wharf steamboat fire at Pittsburgh, May 7, 1859. Dragged away from the other victims she was found to be ablaze in mid-river and was lost. Owned at the time by Andrew Ackley, Capt. Doyle, master.

1362 CREOLE

SW p wh b. Louisville, Ky., 1847. 122 tons. Ran New Orleans-Alexandria, on Red River, Capt. C.H. Wilson. Burned and lost at New Orleans, Dec. 27, 1850.

1363 CREOLE

Stw p wh b. Harmar, Oh., 1853. A rather small cotton packet, one boiler. Machinery by Owen Franks, Marietta, Oh. Off the lists in 1858. Was running Vicksburg-Yazoo River in 1856.

1364 CRESCENT

SW p wh b. Cincinnati, Oh., 1850. 547 tons. First home port, New Orleans. Burned and lost at New Orleans, Feb. 4, 1854.

1365 CRESCENT

Stw p wh b. Ravenswood, Va., 1856. 316 tons. First home port, Cincinnati. Went to Confederate registry 1861.

1366 CRESCENT

Prop packet wh b. New Albany, Ind., 1867. 34 tons. Running New Orleans-Lower Coast in 1869, to Pointe-a-la-Hache, Capt. Charles R. Fagot, master, with Joseph Rither, clerk.

1367 CRESCENT

Rig? b. Burnside, Ky., 1888. 34.82 tons. Owned and operated out of Burnside on the Cumberland River.

1368 CRESCENT

Stw ex wh Originally *JOE FOWLER* (see) made over into an excursion boat at Evansville, Ind., 1919, by the Williams family. Burned in winter quarters, Green River, Ky., Nov. 17, 1920. Two of her boilers and stage-plank went to *BETSY ANN*; the other two boilers to towboat *SCOUT*.

1369 CRESCENT CITY

SW p wh b. Cincinnati, Oh., 1854. 688 tons. Ran St. Louis—New Orleans. Her master 1860 was Capt. H. Thornburg. Sam Clemens stood his first pilot watches on her. Off the lists in 1861.

1370 CRESCENT CITY

Prop packet wh b. Evansville, Ind., 1867. 66 tons. In 1870 Capt. A. Start, master, with Will H. Hugo, clerk. Sold to the U.S. 1873.

1371 CRESCENT CITY

Stw p wh Originally *EVANSVILLE* b. Cincinnati in 1880 (see). The Louisville & Nashville RR. bought *EVANSVILLE* c. 1897, rebuilt her at Madison, Ind., and renamed her CRESCENT CITY. She ran Evansville-Green River, Capt. Dick Williams (no kin to the celebrated Williams family). Lee Howell, president of Evansville & Bowling Green Packet Co., effected a consolidation with the L&N, c. 1903, kept her in the trade with Capt. M.P. Kimbley, master, with T.C. Wesson, clerk. In 1906 again rebuilt at Madison, Ind., and resumed her original name *EVANSVILLE,* documented as a new boat.

1372 CRICKET

Stw p wh b. Cincinnati, Oh., 1860. 67 tons. Went to Confederate registry 1861.

1373 CRICKET

Stw p wh b. Parkersburg, W. Va., 1900. 132.6 x 18.3 x 2.9. Engines, 9″- 2½ ft. One boiler, 43″ by 16 ft., 10 flues. Owned by Capt. Gordon C. Greene and used for low water work. Originally had an open hold and scow bow. She was taken back to Parkersburg in 1902, given a model bow and decked. Ran Catlettsburg, Ky., Big Sandy River in the springs of 1901–1904, Capt. Jesse P. Hughes, master. Original drawings, etc., are presented in *S&D Reflector,* issue June 1964. Was enlarged in 1909 and renamed *GREENDALE* (see).

1374 CRICKET NO. 2

Stw p wh b. California, Pa., 1860. 151 x 27.7 x 4. Engines, 13's- 4½ ft. Owned originally by R. Hamilton, Hanging, Rock, Oh., and John Kyle, Cincinnati. Capt. S.B. Hempstead was master. Ran Pittsburgh-Cincinnati, in summers Cincinnati-Louisville. Sold to the U.S. Nov. 18, 1862, and became U.S. Tinclad *CRICKET,* designated #6. Sold to private owner Sept. 25, 1865, again *CRICKET NO. 2,* and was last owned and operated by Capt. William Durbridge, New Orleans. Dismantled 1867.

1375 CRICKET NO. 3

Stw p wh b. Cincinnati, Oh., 1863. Sold to U.S. on Mar. 8, 1864, and converted into a tinclad, renamed *NYMPH,* designated #54. Sold to Capt. A.M. Hutchinson in the fall of 1865, and resumed original name *CRICKET NO. 3.*

1376 CRICKET NO. 4

Stw p wh b. Cincinnati, Oh., 1863. 171 tons. sold to the U.S. on Dec. 23, 1863, and renamed *TALLAHATCHIE.* Sold to private owners Aug. 25, 1865, and renamed *COOSA* (see).

1377 CROWN POINT

Stw p wh b. Evansville, Ind., 1885. 123 x 25 x 4.2. Engines, 19½'s- 4½ ft. Two boilers each 28″ by 18 ft., four flues. Built for Evansville-Wabash River. Sold to Vicksburg and ran up Yazoo River. Eventually sank in Lake Centennial at the south end of De Soto Island where the old "P" Line boats were laid up. She was raised but the cabin destroyed. Made several trips up Yazoo with no cabin and only a frame of a pilothouse, Capt. Ledbetter. In 1896 Adam Kellogg took her to Lake Palmyra, built a new hull, put the *CROWN POINT* machinery on it, brought this up to Vicksburg where a cabin was built, and the new vessel was named *LAKE PALMYRA* (see).

1378 CRYSTAL CITY

SW p wh b. Jeffersonville, Ind., by Howard, 1887. 234 x 42 x 7.7. Engines, 24's- 8 ft. Four boilers, each 46″ by 28 ft. Paddlewheels 29½ ft. dia. with 14½ ft. buckets. Owned by the Anchor Line. Capt. Horace Bixby came out master when she was new at Jeff, with William Pavy, chief, and William Lind, second engineer. Once sunk at Ivy Landing, July 10, 1889, and finally lost at Jefferson Barracks, laid up for ice, Feb. 15, 1893. This boat and *CITY OF MONROE* (see) were built at the same time at Jeff. The *CRYSTAL CITY* departed the shipyard on a Friday, the *CITY OF MONROE* the next day. The consequent bad luck which befell the former was attributed to starting her out on a Friday, an old river superstition.

1379 CRYSTAL PALACE

SW p wh b. Freedom, Pa., and completed at Pittsburgh, 1853. 279.5 x 33 x 6. Engines, 32⅔'s- 8 ft. Five boilers, 46″ by 30 ft., 5 flues. Paddlewheels 38 ft. dia. by 12′4″ buckets. Extreme width 69 ft. Owned in part by Capt. William J. Kountz, master. Named for the Crystal Palace building, Sixth Avenue and 42nd Street, New York, which opened July 14, 1853, for the first World's Fair in the U.S. First season ran Pittsburgh-Cincinnati, then Louisville-St. Louis. By 1855 was running St. Louis-New Orleans, Capt. R.A. Reilly. A new hull was built for her in 1856, the cabin moved over, and she was renamed *CITY OF MEMPHIS* (see). The cabin mirror, presented to S&D in 1955, is exhibited in the Ohio River Museum, Marietta, Oh.

1380 CUBA

SW p wh b. Jeffersonville, Ind., 1850. 285 tons. 180 x 29 x 7. First owner was Robert Otis, Mobile, Ala. Snagged and lost at Davis Landing, 90 miles above Mobile, Apr. 20, 1856, with loss of seven lives.

1381 CUBA

Stw p wh b. Brownsville, Pa., 1853. 157 tons. Ran in tramp trades on the Ohio and was on Red River in cotton seasons. Struck the wreck of the *FANNY FERN* below Wheeling on Mar. 24, 1854, and sank. Raised. Was in the Louisville-Nashville trade when she was snagged and lost at West Franklin, Tenn., Sept. 29, 1856.

1382 CUBA

Stw p wh b. Wheeling, W. Va., 1864. 149.2 x 27.9 x4.3.

Built for and operated by Capt. William T. Boardman and others. Ran New Orleans-Red River, 1865–1867, owned by A.F. Duncan, Evansville, Ind., and F.T. Hodge and others, New Orleans. Exploded boilers and burned at Alexandria, La., Nov. 11, 1867, with loss of seven lives.

1383 CUBA

Ferry wh b. Ravenswood, W. Va., 1873. 32.78 tons. Advertised for sale at Middleport, Oh., October 1876. Documented at Wheeling, 1886.

1384 CUBA NO. 2

Stw p wh Originally *B. C. LEVI* b. Belle Vernon, Pa., 1862, then USQMD's *GENERAL CROOKS* during the war. Rebuilt at Cincinnati 1865, hull 129.4 x 25.2 x 4.2 and renamed *CUBA NO. 2.* Owned by L.F. Moore and J.S. Nevin of Catlettsburg, Ky., and Capt. John C. Shute and Jasper L. Russ, New Orleans. Capt. Shute commanded and had been interested in Capt. Boardman's *CUBA* (see above). Sold to Capt. George C. Wilkinson, New Orleans, January 1868, running on Red River. Snagged and lost at Shreveport, La., Mar. 9, 1869.

1385 CUMBERLAND

SW p wh b. Smith's Landing, Pa., 1847. 121 tons. First home port, Pittsburgh, Pa. Off the lists, 1851.

1386 CUMBERLAND

SW p wh b. Paducah, Ky., 1855. 408 tons. Operated on Cumberland River. Off the lists in 1859.

1387 CUMBERLAND

Stw p wh Originally *KENWOOD* b. Cincinnati, 1863 (see). She was Tinclad #14 during the war, then renamed *CUMBERLAND* when sold to private hands. Ran Cairo-Tennessee River 1867 with Capt. Ben F. Egan, master, and John H. Triplett, clerk. In 1868 running Evansville-Cairo with Capt. Ben Howard, master, and Marion Wright, clerk. Exploded and lost at Shawneetown, Ill., Aug. 14, 1869, with loss of 18 lives. The wreck lay below the lower corn shed below Raleigh Landing, Ky. The hull was raised and taken to Cairo "scarcely injured but the upper works are entirely blown away far back as the pantry."

1388 CUMBERLAND

Stw p wh Originally *ABNER O'NEAL* b. 1875 (see). Renamed when sold to Evansville, Ind., c. 1885. Still registered at Evansville in 1892.

1389 CUMBERLAND NO. 2

Stw p wh b. Freedom, Pa., 1849. 141 tons. Stranded and lost at Rising Sun, Ind., 1851.

1390 CUMBERLAND VALLEY

SW p wh b. Smithland, Ky., 1842. 176 tons. Ran Cincinnati-Nashville, Capt. David Green. Then went to Upper Mississippi and finally to the Missouri River where she was snagged and lost Oct. 22, 1849.

1391 CUMBERLAND VALLEY

SW p wh b. Ironton, Oh., 1850. 198 tons. Off the lists in 1856.

1392 CURLEW

Stw p wh b. Paducah, Ky., 1860. 150 x 26.5. Owned by Capt. Paul F. Semonin, Henderson, Ky. Snagged in Chenault Reach, Ohio River, above Stephensport, Ky., upbound with 2,700 sacks of corn for Brandies & Crawford, Louisville, on Mar. 4, 1868.

1393 CURLEW

Stw p wh Originally *FLORENCE* b. Elizabeth, Pa., 1861, then became Tinclad *CURLEW,* #12. Sold at Mound City, Ill., Aug. 17, 1865, to James Polakin.

1394 CURLEW

Stw p wh b. Rock Island, Ill., 1902. 79 x 20 x 3.4. Operated by U.S. Bureau of Fisheries 1903–1917. Sold to Capt. Frank Fugina who took her to Wabasha, Minn., rebuilt her, and she emerged as *ALICE F.*

1395 CUSSETA

SW p wh b. Cincinnati, Oh., 1851. 201 tons. Went to Apalachicola, Fla., and was lost in collision with *UNION* on the Apalachicola River on Feb. 5, 1856.

1396 CUSSEWAGO

SW ferry wh b. Pittsburgh, Pa., 1865. 126 tons. Operated in the Pittsburgh area. Removed from the lists in 1879.

1397 CUTTER

SW p wh b. Cincinnati, Oh., 1843. 148 tons. Came out in January 1843 Cincinnati-Maysville, Capt. M. Collins, soon changed to Pittsburgh-Cincinnati, same master. Collapsed a flue and killed engineer Joseph Hughes, Mar. 17, 1843. Trip to St. Louis that fall. Ran Pittsburgh-Cincinnati with some regularity 1844–1845, Capt. M. Collins. Snagged and lost at Ste. Genevieve, Mo., October 1847.

1398 CUTTER

Stw p wh b. Anoka, Minn., 1863. 92 tons. Operated out of St. Paul. Snagged and lost at Stillwater, Minn., October 1869.

1399 CYCLONE

Stw p wh b. Stillwater, Minn., 1891. 121 x 22.6 x 4. Engines, 14's- 5 ft. Ran Wabasha-St. Paul 1900–1907, Capt. Milt Newcomb. Burned on the ways at Wabasha, Dec. 2, 1907, at which time Capt. Newcomb bought the rafter *JUNIATA,* renamed her *RED WING.*

1400 CYMRO GWYILT

Rig? b. Minersville, Oh., 1879. 55 x 12 x 3.8. Still documented on the upper Ohio in 1886.

D

1401 D'ARTAGNAN

Prop yacht b. St. Louis, Mo., 1904. 85 x 10 x 5. Two engines, each 8" x 8". One boiler, 60" dia. by 10 ft. Owned by Rohan Bros., St. Louis. Inspected through 1908.

1402 D. A. GIVEN

Stw p wh b. Paducah, Ky., 1853. 183 tons. First home port, St. Louis. Off the lists in 1859.

1403 D. A. GOODIN

Stw p wh b. Mount Carmel, Ill., 1883. 77 x 14 x 2.8. Built for Wabash River. Listed in 1886, maybe later.

1404 D. A. GOODIN

Stw p wh b. Evansville, Ind., 1889. 103.6 x 20.3 x 3. Documented at Nashville, Tenn., 1892. Renamed *O. E. STOCKWELL* several years later, then became *SYCAMORE* (both see).

1405 D. A. JANUARY

SW p wh b. Cincinnati, Oh., 1857. 440 tons. 225 x 34. Ran St. Louis-St. Joseph, Mo., on the Missouri River, Capt. Patrick Gore. Sold to USQMD on June 1, 1864, and was converted into a hospital boat. Prior to that she had been impressed into U.S. service and was used 1862–1864 handling sick and wounded, a total of 2,692 soldiers transported from battlefields to northern hospitals. Sold to private owners Mar. 14, 1865, and renamed *NED TRACY* on Feb. 1, 1866 (see).

1406 D. B. BURNS

Stw p wh b. Elizabeth, W. Va., 1885. 71.4 x 16.8 x 2.4. Engines 7 5/16"' 24" stroke. One boiler, 36" by 7'8". Built by Capt. W.T. Wilson, Elizabeth, W. Va., and Edward Evans. Certified for operation between Parkersburg and Glenville, W. Va., allowed 20 passengers, Capt. W.T. Wilson, master. In 1889 was run by Capt. S. Walker Litten in the Matamoras-Wheeling area, Ohio River. Documented at Cincinnati in 1896.

1407 D. B. CAMPBELL

Stw ferry wh b. Louisville, Ky., 1859. 109.8 x 21 x 4.2. First enrolled at Evansville, Ind., with Francis Pratt the principal owner. Sold to New Orleans July 1865 to the Blanks family. In 1866 bought by Mississippi Steam Ferry Co., New Orleans. In December 1869 sold to Phillip Drumm and Jerome Hanly, New Orleans. Exploded boiler in 1870s.

1408 D. B. MOSBY

SW p wh b. Cincinnati, Oh., 1849. 164 tons. Built at the Fulton yard and named for a merchant of New Orleans. Designed to run on Red River, Capt. James Cockreel. Burned and lost at St. Patrick, La., Oct. 19, 1854, with loss of one life.

1409 D.C. HORTON

See *DAVID C. HORTON.*

1410 D. F. KENNER

See *DUNCAN F. KENNER.*

1411 D. F. NORTON

Ferry wh b. Evansville, Ind., 1877. 79.9 x 19 x 2.7. Documented at Shawneetown, Ill., in 1886, perhaps later.

1412 D. G. TAYLOR

See *DANIEL G. TAYLOR.*

1413 D. H. BLUNK

Prop p wh b. Portsmouth, Oh., 1863. 98 tons. Ran Louisville-Madison, January 1864, Capt. Henderson. Bought by Capt. Nat Williams, Madison, Ind., February 1864, and continued in same trade. Converted to sternwheel in October 1864. Snagged and lost at Brown's Landing, La., Nov. 19, 1865.

1414 D. H. MORTON

SW p wh b. Cincinnati, Oh., 1856. 173 tons. She was handling supplies for the U.S. on the upper Arkansas, loaded with hay and grain, when she burned near Dardanelle, Ark., at Gay's Landing, head of Prairie Bend, Mar. 11, 1859.

1415 D. H. PIKE

Stw p wh Originally *BENTON McMILLIN* b. Jeffersonville, In., 1883 (see). The *McMILLIN* was lengthened to become 199.6 x 33.5 x 5.5 by Eagle Packet Co., which ran her St. Louis-Peoria in the 1890s. On one occasion the St. Louis firm Scharff & Berneheimer chartered her, loaded her out with groceries, sundries, etc., and went to Knox's Point, Red River, with her. Dismantled in 1898 and parts used in building the *BALD EAGLE* (see).

1416 D. J. DAY

SW p wh b. Cincinnati, Oh., 1852. 212 tons. First home port, Apalachicola, Fla. Off the lists in 1856.

1417 D. L. TALLY

Stw p wh b. Cincinnati, Oh., 1870. 160.8 x 37 x 5. Originally owned in one-third equal shares by W.F. Stanley and W.F. Rudolph of New Orleans and A.R. Pierce, Maysville, Ky. Ran New Orleans-Shreveport 1870–1872, Capt. W.R. Stanley. Sold by U.S. marshal at New Orleans in July 1873 to Mobile Trade Co., Mobile, Ala., and was taken there. Long ran Mobile-Alabama River, Capt. Frank Stone and others. Burned at Mobile on Mar. 29, 1895.

1418 D. M. SECHLER

Stw p wh b. Portsmouth, Oh., 1864. 111 tons. Built for Parkersuburg-Zanesville trade and ran there with some regularity 1864–1866, Capt. Jos. McVay. In 1866–1867 ran Beverly-Zanesville, same master. Burned and lost at Carrollton, Ky., Dec. 4, 1868.

1419 D. R. CARROLL

SW p wh b. Louisville, Ky., 1858. 175 x 34 x 6. Ran New Orleans-Alexandria on Red River, Capt. William Kimball, advertised as a "low water packet." Went to Confederate registry in 1861.

1420 D. S. STACY

SW p wh b. Louisville, Ky., 1852. 376 tons. In 1852 in New Orleans-Vicksburg-Milliken's Bend trade, Capt. J.J. Tyson. Ran New Orleans-Ouachita River, spring 1853. Off the lists 1857.

1421 D. STEIN

Stw p wh b. Cincinnati, Oh., 1877. 124.4 x 25.8 x 3.5. Had one stack. Advertised April 1878 New Orleans-Bayou Bartholomew "Goes thru to Ouachita City," Capt. Wm. Wenzel with J.M. Tindel, clerk. Often used as a "summer boat" during slack times. In 1879, New Orleans-Ouachita River, Capt. Jack W. Blanks, master, with Ben Cornwell, clerk. Still registered at New Orleans in 1896.

1422 D. VAN BUSKIRK

Rig? b. Gosport, Ind., 1872. 69 tons. Was listed at Evansville, 1876. Inspected at Beaumont, Tex., 1881, and in the Galveston, Tex., area, 1882.

1423 D. W. HEWETT

Ferry wh b. Dubuque, Iowa, 1865. 54 tons. Probably a prop ferry of small size. In 1874 was owned by Wiggins Ferry Co., St. Louis, still there in 1876.

1424 DACOTAH

SW p wh b. Freedom, Pa., 1857. 90 tons. Operated by Hannibal & St. Joseph RR at St. Joseph Mo., along with *A. MAJORS* (see). She was the victim of a tornado at St. Joseph on Mar. 15, 1862, with loss of four lives; one was a railroad engineer, another was a conductor.

DACOTAH

Stw p wh b. Belle Vernon, Pa., 1858. (See *DECOTAH,* proper spelling.)

1425 DACOTAH

Stw p wh b. California, Pa., and completed at Pittsburgh, 1879. 252 x 48 x 5.5. Engines, 18's- 7 ft. Four boilers. Made her maiden trip from Pittsburgh to Fort Benton, Mont., arriving there June 20, 1879, with 550 tons of freight. Bettered this record, bringing up 660 tons from Bismarck on July 13, 1879. In 1881 she brought 627 tons to Fort Benton in one trip. On her last appearance at the fort, she took up 700 tons, July 2, 1883. In all, she made seven trips to Fort Benton. She also handled the largest downbound cargo out of the Missouri River, Kansas City to St. Louis, with 16,000 sacks of wheat and 5,000 items of freight; she did this with five ft. on the K. C. gauge and not once was aground. Struck the bridge at Kansas City on Aug. 15, 1889, and part of her cargo was unloaded to keep her afloat while repairs were made. Originally owned by the Coulson Line. Sold later to Capt. Hunter Ben Jenkins and others, and Capt. George G. Keith was master. Snagged at Providence, Mo., Sept. 17, 1884. In 1889 sold to New Orleans, Capt. William T. Boardman, and ran from there up Red River. Again she broke records: took out of Red River the biggest freight trip ever handled by packet, arriving at New Orleans Dec. 3, 1889, with 1,138 bales of cotton and 12, 265 sacks of cotton seed, this bettering the record of the *JESSE K. BELL* (see). Dismantled at Jeffersonville, Ind., in 1893. Capt. Lud Keefer, Pittsburgh, bought the hull. Half was used for a wharfboat at Manchester, Oh., and the other half became the hull for an excursion barge Keefer used at Pittsburgh. The machinery, parts of the cabin, etc., went to building the *IMPERIAL* (see).

1426 DAISY

Rig? b. New Orleans, La., 1880. 33.52 tons. A boat of this name ran New Orleans-Buras, Capt. Oliver Canton, 1885. In the same Line was the *NEPTUNE*, New Orleans-Port Eads.

1427 DAISY

Stw p wh b. Stillwater, Minn., 1887. 122 x 22 x 3.8. Still registered at St. Paul, 1896.

1428 DAISY

Stw p wh b. Antiquity, Oh., 1903. 75 x 14 x 2. Engines, 6"-18". One boiler, 54" by 7 ft. Built for Capt. E.E. Varian. A daylight short-trader. Capt. John S. Faddis ran her between Morgantown and Martin, Pa., on the Monongahela River most of 1907, owned by H.E. and T.B. Eberhart. Capt. William Goudy, Rice's Landing, Pa., took her over in May 1908. He sold her June 1911 to Capt. W.E. McDade, Portland, Oh. He put her on the Enterprise Docks, Pt. Pleasant, and found there was too much work to do on her, so let her back in the river. George P. Gardner and Gordon C. Greene used the pilothouse and some odds and ends building the *HELEN E.* (see).

1429 DAKOTA

Rig? b. Breckinridge, Minn., 1872. 117.75 tons. Documented at Galena, Ill., 1876. Burned and lost two miles below Fort Pembina, Missouri River, Aug. 9, 1879.

1430 DALLAS

SW p wh b. Louisville, Ky., 1843. 244 tons. 169 x 24 x 6.2. First home port, Mobile. She was returned to New Orleans, March 1847, owned by Capt. Hugh D. Cochrane, master. That November ownership transferred to Capt. John W. Cannon and Benjamin B. Meehen, New Orleans, and Capt. John M. Phillips, master. Off the lists in 1849.

1431 DALLAS

Stw p wh Small boat. Sank on a snag at Morgans Island, Missouri River, in the 1870s, and was lost.

1432 DAMSEL

Stw p wh b. Wellsville, Oh., 1864. 191 tons. Ran on the Upper Mississippi, and sprang to fame when Dan Rice, the circus man, bought her to convey his circus around. The troupe was up Missouri River in mid-July 1878 when pilot Charles Davis was landing the boat at Decatur, Neb. A large snag along shore rent the boat's port side, and she was taken across to the head of Onawa Bend where she settled. The circus was not aboard at the time, having gone overland to keep an engagement. It is said that Dan Rice presented the boat's bell to the citizens of Decatur in appreciation for the assistance cheerfully rendered, and it was placed in the belfry of a local church.

1433 DAN ABLE

SW p wh b. New Albany, Ind., 1866. 240 x 35.5 x 5.5. Owned and operated by Capt. Dan Able, Memphis. First master was Capt. J.D. Clark. Joe Curtis, river historian at Memphis, relates that the boat was soon acquired by Capt. James Lee for the Memphis-Friars Point trade. Sold in October 1869 to the Illinois Central RR, which ran her several months in the Cairo-Columbus, Ky., trade competing with the Iron Mountain RR which had placed a transfer boat at Belmont. The attempt was not a success and the *DANABLE* was frequently laid up. She burned at Columbus, Ky., July 21, 1870, in a spectacular fashion. She had steam up. The flames burned the ropes holding up her lever valves, the side-wheels commenced to roll, and she took off down the river with nobody aboard, and burned in midstream.

1434 DAN B. HURLBURT

SW p wh b. Warsaw, Mo., 1881. 62.6 x 11 x 2.4. Documented at St. Louis through 1896, maybe longer.

1435 DAN CONVERSE

Stw p wh b. McKeesport, Pa., at the Coursin yard, 1852. 142 x 27 x 4.10. Engines, 16's- 5 ft. Two boilers. Came out new in May 1852 in Pittsburgh-Zanesville trade, Capt. Charles Gallagher. That summer ran Newport, Oh.-Zanesville trade, Capt. Till Devol. In 1853 in the Marietta-Zanesville trade, Capt. E.C. Granger. Then ran Pittsburgh-Zanesville, Capt. Monroe Ayres, into 1855 when she was sold to the Upper Mississippi. Snagged and lost at Amazonia, Mo., above St. Joseph, Nov. 15, 1858.

1436 DAN MARBLE

Stw p wh b. Cincinnati, Oh., 1844. 21 tons. Dismantled in 1846.

1437 DAN POLLARD

Stw p wh b. McKeesport, Pa., 1857. 77 tons. First home port, Wheeling. Snagged and lost at Cairo, Ill., Aug. 3, 1864.

1438 DANDELION

Stw lighthouse wh Originally rafter *F. WEYERHAEUSER* b. Rock Island, Ill., 1893. 140 x 31 x 4.5. Engines, 15's- 7 ft. The U.S. Lighthouse Service used her on the Upper Mississippi and sold her at Rock Island in October 1927 to boat broker John K. Klein. She was lost in collision with towboat *HERBERT HOOVER* at Cairo in February 1929.

1439 DANIEL

Stw ferry wh b. Clarington, Oh., 1907. 95.3 x 25.7 x 3.3. Cabin lumber, etc., came from former ferry *ORION*. Operated at Sistersville, W. Va., first owned by F.D. McCoy, E.W. Talbott, Elmer C. Tuel, Stafford Tuel, and K. Tuel, all of Sistersville, and C. Tuel, Fly, Oh. In summer of 1912 her pilot died at the wheel coming into the landing at Fly. Later rebuilt into a small towboat *J. H. SHAW*.

1440 DANIEL B. MILLER

Stw p wh b. California, Pa., 1859. 109 x 26.8 x 4. Owned by Daniel B. Miller and S.B. Kitchen, Bloomfield, Mo., Capt. John A. Williams, of Cape Girardeau, Mo., master. Off the lists 1861.

1441 DANIEL BOONE

SW p wh b. Cincinnati, Oh., 1844. 169 tons. This boat was early distinguished when in 1845 she was taken to Marthasville, Mo., where the bodies of Daniel Boone and his wife were placed aboard and brought to Frankfort, Ky., for final burial. The interment took place at Frankfort on Aug. 20, 1845. U.S. President-elect Zachary Taylor boarded this boat at Nashville, Tenn., and rode to just below Louisville, Ky., where he was transferred to the *COURTLAND* (see): this in February 1849. Capt. Grafton Molen built her for the Cincinnati-Maysville trade. Sold to Draper & Leslie, New Albany, Ind., which, in March 1849, loaded her out for Illinois River. Went in the woods at York, Ill., all but 20 feet of her stern. Her passengers were removed by the *HIBERNIA*. Was put back afloat, and finally was lost in collision with the *SOUTHERN BELLE* at College Point, La., Sept. 10, 1853.

1442 DANIEL BOONE

SW p wh b. Cincinnati, Oh., 1848. 196 tons. Capts. Grafton Molen and William McClain were instrumental in forming the Cincinnati & Maysville Packet Co., in 1844, with the *DANIEL BOONE* and *SIMON KENTON*. The registered name of this steamboat was *BOONE*, although often referred to as *DANIEL BOONE*. and she was replaced by the *DANIEL BOONE* in the next listing.

1443 DANIEL BOONE

SW p wh b. Cincinnati, Oh., 1854. 381 tons. She left Cincinnati Monday, Wednesday, and Friday for Maysville, Ky., Capt. H.L. Church, owned by Cincinnati, Maysville & Portsmouth Packet Co. This company broke up in 1859, at which time the *DANIEL BOONE* was sold to Capt. J. Frank Hicks who ran her Memphis-Napoleon, Ark., James Petty, clerk. Snagged and lost above Vicksburg, Miss., Dec. 13, 1859.

1444 DANIEL BOONE

Stw p wh b. Cincinnati, Oh., 1872. 118 x 21 x 3.8. 121 tons. Built for the Gallipolis, Oh.-Charleston, W. Va., trade on Kanawha River, Capt. R.L. Hamilton, master, and J.A. McClurg, clerk. Still documented 1886.

1445 DANIEL G. TAYLOR

SW p wh b. McKeesport, Pa., 1855. 240 x 38. Engines, 24's- 7 ft. Four boilers. This was primarily a freight boat, and odd looking—her wheels were set far aft. Named for the mayor of St. Louis. When about a year old, July 5, 1856, snagged and sunk at the head of Paine's Island, three miles below Rocheport, Mo., on the Missouri River. Raised, and ran profitably in the St. Louis-New Orleans trade, Capt. Robert A. Reilly and others. Burned at Louisville, Ky., with loss of one life, Feb. 5, 1864. Capt. Henry Symmes bought the wreck from the St. Louis underwriters for $1,000 in mid-February 1864 and took out the machinery.

1446 DANIEL HILLMAN

Stw p wh b. Smithland, Ky., 1846. 145 tons. Made trips to Galena, Ill., 1847. Off the lists in 1855.

1447 DANIEL PRATT

SW p wh b. New Albany, Ind., 1847. 293 tons. First home port, Mobile, Ala. Exploded with loss of three lives at Mobile, Oct. 6, 1854.

1448 DANUBE

SW p wh b. Brownsville, Pa., 1847. 156 tons. Came out new in the Pittsburgh-Brownsville trade, Monongahela River, Capt. George D. Cock, three trips a week. Was there in January 1848. Struck rocks, stove and sunk at Port Byron, Ill., Sept. 6, 1852.

1449 DANUBE

Stw p wh b. Cincinnati, Oh., 1877. 175 x 33.8 x 5.1. Left the shipyard for Red River in September 1877, Capt. Charles Thorne, master, and G.A. Ditton, clerk. She operated in the Red River Line 1877–1890, Capt. Thorne. Sank near Natchez, June 9, 1891, raised and rebuilt. Continued in the New Orleans-Shreveport trade until 1894. Broke her wheel shaft in Atchafalaya River, March 1896, and was towed to New Orleans by tug *WILL H. WOOD*. She was dismantled and the hull converted into a garbage barge.

1450 DARDANELLE

SW p wh b. Cincinnati, Oh., 1856. 170 tons. First home port, Memphis. Snagged and lost at Pine Bluff, Ark., Feb. 6, 1859.

1451 DARDANELLE

Stw p wh b. Little Rock, Ark., 1896. 119 x 23.8 x 3.2. In 1903 was being operated by Capt. M.O. Brinkley who later bought the *HENRY SHELDON* for Arkansas River. We have a note in the file that the first *DARDANELLE* (above listing) sank and was lost in Siler Chute, above the mouth of Plum Bayou on the Arkansas, Capt. Levi Chapman, master, and Ed Carter, clerk. The subject of this listing, commanded by Capt. Eugene Smith, sank below Fletcher's Landing, Arkansas River.

1452 DARLING

SW p wh b. McKeesport, Pa., 1863. 180 x 37. Engines, 18's- 7 ft. Four boilers. Paddle-wheels 28′ dia. with 8 ft. buckets. Built for Capt. C.W. Batchelor and commanded by his brother Capt. Frank Batchelor. Ran usually in Cincinnati-Memphis trade. Carried a calliope. In early September 1864 was flagship of Gen. Smith when a flotilla of transports went down the Mississippi in U.S. service. Was joined in to the "Dean Line" in Cincinnati-Memphis trade in latter September 1864. Sank with a full cargo at Plum Point, Mississippi River, December 1865, raised. In 1869 Capt. J. Lawrence Carter, master, with A.F. Power, clerk. Burned in a wharf fire at Cincinnati, May 12, 1869. She was named for Capt. C.W. Batchelor's young daughter Sallie, more often called "Darling" by her Papa.

1453 DARLING

Rig? b. Parkersburg, W. Va., 1871. 12.72 tons. Extremely light draft. Ran in the Wheeling-Steubenville trade, August 1871 in place of the FOREST CITY. Although new, she was described as "an old looking craft."

1454 DART

Prop p wh b. Akron, Oh., 1865. 13.74 tons. 43 x 9 x 1. Originally a canalboat, converted to steam. Capt. J.C. Bryant operated her on the Muskingum River Zanesville-Marietta for four years 1865–1868. She was reported down-bound at Cincinnati Nov. 12, 1872, with three loaded produce boats for the South, and a fourth to be added below.

1455 DART

Rig? b. Lyons, Iowa, 1878. 10.30 tons. Was inspected at Clinton, Apr. 15, 1881.

1456 DART

Rig? b. Camanche, Iowa, 1881. 43 x 9.5 x 1. Documented at Galena, Ill., 1886.

1457 DAVENPORT

SW ferry wh b. Cincinnati, Oh., 1855. 138 tons. Operated as a ferry at Davenport until impressed into U.S. war service 1864. Lost on the upper Arkansas River at the head of Evan's Bar, above Little Rock.

1458 DAVENPORT

SW p wh b. California, Pa., 1863. 340 tons. 203 x 34.3 x 5.2. Built under supervision of Capt. Richard C. Gray, her first master. Owned by the Northern Line Packet Co., and ran on the Upper Mississippi. Made trips to Cincinnati in winter months. Cut down by ice at St. Louis, Dec. 13, 1876. Raised and dismantled.

1459 DAVENPORT

Stw ferry wh b. Rock Island, Ill., 1904. 112.5 x 36.5 x 3.5. Engines, 14's- 5 ft. Ran Davenport-Rock Island. Rebuilt during the latter 1920s and renamed *W. J. QUINLAN* (see).

1460 DAVID C. HORTON

Stw p wh b. Cincinnati, Oh., 1864. 140 tons. Sold to USQMD on Nov. 13, 1864, for war service. Sold to private owners Sept. 8, 1865, renamed *AMERICAN* (see).

1461 DAVID F. THOMAS

Stw ferry wh Originally *ARION* (see). Was renamed when sold to Twenty-Sixth Street Ferry Co., Huntington, W. Va. Burned at Proctorville, Oh., on Apr. 21, 1929. Dave Thomas was son of Capt. Paul F. Thomas who headed the ferry operations.

1462 DAVID GIBSON

SW p wh b. Murraysville, Va., 1854. 414 tons. First home port, Cincinnati. She was built for a Capt. McKinley. Lost in collision with NATHANIEL HOLMES at Petersburg, Ky., Mar. 28, 1859. Low water exposed the wreck late as October 1871.

1463 DAVID HIMROD

Prop p wh b. Youngstown, Oh. (1862), as a canal boat and converted to prop-steam at Rochester, Pa., 1867. 24 tons. Off the lists in 1876.

1464 DAVID HOSTETTER

Prop yacht ih b. Pittsburgh, Pa., 1877. 80 x 8 x 3.6. 19.37 tons. From the Pittsburgh *Gazette,* June 24, 1876: "The iron propeller just about completed at Hartupee & Co. intended for excursion parties has been named *DAVID HOSTETTER* after Dr. Hostetter." This was the Dr. Hostetter of "Hostetter's Bitters" fame. The yacht was documented at Tampa, Fla., 1892.

1465 DAVID LINTON

Rig? b. Madison, Ind., 1876. 84.08 tons.

1466 DAVID LYNCH

Stw p wh b. Elizabeth, Pa., 1854. 47 tons. Reported sold to Capt. James Sentz for the Charleston-Coalburg trade, upper Kanawha, in mid-February, 1869. Coalburg is still on the charts, about two miles above the Cheylan bridge in the Marmet pool. Off the lists, 1871.

1467 DAVID R. POWELL

SW p wh b. Cincinnati, Oh., 1882. 258 x 38 x 7. There exists a photo of her loaded flat with a sign on the roof "OUACHITA RIVER DIRECT—CHARTERED AND LOADED BY SCHARFF & BERNHEIMER." This St. Louis firm occasionally did this—chartered a boat to take a load south.

1468 DAVID STINSON

Stw p wh b. 1876. Ran during low water, summer 1876, Pittsburgh-Cincinnati, Capt. Strider. That fall in Marietta-Gallipolis trade pending completion of *W. P. THOMPSON.* In April 1877 running Yazoo-Sunflower rivers as an opposition packet.

1469 DAVID SWAIN

SW p wh b. Stillwater, Minn., 1906. 136.6 x 26 x 4.5. Swain inclined oscillating engines, 10's, 20's- 5 ft. Two boilers, each 42" dia. by 18 ft. Operated by the Swains on Illinois River, Capt. Percy Swain. She was the last side-wheel packet on the Illinois. Sold September 1922 to Capt. George Prince for Vicksburg-Natchez trade, replacing sunken *PERCY SWAIN.* She was the last packet in that trade. Dismantled at Vidalia, La., early 1930s.

1470 DAVID TATUM

SW p wh b. Jeffersonville, Ind., by Howard, 1854. 373 tons. 220 x 32 x 6. First home port St. Louis. Dismantled 1865 and became a wharfboat at Cairo, Ill., owned by Capt. J.M. Phillips. Sold June 1870 and moved to Waterproof, La.

1471 DAVID TIPTON

SW snagboat wh b. Jeffersonville, Ind., by Howard, 1900. Originally named *COL. A. MACKENZIE* (see). Her skipper, Capt. David Tipton, died at the wheel on Lake Pepin, near Reads Landing, Sept. 22, 1904. The snagboat was renamed in his honor. The U.S. Engineers operated her on the Upper Mississippi until 1920. Capt. Frank Martin was her last master. Sold at public sale conducted at Rock Island, Ill., to Meyer Katz, St. Louis, and John F. Klein, Pittsburgh. Later ran as a packet Memphis-White River renamed *URSIE BOYCE* (see).

1472 DAVID WATTS

Stw p wh b. Paducah, Ky., 1864. 158.8 x 35 x 5.6. Was at Pittsburgh advertised for Virginia City, Hancock City, Deer Lodge, and all points in the Idaho mining district, Capt. Joseph H. Johnson, March 1865. Made a trip to Fort Benton in 1866, Capt. Johnson, a 70-day round trip from St. Louis. Ran New Orleans-Red River that winter, Capt. George Alban. Ran St. Louis-Tennessee River until lost Aug. 27, 1870, at Price's Landing above Cairo.

1473 DAVID WHITE

SW p wh b. Madison, Ind. at A. F. Temple yard, 1853. 287 x 34 x 7. Engines, 30's- 9 ft. Five boilers, each 46" by 30 ft., five flues. Paddlewheels 37 ft. dia. with 12 ft. buckets. Cabin by Horsley & Ealer. She had three centerpole hogchains. Came out in the Wheeling-Louisville Union Line, Capt. William McClain. Returned to Madison and hull changed to 305 x 36 x 7 in 1865, and entered Louisville-New Orleans trade, Capt. Anson McGill. Caught fire downbound at Irish Jimmy Bar on the Ohio River, Carrsville, Ky., Apr. 13, 1856. The fire was in the hold, and she was scuttled and sunk. Successfully raised. Exploded boilers upbound on the Mississippi River at Point Chicot on Feb. 17, 1867, Capt. Dan Kinney. Large life loss. Passengers testified that *MOLLIE ABLE* had left New Orleans same time as the *WHITE,* and there was much racing up the river. The *ABLE* dropped out after she blew a cylinder-head on the port side and lost her pitman, this near Rodney. The EMERALD was close by when the explosion happened and rescued many. David White, Esq., was a native of Madison, Ind, and became quite prominent on the river.

1474 DAWN

Stw p wh b. Madison, Ind., 1875. 160 x 32 x 4. Machinery from *ERA NO. 13.* Owned by Capt. Charles P. Truslow and others, and ran New Orleans-Shreveport. Downbound

Apr. 4, 1878, burned at Whitehead Plantation, 30 miles above New Orleans. The wrecking boat *T. F. ECKERT* removed boilers, machinery, etc.

1475 DAYTON BELLE

SW ferry wh b. Cincinnati, Oh., 1867. 85 tons. Off the lists 1881.

1476 DECALION

SW ferry wh b. California, Pa., 1858. 102 tons. 108 x 29.1 x 3.7. Owned by Decalion Ferry and Land Co., Capt. J.M. Breedin, Keokuk, Iowa. Off the lists in 1869.

1477 DE DE

Stw p wh b. Algiers, La., 1856. 118 x 20.9 x 3.6. Owned new by William S. Lewis, Caddo Parish. Sold April 1857 to parties in Sevier County, Ark., one of whom, Capt. W.H. Ware, was master. Snagged and lost at Black Bayou, La., Mar. 27, 1858.

1478 DEAN ADAMS

SW p wh b. Sewickley, Pa. (hull) and completed at Pittsburgh, 1880. 190 x 29 x 6. Engines, 17's- 7 ft. Three boilers, each 47" dia. by 23 ft. Machinery came from the *LEGAL TENDER* (see). Built for the Arkansas City-Vicksburg trade, Capt. Matt Williams. After the *IDLEWILD* burned she ran Memphis-Arkansas City. Owned by Major John D. Adams and named for a son. When the *KATE ADAMS* was built, the *DEAN ADAMS* was sold to the Lee Line and burned at the Memphis wharf in 1886.

1479 DECLARATION

SW p wh b. West Elizabeth, Pa., 1846. 229 tons. Went to the Upper Mississippi. Collided with and sank the *IOWA*, Oct. 1, 1847. Sank and lost Nov. 12, 1849.

1480 DECOTAH

Stw p wh b. Belle Vernon, Pa., 1858. 230 tons. She was at Florence, Ala., in late January 1861 along with *J. T. McCOMBS*, and both were asked to leave because they were owned in Pittsburgh, and the war was coming on. In the Pittsburgh-Cincinnati trade, February 1861, Capt. Hendrickson. Capt. Theodore Fink owned her later, and sold her to Johnson & Heydock, Cairo, Ill., for Tennessee River cotton trade. She was on the marine ways for repairs at Paducah, Mar. 25, 1864, when the Confederates staged a raid and burned her.

1481 DEER CREEK

Stw p wh b. Jeffersonville, Ind., 1878. 90 x 25 x 4. Ran Vicksburg to Yazoo River. Was still documented in 1886.

1482 DEER LODGE

Stw p wh b. Belle Vernon, Pa. at the L. M. Speer yard, 1865. 165 x 35 x 5. Engines, 17½'s- 5 ft. by Robinson, Rae & Co. Three boilers, each 38" dia. by 26 ft. James Dunbar was the architect. Appeared new at Pittsburgh with Capt. Thomas W. Rae, master, and H.A. Dohrman, clerk. Designed for the Missouri River, and had aboard a portable sawmill to saw her own cord wood en route. In all she made 11 trips to Fort Benton, eight of them all the way from St. Louis. In 1866 and again in 1868 she made two round trips St. Louis-Fort Benton in a single season. She was the first arrival at the fort in 1869. She was sunk by a snag upbound 12 miles below St. Joseph, Mo., in latter 1865, then owned by Capt. John C. Caplin, H.A. Dohrman and Captain Rae. Raised. In 1866 her passage fare, St. Louis to the fort, 3,175 miles, was $300. Freight was taken up at 15¢ per pound. Quit running in 1872 and dismantled summer 1874.

1483 DEFENDER

Stw p wh b. Brownsville, Pa., 1855. 294 tons. First home port, Pittsburgh. Snagged and lost Apr. 13, 1860, at Laconia, Ark., with loss of five lives.

1484 DEFIANCE

Stw p wh b. Shousetown, Pa. (hull) and completed at Pittsburgh, 1845. 130 x 23 x 5. Litch engines. Three boilers, each 38" by 19 ft. Ran with regularity Pittsburgh-Zanesville for four years. Capt. Till Devol, master, 1845–46; Capt. Newton, 1847–48. Lost at Liberty, Ill., 1848.

1485 DEFIANCE

SW p wh b. Cincinnati, Oh., 1849. 178.7 x 29.4 x 11. Our surmise is that this deep draft boat was engaged principally in towing and berthing ships in the New Orleans area. First owner was the Independent Towboat Co., New Orleans, and first master was Capt. John McPhearson. Had various owners in the area, and finally was purposely burned to prevent capture, Apr. 28, 1862.

1486 DEFIANCE

SW p wh b. Zanesville, Oh., 1856. 55 tons. Ran Zanesville-Cincinnati three years until removed from documentation in 1858.

1487 DEKALB

b. West Wheeling, Oh., 1845. 74 tons. Built for low water work. First season ran Wheeling-Cincinnati. Came in collision with CLIPPER six miles below Smithland, Ky., November 1848 and was sunk. Lytle documents loss on Feb. 12, 1849. A boat of this name was sunk at the lower end of Brush Creek Island, Ohio River, and the wreckage was still there in October 1866.

1488 DEKOVEN

SW transfer wh b. Jeffersonville, Ind., by Howard, 1894. 232.3 x 37 x 6.1. Engines, 20's- 6½ ft. Four boilers (two on each guard) each 44" by 24 ft. Built for the Ohio Valley Railroad Co., L.A. Washington, supt., Henderson, Ky. The O.V. RR was sopped up by the Illinois Central and ownership was changed to correspond, Oct. 4, 1897. Ferried railroad cars Paducah-Brookport. Sent to Helena, Ark., to replace *JOHN BERTRAM* in 1912. She was later sold and converted into a sand dredge, renamed *SANDERSON* (see).

1489 DEL NORTE

Stw p wh b. Elizabeth, Pa., 1846, hull, and completed at Zanesville. 136 x 25 x 4.5. Engines, 16's- 6 ft. Capt. Charles Bowen was master, Pittsburgh-Zanesville, first season. She was sold to New Orleans, there owned by Ellmaker & Viosca, with William F. Bowen, of Zanesville, retaining interest. Bowen contracted to deliver her to the Rio Grande River in Texas, and did so in a harrowing voyage. She was snagged on the Rio Grande in 1849.

1490 DEL NORTE

Prop yacht wh b. Zanesville, Oh., 1893. 35 x 8.2 x 4. Built by S.W. Printz, Zanesville, as a pleasure boat, and named for the *DEL NORTE* of yore (prior listing). Printz built the engine and used a Griffith & Wedge boiler. For some years she was perched on shore at Zanesville but was rebuilt 1916 and given a G&W boiler with 96 two-inch flues allowed 150 psi. She then ran through 1942. Printz died in April 1943, aged 81. Dismantled.

1491 DELAWARE

SW p wh b. Cincinnati, Oh., 1851. 220 x 34 x 7. Engines, 18's- 6½ ft. Three boilers. First home port, St. Louis. Ran St. Louis-New Orleans, also Memphis-New Orleans, Capt. W.W. Baker and others. Snagged at Hat Island, Mississippi River in October 1853, raised. In August 1858 took a big load of railroad rails to Shreveport for the Vicksburg, Shreveport & Texas RR. Lost in 1860.

1492 DELAWARE

Stw p wh b. Freedom, Pa., 1862. 168 tons. Engines, 15's- 5 ft. Three boilers, each 40″ by 22 ft. Ran principally Pittsburgh-Cincinnati-Louisville, Capt. Ray W. Harton. Chartered summer 1867 by Capt. C.L. Brennan for Pittsburgh-Wheeling trade. In 1866 made a trip to Dubuque and above towing three barges loaded with railroad iron, etc. She burned on the marine ways at Cincinnati Aug. 16, 1868, along with the *PINE GROVE, POTOMAC,* and *EZRA PORTER.*

1493 DELEGATE

Stw p wh b. Elizabeth, Pa., 1854. 208 tons. Lost in collision with the *ELLA* on the Ohio River at West Franklin, Ind., Jan. 21, 1859, one life lost.

1494 DELIA

SW p wh b. Louisville, Ky., 1851. 157.5 x 29.1 x 5.7. Operated out of New Orleans, Capt. E. Castillo, owned largely by partners of St. Martinsville, La. Sold March 1854 to other St. Martinsville owners, Capt. A. Moynier, master. Off the lists 1858.

1495 DELLA

Rig? A ferry b. Beverly, Oh., 1866. 10.32 tons. Off the lists in 1872.

1496 DELLA

Stw p wh b. St. Paul, Minn., 1890. 58 x 10 x 2.9. Off the lists 1895.

1497 DELLS

Stw p wh b. Osceola, Wis., 1866. 90 x 16.5 x 5.5. Engines, 8″- 2½ ft. One boiler. Was owned 1874 by Kaskaskia River Navigation Co. Snagged above Arago, Neb., on Missouri River, Oct. 26, 1878. Two men jumped overboard and were drowned.

1498 DELTA

Stw p wh b. Batesville, Ark., 1846. 78 x 18.7 x 3.5. Originally owned by James A. Lusk of New Orleans, Capt. Benjamin Orr, master. The hull was built at Batesville and she was completed at New Orleans. She was sold and taken to Matagorda, Tex. Off the lists 1851.

1499 DELTA

SW p wh b. Cincinnati, Oh., 1849. 182 ft. long. Engines, 22's- 8 ft. Three boilers, each 46″ dia. by 24 ft. with five 10″ flues. Capt. Joel Green built her and commanded her the first season, Cincinnati-New Orleans. Capt. Samuel Brickell took charge second year. John T. Brooks was her engineer. Clifford B. Wayne and Thompson Dean were stockholders. Burned and lost at Algiers, La., May 10, 1858.

1500 DELTA

SW p wh b. Chester, Ill., 1856. 119 tons. First home port, St. Louis. Off the lists in 1865.

1501 DELTA

Stw p wh b. Cincinnati, Oh., 1859. 77 tons. First home port, Memphis. Went to Confederate registry 1861.

1502 DELTA

SW transfer wh b. Jeffersonville, Ind., by Howard, 1891. 226 x 45.5 x 7. She was built to replace the *NORTHERN PACIFIC* at Vicksburg for the Vicksburg, Shreveport & Pacific RR. She operated until approx. 1906 and was dismantled. The hull was used as a barge by a local Vicksburg firm, and turned over in the canal. In late December 1908 the snagboat *HORATIO G. WRIGHT* removed the wreckage.

1503 DELTA

Stw p wh b. Jeffersonville, Ind., by Howard, 1900. Originally named *BAYLISS LEE* (see). 190 x 30 x 5. Engines, 16's- 7 ft. Name was changed to *DELTA* in June 1900 when Lee Line sold her to Capt. E.W.B. Nowland who ran her in the Memphis-Vicksburg trade. Sank after hitting an obstruction at Mayersville, Miss., in March 1903, raised. Burned at Harwood Island, below Greenville, Miss., early March 1905.

1504 DELTA QUEEN

Stw p sh b. Stockton, Cal., 1926. 250 x 58 x 11.5. Cross-compound condensing engines, 26's- 52½'s 10 ft. Two water tube boilers burn fuel oil. This and a duplicate sister ship *DELTA KING* were fabricated at Glasgow, Scotland, insofar as all of the steel work is concerned, on the River Clyde at the Isherwood Yard. Both were knocked down, the sections sent by steamship to San Francisco, and from there barged to a yard at Stockton. There they were assembled and completed. The building operations extended from 1924 through part of 1927. The machinery was built at Denny's Shop in Dumbarton, from plans furnished by Charles H. Evans Co., San Francisco. The paddlewheel shafts and cranks were forged at the Krupp Works, Germany, and machined in San Francisco. The upper cabins were built by U.S. shipwrights, four decks high, largely of oak, teak, mahogany, and Oregon cedar. When completed these boats were the most expensive river sternwheelers extant, costing $875,000 each. The original owner was the California Transportation Co., which ran both in the San Francisco-Sacramento trade on regular year-round schedule. Frequent excursions were made to Stockton. Both boats were rated 1,837 tons gross, and 1,318 net; they frequently carried 800 tons of freight. The staterooms slept 200. Rooms and passenger areas were air-conditioned, hot air heat. The cabins were finished in solid oak, with natural mahogany and walnut trim. Plate glass windows surmounted by colored leaded stained glass transoms provided copious forward lounging areas. There was no hull bracing above the main deck, seven watertight compartments divided the hulls thwartship, all hull space usable. Depth of hold at forecastle 16 feet, and at engineroom 13 feet. Overall length, including paddlewheel, 285 feet. Paddlewheel built with 28 arms, 28-inch dip, 19 ft. buckets, entirely of fir. A circular boxing covered the wheel, steel framed, wood covered, with copper-sheathed sides. Kitchen in the hold, pantries and dining room on the boiler deck, with dumbwaiters to convey food and utensils. Main deck entirely of ironwood imported from Siam. One large smokestack aft of the pilothouse baffled internally into two sections, one for each boiler, with protective jacket running full height of the stack. Evans steam steering gear activated the pilot wheel, with electric signal system between pilot house and engineroom. Many rooms had connecting shower or bath, white tiled, and twin beds. All hardware solid brass. The two superlative boats were dedicated at the Banner Island shipyard, Stockton, on Friday, May 20, 1927, and entered service about June 1. They did handsomely, weathered the Great Depression, but a modern highway linking S.F. and Sacramento was too much. The *DELTA QUEEN's* last trip came on the closing day of the Golden Gate International Exposition, Sunday, Sept. 29, 1940. Both were sold to Isbrandston Steamship Lines. The *DELTA KING* was being prepared for transit to New Orleans when came Pearl Harbor, Dec. 7, 1941. Navy took over both and used them in the S.F. Bay area, painted drab gray, designated "Yard Ferry Boats." At war's conclusion they were turned over to the U.S. Maritime Commission. The *DELTA QUEEN* was sold at public sale to Greene Line Steamers, Inc., Cincinnati, Dec. 17, 1946. Capt. Tom R. Greene, president of the Greene Line, at once initiated arrangements for her transfer to New Orleans. She was towed to the Fulton Shipyard, Antioch, Cal., on Feb. 4, 1947, and prepared for sea. Contract was made with the Portland (Ore.) Tug & Barge Co., for the voyage, and their tug *OSAGE* started the trip Apr. 10, 1947. Transit of the Panama Canal was made May 10-11, and delivery was made at Harvey, La., on May 19. The Avondale Shipyard's Repair Plant then put her back in operating condition. She was taken under her own steam to the Dravo Corporation yard, Neville Island, Pa., arriving there on August 10. A complete renovation required three months on the ways and two more at the Dravo outfitting dock. Changes were extensive. Her two cabin decks were extended forward, dining room placed on the main deck, formerly the freight area. The air-conditioning was completely renovated, which meant elimination of the original water spray for cooling; paddlewheel covering was removed; intakes for boiler water (originally through the bottom) were piped out the hull sides; fuel capacity augmented; many new luxury cabins added where the dining room had first been located; new pantries, bar, and toilet facilities appended to numerous staterooms. She left Dravo Feb. 28, 1948, and arrived at Cincinnati March 1 to receive her new furniture, a swinging stage, etc. Since then she has been in tourist service on the Ohio, Mississippi, Tennessee and Cumberland rivers. Following the untimely death of Capt. Tom R. Greene, July 10, 1950, the *DQ* was managed by his widow, Letha Cavendish Greene, until January 1958 when she laid up the boat and advertised it for sale. Destiny played a hand: an ex-passenger, Richard C. Simonton of North Hollywood, Cal., reorganized Greene Line Steamers in 1950 and the *DQ* became a profitable venture. Dick Simonton became ill and on Nov. 21, 1969, Greene Line was transferred to Overseas National Airways, headed by 37-year-old G.F. Steedman Hinckley, with operations based at Kennedy International Airport, Jamaica, N.Y. The *DQ* ran head-on into Public Law 89-777 prohibiting the operation of wooden superstructured overnight passenger vessels. A near miracle happened New Year's Eve, 1971, when President Richard M. Nixon exempted the *DQ* from the terms of the law for three years. Subsequent presidential sanction has kept the boat operative. During the Hinckley regime ownership was changed to Delta Queen Steamboat Co. In April 1976 ownership was passed to the Coca-Cola Co., of N.Y., and soon thereafter Prudential Lines, Inc., of San Francisco became involved. Betty Blake joined the operations while Letha Greene presided and rose to presidency of Delta Queen Steamboat Co. E.J. Quinby, Summit, N.J. and William Muster became executives during the Simonton era. The *DQ* has had various masters during her Mississippi-Ohio career, chief among them. Capts. Paul Underwood, Ernest E. Wagner and Clarke (Doc) Hawley, and in 1977, Capt. Gabriel Chengery. The *DELTA QUEEN* was brought 5,380 statute miles at sea, the most lengthy salt water transit of record for a flat-bottom sternwheeler. She came through unscathed, a tribute to her builder James Burns, Oakland, Cal.

1505 Denizen

SW p wh b. Smithland, Ky., 1841. 326 tons. 168 x 29. First home port, St. Louis. In 1844 running New Orleans-

Columbia, Capt. W. Shrodes. Exploded boilers 30 miles below Vicksburg, Nov. 30, 1845, resulting in death of Capt. Shrodes. Master then became Capt. J.N. Young. Sold October 1846 to Green & Harding and others, New Orleans, Capt. Simeon D. Windover, and in 1847 Capt. R. Parks. Later in 1847, Capt. James W. Riddle, master. Sold in 1849 to T.B. Puller, Pt. Coupee Parish, La., who also was master. Off the lists 1851.

1506 DENMARK

SW p wh b. Shousetown, Pa. (hull), and completed at Pittsburgh, 1856. 171 x 34 x 5.3. A double rudder boat. Built by and for Capt. Richard C. Gray, Pittsburgh. Ran St. Louis-St. Paul. Ran there 1857–1862. She was part of Grant's fleet to Pittsburg Landing, Tenn., in charge of Capt. J.J. (Windy) Robinson. Struck a snag and lost at Atlas Island, downbound, Oct. 8, 1862, below Keokuk.

1507 DENVER

SW p wh b. Madison, Ind., 1862. 225 x 33. Engines, 24's-6½ ft. Three boilers. Owned by the Hannibal & St. Joseph RR, operated between Omaha and St. Joseph principally. Named for the first governor of Colorado. She made trips to St. Louis. Commanded by Capt. Perrin Kay, Capt. John Waddell, and lastly by Capt. Samuel Burke. Burned at the wharf, St. Joseph, Mo., May 16, 1867. A pot of tar was being heated on the kitchen range and was accidentally upset when a young man tried to remove it and burned his fingers. The hull was not badly damaged, and was used later in building a centerwheel ferry (next listing).

1508 DENVER

Centerwheel ferry wh b. Pittsburgh, Pa., 1869. 136 x 24.1 x 6.3. She is said to have been built using part of the hull of the former side-wheel packet *DENVER*, also engines. Operated at St. Joseph, Mo., in connection with the railroad, and later served at Fort Lincoln. Wrecked by ice at Fort Lincoln on Mar. 13, 1880.

1509 DES ARC

SW p wh b. Paducah, Ky., 1862. 276 tons. 205 x 31 x 6. Engines, 19's-6 ft. Three boilers. Capt. Hicks King had her built for the Memphis-Cairo trade. Soon switched to the Memphis-Duvall's Bluff (White River) trade in the Archer Line, with U.S. Mail contract. The following dispatch is from the Pittsburgh *Commercial*, Mar. 31, 1864: "On the morning of March 22, at about 9 o'clock, the White River packet DES ARC was discovered to be on fire in her hull at the stern. The U.S. steamer *COVINGTON*, Capt. Lord, and the *QUEEN CITY*, Capt. Hickey, were at anchor a short distance below the landing, and upon the alarm being given, the *COVINGTON* slipped her anchor and ran up to the steamboat *ARAGO*, lying immediately below the *DES ARC*, hard aground, and after repeated attempts pulled her out in the stream, relieving her from the perilous situation. She then made fast to the *DES ARC* and towed her across the river where she was sunk by shots from the *QUEEN CITY*, not however in time to prevent the fire from consuming the upper works of the boat, and she burned to the water's edge in 15 minutes, after the fire broke through the deck from the hold. There was a number of boats at the landing, all of which would have been destroyed had not the vessels of Capts. Lord and Hickey been at the Bluff to render assistance, as the wind was blowing fresh on shore, and no boat at the landing had steam up except the *ARAGO* which, being aground, could not render any assistance." A second dispatch that day recounted that *DES ARC* was owned by Champion & Ogden, and had aboard about 300 bales of cotton. The *EMMA NO. 2* on July 12, 1864, arrived at Cincinnati with the machinery, etc., from the burned boat.

1510 DES ARC

SW p wh b. Cincinnati, Oh., 1864. The hull from the former *DES ARC* was used, and she got the engines from the *WILLIAM L. EWING*, 21's-6½ ft. New upper works. Ran Memphis-White River, Capt. John D. Elliott, and James Elliott and Matt A. Glass, clerks. In 1865, same trade, Capt. Dick Mason. She was retired at Memphis in 1871 and was towed to Louisville for dismantling.

1511 DES ARC

Stw p wh b. Valley Park, Mo., 1891. 95 x 18 x 3. This location is about 20 miles up Meramec River, and *DES ARC* is the only boat known to have been built there. In May 1892 she was sold to the owners of the burned steamer *JOSIE D. HARKINS* (see) which had burned 20 miles north of Texarkana, Ark. In January 1893 was in Vicksburg-Sunflower River trade.

1512 DES MOINES

SW p wh b. Madison, Ind., 1857. 298 tons. Was in the Keokuk Packet Co., 1857–1861, Capt. J.D. Malin. Capt. John G. Prather was a part owner. Was appropriated by the U.S. for transport service during the war, and was up Red River in 1864. Struck and sank the *KATIE* (see) at Diamond Island, Ohio River, Nov. 22, 1864. Off the lists in 1865. Her machinery went to the *CORNELIA* (see).

1513 DES MOINES CITY

Stw p wh b. Pittsburgh, Pa., 1859. 122 tons. First home port, Keokuk, Iowa. Was running on the Arkansas River during the war. In May 1864 she was hit over 150 times by rifle shots a few miles from Piney when guerillas attacked. A lady aboard was shot through the right breast, the ball passing through. She was taken ashore at Dardanelle in critical condition. Captain Keinser had a narrow escape, a ball ripping his pants below the knee. Snagged and lost on the Arkansas, Jan. 1, 1865.

1514 DE SMET

SW p wh b. Mound City, Ill., 1872. 184.4 x 34 x 5.1. Capt. Joseph LaBarge built and ran her. First mission was taking freight from St. Louis for the building of the Southern Pacific RR in the Louisiana regions of Red River. The water was too low to make delivery and the freight was forwarded by mule pack. Caught in ice that winter at Helena,

Ark. She made a successful trip to Shreveport in 1873, then to Fort Benton, Mont. Capt. Joe LaBarge had enough experiences on this one trip to the mountains to fill a book. At Fort Benton he was arrested for selling alcohol to the Indians, and there was a long delay while he went to Helena, Mont., to be cleared of the charge. Upon return to St. Louis the boat was entered in the St. Louis-Alton trade competing with the Eagle Packet Co. Eagle Packet bought her in 1874 and ran her St. Louis-Grafton, helping out the *SPREAD EAGLE* (see). In 1877 she ran under charter to the Northern Line in the St. Louis-Louisiana, Mo., trade. In 1876 was in the St. Louis-Paducah trade, Capt. John Bruner. Registered at Vicksburg, 1883. Burned June 12, 1886, opposite Newport, Ark. A detailed account of this boat appeared in *The Waterways Journal,* issue of Dec. 13, 1942.

1515 DE SOTO

SW p wh b. Jeffersonville, Ind., 1841. 260 tons. 157.9 x 27 x 6.5. Ran out of New Orleans owned by Peter Dalman and others. In February 1844 sold to Capt. P.F. Kimball, Natchitoches, La. Collided with the *BUCKEYE* Mar. 1, 1844, causing loss of *BUCKEYE* and great loss of life (see *S&D Reflector,* issue December 1971, pages 51–53, for detailed account of this calamity). She had various ownerships, and in May 1848 was bought by Junius Beene, president of Union Towboat Co., New Orleans. When last enrolled, Jan. 19, 1855, was owned by Good Intent Towboat Co., and others, New Orleans.

1516 DE SOTO

SW ferry wh b. Wellsville, Oh., 1859. 104 tons. First home port, Vicksburg. Exploded and lost at Pascagoula, Miss., Dec. 9, 1865 with loss of eleven lives.

1517 DE SOTO

SW p wh b. New Albany, Ind., 1860. 180 x 35 x 7. Built for and owned in whole by Capt. H.H. Beard, New Orleans. Acquired by USQMD in 1861. Captured as a Confederate steamboat Apr. 7, 1862. Later became U.S. *DE SOTO,* renamed *GENERAL LYON* Oct. 24, 1862. Commodore Andrew H. Foote was injured at the Battle of Fort Donelson and, after the Battle of Pittsburg Landing, he boarded *DE SOTO* (one of the boats he captured at Island 10) and went up the Ohio River on her, and thence to Cleveland, Oh., where he died shortly thereafter. After the war she was sold to private owners, and was renamed *ALABAMA* on Oct. 20, 1865 (see).

1518 DE SOTO

Stw p wh b. Cincinnati, Oh., 1863, originally named *SCIOTO* (see), and during the war was a tinclad renamed *METEOR.* Sold to private owners Oct. 7, 1865, and renamed *DE SOTO.* She was a regular weekly packet, New Orleans, Mobile, Selma and Montgomery, Capt. W.C. Diggs, master, 1866. Off the lists in 1869.

1519 DE SOTO

Stw p wh b. Cincinnati, Oh., 1877, originally named *GOLDEN CROWN* (see). 261 x 41.8 x 6.6. Run by the Cincinnati & Memphis Packet Co., with James D. Parker, president, L.R. Keck, secretary, and R.W. Wise, superintendent. This company had four large sternwheelers, the *OHIO, DE SOTO, BUCKEYE STATE,* and *GRANITE STATE* (all see). About 2 o'clock on the morning of Jan. 28, 1890, the *DE SOTO,* upbound with a big trip, landed at John Henning's distillery, a mile below Owensboro, Ky. to unload empty barrels. Fire was detected, and pilot Charlie Owens beached the boat—this was on a big river with the water up to about the top of Kentucky bank. Everyone got off safely and in the morning only the jackstaff and part of the paddlewheel were visible. Crew at the time: Capt. H.H. Deem, master; Harry O. Proctor, head clerk; Frank Parker, second clerk; William Wilson, third clerk; Charles Owens, pilot; Albert Pritchard, pilot; J.T. Frampton, mate; Jerome Clark, second mate; John Wybrant, chief engineer; A. Spangler, steward. Bad luck attended the company with three disasters in a row: *GRANITE STATE* had been lost three months prior, the *OHIO* had been sunk at Louisville the week before.

1520 DE SOTO

SW ex wh b. Jeffersonville, Ind., by Howard, 1898, originally named *JAMES LEE* (see). She was converted into an excursion boat at Memphis, c. 1914, and operated there until lost in ice January 1918. Her roof bell later went to the Thompson Brothers plantation in Arkansas. Also lost in ice at Memphis, same time was the *GEORGIA LEE* (see).

1521 DE SOTO

Stw p wh b. Houma, La., 1915, originally named *DIXIE* (see). Was renamed *DE SOTO,* c 1925, while operating as a short trader out of Memphis. Sank and lost at Tamm's Landing, 150 miles above Memphis, September 1926.

1522 DE SOTO

Stw p wh b. Hermann, Mo., 1918, originally named *LEXINGTON* (see). She was bought by Capt. Peters Lee, Memphis, in 1928, converted into a short trade packet, renamed *DE SOTO,* and burned at Memphis July 15, 1928, before making a trip.

1523 DEW DROP

Stw p wh b. Monongahela, Pa., 1857. 148 tons. First home port, St. Louis, Mo. Burned at the mouth of Osage River, Mo., June 12, 1860.

1524 DEW DROP

SW p wh b. Cincinnati, Oh., 1858. First home port, Vicksburg. 184 tons. Operated Vicksburg-Yazoo River, Capt. S.H. Parisot. Burned by the Federals when U.S. tinclads *FOREST ROSE* and *LINDEN* raided the Yazoo, May 25, 1863. Her wreckage at Quiver River, Miss., was still in evidence in 1959.

1525 DEW DROP

Stw p wh b. Catlettsburg, Ky., 1867. 44 tons. In 1871 was

running up Big Sandy River, Capt. J.M. Jarred, and ran low water trades on the upper Ohio. Off the lists 1871.

1526 Dew Drop

Stw p wh There is evidence of such a boat in the Cincinnati-Pomeroy trade in October 1878, Capt. E. Barringer, master, with H.C. Teeter, clerk.

1527 Dewey

SW p wh b. Jeffersonville, Ind., 1888 as the *KATE ADAMS* (second; see). The Chalmette Packet Co., New Orleans, bought her in September 1898 and changed name to *DEWEY*. She ran out of New Orleans to Grand Lake and the Bends, and also to Vicksburg and Lake Providence. In 1901 ran with *JULIA* (see) Memphis-New Orleans. The Memphis & Vicksburg Packet Co., sold her in July 1902 to Capt. Thomas B. Sims, St. Louis, who renamed her *LOTUS SIMS* (see).

1528 DeWitt Clinton

SW p wh b. Elizabethtown, Pa., 1847. 265 tons. Owned in Steubenville by Capt. Devinney and others. Ran Pittsburgh-Cincinnati, and in 1849 conveyed several large groups from the upper Ohio to St. Louis, bound for the gold diggings in California. In April 1849 she had aboard 52 persons from Boston, Lynn, Lowell, and other eastern points. A month later she conveyed a Marietta group calling themselves the "Marietta Gold Hunters." She was lost by snagging upbound from New Orleans to Pittsburgh at Dismal Point, opposite Presidents Island, below Memphis, Jan. 25, 1852. Thirty six-lives were reported lost, nine of them Negro deckhands.

1529 Dexter

Stw p wh b. Piketon, Ky., 1867. 65 tons. Operated on the Big Sandy River. Off the lists in 1870.

1530 Dexter

SW p wh b. Jeffersonville, Ind. (hull), and completed at New Albany, Ind., 1868. 307 x 40 (floor 36) x 7. Engines, 34½'s- 9 ft. Eight boilers, each 37½" dia. by 28 ft. Paddle wheels, 35 ft. dia. by 15 ft. bckets. The machinery and cabin came from the *ATLANTIC* (see). Built for Capt. J. Ed Montgomery and others, ran St. Louis-New Orleans. Capt. Sam Montgomery, master. In 1869 running New Orleans-Natchez in place of the *WILD WAGONER* with Capt. A.C. Goddin, master, and J.C. Libano and A.J. Reid, clerks. She was taken out on the marine ways at Mound City, Ill, in 1870 and the hull enlarged to 322 x 52 (floor 48) x 7. This was quite an operation; she was split in two, the halves spread, and a center section built in her. She came out as the longest side-wheeler extant. Her cabin furniture and outfit had been stored in a warehouse at St. Louis while this was done. The warehouse burned, and she appeared in 1870 with completely new outfitting. She seemed to be plagued with financial troubles and went to several forced sales. Last sale was in December 1873 at St. Louis, where Capt. Dave Campbell bid her in at $9,050. She burned a month later, January 1874, at St. Louis.

1531 Dexter

Stw ferry wh b. Wellsville, Oh, 1873. 25 tons. Still documented at Wheeling, 1886.

1532 Diadem

SW p wh b. Brownsville, Pa., 1847. 275 tons. Off the lists 1854.

1533 Diadem

Stw p wh b. Monongahela, Pa., 1860. 154 x 33 x 4.9. Built for the Pittsburgh-St. Louis trade, Capt. Rogers. Did transport work for the U.S. during the war 1861-1864. Lost in ice at St. Louis, Jan. 13, 1866, Capt. J. Wolff.

1534 Dial

SW p wh b. St. Louis, Mo., 1845. 139 tons. Off the lists in 1851.

1535 Diamond

Stw p wh b. Jeffersonville, Ind., by Howard, 1855. 155 x 40 x 5.5. A dispatch dated at Cincinnati, Mar. 12, 1865, reports *DIAMOND* sold to Capt. Albert Stein and others, and will take two barges to Nashville. Dismantled in 1866.

1536 Diamond Jo

Stw p wh b. Prairie du Chien, Wis., 1864. 165.5 x 32 x 4. Built for "Diamond Jo" Reynolds. Capt. William Fleming superintended construction and was master, with Charles W. Cowles, clerk. Handled grain on the Upper Mississippi. In 1875 ran Fulton-Burlington, Capt. Ben Congar, with John Carlisle and Al Congar, clerks. This continued until 1878 when the *JOSEPHINE* (see) took her place. She then ran St. Louis-Davenport, Capt. R.F. Isherwood. Dismantled at Dubuque in 1883.

1537 Diana

SW p wh b. New Albany, Ind., 1845. 296 tons. Engines, 30½'s- 8 ft. from prior *DIANA*. Four boilers, each 42" dia. by 28½ ft. Built for and owned by Capt. Joseph Swager, who ran her Louisville-New Orleans. Her hull was recessed at the wheels so she could pass through the Louisville-Portland canal and locks. Lost in collision with the *OHIO* at Pilot Station, New Orleans, Jan. 23, 1850. This was the fourth steamboat of the name owned by Captain Swager. His first one was built at Brush Creek, Oh., in 1828.

1538 Diana

SW p wh b. Cincinnati, Oh., 1849. 187 tons. Ran Cincinnati-Frankfort, Ky., on Kentucky River, Capt. B.H. Perry. Sold spring of 1854 at a sheriff's sale to an iron firm in St. Louis, Bridges & Bros. They towed coal with her to meet their own needs, Pittsburgh-St. Louis. Off the lists 1864.

1539 Diana

SW p wh b. Jeffersonville, Ind., by Howard, 1857. 275 x 37

x 7. Engines, 28's- 9 ft. Paddlewheels 37 ft. dia. with 12½ ft. buckets, 30" dip. Cabin was 220 by 16, 52 staterooms, texas 82 ft. long with 20 rooms. Capt. Edward T. Sturgeon was principal owner and master, Orlando L. Smith, first clerk, and John W. Forsee, second clerk. Left Louisville on her maiden trip in the New Orleans trade, Dec. 24, 1857. Ran celebrated race with *BALTIC* in 1858 (see *BALTIC*). She was at the scene and picked up survivors when the *PENNSYLVANIA* (see) exploded at Ship Island, June 1858. When the war broke out she carried army supplies to Nashville, March 1862. Sold to the USQMD while laid up at New Albany, Ind., Dec. 6, 1862, and saw service as a troop transport. Sold to private owners, Apr. 14, 1866, and renamed *ROSALIE JUDSON* (see). Capt. Fred A. Laidley recounted that he took a barge of salt from the Kanawha River to Smithland, Ky., in 1860 and secured passage back upriver on the *DIANA,* and was so greatly impressed with this fine steamboat, he decided to follow steamboating.

1540 DIANA

SW p wh b. Brownsville, Pa., 1858. 239 tons. First home port, Galveston, Tex. She was captured by U.S. forces Apr. 27, 1862, and used as a U.S. transport. Recaptured by the Confederates Mar. 28, 1863, and was burned on Bayou Teche to prevent capture, Apr. 12, 1863. Her boilers were long visible on shore there.

1541 DIANA

SW ferry wh b. New Cumberland, W. Va., 1865. 40 tons. Operated in ferry service between Wellsburg, W. Va., and Brilliant, Oh. Off the lists in 1878.

1542 DIANA

Rig? b. Cincinnati, Oh., 1870. 452 tons. First home port, Galveston, Tex. Last inspection was at Galveston in 1879.

1543 DIANA

Stw p wh b. Carlisle, Ill., 1894. 53.4x 8.9 3.2. Single deck and carried a swinging stage.

1544 DIANNA

Rig? b. Terre Haute, Ind., 1880. 71 x 15 x 3. Documented at Evansville, Ind., 1892.

1545 DICK BROWN

Stw p wh b. Harmar, Oh., at Knox yard, 1893. 132 x 24 x 4.5. Compound engines, 8½'s 15's- 5 ft. by Marietta Mfg. Co. Operated by the Browns in local trades out of Huntington, W. Va., until sold to White Collar Line, Cincinnati. Originally single deck, and a full cabin was added later. Ran Cincinnati-Kentucky River. Sank at Sedamsville, Oh., June 23, 1900, and her machinery went to the *ROBERT TAYLOR* (see *Towboat Directory*).

1546 DICK FOWLER

Stw p wh b. Evansville, Ind., 1892. 175 x 31 x 6.5. Engines, 16's- 6 ft. Three boilers each 42" dia. by 26 ft. Owned by the Fowlers of Paducah, and ran Cairo-Paducah 1893-1912. Once a special speed trail was run with her Cairo-Evansville to take down the time record set by *IDLEWILD* (see). Capt. Ben Howard was in command, and Wash Phillips and John Newman were the pilots, both veterans of *IDLEWILD.* John Wallace was engineer, Charlie Trantham, second. Left Cairo at 2:00 A.M. and came to Paducah in 3-17 and arrived Evansville in 14 hours 17 minutes, taking down *IDLEWILD* by 42 minutes. Raced the *SPREAD EAGLE* Paducah to Cairo on Apr. 10, 1896, beating her by nine minutes. She was built with a V-bottom hull, the keel line 11 inches deeper than the knuckles. She "wore" the roof bell from the side-wheel *W. P. HALLIDAY* (see), and it went from her to the *KENTUCKY,* then to *SAINT LOUIS* (both owned by St. Louis & Tennessee River Packet Co.), and later to the First Christian Church, Paducah. She had the *IDLEWILD*'s whistle, later on the *GEORGE COWLING* (see) and lost when the towboat *RIVAL* burned in Green River. After her speed trials she wore a huge set of antlers over her roof bell marked "Take Them If You Can." There were no takers. In 1905 Capt. R.D. Crider in command, Lee Rholdes, clerk. Left Paducah 8:00 A.M daily, Cairo 3:00 P.M. She was "crossed out" by the U.S. inspectors in January 1911 for hull repairs which never were made. Sold at U.S. sale at Paducah, June 1911 and bought by Capt. Ralph Emerson. She sank during a windstorm that November.

1547 DICK HENDERSON

Rig? b. Parkersburg, W. Va., 1873. 21 tons. Registered at Wheeling, 1876.

1548 DICK JOHNSON

Rig? b. Evansville, Ind., 1871. 217 tons. Built as a low water boat for the Evansville Cairo trade, Capt. Lee Howell. Running Evansville-Cannelton in 1875, Capt. Robert C. Adams, with John A. Adams, clerk. Same trade, 1877, Capt. John A. Williams, with R.H. Williams, clerk.

1549 DICK JONES

Rig? b. Antiquity, Oh., 1880. 81.5 x 16 x 2.8. Documented at Memphis, 1886.

1550 DICK KEYS

SW p wh b. Cincinnati, Oh., 1853. 177 x 30.5 x 7.2. Sold to New Orleans in March 1856 to Alexander Norton & Co., Capt. J.D. Phelps. Sold that August to R.A. Heirn, with Capt. G. Angelo Blass, master. Off the lists 1860.

1551 DICK NASH

Stw p wh b. Algiers, La., 1856. 133.7 x 21.7 x 4.7. Originally owned by Capt. William Lampton and others, New Orleans. Ran on Red River. Capt. Charles F. Grater later was master and part owner. Went to Confederate registry in 1861.

1552 DICTATOR

SW p wh b. Freedom, Pa. (hull), and completed at Pittsburgh, 1865. 165 x 40 x 8.5. Compound condensing engines, 16's, 36's- 8 ft. by Hartupee. Three boilers, each 44" dia. by 18 ft., twenty 5" flues. Paddlewheels, 35 ft. dia.

with 14 ft. buckets, 30" dip. 1,077 tons. Owned by Capt. W.B. Donaldson and others. Left Pittsburgh on Sept. 21, 1865, on maiden trip to New Orleans. Sam Barr, Jr., was first clerk, assisted by G. Wash Floyd. This was the first compound engine boat to use a condenser. Although she operated but five months and four days, she was quite a success, and led to the construction of the *GREAT REPUBLIC*. She was burned in a steamboat fire at St. Louis on Feb. 26, 1866, along with the *LUNA, PEYTONA* and *LEVIATHAN* (all see). A detailed story of *DICTATOR* appeared in *S&D Reflector,* issue of December 1965.

1553 DIE VERNON

SW p wh b. St. Louis, Mo., 1844. 161 x 25.5 x 5.5. Single engine. She ran St. Louis-Keokuk, the beginning of the Keokuk Packet Co. Owned by John S. McCune, Sam Gaty, Charles Dean, and Capt. Neil Cameron. The *ARKANSAS NO. 4* was lost in collision with her, June 21, 1849 (see). Sold to New Orleans September 1849, owned there by Obidiah Livermoore, and transferred a month later to other New Orleans owners, Capt. Jourdan Martin, master. In March 1850 ownership included Gen. Toutant Beauregard of St. Bernard Parish, La., and Capt. Jacob Smith was master. General Beauregard owned control 5/9 in November 1850, and a month later she was sold to Good Intent Towboat Co. and others. Sold in January 1852 to Laurent Millaudon, New Orleans. Off the lists in 1854.

1554 DIE VERNON

SW p wh b. St. Louis, Mo., 1850. 255 x 31.1 x 5.8. Replaced former boat of the name in St. Louis & Keokuk Packet Co. Capt. S.S. Matson, master, W.H. Osborn, first clerk, and J.L. Hatcher, second clerk. In 1851 bought by Capt. Thomas Baldwin who ran her Peoria-St. Louis. She ran St. Louis-St. Paul in the summer of 1852, Capt. Rufus Ford, competing with steamers of the Minnesota Packet Co. Retired in 1858.

1555 DIE VERNON

SW p wh b. Madison, Ind., 1859. 578 tons. Built for St. Louis-Keokuk trade. She was in U.S. service as a transport during the war. After the war ran in the Vicksburg trade, Capt. Frank Hicks, owned in part by Capt. Dan Able. Sold January 1867 to Capt. John P. Banfil and others of Memphis, and ran Memphis-Napoleon, Ark. She hit a snag Feb. 10, 1867, at Australia, six miles from Laconia, Ark., upbound. The damage was considered slight, and she proceeded to a wood yard just above Australia. She was taking water rapidly, and all of value was removed. As she sank the current pulled her broadside and the cabin floated off the hull. She was owned at the time by Capt. Hicks and McCune & Co., St. Louis, so said the dispatches at the time.

1556 DILIGENCE

SW p wh b. Wheeling, Va., 1845. 124 tons. Owned largely at Wheeling and ran to Cincinnati and Louisville. The Wheeling *Daily News* carried a testimonial Aug. 27, 1845, from grateful passengers commending Capt. Stoneman for "attention and comfort we have received aboard." Of the more than 40 signers among them were John T. Dufour, Vevay, Ind., and Charles W. Russell, Wheeling. Snagged and lost at Fort Coffee, Ark., Feb. 28, 1849.

1557 DILIGENT

SW p wh b. Louisville, Ky., 1859. 140 tons. She was in U.S. service transporting sick and wounded during the war. Made such a trip to Keokuk 1863. She was loaded with medical supplies at Cincinnati and sent to Pittsburg Landing, Tenn., in April 1862. Snagged and lost at Helena, Ark., Jan. 10, 1865.

1558 DIME

SW p wh b. Fulton, Oh. (Cincinnati), 1845. 61 tons. First home port, Vicksburg. Ran on Yazoo River. Off the lists 1852.

1559 DIME

Stw p wh b. Nashville, Tenn., 1847. 54 tons. Off the lists 1849.

1560 DIME

SW p wh b. Louisville, Ky., 1859. 33 tons. Off the lists 1861.

1561 DIME

SW p wh b. Wheeling, W. Va., 1863. 70 tons. Was running on Muskingum River when new. At the time Morgan and his raiders crossed the Muskingum, the 86th Ohio Regiment was brought to the scene aboard *DIME,* but she arrived too late. She loaded at Louisville for Nashville in October 1864 and parted her steam line while descending the Falls. Hit Wave Rock just above Goose Island. The pilot ran her out on a reef at the foot of the Falls where she sank with many crushed timbers. Capt. Caffrey in command at the time.

1562 DISPATCH

Stw p wh b. Freedom, Pa., 1846. 45 tons. Ran local trades out of Elizabeth, Pa., first owned by Andrew Leech, Jr., William Bell, Thomas Smith, and George Bradshaw, all of Allegheny City, Pa. Was running tri-weekly from Pittsburgh to Monongahela City, Pa., January 1848 with Capt. John Nelson commanding. Mr. Leech was associated with the Leechburg coal mine above Elizabeth, and this boat carried passengers and also towed coal flats in connection with the mine. Off the lists 1854.

1563 DISPATCH

SW ferry wh b. Antiquity, Oh., 1893. 86 x 20 x 4. Owned October 1899 by E.C. Cooper and B.F. Pickens, St. Marys, W. Va. In February 1900, Pickens became sole owner. He sold her to P.Q. Shrake, New Matamoras, Oh., and en route there she sank due to "overloading." Still listed at Wheeling 1896.

1564 DIURNAL

SW p wh b. Brownsville, Pa., 1850. 170 x 24 x 5. Engines, 18's- 7 ft. Three boilers, each 40" dia. by 24 ft. 199 tons.

Engines from *LOUIS McLANE* (see). Hull by J.S. Pringle, engines by Samuel Snowden, cabin by Lanning, Johnston & Co., furniture by J.W. Woodwell. Came out November 1850, Pittsburgh-Wheeling in charge of Capt. Willis S. Conwell, with F.H. Williams and Andrew Beers, clerks. A number of prominent Pittsburghers made the initial voyage, headed by Gen. William Larimer, Jr. Same trade 1852 owned by Capt. Thomas D. Calhoon, Georgetown, Pa., and others, master. In 1854 Capt. A.S. Shepard was master, still Pittsburgh-Wheeling, teamed up with *FOREST CITY* (see) on opposite days. Withdrawn from the trade in 1857, then owned by Capt. James H. Sholes and others. Capts. John and David McDonald and others ran her as a towboat, towing coal until she finally burned at St. Charles, Ark., Sept. 12, 1863.

1565 DIURNAL

SW p wh b. Harmar, Oh., at the Knox yard, 1879. Finished at Wheeling, where engines were put on. Made her trial trip at Wheeling in July 1879. 200 x 31.3 x 4. Built for Capt. John K. Booth, and ran Wheeling-Parkersburg, in the Wheeling & Parkersburg Packet Co., three trips a week, Capt. A.B. Booth, master, with E.K. Booth, clerk. When the Ohio River RR opened, she was sold to Capt. J. Mack Gamble, who went master, and with J.P. Goodwin, clerk, continued in the trade fall of 1884 and spring of 1885. Capt. Gamble chartered her to the Louisville & Evansville Packet Co., for low water work. She sank at Peckenpaugh Bar, was raised and bulkheaded, and started up the river. The bulkhead gave away and she sank again at Grassy Flats, above Louisville, and was lost.

1566 DIXIE

SW p wh b. Cincinnati, Oh., 1860. 130.8 x 24.4 x 4.2. 106 tons. First home port was Vicksburg. Built by Capt. S.H. Parisot and others. She carried a calliope, one of the first heard up Yazoo River. Served as a Confederate transport during the war. Rebuilt at New Orleans in 1865 by Capt. J.D. Wilbanks, and was running Shreveport-Jefferson in 1868 connecting with the *BART ABLE* for New Orleans. Had various changes of ownership at New Orleans and was out of service in 1871.

1567 DIXIE

SW p wh b. Louisville, Ky., 1860. 106 tons. Snagged and lost at Campti, La., Oct. 20, 1860.

1568 DIXIE

Stw p wh b. New Albany, Ind., 1904. 108 x 21.7 x 3. She wound up towing *AMERICAN* showboat built by Walter Needham, and was lost by sinking at Cincinnati.

1569 DIXIE

Prop yacht sh b. Huntington, W. Va., 1905. 35.2 x 7.3 x 3.9. Enrolled at Wheeling 1908.

1569A DIXIE

Stw p wh b. Houma, La., 1915. 131 x 24.2 x 3.4. Engines, 10"-5 ft. Two boilers, each 36" by 16 ft. Built by the Bradfords and they ran her as a freight boat. In 1918 ran New Orleans to Donaldsonville, Capt. R.J. Comeaux, master, with J.E. Dicharry, clerk, in place of the *PAUL*. Bradfords sold her October 1920 to Tri-State Packet Co., Memphis, to replace the *HELEN BLAIR* (see). In 1921 in the Cairo-Caruthersville trade, Capt. Charles R. Pierce. The Valley Line, Memphis, acquired her, renamed her *DE SOTO*, and lost her at Tamm's Landing, 150 miles above Memphis, September 1926.

1570 DIXIE BEE LINE

Stw ferry wh b. Jeffersonville, Ind., by Howard, 1891, originally *EMILY* (see). Operated at Henderson, Ky., and burned there in August 1926. She was rebuilt at Paducah and became *OHIO NO. 2* (see).

1571 DO ALL

Rig? b. Vicksburg, Miss., 1883. 45.9 x 10.6 x 2.2. Still listed at Vicksburg 1886.

1572 DOAN NO. 2.

Stw p wh b. Cincinnati, Oh., 1863. 250 tons. She was burned and lost in a Rebel attack at Johnsonville, Tenn., Nov. 4, 1864, owned by Capts. John Kyle and Holloway, Cincinnati. A number of other steamers were lost in this engagement (see *J.B. FORD*).

1572A DONNA MAE

Prop wh Operated at Lake City, Minn., by Capt. E.W. Holstrom. Dates?

1573 DR. BATEY

SW p wh b. Louisville, Ky., 1850. 171 x 28.7 x 6. 281 tons. Ran New Orleans-Bayou Sara, Capt. William C. Wilson, master, and half owner. In 1854 Capt. Adelard Dugas was master and half owner. In 1851 ran as a summer boat New Orleans-Natchez, Capt. T.C. Holmes. In 1855 the Dugas family incorporated as the New Orleans Coast & Lafourche Transportation Co., and ran the boat until April 1860. Sold at that time to Capt. John Hiern, New Orleans. At the outbreak of the war she was taken to Shreveport, converted into a Rebel gunboat, and participated in the capture of the U.S. *INDIANOLA*. The name of this boat in accounts is variouly spelled *DR. BATY, DR. BEATY, DR. BATTIE, DR. BEATTY*; we have accepted *DR. BATEY* from a contemporary freight bill.

1574 DR. BUFFINGTON

SW p wh b. Cincinnati, Oh., 1857. 176 x 32 x 5. Ran New Orleans-Grand Encore, owned by A.J. Buffington, New Orleans. Capt. L.T. Moore was master in 1858. In 1861 owned by A.J. Witherington, Carrollton (New Orleans), who also was master. Made trips up White River, and was lost there, December 1862.

1575 DR. BURLEIGH

SW ferry wh b. Leavenworth, Kans., 1865, and originally named *HIRAM WOOD* (see), which was snagged in

Missouri River 1870. Capt. Grant Marsh bought the wreck, rebuilt it into a ferry, and renamed her *DR. BURLEIGH* in 1877. She sank at Sioux City, Iowa, 1880, cause unknown. Machinery went to the *ANDREW BENNETT*.

1576 DR. FRANKLIN

SW p wh b. Cincinnati, Oh., 1843. 280 tons. Ran Cincinnati-New Orleans, Capt. J.B. Summons, Jr., master. Burned at New Orleans, Mar. 8, 1846.

1577 DR. FRANKLIN

SW p wh b. Wheeling, Va., 1847. 149 tons. 156 x 24 x 4.1. Built by Capt. John McLure, Wheeling, at the Dunlevy & McNaughton yard at West Wheeling, and came out July 17, 1847, in the Wheeling-Cincinnati trade, teamed up with the *MARY STEPHENS* (see). Sold that fall to the Galena, Dubuque & Minnesota Packet Co., and went to the Galena-St. Paul trade, Capt. M.W. Lodwick, master, and R. Blakely, clerk. She is said to have been the first with a steam whistle on the Upper Mississippi. Came in collisions with the *GALENA* (see) at McCartney, Wis., in Moquoketa Chute, May 7, 1854, and was lost.

1578 DR. FRANKLIN NO. 2.

SW p wh b. Wheeling, Va., 1848. 189 tons. 173 x 26.5 x 4.3. Built by Capt. John McLure for Wheeling-Cincinnati trade. He sold her that first winter to the Harris borthers (D. Smith, Scribe, and Meeker Harris), who ran her on the Upper Mississippi in opposition to the original *DR. FRANKLIN*, b. 1847. Burned at St. Louis on July 7, 1853. The appearance of this boat in the famed daguerreotype of Cincinnati was the key unlocking the date the picture was taken, necessarily in the fall of 1848. Also of interest here is that the wreck of the 1847 *DR. FRANKLIN* was revealed in August 1932 when a U.S. dredge doing channel work uncovered and removed it.

1579 DR. FREDERICK HILL

Recess wheel ferry wh b. Metropolis, Ill., 1870. 140.4 x 36.8 x 4. Ran many years at St. Louis. Was owned by the Missouri Pacific RR when sold December 1916 to serve as a ferry between Louisville and Jeffersonville. Was renamed *GEORGE ROGERS CLARKE* (see).

1580 DR. GEORGE MACKEY

Ferry wh b. Cincinnati, Oh., 1874. 66.4 x 18 x 3.3. 49 tons. She long served at Augusta, Ky. Renamed *WELCOME* (see).

1581 DR. KANE

Stw p wh b. Brownsville, Pa., 1857. 191 tons. Ran tramp trades from Pittsburgh, Capt. Samuel Shuman, master, with J.W. Anawalt, clerk. Served as a transport during the war. In early March 1862 was snagged and sunk in very deep water 300 yards below the public wharf at Cairo, Ill.

1582 DR. ROBERTSON

Stw p wh b. Nashville, Tenn., 1854. 226 tons. Off the lists 1860.

1583 DR. SMITH

SW p wh b. Jeffersonville, Ind., by Howard, 1851. 120 x 30 x 5. Was taken to Galveston, Tex. Off the lists 1860.

1584 DR. WATSON

SW p wh b. Smithland, Ky., 1844. 141 tons. 145 x 23.5 x 4.3. Capt. Josh V. Throop and others ran her in Evansville area until sold 1846 to Capt. Willis Main and others at New Orleans, where she sank and was lost Oct. 26, 1846.

1585 DR. YORK

Rig? Ran up Big Sandy River owned by Dr. J.F. York, Kenova, W. Va. Burned at Kenova on Oct. 27, 1904, at 10:00 A.M.

1586 DOLLIE WEBB

Stw p wh b. Wheeling, Va., 1859. 125 x 27 x 4.5. 139 tons. Enrolled at New Orleans Feb. 29, 1860, owned by Capt. James R. Davis, who commanded, and others. Burned at Algiers, La., on May 5, 1861.

1587 DOLPHIN

SW p wh b. Cincinnati, Oh., 1847. 99 tons. Off the lists 1849.

1588 DOLPHIN

Stw p wh b. West Elizabeth, Pa., 1848. 120 tons. Stranded and lost at Hawesville, Ky., Jan. 7, 1850.

1589 DOMAIN

SW p wh b. Wellsville, Oh., 1844. 131 tons. Came in collision with *COLLIER* a few miles above Wheeling on Nov. 7, 1844, in which the *COLLIER* was sunk. Sank in ice five miles below Quincy, Ill. in March 1849, "an old boat owned principally by her officers, insured for $2,500."

1590 DOMINION

Stw p wh b. Wellsville, Oh., 1846. 186 tons. Built at the Robert Rallston yard. Out of service in 1849. The next boat built at this yard was the *UNION* (see).

1591 DON CAMERON

Rig? b. Jeffersonville, Ind., at the Barmore yard, spring of 1877 for Yellowstone River, along with the GENERAL SHERMAN (see).

1592 DONCA

Stw p wh b. Catlettsburg, Ky., 1901. 109.5 x 18.4 x 3. Engines, 8″- 30″ stroke. One boiler, 42″ dia. by 16 ft. Owned by the Cando Packet Co., and operated on Big Sandy River along with *CANDO* (see) during building in the railroad. Was running low water in the Wheeling-Clarington trade 1903. In 1908 was running Louisville-Kentucky River, also 1909. Sank behind the Ohio River dike opposite Madison. The hull was later used as a barge, and engines went to *CHARLEY KREMER*.

1593 DORA

SW p wh b. Monongahela, Pa., 1860, originally named *EMMA DUNCAN* (see). Was renamed *DORA* after having served in the war as gunboat *HASTINGS*. Apparently operated out of St. Louis 1865-1868, then New Orleans-Red River, owned and commanded by Capt. Kennedy Lodwick of New Orleans. Sold February 1870 to Charles P. Cutzer, New Orleans, Capt. P.C. Montgomery. Condemned at New Orleans in 1871.

1594 DORA

SW p wh b. 1872 by J.D. Hibbler and August Wohlt for Missouri River service. Engines, 7"- 34". One boiler. Sunk by ice at the mouth of Charette Creek, Mo., Jan. 22, 1877. Raised and sold to Washington (Mo.) Ferry Co., and burned when a lamp exploded while in Madison Crossing, 17 miles above St. Louis.

1595 DORA

Stw p wh b. Metropolis, Ill., 1880. 199.5 x 25.2 x 4.3. Built for Schwartz Bros., who ran her St. Louis-Illinois River. She was lengthened 50 feet later, after which she ran St. Louis-Clarksville, Mo. Sank 10 miles above St. Louis, December 1894.

1596 DORA CABLER

Stw p wh b. Cincinnati, Oh., 1877. Built for Capt. James W. Lowell and others for the Cincinnati-Evansville trade. W.S. McBride was first clerk. She had the machinery and a calliope from the *JULIA NO. 2* (see). In 1879 in same trade, Capt. T.H. Armstrong, master, with W.E. Byers, clerk.

1597 DORA MARTIN

Stw p wh b. 1864. 156.4 x 32.5 x 5.3. She ran New Orleans-Red River, and was taken by the U.S. to Mound City, Ill., and there sold on Aug. 19, 1865, to Mary Henin, New Orleans, and ran Shreveport-Jefferson into 1867.

1598 DOROTHY

Stw p wh b. Paducah, Ky., 1917. 140 x 28 x 4.1. Engines, 12's- 8 ft. from rafter *CHANCY LAMB*. Two boilers. Owned by Capt. Fred McCandless, and operated Paducah-Golconda. She burned at Golconda on Dec. 1, 1921. The wreck was salvaged for scrap in 1941.

1599 DOT

Rig? b. 1862. On May 17, 1863, Confederate forces ferried across Black River on her, then burned her. The wreck was found by U.S. forces right next to the railroad bridge at Bovina, Miss. The *CHARM* and *PAUL JONES* were burned immediately below the wreck.

1600 DOUBLOON

SW p wh b. Cincinnati, Oh., 1859. 171.8 x 33.6 x 6.6. Built for and run by Capt. W.C. Harrison, New Orleans-Shreveport-Carolina Bluffs. She was scuttled on Red River in May 1864 to prevent capture. Raised, and continued to run Red River, same master and owner until sold February 1867 to Capt. William C. Mitchell who continued her to Shreveport. She burned at New Orleans in the New Basin Canal, June 24, 1867.

1601 DOVE

SW p wh b. New Albany, Ind., 1848. 237 tons. Was in Evansville-Paducah-Cairo trade in 1852, Capt. John Gilbert. Off the lists 1858.

1602 DOVE

Stw p wh b. Louisville, Ky., 1856. 147.6 x 29.3 x 5. Ran Cincinnati-Madison-Kentucky River. Sold to New Orleans in August 1865 owned by A.G. Oba, St. Louis; C.B. Church and W.W. Furnangton, Memphis; and Mary A. Irwin, Madison, Ind., Capt. A.R. Irwin, master. In December 1865 sold to Z.E. Hyde, Mobile, Ala. Snagged and lost in Pearl River, Miss., 1866.

1603 DOVE NO. 2

Stw p wh b. Jeffersonville, Ind., at Howards, 1867. 116 x 26 x 4.5. Owned by Capt. Sam Saunders, and ran Cincinnati-Frankfort. Dismantled 1878. Machinery went to *MAGGIE HARPER* (see), and the hull was used as the wharfboat at Ghent, Ky.

1604 DOVE

Stw p wh b. Sewickley, Pa. (hull), and completed at Pittsburgh, 1880. 132 x 26.5 x 3.5. Built for upper Arkansas River, Little Rock-Webb City. Capt. W.C. Ghriest, master and clerk. Engines 8"- 3 ft. with rotary valves. One boiler, 44" dia. by 20 ft., six flues. Major John D. Adams ran operations. Sold in March 1882 to T.C. and D.S. Butler, Mobile, Ala. Still documented at Pensacola, Fla., in 1896.

1605 DOVER

Stw p wh b. Elizabethtown, Pa., 1847. 80 tons. Ran Pittsburgh-Freeport, Pa. (on the Allegheny River), Capt. Alf Reno, master, the first season. Capt. Grant Marsh relates that he did his first steamboating on her at the time. Ran Pittsburgh-Parkersburg most of 1848 and made one trip, in March, to Lafayette, Ind., on Wabash River. Sold to John Bell who took her to Evansville for Cumberland River trade. Wrecked in a big storm at Evansville on Aug. 9, 1851. She and the *CALEDONIA* both capsized.

1606 DOVER

Stw p wh b. Nashville, Tenn., 1888. 125 x 20 x 3. Capt. Tom G. Ryman built her to run Nashville-Dover to fight competition from the steamer *HENRIETTA*. There is evidence she ran 1890–1891 in Shreveport-Jefferson trade on Red River. Bought by the U.S. Engineers, Nashville District, in 1891 for Tennessee River service, renamed *McPHERSON*. Still there 1915.

1607 DRESDEN

Stw p wh b. Pittsburgh, Pa., 1842. 29 tons. She ran Marietta-Zanesville, Capt. C.C. Morgan, first season. Spring 1843, Pittsburgh-Zanesville, Capt. Frank Cogswell, and ran briefly Zanesville-Dresden. Ran Pittsburgh-

Zanesville the balance of the year, Capts. Brown and Jesse Smith. Pittsburgh-Zanesville-Dresden in 1844, Capt. Brown. In 1845-1846 ran Marietta-Zanesville, Capt. C.C. Morgan. Dismantled 1846.

1608 DRESDEN

SW p wh b. Cincinnati, Oh., 1852. 548 tons. Snagged and lost at New Madrid, Mo., Feb. 15, 1855.

1609 DROVER

SW ferry wh b. Wellsville, Oh., 1847. 27 tons. Dismantled in 1862.

1610 DROVER

SW ferry wh b. Wheeling, Va., 1861. 26 tons Off the lists 1869. A ferry of this name was sunk at Shreveport, May 1864, to block the channel.

1611 DROVER

SW ferry wh b. Pittsburgh, Pa., 1865. 46 tons. Off the lists 1869.

1612 DROVER NO. 2

SW ferry wh b. Davidson, Pa., 1868. 35 tons. Operated at Moundsville, W. Va., in the early 1870s. Dismantled 1873.

1613 DROVER NO. 3

Ferry wh b. Wheeling, W. Va., 1865. 40 tons. Documented at Wheeling 1867.

1614 DUBUQUE

SW p wh b. Elizabethtown, Pa., 1847. 168 tons. 162 x 26 x 5. Ran St. Louis-Galena-Dubuque, Capt. Edward H. Beebe, a regular. Sold May 1853 to St. Louis & Chicago Transport Co., who towed barges with her from St. Louis to the La Salle Basin. Sank above Mundy's Landing, Mo., 1855.

1615 DUBUQUE

SW p wh b. Wheeling, W. Va., 1867 (hull), and completed at Pittsburgh. 230 x 36 x 5.5. Engines, 20's- 7 ft. by Snowden & Co. 602 tons. Paddlewheels 26 ft. dia. with 10 ft. buckets. Dunlevy & Co. built the hull. Capt. Richard C. Gray superintended construction, and W.C. Gray looked after the machinery. Emil Bott decorated the cabin with landscapes. Left Pittsburgh in latter April 1867 for the Upper Mississippi, Capt. J.W. Parker, master with D.W. Danley, clerk. William (Bill) Henderson was barkeep. Ran in the Keokuk Northern Line. On her first trip she hit the Rock Island bridge pier, May 4, 1867, crippling the starboard engine and doing damage to herself. She burned in Alton Slough with *LAKE SUPERIOR* (see) on the afternoon of Mar. 4, 1879, both being readied for the spring season.

1616 DUBUQUE

Stw p wh b. Cincinnati, Oh., 1879, originally named *PITTSBURGH* (see). The *PITTSBURGH* was relieved of her upper works in a tornado at St. Louis, May 1896. The hull was taken to Dubuque, rebuilt 257.2 x 40.6 x 6.1. She got engines 21's- 7 ft. Three boilers, each 47" by 28 ft. Was renamed *DUBUQUE* and ran in the Diamond Jo Line. Sank at Keithsburg, Ill., after ripping a 142-foot hole in her hull, July 1901, raised. Capt. William Burke was her master 27 years under both names. Streckfus Steamers took her over and continued running her. In April 1912 she made a trip St. Louis to Shiloh Battlefield under charter to the St. Louis & Tennessee River Packet Co. Capt. Charles R. Martin, pilot, dropped dead at the wheel as she approached the Alton railroad bridge in November 1914. The engineer on watch noticed the boat was veering, stopped and backed her. Jack Richtman, off-watch pilot, was quickly called. In the winter of 1919-1920 she was converted into an excursion boat at Keokuk and the work finished at Davenport. She was renamed *CAPITOL* (see).

1617 DUCHESS

SW p wh b. Cincinnati, Oh., 1846. 329 tons. Capt. Joel Green, master, testified in the Wheeling Bridge case. Capt. Richard M. Wade recalled this boat was his first charge as master, running up-river from Cincinnati. She collided with the *LUNA* at Donaldsonville, La., May 17, 1850, resulting in loss of *LUNA* and five lives.

1618 DUCHESS

SW p wh b. Cincinnati, Oh., 1853. 226 tons. Lost at Pomeroy, Oh. Her wreck was reported still in the river there, Oct. 31, 1866.

1619 DUCHESS

Stw p wh b. Brownsville, Pa., 1862. 226 tons. Machinery from the *JACOB POE* (see). She departed Pittsburgh new on Dec. 10, 1862, and was taken over by the U.S. at Cincinnati on Dec. 22, 1862. Built by Capt. John L. Rhoads. Capt. J.H. Lightner was master, with T.H. Golding, clerk, on the only trip she ever made as a packet. She became the U.S. tinclad *PETREL* (2nd of the name). Captured and burned by the Confederates on Yazoo River, Apr. 22, 1864.

1620 DUCK

Rig? b. Wheeling, W. Va., 1875. 54 tons. Documented at Memphis, 1876.

1621 DUCK RIVER

SW p wh b. Cincinnati, Oh., 1847. Ran from New Orleans to Red and Duck rivers, Capt. Samuel Applegate, owned by John Thomas, New Orleans. Sold in 1851 to Charles J. Littlefield ½, John Russ ¼ and William R. Dunn ¼, Capt. A.P. Boardman, master. Off the lists in 1853.

1622 DUKE

SW p wh b. Cincinnati, Oh., 1853. 170 x 32.5 x 6.4. Ran Cincinnati-New Orleans, Capt. William Hamilton. Sold December 1856 to Capt. Samuel Applegate for New Orleans-Shreveport trade. He ran her there until 1859 when he built a new hull, transferred cabins and engines over, and brought out the *GRAND DUKE* (see). (For other news of Captain Applegate see *JOHN WALSH* in this volume.)

1623 DUKE

Stw p wh b. New Albany, Ind., 1862. 125 x 26 x 4. Ran Louisville-Troy-Cannelton. She was in U.S. service most of 1864. Burned and lost at Johnsonville, Tenn., Nov. 4, 1864. Was owned at Evansville. Many other boats were lost in this Rebel raid at Johnsonville (see *J. B. FORD*).

1624 DUKE OF ORLEANS

SW p wh b. Cincinnati, Oh., 1842. 307 tons. Ran Cincinnati-New Orleans. She was a five-boiler boat and noted for speed. In March 1844 came up from New Orleans to Cincinnati in 5 days 18 hours, a record never beaten. Her crew at the time: Capt. C.R. Sedam, master; Louis Krouskropp, clerk; E.W. Cunningham, second clerk; Thomas L. Richardson, mate; Thomas M. Rowe, second mate; Isaac West, chief engineer; Wesley Reynolds, Andrew Sweeney and Enoch Clements, assistant engineers. For several years after, a banner of canvas hung on the forward roof rail boasting of the triumph. The *QUEEN OF THE WEST* (see) tried to better the record, failed. She departed New Orleans on Sunday, May 26, 1844, on this exploit. Her fastest downbound time Cincinnati to New Orleans was 3 days 20 hours, probably also a record which endures. Capt. Joel Green was master in 1845. Burned at Ste. Genevieve, Mo., Apr. 29, 1848.

1625 DUNBAR

SW p wh b. Brownsville, Pa., 1859. 213 tons. Named for James Dunbar, noted boat builder of the Pittsburgh area. Bought new by Capt. Gus Fowler, Paducah, for Evansville-Paducah trade, replacing *SILVER STAR* (see), which had become too small for the business. She was continued there until the opening of hostilities in 1861, then taken up the Tennessee River to prevent capture. Did some service for the Confederates when Bragg evacuated Chattanooga, and then the Confederates scuttled her along with the *PAINT ROCK* (see). Capt. Arthur Edwards, asst., QMCD, was detailed to raise and repair her for the U.S., which he did. She then rendered valuable service ferrying troops the day General Hooker gained Lookout Mountain. After the war she was sold at public sale, bid in by an Upper Tennessee party, and later used as a covered barge. This information was supplied by the late Saunders Fowler, son of Capt. Gus Fowler.

1626 DUNCAN F. KENNER

SW p wh b. Jeffersonville, Ind., by Howards, 1859. 493 tons. 215 x 37 x 8. Built for the New Orleans & Bayou Sara Mail Co., three round trips weekly, Capt. Joseph Vincent, master. She was the passenger boat in the trade, and the *GROSSE TETE* was the freight boat. Burned and lost at New Orleans, May 20, 1860.

1627 DUNCAN S. CARTER

SW p wh b. Mound City, Ill. (hull), and completed at St. Louis, 1858. 428 tons. A rather large Missouri River packet. Engines, 20½'s- 7 ft. Three boilers. Owned by William P. Eads, Jr., and Eardly O. Sayle. Snagged in Augusta Bend, Missouri River, Aug. 28, 1859, en route Weston to St. Louis.

1628 DUNKIRK

SW p wh b. Cincinnati, Oh., 1851. 377 tons. Snagged and lost at Ste. Genevieve, Mo., Jan. 7, 1852.

1629 DUNLEITH

Stw p wh b. Shousetown, Pa. (hull), and completed at Pittsburgh, 1856. 155 tons. Owned by David Gibson & Co. Sunk by ice at Cincinnati when the packet *YORKTOWN* jammed into her. Raised. Served as a transport during the war. Was up Tennessee River during Grant's campaign and in 1864 conveyed soldiers up the Kanawha River from Cincinnati, piloted there by James Johnson and Lloyd Case. Snagged and lost at Island 67, Mississippi River, Oct. 31, 1864.

1630 DUNLEITH

SW ferry wh b. Mound City, Ill., 1868. 316 tons. Inspected in the St. Louis District, 1876. Off the lists 1885.

1631 DUROC

SW p wh b. Louisville, Ky., 1847. 220 tons. Ran St. Louis-New Orleans. Rebuilt at Louisville in 1850. On a trip up Missouri River she was snagged at St. Charles Bend in 1852, raised. Was familiar in Red River 1850–1853. Sank three miles above Natchez on Mar. 10, 1854.

1632 DYCUSBURG

Rig? b. Paducah, Ky., 1883. 70 x 14 x 2.8. Still operating in 1886.

1633 DYERSBURG

Rig? b. Dyersburg, Tenn., 1876. 126 tons. Documented at Memphis. Burned with 284 bales of cotton on the Mississippi, Feb. 28, 1884.

1634 DYERSBURG

Stw p wh b. Dyersburg, Tenn., 1887. 93 x 18.4 x 3. Documented at Vicksburg 1892.

E

1635 E.A. OGDEN

SW p wh b. Cincinnati, Oh., 1847. 249 tons. 126 x 29 x 7.5. Ran in a through line from New Orleans to Mobile and Montgomery, Ala. In 1848 owned by Archibald Irwin, New Orleans, Capt. P.O. Wilson. Capt. J.J. Kercheval went master in October 1848. Went to the Brazos River and was snagged there in 1850.

1637 E.A. OGDEN

SW p wh b. St. Louis, Mo., 1855. 399 tons. 280.5 x 36 x 6. Ran on the Missouri River, Capt. Hamilton Lee. Reported snagged in Claysville Bend, Missouri River, September 1859. Lytle says lost at Jefferson City, Mo., Feb. 22, 1860.

Was said to have accumulated enough profit to pay for herself in the first six months of operation.

1638 E.A. PHARR

Stw p wh b. Patterson, La., 1892. 90 x 29.9 x 4.5. Documented at Vicksburg 1896.

1639 E.A. Woodruff

SW snagboat ih b. Covington, Ky. (hull), and completed at Pittsburgh, 1874. Covington Iron Works fabricated her, and Hartupee put on the machinery. Lengthened at the Cincinnati Marine Ways in 1885 to become 226 x 48 x 7.6. She operated the entire length of the Ohio River. First master was Capt. George W. Rowley. Capt. William H. Christian commanded her many years. One of her early jobs was to remove the wreck of the side-wheel *PAT CLEBURNE* (see) in November 1876. When she was retired in the 1920s Capt. Gordon C. Greene bid her in. After he died she was sold to the Louisville & Cincinnati Packet Co., which transformed her into a wharfboat and used it at Louisville. In 1940 a new wharfboat replaced her, and she was sold to The Ohio River Co. She was beached out at Catlettsburg, Ky., and torn up.

1640 E.B. STAHLMAN

Stw p wh b. Jeffersonville, Ind., by Howard 1876. 201.47 tons. 145 x 27 x 3. Built for the Ryman Line on Cumberland River. Went to U.S. marshal sale June 1878 and was sold to Capt. Josh V. Throop, Evansville. He ran her Evansville-Nashville. Sunk by ice upbound at Kuttawa on the Cumberland Jan. 14, 1879. She turned on her side and was lost.

1641 E.B. WHEELOCK

SW p wh b. Jeffersonville, Ind., by Howard 1889. 160 x 30 x 4.9. Owned by Texas & Pacific RR and ran competition with the regular Red River Line. There was a compromise and Red River Line took her over. Sank at Snaggy Point, La., on Red River, May 3, 1895. Capt. H.J. Brinker was master the last year, with Eugene Barrow, clerk. Charles P. Truslow was president of Red River Line, and Charles W. Drown, traffic manager.

1642 E.C. CARROLL JR.

Stw p wh b. Jeffersonville, Ind., 1878. She was built for Capt. S.H. Parisot for the Vicksburg-Yazoo River trade. Inspected at Vicksburg, Oct. 27, 1882.

E.C. WIGGINS

Documented *EDWARD C. WIGGINS* (see).

1643 E.D. WHITE

SW p wh b. Louisville, Ky., 1848. 166 x 28 x 5.7. Ran New Orleans-Red River, first owned by Butler Gilbert, New Orleans. Capt. Eugene Brady took stock in 1850 and went master. In 1853 sold to Prosper Echlard, Pointe Coupee Parish, La. Retired in 1854 at which time was owned by Samuel and Muayer Gwartney, New Orleans.

1644 E.G. RAGON

Stw p wh b. Jeffersonville, Ind., by Howard 1887. 165 x 31 x 5. Named for a wholesale grocer in Evansville, and ran Evansville-Nashville. The Louisville & Evansville Mail Line bought her in February 1893 and ran her until the side-wheel *MORNING STAR* was built in 1901. Her engines, 14½'s- 4½ ft. later were used on the towboat *DUFFY* b. Harmar, Oh., 1909. Capt. F.M. Ryan was master, and W.C. Lepper Jr., clerk, when a good photograph was taken of her loading tobacco hogsheads for export to England at Cloverport, Ky. "Billy" Lepper told this scribe that he does not appear in the view due to having been bitten by a black widow spider, which confined him to his bunk.

1645 E.H. BARMORE

Stw ferry wh b. Jeffersonville, Ind., 1879. 135.7 x 30.1 x 5.4. Went to the New Orleans area, and was still documented there 1896.

1646 E.H. DURFEE

Stw p wh b. Pittsburgh, Pa., 1871. 206 x 35. Engines, 16's-6 ft. Three boilers, each 38" dia. by 26 ft. Built at Eberman & McFall yard. Engines by John Herbertson, Brownsville, Pa. Built for Capt. William Coulson and others for the Pittsburgh-Fort Benton trade. E.H. Durfee, Leavenworth, Kans., presented a fine carpet for the new boat. She made various through trips over the years, leaving Pittsburgh "for Fort Benton direct." In all she made seven trips to the fort. In August 1876 took General Miles and six companies of the 5th U.S. Infantry to the Indian wars. Later owned by Capt. George G. Keith and others, handling wheat from lower Missouri to St. Louis. Was overloaded when she sank at the mouth of the Gasconade River, May 31, 1881, and was lost.

1647 E.H. FAIRCHILD

SW p wh b. New Albany, Ind., 1857. 496 tons. 237 x 31.2 x 7. Named for Elisha H. Fairchild who was one of the first white persons born in Vanderburg County, Ind., a forwarding and commission merchant at Evansville, and later in New Orleans. Capt. J.H. Fawcett, New Albany, was master and part owner. Ran Louisville-New Orleans. Jesse H. Jones, 86, wrote the Paducah *Sun-Democrat* in 1939 to say he remembered a calliope played aboard this boat, about the first he ever heard. She was laid up at New Albany when the war broke out. Taken over by the U.S., fitted with heavy oak siding, and sent to St. Louis for guns, etc. Was in the USQMD in 1864. Sold later to M.S. Mepham and others, St. Louis. She was laid up at Carondelet, Mo., when ice destroyed her early in 1867.

1648 E. HENSLEY

SW p wh b. Leavenworth, Kans., 1865. 213 tons. 141 ft. long. Off the lists 1876.

1649 E.I. FORD

Stw ferry wh b. Cincinnati, Oh., 1890, originally named

NEW RICHMOND (see). Owned by the Manchester (Ohio) Ferry Co., 1929.

1650 E.L. REEL

Stw p wh b. Vincennes, Ind., 1896. 72 x 14 x 3.6. Operated Evansville-Wabash River. She was bought June 1900 by John H. Monsey, Toronto, Oh., and others. They sold her May 1901 to S.A. Devinney and Ralph E. Gaches, Letart Falls, Oh. Commented Capt. Jesse P. Hughes: "A small sternwheel boat that was good for nothing, and Capt. Snell Devinney got her about 1901; don't know what he did with it, but he showed up as captain on the first *EVERGREEN* in the Charleston-Winfield trade in 1902."

1651 E.M. BICKNELL

SW p wh b. Cincinnati, Oh., 1857. 135 x 30 x 5.5. Went to Franklin, La., and in March 1859 sold to William Gwartney, New Orleans, with Capt. Samuel Gwartney, master. In January 1861 sold to Henry S. Whittmore, New Orleans, same master. In April 1861 sold to Holland Coffee, New Orleans. Made a trip to Mobile in December 1865, Capt. Meyers. Ran on Red River into the late 1860s and was off the lists 1871.

1652 E.M. HENSLEY

Stw p wh Ran on Missouri River owned by Capt. Charles Norris, Lexington, Mo., who commanded the *GEN. D.H. RUCKER* (see). One of her pilots was W.L. Heckmann Sr., all of this prior to 1884.

1653 E.M. RYLAND

SW p wh b. Brownsville, Pa., 1857. 267 tons. Burned and lost at St. Louis, Mo., Oct. 8, 1861.

1654 E.O. STANARD

SW p wh b. Metropolis, Ill., 1865. 281 tons. Went to St. Louis. Lost May 13, 1865, by snagging in De Soto Bend, Missouri River.

1655 E.O. STANARD

Stw p wh b. Pittsburgh, Pa., 1873, originally named *PARAGON* (see). When *PARAGON* burned, the wreck was bought by Capt. William J. Kountz. On the hull he built this *E.O. STANARD.* 260 x 44 x 7. Hartupee compound engines, 12's, 24's-5 ft. Three boilers, each 36" dia. by 25 ft. Wheel 18 ft. dia. with 28 ft. buckets. She was a freight boat, no passenger cabin, and one stack. Ran St. Louis-New Orleans, Capt. C.H. Seaman, master, with M.H. Carpenter, clerk. The machinery came from the first *CARRIE V. KOUNTZ* (see). She was sunk in collision near Cairo, Ill., in April 1881. Two years later the wreck was completely exposed in low water at Davis Island, on shore, the machinery still aboard.

1656 E.P. DAWSON

Stw p wh b. Knoxville, Tenn., 1894. 60 x 10 x 2.8. About 1900 rebuilt into the packet *CHAS. H. BACON* (see).

1657 E.P. MCNEAL

SW p wh b. Cincinnati, Oh., 1850. 204 tons. Went to Memphis. Burned and lost at Memphis, Aug. 30, 1851.

1658 E.R. STEADMAN

Rig? b. at or near Jackson, Miss., 1876, on Pearl River. That May she was taken within six miles of Carthage, Miss., 20 miles above Jackson, the highest any steamboat had navigated. Many overhanging or fallen oaks had to be cut away to permit passage.

1659 E.T. HOLLMAN

Stw p wh b. Nashville, Tenn., 1887. 100 x 20 x 3. Still listed at Nashville 1892.

1660 E.W. COLE

Stw p wh b. Jeffersonville, Ind., at Howard 1879–1880. 201 x 31 x 5.4. Engines, 16's-4½ ft. Three boilers, each 42" dia. by 26 ft. Ran Memphis-Vicksburg. Capt. J. Frank Ellison was master, his first command, this in October 1883. Capt. E.W.B. Nowland brought cotton out of Pine Bluff, Ark., with her in 1886. In 1890 was running New Orleans-Bayou Lafourche, Capt. Max Blanchard, master, with George D. Madere, clerk. Snagged and lost at Welham's Landing, Mississippi River, Jan. 1, 1891.

1661 E.W. FULLER

Stw p wh b. Jeffersonville, Ind., 1872. 132.9 x 26 x 4. Ran out of New Orleans. In 1885 running New Orleans-Bayou Lafourche, Capt. John B. Dumestre, master, with John M. Gugel, clerk. Same trade and master 1886, J.B. Crochet, clerk.

1662 E.W. STEPHENS

SW p wh b. Wheeling, Va., 1847. 199 tons. Was running Cincinnati-Nashville, Capt. James Siddall, 1849. Chartered April 1851 to bring Jenny Lind and P.T. Barnum from Nashville to Louisville. Apparently the arrangements were changed, and they went overland via Mammoth Cave where Jenny warbled on a stalagmite. Off the lists in 1853.

1663 EAGLE

SW p wh b. Shousetown, Pa. (hull), and completed at Pittsburgh, 1852. 201 tons. Went to Mobile, and burned below Columbus, Ga., Jan. 29, 1854, with loss of four lives.

1664 EAGLE

SW p wh b. Alexandria, Mo., 1859. 70 x 12, and drew 13" light. Engine was built at the Pennsylvania Foundry, Keokuk. Built by J. Brandom, Alexandria, who ran her Warsaw-Keokuk until June 1861 when he replaced her with the *MENOMINEE* (see).

1665 EAGLE

SW p wh b. Wheeling, Va., 1861. 242 tons. Built for Capt. Charles David, and ran short trades Cincinnati-Louisville; David designed her as a "small edition" of the *JACOB STRADER,* stacks aft of the pilothouse. In 1862 she was bought by Capt. C.H. Booth and others for the Wheeling-Parkersburg trade, and Charles Muhleman was clerk. On Nov. 8, 1871, she landed in at Newport, Oh., and hit a rock. Discovery that she was taking water was not made until she backed away from the landing. Passengers and crew escaped into a flatboat brought alongside and *EAGLE* disappeared in deep water, only the pilothouse showing. Capt. Berry was in command at the time.

1666 EAGLE

SW p wh b. Warsaw, Ill., 1862. 102.5 x 18.7 x 3.7. Engine, 15½"- 4 ft. One boiler, 46" dia. by 14 ft. with 55 three inch flues. Cabin 60 ft. long, berthed 24 passengers, and she carried 24 deck passengers. Built for the Keokuk-Quincy trade. Owned by Henry Leyhe, William Leyhe, J.W. Bishop, G.W. Hill, J.R. Williams, and Claus Albers & Co., Capt. J.W. Bishop, master. Wrecked at Quincy in 1868.

1667 EAGLE

SW p wh b. Madison, Ind., 1868. About the same size and description as the *EAGLE* b. 1862 described above. Owned by William and Henry Leyhe and possibly others. Rebuilt at St. Louis in 1875, 161 tons.

1668 EAGLE

Stw ferry wh b. Madison, Ind., 1879. 85.9 x 20 x 3.3. She served as a ferry at Warsaw, Ill., many years. Engines, 8"- 2 ft. One boiler. Burned at Lexington, Mo., when a gasoline stove exploded, Feb. 26, 1897. The wreck was removed later that year by the *C.R. SUTER*.

1669 EAGLE NO. 2

SW ferry wh b. Pittsburgh, Pa., 1847. 95 tons. First home port, Wheeling. Off the lists in 1854.

1670 EAGLE POINT

SW ferry wh b. Dubuque, Iowa, 1884. 96 x 22 x 3. Burned at Dubuque, June 1894.

1671 EAGLE POINT

Running at Dubuque 1903, presumably a replacement of the former ferry listed above.

1672 EARL

Stw p wh b. Gainesville, Miss., 1884. 116 x 28.7 x 5.1. Listed at Shieldsboro, Miss., 1896.

1673 EARLE

Rig? b. Brownsville, Pa., at Axton yard, 1880. 148 x 34 x 3. Documented at Wheeling through 1886. Said to have been a cotton-type packet which eventually exploded boilers.

1674 EARLY BIRD

SW p wh b. Jeffersonville, Ind., by Howard, 1867. 126.3 x 25.9 x 4.9. Built for and commanded by Capt. J. Poitevent, New Orleans. Was running to Red River 1869. Off the lists, 1878.

1675 EAST ST. LOUIS

Recess wheel ferry wh b. Louisville, Ky., 1868. 178 x 51.4 x 6.4. Owned by Wiggins Ferry Co., St. Louis. Off the lists 1896.

1676 EAST ST. LOUIS

Stw p and ex wh Originally *VIRGINIA* b. 1895 at Cincinnati (see), later *STEEL CITY* (see). The *STEEL CITY* was renamed *EAST ST. LOUIS* in December 1916 when purchased by the St. Louis & New Orleans Navigation Co. Her texas was extended to allow for more passengers and she entered the St. Louis-New Orleans trade, Capt. John Flanigan, March 1917. Capt. Sam G. Smith went master in May 1917. Owned largely by the J.C. Grant Chemical Co., which shipped baking powder south. That winter she was transformed into an excursion boat at Keokuk, and came out May 1918 at St. Louis, Capt. James Robinson. The company name was retained, and officers in 1922 were Edward M. Cody, pres. and treas.; Lester Robinson, vice-pres.; Oscar A. Moore, secy. Capt. Sam G. Smith was passenger agent, located at 4006 N. Broadway, St. Louis. Following the destruction by fire of the *ISLAND QUEEN* (first) and *MORNING STAR* at Cincinnati in 1922, she was acquired by the Coney Island Co., there, renamed *ISLAND BELLE,* and ran to the park. (See *ISLAND BELLE* for more of the story.)

1677 EASTPORT

SW p wh b. New Albany, Ind., 1852. 280 x 43 x 5.5. Engines, 26's- 9 ft. Five boilers, each 42" dia. by 28 ft. Owned by the Florence & New Orleans Packet Co., and operated between Tennessee River and New Orleans. She once went to Nashville, Feb. 10, 1861; had to lower her stacks to get under the suspension bridge. When the war broke out she was up Tennessee River and the Rebels were converting her into a gunboat. She was captured by the U.S., taken to Mound City, Ill., and completed. She was in Porter's expedition up Red River, sank, raised and then sank again. She was stripped, and destroyed with explosives. There is a first-hand diary kept by Capt. William R. Hoel presented in the September 1973 issue of *S&D Reflector* telling much of this Red River expedition and the fate of the *EASTPORT*.

1678 EAU CLAIRE

Stw p wh b. Brownsville, Pa., 1857. 130 tons. Lost in collision with the *SOUTH AMERICA* at Barnhart, Mo., Mar. 25, 1857.

1679 EAU CLAIRE

SW p wh b. Eau Claire, Wis., 1867. 81 tons. Evansville, Green and Pond River packet, Capt. A.E.B. Hall, master, with C.A. Chamberlain, clerk. Sold by U.S. marshal mid-June 1868 to McColly and Covington, Paducah. On the night of June 7, 1869, Capt. Shoemaker, she hit a pier of the Terre Haute, Ind., bridge, Wabash River. She sank four miles above there, at Fort Harrison, in water so deep only the stacks showed. Owned by Capt. U. Shoemaker.

1680 EBAUGH

Stw p wh b. Pekin, Ill., 1902. 94.5 x 17.5 x 3.5. Engines,

10's- 4 ft. Two boilers, 36" dia. by 16 ft. Owned by Spring Lake Packet Co., Capt. Ed Schermerhorn, master, 1908. She was owned in 1930 by Illinois River Packet Co., and sold, July that year, to Ruprecht Sand & Material Co. The Blaske family owned her briefly, sold her November 1932 to R.B. Potashnick Construction Co., which used her on a job at Alton, Ill.

1681 EBENEZER

SW ferry wh b. Brownsville, Pa., 1859. 108 tons. First home port, St. Joseph, Mo. She went to U.S. service May 1863, became tinclad *TAWAH* (#29). Was burned to avoid capture at Johnsonville, Tenn., Nov. 4, 1864.

1682 ECHO

SW p wh b. Cincinnati, Oh., 1850. 161 tons. 130 x 25 x 5.3. Went to New Orleans 1852 and enrolled there Jan. 22, owned there by William W. Withenburg ⅘ of Cincinnati, and L.T. Murdock ⅕, New Orleans. Capt. William Withenburg, master. Sold November 1853 to Jules Augustin Rousseau ½, and Alphonse Frederick Jeanfrau ½, both of New Orleans, Capt. J.A. Rousseau, master. In July 1854 sold to Elijah Cannon, New Orleans, Capt. D. Power, master. Off the lists 1855.

1683 ECHO

Stw p wh b. California, Pa., 1858. 147 x 22 x 3.2. Owned by Alexander Campbell ⅔ of Bradys Bend, Pa., Capt. Ezekiel Gordon, master. First trip Pittsburgh to Franklin, Pa., on Allegheny River in April 1858. When the oil boom hit the Allegheny in 1860 there were four packets operating there, and *ECHO* was one of them. The other three: *ALLEGHENY BELLE NO. 4, VENANGO,* and *LeCLAIRE.* In fall of 1862 she was solely owned by Ben Coursin, and Gordon continued master. Sold Dec. 26, 1862 to Capt. James Walton ⅔ and Josephus Walton ⅓, both of Monroe County, Oh. They ran her in the Pittsburgh-Gallipolis trade briefly. Sold Mar. 31, 1863, to John J. Raiko ½, Newport, Ky., and Henry Schwein ½, Cincinnati. Burned in Cumberland River, Dec. 10, 1864.

1684 ECHO NO. 2

Stw p wh b. California, Pa., 1863. 145 x 26 x 4. Owned by Thomas M. Rees ⅔, Pittsburgh, and F.H. Coursin ⅓, McKeesport, Pa. Capt. Ezekiel Gordon, master. Ran on the Allegheny River. Sold in the fall of 1863 to the U.S. and became a troop transport. She was rounding to at Cairo with a trip of soldiers down from Johnsonville, Tenn., in latter June 1865. She got hooked on the sharp prow of the U.S. monitor *ONEIDA* anchored there. The *ECHO* sank in a few minutes. The soldiers, some 300, were from the 41st and 13th Ohio Veteran Volunteers, commanded by Capt. E.S. Holiday. One soldier was lost, also ten horses, 13 mules, and a quantity of rations. Wilson Dunn, the pilot on watch, was badly beaten by the soldiers who took vengeance on him for the accident.

1685 ECHO NO. 3

Stw p wh b. California, Pa., 1865. 157 x 30 x 2.5. Owned by James Rees 2/3 and Benjamin Coursin 1/3, both of Allegheny County, Pa. Ran on the Allegheny, Pittsburgh-Oil City, Capt. Ezekiel Gordon. Sold entire to James H. Rees, July 1868, Capt. Frederick Ford, master. Went to the Kanawha River that fall to handle salt from there to Nashville and St. Louis. In January 1869 was laid up in quarantine in the mouth of the Kanawha with Capt. Penn Wright aboard taken with smallpox. Was dismantled soon thereafter.

1686 ECLIPSE

SW p wh b. Louisville, Ky., 1842. 530 tons. 228 x 30 x 8. Ran Louisville-New Orleans in summer; Memphis-New Orleans in fall and winter, Capt. Goslee, master. In 1848 owned by John M. Rich, New Orleans, Capt. P.R. Lott, master. Dismantled 1850.

1687 ECLIPSE

Stw p wh b. Brownsville, Pa., 1849. 55 tons. Off the lists 1857.

1688 ECLIPSE

SW p wh b. New Albany, Ind., 1852. 1,117 tons. 350 x 37.4 x 8.4 (Customs measure).

Length on deck	365 ft.
Width of hull	40 ft.
Depth of hull	9 ft.
Paddlewheels	40 ft. dia., working 15 ft. buckets
Extreme width	77 ft.
Engines	36's- 11 ft.
Boilers	16 in number, later 8, 42" dia., 32 ft.
Smokestacks	95 ft. waterline to tops, 85" dia.
Draft	4½ ft. light, 10 ft. loaded
Passenger capacity	140 cabin, 60 on cots
Freight capacity	1,600 tons
Cost	$375,000 complete

Heights:

Between main deck and cabin floor	14½ ft.
Cabin floor to skylight top	14
Skylight to texas roof	10
Pilothouse	8

Pilothouse top 51 ft. above light-load water line.

Her birthplace was Dowerman's Ship Yard at New Albany, Ind., where the hull was floated off on a natural rise in the river, and not launched, this being a considerable talking point in favor of the speed qualities she later developed. A contemporary description:

> Her proportions, symmetry and power are fully up to all of her other excellencies of construction. The pantryware was made in one of the most noted potteries in France, especially for her, while the pearl-handled cutlery was designed and manufactured at Sheffield, England, and

all of the glassware for the tables, bar, and other parts of the boat were designed and made in Switzerland. The carpet reaching from the gentlemen's hall to the large mirror at the end of the ladies' cabin is seamless, and woven at Brussels, with eyelets at the sides, to be buttoned down instead of being laid permanently, consequently always spotlessly clean. The decorations on the *ECLIPSE* cost as much as many of the present-day steamboats cost.

Another description says:

The cabin is Gothic and Norman styles. The ceiling is divided into diamonds and half diamonds by the crossing of Gothic arches, and at the points of intersection hang pendant acorns entwined with oak leaves of rich gilt, the whole giving the appearance of two vast, arched colonades. The intervening spaces in the ceiling are decorated with frescoes; each stateroom door is embellished with a landscape; and over the forward entrance to the cabin are two large paintings of the patron cities, Louisville and New Orleans. The large stained glass skylights above and the six massive and richly gilded chandeliers are objects of wonder as well as sources of light.

Quoting from a letter written on board near Memphis in 1853 by General S.G. French, USA, to his friend A.B. Hamilton of Washington, D.C.:

This is no six-horse stern wheel boat, and the passengers don't all get tipsy and play cards all night long—but on the contrary this boat eclipses all I have ever seen in these parts, and many of the passengers are from Yankee-doodle-dum, on their way south looking out to see the horrors of slavery and new sights, and would as soon spend money for nought as touch a card, or do anything else to militate against their pockets or consciences. Perhaps you would like to know what sort of a boat this is that strikes my fancy so—well I will tell you something about her. She is three hundred and sixty five feet in length, forty foot beam, with two engines with 36 inch cylinders and eleven foot stroke, with sixteen boilers, two doctors, two freight engines, and wheels forty two feet in diameter—burns one hundred cords of wood per day, carries 1,800 tons and I hope won't burst her "bilers" on 120 pounds of steam to the square inch or under any other circumstances. And then, too, she is beautifully finished, perfect in her accommodations, being just about twice as comfortable as Willards's Hotel—her staterooms are about twice as large as some of his, and much better furnished, and then the table! why it would be a good tonic to you, and give you a most excellent appetite to read the "bill of fair"—indeed I would send you one only I fear you would become discontented with your present sumptuous fare spread out all at once before you. But all joking aside, there is more comfort and convenience on this boat than in most of the Hotels as you can judge when I state that she cost one hundred and thirty five thousand dollars—a great deal for a western style of boat. Just imagine our beautiful cabin 110 yards long!

The crew of the *ECLIPSE* composed as many as 121 persons, at times, among them 70 firemen and deckhands, 25 stewards and waiters, five cooks, three mates, five engineers, and clerks, pilots, etc. The monthly payroll came to $4,605.

This boat was designed for the Louisville-New Orleans trade and was given large power with the expectation that she could make the upstream voyage in four days, which she never did. Capt. Edward T. Sturgeon, master and principal owner, of Louisville, Ky., was 35 years old when he brought out this packet in 1852. Her famed speed trial left New Orleans at 10:12 A.M., Saturday, May 14, 1853. Four days, nine hours and thirty minutes later she landed at Portland, Ky., below the Louisville Canal. A day or so later the side-wheel *A.L. SHOTWELL* (see) came up in almost equal time. For years there was bitter debate as to which boat was the faster. The populations of Louisville, Jeffersonville, and New Albany took these matters quite seriously inasmuch as the *SHOTWELL* was owned in New Albany and hence a rival of the Louisville-owned *ECLIPSE.* Extra editions of Louisville newspapers went on the streets when the *SHOTWELL* arrived at Portland. Horsemen did Paul Revere rides between the Portland landing and the printing plants. The Louisville *Democrat* inserted in their June 4, 1853, issue a statement written by Captain Sturgeon justifying the *ECLIPSE*'s claim for having come up in faster time, accompanied with certified statements from official timekeepers.

For those interested in more details of the *ECLIPSE* we refer them to the September 1975 issue of *S&D Reflector* in which a seven-page account appears. Captain Sturgeon sold the boat in early January 1857 to Capt. Lewis W. Broadwell of New Orleans, and ownership was transferred that November to James M. Broadwell of that city. On Apr. 23, 1858, owner became Robert Bell of New Orleans. Her last running perhaps was in the New Orleans-Vicksburg trade, Capt. Harry I. Spotts, spring of 1860. On Feb. 21, 1860, a great storm at New Orleans blew the *ECLIPSE* into midstream. She drifted down coming into contact with shipping, stove in her bow, damaged her starboard wheelhouse and the ladies' cabin. One month later Captain Spotts had her moored at Portland, Ky., and auctioned off the furniture and apparel. Her hull was made into a wharfboat and served at Memphis until the start of the Civil War.

1689 ECLIPSE

SW p wh b. Belle Vernon, Pa., 1853. 216 tons. She was taken to Galveston, Tex., and ran on the Brazos River. Off the lists 1860.

1690 ECLIPSE

Stw p wh b. California, Pa., 1854. 150 x 27 x 4. 156 tons. Built for Capt. George D. Moore, Hancock County, Va., Bazil Doyle, Steubenville, Oh., and William Akley, Allegheny City, Pa. She was sold to Mobile, Ala., there owned by Cox, Brainard & Co., Capt. H.W. Buckley, master. Off the lists 1860.

1691 ECLIPSE

Stw p wh b. Elizabeth, Pa., 1862. 223 tons. Built for Capt. George D. Moore and others. Bought by Capt. James L. Wise, Cincinnati, and was in USQMD service during the war, Capt. William G. Vohris. On Jan. 27, 1865, was at Johnsonville, Tenn., when the boilers exploded, killing 27, and injuring many more. Captain Vohris was in his room, buried his face in a pillow, and came off with body burns. He afterwards stated that he had notified the USQMD that the boilers were leaking and unsafe, and had asked that repairs be made. He was overruled.

1692 ECLIPSE

SW ferry wh b. Ormo, Wis., 1863. 27 tons. 60 x 14 x 3.5. Owned by Capt. Russel Scudder, master, and Lyman Scudder. Documented at Burlington, Iowa, 1867.

1693 ECLIPSE

Stw p wh b. California, Pa., 1878. 180 x 30 x 4. Engines, 13's- 4 ft. Two boilers, each 40″ dia. by 26 ft. Iron paddlewheel 16 ft. dia. with 22 ft. buckets. Owned by A.B. Sheperd, Wellsville, Oh., Alex V. Caughey, Frank S. Moore, and John D. Biggert, all of Allegheny County, Pa., Capt. George D. Moore, master. Built at Ebberman & McFall yard. Advertised at Pittsburgh, June 1, 1878, to leave on first trip to Fort Benton direct, Moore, master, Shepherd, clerk. In all she made 11 trips to the fort between 1878–1887. She was the flagship of a fleet of steamboats in 1881 carrying several thousand Indians from the Yellowstone to agencies in the Dakotas. Was last owned by Montana Transportation Co., Capt. Isaac P. Baker, master. She sank twice in one year, 1887. The first was in June, in shallow water, and quickly raised. She was fatally snagged 15 miles below Sioux City, Iowa, on Sept. 3, 1887.

1694 ECLIPSE

Stw p wh b. Madison, Ind., 1880. 90 x 24 x 2.5. Documented at Louisville, Ky., 1886.

1695 ECLIPSE

Stw p wh b. LeClaire, Iowa, 1882. 124.9 x 24.6 x 4.1. Engines, 13's- 5 ft. Three boilers, each 30″ dia. by 16 ft. She was built for the Lindsay & Phelps Lumber Co., and towed rafts until the mills shut down in 1904. Then Capt. John Lancaster, LeClaire, who held interest in the boat, and had commanded her as a rafter, bought Capt. John Streckfus's warehouses at Davenport and Clinton, and entered *ECLIPSE* in the trade. A street car line had been opened, and so this venture was not a success, but it was the last effort to run a packet between those cities. She later ran in the Dubuque-Prairie du Chien trade, and in 1913 was laid up in Cat Tail Slough south of Albany, Ill., where she sank. Capt. Ralph Emerson Gaches bought her to tow his showboat. He was making a trip with her from Pittsburgh to Sistersville, W. Va., with an Atlantic Refining Co. gasoline barge on the night of Dec. 8, 1917, when she struck the dike at the foot of Neville Island, Ohio River, and burned and sank.

1696 ECLIPSE

Stw p wh b. Higginsport, Oh., 1903. 100 x 21.2 x 3.0. Engines, 10½'s- 3 ft. One boiler 42″ by 18 ft. Ran on Big Sandy River briefly. Machinery came from the *W.H. GRAPEVINE* (see). Capt. Robert Taylor owned her, and sold her to U.S. Hame Co., Tell City, Ind. Later went to St. Louis registry.

1697 ECLIPSE

Stw p wh b. St. Joseph, Mo., 1901, originally named *CITY ST. JOSEPH* (see). The Lee Line at Memphis in latter 1916 changed her name to *ECLIPSE* and ran her Memphis-Caruthersville. She ended up on a snag at 7:00 P.M., Sept. 12, 1925, opposite Osceola, Ark. Crew and passengers got ashore over a sand bar.

1698 ECONOMIST

Stw p wh b. Pittsburgh, Pa., 1868. 128 x 27 x 3.3. Built for Capt. J.H. Porter who loaded her out, new, for Arkansas River. An account said, "she is an odd looking specimen designed to float on 8 inches of water." In August 1869 was sold to Capt. John W. Tobin, New Orleans. Ran Trenton and upper Bayou Bartholomew, Capt. S.A. Whyte.

1699 ECONOMY

Stw p wh b. Shousetown, Pa., 1858. 155 x 30.5 x 4.5. 200 tons. Capt. M.W. Beltzhoover, first master. Owned in shares by him, and Samuel C. Young and Clarke & Thaw, Pittsburgh. Ran on upper Ohio principally. In Pittsburgh-Cincinnati trade, March 1861, Capt. Beltzhoover. Transporting U.S. troops, Pittsburgh to Louisville, January 1862. Lost Oct. 17, 1862.

1700 ED C. KIRKER

SW batwing wh b. Catlettsburg, Ky., 1890. 70 x 17 x 2. Ran on Big Sandy River. Jesse P. Hughes said, "she was gone and forgotten when I came to the Big Sandy in 1900."

ED F. DIX

See *EDWARD F. DIX,* proper spelling.

1701 ED FOSTER

Ferry wh b. Cincinnati, Oh., 1878. 100 x 26.5 x 4. Built to ferry at Little Rock, Ark., and departed Cincinnati in April 1878 for her new home. Documented at Memphis 1886, and is listed as a Lee Line boat.

1702 ED HOWARD

SW p wh b. New Albany, Ind., 1852. 390 tons. 280 x 35 x 8. Ran Nashville-New Orleans. Her master in 1860 was Capt. J.W. Fowler. Rammed and sank the *HENRY LEWIS* (see) Mar. 7, 1856. Also on another occasion rammed and sank the *SWALLOW.* Became the Confederate gunboat *GENERAL POLK.* Burned with others at Liverpool, below Yazoo City, Miss., July 26, 1862.

1703 ED MYER

Stw p wh b. Jeffersonville, Ind., by Howard, 1909. 124.8 x 22 x 3. Two boilers, each 38″ dia. by 18 ft. Operated by Carthage Packet Co., owned by West Williams and Ed Myer, on upper Cumberland. Sold to the Ryman Line, Nashville, 1910. Often chartered out during low water to Louisville-Evansville trade. Was listed at St. Louis, 1915, and lost in ice at Helena, Ark., Jan. 23, 1918.

1704 ED POPE

Stw p wh b. New Matamoras, Oh., 1874. 96.65 tons. Ran low water, Wheeling-New Matamoras in 1875, Capt. Lewis Pope, and named for his eldest son. Towed produce boats to New Orleans. Still listed 1876.

1705 ED R. HART

SW p wh b. Paducah, Ky., 1860. 175 tons. Went to Confederate service in 1861.

1706 ED RICHARDSON

SW p wh b. Jeffersonville, Ind., by Howard, 1878. 309 x 49 (95 over all) x 12. Engines 38's- 10 ft. Nine boilers. Machinery came from *KATIE* (see). Christened by Miss Roberts of Frankfort, Ky., niece of Capt. John W. Cannon. Named for Col. Ed Richardson, senior member of the firm Richardson & May, cotton factors at New Orleans. She was advertised to leave Louisville on her maiden trip south on Jan. 21, 1879. The Howard family went along, and Cap'n Jim, then four, took his first boat ride on this occasion. First crew: Capt. John W. Cannon, master; Tom J. Howard and John Willbank, clerks; John Garrity and William Kelkner, engineers; Moses Gibbs, mate; James Orrill, steward; John Boone, bar; James Buist, carpenter. Her cabin was 250 feet long, 19 ft. wide and 13½ ft. high; texas 165 ft. long; paddlewheels 41 ft. dia., 18 ft. bucket and 28" dip. Had 21 wheel arms. This was a cottonstyle packet and one of the great ones. Colonel Richardson ran the Refuge Plantation about 13 miles below Greenville, Miss., and Refuge Oil Co. (cotton seed oil) was first commenced here, later moved to Vicksburg. The "racer" *NATCHEZ* after dismantling was used here as a wharfboat, in charge of Capt. Thomas W. Wilcox, father of Capt. W.C. Wilcox and grandfather of Capt. Stuart Wilcox. The *ED RICHARDSON* was dismantled in 1888, and the hull was burned to recover old iron.

1707 EDDIE

Stw p wh b. Evansville, Ind., 1864. 50 tons. Snagged and lost at Bogue Phalia, La., Jan. 30, 1869.

1708 EDDYVILLE

Stw p wh b. Evansville, Ind., 1871. 151 x 31 x 3. Ran in the Evansville & Tennessee River Packet Co., Capt. A.J. Duncan, master; Al Maynard and W.A. Page, clerks. Also ran Evansville-Nashville. Owned 1879 by Josie Hughes, and master was Capt. James Hughes. One-half interest was sold to Henry Gannett that year. Went to Jeffersonville for dismantling in June 1880.

1709 EDGAR

Centerwheel ferry wh b. Leavenworth, Kans., 1866. 120.27 tons. Operated at Leavenworth as a ferry. Lost in 1884.

1710 EDGAR CHERRY

Stw p wh b. Harmar, Oh., at the Knox yard, 1894. 152 x 27.4 x 5. Compound engines by Marietta Mfg. Co., 10's, 17½'s- 5 ft. Two boilers. Owned by St. Louis & Tennessee River Packet Co., until Mar. 22, 1900, when sold to the Mason Line for the Pittsburgh-Morgantown trade on Monongahela River. Capt. John G. Britton became master. On Mar. 10, 1904, she left Pittsburgh for Morgantown, Capt. Robert L. Demain, first boat since December 1903, due to an unusually severe winter. At 10:00 that night, entering Lock 4, she hit the upper lock gates, sprung them, and damaged herself. She was backed out of the lock, and sank not far below there. Robert A. Covert was pilot on watch. His partner was W.H. Lloyd. The towboat *SAILOR* took off passengers and crew. The machinery was salvaged and later served on the towboat *COLLIER,* which was renamed *WM. C. SUTHERLAND.*

1711 EDINBURG

SW p wh b. Brownsville, Pa., 1854. 283 tons. Ran on the Missouri River, St. Louis-St. Joseph, 1856, Capt. Dan Able. Ran to New Orleans and made trips up Red River in latter 1850s. Burned at Bloody Island near St. Louis, along with *MONONGAHELA,* May 15, 1859.

1712 EDINBURGH

Stw p wh b. Louisville, Ky., 1865. 210 x 30 x 5. 393 tons. Built for Capt. Steve Thompson and others and ran Wheeling-Cincinnati, and later Pittsburgh-Cincinnati, Capt. I.L. Thompson, master, with G.W. Thompson, clerk. Sold in February 1870 to Capt. F.Y. Batchelor and others. That September she sank at Island 40, Mississippi River, Capt. J.L. Carter in command. Sold Jan. 15, 1871, to Capt. W.W. Fenton who loaded her out for Red River from Cincinnati. That November she was the first boat to pass up through the new Louisville-Portland Locks and canal improvement, followed by the *CHARMER* and *R.C. GRAY.* Was again sold and ran from the lower Ohio to Arkansas River. Sank May 1, 1873, 40 miles below Pine Bluff, Ark. She was dismantled that summer.

1713 EDITH

Stw p wh 45 x 7 x 2. Engines 5"- 9" stroke. Cabin 10 ft. wide. Burned at the mouth of Red River, La., where she was repairing, September 1880.

1714 EDITH

Stw p wh b. Mason City, W. Va., 1885. 101 x 24 x 3.1. Probably handled produce boats, etc. Registered St. Louis, 1886–1896, maybe longer.

1715 EDITH

Stw p wh b. Evansville, Ind., 1890. 67 x 18.3 x 2.2. Probably handled produce boats, etc. Still at Evansville in 1908.

1716 EDITOR

SW p wh b. Brownsville, Pa., 1851. 247 tons. 174 x 27 x 5.5. Advertised New Orleans to Cincinnati, September 1851, Capt. Golding. Ran in the St. Louis-St. Paul trade, Capt. J.F. Smith, and later Capt. Brady, and had a reputation for speed. Sold to New Orleans winter of 1859–1860. Burned at Algiers, La., May 6, 1861, then owned by John E. Hyde, New Orleans.

1717 EDMONIA

Stw p wh b. Belle Vernon, Pa., 1856. 90 tons. First enrolled at Paducah, Ky. Snagged and lost at Leavenworth, Ind., Aug. 20, 1860.

1718 EDNA

Stw ferry wh b. Jeffersonville, Ind., by Howard (hull only), 1914. 64.7 x 19 x 3. In 1929 owned by Robert H. Groh, Chester, Ill.

1719 EDNA ADAMS

Stw p wh b. Evansville, Ind., 1877. Originally named *H.M. SWEETSTAR,* then *TWO STATES,* before becoming *EDNA ADAMS.* Ran Evansville-Owensboro, Capt. James H. Cox. He was on her seven years, then Capt. John A. Adams went master in June 1889. Burned at the upper end of Evansville, September 1889.

1720 EDWARD BATES

P wh b. St. Louis, Mo., 1848. 299 tons. Ran St. Louis-Keokuk, first as an opposition packet to the regular line, then was bought by the line. She was in the head of Westport Chute on the Upper Mississippi between Westport, Mo., and Hamburg, Ill., when two flues in the port boiler collapsed Aug. 9, 1848. Twenty-eight were killed, thirty scalded. Most of these were deck passengers and crew. Some were buried at Hamburg and the others were taken to St. Louis. The *ELIZA STEWART* replaced her in the trade. Burned at St. Louis, May 17, 1849, in a major wharf blaze.

1721 EDWARD C. WIGGINS

Centerwheel ferry wh b. New Albany, Ind., 1865. 164.9 x 46.2 x 5.5. Owned by the Wiggins Ferry Co., St. Louis. Dismantled 1885.

1722 EDWARD F. DIX

SW p wh b. Madison, Ind., 1864. 266 x 40 x 5.5. Caught fire at St. Louis July 15, 1864, and caused a major steamboat fire which burned the *CHEROKEE, NORTHERNER, SUNSHINE, GLASGOW,* and *WELCOME.* Capt. William Fuller was master at the time. Sank and lost on Red River, La., after striking the wreck of the U.S. gunboat *EASTPORT,* June 15, 1865.

1723 EDWARD J. GAY

SW p wh b. St. Louis, Mo., 1859. 277 x 39 x 8.5. Ran St. Louis-New Orleans, Capt. John Brooks. Registration changed to New Orleans in May 1861. She was taken up Yalobusha River to prevent capture, and there was burned July 17, 1863.

1724 EDWARD J. GAY

SW p wh b. Cincinnati, Oh., 1878. 251.3 x 41 x 7.6. Machinery from the *GOVERNOR ALLEN.* She was completed at the Cincinnati Marine Railway Co., in July 1878 and was towed south by the new *J.M. WHITE.* Ran her trials at New Orleans that October. Designed for the New Orleans-Bayou Sara trade, Capt. J.J. Brown. She carried U.S. Mail under contract until January 1880. Her roof bell came from the *BRILLIANT* of 1850 (see). Her master in 1884 was Capt. S.S. Streck and she was managed by Capt. T.P. Leathers. She burned at First Street in New Orleans, laid up, July 30, 1888.

1725 EDWARD MANNING

Stw p wh b. Marietta, Oh., 1851. 112 tons. Built at the Knox yard for Capt. E.A. Davis and first home port was Keokuk, Iowa. Burned and lost at Alton, Ill., Aug. 10, 1858.

1726 EDWARD WALSH

SW p wh b. Madison, Ind., 1854. 597 tons. Primarily a freight carrier, St. Louis-New Orleans. Her master in 1859 was Capt. J.J. Davis. First to the scene of the *R.F. SASS* disaster (see) in May 1860 and brought many survivors to Memphis, Capt. Burk commanding. Was in the Atlantic & Mississippi Steamship Co., line after the war. Dismantled at St. Louis May 2, 1867.

1727 EDWARDSVILLE

Recesswheel ferry wh b. Carondelet, Mo., 1866. 166.3 x 41.8 x 5.9. Owned by the Wiggins Ferry Co., St. Louis. Dismantled 1894.

1728 EDWIN N. BISSO

Catamaran ferry sh b. Nashville, Tenn., by Nashville Bridge Co., 1925. 130.3 x 46 x 7.5. Handled 273 passengers and 50 cars. Owned by Bisso Ferry Co., New Orleans, until sold 1965 to Mississippi River Bridge Authority. Converted to diesel in 1968 and renamed *CITY OF GRETNA.* Off the lists 1976.

1729 EFFIE AFTON

SW p wh b. Cincinnati, Oh., 1855. 430 tons. Probably named for Sarah Harper Monmouth, contemporary writer of stories and verse. Owned in part and commanded by Capt. Jesse Y. Hurd, Portsmouth, Oh. Struck the bridge at Rock Island, Ill., en route Cincinnati to St. Paul on May 6, 1856. Stoves upset setting the boat afire. Many passengers got off on the bridge. No life loss. A lawsuit resulted in which Abraham Lincoln was attorney for the Chicago & Rock Island RR, owners of the bridge. The roof bell is preserved at the U.S. Arsenal, Rock Island, Ill.

1730 EFFIE BOFINGER

Ferry wh 35 x 16 x 4. Operated at Cape Girardeau, Mo., owned by Capt. C.T. King. He sold her in 1871 to Capt. Dave Campbell and replaced her with the *KATIE KEISER* (see).

1731 EFFIE DEANS

Stw p wh b. Madison, Ind., 1863. 157.6 x 33.9 x 5.3. Owned in 1865 by the Keokuk Packet Co. ½, and Capt. Joseph LaBarge, John LaBarge and others. Named for Sir Walter Scott's character Effie Deans in his *Heart of Mid-Lothian.* Capt. Joe LaBarge commanded her on trips to New Orleans and up the Missouri to Fort Benton. Burned and lost at St. Louis on Apr. 7, 1866.

1732 EFFORT

SW p wh b. Algiers, La., 1855. 125 x 25 x 4. First owned and mastered by Capt. William McMillen, Algiers. Ran New Orleans-Shreveport. Sold July 1859 to D. Kernaghan & Co., New Orleans, Capt. William Kernaghan. That December sold to G. L. Kouns & Bros., New Orleans, Capt. Isaac H. Kouns. Went to Confederate registry in 1861. The Kouns' family renamed her *ERA NO. 1* (see).

1733 EFFORT

SW batwing wh b. Big Sandy, Va., 1862. 29 tons. Ran on Big Sandy River. Dismantled in 1865.

1734 EGLANTINE

Stw p wh b. Pittsburgh, Pa., 1861. 25 tons. First owned in part and commanded by Capt. William Lloyd, Allegheny City, Pa. Capt. Josiah King was master summer 1862 when she took empty oil barrels up the Allegheny to the "Land of Grease." Sold that fall to J. T. Deffenbacker, Allegheny City. Dismantled in 1865.

1735 EIGHTH OF JANUARY

SW p wh b. Portsmouth, Oh., 1846. 98 tons. Dismantled 1857.

1736 EL BLANCO

Stw p wh b. Fisk, Mo., 1898. 51 x 21 x 3.3. Owned in 1903 by Capt. G.W. Huff, master, who operated her on the Black and Current rivers out of Pocahontas, Ark.

1737 EL CAPITAN

Stw ferry sh b. St. Louis, Mo., by John Rohan Sons, 1903. 109.8 x 26 x 3.5. Engines 12's- 6½ ft. Owned by Capts. S.B. and C.H. McNeely, Natchez, Miss., and ferried to Vidalia. Later converted into a towboat renamed *JOHN M. WARNER,* then *NORMAN CRAWFORD.*

1738 EL CAPITAN II

Stw ferry wh b. Paducah, Ky., 1925. Owned by the McNeelys, Natchez, Miss. Burned at Natchez, June 1927, drifted down the river and was lost. The *EL CAPITAN* (see above) was damaged somewhat in the blaze.

1739 EL DORADO

SW p wh b. Pittsburgh, Pa., 1843. 284 tons. Operated in the Louisville-New Orleans trade, Capt. Charles Stone. Dismantled 1847.

1740 EL PASO

SW p wh b. St. Louis, Mo., 1850. 180 x 28 (approx.). Engines, 18½'s- 6½ ft. Three boilers. In 1852 ascended the Platte River to Guernsey, Wyo., the only steamboat ever to go there. In 1853 ascended the Missouri to the mouth of Milk River, first steamboat to that place. Snagged and lost at Franklin Island, White's Landing, near Boonville, Mo., on the Missouri River, Apr. 10, 1855. Owned at the time by Bennett, Itzen and Wineland. Her master was Capt. Andrew Wineland, and the pilot was Capt. William R. Massie.

1741 ELON G. SMITH

SW harbor boat wh b. Madison, Ind., 1873. 160 x 32 x 6. Long served as harbor boat at St. Louis. Later renamed *CITY OF ST. LOUIS* (see).

1742 ELAINE

Stw p wh b. Wheeling, W. Va., 1882. 142.5 x 25 x 3.4. Hull and cabin built at Clarington, Oh., and completed at Wheeling. Engines, 12's- 4½ ft. Two boilers. Operated by Capt. G.W. Conant and others in Pittsburgh-Wheeling trade and also Pittsburgh-Parkersburg. Capt. Fred Kimple Jr., was master in her early days. She was dismantled in 1898 and machinery went to the *AVALON* built at Clarington that year.

1743 ELDORADO

Stw p wh b. Cincinnati, Oh., 1879. 235 x 40 (38 ft. floor) x 5. Engines, 16's- 5½ ft. from towboat *BRILLIANT.* Two boilers, each 47" dia. by 26 ft., six flues. Capt. W.W. Little, Portsmouth, Oh., owned in and commanded, sharing duties with Capt. Isaac Miller, also of Portsmouth. Ran Cincinnati-St. Louis, and also made trips to Pittsburgh. Sold at U.S. sale in Cincinnati, Jan. 24, 1880, to Pittsburgh & Cincinnati Packet Line (¾) and Capt. J.M. Kirker. Sank on the falls at Louisville, Feb. 25, 1880. She was en route St. Louis to Huntington, W. Va., Capt. John S. Patterson, with a cargo of iron ore and flour when she was delayed at Portsmouth for ice. Sank there when the gorge went out, Jan. 6, 1881. The wreck lodged below Conoconnique Bar on the Ohio side, and was visible in low water for years after.

1744 ELEANOR

Stw p wh b. Cincinnati, Oh., 1858. 258 tons. 150 x 31 x 4.8. Owned by Capt. Willis Main (½) of New Orleans who commanded, and Edmond Graces, Alexandria, La. Ran New Orleans-Shreveport. Went to Confederate registry 1861.

1745 ELEANOR

Stw p wh b. Madison, Ind., 1889. 63 x 16 x 3.4. Owned and operated by Capt. Joe Williams who was a brother of Capt. R.H. Williams and an uncle of the Williams boys around Evansville, Ind. She ran Bowling Green to Lock 4, at the mouth of Barren River, and in the upper Green to Brownsville, Ky., which then was the head of navigation. Was still listed 1896.

1746 ELEANOR

Stw p wh b. Kilbourn, Wis., 1903. 75 x 16 x 2.3. Still operating 1908.

1747 ELEANORA CARREL

SW p wh b. Cincinnati, Oh., 1865. 1,165 tons. This was a large carrier owned and commanded by Capt. Hercules Carrel, Cincinnati. She was downbound for New Orleans with a heavy cargo when she burned at Louisville, Ky., Jan. 5, 1866. The hull, practically new, was converted into a wharfboat and taken to Evansville, Ind. The dimensions of the wharfboat were 185 x 40 x 5. The Louisville & Evansville Packet Co., used it until it was cut down by ice in the winter of 1904–1905. When the break-up came it was carried off, and lodged behind Wabash Island.

1748 ELEANORE

Stw p wh b. Beardstown, Ill., 1902. 126.8 x 23 x 3.8. Documented at Peoria in 1908.

1749 ELECTOR

SW p wh b. Brownsville, Pa., 1866. 302 tons. Built at the West Brownsville yard for the Peoples' Line which ran competition with the regular Monongahela River packets. First ran Pittsburgh-Greensboro. The two lines combined in 1868 to form the Pittsburgh, Brownsville & Geneva Packet Co. Capt. Doyle Bugher long commanded. He took her to Fairmont, W. Va., in 1875 on high water, and had quite a struggle with the swift current at Maidsville. Ran excursions at Fairmont and people came from far and wide to see the big boat. Capt. R.R. Abrams was master later on. Dismantled 1881.

1750 ELECTRA

Stw p wh b. Jeffersonville, Ind., by Howard, 1897. 170 x 35 x 5.5. Engines 14's- 5 ft. Two boilers, each 44″ dia. by 26 ft. The staterooms were named for flowers. Ran in the Red River Line, Capt. George L. White, New Orleans-Shreveport. Her clerk was H.C. Boazman. The Red River Line failed, and she and *W. T. SCOVELL* and *RED RIVER* were taken to the Cumberland River in 1905, operated there by Cumberland River Packet Co. In 1907 she was in the St. Louis-Missouri River trade. Was taken to Mobile, Ala., in November 1911 and ran Mobile-Montgomery. There was a U.S. sale and she was bought in by Capt. Owen Burke, Mobile, May 1912. In 1912 she made a trip to Columbus, Miss., Capt. M.T. Jackson, and may have been the last packet there. In 1914 she was renamed *SUNNY SOUTH* (see).

1751 ELENORA

Stw p wh b. New Albany, Ind., 1865. 152 x 33.2 x 4.8. Engines, 16's- 5 ft. Three boilers, each 40″ dia. by 26 ft. Ran New Orleans-Shreveport, Capt. Robert Watson. Sold to Mobile, Ala., and Capt. S.C. Abels was her master there. Returned to Red River and sank 12 miles below Shreveport, La., Feb. 23, 1868, Capt. James F. Muse in charge.

1752 ELEONORE

Stw p wh b. Beardstown, Ill., 1902. 126.8 x 23 x 3.8. Owned in her latter years by the Lee Line, Memphis. Burned at Memphis, September 1911, rebuilt. Turned turtle 20 miles above Memphis drowning several passengers and her purser, then in Memphis-Ashport trade, this in June 1916.

1753 ELEPHANT

SW p wh b. West Brownsville, Pa., 1851. 425 tons. 172.5 x 33.1 x 8. In 1853 she came to Pittsburgh and loaded on board the knocked-down steamboat *KATE FRISBEE* destined to New Orleans and California (see *KATE FRISBEE*). Capt. Oscar H. Pratt was master 1854, in the New Orleans-St. Louis trade. Capt. R.J. Underwood was master 1855, and in 1856 Capt. Hull R. Jackson commanded. Dismantled 1857.

1754 ELEVENTH ERA

SW p wh Not documented at New Orleans up through 1870, but said to be 245 feet long, with a cabin 202 feet long, 14½ feet wide, a pretentious steamboat. A daily newspaper was printed aboard, and Capt. Mart H. Kouns was master in the New Orleans-Shreveport trade.

1755 ELFIN

Stw tinclad wh Originally the *W. C. MANN* b. Cincinnati, Oh., 1863 (see). In U.S. service, was sunk and lost at Johnsonville, Tenn., Nov. 4, 1864.

1756 ELI

Stw p wh b. Little Rock, Ark., 1887. 106 x 21.5 x 2.5. Still registered 1892.

1757 ELISHA BENNETT

SW p wh b. Brownsville, Pa., 1867. 165 x 26 x 5. Engines, 20's- 6 ft. Four boilers, each 36″ dia. by 22 ft. Named for Capt. Elisha Bennett who had died Dec. 31, 1863. Artist Emil Bott did the interior decorative work, putting a scene on each stateroom door. An oil portrait of Capt. Bennett was in the office. Owned by the Pittsburgh & Brownsville Packet Co., and came out with Capt. M.A. Cox, master. Carried a calliope brought from St. Louis aboard the *GLASGOW*. She replaced the *GALLATIN* in the Pittsburgh-Brownsville trade. Later masters were Capts. G.W. Clark, Z.W. Carmack, and Peter Donaldson. She was at Brownsville when the ice gorges broke Jan. 13, 1877, and was carried to Charleroi, sinking on the right shore. The cabins floated off and lodged at Neville Island, Ohio River. When new Lock 4 was being built an old steamboat hull was uncovered, thought to have been that of the *BENNETT*.

1758 ELISKA

SW p wh b. Louisville, Ky., 1846. 231 tons. 168 x 25 x 5.8. Ran in the New Orleans and Upper Bends trade, Capt. J.G. Landry, who owned in partnership with William C. Winchester, Donaldsonville, La. Dismantled 1848.

1759 ELITE

Stw p wh b. Brownsville, Pa., 1849. 79 tons. Sank and lost at Smithfield, Tex., Mar. 5, 1852.

1760 ELIZA

SW p wh b. Freedom, Pa., 1848. 115.8 x 25.6 x 5.3.

Originally named *PLANTER* (see) and renamed at New Orleans Mar. 22, 1851. The new owner was Alexander Guy, Newport, Ky., who also was master. He went partners with Benjamin Martin, Warren, Ark. Off the lists 1858.

1761 ELIZA

SW p wh b. Cincinnati, Oh., 1852. 349 tons. Snagged and lost at Plum Point, Tenn., Jan. 25, 1855.

1762 ELIZA BATTLE

SW p wh b. New Albany, Ind., 1852. 316 tons. Went to Mobile and ran there to Montgomery. Burned and lost at Kemps Landing on the Tombigbee River, Mar. 1, 1858. Twenty-nine persons lost.

1763 ELIZA STEWART

SW p wh b. St. Louis, Mo., 1847. 169 tons. Ran St. Louis-Galena, 1848. Running St. Louis-Keokuk fall of 1849 in place of the *EDWARD BATES* which had collapsed flues (see). Trips up Missouri River, Capt. H. McKee, 1848. She was mistaken at Cairo February 1849 for the *TENNESSEE* which was bringing up President-elect Zachary Taylor; guns were fired, etc., until the error was learned. Burned in the great wharf fire at St. Louis, May 17, 1849.

1764 ELIZABETH

SW p wh b. Marietta, Oh., 1842. 85 x 22 x 4.8. Owned by O.A. Miller, New Orleans. Ran New Orleans-Mobile, Capt. Joseph Swiler, Jr., 1843. New Orleans-Ouachita-Black rivers in 1844, Capt. J.W. White. Dismantled 1845.

1765 ELIZABETH

SW p wh b. Pittsburgh, Pa., 1867. 167 x 25 x 5. Rees engines, 18's- 5 ft. Three boilers each 38" dia. by 24 ft. Paddlewheels 24 ft. dia. working 9'10" buckets. Came out in the Pittsburgh-Elizabeth trade, Monongahela River, Feb. 17, 1867, Capt. F. Houghton. She ran in the trade 21 years, and went to the wrecker in February 1888, the machinery to be transferred to a new boat for the trade also named *ELIZABETH* (see next listing).

1766 ELIZABETH

SW p wh b. Belle Vernon, Pa. (hull), and completed at West Brownsville, Pa., 1888. 166 x 26 x 5.5. Machinery from prior boat of the name (see above). Ran Pittsburgh-Elizabeth, Capt. R.M. Boyd. The trade played out about 1900. She was laid up for some time, and in 1902 an independent line was formed called Monongahela River Packet Co., and she was put in the Pittsburgh-Morgantown trade, Capt. Frank L. Ganoe, running opposition to the regular Morgantown line. This didn't work and she was laid up that November. There was a U.S. sale July 22, 1903, and she was bought in by Theodore A. Miller, Pittsburgh. He sold her to Samuel W. Carpenter, a diver with his fleet moored in the Allegheny River above the Sixth Street bridge. She was tied there and the *OLIVETTE*, alongside, caught fire Jan. 24, 1904, setting the *ELIZABETH* ablaze. The latter was turned loose, drifted down under the Union Bridge, a covered wooden structure, set it on fire, and by then the tug *JOHN DIPPEL* shoved her ashore where she burned at leisure. The bridge damage was estimated at $1,000.

1767 ELK

Stw p wh b. Kanawha, Va., 1844. 84 tons. Ran from the Kanawha River to Cincinnati, Capt. Quarrier. Dismantled 1848.

1768 ELK

Stw p wh b. Elizabeth, Pa., 1851. 61 tons. Lost by stranding at Paducah, Ky., Aug. 9, 1851.

1769 ELK

SW U.S. tinclad wh b. Cincinnati, Oh., 1863. First named *COUNTESS* (see) and in U.S. service was *ELK*, renamed Dec. 8, 1863. Sold to private owners Sept. 6, 1865, and resumed her original name of *COUNTESS*.

1770 ELK

Stw p wh b. Peoria, Ill., 1894. 122 x 22 x 4. Capt. Sol York used her with an excursion barge on the Illinois River in 1895. Later she gravitated to Vicksburg and ran to Lake Palmyra. Was there 1905 with Capt. Ben Yeager as master. Finally sank at Vicksburg and the wreck was removed by the U.S. snagboat *MACOMB*.

1771 ELKHORN

Stw ferry wh b. Pittsburgh, Pa., 1866. 524 tons. Built for the Union Pacific RR under supervision of Capt. Adam Jacobs. She was loaded at Pittsburgh by Springer, Harbaugh & Co., with railroad iron, spikes, etc., and departed for the Missouri River with two barges named *HERO* and *HEROINE* in tow similarly loaded. Destination was Omaha, Neb., leaving Apr. 21, 1866. In 1874 owned by Waterloo Turnpike Road & Ferry Co., and registered at St. Louis. Dismantled and hull used as a barge Nov. 28, 1879.

1772 ELLA

Stw p wh b. Elizabeth, Pa., 1854. 173 tons. Built for Capt. Adam Poe and others of Georgetown, Pa., for the Cincinnati-St. Louis trade. On first trip she went to Galena and Dubuque. In a collision resulting in the loss of the *DELEGATE* (see) at West Franklin, Ind., Jan. 21, 1859. Snagged and lost on the Arkansas River near Little Rock, Dec. 13, 1865.

1773 ELLA

Centerwheel ferry wh b. 1858. First documented Jan. 30, 1868. Operated on the Missouri River. Sank and lost at Leavenworth, Kans., on Aug. 3, 1868.

1774 ELLA

SW p wh b. Cincinnati, Oh., 1860. 21 tons. Acquired by USQMD June 4, 1862 and renamed *COL. CHANDLER*. Sold to private hands Dec. 25, 1865, and retained that name. Sank and lost at Sabine Pass, Tex., Jan. 31, 1866, with loss of two lives.

1775 ELLA

Stw ferry wh b. Wheeling, W. Va., 1867. 59 tons. Operated between Wheeling and West Wheeling. Dismantled in 1884.

1776 ELLA

Ferry wh b. Grafton, Ill., 1870. 72 tons. Still documented 1876.

1777 ELLA

Stw p wh Operated on White River, Ark., in 1870s. Capt. E.W.B. Nowland had lost the *LEGAL TENDER* and procured *ELLA* to make trips on the Arkansas using *LEGAL TENDER*'s crew. On the first trip she sank about 25 miles below Pine Bluff at Rowsey's Point. The boat was lost, the cargo saved.

1778 ELLA

Stw p wh b. Jeffersonville, Ind., by Howard, 1881. 148 x 28 x 2.5. Built for Nashville & Burnside Packet Co., and was reputed to be a good money-maker on the upper Cumberland. Was sold February 1884 to Miss Mary C. Pearson, Little Rock, Ark., who ran the boat Little Rock-Fort Smith. Still documented 1886.

1779 ELLA B.

SW ferry wh b. Delhi, Oh., 1897. 57.7 x 19.1 x 3.4. Long operated by the Toronto (Ohio) Ferry Co., owned by S.B. Goucher and others. Was taken to Dravosburg, Pa., for docking in August 1908 and sank there. Raised and repaired but did not resume business. Sold August 1910 to Thomas M. Axton, West Brownsville, Pa.

1780 ELLA DURHAM

Stw p wh b. Knoxville, Tenn., 1889. 37.5 x 7 x 3.7. Still listed in 1892.

1781 ELLA FABER

Stw p wh b. California, Pa., 1862. 198 tons 150 x 32 x 4.5. Built for D.H. Swaney, John Swaney, J.M. and J. Phillis, and others of Beaver County, Pa. Capt. Josiah Murray was the first master. Later ran Louisville-Henderson trade, Capt. J.H. Peckenpaugh, master, with George Patterson, clerk. In the fall of 1867 she sank at Cannelton, Ind., was raised, and placed in drydock at Shippingport, Ky., and burned there at 8:30 P.M., Oct. 9, 1867.

1782 ELLA HECHT

Stw p wh b. Pocahontas, Ark., 1870. 82 x 22. Capacity 125 bales. Machinery from the *MALTA*. Run by Sam and Levi Hecht, Pocahontas, Ark. Sank in Black River, October 1871.

1783 ELLA HUGHES

Stw p wh b. Paducah, Ky., 1867. 212 tons. For the first several years ran on the Cumberland River, Capt. William Dix, master, with W.S. Bowman, clerk. Made an appearance at Louisville, Ky., in April 1873 with the following newspaper comment: "The *ELLA HUGHES* is certainly not the finest passenger steamer afloat. Her stateroom accommodations are limited to a few shelves with curtains suspended in front. A paper of pins lie on the office desk of this fractional steamer. When a guest asks for a key to his room, Johnny Harper, the clerk, blandly smiles and hands the applicant a pin." The Coles Circus Co., bought her in October 1876 and she hauled their circus around in the south that winter. In spring of 1877 sold to Capt. Wm. Wenzel and others for Ouachita River. Sank and lost near New Orleans, Mar. 17, 1880. Called the *"HELLA 'UGHES."*

1784 ELLA JOHNSTON

Ferry wh b. Wellsville, Oh., 1877. 77.5 x 16 x 4.5. Apparently operated in that vicinity. Still listed in 1886.

1785 ELLA KIMBROUGH

Stw p wh b. Jeffersonville, Ind., 1877. 145 x 28 x 4. Engines, 12½'s- 4½ ft. Two boilers. Originally *GENERAL SHERMAN* built at the Barmore Yard for the U.S. for Yellowstone River (see). The U.S. sold her to Capt. Peter M. Manion who in turn sold her to Capt. T.M. Kimbrough who named the boat for his wife. Snagged in St. Charles Chute, Missouri River, Sept. 20, 1884, with big load of wheat. The ferry *JOHN L. FERGUSON* got the wheat off.

1786 ELLA MAY

Stw ferry wh b. St. Louis, Mo., 1903. 99.1 x 27.6 x 3. Operated on the Missouri River. Still registered in 1918.

1787 ELLEN

Stw p wh b. Louisville, Ky., 1845. 98 tons. Built for Cumberland River. May have gone to the Red River. Lost in collision with a barge in 1849.

1788 ELLEN

Stw p wh b. Franklin, La., 1858. 76 tons. Went to Confederate registry in 1861.

1789 ELLEN

Stw rafter wh b. La Crosse, Wis., 1907. 145.5 x 26 x 4.4. Engines, 14's- 6 ft. The original owner was Sawyer Austin Lumber Co., of La Crosse. The boat was named for wife of W.W. Cargill of this firm. Capt. Charles White, Sr., commanded. Ran rafts and also was used for excursions and private parties of firm members. Austen Cargill once was bitten by a rattlesnake below Trempeleau, Wis., where the boat was landed. Capt. White cauterized the wound with a heated slice bar from the furnace. Sold to the U.S. Engineers in 1911 at La Crosse. Capt. Joseph M. Hawthorne was a guest aboard several times in 1935 and 1936, cousin of author Nathaniel Hawthorne, and long an upper Mississippi pilot. He was born in Erie County, Pa., 1839 and came to Le Claire in 1856 to make his home. Died, 97, in 1937. At one time the *ELLEN* was air-conditioned and an elevator installed in preparation for an expected visit of U.S. President Franklin D. Roosevelt which never came to pass. The boat was sold to private owners in 1943 and the following year was converted to diesel by Industrial Marine Service, Inc., Memphis. (See *Towboat Directory*.)

1790 ELLEN GRAY

Stw p wh b. Cincinnati, Oh., 1859. 150 x 24 (25 ft. floor) x 3. Engines by Anshutz of Cincinnati. Two boilers, each 33" dia. by 22 ft. Capt. John Swasey brought her out in the Cincinnati-Charleston (W. Va.) trade, with J.T. Johnson, clerk. In December 1859 Capt. Snelling C. Farley became master. On Nov. 7, 1860, came in collision with the *ARKANSAS* at Walkers Bar, 90 miles below Evansville, and was lost. Capt. Snelling Farley then ran the *KANAWHA VALLEY NO. 2* (see) in the Cincinnati-Charleston trade.

1791 ELLWOOD

SW p wh b. DePere, Wis., 1860. 171 tons. First home port, Mackinack, Mich. 114 x 31 x 3. Hibernated until the war was over and then went to Memphis where Capt. C.G. Bobo ran her up Obion and St. Francis rivers. Burned and lost in Hatchie River, Tenn., Apr. 16, 1865.

1792 ELLWOOD

Ferry wh b. Portsmouth, Oh., 1864. 37 tons. Still documented 1867.

1793 ELMIRA

Stw p wh b. Pittsburgh, Pa., 1858. 139 tons. Owned and commanded by Capt. James J. Smith of New Orleans. In 1860 sold to Nathaniel and William Offutt, Washington, La., and Capt. B.P. Stinson commanded. Went to Confederate registry in 1861. She was captured with others by Porter in 1863.

1794 ELNORA

Stw p wh b. New Albany, Ind., 1865. 332 tons. 152 x 33.2 x 4.8. Built by Capt. John Rickey who sold her at New Orleans August 1865 to Harry V. Rogers and Charles B. Smith, both of Mobile, Ala., and Capt. S.C. Abels took command. She went to Mobile and in 1867 was returned to New Orleans owned by Capt. James F. Muse, master, and Sylvester Crooks, Mobile. Sank and lost in Red River 12 miles below Shreveport, Feb. 23, 1868.

1795 ELOISE

Stw p wh b. Harmar, Oh., 1889. 112 x 22 x 3.4. Originally a towboat named *ELIZA H.* She was bought in May 1898 by S. Brady Morgan, William E. Roe, and Henry C. Roe and renamed *ELOISE.* In early 1900 Capt. Tom Peel, Burlington, Iowa, and some businessmen of that place bought her and ran her Keokuk-Burlington. One season she sank in shallow water at Pontoosuc, Ill., and was afire once at Keokuk. Capt. Walter Blair bought her in October 1907, made some alterations, and renamed her *WENONA* (see).

1796 ELON G. SMITH

SW harborboat wh b. Madison, Ind., 1873. 160 x 32 x 6. She was the city harbor boat at St. Louis. Later renamed *CITY OF ST. LOUIS* (see).

1797 ELVA

Stw ferry wh b. Leavenworth, Ind., 1899. 90 x 20.3 x 3. Operated on Arkansas River for the Dardanelle & Russellville RR which connected across at Russellville with a ferry, and later a pontoon bridge. In times of high water the *ELVA* was used, also *MARTHA,* and the last one there was the *ENQUIRER*. She was taken from the listings in 1915.

1798 ELVIRA

SW p wh b. Brownsville, Pa., 1851. 222 tons. 172 x 26 x 3.5. Capt. James Dozier ran her St. Louis-Missouri River 1852–1855, the boat named for his second daughter. Snagged and lost below St. Louis, Oct. 11, 1863.

1799 ELWOOD

SW ferry wh b. Portsmouth, Oh., 1864. 21 tons. Was recruited into U.S. service during the war on the St. Francis River. Sank there in the fall of 1864 and was repaired at Mound City, Ill. Burned and lost at Sageville, Tenn., Feb. 13, 1866.

1800 EMBASSY

SW p wh b. Wheeling, Va., 1849. 236 tons. Ran Pittsburgh-St. Louis, Capt. E. Bennett. One of her crew was Joe Hall, Cincinnati, who became famed for the manufacture of locks and safes at that city. She collapsed two boiler flues near the mouth of Green River, at Three Mile Bar, June 9, 1849. Ten were killed and 25 injured. Capt. Bennett commanded at the time. The *CHANCELLOR* towed the disabled boat to Evansville. Later ran Nashville-Memphis. Off the lists in 1856.

1801 EMERALD

SW p wh b. Cincinnati, Oh., 1859. 686 tons. Ran Louisville-New Orleans, Capt. O.C. Williamson, 1860. During the war was at St. Louis, a receiving ship attached to the U.S. fleet. Was with Porter on Red River in 1864. Capt. Alonzo F. Batchelor was clerk on her during the war period and recalled exchanging prisoners under flags of truce several times. He was 81 in 1919 living at East Palestine, Oh. Capt. John N. Shunk bought a share and went master. She picked up survivors of the *DAVID WHITE* explosion in 1867 (see). Sank and lost at Cat Island in Turner's Bend, Mississippi River, Jan. 4, 1868. His account: "The *EMERALD* is among the things that were. She sank Saturday evening at 4 P.M. I regret to say that she sank so quickly and unexpectedly that we lost everything except our lives. There was a mother and daughter and washer-woman thrown off the plank as the boat careened and sank, all three lost. She sank until the jackstaff went out of sight. I was in the cabin when she started down, and was looking for a skylight to break through to get to the hurricane roof. Water started to flow through the skylights. I thought goodbye, but fortunately a stateroom door flew open at the stern on the high side. I grabbed it, hauled myself into the room and kicked out the outside door and saw daylight. The yawl was near at hand and picked me up. I would judge not over 60 to 90 seconds elapsed from the time she snagged until she was out of sight." The boat was in the Cincinnati-New Orleans trade at the time.

1802 EMIGRANT

SW p wh b. Cincinnati, Oh., 1856. 343 tons. Capt. William Terrell, owner and master. Ran St. Louis to St. Joseph up Missouri River, a trip every two weeks. Burned and lost opposite Doziers Landing above Port Royal, Mo., Nov. 19, 1860.

1803 EMILIE

SW p wh b. St. Louis, Mo., 1859. 388 tons. Engines, 22's- 6 ft. Two boilers. Ran on the Missouri River owned and commanded by Capt. Joseph La Barge, and named for his daughter. This was the first side-wheeler seen at Fort Benton, arriving there June 17, 1862, the only trip she made there. She had left St. Louis on May 14 with 350 tons of freight and 160 passengers, along with the *SHREVEPORT*. She helped *SHREVEPORT* the last 100 miles and both arrived at the fort at the same time, noon, June 17. She turned right around and was back at St. Louis on July 3, a round trip in 32 days. Later was sold to the Hannibal & St. Joseph RR and was lost in a tornado at St. Joseph on June 4, 1868. She was completely stripped to the hull, and the wreck floated to Atchison, Kans.

1804 EMILIE LA BARGE

SW p wh b. Mound City, Ill., 1869. 218 x 38 x 5.5. Engines, 22's- 6 ft. Three boilers. Built by Capt. Joseph La Barge and others for Missouri River. Sold at St. Louis Apr. 12, 1871, to Capt. David H. Silver and James Gunsolis. George G. Keith had interest when she was snagged and lost in Nashville Bend, eight miles below Providence, Mo., June 6, 1874.

1805 EMILY

SW p wh b. Elizabethtown, Pa., 1845. 144 tons. First home port, Apalachicola, Fla. Exploded and lost at Apalachicola on May 27, 1849, with loss of seven lives.

1806 EMILY

SW p wh b. Jeffersonville, Ind., 1849. 160 tons. Snagged and lost in White River, Ark., Aug. 6, 1852.

1807 EMILY

Stw p wh b. Osceola, Wis., 1868. 137 x 24.4 x 4.2. Engines, 10½'s- 3 ft. One boiler. Originally named *NELLIE KENT*, built by Capt. William A. Kent. Sold and renamed *MARY BARNES* which was sold to the U.S. in the fall of 1884. The U.S. renamed her *EMILY* and she was lost in the ice breakup six miles above Bismarck, N.D., in the spring of 1885.

1808 EMILY

Stw ferry wh b. Jeffersonville, Ind., by Howard, 1891. 89 x 32 x 3. Engines, 8's- 3 ft. One boiler, 40" dia. by 20 ft. Operated at Kenova, W. Va., from a special wharfboat which later was used at Ashland, Ky., by Capt. James Poage. In 1901 ran July-August between Wheeling and Sisters Island where an amusement park was located, operated by Charles Griffith of the Sharpsburg (Pa.) Sand Co. Sold April 1902 to S.B. Goucher, Toronto, Oh., for service between Wellsville and Congo. Sold February 1913 to Capt. William Manley and C.W. Dickens, Bellaire, Oh. Later sold to Capt. John Davis, Fullerton, Ky., and ran there to Portsmouth. Then was sold to Henderson Ferry Co., Henderson, Ky., who renamed her *DIXIE BEE LINE*. She burned at Henderson in August 1926, was taken to Paducah and rebuilt to become *OHIO NO. 2* (both see).

1809 EMMA

SW p wh b. Cincinnati, Oh., 1856. 211 x 35 x 5.5. Engines, 18's- 6 ft. Three boilers. Probably operated Memphis-White River. She became a U.S. transport in September 1861 and was with Porter on Red River in 1864. Was captured and sunk on Red River and part of the crew taken prisoner. The mate, John Price, escaped and returned to St. Louis that November 1864. He made demands on Capt. Aiken, the boat's owner, for the whole of his wages while in prison. The case was tried in the courts.

1810 EMMA

Stw p wh b. New Albany, Ind., 1856, originally named *BLOOMER* (see). Renamed *EMMA* on Apr. 5, 1866. Sold foreign in 1868.

1811 EMMA

SW p wh b. Elizabeth, Pa., 1857. 54 tons. First home port, Omaha, Neb. Off the lists in 1859.

1812 EMMA

Stw p wh b. Freedom, Pa., 1859. 189 tons. Built for Capts. J.H. and Frank Maratta, Beaver County, Pa. Ran in various trades. Was in Louisville-Nashville trade fall 1859. In January 1862 ran Pittsburgh-Cincinnati, Capt. J.H. Maratta and at that same time Capt. Frank Maratta was running the *LACON* in the same trade. Was reported under contract to the U.S. on Cumberland River in 1864. In January 1865 the Louisville ferry *JOHN SHALLCROSS* hit her wheel, disabling her. The towboat *GIPSEY* came to aid with the result that both went over the falls. The *SHALLCROSS* also was carried down the Middle Chute to the Kentucky shore below Corn Island. Capt. Maratta sold her February 1865 to Capts. Vint and Oliver Shinkle, Covington, Ky. She was snagged and lost at Shreveport, La., June 20, 1865.

1813 EMMA

SW p wh b. Lynxville, Wis., 1867. 101 tons. Burned at Shawneetown, Ill., Dec. 9, 1872. This was primarily a freight boat.

1814 EMMA

Rig? b. Decatur, Ala., 1869. 182 tons. The machinery and equipment from *KINGSTON* used in construction. Ran until 1879, dismantled, and machinery went to *ROBERT R. ANDERSON*.

1815 EMMA

Stw p wh b. about 50 miles above Sioux City, Iowa, Missouri River, 1872. 64 x 18 x 3. One engine and one boiler. Engaged in carrying wood, owned by George and Fay Mattison. Sunk during a storm 20 miles above Omaha, Aug. 1, 1873. Later sold to L.C. Lohmen and ran on Osage River. Was stranded opposite Ewing's Landing bound from Osage to Jefferson City to be dismantled on Aug. 18, 1885. River fell and left her there.

1816 EMMA

Stw tb wh b. Clinton, Iowa, 1872. 55 x 13 x 3. Inspectors listed her as a packet 1883.

1817 EMMA

Stw ferry wh b. Lynn Creek, Mo., 1876. 120 x 24.4 x 2.9. Inspected at Osage City, Mo., on Nov. 18, 1880. Still listed 1886.

1818 EMMA

Stw ferry wh b. Algiers, La., 1880. 102 x 32.5 x 6. Still documented at New Orleans in 1896.

1819 EMMA

Stw p wh b. Parkersburg, W. Va., 1885. 72 x 13.3 x 2.3. Capt. S.W. Litten ran her Wheeling-Matamoras low water 1886 with J.L. Cramer as clerk. Did packet service on the Muskingum between Beverly and Zanesville, Capt. James Mason, 1892–1895. Dismantled and machinery went to *LITTLE QUEEN* (see).

1820 EMMA

Stw p wh b. De Vall's Bluff, Ark., 1893. 48 x 10 x 1.7. Still documented 1896.

1821 EMMA NO. 2

Stw p wh b. Freedom, Pa., 1862. 156.7 x 33.7 x 5. Engines, 16's- 5 ft. Two boilers, each 40" dia. by 26 ft. Hull by McKaskey & Kerr, and engines by Robert Lea. Capt. James H. Maratta was first master, with James Dunlap as clerk. Was in the Memphis-White River run in spring 1864, Capt. Millard. She brought the machinery from the burned *DES ARC* (see) to Cincinnati in July 1864 and appeared "considerably tattered and torn." Then ran Vicksburg-Yazoo River 1866, Capt. John O. Page, connecting with *FASHION* and *GEN. QUITMAN* for New Orleans. In 1868 went to New Orleans, owned by John B. Ludgate, with Capt. William Bowen, master. She was taken to Mobile soon after.

1822 EMMA NO. 3

Stw p wh b. Pittsburgh, Pa., 1866. 495 tons. Engines, 18½'s- 5 ft. Built for Capt. J.H. Maratta and departed Pittsburgh on her first trip February 1866 bound for New Orleans. Ran Cincinnati-New Orleans with trips through to Pittsburgh. Capt. J.H. Maratta, at Island 98, Mississippi River, January 1868, was knocked by a tree limb from the roof to the boiler deck down a stairway, sustaining injuries, and thanking his lucky stars he wasn't swept overboard. She was snagged and sunk at Island 35, Mississippi River, Feb. 19, 1870. Sank to the boiler deck, caught fire and burned. Thirty-five or 40 people were drowned. One group of those lost were in a yawl which capsized. Walter Maratta was first clerk, and was lost. Caleb Maratta, the mate, survived, both brothers of Capt. J.H. Maratta. In 1956 Charles T. Jones, Charleston, W. Va., renamed the diesel towboat *COURTNEY H* to *EMMA NO. 3* inasmuch as his great grandfather L.W. Jones lost his life in this sinking.

1823 EMMA BETT

Stw p wh b. Pittsburgh, Pa., 1858. 79 tons. First home port, Memphis. The U.S. tinclad *FOREST ROSE* was taking wood at Garvins Ferry on Sunflower River, May 1863, and a detachment went above there 14 miles to Bayou Quirer, seized this boat and burned her.

1824 EMMA BOYD

Stw p wh b. Wheeling, W. Va., 1863. 172 tons. Snagged and lost at Selma, Miss., Aug. 26, 1864.

1825 EMMA BROWN

Stw p wh b. Memphis, Tenn., 1854. 107 tons. First home port, St. Louis. Dismantled 1857.

1826 EMMA BROWN

SW p wh b. Madison, Ind., 1863. 117 tons. Built for Brown-Dunkerson & Co., Evansville, Ind., and named for young daughter of William Brown of that firm. The U.S. took over the boat immediately upon completion, Nov. 21, 1863, renamed her *GAZELLE*. She survived the war, was sold to private hands, and became the *PLAIN CITY*. Dismantled 1869.

1827 EMMA C. ELLIOTT

SW p wh b. Jeffersonville, Ind., 1871. 214 x 36.2 x 7. Engines, 21's- 6½ ft. Four boilers. Wheels 26 ft. dia. working 12 ft. buckets. A handsome side-wheeler designed for the New Orleans-White River trade by the Elliott brothers who then were running the *LEGAL TENDER* in White River (see). Also ran Memphis-Cincinnati, Capt. John D. Elliott, master, with George Alcoke and Al Croxell, clerks in 1873. Later acquired by the Anchor Line, Capt. George Lennox, master. Her roof bell was cast for the *ROBT. E. LEE* (2nd) but Capt. Cannon got another and sold it to the Elliott family. Later it was on the *GRAND TOWER*. She ran St. Louis-Grand Tower in the Anchor Line. Sold to the contractors building the Merchants Bridge, St. Louis, and later dismantled.

1828 EMMA DEAN

SW p wh b. Cincinnati, Oh., 1851. 212 tons. Ran Cincinnati-Memphis-Arkansas River. Dismantled 1861.

1829 EMMA DUNCAN

SW p wh b. Monongahela, Pa., 1860. 293 tons. 180 x 34 x 5. Engines, 24's- 6 ft. Three boilers. Named for daughter of a furniture manufacturer in Cincinnati. Ran Pittsburgh-Cincinnati, 1861–1862, Capt. F.Y. Batchelor. Acquired by the U.S., Mar. 16, 1863 and renamed *HASTINGS.* After the war sold to private hands and renamed *DORA* (both see).

1830 EMMA FLOYD

Stw p wh b. Freedom, Pa., 1863. 365 tons. Named for a young Pittsburgh lady who in 1868 married Sam Barr, Jr., purser of the *GREAT REPUBLIC* at New Orleans (see). Ran Cincinnati-Nashville, Capt. James C. Chenoweth, master, with Robert W. Wise and John L. McMeens, clerks. Ran Marietta-Cincinnati, Capt. Frank J. Oakes, 1865. Ran in place of the *BOSTONA,* Cincinnati-Portsmouth, summer 1868. Snagged and sunk at Newburgh, Ind., with a full cargo, Nov. 28, 1870. Machinery went to the *JAMES D. PARKER* (see) in 1872.

1831 EMMA GRAHAM

Stw p wh b. California, Pa., 1855. 137 x 28.5 x 4.5. Originally owned by Capt. Monroe Ayres (¼) and N.W. Graham & Co., Zanesville, Oh. Was named for daughter of N.W. Graham. In the ladies' cabin was a painting of Zanesville and in the main cabin one of a storm at sea, these painted by Col. W.C. Wall, the Pittsburgh artist who decorated the *GREAT REPUBLIC.* Ran Pittsburgh-Zanesville, Capt. Ayres and Capt. C.R. Stull into 1861. Dismantled.

1832 EMMA GRAHAM

Stw p wh b. Belle Vernon, Pa., 1861. 173 tons. Ran Pittsburgh-Zanesville 1861–1865, Capt. Monroe Ayres. Ran Parkersburg-Zanesville, Capt. Ayres, 1865–1866. In the fall of 1866 she was laid up, because the locks in the Muskingum seemed to be continually out of order and causing interruptions. She then was entered in the Parkersburg-Gallipolis trade, Capt. Charlie Roberts (of the *MATTIE ROBERTS,* see) and in 1869 Capt. C.B. Smith was in command, with J.N. Williamson and T.J. Wetherell, clerks. In 1870, Capt. J.N. Williamson, master, with Wetherell and Ira B. Huntington, clerks. Last owned by Williamson and Melvin M. and Miles H. Brown. Lost in ice at Antiquity, Oh., 1872.

1833 EMMA GRAHAM

Stw p wh b. Marietta, Oh. at Knox yard, 1872. 165 x 35 x 4.5. Built for the Parkersburg-Gallipolis trade. Capt. J.N. Williamson had a large interest. Capt. J.T. Russell was master. The U.S. Mail clerk was John Roedell, Pomeroy, who had lost one arm in the Civil War. In the fall of 1875 she was entered in the Pittsburgh-Cincinnati trade replacing the burned *JUNIATA* (see). Capt. J.T. Russell was in charge, with Nat Earhart, clerk. She was taken to Cincinnati, fall 1876, and parts used in building the "new" *EMMA GRAHAM* (next listing).

1834 EMMA GRAHAM

Stw p wh b. Cincinnati, Oh., 1877. 220 x 35 x 5. Rees engines, 18's- 6½ ft. Three boilers. Came out new in the Pittsburgh-Cincinnati trade with Capt. Hod Knowles, master; A.J. Slaven, clerk; Tom Monroe and Pete Dillon, asst. clerks; Nick and Joe Witten, pilots. Was in the Pittsburgh & Cincinnati Packet Line with Capt. J.T. Stockdale the manager at Pittsburgh and J.N. Williamson at Cincinnati. The line was formed November 1878 and the original boats were *GRANITE STATE, BUCKEYE STATE, W.P. THOMPSON, KATIE STOCKDALE,* and *EMMA GRAHAM.* When Capt. Williamson died his interest in the *EMMA GRAHAM* was acquired by Capt. E.B. Cooper who took charge. She had several accidents of note: Collided with the *MONTANA* (see) in Beaver Shoals near midnight Mar. 28, 1881, pilot Billy Abrams on watch. Settled in shallow water and passengers were kept aboard until daylight when the ferry *MARY CAMPBELL* came down from Rochester and took them off. In raising her she swung broadside and sunk again, the operation requiring a week. On Nov. 26, 1885, she was leaving the wharfboat at Ripley Landing, W. Va., pilot William F. Brookhart on watch, backed over a stave barge, put a hole in the stern transom, and she sank just above there. The *MINNIE BAY* took the passengers to Ravenswood, W. Va. Everything of value was taken off, including the machinery. These engines were placed in storage at the James Rees shop, Pittsburgh, and were there until 1934 when Capt. Tom R. Greene bought them and took them to Huntington, W. Va., on the *GORDON C. GREENE.* Later they were scrapped. Capt. E.B. Cooper chartered the *GENERAL PIKE* (see) as a replacement in the P&C Line.

1835 EMMA HARMON

Stw p wh b. Clarksville, Mo., 1854. 125 tons. First home port, St. Louis. Lost in ice at Peoria, Ill., Feb. 7, 1857.

1836 EMMA IRVINE

Prop p wh b. Portsmouth, Oh., 1872. 79 x 15 x 4.4. She was documented at Evansville, Ind., into 1892, maybe later. U.S. Inspectors rated her as a "passenger boat."

1837 EMMA LOGAN

Stw p wh b. Pittsburgh, Pa., 1865. 76 tons. Engines, 10½'s- 3½ ft. One boiler, 38" dia. by 18 ft. She made trips to New Orleans towing produce boats. Sank and lost in heavy ice on Feb. 16, 1872.

1838 EMMA MCSWEENY

Stw p sh b. New Orleans, La., 1891. 107 x 20 x 4.2. Engines, 10½'s- 3½ ft. In 1896 in New Orleans-Grand Isle run, Capt. John Parker, master. She left New Orleans Tuesdays and Saturdays via Company canal and Barataria. In January 1898 sold to a Mexican firm by R.W. Wilmot.

1839 EMMA MARIE

Stw p-tb wh b. Catlettsburg, Ky., 1906 using much equipment from *TELEPHONE* (b. Knoxville, Tenn., 1894, see). 93 x 15 x 2.4. Engines, 8"- 32" stroke. One boiler, 42" x 16 ft. Ran through September 1908, maybe later, a combination packet-towboat.

1840 EMMA MAY

Stw pl wh Operated in the Louisville, Ky., area in 1890s. Small, single deck, one stack.

1841 EMMA UHL

Stw ferry wh b. Marietta, Oh., 1880. 72 x 18 x 3.8. Operated Marietta-Williamstown owned by the Uhl family of Williamstown. Retired when her successor, *PIONEER CITY,* was built, in 1903.

1842 EMMA WATTS

Stw p wh b. Paducah, Ky., 1853. 111 tons. On a trip up Wabash River March 1853 was sunk in collision with *HERMANN,* raised. Was taken to Mobile, Ala., and registered there 1854. Snagged and lost at Mobile, Sept. 22, 1858.

1843 EMORY CITY

Stw p wh b. Kingston, Tenn. (year?) 97.57 tons. Owned by Capt. Jacob Fritts and Col. R.K. Byrd. There was no town on the Emory River when this boat was built and so named. Her machinery went to the *P. DICKINSON* (see).

1844 EMPEROR

SW p wh b. Jeffersonville, Ind., by Howard, 1848. 397 tons. 240 x 32 x 8. In the New Orleans-Vicksburg trade, Capt. M.W. Jenks, 1850, same 1851. New Orleans-Bayou Sara, Capt. J.A. Cotton, 1852. Same, Capt. Landry, 1854, teamed with *LAUREL HILL* (see). Sold to Mobile in 1854. Lost there, July 1, 1856.

1845 EMPEROR

Stw p wh b. Murraysville, Va., 1863. 245 tons. Built for W.E. Gibson & Co., Aurora, Ind., and others. They sold one-fourth interest October 1864 to Capt. J.D. Parker who went master in Cincinnati-New Orleans trade. Same trade and master, 1866. Sank at or near Louisville 1866–1867 and raised by Capt. R.W. Dugan's *UNDERWRITER.* Mid-October 1868 sold to Capt. Wash Dickerson and repaired at Pomeroy, Oh. In 1871 owned by Capt. John A. Williamson operating on the lower Ohio. Sold that fall to Capt. G.W. Thompson and others to run Marietta-Cincinnati trade. That November Thompson chartered her to the Metropolitan Circus Co., to tour the south with a circus. She was dismantled and became the wharfboat at Parkersburg, W. Va.

1846 EMPIRE

SW p wh b. New Albany, Ind., 1845. 260 x 32 x 7. Engines, 22's- 10 ft. Four boilers, each 42" dia. by 32 ft. Paddlewheels 32 ft. dia. working 15 ft. buckets. Capt. B.L. Elliott, master; Mr. Chiles and J.M. Moore, clerks when new. Ran Louisville-New Orleans. Sank on the Louisville Falls, upbound, Jan. 16, 1849.

1847 EMPIRE

SW p wh b. New Albany, Ind., 1849. 245 x 33.5 x 7.2. Engines, 22's- 9 ft. Three boilers, each 42" dia. by 32 ft. Built by Tellon & Co. Machinery by Phillips, Hise & Co. Cabin by Story & Hart. Capt. C. Meekin came out on her in Louisville-New Orleans trade. Retired in 1852.

1848 EMPIRE

Stw p wh b. California, Pa., 1854. 152 x 29.5 x 3.6. 152 tons. First owners were A.S. Shepherd, Pittsburgh, and George Doyle, Steubenville, Oh. She was sold to Mobile, Ala., owned 1855 by Cox, Brainard & Co., Capt. Charles Miller, master. Came back to the Mississippi River 1856 owned by Wm. Underwood and A. Palacio, Portland, Ky., and Wm. G. Underwood and J.B. Russell, New Albany, Ind. She was downbound through the chute at Island 37, hit a snag and was lost, Aug. 15, 1856. The *FALLS CITY* brought freight and passengers to Memphis.

1849 EMPIRE

Stw p wh b. Cincinnati, Oh., 1863, originally named *JENNIE HUBBS* (see). Renamed *EMPIRE* on Jan. 27, 1867. Ran Louisville-Memphis, Capt. Hicks King. She laid up for fog Dec. 27, 1868, near Natchez at 5:00 A.M. A large tree toppled from a caving bank and wrecked her. Passengers and crew got ashore and erected tents for shelter until aid came.

1850 EMPIRE

Prop freight boat b. Akron, Oh., 1864. 70 tons. Handled produce boats, probably out of Evansville, Ind. Downbound from Louisville to New Orleans with produce January 1868 below Cairo and collided with *J.N. KELLOGG.* Was raised and brought to Cairo on Jan. 8, 1868, dismantled.

1851 EMPIRE

Ferry wh b. Middleport, Oh., 1865. 12 tons. Operated between Middleport and Clifton teamed up with the *CLIFTON.* In 1872 owned at Proctorville, Oh. 65 x 14 x 2.5. In 1874 owned by Joseph F. Hannan and M.W. Davis, Ironton, Oh.

1852 EMPIRE CITY

Stw p wh b. California, Pa., 1854. 150 x 34.5 x 5.6. 260 tons. First owned by James Vandergrift, Isaac Hamilton, C.P. Caughey, Samuel Barr, Jr., and William H. Stackhouse, of Pittsburgh, and David G. Mulford, New York. Capt P.S. Mulford, first master. Ran Pittsburgh-St. Louis until the outbreak of the war, then commanded by Capt. Ben Way, Wellsville, Oh. Sold to Capt. Jacob Hazlep, St. Louis. She was in U.S. service as a transport 1862–1865, Capt. Hazlep in charge. Lost in ice at St. Louis, Jan. 12, 1866.

1853 EMPIRE PARISH

SW p wh b. New Albany, Ind., 1859. 170 x 32 x 6. Running New Orleans to Lower Coast and Quarantine Station twice weekly, Capt. R. Baldwin, 1859. Owned 1861 by New Orleans & Plaquemine Steamboat Association, Capt. Alexander Grant, Jr., master. In 1862 running New Orleans-Baton Rouge, owned by William J. Reid, New Orleans, Capt. Eugene Morris. Also ran New Orleans-Balize-South-

West Pass and Lower Coast, Capt. A. Grant. Lost in the wharf fire at New Orleans May 28, 1864, when nine steamers burned.

1854 EMPIRE STATE

SW p wh b. West Elizabeth, Pa., 1849. 303 tons. 182 x 36 x 7.3. Engines, 20's- 6½ ft. Three boilers. Dismantled 1857.

1855 EMPRESS

Stw p wh b. Marietta, Oh., by Knox, 1849. 136 tons. Ran Zanesville-Pittsburgh, Capt. George W. Cox, 1849-1852. Snagged and lost below Cincinnati, June 20, 1853.

1856 EMPRESS

SW p wh b. Jeffersonville, Ind., 1850. 304 tons. 179.7 x 28 x 6.3. Went to Mobile, Ala., she was returned to New Orleans in 1856, then owned by Robert S. Kirk, Mobile (¾) and her commander, Capt. John C. Graeff. Sold September 1857 to Capt. William Risher, Concordia Parish, La. Burned and lost at Algiers, La., on June 29, 1858.

1857 EMPRESS

SW p wh b. Jeffersonville, Ind., by Howard, 1853. 285 x 34 x 7.5. 692 tons. Ran Louisville-New Orleans. After Capt. Edward T. Sturgeon sold the *ECLIPSE* (see) he was master of this boat until the *DIANA* came out December 1857. Capt. G.W. Norton replaced him on the *EMPRESS*. Dismantled 1860.

1858 EMPRESS

SW p wh b. Madison, Ind., 1861. 854 tons. Ran St. Louis-New Orleans until the war broke out and then was impressed to U.S. service. In April 1862 she left St. Louis with nurses, hospital supplies, etc., and went to the Tennessee River where she landed alongside the *IMPERIAL* which then was being converted into a floating hospital. Returned with 900 wounded to St. Louis. Capt. John Molloy was decapitated as he stepped from his texas stateroom on Aug. 10, 1863, by a Rebel cannonball. She was rounding to land at Island 34 on Oct. 28, 1864, when she struck a snag, sank, and broke in two.

1859 ENDEAVOR

Stw p wh b. Freedom, Pa., 1854. 200 tons. Advertised Pittsburgh-Memphis, Capt. May, January 1855. Sank the *CALEDONIA* after colliding with her, Feb. 22, 1855. Burned and lost at Pittsburgh, June 14, 1859.

1860 ENDEAVOR

SW p ih b. Cincinnati, Oh., 1871. 173.6 x 41.8 x 7.1. Originally named *JOHN T. MOORE,* see. The *MOORE* was a sternwheeler, and was lengthened to become 234.8 x 41.8 x 7.1, and was documented thereafter as a side-wheeler. The lengthening and conversion took place somewhere between 1886-1892. She was still documented at New Orleans in 1896.

1861 ENERGY

SW p wh b. Hartford City, W. Va., 1868. 75 tons. Came out in the Gallipolis-Syracuse daily trade along with the *SALLIE V.* She was dismantled 1869 and equipment went to building the side-wheel *ORIOLE* (see).

1862 ENOLA

Stw p wh Undocumented. b. about 1900, 38 x 7. Capt. A.D. Elliott, St. Marys, W. Va., owned her during the local oil boom in that region. Once on high water he had her up Middle Island Creek 15 miles, and often ascended the Creek six miles with passengers and freight.

1863 ENOS TAYLOR

Stw p wh b. Higginsport, Oh., 1893. 116 x 20 x 3.5. Engines, 10's- 3½ ft. One boiler 40" dia. by 20 ft. Built by Capt. Robert Taylor of Higginsport, and named for a son. He ran her briefly Madison, Ind.-Monterey, Ky., up Kentucky River. Delivered new barges built at Madison for the U.S. to St. Louis and Natchez fall 1895. Ran Gallipolis-Huntington several years. Capt. E.E. Eisenbarth bought her in February 1902 and towed his showboat with her through the 1904 season, then sold her to the Bruns-Bokersox Lumber Co., Shawneetown, Ill., to tow logs out of Wabash and Saline rivers. Burned at De Koven, Ky., Mar. 15, 1912.

1864 ENQUIRER

Prop p wh b. Covington, Ky., 1877. Originally named *RAPID TRANSIT* (see). Registered as *ENQUIRER* at Cincinnati in 1886.

1865 ENQUIRER

Stw p wh b. Catlettsburg, Ky., 1907. 94.5 x 20.7 x 4.4. Ran as a packet on Big Sandy River when new, Capt. J.M. Hopkins. Later was a towboat. Sold to Dardanelle Lumber Co., in Arkansas December 1915 and was renamed *CITY OF DARDANELLE.*

1866 ENSIGN

Prop p wh b. Cincinnati, Oh., 1897. 41.7 x 12 x 3.8. In December 1901 was running three trips a day Gallipolis-Middleport on the Ohio River. Documented at Vicksburg, 1908.

1867 ENTERPRISE

SW p wh b. Zanesville, Oh., 1848. 199 tons. Capt. Stephen Bishop operated her on trips from Zanesville to Cincinnati and New Orleans, 1848-1849. Briefly in Pittsburgh-Zanesville trade in 1849. She was the largest boat on the Muskingum in her day. Burned and lost in the Licking River, Ky., May 1850.

1868 ENTERPRISE

Stw p wh b. Pittsburgh, Pa., 1849. 38 tons. Sank and lost in the Wabash River, Ind., Nov. 20, 1849.

1869 ENTERPRISE

Stw p wh b. Brownsville, Pa., 1852, originally named *AMERICA* (see). Renamed at New Orleans February 1862, owned by Stephen K. Fowler of that city, with O.A. Pitfield, master. She carried two masts. Went to Confederate service in 1861.

1870 ENTERPRISE

SW ferry wh b. Parkersburg, Va., 1856. 61 tons. Off the lists 1863.

1871 ENTERPRISE

Stw p wh b. St. Anthony, Minn., 1857. 130 x 22. Built by Capt. Augustus R. Young and sold prior to completion to Thomas Moulton who ran her St. Anthony-Sauk Rapids 1859–1861. Sold 1863 to Capts. W.F. and P.S. Davidson who skidded her around St. Anthony Falls and ran her as a freight boat in the Davidson Line, St. Paul-La Crosse. Hit the Rock Island bridge in May 1866, Capt. H. Sperlman, stove and sank. Sold south, and ran New Orleans-Shreveport, Capt. H.L. Lee in February 1868.

1872 ENTERPRISE

Stw p wh b. Wausau, Wis., 1861. 26 tons. She had to pass down over a considerable waterfall at Stevens Point, negotiate many rapids and innumerable shoals to get to the Mississippi. Snagged and lost below Red Wing, Minn., on Oct. 18, 1865.

1873 ENTERPRISE

Prop p wh b. Portsmouth, Oh., 1863. 54 tons. Probably towed produce boats south. Off the lists 1866.

1874 ENTERPRISE

Stw p wh b. Browning, Ill., 1864. 159.5 x 33 x 4.9. Operated on the Upper Mississippi until 1868 when she went to New Orleans, Capt. H.L. Lee. In 1870 running New Orleans-Shreveport, Capt. Charles Thorn, master, with D.E. Grove, clerk. Dismantled 1871 and hull used as a barge.

1875 ENTERPRISE

SW ferry wh b. Guyandotte, W. Va., 1866. 37 tons. Off the lists in 1873.

1876 ENTERPRISE

Ferry wh b. Portland, Oh., 1875. 36 tons. Documented 1876.

1877 ENTERPRISE

Ferry wh b. Algiers, La., 1880. 270.1 x 40.7 x 9. Still listed 1886.

1878 ENVOY

SW p wh b. Jeffersonville, Ind., 1848. 113 tons. Burned and lost at Matagorda Bay, Tex., Oct. 17, 1850.

1879 ENVOY

Stw p wh b. West Elizabeth, Pa., 1852. 178 tons. Collided with *JANE FRANKLIN* in November 1852, sank. On the Upper Mississippi in 1857–1858. Lost in collision with *MILWAUKEE* at Coon Slough, July 21, 1858.

1880 EOLIAN

Stw p wh b. Brownsville, Pa., 1855. 178 tons. Ran on the Monongahela and made trips up the Youghiogheny. In 1857–1859 was a Minnesota River packet, Capt. Troy. Off the lists in 1863.

1881 EQUALITY

Stw p wh b. Paducah, Ky., 1860. 90 tons. Snagged and lost at Golconda, Ill., May 11, 1861.

1882 EQUATOR

Stw p wh b. Beaver, Pa., 1853. 61 tons. Was on the Upper Mississippi 1855–1856 running out of St. Paul, and on Minnesota River in 1857. She was lost in the "great storm" on Lake St. Croix, April 1858, Capt. Asa B. Green. The pilots at the time were Charles Jewell and George B. Merrick.

1883 EQUINOX

SW p wh b. Monongahela, Pa., 1852. 296 tons. Ran Pittsburgh-New Orleans and other tramp trades, Capt. Sam Dean, and Capt. George Rowley. Dismantled 1859.

1884 ERA

Stw p wh b. Freedom, Pa., 1856. 123 x 23.5 x 3. 78 tons. Owned by Capt. Isaac H. Kouns, Shreveport, La. First master, Capt. Benjamin Kouns. Ran New Orleans-Red River. Snagged and lost on Red River, May 12, 1859.

1885 ERA NO. 2

Stw p wh b. Freedom, Pa., 1857. 124 x 27 x 4.10. Owned by Capt. Isaac H. Kouns, Shreveport, La. First master, Capt. A. Bayless. Ran New Orleans-Red River. In 1859 the owners became George L. Kouns, John Kouns, Benjamin Kouns (all of New Orleans), and William T. Scovell, Ironton, Oh. Capt. G.L. Kouns was master at that time. Sold May 7, 1860, to Capt. Thomas Moore, Covington, Ky. Went to Confederate documentation.

1886 ERA NO. 1

SW p wh b. Algiers, La., 1855. 126 x 25 x 4. Originally named *EFFORT* (see). When the original *ERA* was lost in 1859 the Kouns family bought *EFFORT*, renamed her *ERA NO. 1*. She went to Confederate documentation in 1861.

1887 ERA NO. 3

Stw p wh b. Freedom, Pa., 1858. 129 x 28.3 x 4.3. Enrolled at New Orleans July 19, 1859, owned by Benjamin B. Kouns, John Kouns, and George L. Kouns, with Capt. Benjamin B. Kouns, master. She was sold Aug. 2, 1860, to Capt. William Jenkins, Galveston, Tex. Was captured as a Confederate steamer, sold back to the Kouns Line, which renamed her *NEW ERA NO. 3*.

1888 ERA NO. 4

Stw p wh b. Pittsburgh, Pa., 1859. 134 x 22.2 x 3.5. Original owners were John Kouns, George L. Kouns, Benjamin B. Kouns, and W.F. Scovell, all of New Orleans. First master was Capt. W.F. Scovell. Ownership transferred in October 1860 to Red River Packet Co., George L. Kouns, pres. Went to Confederate service in 1861.

1889 ERA NO. 5

Stw p wh b. Pittsburgh, Pa., 1860. Ran New Orleans-Red River, Capt. Noah Scovell. She was captured by *QUEEN OF THE WEST* on Red River near Atchafalaya on Feb. 11, 1863. Lost soon thereafter.

1890 ERA NO. 6

Stw p wh b. Pittsburgh, Pa., 1860. Owned by the Kouns Line. Burned and lost on Arkansas River at Van Buren, Ark., Dec. 27, 1862.

1891 ERA NO. 7

Stw p wh b. Freedom, Pa., 1859, and first named *INDIANOLA* (see). The Kouns family bought *INDIANOLA* on Sept. 26, 1860, ran her New Orleans-Red River and also on the Ouachita to Camden. Apparently the change of name to *ERA NO. 7* was not documented. She was snagged and lost 20 miles below Warrenton, Miss., Feb. 24, 1863.

1892 ERA NO. 8

SW p wh b. Madison, Ind., 1867. 121.9 x 25.3 x 4. Originally owned by Red River Packet Co., G.L. Kouns, pres. First master Capt. S.H. Kouns. Sold Feb. 25, 1869, to Capt. W.H. Blessing, who went master. The minority stockholders were L.A. Campbell and Capt. John W. Cannon, both of New Orleans. Removed from documentation in 1882.

1893 ERA NO. 9

Stw p wh b. Madison, Ind., 1868. 145.6 x 36.8 x 3.8. Engines 12's- 4 ft. Two boilers. Owned by Red River Packet Co. and first master was Capt. George L. Kouns. Ran New Orleans-Red River. Collided with and sank the *ERA NO. 10* at the mouth of Red River on Dec. 17, 1868 and collided with and sank the *TEXAS* on Sept. 1, 1870 on Red River. Sold in Jan. 1873 to Eugene Robinson of circus fame who also owned the Opera House in Memphis. She is reported as arriving in Mobile on Oct. 25, 1875, Capt. Stewart. At a U.S. marshal sale at Cincinnati, July, 1876, *ERA NO. 9* sold to George Williams for $2,000.

1894 ERA NO. 10

Stw p wh b. Madison, Ind., 1868. 136 x 30.8 x 5. Originally owned by John Kouns and W.T. Scovell of New Orleans, I.H. Kouns of Lawrence County, Oh., and James Willard of Ohio. First master, Capt. I.H. Kouns. Ran in the Kouns Line, New Orleans-Red River. Sold at a U.S. marshal sale at New Orleans, June 1873 to Capt. T.L. Taylor, who ran her New Orleans-Boeuf River. Capt. Tom L. Taylor was master, J.P. Mohr, clerk. During her first season she collided with the *ERA NO. 9* at the mouth of Red River and was sunk, this on Dec. 17, 1868. Burned and lost at Rayville, La., January 1892.

Ed. Note: There also were Kouns packets named *ELEVENTH ERA, TWELFTH ERA,* and *THIRTEENTH ERA*; also *NEW ERA* (see).

1895 ERASTUS WELLS

SW harborboat sh b. Grafton, Ill., 1907. 188.5 x 32.2 x 7. Engines, 20's- 6 ft. Four boilers. Operated by the City of St. Louis, and based there. Capt. Tom Garrison was master in 1908. Capt. Roy Parker was harbormaster in 1927, Capt. C.H. Smith, pilot. Sold at public sale at St. Louis, August 1932 for $6,100. Bought by Commodore Edwin C. Koenig, St. Louis, rebuilt and renamed *CITY OF ST. LOUIS* (see).

1896 ESPERANZA

Stw p wh b. Brownsville, Pa., 1871. 177 x 33.5 x 5. Engines, 15's- 5 ft. Three boilers each 46" by 26 ft. She was completed in March 1871 and was announced for St. Louis and the Missouri River, Capt. Dunlevy commanding, and John B. Coombs in the office. Went south in winter and ran New Orleans-Red River. In fall of 1873 lengthened at St. Louis to 228 ft., and got engines 16's- 6 ft. Was operating in the Cincinnati-New Orleans trade in 1874. Burned at Prophets Island, Mississippi River, Oct. 21, 1874. She took fire on the aft starboard guard, was run ashore, and all escaped safely except the chambermaid.

1897 ESSEX

U.S. gunboat, recess wheel, wh b. St. Louis, Mo., 1861 by enlarging hull of former snagboat *NEW ERA* b. New Albany, Ind., 1856 (see). She measured 198.5 x 58 x 6.8. Engines, 23's- 6 ft. During the engagement at Fort Henry a shot exploded the center boiler resulting in 32 casualties. The pilot, James McBride, was found dead at the wheel, his right hand clutching the stopping bell pull. His body was returned to Cincinnati for burial. She was sold at the war's conclusion, lay around at Cincinnati fall of 1866, and in December 1870 the hull was burned on shore near Mound City to recover scrap.

1898 ESSEX

Prop p wh b. Zanesville, Oh., 1863. 56 tons. Owned by Capt. Bill Linton and ran Zanesville-Dresden 1863-1865. Dismantled 1865.

1899 ESTELLA

SW p wh b. Shousetown, Pa., 1862. 205 x 35 x 6. Engines, 20's- 6 ft. Three boilers. Hull by E. & N. Porter, and machinery by James Rees. Built for Capt. William B. Hazlett and others. Trials were made Mar. 11, 1862, and Hazlett sold her at Cincinnati May 14 to Capt. John P. Keiser and others, St. Louis. She burned in the great steamboat fire there on Oct. 27, 1862.

1900 ESTOLA

Stw p wh b. Charleston, W. Va., 1890. 122 x 20.2 x 4. Engines, 11's- 3 ft. Two boilers, each 38" by 18 ft. Owned by John A. Carr, Charleston. Came in collision with *BAXTER* at Dego, Kanawha River, Dec. 6, 1900, at 6:00 P.M. and was sunk. Capt. George E. Colville was in charge. Was raised, rebuilt, and renamed *CALVERT* (see).

1901 ETHEL

Stw p wh b. Olivier, La., 1894. 90.5 x 27 x 3.8. A picture exists of her taken at Abbeville, La., 1896.

1902 ETTA J.

Prop yacht sh b. Charleston, W. Va., by Ward, 1901. Originally *UNIQUE* (see). She was owned as *ETTA J.* in 1929 by Northwestern Terminals Co., Evansville, Ind., Capt. Monroe Smock. In May 1932 was tied up in Green River near Curdsville, Ky., in charge of McDonald Bros. Fred Smith, president of Dixie Greyhound Bus Lines, had her in 1903. Originally a steam yacht, she was converted to diesel by the U.S. Engineers. Delta Transportation Co., of Memphis had her 1935–1939, maybe longer.

1903 EUDORA

SW p wh b. Cincinnati, Oh., 1847. 420 tons. Ran St. Louis to Ouachita River. Burned at St. Louis in the great wharf fire, May 17, 1849.

1904 EUGENE

SW p wh b. Parkersburg, Va., 1860. 298 tons. 183 x 32 x 5.5. Engines, 20's- 7 ft. Ran in the Louisville & Henderson Mail Line, Capt. Anson Ballard; later Capt. A.M. Davidson. She made a special trip Louisville to Savannah (on Tennessee River) in April 1862 with U.S. supplies, and her clerk counted 107 steamboats between Fort Henry and Savannah. Loaded out at Louisville for Memphis June 11, 1862, first packet bound there since the Battle of Memphis was fought. Chartered to two pilots, she made a New Orleans trip, struck the wreck of the *ELIZA* at Osceola, near Fort Pillow, Nov. 14, 1862. Life loss was placed at 15.

1905 EUGENE

SW p wh b. Brownsville, Pa., 1883. 113.7 x 28 x 3.5. She was owned by Shelby & Perkins, Henderson, Ky., when she flopped over at Mount Vernon, Ind., on May 10, 1894, Capt. Harry Campbell in charge. She had been handling corn out of Wabash River. Crew jumped over on a barge she had in tow.

1906 EUGENE

Stw p wh b. Belle Vernon, Pa. (hull), and completed at Pittsburgh, 1887. 170 x 34 x 4.4. Rees engines, 12's- 5 ft. Two boilers, each 48″ by 20 ft. with six 10″ flues. Ran in Memphis-Arkansas River trade. She was towed back to Pittsburgh in March 1898 by the *ALICE BROWN* and dismantled at the Rees shop. Parts were used building the *LUCILLE NOWLAND* (see).

1907 EUNICE

Stw p wh b. Brownsville, Pa., 1855. 231 tons. Built for Capt. Pres Roberts and others of Steubenville, Oh. In 1858 Capt. R.M. Hunter, master, with Wm. B. Collier, clerk. Ran Wheeling-Louisville in 1860, Capt. John McLure as master. In May that year she was caught in a tornado near Vevay, Ind., with C.M. Holloway on watch. The sash left the pilothouse, and the frame of the pilothouse toppled to the hurricane roof. Pilot Holloway was caught by heavy timbers and had to be extricated, but was unharmed. The roof was loaded with buggies, all swept off. This same storm wrecked the Commercial Building, Fourth and Race, Cincinnati, then new. On Apr. 24, 1861, she was in collision with the *COMMODORE PERRY* near Ashland, Ky., and was sunk, nobody hurt. Capt. John McLure was master at the time, and the boat was in U.S. service. She was raised and in July 1861 she led as flagship a fleet of 12 steamboats up the Kanawha, which resulted in the promotion of McLure as commodore of the Kanawha U.S. Fleet, which he held until summer of 1862, when he was ordered to the Tennessee River for war duty on boats. The *EUNICE* was wrecked at Stout's Landing, Kentucky side, above Brush Creek, Ohio River. The wreck was reported October 1866.

1908 EUPHRATES

Stw p wh b. Freedom, Pa., 1848. 136 tons. Stranded and lost at New Albany, Ind., Oct. 30, 1850.

1909 EUREKA

SW p wh b. Cincinnati, Oh., 1845. 110 tons. Snagged and lost at McNiel Bar, Ala., Nov. 6, 1847.

1910 EUREKA

Stw p wh b. Elizabethtown, Pa., 1847. 112 tons. Lost in collision with *CORINNE* on the Tombigbee River, Ala., Nov. 20, 1851.

1911 EUREKA

Prop freight boat wh b. Aberdeen, Oh., 1862. 42 tons. She once brought 300 brls. of flour to Pittsburgh, having loaded it at Pomeroy. "The *EUREKA* is about as long as one of our Allegheny River keel-boats," said the Pittsburgh *Gazette,* "though she will carry a good bit more freight." Out of documentation 1876.

1912 EUREKA

SW ferry wh b. Freedom, Pa., 1866. 65 tons. Operated between Martins Ferry, Oh., and the Top Mill in Wheeling. Off the lists in 1880.

1913 EUREKA

Stw p wh b. Madison, Ind., 1873. 194 tons. She was built for Cincinnati-Kentucky River trade and came out new in September 1872, Capt. King. That November she was advertised to leave Cincinnati for New Orleans but was tied up at Cincinnati by creditors. Still in the Cincinnati-Kentucky River trade in 1875. Running on Ouachita River 1877.

1914 EUROPA

SW p wh b. Cincinnati, Oh., 1849. 176 x 31 x 6.8. Three boilers. Capt. Henry A. Jones of Cincinnati was master and part owner. She was at Hawesville, Ky., the night the *REINDEER* exploded, Mar. 13, 1854, and helped land the wrecked boat. In November 1857 sold to Thomas L. Basley, New Orleans. Lost at Augusta, Ark., in 1858.

1915 EVA

Ferry wh b. Ironton, Oh., 1869. 35 tons. She ferried at that place. Still documented in 1876.

1916 EVA

Stw p wh b. Cincinnati, Oh., 1869. 100.8 x 15.8 x 2.8. In 1870 owned by Sam Block, Trinity, La., and Francis H. Murray, Yazoo City, Miss.; Block was master. In 1877 in New Orleans-Lower Coast trade, Capt. John Taylor, master. In 1879 in New Orleans-Upper Coast trade, Capt. Charles DeDouchel, master.

1917 EVA ALMA

Stw p wh b. Pomeroy, Oh., 1898. 111.2 x 16.6 x 3.1. Owned when new by Stella J. Vanzant, Kyger, Oh., with Capt. W.R. Haptonstall as master. Owned entire after June 7, 1899 by Capt. W.R. Haptonstall.

1918 EVA EVERT

Stw ferry wh b. Vevay, Ind., 1900. 61 x 29 x 4. Still listed in 1908, perhaps longer.

1919 EVANGELINE

Ferry wh b. Berwick, La., 1881. 53.5 x 21.2 x 3.5. Probably operated at Morgan City, La. Still listed in 1886, maybe longer.

1920 EVANSVILLE

Stw p wh b. West Brownsville, Pa., 1854. 155 tons. In 1860 operating Cincinnati-Carrollton, Ky., Capt. Neal. Snagged and lost at Memphis, Tenn., Jan. 28, 1864.

1921 EVANSVILLE

Stw p wh b. Evansville, Ind., 1869. 109.2 x 26 x 3.9. Equipment from *ADA LYON* (see) used in construction. Ran Evansville-Green River, owned by Green & Barren River Navigation Co. Capt. W.S. Vanmeter was master in 1869. Sold in 1880 when new *EVANSVILLE* was built. Went to the Upper Mississippi, there owned by Matt Clark Transportation Co., Stillwater, Minn., Capt. Edward Root, master. This firm failed, and the boat was sold at a U.S. marshal sale to John Robson of the Lansing Lumber Co. Capt. Walter Blair bought her 1889 from them and used her as a raftboat. Dismantled her after two seasons and used machinery and equipment in building the *VOLUNTEER* (see). Blair operated as the Le Claire Navigation Co., and had Capt. Thomas Witherow as master.

1922 EVANSVILLE

Stw p wh b. Cincinnati, Oh., 1880. 120.2 x 30 x 5.2. Engines, 14's- 5 ft. Two boilers, each 40″ by 26 ft., two 14″ flues. Paddlewheel 17 ft. dia. working 21 ft. buckets. Engines by C.T. Dumont. Elias Ealer built the cabin, 22 staterooms. Owned by the Evansville, Green & Barren River Navigation Co., which also owned the locks and dams on Green River. Capt. Elmore Bewley, first master. Sold July 1890 to Capt. Cole Boren and others for Cairo-Tiptonville trade but was returned to Green River that November. In March 1895 sold to Capt. John F. Klein and ran in the Wheeling-Clarington trade about six weeks. Again returned to Green River where Capt. Abbott Veatch commanded. Was renamed *CRESCENT CITY* (see) in 1897 and retained that name in Green River until completely rebuilt at Madison, Ind., in 1906, at which time she was documented as a new boat.

1923 EVANSVILLE

Stw p wh b. Madison, Ind., 1906. 120.2 x 30 x 5.2. This was a rebuilding program as outlined above. Owned by Evansville & Bowling Green Packet Co. Officers of the company in 1912: Lee Howell, president; T.A. Williams, superintendent; Jeff H. Williams, agent at Evansville; Lucian Graham, agent at Bowling Green. (See *S&D Reflector,* March 1978 for complete scheduling.) Sank at Aberdeen, Ky., July 11, 1919, and quickly raised. Burned at Bowling Green, Ky., July 25, 1931. Your scribe visited the wharf at Bowling Green in company with Courtney Ellis, fall of 1949, and found a huge mound of earth containing the bones of the old *EVANSVILLE.* Her wreckage had been scooped out of the river and for all effect she was buried. Her whistle went to the towboat *TOM WILLIAMS.* She carried a "mockingbird whistle" also upon which tunes were played by pilot Gene Lunn.

1924 EVENING STAR

Prop p wh b. Rochester, Pa., 1862. 25 tons. Off the lists in 1867.

1925 EVENING STAR

SW p wh b. Freedom, Pa., 1864. 343 tons. She was completed at Wellsville, Oh., where the cabin was built and machinery placed. Left Wellsville in June 1864 in charge of Capt. Murphy, formerly of the *MILL BOY.* Went to St. Louis to enter the Missouri River trade. She was close by the *W.R. CARTER* when that packet exploded (see) in January 1866, taking many of the survivors to Vicksburg. Running on the Missouri in 1867. Burned and lost at St. Louis, Mo., Aug. 24, 1869.

1926 EVERGREEN

Stw p wh b. Parkersburg, W. Va., 1902. 119.5 x 22.5 x 3.5. She had compound engines. One boiler, 43″ by 20 ft. Much equipment from the *T.D. DALE* (see). Built for Capt. Gordon C. Greene. First ran Winfield-Charleston on Kanawha River, Capt. Ben Wright. Later ran Gallipolis-Charleston, Capt. Bert Higgenbottom, who later was mayor of Nitro, W. Va. She hit a lock wall at No. 7, Kanawha River, late December or early January 1912–13 and caved in one side of her hull. Dismantled at Point Pleasant in 1916 when the *CHRIS GREENE* (first) was built to succeed her.

1927 EVERGREENE

Stw p sh b. Dubuque, Iowa, 1923 as the ferry *KIWANIS* (see). 140 x 29 x 4.2. Engines, 10's- 6 ft. stroke. Two boilers. Bought by the Greene Line in 1930 as *KIWANIS.* Rebuilt at Dravo's marine ways, Neville Island, Pa., in 1936 and name changed to *EVERGREENE.* She ran Cincinnati-

Huntington from June 10, 1933 until Feb. 2, 1943. Capt. Arch Edgington was first master in the trade, and Capt. Wilsie Miller was the last. Sold to Capt. John L. Beatty, Cincinnati, June 1948. Again sold to Merchant Paving Co., which converted her to a dredge.

1928 EXCEL

Stw p wh b. McKeesport, Pa., 1851. 150 x 27 x 5. Engines, 12's- 4 ft. Two boilers. Ran on Cumberland River for W.P. Henry & Co. Then went to the Illinois River owned by a Mr. Miller, St. Louis. Capt. Ben Beasley ran her later Memphis-Hatchie River, and on the Missouri. Snagged and lost in Osage Chute, Missouri River, Mar. 23, 1856.

1929 EXCEL

Stw p wh b. Middleport, Oh., 1901. 95.4 x 14.3 x 2.8. Engines, 8"- 26". One boiler. Came out new in the Millwood-Middleport trade, Capt. S.A. Devinney, clerk. Ran Parkersburg-Creston on the Little Kanawha, J.J. Wright. Sold 1907 to Albert Monteith who converted her to towing and renamed her *ALMA*.

1930 EXCELSIOR

SW p wh b. Brownsville, Pa., 1849. 172 tons. Built for Capt. James Ward and others for the St. Louis-St. Paul trade. Ran there regularly through 1857, maybe later. Off the lists in 1861.

1931 EXCELSIOR

SW p wh b. Cincinnati, Oh., 1858. 141 tons. Off the lists, 1860.

1932 EXCELSIOR

SW ferry wh b. Cincinnati, Oh., 1864. 155 tons. Ran Portland-New Albany, Capt. John Mitchell. The *JOHN M. MARTIN* was her partner ferry, also *THOMAS CONNER, RUSH, BEN SOUTH.* The New Albany Ferry Co., sold her March 1869 to Wm. Clancy and others of Pittsburgh and she went there. Sold to Memphis later, and was to the scene of the *W. R. ARTHUR* explosion in January 1871. Lost in ice at Memphis, Dec. 30, 1872.

1933 EXCHANGE

SW p wh b. Brownsville, Pa., 1849. 110 tons. Burned on Red River at Gordon's Landing, Oct. 21, 1855.

1934 EXCHANGE

Stw p wh b. Brownsville, Pa., 1852. 128 tons. Running New Orleans to Alexandria, La., on Red River, 1855, Capt. John C. Graeff, master. "Draws but 13 inches and freight will be delivered without detention." Snagged and lost on the White River, Ark., Jan. 13, 1858.

1935 EXCHANGE

Stw p wh b. Brownsville, Pa., 1862. 211 tons. 155.2 x 33.4 x 4.9. Engines, 16's- 4½ ft. Capt. John W. Anawalt built her and was the first master. Hull by Cox and Williams; engines by Snowden & Sons. Came out in the Pittsburgh-St. Louis trade, J.A. Bales, head clerk. Sold to the U.S. on Apr. 6, 1863, and retained her name throughout the war. In passing up the Mississippi in June 1864 she got 32 shots in her and was badly damaged. A shell exploded in the pilothouse, tore the clothes off the pilot, but strangely he was uninjured. She was landed at the foot of Island 82 and repaired. Sold Aug. 17, 1865, at Mound City, Ill., to Capt. W.G. Priest for $7,100. Renamed *TENNESSEE* on Sept. 4, 1865 (see), and was snagged and lost at Decatur, Neb., Apr. 25, 1869.

1936 EXCHANGE

Prop freight boat wh b. Belle Vernon, Pa., 1866. 91 tons. Ran in the Muskingum River, Capt. C. Krigbeaum. Appeared at Pittsburgh in mid-November 1866 and was noticed as the first propeller boat seen there with an upper cabin on her. Off the lists 1883.

1937 EXCHANGE

Stw p wh b. Brownsville, Pa., 1869. 159 x 33 x 4.5. Engines, 14's- 5 ft. Three boilers. Built by Capt. John L. Rhoads. Came out in the Pittsburgh-Cincinnati trade, Capt. A.C. McCallum, master, with John Dales, clerk. Capt. McCallum retired in November 1871, and Capt. Sam Shuman took his place with J.M. Vandergrift, clerk. In the spring of 1872 she was running Cincinnati-Guyandotte-Pomeroy, auspices of the Cincinnati, Big Sandy & Pomeroy Packet Co. Then back to the Pittsburgh-Cincinnati trade, Capt. Shuman. In 1876 sold to the White Collar Line and lengthened 31½ feet. They kept her in the Cincinnati-Pittsburgh trade with Capt. Will Kirker, master, and then Capt. George W. Keyes, with Will A. Maddy, clerk. Pilots included George Hughes, George Littleton, James Henderson, and William Abrams. The White Collar Line in 1878 put her in the Cincinnati-St. Louis trade. She burned at St. Louis on June 8, 1878. The *ROB ROY* was nearby and had to be cut loose to save her.

1938 EXCHANGE

SW p wh b. Oshkosh, Wis., 1870. 143 x 20 x 5.8. Engines, 10½'s- 3 ft. One boiler. Lost by sinking at Vermillion Bayou, La., Jan. 3, 1882.

1939 EXIT

SW p wh b. Carroll County, Miss., 1847. 120 x 20.2 x 6. Owned by James Medd and others, and later Capt. George Sweeney and others. Snagged and lost at Campti, La., Oct. 29, 1850.

1940 EXPANSION

Stw p wh b. Bismarck, N.D., 1900. 123 x 26 x 3.5. Owned by the Benton Packet Co. Capt. Grant Marsh was master-pilot for some time. Lost in ice at Bismarck on Mar. 13, 1910. Part of the hull was later used on the motor vessel *EXPANSION.*

1941 EXPORT

Stw p wh b. Hermann, Mo., 1900. 49.3 x 12.3 x 2.3. Built by Hugo Kropp to deliver beer and ice along the Gasconade and Osage rivers. Documented at Vicksburg, Miss., 1908.

1942 EXPORTER

Stw p wh b. Pittsburgh, Pa., 1872. Owned in part by the James Rees family. Ran between Cincinnati and New Orleans, Capt. John A. Williams, and later Capt. John D. Conway. In 1873 brought 5,341 bales of cotton into New Orleans on a single loading. Burned at New Orleans along with the *JOHN KYLE* and *CHARLES BODMAN* in April 1875. A daughter of James Rees Sr., was drowned while escaping the flames.

1943 EXPRESS

SW p wh b. West Elizabeth, Pa., 1850. 192 tons. The Adams Express Co. ran her Vevay-Madison in 1852 to connect with the new Madison & Indianapolis Railway. Went to the Missouri River later, and was snagged and lost in Spar Island, a short distance below Leavenworth, Kans., on July 15, 1855. Lytle reports this date as June 15, 1855.

1944 EXPRESS

SW p wh b. Belle Vernon, Pa., 1862. 200 x 32 x 6. Engines, 24's- 6 ft. Three boilers. She arrived at Keokuk, Iowa, on Apr. 19, 1862, with 300 sick and wounded Civil War soldiers, including four who had died. This was the first of the casualties to come to the Upper Mississippi. Sank near Manchester, Oh., while en route from Parkersburg to Louisville with troops of the 2nd Division of the Fifth Army Corps aboard; the river was dead low, and nobody hurt. Raised by the *UNDERWRITER*, Capt. R.W. Dugan. Settled down to the Wheeling-Parkersburg trade, Capt. Phil Anshutz, master, with E.J. Anshutz, clerk. Dismantled at Wheeling in 1870.

1945 EXPRESS

Stw p wh b. La Crosse, Wis., 1864. 29 tons. Off the lists in 1881.

1946 EXPRESS

SW ferry wh b. Mason City, W. Va., 1865. 30 tons. Operated Mason City-Pomeroy. Off the lists in 1873.

1947 EXPRESS NO. 2

SW p wh b. Wheeling, W. Va., 1870. 500.25 tons. Wheeling-Parkersburg trade, teamed up with the sidewheel *COURIER* (see). Came out new with Capt. Phil Anshutz, master, with E.J. Anshutz, clerk. This team was on her until the 1875 season closed. In 1876 Capt. A.B. Booth became master, with E.J. Anshutz as clerk. In 1877 H.C. Caldwell was clerk, and in 1878 Martin F. Noll replaced him. Dismantled in 1879 and the hull served as the wharfboat at Wheeling until the Crockard & Booth wharfboat was built at Moundsville in 1892. Her machinery and whistle went to the *ST. LAWRENCE* (see).

1948 EXPRESS MAIL

SW p wh b. Cincinnati, Oh., 1841. 164.7 x 25 x 6. 236 tons. Ran Pittsburgh-Cincinnati, Capt. S.J. Halderman, 1841-1843. Then to the St. Louis-New Orleans trade, Capt. William Kountz, master, Henry Ealer, pilot. In 1845 New Orleans-Red River, Capt. John Smoker, master. Also in 1845 Cincinnati-New Orleans, Capt. James Ellis. Snagged and lost at Campti, La., Apr. 27, 1846.

1949 EZRA PORTER

SW p wh b. Shousetown, Pa., 1866. 179 x 36 x 6.8. Engines, 17's- 6 ft. Three boilers, each 40″ x 24 ft. Largely owned by the Porter family of Shousetown, commanded by Capt. J.H. Porter. Ran Pittsburgh-Cincinnati-St. Louis. In the fall of 1867 ran five trips Pittsburgh-New Orleans. Was caught at Cairo upbound in ice and lay there three weeks in January 1868 with full cabin of passengers and a large trip of sugar, molasses and coffee all destined for Pittsburgh. In April 1868 made a trip New Orleans-Shreveport, Capt. H.L. Lee, master, J.H. Porter, clerk. Burned at Cincinnati on Aug. 16, 1868, along with the *PINE GROVE, DELAWARE,* and *POTOMAC* (all see).

F

1950 F. BARKSDALE

Stw p wh b. Jeffersonville, Ind., by Howard, 1884. 155 x 30.5 x 5.4. Two boilers. Run by the Parisot Line, Vicksburg-Yazoo River. Burned on the Yazoo at Hendrick's Landing, Miss., Dec. 15, 1888.

1951 F.A. GOEBEL

Stw p wh b. Freedom, Pa., 1886. Originally named *R.E. PHILLIPS* (see). The *PHILLIPS* sank in ice at the upper wharf, New Matamoras, Oh., in the winter of 1894. She was raised by her insurance company and the upper cabin removed. They sold her to Capt. Will Duffy, Marietta, Oh., who renamed her *F.A. GOEBEL* for a furniture man in Marietta. Charles Menges ran her in the Pittsburgh-Chartiers trade, 1896. In 1897 was chartered to Capt. William Weigel for the Pittsburgh-Elizabeth trade, Monongahela River. Sold April 1899 to Capt. W.O. Rhodes, Webster, Pa., who ran her Pittsburgh-Monongahela City through 1899. In April 1900 sold to William J. Duffy, Marietta, and ran Wheeling-Clarington briefly. Towed timber out of Big Sandy River 1901-1902. In 1904 Duffy went in equal shares with John Prudent, New Richmond, Oh. Later she went south and sank at Monroe, La., on Aug. 23, 1907.

1952 F.M. OWENS

Stw p wh b. Helena, Ark., 1910. 155 x 35.3 x 5. Engines, 14's- 6 ft. Two boilers, each 44″ by 22 ft. She was bought by Bradford Transportation Co., New Orleans, March 1911. Sank at Little Godel Bayou on Grand River between Plaquemine and Morgan City, La., in 35 feet, loaded with sugar, late January or early February 1915.

1953 F.M. STRECK

SW p wh b. Jeffersonville, Ind., 1844. 155 x 24.5 x 5.5. Ran

New Orleans-Bayou Sara, Capt. Ferdinand M. Streck, owner and master. In 1851 owned by Thomas W. Taber, New Orleans. He took William A. Chambers as a partner, and soon bowed out. Chambers ran her until sold April 1856 to Capt. James M. Skinner, New Orleans.

1954 F.W. BROOKS

Stw freight boat wh b. Burlington, Iowa, 1863. 99 tons. Sold July 20, 1867 at sheriff sale on the court house steps at St. Louis for $120 to the plaintiff, Christian Pinkepank. Had been owned by Henry A. Heuffner and William Retter. Place of build also given as Keokuk, Iowa.

1955 F.W. TUCKER

Stw p wh b. Black Rock, Ark., 1897. 98 x 20 x 4. Owned by Inman-Decker Packet Co., and ran on White, Black, and Current rivers. Out of service by 1904. Note: *F.W. TUCKER NO. 2* built at Black Rock in 1912 was a towboat.

1956 F.X. AUBREY

Stw p wh b. Brownsville, Pa., 1853. 247 tons. Ran St. Louis-St. Joseph, Capt. Ambrose Reeder. Capt. Grant Marsh made his first trip on the Missouri River aboard this one in 1854 with Capt. Reeder. After the *WM. GARVIN* sank, she finished out the 1859 season in the St. Louis-Chester trade, Capt. Alex Zeigler. Was sold to Capt. E.N. Johnson who took her to Pittsburgh, dismantled her, and used the machinery on the *ARAGO* (see).

1957 F.Y. BATCHELOR

Stw p wh b. Freedom, Pa. (hull), and completed at Pittsburgh, 1878. 180 x 30 x 3.5. Engines, 13's- 5 ft. Two boilers, 42" x 24 ft. with five 10" flues. Built at the McCaskey & Kerr yard, and Capt. C.W. Batchelor looked after building her. Built complete in 64 days. Machinery by Robert Lea. She was launched on Apr. 8, 1878, and on June 28 she arrived at Fort Custer on the Bighorn River, the only boat arriving there that season. Then she ran back to Fort Buford in quicker time than the *FAR WEST* had made it when carrying out the wounded from the Battle of Bighorn. Her record from Bismarck to Fort Buford was made in August 1878, beating the *RED CLOUD* record by eight hours, Capt. Grant Marsh, pilot. This was an upriver run, 55 hours 25 minutes, 307 miles. Struck rocks 16 miles below Forest City, S.D., in November 1879 and sank. Leighton & Jordan ran her until 1885 when she was sold to Benton Packet Co. Made her last trip to Fort Benton in 1890, Capt. Thomas Mariner, master, with Bob Wright and Ben Jewell, pilots. This was said to be the last commercial freight taken to the fort by steamboat. She worked around Bismarck after that, and was caught in winter quarters at Running Water, S.D., by ice, and was wrecked, this on Mar. 6, 1907. She was owned at the time by Capt. Jos. Leach, Jr., who had bought her in 1906.

1958 FAIRFIELD

Stw p wh b. Freedom, Pa., 1854. 159 tons. First home port, Nashville, Tenn. Went to Mobile, Ala., and was snagged and lost on the Alabama River, Oct. 13, 1858.

1959 FAIRFIELD

Prop p wh b. Chillicothe, Oh., 1864. 62 tons. Built canal boat style. Off the lists 1876.

1960 FAIRMOUNT

SW p wh b. Glasgow, Pa., 1846. 184 tons. Built and operated by the Poe and Ebert clan of Georgetown, Pa. Operated out of Pittsburgh to Louisville, Nashville, and St. Louis. While upbound St. Louis to Pittsburgh she sank on the Ohio River above Brandenburg, Ky., on May 13, 1850, and was lost.

1961 FAIR PLAY

SW p wh b. New Albany, Ind., 1859. 139 x 27 x 4.7. 162 tons. Owned and operated by Capt. George W. Carras, New Orleans. She was captured by U.S. forces on Aug. 18, 1862, with a load of rifles, etc., aboard, destined for the Rebel forces. The U.S. converted her into a tinclad and used her on the Ohio River based at Evansville, Ind., operating between Smithland and Louisville, Lieut. Leroy Fitch U.S.N. commanding. Sold to private owners Aug. 18, 1865, at Mound City, Ill. Purchaser was Capt. Charles C. Duncan, New Orleans, who changed her name to *COTILE* (see).

1962 FAIRPLAY

Stw p wh b. Cincinnati, Oh., 1877. Owned by Capt. S.H. Parisot and operated Vicksburg to Yazoo and Sunflower Rivers, Capt. B.C. Bookout. She was running New Orleans-Ouachita River when she burned at Monroe, La., along with the wharfboat which had been built on the hull of the famous side-wheel *KATIE,* this about 1879-1880.

1963 FAIRPLAY

SW p wh b. Ashland, Ky., 1891. 117.6 x 17.2 x 3. A batwing designed for Big Sandy River service. Still listed 1896.

1964 FAIRY

SW p wh b. Cincinnati, Oh., 1851. 101 tons. Off the lists in 1855.

1965 FAIRY

Stw tinclad wh b. Cincinnati, Oh., 1863. Originally named *MARIA.* 157 x 31.5 x 4.3. Engines, 14's- 5 ft. Bought by the U.S. on Feb. 10, 1864. Sold at Mound City, Ill., Aug. 17, 1865 to James Kiniston. In Navy service she was Tinclad 51.

1966 FAIRY QUEEN

Stw p wh b. Belle Vernon, Pa., 1854. 169 tons. Advertised Pittsburgh to St. Louis, January 1855, Capt. Reno. Capt. John Kyle later commanded. Cincinnati-Maysville in 1859, Capt. Prather. She is noted as arriving at St. Paul in 1856. Stranded and lost at Buffington Island, Ohio River, Oct. 21, 1860.

1967 FAIRY QUEEN

Stw p wh b. Cincinnati, Oh., 1866. 106 tons. First home port, Cairo, Ill. Stranded and lost in Black River, Ark., July 31, 1870.

1968 FALCON

SW p wh b. Freedom, Pa., 1843. 133 tons. A regular in the St. Louis-Galena-Dubuque and Potosi trade 1845-1846, Capt. Legrand Morehouse. Fall of 1846, Galena-St. Peters, also 1847, and then St. Louis-Galena, same master. Sank in heavy ice at mouth of Wood River, Jan. 26, 1849, having been sold shortly before to Capt. Parkinson. She was bound from St. Louis to the Illinois River.

1969 FALCON

SW p wh b. Jeffersonville, Ind., by Howard, 1849. 225 x 29 x 6. Engines, 10½'s- 7 ft. Paddlewheels 27 ft. dia., working 10 ft. buckets. Capt. William Richards commanded. Burned in the wharf fire, New Orleans, Oct. 9, 1849. Other boats destroyed were *NORTH AMERICA, ILLINOIS, MARSHALL NEY,* and *AARON HART.*

1970 FALCON

SW p wh b. Cincinnati, Oh., 1850. 185 tons. First home port, Apalachicola, Fla. Lost by stranding at Apalachicola, Fla., Aug. 23, 1851.

1971 FALCON

SW p wh b. McKeesport, Pa., 1851. 441 tons. Louisville-New Orleans, 1851, Capt. Neale. Renamed *QUEEN CITY* on Dec. 6, 1854 (see).

1972 FALCON

SW p wh b. Memphis, Tenn., 1852. 177 tons. Burned and lost at Algiers, La., Mar. 24, 1855.

1973 FALCON

Stw p wh b. Zanesville, Oh., 1863. 50 tons. Started out as a freight barge, and was given geared engines and made into a steamboat by Capt. Monroe Ayres who ran her McConnelsville-Zanesville-Dresden. Capt. William Bay ran her briefly Ironton-Proctorville in competition with his brother Capt. George Bay's *HENRY LOGAN* (see). Later was sold to the Wabash River. Off the lists 1868.

1974 FALLS CITY

SW p wh b. Louisville, Ky., at Murray & Gay yard, 1853. 308 x 36 x 6.5. Engines, 30's- 9 ft. Five boilers, each 46" dia. by 28 ft., five flues. Cabin 265 ft. long. Came out new in the Louisville-Wheeling trade, Capt. Sam Mason, leaving Louisville Feb. 5, 1853. She was in the Wheeling Union Line. Collided with the side-wheel *PITTSBURGH* at Shift Tail Bar, below New Matamoras, Oh., Feb. 23, 1853, precipitating the first trial before the U.S. Inspectors at Cincinnati. Got aground at the foot of Blennerhassett Island in June 1853 and while perched there a tornado toppled the stacks and wrecked her cabins "from stem to stern." She was transferred to the Louisville-New Orleans trade in January 1854. Then ran St. Louis-New Orleans. Off the lists 1859.

1975 FALLS CITY

Stw p wh b. Wellsville, Oh., 1855. 155 x 27 x 4.5. Three boilers. Engines, 16's- 6 ft. Built for merchants of St. Anthony Falls who proposed to show the upper Mississippi was navigable to their port. Later ran St. Louis-St. Paul. Sunk by ice in Lake Pepin, April 1857. Sold to Mobile, Ala., Capt. Timothy L. Matthews, part owner and master. Sank and lost in Loggy Bayou, La., Apr. 19, 1864.

1976 FALLS CITY

Stw p wh b. Louisville, Ky., 1867. 170 tons. Built for the Louisville-Bowling Green trade, round trip a week, Capt. J.M. Robinson, master, with E.B. Seeley, clerk. Ran there for three years. She collided with the tow of the *JOHN W. GARRETT* at the lower end of the Louisville-Portland Canal on Feb. 3, 1872. She was downbound, pilot George Dolly on watch. Sank and burned.

1977 FALLS CITY

Stw p wh b. New Albany, Ind., 1890. 132.5 x 27. Owned by Kentucky River Packet & Towboat Co., and ran Louisville-Frankfort. She actually wore out in the trade. Capt. George B. Edgington bought her in 1899, took her to Augusta, Ky., and used equipment building the *CHARLES B. PEARCE,* including the engines.

1978 FALLS CITY

Stw p wh b. Cincinnati, Oh., 1898. 132 x 32.6 x 6. Engines, 12's- 4½ ft. Two boilers, each 42½" dia. by 18 ft. Owned by Louisville & Kentucky River Packet Co. Ran Louisville-Frankfort. Capt. Tom Morrissey took her to Vicksburg in February 1908 to replace the sunken *ROSALIE M* (see). Prince and Wilds ran her in trades out of Vicksburg. In 1916 she was at Vicksburg, laid up, falling apart.

1979 FANCHON

Stw p wh b. Brownsville, Pa., 1875. 174 x 35 x 4.7. Engines, 16¼'s- 4½ ft. Two boilers, each 42" dia. by 26 ft. Owned by Capt. Tom C. Sweeney, Wheeling, and others. She was chartered spring 1877 for a trip up the Missouri and Yellowstone. Often ran Pittsburgh-Cincinnati, and out of New Orleans in winter. In 1880-1882 running New Orleans-Opelousas, Capt. H.H. Broad, master, with E. Quatrevaux, clerk. Exploded boilers at New Orleans with life loss and was demolished. Many of the crew had been on the *JOHN WILSON* (see) which had exploded shortly prior.

1980 FANCY NATCHEZ

SW p wh b. Algiers, La., 1858. 24 tons. 69.5 x 12 x 3. Owned and operated by Capt. James Shepherd, St. James Parish, La. Went to Confederate registry in 1861.

1981 FANNIE

SW p wh b. Brownsville, Pa., 1858. 75 tons. First home port, Chicago, Ill. Off the lists in 1862.

1982 Fannie

Stw freight boat wh b. Carmi, Ill., 1881. 85.4 x 18.4 x 3.7. Documented at Paducah 1895 and at Memphis 1896.

1983 Fannie Dugan

SW p wh b. Portsmouth, Oh., 1872. 165.4 x 28.4 x 4.5. Two boilers. Built for Capt. John McAllister for the Portsmouth-Proctorville trade. Came out with Capt. McAllister, master; Frank Morgan, clerk; Carl Mace, mate; Sam Ware and Jim McAllister, engineers; Crate Booth and John McGuire, pilots; and John Steele, steward. In 1873 Frank Morgan sold his interest and built *CITY OF PORTSMOUTH*. After Capt. McAllister's death, Capt. Jack McAllister went master, with Will Waters, clerk. The *CITY OF PORTSMOUTH* and *FANNIE DUGAN* ran hot competition for some time. The *FANNIE* carried locked mail from Portsmouth to Pine Creek, Franklin Furnace, Greenup, Ironton, Ashland, Catlettsburg, and Huntington. Widow McAllister joined with the Bay Line in 1876, forming the Portsmouth & Pomeroy Packet Co., and the *FANNIE* then ran this trade until sold about 1882 to Capts. Tucker and Walker of Jacksonville, Fla. She made the trip around Florida to the St. Johns River and operated there for some time. This scribe visited Sanford, Fla., in 1922 and was taken across to Enterprise where in the clear water the bones of the *FANNIE DUGAN* still were visible. Her roof bell at that time was on the *CITY OF JACKSONVILLE*.

1984 Fannie Fearn

Stw p wh b. Jeffersonville, Ind., by Howard, 1886. 134 x 31.3 x 5.6. Built for Capt. Sam Fearn who also built the *MAGGIE HARPER* (see). Came out in the Louisville-Madison trade, but was shortly sold to Apalachicola, Fla., where she was still documented in 1896.

1985 Fannie Freese

Stw p wh b. Ashland, Ky., 1882. 69 tons. Ran Ashland, Catlettsburg and Big Sandy River along with *JOSIE HOPKINS, KATIE ADAMS,* and others. Renamed *BLUE WING* about 1890 (see).

1986 Fannie Gilbert

Stw p wh b. Evansville, Ind., 1864. 145 tons. Running New Orleans and Red River, November 1867 in the Kouns Line. Off the lists 1868.

1987 Fannie Keener

Stw p wh b. Jeffersonville, Ind., 1872. 426 tons. A large packet with a texas, running St. Louis and Illinois River. T. & F. Keener had a large riverside warehouse at Naples, Scott County, Ill., owned by the St. Louis & Naples Packet Co., and was their low water boat in the trade, otherwise moving apples from Calhoun County. On Dec. 12, 1876, she was moored outside the ferry *JACOB TAMM* at the Naples Packet Co., wharfboat, St. Louis. An ice gorge shoved the ferryboat ashore and demolished the *KEENER*. She sank in 15 feet and a small portion of the cabin remained above water.

1988 Fannie Lewis

SW p wh b. Jeffersonville, Ind., 1871. 210 x 35 x 5.5. Engines, 18's- 6 ft. Three boilers, each 38" dia. by 22 ft. Owned by the Missouri River Packet Co., William M. Ater, secretary, St. Louis. Her masters, in order: Capts. Sam Rider, Robert Wright, Sam Rider, Jud Cartwright, M.H. Crapster, G.F. Shields, R. Porter, George G. Keith, C.B. Tilden, Henry Keith, James A. Yore, Jud Cartwright. Her hull was altered at Madison, Ind. in May 1872, changing dimensions to 224 x 35.4 x 5.2. Went south in winter and made many trips up Red River. Not re-enrolled after Apr. 1, 1885.

1989 Fannie Malone

Stw p wh b. Elizabeth, Pa., 1852. 87 tons. Ran on the upper Tennessee River, owned by James and William Williams. Off the lists in 1854. Machinery went on *ACACIA COTTAGE* built at California, Pa., 1857.

1990 Fannie Moore

Stw p wh b. Madison, Ind., 1876. 200 tons. Owned by Capts. John Woodburn and Capt. Jesse K. Bell. Carried cotton out of Arkansas River and was named for the daughter of a planter in the region. Downbound with a big load of cotton hit the bank head on, at Sarassa, Arkansas River, 50 miles below Pine Bluff, Apr. 12, 1877. The packet *ELLA* had recently sunk in the same area.

1991 Fannie Scott

Stw p wh b. Belle Vernon, Pa., 1866. 253 tons. 157 x 34 x 5. Engines, 16's- 5½ ft. Three boilers, each 42" dia. by 24 ft. Built for M.S. Mepham & Co. for the Little Rock-New Orleans trade. Ran St. Louis-Chester, Ill., trade later, and was partially burned in the fire which destroyed the *M.S. MEPHAM* at St. Louis, Mar. 2, 1868. Burned and lost at St. Louis on Apr. 9, 1869.

1992 Fannie Tatum

SW p wh b. Madison, Ind., 1873 and completed at St. Louis. 177 x 36.5 x 5. Engines, 15's- 5 ft. Three boilers, each 38" dia. by 24 ft., two flues. Built for Capt. John Elwell, J.G. Prather, Boone Allen, John Adkins, and S.B. Gilmore for St. Louis-Arkansas River. She was sold to Capt. John B. Conway, Capt. George Rowley, and others. They ran her Pittsburgh-St. Louis, and made several "mountain trips" with her up the Missouri. Later entered the Paducah-St. Louis trade. Sank near Fort Chartres 50 miles below St. Louis while landing to take on wheat, mid-September 1880, raised. Was still in Paducah-St. Louis trade in 1882 competing with *HUDSON*.

1993 Fannie Wallace

Stw p-tb wh b. Belpre, Oh., 1888. 86 x 13 x 2.9. Originally named *MARY E* (see). Towed for U.S. Gas & Coke Co., which was taken over by West Kentucky Coal Co. When retired after 1908 her pilothouse was used as part of the office at the Ayer & Lord Tie Co., marine ways, Paducah. It was still there in 1935.

1994 FANNY

SW steamship wh b. Cincinnati, Oh., 1847. 166 x 27 x 10. Main mast 72 ft. high from top of keelson. Built for John J. Deshon, New Orleans, who used her in the coasting trade, Capt. Henry E. Scott, master. She was returned to Cincinnati in 1848, masts down, and a new boiler installed. Deshon sold her in 1849 to William H. Simmons and V.F. Wilson, New Orleans. She had various owners until 1853 at New Orleans, and then was sold foreign. She carried a female figurehead.

1995 FANNY

SW p wh b. Cincinnati, Oh., 1864. 195 tons. 179 x 27 x 5.5. Engines, 15's- 5 ft. Two tubular boilers, each 40" dia. by 18 ft., each with 15 five-inch flues. Wheels 20 ft. dia. working 6½ ft. buckets. Graciana did the interior cabin landscapes. Built for Capt. Albert Stein and made trips to Pittsburgh. Sold to the U.S. on Dec. 3, 1864, renamed *GROSBEAK* (see).

1996 FANNY BARKER

Stw p wh b. Cincinnati, Oh., 1863. 174 tons. Built for Barker, Hart & Cook, Cincinnati. Went to U.S. service, renamed *FAWN,* Apr. 10, 1863. Redocumented *FANNY BARKER* on Oct. 19, 1865. C.J. Caffery, Esq., St. Louis, headed a packet line running St. Louis-Johnsonville, Tenn., in 1866, with this boat included. Lost at St. Joseph, Mo., Mar. 24, 1873.

1997 FANNY BELL

Stw p wh b. Letart Falls, Oh., 1884. 106 x 18 x 3. Built out of the *E.M. NORTON,* and towed produce boats south. Documented at Wheeling, 1886.

1998 FANNY BRANDEIS

Stw p wh b. Madison, Ind., 1864. 170 tons. Built for Brandeis & Crawford, St. Louis, to handle grain. Very light draft. Ran to Cincinnati. Several years later went to the Evansville-Nashville trade, Capt. Henry Miller, with Kitt Rudd, clerk. In late 1871 she was en route down the Mississippi from Memphis with a load of cotton and was snagged and sunk at Island 40 on December 8.

1999 FANNY BULLITT

SW p wh b. Jeffersonville, Ind., by Howard, 1854. 245 x 35 x 7. Named for Fanny Smith Bullitt of Louisville and largely owned by Benedict Bros., of that place. Ran Louisville-New Orleans. In 1860 J.A. Lemcke took one-third interest and became head clerk. Capt. Greer, joint owner and master, died of cholera about this time. Capt. Henry W. Smith came aboard as master and part owner. She was laid up at Portland, Ky., in the spring of 1861 when war closed traffic. Came out again as a U.S. transport and took two trips to Keokuk in fall of 1862 with sick and wounded. Was at Fort Donelson and took wounded from there to Paducah, Evansville, and Louisville. Was sold to St. Louis, and snagged and lost at Napoleon, Ark., Mar. 15, 1864. A towhead formed at the wreck, long called Fanny Bullitt Towhead. One of her early masters was Capt. L.B. Dunham.

2000 FANNY FARRAR

Stw p wh b. Paducah, Ky., 1853. 134 tons. Snagged and lost at Canton, Ky., Jan. 24, 1855.

2001 FANNY FERN

SW p wh b. California, Pa., 1853. 153 x 29 x 4.3. Engines from *JOHN QUINCY ADAMS* (see). Three boilers. Named for a Mrs. Farrington of Boston whose pen name was Fanny Fern. Part owner and first master, Capt. M.E. Lucas, Steubenville, Oh. Ran Pittsburgh-St. Louis. Collided with the *THOS. SWANN* at Little Grave Creek on the Ohio River above Moundsville on Mar. 3, 1854, and sank. Lucas and insurance firms involved sued the owners of the *SWANN* and got judgment. A deputy U.S. marshal came aboard the *SWANN* at Wheeling, removed the throttle valve and impounded it pending settlement of the claim. The owners posted bond in amount $60,000, and she was released. The *CUBA* (see) hit the wreck of the *FERN* later that month and sank. Later the *FERN* was raised and repaired. The Wheeling Steamboat Inspectors who tried the case were Capt. A.M. Phillips and Capt. Joseph Wood. The pilots on watch at the time were Thomas Jabens on the *FERN* and Tom Witten on the *SWANN.* The *FERN* once had her cabin blown off during a storm on the Upper Mississippi. Last owners were Mrs. Frances Martin (⅝) of Allegheny City, Pa., George W. Harris (⅛) of Pittsburgh, and Robert Wasson (¼) of Rochester, Pa. Exploded her center boiler at Lawrenceburg, Ind., on Jan. 20, 1858, upbound from St. Louis to Cincinnati. Capt. Ben Woodward, Newport, Ky., was master, and was lost. Moses Scott, pilot on watch, landed between the boilers still holding the pilotwheel and was unharmed. She burned following the explosion and drifted one and one-half miles and sank along the Kentucky shore. Twenty lives were lost.

2002 FANNY FERN

Stw p wh b. in Caddo Parish, La., 1854. 123 x 26.8 x 5. Operated on Red River owned by Thomas Gilmore (½) and the estate of John M. Collins. Capt. Benjamin Farwell, Caddo Parish, first master. Off the lists in 1858.

2003 FANNY GILBERT

Stw p wh b. Evansville, Ind., 1864. 128.9 x 26.1 x 4.2. Named for daughter of Capt. John S. Gilbert, Golconda, Ill., who later lived at Evansville. During the war was in U.S. service. Sold Nov. 9, 1866, to George L. Kouns and Ben B. Kouns who operated her New Orleans-Red River. Dismantled at Madison, Ind., September 1868.

2004 FANNY HARRIS

Stw p wh b. Brownsville, Pa., 1855. 160 tons. Ran Dubuque-St. Paul owned by Dubuque merchants, Capt.

Jones Worden, master. Lost in ice at Point Douglass, Hastings, Minn., Dec. 27, 1862.

2005 FANNY MCBURNIE

Stw p wh b. Harmar, Oh., at Knox Yard, 1860. Built for Capt. Henry H. Drown designed for Marietta-Cincinnati trade. Commanded by Capt. William Knox. In July 1861, upbound, she was hailed in below Green Bottom, opposite Crown City, Oh., where the "notorious" Dr. Jenkins came aboard with 35 armed men, disarmed the passengers, took a case of revolvers and one sword, and departed. In March 1862 made a trip to Pittsburgh with 900 barrels of oil from Marietta. In U.S. service 1863 and took supplies to the Cumberland River. Sold in November 1863 to Capt. Dan Collier and others of Cincinnati. Lost at Island 34, Mississippi River, Dec. 6, 1863.

2006 FANNY OGDEN

SW p wh b. Madison, Ind., 1862. 417 tons. Built for Capt. Jos. Kinney who wished to name the boat for one of the three daughters of L.C. Ogden, St. Joseph, Mo. He had them draw straws; Fanny had the longest. Ran on the Missouri River. In 1863 owned by Capt. John P. Keiser, St. Louis, and advertised a trip to Fort Benton. Sold again in 1864 to Capt. John C. Copelin and others who advertised her for a trip from St. Louis "to the gold mines of Idaho." Burned in a large steamboat fire at St. Louis on Apr. 7, 1866.

2007 FANNY PEARSON

SW p wh b. Madison, Ind., 1860. 123.3 x 26.4 x 4.9. Went to New Orleans owned by Jacob F. Worley, Jefferson Parish. Renamed *JEFF THOMPSON* which see for further details.

2008 FANNY SMITH

SW p wh b. Jeffersonville, Ind., by Howard, 1850. 220 x 32 x 6.5. Ran Louisville-New Orleans, Capt. W. Richards. Named for Miss Fanny Smith, Louisville, who later was Mrs. Fanny Bullitt for whom the *FANNY BULLITT* (see) was named in 1854 when this boat was dismantled at Jeff.

2009 FANNY SPARHAWK

SW p wh b. Cincinnati, Oh., 1852. 259 tons. Off the lists in 1855.

2010 FANNY THORNTON

Stw p wh b. Franconia, Minn., 1863. 119.4 x 24.1 x 3. Operated out of St. Paul briefly, then went to Memphis. Was with the U.S. fleet on Red River in 1864. Capt. John McDonald was master 1865 again out of Memphis. Off the lists in 1868, and may have burned on Red River.

2011 FANNY WEBSTER

Ferry wh b. Cincinnati, Oh., 1870. 213 tons. Inspected regularly in the Cincinnati district through 1882.

2012 FAR WEST

Stw p wh b. Pittsburgh, Pa., 1870. 190 x 33. Engines, 15's-5 ft. Three boilers. Built for Capt. S.B. Coulson and became one of the more famed steamboats on the Upper Missouri River. Had quite a career during the Indian troubles in the Northwest during the 1870s. For those readers interested in true stories, buy, beg or borrow *Conquest of the Missouri* by Joseph Mills Hanson, a factual life-story of Capt. Grant Marsh in which the *FAR WEST* is a principal actor. Marsh commanded the boat during the ill-fated Custer expedition and had her away up Little Yellowstone River and brought out the wounded to Fort Lincoln. General Miles and Buffalo Bill used the boat on a scouting expedition one time. The *FAR WEST* made 18 trips to Fort Benton and for two years was on the Yellowstone on government service 1876–1877. Capts. Mart Coulson and J.M. Belk also commanded at times. Coulson was skipper during the famed race with the *NELLIE PECK,* Sioux City to Fort Benton and return to Sioux City and won by three hours, the time being 17 days 20 hours. Later sold to Victor Bonnet and Capt. Henry M. Dodds. Sank on a snag at Mullanthy Island, seven miles below St. Charles, Mo., Oct. 30, 1883. Part of the cargo was removed to the *FANNIE LEWIS.*

2013 FARMER

SW p wh b. Cincinnati, Oh., 1848. 198 tons. First home port was Mobile, Ala. Snagged and lost at Island 18, below Cairo, Sept. 19, 1853. The *COL. DICKINSON* had been lost there 10 days prior (see).

2014 FARMER

SW p wh b. Brownsville, Pa., 1849. 158 tons. Exploded and lost at Galveston, Tex., Mar. 23, 1853, with loss of 32 lives.

2015 FARMER

SW ferry wh b. Clarington, Oh., 1851. 43 tons. Off the lists in 1856.

2016 FASHION

SW p wh b. Cincinnati, Oh., 1847. 474 tons. Lost by stranding at Louisville, Ky., May 8, 1852.

2017 FASHION

SW p wh b. Shousetown, Pa., 1848. 149 tons. 143 x 22 x 5. Sold to New Orleans in 1850, owned there by Maunsel White & Co., Capt. J. Martin, master. Sold in 1851 to other owners in New Orleans and had nine other ownerships there through 1855.

2018 FASHION

SW p wh b. New Albany, Ind., 1851. 296 tons. 119 x 25 x 9. Apparently built for the U.S. and sold to private owners 1855. Operated out of Mobile. Length was changed 1859 to 190 ft. She was ocean going, two masts. Owned 1859 by New Orleans & Nicaraugua Steamship Co., Capt. John P. Smith, New Orleans, master. This account is subject to further research.

2019 FASHION

SW p wh b. Cincinnati, Oh., 1865. 262.7 x 42.5 x 7.7. Ran New Orleans-Vicksburg, Capt. A.J. May, owned by A.S. Mansfield, New Orleans. Sold June 7, 1866, to Capt. James

F. Tucker, New Orleans, who commanded. Downbound with 250 passengers and 2,700 bales of cotton she caught fire seven miles above Baton Rouge and burned, Dec. 27, 1866. Thomas Montague, pilot on watch, got the boat landed and was not seen afterward. Oliver Fairchild, engineer, stood at the throttle 'til the last bell, then perished. When the cotton burned off the head of the boat she drifted down to the head of the reach above Baton Rouge and lodged. The *MAGENTA,* downbound with cotton, came by and rendered aid, and was afire three times doing so. The body of pilot Thomas H. Montague was found months later, and was brought to New Orleans for burial aboard the *MAGENTA.* The Louisiana legislature voted $300 annually to his widow as a token of respect. Other than pilot and engineer, six of the crew and 35 passengers lost their lives.

2020 FASHION

SW p wh b. Ironton, Oh., 1872. 120 x 20. She was designed by Capt. Uriah Scott and ran Portsmouth-Proctorville owned by the Bay Line. Was replaced by the *SCIOTO* in 1874, and then ran Huntington-Gallipolis. Sold February 1876 to Messrs. Freil and Chester who ran her briefly on the Monon River out of Elizabeth, Pa., and that fall East Liverpool-Steubenville. Capt. Wash Williamson bought her, renamed her *RELIANCE* (see).

2021 FASHION

Stw p wh b. Jeffersonville, Ind., by Howard, 1877. 220 x 36 x 5.5. Engines, 17's- 6 ft. Three boilers. Built for the Louisville & Henderson Mail Line which sold her within a year to Capt. W.S. Packer and others for the trade between Pittsburgh and St. Louis. Then was bought by Capt. E.B. Cooper, who went master in the Pittsburgh-Cincinnati trade with Al Slaven, clerk, also a shareholder, and Capt. Anthony (Tony) Meldahl, pilot, who also held interest. She replaced the *EMMA GRAHAM* (see). Downbound at Riggs Landing, head of Manchester Islands, she hit the bank at night, Kentucky shore, and went down. Pilot Aaron McLaughlin had mistaken a lantern in a house as the government light. The cargo was principally Hostetter's Bitters, a cure-all of high alcoholic content made in Pittsburgh. Bottles were strewn all along the shore and were picked up for years after. She was a double-stage boat. Loss happened in June 1890.

2022 FASHION NO. 2

Stw p wh b. Elizabeth, Pa., 1849. 88 tons. Collapsed a flue at Pittsburgh, Dec. 20, 1850, killing four or five. Ran local trades out of Wheeling later. Off the lists 1856.

2023 FAVORITE

SW p wh b. Cincinnati, Oh., 1859. 252 tons. Ran in Minnesota River trade, Capt. P.S. Davidson 1859–1860. La Crosse-St. Paul, 1860–1861. Minnesota River, 1862. Capt. Davidson and his brother Capt. William F. Davidson were from South Point, Oh., and both were prominent packet operators on the Upper Mississippi. Her forward boiler deck was glass enclosed.

2024 FAVORITE

SW batwing wh b. South Point, Oh., 1870. 102 x 14.8 x 2.2. In 1877 was advertised as a "regular independent Catlettsburg-Piketon packet" up Big Sandy River, Capt. F.M. Spurlock, master, with Tom Dickenson, clerk. In fall of 1895 during low water, ran Wheeling-New Matamoras, Capt. S.W. Litten, master, with Fred Hornbrook, clerk.

2025 FAVORITE

SW ferry wh b. Cincinnati, Oh., 1876. 120.4 x 40 x 5.2. Later renamed *CINCINNATI* (see).

2026 FAWN

SW p wh b. Jeffersonville, Ind., 1848. 85 tons. Ran Vicksburg-Greenwood on Yazoo River. In April 1849 collided with *PATRICK HENRY* at mouth of the Sunflower River. Engineer Jesse Mitchell was killed, and office and staterooms halfway back one side were carried away, and one engine wrecked. Off the lists in 1852.

2027 FAWN

SW p wh b. Louisville, Ky., 1851. 182 tons. Owned by Capt. Stephen Paxton and others who ran her Louisville-Evansville-Henderson. Was called "the squealing fawn." Replaced by the *RAINBOW.* Off the lists 1855.

2028 FAWN

SW p wh b. Jefferson City (now New Orleans), 1863. 101 x 21.2 x 5.4. Owned in part and commanded by Capt. W.R. Greathouse. Ran New Orleans-Bayou Lafourche, twice weekly, with Leo Bayni as first clerk and Joseph P. Winner, second clerk. Said to have been destroyed in the fire at New Orleans May 28, 1864, when nine steamboats were lost.

2029 FAWN

Stw tinclad wh b. Cincinnati, Oh., 1863. 158.7 x 20.5 x 4.2. Engines, 12's- 4 ft. Originally *FANNY BARKER* (see) renamed in U.S. service, Mar. 10, 1863, until Oct. 19, 1865. U.S. Navy sold her at Mound City, Ill., to D. Coughlin (other accounts say B.W. Cobden), and her original name was restored.

2030 FAWN

Stw p wh b. Jeffersonville, Ind., by Howard, 1875. 180 x 34 x 5. Ran Evansville-Louisville-Cincinnati. In 1877 Capt. F.O. Smith, master, with Chas. V. Williams, clerk; then Capt. E.L. Penny, master, with L.W. Whitlow and J.A. Jennings, clerks. Under charter to the St. Louis & Tennessee River Packet Co., she struck a pier of the Johnsonville bridge on Tennessee River, Feb. 13, 1880, and sank with a big load of cotton, etc., aboard.

2031 FAWN

Stw ferry wh b. Hermann, Mo., 1880. 91.9 x 19.1 x 3.4. Operated at Hermann, Mo. Later was sold and sank at St. Charles, Mo., near the wreck of the former ferry *J.P. GAGE.*

2032 FAWN

Stw p wh b. Evansville, Ind., 1896. 95 x 18.5 x 3.3. Built by Capt. William Kratz and T.C. Gillette. Originally had one boiler and carried a calliope. Sold after a year or so to the Marsden Cellulose Co., Owensboro, Ky., which put two boilers on her and towed corn stalks to Owensboro, used in the manufacture of cellulose. She was first built for the Evansville-Spottsville trade, replacing the smaller *LELA*. Houston Bros., Vicksburg, owned her in the 1920s, Capt. J. Warren Kouns, doing towing. Sold to George E. Breece Lumber Co., October 1926, and went to Monroe, La.*

2033 FAWN NO. 2

Stw ferry (?) wh b. Hartford City, W. Va., 1863. 41 tons. Off the lists in 1871.

2034 FAYAWAY

SW p wh b. St. Louis, Mo., 1848. 102 tons. Off the lists in 1857.

2035 FAYETTE

SW p wh b. Brownsville, Pa., 1865. 162 x 27. Engines, 19's-5½ ft. Capt. Adam Jacobs superintended construction. Came out in Monon River trade, Capt. S.C. Speers. The Union Line had two boats a day out of Pittsburgh, at 8:00 A.M. and 6:00 P.M. Partner boats were the *TELEGRAPH, FRANKLIN,* and *GALLATIN* (see). Came in collision with the *GALLATIN* at Coal Valley in August 1865 and was sunk. The Steamboat Inspectors at Pittsburgh suspended Samuel Hughes for six months, pilot on *FAYETTE*. Capt. M.A. Cox went master in May 1866. Entered the Pittsburgh-Parkersburg trade March 1869, Capt. R.C. Mason, with Dan Moore in the office. Only ran a week or so and then sold to the Portsmouth & Big Sandy Packet Co. They sold her September 1869 to Evansville, Henderson & Nashville Railway Co., which shuttled her Evansville-Henderson, Capt. A.O. Durland, with James H. Letcher in the office. In 1874 same trade, Capt. Charles G. Perkins, with Henry S. Mitchell, clerk. Dismantled 1876.

2036 FAYETTE

Freight boat wh b. Terre Haute, Ind., 1879. 16 tons. Inspected in the Evansville District 1881-1882.

2037 FEDERAL ARCH

SW p wh b. Brownsville, Pa., 1850. 195 tons. Tramped between Pittsburgh and St. Louis. Was in process of dismantling at St. Louis when ice smashed her Feb. 28, 1856. The wrecking steamer *SUBMARINE* was shoved into her.

2038 FELIX GRUNDY

SW p wh b. Cincinnati, Oh., 1845. 165 tons. Built for the Pittsburgh-Nashville trade, Capt. Fowler. Snagged and lost in the Grand Chain, Ohio River, Apr. 20, 1847.

2039 FERD HEROLD

Stw p sh b. Dubuque, Iowa, 1890. 244.6 x 34 x 7.2. Engines, 18's- 8 ft. Three boilers. Ferd Herold, Esq., was a St. Louis brewer who financed construction. His likeness, in the form of a magnified bust, was placed on the forward end of the texas, and later removed to the cabin. Her maiden trip was St. Louis-New Orleans, Capt. Henry W. Brolaski. Then Capt. Milt Harry went on her, and she loaded out at St. Louis for Vicksburg. He placed her in the Ouachita River trade in opposition to the regular line, and quit when he was paid off. She then ran St. Louis-Alton, did no good and was sold to the Lee Line, Memphis, for $30,000, having cost $75,000 new. They ran her St. Louis-Memphis. During the last several years of operation her owner was St. Louis-Memphis Transportation Co., which also ran the *GEORGIA LEE* in the trade. S.C. Edgar was president of the Line, G.F. Lee, vice-president, and J.M. Tucker, gen'l agent at St. Louis. Their folder also advertised the steel hull excursion steamer *MAJESTIC* (see). She ran this trade until July 1919 at which time the Halliday wharfboat at Cairo was sold, and the Lee Line wharfboat at St. Louis was discontinued. The *FERD HEROLD* was dismantled. Sugar Products Co., of New Orleans used the hull as a barge, and it foundered in the Gulf of Mexico late 1920.

2040 FERD KENNETT

SW p wh b. St. Louis, Mo., 1861. 238 x 40.5 x 6.5. 591 tons. Part owner and master was Capt. T.H. Brierly, St. Louis. Entered the St. Louis-New Orleans trade, February 1861, with W.S. Harper, head clerk. In 1862 was in the Memphis-New Orleans trade, Capt. Brierly, carrying Confederate States' mail. Taken up the Yalobusha River for safety as the war progressed, she was burned there mid-summer 1863 along with the *EDWARD J. GAY* and *ARCADIA*.

2041 FIFTEEN

Stw p wh b. Yazoo City, Miss., 1893. 103 x 18 x 3.5. Built on the hull of the *GENERAL MILES* (see). Handled cotton out of the Yazoo. Still documented 1897, maybe later.

2042 FINANCIER

Stw p wh b. Pittsburgh, Pa., 1845. 125 tons. Built for Capt. Adam Poe, Georgetown, Pa., and others. Capt. William J. Kountz bought her in 1846. He advertised her Feburary 1848 from Pittsburgh to Lafayette, Ind. Capt. James Ward and others bought her fall of 1849 and took her to the Upper Mississippi. Exploded boilers near Alton, Ill., Oct. 12, 1850, resulting in the death of the captain's son, named King, and the second engineer William Greene. Others scalded.

2043 FINANCIER

Stw p wh b. Freedom, Pa., 1850. 117 tons. Built for Capt. Adam Poe and others of Georgetown, Pa., and ran in tramp trades. Off the lists 1856.

2044 FINANCIER

SW p wh b. Jefferson Parish, La., 1855. 93 x 18 x 3.4. Built by Capt. E.C. Alexander and others of New Orleans. Off the lists in 1857.

2045 FINANCIER

Stw p wh b. McKeesport, Pa., 1864. 153.6 x 35 x 6.4. Engines, 18's- 5 ft. Three boilers each 38" dia. by 26 ft., two 14" flues. Ran Pittsburgh-St. Louis-New Orleans. Master and part owner was Capt. John Darragh and first clerk James Russell. Downbound at Crows Island, Ohio River, near Baden, Pa., caught fire when a passenger, Mrs. E. Rothchild, lit a camphene light and it exploded. The boat was landed at the island. Mr. and Mrs. Rothchild and two children, en route to Texas, lost their lives, plus six other passengers, this on April 12, 1866. The *BAYARD,* upbound, arrived too late to save lives. Capt. Darragh and his son John Jr., built the *BELLE VERNON* as a replacement (see).

2046 FIRE CANOE

SW p wh b. Ironton, Oh., 1854. 166 tons. Went to the Upper Mississippi and was at St. Paul in May 1855, Capt. Baldwin, and again in 1856 and 1857, Capt. Spencer. Spent 1858 in Minnesota River trade. Goddin Bros. Coal Co., Leavenworth, Kans., bought her that fall and she was snagged at Kaw Bend, near Wyandotte, Kans., on Nov. 13, 1858.

2047 FIRE CANOE

A boat of this name was reported sunk in Lake Pepin, Upper Mississippi, three miles below Wacouta, in April 1861. Passengers and crew taken off by *FANNY HARRIS.*

2048 FIRE KING

New at Cincinnati July 1867 operated by a Capt. Sample, fitted out with a boiler using "coal oil" (kerosene) instead of coal. Ran a trial at Cincinnati August 1. Loaded aboard a number of guests late August and headed for Louisville. The burner was called Saroni's Patent Generator. Had to be hauled out at Madison, Ind., for hull repairs and was visited there by many. Ran demonstration trips at Louisville. Reported one spectator: "If petroleum comes into general use on the river instead of coal the occupation of 5/6 of the firemen will be gone at a sweep."

2049 FIRESIDES

Stw p wh b. St. Paul, Minn., 1864. 34 tons. Off the lists in 1866.

2050 FLAG

Stw p wh b. Cincinnati, Oh., 1853. 235 tons. Sank at Flint Island, Ohio River, Oct. 11, 1853. Lost in ice at Covington, Ky., Feb. 24, 1856.

2051 FLAVILLA

Stw p wh b. Madison, Ind., 1869. 129 x 30.2 x 4. Built for Capt. John T. Roots and others of New Orleans. Sold July 1870 to Capt. John L. Maples and others, New Orleans. That fall sold to Shreveport, La., Capt. James Crooks. Took freight from the wrecked *TEXARKANA,* September 1870. Tied up for debt by a U.S. marshal at Shreveport in August 1873 and sank there.

2052 FLEETWING

Stw p wh b. for Capt. Milton Freese c. 1871 for Ironton-Big Sandy trade, Frank H. Freese, clerk. In winter 1875–1876 was on the lower Mississippi with Dan Rice's horse show. Got in financial troubles and was laid up at Catlettsburg, Ky., for about two years. Sold by U.S. marshal to Capt. Freese for $7,525 in February 1878. The machinery later was placed on the side-wheel *LIBERTY* (see).

2053 FLEETWOOD

SW p wh b. Brownsville, Pa., 1850. 212 tons. Arrived at St. Paul, Minn., June 26, 1851. Snagged and lost 25 miles below Terre Haute, Ind., on Wabash River, Feb. 22, 1852.

2054 FLEETWOOD

SW p wh b. Cincinnati, Oh., 1866. 749 tons. 255 x 36 x 6. Built for Capt. Charles M. Holloway and others for Cincinnati-Pomeroy-Parkersburg trade. Joined in the Cincinnati, Big Sandy & Pomeroy Packet Co., when that organization was formed, October 1866. A newspaper was published aboard, the *Fleetwood Reflector,* from which the *S&D Reflector* of the Sons and Daughters of Pioneer Rivermen later took its name. Clerks included William H. Kyle and John Thornburg. In later years Capt. J.T. Campbell was master, and W.C. Vanderbilt, clerk. In later years she ran Cincinnati-Pomeroy. Dismantled at Cincinnati when the new *FLEETWOOD* replaced her (next listing).

2055 FLEETWOOD

SW p wh b. Cincinnati, Oh., 1880. 302.2 x 43.4 x 6.4. Engines, 25 3/8's- 8 1/2 ft. Four boilers, each 47" dia. by 30 ft., six flues. Paddlewheels 27 ft. dia. working 16 ft. buckets, 58 staterooms. Double railroad in the hull same as *BOSTONA* (see). Left Cincinnati on her maiden trip Aug. 26, 1880, in Cincinnati-Huntington trade, Capt. J.T. Campbell, master, John Kirker, mate. A.W. Kidwell was engineer on her 14 years. Fastest upstream time, Cincinnati-Huntington, was 13 hours with four landings. After the C&O was opened to Cincinnati in 1883, this boat and her partner *BOSTONA* ran Cincinnati-Pomeroy. She occasionally went to Parkersburg but never above there. Later ran Cincinnati-Louisville, Capt. John Brennan, master, Henry Thomas and Charles J. Dufour, pilots, William B. Ketchum, chief engineer and Charles C. Langhart, purser. She was retired when the *CITY OF LOUISVILLE* came out. Capt. John Barrett bought the hull for a model barge.

2056 FLETA

SW p wh b. Louisville, Ky., 1859. 112 x 25 x 3.8. Went to New Orleans, Capt. A.A. Barnes, master, owned by W.T. Epperson and T.J. Morris. Ran Shreveport-New Orleans. Was in Red River until after the war. Sold to Galveston, Tex., April 1868. Off the lists in 1870.

2057 FLETA

Stw p wh b. Jeffersonville, Ind., 1869. 131.7 x 30.5 x 3.5. Engines, 12's- 4 ft. Two boilers, each 40" dia. by 18 ft. Built for R.B. Barnes, New Orleans, and master was Capt. A.A.

Barnes. Ran New Orleans-Shreveport. In 1869 Capt. William Gillen, master, with A.C. Greene, clerk. In 1870 was in the Kouns' Red River Line, Capt. George L. Kouns, master, with C.W. Drown, clerk. In 1876 in New Orleans-Opelousas trade, Capt. C.C. Pickett, with A. Menier, Sr., clerk. Sold to Mobile in 1877 and ran on Tombigbee River, Capt. H.R. Johnston. Dismantled at Mobile and machinery went to Rome, Ga., for a Coosa River boat.

2058 FLICKER

Stw p wh b. Pittsburgh, Pa., 1866. 125 x 26 x 3.4. Engines, 10's- 3 ft. She departed for New Orleans, November 1866, Capt. James Taylor. Built for New Orleans-Red River. Sold 1868 to Capt. Joseph F. Aucoin of Assumption Parish, La., for the New Orleans-Lafourche trade, with P.A. Charlet, clerk. In late 1869 still there with Capt. William Taylor, master, and F. Bergeron, clerk. Out of service in 1873.

2059 FLINT HILLS

Stw p wh b. Rock Island, Ill., 1849. 88 tons. First home port, St. Louis. Off the lists 1851.

2060 FLINT HILLS

Steam ferry wh b. Cincinnati, Oh., 1856. 105 tons. Documented at Burlington, Iowa, 1857. Out of service, 1869.

2061 FLORA

SW p wh b. Brownsville, Pa., 1848. 112 tons. Lost in collision with the *TIMOUR* at Tunica, Miss., January 1852. She had been an Attakapas packet, Capt. J.J. Labarthe.

2062 FLORA

Stw p wh b. California, Pa., 1855. 160 tons. 152 x 19.3 x 3.9. First master and part owner was Capt. Samuel Dean. Other shareholders: Mark Sterling, John A. Caughey, and William Rea all of Pittsburgh. Went to St. Paul as one of the Dubuque & St. Paul Packet Co. boats.

2063 FLORA

Stw p wh b. New Albany, Ind., 1864. 112 tons. On Sept. 19, 1864, loaded gas or water pipes at Louisville consigned to the U.S. at Cairo. Off the lists 1869.

2064 FLORA CLARK

Stw rafter-p wh b. Hastings, Minn., 1894. 130 x 25.3 x 4.5. Engines, 12's- 6½ ft. Two boilers, each 43″ dia. by 18 ft. Used as a rafter out of Stillwater, Capt. Elmer Brown, later Capt. Edward Miller. In winter she made trips south with produce and grain in barges. Later was an excursion boat out of Stillwater and St. Paul. Burned May 17, 1900, at South Stillwater, just off the ways. Her engines went to the *LORA* (see) just being built.

2065 FLORA SWANN

Stw p wh b. Knoxville, Tenn., 1896. 98 x 13 x 2.8. Engines, 9's- 3 ft. Firebox boiler. Ran on the upper Tennessee. Rebuilt at Knoxville in 1903 and renamed *JANE AUSTIN* (see).

2066 FLORA TEMPLE

SW p wh b. Monongahela, Pa., 1858. 158 x 30 x 4. Named for a race horse of some fame in the 1850s. Currier & Ives issued a litho of this horse, 1872. First home port was Keokuk, Iowa. In April 1860 running New Orleans-Bayou De Glaize, Capt. D. Glasscock. That November running New Orleans-Big Tensas River, Capt. George R. Caradine. She was in Confederate service during the war, renamed *COTTON PLANT*. As such she exploded boilers on Sunflower River at Lake George, July 24, 1863. Had several owners in 1861, among them Preston Lodwick of New Orleans.

2067 FLORENCE

SW ferry wh b. West Brownsville, Pa., 1857. 64 tons. First home port, Paducah, Ky. Out of service in 1859.

2068 FLORENCE

SW p wh b. Elizabeth, Pa., 1857. 399 tons. 200 x 34. Engines, 22½'s- 6½ ft. Three boilers. Built for Capt. Joseph Throckmorton and others. Ran St. Louis-Sioux City, and made one trip to Fort Stewart 100 miles above the Yellowstone. Snagged and sunk at Port William, Kans., in 1857, raised. Was sold to J.C. Coeplan and others, St. Louis. Snagged and lost at Atchison, Kans., on Mar. 29, 1864, Capt. Coeplan.

2069 FLORENCE

Stw p wh b. Elizabeth, Pa., 1861. 196 tons. Advertised to depart Pittsburgh latter March, 1862 for St. Louis, Capt. Z.C. Brickell. Sold June 1862 to Capt. Will Kyle and others, Cincinnati. Taken over by the U.S. and renamed *CURLEW* Dec. 17, 1862, tinclad #12 (see).

2070 FLORENCE

Stw sawmill boat wh b. Malta, Oh., 1883. 77 x 16 x 3. Operated by Capt. James McCoy. Was still documented in 1896.

2071 FLORENCE

Stw ferry wh b. Jeffersonville, Ind., by Howard, 1889. 134 x 34 x 4.5. Operated by Capt. John Berry, son of Capt. J.H. Berry. Another son was "Dode" Berry, Williamstown, W. Va., associated with the *T.N. BARNSDALL* (see). This ferry operated in the St. Louis locale until wrecked in ice at the foot of Sidney Street, St. Louis, January 1910.

2072 FLORENCE

Prop p sh b. Shreveport, La., 1893. 56.1 x 12 x 5.8. Shreveport-Index trade, 1894.

2073 FLORENCE BELLE

Stw p wh b. Brownsville, Pa., at Axton Yard, 1895. 150 x 27 x 3. Engines, 13's- 4 ft. by Rees. Came out in April 1895 for the Allegheny River trade, Pittsburgh-East Brady, Capt. H.P. Hudson. In May 1897 made a trip to Oil City, Pa., and took out excursions to Indian God Rock, the last steam packet in that area. Her partner in the East Brady trade was the *NELLIE HUDSON NO. 3* (see). Owners were Capt. H. Page Hudson, Freeport, and Capt. T.P. Hudson, Clinton. Transferred to the Pittsburgh-Morgantown trade, Monon River, summer of 1897. Originally had the pilothouse forward on the boiler deck; in spring of 1898 it was raised on the roof and the boiler deck extended forward. Made a special trip to Fairmont, W. Va., arriving there May 18, 1898, Capt. T.P. Hudson. Harry Donaldson was pilot, having been up there before on *WEST VIRGINIA* (see). A number of persons from Morgantown made the trip. Telephone lines and cable wires were cut and parted at several places. Three boats had been to Fairmont prior; the *ELECTOR,* the *WEST VIRGINIA* (in 1872) and the towboat *HARRY.* Cut down by ice at Creighton, Pa., Dec. 20, 1909.

2074 FLORENCE D.

Steam tug wh b. Pekin, Ill., 1908. 60 x 11 x 5. She was licensed to carry passengers. Documented at St. Louis as a towboat, 1918.

2075 FLORENCE LEE

Stw p wh b. Cincinnati, Oh., 1870. 369 tons. Ran Evansville-Paducah-Tennessee River, Capt. Lee Howell, with R.C. McMechan, clerk. Same trade 1872, Capt. Allen Duncan, with Al Maynard, clerk. When dismantled 1878 her machinery went to *SILVER CLOUD* (see) and the hull served as the wharfboat at Vevay, Ind., operated there by William McKinney.

2076 FLORENCE MEYER

Stw p wh b. Cincinnati, Oh., 1876. 246 tons. She loaded at Little Rock, Ark., leaving there Apr. 9, 1877, and went to the mouth of the Bighorn River on the Yellowstone. She was under charter to Capt. W.F. Davidson and John B. Davis. Was at Fort Smith, Ark., Apr. 3, 1878, loading for Pittsburgh with 600 bales of cotton and a good miscellaneous trip. Owned by Capt. James Nichols, who was master, and named for daughter of Gabriel Meyer, Little Rock, Ark., a large cotton shipper. Ran Pittsburgh-Cincinnati in 1878 with James Alexander as clerk, and also pinch-hit for the *HUDSON* in Wheeling-Cincinnati trade. Sank and lost on the Mississippi about 12 miles above Natchez at Bullett's Bayou in mid-September 1880. She was deeply laden, and five lives were lost. Capt. James Nichols then bought the *THOMAS SHERLOCK* (see).

2077 FLORENCE MILLER

Stw p wh b. Cincinnati, Oh., 1862. 165 tons. Taken over by the U.S. and became tinclad #1, renamed *RATTLER,* Nov. 11, 1862. Lost at Grand Gulf, Miss., 1864.

2078 FLORENCE MILLER NO. 2

Stw p wh b. Cincinnati, Oh., 1863. 189 tons. Taken over by U.S. and became tinclad #34, renamed *MOOSE,* May 20, 1863. Sold to private owners Oct. 9, 1865, renamed *LITTLE ROCK* and burned and lost at Clarendon, Ark., Dec. 23, 1867.

2079 FLORENCE MILLER NO. 3

Stw p wh b. Cincinnati, Oh., 1864. 236 tons. Taken over by U.S. and became tinclad #52, renamed *ORIOLE,* Dec. 7, 1864. When taken over she was owned by John Swasey & Co., and others, who also transferred *ALLEN COLLIER* to the U.S. that same day. Sold to private owners Oct. 14, 1865, renamed *AGNES.* Snagged and lost at Warrenton, Miss., Mar. 3, 1869.

2080 FLORENCE SHANKS

Prop p wh b. Mason City, W. Va., 1888. 96 x 16.5 x 3.8. Owned and operated by Paris C. Brown and others. Ran two trips an hour between Cincinnati and Dayton, Ky., stopping each way to handle passengers at Bellevue, Ky. Was too small, and *BELLEVUE* (see) replaced her in 1890. Ran Matamoras-Sistersville during the oil excitement there, but drew five feet and had much trouble. Burned in the mouth of the Little Kanawha River, Parkersburg, W. Va., Aug. 30, 1896, at 11:00 P.M. Owned then by Capts. Cramer and Hutchinson.

2081 FLORENCE TRABER

Stw p wh b. Cincinnati, Oh., 1866. 241 tons. Ran Memphis-Arkansas River. She was snagged below Little Rock in February 1868, raised, repaired, and three trips later downbound from Dardanelle to Memphis she was snagged in Collins Shoal, 130 miles above Little Rock, and sank in nine feet. Reported "badly broken and will be lost."

2082 FLORIDA

SW p wh b. Louisville, Ky., 1856. 546 tons. Ran Louisville-New Orleans, Capt. Smith. Went to Confederate registry in 1861.

2083 FLORIDA

SW ship wh b. Sewickley, Pa., and completed at Pittsburgh, 1880. 184 x 46.2 x 8. Engines, 24's- 8 ft. by Rees. Ran Savannah-Jacksonville. In 1897 these same engines were sent to Cincinnati and placed on the *QUEEN CITY* (see).

2084 FLORIDA

Stw ferry wh b. Dravosburg, Pa., 1914. Originally named *ALBERT* (see). Boat broker John F. Klein bought her June 1923, repaired her at Cairo, renamed her *FLORIDA.* Sold her to Capt. A.C. Johnson, Helena, Ark., August 1927. Still listed 1929.

2085 FLORILDA

SW p wh b. Louisville, Ky., 1857. 304 tons. Built for Missouri River and came out new in the midst of a financial panic, costing about $35,000. Was said to have paid out in the first six months of operation. Off the lists in 1860.

2086 FLYING CLOUD

SW p wh b. Cincinnati, Oh., 1854. 540 tons. 247 x 37 x 7.5. Engines, 25's- 8 ft. Ran Cincinnati-St. Louis-New Orleans.

Capt. Clifford B. Wayne, Cincinnati, owned in her. Was commanded by Capt. Josiah Cressy for a while. Burned Dec. 10, 1860, 15 miles below Memphis, Capt. Swayne.

2087 FLYING EAGLE

Stw p wh b. Rock Island, Ill., 1888. Originally rafter *IRENE D.* 133.5 x 29.6 x 4.8. Operated out of Quincy, Ill., handling an excursion barge. Sank June 3, 1903.

2088 FONTENELLE

Stw p wh b. Brownsville, Pa., 1870. 205.5 x 33.8 x 4.3. Engines, 14½'s- 4½ ft. Three boilers. Built for Capt. John H. Shaw and saw much Missouri River service. Made seven trips to Fort Benton and four to Cow Island and Carroll for the Kountz and Peck Lines. She was the first arrival at the fort in 1874. She was snagged opposite Amazonia, Mo., August 1868 and raised. Again snagged 10 miles above St. Joseph, Mo., Aug. 21, 1871, raised. Made trips up Red River in 1872. In January 1876 was on the Arkansas, Capt. C.L. Brennan. Spent the winter 1876–1877 frozen in at Pascals Island, 60 miles above Fort Sully on the Missouri, and most of the crew were evacuated by wagon to the fort. Cut down by ice at Yankton, S.D., spring of 1881.

2089 FOREST CITY

SW p wh b. Brownsville, Pa., 1851. 207 tons. Operated in the Wheeling Union Line, Wheeling-Louisville, Capt. A. Murdoch, 1853. That fall was bought by Capt. George D. Moore and others who ran her Pittsburgh-Wheeling along with the *DIURNAL* (see). Capt. Benjamin Way, Wellsville, Oh., also commanded. Sold in November 1857 to a Capt. Porterfield of Vicksburg for the Vicksburg-Napoleon, Ark., trade, to handle U.S. Mail. Off the lists 1859.

2090 FOREST CITY

Stw p wh b. Pittsburgh, Pa., 1865. 243 tons. Built for Pittsburgh-Parkersburg trade, Capt. John Gordon. Sold at U.S. marshal sale April 1867 to Capt. B.W. Doyle, Capt. Abner O'Neal and Nate Wintringer who ran her Steubenville-Wheeling. Rebuilt 1875 at Brownsville, Pa. Capt. John A. Edie, Steubenville, bought the Doyle interest later. Following the rebuilding she was renamed *ABNER O'NEAL* (see).

2091 FOREST MONARCH

SW p wh b. New Albany, Ind., 1848. 215 tons. Built for the Tombigbee and Alabama rivers. She is mentioned in Carl Carmer's *Stars Fell on Alabama.* Snagged and lost on the Tombigbee, Apr. 14, 1855.

2092 FOREST QUEEN

SW p wh b. Cincinnati, Oh., 1851. 283 tons. Ran local trades from Cincinnati, probably to Lawrenceburg, Ind. Off the lists 1859.

2093 FOREST QUEEN

SW p wh b. Madison, Ind., 1858. 419 tons. Built for the Cincinnati-Madison trade, Capt. C. Dan Conway. Made a trip to Pittsburgh in May 1862, got stuck in Glasshouse Riffle just below town, and had to reship cargo by wagon. During the war she served the U.S. with her own crew and management. Ran the Vicksburg batteries Apr. 17, 1863, same time the *HENRY CLAY* (see) was destroyed by gunfire, without harm. Gen. Phil Sheridan later wrote a letter of commendation to Capt. Conway for this accomplishment. Burned at St. Louis along with the *CHANCELLOR* and *CATAHOULA* on Oct. 4, 1863, still in U.S. service.

2094 FOREST ROSE

Stw p wh b. California, Pa., 1852. 205 tons. 154 x 28.5 x 5. First master and part owner, Capt. Francis Maratta, Beaver County, Pa. She ran trips Pittsburgh-St. Louis, and was at St. Paul in 1856. She was at St. Louis in February 1856 when ice wrecked many boats, but was protected behind the Keokuk wharfboat and came off unharmed. Owned by Capt. Richard E. Allen of Paducah she exploded boilers near Napoleon, Ark., on Mar. 25, 1857. Was upbound from New Orleans to Arkansas River. Life loss was given between six and 14 persons, one of whom was the seven-year-old son of Captain Allen. This happened about two miles below Napoleon, and the sound was heard there. The *ARKANSAS* went to the scene to render aid.

2095 FOREST ROSE

Stw p wh b. Freedom, Pa., 1862. 203 tons. 155 x 32.2 x 4.7. Engines, 16's- 5 ft. Built for Capt. Francis (Frank) Maratta, designed for Pittsburgh-St. Louis trade. Sold to the U.S. Nov. 15, 1862, and became tinclad #9, retaining her original name. She was with the U.S. expedition up Yazoo and Sunflower rivers in May 1863 seeking out hidden boats and destroying them. On Red River helping build the ingenious Red River dam. Sold Oct. 14, 1865, and was renamed *ANNA WHITE* (see).

2096 FORESTER

Stw p wh b. Brownsville, Pa., 1854. 188 tons. Burned and lost at New Richmond, Oh., Nov. 13, 1854, with loss of three lives.

2097 FORT GAINES

SW p wh b. New Orleans, La., 1863. 69 tons. 100 x 20.4 x 4.3. Went to Confederate service and registry renamed *COMMODORE.* Captured by U.S. forces and commissioned Feb. 5, 1864, using her original name. Sold Aug. 15, 1865 to Capt. J.P. Furlong, master, and W.H.S. Miller, both of New Orleans. Off the lists 1870.

2098 FORT GIBSON

Stw p wh Details of construction not available. A dispatch dated Jan. 1, 1876, states that the boat was sunk at Bayou Metre, about 70 miles up the Arkansas, and cargo for St. Louis and elsewhere was being taken off by the *MAUMELLE.* The stern was in 16 ft. and the bow on logs about six ft. under.

2099 FORT HENRY

Stw p wh b. Wheeling, Va., 1853. 157 tons. Went to Confederate registry in 1861. She ran out of Wheeling the first year or so, Capt. George Johnston, Wheeling-Louisville.

2100 FORT HENRY

Originally the packet *ALECK SCOTT* (see), renamed by the USQMC in May 1862. Later on the U.S. Navy converted her into a ram, renamed *LAFAYETTE* (see).

2101 FORT HINDMAN

SW tinclad wh Originally ferry *JAMES THOMPSON* built 1861. Purchased April 16, 1863 from H. Marburg et al. for $35,000. Converted into Tinclad #13, 150 x 37 x 5.7. Engines 16s- 5 ft. Two boilers. Capt. James Pierce commanded. Sold to Pink Varble Aug. 17, 1865 for $12,000; renamed *JAMES THOMPSON* Dec. 5, 1865. Dismantled 1873. The engines were later on the ferry *Z. M. SHERLEY* and then on the ferry *CITY OF JEFFERSONVILLE.*

2102 FORT PITT

Stw p wh b. Brownsville, Pa., 1848. 130 tons. Built for Capt. A.D. Miller, master and owner, and made trips up the Allegheny River. Pittsburgh-Nashville, early 1850. In Wheeling-Parkersburg trade, Capt. J.C. Jelly, spring 1854. The first person to jump off an Ohio River bridge was a young lady, a seamstress, who leaped over the rail of the Wheeling suspension bridge on Jan. 25, 1854, aged 18. The river was full of floating ice. Two crew members of the *FORT PITT* launched a yawl and rescued her intact, Martin Dana and Ezekiel Doty. A young man named Lemuel Stanley ran a three-time insertion ad in a Wheeling newspaper disclaiming responsibility. The *FORT PITT* was off the lists 1857.

2103 FORT PITT

SW pl wh b. Pittsburgh, Pa., 1865. Started for Oil City up the Allegheny and was turned back at Mahoning Creek by low water, October 1865. Then went up the Monon to mouth of Cheat River on a fishing expedition. Departed Pittsburgh November 1865 to Rochester, Pa., and ascended the Beaver canal to New Castle and Conneaut Lake where she wintered, and returned to Pittsburgh April 1866, moored at the Fort Pitt Foundry. Crew on these adventures included Capt. James Scott, Col. Juskye, and Maj. John Smith. These trips were given generous notice in the Pittsburgh *Commercial* in successive issues.

2104 FORT SMITH

Stw p wh b. Pittsburgh, Pa., 1866. 244 tons. Built for Maj. John D. Adams of the Memphis & Arkansas River Packet Co. Operated Memphis-Arkansas and White rivers. Bound for Memphis with 370 bales of cotton she sank one-half mile below the foot of the cut off on White River, Oct. 27, 1871. Capt. James N. Bolin was master, J.N. Harbin, clerk, and Leland Drake, pilot.

2105 FORT SMITH

Stw p wh b. Fort Smith, Ark., 1881. 100.5 x 20.5 x 2.5. Still listed in 1886.

2106 FORT TOWSON

SW p wh b. Louisville, Ky., 1842. 142 tons. 135 x 23.5 x 4.8. First master, Capt. Joseph Scott, New Orleans, also part owner. Sold August 1843 to Capt. Franklin Keeling and others. Again sold November 1844 to J.W. Rhodes and John A. Stevenson, New Orleans. In April 1845 sold to Sarah Swofford, Catahoula Parish, La., and master was Capt. Samuel Gleen, Jr. Off the list in 1847.

2107 FORT WAYNE

SW p wh b. Cincinnati, Oh., 1844. 243 tons. Hull was built at Murraysville, Va. for Capt. Hicks. Off the lists 1848.

2108 FORT WAYNE

Stw p wh b. California, Pa., 1857. 148 x 41 x 6. 321 tons. First master, Capt. P.S. Mulford who also was part owner along with Sam Barr, Jr., Jacob Hamilton, James Vandergrift—all of Pittsburgh—and Charles W. Talbott of New Matamoras, Oh. In February 1861 sank at Island 16, Mississippi River, Capt. Sam Barr, Jr., master, with Charles Talbott, clerk, assisted by Jacob Hamilton. Was a transport during the war. In spring of 1862 took a fleet of pontoons from Cincinnati to Pittsburg Landing, Tenn. Ran Louisville-Nashville after the war owned by Sherley Woolfolk & Co., and W.C. Hite, both of Louisville, and Barker, Hart & Cook, Cincinnati. Off the lists 1867.

2109 FORTUNE

SW p wh b. Louisville, Ky., 1845. 101 tons. First home port, St. Louis. Made a trip Cincinnati-Nashville, Capt. Clarke. In April 1845 bought at Cincinnati by Capt. Pierce Atchison who ran her St. Louis-Galena. Sank a keelboat loaded with 1,600 pigs of lead in the mouth of Fever River, July 1846. Sank and lost on the upper rapids, September 1847.

2110 FORTUNE

Stw p wh b. Shousetown, Pa., 1857. 85 tons. Built for Capt. William Reno who ran her in the Pittsburgh-Wheeling trade, in place of the *DIURNAL* which had retired (see). Ran there until December 1857, and was replaced by *ROCKET* (see). Went to Confederate registry 1861.

2111 FOUNTAIN CITY

Stw p wh b. Fountain City, Wis., 1905. 99.5 x 23.5 x 4.3. Engines, 10's- 6½ ft. One boiler, 42" dia. by 15 ft. Was built using much from rafter *LAFAYETTE LAMB.* Ran in the Winona-Fountain City trade, proved too large, and was sold to Capt. Frank J. Fugina and Capt. William Henning of Winona. They ran her with an excursion barge on the upper Mississippi for several years, then sold her to James Grasty, Greenville, Miss. The Vicksburg Gravel Co. owned her briefly, and then she went to Pearl River, Miss., to operate out of Columbia. By 1912 she was in the Burnside & Burksville Packet Co., upper Cumberland River, and sank at Mile 17, Robertsport, and was not raised.

2112 FOUR BOYS

Ferry wh b. Pine Bluff, Ark., 1882. 17.82 tons.

2113 FOX

Stw p wh b. Little Rock, Ark., 1855. 74 tons. Destroyed by gunfire above the raft on Red River, Mar. 28, 1861.

2114 FOX

Ferry wh b. Little Rock, Ark., 1876. 34.84 tons. Documented at Memphis.

2115 FRANCES JONES

SW p wh b. Louisville, Ky., 1852. 62 tons. Owned by Capt. Robert E. Jones, a wealthy Red River planter, an Indian. He also owned the *R.M. JONES*. Ran in upper Red River. Dismantled 1857.

2116 FRANCIS

Stw ferry wh b. Manchester, Oh., 1892. 84 x 24.2 x 3. Originally named *LITTLE LAFIE* (see). She was brought to Gallipolis early 1910, burned off her upper works on February 5, was rebuilt and renamed, owned by Capt. Miles H. Brown. Later bought by Capt. Gordon C. Greene and Charles Stalder who continued her at Gallipolis. Sold April 1919 to John W. Lane who renamed her *JOHN W. LANE* (see). She had the whistle from the Kanawha River packets *JOHN MORGAN, CLARIBEL,* and *NEVA*.

2117 FRANCIS FISHER

SW p wh b. Louisville, Ky., 1861. 301 tons. Operated out of St. Louis. When the *BADGER STATE* sank, Dec. 14, 1862, she removed the furniture, etc., and brought it to St. Louis. Sank and lost at St. Louis, Jan. 21, 1873.

2118 FRANCIS J. TORRANCE

SW ex boat wh b. Marietta, Oh., at Knox Yard, 1900. 211.5 x 34.9 x 6.4. Engines, 20's- 7 ft. Four boilers, each 40" dia. by 26 ft. Built for the Monongahela & Ohio Transportation Co., about 60 stockholders, of which F.J. Torrance was president. Ran excursions on upper Ohio and Monon rivers. Capt. R.M. Boyd was first master, with Aaron McLaughlin, pilot. Sold November 1905 to Coney Island Co., Cincinnati, of which Lee H. Brooks was president. Was renamed *PRINCESS* (see).

2119 FRANCIS WRIGHT

Stw p wh b. Madison, Ind., 1869. 129 x 31.7 x 4.6. Operated out of New Orleans, Capt. J.T. Feeder. A stockholder was T.H. Iler of Shreveport. Capt. E.D.G. Smith, master, in 1870. The *Lytle List* reports she originally was *HIBISCUS,* built 1864 at Fairhaven, Conn., and resumed her original name Sept. 14, 1870; lost in 1873.

2120 FRANK B. HAYNE

Stw p wh b. Jeffersonville, Ind., by Howard, 1904. 130.4 x 27 x 4. Built for John P. Parker, Monroe, La., for Ouachita River trade. Had the machinery from *PARLOR CITY*. Sold in 1908, renamed *ALICE B. MILLER* (see).

2121 FRANK BATES

SW p wh b. New Albany, Ind., 1866. 539 tons. Operated out of St. Louis. Burned at St. Louis, new, Apr. 7, 1866.

2122 FRANK BURNETT

Stw p wh b. Quincy, Ill., 1876. 7.61 tons. 50.5 x 9.2 x 2.8. Named for the U.S. Supervising Steamboat Inspector at Quincy, and was designed to carry 80 persons on short excursions. Later was a towboat. Still documented at Paducah 1896.

2123 FRANK FORREST

Rig? wh b. Durand, Wis., 1870. 108 tons. Was running Memphis-Hales Point, Capt. T.B. Sexton, spring 1873. Burned Dec. 12, 1876, at Cottonwood Point, Mo., 60 miles above Memphis. She was laid up at the time, and had not been in service for several months.

2124 JOHN H. KIRBY

Stw pl sh b. Chicago, Ill., by Marine Iron Works, 1902. 82 x 17.6. Overall length, 97.5 ft. and overall beam, 21 ft. Draft 2.6 ft. High pressure engines. One dry back Scotch boiler. She was single deck, one stack, pilothouse forward of the cabin. Delivered under her own steam to Beaumont, Tex., going through the Gulf. Her guards were removed to get her through the narrow Illinois-Michigan Canal locks. See *Way's Steam Towboat Directory,* T1409A.

2125 FRANK KRANZ

Stw p ih b. Pittsburgh, Pa., 1878. 130 x 28 x 3. The iron hull was built by Riter & Conley, and she was taken to Cincinnati for completion. Had Dumont engines, 16's- 4 ft. and the paddlewheel was all iron save the buckets. Designed for the New Orleans-Grand Isle trade, and went there via Harvey Canal and Bayou Barataria. Grand Isle was a watering resort 85 miles southwest of New Orleans. Capt. John Richey took her south. Sank and lost at Stella Plantation, La., November 1878; and loss was placed at $40,000.

2126 FRANK LORENTZ

Prop p wh b. Cincinnati, Oh., 1875. 40 x 10 x 1.7. Upright steam engine, single cylinder, 6" dia. by 8" stroke. One vertical tubular boiler, 38" dia. by 6 ft. with 54 2" flues. Engine shaft ran aft and coupled to it at the rear of the boat was a sheet-iron fan 6'10" dia. with three blades, an airplane prop. Whether this experiment worked is not clear, but little was heard of it after the initial announcements.

2127 FRANK LYON

SW p wh b. Jeffersonville, Ind., by Howard, 1851. 204.8 x 30.3 x 7.5. Went to Mobile, Ala., but returned to New Orleans and 1852 was in New Orleans-Vicksburg trade, Capt. Stone. Sold April 1853 to William C. Harrissson, New Orleans, who put Capt. J.M. White master in summer trade to Vicksburg in place of the *MAGNOLIA*. Out of service in 1857.

2128 FRANK MCHARRY

SW ferry wh b. New Albany, Ind., 1867. Rebuilt at Jeffersonville, Ind., 1876. 125.5 x 34.5 x 4.2. Engines, 14's- 4 ft. Two boilers each 45" dia. by 25 ft. Paddlewheels 16½ ft. dia. working 6½ ft. buckets. Capt. John B. Mitchell, first master, with Ed Key, engineer, and Thomas Conner, pilot. Owned by the New Albany & Portland Ferry Co. Named for the late Francis McHarry. Dismantled 1890.

2129 FRANK MORGAN

Stw p wh b. Sodo Lake, La., 1869. 124.1 x 25.7 x 4.3. 108 tons. Ran New Orleans-Shreveport, Capt. C.W. Tandy. Lost in a storm at New Orleans, Sept. 15, 1875.

2130 FRANK P. GRACEY

Rig? Operated out of Evansville, Ind., in 1872, Capt. Wiley Simms, master, with Fred Jones, clerk. Burned at Dutch Bend laid up for ice, below Evansville, Feb. 14, 1875. Was 29 months old at the time of the fire and was a complete loss.

2131 FRANK PARGOUD

SW p wh b. Jeffersonville, Ind., by Howard, 1868. 255 x 41 x 9.3. Engines, 32's- 9 ft. Seven boilers, each 38" dia. by 28 ft. Named for Gen. Frank Pargoud, wealthy Ouachita River planter. Built for Capt. John W. Tobin, New Orleans, sole owner. Designed for the New Orleans-Ouachita River trade, proved too large, so went to the New Orleans-St. Louis trade. Made several trips there. Then ran New Orleans-Memphis, a round trip a week (something of an accomplishment for a regular packet). Then ran New Orleans-Vicksburg, two round trips a week (the *MISSISSIPPI QUEEN* in 1977-1978 was making one round trip a week in this trade) and then settled down running New Orleans-Fort Adams. At this time the *KATIE* (see) was running New Orleans-Greenville, Capt. J.M. White, met financial troubles, and was laid up. Capt. Tobin hired White as master of the *FRANK PARGOUD* and immediately entered the New Orleans-Greenville trade where the boat made a mint of money. One writer of the time said "a notorious fact is that her last trip was the most profitable one." The *J.M. WHITE* was built to replace her, at which time the *FRANK PARGOUD* was laid up at New Orleans opposite the Ursaline Convent. Her boilers were removed but, otherwise intact, she slumbered there several years. Captain Tobin had put her out to pasture as reward for work well done.

2132 FRANK PRESTON

Stw p wh b. Catlettsburg, Ky., 1884. 120 x 19.3 x 2.9. Ran Catlettsburg-Big Sandy River, owned largely at Paintsville. Capt. Green Meek. In the 1880s carried a delegation up the Big Sandy investigating the Hatfield-McCoy difficulties. Often ran during low water in local Ohio River trades. Running to Racine, Oh., September 1886, Capt. James Welsh, with S.G. Preston, clerk. Still listed 1892.

2133 FRANK S. OWENS

Ferry wh b. Cincinnati, Oh., 1879. 93 x 24 x 3.2. Ferried Maysville-Aberdeen, Capt. William Linton, bucking the *GRETNA GREEN,* Capt. J.C. Powers. Powers then bought the *OWENS.* Went to Bellaire, Oh., and ferried to Benwood, W. Va. The hull for years lay along the Ohio shore below Duffy, Oh., and just below the location of former Lock 15; still visible in low water in 1915.

2134 FRANK SHERMAN

Ferry wh b. Grafton, Ill., 1879. 117.2 x 33.2 x 4.4. Inspected at Quincy, Ill., 1881. Still listed 1896.

2135 FRANK STEELE

SW p wh b. Hampton, Ky., 1857. 136 tons. 175 x 28. Capt. William F. Davidson ran her in the Minnesota River 1857-1859 and in the spring of 1860. Ran La Crosse-St. Paul 1860-1861, and again on the Minnesota River 1862. Exploded at La Crosse, June 2, 1864, with loss of two lives.

2136 FRANK STEIN

Stw p wh b. Belle Vernon, Pa., 1883. 138.6 x 25 x 3.1. Built for the Wheeling-Clarington trade, Capt. J.B. Thompson, with Eb Cline, clerk. Ran Wheeling-Marietta in 1884, same crew. Ran briefly Marietta-Gallipolis, Capt. Wm. Williamson, with Landstron Cook, clerk, both of Racine, Oh. Capt. J.B. Thompson removed his operations to Evansville, Ind., and took the *STEIN* down there. Still listed in 1892.

2137 FRANK VON BEHREN

SW p wh b. Spottsville, Ky., 1896. 116 x 24 x 3.

2138 FRANK WILLARD

Stw p wh b. Ironton, Oh., 1873. 75 tons. In July 1875 under charter to the Pittsburgh Coal Exchange she carried pilots on an inspection trip down the Ohio recommending relocation of the original shore lights just placed by the Lighthouse Service. Was running New Orleans-Ouachita River, January 1876, Capt. Rack Vaughn, with Lew Rice, clerk. Back to the upper Ohio that summer. Ran New Orleans-Red River in 1878. Inspected at New Orleans in 1882.

2139 FRANKIE FOLSOM

Stw p wh b. Stillwater, Minn., 1886. 82.6 x 15.4 x 3. Was running an excursion Peoria-Pekin on Illinois River when she encountered a thunderstorm at Peoria night of July 12, 1892. Capsized and drowned 10 or 12 persons. Capt. Edward Loesch was pilot on watch. Later was renamed *LEO* and ran on the Ouachita River.

2140 FRANKLIN

Stw p wh b. Brownsville, Pa., 1851. 181 tons. Burned on the Apalachicola River, Fla., January 1854 with loss of one life.

2141 FRANKLIN

SW p wh b. Brownsville, Pa., 1860. 181 tons. Ran on Monongahela River in the Pittsburgh, Brownsville & Geneva Packet Co. She was General Grant's dispatch boat at Vicksburg during the war. Back in Monon River trade in 1867. Off the lists 1872 and her engines went to the towboat *ARK.*

2142 Franklin Pierce

SW p wh b. Covington, Ky., 1853. 348 tons. 179 x 32 x 6.1. Capt. W.W. Withenburg, Cincinnati, ran her on Red River. He applied to change the boat's name on the grounds it was unlucky. On Feb. 22, 1855, she became the *TEXANA* by a special act of Congress. On Apr. 18, 1855, she burned in the Yazoo River.

2143 Fred A. Blanks

SW p wh b. Madison, Ind., 1879 at the Dan Morton yard, 1879. 260 x 41 x 9.5. Engines, 26's- 9 ft. Six boilers. 79 ft. overall. The main deck was 15½ ft. high. She had 32 staterooms, each 9 by 12 ft., and the forward panels in the cabin were embellished with scenes in oils along Black River where Capt. Fred liked to shoot alligators. This was the 28th boat the Blanks family had owned in. Ran New Orleans-Ouachita River. She was cut in two during the New Orleans Exposition by a steamship.

2144 Fred A. Blanks

Stw p wh b. Jeffersonville, Ind., by Howard, 1890. Originally named *OUACHITA*. Capt. L.V. Cooley sold her to the Blanks family and she was renamed. Ran New Orleans-Ouachita River. Was at Paducah having work done and couldn't pay the bills, so Henry A. Petter of that place, plus other creditors, had her sold by the U.S. marshal. In March 1901 Capt. Lew Brenner was master, back in her old trade. Again went to U.S. sale and was bid in by Capt. E.W.B. Nowland for $8,500, this in July 1902. He renamed her *VICKSBURG* (see).

2145 Fred Lorentz

Stw p wh b. Belle Vernon, Pa., 1855. 236 tons. Ran St. Louis-St. Paul 1857-1859. Then was in the Northern Line, same trade, 1860-1861. Made a trip to Pittsburgh March 1862, Capt. Isaac M. Mason. Towed some coal from Pittsburgh to Louisville later that month and then was dismantled.

2146 Fred Swain

SW p wh b. Stillwater, Minn., 1900. 142 x 28.3 x 4.5. Swain compound condensing engines, 12's, 20's- 6 ft. One boiler, 44" dia. by 18 ft. Owned by La Salle & Peoria Packet Co. She departed Peoria on a regular trip in August 1909, caught fire 20 minutes later, was safely landed and 25 passengers and crew came ashore safely. Capt. Verne Swain was in command at the time.

2147 Fred Tron

Stw p wh b. Madison, Ind., 1856. 152 x 37 x 5.5. Engines, 18½'s- 6½ ft. Two boilers, each 42" dia. by 26 ft. Ran Pittsburgh-St. Louis. She had made a New Orleans trip and was northbound when she sank at Island 10, Mississippi River, Oct. 22, 1860, Capt. Fenton, owned by Fenton and Kyle, Cincinnati.

2148 Freddie

Stw freighter wh b. Cairo, Ill., 1875. 29 tons. 70 x 16 and drew nine inches light. One engine, 6" bore, 20" stroke flat-belted to jackshaft and chain to sprocket. A flatboat with cargo box and pilothouse. In the hands of a U.S. marshal for debt at Cairo August 1876 and sold to George Carvell & Co., for $75. Said the Memphis *Avalanche,* Oct. 20, 1876: "The little two dollar and six-bitts steamer *FREDDIE* passed here Friday on her way from Cairo to White River. A circus agent was watching for her to offer the owner a bid on her purchase, but the dinky didn't land."

2149 Freddie

Stw p wh b. Rock Island, Ill., 1891. 73 x 16 x 3. Capt. John Streckfus bought this one to operate in the Quad-City area, Upper Mississippi and so started the Streckfus Line. Listed in 1895, maybe later.

2150 Freddie Robinson

Ferry wh b. Jeffersonville, Ind., 1882. 125 tons. 100 x 28 x 4.3. Inspected in the Memphis District through 1886, maybe later.

2151 Frederic Notrebe

Stw p wh b. Cincinnati, Oh., 1860. 190 tons. Burned and lost at Van Buren, Ark., Dec. 27, 1862.

2152 Frederick

Stw p wh b. Tuscumbia, Mo., 1883. 96.4 x 14.3 x 3. Engines, 7½" bore, 2½ ft. stroke. One boiler. Capt. Henry Castrup and Bob Marshall ran her on Osage River along with the *HULBERT* connecting with the MP Railroad at Osage City. Sold in 1889, and towed barges. She sank at Jefferson City, Mo., Aug. 10, 1894, then managed by R.M. Marshall. Dismantled.

2153 Frederick

Stw ferry wh b. Sattes, W. Va., 1922. 62 x 19 x 3.1. Owned by Sattes Ferry Co., Sattes, W. Va. Still listed 1929.

2154 Freedom

Stw freight boat wh b. Freedom, Pa., 1847. 33 tons. Built by Hugh and Andrew G. Smith and Capt. Joe Stephens commanded. Made trips up the Allegheny. Capt. I.N. Hook had her on the Muskingum handling freight 1855-1856. Dismantled 1857.

2155 Freedom

Stw p wh b. Bayou Black, La., 1850. 32 tons. First home port, Franklin, La. Off the lists in 1855.

2156 Freeman Rawdon

SW ocean ship wh b. Shousetown, Pa., 1850. 493 tons. Duplicate of the *MARTIN HOFFMAN* (see). Capt. C. Cadwallader, master. First home port, New York, N.Y. Renamed *CITY OF SAVANNAH* on Sept. 30, 1856. Foundered and lost off Cape Hatteras, Oct. 16, 1856.

2157 Freestone

Stw p wh b. Cincinnati, Oh., 1858. 150 tons. The hull was built at Murraysville, Va. for Garrett & Co. In early summer 1859 ran Parkersburg, Va. to Scotts Landing, Oh. connecting the Marietta & Cincinnati and the Baltimore & Ohio RRs (see *JOHN BUCK*). Once ran from Cincinnati to Buffalo, Va., on Kanawha River in 24 hours, considered a record. One of the pilots was Capt. W.F. Gregory. Sold south and was snagged and lost at Yazoo City, Miss., on Sept. 27, 1865.

2158 FREIGHTER

Stw p wh b. Zanesville, Oh., 1855. 93 tons. Handled freight 1855–1857 between Zanesville, Cincinnati, and Pittsburgh, Capt. William Davis. Went to the Minnesota River in 1857, Capt. John Farmer. Capt. John B. Davis bought her in 1859 and attempted to take her to the Red River of the North via Lake Traverse and Big Stone Lake. He started too late in the season on a falling river, and she was caught about 10 miles from Big Stone Lake and was a total loss. Her timbers remained there for many years.

2159 FRENCH

Stw p wh b. Parkersburg, W. Va., 1903. 104.8 x 22.4 x 4. Engines, 10's- 3½ ft. One boiler, 44″ dia. by 24 ft. Much equipment used from *ONEIDA* (see). Owned originally by Capt. Ben S. Pope and J.D. Robinson for the Parkersburg-Creston trade, Little Kanawha. Named for the skipper J.D. Robinson who was called "French" Robinson. He had her up to Grantsville on several occasions. Sold December 1906 to Capt. E.E. Varian, Pt. Pleasant, W. Va. Sold April 1908 to Albert Monteith and George H. Fritz, both of Parkersburg. They sold her July 1914 to E. Berry and A.J. Jacobs, Paducah. Capt. Rush Burnside took her down, with Earl Bryan, engineer. Burned Nov. 14, 1914, having run Paducah-McGhee's Landing, Capt. A.J. Jacobs. Fire was at the mouth of Sandy, Tennessee River.

2160 FRIENDLY

Stw p wh b. Friendly, W. Va., 1888. 66 tons. 120 x 27 x 3.5. Two boilers. Burned Oct. 8, 1892, at Douglas Plantation above Shreveport, La.

2161 FRIENDSHIP

Stw p wh b. Wheeling, Va., 1847. 98 tons. Ran occasional trips Pittsburgh-Zanesville in 1848–1849, Capt. Wm. Davis. Rebuilt at Wheeling in 1851. Off the lists 1854.

2162 FROLIC

Stw p wh b. Louisville, Ky., 1844. 126 tons. Loaded at Pittsburgh spring 1844, Capt. Baldwin, for Missouri River. Burned and lost at St. Louis, Apr. 17, 1849.

2163 FROLIC

SW p wh b. Wheeling, Va., 1860. 393 tons. Was in Confederate hands when captured by Porter in 1864. In August 1866 owned by Mary Heimes, New Orleans, with Capt. J.J. Compere, master. Ran New Orleans-Alexandria. Sold May 1867 to John Haelierle, New Orleans, with Capt. George Alban, master. Same trade, 1869, Capt. John Heimes, and also in 1870, Capt. Fred Probst with Richard Hawkins, clerk. Off the lists 1873.

2164 FROMAN M. COOTS

SW ferry sh b. Jeffersonville, Ind., by Howard, 1912. 169 x 50 x 7. She was diesel-electric drive to side-wheels, originally the steam side-wheel *W.S. McCHESNEY, JR.* Converted in 1925 by Falls City Ferry & Transportation Co., Jeffersonville, Ind. Operated Louisville-Jeffersonville. When the highway bridge was opened, she was sold to Ohio River Transit Co., and they ran her Louisville-Cincinnati. She had two F-M diesels, 240 hp. each.

2165 FRONTENAC

Stw rafter-ex wh b. Wabasha, Minn., 1896. 138.9 x 29.8 x 5. Engines, 16's- 5 ft. Built for the Laird, Norton Lumber Co., and rafted 11 years. Then was remodeled into an excursion boat and operated out of St. Paul about five years. She handled a large excursion barge named *MISSISSIPPI,* 182 x 45. Was renamed *PRINCE,* and the barge was renamed *PRINCESS*—the *PRINCE* burned while laid up for the winter in Quincy Bay, foot of Chestnut Street on Nov. 6, 1918. The barge *PRINCESS* was sold to the Barrett Line for a store boat at Cairo. Showboatman Otto Hitner bought it and from it built the showboat *COTTON BLOSSOM* which seated 1,200, the largest hull ever used for a showboat, and it had no pilothouse. Hitner operated it until 1929.

2166 FRONTIER CITY

Stw p wh b. Pittsburgh, Pa., 1860. 144 tons. Operated Memphis-Arkansas River, Capt. Sam Houston. In 1860 two packets were sunk on the Arkansas, the *CEDAR RAPIDS* and *A.H. SEVIER*. The *FRONTIER CITY* was sent up to recover the outfits from these two, loaded the stuff aboard, and sank in the head of Smith's Cut-Off near the mouth of the river, Jan. 4, 1861, resulting in the loss of all.

2167 FULTON

SW p wh b. Pittsburgh, Pa., 1839. 122 tons. Ran Pittsburgh-St. Louis, Capt. William Forsythe. Often ran Pittsburgh-Cincinnati. In spring of 1845, in Pittsburgh-Cincinnati trade, Capt. E.D. Collier, with William J. Kountz and C.W. Batchelor as pilots. Dismantled that fall.

2168 FULTON

SW p wh b. Jeffersonville, Ind., 1846. 114 tons. 110 x 25.5 x 4.2. In 1848 Capt. Matthew Woods, master, running Red River. Sold July 1848 to Capt. George H. Clark, master, and Henry Rhine, both of Caddo Parish, La. Snagged and lost at Shreveport, Mar. 15, 1849.

2169 FULTON

SW p wh b. Elizabeth, Pa., 1852. 206 tons. 142 x 29 x 5.4. Owned by Capt. Benjamin Crooks until sold at New Orleans June 1855 to James M. McCandlish, New Orleans. Transferred within a week (June 19, 1855) to John E. Caldwell and Charles Whiting, both of New Orleans, operating as J.E. Caldwell & Co. and sold Dec. 22, 1855, to

Capt. William Gwartney and J.H. Chapman, New Orleans. Later sold to Mobile and lost in 1863.

2170 FULTON CITY

Stw p wh b. McKeesport, Pa., 1857. 199 tons. Snagged and lost at Buffington Island, Ohio River, Nov. 11, 1858 with loss of five lives.

G

2171 G.A. SHELDON

Centerwheel ferry wh b. Algiers, La., 1860. 77 tons. 97 x 12 x 6.8. First owned and run by Capt. G.A. Sanford, New Orleans. Went to Confederate registry in 1861, same owner. Sold in 1863 to U.S. War Department.

2172 G.A. THOMSON

Stw p wh b. Eureka, Wis., and completed at St. Paul, 1865. 366 tons. In July 1866 advertised New Orleans to St. Louis, Capt. C.L. Huntoon, master, "she will take freight low." Capt. James Alexander Frazier, Cincinnati, and James H. Kelly, Racine, Wis., owned her as partners when she was snagged and lost some 50 miles above Pine Bluff, Ark., on the Arkansas River with reported loss of 17 lives, among them clerks George Ely and John Perkins, both of Cincinnati, this on Apr. 9, 1869. The wreck burned.

2173 G.B. ALLEN

SW p wh b. Metropolis, Ill., and completed at St. Louis, 1865. 593 tons. 215 x 34.5 x 5.5. Engines, 18's- 6 ft. from *GENERAL HODGES* (see). Three boilers. Built for Missouri River for John P. Keiser and others. Ran St. Louis-Shreveport. Burned at St. Louis Mar. 29, 1869, along with *CARRIE V. KOUNTZ* and four others. Sometimes referred to as *GERALD B. ALLEN* in accounts.

2174 G.B. KNAPP

Stw p wh b. Osceola, Wis., 1866. 105 tons. 130 x 20 x 4. Engines, 9's- 4 ft. until 1882 when she got 12's- 6 ft. Built by Capt. Oscar Knapp and named for his son. Ran on the St. Croix River most of the time, but made trips on the Minnesota 1866-1867. In May 1876 the *G.B. KNAPP* and *NELLIE KENT* were running hot opposition on the St. Croix with fares slashed to the bone. Oscar Knapp was squeezed out by other stockholders and then built the *JENNIE HAYS*. The son for whom the boat was named became U.S. Hull Inspector at Dubuque. Dismantled at Stillwater 1889 and engines went to rafter *RAVENNA*.

2175 G.B. MONTEITH

Stw p wh b. Long Reach, W. Va., 1885. 103.4 x 18.2 x 2. Often towed produce boats south from Meigs County, Oh., and also ran in the Ravenswood-Middleport trade. Later on c. 1890 was operated by Capt. W.D. Crammond, Hawesville, Ky. Listed 1895, maybe longer.

2176 G.F. TRUESDELL

Recess wheel ferry wh b. New Richmond, Oh., 1882. 79 x 25 x 3. Built by Capt. Henry Green of New Richmond who also was wharfmaster there. Business did not support the ferry so he sold her. The new owners named her *RICHMOND* (see).

2177 G.H. GRAY

Stw p wh b. Stillwater, Minn., 1863. 57 tons. Off the lists 1871.

2178 G.H. VAN ETTEN

Stw p wh b. Little Rock, Ark., 1881. 119 tons. 130 x 24 x 3. Engines, 15's- 4½ ft. Two boilers. Operated by the Memphis & Arkansas River Packet Co., which in 1884 also ran the *IDA DARRAGH, JOE PETERS,* and *KATE ADAMS*. The *G.H. VAN ETTEN* shuttled freight from Little Rock and Pine Bluff to Rosedale. Went to Mobile in 1888 and returned to sink on Red River at Oak Shoals, Jan. 8, 1889.

2179 G.M. SIVLEY

Stw p wh b. Le Claire, Iowa, 1893. 123.5 x 24 x 4.6. Ran on the Illinois River, Capt. G.M. Sivley who in 1900 also ran the *GOLDEN GATE* (see). In the fall of 1901 was at Helena, Ark., towing in daytime and taking out excursions at night.

2180 G.T. THAYER

Stw pl wh b. Charleston, W. Va., 1894. 46 x 9.3 x 2.2. Gunnel hull, main deck in the hold. One stack forward of the pilothouse. Still listed in 1896.

2181 G.W. ANDERSON

Freight boat wh b. Franklin, La., 1881. 81 x 22 x 3. Documented at Brashear, La., 1886.

2182 G.W. BOLTON

Catamaran ferry wh 80 x 12.5 x 4.5. Recessed center paddlewheel. Operated between Alexandria and Pineville on Red River. Made some packet trips Alexandria-Shreveport in 1891.

2183 G.W. CAMPBELL

Stw ferry wh b. West Wheeling, Oh., 1856. 50 tons. Burned and lost, Mar. 29, 1867.

2184 G.W. CHEEK

Stw p wh b. Madison, Ind., 1869. 241 tons. A two-boiler boat with 18" bore cylinders. Lengthened at Madison in 1872. Operated out of Memphis, and went to U.S. marshal sale there January 1877, sold to John J. Darragh. He sold her within 10 days to Perry & Morrow, Warsaw, Ky., for the Vevay-Cincinnati trade. The *BANNOCK CITY* (see) had been in the trade, but had sunk. W.H. Kirby, Warsaw, had ownership in her, and also was a stockholder in the *G.W. CHEEK*. Ran there all 1877.

2185 G.W. COBBETT

Prop ferry wh b. Pittsburgh, Pa., 1914. 58.5 x 12 x 3. Owned by John E. Cobbett, and ran Woods Run-McKees

Rocks. Sank in ice in the Pittsburgh area, January 1928, then owned by Francis G. Powers. She had sunk once before, after hitting a pier at Esplin.

2186 G.W. Forrest

Stw p wh b. Wheeling, Va., 1857. 90 tons. Went to New Orleans, owned there by New Orleans & Algiers Steam Ferry Co., Joseph Ballister, pres. Master in May 1861, Capt. G.W. Forrest. Sold October 1861 to James Wood, New Orleans, with Capt. Vincent Wood, master. Returned to U.S. registry June 1865, described as 100.6 x 30 x 3.4, William Randolph, master. Sold February 1867 to John Kouns, W.T. Scovell and K.L. Robertson, all of New Orleans, Capt. N.T. Scovell, master. Sank and lost in the Mississippi River, December 1868.

2187 G.W. Graham

SW p wh b. Elizabeth, Pa., 1861. 245 x 39 x 6.5. Engines, 25's- 7 ft. Three boilers. Named for G. Wash Graham, Halliday & Co., Cairo, Ill. Capt. C.W. Batchelor superintended construction. Ran St. Louis-Memphis, Capt. Bart Bowen. Sam Bowen was one of the pilots, both of Hannibal, Mo. Amanda Bowen, their sister, was usually aboard, having southern sympathies and banned from Hannibal. In 1867 made a trip up the Missouri to Fort Buford, and shortly after her return to St. Louis burned with *YELLOWSTONE* there, July 11, 1867.

2188 G.W. Hill

Stw p wh b. Jeffersonville, Ind., by Howard, 1909. 190 x 36 x 5. Engines, 16's- 7 ft. Three boilers, each 42" by 24 ft. Named for Granderson Winfrey Hill of Alexandria, Mo., who died at Alton, Ill., in his 87th year, January, 1911. Built by G.W. Hill for the St. Louis-Calhoun County trade. She was converted into an excursion boat in May 1912 owned by Capt. D.W. Wisherd and Sam Gregory. Tramped to New Orleans, Pittsburgh, etc., until 1923 when she was sold to the Coney Island Co., Cincinnati. Renamed *ISLAND MAID* (see).

2189 G.W. Huff

Stw p wh b. Poplar Bluff, Mo., 1904. 81 x 24.5 x 4. Ran on White River, and in November 1905 was running up Black River to Black Rock. Also up there at the time were the *ALMA JANE,* LAKE CITY *and TAYLOR,* running Pocahontas-Poplar Bluff. Still listed in 1918.

G.W. Kendall

See *GEORGE W. KENDALL,* registered name.

2190 G.W. Lyon

Stw p wh b. Tell City, Ind., 1893. 115 x 22 x 4. Built and owned by Capt. G.W. Lyon who soon moved operations to Greenville, Miss., and died there in June 1901. Sold to Capt. Henry Keith and others and was taken to the Missouri River, based at Glasgow, Mo. Still listed in 1908.

2191 G.W. Mayo

Stw p wh b. Fort Smith, Ark., 1888. 109 x 20 x 2.5. Operated on Arkansas River until 1896, and the following year was in upper Red River, Capt. A.P. Seaman.

2192 G.W. Robertson

Stw ferry wh b. Helena, Ark., 1910. 150 x 40 x 4.5. She became the ferry at Paducah, Ky., replacing the *CARRIE OWENS* (see). Left Paducah early 1914 and went to Memphis where she ran excursions along with the *CHAS. H. ORGAN* until replaced 1915 by the new *IDLEWILD.* Sold at U.S. marshal sale, December 1915, to Capt. Henry C. Murnan.

2193 G.W. Sentell

Stw p wh b. Jeffersonville, Ind., 1882. Originally named *HENRY A. TYLER* (see). Running New Orleans-Bayou Lafourche, 1889. Still there 1893, Capt. C.J. Blanchard, with Leo Guillott, clerk. Burned above New Orleans, Dec. 28, 1894. Machinery went to the *COL. T. G. SPARKS* (see).

2194 G.W. Sparhawk

SW p wh b. Wheeling, Va., 1851. 243 tons. Operated on the Upper Mississippi. Carried officials on an excursion incident to the opening of the Rock Island Railroad, June 1854, Capt. Monroeville Green. In St. Paul trade 1855. Lost in ice at St. Louis, Feb. 26, 1856.

2195 G.W. Thompson

Stw p wh b. Harmar, Oh. at Knox Yard, 1882. 114 x 20 x 3. Came out in the Gallipolis-Huntington trade, Capt. C.R. Small, with C.W. Thornily, purser, and Thomas Morton, clerk. Named for a Parkersburg business man. Ran in the Marietta-Parkersburg trade briefly. Sold, December 1883, renamed *BURNSIDE* (see).

2196 Galatea

SW p wh b. Freedom, Pa., 1868. 238 tons. She was at Pittsburgh loading for St. Louis on May 21, 1868, departing June 5. "A rather novel specimen of marine architecture in these waters." She carried but 20 psi. Had to return to Cairo unable to stem the current of the Mississippi, having ascended but 12 miles. She was turning up 30 rpm and couldn't hold steam. How she managed to get to St. Louis is not revealed, but she was there by mid-July advertising "picnic trips" in the harbor. Was sold to Lexington, Mo., and converted into a barge.

2197 Galena

SW p wh b. Madison, Ind., 1854. 296 tons. Built for the Galena & Minnesota Packet Co., Capt. D.B. Morehouse. Took part in the grand excursion incident with the opening of the Rock Island RR, June 1854. Her masters the following years: Capt. Russell Blakeley, 1855; Capt. Kennedy Lodwick, 1856; Capt. W.H. Laughton, 1857. She was the first boat through the Lake in 1857 and got to St. Paul 2:00 A.M., on May 1, having passed the *GOLDEN STATE* and *WAR EAGLE* under way between Lake Pepin and St. Paul—there were 12 boats in sight when she got through the Lake. Burned and sank at Red Wing, Minn., the loss caused by a deck passenger dropping a lighted match into freight. Several lives were lost, this on June 30, 1858.

2198 GALLARDO

Stw rafter-ex wh b. La Crosse, Wis., 1904. 85.5 x 16.4 x 3. Engines, 8″- 3½ ft. One boiler, 40″ by 8 ft. Built by Sawyer Austin Lumber Co., La Crosse. Soon sold to Capt. Sol York and taken to the Illinois River. Sold about 1910 to Frank Gillman, Caruthersville, Mo., and renamed *ADELINE;* used as a towboat. Off the lists c. 1912.

2199 GALLATIN

SW p wh b. Brownsville, Pa., 1860. 200 tons. Ran on Monongahela River, Pittsburgh-Brownsville-Geneva. Collided with the *FAYETTE* (see) at Stone's upper coal works, Aug. 19, 1865. In June 1866, Capt. A.C. Carlisle, running opposition with *ELECTOR* (see). Sank downbound at Braddock's upper riffle, about midway between Dam 2 and McKeesport, Capt. Doyle Bugher in command. The *ELISHA BENNETT* took off the passengers. Raised. Accident happened May 26, 1868. Ran Pittsburgh-Parkersburg in April 1869. Sold to Memphis August 1869 to ply Memphis-Mound City. Got caught on a sand bar at Island 40 and stayed there three months, released in December 1869. Sold at Memphis by a U.S. marshal in June 1870, and went to the Memphis & St. Louis Packet Co. Capt. Postal took her to St. Louis. Off the lists 1872.

2200 GALLATIN

Stw p wh b. Kingston, Tenn., 1864. Originally named *CLINCH* (see). 140 x 30. Engines, 12's- 4 ft. Two boilers. Renamed *GALLATIN* on Apr. 10, 1866. Operated by Capt. Samuel Howe. She ascended the Missouri above Fort Benton 40 miles to High Wood Creek in 1867, a feat not surpassed until the *TOM STEVENS* went above in 1868 (see). She did this on June 8 for the express purpose of beating the peg set by the *PETER BALEN* the year prior, and went two miles beyond the *BALEN*'s mark. Snagged at the mouth of Little Sioux River on Apr. 16, 1868.

2201 GANT

SW p wh b. St. Landry Parish, La., 1847. 69 tons. 98.7 x 17.5 x 4.5. Owned and commanded by Capt. William A. Chambers, New Orleans. Sold Dec. 30, 1848, to Capt. Edmund Burke, New Orleans. In July 1849 sold to Tiner & Conery, New Orleans. Off the lists 1851.

2202 GARDEN CITY

SW p wh b. Shousetown, Pa., 1853. 409 tons. Ran St. Louis-Illinois River, Capt. Herman Price. On a trip St. Louis-La Salle, 302 miles, spring of 1853, went up in 21 hours 55 minutes, fast time. Eli Mills, stockholder, sold his interest in the boat to Isaac Kimber, November 1854. Burned Jan. 14, 1855, 35 miles below Napoleon, Ark., with no life loss.

2203 GARLAND

Stw p wh b. Jeffersonville, Ind., by Howard, 1888. 162 x 30 x 4.5. Built for Capt. G.W. Rea, and named for daughter of H.C. Stringfellow who owned a large plantation near Shreveport, La. Sister boat to *HALLETTE* (see) which also was named for the sister. Sank and lost at Bulah Landing just below St. Maurice, La., c. 1893.

2204 GARRY OWEN

Stw p wh b. Wheeling, W. Va., 1870. 131 x 32.5 x 4.4. First master, Capt. J.W. Carlton of New Orleans who owned a share along with Charles B. Harrington and Nick Benchman, also of New Orleans. Ran New Orleans-Ouachita River, and in 1873 was at Alexandria, La., on Red River. Reported sunk by a tug at New Orleans, Feb. 4, 1876.

2205 GASCONADE

Stw p wh b. Loutre Island, Mo., 1891. 107.4 x 29.3 x 3.5. Engines, 9″- 3½ ft. One boiler. Owned by Capt. W.L. Heckman Sr., and others of the family who operated her on the Gasconade River. She also towed for the U.S. Engineers and private parties on the Missouri. Sold to merchants of Decatur, Ala., early 1901 for the Decatur-Riverton trade.

2206 GATE CITY

Stw ferry wh b. Cincinnati, Oh., 1857. 85.56 tons. 115 x 34 x 4. Owned and operated by Capt. John Van Dyke at Keokuk, Iowa. Apparently had no steam power until 1865. Off the lists in 1883.

2207 GATE CITY

Freight wh b. Cincinnati, Oh., 1859. 297.84 tons. Enlarged at St. Louis summer 1873 and was to depart "for the cotton streams of the south." Owned 1874 by Thomas B. Cabeene, St. Louis.

2208 GATE CITY

Stw p wh b. Winona, Minn., 1900. 73.8 x 13.8 x 3.5. Engines, 7″- 3′. One boiler, 54″ dia. by 18 ft. Came out in Winona-Fountain City trade, Capt. A.B. Robbins. Sold early 1906 to Capt. John A. Armstrong who rebuilt her at Paducah and took her south. Inspected 1907 at Jonesville, La. In 1911 she was sent to Arkadelphia, Ark., on upper Ouachita River and is said to have been the last commercial boat to go there. She sank in the Saline River (trib. of the Ouachita) June 15, 1913.

2209 GAYOSO

SW p wh b. Memphis, Tenn., 1850. 236 tons. 162.1 x 23.7 x 6.4. Capt. Rufus S. Joyner, master and part owner, along with Warren Prescott, both of Memphis. Enrolled at New Orleans. Burned and lost at Memphis, Nov. 30, 1850.

2210 GAYOSO

Stw p wh b. Brownsville, Pa., at Axton yard, 1883. 127 x 28. Ran Memphis-St. Francis River, owned by the Lee Line, Memphis. Sold to Capt. Elmore Bewley in January 1895 for the Evansville-Green River trade. Name changed in November 1897 to *PARK CITY* (see).

2211 GAZELLE

SW p wh b. Cincinnati, Oh., 1853. 38 tons. She ran low water trades for the U.S. Mail Line, Cincinnati-Louisville. Off the lists in 1858.

2212 GAZELLE

Stw p wh b. Brownsville, Pa., 1854. 204 tons. Capt. John L. Rhodes, master, spring of 1854 in Pittsburgh-Louisville trade. Capt. James Grimes, Sewickley, Pa., was on her for some time. Burned and lost at Pittsburgh, Pa. on June 14, 1859.

2213 GAZELLE

SW tinclad wh b. Madison, Ind., 1863. Originally named *EMMA BROWN* (see). Engines, 16's- 5 ft. The U.S. Navy acquired her, new, and made of her a tinclad, renamed *GAZELLE,* and she bore the number 50. Sold at Mound City, Ill., to John Gilbert, August 1865. Was renamed *PLAIN CITY* (see).

2214 GAZELLE

Prop yacht wh b. Nelsonville, Oh., 1887. 47 x 10 x 6.1. Owned by Biddle Bros., Parkersburg, W. Va., when fairly new, and they ran excursions to Blennerhassett Island. Later sold to Anton Reymann, Wheeling, W. Va. Listed at Wheeling, 1896.

2215 GAZELLE

Stw p wh b. Hawesville, Ky., 1899. 102 x 20.7 x 5.1. Engines, 9½"- 3½ ft. One boiler, 40" by 24 ft. Built and owned by Capt. W.D. Crammond, Hawesville. He built her scow bow, and later remodeled her model bow. Ran Owensboro-Hawesville. Was running Evansville-Cloverport in 1909, Capt. Henry January.

2216 GAZELLE

Prop yacht wh b. Allegheny, Pa., 1901. 65 x 10 x 3. Built by R.C. Price. Sold to Harrison P. Dilworth and others who had coal properties on the Monon River in Greene County, Pa. Capt. John Faddis once took her up Ten Mile Creek to Clarksville, Pa., on a high river. Capt. Frank L. Ganoe, New Geneva, Pa., had her briefly in 1908. H.P. Dilworth sold her to Pennsylvania Contracting Co., in 1911.

2217 GAZETTE

Stw p-tb wh b. Allegheny, Pa., 1903. 69 x 15.8 x 1.8. Built for H.T. Newmaker, Franklin, Pa., and he lived there while he ran the boat. Ran Millwood-Ravenswood spring 1904 under lease to Charles Sears, Millwood, W. Va. Named for the Pittsburgh morning daily newspaper, and carried a picture of the paper's insignia, a coon, on the engineroom bulkheads. Later owned by Capt. David Boyles, Parkersburg, W. Va. She had been up Kentucky River and was returning from Irvine, Ky., to Parkersburg when she burst a flue, June 17, 1909, caught fire and sank four miles below mouth of Red River.

2218 GEM

SW p wh b. Cincinnati, Oh., 1850. 298 tons. 211 x 35 x 6.8. Ran New Orleans-Memphis, Capt. Lewis Snapp, who also was part owner (½) with Peter Hanger, Little Rock, Ark. Sold in June 1852 to Capt. Richard Irwin Dyas, New Orleans. Sold five times in 1854 and in December 1855 sold to John E. Caldwell, New Orleans. Went to Shreveport in 1856 with a load of rail for the Vicksburg, Shreveport & Texas RR. Was dismantled that year.

2219 GEM

Stw p wh b. Wheeling, W. Va., 1863. 145 tons. A dispatch from Cincinnati, Apr. 9, 1864: "Captain Hughes will improve the *GEM,* now en route to Pittsburgh, with alterations at Freedom, Pa. Her length will be increased 45 feet, a texas will be added, and she's to have new engines and a new sternwheel." Lost at Nebraska City, Neb., Nov. 9, 1869.

2220 GEM

Stw p wh b. Jeffersonville, Ind., by Howard, 1898. 135 x 21 x 3. Three boilers. Built for Capt. Ben C. Rea to handle cotton above Shreveport on Red River. Sank just above Shreveport in February 1901 with 650 bales of cotton aboard. She was in the Red River Line, Charles P. Truslow, president, and Charles W. Drown, traffic manager. Again sank, Jan. 30, 1908, a mile above Browns Landing, Red River. Sank at Elevator #3 in the New Orleans harbor, Nov. 23, 1910. Sold to the Comeaux family for the New Orleans-Bayou Sara trade and burned at Hahnville Landing, La., Feb. 14, 1914 with loss of five of the crew. Both pilots lost their lives in this blaze, Eddie Comeaux and William E. Barre.

2221 GEM CITY

SW p wh b. St. Louis, Mo., 1881. 303 x 36 x 6. Engines, 28½'s- 7 ft. Paddlewheels 28 ft. dia., working 15 ft. buckets. The hull was built for the Keokuk Northern Line which got into financial troubles, and turned over before completion to the St. Louis & St. Paul Packet Co., which built her under the supervision of R.H. Medill. First skipper was Capt. A.M. Hutchinson, with N.B. Hatcher, clerk. Her first two trips were St. Louis-Keokuk, and then four St. Louis-St. Paul rounds. Then the command went to Capt. Wm. Thompson, with Pole Hatcher, clerk. Pilots were Campbell Hunt and Hi Beedle. Made 14 round trips to St. Paul that first season. Exceptionally fast and in instances made the round trip (1,352 miles) in 5½ days. Once sank after hitting rock about 10 miles above the mouth of the Illinois, with Capt. George W. Jakes, master, and Douglas Roberts and Mills Purdy, pilots. The *GEN. H.F. DEVOL* was brought alongside to assist in raising her. Machinery came from the *ANDY JOHNSON* (see). Burned at the foot of Barton Street, St. Louis, Sept. 22, 1883.

2222 GEM CITY

SW p wh b. St. Louis, Mo., 1884. 263 x 29.8 x 5.6. Engines, 20's- 7 ft. Side-wheels 28 ft. dia., working 15 ft. buckets. She had a new hull, and cabin and machinery from the *ALEX.*

MITCHELL (see). Ran St. Louis-Keokuk in the Davidson Line. Capt. William Burke was master most of the time, with Ceph Gregg, clerk. Her first purser was Charles Berkley who left to go on the new *CITY OF MONROE.* Bought by the Diamond Jo Line in 1891. Was rebuilt into the *QUINCY* at Dubuque in 1895.

2223 GENERAL

Stw ferry sh b. Jeffersonville, Ind., by Howard, 1925. Originally *CHARLES J. MILLER* (see) and renamed when sold to Capt. A.C. Johnson, Helena, Ark. Sold in 1944 to Todd-Johnson Dry Docks Co., New Orleans and renamed *WARREN JOHNSON* (see).

2224 GENERAL ALLEN

Stw U.S. sh b. Jeffersonville, Ind., 1916. Originally the pleasure steamer *MINNESOTA* (see). The *MINNESOTA* was sold to the St. Paul District, U.S. Engineers, in 1922 and renamed. Inspection trips were made, and she usually towed. She pioneered the first commercial tow out of St. Paul and Minneapolis in May 1926, Capt. William Henning. The *WYNOKA* was to have handled it for Federal Barge Lines but got aground. She also brought to St. Paul the first commercial tow from St. Louis for FBL, Aug. 24, 1927. Ascended the Minnesota River to Shakopee, Minn., 30 miles, towing a quarterboat, derrick, and three barges, August 1939. Had to break tow to get around bends. Excursion steamer *THE PURCHASE* had been up the Minnesota years before (see). Sold in 1943 to Central Barge Line, and resumed her original name *MINNESOTA* (see).

2225 GENERAL ANDERSON

SW p wh b. Brownsville, Pa., 1860. 224 tons. Built for Nashville-Cairo trade, Capt. James (Old Gibraltar) Miller, and others. Taken by Union forces early in the war and used on the Cumberland and Tennessee using the same crew. In Confederate service she had been the last boat to leave Fort Donelson, with Generals Floyd and Pillow aboard. Entered the Pittsburgh-Cincinnati trade early 1864, Capt. C.A. Dravo. Later went to the Cairo-Columbus trade connecting with trains. Completely rebuilt at Mound City, Ill., 1869, still in the railroad run. Owned 1874 by Peter Conrad, St. Louis. Dismantled and hull used as a barge 1877.

2226 GENERAL BARNARD

SW snagboat wh b. Jeffersonville, Ind., 1879. 215 x 37 x 5. Owned by U.S. Engineers and used on Upper Mississippi. The *MONTANA,* U.S. Missouri River boat, was dismantled and parts used in building her. Ascended the Galena (or Fever) River and was at Galena, Ill., June 22, 1899. The *HELEN BLAIR* (see) was there in 1913.

2227 GENERAL BEACH

Stw p wh b. Jeffersonville, Ind., by Howard, 1912. Originally named *CORKER* (see). Louisville & Cincinnati Packet Co. sold *CORKER* to Liberty Transit Co. in 1920 and entered her in Pittsburgh-Wheeling trade, and changed her name that summer. Capt. Walter English was master-pilot, with Eb Cline, pilot. Arch Wriggleworth was purser, F. Way, Jr., clerk. In spring and summer 1921 ran Pittsburgh-Zanesville, Capt. Hiram Douglass. Capt. Scott Heatherington was the Muskingum River pilot. The purser was Homer Mozena, with J. Mack Gamble and later F. Way, Jr., clerk. That fall towed pipe in barges from Pittsburgh to Hanging Rock, Oh., and while coaling at Warwood, W. Va., sank at the tipple of the Richland mine. Repaired at Elizabeth, Pa., and November 1920 ran Pittsburgh-Charleston in place of the *GENERAL CROWDER,* Capt. W.L. Guthrie, with Charles Douglass, clerk. Sold to John F. Klein who rebuilt her at Mound City, Ill., into a towboat named *JIM O'SULLIVAN.* She beached out several years later and went to pieces from neglect.

2228 GENERAL BEAUREGARD

SW gunboat wh b. Algiers, La., 1847. 161.8 x 30 x 10. Originally side-wheel towboat *OCEAN,* long owned by Ocean Towboat Co., and Union Towboat Co., New Orleans. She was made into a Confederate gunboat and ram in 1861.

2229 GENERAL BEM

SW p wh b. Paducah, Ky., 1849. 116 tons. Owned by John B. Adams and others. Capt. Lew Kates went master 1849, his first command. Snagged and lost at Walnut Bend, Arkansas River, Jan. 9, 1854, with loss of 10 lives.

2230 GENERAL BRAGG

SW steamship wh b. New York, N.Y., 1850. 208 x 33 x 8.7. Originally named *MEXICO* and first owned by Charles Morgan and others. She was a side-wheel low pressure beam-engine boat with engine 56" bore, 10 ft. stroke. Seized by Confederates 1861 at New Orleans, and made into a gunboat and ram. Captured by the U.S. and sold by them August 1865 to Capt. David White, St. Louis. Resumed her original name *MEXICO* and was sold foreign in 1870.

2231 GENERAL BUELL

SW p wh b. Jeffersonville, Ind., by Howard, 1862. 248 x 36 x 5.5. 743 tons. Owned by the U.S. Mail Line Co. for the Louisville-Cincinnati trade. Came out June 24, 1862 replacing the *JACOB STRADER* (see). Engines, 20's- 7 ft. Four boilers. Capt. Charles David commanded. Gen. U.S. Grant and wife rode her to Cincinnati, June 19, 1866. Sank in ice at Madison, Ind., Dec. 24, 1872. She was dismantled 1876, and the hull was used as a wharfboat at Aurora, Ind., and the engines and boilers were auctioned off.

2232 GENERAL BURNSIDE

SW gunboat wh b. Chattanooga, Tenn., by U.S. Army, commissioned July 1864. 171 x 26 x 4.8. Turned over to U.S. Navy, and at war's conclusion to USQMD. Used on the Tennessee River. Three similar gunboats were built at Chattanooga, *GENERAL GRANT, GENERAL THOMAS,* and *GENERAL SHERMAN* (all see).

2233 GENERAL BUTLER

Ocean ship wh b. Louisville, Ky., "to aid in the prosecution of the Mexican War." Plans furnished by the USQMD. Stephen H. Long had a part in this. 400 tons.

2234 GENERAL CHAS. H. TOMPKINS

Stw p wh b. Pittsburgh, Pa., 1878. 356 tons. 181 x 25 x 3.5. Engines, 11"-4 ft. Two boilers. Built for William J. Kountz and others. Left Pittsburgh May 12, 1878 piloted by Jacob Poe and Andrew Bunton. Went to the Missouri River. In the spring of 1881 she was at St. Stephens Mission, S.D., where ice broke her loose. She drifted 10 miles and lodged at Swan Lake about one mile distant from the river. Took about two weeks to get her back afloat. Later in Memphis-Arkansas River trade, she sank one-half mile above mouth of White River, Capt. Charles Postal, master, with Charles Nixon, pilot. Date of loss?

2235 GENERAL CROOK

Stw p wh b. Belle Vernon, Pa., 1862. Originally named *B.C. LEVI* (see). In 1863 sold to USQMD and renamed. At war's conclusion sold to New Orleans and renamed *CUBA NO. 2* (see).

2236 GENERAL CROWDER

Stw p wh b. Jeffersonville, Ind., by Howard, 1895. Originally named *R. DUNBAR* (see). The Liberty Transit Co., Wheeling, W. Va., bought the *R. DUNBAR* fall of 1918 and renamed her. Ran Pittsburgh-Charleston, Capt. W.L. Guthrie, with Daniel C. Patchell and Monroe (Doggy) Cross, pilots. Extensively repaired at Pt. Pleasant, W. Va., in 1922 and then ran Pittsburgh-Cincinnati teamed up with the *GENERAL WOOD* 1922–1923. Crew at the time, Capt. W.L. Guthrie with pilots E. Dayton Randolph and Wm. F. Brookhart; purser F. Way, Jr. The Liberty Line discontinued, and *CROWDER* was laid up at Wheeling until sold late 1926 to Capt. William F. Bradford, New Orleans. She was repaired at Slidell, La., and in process of being renamed *M.A. GRACE* when she burned at the Canulette Yard, Slidell, January 1927.

2237 GENERAL CUSTER

Stw p wh b. Belle Vernon, Pa., and completed at Pittsburgh, 1870. 182 x 28 x 3.8. Engines 14½'s- 4 ft. Two boilers, each 38" by 24 ft. Built for William J. Kountz. Went to the Missouri River. Snagged and lost near Rule, Neb., between Winnebago Bar and Rush Bottom, Oct. 5, 1879. She was downbound at the time.

2238 GENERAL D.H. RUCKER

Stw p wh b. Belle Vernon, Pa., and completed at Pittsburgh, 1878. 215 x 35 x 4. Engines, 16's- 5 ft. Three boilers, each 40" by 26 ft. Built for William J. Kountz who presented a piano placed aboard before she departed Pittsburgh Apr. 10, 1878, for Missouri River. The engines were built by Ainslee-Cochran and had been exhibited at the Philadelphia Centennial Exposition in 1876, said to have been nickel-plated. Ran one season St. Louis-Rocheport trade, Capt. John Massie. Documented at Sioux City 1886, maybe longer.

2239 GEN. D.M. WHITE

SW p wh b. Evansville, Ind., 1860. 86 tons. Off the lists 1864.

2240 GENERAL DAWES

Stw p wh b. Harmar, Oh., at Knox Yard, 1883. 119 x 26 x 3.3. Named for the father of ex U.S. Vice-Pres. Charles Dawes. Built for Capt. Charles P. Leavitt, Belleville, W. Va., a Civil War vet and son-in-law of Capt. Horatio Nelson Crooks (see *CLIPPER* and *CLIPPER NO. 2*). Other owner was J.E. Mayhew, also a Crooks son-in-law. Ran Martetta-Middleport with C. Barringer, clerk, later H.L. Ritchie. In 1890 ran East Liverpool-Steubenville; also did contract work, and towed salt to Cincinnati from Pomeroy Bend. In 1892 was rebuilt and renamed *U.K. RIGGS* (see).

2241 GENERAL EARL VAN DORN

SW gunboat wh b. Algiers, La., 1853. 182 x 28.3 x 10.7. Originally a side-wheel towboat named *JUNIUS BEEBE* of New Orleans, owned by Good Intent Towboat Co. Went to the Confederate Navy in 1861, a cotton-sheathed gunboat, renamed. She was the only Confederate vessel to escape the Battle of Memphis in 1862. Went up the Yazoo River to escape capture June 26, 1862 and was scuttled. A few moments later she exploded.

2242 GENERAL FRANK M. COXE

Prop passenger sh b. Charleston, W. Va., at the Charles Ward Engineering Works, 1921. 150 x 28 x 13. Triple expansion steam engines. Built for U.S. Navy and was used in the San Francisco area. Owned in 1948 by Golden Gate Scenic Steamship Lines, San Francisco. In 1951 running excursions in San Francisco Bay, privately owned.

2243 GENERAL G.G. TOTTEN

SW snagboat wh b. Cincinnati, Oh., 1866. 348 tons. Originally side-wheel packet *COMMODORE* (see) converted when new by the U.S. She was blasting out wrecks at Cairo, July 1867, among them that of the *JEFF THOMPSON*.

2244 GENERAL GAINES

SW p wh b. Brownsville, Pa., 1849. 159 tons. Out of service 1855.

2245 GENERAL GRANT

Stw p wh b. Monongahela, Pa., 1863. 172 tons. Engines, 13's- 4 ft. Two boilers. Capt. John Woodburn operated her when new, and sold her March 1864 to a Capt. Packard who made a trip to Vicksburg early 1864, bringing up 250 bales of cotton to Louisville, and was back at Pittsburgh March 14, "the first arrival from Vicksburg since the war broke out." Departed Pittsburgh May 22, 1864, "for the gold mines of Idaho" and was compelled to refuse freight. In charge of a Capt. Packard, who had purchased interest, she participated in the General Sully expedition to the

Yellowstone River summer 1864. Wintered three miles below Bellevue, Neb., with 172 tons of freight for Fort Benton, and was cut down by ice there on Mar. 18, 1866.

2246 GENERAL GRANT

SW gunboat wh b. Chattanooga, Tenn., 1864 by U.S. Army. 171 x 26 x 4.7. Used on the Tennessee River in Navy service, and was turned over to the USQMD June 2, 1865 (see *GENERAL BURNSIDE*).

2247 GEN. H.F. DEVOL

Stw p wh b. Harmar, Oh., at Knox Yard, 1879. 130 x 22.5 x 3.8. Named for Gen. Hiram Fosdick Devol, one of the five Civil War generals from Washington County, Oh. Machinery from the *L.C. McCORMICK* (see). Built for Capt. James Martin. Ran Marietta-Zanesville handling the U.S. Mail, then Parkersburg-Zanesville. Capt. George Wallace and Dana Scott bought interest in August 1887 and commanded. In June 1889 got a cargo of nails at Wheeling and delivered it to St. Louis. In December 1889 running out of Memphis, then was chartered to the Greenville Packet Co., where she ran all that winter. Capt. Dana Scott was aboard for all of this. Sold to Miles Orton's Circus in April 1890. Burned in 1895, rebuilt, and was sold to Tampico, Mexico, where she ran on the Panuco River many years, still there in 1934.

2248 GENERAL HALLECK

Stw p wh b. Oquaka, Ill., 1862. 66 tons. 100 x 18 x 3.5. Built by Capt. Albert Eames. After the war she was in the Memphis-Hatchie River trade where she was renamed *MADISON*. Not long thereafter, on Feb. 5, 1867, she was being landed at Memphis and ran afoul of an old cylinder on the wharf, stove and sank. Lost about 30 bales of cotton. The wreck burned.

2249 GENERAL HAMER

SW ocean vessel wh b. Louisville, Ky., 1848. 168 tons. Went to Cincinnati before departing for New Orleans. Built "to aid in the prosecution of the Mexican War." Stephen H. Long had a part in this. First home port was Pensacola, Fla. Off the lists 1854.

2250 GEN. HARRY WHITE

A snagboat of some description. Was snagging on the Allegheny River in 1880 and was nearly destroyed when a dynamite charge placed under a rock slipped from its position and exploded under the boat.

2251 GENERAL J.L. HODGES

SW p wh b. Louisville, Ky., 1860. 162 x 31 x 5.4. Built and operated by Capt. Reuben Slade, New Orleans. Captured by the U.S. as a Confederate steamboat and sold at war's conclusion to Capt. W.D. Wetmore, New Orleans. Sold in February 1866 to Capt. Charles H. Bland, New Orleans. Machinery went to the *G.B. ALLEN* in 1866.

2252 GENERAL JESSUP

SW p wh b. Elizabethtown, Pa., 1847. 374 tons. Stephen H. Long later stated that she was built, along with others, "to further the prosecution of the Mexican War." Ran St. Louis-New Orleans in 1848-1849. Snagged and lost at Chester, Ill., Dec. 10, 1849.

2253 GEN. JOE WHEELER

Stw p wh b. Decatur, Ala., 1899. 132 x 18 x 3. In November 1903 running on White River between Norfolk and McBee, above Batesville, Ark., Capt. Tom Stallings. (Also see *JOE WHEELER*—both ran on Tennessee River at the same time.)

2254 GEN. JOHN NEWTON

Stw inspection boat sh b. Dubuque, Iowa by Iowa Iron Works, 1899. 150 x 28 x 7.5. Cross-compound engines, condensing, 14's, 32's- 6 ft. Built for the Mississippi River Commission. She was a coal burner for 40 years, later oil. Capt. E. Joe Pierce came out master in 1899 and retired aged 70 in May 1936. Sponsons were added to the hull in 1936. She was declared surplus in 1957 and was sold to the University of Minnesota and converted into a showboat called *MINNESOTA CENTENNIAL SHOWBOAT*. Still serving in that capacity 1978. Many details appear in *S&D Reflector,* issue of March 1977.

2255 GENERAL LANE

SW p wh b. Louisville, Ky., 1848. 240 tons. Ran Louisville-St. Louis, Capt. A. McPherson, spring of 1849. Departed Cincinnati November 1850 advertised for Alexandria, La. Snagged and lost at the mouth of the St. Francis River, Ark., Dec. 30, 1851.

2256 GENERAL LYON

SW gunboat wh b. New Albany, Ind., 1850. 390 tons. 182.1 x 35.8 x 7.5. Engines, 23's- 7 ft. Originally named *DE SOTO* (see). The Confederates made of her a gunboat which was captured by U.S. forces at Island 10, Mississippi River in April 1862. They made of her a tinclad, and renamed her *GENERAL LYON* that October. She was with Porter on Red River in 1864. Sold at public sale, Mound City, Ill., Aug. 17, 1865, to Capt. W.H. Thorwegan, St. Louis. She was renamed *ALABAMA* Oct. 20, 1865 (see).

2257 GENERAL LYTLE

SW p wh b. Cincinnati, Oh., 1864. 1,053.25 tons. 270 x 40 x 7. Engines, 26's- 9 ft. Seven boilers, each 37" by 24 ft., two flues. Built for the U.S. Mail Line Co. and ran Cincinnati-Louisville. She exploded boilers upbound about a quarter mile below Bethlehem, Ind., on Monday, Aug. 6, 1866. She had left Louisville at noon, and had landed at Westport where the *ST. CHARLES* (see) caught up and went by. The *LYTLE* was overtaking the *ST. CHARLES* when the explosion occurred. Witnesses aboard the *ST. CHARLES,* still about 150 yards in the lead, said the blast sounded like the discharge of a six-pounder. A cloud of smoke and ashes arose as high as her chimneys, and no steam was visible. The *LYTLE*'s whole front works, from the center of the wheelhouses to about the center of the office, went up about

60 or 70 feet. The debris showered to both sides of her. The *ST. CHARLES* immediately backed down and came along the port side. Passengers were vacated by the back stairs as the *LYTLE* was afire near the port wheelhouse. Flames were quenched by fire hoses from the *ST. CHARLES.* A piece of boiler flue, about eight feet long, lay across the *LYTLE*'s office desk. Capt. Godman, master of the *LYTLE,* resident of Madison, Ind., was on the roof, over the barbershop. He lived about ten minutes, unable to talk. William Miller, chief engineer, was taken to Louisville badly scalded. His son Charles, striker engineer, was not found. Henry Edwards, second engineer, died soon after the accident. The wrecked boat was towed to Cincinnati by the *GENERAL BUELL,* where a reporter wrote: "She is one of the most complete wrecks we have ever seen." The life loss was variously estimated as 30 to 35 lives. Silverware and fragments of dishes, etc., were picked up in the area for many years after. She was completely rebuilt and ran many years. The officers on the *LYTLE* were outfitted in uniforms in November 1876, "made of blue cloth," and uniform caps had a silver plate bearing the designation of each officer. The idea was said to have been introduced by Capt. Richard M. Wade. Capt. Ben M. Merrielees was master in 1877. She was given an electric light plant, probably to run an arc light, in 1875. On June 24, 1879, she hit an obstruction and sank 14 miles below Cincinnati, raised. Dismantled at Ludlow, Ky., in June 1882. Capt. George Anderson, Carrollton, Ky., used the hull as a wharfboat at that place, and parts of the cabin went to building the *BLUE WING* (see) which he owned.

2258 General Meade

Prop p wh b. Malta, Oh., 1863. 31 tons. She ran briefly in the Zanesville-Dresden trade. Off the lists 1865.

2259 General Meade

Stw p wh b. Pittsburgh, Pa., 1875. 192 x 30 x 4.3. Came out with compound engines, 8¾" and 23"- 4 ft. Two boilers. Built for Capt. William J. Kountz and ran on Missouri River. Once broke loose in ice above Fort Randall, S.D., and floated 12 miles to opposite Yankton Agency, S.D. Snagged opposite Jefferson City, Mo., Sept. 5, 1884. Capt. "Steamboat Bill" Heckmann in recollecting her said he did not see any compound engines on her in her latter days, when she ran St. Louis-Osage River-Rocheport. "At that time she had 12's- 5 ft.," he said. Snagged and lost in Pelican Bend, Sept. 4, 1888, with 4,000 sacks of wheat.

2260 General Meigs

Stw p wh b. Wheeling, W. Va., 1864. 144 tons. Built for the USQMD. Sold Sept. 12, 1865, and renamed *ALLENA MAY* (see).

2261 General Miles

Stw p wh b. St. Louis, Mo., 1878. 103 x 18 x 3. Ran on Yazoo River. Dismantled 1893 and parts used building packet *FIFTEEN* (see).

2262 Gen. O.M. Poe

Stw snagboat wh b. Cincinnati, Oh., 1893. 145 x 34 x 4.6. On the Kentucky River, July 1908, Capt. James F. Browinski. In the Cincinnati District, U.S. Engineers, 1908.

2263 General Pershing

Stw p wh b. Stillwater, Minn., 1900. 150 x 30 x 4.5. Originally *LORA, OMAHA* (see). Liberty Transit Co., Wheeling, W. Va., bought the *OMAHA* in 1918, remodeled her cotton-type main deck and cabin at Clarington, Oh., and renamed her. Ran Pittsburgh-Charleston most of her upper Ohio career. In 1921 Capt. W.L. Guthrie, master, with Holly Barr, purser, and F. Way, Jr., clerk. Dan Patchell and Edward Sims were the pilots. She was laid up at the Smith Docks, Pt. Pleasant, W. Va., that November and never again operated.

2264 General Pierson

SW tr wh b. Metropolis, Ill., 1877. 202 x 42 x 7.2. Engines, 20's- 5½ ft. Four boilers (two on each guard) each 48" by 28 ft. Built for the Memphis & Little Rock RR and used at Memphis. Capt. W.W. Maingault was master for 18 years, maybe longer. On Apr. 4, 1892, she was caught in a windstorm at Hopefield, Ark., blown across the river, lost both stacks and a wheelhouse. Her last inspection was July 3, 1906. Sank at Memphis and part of the wreckage may still be there.

2265 General Pike

SW p wh b. Cincinnati, Oh., 1851. 366 tons. Operated principally in the Louisville-St. Louis service for the U.S. Mail Line Co. commanded by Capt. Isaac Jones, formerly of Wheeling, and who graduated later on to the command of the low pressure *SOUTHERN* in the Cincinnati-St. Louis run. Snagged and lost at Cape Girardeau, Mo., Sept. 23, 1853.

2266 General Pike

SW p wh b. Cincinnati, Oh., 1856. 248 tons. Was at St. Paul in 1857 and again in 1859. For a time ran Memphis-White River. In the New Orleans trade, Capt. John Brown, 1858. Burned at Algiers, La., May 6, 1861.

2267 General Pike

Stw p wh b. Madison, Ind., 1877. 220 x 34 x 4.5. Engines, 16½'s- 6 ft. Owned by the U.S. Mail Line Co. Came out new in the Cincinnati-Madison trade replacing the sidewheel *BEN FRANKLIN* (see). Ran Pittsburgh-Cincinnati in 1886, Capt. E.B. Cooper; again in 1887, Capt. Tom Hunter, in place of the sunken *EMMA GRAHAM* (see). Went back to the Cincinnati-Madison trade and sank shortly before noon, Jan. 1, 1891, having backed into a fleet of coal barges when departing the Madison wharfboat. A rising river soon finished her.

2268 General Polk

SW gunboat wh b. New Albany, Ind., 1852. Originally named *ED HOWARD* (see). The Confederates made of her a gunboat carrying six guns. She was taken up Yazoo River to prevent her capture and destroyed by the crew June 26, 1862.

2269 GENERAL PRICE

SW gunboat wh b. Cincinnati, Oh., 1856. 483 tons. 182 x 30 x 9.2. Originally a side-wheel towboat owned at New Orleans named *LAURENT MILLAUDON.* Was in the fleet of the Good Intent Towboat Co. Engines, 25's- 6 ft. In 1861 the Confederates made of her a gunboat, and renamed her. She was captured by the U.S. When first commissioned as a gunboat she was *GEN. STERLING PRICE,* later *GENERAL PRICE.* Served in Porter's Red River expedition and elsewhere. Sold at public sale, Mound City, Ill., Aug. 17, 1865, to W.H. Harrison.

2270 GENERAL QUITMAN

SW p wh b. New Albany, Ind., 1859. 615 tons. 261.5 x 40.2 x 8.4. Engines, 30's- 10 ft. Six boilers. First master, Capt. John W. Cannon, and original owners were Capt. Richard Holmes (½), T.P. Leathers (¼), and Jane Stout (¼). Came out fall of 1859 in New Orleans-Greenville trade, Capt. John W. Cannon. Spring and summer 1860 in New Orleans-Memphis trade. When the war broke out she was taken to upper Red River for safety and did not emerge until hostilities ceased, then, loaded with cotton, took off for St. Louis. Capt. John W. Cannon was master all this while. After the war he owned ¾ (through Jane Stout) and Leathers ¼. Cannon ran her 1866 New Orleans-Greenville. He left her to build the *ROBT. E. LEE* (see) and as of May 30, 1868, ownership in the *QUITMAN* changed to Jane Stout (½) and T.P. Leathers (½), with Capt. Leathers as master. Was then in the New Orleans-Vicksburg trade, with Sam Ayles, clerk. In mid-August 1868 Leathers required each crew member including roustabouts to sign oath of allegiance to the Democratic party and fired those who refused. She was downbound at New Texas Landing, about 20 miles above Bayou Sara, when she struck a snag and sunk with 1,700 bales of cotton and 4,500 sacks of cotton seed aboard, this at noon, Oct. 22, 1868. Went down to the boiler deck. The *CELESTE,* Capt. J.C. Dowty, took passengers and crew to New Orleans. A peculiar quirk here is that the *GENERAL QUITMAN* once came to the relief of one of Captain Dowty's boats, the *MAJESTIC,* when that boat burned at the same location, Texas Landing. For many years after a wooden statue of General Quitman, which had graced the pilothouse-top of the *QUITMAN,* was mounted on the warehouse at New Texas Landing. The loss of the *QUITMAN* is said to have precipitated hard feelings between Leathers and Cannon. When the loss happened, Leathers owned ⅜, and Cannon ⅝. Cannon collected the insurance in full and Leathers sued for his share.

2271 GENERAL RANSOM

Centerwheel ferry wh b. New Orleans, La., 1865. 135.2 x 22.9 x 4.7. Built for the USQMD. Sold to Capt. John M. Prather, New Orleans, May 2, 1867. Burned and lost at Algiers, La., Apr. 10, 1868.

2272 GENERAL RUSK

SW p wh b. Louisville, Ky., 1850. 128 tons. 117 x 22 x 5. First home port, Franklin, La. Sold January 1853 to Capt. George C. Sutherland and Sabine Navigation Co., Texas. Off the lists 1860.

2273 GENERAL SCOTT

SW p wh b. Cincinnati, Oh., 1847. 293 tons. Burned at New Madrid, Mo., May 13, 1853, with no life loss.

2274 GENERAL SHERMAN

SW gunboat wh b. Chattanooga, Tenn., 1864. 168 x 26 x 4.5. Built by the U.S. War Department and transferred to Navy. Used on the Tennessee River. (See *GENERAL BURNSIDE*).

2275 GENERAL SHERMAN

Stw p wh b. Jeffersonville, Ind., at Barmore yard, 1877. 145 x 28 x 4. Engines, 12½'s- 4½ ft. Two boilers. Built for the U.S. for Yellowstone River, along with the *DON CAMERON* (see). Sold to private ownership and renamed *ELLA KIMBROUGH* (see).

2276 GENERAL SHIELDS

Stw p wh b. Nashville, Tenn., 1849. 76 tons. First home port, St. Louis. Snagged and lost on the Arkansas River, June 1851.

2277 GENERAL SIEGEL

Stw p wh b. Burlington, Iowa, 1863. 128 x 22 x 3.5. 91 tons. First owned by A.M. Root and Andrew and Joseph Geiger. After the war ran Evansville-Nashville, Capt. R.H. Brown, with Will A. Duvall, clerk. Off the list 1868.

GENERAL STERLING PRICE

See *GENERAL PRICE.*

2278 GENERAL TAYLOR

SW p wh b. Louisville, Ky., 1846. 199 tons. 180 x 27 x 5.7. Was at Memphis when telegraphic news reached that city of the nomination of Gen. Zachary Taylor for the U.S. presidency. Capt. Morehead raced down the Mississippi to inform the General of the glad news. "He hoisted all the flags he could raise, cheered every boat he met, fired his big gun, and was in as great a state of excitement as though he was racing a fast steamer." Ownership in February 1850: Capt. Peter Meyer, New Orleans. Out of service 1852.

2279 GENERAL TERRY

Stw p wh b. Freedom, Pa., at the McCaskey & Kerr yard, 1878. 178.2 x 31 x 4. Engines, 13's- 4 ft. Two boilers. Second-hand boilers and engines were used. Built for W.A. Burleigh, Miles City, Mont., and John Todd. There was trouble about payment and James Rees & Sons Co. filed a lawsuit and took interest. Her first trip was from Pittsburgh to Fort Benton, Mont., and return to McKenzie's Point.

J.Q.A. Parr was clerk on her the first seven trips. Later was in the Block P Line and made seven trips to Fort Benton in all, the last one in 1887. In 1881 she helped transport Indians from the Yellowstone to Dakota after Sitting Bull surrendered. In June that year she took 10,000 buffalo robes out of the Yellowstone—the load hid the boat except for the pilothouse and stacks. She transferred this cargo to the *C.K. PECK* at the mouth of the Yellowstone. The Benton Packet Co., owned her at the last. While transporting troops from Fort Yates, N.D., to Kansas City, Mo., she took a sheer and hit a pier of the new Union Pacific bridge at Omaha and sank. Capt. R.L. Woolfolk was in command and William Simms was pilot. The Union Pacific paid the loss claims.

2280 GENERAL THOMAS

SW gunboat wh b. Chattanooga, Tenn., 1864. 165 x 26 x 4.5. Engines, 16's- 5½ ft. Built by U.S. Army and served on the Tennessee. (See *GENERAL BURNSIDE.*) She was turned over to Navy and after the war went back to Army. She was bought by Thad Thomas and Steve Thompson in July 1866 and remodeled into a packet they named *INGOMAR* (see).

GENERAL THOMPSON

Confederate gunboat. Also referred to as *JEFF THOMPSON* which see for details.

2281 GENERAL WASHINGTON

SW p wh b. Louisville, Ky., 1847. 124 tons. 182 x 38 x 8.5. Engines, 23's- 8 ft. Four boilers. Ran Louisville-St. Louis in 1849, Capt. F. Shockley. Out of service 1852.

2282 GENERAL WILES

SW p wh b. Zanesville, Oh., 1876. 40 tons. Dispatch from Gallipolis, Oh., June 12, 1876: "The little side-wheel steamer *GENERAL WILES* landed here for some repairs yesterday and was boarded by Capts. Ford and Rodgers who found there was not a licensed officer or any Inspector's papers on board. She was evidently intended to reach the upper Arkansas and avoid inspection. The Inspectors have ordered her to remain here until she complies with the law." She got to Little Rock, and was operated above there on the Arkansas.

2283 GENERAL WOOD

Stw p wh b. Slidell, La., 1913. 181.9 x 29.8 x 6. Compound non-condensing engines, 12's, 24's- 6 ft. Three boilers. Originally named *S.L. ELAM* (see). Bought by Liberty Transit Co., Wheeling, W. Va., in 1918 and made one Pittsburgh-Cincinnati trip under her first name. Then was remodeled into an Upper Ohio packet, cutting off her cotton guards, altering the cabin, etc., and renamed. Entered the Pittsburgh-Cincinnati trade, Capt. William D. Kimble. Capt. W. Ed Dunaway became master with E. Dayton Randolph and Edgar Brookhart, pilots. Charles Douglass was purser, Herbert Worlein, clerk. Lee Markham was chief engineer, Alonzo Sewell, mate, and William H. Jones, steward. Liberty Transit "folded" in 1923 and the *WOOD* was sold to the Pittsburgh, Wheeling & Cincinnati Packet Co., in April 1924. Capt. Fred Hornbrook took charge, with Fred Hoyt, purser, and William S. Pollock, clerk. She was continued in the Pittsburgh-Cincinnati trade. Messrs. Hornbrook and Hoyt sold their interest early 1927 to William S. Pollock and F. Way, Jr. Thenceforth into 1929 she ran P&C trade teamed up with the *BETSY ANN* and managed by Pollock. In June 1929 she was up Monon River to Elizabeth, Pa. Pinch-hit in Cincinnati-Louisville trade that fall, and was laid up at Pittsburgh. Sold to Pete Milliron, East Liverpool, Oh., in November 1934 for use as a wharfboat there. Sank in ice early 1936, and the wreckage was deposited below Lock and Dam No. 8, Newell, W. Va., and burned that summer for scrap.

2284 GENERAL WORTH

SW p wh b. Louisville, Ky., 1846. 125 tons. Regular Cincinnati-Bowling Green packet, fall of 1849, Capt. Megowan. Off the lists 1851.

2285 GENERAL WORTH

SW p wh b. Cincinnati, Oh., 1847. 345 tons. 190 x 29 x 6.6. Built for New Orleans and Vicksburg trade, Capt. Joseph M. Bennett. In 1849, New Orleans-Lake Providence. Capt. Joseph H. Hendrick. Later owned by Fellowes & Co., New Orleans, and then in late 1851 by Capt. Henry Abbott, St. Landry Parish. Off the lists in 1853.

2286 GENESEE

SW p wh b. Brownsville, Pa., 1847. 175 tons. 168 x 24 x 4.5. In 1850 running Pittsburgh-Louisville, Capt. T. Moore. Off the lists in 1854.

2287 GENEVA

Stw p wh b. Brownsville, Pa., 1848. 121 tons. Went to the Upper Mississippi. Was taking wood four miles below Alton, Ill., Dec. 2, 1852, when her three boilers exploded with loss of many lives, among them Capt. Charles Dean of St. Louis, aboard as a passenger. Snagged and lost at Nebraska City, Neb., Sept. 30, 1856.

2288 GENEVA

Stw p wh b. Brownsville, Pa., 1863. 127 tons. Lost in ice at St. Louis on Dec. 16, 1865.

2289 GENEVA

SW p wh b. Brownsville, Pa., 1871. 284 tons. 163 x 30 x 5. Owned by Pittsburgh, Brownsville & Geneva Packet Co., which in 1875 had semi-daily service up Monon River. Capt. M.A. Cox was master, M.G. Bulger, clerk. She ran this trade 14 years. Sold December 1884 to William J. Caskey and Capt. Lew N. Clark. Was taken to New Orleans to run excursions to the Exposition winter 1884–1885. Returned to Pittsburgh April 1885, and in July Capt. Clark became sole owner. She was the flagship in the marine parade celebrating the opening of Davis Island Dam, the first to be completed on the Ohio River, at West Bellevue, Pa., Oct. 7, 1885, with Capt. C.W. Batchelor, master.

2290 GENEVIEVE

Stw p wh b. Pt. Pleasant, W. Va., 1898. 59.9 x 11.9 x 2.6. Ran Sistersville-New Matamoras during the oil boom in 1898. Ran other short trades and did light towing. Owned for a time by Capt. W.R. Haptonstall, Middleport, Oh. Still listed in 1908.

2291 GENOA

SW p wh b. California, Pa., 1854. 227 tons. 170 x 28 x 5. Went to Missouri River in command of Capt. Joseph Throckmorton who owned in her along with Robert Campbell and Joseph E. Gorman, all of St. Louis. Snagged and lost at Nebraska City, Neb., Sept. 13, 1856, same master and owners.

2292 GEORGE

SW p wh b. Burlington, Iowa, 1865. 118.2 x 21 x 3.4. In February 1867 owned at New Orleans by Newton A. Green, with Capt. James Crooks, master. She took off on a trading expedition on upper Red River above Shreveport in 1867 and was said to have gone 100 miles above the mouth of the False Ouachita, then considered the head of navigation. She was caught by low water and didn't get back out to Shreveport until May 1868, 11 months out. Off the lists in 1872.

2293 GEORGE A. MADILL

SW tr wh b. Jeffersonville, Ind., by Howard, 1891. 265 x 45 x 7. Owned by Wiggins Ferry Co., and operated at St. Louis until worn out 1917.

2294 GEORGE C. WOLFF

Stw p wh b. Madison, Ind., 1872. 198 x 37.5 x 5.7. Engines, 17½'s- 6 ft. Three boilers, each 38" by 26 ft. Machinery from *CITY OF PEKIN* (see). Built for Illinois River Packet Co., and named for Claiborne Greene Wolff whose name wasn't George but he was called George. Ran Illinois River-St. Louis and also made trips St. Louis-Shreveport, Capt. Lloyd T. Belt. Exploded boilers at St. Francis Island, near Helena, Ark., Aug. 22, 1873, with loss of 12 lives and 15 injured. The *LADY LEE* towed the wreck to Memphis, and the towboat *FUTURE CITY* towed it above for rebuilding. Was making a Missouri River trip in the spring of 1874 when she was snagged and lost in Bowling Green Bend at Babbler's Wood Yard, Mo., May 2, 1874. Capt. William W. Crapster was master.

2295 GEORGE CAMPBELL

SW p wh b. Louisville, Ky., 1852. 150 tons. Lost at Island 41, Mississippi River, Dec. 27, 1853. She was bound for San Juan, said the St. Louis *Republican*.

2296 GEORGE COLLIER

SW p wh b. New Albany, Ind., 1851. 540 tons. Owned by Capt. J. Goslee, and ran New Orleans-Memphis. She had arrived at Memphis from New Orleans about 12:30 A.M. Dec. 3, 1855, when fire broke out around the forward stairs. A stiff wind fanned the flames in such a way the passengers and crew couldn't get off by way of the forecastle, and were directed down the back stairway out into the wharfboat. Capt. Burdett Paris was in charge, as Captain Goslee was absent. Her burning resulted in the loss of the *MAYFLOWER* (see).

2297 GEORGE COWLING

Stw p wh b. Metropolis, Ill., 1904. 140 x 26 x 4.5. Engines, 14's- 4½ ft. Two boilers. Owned by Capt. E.J. Cowling, Metropolis, son of George H. Cowling. Ran Paducah-Metropolis. Carried the whistle from the *DICK FOWLER*. Was later sold to Miss Annie I. Baker, Paducah, who sold it March 1921 to Capt. George Street for the Paducah-Golconda trade. Rebuilt in 1923 and renamed *ALTON* (see).

2298 GEORGE D. PALMER

Stw p wh b. Cincinnati, Oh., 1863. Originally named *NANNIE BYERS* which was sunk in collision with the *C.E. HILLMAN* at Eagle Hollow, above Madison, Ind., Feb. 23, 1866. She was raised and rebuilt at Madison and renamed Aug. 17, 1866. 158 x 34 x 4.5. She went to New Orleans owned by William Danley and her master Capt. David Lanahan. Upbound on the Arkansas, 50 miles below Pine Bluff, she sank with a cargo of 1,600 barrels of salt in latter January 1868. Raised and entered the St. Louis-Keokuk trade. Partially burned at St. Louis, Apr. 18, 1868, was rebuilt, and hit the Quincy bridge Oct. 2, 1868, with loss of the boat and several lives.

2299 GEORGE H. COWLING

Stw p wh b. Metropolis, Ill., 1896. 120 x 20 x 4. Ran Paducah-Metropolis owned by the Cowling family and preceded the *GEORGE COWLING* (see). Was sold c. 1904 and renamed *JOHN H. LOVE* (see).

2300 GEORGE H. WALKER

SW tr sh b. Neville Island, Pa., by Dravo, 1923. 340 x 56 x 10.9. Engines geared to the paddlewheels, 18's, 36's- 18" stroke. Four boilers, two on each side. Burned fuel oil. Built for the New Orleans, Texas & Mexico RR Co., Baton Rouge. Capt. Charles Street, originally from Paducah, was master a long time. Owned by Gulf Coast Lines in 1931. Withdrawn from service Oct. 1, 1947, and was laid up at the Texas & Pacific incline, Gouldsboro, La. Converted into a barge in 1949.

2301 GEORGE L. BASS

Stw p wh b. Dubuque, Iowa, 1885. 91 x 21 x 3.3. Originally ran on Missouri and Osage rivers. Was sold south and sank on Red River, Sept. 11, 1897, Capt. B. Armistead. In August 1901, New Orleans-Hahnville daily, Capt. R.J. Comeaux, operated by Comeaux-Le Blanc Packet Co. Reported sold to Brown Lumber Co., Monroe, La., May 1911. In August 1911 in Yazoo-Sunflower River. Snagged at Sheppardstown, Miss., Oct. 27, 1911.

2302 GEORGE M. WATERS

Stw p wh b. Lyons, Iowa, 1895. 78 x 21 x 3. Chartered by Capt. Walter Blair in March 1897 to connect with the *WM. J. YOUNG, JR.* and the *CARRIER* from Davenport.

2303 GEORGE McC. PORTER

Stw p wh b. Wheeling, W. Va., 1864. 133 tons. Named for George McCook Porter, Hancock County, W. Va., whose father held interest in the boat. 140 x 22 x 4.5. Engines, 15's-4 ft. First ran on Kanawha River, Capt. Tom Taylor. Ran Pittsburgh-Wheeling, 1865, Capt. Taylor, with H.A. Dohrman, clerk. Sunk in ice at St. Louis, Dec. 18, 1868.

2304 GEORGE N. ROBERTS

Stw ferry sh b. Evansville, Ind., 1912. 160 x 31 x 5. Originally *JOHN L. LOWRY* (see) and later *WM. P. HALL*. Patton-Tully, Memphis, sold the *HALL* to Luling & Destrehan Ferry Co., New Orleans. They renamed her and ran her there. Finally dismantled.

2305 GEORGE PRINCE

Stw p sh b. Nashville, Tenn., by Nashville Bridge Co., 1922. 144 x 29.5 x 6.2. Cross-compound condensing engines, 12", 24"- 7 ft. Owned by the Royal Route Co., Vicksburg, Miss., run by Capt. George Prince. Sold later to Capt. L.V. Cooley, New Orleans, who changed the name to *OUACHITA* (see). Machinery came from the *PERCY SWAIN* (see).

2306 GEORGE ROGERS CLARKE

Recess wheel ferry wh b. Metropolis, Ill., 1870. Originally *DR. FREDERICK HILL* (see), sold December 1916 to operate Louisville-Jeffersonville, renamed. The opening of the Louisville Highway bridge in 1929 ended ferry operations.

2307 GEORGE SPANGLER

Stw p wh b. Madison, Ind., 1873, for Capt. Nat Williams. 124 x 25 x 4.2. Engines, 10½'s- 3 ft. One boiler. Named for the "well known cabin builder and master mechanic of the joining department of R.J. Stuart & Co.'s shipyard." In 1877, New Orleans-St. Martinsville, Capt. W.C. Smith, teamed up with the *CLARKSVILLE* (see). On Sept. 14, 1879, she was moored at Barry's Landing, Missouri River, five miles above Portland, Mo., broke her lines, and drifted upon the wreck of the *MOLLIE DOZIER* (see) in Albert Bend and sank. She was raised.

2308 GEORGE STRECKER

Stw p wh b. Long Reach, W. Va., 1880. 127.6 x 23.8 x 3.9. Ran Marietta-Beverly, 1885–1886 owned by Capt. Seldon S. Stowe. Ran Marietta-Middleport, September 1886. Burned at Beverly in 1887. There is evidence that Capt. W.D. Crammond, Hawesville, Ky., operated her.

2309 GEORGE T. KINNEY

Freight boat wh b. Nashville, Tenn., 1871. 100 tons. Still listed 1876.

2310 GEORGE W. DECKER

Stw p wh b. Black Rock, Ark., 1885. 174 tons. Listed at Memphis, 1886.

2311 GEORGE W. KENDALL

SW p wh b. Wheeling, Va., 1849. 280 tons. 182 x 32 x 8. Engines, 24½'s- 7½ ft. Four boilers, each 40½" by 27½ ft., two 16" flues. Came out in the Cincinnati-New Orleans trade, Capt. George W. Norton. Collided with the *MELODEON* at Plaquemine, La., in December 1850, causing the *MELODEON* to sink with two drowned. Sank a barge of molasses at St. Joseph on the lower Mississippi River, Feb. 6, 1853, losing 1,600 barrels. Ran on the rocks at Louisville, Ky., and was stranded two or three months, and dismantled. Date given was Feb. 27, 1853.

2312 GEORGE W. MILLER

Stw ferry sh b. Jeffersonville, Ind., by Howard, 1926. 138 x 32 x 4.9. Built for the Mississippi River Ferry Co., Vicksburg, and used there until the bridge was built. Her partner was the *CHARLES J. MILLER* (see). Both became excursion boats. The *GEORGE W. MILLER* went to Coosa River and was there in 1944. Later went to Chattahoochee River owned by Hardy Lines. Sold for debt Sept. 4, 1947, to Columbus Bank & Trust Co., Columbus, Ga. Sold June 1950 to Charles E. Gower, Columbus, Ga. Sold 1952 to Thurston C. Crawford, Columbus, Ga. Dismantled.

2313 GEO. W. PARKER

SW tr wh b. Pittsburgh, Pa., 1879. 266 x 46.5 x 7. Originally sternwheel packet *WYOMING* (see). Converted to handle rail cars Kansas City-Leavenworth, so registered 1892–1896, perhaps longer. Eventually dismantled at Kansas City.

2314 GEO. W. THOMAS

Was at Evansville, Ind., Feb. 26, 1872. An old freight bill with her name on it and no further information exists.

2315 GEORGE WASHINGTON

SW p wh b. Cincinnati, Oh., 1845. 303 tons. Exploded boilers near Grand Gulf, Miss., Jan. 14, 1852, with loss of 17 lives and 10 hurt. By coincidence the *MARTHA WASHINGTON* burned at Island 65 the same day.

2316 GEORGETOWN

SW p wh b. Louisville, Ky., 1850. 395 tons. Engines, 24's-8 ft. from *TELEGRAPH NO. 1.* Ran New Orleans-Louisville-St. Louis. Capt. A. McPherson in 1851. Snagged and lost at Grand Tower, Ill., Oct. 12, 1853.

2317 GEORGETOWN

Stw p wh b. Line Island, Pa. (hull), and completed at Pittsburgh, 1852. 183 tons. Engines, 14's- 4 ft. Two boilers. Owned by Capt. Thomas Poe and others, Georgetown, Pa. Snagged in Missouri River, Oct. 12, 1853, and raised. Snagged fatally at Bellefontaine Bluffs, loaded with U.S. supplies, May 11, 1855.

2318 GEORGIA

SW p wh b. Elizabeth, Pa., 1851. 326 tons. Owned in part and commanded by Capt. S.F. Scull, Pittsburgh, and ran on the Alabama River. Sold in fall of 1853 to Capt. John C. Sinnott, New Orleans. Exploded boilers on Lake Ponchartrain, La., Jan. 28, 1854, with loss of 25 lives.

2319 GEORGIA

Prop p ih b. Jeffersonville, Ind., 1892. 120 x 18 x 6.5. This iron hull boat was built for the Bay brothers and they ran her Ironton-Proctorville on the Ohio River. Named for Miss Georgia Bay. Proved too deep draft and was sold south. Capt. Harry Doss took her down the Mississippi.

2320 GEORGIA LEE

Stw p wh b. Jeffersonville, Ind., by Howard, 1898. 178 x 33 x 5. Engines, 18's- 8 ft. Three boilers, each 44" by 32 ft. Owned by the Lee Line, Memphis. Left Memphis Aug. 13, 1898, on maiden trip in Memphis-Cairo trade, Capt. N.B. McNeely, with Jesse P. Irwin, mate, and Charles Conway, pilot on watch. She replaced the *ROWENA LEE* (see) in the trade. Named for Miss Georgia Lee, daughter of Capt. James Lee. Had a narrow shave in May 1909 at the Paducah Marine Ways. She was being hauled out for repairs when the chains gave way, and she took a run for the river and sank. Ran in the Memphis-Cincinnati trade until 1914 when Lee Line abandoned the trade. Her last operation probably was under charter taking the place of the *KATE ADAMS* which had stranded at Helena, Ark., in 1917. Lost in ice at Memphis, January 1918 along with the ex-*JAMES LEE,* both having been built at Howards in 1898.

2321 GERALDINE

Stw p wh b. Catlettsburg, Ky., 1908. 119 x 20.5 x 3.9. Equipment from *CANDO* used in her construction. Owned by Catlettsburg & Warfield Packet Co. Ran on Big Sandy River and locally around Catlettsburg, often laid up. Burned Aug. 2, 1910.

2322 GERM

Stw p wh b. Marietta, Oh., 1871. 19 tons. Ran Marietta-Parkersburg in low water, summer 1871. Ran Marietta-Beverly, Capt. Rudolph Fearing in 1873, then Parkersburg-Lowell in 1874, same master. Still listed 1876.

2323 GERMANIA

SW p wh b. West Brownsville, Pa., 1878. 163 x 32 x 5.5. 339 tons. Owned by the Pittsburgh, Brownsville & Geneva Packet Co. Capt. R.R. Abrams, first master. She ran on the Monon River 20 years and then was dismantled, winter 1897-1898.

2324 GERMANTOWN

SW p wh b. Industry, Pa., 1846. 193 tons. Ran Cincinnati-St. Louis. Hit a rock on the Louisville Falls, August 1848, and was run out on Sand Island where she sank. Downbound on the Ohio River at Raleigh Bar, she burned on Sept. 23, 1849, Capt. Bugher.

2325 GERTRUDE

SW p wh b. New Orleans, La., 1863. 70 tons. 167 x 17.6 x 4.3. Had one stack. Built by Isaac Davis of Brott & Davis, New Orleans. Was running New Orleans-Donaldsonville, Capt. Joseph Aguda, with G.E. Pitcher, clerk, 1864. Foundered at College Point, La., Sept. 21, 1864, with loss of six lives.

2326 GERTRUDE

Stw p wh b. Hawesville, Ky., 1895. 145 x 28.5 x 5.6. 285 tons. Engines, 14's- 4 ft. Two boilers, each 40" by 24 ft. Ran Hawesville-Owensboro, also Evansville-Tell City, Capt. W.D. Crammond. Sold to Monongahela River Packet Co., Charles F. Foster, May 1902. At Pittsburgh a new maple floor was laid in the cabin and staterooms added. The cabin, which had been painted mahogany, was changed to white. A texas was added. Capt. George B. Hendrickson was master, and his father Joe L. Hendrickson was pilot. Ran Monon River in opposition to the regular line. This ended up in a U.S. marshal sale at Pittsburgh July 22, 1903, and high bidder was Samuel W. Carpenter, Allegheny, Pa. The Chitwood & Sanders Transportation Co., bought her October 1903 and took her to the Chattahoochee River. Capt. David C. Keller took her to New Orleans, and turned her over to Capt. Isaac R. Davis. Engineer Jacob Merriman made the whole trip.

2327 GIPSEY

Stw p wh b. Portsmouth, Oh., 1860. 71 tons. 103 x 23 x 3.3. Owned by J.M., L.P. and William Murphy, all of New Orleans. Went to Confederate registry 1861.

2328 GIPSEY

SW p wh b. Cincinnati, Oh., 1863. 336 tons. Documented out of Wheeling until 1867 when she went to Kansas City to assist in the building of the first bridge to span the Missouri, a railroad bridge built by Keystone Bridge Co., Pittsburgh, for the Kansas City & Cameron RR. On this bridge job 1867-1869 her masters were Capts. C. Ryan and J.S. Bellas. The pilots were J.A. Wise, T.J. Boone, and J.M. Montgomery. Engineers were Thomas Newkirk, D.C. Riter and A.W. Hardy. Off the lists in 1871.

2329 GIPSY

SW p wh b. Louisville, Ky., 1848. 298 tons. 198 x 26 x 6. Ran New Orleans-Bayou Sara, Capt. James H. Ure, twice weekly. Continued until burned and lost at Torras, La., Dec. 7, 1854, with loss of five lives.

2330 GIPSY

Stw p wh b. California, Pa., 1855. 132 tons. First master, Capt. John Klinefelter who owned one-fourth along with George Black, Thomas S. Clarke, and David Holmes, all of Pittsburgh. Ran in tramp trades. Was at St. Paul, 1855 and 1856. Sold to Capt. John Thurston and others, all from Van Buren County, Ark., in 1856. Sunk and lost in ice at Cincinnati, Oh., Feb. 7, 1857.

2331 GIPSY

SW p wh b. Baresville, Oh., 1858. 43 tons. 87 x 18 x 3.5. Built and commanded by Capt. W.D. Sanford of the Ouachita River. Baresville is the old name for Hannibal, Oh. Lost by snagging at Black Bayou, La., Feb. 19, 1861.

2332 GLADIATOR

SW p wh b. Freedom, Pa., 1846. 236 tons. Dismantled and hull used as a barge, Nov. 15, 1851.

2333 GLADIATOR

SW p wh b. Belle Vernon, Pa., and completed at Pittsburgh, 1857. 227 x 34 x 5.8. 425 tons. Built by Capt. George D. Moore and others. After the *PENNSYLVANIA* exploded in June, 1858 Capt. John Simpson Klinefelter took stock and became master in the St. Louis-New Orleans trade. During the war served in Grant's Tennessee campaign and the capture of Fort Donelson. Took sick and wounded to Keokuk. Joseph H. Reevey, St. Louis, bought the boat entire, June 1863 at which time Klinefelter retired from the river, and the command went to Capt. Samuel H. Boyce. In February 1864 Capt. Bart N.L. Bowen took command. In July that year he sold his interest and Capt. William S. Hawkins commanded. Sunk and lost at Willard, Ill., 65.6 miles above Cairo on the Mississippi River, Aug. 14, 1864. A full account of ownerships, etc., appears in *S&D Reflector,* December 1977, page 27.

2334 GLADIOLA

Stw p wh b. Jeffersonville, Ind., by Howard, 1869. 277 tons. 136.5 x 34.5 x 4. In 1869 running New Orleans-Minden, Capt. Nat Puckette, with Ed Groves, clerk. In 1870, New Orleans-Shreveport, Capt. H.L. Lee, with Ed Groves, clerk, also New Orleans-Bayou Pierre, Capt. Ben F. Fulton, with Ed Groves, clerk. Sank and lost 17 miles above Grand Encore, La., on Red River, July 14, 1874.

2335 GLADYS

Stw ferry wh b. Jeffersonville, Ind., by Howard, 1911. 93 x 23 x 3.5. Engines, 10"- 42" stroke. One boiler, 44" by 16 ft. Owned by A.C. Jaynes, Cape Girardeau, Mo. Still there in 1925. Owned 1929 by Greenville Bridge and Ferry Co., Greenville, Miss.

2336 GLASGOW

Stw p wh b. Louisville, Ky., 1845. 49 tons. Off the lists in 1851.

2337 GLASGOW

SW p wh b. New Albany, Ind., 1862. 340 tons. 208 x 34.5 x 5. Engines, 22's- 7 ft. Three boilers. Paddlewheels 27 ft. dia. working 11 ft. buckets. She was at St. Louis on July 15, 1864, and was partially burned in the big steamboat fire that day. The Board of Underwriters auctioned off the burned boats and sold *GLASGOW* to Capt. William P. Lamothe for $6,200. Ran principally on the Missouri River and in 1867 was in St. Louis & Omaha Packet Co., Lamothe, master. In 1873 was in Carter's Red River Line, running St. Louis-Shreveport. One season she ran New Orleans-Ouachita River, Capt. Jack Brinker. Sank and lost on Red River after hitting the wreck of the *MONSOON* in Prudhomme Bend, Feb. 22, 1873.

2338 GLASGOW

Stw p wh b. Brownsville, Pa., 1866. 443 tons. 156 x 33 x 5. Engines, 16's- 4½ ft. Three boilers, each 28" by 24 ft., two flues. Designed for Pittsburgh-Cincinnati trade, and came out with Capt. George Johnson, master, with Charles Fairman, first clerk. Made a Missouri River trip that first season. In 1870 Pittsburgh-Nashville, Capt. A. Robinson. On May 12, 1870, came out of the Louisville locks downbound, hit the sand bar below, swung and collided with the bow of the *PALESTINE.* The *GLASGOW* lost paddlewheel, rudders, and stove her hull. In 1873 ran Cairo-St. Louis, Capt. Andy Robinson, Jr., with W.S. Dravo, clerk. Spring of 1876 in Evansville-Cincinnati trade, Capt. Thomas Boluss, with Samuel James, Jr., clerk. That fall, same trade, with Capt. H.A. Lozier, master, with H.S. Mitchell, clerk. She stove on the falls at Louisville, Nov. 9, 1876, was run into shore at the foot of the falls, sank and was dismantled. Owned at time of loss in equal shares by Memphis & Ohio River Packet Co., Louisville & Henderson Mail Line, and U.S. Mail Line. Commented a Cincinnati editor: "She was built in January 1866 and during her career has changed hands so often and has plied so many trades that we are unable to obtain her history definitely." Commented a Pittsburgh editor: "Capt. Pink Varble has the contract for wrecking the *GLASGOW.* That's very appropriate for Pink put her in the condition that she required a job of that kind."

2339 GLAUCUS

SW p wh b. West Elizabeth, Pa., 1849. 154 tons. St. Louis & Keokuk Packet Co. Burned and lost at Montrose, Iowa, Mar. 30, 1852.

2340 GLEANER

Ferry wh b. Cincinnati, Oh., 1860. 74 tons. Capt. James Rowley, Jr., Vanceburg, Ky., informed F. Way, Jr., in a letter dated Feb. 2, 1950, that this ferry long operated Maysville-Aberdeen on the Ohio River. It was on this ferry that a U.S. marshal and deputies went in pursuit of the towboat *KATE DIXON,* resulting in several shootings. Also Capt. Jim believed this ferry conveyed the duelists from Maysville to Straight Creek where on the Kentucky shore Maysville's ex-mayor William T. Casto and Leonidas Metcalfe paced off at 60 yards, fired, and Casto was shot through, just below the heart, and died in a few minutes. This affair, staged May 8, 1862, was said to have been the last formal duel along the shores of the Ohio. In January 1871 the *GLEANER* was shoved high and dry at mouth of Fish Gut Creek (at Aberdeen, Oh.) by ice gorges, and the *LESLIE COMBS* was on Beasley Bar for the same reason. Still listed in 1876.

2341 GLEANER

Stw p wh b. Pittsburgh, Pa., 1865. 322 tons. 165 x 30.

Bought at Memphis 1865 by Capts. Dan Able, R.C. Gray, and others, and operated there to Arkansas River. Snagged 12 miles below Pine Bluff, Ark., bound for Memphis, February 1867, raised. Off the lists 1869.

2342 GLENCOE

SW p wh b. New Albany, Ind., 1846. 428 tons. Ran St. Louis-New Orleans. On Apr. 4, 1852, just in from New Orleans, she landed at the foot of Chestnut Street, St. Louis, and exploded all three boilers. Forty or more lives were lost including a son of the captain, a clerk, a pilot, etc.

2343 GLENCOE

SW p wh b. Shousetown, Pa., 1870 and completed at Pittsburgh, 1871. 275 x 43 (floor 40) x 7. Engines, 23½'s- 8 ft. Six boilers, each 38" by 26 ft. Engines by Inman, Gault & Co., formerly on *MARY T.* (see), rebuilt by Rees. Owned by Capts. Thomas S. Calhoon and Jackman Taylor Stockdale, and designed for the Louisville-New Orleans trade. Left Pittsburgh on first trip, Jan. 19, 1871, and returned to Louisville Feb. 22, 1871, Capt. T.S. Calhoon, with J.Q.A. Parr, clerk. Later switched to St. Louis-New Orleans trade, stock held by the Glencoe Transportation Co., Capt. John Bofinger, president, with T.S. Calhoon, secretary. Snagged and lost at Delta, La., near Vicksburg, Oct. 28, 1877. Much equipment was salvaged including the whistle (later on the *KATIE STOCKDALE* (see) and chairs which had been bought from the Marietta Chair Co.

2344 GLENDALE

SW p wh b. Cincinnati, Oh., 1853. 394 tons. Built for Capt. John W. Bugher and others and ran Cincinnati-Memphis. Machinery came from the *UNITED STATES.* At the outbreak of the war she was impressed into service as a hospital boat on the Tennessee River. Out of service in 1864.

2345 GLENDALE

Prop produce boat wh b. Peninsula, Oh., 1863. 61.65 tons. Probably a converted canalboat. Off the lists 1869.

2346 GLENDALE

Stw p wh b. Freedom, Pa., and completed at Pittsburgh, 1866. 481 tons. 160 x 35 x 6. Hartupee engines, 17's- 5 ft. Three boilers, each 38" by 24 ft., two flues. Built for Capt. John M. Hare, Allegheny, Pa., with James Mellon, clerk. Operated Pittsburgh-St. Louis. In March 1868 advertised at Pittsburgh for a Missouri River "mountain trip," same officers. Same crew and trade, Pittsburgh-St. Louis, January 1870. Lost at Ste. Genevieve, Mo., Dec. 29, 1870. Her machinery was auctioned off on the St. Louis levee, above the bridge, Feb. 1, 1871, and most everything went to Capt. David Campbell. Equipment from the towboat *SHARK* was sold at this same auction.

2347 GLENDY BURKE

SW p wh b. Jeffersonville, Ind., by Howard, 1851. 245 x 33 x 8. 425 tons. Built for Cobb & Manlove, Vicksburg who held three-fourths interest, and Capt. J.M. White who commanded. Named for firm member in Burke, Watt & Co., Carondelet Street, New Orleans (the Burke was Glen D. Burke). Ran Louisville-New Orleans. Sold March 1852 to Capt. Jacob F. Bentley and others of Mead County, Ky., and usually ran in New Orleans-Vicksburg trade, Capt. J.F. Bentley. In 1854 sold to Capt. Henry W. Smith, New Albany, Ind. Fatally snagged at Bird's Point, near Cairo, Ill., in the Mississippi River, May 24, 1855. The wreck caused damage to several boats as late as October 1891. This boat has become legend due to Stephen Collins Foster's popular song of the title.

2348 GLENMORE

Stw p wh b. Jeffersonville, Ind., by Howard, 1897. Originally named *JOHN W. THOMAS* (see) which burned at Evansville Christmas night 1905 and was rebuilt and renamed for a popular bourbon marketed by the Glenmore distillery. She was sold to the Missouri River and while being repaired at the marine ways, North Kansas City, Mo., the shore eroded and let the boat fall into the river, this on Mar. 18, 1909. She became a total loss. Owned at the time by Booth Baughman, J.J. Pryor, Phil McCrory, and Capt. E.H. Matheus, master.

2349 GLENVILLE

Stw p wh b. Burning Springs, W. Va., 1883. 75 x 14.6 x 2.6. Ran on Little Kanawha River. Still listed 1886, maybe later.

2350 GLENWOOD

Stw p wh b. Manchester, Pa., 1857. 145 tons. Was at St. Paul, Minn. first season. Cincinnati-Nashville, Capt. Frazier, January 1861. On the upper Tennessee operated by the Federals, 1862, and dismantled that year.

2351 GLIDE

Stw p wh b. Shousetown, Pa., 1862. 137 tons. Sold to U.S. Navy in November 1862 and was converted into a U.S. tinclad. Burned accidentally at Cairo, Ill., Feb. 7, 1863.

2352 GLIDE

Stw p wh b. Murraysville, W. Va., 1863. 232 tons. 160.4 x 33 x 5.1. Sold to U.S. Navy, November 1863 and was in war service for the duration. Sold by Navy in August 1865. Was converted into a steam diving bell boat at Algiers, La., in 1867, Capt. James McClintock. Sold June 1868 to Capt. Spencer Field, New Orleans. Again sold August 1868 to James M. Middleton, New Orleans, Capt. A.J. Dye. Exploded boilers 59 miles above New Orleans in mid-December 1868 with loss of 15 lives. She was on her way to Shreveport, apparently again a packet.

2353 GLIDE NO. 3

Stw p wh b. Freedom, Pa., 1864. 225 tons. 156 x 33. Engines, 13's- 4½ ft. Two boilers. All three of these *GLIDE* boats were built for Capt. W.C. Anderson. Ran Pittsburgh-Cincinnati and did so well Capt. Anderson added a texas at Pittsburgh in October 1864. Still in P&C trade spring 1865 with John Anderson and Thomas Javens, pilots. Capt. John Claycomb bought interest in latter April 1865 and ran her Cincinnati-Arkansas River, with George N. Baker, clerk. That fall ran Memphis-Arkansas River, same crew. On a trip up Red River she sank and was lost at Madame Roubleau's plantation with 630 bales of cotton aboard, near Shreveport, La., Nov. 15, 1865.

2354 GLOBE

Stw p wh b. Brownsville, Pa., 1849. 54 tons. Off the lists 1856.

2355 Globe

SW p wh b. Paducah, Ky., 1849. 211 tons. Ran on the Upper Mississippi. Was in the Minnesota River 1854–1856. Capt. Edwin Bell was master in 1855 delivering Indian supplies. Partly owned by Capt. Louis Roberts. Off the lists in 1856.

2356 GOLCONDA

Ferry wh b. Evansville, Ind., 1873. 21 tons. 60 x 16 x 2.7. Ran at Golconda, Ill. Still listed 1886.

2357 GOLCONDA

Stw p wh b. Greenfield Landing, Mo., 1890. 89.5 x 25.3 x 4. A boat of this name capsized in a wind squall Aug. 16, 1901, at Livingston Point, above Paducah, Ky., possibly this one.

2358 GOLD

Stw p wh b. Pittsburgh, Pa., 1901. 88 x 16 x 2. Built by W.N. and D.B. Fuller. Ran in Zanesville-Dresden trade, upper Muskingum in 1904–1905 owned by Ohio Canal Transportation Co. Also in McConnelsville-Beverly trade on the Muskingum briefly. Ran Marietta-Matamoras in low water time.

2359 GOLD DUST

SW p wh b. Jeffersonville, Ind., 1877. 245 x 40 x 7. Engines, 22's- 7 ft. Four boilers. Came out in Louisville-New Orleans trade, Capt. R.H. Woolfolk, with E.W. Gould, Jr., clerk. Soon went to St. Louis-New Orleans trade, Capt. E.W. Gould. She was under the management of the Anchor Line when she exploded boilers near Hickman, Ky., Aug. 7, 1882, with loss of 17 lives. Capt. John McCord was master. Mark Twain rode this boat while preparing manuscript for *Life On the Mississippi.*

2360 GOLD DUST

Stw p wh b. Jeffersonville, Ind., by Howard, 1900. 170 x 34 x 5. Machinery from the *E.G. RAGON.* The Louisville & Evansville Packet Co., put her in the Louisville-Evansville trade to pinch-hit for the *TELL CITY* which was being repaired. Was on her third trip when she burned at Gailey's Landing, four miles below Alton, Ind., in 1901.

2361 GOLDEN AGE

SW p wh b. Pittsburgh, Pa., 1858. 180 x 32 x 6.5. Ran New Orleans-Baton Rouge-Fort Adams with Capt. McCombs, master, and later with Capt. Weibling. Did some transport work for the Confederates and then was taken up Yazoo River where she was scuttled and burned to prevent capture in latter May, 1863.

2362 GOLDEN CITY

Stw p wh b. Cincinnati, Oh., 1876. 280 x 40.5 x 6.3. Engines, 22's- 6 ft. from the *LOUISVILLE.* These were exchanged June 1878, and thenceforth she had 22½'s- 8 ft. Originally three boilers, later four. Owned by Capt. J.D. Hegler and Sterling McIntyre, and ran Cincinnati-New Orleans. She was exceptionally long for a sternwheel packet, although the *CHAS. P. CHOUTEAU* (see) exceeded and both were eclipsed by the *MISSISSIPPI QUEEN* (see). Ran in the Southern Transportation Co., along with the *GOLDEN CROWN, GOLDEN RULE, GUIDING STAR, R.R. SPRINGER, WILL S. KYLE* (all see). Capt. Sterling McIntyre was in command when she burned at President's Island, below Memphis, Mar. 25, 1882. She was upbound, a stiff wind blowing, when fire broke out in the tiller room disabling the rudders. Grounded on President's Island. Many of the passengers jumped in the river and were drowned. The complete outfit of Stowe's Circus was on board. Leo, the lion, swam to the Arkansas shore and dragged himself up through the willows. He was not heard from until the following evening. A black revival meeting was in progress, the Rev. Abijah Elongated Flowers conducting. The reverend had his flock warmed up to a good pitch when Leo entered the door and wandered up the aisle. The door to the church later was found a half-mile distant, and fences were knocked down double that distance. Leo curled up in the pulpit-end of the church where he was found by circus officers, none the worse for his excursion. The life loss in this catastrophe reached 30, including wife and three children of Capt. Louis E. Kouns. The wreck was visible into the early 1900s.

2363 GOLDEN CROWN

Stw p wh b. Cincinnati, Oh., 1877. 261 x 41 x 7. Engines, 18's- 7 ft. Originally had three boilers, later four. Built for Capt. Henry H. Drown, Marietta, Oh., and ran Cincinnati-New Orleans. She lost her paddlewheel at Newburgh, Ind., in May 1878 and it sank out of sight. The *CHAMPION NO. 8* was dispatched to the scene and brought the lost apparel to Cincinnati. Capt. Vincent Shinkle, 64, died on board at Cairo, Ill., November 1885. He had suffered a second stroke of paralysis, and had had financial reverses. The Cincinnati & Memphis Packet Co. bought her and changed her name to *DE SOTO* (see) and as such she burned at Owensboro, Ky., Jan. 28, 1890.

2364 GOLDEN EAGLE

SW p wh b. Freedom, Pa. and completed at Pittsburgh, 1864. 506.62 tons. Built for Capt. Wm. B. Donaldson and others for the Cincinnati-Memphis trade. Sold within a month to the Dean Line which continued her there. Capt. Amos E. Davis and others bought her for the Wheeling-Cincinnati trade in the fall of 1868, and she ran low water in

September 1869 in Cincinnati-Big Sandy trade, Capt. Wash Honshell, with George A. Knight, clerk. Off the lists in 1870.

2365 GOLDEN EAGLE

SW p wh b. St. Louis, Mo., 1876. 941 tons. Built by Capts. W.F. (Fuce) and Peyton (Pate) Davidson for the St. Louis-Keokuk trade. Had engines from the *J.H. JOHNSON*, 26½'s- 7 ft. Burned at Thomas Landing, above the mouth of the Illinois River, May 31, 1880, Capt. David R. Asbury. Golden Eagle, Ill., is now nearby. She had a partner side-wheeler in the trade, the *WAR EAGLE*, both much alike in appearance and size.

2366 GOLDEN EAGLE

Stw p wh b. Jeffersonville, Ind., by Howard, 1904. Originally cotton packet *WM. GARIG* (see). The *GARIG* was sold in 1918 to the Eagle Packet Co., St. Louis, greatly altered and renamed. She was entered in the St. Louis-Peoria trade and did well. In 1932 was put in the St. Louis-Cape Girardeau-Commerce trade and after about six months was withdrawn, this spelling the end of the regular passenger and freight packet business for Eagle Packet Co. When Eagle Packet sold the *CAPE GIRARDEAU* to the Greene Line, Cincinnati, in 1935, they renovated the *GOLDEN EAGLE* into a tourist boat and scheduled her to St. Paul, Chattanooga, Cincinnati, Nashville, etc., Capt. W.H. (Buck) Leyhe, and did well. As sort of a presage of coming events, on Apr. 22, 1939, she engaged in a "remote control" race with the *DELTA QUEEN*, which was plying the Sacramento River. The *GOLDEN EAGLE* was judged the winner. Upbound at Chester, Ill., on the night of June 14, 1941, she hit a submerged dike and sank along shore. When the river fell she was raised. She then continued 1942-1943 and was preparing to enter the 1944 season when her old boilers were condemned. Due to World War II replacement was impossible, and she idled at St. Louis 1944-1945. In 1946 she was sold to Mr. and Mrs. Dewey Miller and Mr. and Mrs. E. Willers, together with operating rights, and thus ended the Leyhe management of Eagle Packet Co. She ran all that 1946 season with a final trip to New Orleans and back. Sold in March 1947 to Herman T. Pott of St. Louis Shipbuilding & Steel Co., and on the first trip downbound, about 1:30 A.M., May 17, 1947, she ran aground on Tower Island and sank. All passengers were vacated safely. The *DELTA QUEEN* was then in the Gulf of Mexico headed for New Orleans to become a tourist boat for the Greene Line. The Golden Eagle Club, St. Louis, had its origins from *GOLDEN EAGLE* fans. The boat's pilothouse, rescued thanks to Ruth Ferris, now is the decorative centerpiece in the Missouri Historical Society's exhibits, Jefferson Memorial, St. Louis.

2367 GOLDEN EAGLE

Stw pl wh b. Des Moines, Iowa, 1911. Ran on the Des Moines River locally. Still listed 1918.

2368 GOLDEN ERA

SW p wh b. Wheeling, Va., 1852. 249 tons. In Galena, Dunleith & Minnesota Packet Co., 1856. She was utilized as a troop transport by the U.S. during the war, making at least three trips to Vicksburg in 1863. 178 x 29 x 5.1. Sold in December 1865 to M.W. Wetmore, New Orleans, with Capt. John R. Neeld, master. Sold September 1866 to Michael Purcell, New Orleans, with Capt. Volney Brown, master. Sold November 1866 to Capt. John Kaiser, New Orleans, also part-owner. He owned her entire in 1867. Dismantled 1868.

2369 GOLDEN ERA

Stw p wh b. California, Pa., and completed at Pittsburgh, 1862. 150 x 33 x 4.5. Engines, 15's- 5½ ft. Three boilers. Built in equal shares by Capt. J.J. Blagg, John Heisner, and S. Halliday of Gallipolis, Oh., and R.W. Terry and D.F. Sayres, Millersport, Oh. First master was Capt. R.W. Terry who had been on the *OHIO NO. 2*. Ran Marietta-Cincinnati. In fall of 1864 Capt. Wash Kerr bought control and with W.H. Bryan as clerk put her in the Pittsburgh-Portsmouth trade. Knocked down her stacks on the Wheeling suspension bridge during the big flood March 1865. Sank at Guyandotte, W. Va., Feb. 14, 1866, and running ice badly mauled her. The cabin floated off and furniture stored in the texas was rescued by men in skiffs. During low water in July 1866 the hull was raised and was taken to Cincinnati for rebuilding. (See next listing.)

2370 GOLDEN ERA

Stw p wh b. Cincinnati, Oh., 1866. 155.7 x 32.4 x 4.9. Same hull as former *GOLDEN ERA* (listing above) and new upper works. Capt. A.M. Halliday, master, with J.S. Alexander, clerk, in 1867, and made trips on the upper Ohio. She was taken to New Orleans in the fall of 1868 owned in shares by Capts. Gus Hodge, A.M. Halliday, and J.J. Blagg. Capt. Gus Hodge, master, and he owned 19/20. Sold March 1870 to Warren P. Ketchum, New Orleans, with Capt. B.F. Litterall, master. Broken up for scrap July 1870.

2371 GOLDEN FLEECE

Stw p wh b. Paducah, Ky., 1913. 134 x 26 x 3.9. Built from the side-wheel *LIBERTY* (see). Ran Paducah-Golconda. Came to Pittsburgh August 1919, Capt. William A. Blackstock. Sold to John F. Klein who rebuilt her into a towboat at Mound City, Ill., 1925, renamed *JULIA O'SULLIVAN*, later *FRANK WOODS*.

2372 GOLDEN GATE

SW p wh b. Madison, Ind., 1852. 317 tons. Burned and lost at Sulphur Springs, Mo., Sept. 6, 1857.

2373 GOLDEN GATE

Stw p wh b. Lawrenceburg, Ind., 1863. 45 tons. Off the lists 1865.

2374 GOLDEN GATE

Stw p wh b. Dubuque, Iowa, 1878. 131.4 x 30 x 5. Engines,

14's- 4 ft. Built for J.H.S. Coleman, Davenport, and brothers James and Andrew. J.H.S. had a tenth interest in the Homestake Mine, Deadwood, S.D., and some of the profit went to building this rafter. Had engines from the *JAMES MEANS* (see). Capt. J.M. Turner was on her 1881-1882 running Chippewa Lumber & Boom Co.'s rafts to Hannibal and St. Louis. Mississippi River Commission bought her at Memphis 1895 and by 1900 she was on the Illinois River, Capt. G.M. Sivley. Capt. W.E. Pratt, Madison, Ind., ran her Cincinnati-Madison in 1902 and in May 1903 was running Louisville-Kentucky River three trips a week, to Monterey. Later that year sold to C.F. Disken, Carrollton, Ky., who dismantled her in the Kentucky River at Carrollton.

2375 GOLDEN GIRL

Stw p wh b. Cloverport, Ky., 1911. 93.4 x 28.5 x 3.7. Built from the *R.D. KENDALL* using machinery from the *THOMAS PARKER*. Owned by Capt. and Mrs. Frank T. Rounds, Cloverport. She was primarily an excursion boat, also suitable for towing. Burned and sank at Owensboro, Ky., Easter Sunday, 1916.

2376 GOLDENROD

Stw lighthouse tender sh b. Jeffersonville, Ind., at the Sweeney Yard, 1888. 150 x 26.5 x 3.7. Engines, 12's- 5 ft. Two boilers. An attractive example of marine architecture. Served the government lights on Ohio River and tribs, replacing the *LILY* (see). Capt. Owen F. Jolly was master in early years, then Capt. Leslie T. Hill, native of Aberdeen, Oh., was on her until the end. Harry Layfield, New Richmond, Oh., went striker engineer 1903, became chief 1912 and left her in 1917. William Handley was engineer 22 years. Decommissioned when the *GREENBRIER* (see) was built in 1925, and sold to John Lyons, Middleport, Oh. He moored her under the ice piers there, and in a flood she broke away and was lost.

2377 GOLDEN RULE

Stw p wh b. Cincinnati, Oh., 1877. A large Cincinnati-New Orleans packet built for the Shinkle family, Covington, Ky. Engines 18's- 7 ft. Three boilers. Downbound on the Mississippi she was making Omega Landing 26 miles above Vicksburg, July 19, 1877 at 5:00 A.M. when she struck a snag and was lost. The machinery and boilers were recovered. The engines later went to the *PARIS C. BROWN* (see).

2378 GOLDEN RULE

Stw p wh b. Cincinnati, Oh., 1877. 261 x 41 x 9. Engines, 20's- 7 ft. Four boilers. Owned largely by Capt. Oliver P. Shinkle, who commanded. Ran Cincinnati-New Orleans, with A.L. Shinkle, clerk. Thomas E. Reardon recalled that a special press was carried aboard and a daily newspaper prepared and issued, "real newspaper style and better than those on the first *THOMPSON DEAN* and *RICHMOND*." Truman C. Holmes recalled her whistle which "was like a full orchestra blended into one note." She caught fire at Cincinnati Mar. 31, 1892. The *KEYSTONE STATE*, Capt. T.S. Calhoon, was alongside and many jumped to her decks. Six lives were lost, one of whom was Miss Nellie Maloney who had come aboard to bid good-bye to Capt. and Mrs. Shinkle. She fell between the boats.

2379 GOLDEN STATE

SW p wh b. McKeesport, Pa., 1852. 298 tons. Ran Pittsburgh-St. Louis, owned at Georgetown, Pa. Capt. Joseph M. Calhoon of that place commanded and died aboard at St. Louis. Later in the Galena, Dunleith & St. Paul Line, Capt. N.F. Webb, with Charles Hargus, clerk in 1856. Capt. Scott, master, in 1857, with Frank Ward, clerk. Was at St. Paul in 1859. Off the lists 1860.

2380 GOLDENA

Stw p wh b. Brownsville, Pa., 1862. Originally named *JULIET* (see). Was in U.S. service during the war and sold 1865 and renamed. She was wrecked in the cut-off between Arkansas and White rivers, Capt. Sol Franklin, Dec. 31, 1865. The wrecked *LINTON* (see) was nearby.

2381 GOLDFINCH

Stw p wh b. Wellsville, Oh., 1862. Originally named *NEW ERA* (see). As such she was in U.S. service during the war and was rebuilt at St. Louis 1865 and renamed. In 1866 made a trip to the upper Missouri. On June 3, 1868, she had run a picnic excursion at Evansville, Ind., had unloaded the crowd, and was being dropped down to lay up when fire was discovered. Burned and lost. Owned at the time by Capt. William Karr, Osceola, Ind.

2382 GONDOLA

Stw p wh b. Pittsburgh, Pa., 1883. 120.2 x 23 x 3.2. Originally a towboat, bought by the Mississippi River Commission in 1887 at Jeffersonville, Ind., and renamed *VEDETTE*. Sold privately and resumed her original name. Sold August 1905 to Syl Gardner, Pt. Pleasant, W. Va., and ran Gallipolis-Charleston, Capt. W.L. Guthrie in 1907.

2383 GONDOLIER

SW p wh b. Freedom, Pa., 1847. 198 tons. Came in collision with *JOSIAH LAWRENCE* (see) at Preston's Landing, a short distance below St. Louis, upbound, Nov. 1, 1848. She had been running in the Pittsburgh-St. Louis trade owned by her commander Capt. Lyon and a Mr. Darrow and others of Pittsburgh. Lost.

2384 GOOD INTENT

Stw p wh b. Wheeling, W. Va., 1881. Was inspected at Evansville, Ind., November 1882. Then ran Racine-Middleport owned by the Paden family. She had a full cabin, no texas. Dr. Ben Sibley recalled that she was a favorite with the Racine boys because in the afternoons she coaled at Antiquity, Oh., and they rode up on her. Listed 1884, maybe later.

2385 GOODY FRIENDS

Stw p wh b. Brownsville, Pa., 1857. 195 tons. Was at St. Paul in 1859, and advertised at Cincinnati for Memphis in October that year, Capt. Shuman. In November 1864 the

Rebels made a spectacular attack on Johnsonville, Tenn., and destroyed her along with other boats. She was owned at the time by David Gibson & Co., Cincinnati, and others.

2386 GOPHER

Ferry wh b. Minneapolis, Minn., 1874. 59 tons. Inspected May 25, 1881, at St. Paul and listed as a ferry.

2387 GORDON C. GREENE

Stw p-tourist sh b. Jeffersonville, Ind., by Howard, 1923. Originally named *CAPE GIRARDEAU* (see). Greene Line Steamers, Cincinnati, acquired her from Eagle Packet Co., St. Louis, changed the name, and departed St. Louis with her Mar. 31, 1935. First trip was with tourists, St. Louis-Florence, Ala., and return. Ran Pittsburgh-Cincinnati accepting passengers and freight summers 1935-1936 and ran tours spring and fall. Twice altered; in spring of 1936 a second texas was added and pilothouse raised 28" at Cincinnati; texas again altered and pilothouse upped two ft. in November 1937. Made a Mardi Gras trip from Cincinnati in 1938, and again in 1939, 1941, and in 1947. (Mardi Gras was not celebrated during WW II). Ran a tourist trip Cincinnati-St. Paul in 1944, first Ohio River boat taking passengers there since the *JOE FOWLER* (see) ran one from Pittsburgh in 1914. Went to Knoxville, Tenn., fall of 1949, first packet there in years. She burned coal until four new boilers were placed at Gallipolis in early 1941, prior to Mardi Gras, at which time she was given oil burners. Was the "family boat" with Capt. Tom R. Greene in command, his mother usually aboard, his wife Letha and family frequently, also Capt. and Mrs. Jesse P. Hughes. A bar was provided on the main deck (called "Uncle Tom's Cabin") but no liquor sold. The atmosphere on board was pleasant and healthy, the operation eminently successful in a financial way, and Cap'n Tom and his mother were generous with invitations to "river fans" who rode as guests from here to there, a floating convention center. Hence many youngsters who worked aboard, or who rode for free, grew up better for the experience and opportunity. There never was anything quite like this on the rivers. When the *DELTA QUEEN* arrived on the scene, the *GORDON* was put in the St. Louis-St. Paul trade, cracked the paddlewheel shaft and got a new one at St. Louis, the only accident of this type she ever had. Robert H. McCann, Sewickley, Pa., was her purser over most of this period. She was retired at Cincinnati and sold 1952 to become a floating hotel at Portsmouth, Oh., renamed *SARAH LEE*. This did not work out, and she was sold to Owensboro, Ky., to become a floating restaurant renamed *RIVER QUEEN*. There were problems, and she was taken to Bradenton, Fla., and lavishly outfitted as a tourist attraction which turned sour. By 1960 she was back in New Orleans with talk of a high-class nightclub. She went to Hannibal, Mo., and then across from Hannibal to purvey food and drink. In 1964 she was moved to St. Louis, under the shadow of Eads Bridge, and was, for once, well patronized as a restaurant-bar. Then early Sunday morning, Dec. 3, 1967, she sank. Most of the wreckage was cleared out, but in extreme low water, December 1976, portions of the hull were exposed and photographed. Her whistle, with history back to the side-wheel *CALHOUN*, reposes in the River Museum, Marietta, Oh.

2388 GOSSAMER

Stw p wh b. McKeesport, Pa., 1850. 142 tons. Snagged and lost above Clarksville, Mo., June 19, 1854.

2389 GOSSAMER

Stw p wh b. Pittsburgh, Pa., 1863. 144 tons. 122.5 x 23.1 x 3.3. According to USCG Cmdr. William H. Fuller, who was stationed in the Huntington, W. Va., CG office in 1960, his home in Bradrick, Oh., opposite Huntington, was built in 1863 by Capt. James Forgey and his wife Josephine (who was a Fuller). Capt. Forgey owned in the *GOSSAMER* and in the Civil War had the boat at Franklin, La., where, upon orders of General Banks, it was burned. At the conclusion of the war the hull, practically new, was rebuilt at Cincinnati, and the upper works put on new, and she reappeared still as *GOSSAMER*. She was enrolled at New Orleans owned by the Red River Packet Co., G.L. Kouns, president, Dec. 6, 1866. In 1869 sold to Charles O. Hardy, New Orleans, with Capt. M.M. Dufour, master. Sank and lost in Red River at Campti, La., Sept. 22, 1869, owned at the time by Frank Seuzeneau, New Orleans, with Capt. Phil Crooks, master.

2390 GOULDSBORO

SW tr ih b. St. Louis, Mo., 1863. Originally U.S. gunboat *CHICKASAW* (see) converted into a railroad transfer and renamed for the location of the terminal she served opposite New Orleans. She had been documented as a barge April 2, 1875 and so used until converted into a sidwheel railroad transfer ferry and renamed December 31, 1881. Her dimensions were then 206 x 52.4 x 9. The New Orleans Pacific Railroad owned her and later the Texas & Pacific. Her superstructure was twice rebuilt between 1881 and 1938 and her hull was practically renewed in 1910. This transfer ran, or was in shape to run, until 1941.

2391 GOVERNOR ALLEN

SW p wh b. Jeffersonville, Ind., by Howard, 1867. 217.9 x 40.8 x 10. Engines, 20's- 8 ft. Six boilers, each 44" by 20 ft. Built for and owned originally by Capt. John Smoker, New Orleans. Named for Gov. Henry W. Allen of Mississippi who had been a lawyer at Grand Gulf, Miss., in his earlier days. He and Dr. Marsteller, a local physician, crossed the river and fought a duel in July 1843, using pistols at 10 feet loaded with buckshot. Both were wounded. Dr. Marsteller probed his own wound, dislodged the ball, and never went to bed. Allen then became a sugar planter near Baton Rouge, and had served a term in the Mississippi legislature before the war. In the war he was wounded several times and was on crutches when he ran for state's governor. Years later he met Dr. Marsteller in Mexico and they greeted one another with a handshake. In November 1869 the *GOVERNOR ALLEN* was sold to John C. Sinnott, New Orleans, with Capt. R.

Sinnott, master. Ran New Orleans-Ouachita River to Camden. Collided with *MAYFLOWER* (see) above Davis Landing on the Ouachita July 25, 1869, and *ALLEN*'s pilot got 60 days suspension. Often ran in summer to Vicksburg and Greenville in place of the larger regulars. About her last running was New Orleans-Bayou Sara, Capt. J.J. Brown, with A. Dugas, clerk, this in 1877. Was dismantled and her engines went to the *EDWARD J. GAY* (see).

2392 GOVERNOR ALLEN

SW p wh b. Ironton, Oh., 1874. 136 x 26 x 4. Engines, 14's-5 ft. Three boilers. 206 tons. She lay around Cairo all winter 1875-1876 and then was sold to W.J. Lewis, St. Louis, who had her towed there by the towboat *RAVEN*. She became a shuttle boat connecting with the St. Louis, Kansas City & Northern Railway (now the Wabash) at Dewitt, Mo. On Mar. 13, 1877 en route from Waverly, Mo., to DeWitt with grain and stock for reshipment, she was snagged in Malta Bend (Miller's Island Bend) and lost, also the cargo.

2393 GOVERNOR BENT

SW p wh b. St. Louis, Mo., 1847. 190 tons. Exploded boilers at Island 76, Mississippi River, May 12, 1849. One fireman killed. Many others seated on the boiler deck owed their escape to a rat. They had gotten up to chase the rodent and were out of harm's way when the blast came. Off the lists 1852. 162 x 25.7 x 4.8. The skipper was Capt. David Brandenburg, New Orleans, also part owner. His partner in the boat was Christian Hayes, St. Louis.

2394 GOVERNOR BREATHITT

SW p wh b. Louisville-New Orleans. First skipper was Capt. B.L. Elliott. Snagged and lost at New Richmond, Oh., July 24, 1849.

2395 GOVERNOR BRIGGS

SW p wh b. St. Louis, Mo., 1845. 90 tons. Built for Frank & Walker and first ran Peoria-Peru trade, Illinois River, Capt. C.H. Pratt, master, Henry Detweiller, pilot. Same trade in 1846, Capt. James E. Starr. Transferred to Galena trade carrying U.S. Mail and Detweiller went along. In 1847 St. Louis-Alton, Capt. James E. Starr, with Detweiller, pilot. Sunk at St. Louis July 1849 having hit wreckage of a burned steamboat. Sold to Memphis. Off the lists in 1854.

2396 GOVERNOR GARLAND

Stw p wh b. Belle Vernon, Pa., and completed at Pittsburgh, 1876. 170 x 35 x 4. Rees engines, 13's- 5 ft. from the *FORT GIBSON*. Was built for Memphis & Pine Bluff Mail Line, Capt. E.W.B. Nowland. Burned on the Arkansas above Coos' Ferry, Garland Lake, 3:00 P.M., Mar. 15, 1877. A gentleman passenger lost.

2397 GOV. JOHN C. BROWN

SW wh b. New Orleans, La., 1888. 252.6 x 43.1 x 9.3. Operated by the Texas & Pacific RR. Capt. Wallace Lamb was pilot on her in 1894, a licensed pilot since 1852.

2398 GOVERNOR JONES

SW p wh b. New Albany, Ind., 1844. 396 tons. Off the lists 1847.

2399 GOV. KOSSUTH

Stw p wh b. Keokuk, Iowa, 1852. 89 tons. Off the lists 1854.

2400 GOV. MEIGS

Stw p wh b. Freedom, Pa., 1851. 145 tons. Ran on upper Ohio in short trades. Collided with *HAIL COLUMBIA* in Beaver Shoals, Pa., Apr. 19, 1852, resulting in loss of the latter (see). Several freight bills exist, signed at Pt. Pleasant, Va., and Hannibal, Oh. Off the lists in 1855.

2401 GOVERNOR MOORHEAD

SW p wh b. Madison, Ind., 1841. 122 x 20 x 4.2. Built for Leo Tibbatts, Newport, Ky., with Capt. D.F. Rudd, master. Went to New Orleans. Sold April 1844 to Capt. Roswell R. Frisbee, who commanded. Three weeks later sold to a group in Yazoo City, Miss., and Vicksburg, Capt. James Garland. Capt. William T. Stratton was master, July 1844, in Yazoo River. Off the lists 1846.

2402 GOVERNOR MORTON

Prop p wh b. Lafayette, Ind., 1863. 80 x 12.5 x 4. Went to New Orleans, owned in part and commanded by Capt. G.E. Pitcher. Sold September 1865 to Capt. Henry Gallagher, New Orleans, and sold within the month to Ephriam Knowlton, New Orleans. Sold January 1867 to George P. Deshon, New Orleans with Capt. W.H. Abrams, master. Stranded and lost at Grand Isle, La., Feb. 15, 1868.

2403 GOVERNOR MORTON

SW p wh b. Indianapolis, Ind., 1865. 150 tons. Owned by Indianapolis & White River Steamboat Co. Ran a trial trip Aug. 25, 1865, up White River past mouth of Fall Creek to Crowder's Ford. On Apr. 29, 1866, went to Cold Creek, said to be the highest point a commercial boat ever reached. Sank at Indianapolis, Aug. 6, 1866. During her brief career was in charge of Capt. Henry A. Socwell, Vevay, Ind. Pilots were Michael R. Scudder and Hiram Minick. Dismantled and hull was used as a barge for hauling paving stone by Levi Comegys, Indianapolis.

2404 GOV. PEASE

SW p wh b. Jeffersonville, Ind., by Howard, 1856. 240 tons. 160 x 32 x 6. Built for Galveston, Tex., parties. Burned and lost on Trinity River, Tex., Feb. 26, 1858.

2405 GOVERNOR POWELL

Stw p wh b. New Albany, Ind., 1856. 181 tons. 117 x 32 x 5.5. Showed up at New Orleans December 1858 owned in part and commanded by Capt. Edward Castello, St. Landry Parish. Was running New Orleans-Attakapas via Plaquemine, Capt. P.E. Burke, 1860. Went to Confederate registry in 1861.

2406 GOVERNOR SHARKEY

Stw p wh b. Madison, Ind., 1862. Originally named *ALONE* (see). After war service she was renamed. Many laborers were taken aboard and she departed St. Louis near midnight June 21, 1867, and sank, drowning three. The *KATE PUTNAM* struck this wreck Feb. 22, 1868, and sank, later raised.

2407 GRACE DARLING

Stw p wh b. Madison, Ind., 1855. 261 tons. Was at St. Paul, Minn., 1856. Off the lists, 1858.

2408 GRACE DEVERS

Stw p wh b. Paducah, Ky., 1920. 112.3 x 26.2 x 4.2. Built from the *C. C. BOWYER* (see) including engines. Owned by Capt. F.O. Devers, Dycusburg, Ky., and ran Paducah-Dycusburg. Started towing showboats in 1925, and in 1929 was owned by Capt. D. Otto Hitner, towing showboat *COTTON BLOSSOM*.

2409 GRACE MORRIS

Stw p wh b. Evansville, Ind., 1882. 101.5 x 20 x 3.8. Ran packet trades in Kentucky River and later in Green River. Still listed 1896, maybe later.

2410 GRACE VIRGINIA

Stw ferry wh b. Parkersburg, W. Va., 1900. 99.3 x 28.2 x 3. Served between New Matamoras and Friendly on Ohio River, first owned by Charles W. True and P.Q. Shrake, both of New Matamoras. B.T. Flesher, Middleport, Oh., acquired interest in 1903 and took as partner L.A. Cisty, New Matamoras, this in 1904. Later in 1904 sold entire to Edwin Hornbrook, New Matamoras.

2411 GRACEY CHILDERS

Stw p wh b. Jeffersonville, Ind., by Howard, 1895. Originally named *ROSE HITE* (see). She was bought at Pittsburgh by Capt. J.S. Tyner who took her to Paducah and renamed her to honor Col. Gracey Childers who commanded the 1st Tennessee Regiment in the Philippines 1899 and served there under William Howard Taft. Ran Paducah-Cumberland River and was taken in fall of 1909 to Paducah for a new hull and burned at the foot of Broadway before she got it, this in September. Capt. W.L. Berry acquired the wreck and disposed of it.

2412 GRACIE KENT

Stw p wh b. Stillwater, Minn., 1897. 111 x 20 x 4. Engines, 8"- 2½ ft., later replaced with 12's- 4 ft., and finally by 10's- 6 ft. Started with one boiler, then two, finally three. Built by Capt. John Kent who ran her in trades on St. Croix River. He took a load of potatoes and apples to New Orleans in November 1897. The Burnside & Donaldsonville Packet Co., ran her 1899 and put the two boilers on her. The 10's- 6 ft. were Swain engines, installed prior to purchase in 1908 by Capt. Oscar Blanchard. He used her as a log boat with a tow post behind the pilothouse. Sank on her first trip below Baldwin, La., and was dismantled. The engines were salvaged and used on the towboat *PATRICIA* owned by J.N. Pharr & Sons, Patterson, La.

2413 GRAMPUS

Stw p wh b. Freedom, Pa., 1850. 221 tons. Lost by stranding in USQMD service 1865.

2414 GRAMPUS

Stw p wh b. Brownsville, Pa., 1857. 100 tons. In 1858 William H. Brown, Pittsburgh coal operator, hitched *GRAMPUS* to one side of a coal tow, the *GENERAL LARIMER* on the other, and went to New Orleans successfully. Both were loaded there with molasses and sugar and returned to Pittsburgh. Reported the St. Louis *Republican*, April 1862: "At the banks of Island 10 is the Rebel gunboat *GRAMPUS* so long notorious for reconnoitering purposes last winter at Columbus. On its stern stood Capt. Thomas Chester of Pittsburgh from whom the vessel had been stolen when the war broke out. It was painted dark brown and mounted with two guns. The boat will be raised immediately." Burned in Wolf River, Memphis, Jan. 11, 1863.

2415 GRAMPUS NO. 2

SW p wh b. McKeesport, Pa., 1856. 252 tons. First home port, Brownsville, Tex. Went to Confederate registry 1861.

2416 GRAMPUS NO. 2

Stw p wh b. Brownsville, Pa., 1862. 117 tons. Capt. Luster P. Chester, son of Capt. Thomas Chester (see above) recalled that he and his father operated both *GRAMPUS* and *GRAMPUS NO. 2*, both were seized by the Rebels, and both destroyed during the course of the war. The speculation in Ye Ed.'s mind is whether these primitive towboats were possibly built packet style—serving the double purpose of guiding coal south, and then loading aboard pay cargo for the return North? Seems so.

2417 GRAND

Stw p wh b. Grand Rapids, Mich., 1905. 136 x 32.2 x 5. Engines, 12's- 6 ft. One firebox boiler 54" by 20 ft. Built by merchants of Grand Rapids to run to Grand Haven, Mich., to connect with lake steamers for Chicago. They also built *RAPIDS* (see) same time. Both were bought by merchants of Little Rock, Ark., in 1909 and brought under their own steam through the Fox River improvement to St. Louis. *GRAND* had her guards cut down to fit the Fox locks. Ran Memphis-Little Rock, sometimes going up to Dardanelle, Capt. Henry C. Daniels. Later owned by Capt. R.C. Johnson, Memphis, and ran there to St. Francis River, with Sam G. Smith, clerk. Sold July 1920 to Capt. Jos. Chotin for hauling rice to Morgan City, La. Burned at Bayou Teche, La., May 17, 1921.

2418 GRAND BAY

Stw p wh b. Mobile, Ala., 1857. 121 x 26.5 x 4.5. Transferred to New Orleans October 1858, owned by Daniel L. Shearer, New Orleans. Sold November 1858 to R.J. Fox,

New Orleans, with Capt. D.G. Hill, master. Sold November 1860 to James Lovie, New Orleans, and transferred next day to Benjamin J. Montgomery, New Orleans, with Capt. Julius A. Pratt, master. Sold January 1861 to Samuel F. Rice, New Orleans, Pratt, master. Went to Confederate registry.

2419 GRAND DUKE

SW p wh b. Jeffersonville, Ind., by Howard, 1859. 205 x 35 x 7.5. Engines, 24's- 7 ft. Four boilers. Owned entire by Capt. Samuel Applegate, New Orleans, who commanded. Cabin and engines came from *DUKE* (see) which Applegate had bought 1856. Ran New Orleans-Shreveport in the season, and often to Vicksburg, Lake Providence and Skipworth's Landing in dull season. At outbreak of war sold to Hugh D. McCown, New Orleans, and went to Confederate registry with Capt. Alex Norton, master. Norton was from Steubenville, and turned "Secesh." She was prepared for war at Alexandria, La., and commanded by Capt. J.M. White. Fought the U.S. gunboat *ALBATROSS* at Fort De Russey, a draw. Accidentally burned at Shreveport Sept. 25, 1863.

2420 GRAND ERA

SW p wh b. Louisville, Ky., 1853. Originally named *R. W. McREA* (see). Renamed 1860 and ran New Orleans-Vicksburg 1860, Capt. John H. Kouns. Was in Confederate service in the war, and assisted with capture of *INDIANOLA* (see) Feb. 11, 1863. Ran New Orleans-Shreveport in 1864, Capt. G.L. Kouns, master, with James Kerr, Jr., clerk. Dismantled and machinery went to a Confederate gunboat built at Shreveport in 1864 named *MISSOURI*.

2421 GRAND ERA

SW p wh b. Jeffersonville, Ind., 1869, at the Barmore Yard. 240 x 40 x 7.5. Engines, 25's- 7 ft. Four boilers. A low pressure condensing boat like *RICHMOND* (see), machinery from *GREY EAGLE*. Ran New Orleans-Red River, Capt. John H. Kouns, also Capt. G.L. Kouns, 1870–1871, with James Kerr, Jr., clerk. She had been running New Orleans-Greenville, Capt. J.M. White, master, and was laid up temporarily at New Orleans when she was burned and lost in a wharf fire, January 1871 (see *MAGENTA* for details of the fire).

2422 GRAND ISLE

SW p wh b. Cincinnati, Oh., 1882. 154 x 28 x 5. Engines, 16's- 4½ ft. Built to run from New Orleans to Grand Isle, a pleasure resort in the Gulf with hotels, etc., Capt. John F. Krantz. Burned on Black River, La., near Lismore, just upstream from the Willson property, 12 miles south of Jonesville, La. She had put in the 1883 season in the Grand Isle trade and had been chartered to take the place of a regular packet which had been snagged on the Mississippi. Was on her first trip when she was burned. Had two boilers.

2423 GRAND ISLE

Rig? A regular New Orleans-Grand Isle-Barataria boat, Capt. M. McSweeney, operating in 1904–1911 when McSweeney sold her, replacing her with the *AMERICAN EAGLE*.

2424 GRAND PACIFIC

Stw p wh b. La Crosse, Wis., 1876. Originally named *TIDAL WAVE* (see). Ran in the St. Louis & St. Paul Packet Co., organized by Capts. W.F. Davidson and A.M. Hutchinson, called the "White Collar Line." Their wharfboat at St. Louis was at the foot of Olive Street. This name change came about c. 1883. She hit a pier of the Burlington, Iowa, bridge, Apr. 20, 1884, ripping the hull. Drifted 300 yards and settled in 20 feet.

2425 GRAND PRAIRIE

SW p wh b. Gallipolis, Oh., 1852. 261 tons. Made three trips St. Louis-St. Paul in 1853, and was running to St. Paul in 1855. Off the lists 1857.

2426 GRAND REPUBLIC

SW p wh b. Shousetown, Pa., 1867. Originally the *GREAT REPUBLIC* (see). She was renamed in 1876 following repairs, renovation, and the addition of another boiler at Carondelet, Mo., then owned by Capt. William H. Thorwegan. On her second or third trip, May 1876, she carried Emperor Don Pedro II and retinue, of Brazil, from St. Louis to New Orleans. She was held 24 hours at St. Louis for the emperor to come aboard. He and party occupied 16 rooms. That December she arrived in New Orleans on the sixth of the month with a banner cargo consisting of 8,210 bales of cotton, 525 sacks of cotton seed, 872 sacks of oil cake, 400 sacks of meal, and 350 barrels of oil. Her freight manifest was 45 feet long. Wrote a local reporter: "Her appearance at the wharf presented that of a packet intended to do honors to some Duke, Count or other nobility. Blue streamers were floating from her decks and flagstaffs, and across the cotton foward was a large piece of canvas with the following inscription: CHAMPIONSHIP OF THE WORLD, 8210 BALES. Her deck crew wore blue bands on their hats, while from the jackstaff-holder could be observed two large brooms decorated with blue ribbons. We also noted suspended between her derricks a diminutive bale of cotton, also decorated with ribbons. This trip outranks any previous trip by 509 bales that was ever brought to this port." This was something to see; cotton bales were stowed 11 high on her forecastle, on the roof there were two and three tiers. In the hold were some 2,000 bales. On the way back up the river Mrs. Alex DeValcourt at Gaines Landing presented Capt. Thorwegan with a plate of butter carved into the shape of a basket of flowers, and at Memphis E.S. Levy presented a miniature cotton bale done up in silk. She was laid up at St. Louis when she caught fire at 11:30 P.M. on what was described as "a clear moonlight night with fleecy clouds in the sky," this on Sept. 9, 1877, and was lost. The steamer *CARONDELET* also burned.

2427 GRAND TOWER

SW p wh b. Cincinnati, Oh., 1853. 569 tons. Hit the wharfboat at Warsaw, Ky., Feb. 9, 1853, causing it to sink with loss of much cargo. Collided with *PACIFIC* (see) at Cairo Nov. 23, 1854, resulting in loss of both boats.

2428 GRAND TOWER

SW p wh b. Jeffersonville, Ind., by Howard, 1870. 1,058 tons. 265 x 42 x 8. Operated by the Anchor Line, St. Louis. Collided with and caused the loss of *SHIPPERS' OWN* (see) at Cairo, Ill., between 11:00 and midnight, June 14, 1876. The *GRAND TOWER* was burning her torchbasket under way and the night was black and rainy, confusing the pilots. The *GRAND TOWER* sank and was lost at Goose Island, about 10 miles below Commerce, Mo. Much equipment was salvaged including her roof bell which was much prized and had come from the *EMMA C. ELLIOTT* (see).

2429 GRAND TURK

SW p wh b. Freedom, Pa., 1848. 241 x 30.7 x 7.7. Owned in part and commanded by Capt. Newman Robirds, St. Louis. Ran Louisville-New Orleans. Capt. Clayton was master 1852–1853 with H.S. Phillips, clerk. Burned and lost in the steamboat fire at New Orleans Feb. 6, 1854, which originated on the *CHARLES BELCHER* (see).

2430 GRAND TURK

Stw p wh b. McKeesport, Pa., 1854. 155 x 33 x 5.2. Ran Pittsburgh-St. Louis, Capt. A.B. Gallatin, McKeesport, with George H. Ghriest, clerk. Was sunk near Cloverport, Ky., after hitting a log, Mar. 20, 1857, raised. Was at St. Louis during the wharf fire July 2, 1856, and badly scarred. Off the lists 1862.

2431 GRANGER

Sawmill p wh b. New Albany, Ind., 1874. 26 tons. Apparently ran short trades in the upper Arkansas, and was reported burned four miles above Little Rock on July 9, 1877. Then on July 17, 1878, came a report that "a sawmill boat named *GRANGER,* Capt. Burton, is running on the Yazoo and will cut timber to any dimension."

2432 GRANITE STATE

SW p wh b. West Elizabeth, Pa., 1852. 296 tons. Ran Pittsburgh-St. Louis, Capt. Rodgers in command, 1854. Operating in the Galena, Dunleith & Minnesota Packet Co., 1856, Capt. Jesse Y. Hurd. Same territory 1857, Capt. W.H. Gabbert. Off the lists 1860.

2433 GRANITE STATE

Stw p wh b. California, Pa., 1870. 183 x 34 x 5. Rees engines, 16's- 5½ ft. Three boilers, each 38" by 26 ft. Came out in the Pittsburgh-Portsmouth, Oh., trade, Capt. Wash H. Kerr, master, with T.T. Johnson, clerk. In spring 1872 ran Cincinnati-Pomeroy, Capt. Wash Honshell, master, with George A. Knight, clerk. Then back Pittsburgh-Portsmouth with Capt. Wash Kerr, master, W.C. Anderson, clerk. She continued this trade until retired at Cincinnati July 1878. Joe and Davis Alexander were her pilots at the time. Capt. Wash Kerr gets credit for originating this Pittsburgh-Portsmouth trade with the *LADY BYRON* (see).

2434 GRANITE STATE

Stw p wh b. Cincinnati, Oh., 1879. 221 x 35.6 x 5.7. Rees engines, 16's- 5½ ft. from prior boat of the name. Two boilers, each 42" by 28 ft., with twelve 6" flues. Paddlewheel 22 ft. dia. working 26 ft. buckets. Built for Capt. Wash Kerr, Pittsburgh-Portsmouth. He died March 1880, at which time the boat was in the Pittsburgh-St. Louis trade, Capt. Tom Hunter. Capt. Wash Honshell and T.T. Johnson owned shares in her. Was in the Memphis & Cincinnati Packet Co., 1888, Capt. Don Marr. Sank and lost in the Grand Chain, Ohio River, near Mound City, Ill. The hull served as a wharfboat at Catlettsburg, Ky., under several ownerships, lastly by Capt. Gordon C. Greene who replaced it c. 1913 with the hull of the *CARRIE BROWN.*

2435 GRAPESHOT

Stw p wh b. Louisville, Ky., 1855. 179 tons. Burned and lost in Galveston Bay, Tex., May 8, 1858.

2436 GRAPESHOT

Stw p wh b. California, Pa., 1855. 153 tons. 151 x 29 x 3.7. First owned by the McBride family, Pittsburgh, Capt. A. McBride. Sold to Van Buren, Ark., Capt. Edward C. Carter, and was snagged and lost there June 10, 1859.

2437 GRAY CLOUD

SW p wh b. Elizabeth, Pa., 1854. 245 tons. Went to St. Louis. Was in Confederate registry when captured by the U.S. and had been renamed *COLONEL KINSMAN.* The USQMD renamed her *KINSMAN* Sept. 30, 1862, and turned her over to the Navy. Snagged and sunk in Berwick Bay, La., Feb. 23, 1863, with loss of six lives.

2438 GREAT REPUBLIC

SW p wh b. Shousetown, Pa., and completed at Pittsburgh, 1867. 335 x 51 x 9.5. Compound engines, 28's, 56's- 10 ft. Six boilers. The hull for this river leviathan was built at the E. & N. Porter yard, now Glenwillard, Pa., on the Ohio River about 15 miles below Pittsburgh. The larger timbers were brought in from the upper Monongahela River. She was launched Saturday Nov. 3, 1866, the river at 7½ ft. at Pittsburgh, falling. The hull broke free, went across the river, and lodged on the shore. A worker was killed as she went down the ways, considered an omen of bad luck. She was towed to Pittsburgh Nov. 7, 1866, for completion. Examination showed the hull had been hogged during launch and coal was piled in it at Pittsburgh to straighten it out. The original stockholders were Capt. William B. Donaldson (⅓), Joseph P. Haigh (⅓), Samuel Morrow (⅙), and Andrew Hartupee (⅙). Charles Gearing built the cabin containing 54 staterooms, each eight ft. by eight ft., with 10 more in the texas for passengers. The texas was 166 ft. long. Col. William C. Wall was the artist who decorated the interior with many and varied landscapes. Andrew Hartupee built the engines, and Morrow & Barnhill the boilers. The architecture of the cabin borrowed from many styles was all but overwhelming. There were fluted columns, wooden flounces, frills, fresco and flubdub, floral-bedecked carpeting, and carved and sculptured furniture. She was elegant inside and rather ungainly outside, sort of like the *MISSISSIPPI QUEEN*. Following a public inspection at Pittsburgh, complete with ceremonies and speeches, she departed with a full cabin of passengers on a snowy, blizzardy Mar. 16, 1867, for New Orleans mortgaged for $94,662.79 to William A. Caldwell, Nathan Porter, and George W. Coffin. The river banks were lined with shivering spectators day and night to see her pass down. The crew: Capt. William B. Donaldson, master; Sam Barr, Jr., Charles A. Dravo, Alfred Davitt, and G. Wash Floyd, clerks; Sam McBride and Sam Williamson, pilots; William Patterson, mate; John Hartupee, chief engineer; J.V. Starr, second; Sam W. Morgan, steward, and James Simmonds, bartender. The passenger list reflected the best society of Pittsburgh and environs, among them Capt. and Mrs. C.W. Batchelor, Miss Ann Batchelor, William K. Nimick, Miss Lizzie Nimick, Robert McCutcheon, Mrs. Benjamin Crawford, Mrs. Thomas M. Marshall, Stephen C. McCandless. Louis Dalzell, W.L. Boggs, Jr., Hon. and Mrs. W.R. Boggs, Robert Mackey, A. Tomlinson, Capt. William Hanna, Capt. and Mrs. Frederick Dippold, James H. Parker, Miss E. Zug, Charles Spang, Mr. and Mrs. William S. Bissell, Misses Rebecca and Hannah Shields, Miss Mary Bissell, Dr. Gazzum, W.S. Haven, J.B. Oliver, John McClanahan (New York *Herald*) and William M. Runkel (Pittsburgh *Commercial*). The snow storm stopped her that first night at McKees Rocks, Pa. Next day she landed in at Cable's Eddy to lower her jackstaff to clear the Panhandle RR bridge above Steubenville. The upper sections of her smokestacks had not been placed because of bridges. A visit at Wheeling was thwarted because of the multitude of sightseers swarming the wharf. At Cincinnati so many well-wishers trampled her new carpets, the visit was cut short. At New Albany she came alongside the new and uncompleted *RICHMOND* (see) to get her stacks topped. She got but faint praise from the press at Louisville, noted as "box-like in appearance and devoid of the graceful lines for which our local shipyards are noted." A comprehensive report of her building, the maiden voyage, and press reports appears in *S&D Reflector,* issue March 1867. She was entered in the St. Louis-New Orleans trade. In early January 1868 she loaded at New Orleans for Cincinnati, bringing up 1,097 tons, principally sugar and molasses and upon arrival at Cincinnati was visited by an estimated 20,000 persons. A dispatch from St. Louis dated Nov. 27, 1868: "The *GREAT REPUBLIC* from bad management has resulted most disastrously for her owners. In less than two years she has bankrupted her owners and builders. Her captain is under $10,000 bond for killing a number of his deck crew and the clerk is under $20,000 as an accessory, and today the boat will be sold by the U.S. marshal to satisfy $40,000 lien claims with some $94,000 building bills hanging over unsatisfied." At the sale but one bid was received, in amount $25,000, and was rejected. Through a reorganization of affairs she continued under Capt. W.B. Donaldson. At a sale in May 1871 she was bid in by Capt. William H. Thorwegan and Thomas Morrison for $48,000. They hauled her at the Carondelet Ways in fall of 1872, lengthened the hull, and in 1875 Morrison went bankrupt. Captain Thorwegan bought the boat entire. In March 1876 she was again rebuilt, an additional boiler added, and her name changed to *GRAND REPUBLIC* (see). Of passing interest to whistle buffs, Captain Thorwegan in October 1873 bought the whistle formerly on the *WILD WAGONER* for $206. It was used thenceforth on *GREAT* and *GRAND REPUBLIC.*

2439 Great West

Stw p wh b. California, Pa., 1855. 230 tons. 151 x 34 x 4.3. Ran tramp trades from Pittsburgh owned in part and commanded by Capt. Samuel McCullough, who with James Park, both of Pittsburgh, owned control. She was moored at the docks, Manchester section of Pittsburgh, when the *ARCTIC* caught fire and also destroyed *GREAT WEST,* this on July 15, 1858.

2440 Great Western

SW p wh b. Cincinnati, Oh., 1857. 429 tons. 178 x 45.4 x 8. Engines, 22½'s- 8 ft. She carried supplies and was a transport for the U.S. during the war, and was sold at Mound City, Ill. Nov. 29, 1865, to John Riley for $4,300.

2441 Greater New Orleans

Stw ex wh b. Cincinnati, Oh., 1895. Originally named *VIRGINIA,* then *STEEL CITY,* then *EAST ST. LOUIS,* then *ISLAND BELLE* (all see). Under the latter name was sold in April 1927 to Greater New Orleans Amusement Co., headed by C. Maestri, completely rebuilt at Paducah, and renamed. Ran excursions at New Orleans for a year or so, then was sold to Streckfus Steamers, St. Louis who dismantled her and used the boilers on their excursion steamer *WASHINGTON.*

2442 Greater Pittsburgh

Stw wh b. Jeffersonville, Ind., by Howard, 1914. Originally named *HOMER SMITH* (see). The Pittsburgh Amusement Co., headed by William B. Rodgers, Jr., bought her in 1928 and renamed her. Ran excursions out of Pittsburgh, and carried dignitaries to Cairo during the 1929 celebration for completion of Ohio River locks and dams. Ran up a dock bill at Paducah, had Depression troubles, and burned rather mysteriously while moored at Manchester on Pittsburgh's North Side, April 1931. The watchman was jailed for arson, nothing was proven, and he was released. Two of her boilers went to towboat *JOHN G. BRITTON,* and two to the towboat *SHAWNEE.* The engines were scrapped.

2443 Greek Slave

SW p wh b. Jeffersonville, Ind., 1849. 143 tons. Built for Capt. W.C. Francis for the Louisville-Tennessee River trade. On her wheelhouses were paintings of the celebrated statue "Greek Slave" by sculptor Hiram Powers. These were described by river reporters as "large and as natural as life," and "very neat and chaste and very appropriate; attract the attention of everyone." She made 18 trips Rock Island-St. Paul in 1853, and was in Upper Mississippi trades regularly through the 1856 season. It is said that the noted Louis Roberts, founder of St. Paul, was an owner. Off the lists in 1857.

2444 GREENBRIER

Stw lighthouse tender sh b. Charleston, W. Va., by Charles Ward Engineering Works, 1924. 164 x 32 x 5.5. Engines, 15's- 7 ft. Three boilers. Serviced government lights on the Ohio and tribs. Capt. Leslie Hill was first master and retired in spring of 1938, after which Capt. Arthur J. Schletker had charge. She conveyed U.S. President Herbert Hoover from Cincinnati to Louisville during the 1929 Ohio River locks' and dams' celebration. Long had on board a mascot dog "Shawnee" which had come aboard at Shawneetown, Ill., on Thanksgiving Day 1936. Transferred July 1, 1939, from the U.S. Lighthouse Service to the U.S. Coast Guard. During WW II had an anti-aircraft gun mounted on the roof. She ascended the Kanawha River to Loup Creek, W. Va., five miles from the falls, Feb. 26, 1946, at the prodding of F. Way Jr., and J.W. Rutter who were guests of Capt. "Red" Schletker. Decommissioned Sept. 1, 1947, laid up at Paris, Tenn. Sold to two men of Stillwater, Minn., who resold her March 1948 to Charles G. Smith Co., Houston, Tex. She became a landing boat on the Intracoastal Canal.

2445 GREENDALE

Stw p wh b. Pt. Pleasant, W. Va., 1909. 139 x 26.6 x 3. Engines, 9's- 3½ ft. from *T.D. DALE*. One boiler, and one stack. Owned by Greene Line Steamers, Cincinnati. She was the low water boat. In 1912 tried the Pittsburgh-Fairmont trade, Monon River, Capt. Jack Ward, with no success. In June 1914 tried the Marietta-Gallipolis trade, no success. She carried the roof bell formerly on *C. W. BATCHELOR* which today (1978) is at the Ohio River Museum, Marietta, Oh. Greene Line sold her February 1921 to Capt. John Davis, Fullerton, Ky., who rebuilt her into the *J. P. DAVIS* (see).

2446 GREEN RIVER

Stw p wh b. Hastings, Minn., 1902. Originally named *J.J. HILL* (see) and then *LOUISIANA* (see). J. Porter Hines once told Ye Ed. he was pilot on *SPEED* and raced the *GREEN RIVER* which then, in 1916, was running Evansville-Livermore in opposition to the regular boats. The towboat *WILLIAM EICHEL* was built at Evansville 1924 using parts from her.

2447 GREENLAND

SW p wh b. Harmar, Oh. at Knox Yard, 1903. 210 x 32 x 6.5. Her overall width 49 ft. Engines, 15's- 6 ft. from *ZANETTA*. Two boilers, each 44" by 22½ ft. Designed for Pittsburgh-Charleston trade, Capt. Gordon C. Greene being owner and skipper. Paddlewheels 28 ft. dia. working 6½ ft. buckets. The hull stern was built with a transom, sternwheel style, two rudders. Had 54 cabin staterooms and made four trips from the Ohio River to the World's Fair at St. Louis in 1904. Ran most of her career in the Cincinnati-Pomeroy-Charleston trade. Sometimes chartered to run Cincinnati-Louisville in low water. In 1917 made several trips Pittsburgh-Cincinnati. During her mid-years there was an engine exchange, and she got 16" bore from *HENRY M. STANLEY,* and also three boilers. Injured her hull 1917 grounding on Bonanza Bar, Portsmouth, Oh., and was hauled out on the marine ways at Cincinnati. Severe gorges winter 1917-1918 lifted her from the cradles and she sank and was lost. She carried the whistle from the *COURIER*; it was recovered and went to the first *CHRIS GREENE*. Capt. Tom R. Greene was born aboard while the boat was laid up for ice at Pt. Pleasant, W. Va., Feb. 3, 1904. Capt. Jesse P. Hughes and bride (Telia Vaughn) took their wedding trip aboard to St. Louis 1904. Capt. Mary B. Greene commanded on occasion. A rather full story of *GREENLAND* appears in the *S&D Reflector,* issue March 1977.

2448 GREENVILLE

Stw p wh b. Evansville, Ind., 1857. 105 tons. Ran in Green River, Capt. Tom Ashby, with John Travis, clerk. Sold at a U.S. marshal sale and shortly thereafter ran Evansville-Bowling Green, Capt. Penuel Jones and Noah Rothrock. They took her after several months to the Wabash River where she was snagged and lost at Terre Haute, June 6, 1861.

2449 GREENWOOD

Stw p wh b. Elizabeth, Pa., 1848. 47 tons. Built to carry passengers from Pittsburgh to Manchester (now North Side, Pittsburgh) to Greenwood Gardens, owned by James McKain. Sold fall of 1848 and ran on the Kanawha River to Gallipolis, Oh. Exploded her boiler leaving Kanawha Salines (now Malden, W. Va.) Aug. 23, 1850, with loss of two lives and others hurt.

2450 GREENWOOD

Stw p wh b. Parkersburg, W. Va., 1898. 168.5 x 30 x 4.4. Engines, 14's- 6 ft. Three boilers, each 38" by 18 ft. Originally owned by Capt. Gordon C. Greene (3/4) and Carrie G. Greenwood (¼). The machinery was installed at Ironton, Oh., and on the trial voyage there, Capt. Jesse P. Hughes, pilot on watch, came near sinking her when she hit something and broke floor timbers. Ran Pittsburgh-Parkersburg, then Pittsburgh-Charleston. After the Greene Line became based at Cincinnati she ran Cincinnati-Pomeroy-Charleston. After the loss of the *H. K. BEDFORD* (see) in 1912 Capt. Henry Kraft ran her Pittsburgh-Parkersburg for about a year, then she returned to Cincinnati. In 1925 Captain Greene retired her and was about to start dismantling her at Gallipolis when the *BETSY ANN* had an accident and *BETSY*'s owner D. Grover Gill chartered the *GREENWOOD* and made several Pittsburgh-

Cincinnati trips with her. She was at Cincinnati about ready to leave for Pittsburgh on Nov. 17, 1925, when the *CHRIS GREENE,* departing, backed into her and ripped open the hull. She turned over and landed just below the suspension bridge. Her three boilers went to the towboat *JOHN F. KLEIN.* Captain Greene recalled her as the "goose that laid the golden egg" for the Greene Line.

2451 GRENADA

SW p wh b. New Albany, Ind., 1851. 217 tons. 140 x 28 x 6. Went to New Orleans owned by Capt. Michael Gwartney and others of Grenada, Miss. Sold in 1854 to Capt. Richard P. Crump and others, New Orleans. She made trips to Shreveport and in 1859 was running on Ouachita River, Capt. Cooper, then owned by E.A. Patterson & Co., New Orleans. Burned and lost at Algiers, La., May 6, 1861.

2452 GRETNA

SW ferry wh b. Gretna, La., 1847. 22 tons. Exploded and lost at Lafayette, La., with loss of three lives, June 17, 1851.

2453 GRETNA GREEN

SW ferry wh b. Manchester, Oh., 1875. 120 tons. 91.3 x 27 x 3.6. Operated between Maysville and Aberdeen, Ohio River, Capt. J.C. Powers. Had some lively competition for several years with the *FRANK S. OWENS,* but won out. Still listed in 1892.

2454 GREY EAGLE

SW p wh b. Louisville, Ky., 1840. 352 tons. Operated Louisville-New Orleans, Capt. John Shallcross. Off the lists 1845.

2455 GREY EAGLE

SW p wh b. Cincinnati, Oh., 1847. 177 tons. Ran briefly on Kentucky River out of Frankfort and then sold south. Collided with *SULTANA* on the Mississippi June 13, 1848, two of crew killed, several hurt. In January 1849 owned in part and commanded by Capt. David Robbins Muggah, St. Mary Parish, La., and ran one season on Red River. Snagged and lost at Grand River La., Jan. 18, 1850.

2456 GREY EAGLE

SW ferry wh b. Wellsville, Oh., 1850. 51 tons. Apparently operated in the Wheeling area, and was burned and lost at that place, May 1, 1857.

2457 GREY EAGLE

SW p wh b. Cincinnati, Oh., 1857. 382 tons. 250 x 35 x 5. Engines, 22's- 7 ft. Four boilers. Owned by the Minnesota Packet Co., Capt. D. Smith Harris. In 1858 she carried the news of the completion of the Atlantic Cable from Dunleith to St. Paul, a message from Queen Victoria to President Buchanan, racing the *ITASCA* most of the way, 290 miles, averaging 16½ mph. She long held the record early spring arrival at St. Paul, coming up from Galena, at St. Paul Mar. 25, 1858. This held good until FBL towboat *CAIRO* got to St. Paul Mar. 19, 1947. Hit a pier of the Rock Island bridge May 9, 1861 at 5:00 P.M. and was lost.

2458 GREY EAGLE

SW p wh b. Shousetown, Pa., 1859. 241 tons. First owned at Gallipolis, Oh., by Eugene Donnally and John Hutsimpiller. Ran Marietta-Cincinnati, Capt. A. Donnally. She sported a calliope. In spring of 1861 running Louisville-Evansville-Henderson, one of the regular line. Became known as the *STAR GREY EAGLE* although not so documented. Sold September 1865 to Garland, Thomas & Co., operating the Gallipolis & Portsmouth Packet Co. Ran Gallipolis-Cincinnati, Capt. D.H. Young, 1866. Replaced the burned *WINCHESTER* (see) in the Pittsburgh-Parkersburg trade, Capt. C.L. Brennan. She was being dismantled at Pittsburgh in January, 1870 when a windstorm assisted, taking off the cabin.

2459 GREY EAGLE

SW p wh b. Louisville, Ky., 1860. 230 x 33 x 6.5. Came out Jan. 14, 1860, in Louisville-Henderson trade owned by Anson Ballard and others, Capt. W.H. Daniel. She was a bit too much boat for the trade and soon was run through to New Orleans. Just prior to actual hostilities she took aboard at Louisville some notables, John C. Breckenridge and Humphrey Marshall among them, who spoke to delegations at Owensboro, Evansville, Henderson, and Paducah. They disembarked at Memphis, and the boat went on to New Orleans, Capt. W.H. Daniel, taking a group of legislators down from Baton Rouge. All black cabin crew were impounded at New Orleans and Capt. Daniel had to buy them to get them back aboard. By now the war was on for real and the Rebels were detaining all upbound boats at Napoleon, Ark., and had quite a collection including *OHIO BELLE, MARS, ELEPHANT, HETTIE GILMORE.* Capt. Daniel was wearing a fraternal order pin agreeable to the Rebel leader and his boat was passed on. She was halted at Memphis and was allowed to proceed when Daniel agreed to take aboard two large guns and deliver them at Fort Randolph. She was sold south after the river was freed, and ran New Orleans-Vicksburg, Capt. John S. Woolfolk, Louisville, partly owned by him and largely owned at Vicksburg by Duff Green and J.H. Willis. In May 1866 Capt. John W. Cannon owned in equal shares with A. Lewis Collins, both of New Orleans. By 1868 was in the New Orleans-Bayou Sara trade, Capt. V.B. Baranco, with J. Hodgkinson, clerk, with Capt. Cannon still part owner. In June 1869 owned by Red River Packet Co., Capt. G.L. Kouns. She was returned to Louisville, dismantled, and her engines went to the *GRAND ERA* (see).

2460 GREY EAGLE

SW p wh b. Peninsula, Oh., 1863. 41 tons. First home port, Wheeling, W. Va. Off the lists 1866.

2461 GREY EAGLE

SW p wh b. Warsaw, Ill., 1865. 70 tons. 135 x 21 x 4.5. Engines cast at Vail & Armitage Co., Keokuk. Two boilers. Construction supervised by Henry and William

Leyhe. Ran Keokuk-Quincy, Capt. J.W. Bishop. Capt. John Reid Williams took her to the Peoria-Henry trade, and was president of Eagle Packet Co., 1875–1884, retiring to a farm near Warsaw, Ill., where he lived past the 100 mark. Capt. Sol York bought the boat and ran her Lacon-Peoria. Finally sank at Henry, Ill., and was removed from documentation 1888.

2462 GREY EAGLE

SW p wh b. Jeffersonville, Ind., by Howard, 1871. 238 x 36 x 6. Owned by Louisville, Evansville & Henderson Packet Co. In 1878 the company was headed by W.C. Hite, with A.T. Gilmore, superintendent, and W.W. Hite, secretary and treasurer. Crew in 1873: Capt. E.P.T. Holcroft, with M.D. Warren and J.E. Jones, clerks. In 1875: Capt. A.T. Gilmore, with M.D. Warren, clerk. In 1878: Capt. Jesse C. Berry, with L.T. Whitlow and E.T. Meek, clerks. In 1881: Capt. Jesse Berry, with R.B. Baldwin, clerk. Captain Berry was said to have been a retired minister. Dismantled in 1888 and parts used building *CITY OF OWENSBORO* (see).

2463 GREY EAGLE

SW p wh b. Jeffersonville, Ind., by Howard, 1892. 250 x 40 x 5.5. Overall, 70 ft. Engines 20's- 7½ ft. from *NEW SOUTH* (see). Four boilers, each 40" by 20 ft. Much of the superstructure came from the *CALHOUN* (see). Built for Eagle Packet Co., St. Louis, and designed for the St. Louis-Peoria trade. She was too large to negotiate the turn bridges on the Illinois, and soon went to the St. Louis-Cape-Commerce trade. In 1894 ran under charter to the Anchor Line, St. Louis-Vicksburg. Damaged in the cyclone at St. Louis, May 27, 1896. Participated in the parade welcoming U.S. President Theodore Roosevelt at St. Louis Oct. 2, 1907. Chartered to Kansas City Commercial Club, she participated in the parade down the Mississippi accompanying U.S. President William Howard Taft who was aboard *OLEANDER* (see) leaving St. Louis Oct. 25, 1909. Chartered to Capt. William H. Thorwegan in 1910 to run St. Louis excursions in place of *CITY OF PROVIDENCE* lost in ice (see). She ran excursions thenceforth, and was lost in ice at the Duck's Nest, Paducah, Ky., January 1918.

2464 GREYHOUND

Stw p wh b. Ironton, Oh., 1901. 150 x 23 x 4. Engines, 14's- 5 ft. Two boilers, each 43" by 22 ft. Built by Capts. William and George Bay. Capt. Jesse P. Hughes explains it this way: "The Bays built a 'lighter' flat at the same time they built the *KANAWHA* at Ironton in 1896, using same material. The *KANAWHA* used it for low water work. Capt. William E. Roe bought the *KANAWHA* on Nov. 10, 1899, but the Bays kept the lighter at Ironton. Later they beached it high and dry in a flood, put a model bow on one end, and a shaped stern on the other, and this became the hull of the *GREYHOUND*. She got old engines which had been stored in the Ironton wharfboat." She ran in the Portsmouth-Proctorville trade, was quite fast, and any boat which could lick her was "going some." Capt. Tom Roush was master for a long time, later Capt. Pete Lallance. Chief engineer was Charles L. Brown. She was laid up and in use as a wharfboat at Ironton when lost in ice Dec. 31, 1917.

2465 GRIFFIN YEATMAN

SW p wh b. Cincinnati, Oh., 1847. 286 tons. This was a large, light draft, low water boat. She came down from Louisville to Cairo in September 1849 when many of the regular boats were laid up. Advertised at New Orleans for St. Louis in September 1851, Capt. E. Holister. Off the lists in 1853.

2466 GROSBEAK

SW tinclad wh b. Cincinnati, Oh., 1864. 195 tons. Originally named *FANNY* (see), sold to U.S. Navy Dec. 3, 1864. Converted into a tinclad named *GROSBEAK, #8*. At war's conclusion sold Aug. 17, 1865, to Robert Curran (or Keames) for $11,000. She was then described as 163.8 x 28.4 x 4.7, engines 16's- 5 ft. Renamed *MOLLIE HAMBLETON* (see).

2467 GROSSE TETE

SW p wh b. New Albany, Ind., 1858. 399 tons. 180 x 34 x 7. Built for J.A. Cotton, New Orleans. Ran New Orleans-Bends trade, Capt. Isaac Hopper. In 1860 in the Bayou Sara Mail Co., New Orleans-Coast, Capt. J. McQuoid. She was rebuilt into a Confederate gunboat named *MAUREPAS*, and as such was sunk in White River near St. Charles, Ark., June 16, 1862, to obstruct the channel.

2468 GROVER CLEVELAND

Prop p wh b. New Orleans, La., 1884. 104.4 x 27.7 x 7.1. She ran New Orleans-Port Eads-Pilot Town, three trips weekly, Capt. Charles Musselman, with C.F. Tucker, clerk. By 1896 was running New Orleans-Forts, twice weekly, Capt. C.E. Kouns, with E.J. Reinhardt and James M. Salvant, clerks. Ran New Orleans-Forts-Oakville, three trips weekly, Capt. S.C. Kouns with James M. Salvant, clerk, 1901. She was burning oil for fuel in 1902, the only packet at New Orleans so equipped.

2469 GUADELOUPE

SW p wh b. West Elizabeth, Pa., 1853. 139 tons. 125 x 26 x 4.5. Engines, 14's- 4½ ft. Two boilers, each 40" by 22 ft. Side-wheels 22 ft. dia. working seven ft. buckets. First home port, Galveston, Tex. Sold foreign, 1858.

2470 GUIDING STAR

SW p wh b. Cincinnati, Oh., 1878. 300 x 41.5 x 7.5. Overall 77 ft. Originally had engines from *ROBERT BURNS* (see) which were replaced in 1880 by 26's- 8 ft. Five boilers, each 42" by 28 ft., two flues. Paddlewheels 28 ft. dia., working 14 ft. buckets, 17 arms. Boiler deck 60 ft. wide in front, guards running back 165 ft. on each side. Cabin 235 ft. long, 16 ft. wide, 11½ ft. high with black walnut and birds-eye maple finish. Fifty cabin staterooms, office on starboard side, bar opposite. Pantry on starboard side with kitchen below. Barbershop opposite. Texas 108 ft. long, and captain's room in front 16x16 with open grate stove. Two rooms 8x10 opened off captain's room. Aft came the crew's quarters, freedmen's bureau, then cabin boy's quarters. Pilothouse 14 ft. square. Stacks 85 ft. from light-load line. Roof bell from Vanduzen weighed 1,800 lbs. Col. Thompson Dean selected the furniture in New York. She was of 1,800 tons capacity, drew 33″ light. Came out in Cincinnati-New Orleans trade, Capt. William B. Miller, with John S. Jones, clerk; Charles Owens and George Melona, pilots; Thomas J. Henry and Henry Myers, engineers. Captain Miller lost her at a U.S. marshal sale conducted at Cincinnati, June 1881, the purchaser being Capt. J.D. Hegler who continued her in the trade. In 1883 Captain Hegler bought Parker's Grove above Cincinnati, renamed it "Coney Island of the West" and operated it as a pleasure park. The *GUIDING STAR* and *MINNIE BAY* were the first boats to handle passengers there. Hegler later sold the park to Lee H. Brooks. Was cut down by ice eight miles below New Madrid, Mo., on Jan. 6, 1893. The roof bell was taken to New Albany, Ind., and used on a fertilizer plant where in 1914 C.C. Bowyer "discovered" it and bought it for the *HOMER SMITH*.

2471 GUIDON

Stw p wh b. McKeesport, Pa., 1864. 240 tons. Built under supervision of Capt. C.W. Batchelor and came out in Pittsburgh-Cincinnati-Louisville trade, Capt. J.W. Batchelor. In November 1864, rounding to land at Louisville she got too far out and struck a pair of loaded coalboats stranded on the rocks, stove one of them, and was released next day. Had a replica of the Statue of Liberty on top of the pilothouse. Then ran Memphis-Arkansas River, Capt. I.R. Whittaker, and went to St. Louis to be docked in May 1866. Loaded at St. Louis mid-April 1867 for a trip to Fort Benton, Capt. J.L. Bissell, with Sam D. Booth, clerk. Back to Memphis-Arkansas River, and was snagged and lost 90 miles up Arkansas River at Harris's Crossing, Mar. 23, 1870.

2472 GULNARE

SW p wh b. Cincinnati, Oh., 1849. 347 tons. Machinery from *PIKE NO. 8* (see). Off the list in 1859.

2473 GULNARE

Stw p wh b. c. 1891 at Pittsburgh, Pa. by Charles Rogers, Jr., who built her entire including hull, cabin, machinery, boiler, generator, and light plant. Made his own patterns for the machinery. Sold to Howard Jones, Pittsburgh, who renamed her *BLANCHE EDMUNDSON* (see).

2474 GUS FOWLER

Stw p wh b. Jeffersonville, Ind., by Howard, 1880. 160 x 29.5 x 5.6. Engines, 14 3/4's- 4 3/4 ft. Two boilers. Owned by the Fowler Line, Paducah, and replaced the *JAMES FISKE, JR.*, in the Paducah-Cairo trade, and ran there 17 years until the *DICK FOWLER* replaced her. She carried the whistle from the side-wheel *IDLEWILD*, and it went over to the *DICK FOWLER*. In summer 1897 ran Memphis-Friar's Point, and was returned to Paducah that September. Sold March 1898 to Yazoo City Transportation Co., and her Yazoo pilots were John Hunnicutt and James K. Dent. Sold to H.L. Jones who took her to the Missouri River where Capt. Alex Lamont was master, Hans Chadwick, pilot. Snagged and lost at Mokane, Mo., Aug. 22, 1899.

2475 GUYANDOTTE

SW batwing p wh b. Guyandotte, W. Va., 1896. 104.3 x 16.1 x 2.9. Belt operated from a single steam engine, 8 ¾″ bore, 12″ stroke. One boiler, 46″ by 7½ ft. Once went up the Guyandotte River to Logan, W. Va., taking up material and supplies for a railroad construction job. Sold December 1902 to James F. York, and Albert G. Holt, both of Kenova, W. Va. Sold, March 1904 to William P. Vaughn, Catlettsburg, Ky. Saw service on Big Sandy River. Burned Aug. 13, 1908.

H

2476 H. A. HARVEY, JR.

Stw p wh b. Harvey's Canal, La., 1892. 98.5 x 19.8 x 3.8. Overall was 113 x 25. Made a noteworthy trip to Dallas, Tex., arriving on May 24, 1893, first there since Civil War days and the snagboat *DALLAS* accompanied her. Still documented at St. Charles, La., 1908.

2477 H.A. HOMEYER

Stw p wh b. New Albany, Ind., 1863. 389 tons. 164.7 x 32.5 x 5. Ran Cincinnati-St. Louis, Capt. Hukill. Was operating on Red River 1865–1867. Owned 1867 by Daniel T. Head with E.S. Austin, master. Burned Jan. 13, 1868, on Ouachita River, at Falk's Landing, La., 25 miles above Franklin. She was downbound from Camden, Ark., to New Orleans. Nine hundred bales of cotton were lost.

2478 H.A. MEAD

Recess wheel ferry wh b. Ironton, Oh., 1879. 90 x 26.5 x 3.7. Engines, 10's-3½ ft. One boiler. Ran Ironton-Russell, owned and operated by Capt. J.M. Kirker who lived at Russell, Ky., and later at Catlettsburg. Dismantled 1895 and engines went to *ARGAND* (see).

2479 H. B. SINCLAIR

Stw ferry wh b. McKeesport, Pa., 1886. 88 x 24.4 x 5.4. Ferried at McKeesport, Pa., succeeding the *NORA* (see). When the Dravosburg bridge was opened March 1890 the ferry service was discontinued. Sold September 1890 entire to James B. Patterson, Allegheny, Pa., who planned to revive the Manchester-West End ferry service long handled by *WM. THAW* (see), but he had no success. In spring 1903 she was tied up at the foot of Chartiers Street, Allegheny, in sunken condition.

2480 H. C. NUTT

SW wh b. California, Pa. (hull) and completed at Wellsville, Oh., 1870. 180 x 33 x 5. Engines, 20's- 5½ ft. Four boilers (two on a side). Owned by Missouri River Transfer Co., in which William W. Marsh and H.C. Nutt owned equally. Could handle five cars on a single track. Operated at Omaha, Neb., until 1872 when she went to Arkansas River owned by M.B. Pritchard, Little Rock, Ark., with W.W. Maingault, master. Out of service in 1878.

2481 H. D. BACON

SW p wh b. Cincinnati, Oh., 1851. 576 tons. Built for Capt. Henry A. Ealer and others, and ran St. Louis-New Orleans. Stranded and lost at Island 10, Miss. River, Feb. 18, 1855.

2482 H. D. BACON

SW p wh b. Louisville, Ky., 1860. 370 tons. Burned and lost at St. Louis along with *T. L. McGILL, ESTELLA, A. McDOWELL,* and *W. H. RUSSELL* on Oct. 27, 1862.

2483 H. D. MEARS

SW p wh b. Wheeling, Va., 1860. 338 tons. Ran Wheeling-Cincinnati, Capt. James C. Jelly, with Billy Batelle, clerk. 214 x 34 x 5.5. Engines, 22's- 7 ft. Five boilers, each 44" by 29 ft. Paddlewheels 27 ft. dia. working 11 buckets. Had 42 staterooms. Cabin and office lighted with Johnson's Self Generating Gas. Andrew Marsilliot and Amos Davis, pilots, and T.C. Wheat and Ed Wilson, engineers. She was sold to Memphis-Napoleon trade. Was taken up Sunflower River where she was purposely burned Sept. 25, 1863, to prevent capture by U.S. forces.

2484 H. D. MUNSON

Stw p wh b. Harmar, Oh., at Knox Yard, 1893. 120.6 x 22.3 x 4. Ran Marietta-Zanesville, Capt. Andrew C. Scott, fall 1893. Went to the upper Mississippi River where in 1895 she was bought by the Mississippi River Commission and renamed *SEARCH* (see). Sold at St. Louis in 1921 and was taken to the Panuco River, Mexico. Capt. Ed Nowland, Jr., was in charge to New Orleans. Her original name was restored, and she operated out of Tampico as *H.D. MUNSON.* In March 1924 she was hauled out on the ways at Tampico and an argument ensued about who was to pay the bill.

2485 H. D. NEWCOMB

SW p wh b. New Albany, Ind., 1856. 549 tons. Ran Louisville-New Orleans, Capt. William Hart in 1856. Same trade 1858, Capt. Harry I. Spotts. Snagged and lost at Island 21, Miss. River, Oct. 25, 1858.

2486 H. E. MYRTLE

Stw p wh b. Hermann, Mo., 1911. 104.1 x 19.6 x 3.2. Ran in Missouri River until 1921 when sold to Tennessee River and renamed *SAM CONNER* (see).

2487 H. G. HILL

Stw p wh b. Paducah, Ky., 1918. 165 x 30 x 4.8. Engines, 12's- 6 ft. from *RAPIDS* (see). Owned by Nashville Navigation Co., in which Capts. W.L. Berry and Fred McCandless were owners. Ran Paducah-Nashville, Capt. R.D. Crider, with J. Wylie Leek, purser. Named for a wholesale grocery owner in Nashville. During the 1927 flood she caught out at Wooddale Grove above Nashville and settled across a highway, blocking access to a colony of summer cottages. She was blasted apart to clear the road. Her engines in 1935 went to the *BARBARA HUNT.*

2488 H. H. BENNER

Stw p wh b. Pittsburgh, Pa., by Rees, 1880. 13's- 5 ft. engines. Two boilers, each 42" by 22 ft. Built for the National Board of Health in Washington, D.C., for use in quarantine service on the Mississippi, prompted by the *JOHN PORTER* affair. The towboat *HARRY BROWN* in May 1885 brought her back to Pittsburgh. She had been bought by Capt. Sam Brown.

2489 H. H. DENNIS

SW p wh b. Dunn's Eddy on upper Allegheny River, 1861. 38 tons. Engines, 12's- 3½ ft. One locomotive boiler. Ran on Allegheny River and out of service in 1863.

H. HANNA BLANKS

See # 2511

2490 H. J. DICKEY

Stw p wh b. Memphis, Tenn., 1881. 169.4 x 32.3 x 5.8. Engines, 13's- 4 ft. Three boilers, each 36" by 20 ft. Ran New Orleans to the bayous (Lafourche, Macon, and Tensas). In 1886 her master was Capt. J. B. Sullivan, with Tom Knee, clerk. In 1883 she was sucked into a crevasse 23 miles below Donaldsonville, La., on Bayou LaFourche and lodged halfway through but was recovered. Sank after hitting a snag at Toothpick Point, Bayou Macon, Jan. 14, 1891.

2491 H. K. BEDFORD

Stw p wh b. Jeffersonville, Ind., by Howard, 1885. 149 x 27.7 x 4.1. Built for the upper Cumberland River, Alex. Kendall, superintendent, with Capt. A.T. Armstrong, master, and W.W. Parminter, clerk. In fall of 1886 was running low water trades out of Wheeling, W. Va. Capt. Gordon C. Greene bought her at Nashville and arrived at Pittsburgh with her on Sunday, June 22, 1890, to enter Pittsburgh-Wheeling trade, the beginning of Greene Line Steamers, Inc. Later ran Pittsburgh-Charleston, and a texas was built on her under way in May 1897. Sold 1898 in equal shares to Capt. Henry R. Kraft, Charles and C. Augustus Frantz who ran her Pittsburgh-Parkersburg. In early 1912 she had been laid up for ice at Marietta, and on Feb. 27 started for Pittsburgh, Capt. Kraft in charge. Ice cut her down at Bean's Landing, Oh., at Carpenter Bar, not far above Marietta. The wreck was removed during low water of 1914. As a postscript, in October 1897 under charter to the Louisville & Cincinnati Packet Co., she ran the L&C trade with Capt. Mary B. Greene, master—first time a woman had been in charge of an L&C packet.

H. Kinney

See # 2512

2492 H.L.

Stw p wh b. Clinton, Iowa, 1905. 70 x 16 x 3.5. A small pleasure boat. Capt. Frank J. Fugina bought her to run excursions, changed the name to *IDEAL* because posters advertising *"H. L."* were too easily transformed by boys to "HELL." (See *IDEAL*.)

2493 H. M. Carter

Stw p wh b. Jeffersonville, Ind., by Howard, 1901. 155 x 28 x 3.5. Compound Swain engines on her. Owned by Carter Packet Co., and ran New Orleans-Ouachita-Black rivers. On a trip up Red River sank at Alexandria, La., June 1905. Was in New Orleans-Baton Rouge trade, Capt. H.M. Carter, when she exploded her boilers near Bayou Goula, upbound, Nov. 20, 1908. Capt. E.A. Rucker was pilot on watch. Ten or more were killed.

2494 H. M. Childs

Stw p wh b. Cincinnati, Oh., 1864. 110.3 x 21.6 x 3.9. In the former Hotel Hatcher at Pikeville, Ky., was a printed notice saying that Gen. James A. Garfield was at that place in 1862 aboard this boat (somebody needs mind his dates). Sold to New Orleans spring 1868, owned and commanded by Capt. Kennedy Lodwick. Sold January 1869 to Capt. Gideon D. Warren, Shreveport, La. Off the lists 1869.

2495 H. M. Stafford

SW batwing p wh b. Paintsville, Ky., 1898. 81 x 7.9 x 1.5. In the Big Sany Navigation Co., February 1900 along with *THEALKA, MAXIE YOST,* and *ARGAND.*

2496 H. M. Summers

SW p wh b. Evansville, Ind., 1851. 116 tons. A very light draft boat which ran Evansville-Green River, Capt. J.J. Hugo, then up Wabash and White rivers. Sold by U.S. marshal to Wash and Philo Johnson who sank her in the Grand Chain, Ohio River. Wash sent a telegram to his brother Philo: "DEAR BROTHER PHILO THE H.M. SUMMERS AM NO MORE STOP SHE SUNK IN FOUR AND A HALF FEET OF WATER STOP NO LIVES LOST THANK GOD STOP YOUR BROTHER WASH."

2497 H. M. Sweetster

Stw p wh b. Evansville, Ind., 1877. 104.2 x 24 x 3.1. Owned by Evansville & Terre Haute Railroad Co. They ran her on Wabash and White rivers handling corn, Capt. E.S. Babcock, Jr. Sold to Capt. John Adams who renamed her *TWO STATES* (see).

2498 H. M. Wright

SW p wh b. Jeffersonville, Ind., by Howard, 1852. 366 tons. 188.5 x 29 x 7. Owned by Capt. J.D. Clarke, master, and J.W. Arthur & Co., New Orleans. Sold June 1854 to Capt. Charles H. Manson, New Orleans. Ran New Orleans-Vicksburg. Lost on Red River at Hailey's Cut Off, La., Mar. 1, 1857. The wreck was removed that July by snagboat *ALGERINE.*

2499 H. O. Penick

Catamaran ferry sh b. Jeffersonville, Ind., by Howard, 1916. 115.2 x 28 x 7.2. Engines, 12's- 5 ft. One boiler, 44" by 12 ft. Owned by Ascension Parrish Ferry Co. Handled 250 passengers and 30 cars. Owned later by Napoleon Ave. Ferry Co., New Orleans. Still running 1949.

2500 H. P. Card

Pass. boat wh b. Akron, Oh., 1867. 59 tons. Inspected in the Cincinnati District 1881-1882, maybe later.

2501 H. R. W. Hill

SW p wh b. New Albany, Ind., 1852. 602 tons. Engines, 30's- 10 ft. Ran New Orleans-Memphis prior to the war, Capt. Thomas H. Newell. In a collision sank the *WESTERN WORLD* at Princeton, Miss., Dec. 14, 1852, causing the loss of that boat and 12 persons (see). Brought to New Orleans the largest cotton trip in 1858 with 5,162 bales. At the outbreak of the war title was transferred to Mrs. Jane Newell, and Capt. Tom joined the Johnny Rebs in 1861 and came through unscathed in 1865. The boilers exploded at Baton Rouge in Oct. 31, 1860, with loss of 39 lives. Apparently repairs were not made, and she was towed to Memphis where she was captured by U.S. forces during the Battle of Memphis. Towed to Cairo where the engines were taken off and went to Capt. B. Rush Pegram's *RUTH* in 1865. The hull became a wharfboat at Cairo. Her starboard wheel shaft was planted upright on the wharf grade at Memphis, where it was a "steamboat hitching post" for many years, sticking up nine feet. Workers cut it off flush with the grade, Apr. 12, 1937, the job done by Wolf River Transportation Co.

2502 H. S. Allen

Stw p wh b. Chippewa Falls, Wis., 1855. 41 tons. Ran on the Minnesota River 1856-1859. After 1860 ran in St. Croix River between St. Croix Falls and Prescott, Capt. William Gray. Her pilots were Charles Jewell and George B. Merrick. Dismantled 1866.

2503 H. S. McComb

SW tr wh b. Jeffersonville, Ind., by Howard, 1873. 195.8 x 45.6 x 6.6. 70 ft. overall. Two tracks stem to stern in 25 ft. width area. Built for Illinois Central for Cairo, Ill., service. Completed in November 1873, Capt., McKinney. Stacks 52 ft. high installed in 1880. In 1892 sold to the Ohio Valley RR Co., Evansville, Ind. Registered at Dubuque, Iowa, 1896. Renamed *HENRY MARQUAND* (see).

2504 H.S. Thibodeaux

SW p wh b. Cincinnati, Oh., 1843. 162 tons. Her wreck was noted Oct. 31, 1866, in the W. Milnor Roberts Report at the mouth of Indian Kentucky River, Ohio River. She was off the lists 1844, so apparently came to grief while a new boat.

2505 H. S. TURNER

SW p wh b. Cincinnati, Oh., 1866. 763 tons. Ran in the St. Louis & Omaha Packet Co., Capt. James A. Yore, 1867. In 1869 ran New Orleans-Bayou Sara twice weekly, Capt. V.B. Baranco, with Allen Jumel, clerk. Sank at Island 16, Miss. River, night of Jan. 6, 1871, Capt. W.J. Rusk. Captain Rusk observed that this was the seventh boat he'd been on which came to grief and ticked them off on his fingers: *NANNIE BYERS, CREOLE, WESTMORELAND, W.R. ARTHUR, ST. CLOUD, SUNNY SOUTH,* and now the *H. S. TURNER*; several burned. However in two weeks he had the *TURNER* afloat. He was still running her to New Orleans in 1873. In 1875 she was a regular Cincinnati-Evansville packet, Capt. W.C. Tichenor, with W.R. Shaw, clerk. On May 7, 1876, was at Pittsburgh taking a full load to St. Louis, towing alongside a barge also laden, Capt. Henry U. Hart. Dismantled at Cincinnati, 1877.

2506 H. T. DEXTER

SW p wh b. Sewickley, Pa. (hull), and completed at Pittsburgh, Pa., 1880. 190 x 33 x 5. Engines, 16's- 5 ft. by Rees. Three boilers. Built for the Evansville & Cairo Packet Co. Capt. J.G. Grammar took her down, and when abreast the Barmore shipyard, Jeffersonville, Ind., she caught fire. She was beached at Towhead Island where she burned a total loss, July 25, 1880.

2507 H. T. DEXTER

SW p wh b. Pittsburgh, Pa. (hull), and completed at Evansville, Ind. Built by the Evansville & Cairo Packet Co., to replace the loss of the first of the name (see above). The hull with boiler deck frame up arrived at Evansville Sept. 3, 1880, in tow of the *MATTIE HAYS*. Machinery from *ARKANSAS BELLE* (see). Ran Evansville-Paducah, Capt. James A. Damron, with J. Frank Ellison, clerk. Inspected at Evansville Oct. 31, 1882.

2508 H. T. YEATMAN

Stw p wh b. Freedom, Pa., 1852. 165 tons. Operated out of Pittsburgh first several years and sank in Glass House Riffle, Pittsburgh, Feb. 16, 1855. Sold to Minnesota River and ran there 1855-1856. Wintered 1855-1856 at Point Douglas, mouth of St. Croix River, then loaded at St. Paul and while landing at Hastings, Minn., stove her bow on rocks, drifted down and lodged at the mouth of the Vermillion River, Apr. 10, 1857, lost.

2509 H. W. BUTTORFF

Stw p wh b. Jeffersonville, Ind., by Howard, 1896. 160 x 30 x 4.1. Engines, 13½'s- 4½ ft. Two boilers, 44" by 20 ft. Owned by the Ryman Line, Nashville-Paducah. In 1901 Capt. James S. Tyner, with Al Bishop and George Bitroff, clerks; Bud Yarbrough and B. Collishaw, pilots; Bedford Harris and Allard Jones, engineers. She struck the bridge pier abutment at Clarksville Mar. 5, 1899, looked like a total loss, but was raised. Capt. J.S. Tyner spent his honeymoon aboard, was master 15 years, and his wife lived aboard eight of those years. In 1906 again at the Clarksville bridge an L&N passenger train (No. 102) ran out and dropped the engine and coal car into the Cumberland River, losing the engineer and express messenger. The *BUTTORFF* was getting ready to run the open draw at the time, but was uninjured. The boat was named for the founder of Phillips & Buttorff Co., Nashville. She was bought by the Lee Line, Memphis, January 1911, which renamed her *JOHN LEE* (see).

2510 H. W. LONGFELLOW

Stw p wh b. Excelsior, Minn., 1881. 46 tons. Originally documented as a packet. Later was towing coal out of Illinois River, and dismantled at Kingston Mines, Ill., January 1912.

2511 H. HANNA BLANKS

Stw p wh b. Cincinnati, Oh., 1880. 155 x 34 x 5.5. Engines, 14's- 6 ft. Two boilers, each 42" by 26 ft., two 16" flues. Engines by C.T. Dumont, cabin by Elias Ealer. Owned by Capt. Jack W. Blanks and named for his 32- month-old son. Also named for John H. Hanna, grain merchant in New Orleans, and also for Henry Blanks, younger brother. In 1884 New Orleans-Ouachita River, Capt. L.P. Delahoussaye, with Stonewall Hanna, clerk. In 1886 same trade with Capt. L.V. Cooley, master and H. Molaison, clerk. Sank in the Ouachita River Dec. 29, 1889, and lost.

2512 H. KINNEY

SW p wh b. Pittsburgh, Pa., 1844. 130 tons. Exploded and lost at Wilkin's Landing, Ala., with loss of seven lives, May 28, 1848.

2513 H. WEBER

Stw p wh b. Cincinnati, Oh., 1870. 79 x 13 x 2. Operated out of Evansville to Wabash River points, Capt. Jos. Smith. Sold while stranded on the Wabash, January 1871, to Americus Flesher and Andrew Flesher, both of Noble, Ill. Still documented at Evansville 1886.

2514 HAIL COLUMBIA

Stw p wh b. West Elizabeth, Pa., 1848. 116 tons. Originally named *RHODE ISLAND* (see). Capt. David Green bought her, rebuilt and renamed her. Ran Pittsburgh-Wheeling, and made trips to Wabash River. Capt. George Poe remembered her and said she had a 'scape like somebody beating a pine board. Lost in collision with *GOV. MEIGS* in Beaver Shoals, Pa., Apr. 19, 1852.

2515 HALLETTE

Stw p wh b. Jeffersonville, Ind., by Howard, 1887. 161 x 30.5 x 4.5. Machinery from the *ALEXANDRIA* (see). Owned by the Red River Line and named for daughter of H.C. Stringfellow, plantation owner near Shreveport. The *GARLAND* also was named for a daughter (see). Capt. George W. Rea sold her January 1899 to Capt. Matt Downs of Pine Bluff (Ark.) Paclet Co. In 1902 running New Orleans-Atchafalaya-Des Glaizes trade, Capt. E.A. Rucker, with Oscar Smith, clerk, in place of the *JULIAN*

POYDRAS. In 1905 bringing cotton out of the Yazoo for the Parisot Line.

2516 HAM HOWELL

Stw p wh b. Murraysville, Va., 1857. 144 tons. 120 x 30 x 4.5. Completed at Wheeling. Owned 1858 by Proctor Ankrum, New Orleans. Ran on upper Red River, and burned at Blantons Wood Yard, Jan. 20, 1860, loaded with 750 bales of cotton and 30,000 hides. Crew rescued by the *ERA No. 3* and taken to New Orleans. Note: *Lytle-Holdcamper* lists her as *HENRY HOWELL,* but she appears in U.S. Custom records at New Orleans as *HAM HOWELL*.

2517 HAMBURG

SW p wh b. Elizabeth, Pa., 1849. 206 tons. Ran Dubuque-St. Paul, 1855, Capt. J.B. Estes, with Frederick K. Stanton, clerk. St. Louis-St. Paul, 1856–1857, Capt. Rowe. Lost in ice in Lake Pepin, March 1858.

2518 HAMILTON

Stw p wh b. Cincinnati, Oh., 1867. 123 tons. In January 1871 reported sold to Capt. C.C. Pickett, New Orleans, to run in connection with the *SELMA*. Off the lists 1876.

2519 HAMILTON BELLE

Stw ferry wh b. Cincinnati, Oh., 1857. 133 tons. First home port, Keokuk, Iowa. A dispatch from Vicksburg, Miss., July 14, 1866: "The ferry *HAMILTON BELLE* had her safe broken into and robbed of several hundred dollars Tuesday last. One arrest has been made." Off the lists 1868.

2520 HANCOCK

SW p wh b. Freedom, Pa., 1849. 152 tons. First home port, Savannah, Ga. Off the lists 1855.

2521 HANDY

Stw p wh b. Cincinnati, Oh., 1873. 110.3 x 21.6 x 3. 99 tons. Owned by the Redden family, Vanceburg, Ky., and operated around Portsmouth, Oh. Sold by them to Salt River. Registered at Wheeling 1886.

2522 HANDY

Stw p wh b. Jeffersonville, Ind. by Howard, 1903. 110 x 22 x 3. Engines, 8"- 3 ½ ft. One boiler 42" by 20 ft. A small cotton packet owned at Monroe, La. Lost at Baton Rouge, La., during the big September 1909 storm, along with towboat *HARVESTER* and *CONQUEST*.

2523 HANDY NO. 2

Stw p wh b. Covington, Ky., 1883. 139 x 25.6 x 4.3. Owned by Maysville & Vanceburg Packet Co., David Gibson, pres., Bruce Redden, sec., and L. Redden, superintendent. Sold to L.A. Carr and others, and in 1896 was running on upper Kanawha River, Charleston-Montgomery. Completely rebuilt at Middleport, Oh., in 1897 and came out as *SPEEDWELL* (see).

2524 HANGING ROCK

Stw p wh b. Portsmouth, Oh., 1859. 96 tons. A single engine boat reported sunk and lost at Cannelton, Va., Nov. 14, 1861. The engine was recovered and bought by Capts. William and George Bay who installed it on the *MINNIE,* the first of their fleet.

2525 HANNIBAL

SW p wh b. Elizabeth, Pa., 1844. 463 tons. First home port, St. Louis. Off the lists in 1853.

2526 HANNIBAL

SW p wh b. Belle Vernon, Pa., 1856. 497 tons. 226 x 36 x 7. Engines, 24's- 7 ft. Four boilers. Ran St. Louis-New Orleans, Capt. H.L. Lee, 1861. Sank and lost five miles above Donaldsonville, La., Capt. Terry Bell, Oct. 1863, downbound from St. Louis.

2527 HANNIBAL CITY

SW p wh b. Madison, Ind., 1858. 563 tons. Ran St. Louis-Keokuk. A snag tore her hull from end to end eight miles below Louisiana, Mo., Sept. 4, 1864. Her machinery went to the *J. H. JOHNSON* (see).

2528 HARBOR NO. 25

Stw p wh Capt. Jesse P. Hughes rode her 1900 on a low water Ohio River inspection trip with members of Masters, Mates & Pilots Association Harbor 25, Pittsburgh. "She was of the compound engine type with cylinders near the size of oyster cans operating a sternwheel by means of sprocket chains. An upright boiler supplied the steam, and two stacks of the diameter of a stovepipe gave the boat a real steamboat look of great dignity. The engineer fed in a few lumps of coal occasionally to the little furnace as he watched the water go up and down in the glass gauge and listened to the chatter of the sprockets." She made the 1900 trip faced to a houseboat.

2529 HARD CASH

Stw p wh b. Pittsburgh, Pa., 1876. 170 x 35 x 5. Engines, 18's- 5 ft. Three boilers, each 38" by 26 ft. Built for Memphis-White River trade, Capt. Edward Postal. Departed Pittsburgh September 1876 with Capt. James Rees, Jr., master, and G. Wash Floyd, clerk. Sank on a snag below St. Louis, September 1879, Capt. Ed Postal. Sold to Mobile, Ala., and went there October 1885. Capt. William Pettus was on her as master when she made regular trips during the navigation season to Columbus, Miss. She made her last visit to Columbus in 1909. She was laid up in Bayou Sara Creek, Ala., in 1910, and dismantled in 1914.

2530 HARD TIMES

SW p wh b. Cincinnati, Oh., 1845. 291 tons. In 1846, New Orleans-Vicksburg, Capt. J.M. Broadwell. She is said to have made three New Orleans-St. Louis rounds in a month, 1847. Off the lists 1853.

2531 HARD TIMES

Stw p wh b. Parkersburg, W. Va. (hull) 1864. 228 tons. 159 x 30 x 4.5. Brought to Pittsburgh for completion. Rees engines. Owned by her master, Capt. Perry Brown, with A.J. Hazlett, clerk. Ran Pittsburgh-St. Louis. Was in collision with *MERCURY* below St. Louis in latter May 1865. On Aug. 21, 1865, at Wheeling, sheriff William H. Irwin attempted to attach the boat for $1,000 indebtedness. Captain Brown backed the boat out, the sheriff aboard, and proceeded to Pittsburgh. There he paid the obligation in full, everybody shook hands, and the sheriff returned to Wheeling. Next time *HARD TIMES* landed at Wheeling Sheriff Irwin came aboard armed with a warrant issued by a justice, took Capt. Brown before Squire Johnston, who slapped $1,000 bail on him for appearance before the October term of Circuit Court on a charge of kidnapping. The boat was sold to Savannah, Ga., documented there in 1867, and off the lists 1870.

2532 HARLEM

Stw p-tb wh b. Pittsburgh, Pa., 1844. 56 tons. 117 x 16.5 x 3. Ran short trades on Monon River, Capt. Joel Wall. Also handled loaded coal barges from the mines of Judge Baird, above Monongahela, Pa. Capt. H.H. Finley also was master in packet trades. In 1846 taking coal to Hanging Rock, Oh., in barges and returning with pig metal, Capt. Thomas Carothers. Off the lists 1851.

2533 HARMONICA

Stw p wh b. Elizabeth, Pa., 1856. 151 tons. 149 x 28 x 3.5. St. Louis-St. Paul, 1857, Capt. Allen. Made a trip to Red River 1858. Snagged and lost at Warsaw, Ill., Nov. 10, 1860.

2534 HARRISON BRIDGES

SW p wh b. New Albany, Ind., 1856. 176 tons. Snagged and lost at Cromwell, Ky., June 25, 1859.

2535 HARRY CLYDE

Stw p wh b. New Franklin, Mo., 1889. 60.9 x 23.3 x 3.3. Engines, 6″- 2 ft. One boiler. Owned by F.J. Hawkins & Bros. Burned at New Franklin Aug. 14, 1890. Was rebuilt, and was snagged near Omaha, Neb. Apr. 1, 1891. On Apr. 1, 1892, wind waves swamped her in 20 ft., and she was lost.

2536 HARRY D. KNOX

Stw p wh b. Harmar, Oh., at Knox Yard, 1883. 117 x 20.6. Engines, 9¾″- 3½ ft. Built for Capt. O.J. Stowe who ran her Marietta-Beverly on the Muskingum first two seasons. Then ran Parkersburg-Belleville, Capt. Ed Cooper, until the B&O arrived. Then went in the Parkersburg-Ravenswood trade, Capt. Anthony (Tony) Meldahl, with Tom Monroe, clerk, in 1887. Same trade 1890, Capt. J.E. Wilkinson, with R.W. Kelly, clerk. Owners included Wick Hayman and Lon Ritchie. In 1894 sold to Monongahela River where Capt. Charles Menges was master in Charleroi-Rice's Landing trade, in opposition to *LENI LEOTI* (see). Dismantled 1898. Engines went to ferry *CHAMPION NO. 3* and boilers to *ADMIRAL DEWEY*.

2537 HARRY DEAN

Stw p wh b. Harmar, Oh., 1863. 235 tons. Originally named *OHIO VALLEY* (see) which was sold Dec. 10, 1864, to U.S. Navy, converted into a tinclad (#10) named *IBEX*, and when sold in 1865 to private owners was renamed *HARRY DEAN*. The Dean Line ran her Cincinnati-Memphis, Capt. H. Blasdel, with G.A. Ditton, clerk. Sold July 8, 1867, to run Cincinnati-Marietta, Capt. Daniel F. Sayre, with Horatio Booth and Henry Chapin, clerks, and J.A. Levesay and B.F. Hall, pilots. She exploded her port boiler (she had three) at 10:00 A.M., Saturday, Jan. 4, 1868, at Walker's Landing, two miles below Gallipolis, Oh., downbound. Capt. George W. Norton, Wheeling, former master of the *ALVIN ADAMS*, was reading in the cabin and with him was R.M. Biggs, Ashland, Ky. Both were killed. The *EDINBURGH* (see) upbound, took off survivors and continued up the river. The *OHIO NO. 3* brought relatives down from Marietta, met the *EDINBURGH* at Buffington Island, and took survivors aboard for return to Marietta. James Chamberlain was chief engineer on *HARRY DEAN*, and was suspended one year by Wheeling Inspectors for allowing his boiler water to get too low. The death list came to five persons. Capt. Hiram Burch, pilot on watch at the time, had both legs broken, and had been blown up three times previously. The wreck was raised in March 1868 and towed to Harmar, Oh., by the towboat *TRAVELER*.

2538 HARRY G. DREES

SW tourist boat sh b. Jeffersonville, Ind., by Howard, 1917. Originally named *PILGRIM* (see). She was remodeled into a tourist boat in 1924 by the Mississippi & Ohio Steamboat Co., of St. Louis. Ran St. Louis-St. Paul, this before modern improvements, and often was stuck on sand bars due to her rather deep draft. Sold to Tampa, Fla., shortly thereafter and gradually fell apart. There was talk in 1930 of towing the hull to the Bahamas.

2539 HARRY HILL

SW p wh b. Cincinnati, Oh., 1847. 332 tons. 191 x 29.9 x 6.1. Ran Nashville-New Orleans, Capt. George W. Haygood, 1847. Capt. Thomas H. Newell, master, 1850. In 1852 owned at St. Louis, Capt. John H. Filbrun, along with James McCord. Collided with and sank the *MARENGO* on Aug. 24, 1848 (see). Collided with and sank the *SAM CLOON*, Feb. 14, 1853 (see). Said to have been named for the same gentleman for whom the *H. R. W. HILL* (see) was named. Off the lists 1853.

2540 HARRY LEE

Stw p wh b. Clarington Oh., 1899. Originally named *CITY OF WHEELING* (see). Renamed by the Lee Line, Memphis, Tenn. Sank at Brandywine Landing, 45 miles above Memphis, August 1911, raised. Burned at Memphis, Mar. 19, 1914. She carried the whistle of the Lee Line *ROBERT E. LEE* (see).

2541 HARRY LEE

Stw p sh b. St. Louis, Mo., 1915. 175.5 x 36 x 6.7. Engines, 16's- 6 ft. Three boilers set on her backwards; fired from deckroom. Owned by the Lee Line, Memphis. Ran Memphis-Helena-Friar's Point. In January 1921 she was 40 miles up St. Francis River. She was built at the Phil A. Rohan Boat, Boiler & Tank Works, St. Louis. Last owned by the Valley Line, Memphis, which sold her June 1924 to Sherburne Transportation Co. She served during WWII at Alexandria, La., on Red River, a barracks for soldiers, and was moved from there to Orange, Tex., used to quarter shipyard workmen, and burned May 12, 1942. She was then converted into a showboat at Orange, and was still there in 1951.

2542 HARRY S.

Stw p wh b. Wolf Creek, Ky., 1886. 132.7 x 29 x 4. Documented at Vicksburg, Miss., 1892.

2543 HARTFORD

Stw p wh b. Monongahela, Pa., 1851. 144 tons. A letter received by Ye Ed. in 1973 from Mrs. Alan J. Lieber, Manhattan, Kans., relates that Manhattan was founded, 1855, by a group of Free-Staters who arrived there aboard the *HARTFORD,* and the boat grounded there.

2544 HARTFORD

Stw p wh b. Cincinnati, Oh., 1863. Sold in 1864 to the U.S. and converted into a gunboat named *SIBYL*. At war's conclusion she was sold to private owners who renamed her *COMET* in October 1865. 176 tons.

2545 HARTFORD

Stw p wh b. Evansville, Ind., 1869. 94 tons. Ran local trades at Evansville, Capt. Joseph McReynolds, with W.H. Liter, clerk. Sold at U.S. Marshal sale 1872 to Capt. Sam Van Sant and others. Sank in 1873 and the cabin was skidded on sleds to Le Claire, Iowa, where it was put on the *D. A. McDONALD* which had lost hers in an explosion.

2546 HARTSVILLE

Stw p wh b. Nashville, Tenn., 1853. 107 tons. Lost in ice at Robertson's Island, Cumberland River, Feb. 17, 1859.

2547 HASTINGS

Stw p wh b. Shousetown, Pa., 1857. 191 tons. Went to the Upper Mississippi. Was at St. Paul in 1859. Snagged and lost at Alexandria, La., Apr. 23, 1864.

2548 HASTINGS

SW p wh b. Monongahela, Pa., 1860. Originally named *EMMA DUNCAN* (see). Renamed by the U.S. in war service 1863. After the war she was sold to private owners, renamed *DORA*. Her vitals as *HASTINGS:* 176.5 x 33.5 x 6. Engines, 20's- 6 ft.

2549 HATTIE BLISS

Prop p wh b. Harmar, Oh. at Knox Yard, 1883. 85 x 14 x 3. Named for the two daughters of Capt. T.B. Townsend. Ran occasional Marietta-Zanesville trips 1884, Capt. William W. Brown but primarily handled produce boats south. She was tied up one night when a passing boat made huge swells, upset the stove, and she burned. This happened at Darrensville (State?), Jan. 27, 1887.

2550 HATTIE BROWN

Stw p wh b. Belle Vernon, Pa., 1884. 120 x 20.3 x 3.1. Engines, 10's- 4 ft. Two boilers each 38" by 18 ft. Capt. Dick Brown ran her in the daily Warsaw-Madison trade, Ohio River, many years. Left Warsaw 6:00 A.M., was at Vevay and Ghent 7:00 A.M., Madison at 10:00 A.M. Left Madison 2:00 A.M., returning to Warsaw 6 or 7:00 P.M. Laid up nights at Florence, Ind. Later owned by Louisville & Cincinnati Packet Co. She was caught in a windstorm at Craig's Bar and taken to Jeffersonville for rebuilding. The Howard Yard did the work in 1915 and she was converted into an oil engine boat. Lost in the big ice at Cincinnati, winter 1917–1918. Her machinery went to the *VIM* (see). In his older years, Capt. Dick Brown was clerk in the Farr Hotel, and then in the Frederick Hotel, Huntington, W. Va.

2551 HATTIE MAY

SW p wh b. Wheeling, W. Va., 1864. 230 tons. Lost in ice at St. Louis, Jan. 12, 1866.

2552 HATTIE McDANIEL

Stw p wh b. Gatlinburg, Tenn., 1891. 90.5 x 18 x 2.5. Still documented 1896.

2553 HATTIE NOWLAND

Stw p wh b. Pittsburgh, Pa., 1877. 180 x 35 x 3.5. Engines, 13's- 5 ft. by Rees. Three boilers. Ran Memphis-Little Rock, Capt. John Darragh. Lost in May 1880 at Cooper's Landing on the Arkansas. Broke in two and the hull filled with sand.

2554 HATTIE WELLER

SW ferry wh b. Metropolis, Ill., 1866. 90 tons. Operated in the St. Louis district and was lost in 1873.

2555 HAVANA

Stw p wh b. Parkersburg, W. Va. (hull), and completed at Wheeling, 1863. 390 tons. Built for Louisville-Nashville trade by the Sweeneys of Wheeling. She handled U.S. supplies to the Cumberland River. Sold February 1864 to W.E. Gibson & Co., Aurora, Ind., Capt. Ira Malin. Burned and lost at Parlor Grove in the vicinity of North Bend, Oh., Aug. 16, 1869.

2556 HAVERHILL

SW p wh b. Haverhill, Oh., 1851. 69 tons. Off the lists 1854.

2557 HAWKEYE STATE

SW p wh b. Shousetown, Pa., 1860. 405 tons. Built under direction of Capt. Richard C. Gray for the Northern Line Packet Co. along with the *SUCKER STATE* (see). Ran St. Louis-St. Paul. Departed St. Louis June 11, 1861, Capt. R.C. Gray, and arrived in St. Paul three days, six hours 20 minutes, 54 landings en route, her freight receipts $2,087. Made eight rounds that season in 73 days. In 1867, Capt. Wordon, raced the *PHIL SHERIDAN* (see) to Dubuque, and then continued to St. Paul 2-21-19. On another occasion round-tripped in six days 20 hours. The best time St. Louis-St. Paul lies between the *PHIL SHERIDAN, GEM CITY,* and *HAWKEYE STATE,* all fast nags. Dismantled and her engines went to the *LAKE SUPERIOR* (see).

2558 HAYDEE

SW p wh b. Louisville, Ky., 1847. 144 tons. Snagged and lost on the Ouachita River, June 14, 1851. She was 138 x 22 x 5. Owned 1851 by Pierre Deverges, New Orleans.

2559 HAZEL

Stw ferry wh b. Lake Charles, La., 1888. 84 x 37 x 5. In the 1920s sold to the Baton Rouge Transportation Co., and renamed *PORT ALLEN* (see).

2560 HAZEL DELL

Stw p wh b. California, Pa., 1857. 148.5 x 29.8 x 4.4. Originally owned one-half by the Rees family, and James P. and William F. Richardson, all of Pittsburgh. Ran Louisville-Owensboro, 1858. Pittsburgh-Cincinnati, Capt. Metcalf, 1861. Had been to St. Paul in 1858. During the war did transport service, bringing the 2nd Kentucky Regiment from Charleston, W. Va., to Jeffersonville, Ind., January 1862 along with *MARMORA* and *KENTON.* Overhauled at Madison, Ind., August 1864 when a windstorm took down her stacks and did damage to her cabins. Sold August 1865 to Alabama River, Capt. I.M. Davies of Mobile, master. Snagged and lost at Demopolis, Ala., with loss of four lives, Jan. 5, 1866.

2561 HAZEL L. WATSON

Prop p wh b. Allegheny, Pa., 1901. 70 x 10 x 3. Owned by Capt. John O. Watson, Lock Four on Monon River. Capt. William Syphers bought interest in 1907 and became sole owner 1909. Syphers, who owned the Monongahela Hotel, at Rice's Landing, Pa., ran her Brownsville-Rice's Landing. Later owned by Crosan Construction Co., Brownsville, Pa., and was lost in ice at Rice's Landing, Feb. 10, 1918.

2562 HAZEL RICE

Stw p wh b. Harmar, Oh., at the Knox Yard, 1895. 125 x 22.6 x 4.3. Engines, 12's- 4 ft. from *LIZZIE CASSEL.* Built for J.W. Rice of Zanesville. Frequently leased to the U.S. Engineers, Zanesville District, towing dredges and equipment, Capt. W.W. Richardson. Chicago Mill & Lumber Co., owned her 1916, then Capt. W.L. Berry, Paducah. Capt. Lewis Tanner bought her October 1918 and ran her Madison-Monterey, and took an excursion to Beattyville on the Kentucky in June 1919. Towed for the Flesher Sand & Gravel Co., Mt. Vernon, Ind., in spring of 1926. Evansville & Bowling Green Packet Co., had her in 1929 and in 1930 Capt. Jeff Williams dismantled her and built the towboat *TOM WILLIAMS* using much equipment.

2563 HEAD LIGHT

Stw p wh b. Jeffersonville, Ind., by Howard, 1877. 140 x 24.6 x 3.9. Ran on Yazoo and Sunflower rivers and was brought to Marietta, Oh., in 1887 for dismantling. Engines and other parts used building the *ADDIE E. FAISON.*

2564 HECLA

SW p wh b. New Albany, Ind., 1847. 285 tons. 181 x 27 x 6.1. Went to New Orleans, Capt. Peter Dalman, running New Orleans-Red River. In 1850 sold to Capt. William Kay, New Orleans. In 1851 sold to Scott & Robinson, New Orleans, and then had several owners until 1853 when Ocean Towboat Co., and Star Towboat Co., New Orleans, acquired her, Capt. William Whann. They sold her to Capt. Chenny Johnson, St. Mary Parish in March 1854. Off the lists 1857.

2565 HELEN

SW p wh b. Jeffersonville, Ind., by Howard, 1850. 292 tons. 180 x 26 x 6.5. Went to Mobile, Ala. Burned and lost at Mobile, May 12, 1855.

2566 HELEN

SW p wh b. Marietta, Oh., 1862. 84 tons. Originally named *TRANSFER,* sold to USQMD in 1863 and renamed following sale to private owner Dec. 15, 1865. Off the lists 1867.

2567 HELEN

Stw ferry wh b. Boonville, Mo., 1909. Originally named *DOROTHY* (see). Sold July 1923 to Capt. Ben Flesher, Huntington, W. Va., and renamed. Ran Huntington-Chesapeake until sold March 1932 to Ray E. Maston, Cincinnati.

2568 HELEN BLAIR

Stw p wh b. Harmar, Oh., 1896. Originally named *URANIA* (see). Capt. Walter Blair bought *URANIA* at Cincinnati midsummer 1901 and took her to Burlington, Iowa, to run local trades. Burned her texas and pilothouse off at Muscatine, Iowa, Sept. 5, 1901. Rebuilt that winter and renamed to honor his daughter, later Mrs. Hugh T. Smith, Philadelphia, Pa. Blair, with a penchant for exploring, had this boat to Galena, Ill. on Apr. 27, 1913, first one there in years, and, as matters turned out, the last steamboat to go there. In 1915 ran a special cruise Davenport to Pittsburgh, Pa., arriving Pittsburgh May 14. Among the passengers was Capt. Ben Taber, former master of the *RUTH* (see). Pilots Dayton Randolph and Walter English handled her Cincinnati-Pittsburgh. In November 1915 went to Clarendon, Ark., on White River with a load of potatoes and brought back to Muscatine pearl shells for Henry F. Kath. In October 1916 made a round trip Davenport-New Orleans with 60 passengers, William J. Keith, purser. Capt. Joseph H. Young was long her master on the Upper Mississippi. In September 1919 sold to Memphis and was dismantled there June 1920.

2569 HELEN BROOKE

SW p wh b. Chester, Pa., 1863. 26 tons. Left Baltimore Aug. 9, 1869, then via Chesapeake Bay passed through a canal in Delaware, thence up Delaware River to Trenton. Then through New Jersey by canal and down the Raritan River to New York City. Then up the Hudson to Troy, N.Y., and over the Erie Canal to Buffalo. Thence transited the Great Lakes to Chicago, down the Illinois Canal to the Illinois River, to St. Louis. She was at Napoleon, Ark., Oct. 14, 1869, en route to Bayou Teche, La. Lost in ice at Memphis, Tenn., Dec. 26, 1872. She was 60.4 x 11.2 x 4. Upon arrival at New Orleans in December 1869 was sold to Edwin Walters and Pinkney C. Bethell, equal shares, both of Franklin, La.

2570 HELEN BURKE

Stw p wh b. Mobile, Ala., 1914. Originally the *PEERLESS* (see). The Burke Line of Mobile bought her 1924 and renamed her. Ran four or five years, then was laid up in 12-Mile Marsh, above Mobile, and rotted down c. 1929–1930.

2571 HELEN E.

Stw p wh b. Pt. Pleasant, W. Va., 1913. 105 x 19.7 x 2.8. Engines, 9″-3½ ft. One boiler 40″ by 18 ft. Owned originally in equal share by Capt. Gordon C. Greene, George P. Gardner and W.E. McDade. Ran Gallipolis-Racine, McDade, master, W.R. Barringer, clerk. Named for McDade's daughter Helen Elizabeth. Was carried off by ice from Pt. Pleasant in January 1918, laid up at the time, nobody aboard, to below Madison, Ind., 293 miles. Came to no harm and was returned under her own steam. In June 1918 Capts. James and Sam Williamson bought her, added a boiler deck cabin, and ran her Wheeling-New Matamoras until 1930. She ran Pittsburgh-Parkersburg briefly 1931, Capt. Clayton Adams. Capt. Dan Patchell tried her briefly in Kanawha River. Sold to Ben Raike who rebuilt her into a towboat named *CLAIRMONT* in 1934.

2572 HELEN LANE

Stw p wh b. Dana, W. Va., 1915. 136.3 x 24.8 x 6.1. Engines, 12's- 5 ft. Two boilers. Equipment from *J. Q. DICKINSON.* Built for Capt. John Lane, and ran Charleston-Montgomery on upper Kanawha. Sold to the lower Mississippi summer 1918 and foundered at Berwick, La., June 30, 1919.

2573 HELEN M. GOULD

Stw p wh b. Middleport, Oh., 1897. Originally named *SPEEDWELL* (see). Capt. Sam Parsons bought *SPEEDWELL* in 1902, changed her name. Ran Portsmouth-Cincinnati briefly, then Madison-Louisville competing with *BIG KANAWHA* of Louisville & Cincinnati Packet Co. Commodore Laidley of L&C swapped, accepting the *GOULD.* In 1910 L&C rebuilt her into *LOUCINDA* (see).

2574 HELEN MAR

Stw p wh b. California, Pa., 1852. 140 x 27 x 5.5. Engines, 16's- 4½ ft. Three boilers. Came out in Cincinnati-Zanesville trade, Capt. George W. Cox. Ran Pittsburgh-Zanesville, same master, 1853. Captain Cox, Lowell, Oh., was principal owner. Sank in ice at Maysville, Ky., Feb. 24, 1855, raised. Sold to the lower Ohio and last master was Capt. Josh V. Throop. Dismantled in the fall of 1857 and engines went to the *SAM KIRKMAN* (see).

2575 HELENA

Stw p wh b. St. Louis, Mo., 1866. 199 tons. Engines, 13½'s- 3½ ft. Two boilers. Snagged on the Missouri River at Bonhomme Island, Oct. 16, 1868, upbound from St. Louis to Grand River with U.S. supplies. John Stansberry was the pilot on watch.

2576 HELENA

Stw p wh b. California, Pa., 1878. 194 x 33 x 4.5. Originally owned by T.C. Power & Bros., of Fort Benton, Mont., J.W. Knight of Fort Shaw, John C. Barr, St. Louis, and Capt. James McGarry, master. On first trip loaded at Pittsburgh direct for Fort Benton, arriving there May 14, 1878 with 235 tons of freight and 56 passengers. In 10 years she made over 50 trips to Montana points under many masters associated with the Power Line. In 1884 she was the first spring arrival at the fort, coming in a week ahead of others, May 6. Sold 1887 to A.S. Bryan and others, Washington, Mo. Snagged that year at Lower Bonhomme Island, Mo., raised. Final snagging was at Bonhomme Island, Oct. 23, 1891, Ed Anderson the pilot on watch. Last master was Capt. Geary W. Murray.

2577 HELENA

SW p wh b. Pittsburgh, Pa., 1878. Originally named *J. B. M. KEHLOR* (see). The *KEHLOR* was rebuilt 1881 and renamed. She measured 260 x 50 x 8.5. In 1886 renamed *GRAND REPUBLIC* (see).

2578 HENDERSON

Stw ferry wh b. Evansville, Ind., 1900. 76.5 x 17 x 3.3. Engines, 6″-2 ft. One boiler, 72″ by 6 ft. Owned at Henderson by John Collins. Sold and renamed *SPOTTSVILLE* in February 1908 (see).

2579 HENRIETTA

Stw p wh b. California, Pa., 1853. 179 tons. 143.5 x 25.5 x 4.8. Capt. George B. McClintock first master and principal owner. Ran Pittsburgh-Louisville briefly, then sold to the Upper Mississippi. Was a regular at St. Paul 1853–1859. Off the lists in 1860.

2580 HENRIETTA

Stw p wh b. Stillwater, Minn., 1879. 130 x 24 x 4.3. Originally a rafter on the Upper Mississippi named *J. E. STAPLES,* later *DAVID BRONSON.* As *HENRIETTA* she handled excursions at St. Paul in 1898, later taken to the Missouri River by Berlin and Healy and ran excursions at

Omaha. Spring of 1902 sold to Capt. R.A. Talbot and Myron H. Sherman for excursions at Sioux City. That fall sold to Capt. Shep Green for Dover-Nashvlle trade on the Cumberland River. Owned March 1904 equal shares by John S. Summers, Parkersburg, W. Va., and Arthur A. Peck, Paducah, who converted her into a towboat. She then towed ties out of the Tennessee River, Capt. W.L. Berry. Dismantled in 1910 and machinery went to the towboat *HIBERNIA*.

2581 HENRIETTA

Stw p wh b. Covington, Ky., 1890. 101.5 x 16.3 x 3.6. Owned in 1900 by W.A. Baker, New Matamoras, Oh. Sold and renamed *LOUISE* (see).

2582 HENRY A. JONES

Stw p wh b. Cincinnati, Oh., 1856. 193 tons. Owned by Capt. Knight, and burned and lost one mile below Augusta, Ky., Feb. 27, 1858.

2583 HENRY A. JONES

Stw p wh b. Pittsburgh, Pa., 1869. Built by Capts. Frank and Dan Maratta for use on the Trinity River in Texas. Departed Pittsburgh November 1869.

2584 HENRY A. TYLER

Stw p wh b. Jeffersonville, Ind., 1882. 160 x 30 x 4.7. Engines, 15's- 5 ft. Two boilers. Ran Memphis-Cairo-Paducah in 1883, Capt. Massengale, with Lem Hill, clerk. She became the first packet of the St. Louis & Tennessee River Packet Co. Sold c. 1890 and renamed *G. W. SENTELL* (see).

2585 HENRY ADKINS

Stw p wh b. Portsmouth, Oh., 1867. 328 tons. Went to St. Louis and burned there Mar. 29, 1869.

2586 HENRY AMES

SW p wh b. Carondelet, Mo., 1864. 777 tons. 260.7 x 22.4 x 7.6. Ran St. Louis-New Orleans owned by stockholders of St. Louis and Jefferson City, Mo., Capt. Thomas L. Crawford. Ran the blockade at Columbus, Ky., mid-June 1864 downbound with a gunboat lashed on the shore side, came off unscathed. Hit a snag and sunk seven miles above Cairo July 30, 1864, raised. Capt. Thomas L. Crawford was still master 1866, same trade. Rebuilt 1870, and in 1873 Capt. J. West Jacobs, master, with W.C. Aiken, clerk, same trade. Snagged and lost at Waterproof, La., August 1874 with loss of two lives.

2587 HENRY BURKE

Stw p wh b. Mobile, Ala., 1905. Originally named *MARY E. STAPLES*, then *ALMA*. She ran Mobile-Tombigbee River, Capt. Matt Jackson. The trade played out and she was converted into a ferryboat named *CECIL N. BEAN* (see).

2588 HENRY C. YAEGER

Stw p wh b. Elizabeth, Pa., 1870. 234 x 50 x 8. Hartupee compound engines, 15's- 33's- 6 ft. Four boilers, each 38" by 24 ft. Owned by Capt. William J. Kountz, Pittsburgh. She was too long for Monon River Locks 1 and 2 and cofferdams were built to let her through. The old locks there were 215 by 50. She ran St. Louis-New Orleans, primarily a freight carrier and of odd design. Capt. I.C. Vanhook commanded. She was having engine trouble on Mar. 22, 1880 near Grand Tower, Ill., and while at shore repairing became hooked on a log. The towboat *LIONESS* was called to assist, the log went through the hull, and she was towed across the river where she sank.*

2589 HENRY CHOUTEAU

SW p wh b. Cincinnati, Oh., 1853. 633 tons. 263 x 35 x 7. Engines, 26's- 10 ft. Six boilers. Ran St. Louis-New Orleans, Capt. Dayree. Served as a U.S. transport during the war. Burned at Columbus, Ky., Sept. 26, 1863. Apparently was recovered, and the hull was used as a wharfboat at Natchez, Miss., in 1865.

2590 HENRY CLAY

SW p wh b. McKeesport, Pa., 1858. 181 x 31. Built for the Northern Line on the Upper Mississippi. Capt. James W. Campbell was master first season. Capt. Charles Stephenson, 1858-1859. Capt. C.B. Goll, 1861. Destroyed running the batteries at Vicksburg, burned and lost, Apr. 22, 1863.

2591 HENRY COLE

Stw p wh b. Leavenworth, Kans. 1881. 18 tons. A freight boat on Missouri River.

2592 HENRY FITZHUGH

Stw p wh b. Cincinnati, Oh., 1857. 217 tons. Did service for the U.S. during the war, handling mules, army wagons, etc. Sank Jan. 22, 1864 in ice at Shawneetown, Ill., raised and taken to Green River for protection. She was returned to Cincinnati and laid up in the mouth of Licking River. On Sept. 4, 1864, a freak flood in that stream overturned her and the cabin floated off. She was being dismantled at the time.

2593 HENRY FRANK

Stw p wh b. Cincinnati, Oh., at the Mack Yard, 1878. 276 x 52 x 10.5. Engines, 28¼'s- 9 ft. Six boilers, each 42" by 28 ft. Five flues. Paddlewheel 30' dia. working 39' buckets, 28" dip. Machinery came from towboat *AJAX*. This was a large cotton carrier designed for the Memphis-New Orleans trade, named for a Jew who was a solid businessman of the South. Owned by Capt. J. Frank Hicks who commanded, with Alfred Grissom, clerk. Departed Cincinnati on Oct. 28, 1878 on her first trip. Teamed up with the *CHAS. P. CHOUTEAU*, these were the big cotton carriers of the day. On Apr. 2, 1881, she brought to New Orleans the largest cotton cargo ever handled by a packet, having on her decks 9,226 bales, plus 250 tons of other freight. She made 12 trips that season and brought down a total of 76,009 bales, 28,218 sacks of cotton seed, 13,675 sacks of oil cake, and 1,225 barrels of cottonseed oil. Burned at Davis Creek Island, 22 miles above New Orleans, Oct. 2, 1884.

2594 HENRY GRAFF

Stw p wh b. Belle Vernon, Pa., 1855. 250 tons. Owned by Capt. George L. McClintock who commanded. Ran Pittsburgh-St. Louis and made several trips through to St. Paul (1856–1857). She was at Pittsburgh starting to load on May 7, 1859, caught fire, and in this blaze other boats were also burned.

2595 HENRY HARLEY

Stw p wh b. Jeffersonville, Ind., by Howard, 1898. 160 x 29 x 3.2. Engines, 12's- 4 ft. Two boilers, each 42" by 22 ft. Named for a merchant of Nashville, Tenn. Built for and run by Capt. J.R. Handly and family, Nashville-Burnside. Capt. William T. Hunter was first master. Later in the Ryman Line, and was laid up at Nashville when they took bankruptcy in September 1916. Blown ashore in a storm and heavy ice, Jan. 13, 1917, and lost.

2596 HENRY J. KING

SW p wh b. New Albany, Ind., 1856. 409 tons. Went to Mobile, Ala., and to Confederate registry in 1861.

2597 HENRY L. CLARK

Recesswheel ferry wh b. Jeffersonville, Ind., by Howard, 1891. 172 x 45 x 5. One engine, 28"- 6 ft. Three boilers, each 44" by 18 ft. Owned by Wiggins Ferry Co., St. Louis. Dismantled about 1916 and converted into a wharfboat by the Eagle Packet Co., St. Louis.

2598 HENRY LEWIS

SW p wh b. Cincinnati, Oh., 1854. 480 tons. She was rammed by the *E. HOWARD* (see) on Mar. 7, 1856, sunk. New Orleans-Upper Coast, 1858, Capt. B.F. Orr, with P. Michel, clerk. Off the lists 1860.

2599 HENRY LOGAN

Stw p wh b. Parkersburg, Va., 1860. 75 tons. Ran local trades out of Parkersburg. She and the *R. B. HAMILTON* were racing up the Ohio at Blennerhassett Island Mar. 7, 1862. A downbound keelboat, J.H. Atkinson in charge, and deeply laden with firebrick and clay, was victim of this affair when one racer took up one side of her and the other the other side. The *LOGAN* hit the keel's bow, the *HAMILTON* hit the stern of it, and the keel went down. The keel's crew got ashore in a yawl. Neither racer stopped. The *HENRY LOGAN* was bought in or about 1866 by Capt. George Bay for the Ironton-Proctorville trade. His brother Capt. William Bay was running the *FALCON* in competition. There were hot times, and some shots were exchanged. The *HENRY LOGAN* sank at Coal Grove, Oh., and was dismantled at Parkersburg. The brothers Bay made up, built the *J. C. CROSSLEY* (see).

2600 HENRY LOGAN

Stw p wh b. Murraysville, W. Va. (hull) and completed at Parkersburg, W. Va., 1878. 106.6 x 24.4 x 3.4. In 1882 ran Middleport-Marietta, Capt. C.P. Leavitt, with L.J. McGee, clerk. Went to the Louisville, Ky., area c. 1890 and was lost in Salt River, Ky., May 1894.

2601 HENRY M. SHREVE

SW p wh b. Jeffersonville, Ind., by Howard, 1867. 198 x 35 x 5.5. Engines, 20's- 6 ft. Four boilers. Machinery from *STEPHEN DECATUR* (see). Built for Capt. Henry S. Carter and others, St. Louis. Ran in the "Carter Line" St. Louis-Shreveport, and also made trips up the Missouri. In 1869 she went to Fort Benton and the story of the trip is preserved in a complete log (see *Missouri Historical Review,* XXXI, 1945). Burned at Chester, Ill., Nov. 23, 1872. A contemporary news account relates she had aboard 40 kegs of powder "which exploded and blowed everything to atoms." A number of horses and mules were lost.

2602 HENRY M. STANLEY

Stw p wh b. Murraysville, W. Va. at the Flesher Yard, 1890. 180 x 32.4 x 5.5. Engines from towboat *JOHN HANNA.* Built for the Bay Brothers for Cincinnati-Charleston trade. Ran competition with the White Collar Line's boats, usually *SHERLEY.* Manager Fred A. Laidley of White Collar bought the *STANLEY* in 1895 thus ending the fray. On Feb. 1, 1900, hit the Southern Bridge, Cincinnati, sank, drowning one. Raised March 20, and repaired at Madison, Ind. On Apr. 4, 1900, just off the ways, she collided with the coal tow of the *JOSEPH WALTON* at Rising Sun, Ind., and again sank. She was raised April 10, and returned to Madison to again go on the ways. Sold in 1904 to Greene Line Steamers who ran her Cincinnati-Pomeroy-Charleston. On Sept. 3, 1907, she was downbound in fog at Gallipolis Island and hit the U.S. dredge *OSWEGO* engaged in dredging the channel. She sank and as preparations were under way to raise her she burned. Her wheel shaft and flanges lay in the mud at the Acme Boiler Works, Gallipolis for years. Whistle went to the *ISLAND QUEEN* (first). Machinery went to the *GREENLAND* (see). Capt. Jesse P. Hughes says she was the last boat built at the Flesher Yard, Murraysville. Jack Flesher, who ran it, went to Levanna, Oh., and ran the Barrett Yard thereafter.

2603 HENRY MARQUAND

SW railroad transfer wh b. Jeffersonville, Ind., by Howard, 1873. Originally named *H. S. McCOMB* (see). Engines 22's- 8 ft. Four boilers, two on a side. She was the Iron Mountain RR transfer at Cairo many years, Capt. J.J. Gillespie. Bought by boat broker John F. Klein c. 1925, and was used at Neeley's Ldg., Mo., as a loading barge by Morse Stone & Timber Co. Dismantled at the Mound City Marine Ways in 1927.

2604 HENRY PROBASCO

SW p wh b. Madison, Ind., 1873. 235 x 35 x 6.7. Engines, 22's- 7 ft. Owned by Stuart & Co., Madison, Ind., and others. Ran Cincinnati-St. Louis-Memphis, Capt. Lon Bryson, with Alex Young and Frank Bryson, clerks. Capt. Andy Robinson also commanded. Hit on rocks in the Grand

Chain, Ohio River, and was lost, Nov. 14, 1873, at 6:00 P.M. The *IDLEWILD* took off passengers and crew.

HENRY S. TURNER

See *H. S. TURNER*.

2605 HENRY SACKMAN

SW railroad ferry wh b. Jeffersonville, Ind., by Howard, 1883. 254 x 48 x 6. Engines, 22's- 8 ft. Four boilers, two on a side, each 44" by 22 ft. Owned by Wiggins Ferry Co., St. Louis, Mo. Dismantled c. 1918.

2606 HENRY SHELDON

Stw snagboat wh b. Little Rock, Ark., 1884. 134 x 26 x 3. Operated by U.S. Engineers on White River, Ark. Her pilot in 1900 was Capt. Rees V. Downs. Sold at public sale May 1903 to Capt. M.O. Brinkley. Converted into a packet and renamed *LIGHTWOOD* (see).

2607 HENRY TETE

SW p wh b. Louisville, Ky., 1869. 439 tons. 177 x 34.4 x 6.9. Went to New Orleans owned by Coast & Lafourche Packet Co., R.B. Martin, sec., Capt. Joseph Dalferes, master. Same trade and master 1873, with M.H. Landry, clerk. In 1879, same trade, Capt. J.F. Aucoin, with M.H. Landry, clerk.

2608 HENRY VON PHUL

SW p wh b. Paducah, Ky., 1860. 249 x 39 x 7.2. Ran St. Louis-New Orleans. Served as a U.S. transport during the war. Once passing Bayou Sara was fired upon from the opposite shore and her master, Capt. Patrick Gorman, was killed, and also the barkeeper, when a ball passed through the forward cabin. In March 1865, St. Louis-New Orleans, Capt. James Allen, with Sam Bowen one of the pilots. Owned 1866 by Capt. Frank Hicks, R.P. Walt & Co. (the partners being Martin Walt and Rufus P. Walt), and Daniel Walsh, administrator for the estate of Capt. Patrick Gorman. Caught fire downbound above Donaldsonville, La., with 101 passengers and 3,465 bales of cotton. Five lost their lives, and many of the survivors escaped ashore in nightclothes, this on Nov. 15, 1866.

2609 HENRY WATTERSON

SW ferry sh b. Jeffersonville, Ind., by Howard, 1897. Originally named *ANDREW CHRISTY* (see). Bought by the Falls City Ferry & Transportation Co., and served between Louisville and Jeffersonville teamed up (1924) with *W. S. McCHESNEY, JR.* Later used as their wharfboat at Louisville. When the bridge was opened she became a barge 1940-1941 used to transport beer Evansville-Memphis.

2610 HENRY WOHLT

Stw p wh b. Hermann, Mo., 1900. 97.8 x 20 x 3. Engines, 7"- 3½ ft. One boiler. Owned by Hermann Ferry & Packet Co. Sunk by ice at Boonville, Mo., Jan. 1, 1910. Raised.

2611 HERALD

SW p wh b. Brownsville, Pa., 1852. 295 tons. Off the lists 1858.

2611-A HERCULES

SW p wh b. Cincinnati, Oh., 1858. 186.5 x 32.7 x 9.7. Operated out of Memphis. In November 1865, Capt. John S. Dunham, at New Orleans. Dismantled in February 1868.

2612 HERE I AM

SW ferry wh b. Wellsville, Oh., 1856. 39 tons. Rebuilt at Wheeling, 1863. Served between Bellaire, Oh., and Benwood, W. Va.

2613 HERE'S YOUR MULE

Prop p wh b. Buffalo, N.Y., 1866. 14 tons. Spent much of her career around Coal River and in the upper Kanawha. Item dated June 23, 1871: "Capt. J.T. Daddow has purchased the *MULE,* a Kanawha River steamboat, and is now running her in connection with the *MOCKINGBIRD* in the Brownstown trade." Owned December 1874 by Hugh Snodgrass, Peytona, W. Va. Her dimensions are given as 51.1 x 9.8 x 2.8.

2614 HERMANN

SW p wh b. Louisville, Ky., 1848. 194 tons. Collided with and sank *EMMA WATTS* on the Wabash River, Mar. 3, 1853. Advertised Pittsburgh to St. Louis, Capt. Kinkle, January 1856. Off the lists 1857.

2615 HERMANN

Stw ferry wh b. Hermann, Mo., 1912. 89 x 19.6 x 2.4. Operated at Hermann, Mo.

2616 HERMANN

Stw ferry wh b. Hermann, Mo., 1928. 86.8 x 18.2 x 2.7. Owned by Hermann Ferry & Packet Co., Hermann, Mo.

2617 HERO

SW p wh b. Cincinnati, Oh., by the U.S. and sold February 1866 to private operators. Possibly the *HERO* dismantled at Metropolis, Ill., 1869, and machinery went to *UTAH* (see).

2618 HEROINE

SW p wh b. Brownsville, Pa., 1851. 94 tons. Advertised 1854 Mobile-Demopolis-Bladon Springs, Capt. S.W. Abels, "extremely light draft." Exploded and lost at Blakely Landing, Ala., Mar. 13, 1855, with loss of three lives.

2619 HEROINE

SW p ih b. Glasgow, Scotland, 1862. 178 x 19.2 x 7. Built on the River Clyde designed as a blockade runner and so used, owned by the U.S. Sold December 1866 to Richard H. Porter, St. Louis. Soon transferred to the Good Intent Towboat Co., New Orleans, Capt. Hiram Follett. The late Capt. Vance Higbee recalled her as a walking-beam towboat employed in moving ships between New Orleans and the Jetties. He says about 1880 she was converted into a passenger boat at New Orleans for the New Orleans-Bay St. Louis-Biloxi run. To enter this trade the owners steamed her out through the Jetties and back to New Orleans, about ½ mile as a crow flies, but a voyage of about 250 miles. Capt. John Boardman was master, with John Hall, clerk. Capt. Riddle piloted her around. Off the lists in 1907.

2620 HESPER

Stw p wh b. Cincinnati, Oh., 1866. 184 tons. 127 x 35 x 3.5. Engines, 8″- 3 ft. One boiler. Sank on the upper Arkansas early March 1868 owned by Clayton & Morse, Cincinnati. In the Ouachita River Packet Co., Capt. J. Ferguson, 1870. Sank and lost 60 miles above Alexandria, La., on Red River, Nov. 7, 1872.

2621 HESPERIAN

SW p wh b. Louisville, Ky., 1857. 218 x 33. Engines, 23's- 7 ft. Three boilers. Ran St. Louis-Omaha fall 1857, Capt. F.B. Kercheval, with Grant Marsh, mate. In the St. Louis and St. Joseph Union Packet Line, 1858, same master. Burned at Atchison, Kans., Aug. 19, 1860.

2622 HETTIE

Stw ferry wh b. Cincinnati, Oh., 1879. 124 x 49.3 x 6.6. Documented in the New Orleans area through 1892, maybe later.

2623 HETTIE

Catamaran ferry wh b. New Orleans, La., 1898 111.3 x 40.2 x 6.5. Still listed in 1918.

2624 HETTIE GILMORE

Stw p wh b. Cincinnati, Oh., 1859. 110 x 22 x 3.5. Named for daughter of Capt. A.T. Gilmore identified with the Louisville & Henderson Packet Co. Captured by the Confederates at Clark's Landing, Ky., at the mouth of Barren River, Feb. 21, 1863, loaded with supplies for the U.S. Reportedly burned by the Confederates but if so she made remarkable recovery. Was with Porter on Red River 1864, then owned by Mrs. Agnes Bouchard, New Orleans. Sold Sept. 1865 to two British subjects, David H. Syme and John Syme. Apparently was over on Bayou Lafourche. Had several ownership changes, and was removed from documentation September 1867, "found unfit for service." Seems she was fixed and in April 1868 advertised New Orleans-Lafourche twice weekly, Capt. William H. King, with John A. Labarthe, clerk. Out of service 1869.

2625 HIAWATHA

SW p wh b. Elizabeth, Pa., 1856. 767 tons. 250 x 41. Ran St. Louis-New Orleans in the "Railroad Line," Capt. Edw. F. Dix. Burned at St. Louis along with *IMPERIAL* and *POST BOY* on Sept. 13, 1863.

2626 HIAWATHA

Stw p wh b. Dubuque, Iowa, 1882. 146 x 32 x 5.5. Originally *W. J. YOUNG, JR.* (see). She was converted into an excursion boat in 1906, run by Kentucky & Indiana Bridge Co., and ran usually below the Falls. Harrison L. Kendle, former purser on the *TELL CITY,* was skipper and part owner, Burned at the foot of Broadway, Louisville, Ky., Nov. 30, 1911.

2627 HIAWATHA

Stw p wh b. Harmar, Oh., at Knox Yard, 1890. 140.5 x 30 x 5.5. Built for Capts. Dana Scott and George Wallace, designed for the Pittsburgh-Zanesville trade. She was taken to St. Louis instead, and briefly ran in the wheat trade to Harrisonville, Mo. Sold to the Brazos River, Texas, and ran East Columbia-Velasco in charge of Capt. Thomas L. Smith. Still in documentation 1902.

2628 HIAWATHA

SW wh b. St. Paul, Minn., 1904. 95 x 18 x 4.2. Operated in the St. Paul area. Still documented in 1918.

2629 HIBERNIA

SW p wh b. Pittsburgh, Pa., 1844. 175 x 23.4 x 5. Owned by Capt. John Klinefelter and others of Pittsburgh. Advertised Pittsburgh to Dubuque, Capt. Parker, March 1844. Settled down as a regular Pittsburgh-Cincinnati packet in charge of Capt. Klinefelter until spring of 1847 when replaced by *HIBERNIA NO. 2* (see). She then ran Pittsburgh-Wheeling, Capt. Sam Smith, 1847. Made a trip to St. Louis and burned there Mar. 10, 1848, along with other packets. The wreck was returned to Jeffersonville, Ind., and lay around there until it sank February 1851.

2630 HIBERNIA

Stw p wh b. Elizabeth, Pa., 1856. 179 tons. Burned and lost at Beach Bottom, W. Va., below Wellsburg, Va., on the Ohio River, the fire starting in the cookhouse, Jan. 1, 1858. She had been afire twice in her career and twice sunk.

2631 HIBERNIA

Stw p wh b. Rock Castle, W. Va. (Leon) 1881. 135 x 25 x 4. Engines, 12's- 4½ ft. from the *J. M. CAMDEN.* Two boilers. Ran Gallipolis-Marietta, 1881, Capt. Alf Day, with William Birthisell, clerk; later that year Capt. W.A. Maddy, with J.J. Maddy, clerk. Same in 1882. Same in 1883. In 1885 Gallipolis-Parkersburg, Capt. G.B. McClintock, with J.M. Deem, clerk. Took passengers from the sunken *TELEPHONE* Jan. 2, 1885 (see). Ran out of Kentucky River along with *BLUE WING* and others later, Capt. Joel Wall. Was too long for the locks and her forecastle was shortened. Sold to Vicksburg and went through a sale or so until the Parisot Line acquired her for the Belzoni trade. They sold her to Capt. James Britton who ran her a few trips on the Sunflower River and tied her up at the mouth of the Yazoo Canal where she burned, Kleinston, Miss., Oct. 29, 1899.

2632 HIBERNIA NO. 2

SW p wh b. Shousetown, Pa., 1847. 217 x 27 x 5.4. Owned by David Holmes, William Frampton, George R. Massey, William Bingham, and M. Klinefelter, all of Pittsburgh, and Thomas Arbuckle, Brooke County, Va. Capt. John Klinefelter, master. Ran Pittsburgh-Cincinnati. In July

1849 cholera broke out and Jesse Klinefelter (brother to Capt. John) died as the boat was landing at Pittsburgh. Capt. C.W. Batchelor acquired his stock that summer and went master, remaining in this position until 1852. This boat figures in the famed "Wheeling Bridge Case" as her stacks were damaged in striking that structure, thereby setting off the fireworks culminating in a case heard by the U.S. Supreme Court. Attorney Edwin M. Stanton, Steubenville, was aboard at the time, and many believed he had ordered the accident to produce actual grievance. Later ran out of St. Louis, Capt. Price, and was in the big ice jam there Feb. 3, 1854.

2633 HICKMAN

SW p wh b. Cincinnati, Oh., 1855. 228 tons. Owned by Thompson Dean and others, Cincinnati. Burned below Little Rock, Ark., Mar. 2, 1860. Capt. Andy Byars. Two lives were lost.

2634 HICKORY

Rig? p wh b. Mound City, Ill., 1874. 225 tons. Ran out of St. Louis, Capt. W.D. Chapman. Brought passengers from the wrecked *FANNIE TATUM* (see) from Fort Chartres to Cairo, 1880.

2635 HIDALGO

Stw p sh b. Pittsburgh, Pa., by Rees, 1904. 127 x 24 x 5. Ran her trials in May, destined to Frontera, Mexico. Went to New Orleans on her own steam, and there was boarded up five ft. around her head and three ft. on sides. Tug *MONARCH,* owned by H.H. Thornton, Pensacola, took her across the Gulf successfully, the tow bill $1,150. In Mexican service she was officially named *HIDALGO EL LIBERTADOR*. She normally carried passengers, much lumber on deck and towed a barge alongside loaded with coffee. Became famed when she carried President Porfiro Diaz in his escape during the Mexican revolutionary era.

2636 HIGHFLYER

SW p wh b. Madison, Ind., 1854. 253 x 32 x 6. Engines, 24's- 8 ft. Came out in the Louisville-Cincinnati trade 1854, Capt. Thomas T. Wright. Entered Louisville-New Orleans trade, spring 1855, same master. One of her attributes was a texas 50 ft. long "removable for use as a life raft in case of sinking." Was at St. Louis Dec. 7, 1855, when a wharf fire destroyed three packets; she pulled others out of harm's way and was not hurt. The U. S. Mail Line Co., extended to St. Louis, and had her in the Louisville-St. Louis trade, Capt. Wright. Dismantled 1861 and after the machinery, etc., was removed she was used at the Louisville-Portland Canal as a boarding-house for laborers.

2637 HIGHLAND CHIEF

Stw p wh b. Cincinnati, Oh., 1864. 342 tons. Built for Capt. L. Newt Robinson, and ran in Cincinnati-Marietta trade that summer. That fall was running below Cincinnati, and on Aug. 18, 1864, came in collision with the *MAJOR ANDERSON* above Vevay, Ind., and sank with loss of five lives. In July 1868 a diving bell boat was at the scene taking out the engines, and reported the location two miles above Vevay.

2638 HIGHLAND MARY

SW p wh b. St. Louis, Mo., 1848. 158 tons. Made trips to Wheeling and Pittsburgh when new and in 1849 was stationed at St. Joseph, Mo., serving as a ferryboat, along with *SACRAMENTO,* conveying emigrants and equipment across, and charging $5 to $10 for a two-horse wagon. On Apr. 19, 1850, she and *NOMINEE* were the first to St. Paul, Capt. Jos. Atchison. That year Atchison died of cholera, and the boat was laid up. Bought in 1852 by Capt. Joseph La Barge who ran her on the lower Mississippi entire season 1853. Lost in ice at St. Louis, Feb. 26, 1856.

2639 HIGHLAND MARY

Stw p wh b. Harmar, Oh., by Knox Yard, 1894. 142 x 31 x 5.5. Compound condensing engines by Griffith & Wedge, Zanesville, Oh. Scotch marine boiler. Owned by Capts. William W. Richardson, George Wallace, Dana Scott, Lou Myrick, John Rice and Charles S. Beckwith. Designed for Pittsburgh-Zanesville trade, but made only one trip. That summer was handling excursions at Zanesville. Sold September 1894 to the Magdalena River, South America. She made the Gulf crossing in tow of the tug *B.D. WOOD* and arrived intact.

2640 HIGHLAND MARY NO. 2

SW p wh b. Wheeling, Va., 1848. 158 tons. Burned and lost at St. Louis, July 27, 1853.

2641 HIGHLANDER

SW p wh b. Pittsburgh, Pa., 1842. 346 tons. Ran St. Louis-New Orleans, 1844, Capt. Brother. Also ran on the Upper Mississippi and was one of the largest there in 1848. Capt. Henry A. Ealer was pilot on her in the New Orleans trade. She burned and was lost at St. Louis, June 1, 1849.

2642 HIGHLANDER

Stw p wh b. Elizabeth, Pa., 1847. 126 tons. Snagged and lost at Clinton, Ind. (Iowa?), in March 1850.

2643 HIGHLANDER

Stw p wh b. Wheeling, W. Va., 1864. 241 tons. Lost in ice at Johnsonville, Tenn., Dec. 16, 1865.

2644 HILL CITY

SW p wh b. Madison, Ind., 1897. 327 x 44 x 8.5. Engines, 26's- 9 ft. Five boilers. Paddlewheels 33 ft. dia. working 14½ ft. buckets. Built out of the *CITY OF MONROE* (see). Owned by the Anchor Line and ran St. Louis-New Orleans. Went to U.S. Marshal sale Feb. 7, 1898, and bought by Capt. T.B. Sims, St. Louis who continued her in the trade with Jim Grasty and T.B. (Trim) Wadlington, pilots. Sank below Memphis November 1900, raised. In 1903 she was remodeled into an excursion boat and renamed *CORWIN H. SPENCER* (see).

2645 HINDOO

SW p wh b. Brownsville, Pa., 1849. 199 tons. Ran Pittsburgh-St. Louis. Was twice at St. Paul in 1853. Snagged and lost at Ste. Genevieve, Mo., Jan. 28, 1855.

2646 HIRAM B.

Ferry wh b. Wheeling, W. Va., 1875. 50 tons. 76.8 x 17 x 4.4. Still documented 1886 at Cincinnati.

2647 HIRAM POWERS

SW p wh b. Cincinnati, Oh., 1848. 225 tons. Machinery from *BEN FRANKLIN NO. 7* (see). Owned by Capt. Charles G. Pearce and others, Cincinnati. Ran Cincinnati-New Orleans. Hiram Powers, celebrated sculptor, presented "the veteran Capt. Charles Pearce with a flag and a most complimentary letter upon learning this boat was named for him." Capt. Henry A. Jones who later ran the *NICHOLAS LONGWORTH* was associated with this boat. Burned in the Wabash River, Ind., May 7, 1853.

2648 HIRAM WATSON

Stw p wh b. Olean, N.Y., 1871. 25 tons. Rebuilt at Cincinnati 1876 and tonnage increased to 27.40 tons. Then measured 67 x 13 x 2.5. She was the advance advertising boat for the Castello Circus in fall of 1876, and was snagged above Ironton, Oh., that fall, the river very low. She was repaired at the Ashland Dry Dock Co., and then attached for the bill, $800. Sold November 1876 to a Capt. McDonald, Pittsburgh.

2649 HIRAM WOOD

SW p wh b. Wyandotte, Kans., 1865. 100 x 22. Engines, 10¼"-20 stroke. One boiler. Owned by Crockett, Nelson & Wood, Capt. Alex Crockett, master. Snagged at Bijou Hills, Rosebud Landing, S.D., in 1873 on the Missouri River. Capt. Grant Marsh bought the wreck, rebuilt it into a ferryboat, and in October 1877 renamed it *DR. BURLEIGH* (see). This sinking was at or near Yankton, S.D.

2650 HOCK WHITE

Stw p wh 70 x 15. In Oct. 1898 running Keokuk-Burlington in place of *S. R. VANMETRE.* In May 1902 Caruthersville-Booth's Point, Capt. Frank Shepard, who had just bought her. Sank 15 miles below Dyersburg on Forked Deer River; caught fire and burned, January 1903.

2651 HOLSTON

Stw p wh b. Kingston, Tenn., 1864. 89 tons. Built for USQMD, and sold at public sale, April 1866. Owned by John L Doss & Co. Sank at Luna Landing, Ark., in 40 feet, Dec. 10, 1870. She was owned at Muscatine, Iowa, at the time. Passengers and crew had narrow escapes.

2652 HOME

SW p wh b. Cincinnati, Oh., 1855. 183 tons. 150 x 25 x 5. Originally operated at Vicksburg. In 1860 owned at New Orleans by Capt. Gustavus A. Slife. Sold May 1860 to Joshua Fenimore, New Orleans, Capt. M.N. Wood, master. Ran New Orleans-Red River. To Confederate registry 1861.

2653 HOME

SW p wh b. Cincinnati, Oh., 1877. Built for the Parisot Line operating Vicksburg-Yazoo River. News item dated Aug. 12, 1878: "Mel Shannon and John Roberts have bought the little steamer *HOME* and are fitting her up at New Richmond, Oh., for a southern tributary trade."

2654 HOMER

SW p wh b. Louisville, Ky., 1846. 247 tons. Built for Capt. Jos. Swager and others for Louisville-New Orleans trade. She was following *CAR OF COMMERCE* over the Louisville Falls noon Dec. 17, 1848, when the latter hit rocks (see). Captain Swager retired from the river, 56, in 1848. Off the lists 1850.

2655 HOMER

SW p wh b. Parkersburg, Va., 1859. 194 tons. 148 x 28 x 5. Owned by Capt. Samuel Applegate, New Orleans. Ran New Orleans-Red River June 1860 in place of *GRAND DUKE.* In May 1861, Capt. W.W. Withenbury, master, same trade, also 1862. Capt. Levi H. Hopkins was master 1860 in New Orleans-Ouachita River trade, from Mason County, W. Va. He moved to Gallipolis 1884—spent much of his career on the lower Mississippi on boats owned by Capts. Cannon and Tobin. *HOMER* went to Confederate registry 1861.

2656 HOMER

SW p wh b. Evansville, Ind., 1875. 326 tons. En route from Alexandria to Shreveport on Red River snagged Dec. 14, 1876 at 4:00 P.M. in Tucker's Reach. Keeled over and sank with loss of two passengers and two of the crew.

2657 HOMER C. WRIGHT

Stw p wh b. Tuscumbia, Mo., 1920. 86.8 x 18.5 x 3.4. Engines, 7"- 3½ ft. One boiler. Operated on Missouri River. Later did ferry service for Union Electric at St. Louis and then was an extra boat for the New St. Louis & Calhoun Packet Corp. They owned her when she sank at the foot of Rutger Street, St. Louis in August 1927.

2658 HOMER SMITH

Stw ex wh b. Jeffersonville, Ind., by Howard, 1914. 235 x 40 x 5.9. Compound non-condensing engines, 16's, 32's- 8 ft. Five boilers. Built for the Security Steamboat Co., Pt. Pleasant, W. Va., composed of Homer Smith, John Samuel (Sam) Spencer, C.C. Bowyer and others of that place. Ran excursions on the lower Ohio 1915 and briefly tried the Louisville-Cincinnati trade. Ran a Pittsburgh-New Orleans Mardi Gras trip 1916 and then an Easter Cruise Pittsburgh-New Orleans and return. Capt. Peter Holloway was master 1915, and Capt. W.C. Lepper, Jr., in 1916. She settled down to become a regular excursion boat at Pittsburgh, wintering in the mouth of the Kanawha, and running tramp excursions in the spring. At Pittsburgh she ran day trips to Sewickley, Pa., 12 miles down the Ohio, to Walnut Beach, a resort. Capt. Henry Holloway went pilot on her April 1915 and was on her until she was sold 1928. John Douglass was purser, later master. Jack Smith, son of Homer Smith, was purser. Jimmy O'Brien was mate. A rather full story of this boat appears in the December 1969 issue of *S&D Reflector*. She was sold 1928 to Pittsburgh Amusement Co., and renamed *GREATER PITTSBURGH* (see).

2659 HONDURAS

SW p wh b. Brownsville, Pa., 1853. 296 tons. Engines, 18's- 6½ ft. Three boilers. Ran Pittsburgh-St. Louis-Missouri River. Snagged and lost at Hat Island, Chester, Ill., Jan. 25, 1855, then owned by W.W. Conley and others, Capt. M. Conley, master.

2660 HOOSIER

Freight boat wh b. Toledo, Oh., 1863. 60 tons. Probably of canal origin, and was documented at Evansville, Ind., 1876, maybe later.

2661 HOOSIER STATE

SW p wh b. Cincinnati, Oh., 1850. 344 tons. 220 x 30 x 6. Engines, 24½'s- 8 ft. Four boilers, each 42" by 30 ft., two 16" flues. Ran Cincinnati-Madison. Off the lists 1855.

2662 HOPE

Stw p wh b. Elizabeth, Pa., 1849. 32 tons. 80 x 17.3 x 2.3. Ran in the bayous of Louisiana, Capt. Cleophas Gauthreaux, Lafourche Parish. In 1850 Capt. Justinien Cleophas Gauthreaux. Exploded and lost at Laplace, La., Feb. 27, 1850, with loss of five lives.

2663 HOPE

SW p wh b. Louisville, Ky., 1855. 193 tons. 128 x 34 x 5. Engines, 14's- 4½ ft. Originally owned by W.H. Granger, Louisville, Ky., and M.E. Sheres, Allegheny, Pa., equal share. Capt. Thomas Moore, master. Ran New Orleans Red River. In 1856 owned at Shreveport, La. In 1857 owned at New Orleans and Algiers, Capt. Silas McClure. In 1858 Mrs. M.E. Sheres, then residing in St. Tammany Parish, was sole owner, and Capt. Thomas Moore, master. Burned and sunk in Tallahatchie River to prevent U.S. capture, July 24, 1863.

2664 HOPE

SW p wh b. Cincinnati, Oh., 1859. 218 tons. In 1866 Vicksburg-Yazoo River, Capt. Thomas Metzler, with Charles F. Grater, clerk, connecting with *FASHION* and *GEN. QUITMAN* for New Orleans. Snagged and lost in Yazoo River, Nov. 29, 1867.

2665 HOPE

SW p wh b. New Albany, Ind., 1862. 598 tons. Built on hull of the *T. L. McGILL* which had burned off her upper works at St. Louis Oct. 27, 1862. There was a legal snarl about this name change, but seems she operated as *HOPE* in St. Louis-Missouri River trade, and possibly trips to New Orleans through May 1864. Then original name was restored, *T. L. McGILL* (see).

2666 HOPE

Stw p wh b. Murraysville, Va. (hull), and completed at Marietta, Oh., 1868, Capt. Dawes Davis. Soon entered Wheeling-New Matamoras trade, Capt. J.W. Williamson. Had a steam explosion at New Martinsville, W. Va., Jan. 1, 1872, injuring eight. Later went to the Upper Mississippi under charter to Capt. C.M. Cole, Marietta, who was building wing dams there. In latter days towed railroad cross ties from Parkersburg to Pittsburgh, Capt. Jacob Cramer. Following Cramer's death she was sold to the Kanawha River and dismantled 1885, equipment used building towboat *GATE CITY*.

2667 HOPE

Stw p wh b. New Albany, Ind., 1877. 107 x 20 x 3.5. Engines, 10¼'s- 3½ ft. One boiler, 42" by 22 ft. Capts. August Wohlt and William L. Heckman bought her at New Albany, took her to Hermann, Mo., and worked for the MP Railroad towing ties, handling freight. These two men acquired other boats and in 1881 formed the Hermann Ferry & Packet Co. The *HOPE* later was sold to the Memphis area, still there 1892.

2668 HORACE

Stw p-tb wh b. Murraysville, W. Va., 1881. 90 x 18 x 3. Ran in Little Kanawha River to assist *C. C. MARTIN* and others. Documented at Pittsburgh, Pa., 1892.

2669 HORATIO G. WRIGHT

SW snagboat sh b. Carondelet, Mo., 1880. 187 x 62 x 8. Engines, 18's- 6 ft. Four boilers. Built by the Western Iron Boat Building Co., for the U.S. Engineers. She had been under construction over a year when she was launched in June 1880, christened by Miss Katie Constant, niece of Colonel Allen. She was a "snag extractor" on the Mississippi River many years. An excellent model of her is displayed at the Museum of Science and Industry, Chicago. She was sold 1938 to Patton-Tully Transportation Co., Memphis. They dismantled her fall 1941.

2670 HORIZON

Stw p wh b. California, Pa., 1854. Originally named *JOHN C. FREMONT* (see). Renamed Mar. 1, 1861, owned by Capt. Jackman T. Stockdale and J.N. McCurdy. Ran Pittsburgh-Cincinnati, Capt. Richard Calhoon, with T.S. Calhoon, clerk; Joseph Calhoon, steward (nephew of the captain), and William Briggs, engineer (married to Capt. Stockdale's sister). There was a call for a number of Pittsburgh-based boats to go to Cumberland River to relieve sick and wounded soldiers, early 1862, and *HORIZON* was among them. Ran the Vicksburg and Grand Gulf batteries April 1863 with six other transports. She was transporting troops near Grand Gulf May 1, 1863, when she collided with *MODERATOR* at night, both boats running without lights. Many soldiers were lost when *HORIZON* sank.

2671 HORNET

Stw p wh b. West Point, Ky., 1880. 130 x 27 x 5.4. Ran Louisville-Kentucky River. She got in backlash at Lock 1, Kentucky River, 1885, hit cribbing, stove, and sank.

2672 HOUMA

Stw p wh b. New Albany, Ind., 1848. 55 tons. 97 x 26 x 6. Went to Franklin, La. In September 1850, Capt. Daniel R. Faussett, part owner and master. Off the lists 1852.

2673 HOUMA

Stw p wh b. Madisonville, La., 1906. 136 x 23.8 x 4.8. Engines, 9½'s- 3 ft. One boiler, 44" by 20 ft. Built from *OZARK QUEEN* (see). Owned by Bradford Transportation Co. Ran New Orleans, Lower Terrebonne, Sugar Refinery and Houma, and on Bayou Lafourche to Lafourche Crossing. In 1909 Capt. T.W. Cook, with A. Rodriquez, clerk. She escaped a bad windstorm at New Orleans only to be destroyed by fire soon after, September 1926.

2674 HUDSON

Stw p wh b. Glasgow (Smith's Ferry) Pa., 1846. 94 tons. Capt. George W. Ebert, first master. Ran Pittsburgh-Sunfish (Clarington, Oh.) 1847. Pittsburgh-Bridgeport, semi-weekly, 1847–1848. Sold December 1848 to Capt. James McMillan, who ran her Pittsburgh-Hockingport, Oh. In April 1850 loaded aboard California prospectors from Marion and Wayne Counties, Oh., and at Cincinnati they were robbed of their funds, in amount $2,000, "and all started home without a cent, and in no very sentimental mood." Off the lists 1851.

2675 HUDSON

Stw p wh b. Belle Vernon, Pa., 1857. 172 tons. Went to Confederate service 1861.

2676 HUDSON

Stw p wh b. La Crosse, Wis., 1863. 176 tons. Operated on the Upper Mississippi. Off the lists in 1878.

2677 HUDSON

Stw p wh b. Murraysville, W. Va. (hull) and completed at Wheeling, 1875. 200 x 33.6 x 6.2. Engines, 19's- 6 ft. Four boilers. Owned by Parkersburg & Ohio River Transportation Co., Capts. William and Charles List. Ran Wheeling-Cincinnati. When the Lists built the *ST. LAWRENCE* (see) in 1879 the *HUDSON* was sold to Capt. J.N. Williamson, Wash Honshell and others to replace the *W.P. THOMPSON* they had sold to the Reddens at Vanceburg, Ky. She then ran Pittsburgh-Cincinnati, Capt. Phil Anshutz, with pilots Anthony (Tony) Meldahl and Harry Ollom, and first clerk Al Slavin. Later sold to Capt. J. Frank Ellison, Paducah, who ran her with success Paducah-St. Louis, and returned her to Freedom, Pa. in 1885, using parts in construction of his new *HUDSON* (next listing).

2678 HUDSON

Stw p wh b. Freedom, Pa. (hull), and completed at Pittsburgh, 1886. 225 x 37 x 6. Engines, 20's- 6 ft. Four boilers. Overall width 43 ft. Built for Capt. J. Frank Ellison for Paducah-St. Louis trade. Then ran St. Louis-Grafton. Brought back to the upper Ohio for the Pittsburgh-Cincinnati trade c. 1889, Capt. Ellison, master, with Al Slavin, clerk. Later that year Dan Lacey was clerk. Captain Ellison took stock in Pittsburgh & Cincinnati Packet Line and became the superintendent at Cincinnati. Capt. Robert R. Agnew then was master. Went to Memphis fall of 1898 to fill the trade until *KATE ADAMS* (3rd) was completed at Jeffersonville. Her last running in the Pittsburgh-Cincinnati trade was in spring of 1903 while the *QUEEN CITY* went to Mardi Gras. That summer she ran Cincinnati-Memphis with her regular P&C officers except clerks and pilots. Often helped out at Cincinnati taking people to Coney Island. Sank at Cincinnati at 7:30 P.M. June 25, 1904, laid up at the time. Raised and docked. Burned at Cincinnati Feb. 5, 1905, at 9:00 P.M., having been laid up some months. A rather full story of this boat's career with many pictures appears in the *S&D Reflector,* September 1974 issue. She was a handsome, proudly built boat, and many of her virtues were enhanced in building the *VIRGINIA* and *QUEEN CITY.*

2679 HUGH MARTIN

Stw p wh b. Kingston, Tenn., 1870. The cabin was built at Jeffersonville, Ind., and shipped by rail to Kingston. Designed for the Kingston-London trade, Tennessee River. Parts of *CHEROKEE* used. Capt. Hugh Martin built her and soon sold her to Allison Brothers who got her high and dry on a sand bar, then sold her to Capt. Jacob Fritts. On Aug. 14, 1875, she exploded boilers at Washington Landing killing Capt. Fritts and others. The wreckage was visible in the 1920s in low water.

2680 HUMBOLDT

Stw p wh b. Cincinnati, Oh., 1855. 513 tons. Ran out of St. Paul first season. Lost in collision with the *BELFAST* at Island 75, Miss. River, Feb. 21, 1857, with loss of 15 lives.

2681 HUMMINGBIRD

Prop p wh b. Buffalo, N.Y., 1871. 33 tons. 80 x 12 x 4.5. A regular between Gallipolis and Pomeroy Bend, up to Syracuse, Capt. M. Brown, leaving Gallipolis daily except Sunday at 1:00 P.M. In 1878 a replacement was contracted for, and meanwhile *THREE BROTHERS* took the trade temporarily.

2682 HUMMINGBIRD NO. 2

Prop p wh b. Wheeling, W. Va., 1878. 83 x 12 x 6.5. Replaced the original of the name (see above). Machinery was placed at Gallipolis, Oh., August 1878. Capt. M. Brown ran her in the Gallipolis-Syracuse trade. When the big flood crested at Pomeroy, Oh., Feb. 11, 1884, this boat was tied up to the iron railing on the second floor of the Pomeroy Court House. Capt. Charles Chambers bought her from the Brown family, gave her a larger hull in 1889 and renamed her *CHICOT* (see).

2683 HUNGARIAN

SW p wh b. Elizabeth, Pa., 1850. 279 tons. Owned and operated by Capt. Daniel Collier in tramp trades, Cincinnati-St. Louis-New Orleans. Capt. Horace E. Bixby recalled he had his first pilot's job on her. Dismantled 1859 and machinery went to *A. O. TYLER* (see).

2684 HUNTER

Prop p wh b. Louisville, Ky., 1865. 34 tons. 66.5 x 15.5 x 6. First owner, H. Denseaux De La Croix, New Orleans, with Capt. A. Palms, Jr., master. Ran New Orleans and Lower Coast. In 1872 Capt. Charles R. Fagot, master, with Louis Curien, clerk. Snagged and lost, Dec. 15, 1874.

2685 HUNTRESS

Stw p wh b. New Albany, Ind., 1862. 138 tons. 131.6 x 31.2 x 4.1. Engines, 12½'s-4 ft. Taken over by the U.S., June 9, 1964, and converted into a tinclad (#58) retaining same name *HUNTRESS*. Sold at public sale, Mound City, Ill., Aug. 17, 1865, to Sam Black. Snagged and lost at Alexandria, La., Dec. 30, 1865.

2686 HUNTSMAN

Stw p wh b. New Albany, Ind., 1863. 177 tons. Lost in 1869.

2687 HUNTSVILLE

SW p wh b. New Albany, Ind., 1845. 344 tons. 205 x 29 x 6. Owned 1852 by Charles W. Harrison, James Pell, L.H. Flernoy (all of Paducah), George P. Frazer, Jefferson County, Ky., and George Warren, Alabama. Master was Capt. Charles Pell. Snagged and lost at Ste. Genevieve, Mo., Aug. 21, 1854.

2688 HUNTSVILLE

Stw p wh b. New Albany, Ind., 1864. 358 tons. 159 x 33 x 4.5. Engines, 13's- 4 ft. Two boilers, Ran New Orleans-Shreveport, and made a trip to St. Louis 1871. Downbound on Red River 80 miles below Shreveport she broke her tiller line and hit the bank and sank. Had 180 head of cattle, many of them drowned. No life loss, this on Aug. 26, 1873.

2689 HUNTSVILLE NO. 2

SW p wh b. New Albany, Ind., 1853. 898 tons. 261 x 40 x 9. Owned 1854 by Charles W. Harrison and Charles Pell (of Paducah), George P. Frazer, Jefferson County, Ky., George Warren of Texas, and William R. McClure, Tuscumbia, Ala. Arrived New Orleans from Florence, Ala., with 5,201 bales of cotton, 1,365 sacks of corn, and 486 pieces of freight, the largest to that date, eclipsing the cargo of the *AUTOCRAT* from Memphis in 1849. Got to New Orleans on Feb. 18, 1854, Capt. C.W. Harrison. Burned at Hamburg, Tenn., on the Tennessee River with 4,000 bales, Mar. 24, 1855, Capt. Pell.

2690 HURON

Stw p wh b. Christler's Landing, Pa., 1851. 168 tons. Snagged and lost in Atchafalaya River, Feb. 23, 1855.

2691 HURRICANE

Stw p wh b. Pittsburgh, Pa., 1853. 58 tons. Was running Gallipolis-Kanawha River spring 1859. Off the lists 1861.

2692 HY JACOBS

Catamaran ferry wh b. Berwick, La., 1903. 72 x 34.8 x 4.9. Documented at Morgan City, La., 1918.

I

2693 I. C. WOODWARD

SW p wh b. West Brownsville, Pa., at Axton Yard, 1898. 164 x 42 x 5. Engines, 17's- 6 ft. Three boilers, each 38" dia. by 28 ft. Built for Pittsburgh, Brownsville & Geneva Packet Co., which consolidated July 1902 with the "Mason Line" to become the Pittsburgh, Brownsville & Morgantown Packet Co. Her texas was lengthened aft in November 1898. Named for Capt. Isaac C. Woodward who died at Brownsville September 1898. Ran Pittsburgh-Morgantown, twice weekly, 1898-1911. Ran one trip through to Fairmont 1912. Ran excursions at Fairmont, October 1913, sold to New Albany, Ind., converted into an excursion boat, renamed *VIRGINIA* (see).

2694 I. L. LUDLOW

SW ferry wh b. Cincinnati, Oh., 1860. 52 tons. Off the lists 1870.

2695 I. T. RHEA

Stw p wh b. Jeffersonville, Ind., by Howard, 1888. 149.8 x 30.4 x 3.9. Owned by the Ryman Line and operated on the Cumberland River above Nashville. Sank at Butler's Landing, Apr. 27, 1894, with loss of a large shipment of corn. Named for a Nashville grain merchant. During a storm Apr. 6, 1895, she was blown into Brooks Bluff, near Brooks Island. Sank in 30 feet and was lost. Capt. W.S. Bowman commanded at the time. Parts of the *SAM P. JONES* were used in building her, and after her loss the *R. DUNBAR* was built to replace her.

2696 I GO

Stw p wh b. Antiquity, Oh., 1861. 104 tons. Exploded her boiler at Parkersburg, W. Va. 1861, was rebuilt. Burned and lost at Arkansas Post, Ark., June 12, 1864.

2697 IANTHE

Stw p wh b. Guyandotte, W. Va., 1870. 45 tons. Built for the Guyandotte River. Later bought by Capt. John V. Reynolds and ran on the Kanawha, Charleston-Brownstown. Saw service on Coal River, W. Va., 1873. Still documented 1876.

2698 IANTHE

SW p wh b. Stillwater, Minn., 1902. 66.5 x 12.7 x 3.8. Single deck, one stack, and towed an excursion barge. Later renamed *MARY Mc.*

2699 IATAN

SW p wh b. Cincinnati, Oh., 1858. 221 x 33 x 5.9. Engines, 22's- 7 ft. Four boilers. Built for Capt. H.S. Eaton and others for the Missouri River. Ran Mobile-New Orleans, 1865. Cattle trade out of Shreveport, La., Capt. John Hein, owner-master, and Fred Probst, clerk, 1868. Dismantled 1868.

2700 IBERVILLE

SW p wh b. New Albany, Ind., 1859. 368 tons. 179 x 35 x 6.3. Engines, 22's- 7 ft. Four boilers. Built for the Bayou Sara Mail Co., Eugene Lanone, pres., of New Orleans. Capt. V.B. Baranco, first master. Capt. J.J. Brown, master, 1861. She was used by the Confederates in war service, captured by the U.S. and they used her as a transport. Burned at New Orleans, laid up, July 13, 1866. Rebuilt 1867 to become 189.2 x 36.2 x 7.1. Owned and operated by Capt. A.T. Dunbar, New Orleans. Sold March 1867 to J. Morgan Hall, New Orleans with Capt. Emile F. Gross, master. Sold March 1869 to Capt. Samuel J. Seymour, New Orleans. Ran New Orleans-Bayou Sara in her latter days. Off the lists 1869.

2701 IBEX

Stw p wh b. Harmar, Oh., 1863. Originally named *OHIO VALLEY* (see). Sold to U.S. Navy, December 1864 who renamed her *IBEX* (#10). Sold at public sale August 1865 to Capt. William B. Miller who renamed her *HARRY DEAN* (see).

2702 IDA

SW p wh b. Gretna, La., 1860. 77 tons. She was sold to U.S. Navy March 1863. Torpedoed in Blakeley River at Mobile, Ala., Apr. 13, 1865, with loss of three lives.

2703 IDA

Stw p wh b. St. Louis, Mo., 1866. 326 tons. 172.2 x 32.4 x 4.3. Sold November 1870 to Henry Willoughby, New Orleans, with Capt. B.F. Hargass, master. Last inspected at New Orleans in 1875.

2704 IDA

SW ferry wh b. Le Claire, Iowa, 1866. She was originally a horse-operated craft, side-wheel, built by James Gifford, Nauvoo, Ill. Later converted to steam, run by Leo Hudson and a Mr. Gifford. Off the lists 1874.

2705 IDA CAMPBELL

Stw p wh b. Durand, Wis., 1867. 38 tons. Rebuilt at Reads Landing, Minn., 1872, evidently enlarged, 68 tons, this following a fire at Eau Claire, Wis. Inspected at Reads Landing July 1881.

2706 IDA

Rig ? p wh b. Decatur, Ala., 1869. 118 tons. Owned by Capt. J.H. Johnson who owned Half Moon Island on the Tennessee River, and his brother-in-law John H. Jackson. Still registered 1876.

2707 IDA DARRAGH

Rig? p wh b. Madison, Ind., 1882. 443 tons. Owned by Memphis & Arkansas River Packet Co. Ran Memphis-Pine Bluff, Capt. John J. Darragh, with J.N. Thompson, clerk (1882), in 1883 with Amos S. Day, clerk. In 1884 Capt. E.B. Smith, master, with Charles Musselman, clerk. Burned at the Anchor Line wharfboat. Memphis, foot of Union Street, shortly after 3:00 P.M., Feb. 18, 1885. She set fire to *CITY OF HELENA* (see) causing her loss, also destroying the wharfboat built six years prior on the hull of the *CAPITOL CITY* (see).

2708 IDA ELLIS

Stw ferry wh b. Mound City, Ill., 1864. 71 tons. 86 x 20 x 3. Ran Cairo-Mound City. Sold April 1866 to Upper Mississippi, documented at Keokuk, Jonathan Hewirr, master. Out of service 1871.

2709 IDA FULTON

Stw p wh b. Cincinnati, Oh., 1863. 143 tons. Originally named *CONVOY NO. 2* (see) and sold to USQMD January 1864. 145 x 26.2 x 4.5. Engines, 14's- 4½ ft. Two boilers, each 42" dia. by 16 ft. Sold to private owners and renamed January 1867. The Diamond Jo Line operated her on the Upper Mississippi and Monnseota rivers many years. Documentation removed 1884.

2710 IDA HANDY

SW p wh b. Jeffersonville, Ind., by Howard, 1864. 258 x 45 x 8. Owned by Capt. B. Rush Pegram and others, St. Louis-New Orleans. She was flagship for Gen. A.J. Smith when his command was moved from Eastport, Tenn., to New Orleans February 1865. Capt. John T. Moore was master later; he died at Wauban Plantation, La., May 1909. Burned at St. Louis June 2, 1866, along with *BOSTONA* and *JAMES RAYMOND*.

2711 IDA KING

SW p wh b. Alton, Ill., 1865. 71 tons. Off the lists 1867.

2712 IDA LEE

Stw p wh b. Pittsburgh, Pa., 1880. 110 x 22.5 x 3. Engines, 8" bore, 3 ft. stroke, rotary valves. One boiler, 40" dia. by 20 ft. Owned by St. Francis River Transportation Co., Memphis, Capt. Pete McArthur. Sold to James H. Rees, March 1884. She was built by James Rees & Sons Co. In 1886 was in the Evansville area.

2713 IDA LEON

Stw p wh b. Wheeling, W. Va., 1873. 82 tons. Named for Ida Leon Walton, Clarington, Oh., daughter of Capt. James Walton. Caught on the bank and capsized Aug. 26, 1876, at Coushatta, La. on Red River, lost.

2714 IDA MAY

Stw p wh b. Freedom, Pa., and completed at Pittsburgh, 1858. 157 x 32 x 4.8. 220 tons. Capt. John May, Beaver, Pa., original master and owned 6/16. Other owners: William S. Graham, Freedom, Pa., William Hamilton,

Allegheny City, Pa., and C. Preston and Bernard McDonald, Pittsburgh. Ran Pittsburgh-Cincinnati. Composer Stephen C. Foster rode her Pittsburgh-Cincinnati in November 1858, good friend of the clerk, Billy Hamilton. Sold to David Gibson, Cincinnati, December 1862. Acquired by USQMD in November 1863, and sold December 1865 to James H. Peters, New Orleans, and transferred several days later to Augusta Richards. Sank in Red River c. Dec. 28, 1865.

2715 IDA MAY

Ferry wh b. Grafton, Ill., 1875. 65 tons. 100 x 28 x 3.6. Operated at Muscatine, Iowa. Still listed 1886.

2716 IDA PICKENS

Prop p wh b. Middleport, Oh., 1876. 30 x 8 x 4. Named for youngest sister of Capt. Cornelius Pickens, who owned the boat. He operated it on Coal River, W. Va. Still documented in 1886.

2717 IDA REES

Stw p wh b. Elizabeth, Pa., 1863. 156 x 30 (29 ft. floor) x 4.5. Engines, 13's- 5 ft. Two boilers, each 40" dia. by 20 ft., five flues. Had four rudders. Owned by Thomas M. and James H. Rees, Pittsburgh, and Capt. Ezekiel Gordon, master. Capt. Rees Rees was master later in the Pittsburgh-Oil City, Pa., trade on Allegheny River. In November 1865 took 2,700 brls. oil Pittsburgh to St. Louis for W.P. Logan, Pittsburgh, said to have been the first all oil cargo out of Pittsburgh. Ran Pittsburgh-Cincinnati 1866–1867, Capt. Joe Brown. Spring of 1868 made a trip to Fort Benton, Mont., under management of James Rees. That fall she was taken to Galveston, Tex., and ran on the Sabine River, Capt. Thomas Stubblefield. He was murdered in 1870, and Judge John T. Smith went master. Sank and was lost Feb. 28, 1873, en route out of the Sabine to New Orleans with 500 bales.

2718 IDA REES NO. 2

Stw p wh b. Pittsburgh, Pa., 1865, hull by William Latta. 180 x 30. Engines, 18's- 5 ft. Three boilers. Owned by Thomas M. and James H. Rees. Operated Pittsburgh-Oil City, Pa., on Allegheny River. Arrived at Pittsburgh from Oil City on May 24, 1868, and quit the trade, the last of the Oil City packets. Captain Rees Rees commanded, and Henry C. Frye and Jacob Magee were the pilots. During the summer of 1868 ran Pittsburgh-Brownsville-Geneva on the Monongahela. That fall she made a round trip Pittsburgh-Memphis, Capt. G.W. Albert, with James H. Rees, clerk. Spring of 1869 lengthened 20 feet and departed for Fort Benton, Mont., Capt. Thompson. Sold to Durfee & Peck, and continued on the Missouri. Sank and was lost near mouth of White River, 23 miles below Chamberlain, S.D., June 20, 1871, loaded with furs and buffalo robes, some of which were salvaged.

2719 IDA SMITH

Stw p wh b. Parkersburg, W. Va., 1884. 111.6 x 17.9 x 2.6. Ran Raven Rock, W. Va.-Marietta, Capt. Brady Morgan, with William E. Roe, clerk. Ran Marietta-New Matamoras in low water 1887 connecting with *SAWYER* for Wheeling. Ran various short trades. In 1896 was running Charleston-Pomeroy, owned by Charles Small, Gallipolis, father of Mrs. O.O. McIntyre. Burned at Letart, Oh., about 1902, then owned by Ralph Emerson Gaches.

2720 IDA STOCKDALE

Stw p wh b. McKeesport, Pa. (hull), and completed at Pittsburgh, 1867. Engines, 14's- 4½ ft. Two boilers, each 42" dia. by 24 ft. Built for Capt. Jackman T. Stockdale, Allegheny, Pa., and named for his daughter Ida who later married Homer S. Knowles, potter of East Liverpool, Oh. First trip from Pittsburgh was to Fort Benton, Mont., Capt. Grant Marsh in charge, and Thomas S. Calhoon, clerk. That first season she took Gen. Alfred H. Terry and his staff to Fort Benton. Captain Marsh was on her several seasons on the Missouri, and in one five-month period she cleared $42,500, twice her value. In all she made six trips to Fort Benton. Sunk by ice at Bismarck, S.D., in April 1871, then owned by J. Wesley Jacobs.

2721 IDA STOCKTON

Stw p wh b. Osage City, Mo., 1876. 64 tons. 103 x 20.8 x 3.6. In 1886 documented at Pensacola, Fla.

2722 IDAHO

SW p wh b. Melrose, Wis., 1862. 99.4 x 17 x 3.4. Dispatch dated Apr. 26, 1864: The *IDAHO* recently sunk by a gunboat near Paducah is a little craft from the Upper Mississippi. She was enrolled at New Orleans in October 1865, then owned by Charles Newcome, New Orleans. Exploded and lost at New Orleans, Nov. 26, 1867.

2723 IDAHOE

Stw p wh b. Cincinnati, Oh., 1863. 153.7 x 33.5 x 4.9. Her original builders were Capt. J.N. Newcomb, John Swasey, and David Gibson. She was chartered to the U.S. for hauling army supplies to Nashville. General Rosecrans issued an order banishing whores from Nashville, thereupon many boarded the *IDAHOE* and were taken to Louisville, Ky. Not permitted to land there, the boat continued to Cincinnati and anchored a short distance above town. The reception in Cincinnati was decidedly cool, so Capt. Newcomb returned his charges to Nashville. By 1866 she was running New Orleans-Ouachita River, Capt. Eugene Elliott, with William B. Clarke, clerk. In May 1867 Robert A. Blanks of Caldwell Parish acquired ⅓ ownership and Capt. F.A. Blanks went master. Capt. J.W. Blanks was master 1868. Sank and lost in the Ouachita River, Jan. 10, 1869, at Columbia, La.

2724 IDEAL

Stw p wh b. Clinton, Iowa, 1905. 70 x 16 x 3.5. Originally named *H.L.* (see). Ran excursions along the Upper Mississippi, towing an excursion barge named *ALICE*. In

1917 owned by F.J. Fugina, Winona, Minn. Still documented in 1918.

2725 IDEAL

Stw p wh b. Hermann, Mo., 1906. 53.5 x 10.1 x 2.3. Owned by the Heckmann family, Hermann, Mo., who also ran the *KINGFISHER* and others. Still listed in 1918.

2726 IDLEWILD

SW p wh b. Jeffersonville, Ind., by Howard, 1870. 216 x 35.6 x 6.4. Engines, 22's- 6½ ft. Four boilers, each 38" dia. by 26 ft. Paddlewheels 28 ft. dia. working 12 ft. buckets. Capt. Augustus (Gus) Fowler was master of the Cairo-Paducah-Evansville trade. Named for the home of poet N.P. Willis overlooking the Hudson River. Took pilots out to the *ROB'T E. LEE* and put them aboard at Island 1, below Cairo, during the celebrated race with *NATCHEZ.* Ran a celebrated "speed trial" from Cairo to Evansville later March 1871 and went up in 15 hours 29 minutes, 179.8 miles. Capt. Gus Fowler was master; Wash Phillips and John Newman, pilots; John and Silas Moore, engineers. Sold to the Evansville, Cairo & Memphis Steam Packet Co., July 1872 for $65,000. "She was a beautiful clipper of faultless proportions, proud and jaunty appearance, and as speedy as she was handsome. This boat paid for herself in just two years, and then was sold for just what she cost . . . ." Her last owner was Memphis & Arkansas City Packet Co., and Capt. G.J. (Jack) Grammar long commanded. On Feb. 13, 1876, below Friar's Point, Miss. she knocked out both cylinder heads on one engine when her starboard shaft broke. A tornado whipped across, sinking the *CITY OF QUINCY* nearby. The *IDLEWILD,* in her disabled condition, came alongside and removed the passengers. The *IDLEWILD* and *OSCEOLA BELLE* burned at Memphis on July 31, 1881, at which time the *DEAN ADAMS* took her place in the Memphis-Arkansas City trade. The owning company at time of loss was divided between Major John D. Adams, James H. Rees, Capt. Mark R. Cheek, and A.L. Cummins.

2727 IDLEWILD

Stw p wh b. Cincinnati, Oh., 1879. 200.6 x 35 x 5.5. Originally named *ARIADNE* (see) and ran Cincinnati-Tennessee River. In 1880 was running Evansville-Paducah. Bought by the T.J. Moss Tie Co., and ran St. Louis-Cape Girardeau until she sank at Kimmswick, Mo., c. 1893. The tie company then bought *CITY OF NEW ALBANY* and changed her name to *NEW IDLEWILD* for the trade (see).

2728 IDLEWILD

Stw p-ex sh b. Pittsburgh, Pa., by James Rees & Sons Co., 1914. 157.5 x 36 x 5. Rees engines, 16's- 6½ ft. Three boilers. Built for the West Memphis Packet Co. and departed Pittsburgh on Saturday, Jan. 9, 1915, on her trip to Memphis. She served variously as packet, excursion boat, and ferry. Sold to the New St. Louis & Calhoun County Packet Co., Hardin, Ill., in February 1928. They sold her in April 1947 to J. Herod Gorsage, Peoria, Ill., who renamed her *AVALON* (see) in February 1948.

2729 IDONA

Centerwheel ferry wh b. Cape Girardeau, Mo., 1866. 32 tons. Off the lists 1877.

2730 IKE BONHAM

Stw p wh b. Mason City, W. Va., 1878. 93.4 x 18 x 3.6. Built at the Mees Yard, above the city wharf, for Capt. W.H. Sargent. Ran on Kanawha River 1879. Captain Sargent then took her to Yazoo River. On Mar. 11, 1886, her boiler exploded on the Mississippi 11 miles below Vicksburg with life loss. Captain Sargent was not aboard, but Mrs. Sargent kept a cool head, helped extinguish a resulting fire and aided with the rescue work (see *S&D Reflector,* March 19, 1978, page 5). Sank in the Yazoo River and lost 1893. On occasion she had run excursions, New Orleans-Grand Isle.

2731 ILLINO

Stw ferry wh b. Rock Island, Ill., 1891. Originally named *CANTONIA* (see). Later renamed *ILLINO.*

2732 ILLINOIS

Centerwheel ferry wh b. St. Louis, Mo., 1843 with a double hull. 137 tons. 130 x 30 x 4.5. Built for James Harrison, and in second year owned by Estate of Andrew Christy, Adam L. Mills, Charles Mullikens, J.H. Gay, and Bernard Pratt. Operated at St. Louis, and later was owned by Capt. William C. Wiggins, founder of the Wiggins Ferry Co., at that city. Converted into a wharfboat 1854.

2733 ILLINOIS

SW p wh b. St. Louis, Mo., 1847. 579 tons. Burned in the wharf fire at New Orleans, Oct. 9, 1849, along with *FALCON, NORTH AMERICA, MARSHALL NEY,* and *AARON HART.*

2734 ILLINOIS

SW p wh b. Brownsville, Pa., 1852. 278.5 x 37 x 6.9. 682 tons. Built at the Pringle Yard and was the largest side-wheeler ever built at Brownsville. Owned by James Holmes, Redmund J. Grace, William B. Holmes, J.A. Hutchison, R.S. Hayes, and Capt. D.Y. Smithers, all of Pittsburgh. Ran briefly Pittsburgh-Cincinnati, then in the "Railroad Line" Cairo-New Orleans, Capt. John W. Carroll. She was dismantled at Mound City, Ill., in the early part of the war.

2735 ILLINOIS

Stw p wh b. Sardis, Oh., 1865, 190 x 38 x 6. Engines, 19's- 7 ft. Three boilers, each 42" by 20 ft. Capt. John A. Bruner ran her on the Tennessee River 1867. Bought by the Peoria Packet Co., for the St. Louis-Peoria trade. In 1873 Capt. W.A. Lowth, master; R.M. Ford and James Emerson, clerks. In December 1871 she loaded out at St. Louis for Ouachita River, ran aground at Platin Rock, above Crystal City, Mo., and had to be docked at St. Louis. Dismantled 1874.

2736 ILLINOIS

SW p wh b. Cincinnati, Oh., 1871. 726 tons. First ran Cairo-Columbus in the railroad transfer trade succeeding the *ARLINGTON* (see). Sold at U.S. marshal sale at Memphis January 1877 to Capt. John J. Darragh and others, and had been in the Memphis-Vicksburg trade the year prior. Ran at times in the Anchor Line, Capt. John Molloy, master. Later tried the St. Louis-Keokuk trade. Dismantled c. 1881.

2737 ILLINOIS

Stw p wh b. Dubuque, Iowa, 1888. Originally named *REINDEER* (see) of Illinois State Fish Commission. She was condemned in 1901, and rebuilt at Quincy, Ill., renamed. Hull measured 139 x 26.6 x 4.8. Engines, 12's- 6½ ft. Two boilers. The fish commission operated her until 1913 when Governor Dunn ordered her detached on the grounds that certain convivial politicians and their no less convivial ladies had abused the uses for which the boat had been intended. She was turned over to the Alton Division of the Naval Reserves. In 1925 was owned by the New St. Louis & Calhoun Packet Co., who used her both as packet and towboat. In 1929 sold to Phillips Bros. and on Sept. 30, 1930, she burned in mid-river above the mouth of Wood River, Alton, Ill. There was rumor she had been in use as a distillery with a moonshine still aboard, and had been cut adrift when the Federals were about to arrive.

2738 ILLINOIS BELLE

Stw p wh b. McKeesport, Pa., 1854. 148 tons. 144 x 28 x 3.9. Went to Mobile, Ala., spring of 1855 owned by Jesse Cox and James Brainard. Capt. James Bragdon took her there. Off the lists in 1859.

2739 ILLINOIS NO. 2

Centerwheel ferry wh b. New Albany, Ind., 1860. 255 tons. Operated at St. Louis by the Wiggins Ferry Co. Out of service 1865.

2740 ILLMO

Stw p wh b. Hermann, Mo., 1904. Originally named *W. L. HECKMANN* (see). Still listed on the Missouri River 1918.

2741 IMPERIAL

SW p wh b. Jeffersonville, Ind., 1858. 907 tons. Built for Capt. E.W. Gould and ran St. Louis-New Orleans. Was at the scene of the *PENNSYLVANIA* explosion (see) June 13, 1858, at Ship Island. In the "Railroad Line 1859-1861 with Capt. C.S. Rogers, master. Used as a U.S. hospital boat on the Tennessee River. Burned and lost at St. Louis, Sept. 13, 1863, along with *POST BOY, JESSE K. BELL,* and the *HIAWATHA*.

2742 IMPERIAL

Stw p wh b. Cincinnati, Oh., 1863. 286 tons. Engines, 15½'s- 4½ ft. Three boilers. Was in St. Louis-Nashville trade, spring 1865. She made at least one trip to Fort Benton, Mont., fall 1867. Was caught by low water on the return and her spars were set 132 times out to St. Joseph, requiring eight weeks. Lost in ice at Bonhomme Island, 20 miles above Yankton, S.D., that winter. Owned at the time by David White, W.S. Harper, and A.S. Rowland, with Capt. McComas, master.

2743 IMPERIAL

Stw p wh b. Cincinnati, Oh., 1864. Originally named *ALLEN COLLIER* (see) and in war service as *COLLIER* (see). Sold to private owners and name changed to *IMPERIAL* Sept. 22, 1865. Confusion exists regarding this boat, and the Missouri River trip ascribed to *IMPERIAL* in previous listing may have been this boat, as well as demise. Granted this is so, the fate of the St. Louis-Nashville *IMPERIAL* may have been at Nashville, Mar. 8, 1865, when she hit a pier of the bridge there and sank.

2744 IMPERIAL

Stw p wh b. Jeffersonville, Ind., by Howard, 1894. 210 x 40.6 x 6.6. Engines, 18's- 7 ft. Three boilers. Paddlewheels 22 ft. dia. working 28 ft. buckets. She was a cotton carrier built for the Scovells (W.T., Matt and Noah) to bring cotton out of Red River to New Orleans. The Mississippi Packet Co. acquired her, J.B. Woods, pres. and gen. mgr., and ran her New Orleans-Bayou Sara. Her master in 1902 was Capt. John M. Burgoyne. She ran in the cotton season and often was retired in the summer months, the *ST. JAMES* (see) handling the trade. Made a Mardi Gras trip from Monroe, La., to New Orleans in Feb. 1911, and was laid up some 16 months when she sank from swells of passing tugs June 16, 1912, and burned the next day. She had equipment from the *DACOTAH* which was dismantled at Jeffersonville same time she was built.

2745 IMPORTER

Stw p wh b. California, Pa., at Craft & Lambert Yard, 1866. 150 x 33 (32 ft. floor) x 5. Rees engines, 16's- 5 ft. Three boilers, each 38" by 26 ft. Owned by James Rees and Capt. John Noss. Ran Cincinnati-Memphis, and Pittsburgh-St. Louis, Capt. John Noss. Sold at a public sale at Pittsburgh, Mar. 18, 1868, and was bid in by James Rees. She loaded for Fort Benton, Mont., Capt. John A. Williams, and when she returned to St. Louis in mid-July she was docked and lengthened to measure 183.9 x 33.4 x 4.8. Her boiler deck was extended, and she was given cotton guards, designed for the Arkansas River-New Orleans trade. In 1870 she was largely owned by James H. Pues, New Orleans, Capt. John A. Williams, master. She sank Mar. 12, 1872, 140 miles above Little Rock, Ark.

2746 INDEPENDENCE

SW p wh b. Jefferson City (now New Orleans) 1863. 42 tons. 75 x 17 x 3. Owned by Capt. John Henry, New Orleans. Ran Shreveport-Carolina Bluffs 1867-1868 connecting with the *BART ABLE* for New Orleans. Retired 1869.

2747 INDEPENDENCE CITY

SW p wh b. Cincinnati, Oh., 1857. 68 tons. First home port, St. Louis. Off the lists in 1859.

2748 INDEPENDENT

Rig? p wh b. Ashland, Ky., 1884. Originally named *LIGHTWOOD* (see). Not listed 1895.

2749 INDIA GIVENS

Stw p wh b. Evansville, Ind., 1900. 161 x 29 x 4.6. Engines, 11's- 4½ ft. Two boilers, each 36" by 18 ft. Built from the *P.D. STAGGS* (see). Operating out of St. Louis by Calhoun Transportation Co., 1901. Owned 1906 at St. Louis by H.W. Sebastian. Burned at Hickman, Ky., Jan. 27, 1907.

2750 INDIAN

Stw p wh b. Shousetown, Pa., 1857. 112 tons. 139 x 24.5 x 3.5. Operating New Orleans to Tensas and Bayou Macon, Capt. R. Greenlee, in April 1860. Sold June 1860 to Apalachiocola, Fla., Capt. Andrew W. Wing and others. Went to Confederate registry 1861.

2751 INDIAN NO. 2

Stw wh b. Monongahela, Pa., 1859. 146 tons. 135 x 28 x 4.1. In 1860 running New Orleans to Tensas and Bayou Macon, Capt. L.S. Greenlee. Owned 1860 by Charles W. Greenlee, Allegheny, Pa., and Hugh Slicer, New Orleans, equal shares. Sold March 1862 to E.H. Skaggs, St. Mary Parish, and Capt. Jesse Johnson. Was marooned in upper Red River during the war. Rebuilt into a side-wheeler 1865 by E.H. Skaggs and sold January 1866 to Galveston, Tex., owned by Capt. Byrd M. Grace. Off the lists 1871.

2752 INDIANA

SW p wh b. Cincinnati, Oh., 1850. 369 tons. Off the lists 1857.

2753 INDIANA

SW p wh b. Madison, Ind., 1864. 260 x 44 x 7.5. Engines, 25's- 8 ft. Five boilers, each 40" by 26 ft., two flues. 1,527 tons. Came out in Louisville-New Orleans trade, Capt. R.E. Neal. Capt. J. Stut Neal also commanded, then built the *RICHMOND* (see) in 1867. She was acquired by the Cincinnati & New Orleans Packet Co., George W. Neare, Sr., president, and Capt. W.J. Rusk, master. Rebuilt at Madison in summer of 1874. Sank and lost near Chicot Landing above Arkansas City, Ark., Sept. 7, 1875, and Choctaw Bar built up on the wreckage.

2754 INDIANA

SW p wh b. Jeffersonville, Ind., by Howard, 1900. 285 x 45 x 6. Engines, 25's- 8 ft. from the *BOSTONA* (see). Five boilers, each 42" by 26 ft., two flues. Built for the Louisville & Cincinnati Packet Co. Drew 30" light, and ran Louisville-Cincinnati during low water periods, usually in place of the *CITY OF LOUISVILLE* (see). Her roof bell came from the *TELEGRAPH NO. 3*, and in her early years she carried the whistle from the *MINNIE BAY*. Later she got the *BONANZA's* whistle. She never was below Louisville, and in spring of 1901 ran Cincinnati-Pomeroy. Burned partially at the foot of Main Street, Cincinnati, May 1, 1916. She was taken to the Howard Yard, Jeffersonville, and rebuilt, renamed *AMERICA* (see).

2755 INDIANOLA

Stw p wh b. Freedom, Pa., at the Graham Yard, 1859. 146 tons. 125 x 27.4 x 4.7. Went to New Orleans and ran to Bayou Macon, Capt. James Ransom. Ransom owned stock, as did Thomas Rees, Abner Martin, Horace Beeson, and Lewis Danah, all from the upper Ohio. Her clerks included Beeson, Allen Stockdale, and John H. Stockdale. Sold September 1860 to G.L. Kouns & Bros., New Orleans, and transferred same day to Red River Packet Co., Isaac H. Kouns, master. Snagged and lost 20 miles below Warrenton, Miss., Feb. 24, 1863.

2756 INDIANOLA

SW gunboat wh b. Cincinnati, Oh., 1862. 175 x 52.3 x 7.7. Engines, 24's- 6 ft. Five boilers, each 40" by 26 ft., five flues. She also had two propellers. Two 11" guns forward and two 9" guns aft. Bound up the Mississippi on the night of Feb. 24–25, 1863, she was overtaken by Rebels gunboats above Grand Gulf. Quite an engagment resulted and, in sinking condition, she was surrendered. The Rebels towed her to the eastern shore where she settled. She lay there about a year and finally was recovered by the U.S. and taken to Mound City, Ill., but not repaired. Sold Nov. 29, 1865, to one J. Riley for $8,000, and was broken up for her scrap.

2757 INDIANOLA

Prop canalboat wh b. Nelsonville, Oh., 1866. 65 tons. Conversion to steam probably was made at Chillicothe, Oh., in 1867. In 1873–1874 she made occasional trips between Marietta and Zanesville on the Muskingum River, Capt. James Helmick. Off the lists 1883.

2758 INDUSTRY

SW p wh b. Newport, Ky. (hull), and completed at Cincinnati, 1848. 122 tons. Designed as a Nashville packet. Off the lists 1853.

2759 INGOMAR

SW p wh b. Louisville, Ky., 1854. 730 tons. 275 x 40 x 7.5. Engines, 28's- 7 ft. Built for the Memphis & New Orleans Packet Co. In 1855, Capt. L. McDonough with H.R. McLauglin, clerk; in 1857–1858, Capt. Burdett Paras; in 1860–1861, Capt. Joe D. Clarke who joined up with the Confederates and came through unscathed in 1865. Dismantled at New Orleans 1862 and her engines went to Confederate gunboat *LOUISIANA*.

2760 INGOMAR

Stw p wh b. Wheeling, Va., 1858. 133 x 23 x 4. Machinery from *AURILLA WOOD* (see). She enrolled at St. Louis 1865 and that October was sold to Capt. P.E. Burke, New Iberia, La., and others. Sank and lost in Bayou Plaquemine Aug. 10, 1867.

2761 INGOMAR

SW p wh b. Chattanooga, Tenn., 1864. Originally U.S. gunboat *GENERAL THOMAS.* Sold at war's conclusion to Capts. Fred Kimpel, Steve Thompson, and others who made her over into a packet and ran her Pittsburgh-New Matamoras, Oh., two rounds a week. Sam Glover was clerk. She ran onto a sunken barge at Tomlinson's Run (below Clusters Islands) evening of Mar. 24, 1868, and sank. Upbound at the time. The *GREY EAGLE* took her passengers and *JAMES GILMORE* took off the freight. Raised. She was sold to D.T. Lane, Pittsburgh, and on her way up, Dec. 31, 1868, hit a snag four miles above Wheeling and sank. Mr. Lane took off the machinery and later used it on the towboat *D. T. LANE.*

2762 INGOMAR

Stw p wh b. Harmar, Oh., at the Knox Yard, 1883. 110 x 19 x 3. Built for Capt. Brady Morgan and others and ran local trades in the Wheeling-Parkersburg area. One summer ran Cincinnati-New Richmond, Capt. Mace Agnew with Jim Rowley, Jr., pilot, in opposition with the *T.D. DALE.* Also ran on Big Sandy River with Paintsville, Ky. owners. Name was changed to *JOLLY BROS.,* on Mar. 3, 1891, and thenceforth she was a towboat.

2763 INTERCHANGE

Stw p wh b. Wheeling, Va., 1854. 251 tons. Snagged and lost at Newport, Ark., October 1860.

2764 IONIAN

Stw p wh b. Wheeling, Va., 1850. 167 tons. Off the lists 1855.

2765 IOWA

SW p wh b. St. Louis, Mo., 1848. 454 tons. 220 x 35 x 7. Owned by American Fur Co., and ran on Missouri River. Also made frequent trips St. Louis-New Orleans. Cut down by ice at Marietta, Oh., Mar. 17, 1856.

2766 IOWA

Stw p wh b. Freedom, Pa., 1855. 265 tons. Built for Capt. William A. Moore and others. Ran Pittsburgh-New Orleans; also Pittsburgh-St. Louis. Dan Moore, clerk. Came in collision with *MADISON* (see) at Aurora, Ind., Jan. 3, 1859, resulting in loss of *MADISON.* In December 1862 took Illinois 131st Infantry to Memphis, thence to Miliken's Bend, and to Haines Bluff on the Yazoo. Ended her career in U.S. war service.

2767 IOWA

SW ferry wh b. Savanna, Ill., 1865. 73 tons. 126 x 20 x 3.7. Documented until 1899.

2768 IRENE

Stw p wh b. Elizabeth, Pa., 1850. 124 tons. Built for Capt. G.L. McClintock and others. Snagged at Moscow, Oh., February 1851, raised. Hit another snag Feb. 9, 1857, near Portsmouth, Oh., and was lost.

2769 IRENE

SW p wh b. Cincinnati, Oh., 1858. 158 tons. Snagged and lost on Arkansas River near Little Rock at Sawmill Bend (since called Irene Bend) on Sept. 24, 1859, Capt. John D. Adams.

2770 IRENE

Stw p wh b. Louisville, Ky., 1864. 211 tons. 155.9 x 31.8 x 4.6. Running New Orleans-Opelousas, Capt. O. Hinckley with M. Kenison, clerk, 1866. In February 1867 sold to A. Placio, New Orleans, and William Underwood and John Clark Mitchell, Louisville, who ran her New Orleans-Ouachita River, Capt. H.C. Heath. In 1868 running New Orleans-Red River, Capt. William Underwood, later Capt. John T. Roots. Lost on Red River 20 miles below Shreveport, Nov. 10, 1868.

2771 IRENE

Centerwheel f wh b. Wellsville, Oh., 1867. 117 tons. A double-end ferry used at Omaha, Neb. Lost there in an ice gorge February 22, 1877.

2772 IRENE

Rig? ferry wh b. Metropolis, Ill., 1880. 85 x 24.2 x 4.6. Inspected at Baton Rouge, La., in 1882. Documented 1886, perhaps later.

2773 IRIS

SW p wh b. Rising Sun, Ind., 1852. 86 tons. 115 x 20 x 4. Capt. J.J. Kercheval took her to New Orleans in 1853, selling her to Capt. James T. Cooksey. Sold March 1854 to Capt. Marion N. Wood of Catahoula Parish who ran her New Orleans-Shreveport. Off the lists 1856.

2774 IRMA

Stw p wh b. Little Rock, Ark., 1896. 104 x 24.7 x 2.8. Operated out of Little Rock in Arkansas River short trades. Capt. Dave Chapman, master, 1900.

2775 IRON CITY

Stw p wh b. Pittsburgh, Pa., 1844. 118 tons. Ran most of her career in the St. Louis-Galena trade, Capt. J.C. Ainsworth. She left St. Louis for Beardstown, Ill., on Dec. 31, 1848, and was crushed by ice, sinking within two feet of the hurricane deck. Five lives lost including the steward and cook. Owned at the time by M. Rodgers, Quincy, Ill.

2776 IRON CITY

Stw p wh b. Pittsburgh, Pa., 1864. 150.3 x 28.6 x 3.9. 190 tons. Owned by Capt. John Noss and others. Ran Pittsburgh-Cincinnati, Noss, master, with James L. McCleery, clerk. Entered Pittsburgh-Parkersburg trade April 1865, same officers. A texas was added early that spring. Made a trip to St. Louis that August, and Noss sold her to Mepham & Bros., of that city. Made trips to Arkansas River, Capt. E.A. Sheble, with Bird and Sheble, clerks. Sank four miles below Alexandria, La., on Red River, Feb. 3, 1868, Capt. John Root, and lost.

2777 Iron King

Stw p wh b. Parkersburg, W. Va., 1875. 8.6 tons. Owned by J.R., J.F. and J.K. King. Small single decker in Ohio River short trades a year or so, then used as a towboat. Still documented 1886 at Wheeling.

2778 Iron Queen

Stw p wh b. Harmar, Oh., at Knox Yard, 1892. 237.5 x 37.7 x 6. Engines, 18's- 7 ft. Built for the Pittsburgh & Cincinnati Packet Line. Original crew: Capt. John M. Phillips, master; Robert H. Kerr, purser; Al Voegtly and Gus C. McCullough, clerks; E. Dayton Randolph and William H. Clark, pilots; Al Pennywitt and John Heatherington, mates; Ash Ruth and Kelly Flesher, engineers; Park Allen, carpenter; C.W. Pusey and Harry DeHart, stewards, and Noah P. Pharris, watchman. The Chicago World's Fair attracted many passengers the first season, with river-rail tickets issued. She was landing at Powhatan Point, Oh., 1:00 A.M. July 17, 1892, downbound, hit an obstruction and sank. The *H. K. BEDFORD* brought a pump, the break was battened, and she was floated within hours. Many of the passengers did not know she had been sunk until breakfast time. She landed at Antiquity, Oh., upbound on Apr. 3, 1895 to load hoop-poles. A rouster carrying a bundle of these swung his load and knocked over a lantern setting fire to flammable freight. Breakfast was being prepared in the cabin, and all passengers and crew escaped ashore safely. Mattie Mosby, chambermaid, when told that she must ride the B&O to Parkersburg, remembered she had no hat on, panicked, ran back aboard to get it, and was trapped. She jumped into the river and was drowned. The boat was three years old to the day when she burned. The wreckage was visible in low water late as 1909. A contract was let immediately afterward to build the *VIRGINIA* as a replacement.

2779 Ironton

SW p wh b. Cincinnati, Oh., 1850. 189 tons. 157 x 26 x 5.7. Engines, 24's- 7 ft. Three boilers. Engines from *NORTHERN LIGHT*. In early May 1850 she had loaded lumber at a landing above Vanceburg, Ky., was leaving, and a steam explosion aboard killed three. Snagged and lost at Washington, Mo., Dec. 24, 1854.

2780 Ironton

Recess wheel ferry wh b. Levanna, Oh., 1895. 90.8 x 27 x 3.9. Engines, 10's- 3 ft. One boiler 42″ by 17 ft. Owned by C&O Railroad and operated at Ironton, Oh. Sold August 1910 to P.Q. Shrake, Kenova, W. Va., entirely rebuilt. Sold October 1910 to Charles W. True, New Matamoras, Oh. Sold September 1911 to Bellaire, Benwood & Wheeling Ferry Co., R.M. Gilleland, president. Badly damaged by fire at Moundsville, W. Va., November 1923. Rebuilt and renamed *RUTH ANN* (see).

2781 Ironton

Recess wheel ferry wh b. Pt. Pleasant, W. Va., 1909. 90 x 28 x 3.7. Engines, 10″- 3 ft. One boiler. Owned by C&O Railroad and used at Ironton, Oh. Sank in ice at Ironton on Jan. 28, 1918, raised. Later sold to Fullerton-Portsmouth Ferry Co., and ran that run for many years, still listed 1935.

2782 Iroquois

SW p wh b. New Albany, Ind., 1847. 485 tons. 230 x 30 x 7.8. Ran Louisville-New Orleans, Capt. George C. Taylor. Sold October 1850 to Robinson Yeatman and John Yeatman, New Orleans, Capt. J.B. Weymouth, master. Capt. James Lee, master in 1851. Apparently ran Nashville-New Orleans in latter years. Capt. Charles P. Peterson was last master. Off the lists in 1856.

2783 Isaac Bowman

SW ferry wh b. Jeffersonville, Ind., by Howard, 1860. 152.6 x 39.6 x 5.6. 243 tons. Operated Louisville-Jeffersonville. Sold August 1870 to Crescent Ferryboat Co., New Orleans, Capt. W.W. Freeman. Off the lists 1874.

2784 Isaac M. Mason

Stw p wh b. Brownsville, Pa., at Andrew Axton & Son Yard, 1893. 122 x 22 x 4. Engines, 11's- 5 ft. 114 tons. Built for the Mason Line and ran Belle Vernon-Morgantown on the Monongahela River, Capt. John G. Britton. She carried the U.S. Rivers and Harbors Committee from Point Marion, Pa., to Pittsburgh Mar. 20, 1896, and next day they continued to Parkersburg on the *VIRGINIA*. The Mason Line folded, and she had several owners on Monon River, lastly W.C. McCune, Dravosburg, Pa. Sold in fall of 1906 to Capt. Thomas F. McCleary who used her as a towboat. Burned at Cooks Ferry, Pa., on the Ohio River, Mar. 4, 1913, in early morning hours, having been laid up about two weeks.

2785 Isaac Newton

SW p wh b. Elizabeth, Pa., 1847. 241 tons. 174 x 26.5 x 5.8. Owned by Alex and W.K. Nimick, and C.F. Isreal. Named for Sir Isaac Newton who numbered the stars and died winding his watch. Lincoln's Secretary of War Edwin M. Stanton got his perpetual limp after falling down a hatch aboard this boat at Pittsburgh. Ran Pittsburgh-Cincinnati, later to St. Louis. Dismantled in 1852.

2786 Isaac Shelby

SW p wh b. Cincinnati, Oh., 1844. 158 tons. Ran Cincinnati-Kentucky River, round trip a week, Capt. J.T. Washington, later Capt. J. Wesley Brown. Out of service 1852.

2787 Isaac Shelby

Stw p wh b. Murraysville, Va., 1856. 100 tons. Built for Cincinnati-Kentucky River and drew 11″ light. Soon sold to the Upper Mississippi; was at St. Paul November 1857, and ran in Minnesota River 1858–1859. Snagged and lost at Swan Lake, Ark., June 21, 1860.

2788 Isabel

SW p wh b. St. Louis, Mo., 1850. 326 tons. Ran St. Louis-New Orleans. Capt. William B. Miller, master, in 1853.

Capt. John P. Keiser was cub pilot and got his license aboard her; he later was president of the Anchor Line. Lost in 1854.

2789 ISABEL

Stw wh p b. New Orleans, La., 1876. 136 tons. In 1880 owned by New Orleans & Gulf Transportation Co., handling U.S. Mail and passengers New Orleans to Port Eads and Pilot Town, Capt. James T. O'Pry with Octave Legler, clerk. Also in the Line were the *ALVIN, KITTIE NYE,* and *MARTHA*. John Kouns was president of the line. Still there 1882.

2790 ISABELLA

SW p wh b. Jeffersonville, Ind., by Howard, 1849. 175 x 41 x 6.5. Engines, 18's- 7½ ft. Two boilers, each 42" by 30 ft. Paddlewheels 26 ft. dia. working 13 ft. buckets. Cabin by Hart & Story, New Albany, Ind. Went to Mobile owned by Cox and Brainard. In 1854 returned to Mississippi River owned and commanded by Capt. Charles E. Marshall of that place, and made trips to Louisville. Capt. Edward Phelps owned and commanded after October 1854. She was owned at Selma, Ala., 1855 by Capt. Isaac W. Beebe of that place. F.L. Wooldridge records that she ran New Orleans-Shreveport in 1858. Burned Feb. 1, 1860.

2791 ISABELLA

SW p wh b. McKeesport, Pa., 1857. 361 tons. 211 x 32. Capt. John P. Keiser bought interest in 1858 and was master until 1861. Made trip up Missouri River. Took part in the so-called Yellowstone Expedition under General Sully spring 1864. Was present at the loss of the *JAMES WATSON* (see) at Island 76, Mississippi River, Feb. 25, 1865. Snagged and lost at Dozier Landing, Mo., Apr. 15, 1868; had been owned by Dozier and McPherson.

2792 ISABELLA

SW gunboat ih b. Glasgow, Scotland, 1860. 642 tons. Originally named *GIRAFFE* and was in British registry when converted into a gunboat by the Confederates at the start of the Civil War. They renamed her *R.E. LEE,* or *ROBERT E. LEE,* and as such she was captured by the U.S. at Fort Donelson, January 1864. Sold to private parties 1865, renamed *ISABELLA*. Sold foreign in 1869.

2793 ISLAND BELLE

Stw ex wh b. Cincinnati, Oh., 1895. Originally named *VIRGINIA,* then *STEEL CITY,* then *EAST ST. LOUIS,* and converted to excursions under the latter name. She was entered in the Cincinnati-Coney Island trade in 1923 following destruction by fire of the *ISLAND QUEEN* and *MORNING STAR*. Sold April 1927 to Greater New Orleans Amusement Co., who docked her at Paducah, rebuilt and reboilered her, and renamed her *GREATER NEW ORLEANS* (all see).

2794 ISLAND CITY

SW p wh b. Brownsville, Pa., 1856. 245 tons. Went to Galveston, Tex., and to Confederate registry in 1861.

2795 ISLAND CITY

Stw p wh b. Port Byron, Ill., 1863. 140 x 30. Two boilers. Owned by Adam Heine, with Capt. Alex Lamont, master. She was one of the fleet of eight boats on the Yellowstone Expedition in the spring of 1864 under General Sully. She was snagged directly opposite Fort Buford, N.D., August 1864, the hull loaded with corn and pork for General Sully's troops and animals. All cargo lost. The machinery was recovered and taken to St. Louis on the *BELLE OF PEORIA*.

2796 ISLAND MAID

Stw ex wh b. Jeffersonville, Ind., by Howard, 1909. Originally named *G. W. HILL* (see) and after the destruction by fire of *ISLAND QUEEN* and *MORNING STAR* she was sold to the Coney Island Co., Cincinnati, who renamed her. Caught fire early spring 1929 at Cincinnati and burned off much of her upper works. Rebuilt. Burned on the marine ways at Madison, Ind., on Dec. 7, 1932, and flames also consumed the towboat *FRED HALL*. Coney Island had enjoyed two-boat service until this happened, and thereafter the *ISLAND QUEEN* (2nd) cared for the park business.

2797 ISLAND PACKET

Stw p and ferry wh b. Wheeling, Va., 1846. 89 tons. Made occasional trips Pittsburgh-Wheeling when new. She was owned by the Zane family, Wheeling, and served as a ferry between Wheeling and Wheeling Island until the suspension bridge was opened. There was a bridge across the back channel for many years prior to the opening of the suspension bridge on Nov. 1, 1849. She suffered a steam explosion at Wheeling, Dec. 9, 1847, killing two and injuring two others. Had a pair of slide valve poppet cut-off engines which, after serving their time on this boat, went to Crawford's Flour Mill, Bridgeport, Oh. In 1871 they were put into the *IRON VALLEY,* a towboat later the *BELLE PRINCE*.

2798 ISLAND QUEEN

Stw p wh b. Madison, Ind., 1893. Originally named *ST. JOSEPH* (see). Capt. John F. Klein bought her at Natchez, Miss., early 1905, and brought her to Pittsburgh, Pa., and renamed her. Ran excursions to a park on Neville Island, Ohio River, about where the Dravo Corporation now is located, Capt. B.W. Hebel in charge. On May 10, 1905, she took Theodore E. Burton, chairman of the Congressional Rivers and Harbors Committee on an inspection tour Pittsburgh to McKeesport, Pa., plus ten other members and friends. Sold September 1908 to Harrison P. Dilworth. In July 1912 was renamed *MORNING STAR* (see).

2799 ISLAND QUEEN

SW ex wh b. Cincinnati, Oh., by Cincinnati Marine Railway Co., 1896. 281.4 x 42.6 x 8.5. Compound non-condensing engines, 20's, 35's- 9 ft. Six boilers, each 42" by 24 ft. Owned by the Coney Island Co., Cincinnati and operated between that city of the Coney Island amusement park nine miles upstream on the Ohio side. Tramped in off seasons; was at New Orleans, but never above Pomeroy on the Ohio. Capt. Sterling McIntyre was first master with James DuPuy, mate. DuPuy became master and in all was with the boat 28 years. Capt. Ben I. Pattison succeeded him. Launched May 16, 1896, and christened by Miss Rosa Brooks, daughter of Lee H. Brooks who headed Coney Island. Originally docked at the foot of Vine Street, and later moved to the foot of Broadway. Capt. Harry W. Doss was pilot and Homer Denney played calliope. In winter she was kept in the mouth of Licking River, and later in the mouth of the Kentucky. In January 1918 in Kentucky River she broke loose in ice and drifted below Madison, Ind., where she was safely landed and taken to the Louisville Canal. During an excursion with Gallipolis and Point Pleasant folks aboard she hit a low-hanging wire at Dam 26, knocked down her stacks, and two boys were injured. A marine parade was staged from Cincinnati to Point Pleasant, Oh., Apr. 27, 1922, celebrating the centennial of the birth of General U.S. Grant, and while upbound the forward hurricane deck collapsed injuring 28 boys, one of them permanently. Her partner boat in the Coney run was the *PRINCESS*, ex-*FRANCIS J. TORRANCE* (see), until 1918 and then the *MORNING STAR* (see). Coney Island, which was no island at all, was eminently successful, and on Nov. 4, 1922, when the *ISLAND QUEEN* and *MORNING STAR* burned at Cincinnati, along with the *TACOMA* and *CHRIS GREENE* (1st), two generations of Cincinnatians were stunned.

2800 Island Queen

SW ex sh b. Midland, Pa., by Midland Barge Co. (hull), and completed at Cincinnati by her owners, Coney Island Co. 286.1 x 45.6 x 7.3. Barnes compound non-condensing engines, 22's, 40's- 9 ft. Six boilers. Burned fuel oil. Paddlewheels 30 ft. in dia. working 16 ft. buckets, 20 arms. Construction started in 1923 and she was completed and dedicated Apr. 18, 1925. Carried passengers to and from Coney Island during the season and tramped before and after, Pittsburgh to New Orleans. In October 1929 en route to St. Louis struck Paul Jones Rock, eight miles below there, and had to be docked in New Orleans. She beached out at Coney Island Mar. 11, 1929, with 39.6 on Cincinnati marks, but was freed when U.S. towboats came to the scene with dredge *C.B. HARRIS.* She was taken to Dravo Marine Ways, Neville Island, Pa., in January 1941 for hull work, and the addition of sponsons increased width to 51.6 ft. Capt. Charles N. Hall was long her master; Capt. Harry Doss, pilot; Homer Denney, calliope. George F. Schott, president of Coney Island, died July 25, 1935, and was succeeded by his son Edward L. Schott, then 28. On Sept. 9, 1947, at Pittsburgh, her fuel tanks exploded resulting in the destruction of the boat, and loss of 19 lives. No passengers were aboard at the time. Capt. Ernest Wagner was mate at the time and jumped from the roof to save himself. The *DELTA QUEEN* had just been pulled out on the Dravo Marine Ways that day, fresh from California. The wreck was removed by Crain Bros. Inc., Pittsburgh, on a bid of $28,500. The "Big Liz," as she was called, had license to carry 4,100 passengers.

2801 Issaquena

SW p wh b. Ironton, Oh., 1879. Originally named *CITY OF IRONTON* (see). She was sold in June 1882 to Vicksburg & Greenville Packet Co., and rebuilt at Cincinnati to measure 190.7 x 28 x 4.7, and renamed. Capt. H.C. Marionneaux, master, with Frank Steigelman, clerk, in Vicksburg-Greenville trade. Burned near Vicksburg, April 1887.

2802 Istrouma

Recess wheel ferry wh b. Jeffersonville, Ind., by Howard, 1896. 120 x 25 x 5. Owned by Baton Rouge Ferry Co. Sunk at Baton Rouge in October 1915 during a severe storm.

2803 Itasca

SW p wh b. Cincinnati, Oh., 1857. 230 x 35 x 5.6. Engines, 20's- 7 ft. 340 tons. Paddlewheels 28 ft. dia. working 10 ft. buckets. Four boilers. Capt. David Whitten, master, 1857-1860. Capt. Jesse Y. Hurd, master, 1861-1862. Upper Mississippi packet, teamed up with *KEY CITY* (see). Burned at Paducah, Ky., Dec. 27, 1868. Machinery went to *BELLE OF LA CROSSE.*

2804 Ivanhoe

SW p wh b. Elizabeth, Pa., 1848. 298 tons. Burned and lost at Cincinnati, Oh., Nov. 9, 1849.

2805 Ivy

The wrecking boat *TRAVIS WRIGHT* in November 1873 removed from the Yazoo River near Liverpool landing an interesting relic in the form of a vessel 191 x 28 x 9 powered by a vertical condensing engine, beam type, 44" dia. by 11 ft. stroke. It had been purposely burned by the Confederates in May 1863 to prevent its capture. This 454-ton vessel had been the C.S. privateer *V.H. IVY,* known in the war years as *IVY.*

2806 Izetta

SW p wh b. McKeesport, Pa., 1859. 301 tons. In January 1861 arrived at Cincinnati from Memphis with cotton consigned to Pittsburgh, Capt. William Windsor. She was impressed into U.S. service as a transport 1862-1864, owned by Capt. John Kyle and others. Acquired by USQMD in April 1865. Sold to private owners that fall and renamed *MEXICO* on Nov. 25, 1865. Burned and lost at St. Louis, Jan. 20, 1867.

J

2807 J.A. Cotten

SW p wh b. Jeffersonville, Ind., by Howard, 1861. 549 tons. 229 x 36 x 7. Built for the New Orleans & Bayou Sara Mail Line Co., E. Lanone, president, of New Orleans. Capt.

V.B. Baranco, master. Converted into a gunboat by the Confederates and was destroyed in Bayou Teche by U.S. gunboats on Jan. 14, 1863.

2808 J.A. COTTON

SW p wh b. Jeffersonville, Ind., by Howard, 1861. 177 x 34 x 6.9. Engines, 22's- 8 ft. Four boilers. Originally named *MARY T.* (see). Following the loss of the original *J.A. COTTEN* the *MARY T.* was commissioned as a Confederate gunboat Mar. 19, 1863, renamed. She was captured by U.S. forces at Shreveport, La., in June 1865 and sent to Mound City, Ill. In Confederate service was often referred to simply as *COTTON.* She was sold to private owners at the conclusion of the war and went to Pittsburgh, Pa., under her own steam, where she was dismantled. Capt. Thomas S. Calhoun bought the machinery and used it in building the side-wheel *GLENCOE* (see).

2809 J.A. RHOMBERG

SW ferry wh b. Bellevue, Iowa, 1875. 23 tons. Operated at Guttenberg, Iowa. Still documented 1881.

2810 J.A. TOWNS

Stw p wh b. Jeffersonville, Ind., 1904. Originally named *STELLA* (see). 101.5 x 25 x 3. Engines, 11"- 4 ft. Two boilers, each 44" by 16 ft. The *STELLA* burned December 1906 and was rebuilt, renamed. Operated out of Greenwood, Miss., owned by Montjoy Bros.

2811 J.A. WOODSON

Stw p wh b. Louisville, Ky., 1881. 142 x 30 x 3.7. Engines, 10's- 4 ft. Two boilers. Named for the mayor of Little Rock, Ark., and ran Little Rock-Pine Bluff. Crew 1882: Capt. L.P. Drake, master, with Charles Musselman, clerk. Crew 1884: Capt. L.P. Drake, master; James Bowlin and Rees Pritchard, pilots; Amos Day, purser; Harry H. Edwards, 2nd clerk; George Ivey, mate; Green W. Johnson, chief, and George Ballou, 2nd engineer. She was run to fight railroad rates. Sank at Free Nigger Bend, Ark. River, Dec. 18, 1887. Again sank at Perrine Landing, White River, June 2, 1894. In 1897 started for St. Louis with Capt. David Silver in command, and was snagged and sunk above the elevator at Columbus, Ky. Raised and taken to Mound City, Ill., where she was rebuilt to become the *W.H. GRAPEVINE* (see).

2812 J.B. CARSON

Stw p wh b. Shousetown, Pa., and completed at Elizabeth, Pa., 1855. 186 tons. Lost at Alton, Ill., Feb. 14, 1859, probably in ice.

2813 J.B. FORD

Stw p wh b. Moundsville, Va., 1857. 197 tons. Named for the Wheeling agent of the B&O Railroad. Ran Pittsburgh-Cincinnati, Capt. John S. Devenney, and in February 1862 entered Pittsburgh-Portsmouth trade, Capt. Wash Kerr, with W.H. Bryan, clerk. Soon impressed into U.S. service handling troops and supplies. In the late fall of 1864 the Rebels made a concerted attack at Johnsonville, Tenn., and destroyed a number of boats, the *FORD* among them.

2814 J.B.M. KEHLOR

SW p wh b. Belle Vernon, Pa., by Spear, 1877. 265 x 49 x 8. Single engine, stiff shaft, compound. Two batteries of 2 boilers each, 38" by 24 ft. Primarily a freight boat owned by Capt. William J. Kountz. Unique in construction. The paddlewheels rolled lazily and seemed almost to hang up on center. She was referred to as the "Alphabet Kehlor." Left Pittsburgh in January 1878 in charge of Capt. Daniel Michael Brady, East Liverpool, Oh. Marsh Hays and Jacob Poe piloted her to Cincinnati and said she was easily handled. W.J. Kountz went along, first trip down the Ohio for him in 16 years—said his last trip was on the *PRIMA DONNA* with Capt. George D. Moore. She was operated St. Louis-New Orleans and could load 2,200 tons. Notoriously slow, and a story originating in the St. Louis *Republican* in 1879 went into great detail about her exciting race with the East St. Louis grain elevator, widely copied. Rebuilt in 1881 and renamed *HELENA* (see) and finally *GRAND REPUBLIC* (also see).

2815 J.B. RICHARDSON

Stw p wh b. Jeffersonville, Ind., by Howard, 1898. 165 x 29 x 4.3. Engines, 14's- 4½ ft. Two boilers, each 44" by 20 ft. Built for the Ryman Line, Nashville, Tenn. Named for a shoe merchant of that city. Ran Nashville-Evansville. When the Ryman Line failed in 1910 she was acquired by Cumberland River Steamboat Co., headed by W.W. Parmenter and Tom G. Ryman, Jr. Burned below the wharf at Paducah, Ky., Nov. 18, 1913. Her first master was Capt. W.S. Bowman.

2816 J.C. ABBOTT

SW ferry wh b. Madison, Ind., 1873. 90 x 28 x 3.6. She was the ferry at Madison, Ind., for many years. Upper works burned in 1884 and again in 1893, both times repaired. Replaced by the *TRIMBLE* (see) in 1895.

2817 J.C. CROSSLEY

Stw p wh b. Madison, Ind., 1868. 137 tons. Built for Capts. George and William Bay and named for an iron manufacturer at Ironton, Oh. Ran Ironton-Proctorville. She was lengthened 20 feet at Middleport, Oh., November 1876. She was wrecked along the Ohio shore below Proctorville, opposite the mouth of Guyandot River.

2818 J.C. HOPKINS

Batwing SW p wh b. Paintsville, Ky., 1890. 102 x 16.4 x 3. Operated on Big Sandy River by Capt. William Vaughn and others. Said to have been a double decker.

2819 J.C. HOPKINS NO. 2

Batwing SW p wh b. Catlettsburg, Ky., 1895. 120 x 18.4 x 3.3. Ran on Big Sandy River, owned by Capt. William Vaughn and others. In June 1895 was running low water in

Pittsburgh-Wheeling trade. Sold to Yost Bros. who changed her name to *ALEX YOST* (see).

2820 J.C. IRWIN

Stw p wh b. Wyandotte, Kans., 1864. 145 tons. Wyandotte is on the Missouri River near Kansas City. Completed at Leavenworth, Kans., in June 1864 and sold to Capt. J.D. Smith of Bunker Hill, Ill. She exploded boilers at Big Eddy Towhead, 10 miles above Eddyville, Cumberland River, morning of Oct. 17, 1864. Captain Smith was killed, also John Elliott Hask, pilot, the mate, three deckhands, the watchman and four passengers. Mrs. J.D. Smith was hospitalized at Eddyville. The boat had been landed to repair her doctor pump. Woodwork littered the island and the hull sank.

2821 J.C. KERR

Stw p wh b. Chambersburg, Oh., 1884. 121 x 27.8 x 4. Engines, 10's- 3½ ft. Two boilers, each 36″ by 18 ft. Operated on the upper Ohio until 1892 when sold to Capt. R.H. Williams for Evansville-Green River. He joined her in the Evansville & Bowling Green Packet Co., and took stock in return. In 1897 Capt. Dick Williams, master; T.A. and W.M. Williams, pilots; J. Edgar and Jeff H. Williams, clerks, and J.E. Williams, chief engineer. Renamed *CHAPERON* in 1904 (see).

2822 J.C. SWON

SW p wh b. Louisville, Ky., 1856. 678 tons. She ran St. Louis-New Orleans, Capt. I.H. Jones, master, in the Railroad Line. After the war was in the Atlantic & Mississippi Steamship Co., same trade. Dismantled in June 1867 and her hull was converted into a wharfboat used at Columbus, Ky. This wharfboat was docked and repaired at Mound City, Ill., in 1872.

2823 J.C. THOMPSON

Rig? ferry wh b. De Soto, Wis., 1872. 51 tons. Documented at Galena, Ill., through 1876 and inspected at New Orleans 1881–1882.

2824 J.C. WARNER

Stw p wh b. Chattanooga, Tenn., 1883. 142 x 31.6 x 4.6. Engines, 13's- 4½ ft. Two boilers. Built from *CITY OF KNOXVILLE* (1st). Ran Chattanooga-Kingston owned by Capt. J.P. Kendrick. He sold out winter 1886–1887 and she continued the trade owned by Tennessee River Transportation Co., Capt. W.C. Wilkey. The engines went to the *JOE WHEELER* (see).

2825 J.D. HINDE

Prop p wh b. Portsmouth, Oh., 1863. 126.9 x 22.8 x 4.3. 111 tons. There is evidence she originally was prop, so stated in a contemporary account dated April 1864 when Messrs. Harper & Son bought her at Cincinnati for "the Kentucky River trade." However, when documented at New Orleans in September 1866 she is described as sternwheel. The New Orleans, St. Mary & St. Martin Packet Co., ran her into June 1869. Then sold to Capt. Vincent J. Wood, New Orleans in June 1869 who transferred her within two days to Capt. Thomas R. Muggah, St. Mary Parish, who sold her to Galveston, Tex., that August. She was snagged and lost on the Trinity River, Tex., Nov. 1, 1869.

2826 J.D. SWAIN

SW p wh b. Jeffersonville, Ind., by Howard, 1859. 150.6 x 30 x 5. Built for parties at Franklin, La. This was a lake-type steamer, and was sunk by U.S. forces 1862 and remained on the bottom until the U.S. raised her in April 1864. She was sold at public sale December 1866 to Capt. Edwin F. Saunders, New Orleans. He ran her New Orleans-Mobile. Sank in Escambia River, Fla., 1869.

2827 J.D. WYKER

Stw ferry wh b. Decatur, Ala., 1909. 69.6 x 17.7 x 2.9. Owned by Harry P. Pittman and apparently used at Albany (section of Decatur).

2828 J.D. WYKER

Stw ferry wh b. Albany, Ala., 1920. 63.3 x 22.5 x 1.8. Owned by J.S. Walker, Decatur, Ala.

2829 J.E. RANKIN

Stw p wh b. Metropolis, Ill., at the Alf Cutting Yard, 1871. 142 x 30.5 x 4. Engines, 12's- 4 ft. Owned by C.M. Cole, Cincinnati, who sold her April 1877 to Capt. Sila Hemmway, Chester, Ill., for Missouri River.

2830 J.E. TRUDEAU

Stw p wh b. Jeffersonville, Ind., by Howard, 1889. 160 x 30 x 4.2. 242 tons. Engines, 12's- 5 ft. Two boilers, each 42″ by 20 ft. She and the *WARREN* (see) ran New Orleans-Atchafalaya River under joint management. First master, Capt. A.P. Trousdale. The New Orleans & Washington Packet Co., ran her later. She sank after hitting an obstruction at Alto Landing, La., in Point Coupee Parish, Apr. 20, 1898, then running New Orleans-Melville. The *ELECTRA* took off her passengers. Capt. E.M. Ditch ran her later, New Orleans-Franklin, under Planters Packet Co. Burned Feb. 29, 1912, at Belle River, La., on the lower Mississippi River at 100-Mile Point, St. Gabriel. This same Ditch family bought the replica steamboat *NEW ORLEANS* (see) in 1911.

2831 J.F. HATTEN

Rig? p wh b. Catlettsburg, Ky., 1879. 109.5 x 14.3 x 2.4. Operated by Ohio & Big Sandy River Transportation Co., Capt. T.J. Owens, master, with John W. Culver, clerk. Often ran low water trades on the Ohio. Still listed in 1886.

2832 J.F. JOY

SW transfer boat wh b. Madison, Ind., 1873. 145 x 32 x 5. Operated at Nebraska City, Neb., into mid-1880s and then went to Helena, Ark. Capt. N.E. Tibbals was master in 1899 and had been on her many years. She sank at the incline, Helena, Ark., late January 1895, then operated by Linehan Transfer Co., Dubuque.

J.F. PARGOUD

See *J. FRANK PARGOUD*.

2833 J.G. BLACKFORD

Stw p wh b. Gallipolis, Oh. (hull), and completed at Cincinnati, 1864. 160 x 31 x 5. Machinery came from Pittsburgh, 16's- 4½ ft. Two boilers. Built for Capt. F. Ford whose financial partner was Frank Cathbern, Parkersburg, W. Va. Was at Pittsburgh in March 1865, loading for Cincinnati. Went to St. Louis, and sold thence to New Orleans, Capt. H.L. Lee, November 1867. Sold a month later to Capt. Charles C. Pickett, New Orleans, who ran her New Orleans-Opelousas-Atchafalaya. Sold to Mobile, Ala., December 1870. Burned and lost at Wetumpka, Ala., with a load of cotton, Jan. 13, 1871.

2834 J.G. GARDNER

Rig? ferry wh b. Mt. Vernon, Ind., 1878. 21 tons. Still listed 1882, maybe later.

2835 J.G. MORROW

SW ferry wh b. Brownsville, Pa., 1861. 163 tons. First home port, Memphis, Tenn. Snagged and lost at St. Joseph, Mo., Sept. 1, 1861.

2836 J.H. BALDWIN

SW p wh b. Louisville, Ky., 1861. 173 tons. Built for Louisville-Cumberland River, Capt. McGuire. Captured by the U.S. on Cumberland River spring of 1862 and sold for $12,000 to Wiley Simms and A. Hamilton Co., steamboat agents at Nashville. Sold at Nashville to USQMD Mar. 21, 1864, and redocumented Oct. 4, 1865, as *C.J. CAFFREY* (see).

2837 J.H. BELL

SW p wh b. Jeffersonville, Ind., by Howard, 1853. 171 x 30 x 6.7. First home port, Galveston, Tex. Went to Confederate service 1861 and known as *JOSIAH H. BELL*.

2838 J.H. BEST

Stw p wh b. Harmar, Oh., at Knox Yard, 1865. 227 tons. Operated out of Zanesville, Oh., to Parkersburg, Marietta, and Beverly 1865–1873. First master, Capt. R.N. Cole, with J.H. Barker, clerk. Then Capt. Ed Martin, with Theo. McCadden, clerk. Capt. Sol G. Hoge was on her 1868–1870, then Capt. Jesse J. Barr, with Charles Welch, clerk. Her U.S. inspection was allowed to expire August 1873.

2839 J.H. DONE

Stw p wh b. Shousetown, Pa., 1854. 211 tons. Named for the traffic manager of the B&O Railroad at Wheeling. 155 x 30 x 4. Engines, 15's- 5 ft. Capt. D.B. Herron, first master. Ran out of Wheeling. In 1861 ran Cincinnati-Arkansas River, Capt. L. Davis. Worked for the USQMD during the war, and was lost at Scotia on the Upper Arkansas 1864.

2840 J.H. HILLMAN

Stw p wh b. Jeffersonville, Ind., by Howard, 1882. 149 x 28.5 x 3.7. Built for Capt. Tom Ryman and operated out of Nashville, Tenn. J.H. Hillman, Esq., was a Cumberland River iron operator who in later years migrated to Pittsburgh, Pa., and became an outstanding industrialist. T.T. Hillman (see *T. T. HILLMAN*) was his brother. Last annual inspection was on July 21, 1888. Sold and remodeled into the *J.J. ODIL* (see).

2841 J.H. HUBBELL

Stw p wh b. Beverly, Oh., 1873. 61 tons. She was scow bow, had slide valve engine, and belt to paddlewheel. Ran Marietta-Beverly on the Muskingum 1873–1881, Capt. James Cooney.

2842 J.H. JOHNSON

SW p wh b. Madison, Ind., 1863. 546 tons. 244 x 40.5 x 6. Engines, 26½'s- 7 ft. Four boilers, each 46" by 24 ft. Machinery came from *HANNIBAL CITY*. Capt. J.H. Johnson often was called "Harry" and references to this boat often call her "Harry Johnson." She was in the Keokuk Packet Co., and later in the Keokuk Northern Line. Her skippers included Capt. S.S. Matson, Capt. F.S. Lee, and Capt. Samuel Gray. She hit the Wabash RR bridge above Hannibal, Mo., Apr. 1, 1874, sank, and was raised. Dismantled winter 1876–1877 and machinery went to *GOLDEN EAGLE*.

2843 J.H. LACY

SW p wh b. Madison, Ind., and completed at St. Louis, 1857. 269 tons. Ran St. Louis-St. Joseph trade up Missouri River. She may have been lengthened. Described later as 670 tons, 270 x 41 x 8.2. She was with Porter on Red River, 1864. Snagged and lost at Nodaway, Mo., on Oct. 10, 1867, en route from Omaha to St. Joseph. She was a three-boiler boat with engines 20½'s- 6 ft. Last owned by Hannibal & St. Joseph Railway Co.

2844 J.H. MENGE

Stw p wh b. Jeffersonville, Ind., by Howard, 1910. 188 x 38 x 5.8. Cotton guards, 50 ft. wide over all. Gillett & Eaton compound engines, 13's, 26's- 8 ft. Three boilers, each 44" by 30 ft. Built for the Mississippi Packet Co. and ran New Orleans-Ouachita River, spring 1911, then New Orleans-Vicksburg. Capt. Thomas Morrissey ran her briefly Memphis-Vicksburg with Capt. Ed Nowland, Jr., master, 1914–1915. She was sold to Capt. Owen F. Burke, Mobile, July 1916, and name changed to *M.A. BURKE* (see).

2845 J.H. MILLER

Stw p wh b. Hazelton, Ind., 1863. 68 tons. Hazelton is on White River about 15 miles above the mouth in Gibson County, Ind. Burned and lost at Pine Bluff, Ark., August 1864.

J.H. OGLESBY

See *JOSEPH H. OGLESBY*.

2846 J.H. RUSSELL

SW p wh b. New Albany, Ind., 1850. Originally named

CHEROKEE (see). Rebuilt 1864 and renamed. Ran New Orleans-Bayou Sara, Capt. S. Reno, with E. Burke, clerk, under charter to owners of *MITTIE STEPHENS.* Burned near Plaqumine, La., night of Mar. 28, 1864, downbound from Red River to New Orleans. At a trial held in St. Louis October-November 1865 a document was introduced in which Isaac V. Ayleshire petitioned Hon. S.R. Mallory, Secretary of the Confederate Navy, Richmond, Va., under date of Apr. 13, 1864, for 10% of the value of boat and cargo. He was a hired "fire bug" and had acted on orders from the Confederates. He had boarded the *RUSSELL* at Baton Rouge and at 8:00 that evening when she was landing at Plaquemine, he fired two cotton bales. The cargo comprised 700 bales, 3,000 sacks of seed, 50 mules, 150 hogs and 50 cattle. All passengers got away safely; all cargo was lost.

2847 J.H. SHAW

Stw ferry wh b. Clarington, Oh., 1907. Originally named *DANIEL* (see). Rebuilt at Parkersburg, W. Va., 1916 and renamed, then owned by G.M. Dressel. The highway bridge at Parkersburg opened 1916 put an end to the ferry business to Belpre, Oh. She ran at Ironton, Oh. under charter to the C&O Railroad after ice sunk the *IRONTON* there. Sold 1920 to Richland Coal Co., Warwood, W. Va., and converted into a towboat.

2848 J.H. WHITELAW

SW p wh b. Beardstown, Ill., 1865. 439 tons. Off the lists 1871.

2849 J.J. CADOT

Stw p wh b. Gallipolis, Oh., 1859. 62 tons. 109.6 x 18.9 x 4.5. Owned at Memphis by Capt. P.D. O'Neal 1866-1867. Off the lists 1867.

2850 J.J. HILL

Stw p wh b. Hastings, Minn., 1902. 130 x 25.3 x 4.5. Engines, 12's- 6 ft. Two boilers, each 42" by 18 ft. Ran on the Upper Mississippi until sold c. 1905 and renamed *LOUISIANA* (see).

2851 J.J. ODIL

Stw p wh b. Nashville, Tenn., 1889. 149.5 x 28 x 3.3. Machinery, etc., from the *J.H. HILLMAN* (see). Named for a Nashville merchant and ran Nashville-Burnside, Capt. W.B. Harris. Bought by Capt. Martin Coyne and Capt. Louis Roche and others in June 1894 for St. Louis-Illinois River. Wrecked in the St. Louis tornado, May 27, 1896. Capt. Sim Woods, her purser, lost his life.

2852 J.L. DYKES

Stw p wh b. Kingston, Tenn., 1906. 84.7 x 14 x 3. Owned by Huntsville Navigation Co., Capt. J.L. Dykes. Ran on the Upper Tennessee River. Still registered 1918.

2853 J.L. FERGUSON

Rig? ferry wh b. Grafton, Ill., 1876. 79 tons.

2854 J.L. GRAHAM

Stw p wh b. Pittsburgh, Pa., 1866. 113 tons. Ran Pittsburgh-Smiths Ferry, Pa., spring 1866, Capt. J.C. Rayburn. In December 1867 in the Paducah-Cairo trade, Capt. Ferguson.

2855 J.L. McLEAN

SW p wh b. Elizabeth, Pa., 1849. 271 tons. 167.9 x 24 x 7. Built for Capt. A.W. Tufts, New Orleans. Sold February 1850 to Capt. James Melliger, Pittsburgh, Pa. Snagged and lost at Grenada, Miss., Mar. 4, 1854.

2856 J.M. BOWELL

Stw p wh b. Brownsville, Pa., 1882. 115 x 23 x 3.8. Engines, 13½'s- 6 ft. Built as a short trade packet in the Belle Vernon-Brownsville trade, Monon River, owned by J.M. Bowell and Morgan Bowers. On July 24, 1884, she capsized during a storm below Coal Center with 30 passengers; one drowned. In late October 1889 at Belle Vernon Captain Bowell got into an altercation with Capt. E.D. Abrams of the *R.B. KENDALL* in which Bowell was hit with a rock, fell unconscious, and later died. The *BOWELL* was converted into a towboat, served both on Kanawha and Green Rivers, and burned at Pt. Pleasant, W. Va., March 1909.

2857 J.M. CLENDENIN

SW p wh b. Louisville, Ky., 1852. 276 tons. 200 x 32. Engines, 20's- 7 ft. Three boilers. Owned by Capt. Henry W. Smith, who was master, Lewis Bros., and others. Later on Smith was a founder of the Anchor Line. Capt. John P. Keiser, once president of Anchor Line, started his steamboating on the *CLENDENIN.* She was snagged and lost at Bates Woodyard, 10 miles below Hermann, Mo., on Nov. 1, 1853. Woodyard proprietor Theodore Bates bought the wreck and made a saloon out of the cabin, erected at Berger, Mo.

2858 J.M. CONVERS

SW p wh b. McKeesport, Pa., at Coursin Yard, 1856. 417 tons. 225 x 35 x 6. Engines, 25's- 7 ft. Advertised at St. Louis, Apr. 3, 1856, Capt. George W. Bowman, every other Saturday, St. Louis to St. Joseph, Mo. Lost on March 1857 at Fairy Island. Machinery went in 1859 to towboat *CONESTOGA* which became an early U.S. gunboat in the Civil War (see). Named for Capt. J.M. Convers who commanded the fast *J.M. WHITE* of 1844 (see).

2859 J.M. HARRIS

Stw p wh b. Shousetown, Pa., 1851. 123 tons. Named for Capt. J.M. Harris of Washington, Pa., who married a Shouse. Sank at the foot of Five Islands, upper Arkansas River, loaded with pecans and hides, Capt. Rube Haynes. The second clerk was Capt. W.B. Nowland, doing his first steamboating. Date?

2860 J.M. KERR

Stw p wh b. Chambersburg, Oh., 1876. 152 tons. Named for a Gallipolis, Oh., hardware dealer whose daughter was

NORA BELLE for whom a packet was named (see). Went to U.S. marshal sale at Gallipolis when still new, October 1876, bid in by Dr. W.C. Needham and Daniel Poisley of that city. Came out February 1877 in Pittsburgh-Wheeling trade, Capt. Edwin F. Maddy and ran all year. Sold May 1878 to the Illinois River where one of the stockholders was Swartz Bros. Commission Co., their first river venture—later owned *BALD EAGLE, BELLE OF CALHOUN.* Capt. Alex Lamont was master on the Illinois, with D.M. Morris, clerk. They described her as 110 x 18 x 3.5. Sold to Natchez soon thereafter and was operated by R.F. Learned in his lumber operations to the mouth of Red River. For some years her roof bell has graced the premises of Magnolia Vale, home of Mr. and Mrs. Howard B. Peabody, Natchez.

2861 J.M. McArthur

Rig? wh p b. Cincinnati, Oh., 1875. 45 tons. In June 1876 this boat, plus *MARY KENNER* and *WATER WITCH,* were running between Cincinnati and Dayton, Ky.

2862 J.M. Relf

SW p wh b. Louisville, Ky., 1851. 157 tons. 133 x 27 x 4.2. Owned by Capt. Charles Hall and others, New Orleans. Ran New Orleans-Black River-Tensas-Bayou Macon. By 1855 Captain Hall decided he needed a larger boat and built the *MILTON RELF* (see). He used the engines, etc., from the *J.M. RELF,* and when the *MILTON RELF* came to New Orleans a new boat in 1856 she brought down along the hull of the old boat, which then was used as a lighter barge.

2863 J.M. Richtman

Stw p wh b. Sterling Island, Ill., 1899. 121 x 23.5 x 3.9. Engines, 12's- 6 ft. Two boilers. Owned by Jacob Richtman & Sons, Capt. J.J. Richtman, master. On Sept. 13, 1900, staybolts supporting the crown sheet in her starboard boiler let go, scalding several passengers, this after she left Florence, Neb., on the Missouri River. Capt. Jim Richtman later was commodore for the Drs. Mayo on the *ORONOCO* (see). Name changed in June 1904 to *CONQUEST* (see).

2864 J.M. Sharp

SW p wh b. Jeffersonville, Ind., by Howard, 1859. 218 tons. 147 x 29 x 6.5. Enrolled at New Orleans December 1860, Capt. J.W. White, who owned one-third. Enrolled in Confederate registry Nov. 11, 1861, owned by Eugene Lanone, New Orleans, Capt. Andrew Jackson Dye. She served the Confederates on Yazoo River and tributaries. Lieut. E.K. Owen of the U.S. steamer *MARMORA,* at Greenwood, Miss., reported on Feb. 15, 1864: "The Rebel steamer *SHARP* was burned a few days ago in the Yalobusha River to prevent her falling into our hands." Be this as it may, she was enrolled at New Orleans June 26, 1865 owned by the Bayou Sara Mail Co., J. Morgan, pres., and Capt. A.J. Dye, master. Dimensions changed to 152.1 x 30.5 x 6. In 1866, New Orleans-Bayou Lafourche. In April 1868 New Orleans-Jefferson-Shreveport, Capt. J.M. White, master, with J.L. Russ, clerk. Had various owners in New Orleans and retired in 1871.

J.M. Stockwell

See *JOHN M. STOCKWELL.*

2865 J.M. White

SW p wh b. Pittsburgh, Pa. (hull), and completed at St. Louis, 1842. 233 x 33. Engines 25's- 10 ft. Eight double-flue boilers. Owned by J.M. Convers, J.M. White, and H.H. Beebie, all of St. Louis. She made four trips St. Louis-New Orleans, and was snagged and sunk 35 miles above Cairo, Ill., on Mar. 28, 1843. One woman drowned. George Cable was the pilot on watch and his off-watch partner was Nathan Way.

2866 J.M. White

SW p wh b. Elizabeth, Pa., 1844. 200 x 30.5 x 7.6. Engines, 30's- 10 ft. Seven 2-flue boilers. Paddlewheels 30 ft. dia. working 12 ft. buckets. She was said to be 233 ft. overall, and 62 ft. wide. Owned by J.M. Convers, J.M. White and E.N. Beebie, all of St. Louis and Convers was master. 498 tons. She was designed for speed. A reporter from *Spirit of the Age* interviewed Captain Convers at Pittsburgh who said she would make the run from New Orleans to St. Louis under four days. Captain Convers was a native of Zanesville, Oh., and is buried there. She left Pittsburgh on Mar. 6, 1844, with passengers eating their noon meal and was at Cincinnati next noon, her time 24 hours 5 minutes—470 miles. During the first season she ran a "speed trial" from New Orleans to St. Louis and confirmed all expectations—came up in 94 hours 9 minutes. The pilots on that occasion were Isaiah Sellers and Nathan Way. Later on posts were placed along the shores at the 24-hour mark, 48-hour mark, etc., as brags to all and sundry. She was unequaled for speed; no other boat could touch her; her crew had to content themselves by surpassing their own records from time to time. Mr. W. Few, chief engineer, said she did the Cairo-St. Louis run a few years later in two hours better time. Edward H. Beebie was her clerk on the 1844 run—later lived at Galena, Ill. Jonathan Warden, assistant engineer, was living at Independence, Mo., in 1870 and recalled that the valve packing in her engines was cotton and hemp which had to be constantly screwed up, and replenished every day. He also recalled that her side-wheels had no circles and when running in drift were frequently pushed back on the arms, a circumstance which happened on the fast trip and she was not delayed to fix them. The hull shape was designed by John Wakens from a half-section model whittled by William (Billy) King, Elizabeth, Pa. This half-section was a prized possession of Hon. Edwin M. Stanton, Lincoln's war secretary, and hung over the door of his Washington office. A widely circulated tale was that Billy King destroyed the half-section with an axe to prevent anyone from duplicating the *WHITE*'s superior lines. J.M. White, Esq., died at St. Louis, Sept. 26, 1846. Capt. J.C. Swon afterwards ran the boat and remarked, "Convers has often beaten me in the speed of his boat, but he never before has beaten me half so badly as when he sold me the *WHITE.*" She was more of a plaything; not a commercial success. Speaking of that half-section model, there is record that Gen. James A. Ekin, Elizabeth, Pa., had such a model 10 feet two inches long of laminated pine and black walnut over his home fireplace. William Evans, river reporter for a Pittsburgh daily in 1870 remarked in his column that he owned a "model of the *J.M. WHITE* made by the draughtsman, and the one who superintended the building," and also said he was the possessor of an original daguerreotype of the boat made at St. Louis. The boat was dismantled, her engines went to the *AUTOCRAT* of 1847 (see) and her hull served as a wharf-boat at Memphis until it burned in 1850.

2867 J.M. White

SW p wh b. Jeffersonville, Ind., by Howard, 1878. 312.7 x 47.9 x 11.5 amidship and 17½ ft. at bow and stern. She was 321 ft. overall length and 91 ft. overall width. Engines 43's-11 ft. Ten boilers, each 42" dia. by 34 ft., two 16" flues. Paddlewheels 44 ft. dia. working 19 ft. buckets with eight ft. dip. Owned by Greenville & New Orleans Packet Co., composed of Capt. John W. Tobin, Capt. John W. Cannon, R.H. Woolfolk, Samuel S. Brown, N.M. Jones, Capt. J.M. White, and John Howard. Named for Capt. J.M. White (1823–1880) of Cloverport, Ky. The prior two boats of the name honored a respected merchant of Herculanium and St. Louis, Mo. This boat was the supreme triumph in cotton boat architecture. A description, written by Col. Will S. Hays, appeared in the Louisville Courier-Journal, Aug. 7, 1878, from which we quote:

The *J.M. WHITE* is the 276th boat built by the Howards, and their crowning effort. She is the fourth boat they have built for Captain Tobin. The contract was signed on the 12th of June, 1877, and preparations immediately made to commence the work. She was launched on the 3rd of April and taken over the Falls on May 3rd and steamed out of the Ohio in the latter part of June, receiving her finishing touches at Paducah and Cairo.

Great care was taken in the selection of the timber. The oak was from West Virginia, the pine from Pennsylvania, and the heavy cylinder timbers, wheelhouse chocks, etc. from Scott County, Indiana. Her draft of water is six and a half feet in light-running trim and she is calculated to carry 10,000 bales of cotton.

The work of building the cabin was commenced August 16, 1877 and finished June 13, 1878. The designs and plans were made one year before it was contracted for, and after the contract was awarded the plans were revised and new ones made. It took from 10 to 40 men constantly employed, with the aid of a large lot of machinery invented for the purpose of getting out work for steamboat cabins, ten months to complete the massive work.

The main cabin is 19 feet wide, 233 feet long, 13 feet high in clear on each side; staterooms 8 x 10 and 9 x 12 to aft of the wheels, and from there aft the rooms are 9 x 14, and the two aft rooms, the bridal chambers, are 12 x 14; all the rooms 9 feet high. Office and bar 10 x 12 with octagonal dome over each, each one with 8 skylight sashes and a chandelier. The style of the architecture of the cabin will have to be seen to have any idea of, as it was not taken out of the books; nor was it got up to be like anything that has ever been built before. It was not intended to follow any order of architecture in the building of it. It is an original idea of Mr. Thos. Bell's, who planned the cabins for the following boats: *ROB'T E. LEE* (new), *FRANK PARGOUD, RUTH, JOHN T. MOORE, CITY OF HELENA, CITY OF VICKSBURG, CITY OF CHESTER, GRAND TOWER, BELLE MEMPHIS, JAMES HOWARD, BELLE LEE, SEMINOLE, LESSIE TAYLOR, BEN FRANKLIN,* and who helped build 137 other cabins. Mr. Samuel Coggeshall, who superintended the work of building the cabin, has been a cabin builder for 40 years. This firm built, from 1851 to 1878, 163 cabins, and are at work on more.

One of the most attractive features of this floating palace is the stained glass furnished from the establishment of William F. Blum. The skylights are very chaste in drawing and in execution, one of the main features being the busts and statuary in the center of each light. The statues are painted in pearly gray on a blue ground, inclosed by a wreath of ivy in gray on a white ground, the whole light surrounded by a border of purple and gold.

The front of the cabin is beautiful, being fitted up with 12 doors, all filled with stained glass in blue, purple and gold, of original designs, each pane being variegated in colors and ornamentation. A novel feature of the finish of the cabin is the veneered sunk panels, which are laid in the finest rosewood and walnut burl, and richly polished, which are not only beautiful in themselves, but present a handsome contrast and relief to the usual monotonous white. The doors are veneered with the choicest French burl walnut, inlaid with root ash and ebony, the panels being elaborately engraved in gold with various artistic designs. The large mirror in the ladies' cabin is of enormous proportions, the fine French plate being 5½ by 7½ feet. The frame is pure Gothic in style, very massive, with gold carvings, the whole finished in burnished and dead gold with panels of ebony relief.

One of the bridal chambers is beautifully panelled in mahogany and satinwood, and the other in rosewood and satinwoods, together with graceful engraving illuminated with gold and colors—the whole far surpassing in style and workmanship anything of the kind heretofore attempted. There is a fine oiled walnut Queen Anne suite of furniture in one, and an East Lake suite in the other. Also in each chamber is a large French plate mirror, fancy satin chairs, oiled walnut French dresser.

There are seven sixteen-burner gold-gilt chandeliers in the main cabin, from Cornelius & Co. of Philadelphia, and designed expressly for the *WHITE.* They are made of fine brass, highly polished, and then the surface is covered with pure gold. They are all of Egyptian design and are acknowledged the most costly and elegant on any vessel in the United States.

All silverware is monogrammed "J.M.W." The table china is from Haviland, handsomely ornamented and monogrammed. A full concert grand piano from Chickering & Co. is one of the two grand pianos exhibited in the Centennial Exposition, and was awarded flattering testimonials besides the prize medal.

NOTES ABOUT THE *J.M. WHITE*

The machinery weighed 190 tons; each shaft and wheel weighed 50 tons . . . . Capt. Sam S. Brown of Pittsburgh presented her with a full set of colors . . . . all outfitting bought in New York City, in the East, and abroad, was selected by Col. Thompson Dean . . . . the officers ate and slept in the texas . . . . meals served to colored passengers in the colored cabin in texas hallway . . . . hot and cold water in the bathrooms . . . . 170,000 feet of lumber in building the cabin . . . . engines rated 3,400 hp. . . . . roof bell weighed 2,880 pounds and was made in New Albany, Ind. . . . . throttles were ten feet above the main deck . . . . engines by Ainslee-Cochran & Co. . . . . boilers by Jos. Mitchell. . . . pilotwheel 11 feet in diameter . . . . stacks 75 inches in diameter and 80 feet high above the roof . . . . ornamental leaves on the stack tops each seven feet long . . . . had two 16" flues in each boiler . . . . allowed 173 psi . . . . boilers all steel including heads . . . . boiler diameters smaller than engine diameters . . . . main cylinder timbers 82 feet long . . . . cotton guards extended 22 ½ feet beyond the hull line . . . . from stemband to 25 feet aft she was solid oak . . . . in eight years her insurance premiums totalled over $100,000.

. . . .

On her maiden trip south the *WHITE* towed the partially completed *EDWARD J. GAY* (see). Due to poor times and yellow fever the big boat never carried her cotton capacity; her banner trip totalled 5,067 bales on a trip in 1878. She ran New Orleans-Vicksburg teamed up with the *ROB'T E. LEE* (2nd) and *NATCHEZ* (7th).

The fire which destroyed the *WHITE* was spectacular. She was moored at Blue Store Landing, St. Maurice Plantation, Point Coupee Parish, La. on December 13, 1886 when the blaze was discovered. Several lives were lost, and more would have been save for the cool determination of her clerk G. Wash Floyd, who lost his life saving others. Gunpowder stowed in the boat's magazine in the hold let go and blazing timbers were hurled aloft. The old hulk was bedded in the sand there for many years, grim reminder of the greatest cotton queen of the Mississippi.

For further reading about the *J.M. WHITE* and related topics, see *S&D Reflector,* March 1974, pages 25-38 for a rather full account and many photographs; June 1974, page 10, for story of the two pilots at the time of the fire; a visit to grave of Capt. J.M. White is described in March 1975 issue, page 17; a photograph of Captain White's monument at Cloverport, Ky., see June 1975 issue, page 2; photograph and life history of Capt. John W. Tobin in December 1975 issue, pages 17-28; photograph of Mrs. John W. Tobin and her biography, Sept. 1976 issue, page 16; correspondence when the *WHITE* was built, March 1977 issue, pages 8-12; reproduction of John Stobart's oil painting of the *WHITE,* cover of June 1977 issue; poem "His Last Trip" by Will S. Hays honoring Capt. J.M. White, December 1974 issue, page 4.

The best model of the *J.M. WHITE* was jointly built by John H. Leslie and Ralph C. Hitchcock, first exhibited at Marietta, Oh., in 1972 at the annual S&D meeting. This model now is with the Smithsonian exhibits, Washington, D.C.

Proud monster of the Sunny South,
  Go, bearing proud thy name;
May every trip you make for Tobin
  Add fortune to his fame.
—Will S. Hays

2868 J.N. HARBIN

Stw p wh b. Brownsville, Pa., at Axton Yard, 1895. 154 x 19 x 3.5. Engines, 10's- 4 ½ ft. One boiler, 44" by 24 ft. Owned by Arkansas River Packet Co. Stranded at Lake Landing, Miss., Aug. 25, 1911, sank, and was dismantled a month later where she lay. Capt. J.N. Harbin, long treasurer of Arkansas River Packet Co., died at Cincinnati in October 1902.

2869 J.N. MACOMB

SW snagboat ih b. Covington, Ky., 1874. 177.5 x 62 x 8. This was the first metal hull snagboat built as an experiment, and was used on the Mississippi by U.S. Engineers. The *E.A. WOODRUFF* also was built at Covington, same year (see). Broke up the wreck of the Confederate gunboat *BEAUREGARD* at Memphis, August 1911. Advertised for sale by the U.S. Engineers sans engines, boilers, etc., summer of 1934.

2870 J.N. MCCULLOUGH

SW p wh b. Pittsburgh, Pa., 1867. 518 tons. Engines, 22's-7 ft. Built for Capts. George D. and Dan Moore, and Andrew Ackley. Ran in the Pittsburgh-Cincinnati trade 1867 and in February 1868 ran Pittsburgh-Parkersburg until April, then resumed Pittsburgh-Cincinnati. In May 1868 Captain George Moore's father, 85, made a trip on her, living at Wellsville, Oh. The boat was named for a prominent railroad man at Wellsville. Took the place of the *GEN. LYTLE* in the Louisville-Cincinnati trade for a few weeks summer 1868, then resumed P&C trade in September, Capt. Dan Moore, with A.C. McConnell, clerk. She had gone to Louisville with freight and was returning to Cincinnati on Tuesday night, Nov. 17, 1868, when she hit the loaded tow of the *TIGER* at Eagle Hollow, above Madison, Ind. Sank in three minutes in 17 feet. The *MELNOTTE* took off the people from the hurricane roof and delivered them to Cincinnati. The *TIGER* was rounding to at the time, preparing to deliver coal at Madison. Several of her barges sank. Vance & Armstrong of the Madison Marine Ways agreed to raise her no-cure no-pay for $20,000. They got her up on chains, the head swung downstream, and several chains broke when a Mail Line boat passed making swells. While this was going on the *UNITED STATES* and *AMERICA* collided above Warsaw (see). About Dec. 15 she was floated down to East St., Madison, held up on barges. The hull and machinery were detached from the upper works preparatory to hauling on the ways and then came an ice run-out destroying all. The machinery was not recovered until low water September 1869 and went to the *ARLINGTON* (see). Pilot Carlton Cable of the *McCULLOUGH* lost his license because of this affair.

2871 J.O. HENNING

Rig? ferry wh b. Hudson, Wis., 1868. 17 tons. Operated at Hudson on St. Croix River. Still operating 1881.

2872 J.O. WATSON

Stw p wh b. West Brownsville, Pa., at Axton Yard, 1902. 85 x 18.7 x 3. Engines 9″- 3 ft. Capt. John O. Watson ran a boat store at Lock 4, Monon River. This "daylight" packet ran short trades on Monon River; Lock 4-Donora then Charleroi-Rices Landing, then Morgantown-Fairmont. In this latter trade, made possible by the new slackwater in 1904, Capt. Robert F. Eberhart was master. She also had an excursion barge and took two trips out of Monongah, six miles up West Fork. Sold to Capt. Elmer E. Varian, Pt. Pleasant, W. Va., May 1908. She was used henceforth as a towboat. Sold March 1913 to West Va. & Pittsburgh Coal Co., Wellsburg, W. Va., and turned turtle in a storm there, March 1916.

2873 J.P. DAVIS

Stw p wh b. Pt. Pleasant, W. Va., 1909. Originally named *GREENDALE* (see). Capt. John F. Davis, Fullerton, Ky., bought the *GREENDALE* at Pt. Pleasant in 1920, remodeled her into an excursion boat, and operated her Portsmouth, Oh.-Fullerton, Ky., where the Davis family had an amusement park called Coney Island. In January 1921 entered Big Sandy River trade and made three trips, first to Paintsville, second Prestonburg and last to Pikeville. She sank in shallow water downbound on this last trip near Paintsville, raised. This was the last packet operation on that river. She was sold to the Marietta Packet Co., and ran Wheeling-Marietta briefly with poor results. Was laid up above the upper guide wall at Ohio River Lock 16 where she sank.

2874 J.P. DROUILLARD

Stw p wh b. Jeffersonville, Ind., by Howard, 1881. 165 x 31.3 x 4.9. Equipment from *BOLIVAR H. COOK* (see). Named for an iron industrialist at Nashville, owned by Ryman Line. Ran Nashville-Paducah, Capt. W.R. Gracey. Last inspected at Paducah Dec. 22, 1891.

2875 J.P. GAGE

Stw ferry wh b. Clinton, Iowa, 1884. 114 x 32 x 5. Engines, 16's- 4½ ft. Two boilers. Operated at St. Charles, Mo., owned by St. Charles Ferry & Transportation Co. Snagged and sunk Sept. 7, 1893, raised. In 1898 was transferred to Dardanelle, Ark., from Rock Island, Ill.

2876 J.P. WEBB

Stw p wh b. Newburgh, Ind., 1865. 171 tons. Ran Evansville-Clarksville, Capt. R.L. Lancaster, with Chet W. Bradley, clerk. On a trip to Louisville hit a bridge pier and sank at Sand Island in the Falls with only the pilothouse showing, Sept. 17, 1868. Owned by M.A. Lancaster, Vincennes, Ind.

2877 J.Q. DICKINSON

Stw p wh b. Pt. Pleasant, W. Va., 1906. 135.5 x 24.5 x 5.1. Engines, 12's- 5 ft. Two boilers, each 43″ by 18 ft. Built on hull of the *ZANETTA* (see). Owned by Calvert Bros., and ran Charleston-Montgomery on upper Kanawha. Machinery from *KANAWHA BELLE*. Burned her upper works at Charleston Dec. 28, 1910, rebuilt. On Apr. 22, 1912, a high wind drove her ashore 300 yards above Lock 3 and she sank and was raised. Completely rebuilt at Dana, W. Va., 1915 and renamed *HELEN LANE* (see).

2878 J.R. McMILLAN

Stw ferry wh b. Williamstown, W. Va., 1865. 22 tons. Operated between Marietta and Williamstown replacing earlier *JULIA* (see) and replaced 1871 by *MARIETTA* (see).

2879 J.R. PRATT

Prop canalboat wh b. Massillon, Oh., 1862. 64 tons. Machinery was installed at Wheeling in 1863. John L. Little, Louisville, owned her 1870, selling her to L.W. Harrod, Frankfort, Ky. Sunk and lost at Lock 2, Kentucky River, June 8, 1871.

2880 J.R. WELLS

Stw p wh b. Tuscumbia, Mo., 1897. 110.6 x 20 x 4. Engines, 10's- 4 ft. One boiler. Built for Anchor Milling Co., Tuscumbia, Mo., and named for the head of the firm. Ran in Osage River trade, Capt. John W. Adcock first master-pilot until sold in 1909. Stanton & Jones owned her when she sank in Pelican Bend, near St. Charles, Mo., Jan. 30, 1920.

2881 J. S.

Stw ex wh b. Jeffersonville, Ind., by Howard, 1901. 175 x 33 x 5.5. Engines, 16's- 6 ft. Two fire box boilers. Built for Capt. John Streckfus. Came out new as a morning packet from Davenport to Clinton, and ran "moonlight" excursions out of Davenport and Rock Island. Was too heavy to run the rapids every day, up and down, fair weather and foul, so she was withdrawn and entered the regular excursion business. Scored a great success. Burned with excursionists aboard, Saturday, June 18, 1910, returning to Lansing, Iowa, from La Crosse, Wis., at Bad Axe Island. John

Plein, a passenger, was confined in the boat's jail located in the hold, and set the fire. He lost his life, and a lady passenger also was lost. The passengers were let ashore at Bad Axe Island. The raftboats *NORTH STAR* and *HARRIET* conveyed them home. Details of this fire are presented in *S&D Reflector,* March 1965 issue, pages 4, 5. Capt. John Streckfus, Rock Island, Ill., pres. D.W. Wisherd, Davenport, was passenger agent.

2882 J. S.

SW ex wh b. Dubuque, Iowa, 1896. 264.7 x 42 x 6.8. Originally named *QUINCY.* Entirely rebuilt into a "deluxe" excursion boat by Streckfus Steamers, Inc., St. Louis, and so appeared in 1919. She handled the carriage trade at St. Louis until the *PRESIDENT* came out July 4, 1934. Often tramped on the Upper Mississippi and was well known at all towns to St. Paul. In June 1934 was up the Ohio River to Parkersburg, W. Va., and in 1935 to New Martinsville, W. Va. Capt. Verne Streckfus was master on these Ohio River trips. Dismantled at St. Louis, winter 1938–1939.

2883 J.S. CHENOWETH

SW p wh b. Haverhill, Oh. (hull), and completed at Cincinnati, 1851. 309 tons. Haverhill is opposite Greenup, Ky., on Ohio River. Sank and lost at Algiers, La., Sept. 17, 1855.

2884 J.S. DUNHAM

Stw p wh b. 1870. Machinery from *LINTON,* 12's-4 ft. Two boilers. Ran New Orleans-Arkansas River, Capt. R.L. Desmukes, going to Fort Smith, Ark., teamed up with *JUDGE WHEELER* (see). Sank and lost six miles below Little Rock, Ark., Apr. 14, 1871, upbound with a load of railroad rails which had come in from France. Captain Desmukes was master at the time of loss.

2885 J.S. PRINGLE

Stw p wh b. Brownsville, Pa., 1854. 307 tons. Built for Capt. William Stoops. This was a four-engine low water carrier. Stoops ran a ferry many years across the Ohio, Sewickley-Stoops Ferry, Pa. He sold this boat 1855 to Missouri River where she ran St. Louis-St. Joseph, Capt. William Conley. In 1861 carrying army supplies Cincinnati-Nashville, Capt. George W. Neare, with H.H. Devenney, clerk. Louisville-Tennessee River, spring 1862, Capt. Hazlett. Acquired by USQMD in March 1865.

2886 J.S. WEBB

SW p wh b. New Albany, Ind., 1849. 85 tons. First home port, Memphis. Off the lists 1854.

2887 J.T. DAVIS

Centerwheel ferry wh b. Grafton, Ill., 1880. 122.5 x 32.5 x 4.1. Single engine, 16"- 4½ ft. One boiler, 46" by 18 ft. Owned by Hufner and Morris and ran at Hannibal, Mo. She was still in business in 1917.

2888 J.T. DOSWELL

SW p wh b. Louisville, Ky., 1848. 190 tons. 155 x 25 x 5.1. Operated out of New Orleans with many owners, first being Bonner & Smith of that city. Dismantled in 1856.

2889 J.T. HUSTLER

SW batwing p wh b. Guyandotte, W. Va., 1892. 88 x 12.1 x 2.2. In the U.S. Report of Guyandotte River commerce, year ending June 30, 1895, this boat and *FAVORITE* (both side-wheel) are noticed as the only craft plying that stream.

2890 J.T. REEDER

Stw p wh b. Knoxville, Tenn., 1890. Originally *LUCILE BORDEN.* Rebuilt at Paducah 1902 to measure 98 x 19 x 2.6, renamed. Engines, 7"-30". One fire box boiler, 39" by 12 ft. Owned by Riverton & Florence Packet Co., Capt. Tom Reeder. Ran Florence-Georgetown Landing. Sold to Capt. J.E. Moad, Caruthersville, Mo., spring 1911.

2891 J.T. STOCKDALE

Stw p wh b. West Brownsville, Pa., 1863. 188 tons. Named for Capt. Jackman T. Stockdale, Allegheny, Pa. Loaded out for Cincinnati, Capt. B.M. Laughlin, Oct. 26, 1863, and was sold to the U.S. Nov. 13, 1863. In war service known as *STOCKDALE.* Sold to private owners Sept. 1, 1865, renamed *CADDO* (see).

2892 J.T. WILDER

Stw p wh b. Kingston, Tenn., 1872. 185 tons. 139.6 x 29 x 6.3. Built for Capt. Joe Glover and the Roane Iron Co., Rockwood, Tenn. Machinery from the sunken *R.P. CONVERSE,* later exchanged for engines from the *RESACA.* Ran on Upper Tennessee until sold to Capt. J.P. Kindrick and others who used her to handle pig iron in barges for Roane Iron Co. The *R.M. BISHOP* (see) was in this same traffic. During the yellow fever epidemic at Chattanooga, July 1878 the *WILDER* was taken several miles above there with Capt. and Mrs. Kindrick, Capt. and Mrs. W.L. Dugger and others aboard where they kept isolated several months. Machinery went to the *R.C. GUNTER* in 1886.

2893 J.W. CHEESMAN

Stw p wh b. Cincinnati, Oh., 1856. 215 tons. 165 x 33 x 5.5. Ran Cincinnati-upriver trade, Capt. Andrew Wilson. Upon his death Capt. Jacob Ketchum succeeded as master, both of New Richmond, Oh. She was under contract to the U.S. during the war, and Captain Ketchum was killed aboard on Yazoo River, shot by a Rebel on shore, April 1863. In early November 1864, Capt. Thad Wirthlin commanding, she attempted to run a Rebel battery on Tennessee River when a shot from shore severed the steam line, and the boat was captured. This happened at White Oak Island, Tenn., Nov. 3, 1864. The crew was taken prisoner, and didn't get back to Cincinnati until Mar. 3, 1865. The Rebels burned the boat. See *PRIMA DONNA* and *VENUS,* also in this engagement.

2894 J.W. DILLON

Rig? ferry wh b. Catlettsburg, Ky., 1871. 80 tons. Cincinnati was home port 1876, and in 1881 she was inspected at St. Louis.

2895 J.W. Hailman

Stw p wh b. Elizabeth, Pa., 1855. 267 tons. Machinery from the *BEAVER* (see). Ran Pittsburgh-St. Louis, also Pittsburgh-Louisville. Doctors, nurses and hospital supplies were sent from Pittsburgh after Pittsburg Landing early 1862 aboard *J. W. HAILMAN* and *MERANGO,* and both returned to Pittsburgh Sunday April 27 with wounded soldiers aboard. Capt. J.W. Porter, Sewickley, was clerk on the *HAILMAN,* his first river job. Dismantled 1863.

2896 J.W. Spencer

SW ferry wh b. Jeffersonville, Ind., by Howard, 1882. 131 x 35 x 5. Went to the Upper Mississippi. Still listed at St. Louis, 1896.

2897 J.W. Swayze

Stw p wh b. Jonesville, La., 1898. 110 x 21 x 3.7. Operated on the Ouachita in place of the *AMERICA,* July 1899. Foundered at Jonesville Aug. 20, 1911.

2898 J. Don Cameron

Rig? wh p Built Jeffersonville, Ind. at Barmore yard, 1877, by the U.S. for Yellowstone River. Snagged and lost 40 miles above Sioux City, Iowa, May 19, 1877. She was upbound, loaded with baggage and private property of the Fifth Infantry, bound from Fort Leavenworth to Fort Keogh on the Yellowstone. This was her first trip. The *W. T. SHERMAN* took off 65 passengers including the wife of General Miles and her sister Miss Lizzie Sherman, niece of General Sherman. No life loss. A newspaper dispatch dated Jan. 17, 1878, reports that N.C. Davis has bought the wreck of the *J. DONALD CAMERON* and is arranging to raise the craft and contents bodily from the bottom of the Missouri. NOTE: *DON CAMERON* listed herein as #1591 is same boat.

2899 J. Frank Pargoud

SW p wh b. Jeffersonville, Ind., by Howard, 1860. 219 x 36 x 7. Engines, 24's- 8 ft. Five boilers. 522 tons. Built for Capt. John W. Tobin, New Orleans, sole owner. Ran New Orleans-Ouachita River. Ownership transferred November 1861 to Mary Frances Tobin. Was taken up the Yazoo River during the conflict and scuttled at Greenwood, Miss., May 13, 1863. In July she was burned to prevent capture. (Also see *FRANK PARGOUD.*)

2900 J. Jenkins

SW p wh b. Elizabeth, Pa., 1852. 145 tons. Went to the Apalachicola River, Fla. Off the lists 1859.

2901 J. Luther Troxell

Stw p wh b. Chamberlain, Tenn., 1913. 140.5 x 28 x 3.6. Engines, 11"- 3½ ft. Two boilers, each 36" by 21 ft. Originally named *T.L. BROWN* (see). Renamed in 1910. Owned entire in 1925–1926 by Capt. Paul H. Underwood, Chattanooga, Tenn.

2902 J. McKee

SW p wh b. McKeesport, Pa., 1850. 140 tons. Named for the founder of McKeesport, and ran first season in Pittsburgh-McKeesport trade. Sold April 1852 to Keokuk, Iowa. Ran Keokuk-Davenport, Capt. Leroy Dodge, owner and master of her. The *BEN CAMPBELL,* same trade, was on opposite days. Lost in collision with *CHEROKEE* at Island 92, Miss. River, Feb. 7, 1858.

2903 J. McMurchey

Rig? ferry wh b. Dubuque, Iowa, 1872. 36 tons. Operated Specht's Ferry, Iowa to Potosi Station, Wis. Still there 1881.

2904 J. Morrisett

SW p wh b. Jeffersonville, Ind., 1849. 391 tons. 168.7 x 31 x 8. Documented at New Orleans November 1850 owned by Hill, McLean & Co., of that city and others. The Hill in the firm was Henry R.W. Hill (see *H.R.W. HILL*). She is described as "one deck, cabin on deck," and probably was a freight boat. Ran from New Orleans to Arkansas and White rivers. Had several ownership changes prior to November 1853 when Capt. David Brandenburg became part owner and master, still running New Orleans-Arkansas and White. Off the lists 1857.

2905 J. Rohn

Rig? ferry wh b. Peoria, Ill., 1879. 65 x 22 x 3.9. Operated at Beardstown, Ill. Still documented 1886.

2906 Jack Gumbert

Stw p wh b. McKeesport, Pa., 1875. 64 tons. Ran local Monongahela River trades, an odd looking craft with a single stack behind the pilothouse. Capt. William Caughey of this boat died at home, McKeesport, Pa., Jan. 3, 1878, of lockjaw. Boat was owned by Capt. Jack Gumbert. Still listed 1882.

2907 Jack Hays

SW p wh b. Cincinnati, Oh., 1849. 189 tons. Went to Galveston, Tex. Off the lists 1855.

2908 Jack Porter

Rig? ferry wh b. Little Rock, Ark., 1882. 63 x 25 x 3. Still listed 1886.

2909 Jack Rabbit

Stw p wh b. Mt. Sterling, Mo., 1897. 73.6 x 16.2 x 3.3. Condemned at Memphis December 1904 along with *OZARK QUEEN* (see).

2910 Jackson

Stw p wh b. Brownsville, Pa., 1860. 84 tons. First home port, Apalachicola, Fla. Went to Confederate registry. Burned as a Confederate war boat at New Orleans, Apr. 2, 1862.

2911 Jacob D. Early

SW p wh b. Cincinnati, Oh., 1853. 348 tons. Burned and lost at Alton, Ill., Apr. 29, 1858.

2912 Jacob Poe

Stw p wh b. Freedom, Pa., 1855. 201 tons. Named for Capt.

Jacob Poe, Georgetown, Pa. A tramp packet, and was at St. Paul in 1857. Was running Pittsburgh-Louisville 1860. In 1862 handling army goods Louisville-Cumberland River. Was sold July 1862 to Capt. John L. Rhoads who brought her from Cincinnati to Brownsville, Pa., for dismantling.

2913 JACOB RICHTMAN

Stw ex wh b. Sterling Island, Ill., 1898. 160 x 32 x 5. Engines, 14's-6 ft. Two boilers, each 40" by 26 ft. Owned by the Richtman family. Sold to Missouri River and renamed *UNCLE SAM* (see).

2914 JACOB SASS

SW p wh b. Leavenworth, Kans., 1865. 179 tons. Engines, 12's- 4 ft. Two boilers. Snagged below Decatur, Neb., on Missouri River, 1869, lost.

2915 JACOB STRADER

SW p wh b. Cincinnati, Oh., 1853. 905 tons. 347 x 38 x 8. Engines, 60's- 10 ft. Two boilers, each 11 ft. dia. by 38 ft. long. She was "low pressure," carrying 30 psi or less, and steam was condensed from her huge cylinders. Owned by the U.S. Mail Line Co. and ran Cincinnati-Louisville. Entered the trade June 7, 1853, Capt. John Blair Summons. He commanded until shortly before his death Mar. 3, 1858, at Cincinnati, 47 years on the river, and burial was in Spring Grove Cemetery. Services were held in the Spencer House to contain the multitude. A stockholder's meeting was held to elect his successor, Capt. Charles Dittman, who had served as pilot. Dittman resigned Mar. 17, 1861, and was succeeded by Capt. David Whitten. Her original boilers were replaced 1860 with five 16-flue boilers, each 63" dia. by 38 ft. Originally her stacks were aft of the pilothouse, but were placed forward when this boiler exchange was made. During the early part of the war she often was used to convey wounded and sick soldiers, having a cabin 306 feet long, and 310 available berths. There is strong evidence she once went to Nashville, Tenn., in war service, undoubtedly the largest steamboat ever seen at that city. She was towed from Louisville to Madison, Ind., for dismantling in July 1866. This low pressure machinery went to the *RICHMOND* (see). For an excellent painting of the *JACOB STRADER* by artist Dorothy Frye, a picture of Jacob Strader, Esq. (1795-1860) and related matters see *S&D Reflector,* March 1966 issue, pages 16, 17.

2916 JACOB TAMM

Rig? ferry wh b. Grand Tower, Ill., 1871. 92 tons. 109.5 x 30 x 4.1. Owned 1874 by G.H. Timmerman. Inspected regularly at St. Louis. Still listed 1886.

2917 JACOB TRADER

Stw p wh b. Hampton, Ky., 1856. 238 tons. A large boat operated by double sternwheels having independent engines. Capt. William F. Davidson, later prominent on the Upper Mississippi, was interested in her while still living near Ironton, Oh. Not noted for speed. Burned and lost at Cincinnati, Oh., May 8, 1859.

2918 JAMES B. MCPHERSON

Stw snagboat ih b. Dubuque, Iowa, 1891. 170 x 36 x 5.6. Owned by U.S. Engineers and employed on the Missouri River. Still in service 1925.

2919 JAMES BATTLE

SW p wh b. New Albany, Ind., 1859. 225 x 35 x 7.5. Engines, 24's- 7 ft. Five boilers. In September 1860 running New Orleans-Vicksburg-Upper Bends, Capt. J.H. Estes. In 1863 in Mobile-Montgomery trade, Capt. James A. Greer. This steamboat and *ALICE VIVIAN* were loaded with C.S.A. cotton spring 1864 and started for Cuba. Both were captured 50 miles off Key West by *DESOTO.* Unloaded at Key West and returned to New Orleans. Turned over to USQMD and served the balance of the war in U.S. service. Sold to private owners, October 1865. She came to New Albany, Ind., in June 1867 in the remarkable time of 16 days 5 hours out of New Orleans piloted by W.H. Daniel and David Smith. Dismantled there.

2920 JAMES D. PARKER

Stw p wh b. Cincinnati, Oh., 1872. 505 tons. 185 x 36 x 5.5. Engines, 16's- 5½ ft. Three boilers. Machinery from *EMMA FLOYD.* Owned by Memphis & Ohio River Packet Co. Named for Capt. James D. Parker of Cincinnati, partner in Parker, Wise & Co., boat store (afterwards Consolidated Boat Store) and who managed the J.W. Gaff Estate. Capt. Robert W. Wise was master in 1874, with W.F. McIntyre, clerk. Capt. Charles B. Russell, master in 1878, with G.W. Thompson, clerk. Hit the dam at the head of the Louisville-Portland Canal on Mar. 5, 1882 at 12:30 P.M. Had a full load and 105 passengers aboard. Nobody hurt. Pink Varble was pilot on watch. The hull was raised.

2921 JAMES DEITRICH

Stw p wh b. Pittsburgh, Pa., 1904. Constructed by James Rees & Sons Co., for customer in Nicaragua. Departed Pittsburgh under her own steam for destination in April 1904.

2922 JAMES E. WOODRUFF

SW p wh b. New Albany, Ind., 1855. 612 tons. Operated in the Railroad Line, St. Louis-New Orleans. Capt. C.S. Rodgers, master, 1857. Named for a St. Louis businessman, benefactor to many young men getting started. She was first to the scene of the *PENNSYLVANIA* disaster at Hat Island June 13, 1858 (see), with Capt. E.W. Gould in command. A newspaper was published on board edited and prepared by clerk G.W. Ford, a daily. Lost at Hat Island in ice (above Grand Tower, Ill.) on Feb. 25, 1858.

2923 JAMES FISK JR.

Rig? p wh b. Ironton, Oh., 1870. 160 tons. Built for Capt. W.P. Ripley. Sold mid-January 1871 to Fowler, Lee & Co., Paducah, Ky., for the Paducah-Cairo trade to replace *ARMADA* which was too large. Capt. Joe Fowler commanded and she ran there until the *GUS FOWLER* was built in 1879.

2924 JAMES G. BLAINE

SW p wh b. East Riverside, Pa. (hull), and completed at Brownsville, Pa., 1882. 162 x 34 x 5.5. Engines, 18's- 5½ ft. Three boilers. East Riverside is about 19 miles above Brownsville, Pa., on the east, or right shore. Owned by the Pittsburgh, Brownsville & Geneva Packet Co. She was first through the new slackwater to Morgantown, W. Va., arriving there Nov. 8, 1889. U.S. Engineer Col. William E. Merrill rode up along. In mid-July 1890 struck a rock departing Morgantown and sank. Sank again in first week of January 1896 at Hatfield's Landing, near the Masontown bridge, when wind blew her into a stump. Sank twice in 1900, first on Feb. 12 near the Crescent Coal Works, and on June 28 at Monessen, Pa. She was retired at Brownsville, beached during a flood in December 1902 and dismantled. Machinery went to the *COLUMBIA* (2nd).

2925 JAMES GRAY

Stw p wh b. Grayville, Ill., on Wabash River, 1863. 64 tons. In December 1865 running Evansville-Green-Pond rivers, Capt. Thomas Randall, master, with John M. Reynolds, clerk. Dismantled at Pittsburgh 1872.

2926 JAMES GUTHRIE

SW p wh b. Jeffersonville, Ind., by Howard, 1877. 244 x 37.5 x 5.8. Owned by Louisville & Henderson Mail Line Co. Called "the dandy Jim," built to replace the *TARASCON* (see). In 1881 Capt. David L. Penny, master, with M.D. Warren and R.B. Baldwin, clerks. When dismantled equipment went to *CITY OF NEW ALBANY* (see).

2927 JAMES H. LUCAS

SW p wh b. Jeffersonville, Ind., by Howard, 1854. 230 x 35 x 7. Engines, 25's- 7 ft. Named for a St. Louis banker. Owned by Capt. David Silver and others. Ran St. Louis-St. Joseph, and took down the time of the *POLAR STAR*. Left St. Louis July 19, 1856, at 11:55 P.M. and arrived at St. Joe July 22 at 12:54, time 60 hours 57 minutes. The deer horns she won from the *POLAR STAR* later hung in the Lee Line wharfboat at Memphis. Capt. Andy Wineland was master on the fast trip, with Gates McGarrah and Robert Wright, pilots. Dismantled 1861 and machinery went to the *G. W. GRAHAM*.

2928 JAMES H. TROVER

Stw p wh b. Belle Vernon, Pa., 1864. 241 tons. Originally named *KATE B. PORTER*. 160 x 32. Engines, 12¾'s- 4½ ft. Two boilers. She was tinclad #55 during the war, known as *KATE*. Sold to private hands and renamed Mar. 12, 1866. Upbound from St. Louis to Fort Benton in June 1867 she was aground several times and laid up for repairs five times; she was on fire three or four times; a crew member got smallpox; and a spar fell on another and broke his leg. Commanded by Capt. D. Artee, she got to Trover Point, 30 miles above Musselshell River, Mont., when the doctor pump became deranged. She was landed to make repairs, the river was falling, she got caught high and dry and had to be abandoned June 21, 1867. The *IDA STOCKDALE* took her trip to Benton.

2929 JAMES HALE

SW p wh b. Freedom, Pa., 1860. 173 tons. Went to U.S. war service 1864. Machinery went to the *U.P. SCHENCK* in 1875, later removed.

2930 JAMES HOWARD

SW p wh b. Jeffersonville, Ind., by Howard, 1870. 320 x 53 x 10. Engines, 34⅝'s- 10 ft. Six four-flue boilers, each 46" by 30 ft. Paddlewheels 39 ft. dia. working 16 ft. buckets. Carried 3,200 tons. Built for Capt. B. Rush Pegram and others for the St. Louis-New Orleans trade. Cost $180,000. Made her first trip south from Cincinnati, and again was at Cincinnati Jan. 21, 1871, opened for public inspection. An estimated 45,000 visitors came aboard over one gangway and left by another. Transported the Grand Duke Alexis of Russia and entourage to New Orleans early in 1872 in time for Mardi Gras, at which the Rex organization was formed. Fire was discovered in the hold as she landed at Commerce, Mo., Sept. 9, 1873, and she was purposely scuttled to save her. She sank in shallow water—too shallow to put out the blaze—so was pumped out and moved to deeper water and again purposely sunk. This time she settled below her guards and the fire was extinguished. Her masters over her span of operation were Capt. B. Rush Pegram, Capt. James O'Neal, Capt. James H. Pepper, and Capt. Joseph W. Bryant. Her biggest cotton cargo into New Orleans on a single trip was 7,701 bales, a record to that date, handled in 1875. Biggest trip she took down was in January 1881, 3,200 tons of cargo. Capt. Pegram et. al., sold her to the Anchor Line in 1878. Burned at St. Louis, just in from New Orleans with a large cargo of sugar, Mar. 13, 1881. Crew at the time: Capt. Jos. W. Bryant, with Archie Woods, first clerk; J.C. Elton, 2nd clerk; James Reed and Ned Fulkerson, pilots; James Newell, chief engineer; Eugene Smith, 2nd engineer; Dennis Conner, mate; Patrick Doyle, second mate; and Alf Dickson, steward. All escaped safely ashore, and among the passengers were Mr. and Mrs. John I. Nevin of the Pittsburgh *Leader,* their child and a nurse. The *THOMPSON DEAN* replaced her. The "Oil Cake Jim" was one of the river's great.

2931 JAMES JOHNSON

SW p wh b. Jeffersonville, Ind., 1856. 525 tons. Ran Nashville-New Orleans, teamed up with the *JAMES WOODS* (see). Capt. Jesse Johnson, master. She and the *JAMES WOODS* were set afire and burned at Nashville to prevent their capture by the U.S., Feb. 23, 1862.

2932 JAMES LAUGHLIN

SW p wh b. Gallipolis, Oh., 1853. 188 tons. In 1856 running Memphis-Napoleon-White River, Capt. J.T. Shirley, with W.T. Woods, clerk. Sank and lost at Memphis, Sept. 13, 1856, with loss of six lives.

2933 JAMES LEE

SW p wh b. Sewickley, Pa. (hull), and completed at Pittsburgh, 1879. 241 x 34 x 7.5. Engines, 22's- 7 ft. from the *PHIL ALLIN* (see) powered by four boilers, each 44" dia. by 28 ft., six flues. Paddlewheels 29 ft. dia. with 15 ft. buckets. The hull was built at the Pittsburgh Boat Yard Co., for Major John D. Adams, Memphis, who planned naming her *TROUBADOUR*. The hull stuck on the ways during the launch and Adams sold it to Capt. James Lee, Memphis. A duplicate hull then was built at the same yard for Adams which became the *KATE ADAMS* (1st), see. This was the second boat built at the Sewickley Yard, the first having been the *BUTTE* (see). Ran out of Memphis in the Lee Line. Crew in 1882: Capt. Stacker Lee with Lloyd Whitlow, Platt Rhoads and Arthur Browne, clerks. Her upper works badly burned in a fire Oct. 3, 1883, rebuilt. She was retired c. 1894. The metal from her engines was broken up and recast into cylinders for the U.S. steamer *JOSEPH HENRY* (see).

2934 JAMES LEE

SW p wh b. Jeffersonville, Ind., by Howard, 1898. 230 x 43 x 7. Engines, 24's- 8 ft. Five boilers, each 44" by 30 ft. Built for the Lee Line, Memphis, and ran Memphis-Friar's Point, Capt. John J. Darragh. This was a handsome boat, consistently successful, and outlived her usefulness as a packet. She was converted into an excursion boat at Memphis in 1917, renamed *DESOTO* (see) and was victim of the 1917-1918 ice.

2935 JAMES LYON

Stw p wh b. Belle Vernon, Pa., 1853. 187 tons. She was best known on the Upper Mississippi, St. Louis-St. Paul 1855-1858. Was making a Missouri River trip when snagged and lost at Miami Bend, Dec. 26, 1858.

2936 JAMES M. NILES

SW p wh b. Cincinnati, Oh., 1848. 266 tons. Sank and lost at Louisville, Ky., Feb. 20, 1854.

2937 JAMES MEANS

Stw p wh b. Wheeling, Va., 1860. 140 x 31.5 x 4.5. Engines, 14's- 4 ft. Ran Wheeling-Steubenville until sold, July 1862 to Northern Line Packet Co., which loaded her out at Pittsburgh, Capt. James Robinson, for the Upper Mississippi. Ran Davenport-Galena-Dubuque along with the *BILL HENDERSON* carrying U.S. Mail. Sold 1871 to J.W. Van Sant and son Sam, who removed part of the cabin and made a raftboat out of her. John McCaffrey bought one-half interest and went master of her. Dismantled fall 1877.

2938 JAMES MILLINGAR

SW p wh b. Elizabeth, Pa., 1849. 285 tons. Built for Capt. Alex Norton and his brother Capt. William Norton, and ran Louisville-New Orleans. The *ALERT NO. 2* was lost in collision with this boat at Golconda, Ill., November 1849. Bought 1851 by Capt. Dunning M. Foster (brother of composer Stephen Collins Foster) for Cincinnati-New Orleans trade. Composer Foster and party of friends round-tripped to New Orleans on her March 1852. Burned at Cincinnati, June 14, 1853.

2939 JAMES MONTGOMERY

SW p wh b. New Albany, Ind., 1856. 536 tons. 270 x 36 x 7.5. Engines, 26's- 9 ft. Six boilers, each 38" by 20 ft. Built for Capt. Sam Montgomery and others for the Louisville-New Orleans trade. Capt. J.B. Russell was master 1860. Sank at New Albany, laid up, on Sept. 3, 1860, at 12:30 A.M. in 15 feet. The *CHAMPION NO. 4* succeeded in raising her three weeks later. Sank at Island 10 above New Madrid, Mo., Jan. 2, 1861, and *PRINCE OF WALES* took off the people. Sank and lost at Devil's Island five miles above Cape Girardeau, Mo., Dec. 11, 1861. The *CONTINENTAL* hit the wreck early December 1864 and sank, later raised. The *PARAGON* hit the wreck latter February 1868, tore out her bottom, and was lost. A U.S. snagboat in September 1931 removed a steamboat wreck below Cape Girardeau, and chief Charles S. Henry measured the recovered engines to judge them 26's- 10 ft., surmising this to be the wreck of the *MONTGOMERY*.

2940 JAMES N. TRIGG

Stw p wh b. Decatur, Ala., 1910. 158.2 x 28.2 x 4.1. Engines, 14's- 5 ft. Two boilers. Owned by Tennessee River Navigation Co. In Chattanooga-Kingston trade 1921, Capt. Paul Underwood, with Harris Underwood and Johnny Dobbs, pilots. Got in a storm near Guntersville, Ala., and wrecked, 1921.

2941 JAMES N. WHITE

Stw p wh b. Nashville, Tenn., 1893. 147 x 27 x 3. Ran Nashville-Burnside, Capt. W.D. Cowleshaw, part owner and master. Machinery from *PEARL*. Later owned and operated by Capt. William T. Hunter, who later was U.S. Hull Inspector at Nashville. His father W.A. Hunter was the mate. In September 1898 running excursions at Paducah. Still listed 1902.

2942 JAMES NELSON

Stw p wh b. Elizabeth, Pa., 1848. 182 tons. Named for the early Pittsburgh machinist and engine builder. 150 x 26 x 5. First master and part-owner, Capt. George D. Moore, and his partners were George Ledlie, David C. Herbst, David R. Dale, and James B. Fulton, all of Pittsburgh. Ran Pittsburgh-Wheeling. Sold in fall of 1851 to Capt. Mark Sterling who towed coal with her to St. Louis, and March 1852 sold to Andrew Leech & Co., for same purpose. Dismantled, and engines went to *GEORGE ALBREE*.

2943 JAMES PARK

Stw p wh b. California, Pa., 1853. 258 tons. 151.5 x 34 x 5.5. Owned in part and commanded by Capt. Robert Miller, Pittsburgh. Ran Pittsburgh-St. Louis. She was at Thebes, Ill., May 12, 1856, upbound with cargo of railroad rails and a barge of lumber for Hannibal, Mo., when she caught fire near the boilers. W.J. Montague, the pilot on watch, jumped out of the pilothouse window, onto the barge, and then into the river. Nathan Hart, his partner, followed suit, having been asleep in the pilothouse. The flaming boat hit the Missouri shore head-on, broke loose from the barge, and both swung around and went on down the river. The *SOUTH AMERICA* secured a line to a ringbolt in the hull and towed the burning boat opposite Commerce, Mo., where she sank in 40 feet.

2944 JAMES PAUL
SW p wh b. Fulton, Oh., now a section of Cincinnati, 1853. 70 tons. Sank and lost at Palestine, Ill., Dec. 9, 1855.

2945 JAMES R. GILMORE
Stw p wh b. California, Pa., 1863. 205 tons. 156.5 x 32.1 x 4.4. Capt. D.S.H. Gilmore was master and owned her entire when she was new. Ran Pittsburgh-St. Louis. In U.S. service Evansville-Nashville 1864, and last owned by Capt. R.S. Yerkes, Covington, Ky., and A.C. Carlton, Cincinnati. Snagged and lost at mouth of Cache River, Mound City, Ill., Sept. 18, 1866, Capt. Yerkes in charge and Stanton Batchelor, clerk. She ran afoul of the wrecked *COURIER*, burned there in August 1864 (see).

2946 JAMES RAYMOND
SW p wh b. Cincinnati, Oh., 1853. 274 tons. Best remembered as escort and towboat for the Spaulding and Rogers' *FLOATING CIRCUS PALACE*, and was equipped with "an elegant concert saloon" called the Ridotto, where dramatic performances, vaudeville and minstrel entertainments were staged. The outfit was in New Orleans 1861 when the unpleasantness broke out and the showboat was taken over by the Confederates to become a floating hospital ship. Dan Rice, rival of Spaulding and Rogers, procured the *JAMES RAYMOND* and hustled her north where she is said to have done patrol duty while playing her calliope on moonlight nights. Spent the summer of 1862 perched high and dry on a lower Tennessee River sandbar. Burned at St. Louis along with *IDA HANDY* and *BOSTONA*, June 2, 1866.

2947 JAMES REES
SW p wh b. Elizabeth, Pa., 1862. 302 tons. Built for the Pittsburgh & Elizabeth Packet Line and ran that trade "as regular as clock works" until sold September 1866 to Wheeling & Sun Fish Packet Co., Capt. Steve Thompson and others, and ran Wheeling-Clarington until she was dismantled in 1876 and equipment used in building her successor, the *TELEGRAM* (see).

2948 JAMES ROBB
SW p wh b. Cincinnati, Oh., 1852. 593 tons. Owned by Capt. Hercules Carrel and others for Louisville-New Orleans trade. Named for the "father" of the early railroad connecting New Orleans and Morgan City, La. Also ran St. Louis-New Orleans. Sank and lost at Grand Tower, Ill., Feb. 17, 1855.

2949 JAMES THOMPSON
SW ferry wh b. Jeffersonville, Ind., by Howard, 1862. 280 tons. 155 x 37 x 5. Built for the Jeffersonville Ferry Co., and launched Nov. 1, 1862. Sold to U.S. Navy in March 1863 and renamed *MANITOU* that June. She became tinclad #13, renamed *FORT HINDMAN*, in November 1863, and resumed her original name when sold privately in December 1865. Machinery went to the ferry *Z.M. SHERLEY* in 1873.

2950 JAMES TRABUE
SW p wh b. Cincinnati, Oh., 1854. 244 tons. Snagged and lost at Campti, La., Feb. 16, 1855.

2951 JAMES W. GAFF
Stw p wh b. Cincinnati, Oh., 1876. 600 tons. 230.4 x 25.6 x 5.6. Engines, 16's- 6 ft. Two boilers, each 47" dia. by 24 ft., 10 flues. Owned by Memphis & Ohio River Packet Co. and ran Cincinnati-Memphis. Capt. Robert W. Wise, master, with J.D. Moore, clerk, 1877–1878, and with James Surtees, clerk, 1879. Sank at Marshall's Landing, below Cloverport, Ky., Mar. 21, 1878, at 3:00 P.M., head on shore and stern under water up to the cabin deck. Capt. J.D. Moore later was master, James Surtees, clerk. Still listed 1886.

2952 JAMES WATHEN
Recess wheel ferry wh b. Jeffersonville, Ind., by Howard, 1871. 221 tons. 149.6 x 38.6 x 6.5. Operated Louisville-Jeffersonville. Was renamed *VENICE* and so registered at St. Louis, 1886.

2953 JAMES WATT
Stw p wh b. Monongahela, Pa., 1852. 79 tons. Operated Marietta-Zanesville 1853–1854, Capt. Henry H. Drown. Sold January 1855 to run Cincinnati-Madison, Capt. Harris, and sank opposite Petersburg, Ky., Mar. 8, 1855. Lost in ice at Cincinnati, Feb. 7, 1857, when the *A. W. QUARRIER* jammed into her.

2954 JAMES WATSON
Stw p wh b. Cincinnati, Oh., 1863. 200 tons. She was at Pittsburgh, advertised for Cincinnati, Feb. 24, 1864, Capt. James Watson, with Mr. Sontag in the office. Was in U.S. service most of 1864 in the Vicksburg-Memphis area. She sank and was lost in what now is Lake Whittington, east of the Mississippi River, where Island 76 was located, near Caulk Neck Cut Off. This happened the morning of Mar. 2, 1865, having aboard many passengers, 86 soldiers, a cargo of U.S. freight and Adams Express. Life loss was 35 persons, including 20 soldiers, three ladies, two children, five male passengers and some deckhands. The *ISABELLA* was on hand to care for survivors, as well as a trading boat named *WILLIAM BUTLER*.

2955 JAMES WHITE
SW p wh b. Cincinnati, Oh., 1864. 662 tons. 260 x 40 x 7. Engines, 26's- 8 ft. Four boilers. Launched in May 1864 and

went to St. Louis, Capt. Hugh L. White, master, with J.H. Menge, clerk. Named for Captain White's father, a Missourian who settled there 1810. Owned by Stiiwell, Powell & Co., St. Louis. Snagged and lost at Island 10, Miss. River, Nov. 5, 1864, with loss of 15 lives. The *CONTINENTAL,* upbound, came to the scene finding the boat sunk in 13 feet. Went alongside and took off 60 head of cattle and some hogs. Most of the stock escaped to the Tennessee shore. A large steamboat with a short story.

2956 JAMES WOOD

Stw p wh b. California, Pa., 1856. 154 x 40.4 x 6. 328 tons. Part owner and first master, Capt. James J. Robinson, Pittsburgh. Mark Sterling owned 3/8, of Birmingham (Pittsburgh). When she burned at Pittsburgh, May 7, 1856, she was regarded as one of the largest sternwheelers at Pittsburgh. Capt. Robert Anderson was the last documented master.

2957 JAMES WOODS

SW p wh b. Jeffersonville, Ind., by Howard, 1860. 585 tons. 257 x 37 x 7. Ran Nashville-New Orleans along with *JAMES JOHNSON* and *RED ROVER* (both see). Capt. W. Boyd, master, in 1860. She was purposely destroyed by fire at Nashville to prevent her capture by the U.S., Feb. 23, 1862, along with the *JAMES JOHNSON.* The fire was set by Charles Gallagher, father of Capt. T.M. Gallagher.

2958 JAMESTOWN

SW p wh b. Cincinnati, Oh., 1845. 338 tons. Operated Cincinnati-New Orleans. Capt. David Whitten was master for a time. Dunning Foster returned from the Mexican War on her to Cincinnati, September 1847, brother of composer Stephen Collins Foster. Lost by stranding at Columbus, Ky., Jan. 9, 1853.

2959 JAMESTOWN

SW ferry wh b. Fulton (Cincinnati), Oh., 1850. 89 tons. Off the lists 1853.

2960 JANE

SW ferry wh b. Wellsville, Oh., 1853. 44 tons. Off the lists 1856.

2961 JANE AUSTIN

Stw p wh b. Knoxville, Tenn., 1903. 112 x 18.5 x 2.9. Engines, 10"- 3 ft. One boiler. First owned by D.R. Hicks, who built her from the former *FLORA SWANN* (see). She succeeded the *BILL TATE* (see) and ran in the Dandridge trade, upper Tennessee River. Jake L. Dykes owned her later and lost her by sinking, under the Southern railroad bridge at Knoxville. Lexie Palmore, Austin, Tex., has a cream pitcher and sugar bowl used aboard.

2962 JANE FRANKLIN

Stw p wh b. Freedom, Pa., 1851. 196 tons. Originally owned by Capt. George Benedict and others, Marietta, Oh., with I.N. Cook, first clerk. Ran Marietta-Cincinnati. Ran tramp trades. Off the lists 1859.

2963 JANE NICHOLS

SW ferry wh b. Wheeling, Va., 1851. 68 tons. Exploded and lost at Wheeling, Apr. 24, 1859.

2964 JANIE RAE

Stw p wh b. Jeffersonville, Ind., by Howard, 1890. 110 x 25.9 x 3. Owned and operated by Capt. Robert Hornbrook, Evansville, Ind. She was snagged and lost on the Apalachicola River near Bluntstown, Fla., June 1898.

2965 JEAN WEBRE

Stw p wh b. Elizabeth, Pa., 1853. 101 tons. 115 x 24 x 4. Went to Bayou Lafourche, La., with Capt. Ulysee D. Terrebonne, master and half owner. Had several ownership changes in that area, and John W. Bowles became principal owner, of Franklin, La., with Capts. T.W. Bowles and G.B. Bowles, masters. Off the lists in 1856.

2966 JEANETTE

Stw p wh b. Elizabeth, Pa., 1854. 145 tons. Went to Mobile, Ala. In 1859 running Mobile-Bladen and Cullem Springs, Capt. H.R. Johnson, master, teamed up with the *ADVANCE.*

2967 JEANNETTE ROBERTS

Stw p wh b. Rock Island, Ill., 1857. 111 tons. Ran St. Paul-Minnesota River, Capt. F. Aymond, owned in part by Louis Robert (no "s") who came to Minnesota c. 1838 and returned in 1842 to build a log cabin in what today is St. Paul. He was interested in various packets, *TIME AND TIDE, GLOBE, GREY EAGLE, GREEK SLAVE.* Your scribe had a letter August 1953 from Lilian Lamprey (Mrs. Francis H.) Murray, 80, whose mother was Jeannette Roberts, and eldest grandchild of Louis Robert. Boat was dismantled in 1870.

2968 JEANNIE DEANS

SW p wh b. McKeesport, Pa., and completed at St. Louis, 1852. 485 tons. Operated in the St. Louis & Keokuk Packet Co. Lost in ice at St. Louis, Feb. 26, 1856.

2969 JEANNIE DEANS

SW p wh b. Madison, Ind., and completed at St. Louis, 1860. 503 tons. 244.7 x 39.8 x 6. Engines, 23's- 7 ft. Four boilers, each 46" by 24 ft., five flues. Built for Capt. Joseph Brown and ran St. Louis-Keokuk. Frequently ran in winter months to New Orleans, and once made 12 round trips St. Louis-New Orleans keeping pace of 11 days per round. Once a snag speared through her decks, bent a copper steam line upward into a stateroom where a man was pinned in his berth. This happened 800 miles below St. Louis but the trip was continued without further incident. Burned at Carondelet, Mo., at the Marine Railway Docks, May 12, 1866, also burning the docks.

2970 JEFF DAVIS

SW p wh b. Louisville, Ky., 1847. 107 tons. First home port, Vicksburg, Miss. Snagged and lost at Sartartia, Miss., Oct. 10, 1850.

2971 JEFF THOMPSON

SW p wh b. Madison, Ind., 1860. 137 tons. 132 x 25.5 x 4.2. Originally named *FANNY PEARSON* (see). Renamed at New Orleans at the start of the war. In February 1862 owned by Capt. John Smoker one-half and R.W. Doyle one-half. After the war, in October 1865 she resumed her original name *FANNY PEARSON,* then owned by Jacob F. Worley, Jefferson Parish, La. Transferred in several days to Daniel E. Senigs, New Orleans, also listed as master. Sold Feb. 2, 1867, to James L. Lobdell, New Orleans, Capt. Josiah Triplett, master.

2972 JEFF THOMPSON

Confederate gunboat Also referred to as *GENERAL THOMPSON.* She was on hand at the Battle of Memphis in April 1862. She was run ashore on the Arkansas side, set afire, and abandoned. Next morning about 7:30 she exploded. The *PLATTE VALLEY* hit this wreck in January 1867 near the head of President's Island and was lost (see). The U.S. snagboat *GEN. G.G. TOTTEN* blasted the wreck out in July 1867.

2973 JEFFERSON

Stw p wh b. Wheeling, Va., 1849. 146 tons. Ran on the Upper Tennessee owned by James and William Williams. Sold to John L. Doss Co., July 1855, Capt. Jacob Work. Dismantled 1856.

2974 JEFFERSON

SW p wh b. Newport, Ky., 1851. 232 tons. 154 x 30 x 4.4. Owned by J.W. Arthur & Co., New Orleans, Capt. B. McKinney, master. Was running Memphis-Batesville, and was snagged and sunk at Pine Bluff, Ark., Feb. 26, 1852.

2975 JEFFERSON

Stw p wh b. Elizabeth, Pa., 1851. 74 tons. Snagged and lost at Campti, La., Feb. 26, 1852.

2976 JEFFERSON

SW p wh b. McKeesport, Pa., 1852. 187 tons. Came out new Oct. 17, 1852, in the Pittsburgh-Brownsville trade, Monongahela River, Capt. Morgan Mason. In collision with *COL. BAYARD* on Feb. 6, 1853, seven miles above Pittsburgh, and two lives were lost on the *JEFFERSON.* Off the lists in 1861.

2977 JEFFERSON

SW p wh b. Jefferson City (now New Orleans) 1856. 102 tons. 100.5 x 26.7 x 4.3. Owned at New Orleans by Naamon L. Burgess and Miioyah Felton, Capt. James Roberson, master. Off the lists 1858.

2978 JEFFERSON

Stw ferry wh b. Jeffersonville, Ind., by Howard, 1858. 146 tons. 120.4 x 30.2 x 4.5. Owned by Capt. William Bobb, Jefferson Parish. Went to Confederate registry 1862. Off the lists, 1864.

2979 JEFFERSON

NOTE: Evidence of a steamer *JEFFERSON* on Red River, October 1869 loading at Shreveport for Jefferson, Tex. Also that a boat of the name burned at mouth of Black River with 134 bales of cotton, Mar. 27, 1870. May be the same one listed above, maybe not.

2980 JEFFERSON

Ferry wh b. Brooke County, W. Va., 1870. 28 tons. Operated at Steubenville, Oh., along with *REBECCA* and *UNION* (see). In 1877 owned by Captain W. Stoops, Stoops Ferry, Pa.

2981 JENNIE

Stw p wh b. West Wheeling, Oh., 1859. 40 tons. Off the lists 1861.

2982 JENNIE

Stw p wh Small packet with "a drygoods box cabin" in upper Red River, Capt. George L. White, master, in 1880s. So said Capt. Jesse K. Bell Rea. A *JENNIE* was built at Mobile, Ala., 1871, 42 tons, inspected in the New Orleans area into 1882, maybe later, perhaps the one Capt. Rea recalls.

2983 JENNIE BALDWIN

Prop p wh b. Cincinnati, Oh., 1863. 291 tons. Operated as a barge until 1866 when machinery was added, perhaps a canalboat. William J. Petersen tells of her loading 250 Norwegians at Dunleith for points upstream in June 1866. Was documented at Galena, Ill., 1876, as a towboat. Reported cut down by ice at St. Louis, Dec. 12, 1876.

2984 JENNIE BEALLE

SW p wh b. New Albany, Ind., 1852. 231 tons. Went to Mobile, Ala., and off the lists 1859.

2985 JENNIE BROWN

SW p wh b. Louisville, Ky., 1864. 146 tons. 137 x 23.6 x 4.5. Engines, 14's- 4½ ft. She ran Cincinnati-Chilo during low water, July 1864, Capt. Irwin. Was considered a good boat designed for U.S. express service on the Missouri River but never went there. Was owned by James Rees, Pittsburgh, 1869, and he sold her that July to Capt. W.H. Pierce of Rock Island, Ill., who intended using her in connection with a bridge being constructed there. He ran her Davenport-Clinton-Fulton, with W.P. Hall, pilot, 1870–1872. Sold to John Lawlor, Prairie du Chien, who operated her several seasons. Sold to Isaac Staples, Stillwater, Minn., who used parts building the rafter *ISAAC STAPLES.*

2986 JENNIE CAMPBELL

Stw p wh b. West Brownsville, Pa., at Axton Yard, 1881. 144 x 26 x 4. Sweeney engines, 16's- 6 ft. Two boilers. Named for daughter of Capt. William Campbell of the *ROB'T E. LEE* (2nd). Built for Capt. Ed Hornbrook and others who had previously run the *ARGOSY.* After several years on the Upper Ohio she was taken to Evansville and ran there to Henderson, Ky., until the *ROYAL* was built in 1890. Came back to the upper Ohio, towed coal out of Kanawha River, and for a time was in the Armstrong fleet at Wheeling. Capt. John Barrett recalled he had interest in her at one time, one of the first of the Barrett Line. Sank and lost at Memphis, Nov. 28, 1895. The real-life Jennie Campbell became the wife of Capt. John F. Rust, well known on Kanawha River.

2987 JENNIE GEORGE

Stw p wh b. Farmers, Ky., 1893. 90.5 x 8 x 2.4. Single deck, one stack. Did job towing and ran low water packet trades on the upper Ohio. Still going 1901, maybe later.

2988 JENNIE GRAY

Stw p wh b. Monongahela, Pa., 1857. 161 tons. Capt. Hannah J. Beares was part owner and master when she burned in the steamboat fire at Pittsburgh, May 7, 1859.

2988-A JENNIE HAYES

Stw p wh b. Franconia, Minn., 1879. 117.4 x 14.5 x 3.6. Operated on the St. Croix River. Still listed 1886, maybe longer.

2989 JENNIE HOPKINS

Stw p wh b. Cincinnati, Oh., 1863. 212 tons. In contemporary news items sometimes called *GINNY HOPKINS*. Ran on Ohio River until sold to USQMD in October 1864. Taken to New Albany, Ind., and altered into a hospital tender, associated with the floating hospital *R.C. WOODS*. Sold to private owners 1865 and renamed *LAURA FENTON* Oct. 10, 1865 (see).

2990 JENNIE HOWELL

Stw p wh A cotton-type packet built about 1871 for Capt. A.M. Halliday and others, and he commanded. A photo exists of her with a big cotton trip aboard marked: "A. M. Halliday, master, 2456 bales, Jan. 1873." Ran from New Orleans to Arkansas and Ouachita rivers. She hooked a snag below Shawneetown, Ill., July 26, 1873, upbound. The *ARKANSAS BELLE* took passengers and part of the crew to Evansville and by July 29 officers of the *QUICKSTEP* reported the upper works washed off and only a portion of the stern and the wheel were visible. The wrecking boat *T.F. ECKERT* was sent up from Cairo and from Caseyville on up found natives along shore "in a high state of intoxication" enjoying boxes of wine floated from the wreck. The *BELLE VERNON* hit the wreck about a month later (see) and was lost.

2991 JENNIE HUBBS

Stw p wh b. Cincinnati, Oh., 1863. 220 tons. Built for David Gibson and others and named for his 17-year-old niece. Was at Pittsburgh, Capt. H.H. Devenney, advertised for Cincinnati, Dec. 3, 1863. Sold March 1864 to the Dean Line for Cincinnati-Memphis trade, Capt. James Carroll. The line that July was composed of the *ALICE DEAN, SILVER MOON, GLENDALE, GOLDEN EAGLE,* and *JENNIE HUBBS*. William B. Miller was clerk, and was promoted to master September 1864. Sank at the Falls near New Albany, Ind., November 1864, raised, rebuilt, and in January 1867 renamed *EMPIRE* (see).

2992 JENNIE KIRK

SW p wh b. New Albany, Ind., 1859. 91 tons. Went to Mobile, Ala. 135 x 28 x 3.5. Ran Mobile-Montgomery, Capt. Byrnes Maeher. Went to Confederate registry 1861.

2993 JENNIE LANE

Stw p wh b. Jeffersonville, Ind., by Howard, 1869. Originally *BIG SUNFLOWER* (see).

2994 JENNIE LEWIS

SW p wh b. Paducah, Ky., 1864. 509 tons. Built for Capt. Henry McPherson, part owner and master. William W. Ater, St. Louis, formed the Miami Packet Co., in September 1867, of which he was managing owner. She ran St. Louis-Glasgow-Cambridge. The latter town on Missouri River is no longer there, but once was important. Burned at St. Louis Mar. 29, 1869, Capt. McPherson in charge.

2995 JENNIE MAY

Rig? p wh b. Fort Smith, Ark., 1879. 120 x 24 x 2.4. Rebuilt in 1884 at Fort Smith and documented as a new boat. Still listed 1886.

2996 JENNIE ROGERS

Stw p wh b. Elizabeth, Pa., 1863. 260 tons. 156.7 x 34 x 5.3. Built for C.R. May, New Orleans, Capt. J. McQuoid. Sold to USQMD and sold May 1866 to Joseph Leach, New Orleans, who turned her over to Eclipse Towboat Co., Algiers. Sold to Mobile, and off the lists 1873.

2997 JENNIE WALKER

Stw p wh b. Pittsburgh, Pa., 1874. 65 x 11.5 x 2.5. Operated by Capt. William V. Thompson, Evansville, Ind., who loaded crockery, dishes, etc., procured along the Monongahela River aboard a covered barge and peddled these wares down the Ohio, the *JENNIE WALKER* attending. Housewives looked forward to the arrival of the "dish boat" or "jug boat" and many family heirlooms had origin with this operation. Thompson died at Evansville, 75, on Aug. 1, 1927. His steamboat was still listed in 1886, maybe longer.

2998 JENNIE WHIPPLE

Stw p wh b. Brownsville, Pa., 1857. 138 tons. 135 x 30. Engines, 15½'s- 3½ ft. Three boilers. Built for Chippewa River, Capt. Charles C. Gray, but soon went to the Arkansas 1858–1859, Capt. Ad Storm, running to Memphis. Went to the Fort Madison-Rock Island trade 1861 owned and run by Capt. J.W. Campbell and Capt. Hillhouse. In August 1864 she loaded 7th Infantry Volunteers at Burlington and took them to St. Louis, but usually stayed in her trade. Off the lists 1866.

2999 JENNY LIND

SW p wh b. Cincinnati, Oh., 1847. 246 tons. 162 x 27.5 x 5.8. Built for Capt. George W. Haygood who commanded and Willis Main, both of New Orleans. Sold November 1849 to Capt. James Bercier and others, New Orleans, who sold her November 1850 to Mobile, Ala., Capt. George Cloudes, master. Lost at Savannah, Ga., Sept. 6, 1854.

3000 JENNY LIND

Stw p wh b. Zanesville, Oh., 1848. 107 tons. She operated in the Muskingum River four years running successively to Beverly, Marietta, and Pittsburgh. Capt. Charles Gallagher was master 1848-1849 in the local trades, and Capt. Dan Hurd in the Pittsburgh trade 1850-1851. Sold October 1851 to Spaulding, Rogers & Van Orden circus to replace the *LOYALHANNA*. Off the lists 1854.

3001 JERRY OSBORNE

Batwing p wh b. Pikeville, Ky., and completed at Portsmouth, Oh., 1872. 38 tons. A double-decker built by Capt. O.C. Bowles who had run the *TOM HACKNEY* (see). Still listed 1876.

3002 JERRY OSBORNE NO. 2

Batwing p wh b. Ashland, Ky., 1878. 115.4 x 15.8 x 2.5. Equipment from former boat (see above) used building her. A dispatch from Wheeling dated Oct. 16, 1878: "The *JERRY OSBORN NO. 2* which seems to be a cross between a model barge and a Gulf steamer with uncovered wheels came up from Parkersburg yesterday to take the place of the *MOLLIE RAGON* in the Parkersburg trade. She is especially adapted to low water, drawing only 10 inches, and runs like a greyhound." Designed for Big Sandy River. Still listed 1886, maybe longer.

3003 JESSE K. BELL

SW p wh b. Cincinnati, Oh., 1856. 325 tons. 255 x 40 x 6. Engines, 22's- 8 ft. Three boilers. Apparently ran Louisville-St. Louis. She was at Louisville when the war broke out, April 1861. Rebuilt at Cincinnati, 1862. Gen. Lew Wallace used her as his headquarters during the Tennessee campaign. Burned at St. Louis Sept. 13, 1863, along with *POST BOY, HIAWATHA,* and *IMPERIAL*.

3004 JESSE K. BELL

SW p wh b. Jeffersonville, Ind., by Howard, 1879. 219.4 x 41 x 6.9. Built for Capt. Dick Sinnott and others. In 1880 running New Orleans, Grand Encore, and Alexandria, Capt. Dick Sinnott, with George C. Hamilton, clerk. Jesse K. Bell was president of the New Orleans National Bank and good friend of Dick Sinnott. Later on Dick became Collector of the Port, and sold his boat to Capt. George Washington Rea who ran her a couple of years and by 1893 she was in the Mississippi Packet Co., J.B. Woods, president, running New Orleans-Bayou Sara. Dismantled in January 1897. The hull became a coal barge and ultimately sank just above the mouth of Red River.

3005 JESSE LAZEAR

Stw p wh b. Brownsville, Pa., 1854. 72 tons. Snagged and lost in White River, Ark., January 1858

3006 JESSIE

SW ferry wh b. Maiden Rock, Wis., 1866. 36 tons. 70 x 14 x 3. In 1872 owned by Samuel Wadleigh, Oquaka, Ill., with Capt. John A. Brooks, master. Off the lists 1880.

3007 JESSIE

Stw ferry wh b. Jeffersonville, Ind., by Howard, 1866. 132 x 35 x 5. 187 tons. Owned and operated in the New Orleans area by Capt. William Bobb. Lost at New Orleans, July 3, 1875.

3008 JESSIE B.

Rig? ferry wh b. Wheeling, W. Va., 1873. 67 tons. 101.4 x 28 x 3.7. Operated at Benson's Ferry, not far from Bloch Bros. Tobacco Co. plant, Wheeling. Still listed 1886.

3009 JESSIE BERGER

Stw p wh b. Brownsville, Pa., at Axton yard, 1887. 110.6 x 24.6 x 3.7. Operated between Wheeling and Bellaire, Ohio River. John Long was pilot on her. Still listed 1896.

3010 JESSIE EDGINGTON

Rig? ferry wh b. New Cumberland, W. Va., 1860. 42 tons. Operated between McConnelsville and Malta, Muskingum River, 1860-1867. She was hustled to Eagleport when Morgan and his raiders crossed during the Civil War. Her weapon was a Fourth of July cannon, but she arrived too late with too little. There is evidence she was taken to the Upper Mississippi, rebuilt at Alton, Ill., and served in that area until 1876. Off the lists 1879.

3011 JESSIE WILSON

Stw ferry wh b. Golconda, Ill., 1888. 81.5 x 20 x 3.8. Owned by B.W. McCandless and operated from Livingston County, Ky., across the Ohio to Golconda, Ill. Young Fred McCandless, B.W.'s son, fired the boiler on occasion. Fred afterwards operated the *ROYAL,* built the *DOROTHY,* etc. Still listed 1896.

3012 JEWEL

Stw p wh b. Jeffersonville, Ind., by Howard, 1878. 177.2 x 33 x 5. When new in October 1878, loaded out at Cincinnati for New Orleans, Capt. Charles P. Truslow, master, with Charles W. Drown, clerk. Operated New Orleans-Red River, Lower Coast, Bayou Lafourche, and Upper Coast. Burned at Mobile, Ala., in a cotton shed fire, 1890.

3013 JEWEL

Stw p wh b. Brownsville, Pa., 1892. Originally named *LYDE H.* (see). Renamed while in the Wheeling-Clarington trade owned by Capt. Thad Thomas, George Urpman, and others, upon the persuasion of Capt. Earn Clark who had boated at Evansville and was enamored of the *JEWEL* down there (see next listing). Capt. Oscar Webster bought the boat from these owners, ran her in Muskingum

River, Lowell-Zanesville 1897-1898, then briefly Gallipolis-Charleston. Sold April 1899 to Capt. J. Mack Gamble and others for Wheeling-Clarington run. Sold to John Hyer and Sam Williamson for the Newport-Wheeling trade, and after some stock swapping J. Mack Gamble had her in the same trade, Capt. Mike Davis. In 1903 again in the Muskingum River, Lowell-Zanesville, Capt. Oscar Webster; and occasionally in 1904. Rebuilt at Clarington 1906, sold to Capt. W.H. Smith and others in local Upper Ohio trades. While laid up for ice at Marietta in the mouth of the Muskingum she got caught on shore, and while effort was made to release her she sank, this on Feb. 8, 1908 at 4:00 P.M. Capt. John W. Beaver was master at the time. There came a flood on February 18, but she was salvaged after the water fell. She was the first boat locked at Lock No. 13, Ohio River, September 1909. Ran on the Monongahela River in place of the *COLUMBIA* fall of 1909. In 1914 owned by John W. Hubbard, Pittsburgh, who ran her Pittsburgh-East Liverpool on a hoot owl schedule so East Liverpool patrons could see stage shows in Pittsburgh and go home by night. Capt. Otto Hitner later towed his *COTTON BLOSSOM* showboat with her, and while so engaged cut down by ice at Mt. Vernon, Ind., in January 1918.

3014 JEWEL

Stw p wh b. Evansville, Ind., 1893. 150 x 27.8 x 4.7. Engines, 13's- 4 ft. Two boilers each 44" by 26 ft. Owned by Capt. J.B. Thompson and others, and ran Evansville-Henderson, replacing the *ROYAL*. Burned Feb. 2, 1910, at Evansville.

3015 JEWEL

Stw p wh b. Golconda, Ill., 1899. 102 x 17 x 3.5. Originally *CITY OF GOLCONDA* which capsized drowning 18 (see) in 1901. Rebuilt and renamed 1902, owned by Lyons Brothers, Greenville, Miss. Operated local packet trades out of Greenville. Later sold to Robert P. Wineman, Baton Rouge, and towed lumber to the Wineman mill at Greenville. She was lost in a storm while tied up north of the concrete wharf at Greenville on January 17, 1934.

3016 JEWESS

SW p wh b. Elizabethtown, Pa., 1847. 248 tons. Owned by Capt. John W. Bugher and others. Credit is given to this boat as being first to adopt fancy exterior railing ornamentation, "gothic" style. Downbound on an early trip she cleaned off much of this finery when she side-swiped a tree along the lower Ohio. She proceeded up the Mississippi bound for St. Louis, hooked a snag and cleaned off the other side back to the wheelhouse. Ran principally Cincinnati-St. Louis, and was lost in ice at St. Louis, Jan. 1, 1852.

3017 JEWESS

Stw p wh b. Cincinnati, Oh., 1862. 157.5 x 34 x 4.8. Ran Cincinnati-Memphis, Capt. Alex J. Frazier. Sold September 1865 to Mobile for the trade to Montgomery, Ala., owned there by Henry A. Shillot and others. Snagged and lost at Mobile, Dec. 28, 1868.

3018 JIM BARKMAN

Stw p wh b. New Albany, Ind., 1859. 65 tons. 93 x 23.7 x 3.3. Owned by Capt. James R. Bangs, Arkadelphia, Ark., and others. Operated in Ouachita River. Went to Confederate registry in 1861.

3019 JIM GILMER

SW p wh b. Cincinnati, Oh., 1846. 115 tons. 123 x 25.6 x 4. Built for Capt. J.F. Lodwick of New Orleans. In September 1849 sold to Charles M. Dowd, White Cliffs, Ark. Sold October 1849 to John Thomas, New Orleans, with Capt. R.H.R. McKenny, master. Snagged and lost at Soda Lake, La., with loss of two lives, March 13, 1851. The *NEW LATONIA* went up above Shreveport to take off the cotton.

3020 JIM LEIGHTON

Stw ferry wh b. Sioux City, Iowa, 1880. 119.5 x 30.1 x 3.6. Owned and operated by the Chicago & North Western RR, at Pierre, S.D. Still documented on Missouri River, 1908.

3021 JIM MONTGOMERY

Stw p wh b. Pt. Pleasant, W. Va., 1883. 92.6 x 17 x 2.9. Originally named *DOC HOY,* renamed c. 1890. Ran Madison-Warsaw-Florence on the Ohio River, Capt. Haz Albro, with W.H. Kirby, clerk. Reported sold to Capt. Ralph Emerson Gaches, March 1899.

3022 JIM TURNER

SW p wh b. Louisville, Ky., 1853. 212 tons. Operated on upper Red River above the Raft, Capt. S.B. Allen. Sank and lost at Rowland, La., April 27, 1853.

3023 JIM WILLIAMS

Rig? p wh Ran on the Upper Tennessee River pre-Civil War owned by James and William Williamson. The *Knoxville* (Tenn.) *Register* ran an item July 12, 1855: "John L. Doss & Co. have bought the *JIM WILLIAMS* and that boat, with the well-known *JEFFERSON,* will make regular trips between Chattanooga and Knoxville, carrying both freight and passengers."

3024 JO GALES

SW ferry wh b. Cincinnati, Oh., 1855. 208 tons. She was the ferry at Burlington, Iowa. Dismantled in 1871.

3025 JO HORTON FALL

Stw p wh b. Jeffersonville, Ind., by Howard, 1913. 158 x 28 x 4. Compound engines, 9's, 18's- 5 ft. Two boilers, each 38" by 24 ft. Built for Capt. Tom Ryman, Jr., and others, and ran on Cumberland River. He was shot and killed aboard near Hunter's Landing, Tenn., fall of 1915. The Nashville Navigation Co., headed by H.G. Hill, Nashville, and managed by Capt. W.L. Berry, Paducah, continued her. In November 1921, she went up to Greasy Creek, Capt. Charles Hill, with Dave Martin, mate; Guy Martin, purser; Will Harris and John Gans, pilots; Pat Cox, chief; Fred Shearer, second, and Jack Pride, steward. In May 1922 made a special trip to Burnside, Ky., head of navigation, and aboard as passengers were Donald T. Wright and

Art J. Dyer. Later sold to Capt. Pete Lee, Memphis, who converted her into an excursion boat renamed *VALLEY QUEEN* (see).

3026 Jo Long

Stw p wh b. Lyons, Iowa, 1896. 120.3 x 21.3 x 4. Engines, 12's- 6 ft. by Swain. Ran in the Davenport-Clinton trade by Capt. J.N. Long and skippered by Capt. Ben Congar. On Aug. 8, 1896 there was an argument at the Diamond Jo warehouse, Davenport, in which agent James Osborn was stabbed and Captain Long was arrested and fined $300. She had been running competition with the *VERNE SWAIN* and this about ended the rivalry. Soon afterward the *LONG* was sold for Vicksburg-Lake Providence trade, renamed *PROVIDENCE,* where she capsized and sank (see).

3027 Joab Lawrence

Stw p wh b. Cincinnati, Oh., 1864. 221 tons. Named for skipper of the *LEVIATHAN* (see). Capt. G.B. Russell was master. Sold to Mobile, Ala. and was lost at Red Jacket Bar, Ala., Sept. 28, 1867.

3028 Joan of Arc

SW p wh b. Louisville, Ky., 1852. 148 tons. Capt. J. Frank Hicks, part owner and skipper, his first command. Probably out of Memphis. Off the lists 1860.

3029 Joe Bryarly

Stw p wh Running New Orleans-Shreveport in 1878, Capt. Matt Scovell. Hit an obstruction at the mouth of Red River, December 1878, knocking 700 bales of cotton overboard, killing fifteen, and injuring three others. Burned en route from Shreveport to New Orleans at Barnaby's Landing near Atchafalaya, Oct. 13, 1880.

3030 Joe Curtis

Stw p wh b. Jeffersonville, Ind., by Howard, 1891. Originally ferry *EMILY* (see), then *DIXIE B. LINE,* and *OHIO NO. 2.* Converted into a short trade packet by Capt. Peters Lee who ran her as *JOE CURTIS,* named for the popular river reporter of the Memphis *Commercial-Appeal,* this 1934–1936. Sold March 1936 to the Wolf River Transportation Co., Memphis, thus ending the operation of Lee Line Steamers at Memphis. That fall Capt. Russell Warner ran her as a packet Memphis-Gayoso Bend. Sank in ice and lost at Memphis, Jan. 25, 1940.

3031 Joe Fowler

Stw p wh b. Jeffersonville, Ind., by Howard, 1888. 182 x 31.6 x 5.5. Engines, 16's- 7 ft. Three boilers, each 44″ by 22 ft. In 1913 she received new patent Kidney boilers which were failures, and were replaced 1914 by four new Western style boilers allowed 259 psi, then the highest boiler pressure on Western rivers. These were set to pop at 244 psi, and were 40″ by 22 ft. with four 6″ and four 8″ flues. She was built by the Fowler family for the Evansville-Paducah trade, teamed up with the *JOHN S. HOPKINS.* Capt. James Damron was master when she was new. On May 1, 1895, she had completed in seven years a total of 327,000 miles as a U.S. Mail steamer, and had carried some 152,400 passengers without life-loss. She was continued in this trade until she wore out and was condemned. Capt. Ben S. Pope, Parkersburg, W. Va., bought her early spring 1912, and she came there under her own steam and was completely rebuilt that summer and winter. Her first trip was Parkersburg-Pittsburgh in April 1913 handling huckster business with Capt. Martin F. Noll, purser—his last steamboating. That summer she ran excursions in the Wheeling-Bellaire area. Ran a Mardi Gras cruise from Parkersburg to New Orleans and returned to Pittsburgh in early 1914. Ran a special cruise, Pittsburgh-St. Paul, Minn., and returned to Louisville in June 1914. The details of this unusual voyage are recounted in *S&D Reflector,* June 1867 issue, pages 6–17, with many illustrations. The crew: Capt. Elmer E. Pope, manager; Capt. A.C. Dunbargar, master; Clyde Packard, purser; Clarence L. Cunningham, chief; Bill Sampson, steward; Earl Cooper, electrician. Dayton Randolph piloted to Cincinnati, and Walter S. and Stuart Conner thence to Cairo. She ran excursions at Louisville summer 1914, Capt. W.C. Lepper. In 1915 ran Pittsburgh-Louisville, round trip a week, no mean trick. Crew: Capt. Ben S. Pope, master; Dayton Randolph and Walter English, pilots; Jack Speers and Earl Cooper, clerks; William English, mate; Billy Sampson, steward. She carried a calliope played by Gus Fissmer, Louisville. Average cost per round trip $1,100, and she burned 3,000 bushels of coal weekly. In 1916 ran excursions in the Parkersburg-Pittsburgh area. Came to Ambridge, Pa., January 1917 to get new barges for delivery south. Sold to Capt. John L. Lowry, Evansville, who resold her to Capt. Jeff H. Williams, Evansville. She was converted into an excursion boat and renamed *CRESCENT* (see). The original whistle was transferred to the *RUTH* in the Evansville trade, and Capt. Ben Pope procured from the J. Mack Gamble family of Clarington, Oh., the *COURIER* whistle.

3032 Joe Jakes

Rig? p wh Owned at Arkadelphia City, Ark., by Joe Cossart in the 1850s. When dismantled her engines went to the *ARKADELPHIA CITY* (see).

3033 Joe Kinney

SW p wh b. Madison, Ind., 1872. 739 tons. 231 x 38.4 x 6.8. Engines, 22's- 7 ft. Three boilers. Ran St. Louis-Missouri River, and in off seasons was occasionally sent to Red River. Owned by Kansas City Packet Co., Capt. George G. Keith, master. Once struck the Boonville Bridge, swung under the south span, taking away pilothouse, texas, and chimneys. Collided with a pier of the Kansas City Bridge March 27, 1876, losing a wheel. She was upbound at the Glasgow Bridge April 13, 1882, when her tiller line parted. She swung around and hit a pier, stoving in her side. Then she drifted back and sank to the roof. She had aboard 4,500 sacks of wheat. Tony Schwab was the pilot on watch. Boat and cargo lost.

3034 JOE NEWMAN

Batwing p wh b. Cincinnati, Oh., 1879. 24 tons. Ran Catlettsburg-Piketon. In that run, September 1883 with Capt. Friend, master, and John Culver, clerk.

3035 JOE PETERS

Stw p wh b. Belle Vernon, Pa. (hull) and the Wm. M. McFall yard. Completed at Pittsburgh, 1883. 177.2 x 34.4 x 4.6. Cabin equipment, etc., from the *KATIE HOOPER* which was brought to Pittsburgh at the time for dismantling. Built for Memphis & Arkansas River Packet Co., Capt. John J. Darragh. She was running Memphis-Vicksburg, Capt. J.A. Cummins, when she sank and was lost at Memphis in the late fall of 1895.

3036 JOE S. KINNEY

Stw p wh b. Nashville, Tenn., spring 1871. 160 x 30 x 3. Built by Capt. William Kiber, and launched just below the suspension bridge. She was said to have been the first boat built at Nashville in 30 years.

3037 JOE WEBRE

Rig? p wh b. Bayou Bouef, La., 1878. 41.39 tons. In 1885 running New Orleans-Grand Isle, three trips a week, Capt. A.E. Hotard, with Frank Kraus, clerk.

3038 JOE WHEELER

Stw p wh b. Chattanooga, Tenn., 1898. 155.8 x 33.5 x 3.5. Engines, 13's-4½ ft. Two boilers, each 38" by 20 ft. Owned by Tennessee River Navigation Co., W.C. Wilkie, manager. Ran Joppa, Ill., to Chattanooga until 1907, then Chattanooga-Kingston. She made one trip to Knoxville, taking up government officials. Machinery came from the *J.C. WARNER*. She carried passengers as well as freight until June 1918 when the cabin was cut down. After that time she served as a towboat. Dismantled 1919 and parts used building towboat *CAPTAIN LYERLY*.

3039 JOE WILSON

SW ferry wh b. New Richmond, Oh., 1852. 47 tons. Exploded and burned at Columbus, Ark., Jan. 6, 1853.

3040 JOHN A. FISHER

Stw p wh b. Louisville, Ky., 1859. 122 tons. Operated out of Nashville, Tenn., to St. Louis. Snagged and lost at Carroll Island, below St. Louis, Oct. 27, 1864.

3041 JOHN A. PATTEN

Stw p wh b. Jeffersonville, Ind., by Howard, 1906. 167 x 34.5 x 6.4. Engines, 12½'s-6 ft. Two boilers, each 38" by 26 ft. Owned by Tennessee River Navigation Co., and named for company president Patten. Ran Chattanooga-Decatur trade. In February 1907, while racing with the towboat *PARKER* a few miles above Chattanooga, the *PARKER* exploded boilers. The *PATTEN* burned at Bridgeport, Ala., laid up for low water at the time, night of Nov. 5, 1910.

3042 JOHN A. SCUDDER

SW p wh b. Cincinnati, Oh., at Mack Yard and completed at St. Louis, 1873. 302 x 50.5 (48 ft. floor) x 8. Engines, 28's-8 ft. Six boilers, each 38" by 26 ft., 6 flues. These boilers were said to be from the U.S. gunboats *SANDUSKY* and *MARIETTA*, each of which had three of this description. Paddlewheels 32 ft. dia. with 14 ft. buckets. She had no hull planks under 46 ft. length and many were still in her when she was dismantled in 1885. She was a large cotton carrier for the Memphis-New Orleans trade, partly owned and commanded by Capt. A.J. Carter. Clerk in 1879 was D.A. Wist. She was taken into the Anchor Line for St. Louis-New Orleans service, Capt. W.W. Baker with J.C. Elton, clerk, in 1884. Arrived at New Orleans with her largest freight trip on Nov. 28, 1878: 4,484 bales, 10,055 sacks of cotton seed, 1,069 barrels of cotton seed oil, and 3,509 sacks of oil cake and hulls. When dismantled in 1885 her hull was used at Vicksburg as a wharfboat. Much of the cabin material came from the *MARBLE CITY* which was dismantled in 1873 when the *SCUDDER* was built.

3043 JOHN ADAMS

SW p wh b. Cincinnati, Oh., 1848. 298 tons. Built by Capt. Henry A. Jones of Cincinnati and others for the New Orleans trade. She was upbound at Island 82 above Greenville, Miss., on Jan. 28, 1851, when a snag broke the hull in two and she sank immediately with life loss set at 123 persons. The larger share of the casualties were deck passengers and deck crew. The scene of this tragedy was considerably west of the present course of the Mississippi.

3044 JOHN B. GORDON

SW p wh b. Brownsville, Pa., 1848. 57 tons. Capt. Jacob Poe had a share in building and running her. She had the distinction of making a trip to Chillicothe, Oh., arriving there on Jan. 31, 1849 via the Scioto River improvement from Portsmouth, Oh. Snagged and lost in the Arkansas River, June 8, 1851.

3045 JOHN B. GORDON NO. 2

Stw p wh b. Brownsville, Pa., 1849. 48 tons. Capt. Jacob J. Vandergrift came out master, with B.M. Laughlin, clerk. Several years later she ascended the Des Moines River to Fort Des Moines, arriving on a sabbath while church services were being held at the Fort. The congregation was dismissed for the event. She was in Minnesota River 1855 and dismantled that year.

3046 JOHN B. MAUDE

SW p wh b. Metropolis, Ill., at the Cutting & Wood Yard, 1872. 239 x 37 x 8. Owned by her namesake of St. Louis and others. Ran St. Louis-Memphis-New Orleans. Sank at O.K. Landing 40 miles above Helena, Ark., downbound with 800 bales, Jan. 1, 1875. Capt. John T. Noel was master at the time. She was raised on Jan. 20, and was taken to Mound City for repairs. The Memphis & St. Louis Packet Co. (Anchor Line) bought her at New Orleans in early March 1876. Capt. William H. Blake, master, 1878. Sank Nov. 1, 1880 at Brickley's Landing, Mo., and raised. In 1885 in August was running New Orleans-Plaquemine-

Upper Coast, Capt. J.A. Comstock with W.S. Mayor, clerk. Burned at New Orleans, laid up at the time, Jan. 30, 1886.

3047 John Bell

Stw p wh b. Louisville, Ky., 1855. 209 tons. Snagged and lost at St. Charles, Mo., Sept. 24, 1863.

3048 John Bertram

SW tr wh b. Jeffersonville, Ind., at Barmore Yard, 1880. 180 x 34 x 5.6. Engines, 20's- 6½ ft. Four boilers (two on a side) each 38" by 24 ft., 2 flue 13½". Built for Sioux City & Pacific RR, and her first service was 25 miles below Omaha, Neb., Capt. D.W. Fenton. Rebuilt at the Madison, Ind., ways, summer 1898, Illinois Central RR. Served at various locations. Capt. Sam Dryden was master for some time. She was at Helena, Ark., until replaced by the *DeKOVEN* (see) in February 1912.

3049 John Briggs

SW p wh b. New Albany, Ind., 1856. 352 tons. Operated Louisville-Henderson in 1858. Off the lists 1868.

3050 John Buck

Stw p wh b. California, Pa., 1854. 111 tons. 135 x 23.1 x 3.8. Named for a Morgan County, Oh., pioneer who lived below Big Bottom on the east side of the Muskingum River and was associated with construction of the locks at Taylorsville, Luke Chute, and Lowell. Capt. Henry T. Dexter, Zanesville, first owner and master. She spent six years in Muskingum service, principally Marietta-Zanesville. When the Marietta & Cincinnati RR started regular service June 6, 1857, its trains came to Moore's Run at the head of Muskingum Island where the *JOHN BUCK* made connection to the B&O at Parkersburg, the location then called Scott's Landing. She ran this shuttle service all summer and fall 1857, and again in the early summer 1858. The *FREESTONE* and *VIRGINIA HOME* (see both) ran this trade later on. Her skipper in 1857 was Capt. Joseph McVay, and in 1858–1859, Capt. James Darlington. Off the lists 1861.

3051 John C. Calhoun

SW p wh b. West Brownsville, Pa., 1859. 165 tons. First home port, Apalachicola, Fla. Exploded and lost at Bainbridge, Ga., with loss of six lives, April 28, 1860.

3052 John C. Fremont

Stw p wh b. California, Pa., 1854. 315 tons. 150 x 39.5 x 6. Built for Capt. Jackman T. Stockdale, Georgetown, Pa., and others. Ran Pittsburgh-St. Louis. Collided with *SWITZERLAND* near Vevay, Ind., January 1855, and the U.S. Inspectors handed pilot John Shouse a 30-day suspension of his license. Renamed *HORIZON* on March 1, 1861 (see).

3053 John D. Grace

Stw p wh b. Jeffersonville, Ind., by Howard, 1917. 166.4 x 33 x 5.6. Owned by Bradford Transportation Co., Donaldsonville, La. Engines, 14's- 6 ft. Two boilers, each 44" by 22 ft. Ran New Orleans-New Iberia. This boat was immortalized by Roark Bradford in a series of magazine roustabout stories. Later was in Sherburne Transportation Co., Plaquemine, La. Pilots Hymel and Pintado in June 1921 had been partner pilots for 25 years. Capt. W.A. Bisso, president of Bisso Towboat Co., bought her early spring 1930, dismantled her. The engines went to towboat *TYLER*.

3054 John D. Perry

SW p wh b. Jeffersonville, Ind., by Howard, 1858. 220 x 33 x 6. Engines, 20's- 7 ft. Four boilers, each 38" by 26 ft. First ran St. Louis-Missouri River, Capt. Joe S. Nanson. In 1860, New Orleans-Red River to Alexandria, La., Capt. William Kimball. She left St. Louis latter March 1861 for the south, and was hailed down and stopped at Cairo by the *SWALLOW* in U.S. service, searched, and then escorted to the Cairo wharf where bar lead and shot in her cargo was confiscated. She then was allowed to proceed. The *C.E. HILLMAN* was similarly searched next day and relieved of almost a full cargo of guns and ammunition. She was in the St. Louis & Memphis Packet Co. in the war period and after, Capt. Alex Zeigler with A.E. St. Gemme, clerk. In early April 1868 with an excursion party aboard she ran on a sandbar 12 miles above Batesville, Ark., on White River. The *W.H. BROOKS* took off the excursionists. Sank April 6, 1869 at Devalls Bluff, Ark., on White River, caught fire and burned. Then owned by Capt. Pat H. Wheat of Devalls Bluff.

3055 John D. Scully

Stw p wh b. Freedom, Pa. (hull) and completed at the Rees shop, Pittsburgh, 1878. 215 x 34.6 x 4.5. Engines, 15's- 4½ ft. Three boilers, each 38" by 26 ft. Built for Capt. William J. Kountz. Had one stack and a long, narrow cabin, primarily a freight boat. This machinery may have originated on the *CARRIE BROOKS* (see). In departing Pittsburgh a new boat she knocked down her stack on the Point Bridge and returned for repairs. Kountz used her on the Mississippi, and later she was owned by Capt. W.T. Scovell, New Orleans, who ran her up Red River. She received a new hull at New Orleans 1894, and burned Aug. 20, 1895 at Carrollton, La. Just prior she had been running New Orleans-Bayou Teche, a 10-day round trip to New Iberia and Franklin, Capt. M.N. Wood.

3056 John Darling

SW ferry wh b. Wellsville, Oh., 1864. 36 tons. First home port, Wheeling. Off the lists 1866.

3057 John E. Kenna

Stw p wh b. Charleston, W. Va., 1878. 30 tons. Named for a West Virginia state senator and old-timers around Charleston recalled she once made a trip up Elk River. Was sold to Red River, running out of Shreveport. Sank and lost in the vicinity of New Orleans, Aug. 7, 1883.

3058 JOHN F. ALLEN

Stw p wh b. Cincinnati, Oh., 1884. 130.9 x 37.6 x 4.5. Built for the Yazoo & Tallahatchie Packet Co. Sank six times during a long and otherwise successful career. Burned in Yazoo River near L'Argent, Miss., October 1896.

3059 JOHN F. HALPIN

Stw p wh b. Mason City, W. Va., 1882. 116.2 x 22.4 x 4.3. A short trader bought by Capt. William H. Sargent who used her on the Yazoo and out of Vicksburg, renamed *L.H. SARGENT* (see).

3060 JOHN F. LINCOLN

SW tr wh b. Jeffersonville, Ind., 1881. 155 x 32 x 6.2. Inspected at Sioux City, Iowa, June 2, 1881. Later was operated at Cairo, Ill. until laid up January 1900. The *JOHN BERTRAM* replaced her there. Capt. L.E. Patton bought her, took her to Memphis and dismantled her, February 1902.

3061 JOHN F. TOLLE

Stw p wh b. Elizabeth, Pa., 1871. 237 x 51. Compound Hartupee engines, 15's- 33's- 6 ft. Three boilers, each 40" by 28 ft. Owned by Capt. William J. Kountz, and primarily a freight carrier. Capt. D.M. Brady, master. Ran St. Louis-New Orleans. The *Pittsburgh Commercial* remarked, Oct. 14, 1871: "The *JOHN F. TOLLE* is rapidly nearing completion. Her engines and boilers are in place, and her smokestack, which is located near the stern, is now being raised. She resembles in many respects the picture of Noah's Ark." She burned at Grand Gulf, Miss., 11:45 P.M., Nov. 10, 1877 with 23,000 bushels of wheat aboard. Collided with and wrecked the *BILL HENDERSON* (see) near Port Hudson, Feb. 18, 1876.

3062 JOHN FOWLER

Stw p wh b. Jeffersonville, Ind., by Howard, 1886. 147.5 x 28.5 x 3.5. Owned when new by Alex Kendall and Arch P. Green, and ran in the Nashville-Burnside trade on Cumberland River. Her masters included Capt. W.A. Crawford and Capt. A.T. Armstrong. Still listed 1892.

3063 JOHN G. CLINE

SW p wh b. Madison, Ind., 1853. 295 tons. Operating 1856 in Nashville-Memphis trade with *JOHN SIMPSON, CITY OF HUNTSVILLE,* and *EMBASSY.* Off the lists 1860.

3064 JOHN G. FLETCHER

Stw p wh b. Jeffersonville, Ind., by Howard, 1877. 121 x 26 x 4. Primarily a freight boat which appeared on the Arkansas in January 1878 for the Little Rock-Fort Smith trade, having come from the upper Missouri and Yellowstone rivers. In April 1878 went to Webbers Falls, 75 miles above Fort Smith in Indian country to bring down cotton, seed, and corn. Inspected at Memphis 1881, at New Orleans 1882. Reported sunk on Red River, Dec. 7, 1886.

3065 JOHN GAULT

Stw p wh b. Louisville, Ky., 1857. 198 tons. Ran Cincinnati-Nashville, Capt. Reeder, who was replaced March 1860 by Capt. Bunce. She was seized by the U.S. at Cairo in early 1862, where she caught out on the grade and was lost March 15, 1862.

3066 JOHN GILBERT

Stw p wh b. Sewickley, Pa. (hull) and completed at Pittsburgh, 1881. 220 x 44 x 6. Engines, 18's- 7 ft. Three boilers. Ran Cincinnati-Tennessee River, Capt. James Till. Was making a trip to St. Louis when she was snagged at Liberty Island between Grand Tower and Ste. Genevieve in the "Graveyard Stretch." Owned by the Evansville & Tennessee River Packet Co. of which Mr. Gilbert was president. Rousters called her the "Peanut John." An orchestral work titled *John Gilbert; a Steamboat Overture* by Dr. Claude Almand was conducted by Dr. Almand and played by the Louisville (Ky.) Philharmonic Orchestra on Feb. 8, 1949, and repeated Dec. 10–11 by the Cincinnati Symphony, winning instantaneous reception. The theme was suggested to the composer when he saw the book *Steamboatin' Days* by Mary Wheeler of Paducah, Ky., in which a song of the *JOHN GILBERT* is preserved as chanted by roustabouts.

John Gilbert is the boat,
Di De Oh Di De Oh,
John Gilbert is the boat,
Di De Oh,
Runnin' in the Cincinnati trade.

3067 JOHN GO 'LONG

SW p wh b. Ice Creek, Oh., 1844. 144 tons. Capt. A.P. Kouns brought her to Pittsburgh in January 1844, then ran her on Kanawha River. Sold to the Baker family on Missouri River. Capt. William Baker, master; his father was clerk; Bob, pilot; Tom, engineer, and Charles K. was mate. Ran St. Louis-Weston. Snagged and lost in Malta Bend, Camden, Mo., March 8, 1848. The profits from this boat built the *ST. JOSEPH* (see).

3068 JOHN H. DICKEY

SW p wh b. Madison, Ind., 1858. 403 tons. Built for Missouri River service, one of the "Great Mail and Transportation Company of the West." Capt. Dan Able, master. Other boats in the Line; *WHITE CLOUD, VICTORIA, POLAR STAR, WM. H. RUSSELL* and *ST. MARY.* About 1:00 A.M., Nov. 6, 1862, 10 miles above Ste. Genevieve, she hit the shore on the Illinois side with considerable headway. Passengers were brought awake, many of them in the cabin and on the guards, when a boiler exploded. Fire broke out but was extinguished. Capt. Marcelman was in charge. In early January 1865, the *DICKEY* was downbound loaded with U.S. troops near McCaleb's Point, 20 miles below Vicksburg. The *JOHN RAINE,* upbound, hit the *DICKEY* almost head-on, sheering down the starboard side. Three were killed on the *DICKEY* and twenty injured. It was a moonlight night. The force of the impact knocked down the smokestacks on the *DICKEY,* and they went off the starboard side into the river, causing some of the injuries. Dismantled 1865.

3069 JOHN H. GROESBECK

SW p wh b. Cincinnati, Oh., 1863. 604 tons. Ran Memphis-New Orleans, 1866, Capt. James Ransom, with John Spencer, clerk. Advertised at New Orleans for Cincinnati, 1864, Capt. Robert Baldwin. Capt. Dan Maratta bought control at Cincinnati, October 1866. Advertised at New Orleans for Cincinnati and Pittsburgh, April 1868, Capt. D.W. Maratta, with W.M. Maratta, clerk. She was the last of the short-length sidewheelers styled for passage through the Louisville-Portland locks. Dismantled summer 1872.

3070 JOHN H. HANNA

Stw p wh b. Madison, Ind., 1876. 181.2 x 38 x 6.5. Ran principally New Orleans-Ouachita River. Capt. J.W. Blanks was master, 1877, with J. Holmes, clerk. She was the "summer" boat in place of *OUACHITA BELLE,* connecting with *GOOSE* for Little River; *TOM PARKER* for Boeuf River; *ORA, ACME* and *TIMMIE BAKER* for Bayou Bartholomew, and *BERTHA BRUNNER* for Bayou d'Arbonne. Still in the trade 1885 with Capt. F.A. Blanks, master, and J.S. Holmes, clerk. She was downbound at Plaquemine, La., on Dec. 24, 1888 with 3,000 bales when news came of the burning of the *KATE ADAMS,* and the *HANNA* crew found their own boat afire. There was life loss of 22 persons. This boat had a 5½ ft. high single barrel whistle, one of the largest on the rivers.

3071 JOHN HANCOCK

SW p wh b. Cincinnati, Oh., 1845. 293 tons. She appears in the famed Cincinnati wharf daguerreotype made in 1848. Snagged and lost at Cape Girardeau, Mo., March 25, 1851.

3072 JOHN HECKMANN

Stw p wh b. Hermann, Mo., 1919. 163.6 x 30.5 x 4.2. She had two sternwheels operated by four Gillett & Eaton engines. Two return flue boilers facing aft. A big carrier for her size owned by the Heckmann family, with Capt. Ed Heckmann, master. In April 1922 she made a trip up Cumberland River to Nashville and Burksville, Capt. R.A. Goad. Was rebuilt into an excursion boat for Missouri River and was lost in ice at Hermann in 1928. In 1977 a replica pilothouse was built on the bluff at Hermann using the *HECKMANN*'s old pilotwheel.*

3073 JOHN HOWARD

Stw p wh b. Jeffersonville, Ind., by Howard, 1871. 180 x 36 x 6. Ran New Orleans-Ouachita River, Capt. P.C. Montgomery, with E.R. Perry and V.G. Entriken, clerks. In the cotton season, 1875, she ran White River to New Orleans and was the only through boat; in seven trips she brought down 8,677 bales. She went up White River to Batesville. She was returned to Jeffersonville in 1893 and received a new and larger hull. (See next listing.)

3074 JOHN HOWARD

Stw p wh b. Jeffersonville, Ind., by Howard, 1893. 184.6 x 37.8 x 6.3. Engines, 18's- 6 ft. from former boat. Four boilers, each 38" by 35 ft. Capt. E.R. Perry, master, with M.E. Fahy, clerk. Ran trips from St. Louis to Shreveport, La., Capt. J.W. Carlton, 1894. Burned at Columbia, La., Dec. 17, 1898.

3075 JOHN IVERS, JR.

Recess wheel ferry wh b. New Albany, Ind., 1860. 86 tons. First home port, St. Louis. Off the lists 1862.

3076 JOHN J. ROE

SW p wh b. Cincinnati, Oh., 1856. 270 x 40 x 8. 691 tons. Engines, 24's- 8 ft. Three boilers, each 46" by 28 ft. Primarily a freight boat with little or no cabin accommodations for passengers. Ran St. Louis-New Orleans, Capt. Mark Leavenworth. She carried troops for the U.S. up Tennessee River in 1862 under Major-Gen. Lew Wallace's command. Capt. Grant Marsh was mate on her at the time. She was snagged and sunk at New Madrid, Mo., Sept. 12, 1864, downbound with 2nd Wisconsin Cavalry aboard. They lost 165 horses. She went clear down to the roof. Capt. Ben Taber was master. Mark Twain piloted her before the war.

3077 JOHN K. SPEED

Stw p wh b. Madison, Ind., 1892. 261 x 42 x 8. Frisbie engines, 22½'s- 8 ft. Came out new with Capt. Lew Kates, master, and Joe Conlon, clerk, and made a Mardi Gras trip from Cincinnati to New Orleans. Owned by the Cincinnati, Memphis & New Orleans Packet Co. Capt. M.M. Deem with Charles P. Vinton, clerk in her early career. She sank three times, was afire twice, broke several shafts, and once lost her wheel overboard. Her first sinking was at Belle Grove Plantation, Nov. 29, 1898. Second was at the Louisville Falls, April 9, 1899. The third time at President's Island, below Memphis, Nov. 27, 1901. She threw her paddlewheel in the river upbound at Davall's Landing, 34 miles above Vicksburg, in May 1898 and the *BUCKEYE STATE* took her passengers. At that time she was running St. Louis-New Orleans along with *CITY OF ST. LOUIS* and *HILL CITY.* On June 30, 1901, she stripped her wheel at Island 66 and had it rebuilt at Helena, Ark. Burned at New Orleans, May 22, 1902.

3078 JOHN KILGOUR

SW p wh b. Cincinnati, Oh., 1864. 1,550 tons. 252 x 41 x 7. Engines, 25's- 8 ft. Came out with four tubular boilers, each 46" by 24 ft. with 196" flues. Paddlewheels 32" ft. dia. working 12½ ft. buckets. Built for Capt. William S. Foster and others. When completed in mid-November 1864 she was announced as a regular Pittsburgh-Cincinnati packet, but this did not come to pass. She left Cincinnati, March 1865, for Nashville with U.S. commissary stores including 8,000 boxes of hard tack. The tubular boilers were removed May 1866, and she was given five Western style, each 44" by 24 ft., five flues each. Ran Louisville-New Orleans, Capt. John G. Benson in 1868. In October 1869 in New Orleans-Vicksburg trade, Capt. Benson, with H.E. Fillmore and Ed Shaw, clerks. Sold at U.S. marshal sale at Shippingport, Ky., May 1871, after which Capt. Albert Stein became master, with Ben Merrielees, clerk. Owned then by Charles Kilgour and others, and ran Cincinnati-New Orleans. Dismantled 1874. Machinery went to the *CHARLES MORGAN* (see).

3079 JOHN KYLE

Recess wheel ferry wh b. Ashland, Ky., 1867. 28 tons. Capt. Jim Rowley, Jr., recalled that she ran Vanceburg-Maysville in 1878, three trips a week, Capt. George Kelly. She was primarily a ferry, some accounts saying built at Catlettsburg, Ky. Off the lists in 1881.

3080 JOHN KYLE

SW p wh b. 1870. Ran Cincinnati-St. Louis-New Orleans. Collided with a steamship leaving New Orleans for Cairo Jan. 1, 1871 with 1,000 tons of freight and 75 mules as cargo. Broke steam drum and knocked down her stacks. She was landed at Algiers, hull repaired, and then proceeded to Mound City for cabin repairs. Sank in the Grand Chain, Ohio River, bound Cincinnati to St. Louis, Feb. 23, 1872. Capt. A.M. Hutchinson was master with W.M. Brown, clerk.

3081 JOHN L. AVERY

SW p wh b. Cincinnati (Fulton), Oh., 1853. 323 tons. Hit a snag and sank at Fort Adams, Miss., Mar. 9, 1854. She was downbound with a big trip. Had been operating New Orleans-Natchez. Went down in five minutes with only top of cabin showing. Official report says 40 lives were lost.

3082 JOHN L. FERGUSON

Recess wheel ferry, wh. b. Grafton, Ill., 1876. 111.6 x 25.6 x 3.6. Operated at St. Charles, Mo. Still documented in 1886.

3083 JOHN L. LOWRY

SW saw mill and packet, wh. b. Clarington, Oh., 1893. 108 x 16 x 3.6. Ran low water in the Wheeling-New Matamoras trade, October 1894, with T.S. Hanes, master, and J.A. Voegtly, clerk. Capt. Grover Litton remembers her as a saw mill boat. On the lower Ohio in 1896, maybe longer.

3084 JOHN L. LOWRY

Stw p wh b. Cave In Rock, Ill., 1909. 132 x 22 x 4.5. Engines, 12's- 5 ft. Two boilers, each 40" by 20 ft. Owned by Capt. John L. Lowry and ran Evansville-Paducah. Burned at Hamletsburg, Ill., opposite Smithland, Ky., June 1911.

3085 JOHN L. LOWRY

Stw p sh b. Evansville, Ind., 1913. 160 x 31 x 5. This steel hull packet was built for Capt. John L. Lowry and ran Evansville-Paducah. Sank in a storm at Kincaide Ldg., Ill., Mar. 17, 1919, raised. In June 1920 went to Pittsburgh and towed the hull of the old towboat *MARINER* (iron hull) loaded with automobiles to St. Louis. Returned to her trade and was taking coal at Saline Mines, Ill., near Shawneetown when she burned, Oct. 4, 1920. The hull was taken to Paducah and there sold to Capt. Nettie Johnson, Memphis. Resold to Patton-Tully Transportation Co., who created a combination derrickboat-towboat named *WM. P. HALL*. Sold to Luling and Destrehan Ferry Co. and remodeled into a ferry named *GEO. N. ROBERTS*. Dismantled.

3086 JOHN L. RHOADS

Stw p wh b. Pittsburgh, Pa., 1875. 222 x 36 x 5. Engines, 16's- 5 ft. Three boilers, each 38" by 26 ft. Built for Capt. John L. Rhoads and others of Pittsburgh. In May 1878 she had made 28 round trips to St. Louis and two more to New Orleans from Pittsburgh, then commanded by Capt. J.M. Vandergrift with John C. Fisher, clerk. Sank on the Falls at Louisville, June 1877, raised. Ran low water, Cincinnati-Madison, fall 1877. Captain Rhoads lived in a white frame atop the hill at Haysville, Pa. still standing 1978. Capt. David Silver and others bought the *RHOADS*, renamed her *CHAS. C. CARROLL* (see).

3087 JOHN LADDELL

Stw p wh b. Millersport, Oh., 1860. 160 tons. First home port, Wheeling. Lost in collision at Marietta, Oh., Dec. 15, 1860.

3088 JOHN LEE

Stw p wh b. Jeffersonville, Ind., by Howard, 1896. Originally named *H. W. BUTTORFF* (see) which was sold to the Lee Line, Memphis, and renamed in 1911. Lee Line ran her short trade out of Memphis, and later converted her into an excursion boat named *PRINCESS* (see).

3089 JOHN LUMSDEN

Stw p wh b. 1870 for Cumberland River. In May 1871 downbound at Clarksville she hit the bank in a fog, sinking to the boiler deck. She had 220 hogsheads of tobacco for New Orleans, six race horses for Springfield, Ill., and many passengers. No life loss. Later in the Evansville, Cairo and Memphis Steam Packet Co. running Evansville-Cairo, Capt. Henry T. Dexter, with Pennington and Dexter, clerks. In May 1873 taken to Madison, Ind., and rebuilt to become the *LAURA L. DAVIS* (see).

3090 JOHN M. ABBOTT

Stw ferry (?) wh b. Madison, Ind., 1883. 92 x 20 x 3.6. Went to the upper Mississippi in the area of Muscatine, Iowa; later to the lower Mississippi. Not listed 1895.

3091 JOHN M. CHAMBERS

Stw p wh b. Mound City, Ill. (hull) and completed at St. Louis, 1875. 174 x 32 x 4.7. Built for Capt. Joe La Barge and others for St. Louis-Missouri River. Made one trip, at least, to Fort Benton. Badly burned at St. Louis, laid up, February 1876. Sold 1878 to Capt. L.T. Belt for New Orleans-Bayou Teche trade. Crew in 1880: Capt. T.R. Muggah with T.K. Voohrees, clerk. Struck a snag July 1884 and burned as she sank. Capt. L.T. Belt replaced her with the *TECHE* (see).

3092 JOHN M. MARTIN

SW ferry wh b. New Albany, Ind., 1853. 104 tons. Ran New Albany-Portland until retired in 1860. Also see *EXCELSIOR*.

3093 JOHN M. SANDIDGE

Ferry wh b. Pineville, La., 1881. 23 tons. Inspected at Alexandria, La., 1881; at New Orleans in 1882.

3094 JOHN M. STOCKWELL

SW p wh b. New Albany, Ind., 1853. 352 tons. Often referred to in contemporary news accounts as *J.M. STOCKWELL*. Ran New Orleans-Louisville-St. Louis. Burned and lost at St. Louis, July 2, 1856.

3095 JOHN MATHEWS

Stw p wh b. Madison, Ind., 1890. 140 x 29 x 3.9. Plied between Fort Smith and Pine Bluff on Arkansas River. Struck a pier of the bridge at Van Buren, Ark., 1:00 A.M., June 3, 1892, with such impact that she was crushed and sank. Had 12 passengers and a cargo of cotton and corn. No life loss.

3096 JOHN MCFADEN

Stw p wh b. McKeesport, Pa., 1852. 222 tons. Contemporary accounts spell the name *JNO. McFADDEN*. Lost in collision with the *S. F. J. TRABUE* at Wolf Creek bend, Ohio River, Apr. 3, 1854. Three lives lost.

JOHN MCKEE

See *J. McKEE*.

3097 JOHN OVERTON

Ferry wh b. Memphis, Tenn., 1872. 314 tons. 130 x 28 x 4.8. Still listed with Memphis as home port 1886.

3098 JOHN P. TWEED

SW p wh b. Cincinnati, Oh., 1851. 315 tons. Snagged and lost at Roth, Ill., Aug. 14, 1857. Two lives lost.

3099 JOHN QUILL

Stw p wh b. Jeffersonville, Ind., by Howard, 1907. 168 x 35 x 4.9. Built for Quill and Moore, Mobile, Ala. Ran on Mobile, Tombigbee and Alabama rivers. Hit a rock in Warrior River June 12, 1916, and sank in 15 feet. A tug towed her from Mobile to Twelve Mile Island, February 1928, on what was termed her last trip.

3100 JOHN QUINCY ADAMS

SW p wh b. Brownsville, Pa., 1848. 189 tons. 182 x 36 x 8. Engines, 24's- 8 ft. Four boilers. Ran Pittsburgh-St. Louis. In early spring 1849 arrived at Cairo and had on board John W. Audubon, son of the naturalist John James Audubon, with a party organized by Col. Henry L. Webb, bound for California via New Orleans. They transferred to the *GEN. SCOTT* for the trip south. Running Pittsburgh-Louisville spring 1851, Capt. M.E. Lucas. Dismantled 1853 and machinery went to *FANNY FERN*.

3101 JOHN R. DRACKETT

Catamaran ferry sh b. Morgan City, La., 1928. 127 x 42 x 5.5. Owned by Morgan City-Berwick Ferry Co.

3102 JOHN R. HUGO

Stw p wh b. Evansville, Ind., 1879. 127 x 27 x 3. Engines, 12½'s- 3½ ft. One boiler. Sold to the Missouri River, and there was bought by Capt. R.M. (Bob) Marshall and Capt. Henry Castrup. Burned at Florence, Neb., on May 22, 1900. The hull was floated down to Osage City, Neb., using steering oars by Capt. William L. and Hal Thompson. The machinery was placed on a new boat, the *OSAGE*.

3103 JOHN R. MEIGS

Stw snagboat ih b. South St. Louis, Mo., 1879. 172 x 38 x 5. She snagged on the Mississippi, Arkansas, and once was on the Tennessee. Owned by U.S. Engineers. At the close of the Spanish-American War the *MEIGS* was called to New Orleans to remove mine fields from the Passes, under Capt. Phineas Starr. On the return a mine was struck accidentally and the *MEIGS* was blown to bits, killing all on board save the colored maid and one white man, Jack Lane, who lived in Vicksburg until his death. Capt. Starr is the same person who was sent to investigate the chances of raising the U.S. gunboat *CAIRO* after the Civil War. He sent in an adverse report.

3104 JOHN RAINE

SW p wh b. New Albany, Ind., 1858. 541 tons. 256 x 36.5 x 6. Ran Louisville-New Orleans, Capt. William Underwood. During the Civil War did transport service for the U.S. Burned and lost at Greenville, Miss., Jan. 17, 1867 with loss of 59 lives.

3105 JOHN RAY

Stw p wh b. Wellsville, Oh., 1859. 86 tons. 100 x 24 x 4. Owned by Woodridge & Groves, Trinity. Ran New Orleans-Vermillion, Capt. Thomas E. Kercheval. Snagged and lost at Pine Prairie, La., Aug. 5, 1860.

3106 JOHN ROSS

Stw p wh b. Chattanooga, Tenn., 1905. 121 x 22 x 4.5. Engines, 9″- 3½ ft. One boiler, 42″ by 20 ft. Owned by Tennessee River Navigation Co., Decatur, Ala. Sold in 1919 to Capt. E.P. Matthews, Pt. Pleasant, W. Va. who ran her briefly Gallipolis-Huntington. She did job towing, then was sold to Capt. Otto Hitner in 1923 who towed his showboat *COTTON BLOSSOM* with her. He laid her up above the Spottsville Lock on Green River in July 1925, and she sank there Aug. 9, 1925. Hitner replaced her with the *GRACE DEVERS* (see).

3107 JOHN RUMSEY

Stw p wh b. Waubeck, Wis., 1862. 39 tons. Operated on Chippewa River by Capt. Nathaniel Harris. Lost in 1864.

3108 JOHN S. BRANSFORD

Stw p wh b. Jeffersonville, Ind., by Howard, 1872. 150 x 30 x 4. In the Louisville, Evansville & Henderson Mail Line in 1875, Capt. Frank O. Smith, with Allen Jennings, clerk. Owned 1878 by the Peoples' Line, Nashville, which went to U.S. marshal sale that June, and sold to Alex Kendall of that city. In October 1878, sank on a log at Puppy Creek Bar, Ohio River, raised. Operated out of Evansville, and in mid-

August, 1880, was chartered to run up the Wabash River and sank on a sycamore snag; raised by Robert Hornbrook. In 1885 was at Memphis as part of Capt. Milt Harry's fleet in White River service.

3109 JOHN S. HALL

Stw p wh b. Brownsville, Pa., 1864. 110 tons. 137 x 25. Capt. John Woodburn advertised her from Pittsburgh to St. Louis and St. Paul on her first trip, leaving mid-September, 1864. J.H. Chambers was clerk. She was in U.S. service, principally on the Cumberland, that winter. Returned to Pittsburgh early May 1865 and loaded out for Memphis. Sold there to Little Rock and Fort Smith Packet Co., and was in charge of Capt. W.M. Reasoner, with J.W. Williams, clerk. Sank and was lost at Calla Rock, near Little Rock, June 22, 1866.

3110 JOHN S. HOPKINS

Stw p wh b. Sewickley, Pa. (hull) and completed at Pittsburgh, 1880. 200 x 35.3 x 6. Engines, 16's- 7 ft. Three boilers, each 44" by 20 ft. Owned by Evansville, Paducah & Cairo Mail Line, run by Capts. Joe and Dick Fowler and others. Damaged by fire in 1882 and rebuilt at Cincinnati. Capt. H.C. Gilbert, Evansville, was her master many years, with W.D. Newbill, clerk. Sam G. Smith went clerk of her November 1905. Capt. J.B. Thompson, Evansville, converted her into an excursion boat in April 1912. Burned laid up in Green River, January 1917. Most of her years ran Evansville-Paducah.

3111 JOHN S. MCCUNE

Stw p wh b. Brownsville, Pa., 1862. Originally named *BRILLIANT* (see). Was renamed Oct. 11, 1865 at conclusion of her war service. Owned jointly by Capt. J.H. Duffer and M.C. Espy, she ran DeVall's Bluff on White River to St. Louis. Burned Dec. 6, 1867 at Prairie Landing, Ark., with loss of one life.

JOHN S. PRINGLE

See *J. S. PRINGLE*.

3112 JOHN SCOTT

Built at Madison, Ind., summer of 1871 for Capt. Stanford.

3113 JOHN SHALLCROSS

SW ferry wh b. Louisville, Ky., 1863. 273 tons. Operated Louisville-Jeffersonville. During a regular crossing, January 1865, she was carried down on the falls and lodged in the Indiana Chute. The many passengers aboard were skiffed ashore safely enough. A rising river floated her, and she drifted through the chute and was captured below safe and sound. She ran there until dismantled in 1877.

3114 JOHN SIMONDS

SW p wh b. Freedom, Pa. (hull) and completed at Pittsburgh, 1852. 295 x 40.5 x 8. Engines 38's- 10 ft. Six boilers. 1,024 tons. Capt. Charles B. Church owned stock and was master. Collapsed a boiler flue while rounding out from the Louisville wharfboat, Jan. 7, 1863; no injuries. Ran principally New Orleans-Memphis. In 1859 Capt. J.F. Smith, master. Other skippers were Capt. Newman Robbirds and Capt. J.F. Hicks. When the war broke out she was in service for the South, and was purposely sunk in the chute at Island 10, Mississippi River, to block traffic, along with the *WINCHESTER* (see).

3115 JOHN SIMPSON

SW p wh b. Jeffersonville, Ind., by Howard, 1850. 228 tons. 180 x 30 x 6.5. Capt. Jesse K. Bell put her in the Louisville-Cincinnati trade in June 1851 as opposition to the U.S. Mail Line. In summer of 1856 was running Nashville-Memphis along with the *JOHN G. CLINE* and others. Dismantled that fall.

3116 JOHN SNOWDON

Stw p wh b. Brownsville, Pa., 1876. 302 tons. Built for the Pittsburgh & Brownsville Packet Co., Capt. Peter Donaldson, with G.W. Acklin, clerk. Hull by John Pringle. 150 x 36 x 4.5. Engines, 17's- 5½ ft. Three boilers, each 38" by 24 ft. Cabin by Aubrey & Son. She was the only sternwheeler in the Line. Ultimately dismantled and in 1887 her hull was made into an excursion barge renamed *ALICE*, towed by the *TWILIGHT*.

3117 JOHN STRADER

SW p wh b. California, Pa., 1852. 235 tons. 137 x 28.3 x 5.8. First owner (⅔) Capt. Joseph Losey, Pittsburgh, and Perry Brown of Freedom, Pa. Lengthened in summer of 1853 to measure 154 ft. In 1855, New Orleans and Yazoo River, Capt. J.C. Brown (owner entire) with W.W. Allein, clerk. Brown still owned her when she burned and was lost above Gaines Landing, Ark., Nov. 18, 1857.

3118 JOHN SWASEY

SW p wh b. Cincinnati, Oh., 1851. 274 tons. First year Capt. Pres H. Devol, master, in the Cincinnati-New Orleans trade. Burned and lost at New Orleans Feb. 16, 1853, with loss of three lives. In the same fire *POST BOY* and *TEXAS* also burned.

3119 JOHN SWASEY

Stw p wh b. Cincinnati, Oh., 1864. 236 tons. 157 x 33 x 5. Engines, 15's- 5 ft. Two boilers. Owned by a Captain Carnes, and named for a venerable Cincinnati merchant. Snagged and lost above Cape Girardeau, Mo., Aug. 31, 1864.

3120 JOHN T. MCCOMBS

Stw p wh b. Freedom, Pa., 1860. 209 tons. Built for the Pittsburgh-Wheeling trade by a wholesale grocer of Pittsburgh, John T. McCombs. He died of tuberculosis on March 15, 1862, and the boat was sold to Sherley & Woolfolk and others for the Louisville-Henderson trade, May 4, 1862. While landed at Brandenburg, Ky., on July 8, 1863, she was seized by John Hunt Morgan's cavalry and used as a decoy to flag down the *ALICE DEAN* (see) whereupon the Morgan Raiders crossed the Ohio on the *DEAN* into Indiana. In

1866, still in the Louisville-Henderson Line, Capt. E.P. Crider, with M.D. Warren, clerk. Spring of 1867, she was stranded out on rocks during high water, and stayed there through June. While stranded she was sold to Capt. George McCallum, Louisville, perched 20 feet above the river. These rocks were called "State Rocks," location unknown to this scribe, nor do we know what happened to her. Capt. Thomas S. Calhoon, later part owner and master of the *KEYSTONE STATE, VIRGINIA* and others, had his first river job on this one in the Pittsburgh-Wheeling trade.

3121 JOHN T. MOORE

Stw p ih b. Cincinnati, Oh., 1871. 176.6 x 42 x 7.1. This iron hull packet was built for Capt. W.T. Boardman, New Orleans, for the New Orleans-Red River trade. On the maiden trip she loaded out for Shreveport and Jefferson at Cincinnati. It is said the hull cost $30,000, and the boat entire represented an investment of $80,000. In September 1873 she was in the hands of the U.S. Marshal at New Orleans. Had been running in the Carter Line, St. Louis-New Orleans. Later was enlarged to become 234.8 x 41.8 x 7.1., renamed *ENDEAVOR* (see).

3122 JOHN TAYLOR

Ferry wh b. Madison, Ind., 1875. 87 tons. 115 x 23 x 4.5. Operated at Burlington, Iowa. Still listed in 1896.

3123 JOHN TOMPKINS

Stw p wh b. Jeffersonville, Ind., by Howard, 1855. 160 x 36 x 5. 199 tons. Burned and lost at Louisville, Dec. 13, 1860.

3124 JOHN TRENDLEY

Recess wheel ferry wh b. Cincinnati, Oh., 1860. Built for the Wiggins Ferry Co., St. Louis. Forced out on the Illinois shore by ice at East St. Louis, Jan. 12, 1866.

3125 JOHN TRENDLEY

SW railroad ferry wh b. Madison, Ind., 1881. 205.4 x 36.6 x 5.8. Engines, 22's- 7 ft. Four boilers. Owned by Wiggins Ferry Co., St. Louis. Burned at East St. Louis, Ill., Nov. 11, 1892.

3126 JOHN W. CANNON

SW p wh b. Jeffersonville, Ind., by Howard, 1878. 252½ x 43 x 9½. Engines, 34 ⅛'s- 9 ft. by Ainslee & Cochran. Owned by Capt. John W. Cannon and was perhaps his finest boat. Operated New Orleans-Bayou Sara along with the *EDWARD J. GAY* (see) replacing the *WILLIAM S. PIKE* of former days. This boat had a feature peculiar to her: the boiler deck was extended forward over the forecastle. She was given lavish attention in the cabin outfitting and details, being primarily a carriage horse for the planters of the fabled Upper Coast. Gen. U.S. Grant, guest of Capt. Cannon, once rode out to see the Jetties on this vessel. Dismantled at Jeffersonville in 1886. Machinery, cabin, etc., went to building the *OLIVER BEIRNE* (see).

3127 JOHN W. HART

Stw p wh b. Jeffersonville, Ind., by Howard, 1890. 168 x 29 x 3.1. Owned by Lovell Bros., Nashville, for Cumberland River. She ran in the Nashville-Burnside trade for five years. Sank near Granville, Tenn., April 5, 1897, bow against the shore. The pilothouse stove overturned, setting the boat afire. The blaze was extinguished, but the sinking was fatal.

3128 JOHN W. HUBBARD

Stw p wh b. Jeffersonville, Ind., by Howard, 1910. Originally *J.H. MENGE*, then *M.A. BURKE* (both see). The *BURKE*, a cotton packet, was sold in 1919 to Louisville & Cincinnati Packet Co. and entered the L&C trade Oct. 28, 1919. She ran the balance of the year under that name. That winter she was rebuilt at Mound City, Ill., and greatly altered in appearance The boiler deck was lowered, and the cotton guards removed. She then was renamed *JOHN W. HUBBARD* and re-entered the L&C trade, Capt. Ed Williamson. She and the *QUEEN CITY* were the regulars until 1929, along with the *CINCINNATI* and *KENTUCKY.* When the L&C Packet failed in 1932 the *HUBBARD* went to the Greene Line, who never operated her. She was allowed to beach out at the upper end of Jeffersonville where she littered the landscape several years.

3129 JOHN W. LANE

Stw ferry wh b. Paducah, Ky., 1925. 84.4 x 24 x 3.6. Equipment from the ferry *FRANCIS* used in construction (see). She was the ferry at Gallipolis, Oh., operated by John W. Lane. Upon his death, continued by John E. Evans, Jr. Docked at Parkersburg, W. Va. in 1944 and shortened somewhat. Owned by C.C. Thornton when she burned at Gallipolis Ferry, W. Va., on Jan. 22, 1947.

3130 JOHN W. STONE

Ferry wh b. Middleport, Oh., 1872. 28 tons. Still listed in 1882, inspected in the Wheeling District.

3131 JOHN W. THOMAS

Stw p wh b. Jeffersonville, Ind. by Howard, 1897. 160 x 26.5 x 4.2. Engines, 14's- 5 ft. Two boilers. Built for the Lovell Line, Nashville, and named for the president of the Nashville, Chattanooga & St. Louis Railroad. Often ran during low water in the Louisville-Evansville trade, but regularly Nashville-Burnside. While backing away from the wharfboat at Tell City, Ind., Dec. 21, 1905, she hit the Obrecht dock, damaged her hull, and was landed at the foot of Washington Street where she sank. On Christmas night, at midnight, she burned. The hull was raised by the insurance company, and she was rebuilt to become the *GLENMORE* (see).

3132 JOHN WALSH

SW p wh b. Cincinnati, Oh., 1858. 809 tons. 275 x 38 x 8. Engines, 24's- 7 ft. Built for the St. Louis-New Orleans trade, Capt. John Molloy. In 1861 sold to Capt. Samuel Applegate. She served as a Confederate troop transport, and after the fall of Memphis was taken into Yazoo River and purposely sunk by the Rebels near Fort Pemberton to block the river. In late May 1863, a U.S. party from the *FOREST ROSE, LINDEN* and *PETREL* burned her. Captain Molloy during the war was decapitated by a cannon ball aboard the *EMPRESS* (see). Capt. Applegate lived out his old age at Winona, Minn.

3133 JOHN WARNER

SW p wh b. New Albany, Ind., 1856. 391 tons. 220 x 35 x 6. Engines, 24½'s- 7 ft. Three boilers, each 38" by 28 ft. During the war, in U.S. service, she was downbound on Red River May 5, 1864. She had aboard a load of confiscated cotton from Alexandria, La. At Dunns Bayou she was in advance of two escorts, the *SIGNAL* and *COVINGTON,* when shelled by the Rebels from ashore. She was sunk. The *COVINGTON* was burned in this encounter, and the *SIGNAL* was abandoned to the enemy.

3134 JOHN WILSON

SW ferry wh b. Cincinnati, Oh., 1854. 131 tons. Out of service, 1856.

3135 JOHN WILSON

Rig? p wh Ran New Orleans-Ouachita River, 1878-1879 during the summer seasons, Capt. J.W. Blanks, with B.G. Cornwell, clerk. Ultimately exploded her boilers. Many of the crew transferred to the *FANCHON* (see) and were on her when she exploded.

3136 JOHNNY SCHMOKER

SW p wh b. La Crosse, Wis., 1866. 27 tons. Also spelled *JOHNNY SMOKER.* She may have been used in rafting. She and the *CHIPPEWA* burned at Rumsey's Landing on the Chippewa River, both owned by H.S. Rumsey of La Crosse, Jan. 21, 1871. Documented until 1879.

3137 JONAS POWELL

Stw p wh b. Parkersburg, Va., 1860. 152.4 tons. A Muskingum River packet, Capt. James Darlington. Ran Zanesville-Parkersburg, 1860; Zanesville-Pittsburgh, 1861-1862; Marietta-Zanesville 1863, and Zanesville-Parkersburg in 1864. During the course of the war made a trip for the U.S. to Nashville with Capt. Darlington and his regular pilots along, Aaron and Milt McLaughlin. Sold after the war and ran Pittsburgh-Portsmouth briefly, then was in the hands of a U.S. marshal at Gallipolis in December 1866. Capt. James Rowley (Jr.) recalled to this scribe that his first steamboat ride was on the *JONAS POWELL* from Vanceburg, Ky. to Indian Run (below Portsmouth) to visit an aunt. The boat then was running Maysville-Portsmouth. Ran Big Sandy-Portsmouth spring 1869 in competition with *VIOLA* (see). Off the lists 1873.

3138 JOSE SAN ROMAN

SW p wh b. Brownsville, Pa., 1865. 400 tons. Went to Brownsville, Texas. Off the lists in 1874.

3139 JOSEPH BISSO

Stw ferry sh b. Jeffersonville, Ind., by Howard, 1916. 115.2 x 28 x 7.2. Owned by Bisso Ferry Co., New Orleans.

3140 JOS. E. RANSDELL

Stw snagboat sh b. Jeffersonville, Ind., 1908. 137 x 5. Was in the Vicksburg District, U.S. Engineers, and was usually assigned to work on Red River. She was at Shreveport, La., various times. On July 10, 1928, leaving there, she hit the Cotton Belt draw span and took away her pilothouse top and stacks. In 1927 she was up Yazoo River above Greenwood, Miss., to the falsework for a new bridge. Sold, Oct. 29, 1935 to the Royal Route Co., Capt. George Prince. When the *TENNESSEE BELLE* (see) sank in 1936 the *RANSDELL,* towing a barge, took her place in the packet trade. Sold to the Cincinnati Gymnasium Boat Club, August 1939. Her whistle is in the Ohio River Museum, Marietta, Oh.

3141 JOS. G. SMITH

Ferry wh b. Jeffersonville, Ind., 1867. 49 tons. Still documented at St. Louis, 1876.

3142 JOSEPH H. CONN

Stw p wh b. Shousetown, Pa., 1856. 265 tons. Owned by Capt. James Woodburn and others. She burned and was lost in a steamboat fire at Pittsburgh, May 7, 1859. Other stockholders included Capt. Nelson Crooks, Belleville, Va., B.F. Woodburn, Shousetown, Pa., and J.C. Anderson, Sewickley, Pa.

3143 JOSEPH H. OGLESBY

SW p wh b. Cincinnati, Oh., 1856. 399 tons. 225 x 35. Built for Capt. Henry A. Ealer and others. Running Louisville-New Orleans, January 1857, Capt. Oglesby. Snagged and lost in the Missouri River above Glasgow, Mo., in Euphrashie Bend, Aug. 28, 1858.

3144 JOSEPH HENRY

SW lighthouse tender wh b. Jeffersonville, Ind., by Howard, 1880. 180 x 32 x 5. Engines, 18's- 6 ft. Three boilers, each 42" by 28 ft. Had three longitudinal and five transverse iron bulkheads in the hull. She first served in the old 15th District. Was sold at public sale and became the excursion boat *LOUISIANA* (see), later *PATTONA* (also see).

3145 JOS. HOLDEN

Stw p wh b. Harmar, Oh., at the Knox yard, 1856. Owned in part and commanded by Capt. Owen Franks. Other partners were Wm. F. Curtis and Capt. Horatio Booth, all of Marietta. Made trips to Shreveport, La., and was snagged and lost at Twelve Mile Bayou, La., April 7, 1859.

3146 JOS. L. STEPHENS

Centerwheel ferry wh b. Jeffersonville, Ind., by Howard, 1887. 103 x 29.4 x 4.2. Engines, 10's- 3½ ft. One boiler. Operated at Boonville, Mo., owned by L.E. Mohle, and could handle 12 wagons. Burned at Kansas City, Mo., Oct. 31, 1909, owned by Mary E. Brent. Rebuilt and burned at Cairo, Ill., Jan. 8, 1912.

3147 JOSEPH LANDIS

SW p wh b. Cincinnati, Oh., 1853. 377 tons. 178 x 32.2 x 7. Owned by the Eclipse Towboat Association, New Orleans.

Probably towed ships below New Orleans. She was in Confederate service in the war, and was captured by U.S., April 28, 1862. Served in the U.S. Army service.

3148 JOSEPH PIERCE

SW p wh b. Freedom, Pa. (hull) and completed at Pittsburgh, 1864. 533 tons. 260 x 36 x 6. Engines by Robinson & Rea, 22's- 7 ft. Four boilers, each 40" by 26 ft. Emil Bott decorated the cabin. Built for Capt. S.B. French who planned to run her Pittsburgh-Cincinnati. He changed plans, loaded out for Memphis, and went on to New Orleans. Entered her in the New Orleans-Vicksburg trade with S.C. McKinney as first clerk. This was the first packet in the trade since the war broke out. She exploded boilers and was lost at Palmyra Landing, Miss., on July 31, 1865, with loss of twelve lives. Capt. P.D. Pratt was master at the time, with F.A. Sherman, clerk.

3149 JOSEPHINE

Stw p wh b. Freedom, Pa. (hull) and completed at Pittsburgh, 1873. 183 x 31 x 4. Engines, 15's- 5 ft. Two boilers. Originally owned by J.S. Coulson, Eliza Coulson, Sallie B. Coulson, James C. McVay and Fanny Maratta. Named for the small daughter of Gen. David S. Stanley. Capt. Grant Marsh superintended construction. No steamboat in the Fort Benton trade had a more varied or interesting career than the *JOSEPHINE*. In 1873 she made her first trips to the Yellowstone River under Capt. Grant Marsh for Custer's famed Seventh Cavalry. In 1874 she went into the Fort Benton service and the following year, 1875, was back on the Yellowstone under Captain Marsh to conduct an exploration of that stream. She went further up than any boat before or since, going above Pompey's Pillar to Hell Roaring Rapids, 483 miles above the mouth, where she arrived on June 7, 1875 at 2:00 P.M. The *F. Y. BATCHELOR* (see) later went to Pompey's Pillar and above some distance. Josephine Park at Billings, Mont. is named for this boat. The Canadian northwest was being opened in 1875, following the initial arrival of the Mounted Police the year before. The *JOSEPHINE* transported Canadian troops bound for posts in Alberta and Saskatchewan. Like many another steamboat on the Missouri she went off to the Sioux wars in 1876, ferrying supplies for Terry, Crook, Gibbon and Custer. She was attacked by Sioux at Glendive Creek but went on after two companion boats turned back. Altogether she made about fifty trips to Montana, most of them to Fort Benton, under the Coulson flag. She was sold in the mid-1880's and entered government service as a snagboat. Laid up in the fall of 1889 and idled a year or so until repaired in 1891 for government inspection work under Captain Gould. Thereafter she worked out of Bismarck until sold to Capt. Joseph Leach who planned operating her again as a packet but she was cut down by ice on March 8, 1907, at Running Water, S.D., and sank a loss. The machinery was salvaged and was shipped to Alaska for use on a Yukon River steamer.

3150 JOSEPHINE

Stw p wh b. Dubuque, Iowa, 1878. 155.2 x 28.8 x 5.6. Engines, 16's- 4½ ft. Two boilers. Built by the Diamond Jo Line for the Fulton, Ill.-Burlington, Iowa trade, succeeding the *DIAMOND JO* (see) and there into 1880. Later used in other packet trades, and in her latter days did odd-job towing, Capt. Al Dawley. Dismantled at Dubuque in 1899.

3151 JOSEPHINE

SW ferry wh b. Elizabeth, Pa., 1889. 87 x 23 x 4.8. First boat built at the Wiegel yard of which William Wiegel was superintendent. Operated on the Monongahela. Caught fire at the foot of 22nd Street, South Side, Pittsburgh, March 28, 1896, owned by Holmes Harger, Pittsburgh.

3152 JOSEPHINE SAVAGE

SW p wh b. Paducah, Ky., 1857. 465 tons. First home port, Nashville, Tenn. Burned and lost at Tunica Island, Natchez, Miss., Jan. 8, 1859.

3153 JOSH V. THROOP

Stw p wh b. Evansville, Ind., 1880. 145 x 30 x 3.5. Engines, 12's- 4 ft. Two boilers. Built by Capts. George S. and John H. Throop, sons of Capt. Josh who had died sometime prior to the boat's construction. Ran competition Evansville-Paducah with the *JOHN S. HOPKINS* (see) in 1883. During the 1884 flood she was used by the Red Cross for relief work around Evansville, the boat and crew volunteered by John H. Throop. Clara Barton personally supervised the mission. Later renamed *A. G. HENRY* (see).

JOSIAH H. BELL

See J.H. BELL.

3154 JOSIAH LAWRENCE

SW p wh b. Cincinnati, Oh., 1848. 593 tons. Ran usually St. Louis-New Orleans, Capt. Carrington. While the railroad was being built to connect Louisville and Frankfort, Ky., this boat brought up from New Orleans the first 500 tons of English-made rail. Sank the *GONDOLIER* in collision below St. Louis, November 1848 (see). She was primarily a freight boat, had a mess room for the deck crew and slept them in bunks on the main deck. Off the lists 1853.

3155 JOSIE

Stw p wh b. Madison, Ind., 1873. 146.2 x 28.6 x 4.8. Built by the Diamond Jo Line and used principally on the Upper Mississippi. Later was bought by Eagle Packet Co., who used her as a towboat. Collided with the *L.E. PATTON* at Peters Towhead below Memphis, was run ashore and sank. Capt. Henry Leyhe was master at the time, with pilot Warren Renfrew on watch. Was raised with help of Charles Hunter of the Patton-Tully Company. Operated until 1895, maybe later, and burned at Cape Girardeau, Mo. Master at the time was Capt. Sam Shrodes. The wreck floated down the chute of Bernum's Island.

3156 JOSIE

Prop ferry sh b. Jeffersonville, Ind., by Howard, 1891. 95 x 25 x 9. Engines, 9", 18"- 2 ft. stroke. She was the first steel hull boat built at the Howard Yard. Operated at New Orleans until April 1928, being the relief ferry at Canal Street, owned then by Algiers Public Service Corp. Went from there to Belle Chasse, 18 miles below.

3157 JOSIE D. HARKINS

A small fry, probably batwing, on Big Sandy River, which went to Red River and burned 20 miles north of Texarkana, Tex., March 10, 1892.

3158 JOSIE HARRY

Stw p wh b. Belle Vernon, Pa., and completed at Pittsburgh, 1878. 173 x 36 x 6. Rees engines, 16's- 6 ft. Three steel boilers, 40" by 26 ft. Sported a Brussels carpet in the pilothouse, had a Chickering piano, and the interior decoration done by artist Emil Bott. Built for Capt. Milt Harry and named for his wife. Operated Memphis-White River with J.C. Wykoff and Peter Mitchell, clerks. When she sank on the Mississippi River in 1883 a large towhead formed around and below the wreck long called Josie Harry Towhead.

3159 JOSIE L. K.

Stw ferry wh b. Chamberlain, S.D., 1884. 71.5 x 14.5 x 3.5. Owned by Capt. Joseph Giesler and operated at Yankton, S.D. Cut down by ice and lost at Yankton April 1, 1920.

3160 JOSIE SIVLEY

Stw p wh b. 1896. 88 x 20 x 3. Engines 6"-3'4" stroke. One boiler. Built to bring wheat from Illinois River to St. Louis. Sank in the Sunflower River, Cypress Bend, below Choctaw, Miss., June 1900. One life lost.

3161 JOSIE W.

Stw p wh b. Belle Vernon, Pa., and completed at Wheeling, W. Va., 1885. 140.9 x 30.4 x 4.8. In 1886, New Orleans-Ouachita River in place of the *H. HANNAH BLANKS* (see), Capt. L.P. Delahoussaye, with Stonewall Hanna, clerk. In 1893, Monroe-Camden on the upper Ouachita, connecting with the *OUACHITA* (see) for New Orleans. Her engines came from the *MARY M. MICHAEL* (see), and she was owned by the Blanks interests. Was sold to Mobile, owned there by Capts. Matt Jackson and N.W. Eanes (who also ran the *LIBERTY*) and they dismantled her in 1903.

3162 JUDAH TOURO

SW p wh b. New Albany, Ind., 1854. 332 tons. 175 x 34 x 6. Engines, 23's- 7 ft. Four boilers. Ran New Orleans-Red River first owned by Capt. Samuel Gwathney, New Orleans. In 1856, T.G. Ledbetter, Carroll County, Miss., became a stockholder, and by 1859 he owned her entire. He sold out fall of 1860. In 1861 went to Confederate registry, owned by Edward Schiller, New Orleans, Capt. M. Langhorne. She was burned at Shreveport, La., to prevent capture about July 5, 1863. There was a three-master sailing ship also named *JUDAH TOURO*, in which he was part owner, his address given as New Orleans. Also of interest, in 1855 the steamboat, subject of this sketch, was running in the New Orleans-Ouachita River trade, Capt. G.L. Kouns, with John W. Tobin, clerk.

3163 JUDELLE

Stw p wh b. Madison, Ind., 1881. 100 x 25 x 3. Operated out of Evansville and Hawesville, Ohio River, owned by Capt. W.D. Crammond. Still listed 1895.

3164 JUDGE FLETCHER

SW p wh b. Brownsville, Pa., 1860. 260 tons. Was in the Kouns Line, New Orleans-Red River. In summer 1866, New Orleans-Ouachita River, Capt. John W. Tobin, with G. Pres. Work, clerk, taking the place of the *VICKSBURG* (see). In 1868 transferred from registry at Little Rock, Ark., to New Orleans, Capt. Harrison L. Watts, owner-master. Was sold to Edgar Nott, New Orleans, Oct. 1868, Capt. James E. Phelps. Early in 1869 she hit a rock and stove on Red River.

3165 JUDGE FLETCHER

Stw p wh b. New Albany, Ind., 1877. Was taken to the Missouri River under charter to Capts. W.F. Davidson and John B. Davis along with many others. Gen. Philip Sheridan was taken up to visit the battlefield of Custer's Massacre on this boat 1877.

3166 JUDGE MCCLURE

Stw p wh b. Elizabeth, Pa., 1857. 64 tons. Ran on Monongahela River, and also made trips on the Youghiogheny to West Newton, Pa., while the locks and dams existed. Capt. Joseph Price, killed when the towboat *FRED WILSON* exploded below Louisville in 1904 said he first steamboated on the *McCLURE*. Off the lists in 1860.

3167 JUDGE PORTER

SW p wh b. Jeffersonville, Ind., by Howard, 1859. 203 tons. 135 x 30 x 5.5. First home port was Franklin, La. Sold October 1859 to Capt. Edward F. Shields, master, and William F. James, both of Mobile. Burned in Lake Ponchartrain March 13, 1860, with loss of seven lives.

3168 JUDGE TORRENCE

SW p wh b. Cincinnati, Oh., 1857. 419 tons. 180 x 30 x 7.5. Engines, 23's- 7 ft. Four boilers. Ran Cincinnati-New Orleans, Capt. Richard M. Wade. Sold to USQMD Feb. 10, 1862. She was the powder supply boat for the Mississippi Squadron, and retained her name while in U.S. service. Sold privately and renamed January 1866 to become *AMAZON* (see).

3169 JUDGE WHEELER

Stw p wh b. Memphis, Tenn., 1870. Owned by Capt. W.B. Nowland and others, and ran New Orleans-Fort Smith, Ark. She was downbound with 600 bales of cotton 45 miles above Vicksburg in February 1871 when her boilers exploded and she burned with loss of three deckhands. She had been running but four months when she was lost.

3170 JUDITH

Stw p wh b. Mound City, Ill., 1881. Originally a railroad transfer, *NORTHERN PACIFIC NO. 2* (see). 184.4 x 33.2 x 4.4. Engines, 14's- 5 ft. Two boilers. She was rebuilt into a packet by Benton Transportation Co. who sold her to Capt. John E. Massengale and Augustus W. Block. Snagged in Brickhouse Bend, Missouri River, July 29, 1888, and lost. Capt. Charles W. Able was master, John Gilham, pilot. Had aboard a large cargo of wheat.

3171 JULIA

SW p wh b. Elizabeth, Pa., 1846. 234 tons. Built for Capt. Joe Convers who sold her 1848 to Capt. John W. Keiser, a Missouri River fur trade boatman associated with the American Fur Co. Snagged and lost in Bellefontaine Bend, Missouri River, Sept. 14, 1850.

3172 JULIA

SW p wh b. Louisville, Ky., 1848. 99 tons. Built at the Nadle yard. 112 x 19.9 x 4.8. Owned by Robert Foster, Oldham County, Ky. First master, Capt. Daniel G. Carr, Louisville. Made trips to Red River. Ran New Orleans-Memphis, summer 1856, Capt. Frank Hicks, with W.R. Huls, clerk. Snagged and lost in the Arkansas River, Dec. 17, 1860.

3173 JULIA

SW ferry wh b. Wheeling, Va., 1859. 38 tons. She was the original steam ferry between Marietta, Oh., and Williamstown, Va. Operated by Alfred Kinnaird. Out of service in 1862. Was replaced by the *J.R. McMILLAN* (see).

3174 JULIA

Stw p wh b. Manchester, Pa., 1863. 158 tons. Ran Pittsburgh-Zanesville, Capt. William Coulson, 1863–1865. In summer of 1864 she was in U.S. service, running from the foot of Blennerhassett Island to Pittsburgh, and made several low water trips Wheeling-Parkersburg. Downbound on the crest of the 1865 flood in March she hit a pier of the new bridge at Steubenville at night with such force she had to limp back to Freedom, Pa., for repairs. Was sold soon after this to the Northwestern Line on the Upper Mississippi. In July 1865 took a load of railroad rails to Council Bluffs, Iowa where the Union Pacific was constructing a pontoon bridge. Snagged and lost within four miles of Mankato, Minn., May 10, 1867.

3175 JULIA

SW p wh b. Jeffersonville, Ind., by Howard, 1863. 623 tons. 241 x 41 x 7. Built for Capt. George Pegram and others for St. Louis-New Orleans trade. Was entered in the Atlantic & Mississippi Steamship Co., 1866, Capt. William Thompson, with John S. Lehmer, clerk. Capt. W.C. Blake bought her outright from the Anchor Line January 1873. Dismantled at St. Louis in 1876.

3176 JULIA

Stw p wh b. St. Louis, Mo., 1895. Originally the *BELLE OF CALHOUN* (see). She was renamed *JULIA* in April 1899, when bought by A.E. and Capt. L.P. Cummins for the Memphis-Vicksburg trade, named for Capt. L.P.'s wife. Ran New Orleans-Vicksburg-Grand Lake in 1900, Capt. L.P. Cummins, with F.B. Heiner, clerk. Ran Memphis-New Orleans, February 1901, along with the *DEWEY* (see). Was returned to St. Louis and her original name was restored (see).

3177 JULIA NO. 2

Stw p wh b. Wellsville, Oh., 1865. 322 tons. Operated out of Zanesville, Oh., usually to Pittsburgh, 1865–1872. Built for Capt. William Coulson and others. Capt. Calvin R. Stull was part owner and master 1869–1872. She was sold to Capt. J.V. Reynolds who, with W.H. Truslow, clerk, ran her Cincinnati–Kanawha River until he built the *VIRGIE LEE,* then sold her to Capt. J.W. Lovell who took her to the Cumberland River to run opposition to the boats of the Ryman Line out of Nashville. Lovell put a calliope on her and played it all the way to Burnside, Ky. Dismantled her in 1879, put the engines and calliope on a new boat he built, the *DORA CABLER* (see).

3178 JULIA A. RUDOLPH

Stw p wh b. California, Pa., and completed at Pittsburgh, 1869. 154 x 34 x 5. Engines, 16's- 5 ft. Three boilers. Machinery came from the *NASHVILLE* (see). Built for Capt. Harry G. McComas who ran her New Orleans-Shreveport. She was laid up when she burned at New Orleans, Jan. 1, 1871. Other boats were lost in the fire (see *MAGENTA*). Engines went to the *FANNIE TATUM* (see) in 1873. Clerks on her were James Bell and Fred V. Cellos.

JULIA ANN

See *JULIANNE*

3178A JULIA B.

Steam yacht 70 ft. long. b. Stillwater, Minn., 1899. Owned by George H. Atwood of that place. Handsome lines and finish.

3179 JULIA BELLE SWAIN

SW p and ex wh b. Santa Rosa, Fla., 1913. Originally *CHARLES E. CESSNA* (see). The Swain family, involved in her construction, repossessed her in Florida, 1916, and brought her to the Illinois River, renamed her. She ran as a packet and in excursion work, Capt. Percy Swain in charge, until sold, April 1924, to Edward M. Cody and Capt. Oscar A. Moore. They formed a Delaware corporation, Penn Excursion Co., and brought her to Pittsburgh. Capts. Percy and Verne Swain made the trip. Her forecastle signboards still read *PENSACOLA-MOBILE.* She burned in winter quarters on the Monongahela River in December 1931. This was the last steamboat the Swain family owned. A full account of the family boats and operation is featured in the *S&D Reflector,* issue of June, 1971.

3180 JULIA BELLE SWAIN

Stw ex sh b. Dubuque, Iowa, by Dubuque Boat & Boiler Co., 1971. 108 x 22. Engines, 12's- 5 ft. from ferry *CITY OF BATON ROUGE* (see). One water tube boiler. This delightful excursion boat was planned and built by Capt. Dennis Trone and was christened by Julia Belle Swain Shelton for whom the original boat of the name was called (see above), daughter of Capt. Percy Swain. As this is written, August 1978, the boat is based at Peoria, Ill. The grace and charm of the boat has made her familiar to TV viewers as she appears in movies and commercials. She worked out of Chattanooga for several summer seasons and is very much a Trone family enterprise.

3181 JULIA DEAN

Stw p wh b. McKeesport, Pa., 1850. 117 tons. 138.5 x 24 x 3.8. Ran Pittsburgh-Zanesville, 1850-1853. Built for N.W. and George Graham of N.W. Graham & Co., Zanesville, Oh. Her masters include Capts. Charles Galligher, Jos. McVay, J.J. Binning, Henry S. Pierce and Geo. Russell. Inasmuch as two boats of this name were built in 1850 their careers have become tangled. One of them was on the Upper Mississippi 1855-1856, noticed at St. Paul both years. The subject of the present sketch was lost in collision with the *RAINBOW* at Mount Vernon, Ind., April 26, 1857, with loss of five lives.

3182 JULIA DEAN

SW p wh b. New Albany, Ind., 1850. 145 tons. Stranded and lost at West Franklin, Ind., on the Ohio River, Sept. 29, 1856. One of these boats (see last listing) was on the Des Moines River for a time.

3183 JULIA MAFFETT

Stw p wh b. Cincinnati, Oh., 1860. 56 tons. Built for service on the upper Kanawha River, Charleston and Cannelton, Capt. Johnson. She was burned at Tyler, Va., Aug. 1, 1861 as the forces of Gen. Jacob D. Cox advanced up the Kanawha to clear out the Rebels.

3184 JULIA ROANE

Stw p wh b. California, Pa., 1859. 141 x 21.2 x 4.8. Built for James M. and William Donley, Little Rock, Ark. First master, Capt. James M. Donley. Apparently widened; later documents show width 31.1 ft. Owned 1861 by Capt. James N. Danby and William Danby, both of Little Rock. Burned at Little Rock, Ark., Sept. 10, 1863.

3185 JULIAN

SW p wh b. Parkersburg, Va., 1862. 26 tons. Snagged and lost in Hatchie River, Tenn., Dec. 6, 1866.

3186 JULIANNE

Stw p wh b. Paducah, Ky., 1851. 45 tons. Ran on Cumberland River and sank on a log 70 miles above the mouth Dec. 10, 1851, with a load of groceries. Raised. Sank near York, Ind., on Wabash River, April 20, 1853, and was reported lost. Name also appears as *JULIA ANN*.

3187 JULIEN GRACEY

Stw p wh b. Clarksville, Tenn., 1880. 100 x 22 x 3. Light draft, and operated up Red River, tributary of the Cumberland. Still listed 1886 and perhaps later.

3188 JULIEN POYDRAS

Stw p wh b. Jeffersonville, Ind., by Howard, 1898. 145 x 28 x 4. Built for the Baton Rouge & Bayou Sara Packet Co. Named for the gentleman who developed New Roads, La. The Garig family (see *WM. GARIG*) bought her in 1904, took her back to the Howard Yard, and put the engines, boilers, etc., on the *WM. GARIG*. The hull was used in building the towboat *EAGLE* for Eagle Packet Co. Much of the silverware, etc., on the *GARIG* bore the name of *JULIEN POYDRAS*.

3189 JULIET

Stw p wh b. Brownsville, Pa., 1862. 155.5 x 30.1 x 3.8. Engines, 13's- 3½ ft. Built by Capt. John L. Rhoads. Sold to U.S. Navy Nov. 1, 1862, and became tinclad #4 during the war. Was Porter's dispatch boat 1863-1864. Sold to Phillip Wallack at Mound City, Ill., Aug. 17, 1865. Was renamed *GOLDENA* (see).

3190 JULIUS F. SILBER

Stw p wh b. Hermann, Mo., 1905. 101.8 x 21.3 x 3.7. Ran on Missouri River, and in 1917 operated Omaha-Decatur. In June 1927, the Woods Bros. Construction Co. renamed her *CLARKE WOODS*, used her as a towboat.

3191 JULIUS H. SMITH

Stw p wh b. Paducah, Ky., 1859. 224 tons. Burned and lost at Fort Henry, Tenn., Feb. 6, 1862.

3192 JULIUS H. WALSH

SW ferry sh b. Jeffersonville, Ind., by Howard, 1912. 169 x 50 x 7. Operated by 16 x 24 inch engines geared to the wheels. Two boilers, each 66" by 18 ft. Owned by Wiggins Ferry Co., St. Louis. Ultimately dismantled.

3193 JUNIATA

SW p wh b. Freedom, Pa., at McCaskey & Kerr yard, and completed at Pittsburgh, 1870. 235 x 33.5 x 5.8. Rees engines, 19's- 6½ ft. Four boilers, each 38" by 24 ft. Paddlewheels 25 ft. dia., working 10½ ft. buckets. Capt. Chris L. Brennan brought her out new in the Pittsburgh-Cincinnati trade, with pilots Robert Gordon and W.M. Dever. Pilots Joe and Davis Alexander were her regular pilots into 1873, and then Joe and Nick Witten. Clerk was W.S. Dravo. Burned at the Pittsburgh wharf, evening of May 25, 1875, ignited by flames from the *MOLLIE EBERT* (see).

3194 JUNIUS S. MORGAN

SW tr wh b. Jeffersonville, Ind., by Howard, 1875. 195 x 44.5 x 7. Ran between Cairo and Birds Point for the St. Louis, Iron Mountain & Southern Railway Co. She was a two-track ferry. This operation is investigated with map and pictures in the *S&D Reflector,* issue March, 1966. Sank near Cairo in October 1904.

3195 JUNO

SW p wh b. New Matamoras, Oh., 1864. 94 tons. This peculiar craft had two boilers independent of one another, one on each side. Once near Grandview, Ind., the engineer closed the throttle of one engine to pack an engine. The boiler exploded, killing a fireman and badly scalding another. She proceeded to Evansville using the other boiler and engine. Dismantled in 1866.

3196 JUNO

SW p wh b. Brownsville, Pa., 1877. 3.5 tons. We have the word of C.R. Stull that she was side-wheel, and ran at times on the Muskingum River. Inspected at Pittsburgh through 1882.

3197 JUSTICE

Stw p wh b. West Newton, Pa., on Youghiogheny River, 1851. 75 tons. Owned by John and F. Steiner, West Newton. She ran on the Allegheny River. During low water, 1852 ran in the Wheeling-Wellsville, Oh., trade, Ohio River, Capt. Murdoch, while the *WINCHESTER* and *DIURNAL* were laid up. Sold in July 1854 to the Upper Mississippi. Off the lists 1858.

3198 JUSTICE

SW p wh b. Walton, Oh., 1864. 117 tons. Her first home port, Wheeling, W. Va. Sank and lost between Liberty and Galveston, Tex., June 9, 1870.

K

3199 K & I

Stw ferry wh b. Hawesville, Ky., 1910. 68 x 18.6 x 4. Operated between Hawesville, Ky., and Cannelton, Ind. Capt. W.D. Crammond and crew rode her 49 miles to near Newburgh, Ind., during the ice run-out February 1918; the story appears in *S&D Reflector,* issue March 1978. Owned later by J.W. Pate, Hawesville.

3200 KABEKONA

SW p wh b. Stillwater, Minn., 1907. 112.6 x 22.5 x 4. Swain oscillating engines, 8″, 16″- 4 ft. stroke. One boiler, 40″ by 14 ft. She was built by David Swain for a wealthy lumberman of Minneapolis, Archibald Guthrie, with no expense spared. Had six staterooms each with private bath, leaded *fleur-de-lis* in each skylight glass, etc., a private pleasure boat. In July 1915, Edwin C. Koenig and Andrew J. Franz, St. Louis, bought her from the Swain family and ran her 2½ years handling private parties. In 1917, Ira Davenport, president of Dubuque Boat & Boiler, had new sub chasers to be delivered to New Orleans, and *KABEKONA* towed them south, and was sold there upon arrival to others. Miller & Butterworth, sand and gravel operators at Little Rock, Ark., bought her later, and built the towboat *BONNER* from her in 1919.

3201 KALISTA

Prop p wh b. Geneva, Oh., 1892. 47.9 x 9.3 x 3.9. She was brought to Cincinnati by rail, ran locally for a time, and was taken to Evansville. Ran Evansville-Spottsville, Calhoun-Livermore, then Bowling Green-Morgantown. Capt. John Porter Hines ran her until 1902, then sold half-interest to Walter G. Hougland, this being Hougland's first river venture. She was converted to gasoline in 1905, then run by T.A. Tichnor. Burned Nov. 11, 1917 at Bowling Green, Ky.

3202 KALITAN

Stw p wh b. Rock Island, Ill., 1909. 135 x 32 x 4.5. Engines, 14's- 5 ft. One boiler, 41″ by 24 ft. Built on the lines of a private yacht for the Deere family, Moline, Ill., using the former *C. W. COWLES* (see). Towed the family's private houseboat *MARKATANA*. In the winter 1927–1928, a party toured aboard to New Orleans and back. Later acquired by the showboat Menke brothers for towing their showboat. Laid up in the Atchafalaya River several years (1942–1944) and sold to the Bisso Ferry Co., New Orleans, dismantled.

3203 KANAWHA

Stw p wh b. Ironton, Oh., 1896. 180.6 x 35.2 x 5.2. Came out new with high pressure engines, 15's- 6 ft., and these were replaced in 1909 with compound non-condensing Marietta engines, 10's- 17½'s- 6 ft. Three boilers. She was built by the Bay Line, Ironton, Oh., for the Pittsburgh-Charleston trade. Came out new with Capt. Ira B. Huntington, master, and the pilots were Henry Ollom and Henry Brookhart. In March 1899, Capt. T.T. Johnston became master. On Nov. 10, 1899 Capt. William E. Roe, Williamstown, W. Va., bought the boat and ran her Pittsburgh-Charleston until October 1912. Most famed exploit came in mid-summer 1911, when the Rivers and Harbors Committee from Washington, D.C. rode the *KANAWHA* from Pittsburgh to Cairo during bone-dry weather and the river so low that all regular packets were laid up. She hit bottom every day but one and from Tell City to Owensboro a pilot in a rowboat sounded ahead to find the deepest water. Captain Roe sold her to John W. Hubbard Oct. 20, 1912, but bought her back Dec. 7, 1914, still in the Pittsburgh-Charleston trade. On the evening of Jan. 5, 1916 she landed at Little Hocking, Oh. and in backing out hit a steel pier on the outer lockwall of Dam 19, overturned, and ten lives were lost. The details of this tragedy appear in the *S&D Reflector,* issue June 1966.

3204 KANAWHA BELLE

Stw p wh b. Cincinnati, Oh., 1865. 168 tons. Built for the Gallipolis-Charleston trade, Capt. Sam Christy, with William H. Truslow, clerk. Continued until 1870 when sold to four Gallipolis gentlemen with a partner from Portsmouth, Oh. They tried her in the Cincinnati-Maysville trade with poor luck. In 1876 she was tied up at Maysville "where she had been for some time" and was dismantled. An account and pictures appear in *S&D Reflector,* issue December 1977, page 33.

3205 KANAWHA BELLE

Stw p wh b. Harmar, Oh., 1887. Originally named *BELLAIRE* (see) and was given a cabin and alterations by the Calvert family, Kanawha River, renamed, and ran Charleston-Montgomery. On the night of Dec. 19, 1901, she plunged over the fixed dam No. 3, Kanawha River. Eight were drowned, one died of exposure, and eight were saved. Capt. E.O. Calvert was in charge, and "Musty" Snyder was pilot. The official report says "the pilot thought he was going upstream." This odd statement came about inasmuch as the boat had been proceeding to Montgomery, plans were changed, and she was turned back toward Charleston. "Musty" Snyder came on watch, unacquainted with the switch, and in the darkness thought he was upbound, saw the white light on the lock wall, thought it was on a moored coal fleet, steered out in mid-river to miss it, and went over the dam. The machinery was salvaged and went on the *J. Q. DICKINSON* (see).

3206 KANAWHA VALLEY

Stw p wh b. Wheeling, Va., 1857. 126 tons. Ran Cincinnati-Kanawha River, Capt. Jesse Walton, with William L. Maddy, clerk. She replaced the *AURILLA WOOD* (see). On Aug. 1, 1861 she loaded aboard the outfit of the 22nd Regiment of Kanawha at Charleston to be delivered upstream to Cannelton. The Regiment was encamped along shore, hailed the boat, and when she failed to stop fired into her (somebody did) killing one man aboard. At Cannelton while unloading there arose a commotion about this shooting and General Wise ordered the boat burned. She was taken across the river (to what is now Montgomery) and the torch was set. The hull lay there for years after. Capt. S.C. Farley was in command of the boat; William Hix was pilot; and Joseph Smith was the engineer.

3207 KANAWHA VALLEY NO. 2

Stw p wh b. Wheeling, Va., 1860. 147 tons. Built for Cincinnati-Kanawha River trade, Capt. Jesse Walton, with Thos. Waggener, clerk. In spring of 1861 was taken to the Memphis-White River trade. Was in use as a Confederate transport when she was burned at Island 10, Miss. River, April 6, 1862.

3208 KANKAKEE

Prop p wh b. Joliet, Ill., 1865. 84 tons. 99.4 x 16.8 x 5.7. Sold to New Orleans in November 1869, owned there by Samuel Latta, and in charge of Capt. William Maitland. Sank and lost at New Orleans, June 11, 1871 with loss of one life.

3209 KANKAKEE

Stw Coast Guard cutter sh b. Dubuque, Iowa, 1919. 156.6 x 34.6 x 5.6. Condensing engines 15's- 32's- 7 ft. Designed for flood relief work, etc., and based at Evansville, Ind. Took part in the ceremony when Dade Park bridge was opened at Evansville, July 4, 1932, along with the *SOUTHLAND* (see) and others. Sold to the Barrett Line in 1936 and rebuilt to become the towboat *RICHARD BARRETT.*

3210 KANSAS

SW p wh b. St. Louis, Mo., 1847. 276 tons. Ran on the Missouri River. Capt. Joe La Barge brought a Kentucky delegation aboard to Marthasville, Mo., when the remains of Daniel Boone were to be removed from there to Frankfort, Ky. Snagged and lost in Kansas Bend, above Linden Landing, Brownsville, Neb., April 25, 1853.

3211 KANSAS MILLERS

Stw p ih b. St. Louis, Mo., 1885. 75.3 x 16 x 3. Documented at Arkansas City, Kan., 1886. No further information about this iron hull steamboat has come to hand.

3212 KASKASKIA

SW p wh b. Cincinnati, Oh., 1859. 49 tons. First home port, Evansville, Ind. Lost in the Grand Chain, Ohio River, Feb. 20, 1864.

3213 KATE

SW p wh b. McKeesport, Pa., 1851. 180 tons. Taken to Galveston, Tex. Off the lists 1854.

3214 KATE

Stw tinclad wh b. Belle Vernon, Pa., 1864, originally *KATE B. PORTER* (see). Converted into a tinclad by the U.S. named *KATE* (#55). Sold at war's conclusion to private owners who renamed her *JAMES H. TROVER* (see) March 12, 1866.

3215 KATE ADAMS

SW p wh b. Sewickley, Pa. (hull and framing) and completed at Pittsburgh, 1882. 250 x 37 x 8. Engines, 24's- 9 ft. Five boilers. Boat built entire under contract to James Rees & Sons Co., Pittsburgh. Built for Maj. John D. Adams and named for his wife. He headed the Memphis & Arkansas City Packet Co. Had an Edison electric light system, one of the first so equipped. This boat and the *WILL S. HAYS* (see) were completed side by side at the Rees shop bordering the Allegheny River near the Point, Pittsburgh. The hull originally intended for the *KATE* was sold to the Lee Line, Memphis, to become the *JAMES LEE* (see) whereupon a second hull, almost identical, was built for the *KATE.* These two side-wheelers, alike in many respects, vied for the speed championship between Helena and Memphis, 90 miles. Prior records were:

BELLE LEE	5 hours, 53 minutes
CITY OF CAIRO	5 hours, 52 minutes
CITY OF PROVIDENCE	5 hours, 49½ minutes
JAMES LEE	5 hours, 33 minutes

On Sunday, March 18, 1883, the *KATE ADAMS* "went over the track" in 5 hours 18½ minutes. The owners of the *LEE* handed over an elegant set of deer horns which the *KATE* wore the rest of her career. Capt. Mark R. Cheek was master when the *KATE* was discovered afire at Commerce

Landing, 40 miles below Memphis, early Sunday morning, Dec. 23, 1888. She was on her 602nd trip in the trade, Memphis-Arkansas City. Her cargo included 1,161 bales of cotton, 1,900 sacks of cotton seed, and 87 sacks of seed corn. Thirty-three lives were lost. During the days of this boat, in February 1884, there was a combination of packet lines at Memphis. The *KATE ADAMS* and *R.L. COBB* owned by Major John D. Adams; the *WILL S. HAYS* and *E. W. COLE* owned by James H. Rees, Jr.; the *IDA DARRAGH, JOE PETERS,* and *G.H. VAN ETTEN,* owned by the Memphis & Arkansas City Packet Co., combined into a single Line, capitalized at $250,000. Major John D. Adams was named president; John M. Peters, secy.-treas., and John N. Harbin, general freight and passenger agent. The board was composed of John D. Adams, Mark R. Cheek, James H. Rees, Jr., Edward W. Nowland, and John M. Peters.

3216 KATE ADAMS

SW p wh b. Jeffersonville, Ind., by Howard, 1888. 250 x 36 x 8.5. Engines, 22's- 8 ft. Four boilers, each 40" by 30 ft. Owned by the Memphis & Arkansas City Packet Co. (see above), and ran that trade. Capt. Mark R. Cheek was first master. In October 1896, he was succeeded by Capt. Thomas B. Good, and in March 1898 she was commanded by Capt. "Billy" Hodge. Sold in September 1898 to the Chalmette Packet Co., who changed her name to *DEWEY* (see). The trade was cared for by the *HUDSON* (see) until the third and last *KATE ADAMS* (see) was built. The first two boats looked much alike, and may be identified in photographs by the 'scape pipes. On #1 they were lower than the top of the pilothouse and rather heavy in diameter. On #2 they were slender and slightly higher than the pilothouse top.

3217 KATE ADAMS

SW p sh b. Jeffersonville, Ind., by Howard, 1899. 240 x 7. Rees engines, 24's- 8'8". Four boilers, each 48" by 28 ft. This steel hull side-wheeler had 18 watertight hull compartments. Built under the supervision of the Rees firm, Pittsburgh, Thomas Dunbar, superintendent. Capt. Mark R. Cheek by this time had become superintendent of the Line and the new *KATE* was commanded by Capt. Grant Marsh (1900–1902) and Capt. Robert R. Agnew who became superintendent in 1904 following Cheek's death. The pilots were a father-and-son team, Capts. William and W.J. "Billy" Hodge. The son Billy became master in the fall of 1913 and resigned April 1920 due to ill health which resulted in his death two months later. By 1919 the owning company's name had been changed to the Memphis & Rosedale Packet Co. and the *KATE'S* schedule was stretched to conform. The original schedule adhered to by all three *KATE*s was:

Lv. Memphis every Monday and Thursday 4:00 P.M.

Lv. Arkansas City Tuesday and Friday 6:00 P.M.

The new Rosedale schedule was similar save that the departure hour was set back to 5:00 P.M. Capt. James H. Rees had been the guiding light in all three *KATE*s. He died, 71, Aug. 18, 1920, at Pittsburgh. For all purposes the story of the three boats *KATE ADAMS* is an extension of the steamboat and engine-building firm of Pittsburgh, James Rees & Sons Co. The officers of the Memphis & Arkansas City Packet Co., for many years were James H. Rees, pres.; A.S. Caldwell, vice-pres.; David A. Rees, secy.; and W.M. Rees, treas. These men Rees were brothers, and a fourth brother was Thomas M. Rees who headed James Rees & Sons Co. Major John D. Adams died, 70, while the first *KATE* was in operation, and had been associated with Thompson Dean (operating as Dean & Adams), and it was then that the Rees family became dominant. Mr. A.S. Caldwell succeeded Capt. James H. Rees as president of the line, but he soon sold out to Capt. Jeff Hicks (son of J. Frank Hicks who ran the *HENRY FRANK* et al.) and Capt. Rees V. Downs. On June 29, 1917, the *KATE* stranded at Helena, Ark., on a falling river and remained high and dry until refloated by the John Eichleay Jr., Co., Pittsburgh—this on Oct. 12, 1918. At a meeting held in January 1921, D.A. Rees was elected pres.; Jeff Hicks, vice-pres.; A.A. Powell, secy.; and W. Hamilton Dukes, treas. These officers and Capt. J. Frank Ellison made up the new board of directors, and Capt. Downs was made general manager. The Lee Line of Memphis captured the U.S. Mail contract between Memphis and Rosedale in 1922, and the *KATE*'s schedule was stretched out to Greenville, Miss. In February 1923, she made a Mardi Gras trip from Memphis to New Orleans with new fancy-topped stacks commanded by Capt. Jeff Hicks. The name of the Line was changed to Delta Line that year. In January 1924, Delta Line and the Lee Line consolidated, becoming Valley Line Steamers, with Capt. Hicks as president and Capt. Peters Lee, manager. About the first act of the new regime was to lay up the *KATE* and on Aug. 1, 1924, the mail contract went to the Missouri-Pacific Railroad. In the spring of 1925 the *KATE* was taken to Paducah and her cotton guards were covered over by extending the boiler deck guards, and she got bull rails and stationarys, and hinged stacks. She was entered in the Pittsburgh-Cincinnati trade that summer commanded by Capt. A.A. Powell with W. Hamilton Dukes, purser. The management of this venture was to have been handled by Capt. Jeff Hicks, who suffered injuries in an auto accident and died July 31, 1925. This left the decisions up to 80-year-old Thomas M. Rees of Pittsburgh. The boat was returned to the Pittsburgh-Cincinnati trade in 1926, having made a Mardi Gras trip that spring in command of Capt. Jerry McDavid. In the fall of 1926, she was returned to Memphis and renovated to take part in the filming of *Uncle Tom's Cabin,* during which she was renamed *LA BELLE RIVIERE.* Capt. Gus Phillips commanded during the filming which took her south to the Ouachita and Black rivers in Louisiana. She was returned to Memphis, restored (at enormous expense), and burned at the levee Jan. 8, 1927. The hull was raised and used as a model barge upon which a huge cargo of cotton was loaded. On the eve of departure from Memphis this barge and cargo sank. Later raised, the old hull was abandoned at the foot of President's Island. The Mariners' Museum of Newport News, Va., acquired the roof bell. All of which is a long story and inadequate to those who remember the tremor of her decks and the deep hoot of her bull-frog whistle which could be heard for 30 miles back in the Mississippi delta. Some years later Capt. Dick Hiernaux brought out the towboat *LEONA* with a large single-chime whistle said to have come from the *KATE*; said to have been dug out of the mud at Memphis. I doubted this. One day in the Cincinnati wharfboat an aged "darky" was half-asleep on a freight pile and I was standing nearby. Unexpectedly the *LEONA* blew a prolonged blast of that whistle while coming under the suspension bridge. Quite as unexpectedly I witnessed that old darky man awake and raise his head like a hound dog which has heard a wolf call on a still, moonlit night. As the vibrant, deep note died away in echoes, this old man cried plaintively: "Cotton pile! Cotton pile! Dat's de ol' *KATE* moanin' for cotton. God bless de *KATE ADAMS!*" He shuffled to the doorway to look, half expecting to see two tall stacks, two swinging stages, a blue-domed pilothouse, and Capt. Billy Hodge at the wheel. I walked the other direction a believer.

3218 KATE B. PORTER

Stw p wh b. Belle Vernon, Pa., 1864. 241 tons. 160 x 31 x 4.2. Engines by Robert Lea, 13's- 4½ ft. Two boilers, each 40" by 20 ft. Construction superintended by Nathan Porter, Jr., at the L.M. Speer yard. Capt. Joseph H. Porter, master. Upon arrival at Cincinnati on her first trip she was ordered to Louisville by the U.S. to load out for Nashville with U.S. supplies. She was taken over by the U.S. and became tinclad#55, called *KATE* in the service (see).

3219 KATE BRUNER

Stw p wh b. Frederick, Ill., 1861. 118 tons. She was lost on White River, Ark., by running into the wreck of the *LIZZIE GILL* (see). She broke in two and sank with the bow out of water and the stern in 9½ feet. The crew had to stay with the boat, many of them ill with cholera. Four died soon after she sank. Later two more died and their bodies were found on the wrecked boat, this near St. Charles, Ark., Sept. 15, 1866.

3220 KATE CASSEL

Stw p wh b. California, Pa., 1854. 167 tons. Engines, 14's-4 ft., by Haigh, Hartupee & Co., Pittsburgh. Two boilers. Built by a stock company led by Capt. Joseph McVay. Hull 141 x 29 x 5. Ran Pittsburgh-Zanesville, 1854–1855. Sold to the Upper Miss and ran out of St. Paul with Capt. Sam Harlow, master, and Charles Hargus, clerk. George B. Merrick, who later wrote "Old Times On the Upper Mississippi" had his first river job on her. In 1861 she replaced the *BLACK HAWK* in the Fort Madison-Rock Island trade, then owned by B.H. Campbell of Galena, and W.B. Davis of Rock Island. In 1863 she was sold to a Capt. Hillhouse who transported U.S. troops and supplies into 1864 when in March she returned to the upper Ohio, Capt. Perry Kerr, having been acquired by a group from Wheeling including Capt. Charles Booth, Capt. Charles Muhleman, James Jelly, Jackson Harrison, Wm. Battelle, John Mulrine. Dismantled August 1864.

3221 KATE DALE

SW p wh b. New Albany, Ind., 1855. 428 tons. Went to Mobile, Ala. Captured as a Confederate steamer July 14, 1863, and was turned over to the USQMD Jan. 6, 1864. Burned at Mobile May 25, 1865.

3222 KATE DALE

SW p wh b. Stewart Island, Ky. (hull) and completed at Algiers, La., 1858. 160 tons. 136 x 27.3 x 4.7. Owned by William Dale, Concordia Parish, La. Ran New Orleans-Ouachita River in low water, Capt. Frank Moore, with J.H. Cooper, clerk. Out of service, 1862.

3223 KATE DIXON

Stw p wh b. Pittsburgh, Pa., 1873. 96 tons. Probably towed produce boats. Capt. James Taylor, McKeesport, Pa., commanded. The boat was moored below Aberdeen, Oh., when on June 6, 1876, U.S. Marshal Major Harrington attempted to arrest Taylor, resulting in a shoot-out in which both were killed. The boat had just returned from the south, and had been up Black River and the Yallabusha. Still listed at Cincinnati 1876.

3224 KATE FLEMING

Stw p wh b. West Elizabeth, Pa., 1850. 76 tons. She was downbound below Cave In Rock on Oct. 5, 1850, when the boilers exploded at Walkers Bar. Nine were killed outright and six injured, two of whom subsequently died.

3225 KATE FRENCH

Stw p wh b. Fish Creek, Oh. and completed at Wheeling, 1854. Originally named *BRIDGE CITY* (see). Renamed Nov. 19, 1856. She was at St. Paul from St. Louis in 1857, Capt. French. Burned at Napoleon, Ark., Nov. 29, 1860.

3226 KATE FRISBEE

SW p wh b. California, Pa., at the Wm. McFall yard, 1853. 203 x 32 x 7.3. 456 tons. Engines, 28's- 7 ft. Four boilers, each 42" by 22 ft. The entire boat, new, was shipped "knock down" aboard *ELEPHANT* to New Orleans, thence to San Francisco, intended for the San Francisco-Murraysville trade. Plans were changed and she was shipped back to Gretna, La., and there assembled in 1855. Built for Capt. Roswell Riley Frisbee and named for a daughter. Ran trips out of Pittsburgh in 1856 to St. Louis but was too heavy for regular Ohio River trade so was sold that fall to Memphis where she ran to Friar's Point, Laconia, and Concordia; also Memphis-Napoleon-White River carrying U.S. Mail. She was the first at the scene of the explosion of the *PENNSYLVANIA* (see) at Ship Island, June 13, 1858. Capt. Frisbee 1802–1880 was native of Schenectady, N.Y., lived as a youth in Pittsburgh, went to California in the Gold Rush, returned to reside in Tennessee, then built boats and ran them. A son Jerome Benton Frisbee served on a Confederate gunboat- lived in New Orleans, and had a daughter

Catherine Rolph Frisbee who married Capt. U.G. Jones of the towboat *PERCY KELSEY.* When the *KATE FRISBEE* was dismantled in 1861, her engines went to the *LOUISVILLE* (see).

3227 KATE HART

Stw p wh b. Paducah, Ky., 1864. 279 tons. 153 x 29 x 4. Was doing U.S. transport service on White River, Ark., in 1864. After dismantling, the hull was used at Pittsburgh as a sand barge. In 1873, machinery was placed on it, also a boiler, and she became a mechanized sand-and-gravel dredge in the area.

3228 KATE HENDERSON

SW p wh b. Belpre, Oh. and completed at Parkersburg, W. Va., 1865. 293 tons. Out of service in 1874.

3229 KATE HOWARD

SW p wh b. Ripley, Oh., 1855. 42 tons. First home port, Cincinnati. Off the lists 1861.

3230 KATE HOWARD

SW p wh b. Jeffersonville, Ind., by Howard, 1857. 504 tons. 235 x 35 x 6. Engines, 24's- 7 ft. Three boilers. Machinery came from the *N.J. EATON* (see). Ran on the Missouri River, St. Louis-St. Joseph, Capt. Joseph Nanson. In November 1858 running New Orleans, Bayou Sara and Fort Adams, Capt. E.F. Gross, with W.W. Hilliard, clerk. She was snagged and lost in Osage Chute, Missouri River, Aug. 4, 1859. Was downbound from St. Joseph for St. Louis with tobacco and hemp. Capt. Nanson was master, with Joe Fecto, pilot. W.W. Hilliard recalled some years later that he was on this boat as clerk on her first Missouri River trip and a calliope was placed aboard for the occasion. The natives were of course astonished and the instrument was in such lively demand that Hilliard in desperation poured molten lead over the keys to get relief.

3231 KATE KEARNEY

SW p wh b. St. Louis, Mo., 1847. 304 tons. Owned by the St. Louis & Keokuk Packet Co., and ran that trade until 1853. She was in retirement when one of the other boats of the Line sank. On Feb. 16, 1854, she was loaded at St. Louis and was about to leave for Keokuk pinch-hitting in the trade when the boilers exploded causing the loss of six lives and wounding many. On a prior occasion this same set of boilers had suffered a flue collapse at Canton causing life loss.

3232 KATE KEARNEY

Stw p wh b. Belle Vernon, Pa., and completed at Pittsburgh, 1864. 445 tons. Hull by L. Speer, 196 x 40.4 x 5.5. Engines, 20's- 5½ ft. Four boilers, each 43" by 24 ft. Built for the St. Louis & Keokuk Packet Co. She was primarily a freight boat with but a small cabin. Capt. Grant Marsh bought her February 1870, along with Goodin & Bros., a coal firm of Lexington, Mo. She was lost at Island 82, Mississippi River, Christmas Day, 1871. Three days later only her stacks were showing above water. No life loss.

3233 KATE KEEN

Stw ferry wh b. Clayton, Iowa, 1865. 31.5 tons. 80 x 15 x 3. Served as a barge the first year; machinery placed 1866. Ran at Clayton, Iowa. This long-lived ferry was not removed from documentation until 1901.

3234 KATE KINNEY

SW p wh b. Cincinnati, Oh., 1864. 508 tons. Ran on the Missouri River, St. Louis-Omaha, Capt. Joseph Kinney. Partially burned in the steamboat fire at St. Louis, March 2, 1868. Burned at New Albany, Ind., Oct. 29, 1872.

3235 KATE KINNEY

Stw p wh b. Madison, Ind., 1873. 200 x 38 x 6.5. Engines, 18's- 7 ft. Four boilers, each 38" by 26 ft. Machinery from the *R.P. WALT.* Owned by Capt. Joseph Kinney, Boonville, Mo. His old home opposite Boonville is a popular showplace of Missouri architecture and culture. He ran this boat on the Missouri and often went south with her in winter. She burned at Shreveport, La., Dec. 15, 1883.

3236 KATE MAY

Stw p wh b. Cincinnati, Oh., 1859. 207 tons. Ran Cincinnati-Memphis, Capt. Bugher. Burned and lost at Cannelton, Ind., March 31, 1860.

3237 KATE PUTNAM

Stw p wh b. Brownsville, Pa., 1864. 269 tons. Capt. John L. Rhoads superintended her construction. Came out August 1864 in the Pittsburgh-Cincinnati trade, Capt. J.W. Anawalt, with W. Bennett, clerk. Loaded at Pittsburgh in November 1864 for St. Louis, Capt. Frank Maratta. Made frequent trips Pittsburgh-St. Louis-New Orleans. Sank near St. Louis, Feb. 22, 1868, having struck the wreck of the *GOV. SHARKEY.* Capt. George W. Reed bought an interest at Pittsburgh, May 1868, and took command. She was at New Orleans when Gen. Robert E. Lee died in 1870, in command of Capt. Ed Evans. All boats in the harbor displayed mourning with flags half-masted save the *KATE PUTNAM.* Capt. Evans had been in command of the *WESTMORELAND* (see) when Sumter was fired on and shots were fired at his boat killing one man. Arrived at Pittsburgh Jan. 25, 1871, with a fair trip. Went to Nashville with freight from Pittsburgh, April 1871. Lost in ice at Cincinnati, Dec. 31, 1872.

3238 KATE ROBINSON

Stw p wh b. Parkersburg, W. Va., 1863. 283 tons. Built for Capt. R. Robinson and ran out of Pittsburgh to Cincinnati and St. Louis. Was advertised direct from Pittsburgh to Council Bluffs and Omaha in April 1866. Captain Robinson retired from the river June 1868, and Capt. Marsh Hays succeeded him. Sank on a log near Grand Tower in December 1869, raised. In 1870, Cincinnati-St. Louis, Capt. James Keniston, with John E. Thrasher, clerk. Burned and lost at Cincinnati, March 7, 1872.

3239 Kate Sarchet

Stw p wh b. New Albany, Ind., 1856. 184 tons. Sunk on the Wabash River while jumping a dam, June 1858; raised. Lost by stranding, Feb. 18, 1861.

3240 Kate Swinney

SW p wh b. Jeffersonville, Ind., by Howard, 1852. 280 tons. 180 x 30 x 6.5. Engines, 19's- 7 ft. Three boilers, each 40" by 26 ft. Built for a St. Louis tobacco merchant and named for his daughter. In 1854 was making trips up the Missouri for the American Fur Co., and went to Fort Pierre to bring out practically the whole catch of buffalo hides, silver fox, beaver, etc., for the 1854–1855 season. Joe Fecto was her pilot. Snagged and lost at Kate Swinney Bend above Vermillion River Aug. 1, 1855, loaded with furs. George Anderson and the deck crew started walking to Sioux City and were killed by Indians. In September 1873, the wreck was exposed for the first time in sixteen years, the river having changed and exposed the hull. Often referred to as the *KATE SWEENEY* in error, the builder was W.D. Swinney, Glasgow, Mo.

3241 Katherine

Stw ferry wh b. Jeffersonville, Ind., by Howard, 1889. Originally named *THE NEW IDEA* (see). She was taken to Cairo, Ill., for ferry service. On May 26, 1896, Cairo was visited by a severe cyclone, same as St. Louis, and the *KATHERINE* capsized, drowning eleven persons. Capt. J.S. Hacker operated her, then sold her to the Barrett Line. Capt. I.N. Flesher, Mt. Vernon, Ind., bought her October 1907, took her to Pt. Pleasant, W. Va., and used the hull, etc., building a towboat named *I.N. FLESHER,* using machinery from the towboat *ANNIE L.*

3242 Kathryn

Stw p wh b. Elizabeth, W. Va., 1890. Originally named *W.A. HILTON* (see). Capt. Ben S. Pope, Parkersburg, W. Va., bought *HILTON* in 1897, rebuilt and renamed her, and she ran on Little Kanawha River, Capt. J.H. Page. Capt. R.L. (Dick) Elwood, Monongahela City, Pa., bought the boat and in 1900 ran her Pittsburgh-Monongahela City. In 1901 sold to David H. Waters, then to M.F. Gruber who used her as a towboat until she burned near the foot of Brunots Island, Pittsburgh, Dec. 8, 1907. Capt. Edward J. Hulings was master at the time. Crew of the towboat *M.D. WAYMAN* rescued the crew.

3243 Katie

Stw p wh b. Elizabeth, Pa., 1864. 180 tons. Built for William J. Kountz, and was downbound at Diamond Island, Ohio River, Nov. 22, 1864, when she collided with the *DES MOINES* (see) upbound with U.S. troops aboard. *KATIE* sank in nine minutes. Had aboard a large cargo of cattle, most of which swam ashore. The survivors were taken to Evansville, many shoeless and hatless, aboard the *DES MOINES.*

3244 Katie

SW p wh b. Jeffersonville, Ind., by Howard, 1871. 284 x 43 x 8.7. Engines, 38's- 10 ft. Nine boilers, each 40" by 32 ft, 2 flues. Paddlewheels 39 ft. diameter working 17 ft. buckets. Her engines were made for the famed *ROBERT E. LEE* but Captain Cannon changed his mind and had larger engines made for the *LEE.* Capt. J.M. White, who commanded, wanted to name her *LADY LEE* to honor the widow of Gen. Robert E. Lee, but was outvoted. Built for the New Orleans-Lake Providence trade. She was hard to hold, quite fast, and buried her head under full headway. Hit a snag at Trotter's Point opposite Helena, Ark., on her maiden trip and sank. During summer months ran New Orleans-St. Louis on occasion; was at St. Louis 1871. Downbound in a fog, with 3,000 cotton bales aboard, drifted into a crevasse at Bonnet Carre, La., and lodged 2,200 feet from the Mississippi River, Jan. 23, 1876. Remained there for some time. She was returned to Jeffersonville in May 1878, after quite some struggle over the Falls, ascending the Indiana Chute, assisted by towboat *RESOLUTE.* She was dismantled at Jeff. The hull became a wharfboat on the Ouachita River at Monroe, La., where it served until 1879–1880 when it burned along with the packet *FAIRPLAY* (see). The machinery went to the *ED RICHARDSON* (see).

Had ma pic' of ev'y boat
Sunk, burned o' still uh float,
Side o' sturnwheel, big o' small,
Chim'lys sho't chim'lys tall.
Tek de Katie!

Sets de watah lak uh swan,
Comin' up at urly mo'n,
In dat dress all trim in white,
Sho'ly is a pleasin' sight.
Miss Katie!

If Ole Gab'll hap'in 'roun'
Jedgment trumpet fu' tuh soun'
Dis heah whut ol' Gab'll do—

Please him so he wave his han'
Ax de captain if he can
Tek him back tuh Promis' Lan'
On de Katie!

—*Author unknown.*

3245 Katie

Stw ferry wh b. New Matamoras, Oh., 1895. 75.9 x 16 x 2.5. Owned and operated by Capt. P.Q. Shrake, New Matamoras. Ferried there to Friendly, W. Va. Sank at Marietta in the Muskingum opposite Putnam Street, overloaded with coal, May 5, 1900. Did some ferry work on the Muskingum. Shrake also owned the ferry *MARY C. CAMPBELL* (see) at this time. Sold Aug. 19, 1903, to Capt. Elmer E. Varian, Pt. Pleasant, W. Va.

3246 KATIE HOOPER

Stw p wh b. Pittsburgh, Pa., 1877. 180 x 36 x 6.5. Built for the Little Rock & Memphis Packet Co., and named for the wife of Capt. E.W.B. Nowland, Sr. Capt. John N. Harbin came to Pittsburgh from Memphis and took command on the delivery trip. Left Pittsburgh on Aug. 7, 1877, the river dead low. A number of towboat pilots went along to inspect the channel, among them Capt. Wash Gray and Capt. Sam Dean, Jr. In October 1878, she was at Cincinnati loading for Arkansas River, Capt. Ed Nowland. The *HATTIE NOWLAND* (see) sank on the Arkansas and some time later the *HOOPER* struck the wreck and sank. She was raised, returned to Pittsburgh, and parts were used building the *JOE PETERS* (see), this in 1883.

3247 KATIE KEISER

Ferry wh b. 1870. Owned by a Dr. Willard of Rocheport, Mo. Sold September 1871 to Capt. David Campbell, St. Louis, who took her to St. Louis for docking. He sold her immediately after to Capt. C.T. King, Cape Girardeau, Mo., and took in trade the ferry *EFFIE BOFINGER* which had been working there.

3248 KATIE MAY

Ferry wh b. Griggsville Landing, Ill., 1876. 29 tons. 64 x 20.9 x 2.6. Inspected at Naples, Ill., November 1881. Still documented 1886, maybe later.

3249 KATIE P. KOUNTZ

Stw p wh b. Elizabeth, Pa., at Latta yard, 1871. Hartupee compound engines, 10's- 23's- 4½ ft. Four boilers in two batteries. Built for Capt. William J. Kountz. Made three trips to Fort Benton and two to the rival town of Carroll. A large, slow boat unsuited for the upper Missouri, and never made more than one trip to Montana a year. In 1874 was all season making one trip to Carroll. In fall of 1876 was at Pittsburgh loading for St. Louis. Sank in the Mississippi Oct. 15, 1879, in the crossing from Randolph Point to Island 40. Snagged on the Missouri in 1880. Burned at David Landing on the Mississippi Nov. 1, 1883, with a large cargo of cotton and seed.

3250 KATIE PEASE

Ferry (?) wh b. Blair, Neb., 1884. 60 x 17 x 2.6. Listed 1886, maybe later.

3251 KATIE PRATHER

SW batwing wh b. Cincinnati, Oh., 1881. 91 x 14 x 3.4. One boiler. Built for W.W. Prather, Manchester, Oh. George W. Edgington ran her low water in the Manchester-Maysville trade. Still listed 1892.

3252 KATIE ROBBINS

Stw p wh b. Jeffersonville, Ind., 1884. 141 x 28 x 4.9. Operated by the Parisot Line on Yazoo River. Still listed 1886, perhaps later.

3253 KATIE STOCKDALE

Stw p wh b. California, Pa. (hull) and completed at Pittsburgh, 1877. 228 x 34.5 x 5. Engines, 16's- 7 ft. Four boilers. Originally owned by J.T. Stockdale (one-quarter), Willis Stockdale (one-half), and Thomas S. Calhoon (one-quarter). Named for youngest daughter of J.T. Stockdale. Entered Pittsburgh-Cincinnati trade, December 1877, Capt. T.S. Calhoon. Clerks included Nat Earhart, Martin F. Noll, C.M. Buchanan, C. Barringer, H.C. Caldwell, A.J. McConnell, and Charles W. Knox. Whistle and cabin furniture came from the *GLENCOE* (see). James Rowley, Sr., and George Hughes were the original pilots on her. Came out with plain-topped stacks but had fancy tops added, similar to *SCOTIA* (see) in August 1880. Sunk in collision with the towboat *B.D. WOOD,* Feb. 3, 1882. Started out as the Saturday boat out of Pittsburgh but by 1882 swapped over to become the Monday boat. On Feb. 10, 1884, the pilothouse was sawed off level with the pilotwheel to get her under the Parkersburg bridge. The iron paddlewheel she came out with was not successful and was replaced with a usual one. Dismantled at Harmar in 1890 and equipment went to the new *KEYSTONE STATE* (see). The hull with cabin intact was towed to Pittsburgh and rebuilt into an excursion barge for John F. Klein, renamed *CITY OF PITTSBURGH,* later *IDLEWILD,* neither name approved by U.S. Customs and she again became *KATIE STOCKDALE.* Sprung a leak and sank at the Pittsburgh wharf Aug. 2, 1895, at 5:00 A.M. The wreck was raised, towed to the head of Davis Island, Ohio River, there beached and burned.

3254 KATYDID

SW p wh b. Middleport, Oh., 1873. A single deck, daylight packet with one stack. Built for R.R. Hudson and soon sold to the Parkersburg & Ohio River Transportation Co. Ran in Parkersburg-Gallipolis trade until June 1878 when Capt. John Woodburn took one-half interest and ran her Evansville-Rockport. Sold in October 1878 to Ed R. Thomas and others for the White River-Vicksburg trade. Ed Thomas had been first clerk on the *COAHOMA.* She was considered very fast and made fifteen mph. She was equipped with two Scotch boilers. Along toward the last she was bought by Charles Ward, Charleston, W. Va., and operated Charleston-Gallipolis-Pomeroy, and is said to have made the round trip in fourteen hours making 50 landings. Ward put one of his patent boilers on her at the time. When *KATYDID* was dismantled the Ward boiler and her engines went to the *BEE,* a towboat on Kanawha River, 1881.

3255 KELLEY SAULS

Stw tb-p sh b. Memphis, Tenn., 1917. 64.6 x 15.2 x 3.5. Crushed by ice at Paducah, Ky., Jan. 28, 1918. Rebuilt to become the packet *PEARL CITY* (see).

3256 KELLOGG

SW tr sh b. McKees Rocks, Pa., 1898. 303 x 46 x 9.8. Originally a non-propelled 4-track railroad transfer barge. She was powered when the first railroad transfer steamer *STE. GENEVIEVE* sank in 1918 (see). Owned by William

Edenborn, who operated the Louisana Railway & Navigation Co., Angola, La., with the *WILLIAM EDENBORN* and *SARAH EDENBORN,* both towboats. She sank on Old River, La., March 21, 1928 at 2:15 A.M. Took a forward nose dive, broke in two. Capt. C.M. Guess was in command. She was still there, half covered by mud at the T&P bridge, 1934. The U.S. Engineers were preparing to remove the wreck in the fall of 1945.

3257 KENNEDY

Stw p wh b. Lyons, Iowa, 1901. 121.5 x 24.4 x 3.9. Engines, 10's- 6 ft. Two boilers, each 36″ by 18 ft. Bought new by the Heckmanns of Hermann, Mo., who ran her out of Batesville, Ark., on White River carrying railroad supplies to Buffalo Shoals. They returned her to Missouri River, and had her out to St. Louis during the 1904 World's Fair there. Agents for the Florida East Coast Railroad bought her about 1906 and took her to the Florida Keys. Burned in the St. Johns River, Fla., Feb. 24, 1914, still owned by F.E.C.

3258 KENOIS

Stw tb-p wh b. Metropolis, Ill., 1901. 90 x 20 x 3.5. One boiler, 42″ by 22 ft. Ran in Paducah-Metropolis trade 1902, Capt. William Chesterfield. Owned 1903 by Capt. William F. (Ted) Howell, Evansville. Was at Bowling Green, Ky., in the March 1913 flood.

3259 KENTON

SW p wh b. Cincinnati, Oh., 1848. 271 tons. Ran Cincinnati-Maysville, Capt. R. Cooper, in 1855. There was a *SIMON KENTON* in the trade at the same time (see). Out of service 1859.

3260 KENTON

Stw p wh b. Shousetown, Pa. (hull) and completed at Pittsburgh, 1860.215 tons. Built for Capt. Nelson Crooks and others. Sold in October 1861 to Capt. G.W. Ebert and Standish Peppard who ran her Pittsburgh-Cincinnati-Louisville. They sold her to Capt. J.H. Dunlap, Bridgewater, Pa., in October 1863, and for the continuation of the war she was in U.S. service. While moored at Eastport on the Tennessee River, Oct. 10, 1864, the Rebels attacked from both shores. The *KENTON* was struck 50 times by shells, many exploding on board. One shell exploded a caisson in the engine room, rupturing a steam line, killing a watchman, and causing general havoc. Capt. Dunlap got her away from the landing, the crew extinguished a fire which had broken out aboard, and she was moved out of range. Those who saw the boat afterwards say she was almost completely riddled by shot. Dunlap said later that the zeal displayed by his crew and himself was prompted by visions of spending the rest of the war in Libby Prison if captured. After the war Dunlap ran the *KENTON* from Pittsburgh to Cincinnati and New Orleans, with Sharp Hemphill, clerk. In September 1868 at Cincinnati, Dunlap sold the boat to Capt. Wash Kerr for the Pittsburgh-Portsmouth trade, taking the place of the *ROBERT MOORE* (see), with W.J.C. Anderson, clerk, and later D.S.H. Gilmore. Sold, November 1869 to Capt. Henry U. Hart, Cincinnati, for the Cincinnati-New Orleans trade. Snagged and lost opposite Helena, Ark., May 5, 1870.

3261 KENTON

Stw ferry-tb wh b. Cincinnati, Oh., 1879. 105.2 x 33.4 x 5.2. Operated as a ferry in the Cincinnati area until in the 1890s sold to Capt. John Barrett. He narrowed the hull and converted her into a towboat. Sold later to Paducah Coal & Mining Co. (forerunner of the West Kentucky Coal Co.), for bringing coal from Caseyville to Paducah. Last owner was U.S. Gas & Coke Co., New York, who changed her name to *THOMAS NEVINS.* Finally dismantled at Marietta, Oh., and machinery went to the towboat *REAPER.*

3262 KENTUCKY

SW p wh b. Louisville, Ky., 1845. 134 tons. 135 x 24 x 5.5. Hull by John Cunningham. Went to St. Louis, and used out of Galena. Capt. W.H. Atchison was master, 1847. Out of service 1852.

3263 KENTUCKY

SW p wh b. Wellsville, Oh., 1849. 98 tons. A boat of this name was operating in Kentucky River out of Frankfort in 1850, probably this one. Burned and lost at Rock Island, Ill., Aug. 7, 1855.

3264 KENTUCKY

SW ferry wh b. Newport, Ky., 1852. 118 tons. Ran Cincinnati-Covington along with *QUEEN CITY* (see). Off the lists 1865.

3265 KENTUCKY

SW p wh b. Cincinnati, Oh., 1856. 375 tons. 222 x 32 x 5.5. Engines, 22's- 7 ft. Four boilers. Ran Louisville-Memphis, Capt. John Scott, 1860. She was impressed into U.S. war service 1864, and in June 1865 was chartered to move 800 Confederate troops from Shreveport. Downbound on Red River she hit a snag and sank rapidly. Many were drowned. Feelings ran high that this was not altogether an accident, and one correspondent to the New Orleans *Times* declared he "would hang the captain and pilots to the first tree that I could find." The author was Capt. Stephen J. Webber of the transport *CAROL CHAPIN* assisting in the rescue operations.

3266 KENTUCKY

SW ferry wh b. Aurora, Ind., 1867. 29 tons. Ferried at Aurora, and then at Mt. Vernon, Ind. Sank at Evansville during an ice run-out Jan. 24, 1871. Lost at Cincinnati 1880.

3267 KENTUCKY

Stw p wh b. Jeffersonville, Ind., by Howard, 1904. 176 x 33 x 6. Built for the St. Louis & Tennessee River Packet Co. In the winter of 1922–1923 she was completely rebuilt at Paducah and renamed *TENNESSEE BELLE* (see). Her original roof bell was removed at that time and was presented by Capt. S. King Hale to the First Christian Church, Paducah.

3268 KENTUCKY

Stw p wh b. Madison, Ind., 1907. 185 x 33 x 5. Engines, 15's- 5 ft. Three boilers, 38" by 20 ft. Machinery and boilers came from the *LEVI J. WORKUM* (see). Ran a great while in the Cincinnati-Madison trade, frequently Cincinnati-Louisville. She drove away more business and made more money than any boat of her size and time. For some abstruse reason her cabin was designed in a long wedge shape so that the lengths of the berths got shorter as you proceeded aft, some of them barely 5'6" long, and added to this novelty she one time got in a "breeze" and the cabin was shifted out of plumb and leaned in a uniform stagger creating an optical illusion seen nowhere else except in a "Fun House" of a pleasure park. She was proverbially slow, sloppy, and if her smokestacks ever stood straight I never heard of it. Her redeeming feature was in economy of operation. No money ever was spent on her and it is told a carpenter once was employed aboard and two years later, when asked what he did, said he was saving up to buy a saw and hammer. In several of the after rooms it was possible to look from a berth to the floor and see machinery working in the engine-room below. This scapegrace was pawned off on an unsuspecting public without one whit of apology from the management, nor any warning to brace the unwary, and plodded along making enemies and money. Finally the Louisville & Cincinnati Packet Co., who had owned her, went out of business, and the Greene Line took her over and quietly chloroformed her. She carried three whistles in her time; came out in 1907 with the *TELEGRAPH* whistle, swapped this for the old *BONANZA* whistle when the *CITY OF CINCINNATI* sank. Later she had an imitation of the *T.N. BARNSDALL* whistle. Some of her equipment went to building a little towboat named *ECLIPSE* (later *JOHN G. BRITTON*).

3269 KENTUCKY NO. 2

SW p wh b. Evansville, Ind., 1851. 148 tons. Ran Evansville-Green River, Capt. J.T. Hugo. Sold to the Upper Miss, and in early 1857 she caught fire while landing alongside the *PRAIRIE STATE* at Rock Island, destroying the latter (see). Owned by Capt. Rissue, Prescott, Wis., she was at St. Paul in 1857, and sank on a bar at Pruitt's Island, a mile below Prescott in 1858.

3270 KENTUCKY NO. 2

SW ferry wh b. Aurora, Ind., 1873. 28 tons. Apparently ferried at Aurora. Still listed in 1876, maybe later.

3271 KENTUCKY HOME

Stw p wh b. Elizabeth, Pa., 1855. First owned by Capt. Napoleon B. Fowler and others. She was entered in the Pittsburgh-Louisville trade, and on her second trip collided at Sugar Creek, Ky., on the Ohio River with the *TELEGRAPH No. 3* (see) at 9:00 P.M., July 30, 1855, drowning three. In 1958 your scribe had a letter from Mrs. T.G. Hoyt, Jacksonville, Fla., daughter of Captain Fowler. Captain Fowler died at his home. Cuba, Mo., February 1901. Mrs. Hoyt's mother was Sarah Wilcox Caffrey Hoyt, daughter of Capt. B.J. Caffrey.

3272 KENWOOD

Stw p wh b. Cincinnati, Oh., 1863. 232 tons. Sold before documentation to U.S. Navy and became tinclad #14, still named *KENWOOD*. Sold to private owners 1865 and was renamed *CUMBERLAND* (see). 154 x 33 x 5. Engines, 16's- 5 ft.

3273 KEOKUK

SW p wh b. Metropolis, Ill., 1855. 435 tons. Belonged to the St. Louis-Keokuk Mail Line and in 1855 ran there with *JEANNIE DEANS, DIE VERNON* and *WESTERNER* (all see). The *OCEAN SPRAY* (see) caught fire at St. Louis, April 22, 1858, also burning *KEOKUK* and *STAR OF THE WEST*.

3274 KEOKUK

SW p wh b. Brownsville, Pa., 1858. 220 tons. 177 x 27.5 x 5. Engines, 20's- 5½ ft. Three boilers, each 40" by 26 ft. Built for the Rapids Packet Co., Keokuk, Ebenezer Cook, president. Capt. Silas Heaight was master and owned interest, also in *BLACK HAWK* (see). She soon was sold to Minnesota Packet Co., for the La Crosse-St. Paul trade, then in Davidson Line, same trade. After the war ran in the south. Sank at Baton Rouge in 1866 and was dismantled.

3275 KEOKUK

Centerwheel ferry wh b. Brownsville, Pa., 1867. 178 tons. 144 x 41 x 4.3. Engines, 10's- 4½ ft. Two boilers, each 42" by 20 ft. Built at the J.S. Pringle yard, work superintended by Capt. A.D. Hine. Left Pittsburgh in June 1867 with 2,000 boxes of window glass aboard consigned to Keokuk. Operated at Keokuk, first owned by Louis L. Hine, R.N. Martin, and John Van Dyke. Off the lists 1880.

3276 KEOKUK

Stw p wh b. Mound City, Ill., and completed at St. Louis, 1876. Originally named *C.K. PECK* (see). 211.2 x 36 x 5. She was a "mountain boat" for Missouri River. In 1882 she was streamlined into a typical packet and renamed *KEOKUK*. In 1884 sold to the Bayou Lafourche Packet Co., Capt. Max Blanchard, master, and ran twice weekly New Orleans-Donaldsonville-Thibodeaux-Laurel Valley and made a flatboat connection at Laurel Valley for Lockport. W.G. Coyle was president of the company. In 1885 was the "summer boat" in the New Orleans-Baton Rouge trade in place of the *JOHN W. CANNON* (see) with Capt. W.L. Cannon, master. Much about this boat, plus an oil painting by Joseph Wilhelm, in *S&D Reflector*, June 1978, pages 30–31.

3277 KEOKUK

Stw p wh b. Wabasha, Minn., 1907. 138 x 30 x 4. Engines, 13½'s- 6 ft. Two boilers, each 38" by 30 ft. Built for Carnival City Packet Co., to replace the *SILVER CRESCENT* (see) in the Keokuk-Quincy trade. Much equipment from rafter *MUSSER* used in building her. Capt. Walter Blair headed the ownership. Capt. S.R. Dodds, master. Later ran Quincy-Burlington with much success, Capt. Hugh McKenzie, with Fred Bruegge, purser. In April 1922 was swamped in high waves at Nauvoo, Ill. Burned at Davenport, Iowa, August 1926.

3278 KEY CITY

SW p wh b. Cincinnati, Oh., 1857. 359 tons. 230 x 35 x 5.6. Engines, 20's- 7 ft. Four boilers, each 42" by 16 ft. Paddlewheels 26' diameter working 12 ft. buckets. Built for the Minnesota Packet Co., and ran Galena, Dunleith-St. Paul. Capt. James Wordon was first master, with clerk George S. Pierce. They were on her through 1862 season, with Ned West as pilot. Sank the *BEN COURSIN* (see) in collision near La Crosse, Aug. 24, 1857, with loss of seven lives on the latter. Arrived at Madison, Ind., for dismantling on Dec. 6, 1869, and the *MILWAUKEE* also arrived there for the same purpose.

3279 KEY CITY

Ferry wh b. Dubuque, Iowa, 1876. 94 tons. 100 x 25 x 4.4. Operated at Dubuque, and was still there in 1886, perhaps longer.

3280 KEY CITY

Stw p-tb wh b. Kingston, Tenn., 1891. 80 x 18 x 3.2. Ran between Loudon and Kingston, Tenn., carrying U.S. Mail. Renamed *NELLIE* c. 1910.

3281 KEY WEST

Stw p wh b. Elizabeth, Pa., 1857. 169 tons. This boat and the *CHIPPEWA* were the first to arrive at Fort Benton, Mont., July 2, 1860; closest approach theretofore was when the *CHIPPEWA* on July 17, 1859, had ascended the Missouri to Brule Bottom, Mont., 15 miles below the Fort, and was forced to unload there and return due to rapidly falling stage of water. In off seasons she ran to Arkansas River from New Orleans, and was making such a trip in April 1861, Capt. Jos. Brannon. Burned at Van Buren, Ark., Dec. 27, 1862.

3282 KEY WEST

Stw p wh b. Pittsburgh, Pa., 1871. 200 x 33 x 5.4. Owned by John Todd and Nicholas Buison of Columbiana County, Oh., and by Sanford S. Coulson, William S. Evans, and David S.H. Gilmore, Pittsburgh. Belonged to the American Fur Co., and operated on Missouri River. Capt. Grant Marsh was master in 1873 when Gen. Philip H. Sheridan, commanding the Army's Division of the Missouri, ordered the *KEY WEST* on an exploration trip of the Yellowstone. Went 460 miles to mouth of Powder River. Several years later this mileage was vastly exceeded by the *JOSEPHINE* (see). A report in Sept. 1873 said that pilot Nick Buison of the *KEY WEST* had been granted a first class license to navigate the Yellowstone, the first one granted. This boat made in all 23 trips to Montana points, most of them to Fort Benton, under the Coulson Line. After the 1882 season she was sold and renamed *NEW IBERIA* (see).

3283 KEY WEST NO. 2

Stw p wh b. California, Pa. (hull) and completed at Pittsburgh, 1860. 206 tons. Capt. William S. Evans was master 1861-1862, many trips Pittsburgh-Cincinnati. James Mellon was clerk in 1862. Sold to American Fur Co., in April 1862, for a trip to the Yellowstone. Snagged and lost at Chester, Ill., Oct. 26, 1863.

3284 KEY WEST NO. 3

Stw p wh b. California, Pa., 1862. 207 tons. 156 x 32 x 4.5. Original owners: Capt. William S. Evans, master; Henry W. Oliver, Jr., Erastus St. John and William Coulson (all of Allegheny County, Pa.); William F. McKee of Birmingham, Pa., and Martin Coulson of Westmoreland County, Pa. She was sold to U.S. Navy on March 16, 1863, and became tinclad #32 known as *KEY WEST*. Burned to avoid capture at Johnsonville, Tenn., Nov. 4, 1864.

3285 KEY WEST NO. 4

Stw p wh b. Manchester, Pa., 1863. 91 tons. This small edition of her forerunners was sold to the U.S. and taken to Arkansas River. She departed Little Rock on April 1, 1864, and 20 miles below there, at Paw Paw Landing, she stove on a snag and sank. The crew came to Memphis, and thence to Cincinnati on the *SILVER MOON* (see).

3286 KEYSTONE

SW p wh b. Brownsville, Pa., 1853. 307 tons. Ran Pittsburgh-St. Louis. Was at St. Paul in May 1857. Off the lists 1863.

3287 KEYSTONE STATE

SW p wh b. Freedom, Pa. (hull) and completed at Pittsburgh, 1850. 234 x 26 x 5.7. 337 tons. Built for Pittsburgh-Cincinnati trade, Capt. Charles Stone. Stockholders also included Stephen Stone, Beaver, Pa., and D.H. Stone, William C. Gray, Hays & Black and William Thaw, Pittsburgh. Capt. William J. Kountz took stock in 1853, and she was transferred to the St. Louis-New Orleans trade. Burned and lost at Florence, Ill., May 31, 1855.

3288 KEYSTONE STATE

Stw p wh b. Harmar, Oh., at the Knox Yard, 1890. 225 x 37 x 6. Engines, 16's- 7 ft. Three boilers, each 42" by 24 ft. Built for the Pittsburgh & Cincinnati Packet Line using cabin equipment, etc., from *KATIE STOCKDALE*. Left Pittsburgh on maiden trip March 10, 1890, Capt. Thomas S. Calhoon with Charles W. Knox, purser; Harry Ollom and T.S. Sandford, pilots; George Knox, chief engineer; Ben Baker, and James Martin, mates; George Day, steward; Logan Noll and George Donnelly, clerks. In March 1895, Capt. Charles W. Knox became master. J. Henry Best and William D. Kimble were pursers later. E. Dayton Randolph and "Billy" Anderson were pilots many years. William T. Terry, carpenter, was shot and killed at

Parkersburg, W. Va., while removing the whistle during high water, spring 1901. Sidney Cole, residing on a shantyboat nearby, was convicted and served time in the Moundsville penitentiary. She was the "huckster" boat, leaving Pittsburgh Mondays. In October 1909, she was sold to Levi Sparr, Williamsburg, Blair County, Pa., and was taken to Pt. Pleasant and received a new hull. The Kanawha Dock Co., was not paid, and attached the boat for debt, and she remained there several years in litigation. Dixon & Cohen, wholesale fish merchants of Peoria, Ill., bought her for the St. Louis-Peoria trade where she ran until 1913. Sold to Chicago & Gulf Transportation Co., who put new boilers on her at Paducah, could not pay the bill, and Dixon & Cohen took her back. Andrew J. Franz became manager, put Capt. Milt Harry aboard as master, and ran her St. Louis-Peoria the balance of 1913. That was her final packet career. That winter Capt. D. Walter Wisherd and Sam Gregory bought her and converted her into an excursion boat, renamed *MAJESTIC* (see).

3289 KINGFISHER

Stw p wh b. Mount Sterling, Mo., 1895. 74.6 x 16.1 x 2.5. Engines, 6's- 3 ft. One railroad boiler. Built at Heckmann's Mill on the Gasconade River by William L. Heckmann and his son Bill. They operated her as a packet on the Gasconade three years, then sold her to a Mr. Terrel of Texas who took her to Red River for the fish trade. Documented at Galveston, Tex., 1899. Apparently rebuilt at Fulton, Ark., 1901. Still registered at New Orleans, 1905.

3290 KINGSTON

SW p wh b. St. Louis, Mo., 1849. 142 tons. Ran on the upper Tennessee. Off the lists in 1855.

3291 KINGSTON

Stw p wh b. by Federal forces on the upper Tennessee during the Civil War. She was taken to Decatur, Ala., in 1869 and dismantled. Part of her went to the building of the *EMMA* (see).

3292 KINGSTON

Stw p wh b. Kingston, Tenn., 1893. 55 x 11 x 2.6. One boiler. Single deck, one stack back of the pilothouse, scow bow. Last inspection was on Oct. 19, 1897.

3293 KINSMAN

SW p wh b. Elizabeth, Pa., 1854. 245 tons. Originally named *GRAY CLOUD,* and was captured by the U.S. in 1862 as Confederate steamer *COLONEL KINSMAN.* Turned over to the USQMD and renamed *KINSMAN,* and then went in U.S. service. She was snagged and sunk in Berwick Bay, La., Feb. 23, 1863, with loss of six lives.

3294 KIT CARSON

SW p wh b. Elizabethtown, Pa., 1848. 280 tons. 165 x 28.5 x 6.3. Engines, 22's- 7 ft. Three boilers, each 42" by 26 ft. Designed for the St. Louis-Glasgow trade on Missouri River. Capt. N.J. Eaton superintended construction. Quite elaborately furnished, with pilasters of the cabin doors of curly maple, surmounted with gilded capitals. Furniture in the ladies' cabin of covered rosewood. Marble-topped mahogany tables and "elegant" mirrors. Had initials KC between her stacks. Burned in the great steamboat fire at St. Louis May 17, 1849, along with 22 others.

3295 KIT CARSON

SW p wh b. Hazelton, Ind., 1862. 34 tons. Off the lists in 1863.

3296 KITTIE HEGLER

Stw p wh b. Madison, Ind., 1871. 170 x 32 x 5.5. Engines, 20's- 5 ft. Three boilers. Built at the R.J. Stuart & Co., yard. Built to replace the *ANNIE LAURIE* (see) by Capt. J.D. Hegler for the Cincinnati-Kanawha River trade, Stratton, clerk. Still there, 1873, Wm. Birthisel, clerk. The *JULIA NO. 2* took her place (see), and then she ran Cincinnati-Memphis, and in 1875 was in Pittsburgh-Cincinnati trade, Sterling McIntyre, clerk. In January 1876, taking cotton from Little Rock to New Orleans. She took fire at New Orleans at 9:30 P.M., Feb. 24, 1876, and the flames spread so rapidly that Capt. Hegler and McIntyre had no time to save the books from the office. The burning wreck was secured by the tug *CHARLIE WOOD* and moored on the Algiers side. The towboat *JOHN A. WOOD* towed the hull to Pittsburgh in April 1876, for conversion into a model barge.

3297 KITTIE NYE

SW p wh b. Harmar, Oh., at the Knox Yard, 1872. 125 x 24 x 3.5. Built for Capt. Dode Berry who ran her Marietta-Matamoras, and Parkersburg-St. Marys. Named for Miss Katherine Parr Nye, daughter of Mr. and Mrs. James W. Nye, Marietta, Oh. "Kittie" Nye attended the 1955 annual meeting of S&D at Marietta. Capt. William E. Roe was cabin boy on her. Later sold to New Orleans & Gulf Transportation Co., and ran to Port Eads and Pilot Town along with the *ISABEL, ALVIN,* and *MARTHA.* Burned at Monticello, Miss., Dec. 10, 1880.

3298 KITTY WOODS

Ferry wh b. Gallipolis, Oh., 1871. 30 tons. Operated at Gallipolis until c. 1880, and then was taken to Ravenswood, W. Va., where she did ferry service run by Henry Fleming whose brother George ran the Ravenswood wharfboat. Still operating 1881, maybe later.

3299 KIWANIS

Stw ferry sh b. Dubuque, Iowa, 1923. 140 x 29 x 4.9. Built for the Cairo City Ferry Co. and operated there to Birds Point until the bridge was built. Sold to Greene Line Steamers, Cincinnati, and ran Cincinnati-Huntington until 1936, when she was rebuilt at the Dravo marine ways, Neville Island, Pa. and renamed *EVERGREENE* (see).

3300 KLONDIKE

Stw p wh b. Pt. Pleasant, W. Va., 1897. 110 x 20.8 x 4. Engines, 9½'s- 3 ft. One boiler, 43" by 20 ft. Originally ran in the Gallipolis-Syracuse trade, Capt. M.M. Brown, with N. Stone, clerk. Fred Hornbrook and Harry Donnally ran her Portsmouth-Rome about 1912-1915, and sold her April 1916 to Elmer Varian, Pt. Pleasant. She was sent to Pittsburgh, June 1917, to get new barges for delivery downriver. Reported sold to W.L. Berry, Paducah, September 1917. Sank in the head of Pogue Shoals, Ashland, Ky., and was lost. Equipment from the *VESPER* (see) was used building her.

3301 KNOXVILLE

SW p wh b. Louisville, Ky., 1848. 349 tons. 200 x 28 x 6.5. Owned at Vicksburg and New Orleans, Capt. R.H. Krump. Operated from the Tennessee River to New Orleans. Last documented master was Capt. J.G. Harris. She was departing New Orleans for Tennessee River in December 1850 when her boilers exploded demolishing the boat and causing life loss. Apparently rebuilt, and records show she burned and was lost at New Orleans, July 3, 1855 with loss of four lives.

3302 KOLEGON

Rig? p wh b. St. Louis, Mo., 1878. 44.1 x 11 x 2.1. Built by Capt. Jake Swivel, and was said to have engines 5″- 16″ stroke, and one boiler. She was still documented at Brashaer, La., 1886.

3303 KWASIND

Stw snagboat wh b. Knoxville, Tenn., 1899. 70 x 22 x 6. Operated by the U.S. Engineers on the upper Tennessee and tributaries. Still listed 1905, maybe later.

L

3304 L. C. FERRY

Stw p wh b. New Albany, Ind., 1860. 205 tons. First home port, Mobile. Went to Confederate service in 1861.

3305 L. C. MCCORMICK

Stw p wh b. Pittsburgh, Pa., 1872. Machinery from the *GREENBACK,* 10's- 3½ ft. Owned by William McCormick and J.M. Phillips, Pittsburgh. Capt. John M. Phillips later was identified as master of the *IRON QUEEN* and the *CITY OF PITTSBURG* (both see), and this was his first boat. Ran excursions around Pittsburgh and in October 1873, took pilots from Pittsburgh to Gallipolis on a low water inspection trip. Sold in June 1875 to the Muskingum River, owned there by Capt. James R. Martin and others. Ran Beverly-Zanesville trade. Exploded boilers two miles below Beverly Feb. 16, 1879. Capt. William Richardson was pilot, and some years later a farmer plowing in the vicinity turned up Capt. Richardson's shaving mug and returned it. One man killed. In August 1899, the wreck was exposed in low water on the east shore.

3306 L. H. MARRERO

Catamaran ferry sh b. Jeffersonville, Ind., by Howard, 1905. 118 x 53 x 4.5 Engines, 12's- 5 ft. One boiler. Long operated by the Bisso Ferry Co., and burned Jan. 22, 1946, at the foot of Louisiana Ave., New Orleans.

3307 L. H. SARGENT

Stw p wh b. Mason City, W. Va., 1882, and was originally named *JOHN F. HALPIN* (see). Owned by Capt. William H. Sargent who operated out of Vicksburg to Yazoo River and elsewhere. Sank at Vicksburg in February 1895, the same day the transfer *NORTHERN PACIFIC* sank.

3308 L. M. KENNETT

SW p wh b. Cincinnati, Oh., 1852. 276 x 34 x 6⅔. Engines, 30's- 10 ft. Four boilers. Primarily a freight boat in the St. Louis-New Orleans trade commanded by Capt. John Bofinger in 1864, Capt. H. Switzer in 1859, and Capt. J.R. Kerch in 1861. Dismantled and the hull was used as a wharfboat

3309 L. P. EWALD

Stw p wh b. Jeffersonville, Ind., by Howard, 1881. 149 x 30 x 4. Ran on the Cumberland River, Nashville-Burnside, Capt. A.T. Armstrong, with C.V. Williams, clerk. During low water October 1883, ran local trades out of Wheeling. Was sold and renamed *SAM P. JONES* (see).

3310 L. S. THORNE

SW transfer sh b. Dubuque, Iowa, 1898. 204 x 57 x 7.5. Long operated by the Texas-Pacific Railroad at New Orleans. She carried the last passenger train across the Mississippi when the Huey P. Long Bridge was opened in July 1942. At that date freight cars still were handled at Ste. Genevieve, Helena, Natchez, and New Orleans. Was dismantled several years later.

3311 L. T. ARMSTRONG

Stw p wh b. Jeffersonville, Ind., by Howard, 1888. 154 x 29 x 4.3. Ran on the Cumberland River owned by Major L.T. Armstrong and Thomas H. Armstrong, Nashville-Burnside. Sold to Capt. Thomas G. Ryman in 1890, and was continued in her trade until sold late that fall to Mobile, Ala. Burned at House Bluff, Alabama River, Oct. 28, 1891.

3312 L. T. MOORE

Batwing p wh b. Catlettsburg, Ky., 1874, originally named *SANDY FASHION* (see). When the *SANDY FASHION* exploded her boiler at the mouth of Big Sandy River in 1878, the wreck was rebuilt and boat renamed. She was cut down by ice at Louisa, Ky., in 1881.

3313 L. V. BOGY

SW transfer wh b. Madison, Ind., 1870. 227 tons. Engines from the Federal ram *VINDICATOR* (see). Documented at St. Louis 1876, maybe later.

3314 L. DILLARD

Stw p wh b. Shreveport, La., 1865. 107.3 x 18.9 x 3.5. Owned by John J. Hope, Martin Tally, and W.K. Stevens, all of Shreveport. Left Shreveport Dec. 13, 1865, on first trip to New Orleans, Capt. John J. Hope, master. Sank and lost at Soda Lake, La., between Shreveport and Jefferson, Jan. 31, 1867.

3315 La Belle

Stw p wh b. Wheeling, Va., 1853. 130 tons. Snagged and lost on the Ohio River, December 1854.

3316 La Belle

SW p wh b. Jeffersonville, Ind., by Howard, 1869. 510 tons. 178 x 39.6 x 6.6. Engines, 20½'s-6½ ft. Four boilers, each 26" by 26 ft. Originally owned by J. Fenimore (6/8), A. Dugas and J. Wilson, all of New Orleans. Running New Orleans-Donaldsonville fall 1869, Capt. A. Dugas, with A. Trepagnier, clerk. In 1870, New Orleans-Shreveport, Capt. W.T. Boardman, with M.N. Wood, clerk. Lengthened at Madison, Ind., in 1872, forward of the boilers. Sank at Norman's Landing on Red River, Feb. 8, 1878, with 2,699 bales of cotton aboard, Capt. M.N. Wood as master and part owner.

3317 La Belle

Rig? b. Harmar, Oh. at Knox Yard, 1881. 100.7 x 18.5 x 3.4. 47 tons. Sold to the U.S. Lighthouse Board, Oct. 7, 1881.

3318 La Crosse

Stw p wh b. California, Pa., 1856. 150 x 29 x 4/9". First owned by David Holmes (⅝), Capt. John Klinefelter, and William Frampton, all of Pittsburgh. Loaded out new for St. Paul, Capt. D.Z. Bricker. Again at St. Paul in 1857 with 200 tons of Pittsburgh coal purchased at four cents a bushel and sold there at one dollar a bushel. Again there 1861. She was at Galena when the war broke out and had aboard 224 kegs of gunpowder headed south. The mayor of Galena confiscated the cargo. Burned April 12, 1864, at Egg Bend, La., on Red River, then owned by James A. Cunningham, Madison, Ind., and John Weaver, St. Louis.

3319 La Crosse

Stw p wh b. Stillwater, Minn., 1889, originally named *RAVENNA*, a rafter. She had been renamed *LA CROSSE* at the turn of the century and ran La Crosse-Wabasha trade, Capt. H.C. Wilcox and his son. Later was renamed *ORION*, and towed rafts, logs, etc., for Samuel Peters & Son, Wabasha, Minn. The *ORION* was sold in spring 1917, to Dillman Egg Case Co., Caruthersville, Mo., and was lost in ice at Randolph, Tenn., Jan. 31, 1918. She was 122.6 x 22 x 4.

3320 La Grange

SW ferry wh b. Wellsville, Oh., 1850. 43 tons. First home port, Wheeling. Off the lists 1854.

3321 La Mascotte

Stw p wh b. Evansville, Ind., 1886. 172 x 32 x 6. Owned by O.A. Durland, Evansville, Ind., and C.G. Perkins, Henderson, Ky., equal shares. Capt. J.B. Thompson, master. Built for the St. Louis-Cape Girardeau trade. Exploded or collapsed a flue and burned Oct. 5, 1886, near Crawford's Landing, Mo., with loss of 34 lives. Among those lost was Royal Perkins, son of C.G. Perkins. The Evansville packet *ROYAL* was named in his honor.

3322 La Salle

Stw p wh b. Freedom, Pa., 1860. 196 tons. Built for the St. Louis-Peoria trade, owned by the St. Louis & Illinois River Packet Co. She was sent to Cairo in late September 1864 to bring to St. Louis a cargo. The river was low and she was snagged between Devils Island and the Illinois shore near Cape Girardeau. A gunboat was nearby and came to the scene, but she sank to the boiler deck.

3323 Laclede

SW p wh b. St. Louis, Mo., 1845. 239 tons. 197 x 25 x 5. Owned by Capt. Cameron, John S. McCune, and seven others. Ran in the Keokuk Packet Co. Burned at St. Louis, March 10, 1848, in a wharf fire which also took the *AVALANCHE*, *JOHN HARDIN* and *HIBERNIA*.

3324 Laclede

Stw p wh b. California, Pa., 1855. 197 tons. 152 x 29.5 x 4.3. Original owners were Capt. E.C. Hazlitt and Mark Sterling, both of Pittsburgh, P.A. Alford of St. Louis, and T.B. Rodes from Illinois. Ran principally on the Upper Mississippi and Illinois. Lost by stranding at Chester, Ill., Nov. 19, 1862, then owned by Albert G. Trever, St. Louis, and in command of Capt. Thomas W. Singer.

3325 Lackawanna

Stw p wh b. Donaldsonville, La., 1884. 129 x 24 x 4.4. Soon sold and renamed *ALICE LE BLANC* (see).

3326 Lacon

SW p wh b. Louisville, Ky., 1845. 118 tons. Snagged and lost in the Yazoo River, March 1846.

3327 Lacon

SW p wh b. Peoria, Ill., 1856. 95 tons. Off the lists in 1858.

3328 Lacon

Stw p wh b. Freedom, Pa., and completed at Pittsburgh, 1862. 250 tons. 159 x 28 x 4. Machinery from the *CHALLENGE*, two boilers. Built under supervision of Capt. James Woodburn. She lay around Pittsburgh several weeks with no name on her, the builders holding her for payment. On Jan. 13, 1862, she got her name and was advertised to St. Louis, Capt. Frank Maratta. Owners were Capt. John N. Bofinger and F. Blair Symmes, St. Louis. She made several trips to the mountains, up the Missouri, Capt. Jacob Sedam, and then went to the Illinois River, Capt. Stackpole. In January 1863 her master was Capt. Judson Cartwright. On May 10, 1863 she was taken over for U.S. transport service, St. Louis-Vicksburg. Dismantled at Le Claire, Iowa, 1872, and her machinery went to the rafter *STILLWATER*. The hull officially became a barge Oct. 20, 1876.

3329 LADY

Stw p wh b. Elizabeth, Pa., 1863. 122 tons. First home port, Memphis, Tenn. She appears in a photograph of the *ALICE DEAN* taken at Memphis. Off the lists in 1868.

3330 LADY BOONE

Rig? b. Lead Hill Landing, Ark., 1881. 108 x 22.6 x 3. Probably a ferry. Still listed in 1886, maybe later.

3331 LADY BYRON

Stw p wh b. Elizabeth, Pa., 1846. 145 tons. Capt. W.H. Kerr bought her about 1850 for the Pittsburgh-Portsmouth trade, the first in that run. He afterwards ran the *GRANITE STATE* and others. Off the lists in 1852.

3332 LADY FRANKLIN

SW p wh b. Wheeling, Va., 1850. 206 tons. Ran principally on the Upper Mississippi and her first arrival at St. Paul was on June 19, 1851. Took part in the opening excursion for the Rock Island Railroad, June 1854, Capt. Le Grand Morehouse. In the Minnesota Packet Co., 1855, Capt. J.W. Marlin, with clerks Ed Halliday and Orren Smith. Capt. M.E. Lucas was master in 1856. Snagged and sunk at the foot of Coon Slough, Oct. 23, 1856, at Warren Landing. Five lives lost. The *NOMINEE* (see) also was lost in Coon Slough and these two wrecks lay there some 40 years. The rafter *REINDEER* was sunk on one of them.

3333 LADY FRANKLIN

Stw p wh b. Cincinnati, Oh., 1860. 156.4 x 33.8 x 4.8. Operated by the Dean Line in the Cincinnati-Memphis trade. They sold her in February 1864 to Capt. E.B. Granger who ran her Pittsburgh-Cincinnati-Louisville. Had several other owners and in September 1866 was at St. Louis loading for Pittsburgh. Took on iron ore at Carondelet, and sank. Cargo was transferred to the *BERTHA*. Soon raised. Was at New Orleans in December 1866, then owned by James W. Gaff, Cincinnati, and William T. Pate, Patriot, Ind., equal shares. Master was Capt. W.H. Finkbine. While repairing at Algiers, La., she burned Jan. 31, 1867.

3334 LADY GAY

SW p wh b. Cincinnati, Oh., 1865. 1406 tons. 286.4 x 43.2 x 8.3. Built for Capt. John A. Williamson, Cincinnati, J.D. Isham, and Capt. M.W. Beltzhoover. Cost $120,000. She was entered in the Atlantic & Mississippi Steamship Co., and ran St. Louis-New Orleans, Capt. John A. Burk, with John Tatum, clerk. Capt. A. St. Clair Thomasson commanded several trips that year, 1866. In February 1867, downbound from St. Louis, blew a cylinder head at Carondelet. The piston rod speared through the body of an engineer, killing him. The A. & M.S.S. Co. failed and in May 1869, the *LADY GAY* was sold and was entered in the St. Louis & New Orleans Packet Co., Capt. Isaac H. Jones. On Jan. 17, 1870, downbound near Chester, Ill., she was floating along, about 1:00 P.M., Sneed Strong on watch in the pilothouse. The *W.R. ARTHUR* and *KATE ROBINSON* had been lost in the vicinity just prior and no chances were being taken. She rubbed on an obstruction, punctured the hull, and sank 30 yards from shore, straight fore and aft, but badly careened to port with water on the cabin floor. Nobody was drowned. There are various stories about who "Lady Gay" actually was—her portrait was painted on the wheelhouses. One version is that she was a Kentuckian, the wife of a U.S. Army lieutenant. This boat in 1867 was second largest in point of tonnage on the Mississippi System, surpassed only by the *RUTH* (see).

3335 LADY GRACE

Stw p wh b. Madison, Ind., 1865. 159.8 x 33 x 5.2. Engines, 15½'s- 4½ ft. Three boilers. Possibly built for Capt. Grace of Rising Sun, Ind. (see *LADY WALTON*), but sold June 1866, to W.S. Wheeler, Vicksburg, and ran New Orleans-Shreveport, Capt. S.W. Hammond. In the spring of 1867 she was taken to St. Louis and made a mountain trip up the Missouri and was sold that August to Capt. Dave Haney who loaded her out for New Orleans. In spring of 1868, was in the Cincinnati-Evansville trade, Capt. W.C. Watts, with D. Blackmore, clerk, who had bought her at a U.S. Marshal sale. That fall was running Cincinnati-Madison, and was the first boat to the scene of the *UNITED STATES-AMERICA* disaster at Warsaw, Ky., Dec. 4, 1868. In spring of 1869, loaded at Cincinnati for a mountain trip up the Missouri and when she got to St. Louis the Board of Underwriters refused her insurance. She went to Omaha and ran excursions there that fall. Burned at Omaha Jan. 2, 1870.

3336 LADY JACKSON

Stw p wh b Cincinnati, Oh., 1860. 207 tons. Ran Cincinnati-Memphis, Capt. Samuel Dean, spring 1861. In spring 1862, ran Louisville-Cumberland River, and made a trip to Pittsburgh, Pa., Capt. Kates, in May. Snagged and lost on White River, Ark., Oct. 14, 1863.

3337 LADY LEE

Stw p wh b. Pittsburgh, Pa., 1871. 176 x 35 x 5.5. Engines, 16's- 6 ft. Three boilers. 417 tons. Departed Pittsburgh on April 1, 1871, for St. Louis. Pilots to Cincinnati were John Shouse and Andy Bunting. Ran in the Carter Line, St. Louis to Red River, Capt. G.F. Shields, master. In 1874 was owned by the Illinois & St. Louis Packet Co. She was lengthened out to 227 feet in 1881. Operating in the Star Line, St. Louis-Missouri River. Capt. Bill Ball, master. Backed out of a landing two and one-half miles above Sibley, Mo., in a big wind on March 29, 1882, flanked upon a big snag and sank.

3338 LADY LEE

Stw p wh b. Jeffersonville, Ind., by Howard, 1889. 166 x 35 x 6. Three boilers. She and the *ROWENA LEE* (see) were built about the same time for the Lee Line, Memphis, to run Memphis-Ashport. She carried the whistle from the *COAHOMA* (see). Sank in fifteen feet in the chute at Island 40, July 5, 1895. Sand washed out from under her head, the hogchains parted, and she proved a total loss. Capt. William

J. Irwin relates that Lady Lee Landing was on the Arkansas shore on the Mississippi opposite Island 35 up about the middle bar. After this loss the Lee Line bought the *RUTH* (see) as a replacement.

3339 Lady Madison

SW p wh b. Cincinnati, Oh., 1844. 148 tons. Collided at Shawneetown, Ill., with the *PLYMOUTH* on Oct. 27, 1845, resulting in the loss of the latter and life-loss of 25 persons. Off the lists 1852.

3340 Lady Pike

SW p wh b. Wheeling, Va., 1851. 237 tons. Built by John McLure, Jr., Wheeling. Ran low water for the U.S. Mail Line, Cincinnati-Louisville, and also Louisville-St. Louis for the same company. Capt. Jacob Remlein was frequently her master. John McLure, Jr., was a nephew of John McLure, Sr., builder of the McLure Hotel, Wheeling (still in service, 1978), and after leaving the river he owned the hotel. He sold the *LADY PIKE* to the U.S. Mail Line in order to built the *THOS. SWANN, CITY OF WHEELING* and others.

3341 Lady Pike

Stw p wh b. Cincinnati, Oh., 1860. 207 tons. Operated in the Dean Line, Cincinnati-Memphis as a low water boat. They sold her to the Madison Packet Co., April 1864, to replace the *BRILLIANT* (see) in the Cincinnati-Madison trade. Early skippers were Capt. A.C. Montfort and a Capt. Hamilton. In 1867, she was inspected both at Galena, Ill., and at Dubuque. In the early spring of 1869, she was towing loaded ice barges south from the Upper Mississippi Documented as "lost in Oct. 1872."

3342 Lady Walton

Stw p wh b. Cincinnati, Oh., 1858. 150 tons. She went to New Orleans and was captured by the U.S. as a Confederate steamer June 6, 1863. Sold to private hands March 12, 1864, and then was run by a Capt. Grace, Rising Sun, Ind., in towing produce, etc., to Vicksburg, using four small barges. She was downbound one mile above Warsaw, Ky., on Aug. 2, 1864, when she came in collision with the upbound *NORMAN,* and she sank close to the Indiana shore. She was in the Cincinnati-Vevay trade at the time. The *LADY GRACE*, b. 1865 (see), may have been her replacement.

3343 Lady Washington

SW ferry wh b. Newport, Ky., 1853. 107 tons. She was a regular ferry between Cincinnati and Covington. Document surrendered in 1875, and the hull thereafter used as a barge.

3344 Lafayette

SW p wh b. Gretna, La., 1851. 99.9 x 10.5 x 5.4. This small fry 110 ton craft was owned by William A. High, Gretna. Off the lists in 1853.

3345 Lafayette

SW U.S. gunboat wh b. Carondelet, Mo., using machinery and parts from the *ALECK SCOTT* (see) in 1862, by James B. Eads. This gunboat and the *CHOCTAW* were the giants of 1000 tons each, with independent side-wheels. She carried 10 guns and was clad with 3-inch sheet iron carried to three feet below the water line. Sold at public sale by the U.S. at New Orleans in 1865, and was taken to St. Louis where she was dismantled for scrap. Robert Tate was her chief engineer 1862-1865.

3346 Lafitte

SW p wh b. Louisville, Ky., 1856. 95 tons. 106.5 x 19 x 4.5. Went to New Orleans owned and commanded by Capt. Henry B. Harvey of Jefferson Parish. Sold in January 1857, to James C.B. Harvey, New Orleans. Sold in March 1858, to Capt. J.J. Brown and A.H. Gardner, both of New Orleans, who ran her New Orleans-Upper Coast. In October 1858, sold to Coast & Lafourche Transportation Co., Adelard Dugas, pres., with Capt. John J. Brown, master. Had two other owners before going to Confederate registry, 1861.

3347 Lafourche

SW p wh b. Jeffersonville, Ind., by Howard, 1859. 184.6 x 34.6 x 7.4. Originally owned by New Orleans & Lafourche Transportation Co., A. Dugas, pres. First master, Capt. A. Dugas. She ran New Orleans-Coast-Lafourche until the outbreak of the war, teamed up in 1861 with the *MUSIC* (see). Marooned up Red River during the hostilities. Capt. John J. Brown owned and commanded in 1865, same trade. Her tonnage was increased from 334 tons to 563 tons in the fall of 1866, probably lengthened. Sold to the Bayou Sara Packet Co., H.C. Goddin, pres., in January 1867. Capt. John J. Brown became the Line's president in February 1868. On May 29, 1869, she left New Orleans for New Albany, Ind., to be dismantled, then owned by Charles T. Beard of New Orleans.

3348 Lafourche

Stw p wh b. Jeffersonville, Ind., by Howard, 1888. 166 x 38 x 6.5. Engines, 16's- 6 ft. Three boilers, each 42" by 26 ft. Ran in the New Orleans-Coast-Lafourche trade owned and commanded by Capt. P.A. Charlet. Her long-time clerk was Edw. Nicolle. Burned at Twelve Mile Point, La., Sept. 20, 1907.

3349 Lake City

Stw p wh b. Brownsville, Pa., 1857. 171 tons. Went to the Upper Mississippi, running in trades out of St. Paul. Made a trip to Pittsburgh with freight from St. Louis in May 1862, got aground on White's Riffle below Neville Island, and was sunk when a towboat tried to pull her free. Burned by guerrillas at Carson's Landing, Ark., on Dec. 8, 1862.

3350 Lake City

Rig? b. Yazoo City, Miss., 1885. 44 tons. Documented at Vicksburg, 1886, maybe later.

3351 LAKE CITY

Stw p wh b. Lake City, Ark., 1904. 46.5 x 16.4 x 3.1. Was operating on Black River 1905, along with *G. W. HUFF, ALMA JANE* and *TAYLOR*. Documented at Memphis 1908, maybe later.

3352 LAKE ERIE

Stw p wh b. Pittsburgh, Pa., 1845. 108 tons. 157 x 24 x 3. Ran Pittsburgh-Beaver trade connecting with canalboats on the Beaver River. Owned, 1850, by Clarke & Thaw, Hays & Black, and H. Clarke. Capt. Sharp Hemphill, master. Sold in 1851 to Hugh Smith, Dilles Bottom, Oh., who operated coal mines there. He lashed coal barges alongside and delivered them to Cincinnati and elsewhere, and so became a pioneer in using a steamboat to tow coal down the Ohio. Dismantled in 1853. Her machinery was built by Stackhouse & Nelson, Pittsburgh, 18's- 7 ft. Three boilers, each 40″ by 24 ft. Her paddlewheel was 20 ft. diameter working 19½ ft. buckets.

3353 LAKE OF THE WOODS

SW p wh b. Naples, Ill., 1847. 86 tons. Ran out of St. Louis to Galena and elsewhere, Capt. James Dozier. A steamboat wreck was exposed during extreme low water, November 1884, on Brooklyn Rocks, Ohio River. Pilot Henry Porter of the *CITY OF ST. LOUIS* identified it as that of the *LAKE OF THE WOODS,* and said she was a single engine boat owned in her latter days by Thad Jacobs, Paducah, and in charge of Capt. W. Woods. He also recalled that her engine went to the *EMMA BROWN,* an early Cairo-Paducah packet.

3354 LAKE PALMYRA

Stw p wh b. Lake Palmyra (hull) and completed at Vicksburg, Miss., 1896. 123 x 24.8 x 4.5. Machinery from the *CROWN POINT* (see). She had 16 staterooms for whites and a separate cabin for blacks. She left Vicksburg at noon Mondays for Davis Bend, and at noon Wednesdays for Sunflower River. Owned by Adam Kellogg, and her first crew composed of Capt. J.M. Wilkinson, with George W. Bookout and John Daugherty, pilots; Al Robbins, engineer. She burned July 9, 1900, at the Refuge Oil Mill below Vicksburg.

3355 LAKE SUPERIOR

SW p wh b. Wheeling, W. Va. (hull) and completed at Pittsburgh, 1870. 240 x 39 x 6. Engines, 22½'s- 7 ft., from the *HAWKEYE STATE.* Five boilers, each 38″ by 26 ft. Paddlewheels were 28 ft. dia. working 12½ ft. buckets. The machinery was built by Robert Lea, Pittsburgh. Dunlevy & Co., built the hull. Emil Bott did the landscape painting in the cabin. Richard C. Gray superintended construction, and she was the 14th boat built in the area for the Northern Line Packet Co. Capt. Jones Worden was master 1870–1874. Ran St. Louis-Keokuk-St. Paul. In June 1876, brought 800 tons of silver ore from St. Paul to St. Louis consigned to the St. Louis Smelting Co. The shipment originated in Montana. The *LAKE SUPERIOR* and *DUBUQUE* (see) both burned in Alton Slough on the afternoon of Mar. 4, 1879. They were being readied for the season and the blaze was thought to have started in the barbershop of the *LAKE SUPERIOR.*

3356 LAMARTINE

SW p wh b. Elizabeth, Pa., 1848. 174 tons. Capt. James Patterson, Wheeling, was one of the builders, grandfather of Capt. Ernie Anshutz. Went to the Upper Mississippi in 1850, and was within a mile of the Falls of St. Anthony, Capt. J.W. Marsh, that May. Took up surveyors to establish the northern boundary of Iowa in 1852. Ran Davenport-Muscatine, Capt. Phelps, 1855–1856. Capt. Sam R. Van Sant was "slush cook" on her, his first river job. She was lost in ice at St. Louis, Feb. 26, 1856.

3357 LANCASTER

SW p wh b. Pittsburgh, Pa., 1842. 123 tons. Ran Pittsburgh-Cincinnati during low water, summer 1842. Occasional trips Pittsburgh-Zanesville in 1843, Capt. Klinefelter. Our surmise would be that she wound up in the Cincinnati-New Richmond trade (see *LANCASTER NO. 2*).

3358 LANCASTER

SW p wh b. Liverpool, Ill., 1866. 75 tons. Engines, 12's- 4 ft. Two boilers. Snagged and lost at Smith's Island, above New Haven, Mo., on the Missouri River (date?) and the wreck was still visible during low water in 1927.

3359 LANCASTER

Stw p wh b. Harmar, Oh., at Knox Yard, 1886. 135.6 x 23.5 x 3.8. David Gibson contracted for this boat to be delivered in 60 days and the Knox Yard met the deadline. The *T. D. DALE* had entered the Cincinnati-New Richmond trade and this *LANCASTER* was built to whip her out, which she promptly did. Capt. Mace Agnew was master, and Jim Rowley, Jr., pilot. In 1888, was running Cincinnati-Chilo in the Ohio River Packet Co., along with the *TACOMA* (see). Ran in Kentucky River, c. 1890, operated by a coal dealer, Mr. Gaines. Burned at Golconda, Ill., in late June 1896.

3360 LANCASTER NO. 2

SW p wh b. Cincinnati, Oh., 1848. 168 tons. She was nearing completion at the foot of Ludlow Street, Cincinnati, in September 1848, intended for the Cincinnati-New Richmond trade. She was replaced, 1855, by the *LANCASTER NO. 3* (see).

3361 LANCASTER NO. 3

SW p wh b. Cincinnati, Oh., 1855. 257 tons. 176 x 30 x 5.5. Owned by David Gibson and others. Replaced the *LANCASTER NO. 2* (see). Ran Cincinnati-New Richmond. She had only made a few trips when in latter July 1855, she landed at Stepstone, Ky., to load wheat. A steam line parted killing three deckhands. The *OHIO NO. 2,* Capt. Blagg, took the wounded to Cincinnati. She made a trip to St. Louis in

March 1860, Capt. W.H. Keyt. Ran Louisville-Madison, spring 1861. She was acquired by USQMD and converted into an Ellet ram in April 1862. Sunk by gunfire running the batteries at Vicksburg, night of Mar. 23, 1863.

3362 LANCASTER NO. 4

SW p wh b. Cincinnati, Oh., 1861. 218 tons. Built at Dan Morton's yard and came out in January 1861, Capt. Lew Morris. Built for the Cincinnati-New Richmond trade. David Gibson had interest in all of this tribe. She saw considerable service in handling U.S. troops and supplies during the war. Was handling troops on the Tennessee River, spring 1862. Capt. Lewis Morris lived at New Richmond and served on all of the *LANCASTER* fleet. John Connor was clerk on most, and lived about a mile above New Richmond. Ran New Orleans-Vicksburg starting in June 1864, Capt. M.J. McCullough, with John G. Harrington, clerk. That fall she loaded out for Missouri River. Struck a log below Portland, Mo., on Nov. 18, 1864, and went down in 10 feet, under charter to the U.S. David Gibson & Co., owned her at this time. She proved a complete loss.

3363 LANSING

Stw p wh b. Prairie du Chien, Wis., 1864. 83 tons. She is said to have been the first boat owned by Diamond Jo Reynolds. He soon sold her, and in 1867 she was owned by Rambo & Son, Le Claire, Iowa ("Wes" and his father). They first ran her Davenport-Le Claire, and on May 13, 1867, she was handling railroad passengers between Port Byron, Rock Island, and Davenport, over the upper rapids. That day at Hampton, Ill., her two boilers exploded, wrecking the upper works of the boat, and causing considerable life loss. The clerk's body was blown clear across the Mississippi and was found in Iowa. Bob Smith, the pilot, who went across town in the other direction, was also killed.

3364 LARK

Rig? ferry wh b. Cadgett Hollow, Mo., 1872. 22 tons. The Pittsburgh *Commercial* issue of June 17, 1873, reports that the Osage River steamer *LARK* went up an affluent of the main stream called the Pommedeterre as far as Fairfield a few days since and the natives were astonished at the advent of a steamer, none ever having seen one on these waters. Still listed in 1876, maybe later.

3365 LARKIN EDWARDS

Rig? b. New Albany, Ind., 1857. 57 tons. Went to Red River and arrived at Shreveport on Aug. 18, 1858. She was named for the friend and interpreter of the Caddo Indians, 1835. On April 26, 1861, took the Caddo Sportsmen's Military Co., from Shreveport to New Orleans.

3366 LAST CHANCE

Stw p wh b. St. Louis, Mo., 1865. 142.2 x 30.6 x 3.5. Designed for St. Louis-Missouri River. Owned 1867, by W.G. and M.S. Mepham, St. Louis, and master was Capt. O.B. Hunter. Ran that year St. Louis-Fort Buford. In early January 1870, was bought by Capt. C.S. Peck and others for the upper Tennessee, and ran Chattanooga-Knoxville. John L. Doss was her pilot until he died of pneumonia at Washington where his sister lived. His remains were taken aboard the *LAST CHANCE* to Kingston for burial, a river parade composed of the *RESACA, R.C. JACKSON, CHEROKEE, EMORY CITY* and *EMMA*. Collided with the *R.P. CONVERSE* near Dayton, Tenn., on Mar. 6, 1872, resulting in the loss of the latter (see). She was sold to Hugh Martin, Kingston, Tenn., who used much of her building the *R.M. BISHOP* (see), this in 1873.

3367 LAST CHANCE

Stw p wh b. Burlington, Iowa, 1870. 98.2 x 17.8 x 3. Engines, 11's- 3½ ft. One boiler. Came out with a scow bow and was changed to model bow, c. 1878, by McCaffrey & Rambo. Over her career she had three sets of engines, and above described being the last set. Towed a floating circus to New Orleans one winter. The Le Claire Navigation Co., organized in 1872, and used this boat to help rafts over the rapids above Keokuk. They sold her in August 1886, to Capt. H.J. King, Chamberlain, Dak., where she operated Sioux City-Chamberlain. On one occasion she delivered 8,000 barrels of Ohio River salt to Warsaw, Mo., on the Osage River. Snagged and lost near Omaha in 1899.

3368 LATONA

SW p wh b. New Albany, Ind., 1846. 197 tons. 155 x 25.5 x 5.3. Went to New Orleans replacing the *BOIS D'ARC*, owned by Ralph L. Gillet, Capt. John Smoker, master. She had many owners at New Orleans. The first three seasons she ran New Orleans-Port Caddo, Tex., then head of navigation on the Red. Later ran to Shreveport. Her long-time pilot, Capt. W.H. Daniel said later: "She made barrels of money and was very popular—she was my home and I loved her, and when she was dismantled in 1857 I thought I had lost my best friend." The *NEW LATONA* (see) replaced her in the Red River trade.

3369 LATROBE

Stw p wh b. Brownsville, Pa., 1853. 159 tons. 142 x 26.7 x 4.5. Originally owned by Capt. M.W. Beltzhoover, master, and David Holmes (3/4). This boat and the *ALTOONA* (see) were built same place, same time, to connect the Pennsylvania Railroad with Cincinnati during low water. Beltzhoover was master of the P&C side-wheeler *BUCKEYE STATE* at the time. Made trips Pittsburgh-Nashville, spring 1854. Went to St. Paul in 1855. Sank at Phillis Island, Ohio River, in ice, Feb. 16, 1855. She was sold early 1857 and was en route up the Ohio near Wellsville, Oh., with a cargo of pig iron when she sank in early April, 1857, total loss.

3370 LAURA

Stw p wh b. Elizabeth, Pa., 1855. 83 tons. Went to Apalachicola, Fla., where she was lost in 1862.

3371 LAURA

Stw p wh b. New Albany, Ind., 1864. She was originally

named *MATTIE CABLER* but was sold to the USQMC before documentation, March 21, 1864. Sold to private hands Sept. 28, 1865, and named *LAURA*. C.J. Caffery was running the packet line St. Louis-Johnsonville, on the Tennessee River, bought *LAURA* but his line went broke and to sheriff's sale in July 1866. Lost in ice at Memphis, Dec. 26, 1872.

3372 LAURA

Rig? p wh b. Cincinnati, Oh., 1871. 99 x 24 x 4. Went to Texas, and was inspected at Beaumont, 1881. Still in the area 1886.

3373 LAURA

Steam yacht wh b. Pittsburgh, Pa., 1892. 54 x 8 x 2.5. Still listed 1896, maybe later, at Pittsburgh. A small craft of this name was on the upper Kanawha, June 1900, running Charleston-Paint Creek, said to have been built at the Axton yard, Brownsville, Pa.

3374 LAURA BELL

Stw p wh b. Franklin, Pa., on the Allegheny River, 1862. 27 tons. Off the records in 1869.

3375 LAURA FENTON

Stw p wh b. Cincinnati, Oh., 1863, originally named *JENNIE HOPKINS*. When the USQMD sold her she was renamed *LAURA FENTON*, Oct. 10, 1865. Owned and operated by Archer, Hart & Co., Cincinnati which dissolved partnership July 1866. Capt. Archer took the boat as part of his share of the assets. She burned at the wharfboat, Evansville, Ind., upbound from Memphis, Feb. 27, 1867.

3376 LAURA FILSON

SW ferry wh b. Wellsville, Oh., 1866. 39.97 tons. She operated at East Liverpool, Oh., for some time. Dismantled 1881.

3377 LAURA L. DAVIS

Stw p wh b. Madison, Ind., 1873. 137 x 34 x 4.7. Built for Capt. Owen W. Davis of the steamer *JOHN LUMDSEN* (see) and named for his daughter. New hull, new boilers, and she got cabin and engines from the *LUMSDEN*. Designed for the Nashville-Cape Girardeau trade and ran there with Capt. O.W. Davis, master, with F.R. Davis, clerk. She was chartered by Davis to tow Costello's circus summer of 1876, and in October wound up at Evansville with the outfit broke. Running Pittsburgh-Cincinnati, spring 1877, Davis, master. She was lengthened to become 179 feet long, and in spring of 1878 ran Cincinnati-Tennessee River, Capt. John C. Reno, with Charles Regnier, clerk. Same trade that fall with Capt. Hiram J. Vinton, and M.M. Deem, clerk. In December 1883 was renamed *QUEEN CITY* (see).

3378 LAURA LEE

Stw p wh b. Jeffersonville, Ind., by Howard, 1878. 210 x 38 x 6.5. Engines, 17½'s- 5½ ft. Two boilers. Machinery from the *SEMINOLE* (see). Built for Capt. H.L. Lee who proposed to run her New Orleans-Yazoo River. In 1880 he was master, running New Orleans-Vicksburg-Greenville. In 1885 running New Orleans-Shreveport, Capt. Richard (Dick) Sinnott, with H.C. Boazman and T.J. Dowty, clerks. In 1890, New Orleans-Vicksburg, Capt. Blanche Leathers, with W. Montgomery, clerk. She once was in collision with the *CITY OF GREENVILLE* at Bayou Goula, and was sunk at Conrad's Bar, seven miles below Baton Rouge in 1888. Ultimately was laid up at Algiers, La., for old age, c. 1892.

3379 LAURA MAY

Rig? yacht wh b. Freedom, Pa., 1885. 60 x 15 x 3.5. 11.82 tons. Documented at Rochester, N.Y., 1886, and at Milwaukee, Wis., 1896.

3380 LAURA NO. 2

Stw p wh b. Warren, Pa. (hull) and completed at Elizabeth, Pa., 1864. 60 tons. Built for Capt. R.B. Bell, Venango County, Pa. She ran on the Allegheny River to Franklin, Pa., and in 1869, was in the Wheeling-Clarington trade, and made trips up the Big Sandy from Catlettsburg, Ky. In 1871 was running Wheeling-New Martinsville during August low water, and at this same time the *SCIENCE* and *NEW STATE* were running Wheeling-Parkersburg, and the *W.F. CURTIS* between Wheeling and Sunfish (Clarington). "An old looking craft," the *DARLING*, was running Wheeling-Steubenville. In spring of 1873, was in the Parkersburg-St. Marys trade and was dismantled in 1876.

3381 LAURANCE

Recess wheel ferry wh b. Madison, Ind., 1891. 88 x 26 x 3.8. Engines, 10's- 3½ ft. One boiler, 42" by 17 ft. Built and operated by C.M. Phister between Maysville, Ky., and Aberdeen, Oh., on the Ohio River. Phister had married Miss Florinel Hannan from Swan Creek, Oh., and a baby was expected, hopefully a girl, and the new ferry was to be named *LAURA* in her honor. Phister wired the shipyard: "ADD THREE MORE LETTERS TO THAT NAME, N C E." Shortly before Phister died he sold the ferry to Capt. Gordon C. Greene and Charles Stalder. Capt. William Clephane was on the ferry about 26 years. Burned at Maysville, fall 1930, and was rebuilt and continued running until the bridge was built. Then was sold to the Manchester (Ohio) Ferry Co. and was renamed *COL. W.S. TAYLOR* (see).

3382 LAUREL

SW p wh b. Cincinnati, O., 1844. 113 tons. Built by Capt. James A. Payne, Red House, West Va., for Kanawha River and Cincinnati trade. After running about a year there she was sold to Vicksburg for the Yazoo River trade. Was loaded with U.S. Army supplies and was taken to the Rio Grande. Sank there in 1848.

3383 LAUREL

SW p wh b. St. Louis, Mo., 1846. 78 tons. Sank in collision with the *ANTHONY WAYNE* on the Illinois River at

Chillicothe in the fall of 1848. Sank and lost at Alton, Ill., January 1851.

3384 LAUREL

SW p wh b. Vicksburg, Miss., 1847. 148 tons. Off the lists in 1849.

3385 LAUREL HILL

SW p wh b. New Albany, Ind., 1853. 497 tons. 213 x 32.5 x 7.5. Engines, 30's- 8 ft. Four boilers. Original owners: Joseph Gustave Landry and John M. Hall, New Orleans. First master, Capt. John A. Cotton. She ran New Orleans-Bayou Sara, teamed up with *EMPEROR* (see).

3386 LAUREL HILL

SW p wh b. Jeffersonville, Ind., by Howard, 1859. 199 x 38.7 x 6.8. Engines, 30's- 8 ft. Four boilers. She was originally owned by Capt. John A. Cotton entire. First master, Capt. E.F. Snow. Ran New Orleans-Bayou Sara. During the Civil War she passed to U.S. ownership and was with Porter on Red River in 1864. One of her war exploits was being sent to Port Arthur, Tex., to the mouth of the Sabine, to silence some Confederate batteries. She got in heavy seas off the Jetties, threw her stacks overboard, and had to jettison 200 mules before returning safely to the Jetties, this in September 1863. There is record that she was taken to Mobile in April 1865, Capt. Carter. Off the lists in 1869.

3387 LAURENT MILLAUDON

SW p wh b. Cincinnati, Oh., 1856. 483 tons. 182 x 30 x 9.2. This probably was a towboat used at New Orleans by the Good Intent Towboat Co., Capt. W.S. Whann. She went to Confederate registry, and was converted into a tinclad by the Confederates renamed *GENERAL STERLING PRICE.* Was captured by the U.S., June 6, 1862, and thereafter served as the U.S. gunboat *GENERAL PRICE.*

3388 LAVINA MARIE

Stw ferry wh b. Paducah, Ky., 1861. 225 tons. Operated by the Madison County (Ill.) Ferry Co. Off the lists in 1877.

3389 LAVINIA LOGAN

Stw p wh b. Parkersburg, Va., 1861. 145 tons. Arrived in Pittsburgh from Cincinnati with a good freight trip, Jan. 26, 1862. She became the property of Capt. Pink Varble and others. Ran briefly Louisville-Madison in early 1864, and was sold to the USQMD in April 1864. Went to the U.S. Navy Aug. 31, 1864, and was sunk and lost in the Mississippi River on Sept. 23, 1864.

3390 LAWRENCE

Stw p wh b. Cincinnati, Oh., 1863. 199 tons. Machinery from the *BLANCHE LEWIS* (see). She came to Pittsburgh, Pa., Nov. 17, 1865, with 40 tons of fixed ammunition consigned to the Allegheny Arsenal. A great quantity of ordnance and military stores were on the wharf at that time. Ran Cincinnati-Big Sandy trade in place of the *TELEGRAPH,* fall 1869, Capt. Wash Honshell, with George A. Knight, clerk. In 1871 was in the Nashville & Cincinnati Packet Co., Capt. John H. Farrell, with John L. McMeens, clerk. Off the lists 1875.

3391 LE CLAIRE

Stw p wh b. California, Pa., 1859. 93 tons. 127 x 25 x 3.1. Original owners: Capt. James M. Ross and Hamilton Kelly, Kittanning, Pa. Ran on the Allegheny River to Franklin and Oil City and once knocked a hole in her hull negotiating Catfish Riffle. During summer low water often ran Pittsburgh-Parkersburg. Sold to the Kanawha River April 23, 1864, bought by Capt. Samuel Christy, William T. Thayer, and T.J. Bottsford. Off the lists 1866.

3392 LE CLAIRE NO. 2

Stw p wh b. Pittsburgh, Pa., 1864. 155 tons. Capt. Hamilton Kelly was the sole owner and master. Ran on the Allegheny River, Pittsburgh-Oil City, with William Stewart, clerk. On Sept. 22, 1865, at 9:00 A.M. she and the *ALLEGHENY BELLE* were racing, both upbound, at Indian God Rock below Franklin, Pa. They met the *ALBION* downbound, and *LE CLAIRE NO. 2* and *ALBION* collided, splinters flew, and each continued on its way. Captain Kelly ran her on the Allegheny through the spring season of 1866. Sold her February 1867, to Capt. J.G. Saint who outfitted her for the Missouri River gold regions and departed April 2, 1867. She made several Missouri River trips and returned to the Ohio River to sink at Brandenburg, Ky., on Dec. 15, 1867. Owned by others she was in the Louisville-Tennessee River trade when she sank on the Louisville Falls latter January 1869. Made a trip to the Upper Mississippi and sank below Davenport. Sold in July 1870 to Capt. A. Ballard who ran her Louisville-Evansville with P.B. Branham and L.H. Branham, clerks. They sold her to the Evansville, Henderson & Nashville RR and she was moored at the wharf at Evansville, Ind., on Dec. 29, 1872, when she was cut down by ice. Capt. Robert Hornbrook wrecked her inasmuch as she blocked traffic at his wharfboat.

3393 LE FLORE

Stw p wh b. Jeffersonville, Ind., 1878. A small cotton packet with texas built for the Parisot Line at Vicksburg for Yazoo River. She departed Cincinnati with freight latter October 1878, Capt. S.H. Parisot. Still there in 1882, maybe longer.

3394 LE GRAND

SW p wh b. New Albany, Ind., 1856. 235 tons. 198 x 35.5 x 5.5. Engines, 22's- 7½ ft. Three boilers. Went to the Alabama River, arriving at Mobile Nov. 5, 1856, Capt. George Cloudes. She was back at New Orleans and making trips up Red River in 1858. Went to Confederate registry 1861.

3395 LE GRAND

Prop p wh b. Portsmouth, Oh., 1863. 201 tons. 127 x 27.6 x 4.4. Went to Memphis, and in January 1866, to New Orleans, Capt. Henry Willett. Lost on the Mississippi near New Orleans Oct. 7, 1867, Capt. Milton B. Muncy.

3396 LEAVENWORTH CITY

SW p wh b. Wheeling, Va., 1857. 90 tons. First home port, Kansas City, Mo. Off the lists in 1859.

3397 LEBANON

Stw p wh b. Brownsville, Pa., 1855. 225 tons. Advertised at Cincinnati for New Orleans, Oct. 31, 1859, Capt. Frank Davidson. Running Cincinnati-Arkansas River, January 1861, Capt. Frank Davidson, with H.C. Bruce and Henry Aydelotte, clerks. Handling U.S. Army supplies from Louisville to Nashville in March 1861. Impressed into U.S. service at Cincinnati in early March 1862. She went down the Mississippi and was attacked by guerrillas about 10 miles below Greenville. A shell cut the steam line. Rebels boarded and plundered her, then set her afire and she was a total loss, this on May 27, 1864.

3398 LEBANON NO. 2

Stw p wh b. Cincinnati, Oh., 1862. 254 tons. Milnor Roberts' Report dated Oct. 31, 1866, notes that she burned at the head of Hurricane Island, lower Ohio River, and her wreck, and also the wreck of the burned *THISTLE* nearby, are dangerous to traffic. The loss happened on June 24, 1863.

3399 LECOMPTE

SW p wh b. Louisville, Ky., 1855. 238 tons. 176 x 33 x 5.5. Engines, 22's- 7 ft. Three boilers. Ran briefly New Orleans-Red River, Capt. Cheney Johnson. Was sold to Mobile and spent the balance of her career running to the Alabama River ports. Named for a famous race horse. In 1859 Mobile-Montgomery, Capt. Charles Walker. Burned at Mobile, Mar. 27, 1861.

3400 LECOMPTE

SW p wh b. Cincinnati, Oh., 1856. 250 tons. 155 x 32 x 6.5. Engines, 20's- 7 ft. Three boilers, each 42" by 18 ft. Built for Capt. Cheney Johnson for the New Orleans-Attakapas trade. In 1858 and 1859 ran Red River to Caroline Bluffs above Shreveport. Snagged and lost ten miles above Campti, La., upbound, April 16, 1861. Capt. W.W. Withenbury, Cincinnati, was in command.

3401 LEE H. BROOKS

Stw p wh b. Evansville, Ind., 1890. 140.5 x 23 x 3.4. Engines, 12's- 4½ ft. Two boilers (later three). Built for short trades around Cincinnati by Capt. Ott Hissom, didn't do so well, so he sold her and bought the *T.D. DALE* (see). In May 1896 at Cincinnati the mate on the *BROOKS* was Mrs. Helen M. Young of Ironton, Oh., who had received her license from the U.S. Steamboat Inspectors at Cincinnati just prior. Bought by William Weigel in November 1897 who took her to the Monongahela River and ran her between Pittsburgh and Elizabeth, Pa. Capt. H.L. Johnson was master. Weigel sold her February 1900, to J.K. and Edward Davison who were digging and selling Allegheny River sand and gravel. Capt. Edward J. Hulings went master, and thenceforth she was a towboat. Capt. Tom Hudson was on her later. When Davisons built the *ELIZABETH SMITH* they sold the *BROOKS* to W.L. Berry, Paducah, and she then towed ties and lumber, Capt. Grace Davis, with Henry Carroll, pilot; Elwood Wingfield and Walter Hatcher, engineers. Ran through 1922, maybe longer.

3402 LEE HOWELL

Stw p wh b. Evansville, Ind., 1882. 89.3 x 16 x 2. Sank and lost on the Mississippi three miles above Friars Point, Feb. 2, 1888. Had a full cargo and sank clear out of sight. Was owned at the time by James Bros.

3403 LEE WHITE

Catamaran ferry wh b. Dardanelle, Ark., 1902. 65 x 28 x 2.5. Still listed 1908, maybe longer.

3404 LEGAL TENDER

SW p wh b. New Albany, Ind., 1867. 539 tons. Built for Capt. E.W.B. Nowland who ran her from Memphis to Arkansas and White Rivers. In April 1871, she went up the White on a high stage of water, proceeded into Mittox Bay on the south side and got 95 bales of cotton and 180 sacks of seed some 10 miles in, the first time in 10 years a boat had been there. Sank below Memphis on the night of Nov. 8, 1871. Was finally lost by snagging on the Arkansas about 40 miles below Pine Bluff, at Rowsey's Point, Apr. 16, 1876. Capt. Nowland got the *ELLA* to take her place, and on the first trip the *ELLA* sank several hundred feet from the wreck of the *LEGAL TENDER*, with the same crew aboard.

3405 LEHIGH

Stw p wh b. California, Pa., 1857. 210 tons. 151 x 34 x 4.5. Built by Capt. John N. Shunk and others of Pittsburgh. Was running Cincinnati-St. Louis in fall of 1859. She was laid up in the Fulton district of Cincinnati when she burned at 3:00 A.M., June 23, 1861. The *J. W. CHEESEMAN* nearby was badly scorched but was saved.

3406 LELIA

Stw p wh b. Brownsville, Pa., 1861. 121 tons. First home port, St. Louis. Off the lists in 1863.

3407 LELIA

Prop p wh b. Portsmouth, Oh., 1863. 34 tons. Snagged and lost in White River, 1868.

3408 LELIA NO. 2

Stw p wh b. Cincinnati, Oh., 1851. 134 tons. Burned at Algiers, La., May 4, 1853.

3409 LELA

Stw p wh b. Fords Ferry, Ky., 1888. 70 x 18 x 3. She had been running Evansville-Spottsville until the *FAWN* took her place in 1896, Capt. Gillingham. Sank above Henderson, Ky., mid-December, 1896.

3410 LENA

Rig? b. Nashville, Tenn., 1862. 121 tons. Built by the U.S. and sold to private owner in June 1866. Off the lists 1869.

3411 LENA ARCHER

Steam yacht wh b. Hawesville, Ky., 1892. 45 x 9 x 4. Still listed 1896, maybe longer.

3412 LENA MAY

Stw p wh b. Evansville, Ind., 1908. 113 x 28.5 x 4. Built using engines, etc., from the former ferry *CONVEYOR* (see) by Capt. Robert Hornbrook and his son Sam. In 1914 an insurance inspector looked her over at Evansville and noted that she was laid up, had no trade, and was $9,000 in debt. In 1916 was in the Louisville-Stephensport trade and remained in that run until about the time the Williams brothers, Evansville, bought the *NASHVILLE* in 1919 for the trade. In August 1920 she was sold to St. Louis for the Calhoun County apple trade.

3413 LENI LEOTI

Stw p wh b. Freedom, Pa. (hull) and completed at Pittsburgh, 1863. 174 tons. She was bought by Capts. A.S. Shepard and W.A. Moore in latter January 1864, and they loaded her out at Pittsburgh for Louisville. Made trips to Nashville. In 1865 Capt. William Reno, master, with C.H. Bentel, clerk. Ran Wheeling-Parkersburg 1866, and Pittsburgh-Parkersburg in 1867. Departed St. Louis for the upper Missouri in mid-May 1868. In mid-August a letter filtered back to Pittsburgh which read: "Landing at a wood yard 45 miles above Fort Peck, I discovered the dead bodies of the proprietors, seven in number, supposed to have been killed by the Assonaboine Indians in retaliation for the murder of two of their tribe two months ago by woodchoppers in that same vicinity. The bodies of the whites killed were horribly mutilated and in a state of decomposition. I buried them as well as possible under the circumstances. Three of the bodies were outside the cabin, four within. The entire party came up with me this spring on the *PENINAH* from St. Louis and stopped at that point where they met their sad fate. Nothing was found but a few letters scattered around in the cabin, which I have delivered to W.I. Cullen, Supt. of Indian Affairs." (signed) Capt. Haney. Capt. John D. Adams bought the boat at Little Rock, Ark., on Jan. 18, 1869. She had been making trips to New Orleans from there. She was lost by snagging on the Arkansas at McNeal's Landing, downbound for New Orleans with 200 tons of government freight, May 10, 1869, owned by the Memphis & Arkansas River Packet Co.

3414 LENI LEOTI

Stw p wh b. Brownsville, Pa., at Axton yard, 1891. 90 x 18.4 x 3. Engines, 20's- 3 ft. One boiler, 42" by 20 ft. Owned by Capt. Isaac L. Reno and ran several short trades, for a time between Pittsburgh and McKees Rocks along with *VENICE* and *VENUS*. In 1894 ran Charleroi-Rice's Landing on the Monongahela. In 1906 was owned by the Cando Packet Co., at Catlettsburg, Ky. Dismantled there, 1907, and her engines went in the towboat *ENQUIRER*.

3415 LENORA

SW p wh b. St. Louis, Mo., 1848. 128 tons. 126 x 23 x 4.8. Went to New Orleans April 1849, owned by J.I. Warren & Co., and Catres & Dunnica, Covington, La. Sold in December 1855 to Thomas A. Snow (½) and others, New Orleans, Capt. James P. Whiteny. Had other owners in 1856, and then was sold foreign.

3416 LENORA

Rig? ferry wh b. Henderson, Ky., 1876. 19 tons. Inspected locally through 1882, maybe longer.

3417 LEO

SW p wh b. New Albany, Ind., 1868. 349 tons. 165 x 40 x 6.5. Engines, 20½'s- 7½ ft. Two boilers. Built for the Mobile & Montgomery Railway Co. (later L&N), for transferring passengers from Rachod and Blakely, Ala., to Mobile. She had the machinery from the *VIGO* which had been owned by the same company. She was taken to New Orleans and ran on Red River, 1869, Capt. James M. Tucker. Sold to Texas in September 1871, and was delivered at Galveston on Sept. 20, 1871.

3418 LEO

Stw p-tb wh b. Stillwater, Minn., 1886. She originally was *FRANKIE FOLSOM* which capsized at Peoria, July 12, 1892 (see). Rebuilt and renamed *LEO*. In 1905 owned by Capt. O. Swayzie, operating on the Ouachita River.

3419 LEO B. BISSO

Catamaran ferry sh b. Nashville, Tenn., by Nashville Bridge Co., 1929. 136 x 62 x 8. Engines, 16½'s- 6 ft. Handled 232 passengers and 80 cars. Owned by Bisso Ferry Co., New Orleans until sold 1965 to Mississippi River Bridge Authority. They dieselized her in 1968 and changed name to *GOV. JACQUES P. VILLERE*. She since has been transferred to the Louisiana Dept. of Transportation and still operates in 1979.

3420 LEODORA

SW p wh b. Alton, Ill., 1864. 158 tons. 164 x 25 x 5. Loaded at St. Louis with 164 tons of freight and departed for the upper Missouri, April 1866. Went aground at Elk Point, 20 miles below Yankton, S.D., and burned, May 21, 1866. The boilers were recovered 1870–1871 by digging through sand accumulated over the wreck. Among the cargo were 70 casks of liquor and in 1895 a Mr. Wenner located the wreck with a dip needle, brought a sand sucker to the spot and after considerable probing came up with very little if anything.

3421 LEON

Stw p wh b. Brownsville, Pa., 1859. 87 tons. 126 x 25 x 3. Went to Van Buren, Ark., on the Arkansas River, owned there by a stock company. Capt. William M. Reasner, Dardanelle, Ark., master and part owner. Made trips to New Orleans. Snagged and lost at Barnum, Ark., in March 1864.

3422 LEONA

SW p wh b. Cincinnati, Oh., 1856. 232 tons. 150 x 20 x 5.6. There is evidence that the hull was built on the riverbank where Huntington, W. Va. now is situated. Owned by A. Laidley, Henry Taylor and P.S. Drown, and ran briefly Louisville-Madison, Capt. Henry Taylor in charge, and P.S. Drown, clerk. They took her to Mobile and arrived there Nov. 11, 1856. In December 1858 was back in New Orleans, then owned by Capt. R.B. Roberts of that city who commanded. Snagged and lost at Coushatta, La., Dec. 16, 1859.

3423 LEONIDAS

Stw p wh b. Brownsville, Pa., 1863. 364 tons. Engines, 20's-5½ ft. Four boilers. Ran Pittsburgh-St. Louis, Capt. John W. Anawalt. In 1865, Capt. M.A. Cox, master, came trade. Some newspapers referred to her as the "mammoth" *LEONIDAS.* Captain Cox left her in May 1866 to command the *FAYETTE* on the Monongahela River (see) and Capt. Frank Maratta took his place. Made Pittsburgh-New Orleans trips, Capt. R.H. Greenless, 1867; also in 1868, Capt. James Shedden. Capt. J.H. Maratta took charge spring 1870, after losing his *EMMA NO. 3* (see). Snagged and lost at New Albany, Ind., June 26, 1871. This same snag, a sycamore 30 ft. long and 3 ft. dia. at the butt, had previously been hit by the famed *ECLIPSE.* She was owned by Capts. John L. Rhoads and James H. Maratta at the time of loss.

3424 LEONORA

Stw p wh b. Woodland, Va., 1861. 258 tons. Engines, 15½'s-4½ ft. Three boilers. Built for Capt. Michael Davis, and named for his youngest daughter Leonora. The Davis family owned property thereabouts, and Captain Davis was father of Capt. Mike Davis who was the pilot on watch when the *TELL CITY* (see) was lost at Little Hocking, Oh. Made trips to St. Louis from Wheeling. Sold, November 1862, to Capt. Richard Calhoon, with Thomas S. Calhoon in the office. They sold her at St. Louis for the Missouri River trade. Burned at Ponce Landing, Neb., near Junction City, Iowa, May 29, 1866, Capt. Timothy Packard, master.

3425 LEONORA

Ferry wh b. Henderson, Ky., 1876. 19 tons.

3426 LEONORA NO. 2

Stw p wh b. Fish Creek, W. Va., 1864. 310 tons. The hull for this boat, as well as that of her predecessor (last listing) was built on the bank at Fish Creek. Built for Capt. Michael Davis. She went to U.S. marshal sale at Cincinnati, Apr. 13, 1868, and went to Capt. James Wise of the Nashville Packet Co., for $5,400. Lost in collision with the *MARY HOUSTON* near Louisville, Ky., Dec. 28, 1869.

3427 LEROY

Stw p wh b. Levanna, Oh., 1896. 120.5 x 22.4 x 4. Engines, 12's-4 ft. Two boilers, 38" by 18 ft. Built for Capt. Oscar J. Webster and named for his son Leroy, Beverly, Oh. Ran Wheeling-Parkersburg and occasionally on the Muskingum to Beverly. Capt. Thad Thomas of Clarington, Oh., bought her for the Wheeling-Clarington trade, swapping the *JEWEL* to Capt. Webster in the deal. Ran there a year or so, then was bought by Capt. Henry Roe and others and ran Morgantown-Fairmont on the Monongahela River connecting with the *I.C. WOODWARD* and *COLUMBIA* to Pittsburgh. Fall of 1907 was in Pittsburgh-Fairmont trade, Capt. Jack Ward, with Thomas Jackson and Virgil E. Bennett as clerks. In 1908 ran excursions Pittsburgh to Neville Island until bought that August by the Greene Line, Cincinnati, to replace the *NEVA* in the Winfield-Gallipolis trade. Later they ran her Gallipolis-Charleston teamed up with *EVERGREEN* (see). Docked at Pt. Pleasant in 1910, and hull changed to 126 x 26.6. Capt. Jesse P. Hughes bought her 1919, ran her Gallipolis-Charleston, sold her, fall 1920, to Wm. F. Hammell and George F. Bauersmith, Pittsburgh, who ran her Pittsburgh-Morgantown with Capt. Wm. F. Syphers, master. This didn't work so she went to the Wheeling-New Matamoras trade, Capt. Eb Cline, master. Brady C. Litman, New Martinsville, W. Va., bought her January 1921, and ran her Wheeling-New Martinsville, Capt. Frank Justice. That November he sold her equal shares to Harry C. Donnally and Grover Gill. She was taken to Pt. Pleasant for hull work which—as matters turned out—required an entire new hull. Gill maintained he did not order a new hull, and refused to pay. W.F. Smith, who ran the docks, held her in his fleet for some time, and eventually sold her to a sand and gravel firm at Parkersburg, W. Va., for use as a landing float.

3428 LESLIE COOMBS

Stw p wh b. Madison, Ind., 1860. 199 tons. Ran Cincinnati-Kentucky River, Capt. George Stivors, then Louisville-Madison, spring 1861, same master. Ran Marietta-Zanesville, Capt. A.B. Crane, early 1862. Ran Wheeling-Clarington, Capt. Fred Kimpel, 1866. Went to U.S. marshal sale early 1869 and bought by Clark Hanes, Wheeling. He resold her to Portsmouth, Oh., parties in April 1869. Brought two barges of railroad freight cars Cincinnati to Maysville, Ky., June 1871. Condemned at Ironton, Oh., September 1871, and was beached out on shore of the Kentucky River on Apr. 8, 1872.

3429 LESSIE TAYLOR

Stw p wh b. Jeffersonville, Ind., by Howard, 1870. 157 x 37.8 x 7. Named for daughter of Dr. and Mrs. John A. Taylor, Opelousas, La. Ran New Orleans-Baton Rouge-Plaquemine, owned by Capt. M. Kenison and others. Sank and lost at the mouth of Atchafalaya River, Feb. 3, 1878.

3430 LETTIE

Stw p wh b. New Cumberland, W. Va., 1882. 85 x 14 x 2. Ran East Liverpool-New Cumberland one day, then New Cumberland-Steubenville next day, Capt. T.R. Staney 1888–1890.

3431 LEVI J. WORKUM

Stw p wh b. Levanna, Oh., 1890. 183 tons. 154.5 x 30 x 4.8. Engines, 15's-5 ft. Two boilers, each 38" by 20 ft. She plied between the Workum distillery, Petersburg, Ky., and Cincinnati, transporting their wares, familiarly known as "the whiskey boat." Long commanded by Capt. Henry Bascom Fenton, Newport, Ky., whose sons later ran a chain of Fenton dry cleaning shops in the Cincinnati area. She was taken to Madison, Ind., in 1907, the hull enlarged, and renamed *KENTUCKY* (see).

3432 LEVIATHAN

SW p wh b. New Albany, Ind., 1864. 987 tons. 307 x 49 x 8. Engines, 36's- 11 ft., from the *ECLIPSE* (see). Seven boilers, each 46″ by 28 ft. Paddlewheels 38 ft. dia. working 17 ft. buckets. Overall width 93 ft. Ran St. Louis-New Orleans, Capt. Ambrose Reader. Not noted for speed but quite popular with shippers and passengers. Captain Reader died, and she was bought by the Atlantic & Mississippi Steamship Co., and continued in the trade, Capt. George Pegram. Burned at St. Louis, Feb. 26, 1866, along with the *LUNA* and *DICTATOR* (see). The hull was converted into a large wharfboat which served the Eagle Packet Co., at St. Louis until 1910 when it was destroyed by ice.

3433 LEVINA MARIA

Stw ferry wh b. Paducah, Ky., 1861. 225 tons. Registered at St. Louis, 1876. Also spelled *LAVINA MARIA*.

3434 LEW PRESTON

Ferry wh b. Pine Bluff, Ark., 1882. 70 x 16 x 3.5. Still listed 1886, maybe longer.

3435 LEWELLIN

Stw p wh b. Parkersburg, W. Va., and completed at Wheeling, 1864. 155 tons. Built for Capt. E.P. Chancellor, Parkersburg, for short Ohio River trades and low water work. John M. Sweeney, Wheeling, recalls: "I remember being allowed to build and light the first fire and start the engines for the first time, and I was then about ten years old. She had lever engines, 11's- 4 ft. Jim Chamberlain was her engineer and a good one was he." In 1869 was running Evansville-Tennessee River, Capt. J.L. Davy, with W.D. Covington, clerk. Dismantled in 1870.

3436 LEWIS ADAMS

Stw p wh b. Canton, Mo., 1863. 80 tons. First home port, Quincy, Ill. Off the lists in 1867.

3437 LEWIS ADAMS

Stw ferry wh b. Manchester, Oh., 1925. 64.8 x 22 x 4.4. Owned by Ernest B. Suiter, Manchester, Oh. Later was renamed *NEW RICHMOND,* operated by the New Richmond Ferry Co., Paul Nobis, owner. He retired her in 1949, at which time service was continued with a non-propelled ferry flat named *CLERMONT* handled by a diesel towboat *CAMPBELL*.

3438 LEWIS BURNES

SW p wh b. Brownsville, Pa., 1855. 62 tons. First home port, St. Louis. Off the lists in 1857.

3439 LEWIS F. LINN

SW p wh b. Pittsburgh, Pa., 1844. 163 tons. Departed Pittsburgh March 1844, Capt. M. Kennett, for Dubuque. He operated her on the Upper Mississippi. When the *J.M. WHITE* made her fast run New Orleans to St. Louis in April 1844, the *LEWIS F. LINN* took cargo and passengers from her at St. Louis and delivered at Galena. Reported snagged at the head of St. Charles Island, Missouri River, Capt. W.C. Jewett, 1848–1849.

3440 LEWIS V. BOGEY

Centerwheel ferry wh b. Madison, Ind., 1870. 167.6 x 36 x 5. Owned by Wiggins Ferry Co., St. Louis. Still listed 1886, maybe later.

3441 LEWIS WETZEL

SW p wh b. Wheeling, Va., 1848. 118 tons. Upper Ohio and Kanawha short trades. Off the lists in 1855.

3442 LEWIS WHITEMAN

SW p wh b. Cincinnati, Oh., 1851. 319 tons. 178 x 29 x 6.5. In 1855 was owned by Capt. J.S. Wallace and B.F. Powell, both of Yazoo City, Miss. Ran Ricksburg-Yazoo City. Sold November 1860 to Mobile, Ala. Was captured as a Confederate steamer, May 6, 1862.

3443 LEXINGTON

SW p wh b. Jeffersonville, Ind., 1850. 312 tons. Owned by Capt. Josh V. Throop and Ben F. Egan. Was running St. Louis-Louisville, Capt. Throop, when she exploded boilers at Rome, Ind., opposite Stephensport, Ky., on the Ohio River, June 30, 1855, with loss of 30 lives. She was upbound at the time, under headway. The *D.A. GIVEN* was in the area and came to assist, taking survivors and wounded to Stephensport. The *JOHN C. FREMONT* took some to Louisville. Capt. Throop was precipitated from the upper deck to the forecastle, but the mate caught him in his arms and broke the impact of the fall.

3444 LEXINGTON

SW p wh b. Elizabeth, Pa., 1858. 405 tons. Originally named *VICTORIA,* and as such was captured by the U.S. on June 6, 1862, and was used as a wharfboat called *ABRAHAM* by the U.S. and sold to private hands Mar. 16, 1866. Ran Cincinnati-New Orleans, dimensions then 277 x 41 x 6. Engines, 22's- 7 ft. Four boilers, each 38″ by 26 ft. Was in a tornado at Vicksburg night of Apr. 14, 1868, and was reported to have been literally demolished. Burned at Algiers, La., Feb. 3, 1869.

3445 LEXINGTON

SW p wh b. Belle Vernon, Pa., at the L.M. Speer yard, 1861. 180 x 36 x 6.5. Engines, 20's- 6 ft. Three boilers, each 40″ dia. by 28 ft. Paddlewheels 30 ft. dia. working 7½ ft. buckets, 24″ dip. Built for the Pittsburgh-New Orleans trade, Capt. Asa S. Shepherd. Practically the whole crew from the *SOUTH AMERICA* (see) came aboard to man her, including John Doyle, Jr., clerk, and James Fitzgerald, mate. She was sold to the USQMD practically new, June 1861, and was converted at Cincinnati into a U.S. gunboat carrying the same name. Saw active service throughout the Civil War. She was the first through the break at Bailey's Dam on Red River.

3446 LEXINGTON

Stw p wh b. Pt. Pleasant, W. Va., 1890. 58 tons. 121 x 22.4 x 3.6. Engines, 9"-30". One boiler, 30" by 16 ft. Ran various short trades on the upper Ohio. While in the Wheeling-New Matamoras trade Capt. J.F. Cline was master, with J.A. Voegtly, clerk. Was bought by the Carr Line, Kanawha River, and while racing the *ARGAND* she hit the stone wall at Five Mile, near Scary, W. Va., broke in two and sank. This happened Apr. 7, 1900, and her master was Capt. Thomas Fish, Buffalo, W. Va. The wreck was recovered and machinery, etc., went to building the *BAXTER* (see).

3447 LEXINGTON

Stw ferry wh b. Hermann, Mo., 1918. 94.5 x 26 x 3.6. Owned by Lafayette County Ferry Co., at Lexington, Mo. Capt. Albert G. Wohlt ran her. Capt. Peters Lee, Memphis, bought her in 1928, and converted her into a short-trade packet renamed *DE SOTO* (see).

3448 LIAH TUNA

SW p wh b. Cincinnati, Oh., 1853. 647 tons. 251 x 36 x 7.4. Capt. George W. Haygood, New Orleans, commanded and was part owner. In December 1853, the ownership was changed with 9/16 owned at St. Louis, same master. Burned and lost at New Orleans, Feb. 4, 1854.

3449 LIBBIE CONGER

Stw p wh b. Metropolis, Ill. (hull), and completed at Dubuque, Iowa, 1878. 168 x 29.5 x 4.5. Machinery from *JOSIE* which was hand-me-down from *CITY OF KEITHSBURG* and *FANNIE HARRIS*. Owned by the Diamond Jo Line, and was commanded in early days by Capt. John Killeen. On one occasion she was up the Missouri River to Bismarck. Wrecked at St. Louis during the tornado of May 27, 1896.

3450 LIBERTY

Stw p wh b. Wheeling, Va., 1857. 261 tons. Owned by Capt. Charles Booth and others, and operated Wheeling-Parkersburg with occasional trips to Cincinnati. Sold in April 1862 to Mason City Coal Co., and was snagged and lost at Twelve Pole Creek (below today's Huntington, W. Va.) on Dec. 27, 1862.

3451 LIBERTY

Stw p wh b. Harmar, Oh., 1889. 164 x 34.4 x 5. Engines, 17's- 6 ft. Three boilers, each 42" by 22 ft. Built for Capt. John K. Booth and others for the Wheeling-Clarington trade where she ran several years, proved too big, and was stretched out Wheeling-Parkersburg. Sold fall of 1896 and went to the Memphis-White River trade. In 1902 sold for debt to N.M. Jones, coal dealer at Memphis, and that November was bought by Eanes and Jackson for the Mobile-Demopolis trade in Alabama. She was badly mauled in the hurricane at Mobile, September 1906, then rebuilt. The Montgomery Barge Line operated her in the Mobile-Montgomery trade, 410 miles. Sold at U.S. marshal sale at Mobile, July 1911, to Capt. Ed Peppers of Bay Steamship Co. Sold 1912 to John W. Hubbard, Pittsburgh, Pa. Capt. Henry Kraft and crew brought her to Pittsburgh, and in a rebuilding program at Dravosburg, Pa., she was renamed *CITY OF PARKERSBURG* (see).

3452 LIBERTY

Stw p wh b. Belle Vernon, Pa. (hull) and completed at Marietta, Oh., 1890. Originally named *T.N. BARNSDALL* and then *ROYAL* (both see). Her name was changed again to *LIBERTY* on Dec. 11, 1909, owned by the Liberty Packet Co., of which Frank Humphrey, Clarington, Oh. was secretary-treasurer. She ran Wheeling-Clarington until dismantled in 1912 at Clarington. Her engines, etc., went to the "new" *LIBERTY* being built there. The hull of the old boat, still with cabin intact, was sold to the Muskingum River for use as a boat livery and dock. During the 1913 flood it lodged across the Beverly canal and was lost.

3453 LIBERTY

SW p wh b. Middleport, Oh., 1900. 128.4 x 20.5 x 4.2. Came out with rotary engines and feathering wheels, and was owned by Capt. Asa Booth and others of Wheeling. Only turned up 7 or 8 rpm, so radial wheels were placed, same size, but she did no better. J.J. Wilhelm, who ran a Wheeling saloon, bought her, put on engines formerly on *FLEETWING* (see) which had been stored in a shed many years, 11"- 4 ft. She had two boilers, each 48" by 18 ft. Sold, December 1902, to P.J. Roush and Edw. E. Rouch, Longdale, W. Va., and John J. Dower, Graham Station, W. Va. They sold her May 1903 to Harry Maddy and Samuel A. Dunbar, Gallipolis. They sold her July 1903 to the Charleston (W. Va.) Steamboat Excursion Co., D.W. Patterson, and Capt. Robert F. Wilson was master. She had been tried in various short trades, one of which was Morgantown-Bowling Green on the Green River, prior to purchase by John F. Klein, Pittsburgh in spring of 1905. He ran her in the excursion business on Monongahela River, and sold her 1906 to Wm. M. Sauvage, Alton, Ill., who ran excursions there. She burned in 1907, was rebuilt, and went to Cairo, Ill. Capt. Harry Davis, Brookport, Ill., built the *GOLDEN FLEECE* in 1913 and used the machinery, etc., from *LIBERTY*.

3454 LIBERTY

Stw p wh b. Clarington, Oh., 1912. 141.8 x 28.7 x 5. Engines, 12's- 5 ft., from the *T.N. BARNSDALL-ROYAL-LIBERTY* (see above). Two boilers. Built for the Wheeling-Clarington trade where she ran with Capt. S.W. Litten, master, with Frank Humphrey and Walter C. Booth, clerks. By 1918 she was running through to New Matamoras, then to Parkersburg, and entered the

Wheeling-McConnelsville trade in September 1918, and on December 20 that year she entered the Pittsburgh harbor for the first time, extending her trade Pittsburgh-McConnelsville. She started running Pittsburgh-Zanesville on Aug. 24, 1920, and a texas was added. Left the trade in the fall of 1921, tried it Gallipolis-Charleston, and then came to the Pittsburgh-Wheeling trade where she was quite successful. When the *SENATOR CORDILL* abandoned the Pittsburgh-Charleston trade in 1929, the *LIBERTY* replaced her. In April 1932, she made two trips above Charleston to Boomer, W. Va., with freight. Discontinued her trips in June 1936 and was the last year-around packet to call Pittsburgh home port. Her crew at the last: Capt. Walter C. Booth, master; Wilsie Miller, pilot; Roy Collett, purser; Ross Minard, clerk; Mason Thomas, chief engineer; Walter Webster, 2nd engineer; Harry Elliott, mate; Andy Krull, 2nd mate; Kid Riley, steward; Peter Kollar, 2nd steward; William Colter, watchman; Jim Williams and John Clay, firemen. Captain Booth had been associated with the *LIBERTY* since her blueprint stages; Mace Thomas was engineer on her first trip, and Pete Kollar was aboard 24 years. She then towed the *GOLDENROD* showboat on tour with Major Bowes' Amateurs. Got caught in the lower Ohio in the 1936 flood and was stripped by vandals of whistle, bell, fittings, etc. Walter Webster bought her, put her back together, raised steam, and returned her to the Parkersburg Docks in latter February 1937, having been caught in the 1937 flood en route. She was attached for debt and sold for $195 on July 27, 1938. Capt. Ben Raike took her to Kanauga, Oh., and dismantled her. The engines went to the *VALLEY BELLE* (see). Earl Webster located the whistle, originally from the *BEN HUR,* and put it on his towboat *MILDRED.* One of the events associated with the *LIBERTY* was her voyage to Morgantown, W. Va., in 1936. She was towing the *GOLDENROD* showboat with the Major Bowes' Amateurs, left the showboat at Star City, and proceeded to Morgantown and back advertising the show with calliope music. Joe McLaughlin was her pilot on the occasion.

3455 LIBERTY

SW ex wh Originally *BELLE OF THE BENDS,* renamed *LIBERTY* while running excursion trips at Cairo, Ill., and elsewhere 1918–1919. Dismantled by John F. Klein in October 1919.

3456 LIBERTY NO. 2

SW p wh b. Wheeling, Va., 1861. 373 tons. 225 x 35. Engines, 22's- 7 ft. Three boilers. Built to replace the *LIBERTY* described in listing #3450. Ran Wheeling-Parkersburg but soon was involved as a transport in U.S. service. Ran Louisville-Memphis in 1864. Still there 1866 with Capt. Sam Archer, master, with Ed H. Judge, clerk. Also that year in Memphis-White River trade, Capt. James Rice with Milt Harry, clerk. In spring 1867 she encountered a "terrible breeze" 25 miles above Memphis, was blown ashore, and a log went through the hull aft of a wheelhouse. She sank in seven feet, and the *BELLE ST. LOUIS* took her passengers. Dismantled early in 1871 at Mound City, Ill., and her engines went to the railroad transfer *J.C. McMULLIN* (see) being built there.

3457 LIDA NORVELL

Stw p wh b. Portsmouth, Oh., 1865. 103.7 x 18 x 3.7. Operated in the Cincinnati area until sold January 1869 to Capt. P.R. Byrne, master, and Thomas J. Duggan, New Orleans. Sold in May 1869 to James H. Young, New Orleans, with Capt. Richard G. Rawlings, master. Off the lists 1877.

3458 LIGHTEST

Stw p wh b. Jeffersonville, Ind., 1870. 135.6 x 29.4 x 3. Went to New Orleans owned equally by Capts. A.P. Readman and John T. Roots. Designed for operation in Red River above Shreveport. Reported sunk June 17, 1871 and the location not stated.

3459 LIGHTFOOT

SW p wh b. Cincinnati, Oh., 1846. 145 tons. First home port, St. Louis. Operated on the Upper Mississippi, Capt. M.K. Harris, frequently at Galena. Off the lists 1856.

3460 LIGHTFOOT

Stw p wh b. Freedom, Pa., 1856. 142 tons. First home port, Pittsburgh. Off the lists in 1862.

3461 LIGHTFOOT

SW p wh b. Cincinnati, Oh., 1860. 23 tons. Off the lists 1862.

3462 LIGHT WESTERN

Ferry wh b. Oldenburg, Mo., 1874. 23 tons. Documented at St. Louis in 1876, maybe later.

3463 LIGHTWOOD

Stw p wh b. Portsmouth, Oh. (hull), and completed at Cincinnati, Oh., 1868. 156 tons. 130 x 26 x 3. Ran Middleport-Parkersburg in summer, low water, 1868. Capt. Uriah B. Scott had her running out of Camden on the Ouachita River, January 1869. He built her along with shareholders Perry Scott and Jos. Fisher of Ironton, Oh., and George H. Knight and James M. Kirker of Catlettsburg, Ky. Capt. William Kirker was master, late 1870. Caught fire with 560 bales of cotton above the Louisiana line in Bayou Bartholomew and burned to the water's edge, Mar. 10, 1871. The cotton was insured but the boat was not.

3464 LIGHTWOOD

Rig? b. Ashland, Ky., 1884. 96.1 x 15.9 x 2.9. Built by Capt. John Hopkins and Marcum for Big Sandy operation. Later renamed *INDEPENDENT* (see).

3465 LIGHTWOOD

Stw p wh b. Little Rock, Ark., 1884. Originally named *HENRY SHELDON,* long in U.S. Engineer service on White River. Completely rebuilt at Little Rock, 1904. She was sold to private hands, and after a rebuilding in 1917 was renamed *LIGHTWOOD* by the Pine Bluff and Rosedale Packet Co., headed by John D. Crockett and with Joe C. Meyers, general manager. They quit business October 1920, and sold the boat to Capt. P.N. Joest, Rosedale, Miss. She then ran Vicksburg-Yazoo River.

3466 LILLIAN H.

Stw p-tb wh b. Gallipolis, Oh., 1905. 100 x 18 x 2.5. Built by Ernest B. Suiter and others, Proctorville, Oh. Capt. Jesse P. Hughes recalls her as single deck, half packet, half towboat which "laid around Gallipolis but ran little." She was in the Memphis area 1908, then owned by W.P. Hall and others. Engines, 11"-3 ft. One boiler. In 1917 was laid up for lack of repairs.

3467 LILLIE M. BARLOW

Rig? wh Operated on Cane River, La., 1899. Sank at Derry's Landing, La., and was docked at New Orleans. In 1901 on Red River under charter to Capt. William Maikell, Shreveport.

3468 LILLIE MARTIN

Stw p wh b. Freedom, Pa., 1863. 220 tons. 159 x 33 x 4. Two boilers. Reported sold at St. Louis, March 1864. Had been up Red River prior. Ran St. Louis-Memphis until she broke in two and burned at the mouth of St. Marys River below St. Louis, Feb. 4, 1867.

3469 LILLY

Stw p wh b. Louisville, Ky., 1864. 256 tons. Engines, 15's-5 ft. Two boilers. While upbound on the Missouri from St. Louis to Grand River, Capt. D.R. Risley, snagged at Rush Bottom Bend, one mile below Rulo, Neb., Oct. 24, 1868. The snag came through the bow on the starboard side, and up through the forecastle. Loaded with government supplies.

3470 LILY

Stw p wh b. Brownsville, Pa., 1860. 159 tons. First home port, Mobile, Ala. Went to Confederate registry 1861.

3471 LILY

SW Lighthouse tender wh b. Louisville, Ky., 1875. 178 x 28 x 4. Came out for Ohio River service under Capt. Owen B. Jolly who was succeeded in November 1875 by Capt. William R. Hoel. Later commanded by Capt. George Vandergrift who resigned Nov. 5, 1885, to manage the Burnet House, Cincinnati. Capt. Charles Dufour then took charge. She burned off her upper works in the same fire which destroyed the *MORNING MAIL* and first *BONANZA* (1888) and then was completely rebuilt with new hull and texas. The old hull served as the wharfboat at Madison, Ind., and was there in 1894. The rebuilt *LILY* went to the Upper Mississippi and Missouri rivers where Capt. William Eagon long was master. Snagged near Wellington, Mo., Oct. 17, 1911, and again snagged near St. Albans, Mo., Mile 49, Missouri River, head of Centaur Chute, lost, Nov. 24, 1911.

3472 LILY

Ferry wh b. Gilbert, Iowa, 1877. 48 x 17 x 2. Inspected at Moline, Ill., June 1881. Registered at Lansing, Iowa, 1886, maybe longer.

3473 LILLY MAUD

Stw ferry wh b. De Witt, Mo., 1889. 53 x 11 x 3.5. One engine, 6"-12". One boiler. Owned by Samuel B. Casebolt. Sank at Brunswick, Mo., July 8, 1891. She had been laid up for some time and the hull seams had dried. Raised and dismantled.

3474 LINCOLN

Stw p wh b. Monongahela, Pa., 1850. 94 tons. Built for Capt. John L. Doss who took her to the Upper Tennessee. Captain Doss (1818–1870) was an active operator in the area. Dismantled in 1852.

3475 LIND GROVE

Stw p wh b. Belle Vernon, Pa., 1882. 163 tons. She was completed and the machinery installed at Wheeling. Owned in part and commanded by Capt. Campbell T. Sweeney. This was a cotton packet and was taken to Ouachita River. A son of Captain Sweeney, Charles, died during the delivery trip.

3476 LINDA

SW p wh b. Cincinnati, Oh., 1855. 167 tons. 150 x 27.5 x 4.3. Her master Capt. Willis Main, New Orleans, owned her entire. Later commanded by Capt. D.R. Muggah. Off the list in 1858.

3477 LINDEN

SW p wh b. Gallipolis, Oh., 1853. 140 tons. First home port, Wheeling. 137 x 22.5 x 4.8. She was taken to New Orleans, Capt. Jesse Harlam of Franklin Parish, La. Off the lists in 1858.

3478 LINDEN

Stw p wh b. Belle Vernon, Pa., 1860. 177 tons. Ran Pittsburgh-Cincinnati 1861, Capt. T.M. Harton. Taking U.S. Army wagons, etc., Cincinnati to Louisville, January 1862. Sold to U.S. Navy, November 1862 and became U.S. tinclad #10 in January 1863. Snagged and lost at Carson Towhead, Arkansas River, Feb. 22, 1864.

3479 LINN BOYD

Stw p wh b. Paducah, Ky., 1859. 227 tons. Burned and lost as a Confederate steamer at Fort Henry, Tenn., Feb. 6, 1862, to avoid capture.

3480 LINN CREEK

SW p wh b. Paducah, Ky., 1857. 91 tons. First home port, St. Louis. Off the lists in 1859.

3481 LINNIE DROWN

Stw p wh b. Cincinnati, Oh., 1864. Built for Capt. Henry H. Drown of *WILD WAGONER* fame (see) for the Cincinnati-Marietta trade. Ran there about a year, Capt. J.B. Crawford, master, J.H. Rice, clerk. Sold, and ran

Memphis-Pine Bluff, Capt. Claycomb, with George N. Baker, clerk. Snagged and lost at Helena, Ark., Sept. 7, 1866, owned by David Gibson and the aforementioned crew.

3482 LINTON

Stw p wh b. Brownsville, Pa. (hull), and completed at Pittsburgh, 1867. 145 x 29 x 3.5. Engines, 12's- 4 ft., by J.N. Snowden. Two boilers, each 38" by 20 ft. J.S. Pringle built the hull. Built for Capt. N.F. Drew, and first operated Lock 4 to Brownsville and Rice's Landing on Monongahela River connecting with the *PETROLIA* to Pittsburgh while Lock 4 was out of commission. Went to the Evansville-Nashville trade, Capt. Nat F. Drew, master, with N.B. Hayward, clerk. Sank and lost, Oct. 25, 1869, in the head of the cut-off between Arkansas and White rivers, Capt. William Reasoner. Machinery went to the *J.S. DUNHAM*.

3483 LION

SW p wh b. Beaver, Pa., 1863. 33 tons. Off the lists 1868.

3484 LION

Stw p wh b. Lyons, Iowa, 1875. 86 x 15.6. Engines, 10's- 4 ft. Was rebuilt and enlarged to 101.5 x 19.5 in 1888, owned then by Capt. Hiram C. Wilcox. Up to 1886 she had run in the Wabasha-Alma trade, then known as the Beef Slough trade, two round trips a day. After the Burlington Railroad was built up the east side of the Mississippi, she served three years as a rafter, then was in the Wabasha-La Crosse trade through the 1906 season. Dismantled in 1907 while on the ways at the Kahlke yard. The engines went to Honduras for Ulna River service, having been bought by the Marine Iron Works, Chicago. The Wilcox family then bought the *RAVENNA* from Herb Staples, rebuilt her, and changed her name to *LA CROSSE* (see).

3485 LITTLE ACME

Ferry wh b. 1889 (?). 13.6 tons. Owned by Albert Haigh, New Cumberland, W. Va. She was pulled out for repairs when a sudden rise in the Ohio River overturned and wrecked her, Sept. 9, 1890.

3486 LITTLE ANNA

Stw p wh b. Nashville, Tenn., 1881. 92 x 23 x 2. Ran Wheeling-New Matamoras trade, Capt. H. Seamon, with G.P. Goodwin, clerk, 1883. She and *JOHN LOMAS* ran opposition between Martins Ferry, Oh., and Wheeling for a time. Documented at Pensacola, Fla., 1886.

3487 LITTLE BEAUTY

Stw p wh b. Peytona, W. Va., 1877. 55 x 9.3 x 3.6. Originally named *G. W. BARCUS*. Sort of a combination towboat-daylight packet. Was still documented at Wheeling 1896, maybe later.

3488 LITTLE BEN

SW ferry wh b. Pomeroy, Oh., 1895. 70.6 x 18 x 2.8. Ran Middleport, Oh.-Clifton, W. Va., named for Ben Redmond, Middleport. Owned by Clifton, New Castle & Ohio Ferry Co., Capt. F.B. Wilkinson. Sank at the wharf grade, Middleport, Apr. 14, 1913, and was pumped out by the towboat *VALIANT*. Later owned by H.C. (Clate) Pickens, Racine, Oh., running Racine-Graham Station. Still there 1929.

3489 LITTLE BETTY

Ferry wh b. South Point, Oh., 1863. 42 tons. Off the lists in 1870.

3490 LITTLE BOB S.

Small low water packet in the upper Ouachita River 1879, connecting with the *JOHN WILSON* and taking passengers and freight to Camden, La.

3491 LITTLE BOON

Stw p wh b. Ironton, Oh., 1848. 59 tons. Off the lists 1851.

3492 LITTLE BOONE

SW p wh b. Pt. Pleasant, W. Va., 1880. 125 x 18 x 3. She was double deck, like *MAXIE YOST* (see). The Wheeling & Parkersburg Packet Co., had her in that trade during low water, fall 1883, Capt. John K. Booth, with Ed Dunn and T.J. Martin, clerks. Down past Cairo, Ill., Nov. 26, 1883, with a produce boat in tow. Captain Booth bought the *TELEGRAM* in 1884 for the Wheeling-Clarington trade. The *LITTLE BOONE* was registered at New Orleans in 1886.

3493 LITTLE DICK

Ferry wh b. Rocheport, Mo., 1876. 63 tons.

3494 LITTLE DORRIT

SW ferry wh b. Elizabeth, Pa., 1857. 66 tons. First home port, St. Paul, Minn. Off the lists 1862.

3495 LITTLE EVA

SW p wh b. Parkersburg, Va., 1862. 18 tons. Running Parkersburg-Wheeling in November 1862. A low water packet. Off the lists 1864.

3496 LITTLE FLETA

Stw p wh b. Madison, Ind., 1870. Owned by Capt. John Poff, New Orleans. A dispatch from Brownsville, Tex., dated Sept. 23, 1873, says she was descending the Rio Grande with government stores during high water, went out of control, left the channel, and grounded. As the river fell she broke in two.

3497 LITTLE GREY EAGLE

See *GREY EAGLE* b. Shousetown, Pa., 1859. Was called *LITTLE GREY EAGLE* and *STAR GREY EAGLE*.

3498 LITTLE JACK

Rig? wh b. Tuscumbia, Mo., 1867. 26 tons. A dispatch from St. Louis dated June 22, 1867: "A curious specimen of steamboat, called the *LITTLE JACK*, left today for the Osage River. She has a flatboat hull, saw-mill engine and raft cabin. The painter's skill has been developed by putting the name on in chalk."

3499 LITTLE JERRY

Prop p wh b. Gretna, La., 1865. 32 tons. Built for the U.S. Navy. Sold to Capt. W.B. Robertson, New Orleans, October 1865. Apparently used as a ferry. Capt. John Kouns was master January 1867, and part owner along with William T. Scoville and Richard S. Robertson. Last known document, Jan. 9, 1877.

3500 LITTLE JOKER

SW yacht wh b. Terre Haute, Ind., 1878. 56.2 x 8.6 x 2.2. Registered at Evansville 1896, maybe later.

3501 LITTLE JULIA H.

Ferry wh b. Henderson, Ky., 1872. 12.70 tons. Documented at Evansville, 1876.

3502 LITTLE LAFIE

Stw ferry wh b. Manchester, Oh., 1892. 84 x 24.2 x 3. Capt. Ben T. Flesher, Middleport, Oh., bought her entire in July 1901. She was running at 26th Street, Huntington, W. Va., when the *CHAMPION* (see) burned at Gallipolis, summer of 1903. Capt. Miles Brown bought her, took her to Gallipolis, and changed her name to *FRANCIS* (see).

3503 LITTLE LIZZIE

Stw p wh b. Malden, W. Va., 1871. Owned by Capt. W.G. Norvell. Launched June 30, 1871, and was towed to Charleston and raised steam there. Worked fine and many persons watched.

3504 LITTLE MARTHA

SW p wh b. Beardstown, Ill., 1858. 70 tons. Off the lists 1860.

3505 LITTLE MAUD

Stw p wh b. Sioux City, Iowa, 1882. 92 x 20 x 3.4. Ran on the upper Missouri between Running Water, S.D., and Niobra, Neb., connecting with the *SOUTH DAKOTA* which ran Niobra to Fairfax, 75 miles above. Later acquired by the Benton Packet Co., and renamed *WESTON*.

3506 LITTLE MINNIE

Stw ferry wh b. Madison, Ind., 1884. 60 x 16 x 2.5. She was the Ohio River ferry at Carrollton, Ky.

3507 LITTLE MISSOURI

SW p wh b. Cincinnati, Oh., 1846. 198 tons. Capt. Bob Wright, master. Snagged and lost at Glasgow, Mo., April 1848. The location was later known as Little Missouri Bend.

3508 LITTLE MORGAN

Rig? wh b. 1862 (?). Capt. Granville W. Hill took her up the Des Moines River and arrived at Fort Des Moines on Apr. 5, 1862. Had freight aboard. This was classed as an accomplishment.

3509 LITTLE P.

Stw p wh b. Yazoo City, Miss. (hull), and completed at Vicksburg, 1878. Owned by Capt. S.H. Parisot, and ran Vicksburg-Yazoo River. Said to be his first boat. She burned downbound on Yazoo River not far above Vicksburg, Mar. 24, 1880, Capt. Billy Hines.

3510 LITTLE PIKE

SW p wh b. Wellsville, Oh., 1851. 46 tons. First home port, Memphis. Snagged and lost on the White River, Arkansas, Apr. 15, 1854.

3511 LITTLE PRINCESS

SW p wh b. Louisville, Ky., 1846. 23 tons. First home port, Louisville. Off the lists 1848.

3512 LITTLE QUEEN

Rig? yacht wh b. Covington, Ky., 1880. 7 tons. Inspected in Cincinnati area through 1882, maybe later.

3513 LITTLE QUEEN

Stw p wh b. Middleport, Oh., 1896. 82.2 x 14.3. Owned by Capt. Ben T. Flesher, Middleport. Machinery from *EMMA*. Ran short trades. Later rebuilt and renamed *EXCEL*.

3514 LITTLE ROCK

SW ferry wh b. Louisville, Ky., 1850. 60 tons. 81 x 25 x 3.5. Came to Jefferson Parish, La., in 1852, Capt. William Bobb, who owned in equal shares with Charles P. Bobb. Off the lists 1854.

3515 LITTLE ROCK

Stw p wh b. Cincinnati, Oh., 1858. 183 tons. Enrolled at New Orleans, January 1859, Capt. Jenks Brown, master, who owned in equal shares with Phillip Pennywit, Van Buren, Ark. Burned at Little Rock, Ark., Sept. 10, 1863, along with *CHESTER ASHLEY, ST. FRANCIS NO. 3, PINE BLUFF* and *JULIA ROANE*.

3516 LITTLE ROCK

SW p wh b. Cincinnati, Oh., 1863. Originally named *FLORENCE MILLER NO. 2* (see). In May 1963 she became U.S. tinclad #34, renamed *MOOSE,* and at war's conclusion was sold to private hands October 1865, and her name changed to *LITTLE ROCK*. Burned and lost at Clarendon, Ark., Dec. 23, 1867.

3517 LITTLE ROCK

SW ferry wh b. New Albany, Ind., 1865. 125 tons. Snagged and lost at Pine Bluff, Ark., Dec. 1, 1872.

3518 LITTLE RUFUS

Stw p wh b. Stillwater, Minn., 1903. 130.9 x 29.5 x 5.5. Compound condensing engines by Swain, 12", 24"-6 ft. Owned by R.F. Learned and S.B. McNeeley, Natchez, Miss. Ran from Natchez to Black River principally, also to Melville and Atchafalaya River. Burned soon after her last insurance inspection which was on May 6, 1913.

3519 LITTLE SALLIE

Stw p wh b. Jeffersonville, Ind., by Howard, 1860. 71 tons. 98 x 23 x 3.5. Owned by New Orleans Coast & Lafourche Transportation Co., A. Dugas, president. Capt. Louis Lee, master. Went to Confederate registry 1861.

3520 LITTLE SANDY

Stw p wh b. Louisville, Ky., 1880. 94 x 16 x 3. She was in the Racine-Middleport trade, Ohio River, fall 1890, Capt. Sam DeWolf, with W.M. Longstreth, clerk. Still listed 1896.

3521 LITTLE STAR

SW p wh b. Memphis, Tenn., 1867. 67 tons. Off the lists in 1868.

3522 LITTLE TENNESSEE

Stw p wh Ran in the Kingston-Loudon trade handling U.S. Mail about 1900. A small low water boat operated with a sprocket wheel.

3523 LITTLE TOM

Stw p wh b. Opelousas, La., 1849. 62 tons. 91 x 7.1 x 4.2. Owned by Capt. John Lyons, Opelousas, La. Off the lists 1851.

3524 LIVE OAK

SW p wh b. Paducah, Ky., 1863. 365 tons. 176.4 x 37.2 x 6. Engines, 20's- 6 ft. Three boilers. Operated out of Paducah until sold October 1865 to Capt. Peter Fargarona, New Orleans. Had several changes of ownership at New Orleans. Burned to the hull at New Orleans, Oct. 1, 1867. She frequently ran New Orleans-Red River.

3525 LIVINGSTON

SW gunboat wh originally a ferry across Berwick Bay, La., before the Civil War. 180 x 40 x 9. The Confederates converted her into a gunboat with six guns. On June 26, 1862 the *LANCASTER NO. 3* (see). ascended Yazoo River in search of this craft and others. Burned by the Confederates to prevent capture.

3526 LIZE

Stw p sh b. Pittsburgh, Pa., 1893. 62.1 x 13.1 x 3.6. Engines, 8"- 27". One Scotch marine boiler. Built by James Rees & Sons Co., for Messrs. Krajewski and Peasant, Cuba, and was taken to destination afloat.

3527 LIZZIE

Stw p wh b. Jeffersonville, Ind., 1871. 429 tons. 165 x 35 x 5. Went to Vicksburg for Yazoo River trade. Several changes of ownership. Sold in latter 1870s to Galveston, Tex., and still there early 1880s.

3528 LIZZIE

Stw ferry wh b. Middleport, Oh., 1877. 71 x 16 x 3.5. Operated across the Ohio River from Middleport to Bosworth Landing and West Columbia, W. Va. Still documented 1896.

3529 LIZZIE BAY

Stw p wh b. Madison, Ind., 1886. 150 x 30.8 x 4. Engines, 14's- 5 ft. Two boilers, each 42" by 20 ft. Built for the Bay Line. Came out in the Parkersburg-Middleport trade, Capt. George B. McClintock, with J.W. Deem, clerk. Soon entered the Pittsburgh-Charleston trade. Capt. J.M. Keever was master in 1890. She was lengthened to 181 ft., and a texas added while in this trade. In February 1893 she failed to back while landing at the Parkersburg wharfboat in the mouth of Little Kanawha River and hit the B&O bridge knocking down her stacks and pilothouse. The Bays sold her on Nov. 26, 1895, to the White Collar Line, Cincinnati. They ran her usually Cincinnati-Madison, but sometimes upriver as well. Hit a coal barge at Ludlow, Ky., Dec. 8, 1905, and sank. Again sank at Cincinnati, foot of Main Street, June 1909. Dismantled at the Howard Ship Yard, Jeffersonville, Ind., in 1912, and her engines and part of the cabin went to building the *CORKER* (see). A tradition is handed down that once during high water she was taken up Big Hocking River to Coolville, Oh., for freight, this before lengthening. She was popularly known as the "Lousy Liz."

3530 LIZZIE BAYLISS

SW p wh b. Wellsville, Oh., 1861. 117 x 21 x 3. Started off her career as a ferry and by the mid-1870s was running Cairo-Cape Girardeau, and while in ice harbor at Alton, Ill., she burned Feb. 10, 1877, resulting in the death of her owner Capt. Gruel. She was sold at St. Louis June 19, 1878, to Capt. Peter Manion and J.C. Grace & Co., described as a side-wheel boat with engines 14's- 3½ ft., "two years old" (she had been rebuilt at Quincy, Ill., 1876). In October 1878 running short trades out of Louisville, Ky., and seems to have gone to the Yazoo River from there. Documented at Vicksburg in 1886, maybe later.

3531 LIZZIE C. HAMILTON

Stw p wh b. Gallipolis, Oh., 1864. 60 tons. 108.9 x 20 x 3. Went to Shreveport, La., in 1865 owned there by George W. Warren and others, Capt. John W. Bowles. A tongue-in-cheek dispatch from Shreveport, August 1866, reports her departure for Jefferson, La., "with a load of watermelons to be used for water to float the boat over the sand bars." In 1867 owned by L.D. Judice, St. Martin Parish, with Capt. Abe Smith, master. Off the lists 1869.

3532 LIZZIE CAMPBELL

Stw ferry wh b. Jeffersonville, Ind., 1868. 122 tons. Was the ferry at Nebraska City, Neb. Lost in 1883.

3533 LIZZIE CASSEL

Stw p wh b. Marietta, Oh. (hull), and completed at McConnelsville, Oh., 1873. 141 x 24 x 4. Engines, 12's- 4 ft. Had a lengthy career on the Muskingum River. First master Capt. Jesse John Barr in McConnelsville-Zanesville trade, December 1873. Soon changed to Parkersburg-Zanesville. Other masters: Capt. William Davis, Capt. Lou Myrick, Capt. Ed Martin, Capt. A.J. Hahn, and Capt. John Rice. Martin was brother-in-law of W.C. Cassel who operated a flour mill at Zanesville. Sank of old age at Zanesville July 1895, and was sold for junk, bringing $20. Machinery went to the *HAZEL RICE*. The whistle today is in the Ohio River Musuem, Marietta, Oh., cast by a Beverly foundry in 1873.

3534 LIZZIE GILL

SW p wh b. Cairo, Ill. (hull), and completed at St. Louis in April 1865. 242 x 49 (44½ ft. floor) x 7. Engines, 24's- 7 ft. Three tubular boilers, each 48" by 20 ft., 20 flues to the boiler. Paddlewheels 30 ft. dia. working 13 buckets. Named for Lizzie Tate Gill, for whom the *LIZZIE TATE* also was named (see). Sank at the mouth of White River downbound with a full cargo early January 1866. The *KATE BRUNER* hit the wreck later that year (see) and was lost.

3535 LIZZIE HOPKINS.

Stw p wh b. Racine, Oh., and completed at Cincinnati, 1867. 453 tons. 158.8 x 35.8 x 5.8. Owned by A.B. Hopkins (3/4) and Thomas T. Hopkins, Cincinnati; Capt. John T. Roots. Ran New Orleans-Upper Coast. Also made trips to Shreveport. Off the lists 1875.

3536 LIZZIE JOHNSTON

Stw p wh b. Portsmouth, Oh., 1877. 140 x 23 x 3.5. Built for Capt. William Bay and others and run in the Portsmouth & Pomeroy Packet Co. In 1880 ran Gallipolis-Huntington, Capt. William Birthisell, with C.C. Dusenberry, clerk. Named for a young lady of South Point, Oh., who later married Capt. William Bay. During a rebuilding the boat was renamed *ROSEDALE* (see).

3537 LIZZIE LAKE

Stw p wh b. Smithland, Ky., 1855. 54 tons. First home port, Nashville, Tenn. Snagged and lost in the Guadelupe River, Tex., Dec. 7, 1859.

3538 LIZZIE LEE

SW p wh b. Smithland, Ky., 1856. 101 tons. First home port, Galveston, Tex. Snagged and lost at 12-Mile Bayou, La., Jan. 13, 1857.

3539 LIZZIE MARTIN

Stw p wh b. Belle Vernon, Pa., 1857. 164 tons. A regular in the Parkersburg-Zanesville trade through 1861, Capt. David T. Brown. In 1862 made trips Zanesville-Pittsburgh, same master, with S.G. Hoge, clerk. In April 1862 ran Pittsburgh-Wheeling, that trade having just been vacated by the *JOHN T. McCOMBS* (see) and was still there September 1864. Sold, and in September 1864 made trips Pittsburgh-Cincinnati, Capt. Laughlin, with T.L. Calhoon, clerk. Dismantled 1865.

3540 LIZZIE REA

Rig? wh b. 1875. Ran St. Louis-Red River. On second trip up the Red, Mar. 28, 1875, at night, sank and lost below Shreveport. Her master was Capt. Thomas W. Rea.

3541 LIZZIE REID

Stw p wh b. Forest City, S.D., 1896. Belonged to the Northwestern Transportation Co. Burned at Gettysburg, S.D., July 12, 1901.

3542 LIZZIE SIMMONS

SW p wh b. New Albany, Ind., 1859. 454 tons. 204 x 36.5 x 6.5. Ran New Orleans-Ouachita River, Capt. George Hamilton Kirk, in 1860. In 1862 New Orleans-Memphis, Capt. W.B. Richardson, with W.C. Porter, clerk. Teamed up with the *MARY E. KEENE* (see) in that trade. Converted into a gunboat by the Rebels and renamed *PONTCHARTRAIN*. She was destroyed at Little Rock, Ark., Sept. 10, 1863, by the U.S. gunboat *GENERAL PRICE*.

3543 LIZZIE TATE

SW p wh b. Cincinnati, Oh., 1863. 184 tons. 158 x 30 x 3. She was sold before her original documentation to the U.S. who used her during the war named *VICTORY*. Sold to private hands October 1865, and owned 1866 by Capt. H.L. Lee of New Orleans and Capt. W.H. Thorwegan, St. Louis, now named *LIZZIE TATE*. Miss Lizzie Tate married George Gill, Memphis merchant (see *LIZZIE GILL*). Capt. Joseph W. Barnes was master until 1867, then Capt. Charles W. Stinde. Dismantled at Jeffersonville, Ind., 1869.

3544 LLOYD W.

Prop p wh b. Mt. Vernon, Ind., 1914. 40 x 8.1 x 3.1. Documented at Louisville, 1918.

3545 LODI

SW p wh b. Elizabethtown, Pa., 1843. 93 tons. She was a single engine boat, and ran Pittsburgh-Parkersburg, Capt. Tomlinson, 1844. There is evidence she once ran on the Little Kanawha, Parkersburg-Elizabeth, the first regular packet there. Snagged and lost at Grand River, La., Dec. 27, 1845.

3546 LOGAN

SW p wh b. Louisville, Ky., 1853. 150 tons. Off the lists 1853.

3547 LOIS

Stw ferry wh b. Waverly, Mo., 1896. 75.2 x 18.9 x 3.1. Still documented at Kansas City in 1908, maybe later.

3548 LOLA

Stw p wh b. Peoria, Ill., 1895. 71 x 13.3 x 2.3. Single deck pleasure boat on the Illinois River. Still listed in 1903, maybe longer.

3549 LONE STAR

SW p wh b. Louisville, Ky., 1854. 126 tons. 112 x 26 x 4.7. Built for Capt. J.S. Smith and partners, Jefferson, Texas. In 1856 owned by Amite Pressed Brick Mfg. Co., New Orleans. Sold May 1857 to James N. Sherry, New Orleans. Bought January 1860 by Gilbert V. Gamble, East Baton Rouge Parish, La. Went to Confederate registry in 1861.

3550 LONE STAR

Stw p wh b. Monongahela, Pa., 1859. 121 tons. Built by James Rees & Sons, Pittsburgh, for Trinity River service in Texas. Capt. Thomas Stubblefield commanded. Rees owned two-thirds and Charles Gearing the balance. She got to destination and after only a few trips was snagged and lost.

3551 LONE STAR

Rig? wh b. Lyons, Iowa, 1868. 28 tons. 68.4 x 19.3 x 3.2. Ran Davenport-Buffalo, Iowa trade, Capt. Sam Mitchell. Not very fast and had limited accommodations. At the end of the second season she was withdrawn. In November 1876, Mitchell sold her to Goss & Co., sand dealers at Davenport, and they made a towboat of her. Still listed 1886.

3552 LONE WANDERER

Rig? wh b. Wheeling, W. Va., 1881. 92 x 14 x 2. Capts. Phil and Ed Anshutz put a threshing machine engine on a flat with a shanty on it, got some tarpaulins, and brought out this craft in the Wheeling-New Matamoras trade during the low water season of 1881, ran her from mid-summer until November. Carried the U.S. mail. President Garfield was shot Sept. 29, and this boat arrived at Wheeling that day with 12″ on Wheeling riffle, and with the marks on the Wheeling wharf showing 3″. John Muhleman, John and Sam Lankard, and Lee Anshutz composed the crew. She connected with the *SLIM CHANCE* at New Matamoras for Marietta. Still listed in 1886.

3553 LONGFELLOW

Stw p wh b. Jeffersonville, Ind., by Howard, 1872. 112 x 19.6 x 4.3. Operated around Evansville both as towboat and packet. In August 1897 she was pinch-hitting for the *EVANSVILLE* in the Green River trade. In 1892 she had been in the Illinois River.

3554 LONGFELLOW

Stw p wh b. Cincinnati, Oh., 1876. Originally named *U.P. SCHENCK* (see). She was lengthened at Cincinnati to measure 318 x 42 x 6.5, and ran Cincinnati-New Orleans. Rated 1,450 tons. She was prevented from leaving Cincinnati the evening of Mar. 7, 1895, by a heavy fog. At 7:00 next morning, the captain becoming impatient, she departed, assisted by the *HERCULES CARREL*. Fog again closed down and she went broadside into a pier of the C&O bridge causing her loss. J. Lawrence Carter, head clerk, was drowned, as was Gus Chauvert, barkeeper, and several passengers.

3555 LOOKOUT

Stw p wh b. Monongahela, Pa., 1853. 176 tons. Owned by Capt. J.M. Todd, Knoxville, Tenn., and named for Lookout Mountain. Off the lists in 1859.

3556 LOOKOUT

Stw p wh b. Louisville, Ky., 1867. 27 tons. Apparently towed produce boats south. An item in the Pittsburgh *Gazette* dated Jan. 26, 1871: "The *LOOKOUT* will leave Vevay, Ind., for the south in a few days with hay-boats in tow owned by Frank Dupraz and G. Anshutz." Off the lists in 1876.

3557 LORA

Stw p wh b. Stillwater, Minn., 1900. 150 x 30 x 4.5. Engines, 12's- 6½ ft. Two boilers. Machinery came from rafter *FLORA CLARK*. Originally had no texas and ran briefly on the Upper Mississippi. Took out excursions at St. Paul and elsewhere. Then went to Missouri River and the Heckman family ran her St. Louis-Arrow Rock, and ran excursions at Kansas City. Was renamed *OMAHA* (see).

3558 LORAINE K.

Stw p wh b. Jeffersonville, Ind., by Howard, 1908, originally named *CITY OF MUSKOGEE* (see). Operated out of New Orleans, named for wife of Victor Kurzweg, in New Orleans-New Iberia trade. She was sold July 1924 to Capts. L.V. Cooley and F.A. Bradford who renamed her *OUACHITA* and she burned on her first trip at Helvetia Landing below Donaldsonville, La., in September 1924.

3559 LORENA

Stw p wh b. Pittsburgh, Pa., 1865. 455 tons. Built for Capt. Sam Shuman who originally owned one-half in partnership with J.B. Conway and James Rees. Ran Pittsburgh-St. Louis. Charles H. Wilkins was head clerk. Captain Shuman also ran the *WAUNITA* Pittsburgh-St. Louis at this time and as consequence other masters appeared on the *LORENA* including Capts. John H. Lightner, Charles H. Dravo, and Andy Robinson, Jr. James Rees, Jr., was clerk in 1868. She went to U.S. marshal sale at Cincinnati Nov. 7, 1871 and was bought by Capt. W.S. Evans. Dismantled in 1872.

3560 LORENA

Stw p wh b. Harmar, Oh., 1895 at Knox Yard. 141 x 31.5 x 5.6. Engines, 15's- 5½ ft. by Griffith & Wedge, Zanesville. For some years she had two patented boilers, each 72″ dia. by 12½ ft. long. Came out in the Pittsburgh-Zanesville trade replacing *HIGHLAND MARY* (see). Her crew, May 1896: Capt. George Wallace with George Conant and William Richardson, pilots; Dana Scott and Charles Beckwith, clerks; Clawson and Gordon, engineers. Both these boats named *LORENA* were named for the heroine of a sentimental song, the words by Dr. H.D.L. Webster, and music by J.R. Webster (no relation). During the Civil War it was sung by both armies. Sample:

A hundred months have passed Lorena,
Since last I held thy hand in mine,
And felt thy pulse beat fast, Lorena,
Though mine beat faster far than thine!

A hundred months—'twas flowery May,
When up the hilly slope we climbed
To watch the dying of the day
And hear the distant church bells chimed.

The Reverend Webster preached in Zanesville, Oh., fell in love with Ella Blocksom, and troubles intervened to prevent marriage. The poem and song resulted with "Lorena" substituted for poetic reasons. Railroad engines and babies also carried the name. It was a tear-jerker and still is, if you ponder over the thing.

To get along about the boat: the *LORENA* had triple

tragedy within a short space of time: Capt. George W. Conant died at the wheel of this boat nearing East Liverpool, Oh., in April 1907. Lewis Clark, engineer, dropped dead at the throttle nearing Pittsburgh, January 1908. About this same time Luther Miller, another engineer, also dropped dead on watch. The Old Rule of Three. In later years John W. Rice, long steward on the *LORENA,* dropped dead of heat prostration at his home in Zanesville, July 1914. There was an elderly black chambermaid on the *LORENA* named Eliza who in 1900 was 80, and dated back to the first *EMMA GRAHAM* (see). *LORENA* and *GREENWOOD* (see) were the first packets locked through old Merrill Lock and Dam (No. 6) Aug. 5, 1904. Capt. William Richardson succeeded as master in 1908. The *LORENA* also was first boat through the Taylorsville Lock on the Muskingum in April 1896. In July 1910 she stranded on the bar at Cox's Riffle near Wellsburg, W. Va., and by July 25, was out high and dry. She was not released for some weeks. Sold to the Ohio & Mississippi Navigation Co., John W. Hubbard, pres., in 1912. The great flood of March 1913 ended her trips on the Muskingum. She ran Pittsburgh-Parkersburg, Capt. Henry Kraft, and briefly in 1915 ran Pittsburgh-Cincinnati. Damaged her hull at Possum Bar near Clarington, Oh., mid-1915 and was laid up at Pittsburgh. Capt. Fred Hornbrook bought her early spring 1916, took her to Pt. Pleasant, W. Va., for repairs, and she burned there Groundhog Day, Feb. 2.

The years creep slowly by, Lorena,
  The snow is on the grass again,
The sun's low down the sky, Lorena,
  The frost gleams where the flowers have been:
But the heart beats on as warmly now
  As when the summer days were nigh;
Oh! the sun can never dip so low
  Adown affection's cloudless sky.

3561 LORENE

Stw p wh b. Dubuque, Iowa, 1905. 48.8 x 11.5 x 2.4. Handled an excursion barge on the Upper Mississippi and made trips to the Dales of St. Croix. Single deck, one stack. Burned at Ft. Snelling, Minn., Nov. 23, 1911.

3562 LORNA DOONE

Stw p wh b. Fort Smith, Ark., 1891. 51 x 8 x 2.4. Sank on St. Francis River, Ark., and turned over on her side, late January 1900.

3563 LORNA DOONE

Stw p wh b. St. Paul, Minn., 1895. 64 x 12.3 x 3.5. She was built towboat style and was on the Upper Mississippi. Left St. Louis with a cargo of poultry for Tennessee River, August 1897. Capt. Abbott Veatch was master of her running up Rough River, Ky., March 1898. That September she left Evansville for Red River.

3564 LORRAINE

SW p wh b. Covington, Ky., 1888. 155 x 30 x 4.8. This was the first boat built by the Charles Barnes Co., Cincinnati. Mr. Barnes organized the firm in March 1886, and this boat was his first contract. Built for Capt. Henry Higbee. Still documented at Cincinnati 1896.

3565 LOTAWANNA

Stw p wh b. Marietta, Oh., 1867. 479 tons. 155 x 35 x 5. Engines, 16½'s- 6 ft. Three boilers, each 40" by 24 ft., 4 flues. A cotton style packet designed for 2,200 bales. Built for Capt. H.J. Brinker, and ran New Orleans to Ouachita and Red rivers. Sank and lost at Round's Raft, Red River, Feb. 23, 1874, Capt. John H. White.

3566 LOTTIE

Rig? ferry wh b. Evansville, Ind., 1877. 55 x 16 x 2.3. Still documented at Evansville, 1886, maybe later.

3567 LOTUS

Stw p wh b. Wheeling, Va., 1856. 153 tons. Snagged and lost at Montgomery, La., on Red River, Aug. 18, 1858, Capt. Dowd.

3568 LOTUS

Stw p wh b. Pittsburgh, Pa., 1864. 170 tons. Sold to USQMD, Nov. 28, 1864. Sold at public sale to private owners Oct. 4, 1865 and renamed *MATTIE BURNS* (see). She was at Cincinnati when acquired by the USQMC.

3569 LOTUS

Stw p wh b. Havana, Ill., 1884. 76.5 x 12.1 x 2.9. Originally named *CITY OF HAVANA,* (see). Owned by the Illinois Fish Commission in 1898 and maybe a year or two later. She went to the Ohio River, apparently as a private yacht, documented at Cincinnati 1903, but gone by 1905. Single deck, stage, fancy pilothouse.

3570 LOTUS NO. 2

Stw p wh b. McKeesport, Pa., 1866. 135 x 26 x 4.6. 230 tons. She was loading at Pittsburgh announced for New Orleans, June 23, 1866, with Capt. Shedden, master. Owned at New Orleans by Capt. D.D. Daniels who sold her in 1869 to Capt. Thornton E. Jacobs, New Orleans who in turn sold her May 1870 to J.M. Stone, Mobile. Documented at Apalachicola, Fla., 1896, and dismantled 1897.

3571 LOTUS NO. 3

Stw p wh b. Pittsburgh, Pa., 1869. 160 x 36.5 x 5.2. Built for Capt. D.D. Daniels, New Orleans, replacing *LOTUS NO. 2.* En route from Jefferson, Tex., to New Orleans sank with 1,000 bales on Lake Charles, February 1876. The *COL. A.P. KOUNS* brought 752 of recovered cotton bales to New Orleans. Sank at Waterproof, La., en route to New Orleans with cotton, December 1877, and the U.S. Inspector's report states she burned. There was life loss.

3572 LOTUS SIMS

SW p wh Originally the *KATE ADAMS* (2nd) and then *DEWEY* (both see). *DEWEY* was sold July 1902 to Capt.

Thomas B. Sims, St. Louis. Sims was a Jim Brady diamond-bedecked character who could, and often did, slap big sums of cash on the capstan-head to buy major steamboats. He was owner at various times of the *HILL CITY, DAVID R. POWELL,* and others. She ran St. Louis-Nashville handling corn for I.T. Rhea, and on one trip handled 9,000 sacks. Burned at St. Louis, Oct. 28, 1903. Also just after Sims bought her she ran New Orleans-Vicksburg-Cariola, briefly, Capt. T.B. Sims, master, and George Sims, clerk.

LOU EAVES

See *LUE EAVES.*

3573 LOUCINDA

Stw p wh b. Pt. Pleasant, W. Va., 1910. 158 x 30 x 4.5. Engines, 12's- 6 ft. Two boilers. Built for the Louisville & Cincinnati Packet Co., using engines, etc., from *HELEN M. GOULD* (see). She ran Cincinnati-Madison most of the time. Was chartered in 1914 to the Louisville & Evansville Packet Co., and became stranded high and dry on a sand bar where she remained all summer and fall, not getting off until December. Wrecked at Cincinnati by ice on Jan. 30, 1918. The hull was recovered and the *ANDES* (see) was built on it.

3574 LOUDON

Stw p wh b. Pittsburgh, Pa., 1852. 79 tons. Went to the upper Tennessee River, Capt. Jos. Jacques who afterward became noted in railroad operations. Off the lists 1854.

3575 LOUIS A. SHERLEY

Stw p wh b. Madison, Ind., 1876. 221 x 34.7 x 5.2. Built for the U.S. Mail Line Co., and entered the Cincinnati-Madison trade summer of 1876, Capt. Sam Hildreth, with James Browinski as clerk. Named for son of Capt. Z.M. Sherley who died, 30, several years before the boat was built. By Dec. 13, 1878, she had made 700 trips in the trade, missing only five. The Mail Line placed her in the Pittsburgh-Cincinnati trade later, Capt. James M. Kirker, with Frank Morgan, clerk (1885). Ran Wheeling-Cincinnati spring 1887, Capt. John Brennan, with Charles B. Reeves, clerk. Capt. Tom Hunter became master, 1888, with Mr. Reeves, clerk. Continued Wheeling-Cincinnati with occasional trips to Pittsburgh. Downbound on Sunday, Jan. 19, 1890, got a log in her rudders above the B&O bridge, Parkersburg, and passed under the shore span, Ohio side, which then had an inverted truss. Knocked off the pilothouse, stacks, spars, etc., and landed on the West Virginia shore below. Amos Davis, pilot on watch, sustained injuries and was attended by a Parkersburg physician. She was towed to Cincinnati for repairs by the *W.N. CHANCELLOR* (see). Made her last trip in May 1891, and was taken to Harmar, Oh., and dismantled at the Knox Yard. The hull, etc., was used as a wharfboat at East Liverpool, Oh., owned by Billy Pilgrim. Much equipment went to building her successor, the *SHERLEY* (see).

3576 LOUIS D'OR

SW p wh b. Cincinnati, Oh., 1860. 180.9 x 32.6 x 7.2. 343 tons. Engines, 22's- 5½ ft. Three boilers. First home port, Franklin, La. Capt. Cheney Johnson operated her New Orleans-Red River. Capt. John Smoker bought her in January 1867, dismantled her.

3577 LOUIS MCLANE

SW p wh b. Brownsville, Pa., 1845. 175 x 21 x 4. Engines, 18's- 7½ ft. Three boilers, each 38" by 22 ft. Named for the president of the B&O Railroad. Ran on the Monongahela River, Pittsburgh-Brownsville, Capt. Adam Jacobs. The owners were Capt. Jacobs, James Todd, G.W. Cass, John T. Hogg, Thomas Butcher (all of Brownsville), and King & Holmes, and M.B. Ray & Co., Pittsburgh. Dismantled 1850, and engines went to *DIURNAL* (see).

3578 LOUIS O.

SW ferry wh b. Hudson, Wis., 1909. 65 x 20 x 2.5. Owned by John Tipton. Still there in 1914, maybe later.

3579 LOUISA

Stw p wh b. Paducah, Ky., 1851. 81 tons. First home port, Nashville, Tenn. Snagged and lost at Portsmouth, Oh., June 18, 1857.

3580 LOUISA

SW p wh b. Cincinnati, Oh., 1851. 394 tons. In August 1852 in New Orleans-Grand Gulf trade, Capt. Jackson, in place of *PRINCESS.* In 1855 in New Orleans-Vicksburg trade, Capt. J.M. White, taking place of *NATCHEZ.* Snagged and lost at Harrisonburg, La., Mar. 2, 1855. She was built for and owned by Capt. Franklin Keeling who was master.

3581 LOUISA

SW p wh b. Brownsville, Pa., 1863, originally named *CARRIE JACOBS* (see). During the war was owned by USQMD, and when sold to private hands was renamed *LOUISA,* Sept. 28, 1865. Operated in C.J. Caffrey's "Line," St. Louis-Johnsonville, Tenn. in 1866. In 1869 Capt. Tom Boluss, master with C.H. Crawford, clerk. Off the lists 1870.

3582 LOUISA

SW p wh b. Cairo, Ill., 1864. 209 tons. First home port, St. Louis. 130 x 30. Engines, 12's- 4½ ft. One boiler. Burned at South Point, Mo., on the Missouri River when a cargo of hemp caught fire in the hold. She was scuttled and a rising river ended her, this c. 1868.

3583 LOUISA

Stw p wh b. Quincy, Ill., 1875. 23 tons. 73.5 x 16.6 x 2.8. A short-trader ran Davenport-Buffalo, Iowa trade operated by a Captain Jones, and later was sold to the U.S. Engineers—this may be the one. Still documented at Galena, Ill., 1886.

3584 LOUISA NO. 2

Stw p wh b. Louisa, Ky., 1856. 57 tons. Snagged and lost at Bayou Bartholomew, La., May 1859.

3585 LOUISE

Centerwheel ferry wh b. Sardis, Oh., 1867. 134 tons. 121.7 x 33.5 x 4.6. Operated at New Orleans owned by John Kouns, W.T. Scovell, and R.L. Robertson, Capt. John Kouns, master. Off the lists in 1880.

3586 LOUISE

Stw p wh b. Cincinnati, Oh., 1882. 158 x 28.5 x 5. Engines, 14's- 5 ft. Three boilers. Ran Marietta-Parkersburg-Charleston, Capt. Howard Donnally, with William Armstrong, clerk, this in 1885Collis P. Huntington and party on an inspection tour of the C&O right-of-way from Huntington to Cincinnati; crew at the time, Capt. A.J. McAllister with C.C. Dusenberry, clerk; E.L. Curtis, 2nd clerk; Charles Barton, mate; John Bailey, engineer; John Steel, steward. Owned by the Bay Line she took freight from the sunken *BOONE* (see) at Pine Creek, Oh., in 1888, and took *BOONE*'s place in Cincinnati-Charleston trade, this initiating the Bay operations in that run. Burned and lost at Coal Grove, Oh., Jan. 17, 1893.

3587 LOUISE

Stw p wh b. Covington, Ky., 1890, originally named *HENRIETTA* (see). Operated on Green River, Morgantown-Bowling Green carrying U.S. Mail run by Capt. Bewley, c. 1900-1902. Sold November 1901 to C.D. Dotson, Parkersburg, W. Va. Sold March 1904 to J.L. Cramer, Parkersburg, who transferred her that May to Parkersburg Sand & Dredging Co., David Boyles, agent. Sold June 1905 to Asbury Martin and William C. Mills, Gallipolis, Oh., equal shares. While taking her to Gallipolis she collided with tow of the *IRONSIDES* at Middleport, Oh., and sank. Dismantled shortly thereafter.

3588 LOUISE

Stw p wh b. Parkersburg, W. Va., 1908. 85 x 18 x 3. Built for Capt. Hiram Douglass, Parkersburg, W. Va., and named for his wife. She originally was a gasoline-powered packet and ran Zanesville-McConnelsville on the Muskingum River. Rebuilt at Parkersburg summer 1911, the hull enlarged to 103.6 x 21 x 3 and converted to steam. Ran on the Little Kanawha, Parkersburg-Creston, Capt. Douglass, and sometimes went to Grantsville, W. Va. Tried the Charleston-Montgomery trade, Kanawha River, June 1917, and early 1919 was in Zanesville-McConnelsville trade connecting with *LIBERTY* for Wheeling. Sold July 1920 to Capt. Joe Chotin, Berwick, La., who docked her at Mound City, Ill., and changed name to *JOS. S. CHOTIN,* using her as a towboat.

3589 LOUISE HARVEY

Stw p wh b. New Orleans, La., 1894. 62.2 x 12 x 3.3. Ran New Orleans-Grand Isle-Barataria twice weekly, Capt. H.A. Harvey. There in 1896, maybe later.

3590 LOUISE STECHER

Steam yacht wh b. Judsonia, Ark., 1893. 45 x 8.3 x 3. Still listed, Memphis, 1896.

3591 LOUISIANA

SW p wh b. New Albany, Ind., 1840. 631 tons. 272 x 33 x 9. The largest of her day. Built for Memphis-New Orleans trade owned originally by James H. Leverich and Abijah Fisk, both of New Orleans, Cobb, Bell & Co., Eddyville, Ky., and Jeremiah Echols, Memphis. A steam explosion opposite Baton Rouge killed 23, most of them U.S. soldiers, August 1841. Partly burned Dec. 19, 1842. Collapsed a flue 15 miles above Bayou Sara killing 17, Aug. 12, 1844. Collided with and sank *CITY OF CLARKSVILLE* (see), on Dec. 14, 1844. She was sold to Capt. Joseph H. Lyon who commanded, January 1842. Capt. A.W. Tufts, master, 1846. Capt. P.R. Lott, Jackson County, Ark., bought her entire June 1846. A year later owned by John Jameson and commanded by Capt. Charles H. Moore. Off the lists 1849.

3592 LOUISIANA

SW p wh b. Jeffersonville, Ind., by Howard, 1848. 240 x 31 x 7. Machinery was placed at Cincinnati, using old engines possibly from prior *LOUISIANA*. Owned by Capt. John W. Cannon and others. She was departing at the foot of Gravier St., New Orleans on Nov. 15, 1849, when her boilers exploded killing 86 persons. The boat was demolished and the two packets on either side, *BOSTONA* and *STORM,* also were wrecked.

3593 LOUISIANA

Gunboat wh b. New Orleans, La., 1861-1862. She was built by the Confederacy and resembled an Eads gunboat with sloping sided casemates. She was big—264 ft. long—biggest river gunboat on either side of the fray. Carried two 7″ rifles, seven 6″, three 9″ and four 8″. This made her the most heavily armed gunboat as well. Had two props and also two paddlewheels mounted in a well, one ahead of the other. Engines came from the *INGOMAR* (see). Slow and cumbersome, had to be shoved with aid of two towboats. She was barely completed in April 1862, and served as a floating battery moored near Fort St. Philip during the Battle of New Orleans and was blown up by her own people when the Union fleet won the day.

3594 LOUISIANA

Stw p wh b. Cincinnati, Oh., 1865. She was 203 ft. over all, 40 ft. beam and 7 ft. 2″ depth of hold, same size as *LOUISVILLE,* these two being the longest sternwheelers of their day. Ran Louisville-New Orleans. In 1866 Capt. J.M. Phillips, master with J.A. Lusk, clerk. In 1868, Capt. J.A. Lusk, master, with J.L. Eagon, clerk. Burned at Cairo, Ill., July 1869, along with the *UNDERWRITER* (see).

3595 LOUISIANA

SW ex wh b. Jeffersonville, Ind., by Howard, 1880, originally U.S. Lighthouse tender *JOSEPH HENRY* (see). Sold to private hands, c. 1903, and ran excursions. During the World's Fair at St. Louis in 1904, she ran trips St. Louis-Alton. Operated by Bluff City Excursion Co. In 1906 bought by Capts. Powell, Young, and Patton, Memphis. Renamed *PATTONA* (see) in February 1909.

3596 Louisiana

Stw p wh b. Hastings, Minn. 1901, originally named *J.J. HILL* (see). Ran for a time in the New Orleans-Bayou Sara trade, Capt. Joseph Constantine, this about 1905. Later owned by Merchants Box Co., and Hall Stave Co. She was sold to Evansville, Ind., guards cut down, and ran Evansville-Livermore in 1916 in opposition to the regular line, renamed *GREEN RIVER* (see).

3597 Louisiana

Catamaran ferry sh b. Jeffersonville, Ind., by Howard, 1926. 144.5 x 55 x 9.3. Owned by Baton Rouge Transportation Co. She was rebuilt by Avondale at New Orleans in 1969, and converted to twin-prop diesel, owned by Plaquemines Parish Commission Council, Pointe-a-la-Hache, La.

3598 Louisiana Belle

Stw p wh b. Cincinnati, Oh., 1859. 103 x 24 x 4. Owned by Capt. George Alexander who commanded, New Orleans-Bayou Lafourche. Sold November 1863 to Jules Lepene and Desire Boyer, New Orleans, equal shares. Reported destroyed in a wharf fire at New Orleans, May 28, 1864, in which nine steamers were burned.

3599 Louisville

SW p wh b. Louisville, Ky., 1844. 295 tons. 176 x 26 x 6.8. Ran Louisville-New Orleans, Capt. Thomas C. Coleman. He retired from the river and ran a rolling mill at Louisville, and his son ran the *SALADIN* (see). Also in 1845, Capt. J. Miller was master in New Orleans-Nashville trade. In 1848 her Louisville ownership ended when sold to Robert Murphy and John Hughes, New Orleans. The Independent Towboat Co., of that city bought her June 1848, Capt. William Long, master. Sold October 1850 to Jean Martial Lapeyre, New Orleans, Capt. J.M. McPherson, master. In September 1852 Capt. Thomas McLellan came aboard as master and eventually owned the boat almost entire. Off the lists 1857.

3600 Louisville

Stw p wh b. Brownsville, Pa., 1854. 155 tons. 153 x 30 x 4. Built light draft for a "summer boat" by William Dean and was said to have had a "phenomenally successful career." She was on the upper Illinois River spring of 1861. Last documentation that year.

3601 Louisville

SW p wh b. New Albany, Ind., 1861. 572 tons. 220 x 38 x 8. Engines, 28's- 7½ ft. Five boilers. Machinery said to have come from the *KATE FRISBEE* (see). Came out new in the New Orleans-Louisville trade, Capt. Hollcroft, Feb. 9, 1861. Captured by U.S. forces as a Confederate steamer July 13, 1863, on Yazoo River. Refitted into a U.S. gunboat named *OUACHITA*. At war's conclusion sold to Daniel T. Head, New Orleans, and Capt. John W. Tobin was master, now renamed *VICKSBURG* (see).

3602 Louisville

U.S. gunboat wh b. St. Louis, Mo., 1861. She was one of the Eads' gunboats. 176.8 x 52.0 x 6.6. Engines, 22's- 6 ft. Capt. Robert K. Riley, later well known as an Anchor Line master, served on her, as did Capt. William R. Hoel, who took her past batteries at Island 10. Sold at U.S. sale, Mound City, Ill., Nov. 29, 1865, to D. Jacobs for $3,600.

3603 Louisville

Stw p wh b. Wheeling, W. Va., 1863. 288 tons. 180 x 33. Engines, 14's- 4 ft. Two boilers. Reported sold to Capt. David White in March 1864, for $42,000. She started up the Missouri River for the Yellowstone region and was snagged at Pratt's Cut Off (later known as Louisville Bend) between Sioux City and Fort Randall, Capt. Abe Wolf, master. She gradually sank in the mud, the stacks fell over, and the cabin floated off. Freight was lost. The accident happened in latter May, 1864.

3604 Louisville

Stw p wh b. Cincinnati, Oh., 1866. 200 x 42.5 x 7. Engines, 22's- 6 ft. Three boilers each 42" by 28 ft. Paddlewheel 24 ft. dia., working 30 ft. buckets. This boat and the *LOUISIANA* were the longest sternwheelers of the time. Original owners were B.F. Davidson and F.M. Davidson, Newport, Ky. (one-half) and Godfrey Waterhoff, Cincinnati. Capt. A.Q. Ross commanded in the Louisville-New Orleans trade. Alex F. Powers bought interest and went head clerk in 1871. Sold by U.S. marshal at Covington, Ky., Jan. 4, 1875, to Capt. Powers (or Power) who sold her latter July, 1876, to Capt. J.D. Hegler and others. Dismantled 1876. The machinery, etc., went to the *GOLDEN CITY*.

3605 Louisville Drummer

Stw p wh b. New Albany, Ind., 1875. 19 tons. Probably towed produce boats, etc. Registered 1876, maybe later.

3606 Low Water

Stw p wh b. St. Louis, Mo., 1856. 177 tons. Sank from unknown cause at Mills Landing, Mo., on the Missouri River, Nov. 27, 1857.

3607 Low Water

Rig? wh Isaac York and Wm. J. Bell, Evansville, Ind., were partners until June 1871, when Bell became owner entire. Snagged on the St. Francis River below Madison, Ark., with 250 bales of cotton aboard, Mar. 7, 1877.

3608 Lowell

SW p wh b. Jeffersonville, Ind., 1839. 159 tons. First home port, Apalachicola, Fla. Built for Harry T. Hall, Columbus, Ga., and was taken to the Chattahoochee River under her own steam. Sank and lost below Fort Gaines, Fla., in 1845.

3609 Lowell

Stw p wh b. Brownsville, Pa., 1849. 124 tons. 142 x 24 x 4.5. Hartupee engines. Ran Pittsburgh-Zanesville, Capt.

Henry T. Dexter. On Mar. 24, 1851, collided with *S.F. VINTON* at Captina Island, Ohio River, sank in 30 seconds. Cabin parted from the hull. The crew of the *VINTON* rescued the survivors. The *MESSENGER NO. 2,* Capt. Fisher, took her Cincinnati passengers. Fifteen lives were lost.

3610 LOWNDES

SW p wh b. New Albany, Ind., 1844. 229 tons. Apparently went to Mobile.

3611 LOWNDES JR.

SW p wh b. New Albany, Ind., 1847. 267 tons. Built for Mobile, Ala., parties. Ran out of New Orleans to Grand Lake and Lake Providence in 1851, Capt. Andy Johnston. Dismantled 1852.

3612 LOYALHANNA

Stw p wh b. Elizabethtown, Pa., 1847. 120 tons. Noted principally for having towed the Spaulding & Rogers' Floating Theater in summer of 1851. Sank that fall and *JENNY LIND* was procured as a replacement.

3613 LUCIE MAY

Stw p wh b. West Brownsville, Pa., 1855. 172 tons. Ran St. Louis-St. Paul. Capt. J.B. Rhodes was master 1858–1859. Lost in collision with *CEDAR RAPIDS* near La Grange, Mo., on the night of May 14, 1859. Three deckhands were drowned.

3614 LUCILE

Stw p wh b. Campti, La., 1904, originally named *ANNIE P* (see). Renamed following a rebuilding at Vicksburg, Miss., spring 1909. The Pugh Line ran her in Yazoo River. Sank in the Yazoo, May 24, 1912. Raised, rebuilt, and became a small towboat named *EUTAW.*

3615 LUCILE BORDEN

Stw p wh b. Knoxville, Tenn., 1890. 86 x 14 x 2.5. Owned by Florence Packet Co., and ran Florence-Georgetown Landing. Exploded her boiler at Knoxville in early May 1899. The Alabama Stave Co., bought her, and sold her to Capt. Tom Reeder in August 1902. Name was then changed to *J. T. REEDER* (see).

3616 LUCILLE NOWLAND

Stw p wh b. Brownsville, Pa., Axton yard, 1898. 170 x 33 x 5. Engines, 12's- 5 ft. Two boilers, each 44" by 20 ft. Much equipment from *EUGENE* (see) used in construction. Built for the Memphis & Arkansas River Packet Co. Had cotton guards. In fall of 1901 they ran her Memphis-Vicksburg, Capt. Matt Downs, with James N. Thompson, purser; Clarence Hodge and Rees V. Downs, pilots. Sam G. Smith was her clerk in 1906. Capt. Martin F. Noll became owner in May 1910, and she was taken to Parkersburg, W. Va., and altered into an upper Ohio packet. Entered Pittsburgh-Cincinnati trade July 1910, Capt. J.D. Robinson, and low water laid her up the first trip. Came out again December 1910, Capt. Charles W. Knox, master, and ran through spring and early summer 1911. Was first boat locked at Dam 11, Ohio River, July 1911. Came out again in October 1911, but within a month was sent south to run Cairo-Caruthersville, then Evansville-Nashville. Burned off her upper works at Evansville December 1911 and in March 1912 was towed to Jeffersonville, Ind., where she was rebuilt at the Howard Yard for Capt. Fred Hornbrook who renamed her *ABIGAIL* (see).

3617 LUCRETIA

Prop p wh b. New Albany, Ind., 1866. 428 tons. 177.6 x 30 x 5. Built for the Morgan Line, New York City, and owned by Charles Morgan. Ran New Orleans-Mobile, freight only, Capt. John Davis, with W.T. Mayberry, clerk. Rebuilt at New Orleans, fall 1870, to become 181.8 x 30.5 x 6.2. Had a long career and was scrapped in 1889.

3618 LUCY BELL

SW p wh b. New Albany, Ind., 1853. 170 tons. Went to Mobile, Ala. Last documents date 1859.

3619 LUCY BERTRAM

SW p wh b. St. Louis, Mo., 1847. 268 tons. 198 x 38 x 5. Three boilers. Owned by the St. Louis & Keokuk Packet Co. Burned at St. Louis, Jan. 18, 1853.

3620 LUCY BERTRAM

SW p wh b. Madison, Ind., 1863. 698 tons. 242.1 x 40.5 x 5.5. Engines, 24's- 7 ft. Three boilers, each 46" by 24 ft., 2 flues. Owned by the St. Louis & Keokuk Packet Co. Capt. H.W. Browlaski, Jr., was master in 1864 and part of 1865, succeeded in the fall of 1865 by Capt. William H. Laughton. Capt. David R. Asbury was master several seasons. In 1872 Capt. J.L. Thompson was master with George G. Walton, clerk; James Henry Harris, chief engineer. A new hull was built for her in 1867, and she was dismantled in 1876, the hull used as a barge.

3621 LUCY COKER

Stw p wh b. Knoxville, Tenn., 1869. 138 tons. Capt. W.C. Henegar went to Washington, D.C., called on U.S. President Grant, and got a mail contract on the upper Tennessee for this boat. She was taken over for a while by Hinds Bros., who had a mail contract. This was not so profitable so she was resold, and the machinery, etc., went to building the *CHATTANOOGA* (see).

3622 LUCY E. GASTRELL

Rig? p wh b. Cincinnati, Oh., 1878. 197.6 x 30.4 x 4.6. Left Cincinnati on Christmas Day, 1878, for New Orleans, Capt. J.C. Aust, having been built for the Vidalia & Western Railroad Co. Went to Mobile and was inspected there through 1882.

3623 LUCY GWIN

Stw p wh b. Freedom, Pa., 1859. 152 tons. Departed new from Pittsburgh in November 1859, Capt. Andrew K. McKee, and was taken to the Brazos and Trinity rivers in Texas. Capt. McKee had taken the *ALLEGHENY BELLE*

NO. 3 (see) to Mexico earlier that year. She went to Confederate registry 1861.

3624 LUCY HOLCOMBE

SW p wh b. Louisville, Ky., 1858. 440 tons. 198 x 35 x 6.7. Owned in New Orleans by John W. Langdon, Robert Moody and E. Mason. She ran New Orleans-Shreveport, Capt. William D. Bateman, and was "summer boat" in the Vicksburg trade in place of the *VICKSBURG,* Capt. J.M. White. Sold October 1858, to Richard England, New Orleans and ran New Orleans-Vicksburg with off-season trips to St. Louis. Burned and lost one mile below Helena, Ark., Nov. 11, 1859. The new *EMMA C. ELLIOTT* (see) hit the wreck in December 1871 and broke many hull timbers.

3625 LUCY HOPKINS

SW p wh b. Cincinnati, Oh., 1867. 270 tons. 159 x 36 x 6. Engines, 22's- 7 ft. Ran New Orleans-Upper Coast, also on Red River. Dismantled August 1875, and machinery went to the *ASSUMPTION* (see).

3626 LUCY LEE

Rig? ferry wh b. Grafton, Ill., 1870. 46 tons. Owned 1874 by John and John H. Burress. Still registered 1876, maybe later.

3627 LUCY MCCONNELL

SW ferry wh b. Jeffersonville, Ind., by Howard, 1852. 70 tons. 100 x 28 x 4.5. Snagged and lost at Mt. Carmel, Ill., Mar. 6, 1855.

3628 LUCY ROBINSON

SW p wh b. New Albany, Ind., 1851. 239 tons. 121 x 26.7 x 5.6. Built for Capt. C.J. Puckette and others, Natchitoches, La. She was sold in 1854 to a stock company of New Albany, Ind., persons, Capt. Solomon Malbon. Master in 1857, Capt. Robert S. Livingston. Dismantled in 1859. There was a two-masted schooner of Somerset, Mass., carrying the same name, built also 1851.

3629 LUCY WALKER

SW p wh b. Cincinnati, Oh., 1843. 182 tons. Joe Vann was a Cherokee of Webber Falls on the upper Arkansas River, quite well to do. He acquired the famed racehorse Lucy Walker, considered the fastest quarter-mile horse in the world. This Joe Vann built the steamboat *LUCY WALKER* to run Webber Falls-Louisville, Ky. He procured Capt. Halderman as master for the first trip, then took charge personally for the second. It was on this second trip that the boilers exploded below New Albany, Ind., with loss of 18 lives. Date was Oct. 25, 1844. Joe Vann's remains never were found. Eight of the unidentified were buried in Fairview Cemetery near New Albany.

3630 LUCY WING

SW p wh b. Rumsey, Ky., 1846. 59 tons. She was snagged and lost on the Ouachita River, Jan. 24, 1850.

3631 LUDA

SW p wh b. Cincinnati, Oh., 1844. 286 tons. 176.5 x 25 x 6.6. Owned in part by Capt. Thomas Clark, Iberville Parish, La., who was master. Off the lists 1850.

3632 LUDA

Stw p wh b. Louisville, Ky., 1851. 93 tons. 98 x 22 x 4.7. She operated out of Memphis until sold April 1854 to Richard Walsh, Shreveport, La. Capt. H.G. Sumner, master. Snagged and lost on Red River, Feb. 20, 1855.

3633 LUDLOW

Stw p wh b. Cincinnati, Oh., 1847. 76 tons. Ran Pittsburgh-Zanesville, Capt. Sol Scott until lost in collision with the *ALLEGHENY CLIPPER* (see) at Pittsburgh, Oct. 10, 1849, with loss of two lives.

3634 LUE EAVES

SW p wh b. Evansville, Ind., 1859. 80 tons. Ran Evansville-Green River. Sold to USQMD in 1862, and became tinclad #76 and patrolled the Green River. The Rebels were throwing rock into the upper approach at the Spottsville lock and had effectively blocked it before the *EAVES* arrived. Name sometimes spelled *LOU EAVES.* Off the lists 1867.

3635 LUELLA

Stw p wh b. Freedom, Pa., 1850. 122 tons. Owned by Capt. Wm. J. Kountz and others. She was lost on White River, Ark., in collision with the *JESSE LAZEAR,* Sept. 17, 1855.

3636 LUELLA

Stw p wh b. Nashville, Tenn., 1851. 162 tons. Ran Galena-St. Paul, Capt. D. Smith Harris, 1852. Same trade, Capt. Sam Harlow, 1856. Capt. Joseph Brown, St. Louis, had an interest in her. He recalled that her engines came from a New Orleans boat, too large for the *LUELLA,* but this caused her to be speedy. Off the lists 1856.

3637 LUELLA

Stw ferry wh b. New Haven, Mo., 1860. 135 tons. There was a *LUELLA* sunk in the Yazoo Pass expedition during the war, possibly her.

3638 LUELLA

Stw p wh b. Pittsburgh, Pa., 1866. 258 tons. Built for Capt. H.K. Hazlett and others. She was new at Pittsburgh January 1866, advertising for Nashville. She made three trips to Fort Benton, Mont., and was known as the "treasure ship of the Montana gold rush." In the late fall of 1866 she loaded aboard two-and-one-half tons of gold dust at Fort Benton, Capt. Grant Marsh, having been brought from the Last Chance mines. She also brought 230 miners down at $300 apiece, fare to St. Louis. Captain Hazlett was at the fort with her in 1867, making the trip direct from Pittsburgh. Capt. William J. Kountz had interest in her. Dismantled at Pittsburgh early 1868.

3639 LUELLA

Stw p wh b. Mason City, W. Va., 1875. 105 x 18 x 3. She ran

Syracuse-Gallipolis daily, Capt. M.H. Brown with M.E. Brown, clerk. During the Brown ownership they once had her in the Cairo-Paducah trade in opposition to the Fowler Line. They sold her February 1881 to Capt. C.H. Crow, Capt. W.H. McKay and W.W. Hayman for $5,000. These gentlemen put her in the Ravenswood-Middleport trade. Still documented 1888.

3640 LUELLA BROWN

Stw p wh b. Murraysville, W. Va. (hull), and completed at Wheeling, 1890. 128 x 22.3 x 4.5. Engines, 11's- 4 ft. Two boilers, each 42" by 18 ft. Owned originally by Capt. A.H. (Dick) Brown, Gallipolis, Oh., and named for his sister. Ran local trades out of Gallipolis briefly, then Cairo-Paducah, and by 1902 was owned by the Lyon brothers, Greenville, Miss. They ran her Greenville-Luna, Ark., Capt. William Lyon (Lyons?), master. Still documented 1908.

3641 LULA D.

Stw p wh b. Evansville, Ind., 1867. 245 tons. 135 x 35.3 x 4.9. Engines, 13's- 4½ ft. Two boilers. Owned by William Durbridge, New Orleans. Capt. John M. Grace, master. She was making trips to Shreveport early as February 1868. Went to Brownsville, Tex.

3642 LULA E. WARREN

Stw p wh b. Johnsonville, Tenn., 1896. 122 x 22.5 x 3.2. Engines, 8½'s- 4 ft. Two boilers, each 32" by 14 ft. Built for Capt. Henry E. Warren by Capt. Welton, father of Capt. Peter I. Welton to replace the *WYANDOT* (see) in Duck River trade. Capt. Warren soon died whereupon the boat was sold to a Capt. John Barnes who removed the upper cabin and used her for towing cross ties out of Duck River, this in September 1902. Later sold to Capt. J.L. Kilgour who, in 1906, sold her to Dayton Coal & Iron Co. She still was in "fair condition" as of April 1911.

3643 LULA PRINCE

Stw p wh b. Brownsville, Pa., 1891. 142.5 x 28.2 x 4.2. Ran Natchez-Bayou Sara owned by Capt. Thomas Prince, R.F. Learned, and others, three round trips a week. Sank in the spring of 1897 and was towed by the *ALICE BROWN* to Madison, Ind., for a complete rebuilding. In later years commanded by Capt. Charles Pfaffenbach who had been her first clerk prior. She sank at 3:00 P.M., May 18, 1899 at Fish Pond Landing, lower Mississippi. The tugs *LIZZIE B* and *THOMAS HEIDEL* came to assist but were too late. The *BETSY ANN* made her maiden trip in the trade that same week.

3644 LUMINARY

SW p wh b. Cincinnati, Oh., 1863. 260 x 42 x 7. Engines, 25's- 8 ft. Four boilers, each 44" by 26 ft. 1,023 tons. She carried troops and supplies for the U.S. during the war. On Apr. 2, 1863, came to the rescue of tinclad #19 (see *ST. CLAIR*) above Fort Donelson where Rebels had attacked. Ran St. Louis-New Orleans in the Atlantic & Mississippi Steamship Co., 1865, and was in the Anchor Line after that, Capt. William Blake. In latter January 1867 was ice-bound at Hat Island, aground, in precarious shape along with *ENTERPRISE, ANNA WHITE* and *W.B. DANCE*. Took survivors from the wrecked *CLERMONT* at Helena, Ark., Mar. 8, 1867. Snagged and lost at Montezuma, 10 miles below Helena, Ark., Dec. 18, 1869. The hull was recovered and taken to Jeffersonville, Ind., repaired, and sent to Hickman, Ky., as a wharfboat 1870.

3645 LUNA

SW p wh b. New Albany, Ind., 1846. 321 tons. 207.5 x 26.5 x 6. Built at Dowerman & Humphrey yard for the New Orleans-Upper Bends trade owned by a stock company of New Orleans' gentleman, Capt. N.S. Waring, master. Capt. Jesse Hart was master, and then Capt. Charles H. Fairchild. Quite successful. Sold October 1849 to Capt. Bird L. Elliott, Louisville, Ky. While downbound in vicinity of Donaldsonville, La., she was rammed by the *DUCHESS* on May 17, 1850, and went down with loss of five lives.

3646 LUNA

SW p wh b. New Albany, Ind., 1864. 561 tons. Belonged to the Atlantic & Mississippi Steamship Co., Capt. Patrick Yore. Burned at St. Louis along with the *LEVIATHAN* and *DICTATOR* on Feb. 26, 1866.

3647 LUNA

Originally named *BIG-A-PLENTY* on upper Red River. Repaired at New Orleans, November 1900 and renamed. Sank December 1901, 15 miles above Shreveport, La., with 62 bales and 1,500 sacks of seed.

3648 LUNETTE

SW p wh b. McKeesport, Pa., 1852. 166 tons. Built for and operated by Capt. John B. Davis, Pittsburgh. She was loading at St. Louis for the Upper Mississippi on Oct. 13, 1853, when she was burned along with the *MONTAUK* and *ROBERT CAMPBELL*.

3649 LURA

Rig? p wh b. Rodney, Miss., 1873. 61 x 13 x 5. Advertised at New Orleans 1885, three trips weekly to Lower Coast. Cheap excursion charter. Still listed 1886, maybe longer.

3650 LUZERNE

SW p wh b. Brownsville, Pa., 1852. 180 tons. Ran on the Monongahela River, Pittsburgh-Brownsville, Capt. Elisha Bennett. Was at Manchester, Pa. (North Side, Pittsburgh), when *GREAT WEST* and *ARCTIC* burned July 1, 1858, but was saved by firemen. Lost in ice at Crawfords Landing, Mississippi River, Jan. 28, 1864.

3651 LYDE H.

Stw p wh b. Brownsville, Pa. at Axton yard, 1892. 116 x 22.8 x 3.5. Engines, 10's- 4 ft. Two boilers, each 42" by 16 ft. Built for Capt. Dode Berry, Williamstown, W. Va., and named for Lyde Heatherington, Bellaire. Came out single deck. Went to U.S. marshal sale in August 1894, and sold to Capt. John Hyer who ran her Parkersburg-Long Bottom, and to Marietta twice weekly. About 1896-1897 sold to Capt. J. Mack Gamble, Clarington, Oh., who added a cabin and boiler deck. He sold her to Capt. Thad Thomas, George and A.W. Urpman, who ran her Wheeling-Clarington. Her pilot was Earn Clark who had been to Evansville and knew the *JEWEL* down there (see), and he persuaded the owners to rename her *JEWEL* (also see).

3652 LYDA CROSS

Rig? ferry wh b. Racine, Oh., 1871. 27 tons. Was the ferry at Racine to Graham Station, W. Va. Still listed 1876, maybe later.

3653 LYDIA COLLINS

Stw p wh b. Elizabeth, Pa., 1849. 147 tons. Snagged and lost at Belpre, Oh., Dec. 10, 1851.

3654 LYNX

SW p wh b. Cincinnati, Oh., 1844. 124 tons. Ran on the Upper Mississippi, Galena-St. Peters, Capt. W.H. Hooper (1844) and Capt. Atchison later. She was first through the ice at Lake Pepin, 1846. Sank at the head of Atlas Island, Clarksville, Mo., 1849.

3655 LYONS CITY

SW ferry wh b. Lyons, Iowa, 1864. 142 tons. Regularly inspected until dismantled in 1884.

M

3656 M. A. BURKE

Stw p wh b. Jeffersonville, Ind., by Howard, 1910, originally named *J. H. MENGE* (see). In July 1916 the *J. H. MENGE* was sold to Capt. Owen F. Burke, Mobile, who renamed her, and ran her Mobile-Alabama-Tombigbee Rivers. Sold to steamboat broker John F. Klein in 1919. Ran New Orleans-Vicksburg briefly, and left New Orleans May 2, 1919, headed north. Lay at Mound City, Ill., all that summer, sold to the Louisville & Cincinnati Packet Co. She was entered in the L&C trade Oct. 28, 1919, still the *M.A. BURKE,* cotton guards and all. She was altered to become an Ohio River packet and in February 1920 was renamed *JOHN W. HUBBARD* (see).

3657 M. A. GRACE

Stw p wh Originally *R. DUNBAR,* then *GENERAL CROWDER* (both see). Capt. William F. Bradford, New Orleans, bought the *CROWDER* at Wheeling, W. Va., in 1926, took her under her own steam to Slidell, La., where she was repaired at the Canulette yard. Renamed *M.A. GRACE,* she burned there at Slidell, February 1927.

3658 M. B. HAMER

SW p wh b. Cincinnati, Oh., 1844. 198 tons. Ran New Orleans-Yazoo River, Capt. P.C. Wallace. Off the lists 1849.

3659 M. D. SHANNON

Catamaran ferry wh b. Morgan City, La., 1919. 101.3 x 36 x 4.9. Owned by Morgan City-Berwick Ferry Co. In the 1926 hurricane she was damaged when blown into the S.P. railroad bridge at Morgan City. Operated in 1927 by Capt. John R. Drackett.

3660 M.E. ALLEN

SW p wh b. Paducah, Ky., 1861. 198 tons. 137.8 x 28.3 x 5.7. Owned by Capt. Joseph Boisseau, Shreveport, La., who was master. Went to Confederate registry.

3661 M. G. GOBLE

Stw p wh b. Pittsburgh, Pa., 1885, originally *VENUS* (see). Turned over and sank at Catlettsburg, Ky., and exploded just before she went down, drowning two, March 1904.

3662 M. G. KNOX

Stw p wh b. Harmar, Oh., at Knox Yard, 1881. 110 x 18 x 3. Built for Capt. Dode Berry, Williamstown, W. Va. Sold uncompleted to Morris and Prince, Wheeling, who took her there to receive machinery and outfit. Sold to Pittsburgh, May 7, 1885, and name changed to *TILLIE* (see).

3663 M. J. WICKES

Stw p wh b. Jeffersonville, Ind., 1870. 210 x 45 x 7.5. She was the largest sternwheeler of her day, built for the St. Louis-Memphis trade. She and the *CHAS. B. CHURCH* (see) ran the trade spring of 1870, got into financial troubles, and were tied up by a U.S. Marshal. In mid-August there was a sale at Memphis and both were bid in by Capt. Charles B. Church. Sold summer 1872 to Mississippi Valley Transportation Co., who planned to use the hull for a barge.

M. L. DOUGHERTY

See *MARY L. DOUGHERTY.*

3664 M. P. WELLS

Stw p wh b. Belle Vernon, Pa., 1888. 126.6 x 24 x 3. Engines, 10″- 4 ft. One boiler. Built for Capt. William E. Roe and M. Richter. Named for a Marietta person who lived on Second Street in the 300 block. The two cast-iron lions at the entrance of the courthouse in Marietta came from the Wells's premises. She originally was single deck, and soon was sold to the Brown family, Hartford, W. Va., who ran her Gallipolis-New Haven. Sold 1889 to Capt. George W. Edgington, Augusta, Ky., who ran her Vanceburg-Augusta with Fred Edgington, clerk. Acquired by the Greene Line, Cincinnati, 1904 who rebuilt her into the *CHILO* (see) in 1905.

3665 M. S. MEPHAM

SW p wh b. Elizabeth, Pa., 1864. 683 tons. 236 x 38 (35 ft. floor) x 7.5. Engines, 23½'s- 8 ft. Four boilers, each 40″ by 26 ft. Paddlewheels 30 ft. diameter, working 12½ ft. buckets, 26″ dip. William Latta built the hull, and machinery by James Rees. She was a "no expense spared" boat designed for the St. Louis-Leavenworth trade up Missouri River, Capt. A.A. Shaw. She had a Chickering grand piano of such consequence it was displayed in the C.C. Mellor music store, Pittsburgh, prior to going aboard. Oil paintings over the office and on each stateroom door were the talent of Mat M. Hastings, St. Louis. A large spread eagle adorned the pilothouse-top carved by T.G. Bering, Philadelphia. Chinaware came from Landon & White, New York, each piece done in buffet and gold. Silverware from Rogers & Smith, New York. Rugs, carpeting, bedspreads, sheets and blankets came from A.T. Stewart, New York. Bridal chamber was 16 by 8 ft., two rooms connected by folding doors, mahogany bedsteads, etc. Andrew Ackley superintended the outfitting. She was visited by throngs of people at Pittsburgh and Cincinnati enroute to St. Louis. Ran in the Leavenworth trade until mid-summer 1864, Capt. A.A. Shaw, with Jewett Wilcox, clerk. Ran St. Louis-New Orleans 1865 with Capt. A. St. Clair Thomasson, and John Bird, clerk. Was advertised 1867 as a regular Louisville-New Orleans packet. Burned at St. Louis, Mar. 2, 1868, foot of Carr Street. The *FANNIE SCOTT* also was badly singed. Both were owned by M.S. Mepham & Bro., St. Louis.

3666 M. S. Thanhouser

Stw p wh b. Harmar, Oh., 1875. 133 tons. 120 x 19 x 3.5. Ran Wheeling-Clarington, fall 1875, Capt. Steve Thompson, with C.E. Booth, clerk. She once towed produce boats south from Marietta to Vicksburg, Miss., and amongst her crew was Gordon C. Greene, founder of the Greene Line, Cincinnati. This was his only voyage down the Mississippi. She returned towing a circus. Advertised for sale at Reedsville, Oh., September 1877, owned by Sheperd and Humphrey.

3667 M. T. Bryan

Stw p wh b. Chamberlain, S.D., 1903, originally named *J.H. KEENE,* then *GROS VENTRE,* and was gasoline powered. She was bought by Capt. W.L. Berry and others, Paducah, and rebuilt there into a steamboat, renamed to honor the president of the Cumberland River Improvement Association. Mr. Bryan also was vice-president and general manager of the L&N Railroad. She hauled corn from Wabash River to Nashville, Capt. David Martin, with Billy R. Smith and Tim Armstrong, pilots. Burned Oct. 5, 1922, at Eddyville, Cumberland River.

3668 M. V. Reid

Stw ferry wh b. Chattanooga, Tenn., 1882. 65 x 29 x 3.4. Still listed 1896, maybe later in *Lists of Merchant Vessels.*

3669 M. W. Kelly

Stw p wh b. Jeffersonville, Ind., by Howard, 1900. 140 x 32 x 4. Two boilers. Went to Chattahoochee River. Sank several times in her career, finally at the Columbus, Ga., wharf in 1906 where she was dismantled and parts used building the *CITY OF EUFALA.*

3670 M. Livingston

SW p wh b. Paducah, Ky., 1875. 44 tons. 120 x 20. Engines, 11½ - 4½ ft. Two boilers. Sunk in ice at Running Water, S.D., on the Missouri River, early spring 1878. Again sunk in ice on the Missouri, dismantled, and machinery went to *ANDREW S. BENNETT* (see) in 1880.

3671 Mabel Comeaux

Stw p wh b. Cincinnati, Oh., 1883. 145.2 x 29.8 x 5.8. The hull and cabin framing was built on the wharf at New Richmond, Oh., same time the *TACOMA* (see) was built. She ran New Orleans-Upper Coast-Bayou Lafourche, Capt. E.J. Comeaux, with T.K. Voorhees, clerk. She was dismantled and the hull became a wharfboat at Tell City, Ind., and was there in 1894.

3672 Mabel Comeaux

Stw p wh b. Jeffersonville, Ind., by Howard, 1891. 178 x 36 x 6.5. Engines, 18's- 6 ft. Three boilers, each 42" by 26 ft. Owned by Capt. E.J. Comeaux. Ran New Orleans-Donaldsonville-New Hope, T.K. Voorhees, clerk. By 1902 was running New Orleans-Bayou Lafourche, Capt. E.J. Comeaux, with J.V. LeBlanc, clerk. She was eventually laid up at McDonoughville above Coyle's coal yard. Was caught out there and went over on her side. Dismantled in 1909. Known as the "Fair Mabel."

3673 Madge

Prop launch sh b. Charleston, W. Va., 1897. 65.4 x 10.4 x 3.1. Used as a private yacht by Charles Ward of the Ward Engineering Works, Charleston. He sold her, 1903, to the Vicksburg District, U.S. Engineers who renamed her *OUCHITA.* Later they converted her to gasoline. Was still in their fleet 1918, maybe later.

3674 Madison

SW p wh b. Memphis, Tenn., 1852. 168 tons. 118 x 26 x 6. Went to New Orleans, owned by John J. Kercheval. Sold January 1855 to Capt. W.H. Toomer, Mobile. Back in New Orleans March 1856, owned by J.E. Caldwell & Co. Sold that fall to Amite Pressed Brick Co., New Orleans. Owned in 1857 by Capt. William H. Merritt, Madisonville, La. Lost in collision with *IOWA,* Aurora, Ind., Jan. 3, 1859.

3675 Madison

SW p wh b. Cincinnati, Oh., 1853. 399 tons. Owned originally by H.A. Jones and Thomas Sherlock, Cincinnati, and Capt. Jesse Y. Hurd, Portsmouth, Oh. Came out with but half a cabin which later was extended. Captain Hurd was on her the first three seasons, Cincinnati-St. Louis and elsewhere. Capt. George D. Hoople took charge and she ran Cincinnati-New Orleans eight years. During the war she transported supplies for the U.S. up Cumberland and Tennessee rivers. Capt. Ben F. Davidson acquired her for the Cincinnati-New Orleans trade, Capt. James Chenowith, master. There was a U.S. Marshal sale and she went to George L. Johnson & Co., Cincinnati, who had not owned her long when she sank at Poverty Point, above Vicksburg, latter May 1866, upbound. Burned and lost at Gretna, La., Aug. 6, 1866. Her engines were said to have originated on the *METAMORA* (1844) and then on *CHARLES HAMMOND* (1847) (both see).

3676 MADISON

SW p wh b. New Albany, Ind., 1855. 99 tons. Went to Cedar Keys, Fla. Lost 1859.

3677 MADISON

Stw p wh b. Keokuk, Iowa, 1862, originally named *GENERAL HALLECK* (see). The *HALLECK* burned at Memphis, Feb. 5, 1866, was rebuilt and renamed. Ran Memphis-Hatchie River. Ran afoul of an old cylinder lying on the Memphis wharf and sank on it, early March 1866.

3678 MADISON

Stw ferry wh b. Jeffersonville, Ind., by Howard, 1892. 157.4 x 45.4 x 6.1. She was a centerwheel ferry owned by Madison County (Ill.) Ferry Co. Still listed 1908, maybe later.

3679 MADISON NO. 2

Recess ferry wh b. St. Louis, Mo., 1864. 167 tons. First documented in March 1866. Off the lists 1868.

3680 MADISON BELLE

SW p wh b. Madison, Ind., 1847. 169 tons. Snagged and lost on Salt River, Ky., March 19, 1851.

3681 MADONNA

SW p wh b. Louisville, Ky., 1852. 94 tons. Lost in ice at Covington, Ky., Feb. 24, 1856.

3682 MAGENTA

SW p wh b. New Albany, Ind. at Dowerman & Humphrey yard, 1861. 782 tons. 265 x 40 x 8.5. Engines, 30's- 10 ft. Eight boilers, each 40" by 30 ft. Owned in equal shares by Capt. Richard Holmas and William C. Wilson. Ran New Orleans-Vicksburg, and in off seasons ran to Louisville, Capt. Harry I. Spotts. She was taken up Yazoo River when the war broke out, about 70 miles above Greenwood, Miss., ran into the woods, disabled herself, and burned, this on July 14, 1863.

3683 MAGENTA

SW p wh b. Mound City, Ill., 1863. 424 tons. 215 x 35. Engines, 20½'s- 6½ ft. Two boilers. Built for the Missouri River, owned by F.M. Dozier, C.C. Chouteau, Ben Johnson, and Frank Constant. Snagged and lost in the bend below De Witt, Mo., May 22, 1863.

3684 MAGENTA

SW p wh b. New Albany, Ind., 1864. 848 tons. 288.5 x 40.7 x 7.5. She was said to have had the engines from the *ALVIN ADAMS* (see) built at Brownsville, Pa., by John Snowden & Sons. She was built by Capt. J.B. Ford who sold her at the New Albany shipyard to Capt. David White and others, New Orleans. Left Louisville June 25, 1864, for the south, to enter the New Orleans-Vicksburg trade. Sold November 1865 to Capt. Thomas P. Leathers (5/8) with White remaining as a minority owner. In January 1866 Leathers and Capt. John W. Cannon became equal shareholders, each 5/24. She was placed in the Memphis-New Orleans trade in 1868, with Capt. J. Frank Hicks, master. By December 1869 Hicks owned 10/24 and her tonnage had been increased to 1380 tons. Leathers now was out of her, the other owners being John C. Sinnott, John S. Stout (Cannon's brother-in-law), and John S. Sullivan, Memphis. By 1870 Sinnott had control (15/24), and Capt. J. Stut Neal was her master. At 6:30 A.M., Sunday, Jan. 1, 1871, she burned at New Orleans. Also consumed were the *JULIA A. RUDOLPH, GRAND ERA,* and *THOMPSON DEAN.* A peculiar sidelight to her story is that she came near being named *J.M. WHITE,* the wish of Capt. David White. He applied for the name change at St. Louis in 1864 and ran into legal complications which resulted in the change being denied.

3685 MAGGIE

Rig? ferry wh b. Steubenville, Oh., 1879. 79 x 17 x 4.5. Still documented 1886, maybe later.

3686 MAGGIE

Stw p wh b. Yazoo City, Miss., 1894. 85 x 19 x 3.5. Ran Vicksburg, Sunflower, and Yazoo rivers. Sank Mar. 2, 1903 at Simmons Landing on the Yazoo after striking a snag. Her clerk, J.H. Thompson, was drowned. Rebuilt with but one stack after this sinking, and was lost May 1, 1907, following an accident above Greenwood, Miss.

3687 MAGGIE BELLE

Stw p wh b. Madison, Ind., 1884. 95.6 x 18.4 x 3.6. Ran Alton-Troy trade, lower Ohio, owned by a Capt. Williams and son. She was registered at Paducah 1896. Her cabin is said to have wound up on the *MARY WOODS,* a towboat built 1926 at Paducah.

3688 MAGGIE F. BURKE

Stw p wh b. Jeffersonville, Ind., at Barmore yard, 1878. 176 x 35 x 5.7. Built for Capt. Owen Finnegan who took her to Mobile, Ala. Still there in 1886, maybe later.

3689 MAGGIE HARPER

Stw p wh b. Madison, Ind., 1877. 133 x 32.8 x 5. Ran Louisville-Madison, Capt. Sam Fearn, with Nick Durand, pilot. Machinery came from the *DOVE NO. 2* (see). Everything went along swimmingly until the *MINNIE BAY* came there as an opposition packet making daily round trips. Captain Fearn was building the *FANNIE FEARN* at the time (1886) to replace the *HARPER,* but as matters turned out the *MINNIE BAY* soon had it all, and Fearn sold the *FEARN* (see) to the Chattahoochee River and got rid of the *HARPER.*

3690 MAGGIE HAYS

Stw p wh b. West Brownsville, Pa., 1864. 301 tons. 160 x 34

Photographer not known.

U.S. tinclad **NYMPH** (#4251) in Civil War service. These so-called tinclads, this one built from a packet, retained many packet characteristics. The main, or lower, deck was protected with heavy lumber and iron plating. The pilot looked from narrow slits. The second deck (called the boiler deck in river parlance although it never had a boiler on it) was completely vulnerable, and it was here that the crew slept and ate, and where meals were prepared and served. The second small building on the skylight roof aft of the pilothouse is a chicken coop. It was much simpler to keep poultry on the hoof. The identification of these tinclads in old photographs was something of a puzzle, until many years ago we contacted Capt. Dudley W. Knox, USN (Ret.), officer in charge of Naval Records and Library, Washington. He dug into sources and obliged us with a list identifying the assigned number with the boat's original name.

Taken by commercial photographers Fontayne & Porter, Cincinnati. Copy courtesy of Public Library of Cincinnati and Hamilton County (Ohio).

We have selected this section of the famed Fontayne & Porter daguerreotype, a panorama of Cincinnati, eight plates in all, made in the fall of 1848, inasmuch as two very new packets appear in the foreground, the **EMBASSY** (#1800) and **CAR OF COMMERCE** (#0844). The EMBASSY apparently was not documented until early in 1849, but here she is, sporting a texas, the upper cabin structure upon which the pilothouse rests. This feature had been adopted only a few years before, added to house the boats' officers. Steamboat staterooms were so-called inasmuch as each room was named for a state. When Texas was admitted in 1845 this officer's quarters, adopted about that time, was dubbed "the texas." Note how very little ostentation is visible on these two packets. The day of fancy frills was just dawning. The line of buildings in the right foreground was known as Cassilly's Row. The white awning was known as No. 4, where steamboat agents Irwin & Foster held forth, and where Stephen Collins Foster worked for a time.

Thornton Barrette, photographer.

The **LITTLE QUEEN** (#3513) typifies the daily short-trade packets which connected many river communities before modern highways were built. These single-deckers carried passengers and freight on the main deck with a closed cabin amidships for inclement weather. No sleeping quarters were provided and very little in the way of meals. The captain and crew knew most of the folks in the territory and every farm had a road that led to the river. The wave of a handkerchief was sufficient to attract the pilot's attention, and he answered the hail with a short toot of the whistle. Planks bridged from the boat's forecastle to the farm landing, and most of the ladies and girls were adept at springing across these limber boards. Thirty or forty such stops were often made in the course of a trip.

Photographer not known.

The **ROBERT BURNS** (#4774) typified the "canal" packets, built to fit the locks in the Louisville-Portland canal as she plied between Cincinnati and Memphis. Triple locks, each 183 ft. by 50 ft., overcame a fall of 24 feet around the Louisville Falls, often called the Falls of the Ohio. Larger boats were restricted to navigating over the Falls, both up and down, during periods when freshets "drowned out" the rocks, employing a special Falls pilot. Note the ostentation of this packet as compared to the **CAR OF COMMERCE** and **EMBASSY** in this series. The picture was taken at Memphis when the ROBERT BURNS was fairly new, possibly 1864.

Thornton Barrette, photographer. Print courtesy of Capt. William S. Pollock, Beaver, Pa.

The **QUEEN CITY** (#4615) was the superlative of a fleet of sternwheel packets in the Pittsburgh-Cincinnati trade on the Ohio River in the 1880-1910 period, each making a weekly round trip. The downbound freight traffic was mainly iron and steel products from many independently owned mils in the Pittsburgh area. Much of such tonnage was destined south and west of Cincinnati, reshipped to destination on packets operated to Memphis and New Orleans, and also by rail to Oklahoma and other mid-continent supply centers. The owners of the QUEEN CITY held a virtual monopoly on this freight trade, and also catered to tourists attracted by good food, music, and rather posh surroundings, pampered by uniformed officers.

Photographer not known.

This "batwing" type of steamer was developed to handle traffic into the remote areas of tributary streams. Here is the **THEALKA** (#5355) moored at a Big Sandy River landing in Kentucky, engaged in hauling freight and passengers from Ashland and Catlettsburg on the Ohio River to Louisa (27 miles) and then 88.5 more miles up Levisa Fork to Pikeville, Ky. All surplus weight was dispensed with to keep her afloat, including the paddlewheel housings. Navigation was restricted to three or four months a year, usually in the winter and early spring when the rains came.

Taken by a Mr. Hard who operated a floating photo gallery on the Kanawha River out of St. Albans, W. Va. c. 1882.

Built for the Gallipolis-Huntington trade (40 miles) on the Ohio River, the **B. T. ENOS** (#0425) was typical of the short-trader designed to handle passengers in some comfort, as well as local freight. Very few of the towns in those 40 miles had wharfboats to land against, most of the business being transacted by poling the boat's head into shore and lowering the swinging stage. In the period of her operation, the 1890s, the Baltimore & Ohio Railroad paralleled the West Virginia side. There was no rail service on the Ohio side (still true today), and there were no improved highways on either side. Built light, and narrow of beam, such short-traders did not carry a ''texas'', considering it a wind-catcher.

Photograph believed to have been taken by J. Mack Moore, commerical photographer.

Capt. L. V. Cooley's **AMERICA** (#0240) was typical of the cotton-style sternwheelers inhabiting the lower Mississippi and its tributaries. The cabin structure was somewhat narrowed, and the main deck guards were extended fore and aft so's cotton could be tiered from one end to the other, and across the forecastle, giving the boat the appearance of one huge cotton bale. New Orleans was the outlet for both foreign and domestic cotton. An interesting letter detailing the *modus operandi* of bringing cotton down the Mississippi may be found in these pages following the description of the **THOMPSON DEAN** (#5380).

Photographer not known.

The ''racer'' **NATCHEZ** (#4109) was posed for this photograph early in her career. This is the way she looked as she raced from New Orleans to St. Louis in 1870 trying to overtake the victorious **ROB'T E. LEE** (#4777). In preparing for the race her swinging stages were unshipped and left ashore on the New Orleans levee. Her high smokestacks, aside from artistic effect, were beneficial in aiding natural draught for the furnace fires, and also carried away alive sparks. High winds or gales occasionally toppled such high stacks overboard.

Photographer not known.

Side-wheel packets such as the **ADAM JACOBS** (#0059) predominated on the Monongahela River from Pittsburgh to Brownsville, Morgantown and Fairmont. The size of these boats was restricted to rather small lock dimensions. Many low bridges required that the smokestacks be prepared for tilting back, and the JACOBS is fitted with an A-frame rig for the purpose, called the "telegraph plan" or "telegraphing the stacks" inasmuch as the invention was first adopted on the side-wheel **TELEGRAPH** (#5323) to negotiate the Wheeling suspension bridge.

Photographer not known.

Photographed at Yankton, South Dakota, on the Missouri River, are two "mountain boats," sternwheelers designed to carry maximum freight cargoes on minimum water stages. Scores of these specialized craft plied between St. Louis and Fort Benton, Montana. The wood hulls were full-bodied clear to the stem, giving the bow a sort of bulbous appearance. Elaborate sets of derricks and spars on the forecastle served to lift the boats over numerous shifting sandbars. Frequent stops were made to procure wood to fire the boilers. Living conditions were primitive but comfortable. Profits were high and the risks were great. On the left is the **WESTERN** (#5752) and on the outside is the **E. H. DURFEE** (#1646).

Thornton Barrette, photographer.

The sternwheel ferry **PROCTOR K. SMILEY** (#4600) is seen plying across the Ohio River with Ripley Oh. in the background. She made connections with the Chesapeake & Ohio Railroad at Ripley Station, Ky. Ferries of this type required landing floats at both shores to load and unload wagons and cars. Many of them had pilothouse control to the engines, complete with throttle valve and reverse lever. The fireman, without much undue exertion, doubled as toll collector and handled the lines.

Photographer not known.

The **FAR WEST** (#2012) became the most famed of the Missouri River ''mountain boats'' when in 1876 she brought the wounded from the Custer Massacre from Little Big Horn River to Fort Lincoln, 710 miles. Over the years of her operation the boat had various structural changes, but this is how she looked at the time of the exploit. Note the piles of firewood fore and aft of the boilers on the main deck.

Photo by Henry C. Norman, Natchez, Miss.

The St. Louis & New Orleans Anchor Line thrived with a fleet of many look-alike side-wheelers, this one being the **CITY OF VICKSBURG** (#1142). Practically all of them were built at the famed Howard Ship Yard at Jeffersonville, Ind. Trademark of the fleet was a huge gilded anchor slung between the smokestacks. The snag-infested Mississippi River claimed an unfair share of these floating palaces, but high profits permitted constant replacements until they were outmoded by barge competition and superior rail service.

Photographer not known. Made from a glass plate prepared by Capt. Sam G. Smith, St. Louis.

This dramatically posed picture was taken of the Anchor Line's side-wheel **CITY OF ST. LOUIS** (#1130) plying the St. Louis-New Orleans trade on the Mississippi. Passenger revenue formed an important part of the profit, and great exertion was made by the management and crews to set a table worthy of leading hotels, keep the boat spotless, and to entertain the guests. The Anchor Line is generally credited with having introduced formal uniforms for its officers. Many residents of smaller river towns carried to their graves the impression that Anchor Line packets were the most sublime creations of mankind, and anyone who had poked his nose in the cabin doorway and had seen that entire length of elegance, could command an attentive audience as he told of it.

Photo by Capt. Anthony Meldahl.

At Cincinnati a large amusement center and park had sprung up called Coney Island (although not on an island) about eight miles above town bordering on the Ohio River. A summertime steamboat shuttle service provided transportation to and from, serviced by packets idled by low water from plying their usual trades. The Coney Island people in 1896 built the **ISLAND QUEEN** (#2799) primarily for this park service with a hardwood-floored grand ballroom running the length of the second deck, refreshment stands, orchestra and calliope. She was the darling of Cincinnati and the sensation of the rivers. A second **ISLAND QUEEN** (#2800) replaced her in 1925, equally popular.

Photographer not known.

The racer **ROB'T E. LEE** (#4777) as she looked at the time of her celebrated race with the **NATCHEZ** (#4109) in 1870 is seen here moored at Cairo, Ill. As sometimes happens at Cairo a fast rise in the Mississippi has reversed the current in the Ohio River causing it to flow upstream, explaining why the LEE and **GREAT REPUBLIC** (#2438) are moored in this unusual position, headed downstream. The fancy feathers sprouting from the LEE's stack-tops are fashioned on the pattern of oak leaves. Oak timber was used to construct steamboat hulls, highly regarded for strength and durability. Symbolic of security, the oak acorn was widely adopted as ornamentation. Lathe-turned acorns, pod painted red and berry gold-leafed, graced the tops of steamboat flagpoles, davits, masts and booms.

Marked at lower left of the picture, "Edwards, Photographer."

The levee at New Orleans photographed during Mark Twain's career as a river pilot, taken in 1859. Steamboats were wedged in head-on sometimes extending many city blocks, accepting and discharging freight and passengers. Most of those in this scene are fairly local, advertising for points on the Yazoo, Red, Ouachita and Black rivers. Starting at the right: **COL. T. H. JUDSON** (#1232), **LECOMPTE** (#3400), **MILTON RELF** (#3934), **DR. BUFFINGTON** (#1574), **STARLIGHT** (#5181) and the **MESSENGER** (#3906), the latter having a gilded ball surmounted by an eagle on the pilothouse-top. The outbreak of fire amid such tinder and tinsel all too often resulted in the mass destruction of many such steamboats.

Photographer not known.

The U.S. gunboat **CAIRO** (#0793) was posed for this portrait with crew assembled, ready for Civil War service. A total of seven of this style were built in a crash program, and all seven rendered great service to the Union cause. The CAIRO was the first of these so-called ''Pook turtles'' to be lost, on December 12, 1862. She was torpedoed in the Yazoo River. In 1961, almost one hundred years later, the wreck was located and, in 1964, was brought to the surface badly decomposed and damaged. As this account is written in 1983 the old gunboat is being reconstructed at Vicksburg, Miss. for permanent preservation. A wealth of artifacts found on board will be displayed.

Photo by the author, F. Way, Jr.

The **LIBERTY** (#3454), upon her retirement in 1937, was the last of the manually-steered packets. Your scribe stood many watches in her pilothouse, long enough to develop an admiration for the ease of hand-steering with a large pilotwheel. The LIBERTY had proper rudders, the forward and after blades balanced to prefection, so's the movement of only a spoke or so kept her on course. Steam steering was introduced along in the 1890s wherein the pilot spun the wheel by pushing a lever from side to side, the lever connected by rods to a steam cylinder which actuated the tillers. This, of course, was a vast improvement.

From the collection of photographer J. Mack Moore.

Taken early in 1883 at Vicksburg, Miss., this photograph graphically conveys in interesting detail the scope of river activity. The **WILL S. HAYS** (#5795), smoking at the left, is in the Cincinnati-New Orleans trade, and the high stacks of the **ED RICHARDSON** (#1706) dominate the scene at top center. In the foreground is the small cotton packet **LE FLORE** (#3393) just in from the Yazoo River. At the right, moored below the wharfboat, is the **SALLIE CARNEY** (#4979) with the P between her stacks, emblem of the Parisot Line. In the background, from the left, are the **CLARA S.** (#1165), **DEER CREEK** (#1481), ferryboat **AGLIA** (#0085) and the **HELEN MEAD,** a towboat.

Photographer not known.

The **PELICAN** (#4437) was typical of the railroad transfers operated at many points before the rivers were bridged. In this picture, taken at Helena, Ark., freight cars are being taken up the incline by a hard-puffing engine. On these extremely wide transfers, the boiler plants for each engine were independent of one another and, inasmuch as the engines also were independently operated, each watch required double crews of engineers and firemen. The 'scapement of steam from the high pressure engines on a still night as these behomoths crossed from shore to shore could be heard for miles.

Photographed by Capt. C. C. Bowyer.

The U.S. gunboat **TYLER** (#5481) was one of the first to be commissioned at the commencement of the Civil War, converted from what had been the side-wheel packet **A. O. TYLER** (#0024) in the Cincinnati-New Orleans trade. She was made ready for combat in the fall of 1861 and first served in the engagements at Belmont, Mo. and at Hickman and Columbus, Mo. In February 1862 she and the **LEXINGTON** (#3445) explored up the Tennessee River causing the Confederates to burn a number of steamboats to prevent their capture. She served during the engagements at Fort Henry on the Tennessee, and Fort Donelson on the Cumberland. She threw shells into the Confederate lines during the Battle of Shiloh. In January 1863 she took part in the ill-fated Steele's Bayou operation in the attempt to get behind Vicksburg. Her last engagement with the enemy was on June 24, 1864 on the White River in Arkansas. She was fired upon from shore while acting as a convoy assisting nine transports out of that stream.

Photographer not known; from collection of Capt. Sam G. Smith.

The **LAURANCE** (#3381) ferried between Maysville, Ky. and Aberdeen, Oh. on the Ohio River, typical of the recess or bootjack style sternwheeler. In this view she is departing from Maysville, rounding out below three concrete ice piers. Such piers were installed to afford protection to wooden boats and barges during ice runouts. This recess style not only protected the paddlewheel from drift and ice, but permitted twin rudders to be placed aft of the wheel, of considerable aid in steering and handling.

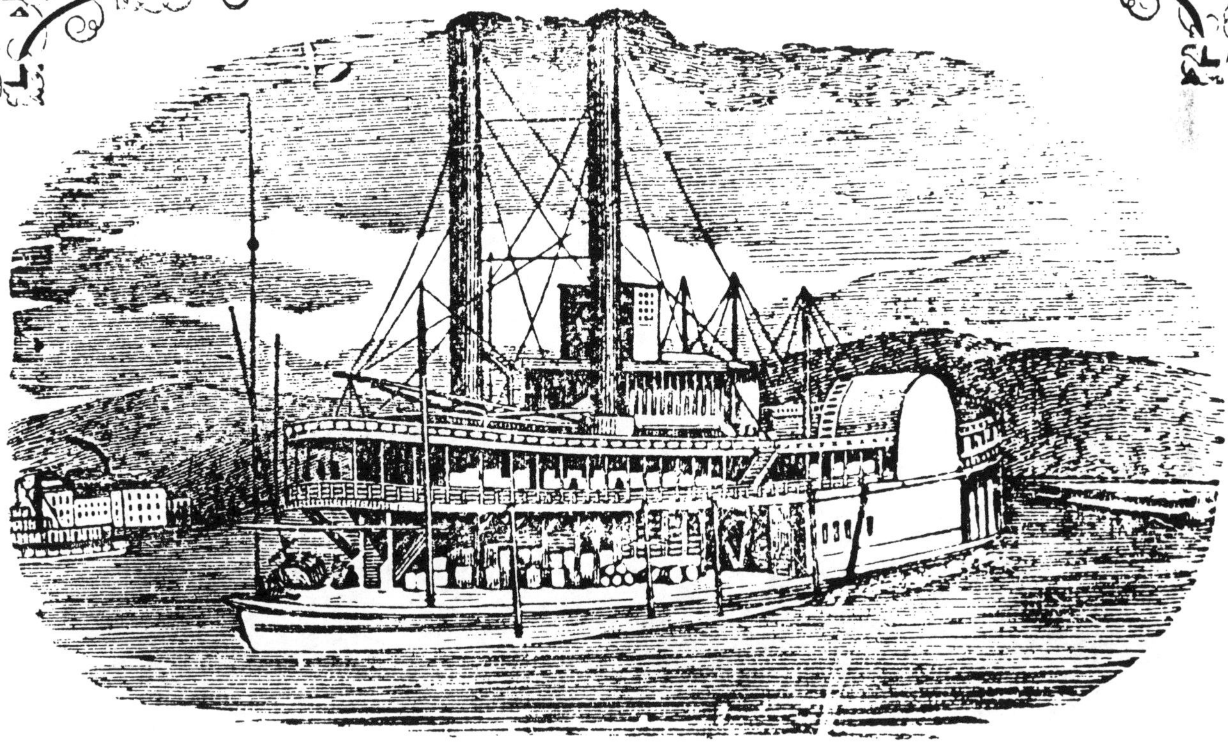

BUCKEYE STATE—#0728—This drawing depicts the boat passing Belpre, Oh. at 5:11 a.m., May 2, 1850, 24 hours out of Cincinnati on her famed ''fast trip'' to Pittsburgh. No photograph of the boat is known to exist but the artist almost surely worked from a daguerreotype; the construction details match those of the Thomas Tredgold plans published in London in 1851.

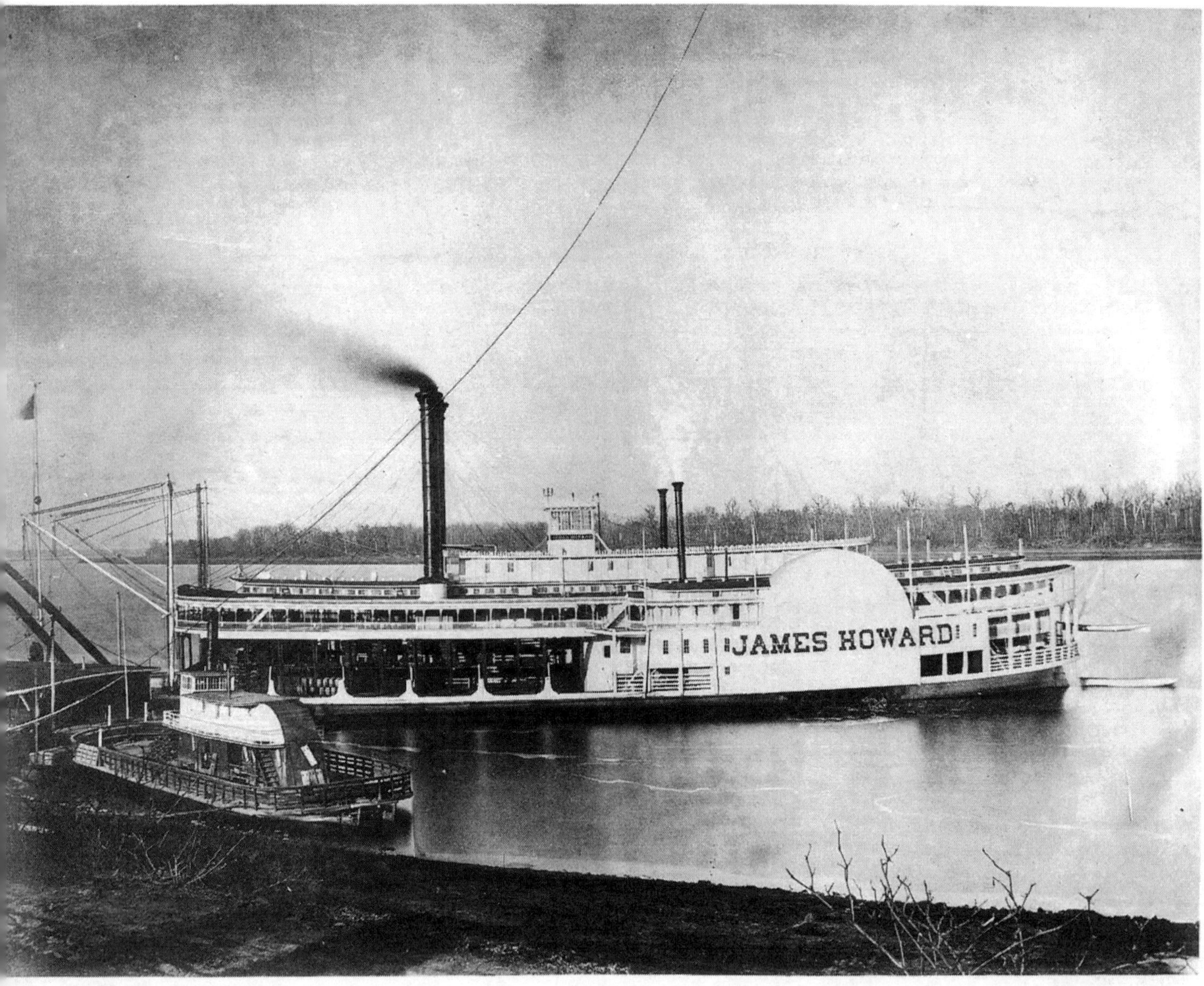

Photo at Cairo, Ill., 1871, from collection of Wm. H. Tippitt.

The **JAMES HOWARD** (#2930) was one of the very grand class of packets built for the New Orleans-St. Louis trade in the first decade after the Civil War. Cotton ruled the economy of the lower valley and boats such as this were designed to carry the crop to the New Orleans market, upwards of 8,000 bales per trip. Size and ostentatious decor in the cabins also attracted the wealthy planters as passengers and at 320 feet in length the **JAMES HOWARD** was one of the largest.

In the left foreground is **NEBRASKA CITY NO. 2** (#4129) an example of a centerwheel ferry. The design was called a "bootjack" on the river because of the shape of the hull, forked toward the stern to accommodate the center-mounted paddlewheel.

THE PILOT HOUSE OF THE "GREAT REPUBLIC."

PILOTHOUSE INTERIOR of the GREAT REPUBLIC—#2438—The original of this engraving appeared in Scribner's Monthly, issue of October 1874. All of the usual haberdashery is there; bell pulls, speaking tubes, etc. The pilot habitually stood at one side or the other of the immense pilotwheel, never at the center. The globular affair on the jackstaff out forward is the nighthawk, used to determine by dark the horizon line in the distance, particularly useful on the Mississippi with its low banks.

Photo by Kay Chandler, Photographer, McConnelsville, Ohio.

Small boats designed for rivers with small locks still followed the typical packet design as witness the **LORENA** (#3560) which operated on the Muskingum River. She had to fit locks 159 feet long by 35.5 feet wide to negotiate the 75 miles from the Ohio River at Marietta to Zanesville, Ohio. The builders contrived with sheer, curves and a modicum of fancywork to produce a boat with good proportions and style. Typical of Muskingum River boats is the cross-braced gate in the boiler deck railing to give access to the lock walls. The **LORENA** ran a round-trip a week in the Zanesville-Pittsburgh trade, here seen when new at the Third Street landing, McConnelsville, Ohio with Malta across the river.

Photographer unknown. From the Murphy Library collection.

Mark Twain described the steamboat cabin: "Inside, a far receding cabin, porcelain knob and oil picture on every stateroom door; curving patterns of filagree-work touched up with gilding, stretching overhead all down the converging vista; big chandeliers every little way, each an April shower of glittering glass drops; lovely rainbow light falling everywhere from the colored glazing of the skylights; the whole a long-drawn resplendent tunnel, a bewildering and soul-satisfying spectacle!" This is the cabin of the **RICHMOND** (#4753) from the Ladies Cabin (no unaccompanied gentlemen allowed) with its upholstered chairs and grand piano looking toward the water cooler and double front doors at the far end. This "resplendent tunnel" was 304 feet long, 13½ feet high with 70 elegant staterooms opening through the doors on either side. Specially designed Brussels carpet covers the floor and chandeliers with oil lamps hang from the ceiling. A waiter stands by the set officers' table just at the edge of the Ladies Cabin.

Photographer unknown. From the Murphy Library collection.

As the trades dwindled in the early 20th century a number of the packets were converted into excursion boats. Streckfus Steamers, St. Louis, was the notable and successful operator of excursion boats up and down the Mississippi and Ohio rivers in the first half of the 20th century. Their **CAPITOL** (#0834) is a good example: A dancefloor has replaced the cabins in the former **DUBUQUE** (#1616) and the outside decoration includes a lattice valance below and a sunshade above the boiler deck, fancy railings and large puddings on the stacks. A calliope, a dixieland band and the promise of cool breezes on the river invited the multitudes until World War II.

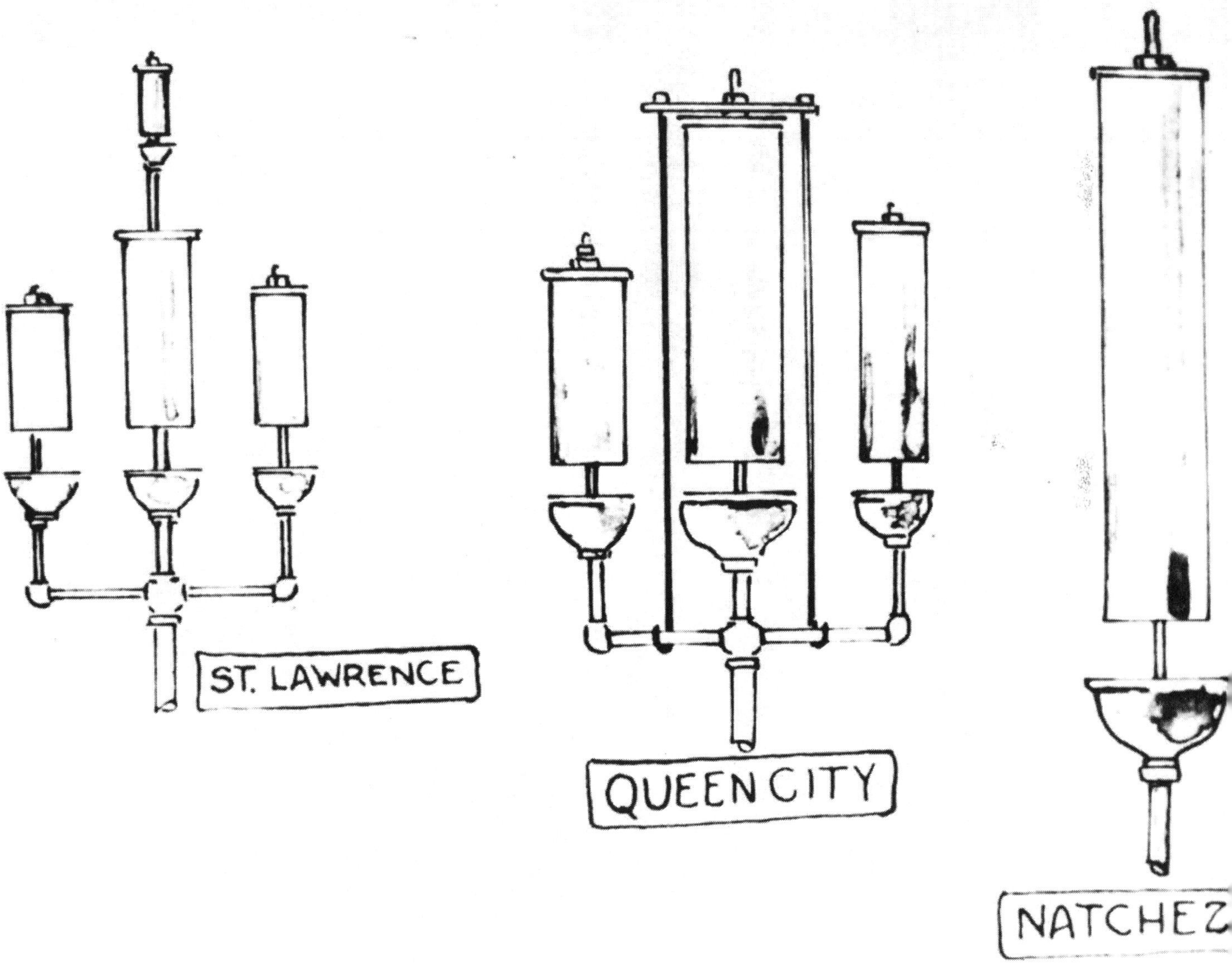

Drawings by Frederick Way, Jr.

STEAMBOAT WHISTLES—Wide variety in the styling is evidenced in these from the *St. Lawrence* (#4945), *Queen City* (#4615), and the "racer" *Natchez* (#4109). The voice of a steamboat was its whistle, although the instrument was a relatively late arrival on the scene, the first one having been used on the *Revenue* (#4741) in 1844.

STEAMBOAT ENGINE—The usual high pressure engine of a sternwheel steamboat, port side, looking aft. This shows the overhead levers, poppet valves, and "outside" cams. The steam-exhaust line (foreground) and the main steam line (aft) apparently are wrapped in metal casing for insulation, a practice which dates back into the 1880s—apparently before asbestos wrapping.

x 5.5. Engines by Rees, 16's- 5 ft. Three boilers, each 38" by 24 ft. Built for Capt. D.L. Hendrickson who was master. Left Pittsburgh June 16, 1864 on her first trip to St. Louis. On May 30, 1867, Capt. Hendrickson sold his interest to James Rees. Although usually in the St. Louis trade, she departed Pittsburgh Jan. 5, 1870, for New Orleans with a big freight trip and towing the model barge *MONARCH,* also loaded. Capt. Barney C. Martin, Sistersville, W. Va., was master. She delivered her trip and was upbound for Pittsburgh when her boilers exploded at Island 66 near Helena, Ark., on Feb. 10, 1870, at 2:30 P.M. Captain Martin was on the roof, seated on the stack shears, and was severely injured. The *COMMERCIAL,* Capt. Matt Glass, rendered aid and brought survivors to Memphis. Captain Martin died enroute. James Dravo, first clerk, had left the boat at New Orleans and had gone by rail to Memphis. James Rees, Jr., second clerk, was slightly scalded. Second engineer, Henry McDermott, died. In all there were six deaths. Pilots Eugene Hammond and Samuel P. Jones survived. Clerk Rees' married daughter Mrs. Doer and her sister-in-law Mrs. Sedam escaped injury. The boat was owned by James Rees (¾) and Benjamin Coursin at time of loss.

3691 MAGGIE P.

Stw p wh b. New Orleans, La., 1869. 53 tons. 84.4 x 19.5 x 4.1. Built for Charles C. Pickett and first master was Capt. John M. Pickett. Sold 1870 to John M. Avery, Iberia Parish. Sold to St. Louis, largely owned by F.M. Briggs, Capt. C.S. Ebaugh, master. Ran St. Louis-Illinois River. Still listed 1886.

3692 MAGGIE PADEN

Stw ferry wh b. Ironton, Oh., 1877. 95.7 x 27 x 4.2. Operated Parkersburg-Belpre many years owned by the Padens and Capt. Shaw. She was cut down by ice at Parkersburg, Jan. 9, 1896. Replaced by the *NINA PADEN* (see).

3693 MAGGIE RANEY

Stw p wh b. Hudson, Wis., 1877. 148 tons. 128.5 x 25 x 4.5. Came originally from Lake St. Croix where she was a packet. Was within five miles of Wapello, Iowa, on the Iowa River in 1882 and again in 1883 bringing out oats and pork, Capt. Thomas Peel. Ran Clinton-Davenport trade, Capt. James Eldridge, frequently towing a barge. Broke down above the Davenport bridge one night, drifted back, hit a pier, turned turtle, and drowned several.

3694 MAGNOLIA

SW p wh b. Cincinnati, Oh., 1845. 596 tons. 274 x 35 (floor 31) x 9. Engines, 31's- 10 ft. Six boilers, each 42" by 30 ft., two 16" flues. Owned by Mary A. Schute and Maria Schute of New York City. Capt. St. Clair Thomasson, master. Ran New Orleans-Vicksburg, and in off seasons to St. Louis and Louisville. "A magnificent boat, well appointed in all respects. It was the fashionable boat of the day, and a great favorite with the ladies and bridal parties. The fashionable crowd seen aboard of her nearly every trip would rival those to be seen at the best watering places. Music and dancing, card playing and flirting would fill up the joyous hours aboard of her." Capt. St. Clair Thomasson was French, very polite and attentive when in a good humor, but highly excitable and would storm and swear when agitated. He specialized in French dishes until the crew paled of such delicacy: a passenger became sick one day and the clerk of the boat consoled him saying, "It's them damn French ducks, and I have to eat them every day." She came in collision with the *AUTOCRAT* at Bayou Goula, La., Feb. 10, 1851, sinking the latter (see). The *MAGNOLIA* was downbound at the time enroute to New Orleans with many notables to hear Jenny Lind, Col. Nicholas D. Coleman and three daughters among them—he later was president of the Vicksburg, Shreveport, and Texas Railroad. Also aboard was a fake count who deceived all and lived high in Vicksburg until exposed. Burned and lost at Baton Rouge, La., July 8, 1855, with loss of eight lives.

3695 MAGNOLIA

SW p wh b. West Elizabeth, Pa., 1850. 160 tons. First home port, Galveston, Tex. A wire from Louisville to the editor of the Pittsburgh *Chronicle* reported her loss below Natchez in a storm, Jan. 13, 1851.

3696 MAGNOLIA

SW p wh b. Jeffersonville, Ind., by Howard, 1852. 325 tons. 180 x 31 x 7.5. Went to Mobile, Ala. Off the lists 1867.

3697 MAGNOLIA

Stw p wh b. Freedom, Pa., 1853. 120 tons. Sank and lost at Shippingport, Ky., Apr. 24, 1856.

3698 MAGNOLIA

SW p wh b. Cincinnati, Oh., 1859. 375 tons. 200 x 31 x 5.5. Engines, 22's- 6 ft. Three boilers, each 46" by 24 ft., 5 flues. Built for Capt. James H. Prather who commanded. Ran Cincinnati-Maysville. Upbound, Mar. 18, 1868, she had landed at California, Oh., and was leaving the landing when the boilers exploded with loss of 35 lives. The towboat *PANTHER* came to assist. The burning wreck floated to Columbia before sinking. Captain Prather's body was never found.

3699 MAGNOLIA

SW p wh b. New Albany, Ind., 1859. 824 tons. 258 x 44 x 7.5. Engines, 28's- 7½ ft. Five boilers, each 45" by 26 ft. Owned by the estate of Maria L. Schute, Theodore Schute, executor, New Orleans, and Mary A. Schute, New York City, equal shares. Capt. J.D. Phelps, master. The boat was, strictly speaking, a cotton and freight boat—she had no passenger cabin although she had a few rooms available. Her largest cotton trip was 6,536 bales on one trip in 1859. John W. Bryant, later the river editor of the New Orleans *Times-Democrat* was clerk on her at the time. She was first to the scene of the *ALFRED T. LACY* disaster (see) at Island 16 on Apr. 26, 1860. Her owners in January 1861 were

William Charles Wilson (¼), Capt. Truman Cook Holmes (¼), Estate of Maria L. Schute (½). Capt. J.D. Phelps still commanded. At the outbreak of the war she was taken up Yazoo River and burned to prevent capture, July 14, 1863.

3700 MAGNOLIA

Prop freight boat wh b. Berlin, Oh., 1865. 73 tons. This sounds like a canalboat and probably towed produce south. First home port, Cairo, Ill. Off the lists 1873.

3701 MAGNOLIA

SW p wh b. St. Louis, Mo., 1865. 1255 tons. The hull was built at the Alph Cutting yard, Metropolis, Ill. Completed above Eads Bridge, St. Louis. Engines, 34½'s- 9 ft. Had an octagonal pilothouse. Ran St. Louis-New Orleans and burned at St. Louis June 13, 1866, just one year old. One heavy loser was George C. Wolfe who had paid $10,000 for the bar privileges for the lifetime of the boat.

3702 MAGNOLIA

SW ferry wh b. Parkersburg, W. Va., 1867. 50 tons. Operated Parkersburg-Belpre until she was capsized in a windstorm. Replaced by the *MAGGIE PADEN* (see).

3703 MAGNOLIA BANNER

Rig? p wh b. Louisville, Ky., 1855. 159 tons. New Orleans-Red River, Capt. Leonard.

3704 MAGYAR

SW p wh b. Smithland, Ky., 1849. 135 tons. First home port, Nashville, Tenn. Exploded and lost 35 miles east of Galveston, Tex., Jan. 4, 1854.

3705 MAID OF PERU

SW p wh b. Peru, Ill., 1865. 37 tons. She was sunk by the *ROBT. E. LEE* in the spring of 1867, on the lower Mississippi. A committee was appointed to determine the damages and $1,000 was agreed upon and allowed. Sank and lost at Helena, Ark., Sept. 6, 1867.

3706 MAID OF THE MIST

SW p wh b. Evansville, Ind., 1859. 40 tons. Sank and lost at Evansville, Sept. 18, 1861.

3707 MAIL

SW p wh b. Cincinnati, Oh., 1844. 211 tons. Burned and lost Apr. 9, 1848 at St. Louis.

3708 MAJESTIC

SW p wh b. Pittsburgh, Pa., 1843. 221 tons. 166 x 25 x 5.6. Pittsburgh-Cincinnati in 1844 and 1845, Capt. Elisha Bennett. In November 1845 sold to Ferdinand M. Streck, Donaldsonville, La. Sold July 1846 to Capt. James H. Ure and others, New Orleans. Sold August 1849 to Capt. Andrew Worley, New Orleans. Sold January 1850 to Capt. R. Cripps and others, Pointe Coupee, La. Last owner, March 1850, was Capt. John B. Evans of Pointe Coupee. Off the lists 1852.

3709 MAJESTIC

SW p wh b. Shousetown, Pa., 1863. 648 tons. Went to St. Louis, owned by Capt. John P. Keiser and others. Burned and lost May 6, 1863, at Island 8 near Hickman, Ky. One life lost.

3710 MAJESTIC

SW p wh b. Cincinnati, Oh., 1864. 201 tons. Built for Capt. Charles M. Holloway, intended for Cincinnati-Pomeroy trade. She burned at Point Coupee, La., Oct. 22, 1865, with 650 bales of cotton, Capt. J.C. Dowty part owner and master. Capt. Charles G. Pearce, Cincinnati owned the balance.

3711 MAJESTIC

Stw ex wh b. Harmar, Oh., at Knox yard, 1890, originally *KEYSTONE STATE* (see). Capt. D.W. Wisherd rebuilt her into an excursion boat at Peoria, early 1914, changed the name. She started out on the Upper Mississippi and was deadheading downbound when she hit an intake tower above St. Louis, at Chain of Rocks, June 1914, and was lost. Crew at the time: Capt. Frank Gill, with Capt. Steve Withrow and John Pearson, pilots; A.J. Mason, chief; Tom Posey, mate, and Edgar Wisherd, purser.

3712 MAJESTIC

Stw ex sh b. Pittsburgh, Pa., 1906, originally *S.S. BROWN*, then *REES LEE* (both see). She was converted into an excursion boat, 1915, by Capts. Peters Lee and D. Walter Wisherd and renamed. On the main deck was a minature scenic railroad and a merry-go-round. She tramped New Orleans to the Upper Mississippi and burned in winter quarters on the Illinois River, May 1922. The steel hull was converted into a cargo barge and George H. Partin loaded it with cotton at Memphis in 1931, and had it towed to New Orleans. On the second cotton trip, towed by the *ROBERT GORDON*, the barge sank fully loaded at New Orleans, this on Dec. 16, 1931. Capt. Peters Lee owned the barge.

3713 MAJOR

Stw ferry wh b. Hawesville, Ky., 1891. 59.9 x 26.5 x 4.3. Engines, 6½"- 18". One boiler, 53" by 10 ft. Owned by W.D. Crammond and operated by Capt. W.W. "Major" Prescott. She was lost in ice at Hawesville, c. 1909, and was replaced by the *K&I* (see).

3714 MAJOR A. DRAIN

Stw p wh b. Freedom, Pa., 1852. 10 tons. Built to run Pittsburgh to Meadville, Pa., via Allegheny River and French Creek Canal, Capt. David Edgar. Whether she ever accomplished even one trip is not recorded. Sold September 1853 and wound up owned by the Guyandotte Land Co., towing coal out of Guyandotte River, and sank in this service, c. 1855.

3715 MAJOR A. HARRIS

SW p wh b. Cincinnati, Oh., 1852. 102 tons. First home

port, Galveston, Tex. Exploded at Galveston, Feb. 6, 1857, with loss of one life.

3716 MAJOR ANDERSON

SW p wh b. Jeffersonville, Ind., by Howard, 1861. 245 x 36 x 5.5. Named for Maj. Robert Anderson of Fort Sumter fame. Built for the U.S. Mail Line Co., and ran Cincinnati-Louisville, teamed up with the *GENERAL BUELL* (see). Capt. Frank Carter commanded and on Jan. 4, 1866, his crew presented him with a silver service as testimonial for their regard for him. Carter was an old U.S. Mail Line man and had been in charge of the *BALTIC* (see) in her race with the *DIANA* (see), and later became superintendent of the Line at Louisville, which position he retained until August 1896, when C.C. Fuller took over. In the cabin was a framed fragment of the flag which flew at Sumter the day the fort was fired upon, presented by Major Anderson himself on one of his visits home in Cincinnati. Rammed and sank *HIGHLAND CHIEF* (see) above Vevay, Ind., August 1864. She and the *ST. CHARLES* (see) collided at Coopers Bar, Dec. 12, 1865, and the pilot on watch on the *ANDERSON* was Napoleon B. Jenkins who later was on watch on the *AMERICA* when she and the *UNITED STATES* collided. In the spring of 1864 she ran regularly Pittsburgh-Cincinnati, Capt. C.A. Dravo, with Andy Robinson, Jr., in the office. Collided with the *NEW STATE* (see) at Rising Sun, Ind., Apr. 5, 1868, and had to be docked at Cincinnati. Sold September 1868 to Capt. Charles Muhleman to replace the sunken *POTOMAC* (see) in Wheeling-Cincinnati trade. When *UNITED STATES* and *AMERICA* collided the U.S. Mail Line chartered the *ANDERSON* from Capt. Muhleman and kept her in the L&C trade until October 1869. Back in the Wheeling trade, she collided with the *ST. CHARLES* at Dewitts Bar during a snowstorm Jan. 1, 1870, and the pilots of both boats got 30-day suspensions from Wheeling inspectors Young and Phillips. Clerk on her in the Wheeling trade was Martin F. Noll, later secretary of the Louisville & Cincinnati Packet Co. Burned at Cincinnati along with the *ST. CHARLES* on Mar. 7, 1872.

3717 MAJOR AUBRY

SW p wh b. Louisville, Ky., 1853. 79 tons. 95.3 x 22.3 x 4.1. Ran New Orleans-New Iberia owned by a stock company with Capt. A.G. Jones, master, and part owner. Snagged and lost at Berwick, La., November 1858.

3718 MAJOR BARBOUR

SW p wh b. Shippingport, Ky., 1848. 133 tons. Ran Cincinnati-St. Louis, Capt. H.I. Spotts. Collided with *PAUL JONES* near Troy, Ind., Feb. 3, 1848. Five were drowned when the *BARBOUR* sank. Was running Cincinnati-Green River in December 1849, Capt. Spotts. Off the lists in 1852.

3719 MAJOR SAUNDERS

Stw U.S. wh b. Tidioute, Pa., 1865, originally named *TIDIOUTE* (see). Renamed in U.S. service on the Ohio River. Capt. George W. Rowley commanded 1871, operating Cairo to Pittsburgh removing snags and assisting in building dikes. That summer they assisted in putting a dike across the back channel of Brunots Island just below Pittsburgh, throwing more water in Glasshouse Chute.

3720 MALLARD

Steam yacht wh b. Terre Haute, Ind., 1887. 46 x 9.5 x 1.8. Still listed at Evansville in 1896.

3721 MALLARD NO. 3

Steam yacht wh b. Terre Haute, Ind., 1893. 60 x 10 x 2. Listed at Evansville in 1896.

3722 MALLIE RAGON

Stw p wh b. Evansville, Ind., 1870. 285 tons. Built for Capt. Josh V. Throop and others, named for daughter of F.H. Ragon of the Evansville firm, Ragon, Dickey & Carson. Ran Nashville-Evansville. She was sold to the upper Ohio and ran Pittsburgh-Wheeling 1873 and in 1875 was there, Capt. J.W. Williamson, with H.C. Caldwell, clerk. In spring of 1876 was back with Capt. Charles Muhleman in charge and with Kirker in the office. Entered Wheeling-Parkersburg trade January 1877, taking place of the *COURIER* which was running Wheeling-Cincinnati. Got stranded on gravel bar at Baresville (Hannibal), Oh., May 1878, and remained for a month or more. She was beached on shore at Wheeling after an ice gorge let go, Jan. 22, 1881, and suffered much injury. Soon thereafter was bought by George Strecker and the Rodick brothers, Marietta, who dismantled her and used the engines on a towboat named *SUCCESS*.

3723 MALTA

Stw p wh b. Monongahela City, Pa., 1849. 114 tons. 140 x 24 x 4.8. Engines, 12's- 4½ ft. Two boilers, each 40" by 22 ft. Built for Capt. Henry T. Dexter who ran her Pittsburgh-Zanesville 1850–1851, and Cincinnati-Zanesville 1852–1854. Snagged and lost at Big Hurricane Island near Paducah, Ky., Sept. 29, 1854. Three lives were lost.

3724 MALTA

Stw p wh b. Marietta, Oh., 1864. 33 tons. Ran with some frequency Marietta-Beverly, on the Muskingum, Capt. Joe Shofield, 1865, and Marietta-Zanesville 1866–1867, same master. Sometimes ran Marietta-New Matamoras. She sank at Marietta, Mar. 30, 1865. In November 1866 she took down from Parkersburg three barges of crude oil to Louisville for the refinery of Skeene & Co., perhaps a first. Went to U.S. Marshal sale at Wheeling January 1869 and sold to William Seawall who took her to Arkansas. She sank on a snag in Current River, fifteen miles above Doniphan, Sept. 10, 1870. Her engines went to the *ELLA HECHT* built at Pocahontas, Ark., 1870.

3725 MAMELUKE

SW p wh b. Cincinnati, Oh., 1848. 570 tons. Ran St. Louis-New Orleans, Capt. Smithers. Burned at St. Louis in the big wharf fire, May 17, 1849.

3726 MAMMOTH CAVE

SW p wh b. Louisville, Ky., 1849. 96 tons. Lost in collision with *GRENADA* on Sunflower River, Miss., May 3, 1852. The *GRENADA* (see) burned three days later at Algiers, La.

3727 MAMMOTH CAVE

Stw snagboat sh b. Jeffersonville, Ind., by Howard, 1908. 141 x 32.8 x 5. Much equipment used from *WM. PRESTON DIXON* (see). Owned by U.S. Engineers, Louisville District, and used on Green and Barren rivers. Sold at public sale, July 31, 1936, to Tom A. and Jeff Williams, Evansville. Sold November 1936 to Capt. Richard Hiernaux, Charleroi, Pa., who rebuilt her at Charleroi into a towboat renamed *RICHARD* which burned same place Dec. 10, 1940.

3728 MANANNA

SW p wh b. Brownsville, Pa., 1859. 205 tons. Went to Apalachicola, Fla., and to Confederate registry, 1861.

3729 MANCHESTER

SW p wh b. Brownsville, Pa., 1853. 293 tons. Ran Pittsburgh-St. Louis. Burned at Manchester, Pa. (north side, Pittsburgh), on July 13, 1853.

3730 MANCHESTER

SW p wh b. Wheeling, Va., 1858. 116 tons. First home port, St. Louis. Off the lists in 1860.

3731 MANDAN

SW p wh b. St. Louis, Mo., 1847. 204 tons. Ran up Missouri River and was once snagged at the mouth of the Gasconade, Capt. Phil Hanna. Burned at St. Louis in the big steamboat fire, May 17, 1849, along with 22 others. Capt. Beers, master at the time.

3732 MANDAN

Stw snagboat ih b. St. Louis, Mo., 1891. 138 x 24 x 4.7. Built for Missouri River service and originally had no machinery, and was towed. When machinery, was installed she was given unusual engines—compounds with the high pressure engine inside the l.p. cylinder, and each had three piston rods. These were built and installed by Charles Wonders, Sioux City, Iowa (still living 1949). She made a trip to Fort Benton, Mont., in 1921, 327.7 miles above present Fort Peck Dam, and on that same trip she was up Yellowstone River 50 miles to where there is a dam with no lock. She was dismantled at the U.S. boatyard, Gasconade, Mo., after 1925. The hull was taken to Bluffton Island Chute and sunk there.

3733 MANHATTAN

Stw p wh A low water boat built by Capt. Lee Anshutz in 1897 for the Sistersville-Wheeling trade. Ran that summer carrying excursions out of Wheeling. In August 1897 she went to Pittsburgh and ran daily trips to Monongahela City, Pa., leaving Pittsburgh at 3:00 P.M. Capt. Leonidas Drake was on her part of the time. Laid up that October by reason of poor business.

3734 MANITOU

SW p wh b. Jeffersonville, Ind., by Howard, 1863, originally named *JAMES THOMPSON*. She was sold to the U.S. Navy in March 1863, and became U.S.S. *MANITOU* June 2, 1863. On Nov. 5, 1863, she was renamed *FORT HINDMAN* (Tinclad #13) and resumed her original name *JAMES THOMPSON* when sold privately Dec. 5, 1865.

3735 MANKATO

Stw freight boat wh b. La Crosse, Wis., 1864. 127 tons. Snagged and lost in the Minnesota River, May 8, 1871.

3736 MANSFIELD

Stw p wh b. Belle Vernon, Pa., 1854. 166 tons. First job was running low water for the U.S. Mail Line, Cincinnati-Louisville, September 1854, Capt. Richard M. Wade. Went to the upper Mississippi and was logged at St. Paul 1856–1857, and was snagged and lost at White Cloud, Minn. Aug. 16, 1858.

3737 MAQUOKETA CITY

Stw p wh b. California, Pa., 1860. 55 tons. 87 x 24 x 3. Original owners, R. Oerham and S. Williams, equal shares. Capt. R. Perham, master. Enrolled Nov. 1862 at St. Louis with Capt. E.P. Lane, master, owning in equal shares with Henry B. Jones, both of Memphis. Dismantled 1864.

3738 MARBLE CITY

SW p wh b. Metropolis, Ill. (hull and framing), and completed at St. Louis, 1864. 272 x 41 x 7.5. Engines, 28's- 8 ft. Five boilers, each 46" by 22 ft. Hull came from Alph Cutting's yard. Owned by Memphis & St. Louis Packet Co., and named for Cape Girardeau, Mo., Capt. James H. Tschudi was master, with Adrian Storm, clerk.

Here comes the *MARBLE CITY* with
  Tschudi in comand,
Looking like a crystal palace just
  arrived from fairyland.
See how she cuts the water and how
  beautiful her form.
She advances like a whirlwind and I
  might add "A. Storm."

Dismantled in 1873, at which time the cabin, etc., went to building the *JOHN A. SCUDDER* (see). The hull was used as a coal float at Baton Rouge by Wood, Widney & Co. It was sunk in the hurricane of September 1879. Al Burris, diver from the *SALVOR NO. 2*, went up from New Orleans on the *FRANK PARGOUD* and dynamited the wreck.

3739 MARCELLA

SW p wh b. Louisville, Ky., 1863. 300 tons. 180 x 32 x 8. Engines, 18's- 7 ft. Four boilers. Advertised "for Fort Benton and the Great Falls of the Missouri" early in 1864. Capt. Sousley was in command, and on board was Grant Marsh taking his first look at the upper Missouri which was to bring him enduring fame. She operated to Missouri River until 1870 when sold in January to Capt. T.G. Ledbetter, New

Orleans. That November, Capt. F.A. Sherman was master. Off the lists 1874.

3740 MARENGO

SW p wh b. Louisville, Ky., 1844. 326 tons. 180 x 28 x 6.8. In October 1846 owned at Memphis by Benjamin F. Ball and Algernon S. Hancock, Capt. Andrew Dunn, master. Sold June 1847 to Crockett, Garland & Co., New Orleans, Capt. A.S. Hancock, master. Ran New Orleans-Lake Providence in 1848 in place of *C.E. WATKINS*. Lost in collision with *HARRY HILL* at Clarksville, Miss., Aug. 24, 1848, with loss of three lives. Her master at the time was Capt. C.J. Brenham who had acquired her two months prior.

3741 MARENGO

Stw p wh b. Brownsville, Pa., 1855. 239 tons. Running Cincinnati-Memphis spring 1860. Trips Pittsburgh-New Orleans, Capt. McAllen, spring 1861. Dismantled 1862. Machinery went to building *ARMENIA* (see).

3742 MARIA

SW p wh b. Cincinnati, Oh., 1844. 692 tons. 265 x 36 x 9.1. Paddlewheels 32 ft. diameter working 15 ft. buckets, 30" dip. Ran St. Louis-New Orleans. Was lost in collision with *SULTANA* in Natchez Island Chute, Nov. 21, 1846, with estimated life loss between 30 and 50. The cause stemmed from a misunderstanding of passing signals. Capt. Isaah Sellers is said to have taken up the matter of adopting uniform rules for tapping the roof bell to indicate in advance such understanding following this tragedy.

3743 MARIA

Stw p b. Cincinnati, Oh., 1863. 173 tons. Built by Capt. Eugene Bowers for low water work. Ran Cincinnati-Memphis in the Dean Line fall 1863. She was bought by the U.S. and became Tinclad #51, renamed *FAIRY* (see).

3744 MARIA

Stw p wh b. Cincinnati, Oh., 1864. 254 tons. Owned by H.A. Jones, Thomas Sherlock, and Charles G. Pearce, Cincinnati. There was note in Cincinnati dispatches Nov. 14, 1864, that *MARIA* would bring to Pittsburgh the immense siege gun "Lady Davis" captured at Vicksburg. She made the trip but no mention in contemporary Pittsburgh papers that this came about. She loaded for St. Louis, Capt. William Dravo. On Dec. 11, 1864, she exploded boilers at Carondelet, Mo., with the Third Iowa and Fourth Missouri Cavalry aboard, Capt. Alex Montgomery in command. The life loss was "immense," giving rise to the expression "hell and maria." Will Dravo, acting clerk, was badly scalded.

3745 MARIA BURT

SW p wh b. Cincinnati, Oh., 1846. 319 tons. 170.3 x 27.6 x 8.1. She was sold to the U.S. and was in government service until January 1849, when sold to N.W. Chittenden, New Orleans. She was altered in January 1850 into an ocean steamship with three masts, then owned by Peter S. Cyphers, New Orleans. Sold July 1850 to Galveston, Tex., Capt. James Emerson. Foundered off Galveston June 25, 1851.

3746 MARIA DENNING

SW p wh b. Cincinnati, Oh., 1856. 691 tons. 275 x 41 x 8. Engines, 26's- 9 ft. Five boilers. Owned by Capt. Hercules Carrel and others, Cincinnati. Built for freight only, the second deck an immense storage room. The original crew: Capt. Hercules Carrel, with Frank Richardson, T.W. Scott and Dick Raymond, clerks; D.D. Blois, pilot; Lew Jewett and Dan Clements, engineers; James Moore, mate. Ran St. Louis-New Orleans. At the outbreak of war this boat was engaged in transporting government stores. General U.S. Grant came aboard at Cairo following the fray at Belmont and there ensued a parley in midstream with Confederate General Cheatham, both of whom had served together in Mexico. Refreshments were served and high brass from both sides visited back-and-forth on the two vessels. At parting time two hours later the boats withdrew from one another to discover that officers from both sides were not sorted out, and a second contact was made to get Yankees and Rebels on board their own boats. This later precipitated something of a scandal, that the war had been suspended, that Grant was drunk, etc. In March 1864, the *MARIA DENNING* was stranded crossways on the Cumberland River. Captain Carrel sold her to Capt. Patrick Yore, St. Louis, with the proviso she be released and delivered to St. Louis, which was done. The reported sale price was $50,000. She acted briefly as a troop transport under Yore's command. Burned at Algiers, La., May 11, 1866.

3747 MARIA LOUISE

Stw p wh b. Jeffersonville, Ind., 1871. 521 tons. 180 x 33.5 x 6. Three boilers. Ran in the Kountz Line, St. Louis-New Orleans, until sold 1875 to Red River Line, Capt. H.J. Brinker, Sr., master. She and *HENRY FRANK* were said to have brought to Alexandria, La. the first Texas & Pacific locomotive, 1881.

3748 MARIAN

SW tr wh b. Jeffersonville, Ind., 1885. 206 x 46 x 6.7. Engines, 24's- 8 ft. Four boilers (two on a side), each 44" by 28 ft. Owned 1902 by Illinois Central Railroad. For quite some time operated in the Paducah, Ky., area.

3749 MARIANNA

Built at Pittsburgh, Pa., 1859, and was leaving that November for Chattahoochee River, a 1500 bale boat, Capt. Vanvecher.

3750 MARIE LOUISE

Stw p wh b. 1871. A cotton packet built for Capt. J.H. Brinker, Sr., operating New Orleans-Red River. 521 tons. Sank in Red River downbound from Shreveport with 1500 bales, March 1880.

3751 MARIETTA

Stw p wh b. Cincinnati, Oh., 1863, originally named *REINDEER* (see). Sold to the U.S. and became Tinclad #57, renamed *PERI*. Sold to private hands and renamed *MARIETTA*, Oct. 3, 1865. She came to Pittsburgh Oct. 26, 1865, and loaded out for Cincinnati, Capt. Ben Hall. with J.F. Wilson, clerk. Owned by Capt. Hoff of Marietta and others. Departed Pittsburgh for New Orleans with loaded barge in tow, Capt. Hoff, Nov. 17, 1865. During 1866 she towed Lipman's Circus from Cincinnati to St. Paul and back to St. Louis. Sold for debt at St. Louis, Jan. 9, 1867, to Willaim C. Daggett for $2,700. Reported sunk at Omaha, Neb., on Jan. 8, 1868.

3752 MARIETTA

Prop gunboat ih b. Pittsburgh, Pa., 1864. 479 tons. 170 x 50. Designed for Civil War, she came too late. Was moored in the Allegheny River at Pittsburgh along with *SANDUSKY* (see) until Feb. 22, 1866, when she was towed south by the *HAWK*. She was single prop. In 1869 briefly renamed *CIRCE*, then back to *MARIETTA*. Disposed of in 1873.

3753 MARIETTA

Stw ferry wh b. 1871. Succeeded the *J.R. McMILLAN* in service Marietta-Williamstown and was replaced later by *EMMA UHL* (see).

3754 MARINER

Stw p wh b. Belle Vernon, Pa., 1856. 193 tons. 180 x 33 x 6. Louisville-Memphis spring 1861. On May 21, 1862, at Wheeling, a tornado took off cabin and pilothouse and the wreck caught fire. On board were 140 soldiers and about 25 passengers. Some were blown overboard, including several ladies, but all were rescued. Got aground on the foot of St. Francis Island, Mississippi River, Capt. John Collier, June 1864. Remained there about a month and was burned by a Rebel raiding party on July 4th.

3755 MARINER

Stw p wh b. Cincinnati, Oh., 1863, originally named *RACHAEL MILLER* (see). Taken over by the U.S. and renamed *REINDEER* on May 25, 1863. Sold to private hands and renamed *MARINER* Oct. 5, 1865. Went to the Missouri River and was snagged and lost in Onawa Bend near Decatur, Neb., May 9, 1867.

3756 MARION

SW p wh b. Louisville, Ky., 1854. 133 tons. 123 x 26 x 4.5. Owned 1855 by Capt. Joseph Boisseau, Shreveport, La., and operating Alexandria-Shreveport. Capt. F.V. Cellos was master later. Snagged and lost at Soda Lake, La., Jan. 7, 1859.

3757 MARION

Stw p wh b. Wellsville, Oh., 1861, originally named *SILVER LAKE NO. 2* (see). Sold to USQMD in 1861. Sold to private hands and rig changed to side-wheel Oct. 7, 1865, renamed *MARION*. Engines, 13's- 3½ ft. Two boilers. Made a mountain trip and sank on a sand bar about 70 miles below Fort Benton, Mont., at Pablo Rapids and was wrecked. Capt. William D. Shanks was master at the time. First news of this came to St. Louis via the *GALLATIN* in August 1866, the officers also reporting loss of the *POCAHONTAS*, 60 miles below Fort Randall (see). The boilers, engines, furniture, etc., were removed on shore. The dispatch from St. Louis telling of this said she was a sternwheeler. The *National Geographic Magazine*, July 1977 issue, included a supplement map "Wild and Scenic Rivers" marking location of the *MARION* wreck at Pablo Rapids.

3758 MARJORIE

Stw ferry wh b. Osage, Mo., 1908. 74.2 x 21.2 x 4. Burned at Lexington, Mo., July 8, 1917.

3759 MARK R. CHEEK

SW ferry wh b. Madison, Ind., 1860. 122 tons. First home port, Memphis. Capt. Mark R. Cheek was master of the *KATE ADAMS (#1, #2)*. Burned and lost at Ouachita City, La., Mar. 31, 1865.

3760 MARK TWAIN

Stw p wh b. Jeffersonville, Ind., 1872, originally named *BUSINESS* (see). She was hauled out on the Covington, Ky., docks, November 1876, lengthened, and renamed *MARK TWAIN*. 111 x 20.4 x 4. Left Cincinnati for Memphis Jan. 27, 1877, Capt. J.L. Randall. Ran Memphis-St. Francis River, Capt. W.P. Hill. Later bought by a Capt. Fogleman, Mound City, Ark., who used her as a ferry there. Exploded her boiler at Mound City Mar. 27, 1885, with loss of six lives. Rebuilt and renamed *ALICE*. Was still listed *ALICE* at Memphis, 1892, maybe later.

3761 MARK TWAIN

SW harborboat wh b. Madison, Ind., 1873, originally named *ELON G. SMITH* (see). She was the harborboat at St. Louis, and was renamed *CITY OF SAINT LOUIS* and so appears in the *Lists of Merchant Vessels 1892–1896*, perhaps later. Samuel Clemens visited St. Louis and for the occasion *CITY OF SAINT LOUIS* was renamed *MARK TWAIN*. He rode in the pilothouse, his last trip on a Mississippi steamboat. She was replaced 1907 by the *ERASTUS WELLS* (see).

3762 MARKET BOY

Centerwheel catamaran ferry wh b. Paducah, Ky., 1858. 113 tons. Off the lists 1860.

3763 MARKET BOY

Stw p wh b. Pittsburgh, Pa., 1862. 70 tons. Handled produce daily with fair regularity between Shippingport, Pa., and Pittsburgh in the summer and fall of 1862. Sold that December to Pomeroy, Oh., for $7,000. Sank and lost at Helena, Ark., May 25, 1866.

3764 MARKET BOY

Stw p wh b. Ashland, Ky., 1870. 94 tons. Handled crude oil

in barrels for the Union Oil Co., between Cannelton, W. Va., on the Kanawha River to Maysville, Ky., refinery. Sold at Cincinnati April 1871 to Capt. William Tawney McKeesport, Pa., and others for $8,000. Ran Elizabeth-McKeesport trade. In 1876 ran in the Wheeling-New Matamoras trade, Capt. William Porter, with L.B. Scott, clerk. Ran low water, Pittsburgh-Cincinnati, September 1877, Capt. Porter. Was towing barges of hickory timber to a mill at New Albany, Ind., spring of 1878.

3765 MARLEN SPEED

Stw p wh b. Pittsburgh, Pa., 1878. 155 x 33 x 3. Engines, 12's-4 ft. Two boilers, each 40" by 20 ft., 5 flues. Built for the Memphis & Arkansas River Packet Co., and named for son of Capt. R.A. Speed. Departed Pittsburgh in July 1878 piloted by James Henderson and Marsh Hays. She was lost on the Arkansas River at Pleasants Landing, Capt. Daragh. Date?

3766 MARMORA

Stw p wh b. California, Pa., 1857. 177 tons. 156.6 x 31.7 x 4.3. Ran Pittsburgh-Cincinnati and elsewhere until the outbreak of the war, and then was under charter to the U.S. in charge of Capt. James McDonald (who later was in charge of the Herron Hill waterworks, in Pittsburgh). *MARMORA* was assigned to the Kanawha River and once took aboard troops at Pt. Pleasant enroute to Red House, W. Va. The soldiers were in charge of Maj. Rutherford Hayes, later U.S. president, and one of the troops was William McKinley, 18-year-old lad with these 23rd Ohio infantry, also to become U.S. president. At another time *MARMORA* was headquarters for General Cox, later Ohio's governor. In 1862 took 2nd Kentucky Regiment from Charleston to Louisville, and then was in the Cumberland and Tennessee campaigns. She ran Pittsburgh-Cincinnati, Capt. C.L. Brennan, after that. Sold February 1866 to Capt. J.E. Streeper, New Orleans, who transferred her that August to Capt. J.T. Burdean, thence to Edward Green, St. Louis. She burned at 3:00 A.M. Feb. 16, 1867, while wooding at Shipland Landing opposite Lake Providence, La.

3767 MARMORA NO. 2

Stw p wh b. Monongahela, Pa., 1862, at the William Latta yard. 155 x 33.4 x 4.8. Engines, 15½'s-5½ ft. Two boilers with six flues each. These boilers, built by Watson & Monroe, were an innovation, having six flues each; three 11" and three 8". Paddlewheel 20 ft. dia. working 24 ft. buckets. Capt. James McDonald built her after leaving the *MARMORA* (see). He had only run her a few trips when the U.S. Navy acquired her. She became Tinclad #2, named *MARMORA*. Sold to private hands at Mound City, Ill., Aug. 17, 1865, for $8,650, bought by D.D. Barr. No record of service thereafter.

3768 MARS

SW p wh b. Cincinnati, Oh., 1856. 329 tons. 180 x 34. Engines, 20's-7 ft. Three boilers. Captured by the U.S. at Island 10, Mar. 7, 1862, during the engagement there. The Rebels had vandalized her, cut her copper steam pipes and so put her on the blitz that she had to undergo major repairs. They had seized her at Memphis June 1861, upbound from New Orleans. Among her freight were the engines from the dismantled *ROBT. J. WARD* (see) consigned to Madison, Ind., for Capt. David White. She became owned by a St. Louis group headed by Capts. E.B. McPherson and H. McPherson. They ran her Memphis-Ohio River, and then on the Missouri. Snagged and lost at Cogswell Landing, Mo., on the Missouri opposite the mouth of Fishing River, July 8, 1865.

3769 MARSHALL NEY

SW p wh b. Louisville, Ky., 1847. 486 tons. 231 x 31 x 7. Owned at St. Louis by John Walsh, Edward Walsh, James B. Hill. Commanded by Capt. Richard J. Lockwood. Ran St. Louis-New Orleans. Observed the Cairo *Delta*, issue, Mar. 15, 1849: "The *MARSHAL NEY* reached this point on the 8th inst. having on board 327 French emigrants, a clean, healthy-looking people, and seemed as if they were accustomed to labor." Burned in wharf fire at New Orleans, Oct. 9, 1849.

3770 MARTHA

SW p wh b. St. Louis, Mo., 1847. 180 tons. Built for Capt. Joseph La Barge and others who ran trades out of St. Louis. Made a trip up the Missouri first season and La Barge took his wife along (Pelagie) who is reputed to have been the first white woman in the Dacotah Territory. Burned in the steamboat fire at St. Louis, May 17, 1849.

3771 MARTHA

Rig? p wh b. Madison, Ind., 1875. 175 tons. Owned by New Orleans & Gulf Transportation Co., operating to Port Eads and Pilot Town. Also in the Line in 1880 were the *ISABEL, ALVIN* and *KITTIE NYE* (all see). Inspected at New Orleans through 1882.

3772 MARTHA NO. 2

SW p wh b. Shousetown, Pa., 1849. 180 tons. Apparently a replacement for the *MARTHA*, b. 1847 (see). She is logged at St. Paul in April 1851 from St. Louis. Off the lists in 1860.

3773 MARTHA E. ALLEN

SW p wh b. Paducah, Ky., 1861. 174 tons. 137.6 x 28.5 x 5.6. Enrolled at New Orleans in December 1865, owned by Capt. M.N. Wood of that city. Sold same date to Capt. James Rudman and associates, New Orleans. Sold entire November 1866 to Capt. Vincent Joseph Woods, New Orleans. Later that month transferred to Capt. William Evans, subject of Great Britain. Last owner was Capt. Patrick Kennan, New Orleans. Dismantled November 1869.

3774 MARTHA JEWETT

SW p wh b. Hannibal, Mo., 1852. 408 tons. Advertised St. Louis-St. Joseph, Capt. David H. Silver, bi-weekly, April 1856. Burned and lost at Cairo, Ill., Jan. 3, 1859. The roof bell was in the belfry of a Presbyterian church at Cairo, Ill., 1895.

3775 MARTHA PUTNAM

Stw p wh b. Cincinnati, Oh., 1857. 225 tons. First home port, Wheeling, Va. Burned and lost at Cairo, Ill., Dec. 29, 1859.

3776 MARTHA STEPHENS

Stw p wh b. Osage, Mo., 1883. 192 tons. Engines, 10's-3½ ft. One boiler. Owned by Capt. Henry McPherson who was master. Snagged on the Missouri River at Sibley, or Turkey Island, Aug. 9, 1884, with a big cargo of sacked wheat aboard. Six lives were reported lost.

3777 MARTHA WASHINGTON

SW p wh b. Cincinnati, Oh., 1847. 299 tons. Ran Cincinnati-New Orleans. She burned at Island 65, Mississippi River, Jan. 14, 1852, under unusual circumstances. Nine lives lost. An examination of the wreck disclosed that the cargo, largely from Cincinnati, was composed of boxes containing scrap paper, etc. Capt. John Cummings, master, was charged with barratry, attempting to collect insurance on a fraudulent cargo. Many of the details are recounted in Gould's *History of River Navigation*, pages 354–55, and again in pages 481–83.

3778 MARTIN BEHRMAN

Catamaran ferry sh b. Jeffersonville, Ind., by Howard, 1917. 126.5 x 31.2 x 7.2. Allowed 200 passengers and 40 cars. Owned by Bisso Ferry Co., New Orleans. Operated until about 1949–1950.

3779 MARTIN HOFFMAN

Ocean steamship wh b. Shousetown, Pa., 1850. 163.1 x 24.2 x 13. 493 tons. Built for J.W. Woodward, New York City, Capt. John T. Smith, master. Also built at Shousetown same year was a similar ocean steamship *FREEMAN RAWDON* (see). Both went to German registry when delivered to salt water. The *HOFFMAN* was renamed *ISLE OF MADEIRA* as of June 18, 1856, and was sold foreign in 1857. These were side-wheelers.

3780 MARTINE

SW p wh b. Hannibal, Mo., 1868. 69 tons. First home port, Quincy, Ill. Off the lists in 1880.

3781 MARY

SW p wh b. Cincinnati, Oh., 1847. 276 tons. First home port, St. Louis. Engaged spring of 1849 taking Mormons up the Missouri River. On one trip that April, 26 Mormons were reported to have died before the boat reached Leavenworth. Burned and lost at St. Louis, July 28, 1849.

3782 MARY

Stw p wh b. Elizabeth, Pa., 1849. 143 tons. First home port, Pittsburgh, Pa. Burned and lost below Fort Gaines, Ga., Feb. 14, 1852.

3783 MARY

Rig? p wh b. Jeffersonville, Ind., 1873. 176.2 x 32.5 x 4. Built for Capt. John Quill who took her to the Alabama River in September 1873. Still listed at Mobile in 1886.

3784 MARY

Stw p wh b. Jeffersonville, Ind., by Howard, 1899. 141 x 28 x 3.6. Built for Alabama River, Joseph T. Spieth and others. Destroyed at Mobile in a Gulf hurricane, Sept. 26, 1906.

3785 MARY AGNES

SW p wh b. Louisville, Ky., 1853. 374 tons. Ran Memphis-New Orleans, Capt. Greenlaw. She burned about thirteen miles above Natchez, at the head of Fairchilds Island, Mar. 1, 1854. The *BELLE KEY* was upriver about a mile, turned back, and rendered aid. Happened just about daylight. The boat was landed and all got ashore.

3786 MARY AMENT

SW p wh b. New Albany, Ind., 1866. 259 tons. Built for David Gibson, Cincinnati, and ran Cincinnati-Chilo spring 1867. She was sold to Evansville and ran Evansville-Cannelton, Capt. John A. Adams, with Dick Morgan, clerk, 1874. Prior to that Adam's brother Robert had been master but retired to Lewisport. Mat Williams served as clerk, later master of the *DEAN ADAMS* (see). Dismantled in 1878.

3787 MARY ANN

Stw p wh b. Elizabeth, Pa., 1846. 142 tons. Owned by David A. Grier with Capt. Hugh Dennison, master. Had 32 staterooms. Ran Pittsburgh-Allegheny River to Franklin, Pa. In the summer of 1848 she made a Missouri River trip, Capt. Robert Duncan, and was snagged on the return near Marietta, Oh. Back in the Allegheny River in December 1848 and on Jan. 19, 1849 she was struck by two loaded coalboats, which had become free-astray, and was sunk. The engines, etc., recovered.

3788 MARY BARNES

Stw p wh b. La Crosse, Wis., 1879. 137 x 24.7 x 4.2. Much equipment from the *NELLIE KENT* went into her (see). Later sold to the U.S. and renamed *EMILY*. Lost in ice six miles above Bismarck, N.D., spring 1885.

3789 MARY BELL

SW p wh b. Metropolis, Ill., at Alph Cutting yard, 1875. 327 x 55.5 x 10.5. Engines, 34's-9 ft. Much equipment from *BELLE LEE* (see) used in construction. Owned by Capt. J. Frank Hicks and others. Named for the wife of Capt. Jesse K. Bell. Ran Memphis-New Orleans. She was downbound on a Mardi Gras trip with 5000 bales of cotton, 8000 sacks of seed, 500 barrels of oil, and had 175 cabin passengers. Arrived at Vicksburg at noon Feb. 27, 1876. Most of the passengers went sight-seeing and with about 30 still aboard she dropped down to the Merchant's Compress Co., landing for more cotton. A large number of Vicksburg citizens had come aboard to visit. Fire was discovered under the front stairway. Many got safely down the burning stairway and across to the packet *TALLAHATCHIE* alongside, and thence ashore. The *YAZOO* also was there, both of these Yazoo River packets transferring cotton to the *MARY BELL*. No lives were lost. The tug *JOHN BIGLEY* pulled the two Yazoo packets to safety, and the *MARY BELL* went up in smoke within 20 minutes from start to finish. In a statement Capt. J. Frank Hicks said. "Never will I give another steamboat a name commencing with an M. I am not superstitious but a strange fatality seems to follow the boats so named. I'll never do so again." He said also that the *MARY BELL* was $20,000 on the profit side on the nine trips she had made, and if she had gotten through this tenth trip she would have added between $8,000 and $10,000 more. Alf Grissom was her head clerk. Salvage was demanded by the owners of the tug *JOHN BIGLEY* for saving the two Yazoo packets and both were libelled by a U.S. Marshal pending decision.

3790 MARY BESS

SW p wh b. Louisville, Ky., 1852. 206 tons. 165 x 33 x 6. Engines, 17½'s- 7 ft. Built for Capt. Sam Montgomery and others and went to Mobile, Ala. Was returned to New Orleans 1853 owned by William Kimball and D.G. Hill. Sold 1854 to Henry J. Muggah, St. Mary Parish, and others, Capt. D.R. Muggah. She was making trips up Red River, 1856, Capt. John Lyons as master. Off the lists 1858.

3791 MARY BLANE

SW p wh b. St. Louis, Mo., 1847. 181 tons. Ran St. Louis-Galena, Capt. J.C. Smith, 1848. Capt. James Dozier ran her out of St. Louis later. Burned and lost at St. Louis, Sept. 10, 1851.

3792 MARY BOYD

Stw p wh b. Cincinnati, Oh., 1869. 159.7 x 33.4 x 5. Engines, 13 ¾'s- 5 ft. Three boilers, 2 flues. Paddlewheel 18½ ft. diameter working 20 ft. buckets. Ran Memphis-Arkansas River, Capt. R.L. Haines. In fall 1870 hit the wreck of the Confederate gunboat *JEFF THOMPSON* four miles below Memphis and sustained damage. Sold April 1876 to Illinois Packet Co., and ran out of Peoria until that October. Sold to Mobile, Ala., soon thereafter and was still documented there 1886, perhaps later.

3793 MARY BYRD

Rig? p wh b. 1866. Owned by Col. R.K. Byrd and Capt. Jacob Fritts. Operated on the Tennessee River. On her first trip she took aboard a party of Congressmen touring the South and had the misfortune to sink. Sank in the "Suck" below Chattanooga in 1870, Capt. Fritts in charge. Said once to have earned $7,777.77 in a single season, with Capt. C.S. Peak in charge. Later owned by the Small brothers who ran her in the North Alabama trade (so called around Guntersville). Lost at Kelly's Ferry, upper Tennessee River, May 9, 1870.

3794 MARY C.

SW p wh b. Rockingham, Iowa, 1852. 157 tons. Was at St. Paul in 1853. Off the lists 1858.

3795 MARY C.

Stw p wh b. Yazoo City, Miss., 1915. 65 x 16.5 x 3.2. Ran to Vicksburg, Capt. John J. Richardson. Still listed 1918, maybe later.

3796 MARY C. CAMPBELL

Stw ferry wh b. Pittsburgh, Pa., 1879. 100 x 28 x 3. Long served as the ferry between Rochester, Pa., and Monaca, Pa., on the Ohio. When the bridge was opened there, 1897, she was retired and sold. In October 1898 she tried the St. Marys-Newport ferry service and ended up in the hands of a U.S. Marshal. Sold to John Swanwecker, St. Marys, W. Va., entire who sold her to P.Q. Shrake, New Matamoras, Oh., Capt. George Kraft, master. She ran 1899, between Grandview, New Matamoras and Friendly, maybe longer.

3797 MARY CLIFTON

SW p wh b. New Albany, Ind., 1849. 206 tons. Went to the Alabama River, first home port, Mobile, Ala. Snagged and lost at Tait Shoals, Ala., Feb. 26, 1855.

3798 MARY COLE

SW ferry wh b. Cincinnati, Oh., 1849. 93 tons. Snagged and lost at Plattsmouth, Neb., Mar. 22, 1855.

3799 MARY COOK

Stw p wh b. California, Pa., 1857. 162 tons. 154 x 29.3 x 4. Original owners: Capt. Hugh Campbell (master), Charles S. Frisbee and William Nelson, all of Pittsburgh, and Ben Coursin, McKeesport. Ran tramp trades, and was in Pittsburgh-Cincinnati trade January 1861, Capt. Frisbee. Transported troops Kanawha River to Louisville in 1862, and then dismantled.

3800 MARY CRANE

Stw p wh b. Madison, Ind. (hull) and completed at Evansville, Ind., 1862. 111 tons. Handled supplies for US-QMC to Cumberland River that year. Landed for wood at Betsy's Landing near Nashville where she was attacked by guerrillas, the pilot killed, and the cargo confiscated. Burned and lost at Lake Cormorant, Miss., Jan. 8, 1863. As of September 1863, Capt. Bob Cully had salvaged the machinery from her and had forwarded it to Louisville.

3801 MARY D.

Stw p wh b. Marietta, Oh., 1870. 55 tons. Ran Vanceburg-Manchester-Maysville. In October 1876 went to Kentucky River and got aground above Lock 1 on a high river and was beached out when the water fell. In latter October a pop rise came along. She floated off, went over Dam 1, and was destroyed.

3802 MARY DISSTON

Recess stw p wh b. Pittsburgh, Pa., 1885. 83 x 18.5 x 3.8. Engines, 8"- 3'9" stroke. One locomotive type boiler with surface condenser. Built by James Rees & Sons for service on the Anclote River, Florida.

3803 MARY E. BENNETT

Stw p wh b. Covington, Neb., 1888. 21 tons. 64 x 14 x 2.5. Owned by Richard Talbot. Sunk by ice at Sioux City, Iowa, Mar. 4, 1894. Snagged and lost at Cook's Landing, Missouri River, Oct. 15, 1898. Note: The character of this boat not known for certain; she may have been a small towboat.

3804 MARY E. FORSYTH

SW p wh b. Shousetown, Pa. (hull), and completed at Pittsburgh, 1862. 621 tons. 254 x 40 x 7. Engines, 25's- 8 ft. Four boilers, each 46" by 28 ft., 6 flues. Wheels 30 ft. diameter working 14 ft. buckets. Built for Capt. Barton Able, St. Louis, who came to Pittsburgh in latter December 1862 and took her to St. Louis. Ran St. Louis-New Orleans in the Atlantic & Mississippi Steamship Co. Named for the wife of the general freight agent of the Illinois Central Railroad, St. Louis. Capt. C.W. Batchelor superintended construction. Was in U.S. transport service during the war, at one time up Red River. In St. Louis-New Orleans trade commanded by Capt. H.H. Symmes, with Jos. Widen, clerk. She was loaded at Mound City, Ill., with a cargo of U.S. ordnance bound for Pensacola, Fla., in latter May 1873, and was caught in a storm off Chandeleur Islands and lost, June 4, 1873. No life loss.

3805 MARY E. GRAY

SW p wh b. Terre Haute, Ind., 1863. 54 tons. 75.9 x 14.2 x 3.3. Enrolled at New Orleans Oct. 2, 1866, owned by R.R. Haynes, New Orleans with Capt. J.A. Henderson, master. Sold Nov. 22, 1866, to Capt. R.B. Hamilton, New Orleans. She was dismantled in Assumption Parish, La., June 1870.

3806 MARY E. KEENE

SW p wh b. New Albany, Ind., 1860. 659 tons. 238 x 38 x 7.7. Engines, 20's- 6 ft. Five boilers. Original owners, Capt. W.B. Richardson (¼) and W.F. Carkey, both of New Orleans. Ran New Orleans-Vicksburg, Capt. Richardson. In 1862 ran New Orleans-Memphis, Capt. W.F. Carkey, with J.M. Renshaw, clerk. An oil painting of the boat hung in the cabin until April 1862 when it was taken to the Keene plantation near Lake Providence, La., in trust of Mary E. Keene for the war's duration. A granddaughter still displayed it in her home in Houston, Tex., in 1949. The *LIZZIE SIMMONS* also ran New Orleans-Memphis, 1862, and Capt. Richardson, named above, was her skipper. She was a Confederate transport until taken up Yazoo River for safety where she was burned to prevent capture, July 24, 1863. S.L. Elam, Natchez, was a soldier aboard when she went up the Yazoo.

3807 MARY E. POE

Stw p wh b. Cincinnati, Oh., 1871. 296 tons. 188 x 33 x 5. Engines, 17's- 5 ft. Three boilers. Built for Capt. Thomas Poe and others. Ran in the Carter Line, St. Louis-Red River. She was downbound Oct. 17, 1873, when she got afire over top of the boilers. Was run aground at Daniels Point near Island 26, about ten miles above Osceola, Ark. William Cohen and Robert Baldwin were her pilots, the latter on watch. Cohen was about to sound the channel when the fire broke out, jumped overboard, and was badly burned by burning oil from 75 barrels stowed aboard. The *CITY OF HELENA* picked up many survivors. Blythe and Holliday, the mates, remained to guard the wreck. A swarm of Tennessee natives arrived to plunder, ran off the mates at gunpoint, and when the *T.F. ECKERT* arrived to salvage the cargo, much had been pilfered.

3808 MARY ELIZABETH

Stw p wh b. Jeffersonville, Ind., 1877. 129 x 25.2 x 4. Departed Cincinnati, Jan. 17, 1878, direct for Pine Bluff, Ark., Capt. J.W. Whipple. In August 1878 sold to Mobile, Ala. Was still listed at Mobile 1886.

3809 MARY ERWIN

Stw p wh b. Cincinnati, Oh., 1866. 308 tons. She departed from Memphis evening of Apr. 30, 1867 for Fort Smith, Ark. with a delegation of Cherokees accompanying the remains of their late departed chief John Ross to be buried at Tallequah. Sank at Rising Sun, Ind. August 1867, upbound from the Tennessee River to Cincinnati on very low water, Capt. George Wolf. The *CHAMPION NO. 6* went from Cincinnati to her aid and raised her. Ran Cincinnati-Marietta in 1868, Capt. J.J. Blagg, with John L. Newsom, clerk. Burned in the Cincinnati steamboat fire May 12, 1869.

3810 MARY F. CARTER

Stw p wh b. Clarendon, Ark., 1893. 77.3 x 22.4 x 3.6. In January 1896 running regularly in the upper White, Indian Bay-West Point, Ark. (255 miles).

3811 MARY F. GOLDEN

Stw p wh b. Millwood, W. Va., 1896. 86.2 x 16.2 x 3.6. Engines, 9½- 3 ft. One boiler. Ran produce boats south, etc. In June 1903 ran Vanceburg-Portsmouth on the Ohio, operated by Frank Agnew and James Rowley, Jr. Capt. William Pell sold her November 1904 to H.A. Harvey, Harvey, La. Burned in Bayou Teche, Jan. 28, 1908.

3812 MARY FOLEY

SW p wh b. Louisville, Ky., 1848. 248 tons. 176 x 20 x 5.5. Ran New Orleans-Bayou Sara, Capt. Celestin Dalfares who owned her entire. Sold, November 1850, to Capt. Antoine Dalfares of Assumption Parish, La. She was sold 1854 to Trudeau, Hutcheson & Co., Baton Rouge. They docked her for repairs, then put her in the New Orleans-Bayou Lafourche trade. In November 1854 sold to Capt. Celestine Moreau, Jr., Avoyelles Parish, La., and others. Sold 1855 to Benjamin F. Coxe, East Baton Rouge. Off the lists 1857.

3813 MARY H.

Stw sawmill boat wh b. Hooksburg, Oh., on the Muskingum River, 1891. 113 x 18 x 3.9. Built by Charles F. Hambleton, Beverly, Oh., and was the third floating sawmill he had built. Sold June 1900 to W.A. Baker, New Matamoras, Oh., and in 1904 Oscie Baker became one-third owner. She was completely rebuilt 1904 at New Matamoras and name changed to *RAY* (see).

3814 MARY H. MILLER

Stw p wh b. Higginport, Oh., 1904, originally named *ADDIE T.* (see). Operated by the Miller Line on Yazoo River. In early Dec. 1910 she sank four miles north of Yazoo City at Whites Bar and was lost.

3815 MARY HEIN

SW p wh b. California, Pa., 1862, originally named *SILVER LAKE NO. 3* (see). Rebuilt and renamed at Cincinnati, 1865, for Capt. John Hein and ran New Orleans-Shreveport. Burned on Red River, Feb. 28, 1866, downbound with 600 bales. Last enrollment dated Sept. 28, 1865, shows Capt. James Keniston, Cincinnati, owner.

3816 MARY HILL

Stw ferry wh b. Jeffersonville, Ind., by Howard, 1899. 100 x 24 x 3. Operated at Burlington, Iowa, Capt. Elmer Hill. Later was renamed *B.B.* (see).

3817 MARY HOUSTON

SW p wh b. Jeffersonville, Ind., 1868. 255 x 39 x 7. Engines, 22½'s- 7 ft. Five boilers. Built for Capt. L.B. Dunham and others, and ran Louisville-New Orleans. In 1870 her clerks were H.H. Walker and Len P. Seabrook. Through tickets were offered New Orleans passengers via Iron Mountain Railroad to St. Louis. She was at New Orleans for the start of the famed race *ROBT. E. LEE-NATCHEZ*, 1870. Dismantled 1877 and much equipment went to building the *NEW MARY HOUSTON* (see). The hull served as a wharfboat at Monroe, La., and sank there Sept. 2, 1880.

3818 MARY HUNT

SW p wh b. New Albany, Ind., 1850, originally named *BRILLIANT* (see). Renamed Nov. 9, 1852. She became a wharfboat at Memphis known as the "Mary Hunt wharfboat" and on Dec. 3, 1855, the *GEORGE COLLIER* (see) took fire while landing at the wharfboat and both were destroyed, also the *MAYFLOWER* (see).

3819 MARY IDA

Rig? p wh b. Paducah, Ky., 1873. 145 tons. Ran New Orleans-Plaquemines daily, 1874, Capt. J.A. Ruiz. In April 1878, New Orleans-Upper Coast, same master, three trips weekly. Also in 1878 New Orleans-Donaldsonville daily, Capt. G.L. Kouns, with Henry E. Kouns, clerk. Inspected at Pensacola, Fla., 1881; in the Mobile district in 1882.

3820 MARY J. ARNOLD

Stw f wh b. Muscatine, Iowa, 1868. 94.4 x 24.8 x 3.7. Engines 9½'s- 3 ft. stroke. Two boilers 38 in. diameter by 14 ft. allowed 150 psi. Owned by Leonard Arnold, Capt. James Tetlow, pilot. Operated at Brownsville, Neb. Sunk by ice March 12, 1875; raised. Sunk by a snag at Brownsville Feb. 20, 1880. Total loss; $2,500.

3821 MARY JOYCE

Stw p wh Built in the latter 1890s on upper White River owned by W.A. Joyce, a Newport, Ark., druggist, along with Capt. Tom Stallings. Stallings left her in 1902 to run the *GEN. JOE WHEELER*.

3822 MARY KENNER

In June 1876 this boat plus the *WATER WITCH* and *J.M. McARTHUR* were running between Cincinnati and Dayton, Ky.

3823 MARY L. DOUGHERTY

SW p wh b. Elizabeth, Pa., 1853. 95 tons. 123 x 18 x 4.5. Ran Memphis-White River owned by John Whiteside & Co., Pocahontas, Ark. She sank on White River Dec. 8, 1854. In 1855 at Memphis owned by W.C. Johnson and others, Capt. Morgan Bateman. Enrolled at New Orleans July 1857 owned by Edmond Castillo. She had run up Red River 1856, Capt. W. Stockman. Off the lists 1859. The partners in John Whiteside & Co., seem to have been Jonathan A. Whiteside and Silas A. Dougherty.

3824 MARY L. HATCHER

Stw p wh b. Pt. Pleasant, W. Va., 1890. 110.4 x 17.5 x 4. Built for Big Sandy River service and frequently ran during low water in Ohio River trades. In December 1897 was operating Syracuse-Gallipolis, Capt. M.M. Brown.

3825 MARY LACY

Stw p-tb wh b. Madison, Ind., 1897. 118 x 22.8 x 4.3. Engines, 13's- 4½ ft. Two boilers, each 44" by 22 ft. One of her first jobs was running Madison-Kentucky River in place of the *FALLS CITY* being repaired. She went to Evansville and was used towing logs, etc., out of Green River. Sold March 1909 to W.J. Duffy, Marietta, Oh. She had been rebuilt 1905 into a full-fledged towboat. Name was changed Apr. 12, 1909, to *DICK C. PAPE*.

3826 MARY MC

SW p wh b. Stillwater, Minn., 1902, originally named *IANTHE* (see). Home port was Burlington, Iowa, in 1908, maybe later.

3827 MARY McDONALD

SW p wh b. St. Louis, Mo., 1866. 563 tons. Engines, 20's- 5 ft. Three boilers. Ran in the St. Louis & Omaha Packet Co., 1867, Capt. John Greenough, owned in part by Capt. James Gunsollis. By 1870 making trips to Ouachita River, Ouachita River Packet Co., Capt. Greenough. Returned to the Missouri River and burned at Gilham's Landing, Mo., on June 12, 1873, Capt. George Keith, master, with Henry Keith, pilot. Her hold was filled with hemp at the time, downbound Kansas City for St. Louis.

3828 MARY McGEE

Rig? ferry wh b. Nordaway Slough, Mo., 1869. 135 tons. Reported cut down by ice at Plattsmouth, Neb. April 6, 1877.

3829 MARY McKINNEY

Stw p wh b. Elizabeth, Pa., 1849. 48 tons. Went to the upper Tennessee River, out of Knoxville. Capt. John L. Doss more than once had her up Holston River to Kingsport, near the Virginia line. Finally sank Dec. 3, 1853, in Meigs County, Tenn., Capt. Jake Lacy.

3830 MARY MILLER

Stw p wh b. Millersport, Oh. (hull and framing by Joel Wall), and completed at Pittsburgh, Pa., 1862. 158 x 30 x 4.5. 170 tons. She was new in April 1862. Sold to the U.S. Navy, Dec. 19, 1862, and became Tinclad #11, named *PRAIRIE BIRD*, in Jan. 1863.

3831 MARY MILLER

Stw p wh b. Dover, Tenn., 1870. 411 tons. Sold at auction Mar. 4, 1871, to W.F. Nisbet, president of Evansville & Memphis Packet Co. Sold mid-June 1871 to Capt. James Paul, late of the *PINK VARBLE*. Made a low water run from Louisville to Cairo in November 1871, taking eleven days. Swapped around a good bit, and in March 1876 owned by Capt. John M. Shunk. Made a trip to Pittsburgh and then settled down in the Cincinnati-St. Louis trade, Captain Shunk, master, with J.H. Griffith, clerk. Still there in October 1878.

3832 MARY MORGAN

Stw p ih b. Pittsburgh, Pa., 1878. 166.5 x 28 x 8. Her home port in 1886 was Philadelphia, Pa.

3833 MARY MORGAN

Stw p wh Ran Little Rock to upper Arkansas River, Capt. Ed Houston, 1898. Her engines, 9″- 26″ stroke, went to the *RUBY* (see), 1900.

3834 MARY MORTON

Stw p wh b. Dubuque, Iowa, 1880. 210 x 32.5 x 6. Engines, 17's- 5½ ft. Owned by the Diamond Jo Line and named for wife of Diamond Jo Reynolds. Built under supervision of Capt. John F. Killeen. Ran upper Mississippi trades. In November 1896 ran St. Louis-Memphis, Capt. Milt Harry, and summer 1897 same trade under charter to the Anchor Line. Anchor Line bought her that fall and lost her at Crain's Island, near Grand Tower, Ill., that October. She once sank at Clarksville Island (Sept. 10, 1892) while in Diamond Jo service. A model of her in a glass case long graced the offices of The Waterways Journal, St. Louis, presented by Capt. John F. Killeen.

3835 MARY PATTERSON

Stw p wh b. Grand Glaize, Ark., 1859. 105 tons. Operated on upper White River by Capt. Morgan Bateman. Was at Jacksonport, Ark., on May 5, 1861, to take out the Jackson Guards to the lower river. Today there is a monument at Jacksonport State Park commemorating the event. Carried troops and supplies for the Confederacy during most of the balance of 1861. Sunk purposely at St. Charles, Ark., in June 1862 along with Confederate gunboat *MAUREPAS* and small packet *ELIZA G.* to block the river.

3836 MARY PELL

SW p wh b. Cincinnati, Oh., 1845. 159 tons. Ran Cincinnati-Aurora, Capt. Pratzman. Was still in the trade when she and *PENNSYLVANIA* collided Apr. 12, 1851, at Lawrenceburg, Ind., causing her loss.

3837 MARY RUBLE

SW p wh A small single deck packet with one stack aft of the pilothouse in the Paducah-Eddyville-Canton trade, spring 1891, Capt. Lee Bauer, with Phil Bauer, clerk. Not listed in 1892.

3838 MARY S. BLEES

Stw p wh b. Mobile, Ala., 1899. 170.2 x 34 x 4.6. Engines, 16's- 7 ft. Built for Mobile-Tombigbee River trade, an adornment to any river. Steamboat broker John F. Klein brought her to New Orleans. Ran briefly New Orleans-Baton Rouge, fall 1914. Sold to William Ruprecht, St. Louis, June 1915. Her cotton guards were removed, etc., and she ran St. Louis-Illinois River, Capt. Milt Harry, summer 1915. Sold to Eagle Packet Co., February 1917 and renamed *PIASA* (see).

3839 MARY STEPHENS

SW p wh b. West Wheeling, Oh. (hull), at yard of McNaughton & Dunlevy and completed at Wheeling, 1847. 224 tons. 191 x 28 x 6. Engines, 20's- 7 ft. Three boilers. Built for Capt. M.E. Lucas, Steubenville, Oh. Reported the Wheeling *News*: "On the hurricane deck there is a cabin which the officers of the boat call the Texas (probably because it is annexed containing eight rooms of great convenience." Came out new in the Wheeling-Cincinnati trade, still there March 1848, then owned by Capt. G.W. Norton and others. Made a trip Cincinnati to New Orleans August 1848. Ran opposition to the regular St. Louis & Keokuk Line boats, 1850, along with *MONONGAHELA* and *NEW ENGLAND,* a financial disaster. Capt. J.W. Malin entered her as opposition to the regular U.S. Mail Line Louisville-Cincinnati in March 1851. Off the lists 1855.

3840 MARY SWAN

Stw p wh b. Cincinnati, Oh., 1866. 169.4 x 30.2 x 4.1. Winter of 1866–1867 she wintered under the wharfboat at Rockport, Ind. Cut down by ice mid-January 1867 while there. Water went over the main deck and the hogchains parted. The *UNDERWRITER,* Capt. R.W. Dugan, raised her. Capt. Samuel Archer was her skipper. Owned, 1868, by Alexander M. Halliday, Cincinnati. He sold her to Capt. John Quill and she went to Mobile, Ala. Off the lists 1875.

3841 MARY T.

SW p wh b. Jeffersonville, Ind., by Howard, 1860. 185 x 34 x 8. Engines, 22's- 8 ft. Four boilers, each 40″ by 26 ft. Built for the New Orleans Coast & Lafourche Transportation Co., New Orleans. First master, Capt. Joseph D. Phelps. She pinch-hit for the *CHARMER* in the New Orleans-Vicksburg trade, and was there 1861, Capt. Richard Holmes, carrying Confederate States Mail. In spring 1863 she was outfitted to become a Confederate gunboat, renamed *J.A. COTTON*. The U.S. captured her at Alexandria, La., June 1865, and despite pleas from the original owners to the effect that the boat had been confiscated from them by the Rebels, she was sent to Mound City, Ill. Sold, and in early 1866 she was stemming her way to Pittsburgh for dismantling. The engines were sold to Capt. Thomas Calhoon and used on his *GLENCOE* (see). The old hulk was moored at McKees Rocks, Pa., and in February 1867 was swept away by ice, then owned by Capt. R. Fisher.

3842 MARY Z. COMEAUX

Stw p wh b. Pittsburgh, Pa., 1883, originally named *ALABAMA* (see). Bought by Capt. F.J. Comeaux and others 1887–1888 and renamed. In 1890 ran New Orleans-Bayou Goula, Capt. F.J. Comeaux, teamed up with the *BELLE OF THE COAST* and *WHISPER* (both see). President of the Line was M.N. Wood, 2 Canal St. She is not listed in *List of Merchant Vessels* after 1890.

3843 MARYLAND

Stw p wh b. Louisville, Ky., 1857. 118 tons. First home port, Nashville, Tenn. Burned and lost at Louisville, Ky., Oct. 24, 1857.

3844 MASCOT

Stw p wh b. Evansville, Ind., 1886. See *LA MASCOTTE*, the enrolled name.

3845 MASCOT

Prop launch sh b. Charleston, W. Va., by Ward Engineering Works, 1893. 61 x 8.1 x 3.3. She was acquired by the U.S. Engineers and used on Kanawha River. Sold later to Capt. E.A. Burnside, Pt. Pleasant, W. Va., who used her for private excursions. He sold her 1912 to St. Louis and in 1918 was owned at Kansas City, Mo.

3846 MASON

SW p wh b. Maysville, Ky., 1863. 57 tons. A dispatch from Cincinnati, Apr. 9, 1864, says she has been acquired by the U.S. Engineers for service on the Big Sandy River. In 1869 she was at Evansville, Capt. James Van Eaton, Jr. Lost on the St. Francis River, Ark., in June 1870.

3847 MASONIC GEM

Stw p wh b. Mound City, Ill. (hull), and completed at Evansville, Ind., 1859. 125 x 26 x 4. She was the pioneer U.S. Mail packet on Green River, running Evansville-Bowling Green. During the war she transported troops. In October 1863 took the 131st Illinois Infantry from Calloway Landing on the Tennessee River to Vicksburg. Machinery came from *RAVEN*. Off the lists 1866.

3848 MATAMORAS

Stw p wh b. Shousetown, Pa., 1860. 172 tons. First home port, Point Isabel, Tex. Sold to the USQMD during the war. Redocumented 1866. Off the lists 1867.

3849 MATE

Stw p wh b. Edwardsport, Ind., 1865. 59 tons. Operated on Wabash River both above and below Vincennes, Capt. B.F. Cunningham. She was snagged below Palestine, Ind., in July 1866. Lost May 17, 1873.

3850 MATHILDA JANE

SW ferry wh b. Cincinnati, Oh., 1845. 87 tons. Snagged and lost at New Orleans, March 1849.

3851 MATILDA

SW p wh b. Cincinnati, Oh., 1859. 41 tons. First home port, New Orleans. Went to Confederate registry 1861.

3852 MATT F. ALLEN

Stw p wh b. Jeffersonville, Ind., by Howard, 1887. 149.5 x 28.3 x 4. Built for the Lovell Line on Cumberland River and ran Nashville-Burnside. Came to the upper Ohio in 1891, run by Capt. Henry R. Kraft and others, with W.M. Goodwin, clerk, Wheeling-Parkersburg. Sold in April 1896 to Capt. Walter Blair who took her to the Upper Mississippi and changed her name to *CARRIER* (see).

3853 MATT F. GRACEY

Stw p wh b. Clarksville, Tenn., 1874. 55 tons. Primarily a freight boat. Involved 1879 in an attempt to run "line" packets to Port Royal, Tenn.

3854 MATTIE

Stw p wh b. Paducah, Ky., 1863. 134 x 30 x 4. Did transport service during the war. Ran on St. Francis and White rivers owned by Preston and Kennedy Lodwick. Snagged and lost at Cut Off, Ark., May 14, 1867, with loss of two lives.

3855 MATTIE BELL

Rig? p wh b. in Ohio 1869. 41 tons. Sounds like a canalboat with steam power. Came out in the Ripley-Concord trade, upper Ohio, round trip daily. Sold by U.S. Marshal at Helena, Ark., in October 1871 to Capt. C.A. Walterhouse for $405. Documented at Memphis 1876.

3856 MATTIE BELL

Stw p wh b. Rocheport, Mo., 1875. 173.2 x 26.2 x 4.2. Engines, 13's- 4½ ft. Two boilers. In the Star Line, St. Louis-Kansas City, Capt. Ralph Whitledge. Ran competition with the *R. W. DUGAN*, Capt. W.L. Heckmann, Sr. The result was a rate war during which wheat was carried at three cents a sack and the *DUGAN* was whipped out. The Star Line folded later. Capt. E.W. Gould was master when she snagged at the foot of Cora Island, Missouri River, Aug. 25, 1879. Sold to St. Louis, Naples & Peoria Packet Co., Capt. James Abrams, and sank in winter quarters at St. Louis, Jan. 30, 1888.

3857 MATTIE BURNS

Stw p wh b. Pittsburgh, Pa., 1864, originally named *LOTUS* (see). When *LOTUS* was sold to private owners at war's conclusion she was renamed Oct. 4, 1865. Ran St. Louis-Tennessee River. Lost by snagging at Bird's Bend, five miles above Cairo on the Mississippi River, upbound for St. Louis, Capt. H.G. McComas. This happened about 9:00 P.M. She had 1400 barrels of cement aboard and broke in two. Engineer Thomas Blanton swam to Cairo. William Nelson, carpenter, clung to a fender and drifted seven miles before landing on the Missouri shore. The *RUBICON*, Capt. Balek, came along to take off passengers and delivered them to St. Louis next day. Among the passengers was a German mother with two children who resisted rescue, convinced that inasmuch as she had paid passage on the *MATTIE BURNS* she should stay with the boat. An interpreter finally convinced her to the contrary and she boarded the *RUBICON* with her children.

3858 MATTIE CABLER

Stw p wh b. New Albany, Ind., 1864. 128 tons. Sold to USQMD when new, and when sold to private hands was renamed *LAURA*, Sept. 28, 1865 (see).

3859 MATTIE COOK

Stw p wh b. Madison, Ind., 1860. 120 tons. 124.2 x 23.8 x 4.5. Built for Evansville-Green River trade, and named for a young lady of Bowling Green, Ky. Owned originally by Capt. Vanmeter and brother and Capt. Adam Liter, South Carrollton, Ky. Sold to a New York firm headed by Morris Ranger who handled tobacco at South Carrollton. In the summer of 1861, Brown's Lock was destroyed by Rebel raiders trapping *MATTIE COOK* above. In March 1862, in high water, she was jumped over the dam and returned to Evansville. Ran Cairo-Evansville that fall and on September 16, was captured by the Rebels, and next shows up at Memphis in November 1864. She was owned by Capt. James Sydney Smith, New Orleans, and George M. Gill, Memphis. Last owner was Horace S. Fulkerson, New Orleans. Off the lists 1867.

3860 MATTIE HAYS

Stw p wh b. Jeffersonville, Ind., by Howard, 1877. 100 x 20 x 3.4. Built for the Louisville & Henderson Packet Co., and named for daughter of Will S. Hays. Did low water work. Made frequent trips on Salt River to Shepherdsville and once at least was up Rolling Fork to Woolridge Ferry. Carried Clara Barton to West Point, Ky., in February 1884, for flood relief work. Lost at mouth of Mill Creek 1891.

3861 MATTIE K.

SW sawmill boat wh b. New Martinsville, W. Va., 1891. 110 x 20 x 3.5. Writes Jesse P. Hughes :"The smallest sawmill boat was this *MATTIE K.* owned by a man named Knapp who lived at Duffy, Oh." Sold July 1902 to Harry E. Cole who lived at Neville Island, Pa. Still listed at Pittsburgh 1908.

3862 MATTIE LEE

Centerwheel f wh b. Grafton, Mo., 1881. 110 x 28 x 4. Owned by Burruss Brothers and operated at Miami, Saline County, Mo. 1881–1894.

3863 MATTIE M.

Stw ferry wh b. Memphis, Tenn., 1894. 95 x 24 x 2.8. Operated in the Memphis area. She sank six miles above Natchez drowning six of her crew in December 1903, owned by Dixie Transportation Co., New Orleans.

3864 MATTIE ROBERTS

Stw p wh b. Cincinnati, Oh., 1863. 147 tons. Ran Parkersburg-Gallipolis. Spent the summer of 1867 stranded in Blennerhassett Island. Hit a rock backing out from a landing at Newberry Island, September 1867, and sank in four feet. Many rivermen were associated with her, Capts. W.T. Hayman, Charles Smith, and Mel Brown among them. The Big Etna Furnace Co., bought her with plans to convert her to towing, but instead sold her to Capt. Jack McAllister. He ran trips to Nashville. Sold to Capt. Taylor Higgins, Portsmouth, Oh., who dismantled her in 1875 using the engines on a new hull and sold her before completion to Jacksonville, Fla., for use on the St. Johns River. What name she bore your deponent knoweth not.

3865 MATTIE WAYNE

SW p wh b. Cincinnati, Oh., 1852. 335 tons. Was badly damaged in the steamboat fire at St. Louis Dec. 7, 1855. Checked in at St. Paul, 1856. Horace E. Bixby piloted her at one time. Dismantled 1858.

3866 MAUD F.

SW ferry wh b. Piney, Ark., 1905. 66 x 26 x 4.4. Still listed with Memphis registry 1908.

3867 MAUMELLE

Rig? p wh b. Madison, Ind., 1874. 299 tons. The Arkansas River Packet Co., bought her at Memphis, December 1876, and Capt. James Rees, Jr., took charge. At Cincinnati advertised for Memphis and Arkansas River, Capt. Thomas J. Darragh, September 1877.

3868 MAUREPAS

SW gunboat wh b. New Albany, Ind., 1858, originally *GROSSE TETE* (see). She was converted into a gunboat by the Rebels 1861 and renamed. She was purposely sunk on White River at St. Charles, Ark., along with *MARY PATTERSON* and *ELIZA G.* to blockade the river, this in June 1862.

3869 MAXIE YOST

Sw batwing wh b. Guyandotte, W. Va., 1897. 117.6 x 15.6. Owned by W.B. and A. Yost, Catlettsburg, Ky. Named for daughter of Capt. W.B., a grocer. Maxie became a school teacher and one of her pupils was Lillian Hughes, daughter of Capt. and Mrs. Jesse P. Hughes. The Big Sandy Navigation Co., was formed 1900 and this boat was one of the fleet composed to the *THEALKA, H. M. STAFFORD* and *ARGAND*. Ran Ohio River low water trades.

3870 MAY A. BRUNER

Stw p wh b. Liverpool, Ill., 1865. 172 tons. First home port, St. Louis. Burned and lost at the mouth of Red River, La., Feb. 3, 1866.

3871 MAY B.

SW p wh b. Ravenswood, W. Va. (hull), and completed at Wheeling, 1877. 18 tons. 66 x 9.5 x 2.6. Ran short trades, for a time between Racine and Pomeroy, Capt. Morris Greenly. Showed up at Cairo, Ill., in 1880, "a pretty little boat that eight good men could carry." Inspected in the Evansville district 1881, and in the Wheeling district 1882.

3872 MAY B.

Stw p wh b. Indianapolis, Ind., 1901. 68 x 20 x 3.5. Still documented 1908.

3873 MAY BELLE

Rig? p wh b. Calhoun, Tenn., 1875. 55 tons. Built for Hiwassee River, single stack, and did quite a bit of business for a time. She ran alternately Charleston-Knoxville, and Charleston-Chattanooga.

3874 MAY BELLE

Stw p wh b. Terre Haute, Ind., 1892. 40.8 x 8.1 x 2.5. Renamed *R.P. HOBSON* (see).

3875 MAY BRYAN

Recess wheel ferry wh b. Jeffersonville, Ind., 1875. 115 x 28 x 4.5. Operated at Washington, Mo., on Missouri River, succeeding the *BRIGHT STAR* (see). Still listed 1896.

3876 MAY DUKE

Stw p wh b. Brownsville, Pa., 1860. 64 tons. 148 x 25.3 x 4.8. First home port, Nashville, Tenn. In late November 1862, at Henderson, Ky., having been in Rebel service and hence liable for confiscation. Sold at Cincinnati, May 1864 to Messrs. Morse, Classon and others for Arkansas River. Advertised October 1865 Memphis-Little Rock with alternate White River trips, Capt. Houston. At New Orleans October 1866 Capt. Waddy Thompson who owned ⅓ along with James T. Fleming and John D. Adams. Ran up Red River, Capt. C.L. Sweet. Dismantled 1867.

3877 MAY FLOWER

SW ferry wh b. Le Claire, Iowa, 1888. 66.9 x 22.4 x 3.9. Still listed in 1908.

3878 MAY LOWERY

Rig? p wh b. Pittsburgh, Pa., 1871. 210 tons. 196 x 31 x 5. Departed Pittsburgh on first trip to New Orleans, Jan. 26, 1871, owned by William J. Kountz. Kountz ran her as owned by M. Lowery Transportation Co., in St. Louis-New Orleans trade. She had made a trip up Red River and burned at New Orleans on Feb. 20, 1876, Capt. W. Breathwaite, Brownsville, Pa., master.

3879 MAY QUEEN

Stw p wh b. Monongahela, Pa., 1850. 68 tons. Collapsed a flue on the Arkansas River, Feb. 16, 1852, twelve persons killed, seven injured. Snagged and lost 45 miles below Little Rock, Ark., Aug. 13, 1852.

3880 MAYFLOWER

Stw p wh b. Freedom, Pa., 1849. 140 tons. Ran Pittsburgh-Louisville, Capt. A. Devenney. Off the lists 1855.

3881 MAYFLOWER

SW p wh b. Pittsburgh, Pa. (hull), and towed to St. Louis for completion, 1855. Towed to Cincinnati by *BUCKEYE STATE,* arriving there at the foot of Broadway Jan. 1, 1855. Delivered to St. Louis by the *NATCHEZ*. This boat was listed at 890 tons. She and *JOHN SIMONDS* (see) were the only two-passenger-deck boats of the time. She was built for Capt. Joseph Brown and others, St. Louis, for the St. Louis-New Orleans trade. In the fall of 1855 this middle cabin deck was removed when she ran Memphis-New Orleans to permit greater freight capacity. She was downbound, moored at Memphis, Dec. 3, 1855, when the *GEORGE COLLIER* (see) took fire, resulting in the loss of both boats and the wharfboat. Owned at the time by McEwin and McAlister, St. Louis, and Captain Brown. Brown later was mayor of St. Louis.

3881A MAYFLOWER

SW p wh b. Cincinnati, Oh., 1867. 564 tons. 212 x 34.5 x 5.5. Engines, 20½'s- 7 ft. Four boilers. Built for Capt. Josh V. Throop and others for Evansville-Paducah-Cairo trade. Captain Throop commanded with William Dunn, clerk. She is said to have lost a great deal of money in this trade and was sold for the Memphis-Evansville trade and then in February 1869 to J.G. McCullock, New Orleans, who ran her New Orleans-Shreveport. Sold October 1869 to Edgar Nott of New Orleans, Capt. W.W. Risher. She made one trip for the Anchor Line, Memphis-New Orleans in 1873 and was dismantled at St. Louis October 1874.

3882 MAYFLOWER

SW p wh b. Catlettsburg, Ky., 1868. 40 tons. First home port, Cincinnati. Dismantled in 1873. Note: Documented *MAY FLOWER,* and some others listed here may be likewise.

3883 MAYFLOWER

Rig? p wh b. Aurora, Ind., 1884. 5.93 tons. This may have been a Big Sandy boat.

3884 MAYFLOWER

Stw p wh b. Pittsburgh, Pa., 1887. 187 x 44 x 5.5. Owned by Wilson & Bailey, a boat store on Water St., Pittsburgh, and commanded by Capt. Lew Clark. She came out as an excursion boat, principally on Monongahela River. The owners of the *KATE ADAMS* bought her June 1895 to take the *KATE*'s place in the Memphis-Arkansas City trade temporarily. Sold, October 1895 to Tennessee River Packet

Co., a firm then bucking the regular St. Louis & Tennessee River Packet Co. She was upbound at the foot of Kaskaskia Island near Chester, Ill., with a cargo of lumber and livestock Apr. 17, 1898, when she sank. The *CITY OF PADUCAH* took off the people and some of the freight. Sold September 1899 to John F. Klein who brought her to Pittsburgh in September 1899. She ran excursions, Capt. Ben Hebel, with Joe McLaughlin, pilot. Burned at 3:00 P.M. Oct. 3, 1904, at the B&O depot along the Monongahela River, Pittsburgh. Fire was discovered on the roof and she soon went. Capt. W.O. Rhodes, Pittsburgh, was master at the time.

3885 MAZEPPA

SW p wh b. Louisville, Ky., 1842. 347 tons. 174 x 28 x 7.5. Came out in the New Orleans-Vicksburg trade, Capt. Abram Auter, continued through 1843. Captain Auter lived in Vicksburg and survived into his 80's still there. In December 1843 sold to Capt. William Enders, Paducah, Ky. Sold September 1845 to Capt. P.C. Shannon, New Orleans. Sold March 1846 to Capt. Edward S. Johnson, New Orleans. She was taken to Cairo, dismantled, and used as a wharfboat, 1848. Newspapers at the time spoke of the "Mazeppa wharfboat."

3886 MAZEPPA

Stw p wh b. Cincinnati, Oh., 1864. 184 tons. She was at Fort Helman (Harmon?), Tenn., Oct. 29, 1864, when Rebels attacked and destroyed her. Dispatch from Cincinnati, Nov. 6:- "The crew of the *MAZEPPA* arrived here yesterday, except Capt. Lee Pettit, master, and Sam Pence, the mate. They were last seen going up over the bank on the opposite shore amid a rain of shot. Captain Pettit resides in Cincinnati and mate Pence is from Middleport, Oh."

3887 MEDIATOR

SW p wh b. Cincinnati, Oh., 1852. 421 tons. Ran New Orleans-Cincinnati, Capt. John A. Williamson. Burned at St. Joseph, La., Jan. 4, 1856.

3888 MEDORA

SW p wh b. New Albany, Ind., 1845. 196 tons. 155 x 24.5 x 5.5. Owned in part and commanded by Capt. Silas F. Miller, New Orleans. Steam explosion at Port Hudson, Feb. 12, 1847, en route New Orleans to Natchitoches. Sold March 1847 to John C. Shannon and Francis Whipple, New Orleans and registry transferred to Mobile, January 1848. Enrolled at Vicksburg, November 1849, owned by Thomas Porterfield, that city. Sold June 1850 to John Thomas, New Orleans, Capt. Samuel Applegate, master. Ran New Orleans-Shreveport thereafter. Off the lists 1852.

3889 MEDORA

Stw p wh b. Brownsville, Pa., 1856. 101 tons. Went to the Upper Mississippi. At St. Paul in 1857 owned by William Constans. In Minnesota River trade 1858, Capt. Ed McLagen. Burned at Jeffersonville, Ind., July 20, 1861, Capt. B.F. Beasley.

3890 MEEKER

Stw ferry wh b. Chester, Ill., 1897, originally named *BELLE OF KASKASKIA* (see). Was renamed *MEEKER* and served at Alexandria, Mo. There in 1908, maybe later.

3891 MEGIDDO

Stw gospel boat wh b. Lyons, Iowa, at Godfrey Marine Ways, 1901. 175 x 33 x 5. Owned by a religious sect known as the Megiddos. Founder was a bearded, astute man named L. (for nothing) T. (for nothing) Nichols who examined many a religion in his youth, found none that he liked. In 1880 he started one for himself, and preached it throughout the midwest. In 1901 he launched the *MEGIDDO,* with 95 followers, and plied up and down the Mississippi and the Ohio making new converts. Later he sold the boat, settled his mission at Rochester, N.Y. Founder Nichols died in 1912. The boat was rebuilt into a packet at Paducah, and renamed *CHATTANOOGA,* March 1904 (see).

3892 MELNOTTE

Stw p wh b. California, Pa., 1856. 160 x 37 x 6. Engine, 20's-5½ ft. Three boilers, each 40" by 28 ft. Original owners included her master, Capt. E. Gordon, Pittsburgh. Ran tramp trips Pittsburgh-Louisville-New Orleans. In March 1861 was at Wheeling, Capt. John T. McCombs, sporting a calliope noticed by a local editor who recognized "Dixie's Land, the Old Grey Horse, Pop Goes the Weasel and Katy Darling." The calliope is mentioned by a Cincinnati editor at Cincinnati on Oct. 31, 1859. Sold in latter May 1862 to Capt. R.D. Cochran of Pittsburgh. Loading at Pittsburgh mid-December 1862 for St. Louis, Capt. Charles A. Dravo. Had several owners after that. Capt. John Grace, late of the *LADY GRACE,* advertised her Cincinnati-New Orleans in mid-September 1865. She was sold at a U.S. Marshal sale at Cincinnati, December 1866. Last owners were James Keniston, John A. Williamson (of Newport, Ky.) and John G. Isham, Cincinnati. Capt. John Keniston was master. They ran her Cincinnati-St. Louis. Burned at Cincinnati, May 12, 1869. Six boats were burned that day between 2:00 and 2:30 A.M., the *DARLING, WESTMORELAND, MARY ERWIN, MELNOTTE, CHEYENNE* and *CLIFTON.* Lying above them, unharmed, were the *SILVER SPRAY, SHAMROCK, ALICE DEAN, SWALLOW,* and the hull of the *UNITED STATES* just repaired from the fire and collision with the *AMERICA* at Sugar Creek. The fire originated on the *CLIFTON,* probably from the upsetting of a lamp.

3893 MELODEON

SW p wh b. Cincinnati, Oh., 1849. 244 tons. Ran Louisville-St. Louis spring of 1849. She was upbound from New Orleans for Nashville on Dec. 14, 1850, when she came in collision with the *G. W. KENDALL* (see) and was sunk near Plaquemine, La., with loss of three lives.

3894 MELROSE

Stw p wh b. Monongahela, Pa., 1856. 177 tons. Ran Cincinnati-Nashville 1861, Capt. William Metcalfe, with

Bradford, clerk. She and *PACIFIC* came in collision at Shawneetown, Ill., Jan. 29, 1861, resulting in her loss. Her wreck was reported still in the channel as of Oct. 31, 1866, with the *BALTIC* wreck just above her.

3895 MEMPHIS

SW p wh b. Cincinnati, Oh., 1848. 196 tons. Ran Cincinnati-Memphis operated by Clifford B. Wayne and Thompson Dean. A severe windstorm encountered fifteen miles above New Madrid, Mo., in June 1849, relieved her of cabin, texas, and pilothouse, with twelve deaths, among them the two pilots and cub pilot. Burned and lost at Cincinnati June 14, 1853.

3896 MEMPHIS

SW p wh b. Cincinnati, Oh., 1852. 319 tons. Replaced the former *MEMPHIS* (see above) in the Cincinnati-Memphis trade. Sank below Madison, Ind., Feb. 12, 1853, with loss of considerable cargo. Off the lists 1860.

3897 MEMPHIS

SW p wh b. Jeffersonville, Ind., by Howard, 1860. 645 tons. 263 x 38 x 7. Ran St. Louis-Memphis-New Orleans. In *Transactions of Naval Architects,* Vol. 2, 1861, there is a paper on American river steamers by Norman S. Russell. Three detailed drawings of *MEMPHIS* are included. Her profile is much like the *JACOB STRADER* (see) with texas well forward, the pilothouse aft of the stacks, set well forward. No hogchains fore and aft. Instead the hull contains five arched bridge trusses, around and over which was the center keelson. Two tall kingposts rise from the center keelson from which iron rods support the paddlebox extremities. Four five-flue boilers appear. In contemporary newspapers she is usually referred to as *BELLE MEMPHIS,* although documented simply *MEMPHIS.* She was owned by the St. Louis & Memphis Packet Co. She had engines 27's- 8 ft. and her four boilers were each 44" by 24 ft. She was in U.S. transport service at frequent intervals during the war. In February 1862 carried the 66th Illinois Infantry, St. Louis to Fort Henry where the troops occupied the vacated premises. She spent most of March and the first week of April 1864 on a sand bar opposite Tiptonville, Tenn. She was anchored at St. Louis at the location of the east pier of the Eads Bridge in the winter 1865–1866, and test borings were made from her forecastle. While so employed she was solidly frozen in ice, which later gorged, resulting in her loss on Jan. 12, 1866. She had a full crew aboard, headed by Capt. Dan Musselman, with Harry Matson and J.H. Parker, pilots. They had adventures getting ashore. The wreck lodged near Duncan Island and on Feb. 13, 1867, the *WHITE CLOUD NO. 2* (see) struck it and was lost.

3898 MEMPHIS

Stw p wh b. Brownsville, Pa., 1863, originally named *COLOSSUS* (see). She became Tinclad #25 in U.S. service during the war and when sold to private hands was renamed *MEMPHIS* on Sept. 27, 1865. Snagged and lost at Pine Bluff, Ark., Dec. 17, 1866.

3899 MEMPHIS

Stw p wh b. Memphis, Tenn., 1895. 111 x 26.6 x 4. Owned by Vicksburg & Yazoo River Packet Co., when she burned at Vicksburg in April 1898.

3900 MENDOTA

SW p wh b. Cincinnati, Oh., 1844. 157 tons. Ran on the Upper Mississippi River out of Galena, Ill. Capt. Robert A. Reilly, master, 1844. Snagged opposite Cat Island, October 1847. Snagged and lost at Ste. Genevieve, Mo., on Jan. 29, 1848.

3901 MENOMINEE

SW p wh b. Fond du Lac, Wis., 1856. 55 tons. 100 x 16. Originally ran on Fox River, but had wandered to Lake Pepin by 1860. Capt. J. Brandon who had been running *EAGLE* in the Warsaw-Keokuk trade bought her June 1860 as a replacement. Had a commodious cabin with rooms. Off the lists 1865.

3902 MENOMONIE

Stw p wh b. Menomonie, Wis., 1855. 41 tons. First home port, St. Paul. Off the lists in 1866.

3903 MERANGO

Stw p wh b. Brownsville, Pa., 1855. 239 tons. 155 x 35. Engines, 18's- 5 ft. Built under supervision of Capt. Adam Jacobs for Capt. A.C. McCallum, Pittsburgh. Ran Pittsburgh-New Orleans. She was at New Orleans when Louisiana seceded and cleared for St. Louis. Her clerk at the time was A.C. McCallum, Jr., who still had these clearance papers in 1904. Handled troops and supplies for the U.S. during the war. She and *J. W. HAILMAN* took doctors, nurses and medical supplies from Pittsburgh to Pittsburg Landing, Tenn., after the battle there, and returned to Pittsburgh with wounded. Off the lists in 1862. Note: Lytle-Holdcamper lists spelling as *MARENGO.*

3904 MERCURY

Stw p wh b. Brownsville, Pa., 1862. 184 tons. Carried troops and supplies for the U.S. during the war. In latter May 1865 came in collision with *HARD TIMES* at Harrisons Landing not far below St. Louis and was beached and sunk. Had aboard wounded soldiers from Vicksburg, all transferred to *HARD TIMES* which turned back and delivered them to St. Louis. She was lost in the Cut Off between White and Arkansas rivers Mar. 13, 1867. Had aboard a cargo of cattle. Went down in 50 feet, 15 feet over top of the roof. Much of her cotton cargo was lost. Two were drowned.

3905 MESSENGER

SW wh b. Pittsburgh, Pa., 1844. 236 tons. 172 x 25 x 5.7. Built for Capt. James J. Perry who commanded and a group of stockholders including A. and W.K. Nimick, Pittsburgh. Ran Pittsburgh-Cincinnati, and occasionally loaded out for New Orleans. She was succeeded in 1849 by the *MESSENGER No. 2* (see).

3906 MESSENGER

SW p wh b. Jeffersonville, Ind., by Howard, 1852. 389 tons. 190 x 30.8 x 7. Built for Robert S. Kirke, Mobile, Ala. Due to a falling river the Howards attempted to take her below the falls to complete her. She stuck on Wave Rock just off Whirlpool Point and became high and dry, but was successfully floated and completed there. In June 1858 she was bought by W.L. Miller, New Orleans and ran Memphis-New Orleans and Ouachita River. She was pinch-hitting for the *INGOMAR,* New Orleans-Memphis when she took fire nine miles above Bayou Sara, Aug. 30, 1859, and was lost.

3907 MESSENGER

Stw p wh b. Belle Vernon, Pa., 1855. 254 tons. 154 x 35 x 5.2. Engines, 20's- 5 ft. Ran Pittsburgh-Cincinnati. Original crew: Capt. Martin Mellinger, with C.L. Brennan and John Gallagher, clerks; James G. Caldwell and Baker Reynolds, engineers; Alfred Moore (of Beaver, Pa.) and Wash Kerr (of Ironton, Oh.) pilots, and William Ryster, steward. Was on the Upper Mississippi, 1857, in opposition to the Minnesota Packet Co. Ran Louisville-Memphis, Capt. John Kyle, fall of 1859. Lost by stranding at Rochester, Pa., Dec. 7, 1861.

3908 MESSENGER

Stw p wh b. Brownsville, Pa., 1865. 436 tons. 157 x 34.5 x 5. Engines, 16's- 5 ft. Three boilers, each 38" by 24 ft. Built for Pittsburgh-St. Louis trade, Capt. William Dean. In the fall of 1866 she was making her third trip to New Orleans, Capt. Jesse Dean, when she sank at the crossing below Island 26. The *UNDERWRITER,* Capt. R.W. Dugan, went to the scene and raised her. In 1871 making Pittsburgh-New Orleans trips, Capt. Robert Greenlee, "one of the oldest steamboatmen in the country having been on the river 40 years." Rebuilt at Brownsville, Pa., summer 1873, during which time her texas was removed "distracting somewhat from her proportions but it was not needed, we presume, otherwise it would not have been dispensed with," said one Pittsburgh editor. Pittsburgh-Cincinnati, 1875, Capt. J.M. Vandergrift, with John C. Fisher, clerk. She was dismantled that year, the hull serving as a barge.

3909 MESSENGER NO. 2

SW p wh b. Freedom, Pa. (hull), and completed at Pittsburgh, 1849. 368 tons. 230 x 30 x 5. Engines, 28's- 7½ ft. Five boilers, each having two 16" flues. Pittsburgh-Cincinnati, Capt. I.C. Woodward, with Alexander Ingram, clerk. Often went through to Louisville. She once ran from Rochester, Pa., to Pittsburgh (25 miles) in 2 hours 34 minutes, with John Shouse and James Witten in the pilothouse and General O'Neal at the throttle. In mid-May 1849 ran Cincinnati to Pittsburgh in 44 hours 14 minutes (470 miles) a record soon bettered by the *BUCKEYE STATE* (see). Capts. John Klinefelter and J.B. Davis commanded later. Off the list in 1856. Klinefelter was skipper in 1851 when showman P.T. Barnum brought Jenny Lind aboard at Cincinnati for the trip to Pittsburgh while the entire population of the upper Ohio Valley stood on the shores and watched.

3910 METAMORA

SW p wh b. Peoria, Ill., 1864. 190 tons. Engines, 15's- 4½ ft. Three boilers. She was first on the Illinois River, and then went to Omaha for use transporting railroad passengers. In 1873 bought at Omaha by Capt. J.A. Ware, docked at St. Louis, and then used between Boonville and Kansas City handling railroad ties, etc. She was snagged on the north side of Franklin Island just below Boonville, Mo., Sept. 27, 1875, and lost. Owned then by A.A. Hibbard and others.

3911 METEOR

SW p wh b. New Albany, Ind., 1847. 162 tons. 154.5 x 23 x 4.5. She is noticed at Cairo, Ill., Feb. 29, 1849, bound from Cincinnati to the Missouri River "in which trade she designs running." A company of California emigrants were on board, numbering about 150, principally from Bedford, Ky., and the neighborhood of Louisville. "She is a light boat, well furnished in the cabin, and of medium speed commanded by Capt. Turner." In March 1848 Capt. James Seabrook, New Albany, Ind., was master, and she was owned by him in shares with Daniel Seabrook, same city. Capt. Henry C. Turner later became two-thirds owner (1850), and the boat burned and was lost at Long Vue, La., (about 50 miles above New Orleans) on Oct. 2, 1850. Three lives lost.

3912 METEOR

SW p wh b. Louisville, Ky., 1857. 417 tons. 233 x 36 x 6. Four boilers, each 40" by 30 ft. In 1864, New Orleans-Natchez, Capt. C.L. Salisbury. Transferred to U.S. War Dept., in 1864. Reported lost in the wharf fire at New Orleans, May 28, 1864.

3913 METEOR

Stw tinclad wh b. Portsmouth, Oh., 1863, originally named *SCIOTO* (see). Sold to U.S. Navy Jan. 23, 1864, and became Tinclad #44, named *METEOR,* Mar. 8, 1864. When sold to private hands Oct. 7, 1865, renamed *DE SOTO* (see).

3914 METROPOLIS

SW p wh b. California, Pa., 1855. 254 tons. 149 x 36.1 x 5.2. First master was Capt. C.E. Haslet, Allegheny County, Pa., who owned control. She exploded one boiler at West Columbia, Va., at 6:00 A.M., one morning in March 1856 killing Captain Haslet and several others. She then was sold to Capt. Richard Calhoon, Georgetown, Pa., and others, and under his command ran Pittsburgh-New Orleans principally. Downbound from Cincinnati she hit the bank at Sugar Creek, Ky., in fog, Dec. 26, 1858, and was wrecked. Among the stockholders at the time were John A. Trimble and William R. Trimble, both of Beaver County, Pa.

3915 METROPOLIS

Rig? p wh b Metropolis, Ill., 1882. 78 x 12 x 4. Ran

Metropolis-Paducah. She was in a storm near Brookport, Ill., Sept. 30, 1884, and turned over in eight feet. Her machinery, being set down in the hull, made her vulnerable to the waves.

3916 METROPOLITAN

SW p wh b. McKeesport, Pa., 1856. 313 tons. Built for the Northern Line on the Upper Mississippi. Ran St. Louis-St. Paul, Capt. Thomas B. Rhodes in 1856–57. In Northwestern Line, same master in 1858–1859. Capt. Thomas B. Buford, same line and trade, 1861. Transferred to the War Dept., in 1865 and was lost in the ice break-up at St. Louis, Dec. 16, 1865.

3917 MEXICO

SW p wh b. Wheeling, Va., 1859. 120 tons. First home port, La Salle, Tex. Burned and lost at Point Isabel, Tex., Mar. 18, 1865.

3918 MEXICO

SW p wh b. McKeesport, Pa., 1859, originally named *IZETTA* (see). She was acquired by the USQMC at war's outbreak and carried her name until sold to private hands and renamed *MEXICO* on Nov. 25, 1865. Burned and lost at St. Louis, Jan. 20, 1867.

3919 MIAMI

Stw p wh b. Cincinnati, Oh., 1863. 175 tons. 159 x 32. She was about six miles above the mouth of the Arkansas River on Jan. 28, 1866, when she exploded boilers with many troops aboard said to have been with the 13th U.S. Cavalry, Company B. Forty lives were lost. The accident happened about 7:00 P.M. She had been owned at St. Louis by Samuel McCarthy and was sent to Memphis August 1865 for short trade work. Capt. Sol Franklin was named as master at the time of the loss. When new in spring of 1864 she made Pittsburgh-Louisville trips, Capt. Lon Bryson, with J.J. Robinson, clerk, and was sold March 1864 to Capt. George W. Wolff, St. Louis.

3920 MICHIGAN

SW p wh b. Elizabeth, Pa., 1853. 482 tons. First home port, St. Louis. Ran St. Louis-New Orleans. Her master, 1856, was Capt. R.A. Reiley. Exploded and lost at New Madrid, Mo., Dec. 9, 1859, with loss of two lives.

3921 MICHIGAN NO. 2

Stw p wh b. Shousetown, Pa., 1847. 103 tons. Ran Pittsburgh-Beaver-Wellsville, Capt. Wolf. She replaced an earlier *MICHIGAN* in the same trades, b. 1842, and dismantled when this one was built. She stopped in at Freedom, Pa., and gathered up the uncompleted *CRYSTAL PALACE* on Jan. 20, 1853, and towed her to Pittsburgh for completion. On the way, at Shousetown, she came in collision with *AUSTRALIA* (see) which was downbound for New Orleans sustaining a broken engine and other damages. Nobody was seriously hurt. The famed Capt. Grant Marsh was the watchman on her in the Pittsburgh-Beaver trade, 1855. Dismantled 1856.

3922 MIDAS

SW p wh b. Cincinnati, Oh., 1851. 307 tons. 180 x 33 (30 ft. floor) x 6.3. Engines, 20's- 6½ ft. Ran Cincinnati-New Orleans, Capt. Charles Davis. Other shareholders: Taylor & Cassilly and M.L. Virdin. Sold 1856 largely owned by Stanley Brown, Paducah, Ky. Master, Capt. J.M. Smith, Paducah. Off the lists in 1859.

3923 MIKE DAVIS

Stw p wh b. Wheeling, W. Va., 1878. 105.3 x 18 x 3. Short trader and low water boat owned by Capt. Michael Davis, Sr., who lived near Fish Creek, W. Va., and who also built *LEONORA* and *LEONORA NO. 2* (see). Sold to the lower Ohio and when the *JOSH V. THROOP* sank September 1883 between Evansville and Paducah the *MIKE DAVIS* took off passengers and freight. Documented at Golconda, Ill., 1886.

3924 MILBREY

Stw p wh b. Mound City, Ill., 1863 originally named *ANNIE JACOBS* (see). Sold to USQMD on Oct. 15, 1864, and when sold to private hands was renamed *MILBREY* Oct. 2, 1865. C.J. Caffrey, St. Louis, formed a "Line" to operate a fleet of packets St. Louis-Johnsonville, Tenn., which went flat, resulting in a sale at St. Louis July 24, 1866, including *MILBREY, LOUISA, LAURA, GRAY EAGLE, M. BURNS, NORTH ALABAMA, FANNIE BARKER* and *C.J. CAFFREY*. She was attached by a U.S. Marshal at Paducah about May 1, 1868. The captain sweet-talked the marshal into letting the boat handle a local Sunday school excursion after which the *MILBREY* took off and was next heard from at Memphis. She caught fire there and the law caught up with her. Sold to Capt. Robert Wood, Paducah, who repaired her and ran her Louisville-Cairo with R.G. Ferguson, clerk. Still there September 1868.

3925 MILES H.

Stw p wh b. Sistersville, W. Va., 1902. 96.4 x 18.4 x 3.3. Built by Charles A.F. Hubbard and T.B. Hubbard, Sistersville, and named for son of Charles. Ran short trades. Sold January 1903 to O.J. and W.B. Webster, both of Marietta, Oh., equal shares. On Mar. 24, 1903, at 7:00 P.M., towing a loaded barge and herself also loaded with freight, she sank in a storm at Mile 10.1 on Tug Fork of the Big Sandy, Capt. Elias Ward, Catlettsburg. She had been sold 30 days prior to J.F. York, Kenova, W. Va. who was operating the Huntington. Ashland & Big Sandy Transportation Co. She was raised, and apparently the Websters took her back. She ran occasional trips Marietta-Zanesville 1903–1904.

3926 MILL BOY

SW p wh b. Brownsville, Pa., 1857. 86 tons. Owned and operated by Capt. Josiah Cornwall, Chambersburg, Oh. He built her as a floating grist mill, and ran a general store aboard plying between Crown City and Gallipolis. Until 1860 she was horse-powered, the steeds operating a treadmill attached to side-wheels. He added a boiler and a small slide-valve engine in 1860. At the outbreak of the war he sold her to others. She was moored at Jacksonport, Ark., on Jan. 31, 1864, when a high wind parted her lines. She drifted against a snag, sank, and later drifted nine more miles and turned bottom side up. Owned then by Mitchell and Johnson, and was grinding grain for the U.S.

3927 MILL BOY

Rig? p wh b. Little Rock, Ark., 1881. 102 x 19.5 x 2.5. Ran Little Rock-Dardanelle, Capt. Dave Pearson. Still listed 1886.

3928 MILL BOY

Stw ferry wh b. Hermann, Mo., 1893. 41 tons. 89.2 x 18.8 x 2.8. Engines, 8″- 2 ft. One boiler. Owned by Frank Blaske and others. Destroyed by ice in winter quarters at the head of the chute opposite South Point, Mo., on Missouri River, Jan. 1, 1910.

3929 MILLIE HIGGINS

SW ferry wh b. Chattanooga, Tenn., 1866. 22 tons. Lost Oct. 20, 1868, at St. Louis.

3930 MILT HARRY

Stw p wh b. Cincinnati, Oh., 1877. 80 tons. Built for Capt. Pete McArthur who was associated with Capt. Milt R. Harry at Newport, Ark., on White River and on Black River at Pocahontas. She burned 20 miles above Batesville, Ark., on White River, Mar. 6, 1885.

3931 MILTON

Stw p wh b. Freedom, Pa., 1850. 158 tons. Ran Pittsburgh-Louisville, Capt. John B. Davis in charge. On a downbound trip she burned at Wittens Towhead above Sistersville, W. Va., Mar. 11, 1853.

3932 MILTON BROWN

SW p wh b. Pomeroy, Oh., 1859, originally named *B. P. CHENEY* (see). She was in Confederate service, apparently renamed at the time, and was burned by U.S. troops at Donaldson's Point on Arkansas River. Lytle-Holdcamper burns her at Yazoo City, Miss., July 14, 1863.

3933 MILTON H. SMITH

Stw p wh b. Jeffersonville, Ind., by Howard, 1885. 111 x 25 x 5. Went to the Chattahoochee River. Dismantled there 1891 and her cabin used in building the *FLINT*.

3934 MILTON RELF

SW p wh b. Louisville, Ky., 1856. 279 tons. 130 x 34 x 6. Engines, 18's- 6 ft. Three boilers, each 36″ by 24 ft. Built for William L. Hall, New Orleans, with Capt. Charles Hall, master. Beautiful view of Niagara Falls in the ladies' cabin and a correct view of Lake Tensas forward "on which she is to run." Her first clerk was S.A. Whyte. Ran New Orleans-Bayou Macon. By 1859 ownership was changed to Capt. Charles Hall. She ran Ouachita, Bayou Macon, Tensas, and Red rivers. Sold 1861 to Capt. Charles C. Pickett, St. Landry Parish, who ran her Bayou Courtableau and Atchafalaya trade as an Opelousas packet. Went to Confederate registry and fate is not known.

3935 MILWAUKEE

SW p wh b. Shousetown, Pa., 1845. 153 tons. Ran Pittsburgh-Marietta, Capt. Clark, spring of 1846. That fall made trips Pittsburgh-Nashville, Capt. Fowler. In passing over the falls at Louisville, July 15, 1848, hit Lower Wave Rock and sank, Capt. McComas, who had just bought and refitted her. Lost in ice at Naples, Ill., Jan. 1, 1849.

3936 MILWAUKEE

SW p wh b. Cincinnati, Oh., 1857. 402 tons. One of the crack packets of the Minnesota Packet Co. Prairie du Chien-St. Paul, 1857–1859, Capt. S. Hewitt; Dunleith-St. Paul, 1860–1861, Capt. John Cochrane; Dunleith trade in 1861, Capt. E.V. Holcombe. Off the lists in 1870.

3937 MILWAUKEE

SW p wh We have mention of her in the White Collar Line, St. Louis-St. Paul, 1879, Capt. W.H. Laughton, with C.T. Spencer and S.R. Spaulding, clerks.

3938 MILWAUKEE

Stw tr. wh b. Jeffersonville, Ind. by Howard, 1880. 136.5 x 30.3 x 5.3. She is documented at Prairie du Chien in 1886. Still listed with Dubuque registry 1896.

3939 MINER

SW p wh b. Bridgeport, Ala., 1864, originally named *BURNSIDE* (see). Built for the USQMD and when sold to private hands was renamed *MINER*, June 7, 1866. She had engines 16½'s- 5 ft., and three boilers. She was sent up Skunk River, near Burlington, Iowa, with a load of piling and contractor's supplies for the building of a bridge for the C.B. & Q. Railroad when snagged and lost June 8, 1869.

3940 MINER

Stw p wh b. Pittsburgh, Pa., 1866. 299 tons. Left Pittsburgh, April 1866, new, Capt. J.H. Porter, bound for the upper Missouri River with 1,187 rails and 20 tons of "connection bands" consigned to Point of Rocks above Fort Benton, Mont., for the Union Pacific RR. Sold by Capt. Porter to the Northwestern Fur Co., and remained on the Missouri.

3941 MINERVA

Stw p wh b. Brownsville, Pa., 1854. 177 tons. Built for the Pittsburgh-Wheeling trade, Capt. John Gordon, with George W. Johnston, clerk. She ran this trade with regularity for 10 years or more. A.R. Bunting was head clerk during the latter war years. She ran Pittsburgh-Parkersburg spring 1865, and when dismantled much equipment went to building the *GLASGOW* (see).

3942 MINK

Stw p wh b. Pittsburgh, Pa., 1865. 165 tons. 125 x 20.5. Ran on Muskingum River, Zanesville-McConnelsville. Capt. William Davis, master, 1865–1871. Capt. Charles C.

Morgan, master, 1872-1877. Howard M. Jenkins, Cambridge, Oh., informed us in 1952 that his father and William Freeman, New Cumberland, W. Va., took *MINK* south in 1877, towing flats of fire clay, brick, etc. They chartered her to a lumber firm which ran her around New Iberia, Franklin, and Morgan City, La., for six months, then purchased her. She is off the lists in 1878.

3943 MINK NO. 2

Stw p wh b. Harmar, Oh., at Knox Yard, 1877. 132 x 21 x 3.5. Ran Zanesville-McConnelsville daily, 1877-1883, Capt. Carlton C. Morgan. Same trade, Capt. Diodate Morgan, 1884-1886. She then towed salt and coal for the Pomeroy (Oh.) Towboat Co. Sold later to Capt. W.L. Cavett, Pittsburgh. She collapsed a flue at 26th Street, Pittsburgh, Sept. 30, 1894, and one man died. Was rebuilt and renamed *CLARA CAVETT* (towboat).

3944 MINNEAPOLIS

SW p wh b. Wheeling, W. Va. (hull and framing), and completed at Pittsburgh, 1869. 233 x 36 x 5.8. Engines, 30's- 7 ft. Four boilers, each 38" by 26 ft. Capt. T.R. Rhodes superintended construction for the Northern Line. Ran on the Upper Mississippi. Mark Twain in May 1882, came from St. Louis to Hannibal on *GEM CITY,* thence to St. Paul on *MINNEAPOLIS.*

3945 MINNEHAHA

SW ferry wh b. Wellsville, Oh., 1856. 33 tons. First home port, Wheeling. Off the lists 1861.

3946 MINNEHAHA

SW p wh b. Guyandotte, Va., 1857. 531 tons. 236 x 36.5 x 6.5. Engines, 25's- 7 ft. Four boilers, each 46" by 30 ft. Ran on the Missouri River, St. Louis-St. Joseph, Capt. C. Baker. The *Louisville Democrat* reported Feb. 2, 1862 that Capt. David White had bought her and would run her Paducah-St. Louis. She burned at New Orleans, May 13, 1865.

3947 MINNEHAHA

Stw p wh b. Canton, S.D., 1894. 40 x 9 x 5. The long and the short of it is she still was documented at Sioux City, 1908.

3948 MINNEOLA

SW p wh b. Cincinnati, Oh., 1865. b. Parkersburg, W. Va., and completed at Cincinnati, 1865. 708 tons. Ran Cincinnati-Memphis in the Dean Line, Capt. Lew Kates. Later commanded by Capt. W.B. Miller who started out clerk on her. In March 1868 she brought to Cincinnati one trip 1,914 bales of cotton, the largest cotton trip ever brought to that city. Sank and lost Dec. 27, 1875, 18 miles above Memphis at Foghuman's Outlet. No life loss.

3949 MINNESOTA

Stw p wh b. Louisville, Ky., 1848. 74 tons. First home port, St. Louis. Off the lists in 1850.

3950 MINNESOTA

SW p wh b. Elizabeth, Pa., 1849. 149 tons. Built under direction of Capt. Richard C. Gray for the Northern Line and went to the Upper Mississippi. Ran Galena-St. Paul, and later in the Minnesota River. Off the lists 1862.

3951 MINNESOTA

Stw p wh b. California, Pa., 1857. 142 tons. 131 x 30 x 4. Built for Capt. Charles A. Hay. Ran New Orleans-Red River to Alexandria, La., Capt. A.D. Glasscock, 1859. Burned at Greenville, Miss. under charter to USQMD on May 3, 1863.

3952 MINNESOTA

SW p wh b. Wheeling, W. Va., 1866. 482 tons. Came to Pittsburgh, new, Mar. 15, 1866. "She is a very pretty sidewheeler," said the *Pittsburgh Gazette.* She was advertised out of Pittsburgh, Apr. 3, 1866, Capt. Thomas B. Hill, with Charles C. Carrell, clerk. Was in the Northern Line. Hit the Clinton bridge May 18, 1867, and was drydocked at Le Claire. In summer of 1881 she was rebuilt into a railroad transfer and renamed *TRANSFER NO. 2* (see).

3953 MINNESOTA

SW p wh b. Prescott, Wis., 1907. 84 x 12.4 x 3. Single deck with one stack aft of the pilothouse.

3954 MINNESOTA

Stw pleasure boat sh b. Jeffersonville, Ind., by Howard, 1915. 115.9 x 30.2 x 5.2. Built for the celebrated Drs. Mayo, Rochester, Minn. (Charles Horace and William James), to replace their pleasure steamboat *ORONOCO* (see). They sold her at Fountain City, Wis., 1922, to the U.S. Engineers who renamed her *GENERAL ALLEN* and added towing knees. She eventually wound up as a posh floating restaurant at St. Louis renamed *COTTON BLOSSOM* which sank and was lost there Jan. 24, 1978. See *S&D Reflector,* March 1972 issue, page 14, for picture and write-up. Also June 1978 issue, page 21, for run-down of her career.

3955 MINNESOTA BELLE

SW p wh b. Belle Vernon, Pa., 1854. 225 tons. Ran St. Louis-St. Paul, Capt. Thomas B. Hill, 1857. In the Northern Line, same trade, same master, 1859. Snagged and lost at Liverpool, Ill., Mar. 28, 1862.

3956 MINNETONKA

Stw p wh b. California, Pa., 1857. 158 tons. 141 x 26.6 x 4.5. Built for Capt. W.W. Williamson and others, Pittsburgh. She was victim of Morgan's Raiders who descended on Nashville, Tenn., Feb. 23, 1862. She was moored in midstream a few hundred yards above the Federal fleet when Morgan's men fired her. Owned at the time by James Miller, George Stacker, and B.M. Runyan; Capt. John S. Dashields, master.

3957 MINNIE

Stw p wh b. Indian Guyan, Oh., 1864. 84.4 x 14.3 x 3. 31

tons. She was built on the lower side of the creek, where Bradrick, Oh., is today, opposite Huntington, W. Va. Owned by Capts. William and George Bay, their first boat. While they were building her the Confederates made a raid, shot George twice, and wounded his sister Sallie in the ankle. Will Bay, hearing the racket, killed two of the Confederates and wounded another. The boat ran Ironton-Proctorville. They sold her south in 1867 to Capt. Samuel R. Bell, St. Martin Parish, La. Off the lists in 1869. Named for the eldest daughter of Capt. George Bay.

3958 MINNIE

Stw p wh b. McKeesport, Pa., 1865. 445 tons. 156 x 32.5 x 5. Engines by Rees, 15's- 4 ft. Two boilers, each 40″ by 24 ft. Built for Capt. A.H. Shaw and Mepham & Bros., St. Louis. She had an octagonal pilothouse with a lighthouse-top (like the *DICTATOR*). Designed for St. Louis-White River trade. While nearing completion at Pittsburgh she was endangered when the *RIVER QUEEN* (see) burned alongside. On Jan. 5, 1866, she had just left Cairo en route to St. Louis when she was struck by a U.S. monitor. The *GEN. ANDERSON* came alongside and took off her passengers. She sank slowly, clear down to the pilothouse. Raised by the *UNDERWRITER*, Capt. R.W. Dugan. The *Louisville Democrat* reported, May 14, 1867: "She has a sugarloaf pilothouse on her, with the Goddess of Liberty with a dirty dress on her; ought to give the old girl a new frock." In March 1868 at St. Louis she was prepared for a Missouri River trip. Aft staterooms were removed to reduce exposure to wind, and the fancywork was removed from the top of the pilothouse. Snagged and lost at Leavenworth, Kans., Nov. 18, 1873.

3959 MINNIE

Stw p wh b. California, Pa., 1869. 40 tons. 83.2 x 18 x 3.3. Built for Capt. Samuel R. Bell, Franklin, La. This small-fry had a long career in the southland. First ran Minden-Loggy Bayou connecting with the *LA BELLE* for New Orleans. In 1896 she was owned by the New Orleans & Washington Packet Co., with Capt. J.E. Trudeau listed as master.

3960 MINNIE

Stw p wh b. Cincinnati, Oh., 1874. Ran Cincinnati-Aurora, Capt. Henry B. Fenton, with Sam Montgomery, pilot. This was the same Captain Fenton who later skippered the *LEVI J. WORKUM* (see) and the same Capt. Montgomery who, then up in years, had been on the *JAMES MONTGOMERY, DEXTER,* and others. Later she was sold to Evansville and burned at Newburgh, Ind., Oct. 17, 1887.

3961 MINNIE

Stw p wh b. Gallipolis, Oh., 1904. 94 x 18 x 3. Built by W.A. Thornily, Gallipolis, and Ed Graham, Raccoon Island, Oh. Raised steam for the first time at Gallipolis, October 1904, and burned at Crown City, Oh., Nov. 27, 1904. The Gallipolis Foundry & Machine Co., bought the wreck.

3962 MINNIE

Stw ferry wh b. Osage City, Mo., 1904. 71.5 x 17.5 x 3. Still listed in the Memphis area, 1918.

3963 MINNIE NO. 2

SW p wh b. Cincinnati, Oh., 1877. 312 tons. 125 x 39 x 5.2. Originally named *ELLEN M. McCOY,* renamed, c. 1880. Still listed at Cincinnati 1896. This possibly may have been a forerunner of the *LEVI J. WORKUM* (see above under *MINNIE,* b. 1874).

3964 MINNIE AVERY

SW p wh b. California, Pa., 1869. 92 tons. 118.4 x 26.4 x 3.3. Built for the Atakapas Mail Transportation Co., New Orleans, Capt. N.P. Millard. Capt. John A. French was master in 1875. Lost 1875.

3965 MINNIE BAY

SW p wh b. Belle Vernon, Pa. (hull), and completed at Wheeling, W. Va., 1883. 182 x 27 x 4.7. Engines, 15's- 5 ft. Three boilers, each 40″ by 24 ft., two flues 14″ dia. Came out with staggered buckets 18 ft. dia. wheels, working buckets 12 ft. across, 24″ dip. She was built at the Wm. McFall yard and engines, etc., from A.J. Sweeney. Built for the Bay brothers for Portsmouth-Proctorville trade and named for George Bay's daughter Minnie (also see *MINNIE*). Minnie married Don Eaton, Proctorville, and died there, 74, October 1938, her husband surviving. In 1885 and 1886 ran Parkersburg-Gallipolis, Capt. G.B. McClintock, with John M. Deem, clerk. She later ran Cincinnati-Madison, Capt. Edwin F. Maddy, competing with the Mail Line, which ended with the Mail Line buying her. They ran her Cincinnati-Maysville. She was downbound Manchester, Oh., to Cincinnati with an excursion party aboard when she was snagged and sunk opposite Moscow, Oh., on Oct. 15, 1889.

3966 MINNIE HARRIS

Prop p wh b. Buffalo, N.Y., 1868. 6 tons. Carried passengers in Belle Vernon-Brownsville trade on the Monongahela River, Capt. McGinnis, in early 1870s. Still documented at Pittsburgh 1876.

3967 MINNIE HEERMAN

Stw p wh b. Reeds Landing, Minn., 1879. 161 tons. 131 x 30 x 2.6. She was snagged and lost below St. Stephens Mission, S.D. on Aug. 23, 1887. Had aboard a cargo of bacon for the Standard Rock Agency at Fort Yates. The *GENERAL CHAS. H. TOMPKINS* (see), Capt. John Belk, salvaged cargo and brought crew to Bismarck.

3968 MINNIE WOODWARD

Prop yacht wh b. Cincinnati, Oh., 1871. She "is a beautiful pleasure boat" reported the *Pittsburgh Gazette* in early February that year.

3969 MINNIETA

Stw p wh b. La Crosse, Wis., 1871. 70 tons. First operated

on the Chippewa River as a packet, and Capt. E.E. Heerman used her as a rafter later on. Listed at Galena, Ill., 1876.

3970 Minnow

Stw p wh b. Ste. Genevieve, Mo., and completed at St. Louis, 1865. 96.8 x 22.6 x 4.1. 69 tons. Owned by Joseph H. and A.W. Leavenworth of New Orleans and St. Louis respectively. Capt. N.H. Leavenworth, master. She had several ownership changes at New Orleans and in 1869 was rebuilt with a recess wheel, owned by Capt. Peter A. Fronty, master, and Joseph Cararas, both of New Orleans. Off the lists 1883.

3971 Minstrel

SW p wh b. Belle Vernon, Pa. and on launch day, April 1842, she fell from the blocks killing Robert Winters and injuring others. Speer and Gaskill were running the yard. She ran trips Pittsburgh-Zanesville in 1843, Capt. McComas. Pittsburgh to St. Louis, Capt. Ingram, September 1843. Downbound Cincinnati to Nashville snagged 10 miles below Madison, Ind., Feb. 3, 1844, one drowned. A memorial was published in Wheeling *Daily News* July 21, 1845, in which passengers en route Cincinnati to Wheeling were grateful to the boat's clerk John Burns who during a storm swam ashore with a rope and got the boat secured to a tree. Dismantled 1847.

3972 Mirror

Stw p wh b. St. Louis, Mo., 1847. 75 tons. Off the lists 1849.

3973 Missionary

Stw p wh b. Bridgeport, Ala., 1864. 86 tons. Built by the USQMD for Tennessee River. Went to private owners June 1866. She entered service as a ferry at Cairo, Ill. The *VIRGINIA* (see) was aground near New Madrid, Mo., and the *MISSIONARY* went there and lightered off some 50 tons of freight, Oct. 24, 1868. The *VIRGINIA* floated free and dragged *MISSIONARY* over a snag, causing her loss.

3974 Mississippi

SW p wh b. Cincinnati, Oh., 1864. 856 tons. 304 x 41.5 x 7. Engines, 30's- 10 ft. Five boilers, each 46" by 24 ft. Capt. James Good came out on her, Cincinnati-New Orleans. She went to the Atlantic & Mississippi Steam Ship Co., St. Louis-New Orleans, Capt. Jesse Y. Hurd, with J.D. Malin, clerk, 1866. Previous to that, in the war period, she was fired upon at Tunica Island by the Rebels and was struck by seven shells, one of which landed in the pantry and as it spluttered flame a young man of Ripley, Oh., Christopher C. Copenhaner, flung it overboard. When the owning firm failed she was auctioned at St. Louis, May 25, 1868. Capt. David Campbell bid $5,000 (faintly). Capt. W.J. Lewis announced $15,000 (loudly). Capt. W.R. Carter took her for $17,800—a boat barely four years old built at a cost of $100,000. Snagged and sank Feb. 28, 1870, at Waterproof, La., downbound. The hull and cabin separated and stories were told that the cabin, its fancy chandeliers burning brightly, drifted past Natchez and many shore dwellers saw the sight.

3975 Mississippi

Stw inspection ih b. St. Louis, Mo., 1882. 174 x 32 x 6. Was purchased partly completed in 1882 by the U.S. Mississippi River Commission. Was used for inspection work on the Mississippi River. Partly burned at Paducah in January 1893 and rebuilt. She was in the tornado at St. Louis, May 1896, Capt. Grant Marsh, and came through okay. U.S. President Theodore Roosevelt boarded her at Keokuk in October 1907 and rode her to Memphis accompanied by many other steamers. Capt. Greenwell was master, and L.H. Sanders was pilot. She was transferred to the U.S. Engineers, West Memphis, Ark., in 1919. Was renamed *PIOMINGO*. Sometime after 1925 she was sold to Warner & Tamble, Memphis, stripped to the hull, and used as a barge. Still there 1961.

3976 Mississippi

Stw inspection sh b. Dubuque, Iowa, 1899, originally towboat *LEOTA*. When the prior *MISSISSIPPI* (see above) was retired, the *LEOTA* was rebuilt at New Orleans, made some larger, and christened *MISSISSIPPI*. 199.2 x 36 x 5.5. Engines, 15's, 32's- 7 ft. She served as the U.S. Mississippi River inspection boat until taken to the Ayer & Lord Marine Ways, Paducah, spring of 1927, and cabins, etc., placed over on a new hull. (See next listing.)

3977 Mississippi

Stw inspection sh b. Jeffersonville, Ind., by Howard (hull) and completed at Paducah, Ky., 1927. Got new engines, 15's, 32's- 7 ft. Also got new water tube boilers, burning fuel oil. Hull measured 185 x 38 x 7.2. Used in inspection and levee work on the Mississippi. In 1961 the U.S. Engineers, Memphis, accepted a new diesel-prop inspection boat built at Pascagoula, Miss., and sold the subject of this sketch. She was moored at the St. Louis levee to become a floating restaurant-museum, renamed *BECKY THATCHER*. Ruth Ferris, Ferguson, Mo., was museum custodian. Financial troubles followed and she was sold by the Bank of St. Louis to Ohio Showboat Drama, Inc., Marietta, Oh., headed by Harry Robinson, summer of 1975. She was moored in the Muskingum River that fall and renovated to become a combination restaurant and showboat, still *BECKY THATCHER*. The engines had been removed at St. Louis, sold to Wilbur Dow, Jr., who removed them to storage at Slidell, La. Still operating as these lines are typed Feb. 17, 1979. Some details and photographs of these Mississippi inspection boats appear in *S&D Reflector,* issues of December 1975, pages 34–35; also September 1975, page 36.

3978 Mississippi Queen

Stw tourist boat sh b. Jeffersonville, Ind., by Jeffboat, Inc., 1973–1975. 379 x 68, over all; 345 x 67, hull. Engines, 16's, 32's- 10 ft., condensing. Two water tube boilers allowed 390 psi. Double stepped paddlewheels on a common shaft. Designed to sleep 400 tourists. Operated by Delta Queen Steamboat Co., Cincinnati, Oh. Steedman Hinckley, chairman of Overseas National Airlines, set construction in motion and tabbed James Demetrion to work out mechanical details and his brother Albert Hinckley to plan the architecture and decor. They went to London, enlisted Three Quays Marine Services Ltd., subsidiary of P&O Lines, who drew hull lines and firmed engine and paddlewheel design. A 20 ft. model of the hull was tank-tested in Holland. Much of the interior decor was contracted in England. The engines were contracted to Pine Tree Engineering Co., U.S.A. Jeffboat, Inc., accepted the contract to build the boat complete. Work was commenced at Jeffersonville, Ind., in summer of 1973, and the first hull section was completed that November. Launching date was Nov. 30, 1974, and she was christened Apr. 30, 1975, at Louisville, Ky. Prior to this time she was unnamed, going by "Hull 2999." Her first shakedown cruise with invited guests came July 20–21, 1976. Many bugs had to be worked out, and there was a second "shakedown" and finally a third, staged at New Orleans, Feb. 26–27, 1977. Prior to the first shakedown, Steedman Hinckley had sold the boat, plus the *DELTA QUEEN,* to Coca-Cola Bottling Co., New York. Her master on the first shakedown was Capt. Ernest E. Wagner with pilots Harry Louden and Art Zimmer. Mates were Joseph "Ted" Davisson and Willard Lockhart. By the time of her third shakedown, Capt. Carl A. Shelton was master, and upon his resignation she was entrusted to Capt. Gabriel Chengery who continues to command as this is typed Feb. 17, 1979. Much credit is due Kenneth Howe, Louisville, for assembling the machinery and making it operative. The *S&D Reflector* since the initial announcement (June 1973, page 4) and an artist's conception (December 1973, page 3) and an architectural profile (December 1973, page 48) has followed in detail the story above both in photographs and text. The *MISS-Q* story rated the front cover in the issues of September 1974, March 1975, and September 1976. The ceremony incident with the completion of the first hull section appears in the March 1974 issue, pages 28–29; of the launching, March 1975 issue, pages 22–27; of the christening, June 1975 issue, pages 39–43; of the initial shakedown, September 1976 issue, pages 7–11; of the final shakedown, June 1977 issue, pages 27–29.

3979 MISSOURI

SW p wh b. Cincinnati, Oh., 1845. 886 tons. 304 (on deck) x 38 x 9. Built at Burton Hazen yard and was the largest boat below the Louisville Falls when built, but was surpassed by the *SULTANA* (see) in 1848, which was 924 tons. Frequently referred to as the *BIG MISSOURI.* First home port, St. Louis. Ran St. Louis-New Orleans. Reported sold at sheriff's sale at St. Louis summer 1848 for $8,900 cash. Sold to "Messrs. Gaty, McCune and Glasby for but a trifle of the sum she cost or ought to have brought at this time." Burned and lost at St. Louis, July 8, 1851.

3980 MISSOURI

SW gunboat wh b. Shreveport, La., 1863. She was built for the Confederates by Capts. John Smoker and Tom Moore, using machinery from the *GRAND ERA* (see). 188 x 50.7 x 7.5. Engines, 24's- 7 ft. Four boilers, each 30" by 26 ft. Casemates were railroad rails. She was captured by U.S. forces on Red River June 14, 1865, and taken to Mound City, Ill. Sold to J. Riley Nov. 29, 1865, for $2,300.

3981 MISSOURI

SW p wh b. Cincinnati, Oh., 1864. 856 tons. 306 x 42 x 8. Engines, 30's- 10 ft. Five tubular boilers, each 46" by 24 ft. having 21 6" flues. Paddlewheels 37 ft. dia., working 15 ft. buckets. Hull by Leatherbury, machinery by C.T. Dumont, and cabin built by Johnston, Morton & Co. Ran St. Louis-New Orleans, and made trips to Louisville. She exploded boilers upbound at the mouth of Green River, on the Ohio, Jan. 30, 1866, said to have been racing the *DICTATOR* (see) at the time. Capt. Jesse Y. Hurd was master, native of Franklin Furnace, Scioto County, Oh., and who attended Marietta College. The explosion killed his wife Catherine and resulted in the death of his son Henry, one of the pilots. Three days later the *W.R. CARTER* exploded (see) killing his brother Capt. Jacob S. Hurd, whose body was not recovered. To pursue this all-nigh incredible sequence, on Sept. 28, 1867, his son Arthur (who was badly burned in the explosion) died of swamp fever in Louisiana. Capt. Jesse, the father, went there and brought back to Portsmouth, Oh., the remains for burial. Immediately thereafter Capt. Hurd became ill, dying on Oct. 23, 1867. Thus within 21 months five of the family died; Capt. Jesse Y. Hurd, wife, two sons, and his brother Jacob S. Surviving was Col. John R. Hurd of the U.S. 2nd Infantry, son of Capt. Jacob S. Hurd. The official report lists 65 killed in this explosion. One was Jim Phillips, chief engineer, who had run the Phillips Machine Shop, Wheeling, and later a machine shop at New Albany, Ind. He had written his brother in Wheeling shortly before, saying he felt the boilers to be unsafe and he planned resigning at Louisville. Capt. J.A. Lemcke wrote: "The explosion happened about 2 in the morning. One of our packetboats [the *ARMADA,* see] was just in from Cairo at the Evansville wharf, early, so we went to the wreck and found it submerged to the hurricane deck, deserted. A steamer which had passed in the night had taken off the survivors [*DICTATOR*] including the captain, and had continued its voyage to Cincinnati. In the wreck we found, lying on her bed and submerged in the water, the steam-scalded body of the captain's wife, which we properly cared for. From under the debris of the office we secured the safe containing a large amount of money. All else was abandoned to the waves, a boat valued at over $100,000, so badly shattered that no attempt was ever made to raise the wreck." The large sum of money in the safe afterwards was counted and amounted to $10,896.05. This tragedy, so closely followed by the explosion of the *W.R. CARTER,* had great consequences. Both were equipped with tubular boilers then quite the rage because of their fuel-saving attributes. The U.S. Steamboat Inspection Service outlawed them almost overnight. Many steamboats were withdrawn from service and were given regular Western-type boilers immediately thereafter. The *MISSOURI* wreck lay in the channel until the fall of 1873 when the *HIRAM C. CAMPBELL* with two wrecking boats and a diver went to the location and removed it. Said to have been "opposite Robertson's saw mill, about a half a mile below the mouth of Green River."

3982 Missouri

SW tr wh b. Metropolis, Ill., 1879. 191.7 x 31.7 x 6.3. A railroad transfer. In 1898 at Carondelet, Mo., along with *PACIFIC* (see). Exploded a boiler in 1897.

3983 Missouri

Stw p wh b. Reeds Landing, Minn., 1880. 133 x 25 x 3. Originally named *MINNIE H.* which went to the Missouri River. She became a U.S. Army survey boat renamed *MISSOURI.* In 1885 left Fort Benton, Capt. Joe La Barge on July 20, for an extended survey of the river. Later in the Power (Block P) Line and made three trips to Fort Benton in 1887, and another in September 1888. Hit a rock at Blue Blanket Island, N.D., Oct. 4, 1889, and was lost.

3984 Missouri

SW snagboat ih b. Pittsburgh, Pa., 1888. Originally named *C.R. SUTER.* Under both names she snagged on Missouri River. Capt. John S. Campbell was master in her latter days with Gerald H. Friemonth, pilot. She burned at Gasconade, Mo., July 29, 1928, and the wreck was dragged down about two miles behind a dike. The dike broke off, exposing the wreck, and the dredge *KAPPA* disposed of it in 1929.

3985 Mist

Stw p wh b. Allegheny, Pa., 1864. 232 tons. 157.2 x 30.2 x 4.3. Engines, 12's- 5 ft. Sold to U.S. Navy, Dec. 23, 1864, and became Tinclad #26, still *MIST.* Sold at Mound City, Ill., on Aug. 31, 1865 to C.C. Hutchinson for $11,500. Sold to Charles C. Hudson and George W. Graham and was taken to Mobile, Ala., Capt. James P. Jack. Off the lists 1874.

3986 Mittie Stephens

SW p wh b. Madison, Ind., 1863. 224 tons. 170 x 29 x 4. Engines, 17's- 5 ft. Three boilers. Machinery from towboat *GRAMPUS.* Her builders were Capt. C.A. Goddin, I.L. Stephens, and A.T. Tample, designed for Missouri River. Documented at New Orleans, June 15, 1864. Rebuilt 1865 to measure 168.8 x 29.8 x 4.7. Ran New Orleans-Bayou Sara in 1864. Sold March 1866 to Capt. Maurice Langhorne who ran her up Red River from New Orleans with M.N. Carpenter, clerk. Had several more ownerships, with Capt. Homer Kellogg, master. Burned on Caddo Lake, Tex., about two miles below Swanson's Landing, Feb. 11, 1869, with life loss described as "many."

3987 Mocking Bird

Prop p wh b. Buffalo, N.Y., 1870. 17 tons. 48 x 10 x 3. Ran from Charleston to upper Kanawha River, Capt. J.T. Daddow, 1871. Sold later to J.E. Jefford who operated her 1873. Sold February 1874 to George Rhodes, Peter Lallance and Edward Layman, all of Syracuse, Oh., and D.D. Rhodes, Cottageville, W. Va. In 1876 running Cincinnati-Ludlow, Ky., competing with *WATER WITCH.*

3988 Moderator

Stw p wh b. Brownsville, Pa., 1856. 231 tons. Capt. William Dean superintended construction. Handling U.S. Army supplies on the Ohio River 1862. Much freight from Louisville was reshipped by B&O at Parkersburg for the East. Collided with and sank the *HORIZON* (see) near Grand Gulf, Miss., May 1, 1863. Owned then by Capt. O.C. Williamson and others. Lost in ice at St. Louis, Jan. 28, 1864.

3989 Mogul

SW p wh b. Louisville, Ky., 1847. 292 tons. Operated by Capt. Dunning who later ran the *COURTLAND* (see). Ran St. Louis-Louisville. Sank and lost at Cloverport, Ky., Sept. 30, 1848.

3990 Mohawk

SW p wh b. Cincinnati, Oh., 1847. 394 tons. 232.1 x 31.4 x 5.6. Ran Louisville-New Orleans, Capt. Maurice Langhorne, with Louisville owners. Sold March 1850 to William Y. Cobb, Vicksburg, and others, Capt. O.B. Cobb. That December, Capt. George R. Price took command as part owner. By 1852, owned and commanded by Capt. Willis Main, New Orleans. Off the lists 1853.

3991 Mohican

SW p wh b. New Albany, Ind., 1848. 398 tons. Ran New Orleans-Tennessee River. She was owned in Louisville until sold to New Orleans in March 1853, Capt. James F. Irwin, owned by many shareholders. Burned at New Orleans Feb. 4, 1854.

3992 Moline

Stw ex wh b. Cincinnati, Oh., 1880. 140 x 26.2. Originally a rafter on the Upper Mississippi owned by Dimock, Gould & Co., Moline, Ill. Kansas City Navigation Co., made an excursion boat of her summer 1900 and ran her at Kansas City. Bought by Capt. Ralph Emerson Gaches and Edwin A. Price at St. Louis December 1907. They renamed her *EMERSON* in February 1908 and she towed the showboat *GRAND FLOATING PALACE.* She got tangled with a cable at Osceola, Ark., October 1908, turned over and was lost.

3993 Mollie Able

SW p wh b. Jeffersonville, Ind., 1864. 873 tons. 295 x 53 x 6. Engines, 32's- 8 ft. Five boilers, each 46" by 26 ft. Ran St. Louis-New Orleans. Capt. Charles P. Warner first commanded, with William H. Rhodes, first clerk. She was entered in the Atlantic & Mississippi Steam Ship Co., Capt. Henry Symmes. Her tubular boilers were removed at St. Louis and replaced with Western-style. Capt. Jesse Y. Hurd went master of her when she resumed her trips (see *MISSOURI,* b. 1864). Her owners failed and she was sold July 1867 to Martin, Walt & Co., for $35,000, who converted her into a cotton carrier. She was racing with the *DAVID WHITE* when the latter exploded boilers in 1869 (see). She was at St. Louis when a tornado struck on Mar. 8, 1871. The pilothouse, texas, and chimneys went down. The ladies cabin was stripped off, including furniture. A bucketplank stove through the hull and she went down "the most complete wreck of a steamboat we have seen for some time," reported a newspaper editor. A lifeboat was blown out on the levee where it wrapped itself around a pole.

3994 MOLLIE DOZIER

SW p wh b. St. Louis, Mo., 1865. 384 tons. 225 x 34. Engines, 17½'s-5 ft. Three boilers. Owned and commanded by Capt. Frank Dozier, with George Keith, pilot. She was snagged at Council Bluffs, Iowa, and on her way down the Missouri for repairs she hit a snag in the chute opposite Chamois, Mo. (Mile 120), on Oct. 3, 1866, back of Stoner Island. The location later was called Mollie Dozier Chute, once the main channel. The *GEORGE SPANGLER* later sank on top of the wreck.

3995 MOLLIE EBERT

Stw p wh b. Pittsburgh, Pa., 1869. A modest sized boat, Capt. George W. Ebert, with Standish Peppard, clerk. She made a "mountain trip" to the headwaters of the Missouri in the summer of 1869, also a trip Pittsburgh to New Orleans that year. She was widened eight ft., and the forecastle lengthened at Reed & Co. docks, Manchester, Pa., in fall of 1870. Capt. Frank Y. Batchelor was master in 1874, with Charles Regnier, clerk; also in 1875 with J.W. Batchelor, clerk. Burned at the Pittsburgh wharf on the evening of May 25, 1875. The blaze also consumed the side-wheel *JUNIATA* (see) and several barges. The hull remained afloat and was taken into the Allegheny River several days later.

3996 MOLLIE FELLOWS

SW p wh b. Cincinnati, Oh., 1864. 224 tons. 138.9 x 24.6 x 4.6. Originally built as a non-propelled barge called *ANDY MACK* used by the USQMD during the war. Built into a steamboat, 1866, owned by Capt. Hugh Derby and S.E. Rundle, New Orleans. Had several changes of ownership in the New Orleans area, and last owner-master was Capt. Adolph Pointevant. Retired in 1870.

3997 MOLLIE FUNK

SW p wh b. Dycusburg, Ky., 1863. 50 tons. First enrolled at Evansville, Ind. Was renamed *R.B. SPEED* and ran Evansville-Pond River (see).

3998 MOLLIE GRATZ

Stw p wh b. Madison, Ind., 1867. 147 tons. Ran Louisville-Evansville in low water 1870, Capt. James Paul, with Samuel Paul, clerk. Capt. Paul and son Sam took her to New Orleans early 1871, sold her down there, and came back to Evansville on *CITY OF QUINCY*. Lost in 1877.

3999 MOLLIE HAMBLETON

SW p wh b. Cincinnati, Oh., 1864. 195 tons. Originally named *FANNY* (see) which was sold to U.S. Navy, 1864, to become Tinclad #8, renamed *GROSBEAK*. Sold to private hands and renamed *MOLLIE HAMBLETON*, Oct. 11, 1865. Ran Memphis-St. Francis River, Capt. T.R. Bowman, with Sam C. Paine, James B. Shell, and W.H. Clark, clerks. Once on high water she ran up to Hornersville, Mo. She was sold to the Trinity River, Texas. Sank and lost at Galveston, Tex., June 9, 1871.

4000 MOLLIE MCPIKE

Stw p wh b. Madison, Ind., 1864. 180 x 27 x 5. Engines, 18's-5½ ft. Although destined to the upper Mississippi, her first job was running low water Louisville-Cincinnati in August 1864. A former commander, Capt. Moses S. Hall, died at Quincy, Ill., 82, March 1902. Lost at Turners Landing, Nov. 8, 1871.

4001 MOLLIE MOORE

Stw p wh b. Elizabeth, Pa. (hull), and completed at Pittsburgh, 1870. Compound engines, 12's- 26's- 5 ft. Three boilers. Primarily a freight boat, the boilers set away aft similar to the *J.B.M. KEHLOR*. Built for Capt. George D. Moore and others and made her first trips Pittsburgh-Louisville. Capt. William J. Kountz bought interest in her. Ran St. Louis-New Orleans, summer 1871, Capt. Moore, with Sam Barr, Jr., clerk. Her pilot in this trade was Capt. Sam Bowen, brother to Capt. Bart Bowen, Hannibal, Mo. He died of yellow fever and was buried along the Mississippi. Caving banks exposed the coffin some years later. It was pointed out to Mark Twain who paid the expense of proper reburial. She made Missouri River trips and was caught on a falling river at Chamberlain, S.D., in 1881. Rocks stabbed up through the hull and she was lost.

4002 MOLLIE NORTON

SW p wh b. Cincinnati, Oh., 1866. 276 tons. Henderson-Evansville packet handling railroad transfer passengers and freight, Capt. Charles G. Perkins, with A.O. Durland, clerk. Dismantled 1869, and machinery went to *SHANNON*, b. Ironton, Oh., 1870 (see).

4003 MOLLY GRATH

Stw p wh b. Elizabeth, Pa., 1851. 75 tons. Collided with *PONTIAC NO. 2* below Owensboro, Ky., Nov. 29, 1851, with loss of twenty lives.

4004 MONARCH

SW p wh b. Louisville, Ky., 1844. 398 tons. 192 x 29 x 7.5. Owned by John Hulme and others, running Louisville-New Orleans. Sold to Capt. Andrew J. Dunn and others, Memphis, January 1846. Dismantled 1848.

4005 MONARCH

SW p wh b. Fulton, Oh. (Cincinnati), 1853. 406 tons. Built for Capt. John A. Williamson, Cincinnati, and others, and ran Cincinnati-New Orleans. In 1861 John S. and Frank Patton were her clerks. On Mar. 5, 1861, she sank at Louisville, downbound with a big cargo for New Orleans,

Capt. Williamson. After repairs she was up Cumberland River soon after the Fort Donelson engagement. In descending, hit the Clarksville bridge, tore off her port paddlewheel and three were drowned. She was taken to New Albany, Ind., where she was sold Apr. 23, 1862, to the U.S. and converted into an Ellet ram. In the Battle of Memphis she rammed the *GEN. PRICE* to great effect, disabled the *BAUREGARD,* shoved the *LITTLE REBEL* aground, returned to the *BAUREGARD,* took the crew as prisoners, and then shoved the *BAUREGARD* out on a bar. She was sunk and lost below St. Louis by ice in latter December 1864, laid up at the time.

4006 MONDIANA

SW p wh b. St. Louis, Mo., 1847. 152 tons. 154 x 23 x 4.5. Owned at St. Louis, 1848, by Cornelius R. Garrison, Daniel R. Garrison, and W.E. Saltmarsh; also T.H. Brierly, Iowa Territory. Sold May 30, 1849, with Daniel R. Garrison retaining interest to Aristide Delahoussaye (9/16), and enrolled at New Orleans. The latter bought her entire Sept. 14, 1849, and sold her same day a year later to Capt. Rufin B. Ratliff, West Feliciana Parish. Off the lists 1852.

4007 MONITOR

Stw p wh b. Reeds Landing, Minn., 1863. 16 tons. Ran on the Chippewa River. Still listed in 1876 at Galena, Ill.

4008 MONITOR

Rig? p wh b. Lafayette, Ind., 1880. 79 tons. Listed as a freight boat. Inspected at Glasgow, Mo., Mar. 16, 1881. Owned by A.J. Dougherty, she sank in the Mississippi River above Cairo, winter 1883-1884. The wreck came to view early September 1884, and the *HUDSON* stopped, took aboard the engines, and delivered them to Mound City, Ill. She had been handling timber to a stave factory.

4009 MONONA

SW p wh b. St. Louis, Mo., 1843. 173 tons. St. Louis-Galena, 1845, Capt. Nick Wall. Sank on the Missouri opposite Little Washington, Oct. 30, 1846. Galena-St. Peters, Capt. E.H. Gleim, 1846. St. Louis-Galena, Capt. Ludlow Chambers, spring 1847. Snagged and lost at Chester, Ill., Oct. 24, 1847.

4010 MONONGAHELA

SW p wh b. Pittsburgh, Pa., 1845. 200 x 24.5 x 5. 238 tons. Owned by Capts. Daniel, Stephen and Charles Stone. Engines, 17's- 8 ft. from prior *MONONGAHELA,* b. 1839. These were replaced later with 23's- 8 ft. Ran in the Pittsburgh-Cincinnati trade, called "the long Monongahela." She also had the cabin, etc., from the 1839 *MONONGAHELA,* lengthened. Jefferson Davis, en route to Washington, D.C., rode her in November 1847. Henry Clay rode her from Pittsburgh to Maysville, Ky., March 1848; at Wheeling "thousands lined the wharf to see Clay." Clerk was Isaac Jones who later was master of the *LADY GAY.* In 1850 ran St. Louis-Keokuk in opposition to the regular line. The fray lasted a season or so with great loss to the owners. Dismantled in 1854.

4011 MONONGAHELA

SW p wh b. Brownsville, Pa., 1855. 174 x 34 x 6.5. Engines, 24½'s- 6½ ft. Four boilers, each 42″ by 28 ft. 335 tons. Left Pittsburgh on first trip to New Orleans, Feb. 19, 1855. Also ran St. Louis-New Orleans. Capt. M.A. Cox was master. Burned at East St. Louis (Bloody Island), May 15, 1859.

4012 MONONGAHELA

SW p wh b. Pittsburgh, Pa., 1863. 74 tons. Engines, 13½'s- 4½ ft. Two boilers. Went to the Missouri River and died of old age at Leavenworth, Kan., Feb. 11, 1870, then owned by Henry J. Hanley and others.

4013 MONONGAHELA BELLE

Stw p wh b. Morgantown, Va., 1854. 74 tons. Ran Marietta-Zanesville, 1855, Capt. Milton Seaman; same 1856, Capt. John H. Lyons. Snagged and lost at Austin, Miss., Mar. 8, 1859.

4014 MONROE

SW p wh b. New Albany, Ind., 1848. 183 tons. 127 x 25 x 5.3. Went to New Orleans owned in large share by Isaiah King & Co., New Albany, Capt. Samuel Gwartney. Made a disastrous trip up the Missouri, St. Louis to Jefferson City, April 1849. Had aboard a group of Mormon emigrants. Cholera claimed loss of many aboard, including Joe Ponto, pilot, and other crew members. In all there were some 40 deaths. The passengers and crew deserted her at Jefferson City. She was upbound from New Orleans for Yazoo River and struck a log at Cowpen Point above Natchez, Mar. 20, 1854, and sank with loss of 30 lives, most of them deckhands and firemen. There were no passengers aboard.

4015 MONROE

Centerwheel ferry wh b. Centreview, Oh., 1860. 44 tons. First home port, Wheeling, Va. Sank and lost at New Orleans, July 21, 1866. Custom records at New Orleans give place of build as Center Run, Oh. She was 99.6 x 17 x 2.9. Owned December 1865 by Capt. Charles Donnelly, New Orleans, who sold her July 1866 to Constantine McPhelin. Sank at the foot of Jackson Street, New Orleans.

4016 MONROE

Stw p wh b. Freedom, Pa. (hull), and completed at Wheeling, W. Va., 1886, originally named *NETTIE QUILL.* She was transferred from Mobile to New Orleans, 1915, and operated to Ouachita River, renamed. Was lost at New Orleans in a storm that year.

4017 MONSOON

SW p wh b. Cincinnati, Oh., 1863. 267 tons. 180.4 x 34 x 6.2. Engines, 18's- 7 ft. Three boilers. She made Cincinnati-Nashville trips, then was bought by Capt. E.A. Sheble, St. Louis. He added another boiler at Cincinnati spring of 1864. "She looks gay as a peacock with her new and graceful chimneys and fancy pilothouse," wrote a Cincinnati editor as he saw her at the foot of Broadway loading for the Missouri River. In 1865 owned by David Gibson & Co.,

Cincinnati, Capt. C.W. Stinde, enrolled at New Orleans. Sold in September 1868 to Joseph A. Aiken and John H. Menge, equal shares, Capt. John H. Menge, master. She was downbound at Prudhomme Bend, Red River, having a large cotton cargo, Dec. 21, 1868, when snagged and lost. The *GLASGOW* (see) hit the wreck in February 1873.

4018 MONTANA

SW p wh b. Shousetown, Pa., 1864. 431 tons. 210 x 33 x 5.7. Engines, 20's- 6 ft. Five boilers, each 40" by 20 ft., three flues. Paddlewheels 25 ft. dia. working 10 ft. buckets. Built for Capt. David Throckmorton and J.E. Gorman "both well known on the Missouri" and ready to leave Pittsburgh first week in May 1864. She was sold to the U.S. in August 1867 along with *C.J. CAFFREY* and *SILVER WAVE* for Upper Mississippi River work. Also served the U.S. on the Missouri. Dismantled in 1879 at La Crosse, Wis., and parts went to building the *GEN. BARNARD.*

4019 MONTANA

SW p wh b. New Albany, Ind., 1865. 231 tons. First home port, Louisville, Ky. Off the list in 1872.

4020 MONTANA

Stw p wh b. California, Pa. (hull), and completed at Pittsburgh, 1879. 959 tons. 250 x 48.8 x 5.5. Engines, 18's- 7 ft. Four boilers, each 42" by 26 ft. Paddlewheel 18.2 ft. dia., working 26 ft. buckets. Original owners were Nicholas Buisson, St. Louis; Sallie B. Coulson and J.C. McVay, Yankton; G.C. Evans and M. Coulson, Allegheny, Pa.; D.W. Maratta, Columbus, Oh.; and Capt. John Todd, Wellsville, Oh., who commanded. First trip was from Pittsburgh to Evansville and return, and then loaded at Pittsburgh for Fort Benton, Mont., Capt. Nicholas Buisson. Arrived there May 28, 1879, with 550 tons, and again June 23 with 600 tons and had discharged a large cargo at the Coal Banks (near present-day Virgelle, Mont.), "the greatest cargo ever brought to Montana by a single boat." She was back at Bismarck, D.T. on June 30, 1879, preparing to reload for a third trip to Fort Benton when at 8:30 P.M. a tornado completely stripped the cabin off. Her sister boat *DACOTAH* also was there but was relatively unharmed. She continued making Missouri River trips but never again was at Fort Benton. Also ran to New Orleans in the winter months. Capt. Edward A. Phillips was master later, and last of all Capt. George G. Keith. She was upbound June 22, 1884, half way through the St. Charles bridge, William Rodney Massie at the wheel, when she veered, hit a pier, and sank. The ferry *JOHN L. FERGUSON* came to the scene.

4021 MONTAUK

SW p wh b. St. Louis, Mo., 1847. 175 tons. Ran St. Louis-Galena, Capt. John Lee. Burned at St. Louis in a large wharf fire on May 17, 1849.

4022 MONTAUK

SW p wh b. California, Pa., 1853. 167 x 21.9 x 5.1. Owned by Henry Corwith, Galena, Ill., Capt. E.H. Gleim. Operated St. Louis-Galena. Burned at St. Louis, Oct. 13, 1853.

4023 MONTAUK

George B. Merrick in *Old Times on the Upper Mississippi,* page 281, records a boat of this name St. Louis-St. Paul, 1855-1857.

4024 MONTEREY

SW p wh b. Cincinnati, Oh., 1846. 143 tons. 135 x 24.7 x 4.8. Enrolled at New Orleans, Nov. 28, 1848, owned by Loring T. Murdock and Samuel B. McConico, both of New Orleans, Capt. W.W. Withenbury, master. As of May 8, 1849, Capt. Withenbury (of Cincinnati) and S.B. McConico owned her jointly. She operated New Orleans-Red River. Snagged and lost Apr. 24, 1850.

4025 MONTEREY

Stw p wh b. Fredericktown, Pa., 1847. 65 tons. Nine of the original owners were from Greene County, Pa., and the other two from Washington County, Pa. Built for the Pittsburgh-Fredericktown trade. Sold Nov. 17, 1847, and was snagged and sunk in the Kentucky River near mouth of Paint Lick Creek. Burned on Red River, La., at Duncan's Point downbound for New Orleans with cotton, Mar. 29, 1849.

4026 MONTEZUMA

SW p wh b. Pittsburgh, Pa., 1841. 170 tons. Pittsburgh-Cincinnati, Capt. Nelson Crooks, spring 1842.

4027 MONTEZUMA

SW p wh b. Madison, Ind., 1843. 170 tons. Went to Mobile, Ala. This boat likely is the same as last listing, rebuilt. 150 x 20 x 6. She was back in New Orleans September 1849, owned by her master, Capt. John Choat, and Victor T. Wilson, both of New Orleans. Wilson sold his share to Andrew W. Smith, New Orleans, Dec. 20, 1850. Off the lists 1852.

4028 MONTGOMERY

SW p wh b. New Albany, Ind., 1843. 407 tons. Went to Mobile, Ala. Returned to New Orleans February 1850, Capt. J.H. Estes, Mobile, master, and owned at Mobile by John G. Owen and F.M. Johnson. Ran New Orleans-Vicksburg. Burned at New Carthage, Miss., 33 miles below Vicksburg, Nov. 7, 1851.

4029 MONTGOMERY

SW p wh b. Cincinnati, Oh., 1854. 315 tons. Went to Mobile, Ala. and ran Alabama River trade, Capt. Joseph L. Harris. Burned and lost at Algiers, La., Feb. 20, 1858.

4030 MONTGOMERY

Stw p wh b. Cincinnati, Oh., 1863, originally *NAUMKEAG* in U.S. war service. Sold to private hands Apr. 16, 1863, and renamed. Burned and lost at Erie, Ala., Jan. 19, 1867, with loss of three lives.

4031 MONTICELLO

Stw p wh b. Freedom, Pa., 1852. 116 tons. First home port, Pittsburgh, Pa. Off the list in 1855.

4032 MOOSE

Stw tinclad wh b. Cincinnati, Oh., 1863, originally *FLORENCE MILLER NO. 2* (see). She became Tinclad #34, renamed *MOOSE,* May 20, 1863. This is the U.S. tinclad which played so important a part in Morgan's Raid. She was below Ravenswood, W. Va., at the foot of Sand Creek bar the night of July 18, 1863, and to mount the bar (for the Ohio was low) she sparred until 2:00 A.M., and succeeded only to have a fog close down until 7:00 A.M. When the fog lifted, Morgan's men were spotted and shelled, and *MOOSE* pursued upriver and prevented the intended crossing at Buffington Island. She was 154.2 x 32.1 x 4.5. Engines, 14's- 4½ ft. When sold Aug. 17, 1865, at Mound City, Ill. she went for $10,100 to Capt. David White, and about a month later was renamed *LITTLE ROCK* (see).

4033 MORGAN

SW p wh b. Mobile, Ala., 1861. 558 tons. She was marooned up Red River during the war, and was captured by the U.S. Sold to private hands January 1866, took aboard a cargo of lumber at Memphis and was heading for Galveston, Tex., with the idea of bringing back to Memphis several hundred head of cattle, when she was lost en route, Oct. 10, 1866, owned by Sands & Co., Memphis. "The old boat has had her day and her career in the service of the 'so called' will perpetuate her name in history," mused a Memphis editor.

4034 MORGAN NELSON

Stw p wh b. Middletown, Pa., 1859. 109 tons. 120 x 21.8 x 4.4. She appeared at New Orleans Jan. 24, 1861, owned by Josiah and James Dillon of Wheeling, Va., with Capt. Joseph Richardson, also of Wheeling, in charge. She had seven changes of ownership at New Orleans 1861–1868, when dismantled.

4035 MORNING LIGHT

SW p wh b. Belle Vernon, Pa., 1858. 198 tons. Said a Wheeling editor, Dec. 2, 1858: "The great high-headed double cabined steamer *MORNING LIGHT* with her tenor-based typanum-destroying whistle, and powerful engines, is getting ready to leave for New Orleans." Actually she was 144 x 30 x 5. She was owned and commanded by Capt. William Dillon and did indeed go to New Orleans. Captain Dillon ran her New Orleans-Red River and Lake Bisteneau. In 1862 was running New Orleans-Tensas-Macon and Black rivers owned and skippered by Capt. Hugh Slicer. In January 1863 sold to C. Rodney May, New Orleans, and as of Feb. 19, 1863, a one-half interest went to Thomas C.A. Dexter, New Orleans. Thenceforth she fades into the *"Gone With the Wind."*

4036 MORNING MAIL

SW p wh b. Cincinnati, Oh., 1881. 225 x 35. 467 tons. Engines, 21's- 6 ft. Three boilers each 45" by 28 ft. She ran Cincinnati-Maysville, Capt. Evan S. Morgan. The forward skylight panel in the cabin was graced with a painting of Logan's Gap, and the one at the rear of the ladies's cabin was a panorama of the river at Maysville, also showing Aberdeen. Captain Morgan's crew on the first trip: John Henderson and Sam Hamilton, pilots; Frank Bryson, Floyd Morgan, and Roby McCall, clerks; Col. Gus Simmons, steward; Will Hanley, chief engineer; George Korns, mate. Capt. Jim Rowley, Jr., once described her "as a small edition of the *CITY OF CINCINNATI* and a handsome boat." She burned in the East End, Cincinnati, on Sept. 20, 1884, along with the *BONANZA* and *LILY* (both see). She was built to replace the *WILDWOOD* and was in turn replaced by the *ST. LAWRENCE.*

4037 MORNING STAR

SW p wh b. Elizabeth, Pa., 1856. 465 tons. 230 x 34 x 5.5. Built for the St. Louis & St. Joseph Union Line. Ran her maiden trip at Pittsburgh, Apr. 2, 1856, Capt. Thomas H. Brierly. Capt. William Rodney Massie later said this was "the most elegant boat he ran on in his sixty years of boating on the Missouri River." He went up on her in command of Capt. Thomas Brierly in 1858. Burned at St. Louis, June 21, 1859.

4038 MORNING STAR

SW p wh b. West Wheeling, Oh., 1860. 53 tons. Ran on Big Sandy River and burned partly at Catlettsburg, Ky., Jan. 6, 1861. Burned and lost at Mound City, Ill., May 23, 1866.

4039 MORNING STAR

SW p wh b. Jeffersonville, Ind., by Howard, 1864. 265.3 x 35.6 x 6.2. Built for the Louisville & Henderson Mail Line Co. Arrived at Evansville on her first trip, Dec. 22, 1864, and next day at Lewisport she was boarded by guerrillas who robbed the safe and passengers of $2,700, broke open the bar and helped themselves to whiskey and cigars, and then killed two unarmed sick soldiers. Capt. Anson Ballard was in command at the time. They required transportation to Hawesville and left the boat there. Capt. Ballard's crew in those troubled times: John Gwathney, head clerk; G.W. Patterson, 2nd clerk; H.S. Mitchell, 3rd clerk. Wages at the time were $150 a month for the captain; $125 for the 1st clerk; $100 for 2nd, and $50 for 3rd. In 1872 Capt. John Triplett was master, with Phil Beverley, first clerk. In 1878 Capt. E.P. Crider, master, with L.W. Whitlow and E.T. Meek, clerks. She was retired in the fall of 1879.

4040 MORNING STAR

Stw p wh b. Boonville, Mo., 1877. 66 tons. Engines, 10"- 3 ft. One boiler. Owned by D.A. Stine and R.D. Willis. Snagged four miles below Jefferson City, Mo., Feb. 23, 1880. Ran on the Osage River, season 1880–1881. Lost in ice at Jefferson City, Feb. 5, 1881, laid up for the winter.

4041 MORNING STAR

Prop p wh b. Mason City, W. Va., 1879. 95 x 12 x 5.5.

Engine by Enos & Hill, Gallipolis, and boiler by J.H. Williams, Middleport, Oh. Hull came from John Young's yard. Built for Vanceburg-Augusta trade, Capts. Henry and Mark Pennywitt. She burst a steam line so badly scalding Mark Pennywitt he died. Henry Pennywitt sold the wrecked boat and died soon after in New Orleans. She then ran Baton Rouge-Bayou Sara before the *JULIAN POYDRAS* was there, recalls Capt. A.D. Butler. Inspected at Baton Rouge 1881, at New Orleans 1882, and was documented at Cincinnati 1886.

4042 MORNING STAR

Stw ex wh b. Madison, Ind., 1893 originally *ST. JOSEPH* (see) and then *ISLAND QUEEN* (also see), and was renamed *MORNING STAR* at Pittsburgh, Pa., in July 1912. She was being operated by John F. Klein. On Aug. 29, 1913, she was running an excursion between Charleroi and Monongahela City on the Monongahela River, Capt. Charles E. Daily. Having landed at the latter city, the passengers went ashore when fire was discovered in the check room. She burned to the water's edge.

4043 MORNING STAR

SW p wh b. Jeffersonville, Ind., by Howard, 1901. 225 x 38 x 6. Engines, 18's- 8 ft. Four boilers, each 42" by 26 ft. Built for the Louisville & Evansville Packet Co. Her first crew in the Louisville-Evansville trade: Capt. F. Marion Ryan, with W. Scott Paris and James Kay, pilots; William C. Lepper, Jr., purser; Ben Bridges and James Gresham, clerks; "Lum" Stapleton and Tom Grimes, mates; James Nunnemacher and Robert (Bob) Lloyd, engineers; George Voll, steward, and Robert Trebu, carpenter. One of her early relief pilots was Capt. Wes Conner who had helped pilot the *ROB'T E. LEE* in her race with the *NATCHEZ.* He stood his last watch on the *MORNING STAR* in 1902, aged 78, and was taken ashore at New Albany, Ind., stricken with paralysis. Capt. Walter Blair bought her in April 1910 at Jeffersonville, Ind., hauled her at Cincinnati on the ways and added 25 feet to her length forward of the boilers to make her 250 x 38 x 6. He then entered her in the St. Paul-Davenport-Stillwater trade under his command. In summer of 1911 ran a special cruise Davenport to New Orleans and out to the Jetties and return. Pilots were J.H. Young, J.E. McCullough, Steve E. Greenwell, J.M. Richtman, and J. Warren Kouns. Engineers were S.B. Burtnell and J.V. Pollock, with J.W. Young and Ewald Von Hein, strikers. W.H. Forrest was purser; Arthur Langford, mate; F.R. Condit, steward; and Fred Vetter, chef. Included in the passenger list were W.H. Lehman, Des Moines, Iowa; Governor and Mrs. S.R. Van Sant of Minnesota; the Bowmans of Davenport (John G. Bowman later became chancellor of the University of Pittsburgh and built the Cathedral of Learning); Miss Helen Gertrude Blair and George W. Blair. A similar excursion was announced for April 1912 but was cancelled due to extremely high water; instead she round-tripped Davenport-Cincinnati with tourists. In May 1914 she made a special trip, Davenport-Tennessee River, and was back in her usual trade that June with F.S. Ratterman as purser, and Donald T. Wright, clerk. Fred Bynum was steward. In September-October 1915 she made a tourist trip St. Louis-New Orleans, and the pilots were John Hottell and J. Harvey Brown. Wm. J. Keith was purser for the full season of 1915–1916, and in May 1916 she made a Davenport-Florence, Ala., trip. Sold early spring 1918 to the Coney Island Co., Cincinnati, to replace the *PRINCESS* (see) lost in ice and ran that season with all her staterooms. She was made into a full-scale excursion boat and continued in the Cincinnati-Coney Island trade until she burned at Cincinnati along with the *ISLAND QUEEN, TACOMA* and *CHRIS GREENE* on Nov. 4, 1922. A heedless watchman boiling tar on the galley stove for roof repairs caused the blaze. Her roof bell went to the *GENERAL WOOD* while she was in the Coney trade, and she got the famed bell from *CITY OF CINCINNATI.*

4044 MORO

SW p wh b. Louisville, Ky., 1858. 132 tons. 122 x 24.8 x 4.7. Owned 1861 by George Merz, New Orleans. In Confederate service 1862–1863 taking supplies from Red River to Port Hudson. Captured by U.S. forces on *QUEEN OF THE WEST* above mouth of Red River, Feb. 8, 1863. They burned her.

4045 MORO CASTLE

SW p wh b. Cincinnati, Oh., 1847. 298 tons. 180 x 33 x 7. Engines, 18½'s- 9 ft. Three boilers. Ran Cincinnati-New Orleans. On the morning of Jan. 5, 1850, upbound New Orleans to Cincinnati, she stove on a rock while ascending the Louisville Falls. On the 7th, with the river rising, a New Albany ferry and the *EMILY* unloaded freight from her and delivered it at Shippingport. Owned by her commander, Capt. Scott. Prospects were that the machinery and cabin equipment could be saved. Also spelled *MORRO CASTLE* in old accounts.

4046 MOSES GREENWOOD

SW p wh b. Cincinnati, Oh., 1852. 268 tons. 175 x 29 x 5.6. Owned by Capt. Albert Thomas, Newport, Ky., who commanded. Documented at New Orleans, February 1853. Off the lists 1855.

4047 MOSES MCLELLAN

Sw p wh b. Cincinnati, Oh., 1855. 398 tons. Low water boat for the U.S. Mail Line, Cincinnati-Louisville, November 1855, along with *CITY OF WHEELING.* Ran with some regularity in the Cincinnati-Memphis trade, Z.M. Sherley, manager, into 1860. Named for Capt. McLellan who was master many years on *TELEGRAPH NO. 3* (see). Made a trip to Pittsburgh with cotton January 1861, Capt. Knight. Delivered U.S. Army supplies to Camp Piatt, above Charleston on the Kanawha River, 1861, and attracted much attention due to her size. Departed Pittsburgh Apr. 1, 1862, with passenger and freight for the Upper Mississippi, having been sold there. Rebuilt at Madison, Ind., 1862. Renamed *CITY OF ST. PAUL* on June 7, 1866 (see). Camp

Piatt, mentioned above, was about where Port Amherst is today. Capt. William Knight was master on the Kanawha trip, and William F. Gregory, pilot (brother-in-law of the late Capt. John F. Rust, well-known Kanawha boatman).

4048 MOUND CITY

Recess wheel gunboat wh b. Mound City, Ill. by James B. Eads, 1861. 175.5 x 52 x 6.5. Engines, 22's- 6 ft. She was rammed by the Confederate gunboat *GENERAL BRAGG* in the engagement at Craigshead Point, April 1862, and again by the *GEN. VAN DORN,* but did not sink. She was auctioned off at Mound City, Ill., Nov. 29, 1865, to Frank Burnet for $3,700. She was beached at the mouth of the Cache River and dismantled in 1866.

4049 MT. STERLING

Stw p wh b. Hermann, Mo., 1910. 60.3 x 12.3 x 2.2. 22 tons. Owned by the Heckman family at Hermann, handling wheat, etc. Engines 6″- 2 ft. One boiler. At time of loss, May 8, 1918, was owned by Buchanan Sand & Supply Co. A windstorm swamped her—laid up at St. Joseph, Mo.

4050 MT. VERNON

SW p wh b. Elizabethtown, Pa., 1847. 177 tons. Built to run low water Pittsburgh-Cincinnati, Capt. Hiram Kountz. Owned largely by William J. Kountz. She rendered aid when the *VIRGINIA* (see) exploded at Rush Run, spring 1849. Pittsburgh-Louisville, Capt. Hiram Kountz, spring 1850. Off the lists 1852.

4051 MOUNTAIN BELLE

Stw p wh b. Brownsville, Pa., 1869. 140 x 27. Owned largely by Capt. A.J. McAllister who ran her Portsmouth-Proctorville on the Ohio River, with Chris Young, clerk. First season she brought up in her safe the money which paid for the land upon which Huntington, W. Va., is located, then a farm known as Holderby's Landing. Her machinery came from the *COTTAGE NO. 2* (see). In January 1870 she became part of the Portsmouth & Big Sandy Packet Co. In September 1871, running Cincinnati-Portsmouth, 18-year-old son of Capt. McAllister shot and killed a youth on the Cincinnati waterfront during a fray involving "teen-agers." In March 1873 the boat was sold to the Upper Mississippi where she was converted into a rafter owned by Hewitt & Wood, La Crosse, Wis. Later in same service owned by G.C. Hixson, La Crosse, and then the McDonald Bros., of same place. She became an excursion boat at St. Paul named *THE PURCHASE* (see).

4052 MOUNTAIN BOY

Stw p wh b. Brownsville Pa., 1868. 198 tons. 135 x 26 x 4. Engines, 14's- 5 ft. Two boilers, each 40″ by 26 ft., with two 9″ and two 10″ flues. Built for the Kanawha & Gallipolis Packet Co., J.W. Oakes, pres., and John A. Robinson, secy.-treas. Capt. James Newton was first master in Gallipolis-Charleston trade, and later Capt. R.L. Hamilton with J.A. McClurg and A.J. Bickett, clerks. In March 1870 went to Wheeling, Capt. James Newton, and transferred the West Virginia state capitol to Charleston. She was at Cincinnati when demolished in an ice gorge latter December 1873. While taking out the boilers that June, workmen discovered a large catfish in one of them which weighed in at 40 pounds. The *KATE PUTNAM* was lost in the same gorge (see).

4053 MOUNTAIN BOY

Stw p wh b. Cincinnati, Oh., 1881. 87 tons. Lost at Owensboro, Ky., rounding to in wind swells, Apr. 6, 1886, Capt. John James. She was running in a local trade, and turned bottom side up.

4054 MOUNTAIN GIRL

Stw p wh b. Ashland, Ky., 1880. 115 x 24 x 3. Capt. George W. Anderson, Carrollton, Ky., used her in Kentucky River. Capt. Willaim C. Lepper, Jr., told of being aboard 1885 when she was handling empty whiskey barrels Frankfort to Tyrone. Came in collision with *J. W. GAFF* (see) at Laughrey Island, Ohio River, Nov. 6, 1885. There was a circus aboard and many of the animals were lost. The *GAFF* brought the crew to Cincinnati.

4055 MOUNTAIN LILY

SW p wh b. Horse Shoe, N.C., 1878. 55 x 18 x 3. Horse Shoe is near Hendersonville in Henderson County, N.C., on the upper reaches of the French Broad River. She was built to ply Asheville-Brevard, and Asheville is 1,985 ft. above sea level. The French Broad Steamboat Line was the brainchild of Col. Sidney Vance Pickens, Hendersonville, who imported a boat builder from Norfolk, Va., to build *MOUNTAIN LILY.* The craft actually ran several seasons when the water was plentiful but was far from a financial success. She retired along shore at King's Bridge, near the Haywood Road Crossing, and gradually disintegrated. [For the benefit of altitude conscious readers, steamboats at Fort Benton, Mont., were 2,820 ft. above sea level. And for geographical readers, the French Broad joins the Holston east of Knoxville, Tenn., to form the Tennessee.]

4056 MOUNTAINEER

SW p wh b. Jacksonville, Pa. (hull), and completed at Pittsburgh, 1844. 212 tons. Jacksonville was just above Webster, Pa., on the Monongahela River. Said to have had a Litch compound engine, stiff shaft. Also named as one of the first to have a full length passenger cabin with the gentlemen's quarters forward and the ladies' aft. In earlier times the gent's cabin was aft of the wheelhouses on the main deck. Capt. Jonathan H. Barker in May 1847 entered this boat in the Louisville-Cincinnati trade in opposition to the U.S. Mail Line, leaving Cincinnati at 10:00 A.M. on alternate days with the *NORTH AMERICA* (see). In spring 1849, was running Louisville-St. Louis, Capt. Charles F. Reynolds. On Mar. 15, 1849, was in collision with *PIKE NO. 9* in a fog near St. Louis, which took away the starboard guard and wheelhouse. She was back in business within a month. Off the lists 1854.

4057 MOUNTAINEER

Stw p wh b. Cairo, Ill., 1864. 211 tons. She was at Johnsonville, Tenn., Nov. 4, 1864, when the Rebels attacked and burned her. She was owned by Capt. O.C. Williamson, Cincinnati, and others at the time. Capt. Abner Martin and others of the crew escaped overland to Nashville and had a lively time en route.

4058 MOUNTAINEER

SW p wh b. Metropolis, Ill., 1867. 584 tons. 205 x 34.5 x 5.5. Engines, 20's- 7 ft. Three boilers. Built for Duncan S. Carter, St. Louis, for the St. Louis-Omaha trade. In the summer 1867 went to the upper Missouri and ran aground near the mouth of Heart River on a falling river. Capt. Woolfolk had his crew dig a channel through the bar and funneled water into it by means of two willow wing dams. The current washed out the sand and released her. Made trips New Orleans-Shreveport in winter seasons. She was twice sunk on the Missouri. Owned in 1874 by William J. Lewis, St. Louis. Off the lists 1875.

4059 MOUNTAINEER

Stw p wh b. Harmar, Oh., at the Knox Yard, 1890. 122 x 20.2 x 4. Owned by George Stone, Winfield, W. Va., and William Stone, Pt. Pleasant, W. Va. On one occasion was running in competition with *T.D. DALE,* Charleston-Winfield on Kanawha River. Capt. James Wright, master, said fares got down to ten cents, and she was liberally patronized with folks from Hurricane, 18-Mile Creek, Seldom Seen, and Paradise arriving at Winfield by horseback and wagon, going to Charleston. Jim Wright was piloting when she and the *DALE* collided, ending the fray. Henry Wright, his cousin, was piloting the *DALE* at the time. Later ran Charleston-Montgomery, Capt. George Colville, master. Hit a log at Ruffner's Landing, a mile above Charleston, downbound, July 18, 1899. Telephoned the *T.D. DALE* to come up and assist, but *MOUNTAINEER* sank before the *DALE* got there. Dismantled.

4060 MOVASTAR

SW p wh b. Naples, Ill., 1849. 140 tons. Off the lists 1858.

4061 MUD HEN

Centerwheel ferry wh b. Nebraska City, Neb., 1869. 30 tons. One engine, 12½"- 3½ ft. One boiler. Owned by F.F. Pratt and others. Exploded her boiler July 24, 1872, and lost.

4062 MULTUM IN PARVO

SW p wh b. Gasconade, Mo., 1866. 44 tons. Off the lists 1869.

4063 MUNNERLYN

Stw p wh b. Monongahela, Pa., 1859. 106 tons. First home port, Apalachicola, Fla. Went to Confederate registry 1861.

4064 MUSCATINE

SW p wh b. Wheeling, W. Va., 1863. 322 tons. Built for the Northern Line Packet Co., under the supervision of Capt. Richard C. Gray. Advertised at Pittsburgh, Capt. J.J. Robinson, for St. Louis and Dubuque, Mar. 11, 1864. He commanded until June 1865 when he died at the Olive Street Hotel, St. Louis; had been on the *DENMARK, SUCKER STATE,* and others. His body was returned to Pennsylvania for burial, attended by his brother Capt. Andrew Robinson. Later ran St. Louis-St. Paul, Capt. M. Green, with Wm. R. Wells, clerk. Lost by stranding at North La Crosse, Wis., 1880.

4065 MUSIC

SW wh b. Jeffersonville, Ind., 1843. 198 tons. 158 x 24 x 5.5. Built for Capt. Ferdinand Shreck, Donaldsonville, La. Sold March 1847 to Capt. Celestin Dalferes, Assumption Parish, La. Off the lists 1849.

4066 MUSIC

SW p wh b. Jeffersonville, Ind., 1850. 273 tons. 172 x 29 x 6. Ran New Orleans-Upper Coast, Capt. F.M. Schreck. Off the lists in 1859.

4067 MUSIC

SW p wh b. Jeffersonville, Ind., by Howard, 1857. 330 tons. 175 x 32.3 x 6.2. Owned by New Orleans, Coast and Lafourche Transportation Co., Adelard Dugas, pres., with Capt. Henry Streck, master. Capt. J.J. Brown was master in New Orleans-Upper Coast trade until she went to Confederate registry. Said to have been taken up Red River for the war's duration.

4068 MUSIC

SW ferry wh b. Jeffersonville, Ind., 1873. 150 x 36 x 6. Engines, 17's- 6 ft. Operated at Louisville, Ky.

4069 MUSIC

Stw ferry wh b. New Albany, Ind., 1880. 150 x 47 x 4.5. Engines, 17's- 6 ft. Operated at Louisville, Ky. Her machinery was used on the towboat *G.W. THOMAS* in 1901.

4070 MUSTANG

SW p wh b. St. Louis, Mo., 1848. 128 tons. Snagged and sunk four miles below Brunswick, Mo., Oct. 9, 1850.

4071 MUSTANG

SW p wh b. Jeffersonville, Ind., 1848. 136 tons. Stranded and lost at Paducah, Ky., Aug. 9, 1851.

4072 MUSTANG

SW p wh b. Marietta, Oh., 1849. 67 tons. 108 x 20 x 3.3. Owned by Capt. N.G. Prescott of Shreveport, La. Burned and lost at Alexandria, La., Jan. 1852.

4073 MUSTANG

SW p wh b. Pittsburgh, Pa., 1860. 172 tons. Sold to USQMD May 31, 1864. Sold to private owners Apr. 11, 1867. Lost on the Trinity River, Tex., June 24, 1869.

4074 MUTA

Stw p wh b. Parkersburg, W. Va., 1865. 149 tons. 110 x 20 x

3.6. Owned by Capt. Andrew P. Kerr, Millersport, Oh., and others, and was operated out of Franklin, La. Off the lists in 1875.

4075 MYRTLE

SW p wh b. Cincinnati, Oh., 1866. 183 tons. 137 x 20.6 x 4. Ran Evansville-Cumberland River, 1866, Capt. John McClain, with Billy Conant, clerk. Went to Vicksburg, thence to New Orleans owned 1869 by James M. Peterson, New Orleans, Capt. William S. Bassett, master. Lost in 1871.

4076 MYRTLE

Stw p wh b. Yellville, Ark., 1893. 64 x 14. Carried a few passengers and towed a 30-ton barge. Owned by W.C. McBee and ran in the upper White. Capt. Tom Stallings later was her skipper, and took her to Black River. Was returning to McBee's Landing on the White when the cookhouse caught fire Mar. 1, 1895, and she was lost.

N

4077 N.B. FORREST

Stw p wh b. Chattanooga, Tenn., 1897. 134 tons. 135 x 25 x 4.5. Engines, 13's- 4 ft. Two boilers, each 34" by 18 ft. Owned by the Chattanooga & Decatur Packet Co., headed by R.C. Gunter. Later in the Tennessee River Navigation Co. She may have had an engine change inasmuch as her machinery is said to have gone into the *JAMES N. TRIGG* which had 14's- 5 ft. Dismantled 1910.

4078 N.D. MUNSON

Rig? ferry wh b. Quincy, Ill., 1867. 165 tons. 137.2 x 45.9 x 4.3. Owned in early days by Waterloo Turnpike Road & Ferry Co., Waterloo, Monroe County, Ill. Later went to the Arkansas River. Dismantled 1883.

4079 N.J. EATON

SW p wh b. Louisville, Ky., 1856. Advertised at St. Louis, Apr. 3, 1856, St. Louis-Brunswick, up Missouri River, Capt. Joseph S. Nanson, every Tuesday. She was snagged and lost on her first trip, Apr. 9, 1856. John P. Keiser, later president of the Anchor Line, was pilot on her. The fatal stabbing happened in Augusta Bend. Her engines, 24's- 7 ft., went to the *KATE HOWARD* in 1857 (see).

4080 N.W. CASEY

SW p wh b. Evansville, Ind., 1865. 109 tons. Off the lists 1873.

4081 N.W. GRAHAM

SW p wh b. Covington, Ky., 1853. 287 tons. In December 1855 arrived at St. Louis from Vicksburg minus 700 bales of cotton from her cargo. Her side chains and guards gave way, spilling the cotton in the river. The crew rescued 50 bales and reward was offered for the balance. Sold and renamed *SELMA,* Oct. 22, 1856 (see).

4082 N.W. HUGHES

Stw p wh b. Memphis, Tenn., 1866. 180 tons. Exploded her boilers near Randolph, Tenn., May 2, 1866. She was upbound, with the *PRIMA DONNA* (see) in tow. Nine were killed, including Capt. Van Dorn, his wife, and the chief engineer Frank Manso. John McLean, formerly on the Evansville-Cairo boats, was pilot at the time and unhurt. Some accounts refer to her as *NICK HUGHES.*

4083 N.W. THOMAS

SW p wh b. Cincinnati, Oh., 1853. 419 tons. 178 x 35 x 7.2. Owned and operated by Capt. William Shorpshire, New Orleans. Capt. John A. Duble commanded, c. 1858, Cincinnati-New Orleans. Same trade 1861, Capt. W.B. Phillips. In April 1861 he was presented with a fine silk "Sesesh" flag which he refused to fly. She was involved in war service on the lower Ohio. Some accounts refer to her as *NICK THOMAS.*

4084 NADINE

Stw p wh b. Howards Ferry, Mo., 1872. 23 tons. Engines, 8"- 3 ft. Owned by Nicholas W. Smith. She was en route from St. Charles, Mo. to St. Louis with grain when snagged three miles above the mouth of the Missouri, Sept. 10, 1878. A contemporary account names Capt. J.A. Stein as owner at time of loss, Roy Coulter, pilot.

4085 NAIAD

Stw tinclad wh b. Freedom, Pa., 1863, originally named *PRINCESS* (see). *PRINCESS* was sold to U.S. Navy, Mar. 3, 1864. Became Tinclad #53, renamed *NAIAD,* Apr. 3, 1864. 156.9 x 30.3 x 4.4. Engines, 13's- 3½ ft. Sold to B.F. Beasley and others, Aug. 17, 1865 and renamed *PRINCESS.*

4086 NANCY

Stw p wh b. Huntington, W. Va., 1894. 98.5 x 16.8 x 3. 36 tons. Ran local trades on the upper Ohio, Pomeroy-Ravenswood (competing with *LITTLE QUEEN*), and 1896 Parkersburg-Long Bottom. Still listed 1897, maybe later.

4087 NANIOPE

SW p wh b. Louisville, Ky., 1850. 114 tons. 120.7 x 21.8 x 4. Owned by A. Lastrapes (7/8) and E. Castillo, St. Martinsville, La., Capt. D.C. Daniel, master, Atakapas, La. (now Franklin). Snagged and lost at Atchafalaya Bayou, La., Sept. 15, 1852. No life loss.

4088 NANNIE BYERS

Stw p wh b. Cincinnati, Oh., 1863. 199 tons. Built for Capt. A.N. Byers and others. Tramped Pittsburgh-St. Louis-New Orleans. Left Pittsburgh, new, for St. Louis, May 10, 1864. On Feb. 23, 1866, downbound, she and *C.E. HILLMAN* (see) came in collision a short distance above Madison, Ind., about 3:00 A.M. The *BYERS* was struck on her port side forward of the engines. As she sank the cabin separated from the hull, was caught and towed into the Madison marine ways. The hull landed at the foot of Church

Street, Madison. Fifteen passengers were drowned and two of the crew. The *HILLMAN* got off almost scott-free, losing her jackstaff. The *BYERS* was in charge of Capt. W.J. Rusk, a former stockholder. A.N. Byers and James K. Cullam were in the office. W.H. Keyt, former clerk, had left her at Cincinnati. She carried as cargo a large shipment of boiler and bar iron from Gaylord & Son, Portsmouth, Oh., which had come to Cincinnati on the *ST. CLOUD* and had been reshipped at Cincinnati to the *BYERS* "without the usual privilege of reshipment" which made the *ST. CLOUD* liable "according to a recent decision." Capt. W.J. Rusk was somewhat accident-prone (see *H.S. TURNER*). That spring and summer the wrecked *BYERS* was completely rebuilt at Madison and renamed *GEORGE D. PALMER* (see).

4089 NAOMI

SW p wh b. Pittsburgh, Pa., 1839. 165 tons. First home port, St. Louis. Snagged and lost on the Missouri River at the mouth of the Grand, Brunswick, Mo., 1840. A man digging a well three miles from the river about 1924 found a Bible from her. The Keytesville cut-off left Brunswick about four miles inland. This Bible story was used in the *National Geographic Magazine,* issue November 1945, in an article "Taming the Outlaw Missouri River," by Frederick Simpich.

4090 NAOMI

SW p wh b. Louisville, Ky., 1849. 134 tons. First home port, Memphis, Tenn. Off the lists in 1856.

4091 NAOMI

Rig? p wh b. Parkersburg, W. Va., 1868. 81 tons. Operated out of Parkersburg. In August 1870 she went to North Bend, Oh., got the engines from the towboat *NEVILLE* which had exploded there, loaded them on a flat, and towed them to Parkersburg. In August 1871 during low water ran Pittsburgh-Parkersburg. Still listed 1876, maybe later.

4092 NAOMI

Stw p wh b. Antiquity, Oh., 1882. 68 x 13.8 x 6. Built on a scow, with cabin. Sawmill engines. Leather belt from engine to jackshaft operating twin sternwheels. Ran Racine-Middleport, round trip a day. Evidently towed produce boats south; listed at Vicksburg 1884; at Wheeling 1886–1896.

4093 NAPOLEON

Stw ferry wh b. Patterson, La., 1894. 50 tons. Originally U.S. steamer *HYACINTH.* Owned 1925 by Kenner Ferry Co., New Orleans. In 1929 owned by N.W. Moody at New Orleans, still in ferry service.

4094 NAPOLEON MULLIKIN

Stw ferry wh b. Jeffersonville, Ind., 1880. 165 x 42.5 x 6. 354 tons. Operated at St. Louis. Still documented 1896; probably lost May 27, 1896 in the St. Louis tornado.

4095 NASHOBAH

SW ferry wh b. Cincinnati, Oh., 1855. 137 tons. First home port, Nashville, Tenn. Went to Confederate registry 1861. She was a ferry at Memphis in 1860 and when the *PERSIA* (see) burned March 23, steam was raised on her and she beached the wreck about a mile below on the Arkansas shore.

4096 NASHVILLE

Stw p wh b. Freedom, Pa., 1846. 93 tons. Burned at the Allegheny wharf, Pittsburgh, in July 1847, owned by Frisbee, Miller & Co.

4097 NASHVILLE

SW p wh b. New Albany, Ind., 1849. 497 tons. 250 x 40 x 7.5. Engines, 23's- 10 ft. Five boilers. Hull by Dowerman & Humphries. Engines by Phillips, Hise & Co. Ran Nashville-New Orleans, Capt. Thomas Bellanyder, with John Orr, clerk. At the outbreak of the war she was converted into a U.S. hospital ship, her two decks berthing 1,000 wounded, called *NASHVILLE.*

4098 NASHVILLE

Stw p wh b. Cincinnati, Oh., 1860. 211 tons. Ran Cincinnati-Nashville, Capt. P.K. Barclay, in the Pioneer Line comprised 1861 also of the *MELROSE, GLENWOOD, CLIPPER, EMMA, IDA MAY, SWALLOW* and *COMMODORE PERRY.* Was in U.S. service handling supplies to Nashville 1862. Reported sold to F. Beatty, Ironton, Oh., May 1864. Dismantled 1869 and engines went to the *JULIA A. RUDOLPH.* Paris C. Brown, Esq., started his boating on her.

4099 NASHVILLE

Stw p wh b. Cincinnati, Oh., 1871. 396 tons. Ran Cincinnati-Nashville, Capt. P.K. Barclay, with C.S. Hart, clerk. In spring 1872 owned by Cincinnati, Big Sandy and Pomeroy Packet Co., Capt. Kerr, along with *EXCHANGE* and *GRANITE STATE.* Running Evansville-Memphis, 1873, Capt. A.E. Drankwater. In 1877 Cincinnati-Tennessee River, Capt. Jack Sleeth.

4100 NASHVILLE

Stw p wh b. Jeffersonville, Ind., by Howard, 1910. 155 x 34 x 4. Compound engines, 11's, 22's- 5 ft. by Gillett & Eaton. Built for the Parminters of Nashville for Evansville-Nashville trade, later Paducah-Nashville. Capt. Shep Green, master, with Harry D. Sayre, clerk in 1917. She was retired June 1918 due to high labor costs and scarcity of coal. Nashville Trust took her in at a forced sale Dec. 21, 1918. Williams Bros., Evansville, bought her April 1919 and ran her Louisville-Stephensport-Evansville. They rebuilt her, 1922, and renamed her *SOUTHLAND* (see).

4101 NAT F. DORTCH

Stw p wh b. Jeffersonville, Ind., by Howard, 1889. 302 tons. 160 x 29.7 x 3. Built for the Lovell Line, Cumberland River, and ran Nashville-Burnside. Named for a tobacco merchant in Nashville. Was sold south and in 1894 running New Orleans-Red River, Capt. Matt F. Scovell. Sank and lost in Red River, March 1895, in Lake Ninock, 28 miles south of Shreveport. The wreck was still visible 40 years later in low water.

4102 NATCHEZ

SW p wh b. New York, N.Y., 1823. 206 tons. First home port, New Orleans. A heavy boat with Watt & Burton type low pressure engine, condensing, with walking beam. Ran New Orleans-Natchez. General Lafayette and party embarked at New Orleans March 1825 and went to St. Louis on her, Capt. Robert Davis. Thence to Nashville where they transferred to *MECHANIC* for trip up the Ohio River. Ran New Orleans-Vicksburg, 1828, Capt. R. Leech. Burned at New Orleans Sept. 4, 1835.

4103 NATCHEZ

SW p wh b. Baltimore, Md., 1838. 792 tons. A heavy seagoing boat intended for the New Orleans-Natchez trade. Once went aground on Natchez Island drawing 12 ft. She was reportedly sold to the Brazilian government and converted into a war vessel. Lost in collision, Nov. 21, 1842.

4104 NATCHEZ

SW p wh b. Cincinnati, Oh., 1846. 280 tons. 174.8 x 25.8 x 6.5. Engines, 20's- 8 ft. Two boilers. Hull by Saunders W. Hartshorn. Engines by Anthony Harkness. Built for the New Orleans-Vicksburg trade, owned entire and commanded by Capt. Thomas P. Leathers. Sold 1849 to Capt. John Pierce, Newport, Ky. Off the lists 1852.

4105 NATCHEZ

SW p wh b. Cincinnati, Oh., 1849. 388 tons. 191.1 x 31 x 6.1. Engines, 24's- 8 ft. Three boilers. Ran New Orleans-Vicksburg owned entire and commanded by Capt. Thomas P. Leathers. Sold September 1853 to James Clark and Charles Morgan, equal shares, Pointe Coupee Parish, La. In January 1854 Clark sold his one-half to Arthur Adams, Pointe Coupee Parish. She ran New Orleans-Fort Adams. In June 1854 a dealer in old boats, Roger A. Heirn, advertised her for sale. Went to Mobile, used as a wharfboat, and foundered in Mobile Bay, Mar. 10, 1866.

4106 NATCHEZ

SW p wh b. Cincinnati, Oh., 1853. 698 tons. 270 x 34 x 8. Engines, 34's- 9 ft. Six boilers. Built for and commanded by Capt. Thomas P. Leathers, Natchez, Miss., New Orleans-Vicksburg. Designed for 4,000 bales. Came in collision with *PEARL* below Plaquemine resulting in loss of *PEARL* and eight lives, Jan. 1, 1854. Burned at New Orleans Feb. 5, 1854 with loss of three lives, one of whom was Leathers's brother James, asleep in the texas. This fire originated on the *CHARLES BELCHER* (see) and consumed many steamboats. She had run only six weeks when lost.

4107 NATCHEZ

SW p wh b. Cincinnati, Oh., 1854. 714 tons. 270 x 34 x 8. Engines, 34's- 9 ft. Six boilers. Owned entire and commanded by Capt. T.P. Leathers, New Orleans. Ran New Orleans-Vicksburg. The well-known trademark of Leathers's boats, a cotton bale emblem swung between the stacks, appeared on this one (mention of its use on his earlier boats is lacking). Capt. Truman C. Holmes and Leathers procured a U.S. Mail contract New Orleans-Vicksburg "three times a week by steamboat—397 miles and back" for which service they received $40,000 annually until the outbreak of the war. This required three packets in the trade. The *NATCHEZ* was the Saturday boat out of New Orleans and the Tuesday and Thursday boats were *PRINCESS, C.D. JR., R. W. McREA, CAPITOL,* and others from time to time. At the conclusion of the cotton season spring of 1860 *NATCHEZ* was sent to Louisville and brought to New Orleans the uncompleted "new" *NATCHEZ* (next listing), after which she was taken to Baton Rouge where she served as a wharfboat.

4108 NATCHEZ

SW p wh b. Cincinnati, Oh., 1860. 800 tons. 273 x 38 x 8. Machinery from *NATCHEZ,* b. 1854. Six new boilers. She was taken unfinished from Cincinnati to Louisville by *TELEGRAPH NO. 3,* and thence to New Orleans by her predecessor (see above), and was not commissioned until Aug. 16, 1860. Had capacity for 5,000 bales. Owned and commanded by Capt. T.P. Leathers. Louisiana and Mississippi joined with four other southern states to form the Confederate States of America, Feb. 8, 1861. The *NATCHEZ* continued her trade but by April cotton had almost ceased as cargo, and New Orleans was blockaded from the sea. She was advertised henceforth as a Confederate States Mail Packet. That fall she ran New Orleans-Memphis. Jefferson Davis and Leathers were close friends. Davis had boarded the *NATCHEZ* at his Brierfield plantation, February 1861, en route to Montgomery where he was sworn in as Confederate president. Davis wanted Leathers to head up the Confederate River Defense fleet but this did not come about. By mid-1862 Memphis had fallen and the lower Mississippi below Vicksburg, was in U.S. control. The *NATCHEZ* in April 1861 had been sent up the White River to transport Confederate troops to Memphis, her last duty. Leathers took her 25 miles above Yazoo City for safety, and there she was torched and destroyed to prevent her capture, Mar. 13, 1863. After the war a U.S. wrecking crew, acting on instructions from James B. Eads, removed the wreck and appropriated the machinery and salvage. Leathers instituted suit, got judgment, but failed to collect.

4109 NATCHEZ

SW p wh b. Cincinnati, Oh., 1869. 1,547 tons. 301 x 42.6 x 9.8. Engines, 34's- 10 ft. Eight boilers, each 2-flue. Niles engines. Dumont boilers. O. Perry Tharp of the Cincinnati Marine Ways superintended construction. Elias Ealer built the cabin, severely plain, no ornamentation. Built for Capt. T.P. Leathers for the New Orleans-Vicksburg trade. Departed Cincinnati on maiden voyage south on Dec. 6,

1869. Said an editor of the Natchez "New South" upon her initial arrival there: "The new boat has been so puffed up we really expected to see a fine steamer. But we are disappointed. She may be substantial and fast but is decidedly plain and ungainly. She lay looped-up over against the shore like a sick mule to a board fence, looking anything but graceful. In our opinion she is not to be compared with the *THOMPSON DEAN, LEE* or *WILD WAGONER.*" Archie Frame and Joe McCamment piloted her out of the Ohio River, and Pink Varble took her over the Louisville Falls. Samuel Ayles (described as a "big fat man") was head clerk assisted by Charles Grice. Johnny Hawkins, a firm friend of Leathers, owned the bar. In off-cotton seasons the *NATCHEZ* made trips to St. Louis, and so it was in June 1870 she sprinted north to that port breaking the long-standing *J.M. WHITE* record by one hour 12 minutes. The businessmen of St. Louis presented a fine set of deer horns to Leathers and much printers' ink was expended in laudation. This achievement set the stage for the celebrated race run several weeks later, New Orleans to St. Louis, between the *NATCHEZ* and the *ROB'T E. LEE.* It is said of her that she went through the water like a swan. She had a half-round groove in her stemband that spurted up water like a fountain-jet when under full headway. Smokestacks were red, and she wore the cotton bale symbol between them. The whistle, a huge, single-chime affair, was mounted inside one of the smokestacks, Capt. Leathers remarking: "The whistle is for awakening persons on shore; not on the steamboat." Observers said it had the sound of a big bumblebee. In addition to crew personnel already noted, these others shared for the Great Race: Frank Clayton and Mort Burnham, pilots; Andy Pauley, John Farwell, Pat Nolan, John Montreville, John Montague and Alexander Meeha in the engineroom; Ovid Bell and Fred Kentham, assistant clerks, and E. Cummings and James Dillon, mates. For details of the *LEE-NATCHEZ* race (which the *NATCHEZ* lost) see *The Great Steamboat Race* by Roy L. Barkhau, 1952, the book printed by Young & Klein, Cincinnati, who reprinted a second edition, 1962. For factual background of Capt. T.P. Leathers see *S&D Reflector,* June 1970, pages 7–13, by Dewey A. Somdal. Also see issue June 1976, page 21, for details of his New Orleans home; Sept. 1976 issue for photograph of his monument; March 1977 issue, page 23, for bronze marker at his home and occupant, and March 1979 issue for full color front page of his Natchez home. The "racer" *NATCHEZ,* subject of this sketch, never flew the American flag. Her die-hard owner refused succor to dispossessed residents of Chicago following the great fire Oct. 8–11, 1871, when Leathers saw that the passes were signed by Gen. Phil Sheridan. "That—that—why that (bleep-bleep-bleep) fiend—he burned out more Southern families than are houseless in Chicago today," he blazed. Workers at the Cincinnati Marine Ways were stone broke after *NATCHEZ* lost the race with the *LEE.* On one trip in 1874 she brought to New Orleans 5,511 bales, her record, Peter Peppers, mate. On June 6, 1879, she was noticed upbound at Louisville, Capt. Harry Stein, bound for Cincinnati to be dismantled, still with her tall red chimneys. She became stranded at Rising Sun, Ind., en route, giving rise to this:

She sticks on Rising Sun Bar
With her chimneys high up in the skies;
While Cons waits to give her a blow,
The Natchez will wait for a rise.

So wrote Will S. Hays in the *Louisville Courier-Journal,* with a sly dig toward Cons Millar, news reporter in Cincinnati. Said Capt. T.P. Leathers: "It would be a damn sight more romantic for the old craft to die and be dismantled 'midstream, with colors flying and the elements she has so bravely ploughed for ten years rippling 'round her, and not in the bone-yard, but," he added, "it's too damn troublesome and expensive that way. Besides I'm anxious to get back to my wife and get rested. Mrs. Leathers has born me children, nine living and several buried, and I aim to get back to her." The towboat *IRON MOUNTAIN* tugged at the stranded side-wheeler to no avail. Finally on July 13, 1879, she was at the foot of Ludlow Street, Cincinnati "sans chimneys, wheels and machinery but still a good looking boat." She was moved up under the marine ways and there remained until early in 1881 the *R.R. SPRINGER* took her in tow to Jeffersonville, Ind., and left her at the Howard Yard. Later the hull was taken south to become a wharfboat at the Refuge Oil Mill below Vicksburg.

4110 NATCHEZ

SW p wh b. Cincinnati, Oh., 1879. 303.5 x 46.5 x 10. Engines, 34's- 10 ft. Eight boilers. Paddlewheels 42 ft. dia. working 18 ft. buckets. C.T. Dumont built boilers, doctor and chimneys. Her cylinder timbers were cut in Kentucky 37 miles off the Big Sandy River, hauled to that stream and delivered to Cincinnati. Stem band and other iron work came from Pittsburgh. Elias Ealer built the cabin. Skylight glasses depicting 22 Indian portraits were from Coulter & Son, Cincinnati. On the wheelhouses were semi-circular landscapes by artist Gordon Blentlinger, Cincinnati. In the cabin painted on the forward skylight bulkhead was a scene at Natchez with Indians worshiping the rising sun, and on the aft bulkhead an Indian queen was leaping from a bluff, both the work of artist Dwight Benton, Covington, Ky. Saunders Hartshorn gets credit as the architect for all seven of Leathers's *NATCHEZ* packets (also the *PRINCESS* fleet, see). Dan Morton employed him. Launched Saturday Aug. 2, 1879, at 4:30 P.M. drawing 3′1″ forward and 2′11″ aft. The traditional smashing of champagne was dispensed with and the launch "was effected without any nonsense." Robert McGregor did the cabin interior scenes. The new boat left Cincinnati towed by two *CHAMPION*s on Sept. 9, Capt. Pink Varble in charge, was taken through the Louisville Canal to New Albany, and thence to Cairo. Departed Cairo on Sept. 21, under her own steam for the South. A huge crowd congregated at New Orleans to witness her arrival there Sept. 29. When she was seen upriver, a dense pall of smoke was coming from her port side, amidships. Her cargo of cotton was on fire, and 246 bales were lost, also 38 sacks of seed. Pilot Smeed Strong rounded her to in order to keep the wind from fanning the blaze. It was a narrow shave. Nevertheless when she landed the reception was a royal one. The Cincinnati *Commercial* carried two columns of description of the event in their Oct. 3 issue. There was a large and grand hickory chair in the cabin marked "Presented to Capt. Thos. P. Leathers of the steamer *NATCHEZ* by his friend C.H. Kilgour on the launching of the boat at Cincinnati, Ohio, July 29, 1879." Entered the New Orleans-Vicksburg trade. In early May 1880 conveyed a large party of notables down to the Jetties. As a sidelight on Capt. Leathers, a die-hard of the first waters, in 1860 he hauled down the American flag from the jackstaff of the *NATCHEZ* (5th) and never again flew the stars-and-stripes until Mar. 4, 1885, which was election day and the Democrats were back. The *NATCHEZ* of this sketch was at Vicksburg that day. Leathers announced he was going to bury the hatchet. A big gun was fired from the forecastle, declaring that the war was over, and the flag was hoisted. Business became slack and the *NATCHEZ* went to the bank in 1887 and remained tied up for two years. She was brought out to run to Greenville and sank at Stack Island on Jan. 1, 1889. Capt. Jeff Hicks was the pilot on watch. Much of her cabin equipment was recovered before the sand washed out from under the hull and broke her up. Jeff Hicks once told this scribe that he wept openly and unabashed at having been party to this loss. "I felt greater pride piloting the *NATCHEZ* than on any other boat," he added.

4111 NATCHEZ

Stw p wh b. Jeffersonville, Ind., by Howard, 1891. 225 x 40 x 8. Engines, 20's- 8 ft. Three boilers, each 46" dia. by 32 ft. Capt. T.P. Leathers was well up in years and the command fell to Capt. Bowling S. Leathers, his son, who had a steamboatin' wife, Capt. Blanche Douglass Leathers who got her license August 1894 and used it. Capt. Blanche, a no-nonsense executive, ran a tight ship, and when her father-in-law, Capt. Thomas P., 80, died in New Orleans from injuries sustained after being struck by a bicyclist, June 1896, she perpetuated the family steamboatin' tradition. Advertisements for *NATCHEZ* in New Orleans newspapers, 1900, listed Capt. B.D. Leathers, master; B.S. Leathers, clerk; no apology, no explanation. This last (and only sternwheel) *NATCHEZ* of the Leathers's fleet survived some near-misses; sank about three miles above Natchez, November 1896, with 1,700 bales of cotton and 8,757 sacks of seed, due to dried hull seams. In early February 1897, hit the shore at Cottonwood, 20 miles below Vicksburg, tore away the jack-staff and stages and toppled her chimneys. Sank at Ford's Crossing, 12 miles below Natchez, November 1899. Capt. William A. Duke became associated with the operation of this boat and also the *T. P. LEATHERS* (see) and was master of *NATCHEZ* in 1902 with T.C. Sachse, clerk. She got new boilers July 1914, and less than a year later was in the hands of a U.S. marshal who sold her for $6,500 to Capt. W.A. Duke, May 1915. He ran her New Orleans-Cariola-Grand Lake with indifferent success, often laid up for long periods, and she was dismantled 1918.

4112 NATCHEZ

SW p wh b. Catlettsburg, Ky., 1903. 81.5 x 8.9 x 1.9. Said Capt. Jesse P. Hughes: "This was a small one, and don't know what ever was done with it." Still listed 1908.

4113 NATCHEZ

Stw excursion sh b. Braithwaite, La., by Bergeron Machine Shop, 1975. 236 x 38. Compound condensing engines, 15's-30's- 7 ft. Two Cleaver Books firetube boilers, oil fired. Built for New Orleans Steamboat Co., headed by Wilbur Dow, Jr., of New York, and managed by his son William P. Dow of the Lake George (N.Y.) Steamboat Co. Architect was Alan L. Bates, Louisville, Ky., previously associated with *BELLE OF LOUISVILLE.* Launched Mar. 8, 1975, and had her trial run April 2. Came out in charge of Capt. Clarke (Doc) Hawley, with Robert (Roddy) Hammett, mate; Gilbert Manson, pilot, and Robert (Bob) Brewer, chief engineer. The engines came from U.S. Steel's towboat *CLAIRTON* (originally *YOUGHIOGHENY,* b. 1927). See *S&D Reflector,* December 1972 for background of *CLAIRTON*; March 1973, page 10, for removal of *CLAIRTON* to Violet Canal; December 1973, pages 36–37 for hull construction views; June 1974, pages 5–8, for superstructure construction views; June 1975 for full color front cover of completed boat, same issue, page 15, for story; September 1975, pages 9–15, for detail views and race with *DELTA QUEEN*; December 1976, pages 20–21, for trip carrying U.S. President Gerald Ford; March 1977, pages 39–41, for Presidential Trip told by William P. Dow, and September 1978 issue, front page, for full color oil painting of *NATCHEZ* by Joseph Wilhelm.

4113A NATHALIE HAMILTON

Stw ferry wh b. New Orleans, La., 1879. 148 tons. 165 x 24.6 x 6.3. Listed 1896, maybe later.

4114 NATHANIEL

SW ferry wh b. Steubenville, Oh., 1887. 85 x 20.3 x 3.9. She was the ferry at Steubenville prior to the opening of the bridge there in 1905. Owned 1899 by Will H. Wells, three-fourths, and Joseph M. Browning, both of Jefferson County, Oh.

4115 NATHANIEL HOLMES

Stw p wh b. Belle Vernon, Pa., 1856. 215 tons. Lost in collision with *DAVID GIBSON* at Petersburg, Ky., Mar. 28, 1859. Charles and Jim Hunter, brothers, of Williamstown Va., were on her at the time. Fifteen lives were lost.

4116 NATHANIEL P. BANKS

Prop steamship wh b. Boston, Mass., 1863. In 1864 running New Orleans-Baton Rouge, Capt. R.P. Blaisdell, three trips a week. "This steamer is entirely new, having been completed in August last [1863]. She has a low pressure engine and makes her trips by daylight, adopting the time and usual landings of the former favorite packet *D.F. KENNER.*" 399 tons.

4117 NATIONAL

SW p wh b. Louisville, Ky., 1854. 248 tons. 173 x 30 x 6. Engines, 18's- 7 ft. Three boilers, each 42" by 24 ft. Ran Memphis-White River, Capt. J.S. McManus. Sank January 1855. Sold to Capt. P.C. Montgomery, New Orleans, and ran New Orleans-Shreveport. Dismantled 1860 and engines, etc., went to new *NATIONAL* (see).

4118 NATIONAL

SW p wh b. Jeffersonville, Ind., 1860. 379 tons. 184 x 33 x 6.7. Machinery from former *NATIONAL* (see above). Built for Capt. P.C. Montgomery for Red River trade. Sold May 1865 to John S. and Richard Sinnott (3/4) and James McClosky, New Orleans. They continued her New Orleans-Red River, Capt. Richard Sinnott, with F.C. Findren, clerk. Retired 1873 and was taken to Cincinnati. She was wrecked on the wharf at Covington, Ky., and the high water that October carried her away.

4119 NATIVE

SW p wh b. Jefferson City (now New Orleans) 1868. 121 tons. 102.8 x 20.4 x 3.6. Owned by Capt. H.A. Jolle, New Orleans.

4120 NATRONA

Stw p wh b. Wellsville, Oh., 1863. 111 tons. Built for Pennsylvania Salt Mfg. Co., Natrona, Pa., on the Allegheny River. This firm marketed "Natrona oil" and had a large refinery. The *NATRONA* operated to Franklin and Oil Creek until sold early 1867 to Allegheny Valley RR who used her while building their line up the Allegheny at Red Bank and elsewhere. Capt. James Lee, Memphis, bought her April 1868 to replace *PRINCE OF WALES* (see) and ran her Memphis-St. Francis River. Later she became a rafter on the Upper Mississippi and served many years. Finally sank near East Dubuque and the wreck was removed by a U.S. snagboat in April 1892.

4121 NAUGATUCK

Stw p wh b. New Richmond, Oh. (hull and cabin), and completed at Cincinnati, 1864. 157 x 37 x 5.5. Engines, 16's- 5 ft. Three boilers. Construction supervised by Capt. Isaac B. Davis. Came out new September 1864, Capt. A.Q. Ross. Ran Cincinnati-Memphis. Sold 1866 to Capt. James W. Gaff and others. Was bound from St. Louis for Cincinnati when she snagged in St. Mary's crossing, Mo., Dec. 31, 1866, Capt. T.K. Barclay. Settled with the bow on shore and the stern down 20 feet. Lost.

4122 NAUMKEAG

Stw p wh b. Cincinnati, Oh., 1863. 326 tons. 154.2 x 30.4 x 4.5. Engines, 14's- 5½ ft. Sold to the U.S. Apr. 14, 1863, before documentation. Command went to Capt. John Rogers who took her to Cape Girardeau, Mo., thence to Parkersburg, W. Va., where Rebels threatened invasion. Then up the Kanawha to procure salt, after which chased Morgan's Raiders up to Buffington Island. In Feb. 1864 with *LINDEN* to Pine Bluff and Little Rock, bringing out cotton. Thence with Federal fleet to Clarendon, Ark., on White, raising the blockade. Retired at Mound City, Ill., and sold August 1865. Was renamed *MONTGOMERY* Sept. 16, 1865, and went to Mobile. Burned at Erie, Ala., Jan. 19, 1867, with loss of three lives. Capt. John Rogers was born near London, England, 1823, came to the U.S., aged 11, joined the U.S. Navy, was married in Pittsburgh, Pa., 1850, and then followed the sea several years prior to the war. Following his river war service he lived many years in West View, Pittsburgh.

4123 NAVIGATOR

Stw p wh b. Brownsville, Pa., 1850. 154 tons. Owned by Capt. William Dean and others. U.S. President Zachary Taylor died in Washington, D.C., July 9, 1850, of typhus and his remains were transported to Louisville, Ky., for burial. The casket arrived at Pittsburgh, Pa., Sunday Oct. 27, and on Monday forenoon the casket was escorted from the canal basin to the *NAVIGATOR* moored at the Monongahela wharf. Departure was made that evening, Capt. Dean commanding, and stops were made at the principal cities en route. J.A. Howells, editor of the *Ashtabula* (Oh.) *Sentinal* wrote in 1902: "Four of my uncles were steamboatmen. The oldest, Capt. William Dean, was first a boy on a keelboat prior to 1820, grew up with the first steamboats on the Ohio, became a pilot and was for 40 years a captain. In January 1852 I shipped aboard the sternwheel *NAVIGATOR* at Wheeling, unique in the respect that Capt. W. Dean was a devout Presbyterian and would not run his boat on a Sunday." Sold, and in 1854–1855 ran St. Louis-St. Paul, Capt. A.T. Chamlin. Off the lists 1856.

4124 NAVIGATOR

Stw p wh b. Brownsville, Pa., 1862. 243 tons. 153.6 x 38.8 x 5.3. Engines, 18's- 4½ ft. Three boilers, each 40" by 22 ft. Very small passenger cabin, built principally for freight. Machinery, etc., from the *BAY CITY* (see), owned by Capt. William Dean and others. Ran Pittsburgh-St. Louis. Capt. John Shouse bought interest that fall. David Gibson, Cincinnati, ran her later. Sold September 1866 to the Red River Packet Co., New Orleans, Capt. G.L. Kouns. Lost on Red River 30 miles below Shreveport with 700 bales aboard, at Loggy Bayou, La., Feb. 6, 1867.

4125 NE PLUS ULTRA

SW p wh b. Cincinnati, Oh., 1847. 248 tons. Engines, 28's- 7 ft. Three boilers. Ran New Orleans-St. Louis, 1851, Capt. Robinson. Was snagged on the Missouri at Council Bluffs, Iowa, May 6, 1854, Capt. Richard Phillips. Was dismantled in 1855.

4126 NEBRASKA

Stw p wh b. Kittanning, Pa., 1853. 39 tons. 101 x 13.5 x 3.1. One cylinder, cogwheels, flywheels, belts, and other fixings. Built by J.K. Wright, Kittanning. In 1855 owned by

Walter A. Burleigh and William L. Greenhill, both of Kittanning, and late that year Greenhill became owner entire. Summer 1856 ran in Pittsburgh-West Newton trade up Youghiogheny River. Apparently gravitated to the St. Louis area in war time, from whence she was transferred to New Orleans February 1864, owned by Vincent J. Wood of that city, with Capt. John Olivate, master. Lost in ice at St. Louis, Jan. 13, 1866.

4127 NEBRASKA

SW p wh b. Cincinnati, Oh., 1854. 683 tons. 285 x 38 x 8. Engines, 32's- 9 ft. Six boilers, each 32" by 30 ft. Ran St. Louis-New Orleans, Capt. G.W. Ford, 1856. In 1857 in the New Orleans & Memphis Packet Line, Capt. A.R. Irvin, master, along with *BEN FRANKLIN, JOHN SIMONDS, INGOMAR, H.R.W. HILL,* and *BELFAST.* Became a troop transport during the war. Took the 91st Infantry Volunteers, Illinois, St. Louis to Vicksburg, July 1863. On Jan. 12, 1866, she was at St. Louis removing furniture, etc., from the sunken *MEMPHIS* (see) in midstream and two days later became victim of the ice.

4128 NEBRASKA CITY

SW ferry wh b. Wellsville, Oh., 1859. 70 tons. Operated at St. Joseph, Mo., Capt. Ebenezer Blackison. Off the lists 1869.

4129 NEBRASKA CITY NO. 2

Centerwheel ferry wh b. New Albany, Ind., 1864. 87 tons. Went to Missouri River, owned 1874 by Marshall Brotherton and J.L. Ferguson in equal shares. Dismantled 1876.

4130 NED TRACY

SW p wh b. Cincinnati, Oh., 1857, originally named *D.A. JANUARY* (see). She was sold to USQMD June 1, 1864. On Feb. 1, 1866, renamed *NED TRACY* back in private ownership. Snagged and lost at Chester, Ill., Dec. 18, 1867.

4131 NELLIE

Stw p wh b. Wabasha, Minn., 1880. 86 x 16 x 3. 76 tons. Built for A.J. Whitney & Son, Rock Island, Ill. Ran Davenport-Clinton 1883, Capt. H.B. Whitney, with Dols Holsapple, pilot, Pern Lancaster, mate. Was sold south, renamed *DICK CLYDE,* and became a towboat on Tennessee River.

4132 NELLIE

Stw p wh b. New Albany, Ind., 1904. 112 x 23 x 3.8. Engines, 7"- 3 ft. Two boilers, each 38" by 18 ft. Originally a towboat owned by J.S. Goulding named *MARIE.* Walter P. Needham bought her, engines were changed to 12's- 3 ft., and she towed a cowboy baseball team showboat operated by Needham and Harry Steiner, renamed *NELLIE,* 1908. Sank at Industry, Pa., that winter, raised, and towed to Cincinnati from Ambridge, Pa., hull of the towboat *SARAH EDENBORN.* Ran Louisville-Kentucky River, Selby Turner as clerk, 1909–1910. Walter Needham built *AMERICAN* showboat at Cincinnati 1911, renamed *NELLIE* to *DIXIE,* and she towed it until she sank and was lost at Cincinnati.

4133 NELLIE BLY

Small low water steamer used 1897 by Harbor 25 Masters, Mates & Pilots Assn., for channel inspection, from Pittsburgh, Pa., down the Ohio.

4134 NELLIE HUDSON

Stw p wh b. Clinton, Pa., on Allegheny River (hull), and completed at Pittsburgh, 1886. 141.3 x 25 x 3.4. Engines from *WILLIAM R. JONES.* Built by H.P. and John S. Hudson. Came out in October 1886 and took pilots on a low water inspection trip down the Ohio, and then ran Wheeling-Parkersburg trade. Spring of 1887 entered Pittsburgh-Kittanning trade on the Allegheny, first packet there in 18 years. Sold to Capt. Lewis Vandergrift, New Harmony, Ind., who took her to Wabash River, and about a year later went to the Parisot Line, Vicksburg, for Yazoo River. Sank at Vicksburg late in 1890.

4135 NELLIE HUDSON NO. 2

Stw p wh b. above Freeport, Pa., on the Allegheny River (hull), and completed at Pittsburgh 1889. 158 x 28.6 x 3.4. Engines, 12's- 5 ft. Two boilers. Built by John S. and H.P. Hudson for Pittsburgh-East Brady, Pa., trade on the Allegheny. Made occasional trips to Oil City, Pa. In low water seasons she ran on the Monongahela to Elizabeth, Pa., and served as a shuttle ferry for people attending the Exposition at Pittsburgh. Sold in 1892 to Henry M. Flagler who was building the Florida East Coast Railroad. Capt. Fred W. Swerger, Brentwood, Pa., took her to Indian River, Fla., renamed *SANTA LUCIA* before departure. She was 50 days en route New Orleans to Indian River but made safe arrival.

4136 NELLIE HUDSON NO. 3

Stw p wh b. Brownsville, Pa., at Axton yard, 1893. 141 x 25 x 5. Engines, 13's- 5½ ft. Three boilers, each 38" by 28 ft. Capt. John S. Hudson, Kittanning, Pa., owner and master. All three of these boats were named for daughter of Capt. John. Ran on the Allegheny until entered in Pittsburgh-Brownsville trade on the Monon, July 1897. Sank mid-March 1898 below Lock 4, Monon River, raised. Later was returned to the Allegheny and ran excursions out of East Brady and Parker, Pa., sometimes going up to Emlenton, Pa. See *S&D Reflector,* September 1970, page 23, for photo of her so engaged in 1905. Later she made trips up the Allegheny to bring out new barges. Cut down by ice at Ford City, Pa., 1913.

4137 NELLIE KENT

Stw p wh b. Osceola, Wis., Mile 45.4 on the St. Croix River (hull), and completed at La Crosse, Wis., 1868. 89 tons. Ran tri-weekly, St. Paul-Taylors Falls, Capt. W. Kent, later Capt. Russ Ruley and Capt. Oscar Knapp. Dismantled 1879 and equipment went to building *MARY BARNES* (see).

4138 NELLIE MILLER

Stw p wh b. Smithland, Ky., 1854. 146 tons. First home port, Louisville, Ky. Snagged and lost at Nashville, Tenn., Feb. 4, 1858. See *NETTIE MILLER*.

4139 NELLIE MOORE

Stw p wh b. Cincinnati, Oh., 1863. 226 tons. Was bound from Nashville, Tenn., to Cincinnati when she sank and was lost at Cumberland Island, Ky., Nov. 25, 1863.

4140 NELLIE PECK

Stw p wh b. Brownsville, Pa., 1871. 201.4 x 35.2 x 4. Construction superintended by Capt. Grant Marsh who was master 1871-1872. See Hanson's *Conquest of the Missouri*, pages 130-136. Built for Durfee & Peck, and first arrived at Fort Benton, Mont., in 1871, and in her career made 13 more trips to the fort. In 1872 she and *FAR WEST* competed in a 2,800-mile race from Sioux City to the fort and return, which the *FAR WEST* (see) won. She was the first arrival at the fort, 1872, and again in 1875. Was above Little Rock, Ark., January 1876, loading cotton for New Orleans. When she got to the fort in mid-June 1876, she couldn't unload due to a flood which had all but submerged the town. Still listed 1892.

4141 NELLIE ROGERS

Stw p wh b. California, Pa. (hull), and completed at Pittsburgh, 1862. 178 x 32 x 4.6. 249 tons. Built for Illinois River and first commanded by Capt. E.W. Gould, part owner, the other shareholders being C.S. Rogers and T.B. Chipley, St. Louis; James Abrams, Naples, Ill.; and Samuel Rider, Griggsville, Ill. Ran St. Louis-Naples. Made trips up the Missouri (see Gould, pages 423-424). Was at Pittsburgh loading for St. Louis, Jan. 5, 1870, in charge of Capt. Thomas Rogers. Owned for a time by Huntsville Transportation Co., John N. Bofinger, St. Louis, president. Dismantled 1872 at Jeffersonville, Ind., and the hull used as a barge.

4142 NEPTUNE

Stw p wh b. Brownsville, Pa., 1852. 214 tons. Advertised in the Wheeling *Intelligencer* Nov. 12, 1852, for New Orleans and Galveston, Tex., Capt. Stener. Off the lists at Galveston in 1858.

4143 NEPTUNE

Stw p wh b. California, Pa., 1857. 211 tons. 150 x 39.5 x 4. Built for Adam, Thomas, Jacob, and George Poe, Georgetown, Pa. Ran Pittsburgh-St. Louis and elsewhere. At the outbreak of the war sold to Capt. John Kyle, Cincinnati, March 1861. He entered her in the Cincinnati-Memphis trade. Downbound on the Cumberland River, Mar. 19, 1862, she hit the Clarksville bridge and was lost. Other victims at the bridge that day were *MONARCH* which tore away her port paddlewheel, and *GREY FOX* lost her stacks.

4144 NEPTUNE

Prop p ih b. Philadelphia, Pa., 1879. 84 tons. 106.4 x 20 x 6.7. Ran New Orleans-Lower Coast-Port Eads, Capt. W.S. Bassett, with John F. Aiken, clerk, thrice weekly. The same line ran *DAISY*, New Orleans-Buras. In 1893 the New Orleans & Southern RR ran her New Orleans-Lower Coast to the Forts, Capt. C.S. Kouns. Still listed 1895, maybe longer.

4145 NETTIE HARTUPEE

Stw p wh b. Allegheny, Pa., 1863. 81 tons. Construction superintended by Capt. James Shedden, and departed Sept. 16, 1863, for Cincinnati. In mid-March 1864 near Nashville some "pirates" stole her, the *NEWS BOY* in hot pursuit. When it became apparent they were being overtaken the "pirates" landed *NETTIE* at shore and leaped into the woods and vamoosed. The *NEWS BOY* shelled the vicinity to no effect. She was in the Gallipolis-Pomeroy trade when she burned at Pomeroy, Oh., Mar. 2, 1865.

4146 NETTIE JOHNSON

Stw p wh b. Memphis, Tenn., 1905. 116 x 28 x 5. Engines, 12's- 4 ft. Two boilers, each 38" by 22 ft. Owned by Capt. Nettie Waldron Johnson, Memphis, wife of Isadore S. Johnson. Ran Memphis-St. Francis and White rivers. She was up the St. Francis River and had left Marianna, Ark., with a log camp outfit aboard, when she sank, Jan. 4, 1912. Capt. (Mrs.) Johnson and son Emory were marooned for a time in a steel lifeboat but got safely ashore. Capt. W.P. Weld ran the boat later, selling her to Capts. J.A. Crouch and H.C. Williams, August 1914, for Memphis-Fritz Landing trade. Capt. W.L. Berry, Paducah, bought her, put her in tow of the *GLEANER*, and gave her a new hull at the Paducah Marine Ways. She then was used to tow railroad cross ties until dismantled, 1923. The towboat *INDIANA* was built at this time using the machinery, etc. See *S&D Reflector*, June 1977, page 32, for picture and story of this boat.

4147 NETTIE MILLER

Stw p wh b. Smithland, Ky., 1854. 146 tons. First home port, Louisville, Ky. Snagged and lost at Blankenship Island, Cumberland River, Feb. 4, 1858. The pilot on watch was Matt F. Dortch who there-and-then quit steamboating and long served as clerk in the Circuit Court, Nashville. In April 1864 *NAVIGATOR* brought the salvaged engines to Cincinnati where Capt. Varner offered them for sale, 11"- 3½ ft.

4148 NETTIE QUILL

Stw p wh b. Freedom, Pa. (hull), and completed at Wheeling, W. Va., 1886. 178.4 x 33.4 x 5.6. Built under supervision of Tom Dunbar. Machinery by A.J. Sweeney & Son, Wheeling. Built for Capt. John Quill, Mobile, Ala., and went there. Was returned to New Orleans, 1915, and renamed *MONROE*, placed in New Orleans-Ouachita River trade, Capt. Swayzie and others. She was lost in the Sept. 29, 1915 hurricane at New Orleans.

4149 NEVA

Stw p wh b. Pt. Pleasant, W. Va., 1898. 117 x 21.6 x 3.4.

Engines, 9″- 3 ft. Two boilers, each 36″ by 14 ft. Ran Winfield-Gallipolis, Capt. W. Austin Barrows, with Charles Stalder, clerk. Sold Sept. 24, 1904, to Capt. Mary B. Greene and C.F. Stalder who continued her in the trade connecting at Winfield with the *EVERGREEN* for Charleston. Burned at Buffalo, W. Va., July 26, 1908, at 11:00 A.M. Capt. Gordon C. Greene bought the *LEROY* to replace her (see). Machinery went to *C.C. BOWYER*.

4150 NEVADA

SW p wh b. Keokuk, Iowa, 1861. 75 tons. 116 x 24 x 3.5. Owned by W.H. Farris (three-fourths) and Robert E. Ventress in 1864, enrolled at Keokuk. Off the lists 1871.

4151 NEVADA

Stw p wh b. Belle Vernon, Pa., 1863. 299 tons. Owned in Pittsburgh, and ran to St. Louis. Was at St. Louis, Apr. 7, 1866, and was burned in a big steamboat fire, Capt. W.S. Evans, with James S. Mellon, clerk. There was very little cargo aboard.

4152 NEW ALBANY

SW ferry wh b. New Albany, Ind., 1849. 57 tons. Off the lists 1851.

4153 NEW BON ACCORD

SW p wh b. Madison, Ind., 1856. 142 tons. Built to replace *BONACCORD* (see). Owned 1874 by Jacob Conrad. Off the lists 1876.

4154 NEW BOSTON

Stw p wh b. Port Byron, Ill., 1864. 234 tons. Partner boat to the *CITY OF KEITHSBURG,* Fort Madison-Rock Island trade, operated by B.H. Campbell, Galena, and B.W. Davis, Rock Island. Capt. Melville, first master. Sold to the Northern Line at close of 1864 season and continued in the same trade. Off the lists in 1873.

4155 NEW CASTLE

Rig? ferry wh b. West Columbia, W. Va., 1871. Ferried Middleport, Oh.-West Columbia on Ohio River. Cut down by ice at Middleport Jan. 15, 1877, owned by Capt. Joe Martin and Middleport Ferry Co. The towboat *LIBERTY NO. 4* ran afoul of the wreck and sank on it in May 1877, and was raised.

4156 NEW CASTLE NO. 2

Rig? ferry wh b. Middleport, Oh., 1873. 29 tons. The Frampton brothers ran her between Frampton's Landing, Oh., and 7th Street, Huntington, W. Va. Replaced in 1880 by the *TRANSFER* (see).

4157 NEW CUMBERLAND

SW ferry (?) wh b. New Cumberland, Va., 1857. 32 tons. Off the lists 1860.

4158 NEW ELLA

Rig? ferry wh b. Leavenworth, Kan., 1868, to replace *ELLA* (see). 201.4 x 35.2 x 4. Inspected at Plattsmouth, Mo., June 1881. Lists of Merchant Vessels carried her as built at Pittsburgh, Pa., 1871. Still documented 1886.

4159 NEW ENGLAND

SW p wh b. Pittsburgh, Pa., 1844. 190 tons. 175 x 24 x 4.8. Capt. Samuel B. Page, master and part owner along with James Holmes, both of Pittsburgh. Ran Pittsburgh-Cincinnati. A Wheeling dispatch regarding this boat, dated Oct. 18, 1845, notes that her staterooms "are named after the several states and, after these are exhausted, other names of places." She had a "clipper" or Litch compound engine (see *CLIPPER*). Starting March 1847, ran Pittsburgh-Wheeling, Capt. G.W. Ebbert, with *HIBERNIA* on opposite days. Prior to this, she was the flagship of a fleet departing Pittsburgh with soldiers bound for the Mexican War, Capt. William J. Kountz. Off the lists 1849.

4160 NEW ENGLAND NO. 2

SW p wh b. Shousetown, Pa. (hull), and completed at Pittsburgh, 1847. 306 tons. 213 x 27.2 x 5.5. Engines, 24's- 8 ft. Four boilers, each 40″ by 28 ft., two 14½″ flues. Owned in part and commanded by Capt. Samuel Dean, Pittsburgh-Cincinnati. Other shareholders: William Bingham, James Holmes, Hays & Black, and Clarke & Thaw. She hooked a snag backing out from Haverhill, Oh., opposite Greenup, Ky., Mar. 17, 1850, floated some ten miles gradually sinking, then sank to her roof. She had been upbound with many passengers and this happened about 4:00 A.M. The *SCHUYLKILL* rescued passengers and crew. She was raised and was sold to St. Louis where she joined a "line" running opposition to the Keokuk Packet Co. Burned at St. Louis, Jan. 18, 1853. Capt. Sam Dean went master of *BUCKEYE STATE* (see).

4161 NEW ERA

Centerwheel snagboat wh b. New Albany, Ind., 1856. 251 tons. Went to St. Louis where, in 1861, she was greatly enlarged, using same engines, and became U.S. gunboat *ESSEX* (see).

4162 NEW ERA

SW p wh b. New Albany, Ind., 1860. 259 tons. 162.1 x 32.2 x 6.7. Went to Red River and was captured from the Confederates and used as a U.S. transport. After the war sold to Red River Packet Co., G.L. Kouns, president. Sold that November to Joshua Fenimore, New Orleans, with Capt. M.N. Wood, master, and ran on Red River. She continued the trade with several adjustments of ownerships, Capt. A. Dugas, master, until dismantled November 1869.

4163 NEW ERA

Stw p wh b. Wellsville, Oh., 1862. 157 tons. Sold to U.S. Navy, Oct. 27, 1862, and became Tinclad #7, known as *NEW ERA*. At the time of her sale at Mound City, Ill., Aug. 17, 1865, she is described as 137.1 x 29.5 x 4.5. Engines, 10″- 4 ft. She brought $5,000 and went to M.S. Mepham, St. Louis. Was renamed *GOLDFINCH* (see) Nov. 27, 1865.

4164 NEW ERA

Rig? ferry wh b. Guyandotte, W. Va., 1874. 32 tons. Continued to be inspected in the Wheeling District through 1882, perhaps longer.

4165 NEW ERA

Stw ferry wh b. Clarington, Oh., 1918, originally named *TRANSIT*. See *THE NEW ERA*.

4166 NEW FALLS CITY

SW p wh b. Paducah, Ky., 1858. 880 tons. 301.3 x 39.7 x 7.6. Engines, 30's- 9 ft. Six boilers, each 46" by 28 ft. Ran St. Louis-New Orleans, Capt. Wm. H. Scudder (1858), Capt. James B. Woods (1859–1861), and Capt. Henry Switzer (1862). She was in the "Railroad Line" prior to the war, connecting with the Illinois Central at Cairo, along with the *IMPERIAL, WM. M. MORRISON, CITY OF MEMPHIS, JAMES E. WOODRUFF, PENNSYLVANIA, ALFRED T. LACY, NEW UNCLE SAM, J.C. SWON* and *ALECK SCOTT* (all see). These were the palaces Mark Twain knew. Owned 1862 by Capts. Henry Switzer and James B. Woods; also William J. Lewis and Archie Woods. During the course of the war she was taken up Red River and purposely sunk by the Confederates to block the channel. In 1880 John A. Bofinger, St. Louis, contracted to clear the Red River of wrecks, this one among them.

4167 NEW HAVEN

Stw ferry wh b. Grafton, Ill., 1882. 94 x 24 x 3. Engines, 10's- 3½ ft. Two boilers. Owned by New Haven (Mo.) Ferry Co. Sank Feb. 25, 1885, in winter quarters at New Haven, Mo., raised. In 1888 she was lengthened to 136.1 ft., acquired a cabin and two stacks (originally had one aft of the pilothouse), and in 1892 the U.S. Engineers, Mobile, bought her at New Orleans, changed her name to *COOSADA* and used her on the Alabama River. Sold to Capt. John Baker, Mobile, 1906, and resumed her original name. Snagged and lost downbound on the Tombigbee River bound from Demopolis to Mobile in January 1910.

4168 NEW HAVEN

Stw ferry wh b. New Haven, Ill., 1902. 76.5 x 18.5 x 4.2. Sank on Wabash River, July 1902, raised that November, and became a ferry at Uniontown, Ky. Still listed 1908, maybe some later.

4169 NEW IBERIA

Stw p wh b. Pittsburgh, Pa., 1871, originally named *KEY WEST* (see). After the 1882 season on Missouri River sold and renamed. In 1885 running New Orleans-Bayou Teche, Capt. T.R. Muggah, with George W. Belt, clerk. Advertised as "the electric light steamer."

4170 NEW IDLEWILD

SW p wh b. Jeffersonville, Ind., by Howard, 1893, originally named *CITY OF NEW ALBANY* (see). Sold, new, and renamed. T.J. Moss Tie Co., ran her St. Louis-Cape Girardeau, replacing the *IDLEWILD* which had sunk in ice. She was in the trade several years. Bought by Eagle Packet Co., and renamed *SPREAD EAGLE* (see). Capt. Byrd Burton was master, and her pilot in 1894 was John N. Hamilton formerly a typesetter on the Hannibal, Mo., *Journal* when Mark Twain worked there.

4171 NEW LATONA

SW p wh b. New Albany, Ind., 1850. 396 tons. 199.6 x 28.5 x 7.1. Engines, 20's- 7½ ft. Owned by Capt. Joseph Gustave Landry who also commanded, New Orleans-Upper Coast to Donaldsonville twice weekly. Sold February 1853 to Capt. Emile Francois Gross, New Orleans-Port Hudson. She frequently ran in Red River, Capt. John Smoker, and was perhaps the largest boat seen at Shreveport in her day. She once went above to Soda Lake to get 800 bales of cotton from the sunken *JIM GILMER*. The river was high and in 12-Mile Bayou, a narrow hole, they met the wreck of the *COTTON PLANT* sunk three or four years prior, carried by the current, rolling over and over, the engines and boilers still on the old hull. It was a narrow miss. W.H. Daniel, Troy, Ind., piloted her for a time and says she also on occasion ran on the Ouachita. Dismantled 1855.

4172 NEW LUCY

SW p wh b. St. Louis, Mo., 1852. 225 x 33. Engines, 22's- 8 ft. Four boilers. Built for Keokuk Packet Co. and ran there with the *JEANNIE DEANS* and *NEW ENGLAND*. Sold to others and ran on the Missouri and gained the reputation of being the best "floating palace" on the stream in her time, and exceptionally fast. Burned while laid up for ice opposite DeWitt, Mo., Nov. 22, 1857.

4173 NEW MARY HOUSTON

SW p wh b. Jeffersonville, Ind., 1877. 287 x 41 x 7.3. Engines, 22½'s- 7 ft. Four boilers. Paddlewheels 30 ft. dia. working 11½ ft. buckets. Launched Oct. 28, 1877 at the Barmore yard and came out Dec. 14, Cincinnati-New Orleans, Capt. Charles Miller. Known as the "Sloppy Molly." In 1880 her clerks were A. Elliott Miller and Charles C. Stowell. Equipment from *MARY HOUSTON* (see) used in construction. Charles Dowerman was mate; Jim (Colonel) Pell and John Morledge, pilots; George Wile, chief engineer and Frank Neal, 2nd engineer. This was the same Jim Pell who piloted the *ROB'T E. LEE* in 1870 race. William Bryant was steward. Said the *Pittsburgh Gazette*, Mar. 6, 1878: "The *NEW MARY HOUSTON* will carry an electric light this trip which will illuminate the river almost bright as day for a distance of five miles ahead. Farmers along the river need not be surprised to hear the 'barnyard lords' crowing for daylight at the dead hour of night. This light is new and is cheaper and more brilliant than any light in existence outside of the sun and will supersede gas and come into general use throughout the world." Capt. Lew Kates was master in later years. She had just come into Cincinnati from New Orleans with a big cargo Jan. 10, 1893, when an ice gorge broke above. She and the wharfboat were carried away. She hit a pier of the C & O bridge, knocked down her stacks, and drifted opposite Petersburg, Ky., where the *LEVI J. WORKUM* landed her. The wharfboat sank at the Big Miami River. She was dismantled soon thereafter, and the hull became a barge.

4174 NEW MARY MORGAN

Stw p wh b. Little Rock, Ark., 1892. 112 x 22.8 x 3.3. See *MARY MORGAN.*

4175 NEW MATTIE

Stw p wh b. Jeffersonville, Ind., 1886. 130 tons. 130 x 34.3 x 5.8. Originally named *MATTIE,* renamed after a rebuilding. She was lost in White River on the east shore in Desha County, Ark., about abreast of the Norrell Cut Off Lock and Dam. The wreck was uncovered by low water in October 1976. The U.S. Engineers took pictures and called in Duane Huddleston, North Little Rock, local historian who made identification. His records show that she had been running out of White River, probably to Memphis, season 1897-1898. She stabbed a snag downbound with 356 bales and 1,000 sacks of seeds Feb. 17, 1900, and was lost. There were 35 persons aboard, and two of the deck crew drowned.

4176 NEW MOON

SW p wh b. Louisville, Ky., 1860. 120 tons. First home port, Memphis. Went to Confederate registry 1861.

4177 NEW MUSIC

SW p wh b. Algiers, La., 1864. 68 tons. 85.5 x 14.7 x 3.4. Captured by the U.S. during the war and sold July 12, 1865, to A.S. Mansfield, New Orleans. Capt. Charles Ford, master. Lost in 1868.

NEW NATIONAL

See *NATIONAL.*

4178 NEW ORLEANS

SW p wh b. Cincinnati, Oh., 1848. 299 tons. 182 x 36 x 8. Engines, 24's- 8 ft. Four boilers. Ran Cincinnati-New Orleans, Capt. David Whitten. Sank and lost at Cairo, Ill., Jan. 28, 1855.

4179 NEW ORLEANS

Stw ferry wh b. Jeffersonville, Ind., by Howard, 1858. 120.5 x 30.2 x 4.5. Owned by William Bobb, Jefferson Parish, La., Capt. C.P. Bobb, master. Documents state she had "double stern" so likely recess-wheel. Went to Confederate registry 1861. In Confederate war service renamed *W.H. IVY,* lost in 1864.

4180 NEW ORLEANS

SW p wh b. Belle Vernon, Pa., 1858. 198 tons. 154 x 34 x 4. Rebuilt in Louisiana and in 1863 owned by C.R. May, New Orleans, Capt. A.J. May, master. Ran New Orleans-Bayou Sara. Reported lost in wharf fire at New Orleans May 28, 1864.

4181 NEW ORLEANS

SW p wh b. New Albany, Ind., 1863, originally named *VINDICATOR* (see). As such she was a ram in U.S. service. Renamed Feb. 27, 1866. Off the lists 1869.

4182 NEW ORLEANS

SW p wh b. Elizabeth, Pa., 1911. 138 x 26 x 6. Built for Historical Society of Western Pennsylvania under supervision of Capt. James A. Henderson to imitate the original Western steamboat *NEW ORLEANS.* In that centennial year this replica retraced the maiden voyage of Nicholas Roosevelt's pioneer side-wheeler, Pittsburgh to New Orleans. Crew: Capt. Melvin O. Irwin, New Matamoras, Oh., master; Thomas Walker, Bellevue, Pa., engineer; Robert Kimble as clerk, and J. Orville Noll, steward. She had a slide valve engine 12"- 26" attached to each paddlewheel by gearing. Two boilers, each 36" by 22 ft. Electric lights and a steam capstan. See *S&D Reflector,* issue June 1969, pages 21-35, for pictures and detailed account of the 1911 voyage. When the replica reached New Orleans she was sold to Capt. Willie Ditch, Morgan City, La., who converted her into a gas-powered twin prop freight boat, to run New Orleans-Abbeville, La., on Bayou Vermillion. The venture was not successful.

4183 NEW ORLEANS

Catamaran ferry sh b. Jeffersonville, Ind., by Howard, 1925. 144 x 55 x 7. Overall width 67 ft. Engines, 18's- 6 ft. Two boilers. Allowed 800 passengers and 40 cars. Engines from Iowa Machine Works. Came in collision with ocean freighter *EDGAR F. LUCHENBACH* July 21, 1939, resulting in the sinking of the latter. Owned by Algiers Public Service Co., and ran New Orleans-Algiers along with *ALGIERS* (see). Sold 1962, dieselized, twin props, renamed *BELLE CHASSE,* owned by Plaquemines Parish Commission Council, Pointe-a-la-Hache, La. Still operating 1979.

4184 NEW PIKE

Stw ferry wh b. Madison, Ind., 1887. 115 x 25 x 3.5. Owned by Louisiana (Mo.) Ferry Co. Went to Huntington, W. Va., in 1918 and renamed *CITY OF HUNTINGTON* (see).

4185 NEW RICHMOND

Stw ferry wh b. Cincinnati, Oh., 1890. 86 x 22.5 x 4.3. Engines, 10½'s- 14". One boiler, 48" x 15 ft. Owned by C&O Railroad and was the ferry at New Richmond, Oh. Owned 1925 by Maysville & Big Sandy Railroad Co. Her pilot many years was John B. Prudent who later leased her for same service. Sold to Manchester, Oh. and renamed *E.I. FORD* (see).

4186 NEW ST. PAUL

SW p wh b. Wheeling, Va., 1852. 265 tons. Apparently rebuilt at New Albany, Ind., 1855-1856 and paddleboxes were lettered *NEW ST. PAUL.* Engines, 18's- 6 ft. Three boilers. Owned by her master, Capt. James Bissell. She was snagged and lost at Auberts Island, below St. Auberts, Mo., on Missouri River, Aug. 9, 1857. See *ST. PAUL.*

4187 New Sam Gaty

SW p wh b. Louisville, Ky., 1860 from *SAM GATY* (see). 367 tons. Engines, 26's- 6 ft. Three boilers. Owned by Capt. F.P. Johnson, master, along with John M. Baldwin and B.L. McKnight. She was downbound on Missouri River opposite Arrow Rock, Mo., June 28, 1868, took a sheer on the pilot, hit the shore where a projecting log listed her, shifted the boilers, set the boat afire, and she was lost. See *SAM GATY*.

4188 New Shallcross

SW ferry wh b. Jeffersonville, Ind., by Howard, 1878. 160 x 36.9 x 6.1. Owned by the Louisville & Jeffersonville Ferry Co., E.L. Dorsey, superintendent. Engines, 20's- 6 ft. went to ferry *COLUMBIA* (see) in 1891.

4189 New South

SW p wh b. Jeffersonville, Ind., by Howard, 1887. 257 x 42.6 x 7. Engines, 20's- 7½ ft. Four boilers. Built for Shelby & Perkins, wealthy Henderson, Ky., firm for Evansville-St. Louis trade, proved too large. C.Y. Perkins of the owning firm also owned in Henderson-Evansville railroad transfer steamers *MOLLIE NORTON, SUNBEAM,* and others. In 1890 she was entered in the Louisville-Cincinnati trade in opposition to *FLEETWOOD* of the U.S. Mail Line. Made only one stop, at Madison, Ind. These two rivals attracted enormous attention, were often in sight of one another, and passenger fare dropped to fifty cents a round trip including meals and berth. Low water laid both boats up and during the summer lull the Mail Line bought *NEW SOUTH* and put her Cincinnati-Memphis. Ran a Mardi Gras trip Cincinnati-New Orleans February 1896. In October 1896 on a trip to St. Louis got in a windstorm near Harrisonville, Ill., and disabled a wheel when she hit some piling. The *C.W. BATCHELOR* took off her passengers and freight. Ran a Mardi Gras trip from Cincinnati in 1902, hit an obstruction downbound on the Ohio River, and sprung her cabin so badly that hundreds of blankets were bought at Cairo to stuff in the cracks. When the ice gorge broke at Cincinnati, Feb. 12, 1905, she broke loose and was so badly damaged she was dismantled at Madison, Ind. There are indications that her original engines went to the *GREY EAGLE* (b. 1892, see), and thereafter she had compound machinery. She spent the summer of 1894 in the Cincinnati-Coney Island trade, Capt. Robert W. McCoy, teamed up with *BOSTONA,* Capt. John Newton. Capt. E.H. Matheus and Capt. W.P. Norwood were masters on her at various times.

4190 New State

Stw p wh b. Wheeling, W. Va., 1865. 398 tons. 157 x 32 x 5. Named for West Virginia. Capt. John McLure, Wheeling, ran her Wheeling-Cincinnati, also Wheeling-Gallipolis. In July 1866, Booth, Battelle & Co., who ran the Wheeling wharfboat, bought her for $24,000, and put her in the low water trade to Pittsburgh, Capt. W.H. Harlan. In January 1867 an ice gorge took her away and although she was safely recovered, "shore pirates" had skinned her of bedding and tableware. She ran Wheeling-Parkersburg 1867, Capt. C.H. Booth, with Jules Wehrman, clerk. Went to Wabash River spring 1868 bringing corn from there to Parkersburg for B&O reshipment East. Capt. Jack Harrison, Belpre, Oh., master in Pittsburgh-Louisville trade April 1868. That fall she commenced as a Pittsburgh-Wheeling regular. Sank in ice at Cox's Riffle, Wellsburg, W. Va., Christmas Day, 1868, and her cabin was demolished. Raised and rebuilt at Parkersburg and was given new engines. Continued Pittsburgh-Wheeling, and went to Parkersburg December 1869, to dismantle sunken *REBECCA* (see). Collided with towboat *EAGLE,* Apr. 7, 1873, in Glasshouse Riffle (Brunots Island) near Pittsburgh, and was sunk. High water submerged the wreck and not until April 21 was the freight recovered by the *L.C. McCORMICK*. Pilot Nathan Potts had his license lifted at a U.S. Inspector's hearing.

4191 New Ulm Belle

Stw p wh b. St. Paul, Minn., 1862. 50 tons. Snagged and lost on the Minnesota River, August 1862.

4192 New Uncle Sam

SW p wh b. New Albany, Ind., 1857. 902 tons. 285 x 38 x 6.5. Engines, 28's- 10 ft. Six boilers, each 42" by 26 ft. Ran Louisville-New Orleans, also St. Louis-New Orleans as part of the "Railroad Line" for several years commanded by Capt. A.R. Irwin. Was sent up Cumberland River, March 1862, went in the woods and knocked down her stacks. Sold to U.S. Navy Dec. 6, 1862, and was renamed *BLACK HAWK* in war service (see).

4193 New World

SW p wh b. Cincinnati, Oh., 1849. 199 tons. 161 x 26 x 5. Went to New Orleans owned in part by Capt. L.G. Moore, master, of Union County, Ark., who was associated with the boat until 1853. Thenceforth control was in the hands of Samuel Ayles, New Orleans, Capt. A.P. Hyatt, master. Off the lists 1856.

4194 New York

SW p wh b. Monongahela, Pa., 1852. 287 tons. Noted at St. Paul, Minn. 1856. In May 1859 the towboat *SAM CLARK* towed the old *NEW YORK* from Pittsburgh to McKeesport, Pa., so that her cabin, etc., could be put on a new hull just completed at the Coursin yard.

4195 New York

Stw p wh b. Belle Vernon, Pa., 1862. 199 tons. 155 x 33 x 4.5. Engines, 15's- 5 ft. Two boilers. Hull by L.M. Speer; engines by Robert Lea. Built for Capt. D.H. Gilmore and others for Pittsburgh-St. Louis trade. Sold at Cincinnati mid-December 1862 to Capt. John R. Rhodes and others for $20,000. Capt. J.H. Lightner took command and was on her during the war years when she frequently was handling U.S. supplies and troops. T.H. Golding was clerk 1862; J.B. Dale in 1864. In October 1864 she brought to Pittsburgh cannon, ammunition, gun carriages, caissons, etc., captured at Vicksburg. In March 1865 at Chickasaw, Ala., in U.S. service on Mobile River. April 1865 grounded in a cornfield below Shawneetown, Ill., and was high and dry. Capt. W.G. Coffin was master 1866. Barker, Hart & Cook, Cincinnati, sold their interest plus that of Capt. J.R. Rhodes, February 1867, to Capt. H. Clay Richmond later of the *ARGONAUT NO. 2,* and A.J. Hazlett became first clerk. In February 1869 made a trip to Pittsburgh with 465 bales of cotton, plus other cargo, William Goslee and Barney Givens, pilots. Left Cincinnati for Memphis Aug. 1, 1868, with full cargo and two loaded barges in tow, best trip of the year, pilots James Madison and I.D. Gough. Sold December 1869 to New Orleans owners, Capt. R.S. Livingston. On February 1, 1870, with big cotton trip from Bayou Bartholemew her cargo became afire as she reached New Orleans, and 150 bales were jettisoned, the boat unharmed. In spring and summer 1869 she toured New Orleans to Pittsburgh with *CRESCENT CITY CIRCUS* featuring Noyes' Circus Troupe. Burned and lost at New Orleans, Mar. 21, 1870.

4196 NEWPORT BELLE

SW ferry wh b. Cincinnati, Oh., 1853. 176 tons. Operated Cincinnati-Newport, Ky., along with *BELLE OF CINCINNATI.* Off the lists 1877.

4197 NEWS BOY

Stw p wh b. Brownsville, Pa., 1859. 115 tons. 133 x 27.3 x 3.4. Went to Red River. Owned 1861 by Capt. John Smoker and R.W. Doyle, equal shares, New Orleans. Capt. Allen Fowler, St. Mary Parish, La., and others bought her February 1862. They ran her New Orleans-Attakapas after the war.

4198 NEWSBOY

Stw p wh b. Brownsville, Pa., 1862. 53 tons. Ran Bellaire-New Martinsville on upper Ohio as a regular, fall 1862. Sold to USQMD late 1862. Back to private ownership Mar. 20, 1866. In Evansville-Henderson trade, Capt. C.G. Perkins, with C.E. Terry, clerk, September 1867, one daily round trip. Out of service 1870.

4199 NEWTON WAGGONER

Stw p wh b. Elizabeth, Pa., 1848. 105 tons. Went to St. Louis area. Off the lists 1855.

4200 NIAGARA

SW p wh b. Brownsville, Pa., 1847. 213 tons. Ran Pittsburgh-St. Louis, Capt. John Shrodes. Joe Hall, later manufacturer of safes and locks at Cincinnati was steward. Sold to Capt. E.W. Gould and C.S. Rodgers c. 1850, St. Louis-Illinois River to connect with a new railroad. Grounded and lost at Randolph, Tenn., January 1856.

4201 NIAGARA

SW p wh b. New Albany, Ind., 1855. 798 tons. In summer season 1856, New Orleans-Louisville, Capt. Harry I. Spotts.

4202 NIAGARA

Stw p wh b. Brownsville, Pa., 1859. 176 tons.

4203 NIAGARA

SW p wh b. Cincinnati, Oh., 1864. 797 tons. Built by Capt. Henry A. Jones and others. Ran St. Louis-New Orleans in the Atlantic & Mississippi Steamship Co., valued $120,000. She was upbound above Helena at the mouth of the St. Francis River on the clear night of Oct. 20, 1865, Capt. William Fitzgerald, with John Greenough, clerk. Met the *POST BOY* which veered and rammed *NIAGARA* with such force that the engineer stepped off his foot-board on to the forecastle of the *POST BOY. NIAGARA* had on board many black soldiers en route home. Holes were cut through the cabin floor to rescue 30 of them. Death toll was set at seventy-five. The *KATE HART,* White River to Memphis, brought up survivors.

4204 NICHOLAS LONGWORTH

SW p wh b. Cincinnati, Oh., 1864. 534 tons. Ran Cincinnati-New Orleans, Capt. Joseph H. Williams. In Columbia Bend, Mississippi River, late May 1864 eight Rebel artillery shells struck her. One went through Capt. Williams's room, two through the cabin, and another through the pilothouse. In July 1864 bringing north sick and wounded to Cairo, July 1864. After the war, ran Cincinnati-Memphis-New Orleans, Capt. A.R. Irwin, then Capt. Lewis Kates, with Eugene Bowers, clerk. Owned 1870 by Henry A. Jones, Thomas Sherlock, J.H. Barker, Thomas Cook, James Hart, and Lewis Kates. Dismantled 1875 and her hull became a wharfboat at Cincinnati, used by the newly formed Pittsburgh & Cincinnati Packet Line. John Shearer was the first clerk on it.

NICK HUGHES

See *N. W. HUGHES.*

4205 NICK SAUER

Stw tb wh b. Chester, Ill., 1882. 100 x 18.2 x 4. Owned by Capt. Harvey Neville who at one time operated her out of Chester, Ill., on a regular schedule up the Kaskaskia (Okaw) River to Evansville, Ill., twice weekly. He also ran *CONQUEST* and *LITTLE NICK* in the same trade. Excursions were run high as New Athens, Ill., in St. Clair County. More often towed wheat, etc. Still listed 1908.

NICK THOMAS

See *N. W. THOMAS.*

4206 NICK WALL

Stw p wh b. Pittsburgh, Pa., 1869. 338 tons. 180 x 33 x 5. Machinery from *PEERLESS* (see). Named for a Missouri River captain. Owned by Capt. J.T. Stockdale and others, and ran up the Missouri. Capt. Thomas Poe, Georgetown, Pa., bought one-half interest mid-February 1870, loaded for Fort Benton, Mont., and was the first arrival that spring. Gen. Philip Sheridan and party came aboard for the down trip. Was downbound near Napoleon, Ark., St. Louis to

New Orleans when snagged night of Dec. 18, 1870, with 15 cabin passengers and 135 on deck, many of whom were Texas-bound from North Carolina and Georgia having boarded at Memphis. The wreck floated three miles when the *SEMINOLE* happened along and took off survivors. Capt. Poe, to rescue his wife trapped in a stateroom filled with water, seized an axe, chopped a hole in the roof overhead, and in doing so gashed Mrs. Poe's head and brought her out unconscious. She died. Her remains were returned to Georgetown, Pa., for burial. Mark Twain reported this incident in *Life On the Mississippi*. Thirty-nine lives were lost. A peculiar aftermath followed in October 1871, when Capt. Poe's *MARY E. POE* broke an engine. He limped her to the *NICK WALL* wreck, dug out of the mud a replacement, and her engineers successfully installed it.

4207 NIGHTINGALE

Stw p wh b. McKeesport, Pa., 1863. 228 tons. Built for Capt. Jeff Dickerson and others for Cincinnati-St. Louis trade. Capt. J. Lawrence Carter, Cincinnati-Memphis, 1865; same master 1866, Cincinnati-Arkansas River, with J.C. Bower, clerk. Ran Louisville-Henderson, Capt. James Mather, with M.D. Warren, clerk, 1869. Cincinnati-Arkansas River 1870, Capt. U.B. Piersel, with J.S. Alexander, clerk. Retired in 1872. Capt. Jeff Dickerson, 94, was at Fort Wayne, Ind., in 1903.

4208 NILE

SW p wh b. Brownsville, Pa., 1859. 149 tons. Burned and lost at Benton, Ala., Nov. 5, 1859.

4209 NILE

SW p wh b. Pittsburgh, Pa., 1866. 454 tons. Loading on first trip at Pittsburgh April 1866 for Council Bluffs and Omaha, Capt. William Haslett. Due to slack business this trip was cancelled until latter April. Capt. Frank Maratta took command, with Asa Shepard, clerk, and she loaded for Missouri River. In 1867 loaded at St. Louis for Fort Benton, Capt. James F. Luker, made the round trip in 73 days. She had but one pilot on the downbound leg, Wirt Ashby, who did all the work and was on watch ten and one-half days doing it, something of a record. Capt. Grant Marsh had her to the fort in 1868, John Greenough in the office; again in 1869. Sank and lost at St. Louis, Apr. 8, 1874, owned then by Daniel S. Stover, M.D. Munson and James H. Hamilton, equal shares. She was described at the time as 200 x 34 x 5. Engines, 22's- 7 ft. Four boilers. At time of loss was acting as a railroad transfer at South St. Louis and was victim of a night storm, blown into a coal barge.

4210 NIMROD

SW p wh b. St. Louis, Mo., 1844. 210 tons. 156 x 25.8 x 5.7. Built for Capt. Joseph Throckmorton, Pierre Chouteau, Jr., and John B. Sarpy. First season made a "mountain trip" up the Missouri for American Fur Co. Details appear in Dunbar's *History of Travel in America*, page 1158. Owned December 1846 by Capt. Charles M. Olivier, Atakapas County, La. (now St. Mary, Iberia, St. Martin, Lafayette, and Vermilion Parishes). Sold March 1847 to George Pardow, New Orleans, Capt. Pierre Renaud. Sold September 1847 to Philippe Millaudon, New Orleans, Capt. Jacob Miller. Lost at New Orleans Aug. 6, 1850.

4211 NIMROD

Stw p wh b. Pittsburgh, Pa., 1865. 30 tons. Exploded and lost at Pittsburgh, Sept. 22, 1865, loss of five lives.

4212 NINA HOUSMAN

Prop ferry wh b. Prairie du Chien, Wis., 1888. 40 x 9 x 4.8. 19 tons. Also listed *NINA DOUSMAN*. Still listed 1908.

4213 NINA PADEN

Recess wheel ferry wh b. Marietta, Oh., 1896. 103 x 26.8 x 4.5. Engines, 12's- 4 ft. Two boilers, each 42" by 16 ft. Owned by J. Henry Shaw, Belpre, Oh., and others, and served Parkersburg-Belpre until February 1917 when sold to Ashland, Ky., to become *CITY OF ASHLAND* (see). She was built to replace earlier *MAGGIE PADEN* (see).

4214 NINA SIMMES

SW p wh b. New Albany, Ind., 1860. 327 tons. 178.8 x 35.5 x 6.7. Built for Capt. G.E. Lenaillier and others. Ran New Orleans-Opelousas weekly. She was hidden in upper Red River during the unpleasantness and reappeared December 1865, Capt. W.R. Greathouse, New Orleans-Bayou Sara, with George Troxler and H.H. Miller, clerks. In 1868 New Orleans-Lafourche twice weekly, same master, with Jos. Dalferes, clerk. On night of Apr. 17, 1869, snagged near Baton Rouge, La., and lost.

4215 NIOBARA

SW p wh b. Wellsville, Oh., 1878. 251 tons. 140 x 25 x 3.5. Engines, 11's- 4 ft. One boiler, 46" by 25 ft. Built for Capt. Andrew M. Haley, Sioux City, Iowa, and others. Built to run Sioux City-Niobara. Sold to Mobile, Ala., and renamed *W.G. LITTLE* May 16, 1885. Owned 1888 by The Red River & Coast Line, New Orleans, Capt. Thomas Carroll. Lost that year.

4216 NIOTA BELLE

SW ferry wh b. Brownsville, Pa., 1858. 75 tons. 102 x 31.5 x 3.5. First home port, Keokuk, Iowa. In 1865 owned by the Cattermole family, Capt. Oscar F. Chambers. Off the list in 1881.

4217 NOMINEE

SW p wh b. Shousetown, Pa. (hull), and completed at Pittsburgh, 1848. 212 tons. Capt. Joseph Smith built her for Pittsburgh-Cincinnati trade replacing *ALIQUIPPA* (see) and ran her there 1849 season. One of her pilots was C.W. Batchelor. That winter she was sold to the Upper Mississippi and went in the St. Paul trade, 1850, Capt. D. Smith Harris. She and *HIGHLAND MARY* were first arrivals at St. Paul, Apr. 19, 1850. Was the first boat through the lake Apr. 16, 1852 at 8:00 P.M., Capt. Orrin Smith. Made 29 trips Galena-St. Paul in 1853, Capt. Russell Blakeley. First boat to St. Paul on Apr. 8, 1854. Snagged and lost at Britts Landing 1854. When Capt. Orrin Smith commanded he laid her up Sundays (see Capt. William Dean on *NAVIGATOR,* another Sabbath observer).

4218 NORA

Stw p wh b. California, Pa., 1864. 214 tons. 159 x 30.5 x 4.8. Owned by James Rees, Pittsburgh (5/8) and Samuel Shuman; Capt. Thomas Shuman, master. Ran Pittsburgh-Cincinnati, Wm. Blackstock, clerk. Capt. H.H. Devenney usually commanded. James and John Shouse, pilots. She made a Missouri River trip spring 1867 and was snagged and lost at Pratt's Cutoff in Louisville Bend, May 28. *SILVER LAKE NO. 4* took passengers to Sioux City without charge. Capt. William Shedden was master, and Henry Keith, pilot.

4219 NORA

SW ferry wh b. McKeesport, Pa., 1869. 72 tons. Open end, one boiler. 86 x 23 x 5.8. Long operated at McKeesport. Replaced 1886 by *H.B. SINCLAIR* (see).

4220 NORA

Stw p wh b. Friendly, W. Va., 1890. 120 x 26 x 4. Ran low water, Wheeling-New Matamoras at various times, Capt. A.J. Monteith, with C.B. Monteith, clerk. Pilothouse on the roof. John Muhleman placed her machinery and was engineer. Named for George Monteith's wife. Towed produce boats south in winter, and was sold down there. Documented at Brashear, La., 1896.

4221 NORA BELL

Stw p wh b. Chambersburg, Oh., 1883. 114 x 20.6 x 3.6. Ran Gallipolis-Huntington. Named for daughter of J.M. Kerr, Gallipolis hardware merchant. Also ran in Kanawha River. Listed 1886, maybe later.

4222 NORA BELLE

Stw ferry wh b. Antiquity, Oh., 1924. 31 tons. 64.6 x 20 x 3.1. Built for Glenwood (W. Va.) Ferry Co., W.W. Cornwell, president. Owned 1929 by Manchester Ferry Co., Manchester, Oh.

4223 NORMA

SW p wh b. Cincinnati, Oh., 1852. 188 tons. 178 x 31 x 7.5. Capt. Dunning M. Foster commanded her spring 1853 and more or less continuously for the next year or so. He was a brother of Stephen Collins Foster, the composer. Prior to running *NORMA* was on the *JAMES MILLINGAR* (see). He died at the Broadway Hotel, Cincinnati, Mar. 31, 1856, and his body was returned to Pittsburgh on the *PHILADELPHIA. NORMA* was lost at President Island, Princeton, Miss., Feb. 11, 1855.

4224 NORMAN

Stw p wh b. McKeesport, Pa., 1863. 238 tons. Construction superintended by Capt. C.W. Batchelor for Memphis parties who ran her on the Arkansas and White. In collision with the *LADY WALTON* at Warsaw, Ky., Aug. 2, 1864, causing loss of the latter. Later ran Cincinnati-Evansville, Capt. P.K. Barclay, with J.H. Triplett and Lew Morris, clerks. Capt. P.K. (Pete) had a brother on the Sacramento River who ran a side-wheeler named *QUEEN CITY* built 1854 honoring Cincinnati. Took fire at Evansville 4:30 A.M., Nov. 21, 1870. Flames spread to *PINE BLUFF* alongside, thence to the new *CITY OF EVANSVILLE,* all burned.

4225 NORTH ALABAMA

SW p wh b. Louisville, Ky., 1844. 172 tons. Operated on Tennessee River. In August 1848 taking cedar logs Cairo, Ill., to Naples, Ill. Later that fall, St. Louis-Memphis. Then back in Tennessee River. Off the lists 1851.

4226 NORTH ALABAMA

SW p wh b. Brownsville, Pa., 1864, originally named *VIRGINIA BARTON* (see). Following service in USQMD she was renamed Jan. 27, 1866, and ran in C.J. Caffrey's "Line" St. Louis-Johnsonville, Tenn. Made a Missouri River trip 1869 with Capt. Grant Marsh at the helm (see Hanson's *Conquest Of the Missouri,* page 126). On another Missouri trip she was snagged and lost, Oct. 27, 1870, in Bow River Bend, above Vermillion, S.D. Capt. A. Townsend was master, and she was owned by Barton Able and others. The sunken boat caused the channel to change and the wreck was completely covered by sand. In July 1906 another change exposed the wreck, then swallowed it up again.

4227 NORTH AMERICA

SW p wh b. Pittsburgh, Pa., 1844. 273 tons. In May 1847, went in Cincinnati-Louisville trade opposition to the U.S. Mail Line, Capt. J. Ed Montgomery, with John N. Bofinger, clerk. Teamed with her was *MOUNTAINEER* on opposite days. Burned at New Orleans in the big wharf fire, Oct. 9, 1849. Others burned were *FALCON, ILLINOIS, MARSHALL NEY* and *AARON HART.*

4228 NORTH AMERICA

SW p wh b. Elizabeth, Pa., 1852. 270 tons. Ran Pittsburgh-St. Louis. Four Catholic sisters took passage at St. Louis, arriving at Wheeling on Apr. 13, 1853, and there established the Sisters of Saint Joseph which continues today at Mount Saint Joseph, Pogue Run Road, Wheeling. Burned at Cincinnati, Oh. on Sept. 8, 1853.

4229 NORTH CAROLINA

SW p wh b. Pittsburgh, Pa., 1845. 190 tons. W.A. Devenney, Steubenville, Oh., later said he was an engineer on her 1847 when she went from Pittsburgh to New Orleans in five days 19 hours, something of a feat. Off the lists in 1852.

4230 NORTH MISSOURI

SW transfer wh b. Jeffersonville, Ind., by Howard, 1865. 160 x 30 x 5.3. 348 tons. She was a single track transfer ferry used at St. Charles, Mo. In the Howard records she is noted as "the first railroad transfer in the West." Lost at Ingleside, Ark., May 25, 1872.

4231 NORTH RIVER

SW p wh b. Shousetown, Pa. (hull), and completed at Pittsburgh, 1847. 242 tons. Built for Capt. William Dean and others, and ran Pittsburgh-Louisville. Described as 182 ft. long. Engines, 18's- 7 ft. Three boilers. Pittsburgh-St. Louis, Capt. C. Verlin, 1849, and that fall ran Cincinnati-Louisville, Capt. Catterlin, in opposition to U.S. Mail Line along with *PIKE NO. 9.* Was acquired by Spaulding & Rogers and towed their "Floating Palace" showboat, renamed *CIRCUS FLEET.* Off the lists 1855.

4232 NORTH STAR

Stw p wh b. Elizabeth, Pa., 1855. 268 tons. Was running White River, Ark., to New Orleans when sunk and lost on the lower Mississippi River near mouth of Big Black Bayou, two miles above Grand Gulf, Miss., Nov. 21, 1857.

4233 NORTH STAR

SW p wh b. St. Anthony, Minn., 1856. 82 tons. Capt. John Rawlins built her above the Falls of St. Anthony and ran her to Sauk Rapids several seasons. Lost in 1858.

4234 NORTH STAR

Prop freight boat wh b. Peninsula, Oh., 1865, as a canalboat, 39 tons. Towed produce boats south. Snagged and lost at Jackson, Miss., Feb. 1, 1867. This sounds like she was on Pearl River.

4235 NORTH WESTERN

SW p wh b. Cincinnati, Oh., 1870. 802 tons. 245 x 38.5 x 5. Engines from *JAMES WHITE.* Four boilers, each 41" by 26 ft. Built for the Keokuk Northern Line, Upper Mississippi River. Capt. Thomas L. Davidson, with F.E. Snow, clerk, for first five years. In spring 1873 was first through Lake Pepin. Burned at the foot of Alma St., St. Louis, July 12, 1882, Capt. Al Haycock. The *BELLE OF LA CROSSE* was lost in the same blaze. The engines referred to above were 26's- 8 ft.

4236 NORTHERN BELLE

SW p wh b. Cincinnati, Oh., 1856. 329 tons. 226 x 29 x 5. Built for the Minnesota Packet Co., Capt. Preston Lodwick. Capt. Jesse Y. Hurd was master 1858–1859, running to Dunleith and La Crosse. Capt. M.L. Virden, later the master of *THOMAS SHERLOCK,* was clerk on her two seasons, likely 1856–1857. Capt. W.H. Laughton in 1861. Transported troops during the war. Off the lists 1870.

4237 NORTHERN ILLINOIS

Stw ferry wh b. Wellsville, Oh., 1864. 139 tons. Operated by Northern Illinois Railroad, ferry service at Muscatine, Iowa. Later sold to Capt. Leonard, Prescott, Wis., and thence to Hersey, Staples & Co., who used engines, etc., building rafter *BUN HERSEY* in 1876.

4238 NORTHERN LIGHT

SW p wh b. Elizabethtown, Pa., 1847. 241 tons. Burned at Cincinnati, Oh., Jan. 18, 1849, and engines went to *IRONTON,* built 1850 (see).

4239 NORTHERN LIGHT

SW p wh b. Madison, Ind., 1857. 414 tons. 240 x 40 x 5. Engines, 22's- 7 ft. Eight boilers, each 46" by 17 ft. Paddlewheels 31 ft. dia. working 9 ft. buckets, 30" dip. Came out spring 1857, Capt. Preston Lodwick, with clerks J.D. DuBois and K.C. Cooley. There were oil paintings of St. Anthony's Falls, Dayton Bluffs and Maiden Rock in the cabin, and paddleboxes were graced with paintings of aurora borealis. She was in the Minnesota Packet Co. Same master through 1860, running St. Louis-Galena-St. Paul. Capt. John B. Davis, 1861; Capt. Gabbert, 1862. She was running Coon Slough when her stern struck a pile of ice, Apr. 11, 1866, and she went down in 30 feet.

4240 NORTHERN PACIFIC NO. 1

SW rail tr wh b. Mound City, Ill., 1879. She was used at Bismarck, Dak. In later years was at Vicksburg, Miss., operated by Vicksburg, Shreveport & Pacific RR. She and the packet *R.L. COBB* were beached out in a flood at Vicksburg and both rotted down on shore, this early in 1895. Replaced by the transfer *DELTA* (see).

4241 NORTHERN PACIFIC NO. 2

SW rail tr wh b. Mound City, Ill., 1881. 354 tons. Inspected on Big Horn River, May 21, 1881. Name changed to *TRANSFER NO. 2,* (see).

4242 NORTHERNER

SW p wh b. Cincinnati, Oh., 1853. 399 tons. Built primarily for passengers, operated by the U.S. Mail Line. They ran her Cincinnati-Louisville in 1854, Capt. Fuller, teamed up with *SOUTHERNER.* She more often made trips Cincinnati-St. Louis, Capt. Erwin. Said to have had low pressure engines and boilers. Stove on a rock in Grand Chain, Ohio River, and ripped an 18 ft. wound, Nov. 8, 1857. Much equipment salvaged and the hull abandoned. The wreck was still there in 1873 when the *HENRY PROBASCO* was lost within 200 yards.

4243 NORTHERNER

SW p wh b. Elizabeth, Pa., at Ekin yard, 1858. 332 tons. 210 x 33 x 5.5. Ran St. Louis-St. Paul, Capt. Pliny A. Alford, in the Northern Line. Competed with *KEY CITY* for the championship speed record on the Upper Mississippi and lost. Burned at St. Louis, July 13, 1864.

4244 NORTHWEST

Stw p wh b. Cincinnati, Oh., 1863. 88 tons. Went to St. Louis area. Off the lists 1868.

4245 NORWAY

Prop p wh b. Spottsville, Ky., 1904. 58 x 10 x 4. Still in the area 1908, maybe longer.

4246 NOVELTY

SW p wh b. Wheeling, Va., 1859. 64 tons. Went to Confederate registry 1861.

4247 NOVELTY

Stw ferry wh b. Manchester, Oh., 1886. 76.4 x 16.4 x 3. Operated by a single engine with belt drive to paddlewheel. Capt. William Morgan ran her Vicksburg-Delta Point. She proved too small so he moved engine, etc., to a new and larger hull in 1894 and brought out a new *NOVELTY* (see next listing).

4248 NOVELTY

Stw ferry wh b. Vicksburg, Miss., 1894. 107.5 x 24 x 3.2. Machinery from prior boat of the name (see above). Ran Davis Bend-Vicksburg trade spring 1898. In January 1899 she was chartered to the Parisot Line for Yazoo River. Laid up for ice Feb. 12, at Vicksburg and burned about midnight.

4249 NYANZA

Stw p wh b. Belle Vernon, Pa., 1863. 203 tons. Sold to U.S. Navy, Nov. 4, 1863. Sold to private ownership and redocumented same name Aug. 26, 1865. Off the lists 1873.

4250 NYMPH

Stw p wh b. Portsmouth, Oh., 1862. 35 tons. Ran low water July 1864 Gallipolis-Portsmouth, Ohio River, connecting with *BOSTONA NO. 3* for Cincinnati. Sank and lost at Louisville, Ky., Dec. 1, 1864.

4251 NYMPH

Stw tinclad wh b. Cincinnati, Oh., 1863, originally *CRICKET NO. 3* (see). Sold to U.S. Navy Mar. 8, 1864, and became Tinclad #54 named *NYMPH*. Sold to private hands and resumed her original name. The public sale was held at Mound City, Ill., Aug. 17, 1865, and she went for $9,000 to A.W. Hutchison. She was described as 161.1 x 30.3 x 4.1. Engines, 14's- 4 ft. No record of service thereafter.

4252 NYMPH NO. 2

Stw p wh b. Portsmouth, Oh., 1864. 149 tons. 147 x 24.9 x 4. Engines, 10"- 4'8". Three boilers, each 18 ft. long, the center one being 42" dia., the side ones 22" dia. There were two 14" flues in the center boiler, and one 14" in the side boilers. Built by Capt. Henry Davies, Portsmouth. Said a dispatch from Cairo dated May 18, 1864: "She is an attractive feature at our levee from the peculiarity of her machinery, build, etc. She is a combination of patents—all of them inventions of her projector and owner, a celebrated mechanic and worthy citizen of Portsmouth, Oh." Disposition unclear. There is record that a boat named *NYMPH* sank at Chain of Rocks on the Missouri River at Sibley, Mo., Mar. 3, 1868, but whether this one or not is not known.

O

4253 O. G. WAGNER

Stw snagboat ih b. South St. Louis, Mo., 1875. 130.5 x 36 x 4.8. Belonged to the U.S. Engineers, used on Lower Mississippi and tributaries. Still serving 1895.

4254 O.K.

Stw p wh b. Cincinnati, Oh., 1899, originally named *BURKESVILLE* (see). Capt. Oscar Knapp (hence the name *O.K.*) bought *BURKESVILLE* at Burnside, Ky., bought and renamed her, figuring on running her in St. Croix River but never did so. He sold her June 1905 to Charles Stevens Transportation Co., Mondak, Mont., and she left Dubuque July 5, 1905, for the upper Missouri. Pilot Arthur Miller took her to Kansas City where Capt. John Marsh took over the wheel—son of Capt. Grant Marsh. That fall she made trips up the Yellowstone to Glendive, Mont. In spring 1906 made her first appearance at Fort Benton. Summers 1906 and 1907 ran between Milk River and the fort, handling boatloads of groceries, hardware, etc., for trading with ranchers and Indians, and did a thriving business. Burned at Fort Benton on June 30, 1908.

4255 O. M. LOVELL

Stw p wh b. Harmar, Oh., 1883, at Knox Yard. 125 x 24 x 3. Capt. Dode Berry, Williamstown, W. Va., built her for Wheeling-New Matamoras trade where she ran while the Ohio River Railroad (later B. & O.) was built, after which she ran four trips a day Marietta-Parkersburg. Sold south prior to 1886, renamed *WILLIAM D. ELLIS*, and documented at Apalachicola, Fla. Still listed as such 1892.

4256 OAKLAND

SW p wh b. California, Pa., 1853. 141 tons. 142 x 26.7 x 4. Built for Capt. J.N. Shunk and others, Pittsburgh. Operated on the Upper Mississippi, St. Louis-St. Paul. Last owner was Thomas H. Williams, Memphis who ran her spring 1859. When inspection came due she was laid up and dismantled.

4257 OASIS

SW ferry wh b. Dardanelle, Ark. (hull), and completed at Little Rock, Ark., 1878. 98 x 26.5 x 3.4. (56 ft. wide over all). Was the ferry at Dardanelle. Still listed 1886.

4258 OBION

SW p wh b. Christler's Landing, Pa., 1861. 62 tons. Came in collision with *NIAGARA* at Liverpool, Ill., Jan. 21, 1856, and was lost.

4259 OCEAN SPRAY

SW p wh b. Elizabeth, Pa., 1857. 371 tons. Ran St. Louis-Peoria. On her second trip she left St. Louis with *HANNIBAL CITY* in hot pursuit. A barrel of turpentine was appropriated from the freight to prod the steam pressure, the contents took fire, attempt was made to jettison it, and it overturned on deck. The boat burned within the city limits of St. Louis at Sawyer's Bend with loss of 23 lives and also burned the *KEOKUK* and *STAR OF THE WEST*, this on April 22, 1858. See *S&D REFLECTOR*, Mar. 1979, issue for details.

4260 OCEAN WAVE

SW p wh b. St. Louis, Mo., 1845. 205 tons. Built for St. Louis-Keokuk trade, Capt. Barton Able. In fall 1848 running Louisville-St. Louis under charter. U.S. President-elect Zachary Taylor, en route to his inauguration, arrived at Louisville Feb. 11, 1849, aboard the *COURTLAND* (see) with *OCEAN WAVE* lashed alongside loaded with dignitaries. Burned Aug. 12, 1851, at Louisville, Ky.

4261 OCEAN WAVE

SW p wh b. Elizabeth, Pa., 1854. 235 tons. Built for Capt. Waldo P. Marsh who ran her in St. Louis-Illinois River trade. Bought by the Minnesota Packet Co., in 1856 and ran various Upper Mississippi trades, remembered as a short boat hard to steer. Winter 1867–1868, she made a trip Dubuque to New Orleans with barges "and was so long upon the way that relatives did not recognize the crew when they got back." Burned on Lake Pepin, Wis., June 11, 1868.

4262 OCEAN WAVE

Stw p-tb wh b. Elizabeth, Pa., at Wiegel yard in 1891. 89 x 15 x 3.5. In April 1895, owned by L.E. Somerville, Pt. Pleasant, W. Va., she was hitched to a coal tow and delivered it at Greenville, Miss. where she burned Apr. 24, 1895, at 12:15 A.M., Capt. Frank Coos, Wheeling, W. Va., in charge.

4263 OCEANA

SW p wh b. St. Louis, Mo., 1854. 607 tons. St. Louis-New Orleans, 1855, Capt. J.T. Burdeau. Off the lists 1860.

4264 OCEANUS

Stw p wh b. California, Pa., 1870. 365 tons. 180 x 40.5 x 5.5. Engines, 18's- 6 ft. Three boilers, each 40" by 28 ft. New at Pittsburgh December 1870, advertised to St. Louis and Arkansas River, Capt. M.A. Cox, with Adam Jacobs, Jr., clerk. Sold to the Carter Line, St. Louis, 1871, and ran St. Louis-Shreveport. Capt. Horace Bixby was on her 1871. She was upbound 20 miles above Cairo in Dog Tooth Bend near Brook's Point at 4:00 A.M., Apr. 11, 1872, the boilers exploded with loss of 34 lives. The *JOHN LUMDSEN* (see) was moored two miles below cooled down. Her pilot Thompson manned a yawl and rescued many. The *BELLE ST. LOUIS* came up, assisted, and delivered survivors to Grand Tower, Ill. Capt. Alhambra Reeder was master, native of Glasgow, Mo., and originally an engineer, married and no children. He lost his life, as did first clerk Henry M. Worsham, 40 years resident of St. Louis, and Charles Worsham (son), 2nd clerk. The wreck burned, taking the life of Harry Tripp, pilot, from Memphis, and also lost was George Wiggins, New Orleans, the Red River pilot. Four lions belonging to James Robinson's Circus were lost. The wreck lay in the middle of the river.

4265 OCOEE NO. 2

Stw p wh b. Chattanooga, Tenn., 1895. 85 x 12. Owned by Capt. Ben H. Ferguson, Chattanooga, who ran her up Hiwassee River making connection at Blythe's Ferry with *CITY OF CHARLESTON* for Chattanooga and Kingston. He had run another small fry prior to 1895 named *OCOEE*, and also was associated with the *J.R. HUGHES* and *CITY OF CHARLESTON*. Still running, 1900, maybe later.

4266 OCTAVIA

SW p wh b. Jeffersonville, Ind., by Howard, 1852. 189 tons. 180 x 30 x 6. Went to Mobile and ran on the Alabama River. Mention is made of her in Carl Carmer's *Stars Fell on Alabama*. Off the lists 1859.

4267 OCTAVIA

SW p wh b. St. Louis, Mo., 1866. 595 tons. Capt. Joe La Barge ran her in the south first fall and winter, returned her to St. Louis and departed May 7, 1867, for Fort Benton. On this trip to the mountains the boat cleared him a reputed $45,000. Made another trip to the fort in 1868. That fall the boat was sold to the U.S. In August 1871 was attempting to get the wheel shafts lifted from the wreck of the *BLACK HAWK*, Porter's old flagship (see), but without success.

4268 ODD FELLOW

SW p wh b. Wheeling, Va., 1862. 70 tons. Ran Gallipolis-Syracuse daily, Ohio River, in 1864. Went from there to Cairo-Columbus trade and was caught in ice at Columbus 3:00 A.M. Jan. 6, 1865. Went down in deep water, head foremost.

4269 OELLA

SW p wh b. Cincinnati, Oh., 1848. 77 tons. 125 x 20.5 x 3.1. Owned 1850 by Capt. William L. Williams, Cincinnati. She was on the Lower Mississippi River en route from Field's Mills with sugar and molasses when she hit the bank at Madame Rosina Lathrane's plantation, a mile above Red Church, La., about 8:30 A.M., Dec. 22, 1850, and was lost.

4270 OELLA

Stw p wh b. Harmar, Oh., 1871, at Wm. Knox & Son yard. 110 x 20 x 3. Built for Capt. George M. Berry who had been running *EAGLE* (see) Marietta-New Matamoras. Owned 1875 by S. Scott, Wm. W. Richardson, and George S. Scott. Winter of 1875–1876 made a trip Marietta-New Orleans with a barge in tow loaded with stoneware, potatoes, beans, oats, oil, grindstones, coal, etc., Capt. Sextus Scott. The diary of this voyage, kept by Dana Scott, nephew, is in Ohio State Museum, Columbus, Oh. Later ran Brownsville-Monongahela City, Capt. Steve Loomis. The *L.W. MORGAN* ran opposition and Capt. L.W. Morgan bought the *OELLA* and continued her in the trade, with Capt. Latta, California, Pa., in charge. Low water August 1878 ran Steubenville-Wheeling, later Wheeling-Sunfish. Dismantled at Marietta, 1880.

4271 OHIO

Stw p wh b. Shousetown, Pa., 1849. 121 tons. Off the lists 1856.

4272 OHIO

SW p wh b. Cincinnati, Oh., 1849. 348 tons. Events concerning this boat and the *OHIO* listed above are confused. The likelihood is that the Shousetown *OHIO* was the original of the name in the Marietta-Cincinnati trade (see *OHIO NO. 2, OHIO NO. 3,* and *OHIO NO. 4.*) The Cincinnati-built *OHIO,* much larger, ran St. Louis-New Orleans, Capt. J.L. Black, 1851. Reported in collision with *W.B. CLIFTON* near Columbus on the Mississippi, Apr. 2, 1854, sinking the latter and causing loss of seven deck passengers. Off the lists 1857.

4273 OHIO

Stw p wh b. Cincinnati, Oh., 1879. 251 x 39 x 5.5. Originally named *CLIFTON* (see). Owned by Cincinnati, Portsmouth, Big Sandy & Pomeroy Packet Co., who ran her 1882, Cincinnati-Pomeroy with Capt. John Livesay, master, and clerks T. Kendall Morgan and C.H. Holloway. She replaced the *OHIO No. 4* (see). Later ran Cincinnati-Memphis, Capt. John Newton, with Harry O. Proctor, clerk. Sank on the "old mill foundation" while ascending the Louisville Falls, Capt. Don Marr, master, 1890. Settled below the K&I bridge along the Kentucky shore, Pink Varble at the wheel. Was loaded deeply at the time, and was raised. Sank Feb. 17, 1894, at Cottonwood Point, Mo. Sam G. Smith, later an editor of *The Waterways Journal,* was clerk on her at the time.

4274 OHIO

Stw p wh b. Clarington, Oh., 1898, originally named *AVALON* (see). The *AVALON* was lengthened at Parkersburg, W. Va., summer 1901, to measure 199.2 x 33.4 x 4.4. Sold at U.S. Marshal sale at Parkersburg on Aug. 21, 1907, to Capts. William E. Roe, Martin F. Noll, and Ben S. Pope, equal shares, for $9,800. Ran Pittsburgh-Charleston in 1908, then Pittsburgh-Cincinnati trade Jan. 18, 1909, Capt. Edwin F. Maddy, with Harry Maddy and Ed Dunaway, clerks. Later (1911) clerks were Charles W. Knox and G.M. Knox. Light draft, she once made five round trips with two inches on the marks at Franklin, Pa. In 1909 went up the Monongahela to McKeesport, Pa., for a cargo of oil well casing. Discontinued the trade in fall of 1913. Handled excursions in the Wheeling area summer 1914 and that September made a "Booster Trip" auspices of the Pittsburgh Chamber of Commerce Pittsburgh-Huntington. Made a Pittsburgh-New Orleans Mardi Gras trip early 1915, Capt. W.C. Lepper, and then loaded out for Memphis. Ran Cincinnati-Memphis that summer, Capt. Billy Stapleton, and later Capt. Connie McGee, connecting with the *JOE FOWLER* for Pittsburgh. Was returned to Parkersburg and burned in the mouth of the Little Kanawha River, night of Feb. 2, 1916.

4275 OHIO

Stw p wh b. Marietta, Oh., 1909. 118.8 x 24.4 x 4. Owned equal shares by Capt. Fred McCandless and Oliver Keibler, Golconda, Ill., and L.C. Hibbs, Smithland, Ky. Replaced the *ROYAL* in Paducah-Golconda trade. Sold about 1916 to Capt. Selby Turner and George Ashby for Madison-Louisville trade, and that December sold to Capt. Lewis Tanner. Later sold to Penick & Ford, Vicksburg, and did work for the Royal Route at times. Dismantled 1924 and equipment went to building another *OHIO* (see next listing).

4276 OHIO

Stw p wh b. Vicksburg, Miss., 1924. 124 x 30 x 4.2. Owned by the Royal Blue Route Co., Vicksburg, 1929.

4277 OHIO

Stw ferry wh b. Paducah, Ky., 1924. 64.7 x 30 x 3. Built in shares by Capt. W.L. Berry and Annie I. Baker for local service. Sold to Mary Jo Ferry Co., Carrollton, Ky., and operated there to Lamb, Ind. Burned at Carrollton on May 15, 1936, owned by Capt. C.D. Wilhoite.

4278 OHIO NO. 2

SW p wh b. Marietta, Oh., at the Knox Yard, 1855. 196 tons. Ran Marietta-Cincinnati, Capt. J.J. Blagg, with John Heisner, clerk. Backed on a snag at the head of Blennerhassett Island, Sept. 6, 1860, and sank. She was used by the U.S. at Cincinnati in 1861 as a receiving ship for gunboat recruits.

4279 OHIO NO. 2

Stw ferry wh b. Jeffersonville, Ind., by Howard, 1891, originally named *EMILY.* (see). Then was renamed *DIXIE BEE LINE* (also see). In 1929 owned by Paducah-Ohio River Bridge Co. Later sold to Memphis and became packet *JOE CURTIS* (see).

4280 OHIO NO. 3

SW p wh b. Marietta, Oh., at Knox Yard, 1858. 264 tons. 218 x 35 x 5.5. Built for the Marietta-Cincinnati trade and came out new with Capt. J.J. Blagg, master; John Heisner, clerk; T. Odlum, 2nd clerk; John Levesay, mate; W. Davis and W. Duncan, pilots; H. Holliday, chief engineer, and T. Burlingame, 2nd engineer. She was dismantled at the time the *OHIO NO. 4* was built at Marietta (1868) and was cut down by ice at the lower end of the Harmar Yard. The hull was buried in sand and Col. Harry Knox noted in 1942 that it still may be there.

4281 OHIO NO. 4

SW p wh b. Harmar, Oh., at Knox Yard, 1868. 242 (on deck) x 37 x 6. Engines, 22's- 7 ft. Four boilers. Built for Marietta-Cincinnati trade. Original crew: Capt. J.J. Blagg, master; J.L. Newsome, 1st clerk; F.J. Donnelly, 2nd clerk; Samuel Dunbar, 3rd clerk; Ellis Mace and James Mace, pilots; Lyman Holliday and Thomas Hancock, engineers; Edward Knox, mate, Levi Blagg, steward. In 1872 was sold to the White Collar Line for the Cincinnati-Pomeroy trade, Capt. F.Y. Batchelor, master, with Charles Regnier, clerk. In 1873 Capt. Alex M. Halliday bought interest. Had several masters including Capt. Pres. Lodwick,

Capt. Dan Moore, and Capt. John Levesay. Wrecked at Cincinnati and replaced by the *OHIO* (see). Capt. J.J. Blagg, original master, died at Gallipolis, Oh., 1881.

4282 OHIO BELLE

SW p wh b. Cincinnati, Oh., 1855. 406 tons. Ran Cincinnati-New Orleans, Capt. John Sebastian. Went under charter to the U.S. spring of 1862 after Island 10 engagement, Capt. John Sebastian and crew remaining aboard. Sold to USQMD June 8, 1864. Sold February 1866 to W.H. McAllister, New Orleans, who changed her name to *ALABAMA BELLE.* Sold February 27, 1866, to Charles Newman (three-quarters) of New Orleans and Bernard Moses. Dismantled spring 1867. Her last enrollments rated her 578 tons, hull 185.8 x 39.6 x 7.8.

4283 OHIO MILLS

Freight boat wh b. Metropolis, Ill., 1876. 78 tons. Documented at Evansville, Ind.

4284 OHIO VALLEY

Stw p wh b. Marietta, Oh., at Knox Yard, 1863. 235 tons. Built for Capts. Chapin, Wells, and others. Tramped Louisville-Nashville, Pittsburgh-Cincinnati, Capt. Chapin, spring-summer 1864. Ran Wheeling-Cincinnati, Capt. Amos Davis, with C.W. Davidson, clerk, Sept. 1864. Sold to the U.S. on Dec. 10, 1864, converted into a tinclad (#10) renamed *IBEX.* Sold fall of 1865 to Capt. W.B. Miller who renamed her *HARRY DEAN* (see) Oct. 5, 1865.

4285 OIL CITY

Stw p wh b. Wellsburg, Va., 1863. 59 tons. Built for the Allegheny River by George W. Morton, William Anderson, Dan O'Neil, and O. King, Capt. John Noss, master. Sold to Wheeling parties late that fall. Ran over a sunken coal barge at Wheeling night of Mar. 30, 1865, and ripped out her bottom. Cabin was smashed and went off in the current. Machinery and hull were saved and she was rebuilt. In 1866–1876 ran on the Muskingum, Capt. Reason Ong, Capt. J.A. Penrose, and Capt. D. Lyne Dismantled 1876.

4286 OIL EXCHANGE

Stw p wh b. Allegheny, Pa., 1863. 40 tons. 83.5 x 15.7 x 3.3. Owned by Capt. John Steiner, Venango County, Pa. Sold to Cincinnati and thence to New Orleans February 1867. Owned in New Orleans by her master, Capt. Mortimer Turner (one-third) and others. Had several changes of ownership in that area, lastly owned by Frederick Arbour and Alfred Delahay, equal shares, both of Baton Rouge. Off the lists 1872.

4287 OIL HUNTER

SW p wh b. Catlettsburg, Ky., 1865. 22 tons. Ran up Big Sandy River. Off the lists 1872.

4288 OKAW BELLE

SW p wh b. Chester, Ill., 1859. 73 tons. May have been a ferry. Off the lists 1861.

4289 OLD HICKORY

SW p wh b. Louisville, Ky., 1845. 445 tons. 250 x 33 x 7.5. Commanded for a time by Capt. James Lee, Memphis. Off the lists 1850.

4290 OLD HICKORY

SW sawmill wh b. Leavenworth, Ind., 1896. 125 x 30 x 4.4. Owned by Falls City Lumber Co., Louisville, Ky.

4291 OLD HICKORY No. 2

Rig? wh b. West Point, Ind., 1876. 97 tons. 109 x 28.6 x 4.7. Documented at Louisville in 1886.

4292 OLEANDER

Stw lighthouse tender sh b. Dubuque, Iowa, 1903. 165 x 34 x 7. Came out new with a set of Hopkins patent boilers and "horizontal steeple compound engines . . . different than anything on the river." She long served in the U.S. Lighthouse Service, Capt. Thomas B. Good. Took U.S. President William Howard Taft down from St. Louis to Memphis in 1909. She was retired in 1926 and replaced by *WILLOW* (see). Capt. Russell Warner, Memphis, bought her in 1930, and stripped off the cabin during the winter of 1930–1931. The steel hull later was acquired by The Ohio River Company and was used by them at Huntington, W. Va., as a coal fueling barge with a steam hoist aboard.

4293 OLIVE

SW p wh b. New Albany, Ind., 1847. 115 tons. Built for Mobile, Ala. Exploded and lost at Chehaw, Ala., Sept. 2, 1848, with loss of one life.

4294 OLIVE

Stw p wh b. Ironton, Oh., 1849. 64 tons. Owned and operated by Capt. W.G. Whitney, Portsmouth, Oh., in the Cincinnati-Portsmouth trade. Named for Olive Whitney McArthur. Off the lists 1854.

4295 OLIVE

Stw p wh b. California, Pa., 1863. 220 ton. 157 x 32 x 4.8. Original owners were T.M. Harton (one-half), J.A. Harton, and H.A. Andrews, all of Pittsburgh. First master, Capt. J.M. Andrews. Bound from Pittsburgh to Cincinnati in June 1864 barrels of coal oil stowed in the hull caught fire at Buffington Island, and she was purposely scuttled to extinguish the flames. Snagged and lost at Golconda, Ill., June 28, 1865, with loss of seven lives.

4296 OLIVE BRANCH

SW p wh b. Jeffersonville, Ind., by Howard, 1863. 697 tons. 283 x 42 x 8. Engines, 30's- 9 ft. Six boilers. Built for Capt. B. Rush Pegram and others for the St. Louis-New Orleans trade. Other than Capt. Pegram her masters included Capts. Ben F. Taber, J.T. McCord, and J.H. Jones. Carried stores to Randolph and Fort Pillow during the war. Was in the Atlantic & Mississippi Steam Ship Co., until that line failed. At time of loss she was owned by Capt. John T. McCord and others. She was downbound at Liberty Island below St. Louis on July 22, 1871, drawing seven ft. Hit a stump at the bow and it about raked the bottom out of her, causing her to sink in one and one-half minutes.

4297 OLIVER BEIRNE

SW p wh b. Jeffersonville, Ind., by Howard, 1886. 260 x 44 x 9 (80 ft. wide over all). Engines, 30's- 9 ft. Paddlewheels 37 ft. diameter working 15′ buckets, 28″ dip. Owned by Planters & Merchants Packet Co., John J. Brown, pres., and ran New Orleans-Bayou Sara. She had a painting of the Howard Ship Yard in the forward cabin. Oliver Beirne, Esq., owned Old Sweet Springs, Va., was a wealthy planter, and operated the Burnsides plantation on the Upper Coast above New Orleans. Capt. John J. Brown was master, with Jesse Youngblood, chief engineer. Much equipment from the *JOHN W. CANNON* used in her construction (see). She ran excursions at St. Louis, Capt. Harry W. Brolaski, with the dancefloor on the main deck. Isaac W. (Ike) Betts was second engineer on her there. Burned at Millikens Bend, La., Oct. 28, 1891.

4298 OLIVETTE

Stw p wh b. Harmar, Oh., at Knox Yard, 1882. 120 x 22 x 3. Engines, 10's- 3 ½ ft. from the *SCIENCE* (see). Built as a low water packet by George Strecker and Rodick Bros., Marietta. Spent most of her first five years running various trades on the Muskingum out of Zanesville, Capts. Ed Martin, Lou Myrick, and James McCoy. Running Parkersburg-Middleport in 1887 with Capt. George B. McClintock, master, and J.M. Deem, clerk. Shortly thereafter sold to J.C. Dueber of the Dueber Watch Works who used her as a pleasure boat in the Cincinnati area and once made a trip with guests to the Upper Ohio. Dueber sold her to Biddle Bros., Parkersburg, W. Va. Ran briefly in the East Liverpool-Steubenville trade, Capt. Logan Noll with Wm. Wilkin, clerk. In 1894–1895 ran in Pittsburgh-Elizabeth, Pa., trade, Capt. Joseph C. Ketchell with H.M. Lowe, clerk. Converted into a towboat fall of 1896, at which time C.W. Posey bought her entire. Her last owner was Samuel W. Carpenter, a marine diver with headquarters in the Allegheny River, Pittsburgh. She caught fire at his landing Jan. 24, 1904, speading the flames to the packet *ELIZABETH* moored alongside (see), resulting in the loss of both.

4299 OLIVIA

SW p wh b. Vintroux Landing, W. Va., on the Kanawha River (hull) and completed at Cincinnati, 1847. 134 tons. Ran Cincinnati and Kanawha River, Capt. J.B. Parker, with John W. Wyatt, clerk, and Riley Finney, pilot. Her mud clerk was Horace E. Bixby, later of Mark Twain fame, who was advanced to pilot on her. In the 1880s while Bixby commanded the Anchor Line side-wheel *CITY OF ALTON* his first clerk was P.W. Sheckley who had been 2nd clerk on the *OLIVIA*. Sank with a cargo of Kanawha salt near Quincy, Ky., early April 1853, raised. Collapsed a flue at Tinkersville, above Charleston, W. Va., causing the death of Charles H. Parker, brother of Capt. J.B. Parker. She was sold to Jerry H. Baldwin, St. Louis, and went there. Off the lists 1855.

4300 OLIVIA

SW p wh b. Louisville, Ky., 1847. 231 tons. 149 x 24 x 6.8. Built for William T. Hepp, New Orleans. First master, Capt. Warren A. Grice. Sold June 1850 to Lake Steam Navigation Co., Mandeville, La., Capt. I.W. Hoffman, master. Sold March 1851 to Capt. Alexander J. Whitmore of New Orleans. Off the lists in 1853.

4301 OLLIE

Prop ferry wh b. Jeffersonville, Ind., by Howard, 1896. Owned by Union Ferry Co., New Orleans. Dismantled about 1909. 105 x 26 x 5.5.

4302 OLLIE B.

A small packet which burned 120 miles above Monroe, La., on Bayou Bartholomew at Alexander's Landing, Mar. 8, 1881. She had been connecting with the *LAURA LEE* for below.

4303 OLLIE BELL

Prop p wh b. St. Paul, Minn., 1902. 50 x 9.6 x 3.5. Still documented at St. Paul 1908, perhaps later.

4304 OLLIE NEVILLE

Stw ferry wh b. Brownsville, Pa. at Axton yard, 1887. 92.9 x 26.5 x 3.4. Engines, 10's- 4 ft. Originally operated East Liverpool-Chester on Ohio River until the bridge was built. Then served at Wellsville, Oh. Capt. Lewis Tanner had her later at Ripley, Oh. She coaled there and started for New Richmond, Oh. but sank about 600 yards above Dover, Ky., early 1905.

4305 OLLIE SULLIVAN

Stw p wh b. New Albany, Ind., 1862. 91 tons. Was under charter to the U.S. handling troops and supplies on Green River during the war. Saw most of her service on the Tennessee, Cumberland and lower Ohio. Capt. J.T. Hugo operated her several years. Collided with the *QUICKSTEP* at Diamond Island, Ohio River, 8:00 P.M. Apr. 10, 1869, and sank to the roof. A lady and two children lost their lives. Sank and lost on the Tennessee River 30 miles above Paducah, June 8, 1870.

4306 OMAHA

SW p wh b. Madison, Ind., 1856. 307 tons. 206 x 30 x 5. Engines, 21's- 6 ½ ft. Three boilers, each 38″ by 28 ft. Sioux City, Iowa got its start, 771 miles above St. Louis, with the arrival of the *OMAHA* loaded flat with lumber, drygoods, hardware, a sawmill, etc., worth $70,000, for which delivery the freight bill was $24,000. The boat made weekly trips between St. Joseph and Council Bluffs, Capt. J.E. Barrow. Said to have been Capt. William Rodney Massie's favorite boat. Lost in ice at St. Louis, Dec. 16, 1865.

4307 OMAHA

Stw p wh b. Stillwater, Minn., 1900, originally named *LORA* (see). She was docked at St. Louis in 1908, completely rebuilt, and renamed *OMAHA,* then owned by Eagle Boat Store Co. The Carter Packet Co., New Orleans, acquired her Aug. 3, 1912, placed an entire new cabin, and 80% of the hull, and ran her New Orleans-Red River. In a staged race May 30, 1914, she beat the *MARY S. BLEES* (see). Sold to Liberty Transit Co., Wheeling, W. Va., in May 1918 and was brought up in command of Capt. Fred Ketchum. That summer was converted for upper Ohio service and was renamed *GENERAL PERSHING* (see).

4308 OMAHA CITY

SW p wh b. Freedom, Pa., 1857. 147 tons. First home port, Omaha, Neb. Lost in ice at St. Louis, Jan. 12, 1866.

4309 ONEGA

Stw p wh b. Knoxville, Tenn., 1891. 104.7 x 18 x 2.5. One boiler, one stack. Ran Knoxville-Chattanooga, built by D.M. Rose and others, Capt. Jacob L. Dykes. On one occasion carried Admiral Dewey from Knoxville to Concord, old home of Admiral Farragut. Natives of the region pronounced the boat's name with a slurring which sounded like "Ol' Nigga" and occasionally she got into the public print as *OL' NIGGER*. Ran about ten years and while hauled on a marine ways a flood lifted her off and wrecked her. The machinery went to a towboat named *CHEROKEE* at Knoxville in 1921.

4310 ONEIDA

Stw p wh b. Harmar, Oh., at Knox Yard, 1881. 104 x 19.7 x 4. Built by a man named Murray who had come to Parkersburg, W. Va., from Oneida County, N.Y., a machinist; he built her engines. Capt. Samuel B. Rathbone operated this boat and the *CARRIE M. KRAFT* in the Little Kanawha in the 1880–1890 period. In early January 1895, moored at the Juliana Street bridge, Parkersburg, she became speared on a piling when the river fell rapidly due to the breaking of an ice gorge at the head of Blennerhassett Island. Rolled over on her side, and while being pumped out rolled over a second time. Exploded her boiler while racing another boat at the mouth of Hughes River, possibly the *W.A. HILTON* or *C.C. MARTIN,* and the cabin forward of the pilothouse was taken away. Sank at Creston, W. Va., on Jan. 26, 1902, at 7:00 A.M., about an hour after arrival, the hull seams cut by ice. Capt. John Stone, Belpre, Oh., was master at the time, and she then was owned by D.M. Miller and M.R. Lowther, Parkersburg. She was raised and returned to Parkersburg under her own steam to go on the docks. While waiting her turn at the docks she sank and turned over. Her machinery was put on the packet *FRENCH* (see). There was much swapping of ownership during her career, once owned, c. 1899, by C.H. and E.E. Varian, equal shares, both of Letart, W. Va.

4311 ONEIDA

Stw ferry wh b. Cincinnati, Oh., 1883. 111.3 x 35 x 5.5. Sold to Morton & Jones, Cincinnati, October 1899, who dismantled her and used the machinery on a towboat they were building for Big Sandy River.

4312 ONLY CHANCE

SW p wh b. Alton, Ill., 1865. 219 tons. Ran St. Louis-Missouri River, and reputed to have made two trips to Fort Benton, Capt. Gilham. Damaged in the steamboat fire at St. Louis, March 29, 1869. Sank and lost at Douglas Landing, Ark., Nov. 23, 1869.

4313 ONTARIO

Stw p wh b. California, Pa., 1864. 265 tons. 156.3 x 32 x 5.8. Engines, 15's- 5 ft. Three boilers. Originally owned by J.A. Harton, A.C. Harton, H.A. Andrews, and George C. McMurtrey, all of Allegheny County, Pa. Ran Pittsburgh-St. Louis. In summer 1864 more cash was subscribed by her owners and crew for the Sanitary Fair held at Pittsburgh to raise money for U.S. medical supplies than any other steamboat. She was awarded a handsome set of colors. She was sold to St. Louis, owned there by John C. Copeland and others, Capt. David Haney. They ran her up Missouri River. An extensive description of this boat and a Missouri River trip appears in *Life, Letters and Travels* authored by Father Pierre-Jean De Smet. Snagged and lost fifteen miles below Nebraska City, Neb., Sept. 25, 1866.

4314 ONWARD

Stw p wh b. Brownsville, Pa., 1864. 241 tons. Ran trips Pittsburgh-Nashville, Capt. S.B. French, 1865. Sold at Cincinnati August 1865 to a Capt. Blackston and others who took her to Mobile, Ala. Burned and lost at Bells Landing, Alabama River, Nov. 17, 1867, with loss of eleven lives.

4315 OPELOUSAS

SW p wh b. New Albany, Ind., 1852. 113 tons. 102 x 22 x 4.5. Ran out of New Orleans owned by John H. Gordon and others, St. Landry Parrish. In 1856 New Orleans-Grosse Tete, Capt. W.C. Neal. Sold entire to Offutt Bros., St. Landry Parish, May 1857. Came in collision with the *GALVESTON* at Galveston, Tex., Nov. 12, 1857, and sank with loss of eighteen lives.

4316 OPHELIA

SW p wh b. New Albany, Ind., 1850. 289 tons. 165.3 x 28.5 x 6.5. Owned in part by Offutt Bros., St. Landry Parish, La., and in 1855 was running one trip a week New Orleans-Pointe-a-la-Hache, Capt. John Dimitry. Had various owners in the New Orleans area, among them Robert Morris of Pope County, Ill., who changed his residence to Jefferson City (now New Orleans). Last owned by Eclipse Towboat Co., in 1860. Off the lists 1861.

4317 ORA

A low water boat on the lower Mississippi built, c. 1872. While ascending the Ouachita River bound from Trenton to Bayou Bartholomew May 23, 1877, she caught fire in her wood pile and burned. Had been connecting with the *JOHN*

H. HANNA. Capt. Elias Cryer is mentioned as sole owner in 1873.

4318 ORA LEE

Stw p wh b. Jeffersonville, Ind., by Howard, 1891. 140 x 32 x 4.4. Owned by the Lee Line, Memphis, and ran short trades. In July 1900 hauled on the Mound City marine ways, and was sold soon thereafter to White River, her name changed to *ORLANDO* (see).

4319 ORB

Stw p wh b. Wheeling, Va., 1854. 226 tons. 150 x 30 x 5. Engines, 20's- 4 ft. Three boilers. Built for Capt. William Dillon who ran her Pittsburgh-Louisville. On the Upper Mississippi in 1857, St. Louis-St. Paul, Capt. Spencer, and ran excursions to Falls of St. Anthony. She was downbound on the Mississippi with a load of railroad iron for Red River when she snagged near Caruthersville, Mo., May 19, 1860, and was lost.

4320 OREGON

SW p wh b. Pittsburgh, Pa., 1844. 181 tons. Ran Pittsburgh-Louisville, Capt. Jabez Smith. Joe Hall, later the safe and lock manufacturer at Cincinnati, was steward on her. Later sold to run St. Louis-Cape Girardeau under several ownerships. Ran through 1848, possibly longer.

4321 OREGON

SW p wh b. New Albany, Ind., 1849. 582 tons. 275 x 35 x 8. Engines, 28's- 8 ft. Five boilers, each 42" by 32½ ft. Paddlewheels 32½ ft. diameter working 14 ft. buckets. Hull by Isaiah King & Co., engines by Phillips, Hise & Co. Owned and commanded by Capt. Ed Montgomery in Louisville-New Orleans trade. She was downbound at Island 82, Mar. 2, 1851, the passengers just finishing noon dinner, when she exploded, took fire, and sank in the channel. The *IROQUOIS* was wooding about a mile distant and came to aid, taking dead and wounded to Memphis. Twenty-one lives were lost. Capt. Montgomery was in command.

4322 ORIENT

Stw p wh b. California, Pa., 1862. 222 tons. 154 x 33 x 4.8. Built for and owned largely by Capt. J.A. Harton, Pittsburgh. Ran Pittsburgh-St. Louis. Snagged and lost at Commerce, Mo., Feb. 17, 1864, with loss of fourteen lives.

4323 ORIENTAL

SW p wh b. Brownsville, Pa., 1848. 249 tons. Capt. J.C. Vanhook and others built her for the St. Louis-Illinois River trade. Left Pittsburgh Mar. 17, 1848, on her first trip. Off the lists in 1853.

4324 ORIOLE

Prop freight boat wh b. Muscatine, Iowa, 1863. 25 tons. In 1874 owned equal shares by Morris Waerpel and Oscar Schultz, St. Louis, then rated 44 tons. Documented at Galena, 1876, as a packet. Off the lists 1881.

4325 ORIOLE

Stw tinclad wh b. Cincinnati, Oh., 1863 as the *FLORENCE MILLER NO. 3* (see). Taken over by the U.S. to become tinclad #52, renamed *ORIOLE*. At the time of sale to private owners Oct. 14, 1865, she was described as 160 x 33.5 x 5. Engines, 14's- 5 ft. Renamed *AGNES* Oct. 14, 1865 (see).

4326 ORIOLE

SW p wh b. Murraysville, W. Va. (hull) and completed at Middleport, Oh., 1869. Came out in Gallipolis-Racine trade, Capt. A.J. Branch with Nat Earhart, clerk. In 1871 ran Pomeroy-Ironton, Capt. Silas P. Coe (who later built and named a towboat for himself), with Edwin F. Maddy, clerk, his first river job. Capt. T. Spence Sandford was master later, his first command. Also ran Portsmouth-Gallipolis. There was an *ORIOLE* in the New Orleans-Lower Coast trade January 1876, Capt. James T. O'Pry, possibly another steamboat, possibly this one. Parts of the *ENERGY* (see) were used in building her.

4327 ORIOLE

Stw p wh b. Pt. Pleasant, W. Va., 1901, originally named *BAXTER* (see). Name was changed to *ORIOLE* Dec. 2, 1907, owned then by Huntington and Point Pleasant Packet Co., J.F. Klenzing of Huntington managing owner. Ran Gallipolis-Huntington, Capt. William D. Kimble and soon James H. Miller took an interest. Ran excursion at Frankfort, Ky., in 1910 and in May 1911 Miller again took interest and returned her to Huntington. In May 1912 sold to the Beaver family (Elmer, H.M., George S., and Charles) of St. Marys and New Matamoras, and ran local trades above Marietta. In August 1912 Clermont C. Green, St. Marys, became ½ owner. Sold to Capt. David Boyles and Charles N. Buckley, Parkersburg, January 1913, and she was given a new hull and converted into a towboat at Parkersburg fall of 1914. Sold to Capt. William F. (Buck) Muller, Ambridge, Mar. 1915, who turned her over within a week to C.P. Krantz, Pittsburgh. Burned along with the towboat *FORD CITY* at 9th Street, Pittsburgh, in the Allegheny River, Mar. 27, 1915.

4328 ORION

Stw p wh b. Wheeling, Va., 1851. 138 tons. 123.5 x 25 x 4.5. Ran Wheeling-Marietta, Capt. William Dillon. Sold October 1853 to Capt. Alonzo D. Denslow, St. Mary Parish, La. Ran in Yazoo River 1855, Capt. Charles L. Hardie, and New Orleans-Attakapas, Capt. Denslow, 1856. Sold March 1857 to Capt. Darning Glasscock, New Orleans. Off the lists 1863.

4329 ORION

Stw ferry wh b. Belle Vernon, Pa., 1884. 110.5 x 24 x 3. Engines, 10's- 4 ft. Two boilers, each 38" by 18 ft. Operated across the Ohio River at Sistersville, W. Va. owned by E.W. Talbott. A new hull was built in 1907 and the cabin, etc., transferred over to become the ferry *DANIEL* (see). The old hull of the *ORION* lay a long time at Sistersville between the ferry landing and the mouth of Miller's Run. Note: there is evidence of a prior *ORION* built at Parkersburg in 1874, 42 tons.

4330 Orlando

Stw p wh b. Jeffersonville, Ind., by Howard, 1891, originally named *ORA LEE* (see). Memphis and White River, weekly, April 1901. Struck a snag two miles above Peach Orchard Bluff on the White, July 5, 1901, en route from Memphis to Newport, Ark., and was lost.

4331 Orleans

SW p wh b. New Albany, Ind., 1852. 401 tons. Commanded by Capt. John Molloy in the St. Louis-New Orleans trade. 219 x 29 x 6. The original owners were James L. Day, Norwich, Conn. (one-quarter), along with Robert and John Geddes (who owned 30%) of New Orleans and others. Sold to C.H. Saltmarsh, St. Louis. Off the lists 1860.

4332 Orleans

Stw p wh b. Mobile, Ala., 1862. 178 tons. Originally named *LIZZIE DAVIS* (see). She was captured by the U.S. and turned over to USQMD. She was not renamed *ORLEANS* until sold to private owners Jan. 13, 1866. When enrolled at New Orleans that date she is described as 115.2 x 25.7 x 6.9 and side-wheel. She was owned by Capt. Thomas E. Henthorn and others of Mobile. Sold March 1866 to Capt. David Sinnott and John A. Wayne, New Orleans, and was taken to Galveston, Tex., in May 1866. Document surrendered at Galveston, May 31, 1867.

4333 Orline St. John

SW p wh b. Louisville, Ky., 1847. 349 tons. Burned and lost at Bridegeport, Ala., with loss of 41 lives, Mar. 4, 1850.

4334 Oronoco

Stw pl and p wh b. Rock Island, Ill., 1892, originally named *E. RUTLEDGE* and then *JOHN H. RICH*, rafter. 132.7 x 30.5 x 4.7. Engines, 15's- 5 ft. Three boilers, each 38" by 18 ft. This was the first of the pleasure boats owned by Drs. Mayo of Rochester, Minn. These celebrated MDs (Charles Horace and William James Mayo) had invested in a lumber firm which went bankrupt and their share of the assets was this steamboat *JOHN H. RICH*. They converted her into a private pleasure boat about 1913 and called her *ORONOCO*. They sold her fall of 1917 to Capt. S.C. Edgar. Two years later she was at Greenville, Miss., in the Greenville-Luna, Ark., trade, owned by Capts. Frank and William Lyons. Sold to Ben Franklin Coal Co., Moundsville, W. Va. and renamed *BEN FRANKLIN*. (see Towboat Directory). While the Mayos owned her she was commanded by Capts. R.N. Cassidy and James J. Richtman. See *S&D REFLECTOR*, March 1972 issue, pages 6–22, for account of the Mayo pleasure boats and others.

4335 Osage

U.S. monitor b. Carondelet, Mo., 1863, 351 tons. Both *OSAGE* and *NEOSHO* (see) were much alike, created by James B. Eads. They were extremely shallow draft ironclads, drawing about three feet. She was commanded by Thomas O. Selfridge USN (later Rear Admiral) and spent most of 1864 hard aground on a sand bar. Her engineer Tom Doughty built a primitive periscope for looking over the turret in 1863, the first. Sunk in the Battle of Mobile, April 1865 but raised. When sold to private owners Nov. 22, 1867, she was described as 180 x 45.8 x 5.4., recess wheel. She was sold to Capt. John Armstrong, New Orleans, and one month later transferred to New Orleans Wrecking & Salvage Co., Capt. Greenleaf Andrews. Same owner and master, May 1870. One account says she sank in Sodo Lake near Shreveport, La.

4336 Osage

SW p wh b. Castle Rock, Mo., 1865. 147 tons. First home port, St. Louis. Off the lists in 1874.

4337 Osage

Stw p–tb wh b. Osage City, Mo., 1900. 100 x 19.8 x 3.5. Engines 12½'s- 3½ ft. from *JOHN R. HUGO*. One boiler, 42" by 24 ft. After a brief career on Osage and Missouri rivers she was sold to Houston Lumber Co., Vicksburg. In 1909 was bought by Mississippi, Yazoo & Sunflower River Transportation Co., and given a new hull. Dismantled about 1917.

4338 Osceola

SW p wh b. West Elizabeth, Pa., 1849. 125 tons. 125 x 23 x 4.7. Original owner was D.G. Hill, New Orleans. First master, Capt. George W. Haygood. In 1851 was owned in Port Caddo, Tex., Capt. Robert H. Martin. Had several ownership changes in the New Orleans area until 1854 when enrolled at Pascagoula, Miss., Capt. William C. Degges. Snagged and lost at Mobile, Ala., Dec. 8, 1859.

4339 Osceola

SW p wh b. Osceola, Wis., 1854. 65 tons. Built for St. Croix River trade and frequently at St. Paul. Off the lists in 1857.

4340 Osceola

SW p wh b. Louisville, Ky., 1858. 157 tons. Running New Orleans to Jefferson and upper Red River spring 1860, Capt. McMillan. To Confederate registry 1861. F.L. Wooldridge reports she later went to Mobile where she served until dismantled in 1873.

4341 Osceola

Stw p wh b. Cincinnati, Oh., 1866. 267 tons. Off the list in 1872.

4342 Osceola

Stw p wh b. Osceola, Wis., 1874. 130 x 22 x 4. Engines, 10's- 4 ft. Two boilers. Built by Emil Munch. Sank at Peters Landing 40 miles below Memphis upbound from St. Francis River to Memphis with 300 bales, Feb. 27, 1876, and *CITY OF AUGUSTA* brought in the passengers and *ELLA* took off the cotton. The *T. F. ECKERT* was sent to raise her. Bought in spring of 1877 by Gen. Mark D. Flower for a trip up Yellowstone River. En route, near Glendive, Mont., a beautiful white stallion was spotted, and the boat was landed. In pursuit went a number of cowboys who had taken passage, and observing from the boat's deck was a preacher and family. During the two hours spent in pursuit of the nag a tornado came along and demolished the steamboat. Those who told the story were quick to add that the preacher's wife was red-headed, confirmation that a white horse, a preacher, and a red-headed woman on a steamboat bodes no good. Loss occurred June 22, 1877.

4343 OSCEOLA BELLE

SW p wh b. Jeffersonville, Ind., 1875. 372 tons. Operated out of Memphis. She went out in the timber above Vicksburg on a falling river early 1876 and was stranded good and proper. A rise came along and *QUICKSTEP* and *WEST WIND* went to the scene with two empty barges, partly filled them with water, placed them under the stranded boat's guards, and pumped them out. In such manner she was jerked back afloat. Burned at the Memphis wharf along with the side-wheel *IDLEWILD* (see) in 1880.

4344 OSSINING

Prop tug ih b. Linwood, Pa., 1885. 128 x 26 x 8. Originally named *SARAH A. JENKS* which operated out of New York City carrying prisoners to Sing Sing prison. Renamed by the Lower Hudson Steamboat Co., of Ossining, N.Y. After 1925 sold to Lyons Bros., of Greenville, Miss., who ran her to Luna Landing, Ark., carrying U.S. Mail. In 1927 sold to Warner & Tamble, Memphis, who ran her in local U.S. Mail trades until 1931. They stripped her down, converted her to diesel, placing a 350 hp. Atlas in her, and renamed her *MARY ELIZABETH.* Sold June 1973 to Murphy Marine Service, Memphis.

4345 OSPREY

Stw p wh b. Franklin, La., 1855. 110 tons. 115 x 24 x 4.3. In July 1856 managing owner was J.W. Barols, New Orleans, with Capt. Samuel Carey, master. An advertisement in New Orleans newspapers July 1858 announced that she now is the property of J.B. and S. Cary, who operate a lumber mill, and she would deliver lumber on the Attakapas waters to Bayou Sale, Vermillion, over the Lake, or anywhere to accommodate customers. Off the lists 1858.

4346 OSWEGO

SW p wh b. Brownsville, Pa., 1847. 187 tons. Downbound at Wheeling, first trip, July 25, 1848. At St. Paul, Nov. 13, 1851. Snagged and lost at Chester, Ill., Feb. 4, 1852.

4347 OSWICHEE

SW p wh b. Elizabeth, Pa., 1853. 212 tons. Went to Apalachicola, Fla., and was snagged and lost on the Chattahoochee River, Mar 1860.

4348 OTIS WEBB

SW p wh b. Wellsville, Oh., 1857. 64 tons. Documented at Wheeling, W. Va. Off the lists in 1859.

4349 OTTO

SW ferry wh b. Cincinnati, Oh., 1849. 59 tons. Documented at Louisville. Off the list in 1854.

4350 OUACHITA

U.S. gunboat sw wh b. New Albany, Ind., 1861 originally packet *LOUISVILLE* (see). Converted into a gunboat by the Confederates, and captured by U.S., May 18, 1863. She was pressed into U.S. service bearing the name *OUACHITA.* Sold at war's conclusion to Daniel T. Head, New Orleans, and refitted as a packet named *VICKSBURG* (see).

4351 OUACHITA

Stw p wh b. Jeffersonville, Ind., by Howard, 1890. 189 x 38 x 6.5. Had cotton guards making her 52 ft. over all width. Often called the "Big *OUACHITA.*" Built for Capt. L.V. Cooley for New Orleans-Monroe trade, connecting with *JOSIE W.* for Camden. W.B. Foulke was clerk. She was bought by Capts. A.E. and L.P. Cummins for the Memphis-Vicksburg trade after the *CITY OF SAVANNAH* (first) burned in 1898. The *WARREN* (see) was there until the big *OUACHITA* arrived. She burned at Memphis on Jan. 19, 1899, at 1:30 A.M. Mr. and Mrs. E.A. Keith and a Dr. Murray lost their lives in the blaze. The hull was towed to Paducah and rebuilt to become the sternwheel *FRED A. BLANKS* (see). Cummins Brothers got the *BELLE OF CALHOUN,* renamed *JULIA,* to replace the *OUACHITA* in the trade.

4352 OUACHITA

Stw p wh b. Jeffersonville, Ind., by Howard, 1899. 140 x 32 x 4. Engines, 10's- 5 ft. One boiler, 44" by 28 ft. Owned by Capt. L.V. Cooley, New Orleans. He sold the boat, c. 1906, to Alabama River Packet Co., Mobile. She was laid up about 1909 and was inactive almost five years until disposed of.

4353 OUACHITA

Stw p wh b. Jeffersonville, Ind., by Howard, 1908. Originally named *CITY OF MUSKOGEE* (see) and then *LORAINE K.* (also see). Capts. L.V. Cooley and M.T. Bradford bought her in July 1924, repaired her and renamed her *OUACHITA,* and she burned on her first trip, Sept. 12, 1924.

4354 OUACHITA

Stw p sh b. Nashville, Tenn., 1922, originally named *GEORGE PRINCE* (see). 144 x 29.5 x 5.2. Machinery from the *PERCY SWAIN,* cross-compound, condensing. Owned by Capt. L.V. Cooley, New Orleans-Monroe. Captain Cooley suffered a stroke aboard, up Ouachita River loading cotton, late 1931. He was removed from the boat at New Orleans and died less than two weeks later, 76, on Dec. 19, 1931, in a hospital. He was survived by his wife, the former Miss Sophie Bell, and by four children: Miss Sophie Cooley of New Orleans, Miss Esther Cooley, Natchetoches, La., L.V. Jr., Slidell, La., and Henry B., Baton Rouge, La. He stood 6′4″ in his socks, and proverbially wore a high standing collar and a Panama hat. He had become a river captain at 19, and was married at 31. He revived Ouachita River packet traffic in 1924 with the *AMERICA* (see) after a 20-year lapse and had continued going there since. Capt. Sam Cotton replaced him on the *OUACHITA*. Capt. Fred Hornbrook and others bought the boat in 1934 and ran her Pittsburgh-Cincinnati. Sold to Ohio River Transit Co., and ran Cincinnati–Louisville, Capt. Hornbrook in charge, 1935. Sold to Greene Line Steamers of Cincinnati November 1936. Dismantled in January 1940 and the hull was used as a cargo barge named *STOGIE WHITE*.

4355 OUACHITA BELLE

SW p wh b. Jeffersonville, Ind., 1870. 218 x 38 x 6. Built for Capt. F.A. Blanks and C.N. Breurd, New Orleans, equal shares. Usually ran New Orleans-Bayou Sara, Captain Blanks, with J.H. Mossop, clerk. Later Capt. John C. Libano was master. Capt. John W. Cannon ran her under lease one cotton season. In the fall of 1878 sold to Maj. John D. Adams, Memphis. Sank at Fox Island in late November, 1880 within 100 yards of where the *ROBERT MITCHELL* (see) had sunk on Nov. 3.

4356 OUCHITA

Prop launch sh b. Charleston, W. Va., by Ward in 1897, originally named *MADGE* (see). Was renamed when sold to the U.S. Engineers, Vicksburg, in 1903.

4357 OWEVA

Stw ferry wh b. Huntington, W. Va., 1921. 97 x 28 x 2.8. Engines from *CARRIE BROWN* (see). Owned by Paul F. Thomas and served at 26th Street, Huntington. Replaced in 1934 by the *PAUL F. THOMAS* (see).

4358 OZARK

Prop U.S. monitor b. 1863. 178 x 50 x 8. Twin props. Had an Ericsson turret. "She is a miserable vessel," wrote Admiral Porter in 1864. She was never tested in any serious action. Sold at Mound City, Ill., to T.B. Ellis, Nov. 29, 1865, for $3,300.

4359 OZARK

Stw p wh b. Cincinnati, Oh., 1866. 281 tons. 152.7 x 29.8 x 3.8. Engines, 12's- 3½ ft. Two boilers, each 38″ by 18 ft. Owned by Stephen Morse and Lewis Clason, Cincinnati, equal shares. Capt. Samuel Houston, master. Operated to Arkansas and Red rivers. Went to U.S. Marshal sale at New Orleans May 1873, sold to Watson, Bacon & Co., for $1,410. Dismantled soon thereafter.

4360 OZARK BELLE

Ferry wh b. Jeffersonville, Ind., 1873. 69 tons. Registered at Memphis 1876.

4361 OZARK QUEEN

Stw p wh b. Batesville, Ark., 1896. 133 x 25.6. Owned by Capt. C.B. Woodbury for service on White River, Ark. In May 1903 in the Batesville-McBees trade, Capt. Will Shipp. Condemned at Memphis December 1904 and later that month Capt. M.F. Bradford bought her and she became the *HOUMA* (see).

P

4362 P. C. WALLIS

SW p wh b. Louisville, Ky., 1855. 230 tons. 159 x 31 x 5. Came out in the New Orleans-Vicksburg trade, Capt. J.H. Hendrick, with Henry Devine, clerk. Sold May 1856 to Cox, Brainard & Co., Mobile, Capt. George M. Kirk. Went to Confederate registry 1861.

4363 P. D. STAGGS

Stw p wh b. Jeffersonville, Ind., by Howard, 1893. 161 x 28.6 x 4.4. Ran Nashville-Burnside on Cumberland River owned by Alex Kendall and Capt. A.T. Armstrong. Captain Armstrong died of a knife wound he had received on this boat when he tried to stop trouble caused by drinking, Feb. 2, 1895. The Louisville & Evansville Mail Line acquired her, and she was making trips Louisville-Kentucky River 1896–1897. Sold to Capt. Tom G. Ryman April 1897, and that November Capt. Douglas Jones, having sold his *ASHLAND CITY* (see) ran her Paducah-Danville. Sank at Metropolis, Ill., and sold to Capt. Lee Howell and others who refloated her, rebuilt the wreck, and so brought out the *INDIA GIVENS* (see).

4364 P. E. BONFORD

SW p wh b. Madison, Ind., 1860. 231 tons. 140 x 30 x 6. Owned by Capt. J.F. Worley and others of the family, Jefferson Parish, La. Ran New Orleans-Shreveport. Went to Confederate registry 1861.

4365 P. F. GEISSE

Centerwheel f wh b. Belle Vernon, Pa., 1869. 172 tons. Used at Omaha, Neb. Named for P.F. Geisse, Wellsville, Oh., who specialized in building transfer boats. A photograph of her shows signs in the background, "Kansas City, St. Joseph and Council Bluffs Railroad" and "Rock Island and Pacific Railroad." Inspected New Orleans Dist. 1876.

4366 P. F. KIMBALL

SW p wh b. New Albany, Ind., 1851. 312 tons. 184.5 x 28.3 x 6.2. Owned by Capt. William Kimball of Jefferson Parish (now New Orleans) La. (three-fourths) and C.B. Cook, Natchitoches, La. Ran New Orleans-Grand Encore. Sold December 1857 to John F. Hall, New Orleans, then had several changes of ownership until sold September 1858 to James A. Green, Mobile. Returned to New Orleans May 1859, owned in Algiers, La. Off the lists by 1861.

4367 P. H. KELLEY

Ferry wh b. Sioux City, Iowa, 1883. 90 x 18 x 2.9. Capt. Grant Marsh operated her at Memphis, 1884–1885.

4368 P. T. MILLER

Rig? wh b. Metropolis, Ill., 1867. 67 tons. Owned 1874 by Jefferson City Steam Ferry Co., and documented at St. Louis.

4369 P. W. STRADER

SW p wh b. Cincinnati, Oh., 1866. 735 tons. 230 x 36 x 6. Engines, 18½'s- 7 ft. Three boilers, each 46" by 28 ft. Machinery from the *DIAMOND*. Ran Cincinnati-Louisville, Capt. Albert Stein, 1866. Owned 1870 by Memphis & Cincinnati Packet Co. Made a trip to Alexandria, La., arriving there Dec. 8, 1873. There was a report she was sold to St. Louis & Peoria Packet Co., latter August 1871. Burned at New Orleans Mar. 9, 1874.

4370 P. DICKINSON

Stw p wh b. Kingston, Tenn., 1881. 122 x 28 x 4. Equipment from former *EMORY CITY* (see) used in construction. Ran Kingston-Loudon on Tennessee River. P. Dickinson was a wealthy citizen of Knoxville. She once got caught up a tributary on a falling river and stayed until the following year. Dismantled in 1888.

4371 PACIFIC

Stw p wh b. Freedom, Pa., 1846. 137 tons. Off the lists in 1853.

4372 PACIFIC

SW p wh b. Elizabeth, Pa., 1850. 572 tons. Operated out of St. Louis. Came in collision with *GRAND TOWER* near Cairo, Ill., Nov. 23, 1854, resulting in loss of both boats.

4373 PACIFIC

SW p wh b. New Albany, Ind., 1857. 603 tons. 290 x 40 x 8. Engines, 28's- 9 ft. Six boilers, each 40" by 28 ft. Owned by J. Bragdon & Co., Louisville. Ran Louisville-New Orleans, Capt. William Lamb. Other masters were Capts. Anson McGill and Jesse K. Bell. Clerks included W.P. Halliday and R.A. Barclay. She was coaling at Uniontown, Ky., Nov. 18, 1860, when she burned with loss of eight lives.

4374 PACIFIC

SW tr wh b. Metropolis, Ill., 1878. 222.8 x 35.8 x 6.1. Engines, 24's- 7 ft. Four boilers. Operated by Waterloo and Carondelet Turnpike & Ferry Co., subsidiary of the Iron Mountain Railroad, at Carondelet, Mo. Her partner ferry was the *MISSOURI* (see). In 1911 she was taken to Cairo and used as a wharfboat for the ferry *HENRY MARQUAND* (see) which the Cotton Belt was running there. In 1913 she was purposely beached at Birds Point and burned for scrap.

4375 PACTOLUS

Stw p wh b. Jeffersonville, Ind., by Howard, 1886. 137.4 x 28.5 x 4.8. She went to the Chattahoochee River and ran there until worn out in 1892.

4376 PADUCAH

SW p wh b. Paducah, Ky., 1847. 99 tons. First home port, Louisville, Ky. Off the lists in 1851.

4377 PADUCAH

Stw p wh b. Jeffersonville, Ind., by Howard, 1916. 170 x 33 x 5. Engines, 14's- 5 ft. Two boilers. Paddlewheel 18 ft. diameter working 24 ft. buckets. Owned by St. Louis & Tennessee River Packet Co. Ran Paducah-Florence. Struck a rock and sank seventeen miles above Paducah in October 1922. Sold in 1928 to Bladgett Construction Co., who used her as a quarterboat at Hickman, Ky. They started to dismantle the cabin and she buckled. Towed across the river behind Island 6 and burned.

4378 PAINT ROCK

Rig? p wh b. upper Tennessee River. Operated by Capts. J.M. Todd and C.C. Spiller. She was sunk along with the *DUNBAR* (see) at Chattanooga when General Bragg evacuated the city. Raised and repaired by the Federals later. Eventually sank near the location of her earlier sinking and was lost.

4379 PALESTINE

SW p wh b. Pittsburgh, Pa., 1844. 172 tons. Had a "Clipper" engine installed by Litch at Pittsburgh. Caught fire June 19, 1844, on the Mississippi just above Cairo. Fourteen persons crowded into the stern yawl still on its davit. It fell drowning twelve. The fire was extinguished. Dismantled in November 1848.

4380 PALESTINE

Stw p wh b. Louisville, Ky., 1864. 183 tons. 155 x 33 x 4.5. Built for Louisville-Nashville trade. Ran low water in the Louisville-Evansville trade 1867, Capt. E.P.T. Hollcroft, with M.D. Warren, clerk. Lost after she hit a pier of the Danville, Tenn., railroad bridge, 1873.

4381 PALMETTO

SW p wh b. Brownsville, Pa., 1848. 136 tons. Went to Apalachicola, Fla., where she sank and was lost Oct. 9, 1852.

4382 PALO ALTO

SW p wh b. Industry, Pa., 1846. 155 tons. Documented at Pittsburgh. Off the lists 1850.

4383 PANAMA

Stw p wh b. Stratton, Oh., 1913. 45 x 8 x 2. Built by John W. Ekey, Stratton, Oh. One upright boiler. One vertical engine flatbelted to an aft jackshaft, thence link-chain to the paddlewheel. Picture appeared in *S&D REFLECTOR*, March 1978, page 34.

4384 PAN HANDLE

SW ferry wh b. Steubenville, Oh., 1854. 46 tons. Documented at Wheeling. Off the lists in 1861.

4385 PANOLA

Stw p wh b. Brownsville, Pa., 1858. 199 tons. Lost in a steamboat fire at the wharf, Pittsburgh, May 7, 1859. At time of loss was commanded by Capt. Harry Mason.

Owners were John W. Mason, J.S. Pringle, W. Buffington, and A.J. McDougal.

4386 PANOLA

SW p wh b. Aberdeen, Oh., 1863. 89 tons. 132 x 22 x 3.9. Robert Moore sold her at Cincinnati January 1865 to A.W. Johnson, Peoria, Ill., who loaded her out for Memphis in charge of Capt. Eugene F.D. Johnson. She was in New Orleans under same ownership and command that September. Snagged and lost at Bayou Goula, La., Oct. 3, 1865.

4387 PARAGON

SW p wh b. Elizabeth, Pa., 1863. 495 tons. The hull was under contract when bought by Capt. C.W. Batchelor, Pittsburgh, who then built the boat complete and sold her before she left Pittsburgh to a Capt. Donnally of Cincinnati. Was advertised Pittsburgh to Cincinnati, Mar. 18, 1864, Capt. Donnally, with A.J. McConnell, clerk. She was upbound from Memphis to St. Louis, Feb. 28, 1868, when she hit the wrecked *JAMES MONTGOMERY* (see) at Devils Island near Cape Girardeau. Water was two feet deep in the cabin and the hull badly twisted. Passengers remained on the roof five hours until the *POST BOY* came along and took them to the Cape.

4388 PARAGON

Stw p wh b. Belle Vernon, Pa. (hull), and completed at Pittsburgh, 1873. 260 x 48 x 8. Rees engines, 22's- 8 ft. Five boilers, each 40" by 26 ft., two flues. Built for Rees & Thorn, and John J. and Thomas J. Darragh, all of Pittsburgh. The hull was floated broadside over Dams 2 and 1 in the Monongahela to get it out to Pittsburgh. Capt. John J. Darragh was in command, and James H. Rees, clerk. She was the longest sternwheeler on the rivers in her day. Ran Cincinnati-New Orleans. In 1874 came to Wheeling in 48 hours from Cincinnati with 1400 tons of freight on a six ft. stage. She burned at St. Louis Apr. 6, 1875. Capt. William J. Kountz bought the wreck, hauled the hull on the St. Louis Sectional Docks and built the *E. O. STANARD* (see) from it.

4389 PARGOUD

Stw p wh b. Jeffersonville, Ind., by Howard, 1884. 242 x 43 x 7.6. Ran New Orleans-Greenville 1886, Capt. J.W. Carlton. Brought 5,662 bales and 546 sacks of seed to New Orleans on a single trip, arriving Dec. 29, 1886. She was the "summer" boat in place of the *J.M. WHITE* in 1885, Capt. John W. Tobin, with Curt Holmes as clerk. She was taken to St. Louis and ran excursions 1893-1894, Capt. Sterling McIntyre, with indifferent success, winding up with a U.S. Marshal sale in August 1894 at St. Louis. After an overhaul at Mound City was returned to New Orleans. The *PARGOUD, NATCHEZ, T.P. LEATHERS, PAUL TULANE,* and others depended heavily on the cotton season. In October 1897 a rate war between them resulted in the *PARGOUD* bringing bales to New Orleans for 35 cents a bale, Capt. Mike Carbine. She was lost above the mouth of Red River on the lower Mississippi early 1898.

4390 PARIS

SW p wh b. Freedom, Pa., 1848. 242 tons. Struck the *METEOR* (see) and sank her near Stephensport, Ky., Aug. 24, 1848. Ran Pittsburgh-St. Louis. Off the lists in 1853.

4391 PARIS C. BROWN

Stw p wh b. Cincinnati, Oh., 1878. 262.5 x 39 (38 ft. floor) x 6.5. Engines, 18½'s- 7 ft. from first *GOLDEN RULE* (see). Four boilers, each 42" by 28 ft., two flues. 904 tons. Came out in Cincinnati-New Orleans trade fall of 1878, Capt. J.V. Reynolds, with Chris Young, clerk. In 1880 in the Southern Transportation Co., Capt. A.M. Halliday, with Chris Young, clerk. In later years Chris Young became master, with A.M. Halliday as a principal owner. She was lost at Hermitage, La., after spearing a snag, Jan. 1, 1889. Crew at the time of loss: Capt. Young, master; Pres Ellison, 1st clerk; I.M. Young, 2nd clerk; James Steen, chief engineer; George Trunnell and Wash Kinley, pilots. Within a year the *CITY OF BATON ROUGE* (see) was lost at the same location. Paris C. Brown was a Cincinnatian connected with the Marine Railway Co., where the boat was built, and also with the boat store Parker, Wise & Co. He was said to resemble Capt. Sam S. Brown of Pittsburgh.

4392 PARK CITY

Stw p wh b. Brownsville, Pa., 1883, originally named *GAYOSO* (see). Renamed in November 1897. Owned by Capt. E.W. Bewley and ran Evansville-Green River. Jake Kittinger was clerk on her, then J. Edgar Williams. Jett Hines clerked her for a while, practically the only boating he ever did. He married Ida Williams, sister of the Evansville Williams boys, and was county clerk of Butler County, Ky., at Morgantown for 24 years (maybe more) and his sons were the men who ran James R. Hines Co., at Bowling Green. The *PARK CITY* went to the Kentucky River in her latter days and was lost by reason of an accident most peculiar. She was rounded to, to make Lafe Mahonery's landing near Mussel Shoals in Owen County. She had aboard a large shipment of whiskey contained both in barrels and cases. One of the barrels tiered high on the main deck lost its balance as the boat rolled, crashed through the deck into the hold, went on through the bottom planking and sank her. This happened on Dec. 6, 1909, within a few miles of where the *SONOMA* (see) turned over and sank.

4393 PARKERSBURG

Stw p wh b. Cincinnati, Oh., 1857. 204 tons. Ran Cincinnati-Parkersburg, Capt. J.M. Vaughan, with E.P. Chancellor, clerk. Was sold south and went to Confederate service 1861.

4394 PARLOR CITY

Stw p wh b. Jeffersonville, Ind., by Howard, 1892. 125 x 25 x 3.7. Capt. L. Brunner built her for the Ouachita River, connecting at Monroe for D'Arbonne and Bartholomew. Capt. L.V. Cooley bought her in 1895 and used her as the off-season or "summer" boat New Orleans-Ouachita River. Sold back to Capt. L. Bruner in 1900 who connected at Monroe with the *FRED A. BLANKS*. She was lost at New Orleans in late October 1902 when struck by the *NATCHEZ* as she was making the landing. The machinery went to the *FRANK B. HAYNE* (see).

4395 PARTHENIA

Stw p wh b. California, Pa., 1854. 154 tons. 150 x 28.8 x 3.9. Owned by her master, Capt. J.J. Robinson and others of California and Pittsburgh. Ran Pittsburgh-St. Louis. Capt. W.H. Reed was master when she burned at St. Louis on Dec. 7, 1855, while loading for the Illinois River. The blaze which originated on the *PARTHENIA* also consumed the *TWIN CITY* and *PRAIRIE CITY*. She was owned by Wall & Wider and Reid & Vohries at the time.

4396 PARTHENIA

Stw p wh b. Freedom, Pa., 1862. 261 tons. Built for Capt. Perry Brown and others. He was master, with Andrew Robinson, clerk. Her first trip was Pittsburgh-St. Louis, and then she advertised Pittsburgh-Memphis, June 17, 1862, "the first packet to load for that port at Pittsburgh since the war started." She was impressed into war service and was burned by the Rebels at Harpeth Shoals, Tenn., Jan. 14, 1863. Owners collected $32,500 for their loss from the U.S. in April 1864.

4397 PASTIME

Stw p wh b. Pittsburgh, Pa., 1900. 58 x 9 x 2.3. A single decker built for Charles G. Rogers, Esplen, Allegheny County, Pa. Harry M. Rogers, Allegheny, Pa., bought her, 1902. John E. Leonard, Brownsville, Pa., came next, who sold her to W.N. Acklin, West Brownsville and in 1905 she went to Samuel Y. Anderson, Sewickley, Pa. After several other swaps she went to Fred A. Heperline, Beaver County, Pa., who formed the Ambridge Transportation Co., and used her to deliver the Ambridge *Citizen* to Woodlawn, Pa. Jerry Gumbert, calling himself the Return Towing Co., bought her 1908 and sold her 1909 to Jesse Klinefelter, Sharpsburg, Pa. Lastly she went to John J. Lemley, Point Marion, Pa., who coaled her head too heavy at a tipple above Lock 5, Monon River, and she sank, Sept. 5, 1910. Burned at Joe's Run, one-half mile above Lock 12, Monon River, 3:00 A.M., Nov. 6, 1910. The wreck was still there in 1917 and your scribe saw it.

4398 PAT CLEBURNE

SW p wh b. Cincinnati, Oh., 1870. A fair sized boat, dimensions not at hand. Engines, 20's- 7 ft. Four boilers, each 37″ by 24 ft., two 14″ flues. Built for the Memphis & White River Packet Co., Capt. W.J. Ashford, with D.P. Davis, clerk. She and *ARKANSAS BELLE* were partner boats and both came to the Evansville-Cairo trade owned by Evansville, Cairo and Memphis Steam Packet Co. In 1875 Capt. John Goff, master, with Mat. Williams, clerk. On a downbound trip she was landed opposite Weston, Ky., May 17, 1876. The *ARKANSAS BELLE* came up and was landing alongside when the boilers of the *PAT CLEBURNE* exploded. Capt. Dick Fowler was in command at the time, asleep in the texas, and was burned in the ensuing fire. The death toll was given as fourteen persons. A Banca boiler plug was later found, melted. The snagboat *E.A. WOODRUFF* removed the wreck.

4399 PAT ROGERS

SW p wh b. Cincinnati, Oh., 1872. Engines, 22½'s- 7 ft. Owned by the U.S. Mail Line Co., and ran Cincinnati—Louisville. She caught fire Aug. 5, 1874, at Laughrey Creek and was lost. Capt. Charles David was in command, and Charles J. Dufour was pilot on watch. Some 30 lives were lost inasmuch as she stuck on a bar and many were forced overboard and drowned. Her machinery later went to the *U.P. SCHENCK* (see). Patrick Rogers, Esq., was a founder of the Cincinnati Marine Ways Co., in pre-Civil War days.

4400 PATIENCE

Stw p wh b. Rock Island, Ill., 1882. 76.3 x 15.7 x 3.2. Originally ran Keokuk-Warsaw until 1894 when sold to Capt. Jack McCaffrey, Claire, Iowa, who made a towboat of her. Later renamed *DUKE*, then *SAMUEL*.

4401 PATRICK HENRY

SW p wh b. Cincinnati, Oh., 1840. 161 tons. Ran Louisville-New Orleans. Her part owner and master in 1842 was a Capt. Bradford, Augusta, Ky., with William Pegman, clerk. She measured 144 x 21 x 5.7. Sold to New Orleans in March 1843, Capt. Robert Dorsey. Had several ownership changes in the New Orleans area and finally in June 1848 went to the Independent Towboat Co., of that city. Foundered and lost at Algiers, La., Feb. 18, 1850.

4402 PATRICK HENRY

SW p wh b. Cincinnati, Oh., 1846. 298 tons. 120 x 30 x 6.1. Built for and commanded by Capt. Robert C. Young, New Orleans. In 1848 she was sold to a number of firms along the Yazoo River including Allen & Barksdale. In descending the Yazoo at the mouth of Sunflower River collided with *FAWN* (see), wrecked the cabin of the latter and her engineer was killed, this in April 1849. Sold August 1850 to Capt. Joseph G. Landy, New Orleans, and then ran New Orleans-Bayou Sara. Dismantled and the hull became a wharfboat in 1854.

4403 PATRICK HENRY

SW ferry wh b. Wheeling, Va., 1862. 66 tons. Off the lists in 1865.

4404 PATROL

Stw p wh b. Sewickley, Pa. (hull), and completed at Pittsburgh, Pa., 1883. 135.5 x 28.8 x 4.2. Rees engines, 12's- 5 ft. Two boilers each 44″ by 20 ft. Built for the Mississippi River Commission and long served on the Mississippi River. Sold at public sale and went to upper Cumberland River as a packet. Lost by stranding in Harmons Shoals, upper Cumberland, Sept. 8, 1918. Wreck still was visible in 1941.

4405 PATTONA.

SW sh b. Jeffersonville, Ind. 1880, originally U.S. Lighthouse tender *JOSEPH HENRY,* then excursion steamer *LOUISIANA*. She was renamed *PATTONA* at Memphis in February 1909, and was the local excursion boat. Capt. Ed Nowland commanded 1914. Caving shores on Mud Island exposed a side-wheel wreck March 1967, identified by local river authorities as that of the *PATTONA*.

4406 PAUL ANDERSON

Stw p wh b. Brownsville, Pa., 1850. 170 x 29 x 6.7. Engines, 22's- 6½ ft. Three boilers, each 40" by 26 ft. Built by Capt. Richard C. Gray who commanded and was principal owner, along with Clarke & Thaw and R.S. Hays. Made two trips Pittsburgh-New Orleans, then ran Pittsburgh-Cincinnati 1851, then many trips Pittsburgh-Cincinnati-St. Louis. Burned in the steamboat fire at St. Louis on Dec. 7, 1855 (see *PARTHENIA*). Gen. Paul Anderson, 1782-1861, took part in War of 1812 and Mexican War and was uncle of Capt. R.C. Gray whose mother was Sarah Anderson. Paul's sister Mary Ann was great-grandmother of your scribe.

4407 PAUL F. THOMAS

Stw ferry wh b. Madison, Ind., 1934. 107 x 30 x 4. High pressure engines from ferry *OWEVA* (see). One boiler. Owned by Twenty-Sixth Street Ferry Co., Huntington, W. Va. Dismantled at Huntington in February 1948, and the wreck burned at Hanging Rock, Oh., May 1950. The engines originally on packet *CARRIE BROWN* are today preserved at the Ohio River Museum, Marietta, Oh.

4408 PAUL JONES

SW p wh b. Cincinnati, Oh., 1843. 232 tons. Owned 1845 by Thomas F. Eckert, Cincinnati, and Simeon Doyle and Nathaniel Montgomery of Kentucky. Ran New Orleans-Waterproof, Capt. James Walworth, 1844-1845, maybe longer. Sank the *MAJOR BARBOUR* in collision near Troy, Ind., Feb. 3, 1848, causing five deaths. Sank in Grand Chain, Ill., and lost, March 1848.

4409 PAUL JONES

SW p wh b. McKeesport, Pa., 1855. 353 tons. 172 x 34 x 6.5. Engines, 21's- 7 ft. Owned in Pittsburgh and ran to New Orleans. Samuel Clemens boarded her at Cincinnati and took passage to New Orleans, thus commencing his river career. In 1858 sold to three towboat concerns in New Orleans who transferred her October, same year to Capt. Franklin Keeling who operated her New Orleans-Camden on the Ouachita. Burned to prevent capture on Big Black River, Miss., July 1863. The wrecks of *PAUL JONES* and *CHARM* were found side by side in August 1962 by skin divers and many souvenirs were brought up.

4410 PAUL TULANE

Stw p wh b. Jeffersonville, Ind., by Howard, 1888. 212 x 41.4 x 7.4. A cotton packet in New Orleans-Upper Coast trade. Ran excursions at St. Louis along with *WAR EAGLE* in 1892. Owned by Mississippi Packet Co., 1896, running New Orleans-Bayou Sara, two trips weekly. Sank and was lost above Donaldsonville, La., at Cora Plantation, July 1896.

4411 PAUL WILCOX

Stw ferry wh b. Boonville, Mo., 1860. 46 tons. Not documented until 1867 and off the lists 1868.

4412 PAULINE

Stw p wh b. Stillwater, Minn., 1878 as a raft boat. 112 x 21 x 3.5. Engines, 12's- 6 ft. (See *Towboat Directory* for rafting career.) Converted into a packet for the Keithsburg-Burlington trade, Capt. Thomas Peel, 1891-1892. Ran competition with the *SILVER CRESCENT* (see). Proved too small, so owners bought the *MATT F. ALLEN* (see) and was sold. Running excursions at Dubuque, 1898. Rebuilt 1900 and renamed *COLUMBIA* (see).

4413 PAULINE

Stw p wh b. Alexandria, La., 1880. 112.6 x 23.7 x 3.2. In the book *A Wandering Showman* by David Lano (Michigan State University Press 1957) the author relates loading a circus on this boat and touring the south country. Documented at Morgan City, La., 1886.

4414 PAULINE

Prop p wh b Petersburg, Ky., 1896. 45.7 x 11.3 x 4.6. Operated Lawrenceburg-Aurora.

4415 PAULINE

Prop p wh b. Petersburg, Ky., 1905. 52 x 12.5 x 5. Ran Lawrenceburg-Aurora on the Ohio River, Capt. E. Alden. Had a single 9" by 9" engine and one boiler. Still listed 1918.

4416 PAULINE CARROLL

SW p wh b. Cannelton, Ind., 1864. 714 tons. 256 x 42 x 7.7. Engines, 26½'s- 8½ ft. Four boilers, each 46" by 30 ft. Built for Capt. John W. Carroll and others. Ran St. Louis-New Orleans. Was sold to Atlantic & Mississippi Steam Ship Co., 1867, Capt. Hugh L. White. Her staterooms were equipped with an annunciator system; a knob pulled in the room rang a corresponding bell in the clerk's office. Was sold May 1869 to St. Louis & New Orleans Packet Co., Capt. John N. Bofinger, president, Capt. J.A. Yore, with C. Miltenberger, clerk. Dismantled at St. Louis 1875 and the hull was converted into an ice barge.

4417 PAVONIA

Stw p wh b. Madison, Ind., 1892. 120 x 26 x 4. Engines, 12's- 5 ft. Two boilers, each 42" by 20 ft. Short trade packet. William Kirk, Madison, Ind., bought her Sept. 1897 at New Albany, Ind. and ran her up Kentucky River where she was sunk in ice that December. Sold to Ayer & Lord Tie Co., Paducah and converted for towing c. 1903. Sank in ice in the Little Chain, Ohio River, Jan. 29, 1918. Her pilotwheel was mounted on the river front at Paducah on Labor Day 1943 with ceremonies.

4418 Pawnee

SW p wh b. Cincinnati, Oh., 1850. 477 tons. 225 x 34 x 7.5. Ran St. Louis-New Orleans. Stranded and lost at Island 18, above Cairo, Mississippi River, Oct. 8, 1853.

4419 Paw Paw

Centerwheel U.S. tinclad wh Built as ferry *ST. CHARLES* at St. Louis, Mo. 1862, 120 x 34 x 3.7. Engines 20's- 6 ft. Two boilers. Purchased by U.S. from J. Van Vortwick for $8,000, April 9, 1863 at St. Joseph, Mo. Became Tinclad #31. Sold to Samuel Nanell Aug. 17, 1865; dismantled.

4420 Paynswick

Prop freighter wh b. Portsmouth, Oh., 1864. 37 tons. 78.6 x 14 x 4.2. Owned at New Orleans 1867 by her master Capt. C.A. Shepard and John M. Curtis, equal shares. They sold her to Capt. William H. Hannon, New Orleans, who converted her into a steam prop tug, and sold her June 1868 to Capt. Ruffin C. Barrow, New Orleans. Off the lists 1876.

4421 Peankishaw No. 108

Stw p wh b. Russellville, Ill., 1891. 80.9 x 20.2 x 3.6. Handled excursions from Vincennes, Ind., to old Fort Knox on the Wabash. Later in Green River running Evansville-Hartford. In winter 1896 most of the floating equipment at Evansville was moved into the mouth of Green River due to impending ice. This craft went along under her own steam and when abreast of the I.C. incline, six miles above Evansville, ice cut her down. Her engineer was drowned.

4422 Pearl

Stw p wh b. West Elizabeth, Pa., 1845. 64 tons. Running St. Louis-Galena first year, same through 1847. Galena-St. Peters 1848 and made trips to St. Croix Falls. She was the smallest packet on the Upper Mississippi. Off the lists in 1852.

4423 Pearl

SW p wh b. Cincinnati, Oh., 1851. 184 tons. 126 x 29.5 x 5.5. Went to New Orleans owned by J.W. Arthur & Co., and others, Capt. Abraham P. Boardman. Sold June 1853 to Bates, Benson & Co., Atlanta, Ga. Sunk and lost at Bayou Sara, La., in collision with *NATCHEZ*, Jan. 1, 1854. Seven lives were lost.

4424 Pearl City

Stw p wh b. Memphis, Tenn., 1917. 64.6 x 15.2 x 3.5. Originally named *KELLEY SAULS* (see). Owned by C.W. Hunter, Memphis, who sold her 1920 to James Grasty, Greenville, Miss., for Black River. Later acquired by Capt. Leslie McCandless who ran her Paducah-Golconda. She was backing away from Roper's Landing, four miles below Golconda, June 10, 1927, when she hooked a snag and went down in 35 ft. Les McCandless was brother to Capts. Fred and Carl McCandless and died, 47, Dec. 18, 1937.

4425 Pearl Plant

Stw p wh b. Louisville, Ky., 1849. 67 tons. 101.5 x 17.5 x 6.3. Owned by Capt. David Brandenburg, New Orleans, Off the lists 1857.

4426 Peerless

SW p wh b. Louisville, Ky., 1858. 349 tons. 209 x 31.8 x 6.5. First ran St. Louis-St. Joseph in the Union Packet Line, Capt. Bissel. This ambitious line comprising some eleven steamers lasted a year. In January 1860 was sold to Samuel L. Butler, New Orleans, and ran to Ouachita River, Capt. Len F. Moore. Sold April 1860 to Capt. Edward N. Woodland, Camden, Ark., and burned at New Orleans May 27, 1860.

4427 Peerless

SW p wh b. Cincinnati, Oh., 1864. 227 tons. 182 x 34 x 5.8. Two tubular boilers with twenty-one 6" flues. Built for Capt. Frank J. Oakes who had just built *REBECCA* and *ROWENA* (both see). Designed for Cincinnati-Wheeling trade. She was downbound at Rising Sun, Ind., in low water (46" on the bar) and came to so sudden a stop her stacks toppled overboard and had to be fished out. Hit the wreck of the *BLACK HAWK* (see) three miles above Cairo at 9:00 P.M. Dec. 15, 1865, careened over, stoves and lamps upset, and she burned. As a sequel to this, the *JAMES R. GILMORE* (see) hit the *COURIER* wreck in this same area September 1866, and was driven to the Illinois shore almost at the same spot where the *PEERLESS* had wrecked, where she sank.

4428 Peerless

Stw p wh b. California, Pa., 1865. 275 tons. 157 x 30 x 4. Owned by her master Capt. A.D. Russell and others of Allegheny County, Pa., and entered the Allegheny River trade, Pittsburgh-Oil City, with Albert Hancock, clerk. She was withdrawn late 1866. T.H. Williams took the boilers out of the hold, decked her, and raised the cabin "materially improving her appearance." Brought her out May 1867 in the Pittsburgh-Cincinnati trade, selling her in mid-May to Capt. J.B. Coffman who put her in the Cincinnat-Chilo trade in opposition to the *MARY AMENT* (see). Sold August 1867 to Capt. Sam Houston who put on smaller engines, gave her a texas and lengthened the stacks for Arkansas River. Sold October 1868 to Tracy J. Bronson, Franklin, La., Capt. Jesse P. Forgay. Transferred October 1869 to Atakapas Mail Transportation Co., Franklin, La., Capt. H.H. Broad, master. Ultimately she gravitated to Pensacola, Fla., owned by a stock company. The machinery was taken out and she was broken up there in December 1886.

4429 Peerless

Rig? w b. Little Rock, Ark., 1882. 80 x 24 x 2.8. Still listed 1886.

4430 Peerless

Stw p wh b. Hermann, Mo., 1893. 96.6 x 21.4 x 3.5. Engines, 8" - 3 ft. One boiler. Owned by Hermann Ferry & Packet Co. Sunk by ice at St. Charles, Mo., Dec. 30, 1903. Went to the Illinois River 1905 and then for a long time was in the Vicksburg area. Owned by Hugh Stubbs, Friars Point, Miss., 1924-1925, maybe later.

4431 PEERLESS

Stw p and tb wh b. Morgantown, Ky., 1903. 100 x 20 x 4. Much equipment from the former *PILOT* went into her. Owned by Capt. Charles McNutt. Listed at St. Augustine, Fla., 1908.

4432 PEERLESS

Stw p wh b. Mobile, Ala., 1908, originally the *JAMES T. STAPLES* (see) which exploded at Poe's Landing, rebuilt by Capt. J.E. Baker. 200 x 40 x 5.1. W. N. Little and Martin Van Heuvel later ran her Mobile-Alabama River. Sold October 1917 to Capt. Owen F. Burke who after 1921 renamed her *HELEN BURKE*.

4433 PEERLESS

Stw ferry wh b. Jeffersonville, Ind., by Howard, 1910. 99 x 34 x 3. Operated at Portsmouth, Oh. Later was renamed *RUSSELL* (see) and served at Ironton, Oh. She was built by Capt. John F. Davis.

4434 PEKIN

SW p wh b. St. Louis, Mo., 1848. 107 tons. Off the lists 1850.

4435 PELICAN

SW p wh b. Elizabethtown, Pa., 1847. 260 tons. 154 x 28 x 7.7. Owned in part by her master Capt. Louis F. Hermann, New Orleans. Burned and lost at Biloxi, Miss., Aug. 23, 1856.

4436 PELICAN

SW p wh b. New Albany, Ind., 1856. 362 tons. 176 x 33.8 x 6.8. Built for a group of New Albany citizens, with Capt. George H. Ashton, master. Enrolled at New Orleans Oct. 27, 1857. Burned at Francis, Miss., Feb. 24, 1858.

4437 PELICAN

SW tr sh b. Dubuque, Iowa, 1902. 306 x 52.5 x 7.3. Had eighteen ft. guards, making over all width 88½ ft. Engines, 26's- 10 ft. Six boilers (three on a side), each 44″ by 26 ft. Served at Vicksburg until the bridge was built, owned by Queen & Crescent Railroad. Went to Helena, Ark., where she transferred for Louisiana & Mississippi Railroad (I.C.). Plans were under way to convert her to diesel in 1956 but the scheme was discarded. Instead she was stripped into a transfer barge shoved by a towboat.

4438 PEMBINA

SW p wh b. Brownsville, Pa., 1857. 264 tons. Construction superintended by Capt. James Ward. Operated St. Louis-St. Paul in the Northern Line and Northwestern Line. Capt. Thomas H. Griffith, 1857–1859; Capt. John B. Hill, 1860–1861. Ultimately dismantled at Quincy, Ill., spring 1872, and her hull was converted into a cargo barge.

4439 PENGUIN

Stw p wh b. Burlington, Iowa, 1877. 61 tons. 80 x 16.6 x 3.4. Originally built as a rafter by James L. and Silas Harris. In 1878 ran in Winona-Alton trade. Capt. A.J. Whitney, contractor, operated her through 1886, sometimes on the Missouri. By 1891 she was classed as a towboat and had gone to the Ohio River by 1895 operating near Paducah. Based at Evansville 1905 and was sunk there by the big towboat *PITTSBURGH* on Christmas Day 1907, during high wind. Burned at Evansville Aug. 28, 1908.

4440 PENINAH

Stw p wh b. Pittsburgh, Pa., 1868. 421 tons. 180 x 30. Engines, 14's- 4½ ft. Three boilers. Owned by Capt. William J. Kountz and others, and named for his wife. She departed Pittsburgh, Mar. 15, 1868, direct for Fort Benton, Mont. In all she made 20 trips up the Missouri into Montana, most of them to the fort. Sank at Sioux City, Iowa, Capt. David Haney, master, Apr. 5, 1875. Raised and was taken to Yankton for repairs, but broke loose in high water and drifted two miles to Stone's farm where she lodged on shore. Nat Sykes, a boat-builder, spent three weeks getting her back in the river and when he did so a cyclone came along and tore off her cabin.

4441 PENINAH NO. 2

Stw p wh b. Pittsburgh, Pa., 1876. 205 x 33 x 5. Apparently the same engines which were on *PENINAH* (see above) 14's- 4½ ft. Three boilers, each 38″ by 22 ft. Capt. William J. Kountz owned her. She is reputed to have been five miles up Marias River, tributary of the Missouri, to pick up buffalo robes in 1877, the sole commercial navigation on that stream. Snagged 1879 at Bon Homme Landing. Last appeared at Fort Benton in 1880. Wound up on Red River in Louisiana, burned Nov. 7, 1887.

4442 PENNSYLVANIA

SW p wh b. Brownsville, Pa., 1847. 242 tons. 172 x 27 x 5.6. Pittsburgh-Cincinnati, Capt. R.C. Gray 1847–1848. Later ran Pittsburgh-St. Louis. Stockholders in 1850: R.C. Gray, Wallingford & Co., David Holmes, J.O. H. Scully, James Park, Jr., and W.C. Gray. Sold for Louisville-Nashville trade 1851, Capt. Yocum. Demolished the *MARY PELL* (see) in collision at Lawrenceburg, Ind., Apr. 12, 1851. Off the lists 1852.

4443 PENNSYLVANIA

SW p wh b. Shousetown, Pa. (hull), and completed at Pittsburgh, 1854. 486 tons. 247 x 32 x 6.3. Originally ran Pittsburgh-Cincinnati, Capt. John Klinefelter. The Wheeling suspension bridge was demolished in a windstorm May 18, 1854, and next day the *PENNSYLVANIA* came by with her stacks lowered, a gesture the Wheeling citizens interpreted as a slap in the face. Tempers were hot inasmuch as Pittsburghers had gone to the U.S. Supreme Court to have the bridge declared a hazard to navigation, dangerous to high steamboat smokestacks. When the Pittsburgh-owned *PENNSYLVANIA* put on this exhibition of lowering her stacks, with no bridge there to lower them for; a mob gathered and stones and brickbats flew. The *CITY OF WHEELING* (see) was also at the Wheeling wharf when these fireworks erupted, and both departed forthwith. The

Wheeling *Intelligencer* issue, May 27, 1854, ran a scathing editorial denouncing Capt. John Klinefelter and his tactics headed "Pittsburgh Outrage." Inasmuch as railroads had bonded Pittsburgh and Cincinnati and had drawn away much of the passenger traffic previously handled by the Pittsburgh & Cincinnati Packet Line, the *PENNSYLVANIA* went to the St. Louis-New Orleans trade, owned in 1858 by George Black, R.S. Hayes, Clarke & Thaw, M.W. Beltzhoover, John Klinefelter, and William Bingham, Pittsburghers all. Capt. John Klinefelter continued to command. She exploded her boilers between Helena and Commerce at Ship Island, upbound, Sunday morning, June 13, 1858. The *DIANA, KATE FRISBEE* and *IMPERIAL* rendered aid. The catastrophe is reported in Twain's *Life On the Mississippi* inasmuch as Twain's younger brother Henry was scalded fatally. U.S. Customs set the death toll at 20, but contemporary accounts were not so sanguine. An on-the-spot check estimated 154 lost or missing.

4444 PEOPLE'S FERRY

Stw ferry wh b. Madison, Ind., 1889. 125 x 34.6 x 4.3. Operated at Quincy, Ill., until September 1906 when sold to the Missouri River Packet Co., and renamed *THOMAS H. BENTON* (see).

4445 PEORIA

Stw p wh b. Jeffersonville, Ind., by Howard, 1914. 242.2 x 37.8 x 6.3. Engines, 22's- 7½ ft. Four boilers, each 44" by 30 ft. She was taken away from Howards incomplete, towed by the *DOROTHY BARRETT* to St. Louis where she got her engines and finishing. Made her trial trip at St. Louis, October 1914. Owned by Eagle Packet Co. Capt. W.H. Thorwegan was on the roof for this trial trip, former owner of the *GRAND REPUBLIC* and others. She proceeded to Alton, Ill., and there, in full view of the Leyhe homestead, was put through her paces as elder Commodore Henry Leyhe watched from the porch in a wheelchair (he died within the month.) Ran St. Louis-Peoria and made Mardi Gras trips, Capt. Buck Leyhe, 1916 and 1917. In January 1918 was in the Docks Nest, Paducah, winter quarters. Ice gorges threatened and steam was raised. As the ice broke, the paddlewheel was rolled to offset the strain on the mooring lines. The pressure was too great and the lines commenced snapping. The crew jumped ashore to safety and the *PEORIA,* still working ahead, rounded out into the river, headed downstream, her electric lights ablaze in the darkness. She disappeared in the distance downriver, one of the more dramatic conclusions to a Mississippi steamboat. Nobody knew where she went until some while later when Capt. W.C. Lepper found the capsized hull several miles away. The boilers were recovered and went to the *GOLDEN EAGLE* (see). The machinery was lost, originally from the towboat *ED ROBERTS.*

4446 PEORIA BELLE

Rig? wh b. Peoria, Ill., 1882. 70.3 x 12.6 x 4.4. Still documented 1886, perhaps later.

4447 PEORIA CITY

SW p wh b. Sardis, Oh., 1864. 459 tons. 231 x 35 x 5. Engines, 22's- 7 ft. Three boilers. The hull was built at Sardis and taken to Wheeling for completion. In 1868 she was enlarged at Madison, Ind., to rate 951 tons. Ran St. Louis-Peoria originally. Capt. J. Cartwright was master at one time. Ran in the Missouri River "Railroad Line" 1869. Snagged and lost at Coles Creek, Miss., Feb. 21, 1869.

4448 PEOSTA

SW p wh b. Cincinnati, Oh., 1857. 204 tons. 151.1 x 34.2 x 5.1. Engines, 18's- 5½ ft. Owned in Dubuque, Iowa, and named for the Indian wife of Julien Dubuque. Took Dubuque citizens to Galena to hear Stephen A. Douglas, Aug. 25, 1858. Ran a July 4th excursion to Cassville, Capt. Tom Levens, 1860. Bought by U.S. Navy at Dubuque, June 1863. Became Tinclad #36. Sold at public sale to John W. Waggener, Aug. 17, 1865. Was dismantled to become a wharfboat at Memphis and burned there, foot of Washington St., Dec. 25, 1870, with a big load of cotton on board.

4449 PERCY SWAIN

Stw tb wh b. Reads Landing, Minn. (hull), 1882. 129.8 x 19.7 x 3.5. Originally *MINNIE* which was dismantled fall 1882 and all but hull shipped to Devil's Lake, N.D. Capt. David Swain bought the hull and on it built the *PERCY SWAIN,* subject of this sketch. Engines, cross-compound condensing, the first of a type built by Swain (see *S&D REFLECTOR,* June 1971, page 16). This was a rafter until sold to E.H. Kirchner & Sons, Fountain City, Wis., river contractors, who used her building wing dams, etc. Later sold to Memphis and renamed *PROGRESS.* This information is inserted here to simplify the record of Swain steamboats for the reader.

4450 PERCY SWAIN

Stw p wh b. Stillwater, Minn., 1910. 146 x 27.6 x 4.6. Owned by Capt. David Swain for the Peoria-La Salle trade on Illinois River. Cross-compound condensing engines. This was the best sternwheeler of the Swain fleet. She was sold in 1913 to the Royal Route Co., Vicksburg, Miss. Ran Natchez-Vicksburg, and was lost at Rifle Point, La., July 23, 1922. Capt. George Prince, who had been operating her, bought the *DAVID SWAIN* to replace her. (see *S&D REFLECTOR,* June 1971, page 27).

4451 PERI

Stw U.S. tinclad wh b. Cincinnati, Oh., 1863. 155 tons. 147.5 x 28.1 x 4.5. Engines, 13½'s- 4 ft. Originally packet *REINDEER* (4717) acquired by the U.S. to become Tinclad #57, renamed *PERI,* Apr. 30, 1864. Sold to private owners at Mound City, Ill., Aug. 17, 1865, and redocumented *MARIETTA* on Oct. 3, 1865 (see).

4452 PERRY SMITH

Prop p wh b. Peninsula, Oh., 1866. 67 tons. A converted canalboat. Ran Muskingum River trades ten years, Capt.

James R. Martin, out of Zanesville. Capt. William T. Dawson bought her at Zanesville, July 1876, and put her in the Steubenville-New Cumberland trade in opposition to *IDA*. Off the lists 1878.

4453 PERRYVILLE

Stw ferry wh b. Jeffersonville, Ind., by Howard, 1904. 100.5 x 27 x 3. Engines, 14's- 4 ft. One boiler, 44" by 16 ft. Had a recessed paddlewheel. Operated at Chester, Ill., by Wallace Neville. The Falls City Ferry & Transportation Co. was organized at Louisville in December 1920, and started operations with the *ANDREW CHRISTY* (see) and *PERRYVILLE*, the latter being the night boat, Capt. Milton Campbell. She later went to the St. Clair Ferry & Transfer Co., East St. Louis, Ill. Still listed 1925.

4454 PERSIA

SW p wh b. California, Pa., 1852. 255 tons. 171 x 28.1 x 5.6. First boat built at the McFall yard, California. Built for Capt. Ben F. Hutchison and James A. Hutchison, Pittsburgh. Ran tramp trades Pittsburgh, St. Louis and New Orleans. Burned at the foot of Court Street, Memphis, 8:30 P.M., May 23, 1860. She had come down from Cincinnati and was loading for the return trip, Capt. R.D. Cochran, master, of Pittsburgh. Owned at the time equal shares by Cochran and James Nimick, New Orleans. The ferry *NASHOBA* towed her about a mile downriver, cut her loose, and officers of the *QUEEN OF THE WEST* and *GENERAL PIKE* later reported meeting the hull 20 miles below, on fire.

4455 PERSIAN

SW p wh b. Cincinnati, Oh., 1836. 430 tons. 165 x 28 x 10. Built for New Orleans-Bends trade, Capt. Jesse Hart. Made trips to Shreveport, La. Was reported to have exploded her boilers at Napoleon, Ark., Nov. 1, 1840, with loss of 23 lives and 30 others scalded. In 1843 owned by Capt. James W. Riddle and others of New Orleans. In 1846 Junius Beebe, New Orleans, became involved in ownership and she was in the Union Steam Towboat Co., and in 1850 in the Good Intent Towboat Co. In 1855 owned by the Board of Health, New Orleans and last owner was Capt. William H. Limbert, New Orleans. Off the lists 1859. This was record longevity for a steamboat of her time.

4456 PERU

Stw p wh b. Freedom, Pa., 1848. 128 tons. Operated by Capt. Sharp Hemphill, Pittsburgh. Lost in ice below Wheeling, Feb. 3, 1852.

4457 PET

According to the Marietta, Oh. *Register*, a small boat named *PET*, about 40 feet long, passed out of the Muskingum in latter September 1870. She had been built at Brooklyn, N.Y., and came by way of the Hudson River, Erie Canal, Lake Erie to Cleveland, thence through the Ohio Canal to the Muskingum. She was bound for the Kanawha River to become a salt boat.

4458 PETE WHETSTONE

SW p wh b. Jeffersonville, Ind., by Howard, 1856. 487 tons. 198 x 36 x 6. Louisville-New Orleans, 1857, Capt. Greenlee. She had owners in New Orleans 1858–1861 when she went to Confederate registry. Last known owner was Capt. Joseph R. Shannon, New Orleans.

4459 PETER BALEN

Stw p wh b. Pittsburgh, Pa., 1866. 545 tons. Engines, 16's- 4½ ft. Three boilers. She was advertised at Pittsburgh on her first trip direct to Fort Benton, Mont., where she arrived June 11, 1866, loaded with gold mining equipment. Her passengers had paid $300 each for the trip St. Louis-Fort Benton. Total receipts for the trip were $102,690, of which $70,690 was net profit. As a stunt, she was taken above Fort Benton about 38 miles on June 18, 1866. No steamboat had been that far. Two years later the *GALLATIN* went two miles further, and in 1868 the *TOM STEVENS* did even better. In 1869 was again at Fort Benton, arriving June 18. She returned to Dauphin's Rapids and brought up the balance of her cargo and, after that had been accomplished, started back to St. Louis. Burned on the return at Dauphin's Rapids on July 22, 1869, owned by M.S. Mepham and others.

4460 PETER DALMAU

SW p wh b. Jeffersonville, Ind., by Howard, 1851. 364 tons. 200 x 30 x 6. Apparently went to Mobile, Ala. Does not show up in New Orleans registry. Off the lists 1861.

4461 PETER J. CLARK

Stw p wh b. Lafayette, Ind., 1892. 82.5 x 17.4 x 3.2. Built for Wabash River. Later owned by Capt. J.H. Peckenpaugh, Evansville, Ind., who sold her to Capt. Joseph E. Hogg who had been on the U.S. Lighthouse Tender *JOSEPH HENRY*. She was running Caruthersville-Booth's Point, Capt. George Hogg, when she burned in late January 1900.

4462 PETER TELLON

SW p wh b. New Albany, Ind., 1853. 738 tons. Ran St. Louis-New Orleans. Engines, 27's- 9 ft. Sank and lost at Greenville, Miss., Dec. 22, 1858. Machinery went to the *RUTH* (see). Also spelled *PETER TELLEN*.

4463 PETERS LEE

Stw p wh b. Jeffersonville, Ind. by Howard, 1899. 681 tons. 220 x 42 x 7. Engines, 18's- 8 ft. Three boilers, each 44" by 32 ft. Owned by the Lee Line, Memphis. Built for the Memphis-St. Louis trade. The *BONANZA* (see) ran Cincinnati-Memphis until early 1904, then was refused insurance and discontinued the run. The Lee Line stepped the *PETERS LEE* into the trade, making her first arrival at Cincinnati early April 1904. She brought 100 bales of cotton to Louisville and unloaded them on the wharf, first seen in years, April 1911. The *GEORGIA LEE* replaced her in the trade, and she sank at Lake Providence, La., after hitting a barge as she backed out, August 1913. Capt. William

Stapleton was master, Al Pritchard and Mose Smith, pilots, and William J. Keith, purser. Sank over the hurricane roof.

4464 PETERSBURG

Rig? b. 1866. A small steamboat for service on White and Wabash rivers and named for Petersburg, Pike County, Ind., on the White. She broke her moorings, floated down the Wabash to Hazelton, Ind., and capsized in February 1867.

4465 PETERSBURG

Stw tb wh b. Hazelton, Ind., 1878. 100 x 30 x 3. Enrolled at Evansville, Aug. 10, 1878, owned by Evansville & Terre Haute Railroad Co. Sold to the U.S. Engineers at Hazelton, Ind., in 1881. She was converted into a snagboat, renamed *OSSEO*.

4466 PETREL

Stw U.S. Tinclad wh b. Brownsville, Pa., 1862, originally *DUCHESS* (see). 226 tons. Captured by the Rebels on Yazoo River and they burned her Apr. 22, 1864.*

4467 PETROLIA

Stw p wh b. Allegheny, Pa., 1864. 100 tons. Built for Allegheny River service owned principally by Hamilton McClintock, with Capt. W.H. Kinter, master. Capt. John Gordon took charge soon afterward. On Nov. 18, 1864, while passing under the Freeport, Pa., aquaduct which carried the Pennsylvania Canal over the Allegheny, she lost her pilothouse, but the pilot and pilotwheel were left intact. On Dec. 20, 1864, while leaving Parker's Landing, Pa., a steering oar from a raft came in a stateroom injuring the occupant. Still running to Oil City, Pa., October 1865. Summer 1867 ran on the Monongahela Pittsburgh to Lock 4, Capt. P. Donaldson. The *NEW STATE AND PETROLIA* were the Pittsburgh-Wheeling packets summer 1869, and continued 1870. Sunk in ice at Pittsburgh Jan. 3, 1873.

4468 PETROLIA NO. 2

Stw p wh b. Manchester, Pa., 1864. 91 tons. Owned principally by Hamilton McClintock of Venango County, Pa., an oil operator. First master, Capt. Uriah Walton. Made her first trip to Oil City, Pa., in August 1864 taking advantage of a freshet. She ran up the Allegheny through 1865 and on Dec. 5 that year was advertised to Oleopolis, Pa. Sold to the Allegheny Valley Railroad spring 1866 making connections between Mahoning and Bradys Bend. On Mar. 5, 1868, sank on Wabash River, Ind., laden with flour and corn, and with a loaded barge in tow. Running Evansville-Owensboro-Cannelton in 1869, Capt. John H. Triplett, with John A. Adams, clerk. Snagged and lost fifteen miles below Pocahontas, Ark., on White River on Feb. 14, 1871. A rising river covered the wreck. Then owned by Ellis Bros., Cairo, Ill.

4469 PEYTONA

SW p wh b. Elizabethtown, Pa., 1845. 138 tons. Went to Apalachicola, Fla. Off the lists 1850.

4470 PEYTONA

SW p wh b. Louisville, Ky., 1846. 548 tons. 266 x 34 x 8. Engines, 30½'s- 10 ft. Six boilers. Ran Louisville-New Orleans, Capt. John Shallcross, native of Louisville, who worked his way up being a river engineer. He was active in getting up the original steamboat inspection laws in 1851. On Apr. 30, 1846 she arrived in Louisville with news of the war with Mexico. The *YORKTOWN* carried the dispatches to Cincinnati, and the *CAMBRIA* on to Pittsburgh. The *J.M. WHITE* took the news to St. Louis. In 1848 she once left Louisville at noon and at 8:00 P.M. was landed at Evansville. That same trip she left Paducah at daylight and long before dark was tied up in Memphis. Dismantled in 1852 and her machinery went to *TELEGRAPH NO. 3* (see).

4471 PEYTONA

Stw p wh b. Elizabeth, Pa., 1848. 38 tons. Owned in part by Capt. James Gordon. Made trips Pittsburgh-McKeesport, Capt. Joseph Hendrickson. She was rounding to, to land at Cincinnati May 2, 1852, and overturned. All on board escaped.

4472 PEYTONA

SW p wh b. New Albany, Ind., 1859. 685 tons. 268 x 33 x 8. Engines, 27½'s- 9 ft. Five boilers, each 42" by 32 ft. Ran Louisville-New Orleans, Capt. J.F. Leyden, with Henry C. Landrum, clerk. Landrum later owned her entire. She was taken to Eureka Plantation, 24 miles above Yazoo City, Satartia, Miss., by her Confederate owners at the outbreak of the war. She was burned there by the Confederates to prevent her capture, July 14, 1863.

4473 PEYTONA

SW p wh b. Cincinnati, Oh., 1864. 747 tons. 265 x 42 x 7. Built for Capt. E. Eugene Bowers and variously ran Cincinnati, St. Louis, and Memphis to New Orleans. T. Finnie Smith, Jr., was clerk. Became one of the fleet of the Atlantic & Mississippi Steam Ship Co., and burned at St. Louis, Feb. 26, 1866, along with *DICTATOR, LEVIATHAN,* and *LUNA* (all see).

4474 PHANTOM

Stw p wh b. Madison, Ind., 1864. 179 tons. Running Evansville-Eastport April 1867, Capt. Hodge Brown, with Tom Wilson, clerk. She was taken in the Evansville, Cairo & Memphis Steam Packet Co. On a downbound trip, Sept. 15, 1869, exploded boilers at New Liberty, Ind., fourteen miles above Paducah. Capt. Henry T. Dexter was master. She was reported to have been racing a rival boat, the *CLARA SCOTT*. Five lives were lost, among them George Nicholson, first clerk. This was the first serious accident to boats of the line.

4475 PHAETON

SW p wh b. Freedom, Pa., 1877. 135 x 33. Built for Capt. John McLure, Wheeling, and soon sold to Capt. Steve Dillon and others. Ran Wheeling-Sistersville, a round trip a day. Sold Feb. 10, 1881, to Capt. Pres Ellison who ran her

Manchester-Ripley on the Ohio River. On June 28, 1881, while racing with the *HANDY,* she exploded her boiler at Brooks Bar above Maysville, Ky., with three killed and one drowned.

4476 PHIL ALLIN

SW p wh b. Memphis, Tenn., 1871. 463 tons. 181 x 38 x 6. Engines, 22's- 7 ft. Three boilers. Ran Memphis-Friar's Point, Capt. James Lee. Machinery came from the *C.E. HILLMAN* (see). Dismantled when the *JAMES LEE* (first) was built and the engines went to that boat. Her jackstaff went to the towboat *DICK FULTON* and in 1920 there still was a set of solid walnut furniture on the Lee Line wharfboat at Memphis which had come from her.

4477 PHIL ARMOUR

Stw p wh b. Jeffersonville, Ind., 1880, originally named *THOMAS D. FITE* (see). 149 x 29 x 4.3. Documented at Nashville, Tenn., in 1886, perhaps later.

4478 PHIL E. CHAPPELL

Stw wh b. Grafton, Ill., 1877. 165 x 29 x 4.5. Engines, 15's- 5½ ft. Two boilers. Machinery from *TOM STEVENS* (see). Ran on the Missouri and Osage rivers. Then went to Red River in the Shreveport trade. Sank and lost on Red River, Mar. 10, 1888.

4479 PHIL MORGAN

Rig? p wh b. Charleston, W. Va., 1871. 47 tons. Capt. W.H. Sargeant was bringing cotton seed out of Yazoo River spring 1878 when she exploded her boiler at Reality on Deer Creek and sank immediately. The accident happened Apr. 28, 1878. Mrs. Sargeant and her three children were aboard at the time, uninjured. Three black deckhands were killed and two others injured. Captain Sargeant later ran the *IKE BONHAM* (see).

4480 PHIL SHERIDAN

SW p wh b. Cincinnati, Oh., 1866. 728 tons. 227 x 36.5 x 6. Engines, 22's- 7 ft. Four boilers, each 40″ by 26 ft., with five 9″ flues. Came out in the Wheeling-Cincinnati trade, Capt. Charles Muhleman, with Chris G. Young and Charles Knox, clerks; George Wright and James Hall, engineers; Amos Davis and Phil Anshutz, pilots; Col Harlan, mate, and Henry Habermehl, steward. Left Wheeling on Saturday in competition with *C.E. HILLMAN* (see). Made her trial trip in the Cincinnati harbor Jan. 20, 1866. Capt. Muhleman sent a wire to the wharfboat agent, Wheeling, dated Mar. 7, 1866: "SHERIDAN PASSED TELEGRAPH NO. 3 UNDER WAY FAIR AND SQUARE," a fair show of speed. Capt. P.S. Davidson came aboard at Cincinnati and put money on the barrelhead to buy the *SHERIDAN.* Capt. Muhleman asked for one week's time so he could get another steamer to take the trade. On this last round to Wheeling the *PHIL* got in a storm at Straight Creek below Dover, Ky., lost her stacks overboard, and the damage came to $1,500, this on Mar. 20, 1866. She was delivered to the Davidson Line the next week following repairs. The *POTOMAC* (see) took her place in the Wheeling-Cincinnati trade and the *SHERIDAN* was taken by her purchasers to the Upper Mississippi. There she proved a stepper, vying for the speed supremacy St. Louis-St. Paul. She came back once afterward to the upper Ohio, arriving in Pittsburgh, Mar. 25, 1870, loading out direct for St. Paul. Capt. E.V. Holcombe was her master on the occasion, with Lon Bryson and John Shouse, pilots. While being hauled on the marine ways at La Crosse for repairs, the cradles let go and she sank, this in 1876, and she was dismantled there. Her machinery went to the *BELLE of MINNETONKA* on Lake Minnetonka, and after that to the Yukon River packet *SUSIE.*

4481 PHILADELPHIA

SW p wh b. Shousetown, Pa. (hull) and completed at Pittsburgh, 1854. 504 tons. 252 x 33.5 x 6.1. Engines, 26's- 8 ft. Six boilers each 36″ by 28 ft. Paddlewheels 37½ ft. diameter, working 12 ft. buckets. Built for the Pittsburgh-Cincinnati trade, Capt. Redmund J. Grace part owner along with R.S. Hayes, William Frampton, Clarke & Thaw, William Bingham, M.W. Beltzhoover, and James Holmes. Dunning Foster, brother of composer Stephen Collins Foster, died at the Broadway Hotel, Cincinnati, Mar. 31, 1856. He had lately commanded the *NORA* (see) and his remains were brought to Pittsburgh aboard the *PHILADELPHIA* for burial. David Holmes, R.J. Grace, and Hervey Allen, three of his river friends, prepared Resolutions of Respect in the name of the Pittsburgh Marine Association. She sank at Steubenville, Oh., upbound, May 28, 1856 while unloading sugar, and was quickly raised. Capt. Clifford B. Wayne bought her for the St. Louis-New Orleans trade, ran her briefly, selling her to the St. Louis & Memphis Packet Co. In 1861 making St. Louis-New Orleans trips, Capt. George Willard. Went to U.S. war service 1862.

4482 PHILIP DODDRIDGE

Stw p wh b. Zanesville, Oh., 1848. 116 tons. Came out in the Pittsburgh-Beverly (Muskingum River) trade, Capt. E.F. Moore, with W.D. Meeks, clerk. Ran there regularly 1848–1849, and in 1850, same master, ran Beverly-Zanesville. At odd times ran excursionists from Pittsburgh to Greenwood Gardens (located in the Manchester section). Off the lists 1852.

4483 PHILIP PENNYWITT

SW p wh b. Cincinnati, Oh., 1849. 246 tons. 180 x 33 x 6.3. She was outfitted at Louisville, and then made a trip from Cincinnati to New Orleans, Capt. Robert Beatty, part owner, along with Philip Pennywitt, Van Buren, Ark., Snagged and lost at Van Buren, May 13, 1851.

4484 PIASA

Prop yacht sh b. Alton, Ill., 1895. 44.4 x 6.7 x 3.3. Documented at St. Louis 1896, maybe later.

4485 PIASA

Stw p wh b. Mobile, Ala., 1899, originally named *MARY S. BLEES* (see). She arrived at New Orleans fall 1914 with original name, ran to Baton Rouge briefly, and then was sold June 1915 to William Ruprecht, St. Louis. She was altered by removing the cotton guards, etc. and was entered in the St. Louis-Beardstown, Ill., trade, Capt. Milt Harry. Sold February 1917 to Eagle Packet Co., St. Louis, who changed her name to *PIASA* and used her as an extra boat. After the 1918 ice had wrecked other Eagle Packet boats, she ran St. Louis-Peoria until replaced by *GOLDEN EAGLE* (see) and then ran St. Louis-Alton until 1927, the last regular in that run. She was retired at St. Louis and dismantled in 1934. Capt. Aubrey D. Haynes II, bought parts for souvenirs and took them to his home near Mound City, Ill.

4486 PICAYUNE

Stw p wh b. Wheeling, W. Va., 1846. 48 tons. A small passenger carrier, no guards, built for Bayou Teche, La., Capt. Samuel Irwin. The editor of the *Wheeling Daily News* went aboard to procure details, was warmly received, and the boat's skipper spoke only French. But, to be agreeable, the skipper wrote out all of the information in French, handed it to the editor, who accepted it with a flourish and printed it in entirety in his paper—still in French—headed TABLEAU. Off the lists 1851.

4487 PICAYUNE

From the *Pittsburgh Gazette,* July 2, 1878: "They have a river craft at Pine Bluff (Ark.) called the *PICAYUNE.* It is ready at all times to carry people or freight up and down the brown-colored Arkansas. She runs to Wildcat above and Swan Lake below Pine Bluff."

4488 PICAYUNE NO. 2

Stw p wh b. Franklin, La., 1856. 221 tons. Off the lists 1859.

4489 PICAYUNE NO. 3

Stw p wh b. Elizabeth, Pa., 1859. 136 tons. Went to Franklin, La. Running New Orleans-Attakapas, Capt. H.M. Broad, 1861. To Confederate registry that year.

4490 PIKE

SW p wh b. Cincinnati, Oh., 1852. 245 tons. Owned by the U.S. Mail Line Co. and succeeded *PIKE NO. 9* (see), Louisville-St. Louis, Capt. Pat Rogers, who was in addition a considerable mechanic. He was a double-ender, both captain and engineer. Ran an engine works in Cincinnati and was a founder of the Cincinnati Marine Ways there. He died December 1870 and a side-wheeler was named for him (see). *PIKE* was lost by snagging at Wilkinson's Landing, Big Eddy, near Cape Girardeau, Mo., May 10, 1854, with loss of ten lives.

4491 PIKE

Prop p wh b. Peninsula, Oh., 1864. 38 tons. Probably handled produce boats, and was long documented at Cincinnati. Off the lists in 1884.

4492 PIKE NO. 7

SW p wh b. Cincinnati, Oh., 1844. 480 tons. John A. Roebling, the bridge builder, measured her at Cincinnati in the summer of 1846, and remarked that she was the largest boat then operating in the Cincinnati-Louisville trade. Owned by U.S. Mail Line Co. From waterline to stack tops she was 69 ft. In February 1845 President-elect James K. Polk came up on her Louisville to Cincinnati en route to his inauguration. She was the last command of Capt. John Armstrong, who lived many years on a farm abreast of Locust Bar, above Madison, Ind. He lived to be 90, and died there Feb. 2, 1880. He retired from *PIKE NO. 7* in 1847 at which time Jacob Strader and James Gorman sold their interests in the Mail Line. A reorganization was brought about as the result of a "hot" competition battle between the Mail Line and Capts. Ed Montgomery and J.H. Barker who ran *NORTH AMERICA* and *MOUNTAINEER* in the Louisville-Cincinnati trade. The Mail Line absorbed the competition, thus introducing Pat Rogers, Thomas Sherlock, Charles G. Pearce, Ed Montgomery, J.B. Summons, and J.H. Barker as stockholders. *PIKE NO. 7* was dismantled in 1849.

4493 PIKE NO. 8

SW p wh b. Cincinnati, Oh., 1845. 238 tons. Owned by the U.S. Mail Line Co. Used as a summer low water boat. Dismantled 1850 and her machinery went to *GULNARE* (see).

4494 PIKE NO. 9

SW p wh b. Cincinnati, Oh., 1847. 239 tons. 178 x 26 x 6.5. Engines, 24's- 8 ft. Four boilers. Her complete measurements appear in *Wheeling Bridge.* She came out new owned by M.G. Anders, Z.M. Sherley, P.W. Strader, and Thomas Fitzgerald. This group entered her, and also the *FASHION* (see) in the Louisville-Cincinnati trade in competition to the U.S. Mail Line boats, evening departures. Soon this was changed to morning departures, the one-way fare dropped to one dollar and the fight continued six weeks. The Mail Line gave in and Capt. James Montgomery, New Albany, Ind., became first president of the formal U.S. Mail Co. Z.M. Sherley soon succeeded him. *PIKE NO. 9* ran Louisville-St. Louis, the first venture of the line in that trade, later expanded to daily departures. Commanded by Capt. J.E. Montgomery, she took many Louisville citizens on their way west to the gold fields. Off the lists in 1850.

4495 PIKE UNION NO. 1

SW ferry wh b. New Albany, Ind., 1860. 94 tons. Operated in the St. Louis area until replaced by *PIKE UNION NO. 2* (see).

4496 PIKE UNION NO. 2

SW ferry wh b. New Albany, Ind., 1868. 50 tons. Operated in the St. Louis area. Off the lists 1871.

4497 PIKETON

SW p wh b. Piketon, Oh., 1862. 52 tons. Piketon is on the

Scioto River about midway between Portsmouth and Chillicothe, Oh. Off the lists 1864.

4498 PIKETON

Built for Big Sandy River, c. 1870. Sunk at Ironton, Oh., latter April 1871 by the *FLEETWOOD* and was raised at the expense of the Cincinnati, Big Sandy & Pomeroy Packet Co. A new hull was being built for her at Newman's yard, Ironton, June 1871.

4499 PILGRIM

Stw p wh b. Belle Vernon, Pa., 1864. 139 tons. New at Pittsburgh in September 1864 loading for St. Louis and Keokuk, Capt. D.Z. Brickell. Bought by Capt. J.C. McVay and others in April 1865 for Pittsburgh-Zanesville trade replacing *JULIA* (see). Snagged and lost 30 miles below Helena, Ark., Dec. 6, 1867.

4500 PILGRIM

Prop p wh b Mason City, W. Va., 1891. She was built by Capt. Marlin Brown and others for short trades in the Gallipolis-Pomeroy area on Ohio River. Off the lists 1895.

4501 PILGRIM

Sw ex sh b. Jeffersonville, Ind., by Howard, 1916. 202 x 36.4 x 6.1. Machinery from *CORONA* (see). Ran excursions in the Louisville area. Sold 1924 to St. Louis and rebuilt into a tourist boat named *HARRY G. DREES* (see).

4502 PILOT

Stw p wh b. Freedom, Pa., 1845. 72 tons. Said to have been the first boat built by William J. Kountz, Pittsburgh. Was at Galena in September 1846. Off the lists 1848.

4503 PILOT

Stw p wh b. Le Claire, Iowa, 1882. 116.8 x 21.2 x 3.7. Built as a rafter, she ran the Davenport-Clinton trade on occasion, and after 1900 made trips Nashville-Burnside on the Cumberland and ran short trades on the lower Ohio. Engines, 10½'s- 4'4". Rebuilt late in 1903 and documented as a new boat named *PEERLESS* (see).

4504 PILOT NO. 2

Stw p wh b. Christler's Landing, Pa., 1847. 93 tons. Capt. William J. Kountz ran her that summer on the Allegheny, Pittsburgh-Freeport, after the Freeport aqueduct burned. In 1850 running Pittsburgh-Point Pleasant, Capt. Shunk. Snagged and lost at Wheeling, Va., Aug. 22, 1852.

4505 PIN OAK

Stw p wh b. Hermann, Mo., 1888. 95 x 17.5 x 2.2. Engines, 8"- 2½ ft. One boiler. Owned by Hermann Ferry & Packet Co., for Gasconade River. Sold 1896 to Archie Bryan and E.W. Wild. Turned over and sank in Sandy Hook Bend on July 29, 1896, this near Wyss Landing, Mo.

4506 PINE BLUFF

Stw p wh b. Elizabeth, Pa., 1859. 153 tons. Running Arkansas River-New Orleans, Capt. L. Wilson, 1862. Was at Pittsburgh, Pa., loading for Arkansas River, Capt. Taylor, June 16, 1866. Burned Dec. 16, 1866, in the mouth of Licking River, opposite Cincinnati. Rebuilt, and in 1870 was running Evansville-Owensboro-Rockport-Grandview, Capt. Lafayette Elder, with John A. Adams, clerk. Burned at Evansville Nov. 21, 1870, along with *NORMAN, CITY OF EVANSVILLE* and the wharfboat.

4507 PINE BLUFF

Stw p wh b. Little Rock, Ark., 1876. 178 tons. Capt. Thomas J. Darragh and others ran her Little-Rock-Fort Smith, connecting with *ROSA MILLER* to Pine Bluff. Sank downbound at Tindell's Landing, 40 miles above Little Rock, Feb. 14, 1877.

4508 PINE GROVE

Stw p wh b. Cincinnati, Oh., 1864. 247 tons. 164 x 32 x 4.5. Dumont engines, 14½'s- 4½ ft. Two boilers. Owned by Capt. Robert Hamilton and Capt. Lon Bryson. Named for Pine Grove Furnace operated by Means, Kyle & Co. Ran Cincinnati-Pittsburgh through spring of 1865, then made trips Pittsburgh-St. Louis. Capt. John W. Anawalt with Lon Bryson, clerk, in the Pittsburgh-Cincinnati trade in June 1866. Sold to Nashville & Cincinnati Packet Co., in 1867, with Capt. S.F. Hildrith, master, and R.W. Wise, clerk. Burned at Cincinnati Aug. 16, 1868, along with *POTOMAC, EZRA PORTER,* and *DELAWARE.*

4509 PINEKNOT

Stw p wh b. on Pearl River, Miss., 1879. 83.6 x 17.4 x 3.7. 28 tons. Owned by B.D. Mitchell, St. Tammany Parish. First master was Capt. B.D. Mitchell.

4510 PINK PONEY

SW p wh b. Louisville, Ky., 1852. 205 tons. 142.5 x 32 x 5. Apparently went to Mobile, also called *PINK TONEY.* Documented at New Orleans July 1858 owned by Emile LaSere of that city, Capt. J.B. Lockwood, master. Lost in the Gulf of Mexico at a point about midway between Brownsville, Tex., and Tampico, Mex., at 20°40′ N, 90°12′ W, Aug. 28, 1858. Also known as *POYDRAS.*

4511 PINK VARBLE

Stw p wh b. Louisville, Ky., 1865. 320 tons. Ran on the lower Ohio, Cumberland, and Tennessee. Running Louisville-Tennessee River in 1870, Capt. N.C. Selby, with John Briggs, clerk. Sunk and lost spring 1873 just above Auburn on the Arkansas River, having made a trip there from Louisville, Ky. Her machinery was recovered and sold at Memphis that September for $300.

4512 PIOMINGO

Stw U.S. inspection sh b. Carondelet, Mo., 1882, originally *MISSISSIPPI* (see), which was transferred from the Mississippi River Commission to the U.S. Engineers, West Memphis, 1919, and renamed. Still in their fleet 1925. Later sold and was stripped to the hull, used as a barge in the Warner & Tamble fleet, Memphis, late as 1961.

4513 PIONEER

SW p wh b. Elizabethtown, Pa., 1846. 209 tons. Off the lists 1852.

4514 PIONEER

SW p wh b. Louisville, Ky., 1848. 89 tons. Off the lists 1850.

4515 PIONEER

Stw p wh b. New Albany, Ind., 1863. 141 tons. 129 x 28.8 x 4.3. Bought in 1865 by Red River Packet Co., G.L. Kouns, pres., Capt. W.T. Scovell. Sold March 1869 to Capt. George E. Wilkerson, New Orleans. Sold that December to Amelie Laurent, Plaquemine, La., Capt. J.L. Petit. Sold March 1870 to Capt. Abraham Samuels, who commanded, and Richard A. Kearney, both of Plaquemine, equal shares. Off the lists 1873.

4516 PIONEER

Stw p wh b. Wilmington, Ill., 1864. 21 tons. 60.1 x 15.6 x 3.7. Had been operating out of Vicksburg when bought March 1868 by Capt. John Delaney, New Orleans. Had several changes of ownership at New Orleans, last being Capt. C.D. Bunce. Off the lists 1871.

4517 PIONEER

Stw p wh b. Gasconade, Mo., 1866. 50 tons. 102.8 x 20.4 x 3.5. Made a trip to New Orleans owned in part by W.O. Clark and F. Thurman, St. Louis. Sold December 1866 to Capt. William H. King, New Orleans. Sold to Capt. J.W. Carlton and others, New Orleans. Sold June 1868 to John R. Clarke, Union Parish, La. Sold March 1869 to Capt. James Edmunds, New Orleans. Sank and lost at Trenton, La., Sept. 14, 1870.

4518 PIONEER

Prop p wh b. Portsmouth, Oh., 1867. 63 tons. Went to the Memphis area. Burned at New Orleans in 1872.

4519 PIONEER CITY

Stw ferry wh b. Marietta, at Knox Yard, 1891. 90.4 x 24.5 x 3. Engines, 9" - 3 ft. One boiler, 42" by 16 ft. Replaced *EMMA UHL* in ferry service Marietta-Williamstown. When the highway bridge was completed 1903 she was owned by Beman Dawes, Capt. John W. Ryder, master. Sold Nov. 1905 to Martin F. Noll and was leased to tow railroad transfer barge at Parkersburg in the Little Kanawha for the B&O. Had her guards cut off and was given tow knees for this service. Sold April 1907 to Central Wharf & Ferry Co., Central City, W. Va., Ellis C. Mace, managing owner. Rebuilt at Pt. Pleasant, W. Va., and renamed *CENTRAL CITY* (see).

4520 PIOTA

SW p wh b. New Albany, Ind., 1852. 250 tons. 129 x 27.8 x 5.2. Owned by Silas F. Miller, New Albany, with Capt. Edward Parker, master. Ran Alexandria-Natchitoches. Burned at Algiers, La., on her second trip in 1856.

4521 PIOTA

SW p wh b. New Albany, Ind., 1858. 293 tons. 187 x 30 x 5.5. Capt. Edward Parker, master and part owner. Enrolled at New Orleans in March 1859. Burned at Carrollton, La., June 4, 1859.

4522 PITSER MILLER

SW p wh b. Freedom, Pa., 1848. 158 tons. 126 x 26 x 5.2. Went to Memphis. Exploded boilers at the mouth of White River, Jan. 23, 1852, with loss of three lives. Capt. J. Frank Hicks started steamboating on her in 1848. Sold to New Orleans January 1853, owned by Sidale, Greene & Co., Capt. C. Alexander. Sold June 1853 to Alexander Landry, St. Martin Parish. Off the lists 1857.

4523 PITTSBURGH

SW p wh b. Shousetown, Pa., 1851. 509 tons. 267.9 x 30 x 6.1. Engines, 31½'s- 8 ft. Five boilers, each 42" by 30 ft. Built for Pittsburgh-Cincinnati trade, Capt. William J. Kountz. Later masters: Capt. Hugh Campbell and Capt. James O'Neal. Left Pittsburgh Apr. 23, 1852, and ran to Cincinnati in 25 hours 3 minutes (470 miles) making seven stops en route and burned coal only, fastest since the *J.M. WHITE* of 1844 (see). Knocked down her stacks on the Wheeling suspension bridge Mar. 16, 1855, with damage to pilothouse and texas and no injuries. Dismantled 1857.

4524 PITTSBURG

U.S. gunboat wh b. Carondelet, Mo., 1861 by James B. Eads. 176.5 x 52 x 6.5. Engines, 22's- 6 ft. Recess wheel. Sold at public sale Nov. 29, 1865, at Mound City, Ill., to J. Ellis for $3,100. Used as a wharfboat and was abandoned on the rock bar above Smithland, Ky., in June 1870.

4525 PITTSBURGH

Stw p wh b. Cincinnati, Oh., 1879. 250 x 39.2 x 5.8. Engines, 21's- 7 ft. Three boilers, each 47" by 28 ft., 6 flues. Paddlewheel 21 ft. dia. working 28 ft. 6 flues. Paddlewheel 21 ft. dia. working 28 ft. buckets. Drew 24" light when new. Built at the Cincinnati Marine Ways for the Cincinnati & Pittsburgh Packet Co., David Gibson, president. Original crew: Capt. John Thornburg, master; Frank Shunk, clerk; Joe and Jim Witten, pilots; Buck Nye and Dore Moore, engineers; David Little, mate, and Garrett Sellman, steward. Buck Nye was father of Capt. Henry Nye. Once ran from Wheeling to Pittsburgh (90 miles) towing model barge *BUTTERCUP*. Capt. Jim Rowley (Jr.) was cub pilot on her when she ran Huntington to Cincinnati in seven hours on 30 ft. in the river; no landings below Ashland. Ran Pittsburgh-St. Louis by 1882. Sold to the Diamond Jo Line on the upper Mississippi and ran St. Louis-St. Paul until demolished in the St. Louis tornado, May 1896. A new upper works was built on the hull and she emerged as the *DUBUQUE* (see).

4526 PLAIN CITY

SW p wh b. Madison, Ind., 1863, originally named *EMMA BROWN* (see) and later U.S. tinclad #50 named *GAZELLE*, which was sold to private owners and renamed *PLAIN CITY,* Oct. 23, 1865. Ran Louisville-Bowling Green, Capt. W.S. Van Meter, with E.C. Jenkins, clerk. Later was sold South and off the lists 1869.

4527 PLANET

Stw p wh b. Pittsburgh, Pa., 1844. 121 tons. At Galena from St. Louis, May 1847. Off the lists 1850.

4528 PLANET

SW p wh b. Cincinnati, Oh., 1856. 604 tons. Built for Capt. Henry A. Ealer and others. Primarily a freight boat. Her lengthy cabin had no staterooms. Capt. John Molloy commanded in the late 1850s. She was in the flotilla to Pittsburg Landing, Tenn., during the war. Ran St. Louis-New Orleans, Capt. J.T. Burdeau in 1861. Stranded and lost at College Point, La., Feb. 1, 1864.

4529 PLANTER

SW p wh b. New Albany, Ind., 1846. 199 tons. Bought in 1847 by Capt. L.T. Belt and his brother Francis T. Belt. On Jan. 5, 1848, she exploded boilers while loading grain at Jones Ferry, Twelve Mile Island, on the Illinois River, demolishing the cabin. Five lives were lost. Capt. Francis T. Belt was in command at the time, later killed when the *SALUDA* (see) exploded. Claiborne Wolff was steward. She was rebuilt. Often made St. Louis-New Orleans trips. Lost in a tornado at St. Louis summer 1851.

4530 PLANTER

SW p wh b. Freedom, Pa., 1848. 128 tons. In October 1848 at Cairo bound for New Orleans with 103 slaves owned by two firms at Louisville. Added six more at Cairo, "a hearty lot happy and careless of the future" to be sold South. Renamed *ELIZA* (see) Mar. 22, 1851.

4531 PLANTER

SW p wh b. New Albany, Ind., 1852. 182 tons. Running Yazoo River-Vicksburg 1855, Capt. Edward Phelps. In 1856 New Orleans-Jefferson, Capt. D.D. Atkinson. Rescued passengers from the sunken *ST. CHARLES* at Devil's Elbow near Shreveport, June 5, 1857. Snagged and lost at Fort Adams, Miss., Dec. 30, 1857.

4532 PLANTER

SW p wh b. Wheeling, Va., 1860. 343 tons. Owned in part by Capt. Charles V. Wells, Sistersville, Va., who was master of Wheeling Union Line's *VIRGINIA* (see) prior. He cast his lot with the Lost Cause and *PLANTER* was captured by the U.S., June 15, 1863, and served in USQMD. Sold to private hands March 1866 and served out of Mobile. Went to U.S. Navy in 1875.

4533 PLANTER NO. 2

SW p wh b. Baresville, Oh., 1860. 58 tons. Marooned up Red River during the war. She was approaching the wharf at New Orleans July 8, 1864, and failed to back; some say she never slowed down. Crashed the dock and was a complete wreck.

4534 PLATTE VALLEY

SW p wh b. Jeffersonville, Ind., by Howard, 1857. 220 x 33 x 5. Engines, 22's- 7 ft. Three boilers, each 44" by 26 ft. Paddlewheels 32 ft. dia. working 8½ ft. buckets. Built for Missouri River service. In 1859 running St. Joseph-Kansas City connecting with Hannibal & St. Joe Railroad, Capt. W.C. Postal. She then entered St. Louis-Vicksburg trade, Capt. William H. Blake, the first of several packets he commanded in that trade (others were *RUBIGON, BELLE ST. LOUIS, JOHN B. MAUDE).* Sank at Devils Island near St. Louis September 1864, soon raised. Was in U.S. transport service during the war. Struck the wreck of the Confederate gunboat *JEFF THOMPSON* just below Memphis, Jan. 18, 1867, and tore out her bottom and sides. Sank broadside to the current. Life loss was not accurately determined, but called "considerable," first estimates said 60.

4535 PLATTE VALLEY

Center wheel ferry wh b. Farley, Mo., 1872. One engine, 10"- 3 ft. Owned by T.W. Nolan. Snagged above Leavenworth, Kans., Mar. 29, 1876, and went down opposite the town, lost.

4536 PLOUGH BOY

SW p wh b. St. Louis, Mo., 1848. 248 tons. 165 x 29. Three boilers. Ran St. Louis-Missouri River. Snagged and lost above Providence, Mo., Oct. 6, 1848.

4537 PLOW BOY

Stw p wh b. Stillwater, Minn., 1876. 36 tons. Burned at Arrow Rock, Mo., on the Missouri River, July 7, 1877.

4538 PLOW BOY

Rig? wh b. Pittsburgh, Pa., 1879. 185 tons. Documented at Memphis until lost in 1882.

4539 PLOW BOY

Center wheel p wh b. Sioux City, Iowa, 1884. 29 tons. 70 x 18 x 3. One engine, 7" by 12". One boiler. Sank at Rocheport, Mo. loaded with corn, Sept. 3, 1885. Snagged three miles below Rocheport, Oct. 29, 1890. Snagged between mouth of Grand River and DeWitt, Mo., May 6, 1897. Boiler and engines salvaged.

4540 POCAHONTAS

SW p wh b. Cincinnati, Oh., 1849. 397 tons. Went to St. Louis. Reported collapsing a flue on the Arkansas below Dardanelle, Mar. 14, 1852, killing eight and scalding many. Burned and lost at Island 78, Mississippi River, Apr. 16, 1852, with loss of ten lives.

4541 POCAHONTAS

SW p wh b. Cincinnati, Oh., 1857. 163 tons. 180 x 32. In latter March 1862 at Pittsburgh, Capt. Henry B. Staines, running to Cincinnati during low water. Louisville-Nashville, April 1862, Capt. Staines. Snagged and lost near Fort Randall, S.D., on the Missouri River, Aug. 9, 1866, and had been carrying Indian supplies there. An island at the scene was called Pocahontas Island thereafter.

4542 POLAND

Stw p wh b. Elizabeth, Pa., 1857. 161 tons. Ran Louisville-Nashville, Capt. Gracey, with Ed J. Frisbie, clerk, 1859. Louisville-Tennessee River to Florence, Ala., Capt. Gracey, February 1861. Taking U.S. army wagons, etc., Cincinnati to Mount Vernon, Ind., January 1862. At Cincinnati June 1, 1864, having been absent from that port since the prior September, having been in U.S. service on the Cumberland, Tennessee, White, and lower Mississippi. A Cincinnati dispatch dated Mar. 3, 1865, reports that David Gibson & Co. had sold her to Henry Ames & Co., St. Louis for $16,000. She was lost on Yazoo River in collision with the *IDAHO* with loss of twelve lives, 1865.

4543 POLAR STAR

SW p wh b. St. Louis, Mo., 1852. 309 tons. Built for St. Louis-Missouri River. Running to St. Joe, 1853 "the holder of a set of polished deer antlers" which she held until 1855 when *JAMES H. LUCAS* bettered her time. Was in U.S. service during the war and spent the spring season of 1862 "tied to one tree at Pittsburg Landing for some reason or other." Off the lists 1865.

4544 POLLY SOUTH

Rig? ferry wh b. Belle Vernon, Pa., 1858. Was the ferry at Belle Vernon, having succeeded the horse ferries *SWAN* and *BELLE VERNON.* Run by James French and sons Willie and Sylvester. "The boat becoming more or less unfit for duty, and always an expense to the owner, gave way to a rope ferry." The engine in 1880 was in use at Mapleton, Pa., on the *PRR,* 159 miles east of Pittsburgh, at the plant of the Speer White Sand Co.

4545 POMEROY

Stw p wh b. Parkersburg, Va., 1857. 127 tons. Ran Parkersburg-Pomeroy, spring 1858. Cincinnati and Kanawha River, Capt. H.W. Bayes, with W.J. Carroll, clerk, 1859. Was running in the Minnesota River, 1861, Capt. Bell. Off the lists 1864.

4546 PONTCHARTRAIN

SW gunboat wh b. New Albany, Ind., 1859, originally *LIZZIE SIMMONS* (see). In early 1862 the Confederates made of her a gunboat and changed her name. Burned opposite Little Rock, Ark., by U.S. gunboat *GEN. PRICE,* Sept. 10, 1863. In July 1871 low water bared the wreck for all to see.

4547 PONTIAC

SW p wh b. Cincinnati, Oh., 1846. 184 tons. Snagged at Smith's Bend, above Doniphan, Mo. on the Missouri River, with cargo of whiskey, Capt. Tom Baker, Apr. 10, 1852.

4548 PONTIAC NO. 2

SW p wh b. Cincinnati, Oh., 1850. 269 tons. Advertised at New Orleans for Louisville and Cincinnati, September 1851, Capt. Warden. Came in collision with *MOLLIE GARTH* below Owensboro, Ky., Nov. 29, 1851, with loss of twenty lives and destruction of both steamers.

4549 POPLAR BLUFF

Rig? wh b. Jeffersonville, Ind., 1883, originally named *WEBB CITY.* Renamed prior to 1886.

4550 PORT ALLEN

Stw ferry wh b. Lake Charles, La., 1888 originally named *HAZEL* (see). Renamed by Baton Rouge Transportation Co., prior to 1925, and still serving 1929, perhaps later.

4551 PORTER

Stw p wh b. Shousetown, Pa., 1860. 65 tons. Went to the St. Louis area. Off the lists in 1873.

4552 PORTIA

Stw p-tb wh b. Portia, Ark., 1890. 76 x 20 x 2.6. Ran on White River, Ark., Capt. Frederick L. Inman. Still listed 1896, maybe later.

4553 PORTLAND

SW p wh b. Louisville, Ky., 1847. 57 tons. Burned and lost at Portland, Ky., May 6, 1851, with loss of one life.

4554 PORTSMOUTH

Stw p wh b. Ravenswood, Va., 1857. 169 tons. Snagged and lost at Weston, Mo., Feb. 26, 1860.

4554A PORTSMOUTH

Recess wheel ferry wh b. Pt. Pleasant, W. Va., 1895. 95 x 31 x 4.5. Operated by the Chesapeake & Ohio Railroad at Portsmouth, Oh. In summer of 1904, towing Newman's Water Circus she sank near Pittsburgh and had to be docked. The *KATIE Mc* took the circus back down the river. While in the Pittsburgh area she was acquired by a group of Sewickley, Pa. gentlemen, Edward and Chris Becker, and Samuel Anderson, plus H.B. Parker of Bellevue, Pa. They entered her in the ferry trade Sewickley-Stoops Ferry, July 10, 1904, Capt. Joe Briggs, master. Two old-time Sewickley rivermen came aboard to take a hand at the wheel, Capt. John Clarke Anderson, then 76, and Capt. John Bevington. Although the project was short-lived, this was the only steam ferry ever to ply at that crossing. Lost in ice that winter opposite Sewickley, Pa.

4555 PORTSMOUTH & SPRINGVILLE

SW ferry wh b. Portsmouth, Oh., 1865. 44 tons. Served between Portsmouth and Springville. Off the lists 1875.

4556 POST BOY

SW p wh b. Cincinnati, Oh., 1851. 158 tons. 140 x 24 x 5. Ran New Orleans-Grand Encore, 1852. Burned at New Orleans along with *JOHN SWAZEY* and *TEXAS,* Feb. 15, 1853. Rebuilt by William S. Wright & Co., New Orleans, who sold her to Capt. A.P. Boardman, Nov. 29, 1853. Sold to Capt. Paul Lacroix, New Orleans, May 1856. Sold July 1857 to C. Meranne, New Orleans, Capt. Frederick Probst, master. Exploded and lost at New Orleans, Jan. 10, 1858, with loss of three lives.

4557 POST BOY

SW p wh b. Elizabeth, Pa., 1859. 348 tons. 215 x 33 x 5.5. Owned by Capt. E.W. Gould and ran St. Louis-Naples on Illinois River. Her crew: Capt. James Abrams, master; O.S. Watt and L.M. Chipley, clerks; Enoch P. King and T.B. Chipley, pilots; Wash McCann and William Mitchell, engineers; Hugh Davis and Hosey Densmore, mates; Fielding Corbin, steward. She was in U.S. service during the war, was dispatch boat for the Vicksburg fleet and also at Arkansas Post, and on White River at Clarendon and De Vall's Bluff. Returned to St. Louis and was burned in the fire Sept. 13, 1863, along with *JESSE K. BELL, HIAWATHA,* and *IMPERIAL* (all see). Confederate spies were the arsonists by their own later admissions. Captain Gould later published *Gould's History of River Navigation.*

4558 POST BOY

SW p wh b. Pittsburgh, Pa., 1864. 475 tons. Capt. Pink Varble took her over the falls at Louisville downbound on her first trip with three ft. on the marks, a feat. Went to St. Louis and ran to New Orleans. In collision with the *NIAGARA* at the mouth of the St. Francis River, Oct. 20, 1865, resulting in loss of that boat (see) and seventy-five lives. In 1869 running New Orleans-Bayou Sara, and also up Red River. Brought a load of iron ore up the Ohio, November 1871. Dismantled at Memphis 1872.

4559 POTOMAC

Stw p wh b. Freedom, Pa., 1857. 173 tons. Ran Pittsburgh-St. Louis, Capt. W.C. Harry. Burned at St. Louis May 7, 1859, along with others, owned by Capt. Harry and Jonathan Crane, Rochester, Pa. Harry was father of Capt. Milt Harry (see *JOSIE HARRY,* etc.).

4560 POTOMAC

Stw p wh b. Wheeling, W. Va., 1865. 974 tons. 180 x 33.5 x 5.5. Engines, 18's- 5½ ft. Three boilers, each with five 10″ flues. Owned by Capt. Theodore Fink and others, Wheeling. Ran Cincinnati-Wheeling. Sold to Capt. Charles Muhleman who had just disposed of the *PHIL SHERIDAN* (see) and was continued in the trade, Muhleman, master, with Chris Young, clerk. Burned at the Cincinnati Marine Ways, Aug. 16, 1868, along with *PINE GROVE, EZRA PORTER,* and *DELAWARE.* Captain Muhleman then bought the *MAJOR ANDERSON* for the trade (see).

4561 POTOMAC

SW p wh b. Cincinnati, Oh., 1870. 833 tons. Built for Capt. Theodore Fink, Wheeling, and entered Wheeling-Cincinnati trade. Made only a trip or so when low water shut her out, in spring of 1870. Sold to Capt. John N. Shunk and others for Louisville-New Orleans trade. Rammed and sank the "racer" *ROBT. E. LEE* opposite Natchez, Miss., Dec. 21, 1870. Was in St. Louis-New Orleans trade June 1872, Capt. J.W. Batchelor, master, with S.J. Batchelor, clerk. Bought by Capt. Wash Honshell and others when the C&O reached Huntington and she and *FLEETWOOD* ran Huntington-Cincinnati. The *POTOMAC* proved too slow, and went to the Cincinnati-Pomeroy trade along with *OHIO NO. 4* and *TELEGRAPH.* In 1881 Capt. Will Kirker, master, with C.M. Phister, clerk. In 1882, same, with James A. Wirthlin, 2nd clerk. She was dismantled soon after, and the hull served as a salt barge, finally sinking above Hartford City, W. Va., where it lay for some time. Ice turned it bottom side up. The *E.A. WOODRUFF* removed the wreckage.

4562 POTOSI

Stw ferry wh b. Dubuque, Iowa, 1893, originally named *TEAL* (see). Rebuilt in 1905 to measure 85 x 19.6 x 4. Potosi Brewing Co. bought her and changed the name, 1905. Capt. George Krubb was master later. Sold to city of St. Charles, Mo., and was renamed *ST. CHARLES* for ferry service there. Later sold to a lumber firm in Louisiana. Snagged and sunk in 1917.

4563 POTOWONOK

Rig? ferry wh b. Fort Madison, Iowa, 1880. 74 tons. 109.5 x 22.4 x 3.2. She was the ferry there, still going in 1886, maybe later.

4564 POUNDER

SW p wh b. Marietta, Oh., 1853. 31 tons. First home port, Cincinnati. Off the lists in 1855.

4565 POYDRAS

SW p wh b. Louisville, Ky., 1852. Also known as *PINK PONEY* (see).

4566 PRAIRIE BIRD

Stw p wh b. Pittsburgh, Pa., 1845. 83 tons. Owned by Capt. John Vandergrift. Ran Pittsburgh-Cincinnati summer 1845 during low water, with Capt. Vandergrift, master, and William J. Kountz and C.W. Batchelor, pilots. The mate was Jacob Jay Vandergrift, nephew of Capt. John. Sold to Capt. Levi Miller, Wheeling, and others. Off the lists 1848.

4567 PRAIRIE BIRD

SW p wh b. St. Louis, Mo., 1845. 213 tons. Snagged and lost at Keithsburg, Ill., May 21, 1851.

4568 PRAIRIE BIRD

Stw ferry wh b. Jeffersonville, Ind., 1851. 65 tons. This was the first steam ferry between Madison, Ind., and Milton, Ky. See *S&D Reflector,* March 1980. Off the lists 1860.

4569 PRAIRIE BIRD

Stw U.S. tinclad wh b. Millersport, Oh., 1862, and originally *MARY MILLER.* Sold to U.S. Navy Dec. 19, 1862, to become Tinclad #11, renamed *PRAIRIE BIRD.* Described at that time as 159.9 x 29.2 x 4.1. Engines, 14's- 4 ft. Sold at public sale to Henry Morton, Aug. 17, 1865.

4570 PRAIRIE CITY

Stw p wh b. California, Pa., 1852. 198 tons. 151 x 28.4 x 5.5. Designed for the Pittsburgh-St. Louis trade, and was the largest sternwheeler of her day. Originally owned in part by her master, Capt. Mark Sterling, along with Henry Mason and Evan Evans, all of Pittsburgh. Sold that fall to Capt. Pleasant Devinny and others of St. Clair County, Ill. Fire broke out in the hold of *PARTHENIA* (see) at St. Louis, Dec. 7, 1855, consuming her and also *TWIN CITY* and *PRAIRIE CITY*.

4571 PRAIRIE CITY

Stw p wh b. Cincinnati, Oh., 1873. 122 tons. Ran Parkersburg-Zanesville, Capt. Jesse John Barr, fall and winter 1873. That spring she had run Evansville-Wabash River, Capt. H.H. Flesher, with E.B. Aumiller, clerk. Went back to Wabash River and in 1879 was running between New Harmony and Wabash Station. Exploded boilers at Hodge's Landing, Dec. 27, 1879.

4572 PRAIRIE ROSE

Stw p wh b. Brownsville, Pa., 1854. 247 tons. Capt. Maratta had her in St. Louis-St. Paul trade, 1855. Ran Cincinnati-Memphis, Capt. James S. Wise, 1861. Was in U.S. service during the war, and was up Missouri River May-June 1864 to Leavenworth, Kans. Sunk by ice at foot of Biddle Street, St. Louis, Jan. 12, 1866.

4573 PRAIRIE STATE

SW p wh b. Shousetown, Pa., 1849. 314 tons. Loaded at Pittsburgh for New Orleans on her maiden trip, Capt. Thomas Baldwin. "We admire her name exceedingly," said the editor of the Cairo *Delta* in latter February 1849. "It must mean Illinois, as that is the great Prairie State of the Union." She entered the Illinois River trade later that spring and was burned and lost at St. Louis in the large fire of May 17, 1849.

4574 PRAIRIE STATE

Stw p wh b. Griggsville, Ill., 1850. 287 tons. Ran St. Louis-Illinois River. Exploded boilers just below Pekin, Ill., while racing *AVALANCHE,* Sunday, Apr. 16, 1852, with loss of 20 lives. Capt. Samuel Rider was one of the stockholders. She was in the St. Louis and Keokuk Packet Co. She was at the Rock Island boat yard tied alongside the *KENTUCKY NO. 2* on July 4, 1855. Ben Howard, her mate, went uptown and left Sam R. VanSant (then a youngster) in charge. The latter took fire and both burned, also a sawmill nearby. The burned sawmill was later bought by two thrifty Germans, Frederick Weyerhauser and Frederick C.A. Denkmann, and they started business there.

4575 PRAIRIE STATE

SW p wh b. Wellsville, Oh., 1863. 184 tons. Went to St. Louis. Bought March 1864 by Capt. Frank Dozier, Samuel Jacoby, and C.C. Ferguson for $30,000. She drew but 17 inches light, and a Missouri River mountain trip was planned. She wound up at Mobile, Ala., and off the lists in 1872.

4576 PRES ELLISON

Stw p wh b. Portsmouth, Oh., 1879. 108.6 x 17.3 x 3.6. Ran Manchester-Maysville-Vanceburg for about a year, then was a local out of Wheeling. Capt. George W. Edgington was original owner. Named for Pres Ellison of Manchester, Oh. Sold to the Cincinnati area and was renamed *MAUD S.*

4577 PRESIDENT

SW ferry wh b. Madison, Ind., 1864. 258 tons. 138 x 36 x 5. Owned by the C.B.& Q. Railroad, Burlington, Iowa. First master was Capt. C.E. Burtcht. In the 1880s she was on the Missouri River. Off the lists 1889.

4578 PRESIDENT

SW ex sh b. Midland, Pa. (hull), 1924, originally named *CINCINNATI* (see), she was sold to Streckfus Steamers, Inc., St. Louis in 1933. Received an entire new superstructure and came out July 4, 1934, as the best excursion boat on the rivers. Over all measurements: 291.5 x 84 x 7.5. Barnes compound non-condensing engines, 22's, 40's- 9 ft. Her six boilers were set down in the hold, oil burners. Allowed 3,100 passengers. After she settled down as the full-time excursion boat at New Orleans her guards were glass-enclosed in 1944. Converted to diesel in 1978, powered by three Murray & Tregurtha prop units (one on each side and one at the stern) delivering 2,000 hp. Capt. Verne Streckfus, as these lines are written, has been manager-master so many years that but few persons remember when he wasn't. Sold, 1981, to New Orleans Steamboat Co. and continues to operate in 1983.

4579 PRESTON

SW p wh b. Louisville, Ky., 1852. 144 tons. Built for parties at Galveston, Tex., but was snagged and lost at White Oak Shoals, Red River, Ark., May 4, 1853. She was loaded deep and the loss of cargo was considerable.

4580 PRIDE OF THE WEST

SW p wh b. Cincinnati, Oh., 1846. 321 tons. Ran St. Louis-New Orleans, Capt. E. Williamson with B.F. Ogleby, clerk. Same trade 1851, Capt. Rogers. Lost in ice at Cincinnati, Feb. 13, 1853, with loss of six lives.

4581 PRIMA DONNA

Stw p wh b. New Albany, Ind., 1856. 79 tons. 112.5 x 20 x 3.8. Half-owner and master was Capt. Louis Hernest Trudeau, with Claude Favre as partner. Off the lists 1858.

4582 PRIMA DONNA

Stw p wh b. California, Pa., 1856. 304 tons. 151 x 37.3 x 6. Built by stockholders of Pittsburgh and Allegheny City, Pa., Capt. Alexander McGowan, master. Engines 22's- 5½ ft. Three boilers, each 40″ by 26 ft. Ran Pittsburgh-Cincinnati-St. Louis. She was impressed into U.S. service and loaded with heavy guns, etc., at Pittsburgh in February 1862, Capt. George D. Moore. Capt. William J. Kountz went along, his last trip down the Ohio until January 1878 when he rode the *J.B.M. KEHLOR* to Cincinnati (see).

Later in the war she was captured by the Rebels on Cumberland River, then in charge of Capt. Joseph Scott, Covington, Ky. The crew became prisoners and on Mar. 3, 1865, arrived at Cincinnati aboard the *PEYTONA*. "Captain Scott has suffered much; also here are W.R. Shaw and William McKinley, clerks; mate W.A. Henderson; engineer J.W. Clemens; carpenter D. Wald; also firemen, watchmen, and deckhands. For days they had no rations, and other days were handed one ear of corn apiece. Banquets were a pint of corn meal and a small piece of stale meat." As late as March 1865, *PRIMA DONNA* was in U.S. service, towing two monitors to Mound City. When condemned at Memphis early 1866, she was still owned by Capt. Joseph Scott and others. She was put in tow of the *NICK HUGHES* to be returned to Cincinnati, and the *HUGHES* exploded boilers near Randolph. Finally made it to Cincinnati and was sold that September to two gentlemen of Helena, Ark., who put her in tow of the packet *CHARLESTON* late October 1866 and took her there for use as a wharfboat.

4583 PRINCE

SW p wh b. Cincinnati, Oh., 1859. 223 tons. Built for Vicksburg-Yazoo River, connecting with *CHARMER* and *PRINCESS* for New Orleans. Went to Confederate registry 1861. Snagged and lost at Hickman, Ky., Feb. 27, 1862, with loss of 74 lives.

4584 PRINCE

Stw p wh b. Harmar, Oh., at Knox Yard, 1881. 120 x 21 x 2. Originally named *C. Y. LUCAS* (see). As *PRINCE* owned by Capt. Thomas Prince and others, Wheeling. Ran short trades out of Wheeling. In 1883 ran Wheeling-Clarington in low water with *TELEGRAM*'s crew, Capt. James H. Gatts, with C.E. Booth, clerk. The Prince family moved operations to the lower Mississippi and took *PRINCE* along. Lost at Troyville, La., Nov. 17, 1892.

4585 PRINCE

Stw ex wh b. Wabasha, Minn., 1896, originally named *FRONTENAC* (see). She operated out of St. Paul towing a large excursion barge named *PRINCESS*, 183 x 40, the outfit run by Capt. D.W. Wisherd. The *PRINCE* burned laid up for the winter in Quincy Bay, foot of Chestnut Street, Nov. 6, 1918.

4586 PRINCE OF WALES

SW p wh b. Cincinnati, Oh., 1860. 572 tons. Built for Nashville-New Orleans trade, Capt. James Lee, Memphis. 248 x 40 x 7. Upon the advent of hostilities sold to Preston Lodwick and others, New Orleans, and ran Memphis-New Orleans, Capt. James Kenniston. She was taken up Yazoo and Tallahatchie rivers to avoid her capture, where she was purposely burned by the Confederates, July 14, 1863.

4587 PRINCESS

SW p wh b. Cincinnati, Oh., 1839. 216 tons. 140 x 25.3 x 6.5. Capt. Cassius B. Sandford was master. First ran in Yazoo River, and then Natchez-New Orleans. She was lengthened in fall of 1842 to become 155.5 ft. long, and tonnage was increased to 242. Owned by William Leathers, Campbell County, Ky., and James W. Conlan, New Orleans. In the spring of 1844, upbound, got lost in a fog, turned around, rammed and went through a levee. The crew of the *REPUBLIC* heard the crash and took off the passengers.

4588 PRINCESS

SW p wh b. Cincinnati, Oh., 1844. 335 tons. 203 x 29 x 7. Engines, 24's- 9 ft. Four boilers, each 42" by 30 ft., two 16" flues. Capt. Cassius B. Sandford, Covington, Ky., part owner and master. Ran Natchez-New Orleans, and made trips to Louisville. She was one of the faster nags of her time, and she was never passed under way. The *J.M. WHITE* tried to on one occasion, a race all the way from New Orleans to Natchez. William Leathers was part owner. Sold June 1847 to Capt. C.H. Fairchild and others, and last owner was Joseph D. Foster, New Orleans who acquired sole ownership April 1849. Downbound with cotton she came in collision with *ALAMO*, January 1851, and was sunk. The *Louisville Journal* issue of January 23, reported that "furniture and a portion of the machinery will be recovered."

4589 PRINCESS

SW p wh b. Paddy's Run, Ky. (hull), and completed at Jeffersonville, Ind., 1852. 687 tons. 260 x 34 x 8. Owned in equal shares by Capts. Truman C. Holmes and Thomas P. Leathers. Burned Oct. 6, 1854, two miles below Fort Adams, Miss., with a large cotton cargo, downbound for New Orleans. Several lives were lost.

4590 PRINCESS

SW p wh b. Cincinnati, Oh., 1855. 715 tons. 270 x 34 x 8. Engines, 35's- 9 ft. Six boilers, each 40" by 34 ft. Ran New Orleans-Vicksburg, Capt. Truman C. Holmes, through 1856. Capt. William C. Wilson, Natchez, took command January 1857. An engraving of this boat showing her full broadside under way was widely reproduced and became standard ornamentation on bills of lading, freight bills, etc. The original carried the boat's name on the wheelhouse, but repros did not. Exploded her boilers below Baton Rouge, Feb. 27, 1859, with loss of 70 lives.

4591 PRINCESS

SW p wh b. Louisville, Ky., 1856. 139 tons. Owned in Nashville, Tenn., and was lost on the Ohio River at Raleigh, Ky., Mar. 4, 1858. She was en route from Nashville to Cincinnati with a pleasure party aboard, and came in collision with the *GREAT WESTERN*. A woman and two children, deck passengers, were lost; also three of the deck crew. On March 29, the cabin was floating by Shawneetown, Ill., and the officers of the *ALVIN ADAMS* reported seeing scavengers in yawls, armed with tools, prying up boards, etc.

4592 PRINCESS

Stw p wh b. Freedom, Pa., 1863. 185 tons. 156.9 x 30.3 x 4.4. Engines, 13's- 3½ ft. Two boilers. Built for Capt. Frank Maratta and Capt. George W. Cullen. They sold her to U.S. Navy on Mar. 3, 1864. Converted into Tinclad #53, renamed *NAIAD.* Sold in 1865 to B.F. Beasley and others for $8,100. They rebuilt her, changed name back to *PRINCESS* Oct. 21, 1865. A boat named *PRINCESS* was reported to have exploded boilers above Alexandria, La., in 1866 with loss of life. Capt. F.P. Voohries ran her St. Louis-Arkansas River and he was in command when she was fatally snagged one mile above Fire Creek, above Napoleon, Mo., on the Missouri River, June 1, 1868. Was en route to Fort Benton.

4593 PRINCESS

Stw p wh b. Harmar, Oh., at Knox Yard, 1882. 115.5 x 20.6 x 3.5. Capt. Thomas Prince owned her and ran her Wheeling-Bellaire, Capt. James B. Campbell. She sank at Bellaire, May 1, 1887, and was altered into a towboat. Capt. Brady Morgan ran her on the Muskingum in 1888, and owned her in partnership with Capt. Gordon C. Greene. She was caught in a storm in Beaver Shoals, Ohio River, June 22, 1901, and sank. The wreck was bought by Capt. T.J. Garlick, Pittsburgh, who dismantled her.

4594 PRINCESS

SW ex wh b. Jeffersonville, Ind., by Howard, 1888, originally named *SUNSHINE* (see). Sold to John W. Hubbard in 1921, renamed, and ran excursions at Louisville and elsewhere. Burned while laid up at Jeffersonville, Ind., January 1928.

4595 PRINCESS

Stw ex wh b. Jeffersonville, Ind., by Howard, 1896, originally packet *H. W. BUTTORFF* (see) and later *JOHN LEE* (also see). The Lee Line, Memphis, made of her an excursion boat renamed *PRINCESS.* She was sold to Pittsburgh, owned there by Edgar E. Eaton, and in 1928 was taken over by Morgan-Davis Dock Co., at Glenwood, Pa. She lay around in their fleet until scrapped in 1934.

4596 PRINCESS

SW ex wh b. Harmar, Oh., at Knox Yard, 1900, originally named *FRANCIS J. TORRANCE* (see). As such she was sold to Coney Island Co., Cincinnati, November 1905, and was renamed. She and *ISLAND QUEEN* teamed in this Cincinnati-Coney trade 1906–1917. Capt. Jim Mace was her pilot through 1914 when he retired in favor of Capt. Harry Doss. Mace dated back to the *FANNIE McBURNIE, OHIO NO. 3,* and first *EMMA GRAHAM,* and died at Burlington, Oh., January 1915. She was being wintered in the mouth of the Kentucky River 1917–1918, when ice broke her loose. Landed above Madison, Ind., hull upside down. Her roof bell, marked *FRANCIS J. TORRANCE* went to the L&C packet *KENTUCKY,* later to towboat *JOHN G. BRITTON.*

4597 PRINCESS JR.

SW p wh b. Cincinnati, Oh., 1848. 336 tons. 201 x 27 x 6.4. Owned by Thomas P. Leathers, Cincinnati, and Peter C. Cregier, Natchez, Miss., Capt. Truman C. Holmes, master. Engines, 24's- 8 ft. Three boilers, each 42" by 32 ft., two 16" flues. Ran New Orleans-Natchez. Carried U.S. President-elect Zachary Taylor from Baton Rouge to his plantation when he was en route to the inauguration, early 1849. Capt. Leathers sold his interest April 1852, at which time Capt. J.D. Phillips went master. Capt. J.M. Broadwell went master in January 1853. Boat was retired in 1855.

4598 PRINCETON

SW p wh b. New Albany, Ind., 1847. 251 tons. Ran New Orleans-Ouachita River. Henry A. Ealer was her pilot for a time. Sank and lost in Ouachita River following collision with *ALAMO,* Jan. 5, 1851. One life lost.

4599 PRIORESS

SW p wh b. Cincinnati, Oh., 1859. 393 tons. Running Cincinnati-Madison, Capt. David, 1861, along with *FOREST QUEEN* (see). Named for a racehorse. Burned at Cincinnati Apr. 16, 1863, with loss of one life. Her machinery was said to have been used on the *C. T. DUMONT.*

4600 PROCTOR K. SMILEY

Stw ferry wh b. Catlettsburg, Ky., 1895. 92 x 30 x 3.2. Sweeney engines, 9"- 4 ft. One boiler, 42" by 18 ft. Named for a resident of Catlettsburg, son of Capt. William Smiley who built the ferry to operate South Point, Oh.-Catlettsburg. Later taken to Ripley, Oh., owned by Sara Barrett (mother of Harry L. Flesher) and later owned by Robert Corbin. An improved highway was built in the South Point-Chesapeake stretch, and the old ferry route there was revived, so the *SMILEY* wound up within sight of her original run. She was caught on shore at Kenova, W. Va., in high water early spring 1932, later dismantled there.

4601 PROGRESS

Stw p wh b. Shousetown, Pa., 1854. 217 tons. Ran Pittsburgh-St. Louis, and was at St. Paul in 1857. Arrived at Pittsburgh, Dec. 29, 1862, with 775 bales of cotton, considered a most valuable cargo.

4602 PROGRESS

Stw p wh b. Zanesville, Oh., 1862. 59 tons. Ran Parkersburg-Zanesville with some regularity through 1865. Also 1864–1865 ran Marietta-Parkersburg, Capt. John Henderson, connecting with B&O trains, Robert Leslie, clerk. Sank and lost on Arkansas River, Dec. 1, 1865, with loss of 20 lives.

4603 PROVIDENCE

Stw p wh b. Lyons, Iowa, 1896, originally named *JO LONG* (see). She was sold to Vicksburg, renamed, and ran to Lake Providence and Davis Bend, c. 1897–1900. Eventually capsized and sank.

4604 PUTNAM

Rig? ferry wh b. Pt. Pleasant, W. Va., 1877. 65 x 18 x 3. Regularly documented in the Wheeling district through 1886, perhaps longer.

Q

4605 QUAKER CITY

Stw p wh b. California, Pa., 1853. 214 tons. 152 x 28 x 5.2. Built for a group of Pittsburghers; Martin Mellinger, Lewis H. Davis, Robert Robinson, James Parks, John Dilworth, and James Caldwell. First master, Capt. John N. Shunk. Ran Pittsburgh-Cincinnati-Nashville. Burned and lost at Nashville on Feb. 17, 1859, then owned by her master, Capt. A. McDaniel of Pomeroy, Oh., and others.

4606 QUAPAW

Stw p wh b. California, Pa., 1857. 245 tons. 152 x 31.9 x 5.4. Built for Capt. James W. Danley, Little Rock, Ark. In 1858 was transporting Seminole Indians from Florida from New Orleans to Fort Smith, Ark. In March 1860 sold to P.C. Adams, Little Rock, Capt. David Thomas, master. Last owner was Capt. A. Byers and she was snagged and lost Feb. 11, 1861, near Little Rock, Ark.

4607 QUAPAW

Stw snagboat wh b. Little Rock, Ark., 1893. 147.5 x 30 x 4.3. Originally named *BEAUREGARD* and used by U.S. Engineers on Arkansas, White, Black, and Current rivers. Rebuilt at Jeffersonville, Ind., 1903, and again at Batesville, Ark., in 1915. Capt. Tom Stallings was master of her, his last boating; became sick on board and was taken home to Newport, Ark., where he died Nov. 18, 1911. Capt. J. Elmer Broadway, Paducah, bought her January 1929, and she was towed there by *CHARLES F. RICHARDSON*. He sold her to Kansas City Bridge Co., August 1932.

4608 QUEEN

Stw ferry wh b. Tieville, Iowa, 1877. 44 x 12 x 2. Operated at Decatur, Neb. Still on the lists 1896, maybe longer.

4609 QUEEN NO. 2

Stw ferry wh b. Tieville, Iowa, 1877. 70 x 18.5 x 3. Operated at Decatur, Neb. Listed in 1886, maybe longer.

4610 QUEEN CITY

SW p wh b. Cincinnati, Oh., 1843. 318 tons. Collapsed a flue while at Natchez, Miss., May 24, 1846, resulting in 12 deaths, many of them German emigrants. Was not rebuilt.

4611 QUEEN CITY

SW p wh b. McKeesport, Pa., 1851, originally named *FALCON* (see). 441 tons. Renamed Dec. 6, 1854. Ran Cincinnati-New Orleans, Capt. Henry A. Jones and Capt. J. Stut Neal. Off the lists 1859. The snagboat *E.A. WOODRUFF* was engaged at Portsmouth, Oh., raising the hull of "the old *QUEEN CITY* which has laid at the mouth of Scioto Chute and has been a dangerous obstruction for a long time." This in August 1878.

4612 QUEEN CITY

SW ferry wh b. Newport, Ky., 1853. 107 tons. Operated Cincinnati-Newport. Off the lists in 1855.

4613 QUEEN CITY

SW ferry wh b. Cincinnati, Oh., 1863. Sold to U.S. Navy, Feb. 13, 1863, and was rebuilt to become Tinclad #26, still called *QUEEN CITY*. She was captured by the Rebels at Clarendon, Ark., June 12, 1864. She was stripped of guns and anything worth the taking, and burned.

4614 QUEEN CITY

Stw p wh b. Madison, Ind., 1873. 179 x 34 x 4.7. Originally packet *LAURA L. DAVIS*, renamed in 1883. Made a trip to New Orleans, winter 1883–1884. Still listed 1886, maybe longer.

4615 QUEEN CITY

Stw p wh b. Cincinnati, Oh., 1897. 236 x 44 x 7. Engines, 24's- 8 ft. Four boilers, each 42" by 26 ft. Engines, by Rees, were built 1880 and served on *FLORIDA*, a side-wheeler out of Jacksonville, Fla. (see). She was built by the Cincinnati Marine Railway Co., under supervision of Capt. J. Frank Ellison for Pittsburgh & Cincinnati Packet Line. Launched fully built save for bucketplanks, June 5, 1897; ran her trials June 10, and departed for Pittsburgh June 19, with this crew: Capt. Robert R. Agnew, master; James S. Gardner, purser; Will Chapman, 2nd clerk; Anthony Meldahl and Phil Anshutz, pilots; John Leonard, mate; Willard Alexander and Marsh Ellis, engineers; Charles J. Hall, steward, and Henry Grear, carpenter. Pilot Meldahl backed her away from the shipyard and never missed a trip on her for the next ten years. This deluxe packet was designed to cater to a rather high class patronage. Her mahogany cabin was finished in gilt trim, and the ceiling was of pressed metal sheets with ornate design. She had wire mesh railings studded with rosettes. This boat and her sister *VIRGINIA* (see) were advertised in Pittsburgh's social register, to good advantage, as many fashionable Pittsburghers trod her decks. The *QC*'s hull was heavily planked and she had an unusually high head and forecastle, too high for conducting business at most wharfboats. She ran Pittsburgh-Cincinnati as water permitted until June 1913. Her owners sent her on a Mardi Gras trip in 1903, such a success that others were made in 1908, 1909, 1910, 1911, 1913, and on the downbound leg of the 1914 trip she sank on the Falls at Louisville, Feb. 17, in charge of Capt. William C. Lepper. In June 1905 the Ohio Valley Improvement Association was host to the Rivers and Harbors Congressional Committee, and en route the National Rivers and Harbors Congress was organized with J. Frank Ellison, secretary, the trip made from Pittsburgh to Cairo, Ill. The owning company was forced into receivership but continued operating until 1912 when the assets were sold to John W. Hubbard, Pittsburgh, who formed the Ohio & Mississippi Navigation Co. Capt. Robert Agnew resigned 1900 to command *KATE ADAMS,* and was succeeded by Capt. Thomas S. Sandford, then Capt. John Sweeney, and when she quit the Pittsburgh-Cincinnati trade June 1913 she was in charge of Capt. Edwin F. Maddy. After the ill-starred Mardi Gras, 1914, she was laid up in the Kanawha River, Pt. Pleasant, W. Va., and hibernated until early summer 1916 when she went to Louisville and ran excursions. Then back to Kanawha River to idle the time until spring of 1918 when Louisville & Cincinnati Packet Co., acquired her for the L&C trade. In tow of *SPRAGUE* she was taken to Mound City, Ill., May 1920, and received virtually a new hull. L&C made Mardi Gras trips with her in 1921, 1922, 1923, and 1925, the first originating at Pittsburgh, the second and third at Cincinnati, and the latter one at Louisville. She was transferred 1929 to the Ohio River Transportation Co., Pittsburgh, a Hubbard inspired organization, and resumed the Pittsburgh-Cincinnati trade, making a Mardi Gras trip early 1930. In the L&C trade her masters were Capt. Ed Williamson and Capt. Jack Lindenburn; and in the final Pittsburgh days by Capt. Ed Dunaway and Capt. Ralph Emerson. She finally was laid up at Pittsburgh in September 1933 with Capt. William S. Pollock ringing the last pilothouse bells.

Fans and devotees of the *QC* are recommended to the files of *S&D Reflector.* In issue of December 1964 is a detailed report of the "Congress Trip of 1905." The September 1967 issue is devoted to an in-depth illustrated story of the *QC*'s career. The December 1976 issue contains ten superb *QC* photographs. This lovely lady had profound influence on river people. She was built at a time of affluence. Her architect, Capt. J. Frank Ellison, admired the side-wheel *IDLEWILD* (see) and the influence is there; also he had made a study of Great Lakes steamers to good advantage. When Harriet Henderson, daughter of Capt. James A. Henderson (president of the P&C Line) broke champagne to christen this boat, she splashed the ultimate of Ohio River packets. As was discovered and stated 500 B.C., "Beauty is proof against spears and shields; she who is beautiful is more formidable than fire or iron." The perfection of the *QC* counted in great measure for her long life. Practical reasons would have pushed her into discard about 1910, or would have dictated her conversion into an excursion boat; but no, with pomp and circumstance, with hauteur and elegance, this queen projected herself 20-odd years beyond her allotted span. John W. Hubbard's checkbook saw her through 1912–1933, and when he tired of the exercise a U.S. marshal stepped in, and the *QC* became a wharfboat at the foot of Wood Street in the Monongahela River at Pittsburgh. Rivermen and boat fans trod her aging decks and musty halls to beg, buy, or borrow souvenirs. She later was moved down to the foot of Liberty to make way for wharf improvements and there sank in January 1940. The wreckage was burned Feb. 17, 1940, a grizzly, smoggy day.

Notes: Her roof bell originated on the Anchor Line side-wheeler *CITY OF ST. LOUIS* and was on the *QC* as long as she ran. Later it was briefly on the towboat *MILDRED,* the packet *OUACHITA,* the towboat *JOHN W. HUBBARD,* and was placed on the *DELTA QUEEN* in 1947 where it does service today. Her whistle quite likely came from Ellison's *HUDSON*; she came out with it and it blew her final landing signal; then it went to the towboat *JOHN W. HUBBARD,* and lastly on the towboat *JOE COOK.* She came out with a Crawley & Johnston "booster" steering rig, which was changed in her L&C days for a Gardner rig. Her fastest time, Cincinnati to New Richmond, Oh. (22.5 miles), was 1 hour 50 minutes, December 1897. When the *CHRIS GREENE* and *BETSY ANN* made this run in 1928 they required 2 hours 25 minutes. She came out new with stepped paddlewheel; after 1920 had an orthodox wheel. Many of her mahogany, glass-paneled stateroom doors went to the *LIBERTY,* and others to the "Boat Hotel," New Martinsville, W. Va. (which ultimately burned). Her roof 'scapes could be heard four miles on a still night, until later days when her heaters were changed. She had a carved figurehead rising from her stem, and retained it until rebuilt at Mound City. Had a *tete-a-tete* in her ladies' cabin. A metal *QC* emblem in gold appeared on each stateroom door. Her grand piano was presented by the Cincinnati Chamber of Commerce. She had oil paintings on the rounded cabin bulkheads. A notorious coal hog, she consumed 3,200 bushels of run-of-mine a week.

Your scribe fell for the wiles of the *QC* in 1911 standing in the forward end of the main cabin gazing aft at her multitude of repititions; repitition of doors, of shining brass oil lamps in their swinging brackets, of overhead lights coming from twined oak leaves of metal, of chairs soldiered in parade, and her dining tables the same way—all of these things as trim as West Point cadets, sweeping in a dip downward to the midship gangways, then up again to the immense mirror in the distance—an unbelievable distance—twice as wonderful as anything military; a person could wear out his eyes looking for a single straight line; there wasn't one anywhere; all was cadence and curve, an immense arc. A lady at the grand piano played. She sang in a dusky voice "Oh Beautiful Lady" and "Chocolate Soldier." She had too much powder and paint for my mother's standards, but I thought she was a blessed angel, and shall expect all honest angels to resemble her in the Hereafter. I was 10 years old when this indelible tattoo creased my imagination. The *QC* did this to adults as well, so I learned later, beholding this man-made art—art in fluidity. From shore the *QC* was completely photogenic; you could attack her with a camera from any angle with pleasing contours.

For accurate drawings and technical details of the *QC,* see *Marine Engineering,* issue of October 1897, *et seq.*

4616 QUEEN CITY NO. 2

SW ferry wh b. Cincinnati, Oh., 1856. 171 tons. Came out 1857 and ferried Cincinnati-Newport. Off the lists 1873.

4617 QUEEN OF DYCUSBURG

Stw p wh b. Paducah, Ky., 1928. 64.9 x 21 x 4.1. Owned by

Fred Joyce, Paducah, and ran Paducah-Dycusburg. By 1934 was at Memphis, making trips downriver, in charge of Capt. Ad A. Powell. Owned 1936 by Kennedy Dry Dock Co., who sold her to James R. Hines Co., Bowling Green, Ky. The towboat *J.B. SMITH* delivered her. She needed docking in 1941 and Hines pulled her on a barge. Sold in 1947 to the Idle Hour Boat Club, Cincinnati, and was taken to their harbor at Bellevue, Ky., and converted into a yacht club.

4618 QUEEN OF ST. JOHNS

Prop p wh b. Cincinnati, Oh., 1885. 192.5 x 36.3 x 7.4. Built by Covington Machine Works. Went to the St. Johns River, Florida, and was converted into a side-wheeler. In 1888 went to the Cape Fear River, N.C. Burned at Wilmington, N.C., July 10, 1889. For story and pictures, see *S&D Reflector,* issue of September 1972, pages 6–7.

4619 QUEEN OF THE WEST

SW p wh b. Cincinnati, Oh., 1843. 328 tons. Cincinnati-New Orleans, Capt. S. Brickle. Off the lists 1848.

4620 QUEEN OF THE WEST

SW p wh b. Cincinnati, Oh., 1854. 406 tons. 181 x 36 x 6. Three boilers. Capt. J. Phil Wade, in Cincinnati-New Orleans trade. He was succeeded by Capt. Jos. Scott, with clerks Malen Scott and John McLeod. At outbreak of the war, Capt. Richard M. Wade. She was converted into an Ellet ram 1862, quite active in Battle of Memphis. Rammed and sank the *GEN. LOVELL,* and when one of her paddlewheels was disabled she was run ashore and there captured the *GEN. PRICE* and entire crew. On Feb. 11, 1863, raided lower Red River capturing *A.W. BAKER, BERWICK BAY, ERA NO. 5,* and one other. Was run aground (accidentally?) and captured—to become a Confederate gunboat, this on Feb. 19, 1863. During the Battle of Grand Lake, Mar. 14, 1863, she was struck with a percussion shell which set afire cotton bales piled aboard for protection, set the bales afire, and she burned and her magazine exploded, with loss of 26 hands.

4621 QUICKSTEP

SW p wh b. Murraysville, W. Va. (hull), and completed at Pittsburgh, 1866. 456 tons. 200 x 29 x 5.4. Hartupee compound engines. Original owners, equal shares, Andrew Hartupee and Samuel Morrow, Pittsburgh. First master, Capt. William B. Donaldson. Entered the Pittsburgh-Cincinnati trade, fall 1866 with Sam Barr, Jr., clerk. Donaldson left her after a week or so to superintend building the *GREAT REPUBLIC* (see) and Barr became master, but fell ill, and Capt. John Shouse commanded until the boat was sold first week of December 1866. Purchaser was Capt. Henry T. Dexter who ran her Evansville-Paducah, then Cairo-Evansville, with Jack Grammar and Walter Pennington as clerks. Collided with and sank *OLLIE SULLIVAN* at Diamond Island, April 1869. During a storm at Evansville July 7, 1873, she lost her stacks and was blown from the landing. When dismantled at Metropolis, Ill., 1876, her machinery went to *COAHOMA* (see). Her oil headlight still was in the Lee Line wharfboat at Memphis 1920.

4622 QUINCY

SW p wh b. Cincinnati, Oh., 1847. 157 tons. Went to Apalachicola, Fla. Off the lists in 1850.

4623 QUINCY

SW p wh b. Jeffersonville, Ind. (hull), and completed at St. Louis, 1856. 427 tons. Owned by St. Louis & Keokuk Packet Co. Ran with *WESTERNER, KEOKUK,* and *SAM GATY.* Off the lists in 1860.

4624 QUINCY

Stw ferry wh b. Madison, Ind., 1859. 125 tons. Operated at Quincy, Ill. Off the lists in 1869.

4625 QUINCY

SW p wh b. Dubuque, Iowa, 1896. 264.7 x 42 x 6.8. Engines, 23's- 8 ft. Two Scotch marine boilers, each 84" by 14 ft. Built by the Diamond Jo Line, and ran St. Louis-St. Paul. Equipment from *GEM CITY* used in construction. Original crew: Capt. John F. Killeen, master; Charles Mather and Ed Paul, clerks; Thomas E. Reardon, steward. Ran her trade until close of the 1917 season. Engineers for the last season were Courtney M. Ellis and Ashley Foster. In the fall of 1911 she tried the St. Louis-New Orleans trade, then owned by Streckfus Steamers, Inc., and made several trips, the last side-wheeler in that run. Sank at Trempeleau Mountain, Wis., July 1906, raised. The Scotch boilers were removed, and she later had four Western boilers. The *QUINCY* was the brag packet of the Streckfus fleet, so popular that extra rooms were built fore and aft of the wheelhouses on the roof. She was converted into a handsome excursion boat, renamed *J.S.* (for John Streckfus), 1918–1919 (see).

R

4626 R.A. LEE

Stw p wh b. Farmersville, La., 1869. 30 tons. 80 x 18.3 x 2.7. Built by Capt. James Harris of Union Parish, La. Soon sold to Capt. G.P. Work, New Orleans, and resold within days to Capt. McWilliam Wright, New Orleans.

4627 R.B. HAMILTON

Stw p wh b. Symmes Creek, Oh., 1858. 175 tons. Ran local trades, upper Ohio. Was impressed to U.S. service summer 1862, but went back to Pittsburgh-Cincinnati trade that November, Capt. John Bradley. Bought by the U.S. in 1864 for war service.

4628 R.B. KENDALL

Stw p wh b. Pittsburgh, Pa., 1881, originally *JOHN LOMAS* (see). Renamed in 1885, owned by R.B. Kendall and Henry C. Rankin, both of Allegheny County, Pa. John E. Cochran bought Rankin's interest, April 1885. In August 1885 sold to Capts. E.D. Abrams and P.C. Williams of Brownsville, Pa. They ran her Brownsville-Geneva, the trade for which *JOHN LOMAS* was originally built. In 1889 running Brownsville-Belle Vernon, Capt. E.D. Abrams. Abrams had an argument with Capt. Jesse M. Bowell of the *J.M. BOWELL* (see), hit him with a rock, and as a result Capt. Bowell died; this in late October 1889. Capt. Abrams was jailed at Uniontown, Pa., and released on $1,000 bond, later was acquitted. Sold the *KENDALL* to Capt. Mel Brown, Hartford City, W. Va., who sold her to Mohler Lumber Co. on the Kanawha River. She ran Marietta-Beverly on the Muskingum, Capt. E.W. Webster, 1892. Dismantled at Charleston, W. Va., 1897 and equipment went to building towboat *REBA REEVES*.

4629 R.B. SPEED

SW p wh b. Dycusburg, Ky., 1863. 50 tons. Originally *MOLLIE FUNK* (see). Ran Evansville-Pond River. Off the lists 1865.

4630 R.C. GRAY

Stw p wh b. Shousetown, Pa., 1866. 427 tons. 156 x 32 x 5.2. Capt. William B. Anderson was master and part owner along with Ezra P. Young and John C. Anderson, J.N. and Nathan Porter, and E. & N. Porter. Ran tramp trades, frequently Pittsburgh-Cincinnati, St. Louis, and several times to St. Paul. She was on the Arkansas April 1870, running Little Rock-Fort Smith. Louisville & Arkansas River Packet Co., operated her 1871. Dismantled 1874. Named for Capt. Richard C. Gray, Pittsburgh, who ran Gray's Iron Line.

4631 R.C. GUNTER

Stw p wh b. Chattanooga, Tenn., 1886. 153 x 28 x 4. Machinery from *J. T. WILDER*. Built by Chattanooga & Decatur Packet Co., headed by Capt. R.C. Gunter who was master. Crew of first trip: M.W. Sams, 1st clerk; John H. Jackson, mate; Chris Short and Buck McKey, pilots; George and Henry Pittman, engineers. Later went to the Illinois River, owned 1896 by St. Louis, Hardin & Hempsville Packet Co. In 1900 Capt. Alex Lamont commanded, with pilots W.C. Colvin and Frank Ebaugh, and engineers John and Allie McCann. Bought February 1901 by Eagle Packet Co., and in spring 1902 was at Kansas City running excursions, Capt. Harry H. Monaghan. While on the Illinois she was snagged and sank to within two feet of the roof, March 1900, at Wetzel's Landing. Dismantled at St. Louis winter 1907-1908.

4632 R.C. JACKSON

Stw p wh b. Loudon, Tenn., 1871. 146 tons. Operated by East Tennessee, Virginia & Georgia RR, and named for the president of the line. Built from *ALERT* (see). Dismantled and machinery went to *ROCKWOOD* (see) in 1882.

4633 R.C. MCCALLA

Stw snagboat wh b. Jeffersonville, Ind., by Howard, 1909. 129.2 x 28 x 5. Engines, 10's- 5 ft. Three boilers. Owned by U.S. Engineers who used her on Tombigbee and Warrior Rivers. Sold at public sale September 1950 to J.F. Fritzel, Mobile. Dismantled 1952.

4634 R.C. OGLESBY

SW p wh b. New Albany, Ind., 1849. 115 tons. 126 x 22.7 x 4. Owned in part by her master, Capt. E.S. Blackstone, Natchitoches Parish, La. Snagged and lost at Lake Bistineau, La., Feb. 7, 1851.

4635 R.C. WOOD

U.S. hospital boat wh b. Madison, Ind., 1857 originally packet *CITY OF LOUISIANA* (see). She was outfitted as a floating U.S. hospital early in 1862, renamed to honor Dr. R.C. Wood who was a pioneer of the Sanitary Commission and asst. surgeon general of U.S. Army. Non-propelled.

4636 R.E. HILL

Stw p wh b. Warsaw, Ill., 1863. 103 tons. 128 x 22 x 4. Part owner and first master was Capt. G.W. Hill, in partnership with Henry Leyhe, W. Leyhe, and two others. She was in war service on Red River 1864. Snagged and lost at the Oxbow, Greenwood, Miss., Aug. 26, 1865.

4637 R.E. LEE

SW gunboat ih b. Glasgow, Scotland, 1860. 642 tons. Originally named *GIRAFFE,* and was in Confederate service when captured at Fort Donelson Nov. 9, 1863, then renamed *R. E. LEE.* Was taken to Louisville and there sank. In May 1864 her wreck was showing as the river fell. Renamed *ISABELLA,* Dec. 16, 1865. Sold foreign in 1869.

4638 R.E. PHILLIPS

Stw p wh b. Freedom, Pa. (hull), and completed at Wheeling, 1886. 110.8 x 20.2 x 3. She was built for Marietta-Parkersburg trade, Capt. G.M. Berry, with G.E. Berry, clerk. Still there, November 1889. Sank in ice under the upper wharf at New Matamoras, Oh., winter of 1894. Raised, and the upper cabin removed by the insurance company, and renamed *F.A. GOEBEL* (see).

4639 R.E. WATKINS

Stw p wh b. Marianna, Ark., 1908. 55.4 x 17 x 2.8. This may have been a job boat of some type. Sank June 5, 1914, at Cape Girardeau, Mo.

4640 R.F. SASS

Stw p wh b. California, Pa., 1855. 238 tons. 150 x 30.3 x 5.7. Ran Cincinnati-New Orleans. When new she was owned in large share by men from New York City, D.G. Mulford (or Murford) and Charles Van Blau Kensteyer. Pittsburghers who held shares were James Vandergrift, William Stackhouse and William Latta. J.R. Shaley, St. Louis, held a one-sixteenth share. First master was Capt. P.S. Murford. By February 1860 master was Capt. R.F. Sass. A gentleman of that name was a steamboat agent at St. Louis in 1889 but whether the same R.F. Sass we know not. Most of these original shareholders still participated when she was lost 15 miles below Memphis at Clark's bar, Glover, Miss., May 9, 1860, with loss of seventeen lives. The crew at the time: Capt. William B. Phillips, master; A.L. Montfort, purser; Andrew Wilson, Jr., 2nd clerk; David Hiner and William M. Allenton, pilots; John Cox and J.A. Phillips, engineers; Andrew Staples, mate, and Fred Kushman, steward. She was upbound when she stove. The *EDWARD WALSH* brought survivors to Memphis. The boat's safe was not recovered, and contained about $6,500, of which $2,500 belonged to the boat. The *NATCHEZ* later reported having met the wreck near Helena, Ark., still partly afloat.

4641 R.G. PARKS & CO.

SW p wh b. Freedom, Pa., 1851. 218 tons. Off the lists in 1854.

4642 R.H. LINDSEY

Stw p wh b. Brownsville, Pa., 1850. 52 tons. 108 x 20 x 3.2. Apparently ran short trades in the Wheeling area until sold April 1856 to Capt. George L. Kouns, New Orleans. He transferred her a month later to A.D. Denslow of St. Mary Parish and William C. Smith, New Orleans, equal shares. Off the lists 1858.

4643 R.H. WINSLOW

SW p wh b. Newport, Ky., 1851. 335 tons. Sank and lost in mouth of Licking River, opposite Cincinnati, June 2, 1859.

4644 R.J. LACKLAND

SW p wh b. Cincinnati, Oh., 1857. 710 tons. 265 x 40. Engines, 28's- 8 ft. Ran St. Louis-New Orleans. Capt. William B. Miller was her master. Went to Confederate registry 1861. The Confederates purposely sank her on Yazoo River about 15 miles below Fort Pemberton to block the river, along with *JOHN WALSH, GOLDEN AGE,* and *SCOTLAND.* A U.S. expedition in May 1863 comprising *FOREST ROSE, LINDEN,* and *PETREL* encountered these sunken steamboats and burned them, May 22, 1863.

4645 R.J. LOCKWOOD

SW p wh b. New Albany, Ind., 1858. 220 x 33 (31 ft. floor) x 6. Built expressly for the Missouri River, Capt. Lamothe. On Mar. 4, 1858, Capt. Lamothe invited guests aboard, 60 or 70 in all, and ran an excursion to the wood-yard as a trial trip. She caught fire in the cookhouse, and was run ashore on the Kentucky side, where everybody got off. As she burned, the boat left the bank, floated some distance down the Ohio, and sank along the Kentucky shore. Total loss. The excursionists waited until evening when the Portland ferry came down and took them back to New Albany. Capt. Lamothe owned her entire, and had no insurance.

4646 R.J. LOCKWOOD

SW p wh b. St. Louis, Mo., 1864. 418 tons. 210 x 34 x 5. Engines, 15's- 5 ft. Three boilers. Operated on Missouri River, and was used for U.S. transport service 1864–1865. With Porter on Red River, 1864. Made a trip to Mobile with troops, arriving there Apr. 14, 1865. On Mar. 4, 1866, exploded boilers at President's Island below Memphis, Capt. Ben Howard in command. He and Capt. George Willard (a passenger) were seated at the cabin stove, about tea time, and were lifted to the roof and bruised. She was upbound from New Orleans and had but 20 cabin passengers. Life loss was set at 25. She was taken to Pittsburgh in 1870 and dismantled.

4647 R.J. LOCKWOOD

Stw p wh b. Freedom, Pa. (hull), and completed at Pittsburgh, 1870. 175 x 33 x 4.5. Engines, 15's- 5 ft., from former boat of the name. Cabin by Wm. F. Richardson. She was contracted by Albert Conkel and William Kimber who defaulted on payments, whereupon James Rees took her over and operated her for the creditors. Three boilers, each 36" by 24 ft. Sternwheel 17½ ft. dia. working 23½ ft. buckets. She was operated in the Carter Line, St. Louis-New Orleans-Shreveport 1870–1872, Capt. James Caghill. Lost in ice at St. Louis, Feb. 26, 1872.

4648 R.K. DUNKERSON

Stw p wh b. Parkersburg, W. Va., 1863. 115 tons. 119.8 x 27.2 x 4. Built for Evansville and Green River trade, and named for a prominent Evansville citizen. Owned largely by Thomas and A. Drinkwater. After the war they took her to New Orleans, Capt. G.E. Boley, and had made but several trips up Red River when she was fatally snagged near Shreveport, Mar. 22, 1866.

4649 R.L. COBB

Stw p wh b. Louisville, Ky., 1855. 197 tons. 158 x 29.5 x 4.5. Enrolled at New Orleans, March 1856 owned by Reuben A. Clark of that city, with Capt. G.L. Cobb, master. Sold in June 1856 to Capt. G.L. Cobb, entire, of Eddyville, Ky. Off the lists 1859.

4650 R.L. COBB

Stw p wh b. Little Rock, Ark., 1883. 145.1 x 28.5 x 3. Maj. John D. Adams connected with the *KATE ADAMS* at the mouth of the Arkansas River with her, accepting reshipping and passengers for Pine Bluff and Little Rock. She was ultimately beached out at Vicksburg in high water, alongside the old transfer boat *NORTHERN PACIFIC* (see) and both rotted down. The *COBB* had been plying in Yazoo River prior.

4651 R.L. WOODWARD

Stw p wh b. Evansville, Ind., 1865. 349 tons. Tramped to St. Louis and elsewhere, Capt. B.F. Woodward, master, with S.B. Leonard, clerk. Off the lists 1867.

4652 R.M. BISHOP

SW p wh b. Cincinnati, Oh., 1866. 298 tons. Went to Missouri River. She was loaded with 3,000 sacks of corn, coming out of Old River, 25 miles below Nebraska City, Neb., July 15, 1867, met a strong current in a cut-off just formed at the head of Peru Cut-Off, capsized, drowned the mate Andy Goff, and was lost.

4653 R.M. BISHOP

Stw p wh b. Kingston, Tenn., 1873. 255 tons. 155 x 28 (34 ft. on deck). Built by Hugh Martin from the *LAST CHANCE* (see) a businessman of Kingston. Named for the mayor of Cincinnati due to the imminence of building the Queen & Crescent RR; Bishop went on to be the governor of Ohio. Ran Chattanooga-Kingston. Sold to Robert Kindrick, then postmaster at Chattanooga, who soon died, and his boat was taken over by his brothers Capt. J.P. and W.E. Kindrick. They operated iron deposits, and the *BISHOP* was used to tow the ore to Chattanooga furnaces. They also got the *J. T. WILDER* (see). She again ran her packet trade summer 1878 during a yellow fever epidemic, Capt. W.C. Wilkey, with Jim Sims, pilot, and W.L. Dugger, Jr., engineer. She was dismantled and engines went in 1881 to the *W.L. DUGGER*.

4654 R.M. JONES

SW p wh b. Newport, Ky., 1851. 193 tons. 136 x 27 x 5.7. Ran New Orleans-Red River owned in part by Berthelet & Jones, Fort Towson, Ark., and her master, Capt. John Ankrin. Named for Robert M. Jones, a wealthy Red River planter, an Indian. He also owned in the *FRANCES JONES*, named for his only daughter (see). Ankrin continued to hold interest until 1854 when Capt. Sidney Relf took command for new owners William H. Chambers and others. Last recorded master was Capt. James Robinson. She was wrecked on Red River and her remains were removed by snagboat *ALGERINE* July 1857.

R.M. PATTON

R.M. PATTON NO. 2

See *ROBERT M. PATTON*, registered name.

4655 R.P. HOBSON

Stw p wh b. Terre Haute, Ind., 1892. 40.8 x 8.1 x 2.5. Originally named *MAY BELLE*. She was still listed at Evansville in 1908.

4656 R.P. WALT

SW p wh b. Cincinnati, Oh., 1870. 202 x 34.5 x 6. Engines, 18's- 7 ft. Four boilers, each 38″ by 22 ft. Paddlewheels 28 ft. dia. working 10 ft. buckets. Owned by Memphis & Arkansas River Packet Co., Maj. John D. Adams, pres. First master was Capt. Morgan Bateman who died aged 43 while commanding her, at Memphis, Apr. 23, 1870. First trip was Memphis to Batesville, Ark., Mile 300.9, on the White River. Carried a gilded cotton bale on top of the pilothouse. Rufus Putnam Walt was born at Petersburg, Va., 1824, became clerk on *GEORGE W. CHEEK*, then he and a brother Martin ran a commission house in Memphis on Front Street and owned in boats. His wife was Rebecca Jane Dillman born near Augusta, Ky., then moved to Higginsport, Oh., where she married R.P. Walt. Later in their married life they moved to Des Arc, Ark., where he died November, 1883. The *R.P. WALT* was cut down by ice at Memphis Dec. 27, 1872, along with *BELLE PIKE, HELEN BROOK, LAURA, SUMMER COON,* and *UNDINE*. Her engines went to the *KATE KINNEY* built at Madison, Ind., 1873. During most of the boat's brief career her master was Capt. "Ad" Storm, with Charles Smith, first clerk.

4657 R.R. HUDSON

Stw p wh b. Murraysville, W. Va. (hull), and completed at Wheeling, 1866. 169 x 33 x 5.5. Engines, 17's- 5½ ft. Three boilers, each 40″ by 20 ft., seven flues. Came out in the Wheeling-Cincinnati trade, Capt. J.T. Russell, with William M. List, clerk. The forward end of the cabin was decorated with a painting of Wheeling, and the aft end showed Blennerhassett Island, both by artist Emil Bott. R.R. Hudson, Esq., was prominent in Pomeroy and Middleport, Oh. (coal, salt, rolling mill), and he presented his namesake boat with a pianoforte at Cincinnati. This boat had a successful career, often going through to Pittsburgh, and accepting freight to Louisville. She was lost in ice at the Belmont landing, Wheeling, Jan. 27, 1875. Her owners at the time were William List, Ed Hornbrook, Charles List, Alex Laughlin, John Mulrine, Alex Heatherington, and James McMillan. A new boat was being built at the time to replace her, lying at Wheeling, and had been named *HUDSON* (see) named for the same Pomeroy Bend businessman. R.R. Hudson, Esq., failed in business due to prolonged low water in the Ohio River summer 1884, unable to ship goods to market. He removed to Canada. Various of his enterprises were reorganized and saw many prosperous years thereafter but Mr. Hudson was unable to do likewise. A street in Middleport, Oh., was named for him.

4658 R.R. SPRINGER

SW p wh b. Cincinnati, Oh., 1879. 294.5 x 41.5 x 8.3. Engines, 24's- 8 ft. Six boilers, each 41″ by 30 ft., two flues. Paddlewheels 32 ft. dia. working 13 ft. buckets with 26″ dip. Ran Cincinnati-New Orleans, Capt. Henry U. Hart. Named for a prominent Cincinnatian who had started his career on steamboats. A large oil painting of Mr. Springer graced the forward cabin, the work of McGreggor, a young Cincinnati artist. Mr. Springer presented the boat with a piano. In late 1879 an electric arc light, called a Brush light, was installed on top of the pilothouse by W.H. Lawrence, Cleveland, Oh. This innovation was supposed to turn night into daylight but blinded the pilots to such a degree that it was soon transferred to a position over the forecastle. She made a "fast trip" in May 1881, leaving New Orleans at 5:30 P.M., April 30, and arriving in Cincinnati May 6, at 7:40 P.M., 6 days, 2 hours, 10 minutes. In May 1884 she made a St. Louis-St. Paul round trip, Capt. A.M. Hutchinson, with Frank King and Willis Blakelee, pilots, and J.S. Jones, clerk. At daybreak, 30 miles above Natchez, the *SPRINGER* was downbound, Monday, May 30, 1885, about to enter Waterproof Cut-Off. On watch at the wheel was 26-year-old Royal Hart, the captain's son. He had been dancing until a late hour and the surmise was that he fell asleep. The boat plowed full head into the point at the head of the Cut-Off and was wrecked. Royal's father had died suddenly at New Orleans a short while prior. Both father and son were highly regarded. Those who knew Royal say that the trauma of this disaster changed him into a silent person and although he continued piloting he worked on towboats. His wife was daughter of congressman J.H. Bromwell, Cincinnati, and when Royal died, Oct. 6, 1895, the funeral, "one of the largest in years," was held from the Bromwell home.

4659 R.S. TRIPLETT

Stw ferry wh b. Owensboro, Ky., 1876. 68 x 20.2 x 3.2. New in November 1876 owned by Capt. John S. Brown, Owensboro. Sold September 1877 to R.S. Triplett and George A. Williams, Owensboro, equal shares. Sold August 1878 to Capt. G.W. Lyon and two others, equal shares, all of Tell City, Ind. Sold November 1879 to Capt. G.W. Lyon, entire, who used her in local packet service prior to acquiring the *G.W. LYON* (see). In July 1880 transferred to James W. Robinson, Pt. Pleasant, W. Va. Said to have had engines from *BENWOOD*.

4660 R.T. BRYARLY

Stw p wh b. Jeffersonville, Ind., by Howard, 1872. 331 tons. 150 x 33 x 3.5. Engines, 13's- 4 ft. Three boilers, each 38" by 22 ft. Built for New Orleans-Shreveport trade. Hit an obstruction, sank, broke in two, and was lost Sept. 19, 1876, on Red River at Picon Point. The wrecking steamer *TRAVIS WRIGHT* was sent to the scene to salvage cotton, hit an obstruction also at Picon Point and went down with 173 bales aboard, Oct. 7, 1876.

4661 R.T. COLES

Stw p wh b. Kingston, Tenn., 1889. 118 x 24.6 x 4.2. Regularly employed on upper Tennessee River. Was brought to the upper Cumberland in early 1897 and after having made but a few trips struck a bluff near King's Eddy and was lost. Two days later the *JOHN W. HART* (see) sank and was lost near Granville, Tenn., on the Cumberland.

4662 R.T. GRAHAM

Rig? ferry wh b. Vevay, Ind., 1880. 58.6 x 18.2 x 3.3. Still documented 1886, perhaps later.

4663 R.W. ADAMS

SW p wh b. Madison, Ind., 1857. 399 tons. 260 x 36 x 5.5. Engines, 25's- 9 ft. Five boilers, each 38" by 28 ft. Went to New Orleans, Capt. C. Marshall, and entered Red River trade, owned by John C. Graeff, New Orleans. Lost at Alexandria, La., Dec. 15, 1858.

4664 R.W. DUGAN

Stw p wh b. Cincinnati, Oh., 1873. 160 x 32 x 3. Engines, 13½'s- 4 ft. Two boilers, each 40" by 26 ft. Engines from *SPRAY*. Originally ran Cincinnati-Memphis, Capt. Lon Bryson, with Frank Bryson, clerk. Acquired early in her career by Capt. Jos. Kinney who ran her St. Louis-Kansas City. Capt. William L. Heckmann, Sr., acquired her 1874, and ran her St. Louis-Rocheport in competition to *MATTIE BELLE* (see) resulting in a ruinous rate war with wheat carried at three cents a sack. Capt. Jos. Kinney again acquired her, March 1876, and ran her St. Louis-Jefferson City. Snagged and lost at DeWitt, Mo., Oct. 31, 1878. Sank to the roof with heavy loss of cargo, mostly flour and grain.

4665 R.W. MCRAE

SW p wh b. Louisville, Ky., 1853. 323 tons. 171 x 33 x 6.1. Originally owned at Louisville, Ky., Capt. Samuel Applegate. Ran New Orleans-Shreveport. Sold December 1854 to L.L. Powell (three-quarters) and N.A. Delaney, both of New Orleans, Capt. Richard Holmes, master. Sold, January 1855 to N.A. Delerne, New Orleans, with Capt. John W. Cannon, master. Sold November 1857 to Capt. John W. Tobin, New Orleans, with Capt. Leander J. Moore, master. In May 1858 made a round trip, New Orleans-Camden in 5 days 12 hours. She was at the scene of the *PRINCESS* disaster and carried many of the wounded to hospitals, February 1858. Sold to Red River Packet Co., Capt. George L. Kouns, December 1860. Was rebuilt into the *GRAND ERA* (see).

4666 R.W. POWELL

SW p wh b. New Albany, Ind., 1855. 349 tons. 175 x 33 x 6.5. Operated out of New Orleans. Originally owned (one-half) by her master, Capt. R.H. Martin. Capt. James Henry Martin was master, October 1856, then Capt. James H. Estes, 1857. Was owned (one-half) and commanded by Capt. William M. Weibling when snagged and lost at Plaquemine, La., Aug. 20, 1861.

4667 R.W. SKILLINGER

Stw p wh b. Murraysville, W. Va. (hull), and completed at Wheeling, 1871. Named for the superintendent of the Murraysville yard. Came out Pittsburgh-Portsmouth, Capt. F.M. Flesher spring 1871. Sold to Capt. S.C. Farley and others for Kanawha River trade. Lengthened at Madison, Ind., summer 1872. Made a trip from Pittsburgh to Shreveport, La., spring 1873, Capt. McCoy. Later ran Wheeling-Cincinnati, then Pittsburgh-Cincinnati, Capt. J.T. Russell. Burned at Cincinnati while laid up for low water, June 21, 1875, during a thunderstorm, perhaps struck by lightning. For a photograph and more details, see *S&D Reflector* December 1977, page 31.

4668 R. DUNBAR

Stw p wh b. Jeffersonville, Ind., by Howard, 1895. 160 x 29.4 x 6.4. Engines, 12½'s- 4 ft. Two boilers, each 42" by 18 ft. Built for the Ryman Line to operate upriver trades on the Cumberland above Nashville. She was very light draft and a big carrier. Named for the storekeeper at Greasy Creek, Ky., Reuben Dunbar (see *S&D Reflector*, issue June 1969, full color front page). Capt. Tom Ryman took religion, having been exposed to revivalist Sam Jones, and there were Biblical inscriptions in the boat's cabin and a large picture of Christ in the ladies' cabin (see *S&D Reflector*, issue June 1972, page 5). Following the death of Capt. Tom Ryman, Dec. 23, 1904, son Tom Jr., ran the line until he was shot and died aboard the *JO HORTON FALL* (see). The timber for the *DUNBAR*'s hull was cut on the farm of Albert Pardue, 40 miles below Nashville, barged to Jeffersonville, aged one year, and creosoted—this being an early use of such preservation. She carried some notables on the upper Cumberland, not the least of whom was Hon. Cordell Hull, U.S. Secretary of State 1933–1944. In a letter to this scribe Mr. Hull said he had made frequent trips on the packet Celina-Nashville. Once ran a race with the *WILL J. CUMMINS* (see), Nashville to Burnside and was the winner, Capt. Tom Ryman, Jr., master. The Ryman holdings went to forced sale, the *R. DUNBAR* bought by Capt. Ralph Emerson who soon sold her to John W. Hubbard, Pittsburgh, 1914. She ran Pittsburgh-Charleston managed by Capt. William E. Roe until the *KANAWHA* sank, at which time Capt. Fred Hornbrook took over the trade. Sold to Liberty Transit Co., Wheeling, in 1918, and they renamed her *GENERAL CROWDER* (see).

4669 RACHAEL MILLER

Stw p wh b. Cincinnati, Oh., 1863. 212 tons. Sold to the U.S. May 25, 1863, and served during the war renamed *REINDEER* (see). After the war sold to private hands, renamed *MARINER* (see) which was lost on Missouri River.

4670 RACKET

Stw p wh b. Manchester, Oh., 1883. 99.1 x 16.2 x 3.6. Originally a single deck packet in local trades above Cincinnati. Rebuilt in winter 1895–1896, hull altered to 97 x 20 x 3, and towed out of Green River to Evansville, Capt. Porter Hines. Still documented 1903, maybe later.

4671 RAINBOW

SW p wh b. Cincinnati, Oh., 1842. 221 tons. 175 x 24 x 5.5. Pittsburgh-Cincinnati in May 1842, Capt. A.C. Montfort. Was sold to New Orleans-Upper Bends trade 1844, Capt. S.S. Selleck. Sold to Mobile, Ala., November 1847, owned and commanded by Capt. William McConaghy. Off the lists 1849.

4672 RAINBOW

SW p wh b. New Albany, Ind., 1854. 486 tons. Entered Louisville-Henderson trade, Capt. Holcroft, and later ran Louisville-New Orleans under his command. Burned 10 miles above Napoleon, Ark., night of Nov. 26, 1857, with large life loss, 75 or more.

4673 RAINBOW

SW p wh b. Jeffersonville, Ind., by Howard, 1879. 264 x 39 x 6. Belonged to the Louisville & Henderson Mail Line. Commanded in 1880 by Capt. Ed Crider, in 1881, by Capt. A.T. Gilmore, and in 1884 by Capt. J.K. Westfall. Another master was Capt. John K. Webster who later superintended the Louisville Orphans Home. M.D. Warren was clerk for some time. Capt. Chris G. Young, Portsmouth, Oh., bought the boat at a sale in 1889 for $8,000 and entered her in the Pittsburgh-Cincinnati trade, Charles W. Knox, purser. One night going down under the railroad bridge at Beaver, Pa., a low hanging lantern swung into the pilothouse, striking pilot Harry Ollom in the face, so badly injuring him that the boat was returned to Rochester, Pa., where he received medical attention. After the *LOUIS A. SHERLEY* hit the Parkersburg railroad bridge (see), the White Collar Line bought half interest in the *RAINBOW* and continued her in the Pittsburgh trade. She burned, laid up for low water, near the location of the old Crane Lumber Co. yard, below and opposite Coney Island Dike, Cincinnati, summer 1890.

4674 RALPH

Stw p wh b. Pittsburgh, Pa., 1887. 115 x 18 x 4. A combination packet-towboat which in the 1890s was at Memphis, Capt. Ed C. Postal. He sold her to the New Orleans & Red River Packet Co., and she sank at Norfolk Landing, 25 miles below Memphis, on her delivery trip, September 1900.

4675 RALPH HICKS

Stw pl and towboat sh b. St. Louis, Mo., 1902, originally named *ALBERMATLA,* a gasoline powered sternwheel pleasure boat. 110.8 x 20.1 x 3.4. Owned by Capt. Jeff Hicks, Pine Bluff, Ark., and had engines, 10's-5 ft., and one boiler allowed 220 psi. Conversion was made, c. 1914. Capt. Hicks died following injuries in an auto accident in 1925. The Fruin-Colnon Contracting Co., sold her July 1927 to the Kansas City Bridge Co. Capts. Roy A. Miller and Robert Roehrig acquired her spring of 1935 and cut her down single deck for job towing. Crew on the Illinois River November 1939: Capt. Ben J. Winters, master; Tom Critchfield, chief, and Ed Richey, mate. Roehrig's partners then were R.J. Schultz and Edgar S. Albrecht. Sold to Charles N. Drake, St. Louis, January 1940. By 1944 she was beached out on the wharf at St. Louis and dismantled. As the gas-powered *ALBERMATLA* she was a handsome boat owned at St. Louis by George S. Johnston.

4676 RAMBLER

Prop yacht wh b. Pittsburgh, Pa., 1891. 37 x 6.7 x 3. Used as a private pleasure boat on the Monongahela and upper Ohio, owned by principals of the Large Distillery and others; Henry Schutz, Jr., Frederick Renziehausen, Henry Studoewith, William H. Jacob, Arnold Schneider, Frederick Fischer, and George Bolland. She was swapped around several times, and was owned for a time by J. Conrad Hahn and Joseph H. Hahn; also by Arthur Moren, Jr. Still documented 1899, maybe later.

4677 RANCHERO

SW p wh b. Freedom, Pa., 1854. 206 tons. Off the lists 1860.

4678 RANGER

Stw p wh b. New Albany, Ind., 1856. 86 tons. Burned at Carthage, Miss., Feb. 15, 1859.

4679 RANGER

Rig? p wh b. Perryville, Ark., 1882. 95 x 17 x 2.2. Made

trips New Orleans-Shreveport in 1883. Documented at New Orleans 1886, maybe later.

4680 RAPID TRANSIT

Prop p wh b. Covington, Ky., 1877. 153 x 28 x 5.5. Twin props driven by four vertical engines. Her owner Capt. Oakes took her to New Orleans where four months later she was in the hands of a U.S. marshal. Val P. Collins of Covington, Ky., bid her in for $3,200, put her in tow of the *LIBERTY NO. 4* and brought her home. In 1879 ran Memphis-Commerce for a few months, Capt. William Ashford, with J. Frank Ellison, clerk. Inspected in the Cincinnati District 1881 and 1882. When dismantled her engines went to *QUEEN OF ST. JOHNS* built at Cincinnati summer 1884.

4681 RAPIDAN

Stw p wh b. Pittsburgh, Pa., 1866. 236 tons. She left Pittsburgh, new, June 1866 for the Tennessee River, celebrated as an extremely light draft packet designed to get over Colbert Shoals and maintain traffic to Florence, Ala. The original news account erroneously called her the *RAPID ANN.* She was lost on the Tennessee 40 miles above its mouth, Mar. 6, 1870. The dispatch was brief: "She is a total loss; its value small."

4682 RAPIDAN

Stw p wh b. (?), 1875–1876. 405 tons. 172 x 32 x 5. Engines, 14½'s- 4½ ft. Two boilers. Owned by Evansville & Tennessee River Packet Co. In 1877 crew was headed by Capt. H.D. Evetts, with R.D. Morrow, clerk. She sank and was lost at Diamond Island Chute, below Pittsburg Landing, Tenn., downbound for Cairo, Ill., Oct. 1879.

4683 RAPIDAN NO. 2

Stw p wh b. Pittsburgh, Pa., 1867. 248 tons. Built for Tennessee River. In 1869 running Evansville-Florence with Capt. Lee Howell, master, and Si Hughes and Billy Williams as clerks. The Evansville & Tennessee River Packet Co. was organized 1870, John Gilbert, president, operating this boat along with the *SAM ORR* (see). They built the *FLORINA LEE* in 1870, the *RED CLOUD* in 1873, the *RAPIDAN* in 1875 (prior listing), and *SILVER CLOUD* in 1878. The *RAPIDAN NO. 2* was dismantled 1875.

4684 RAPIDES

SW p wh b. New Albany, Ind., 1855. 414 tons. 199 x 32.9 x 6.9. Built for C.J. Barston, Rapides Parish, La., Capt. J.C. Dowty, master. New Orleans-Donaldsonville, 1856. Later in New Orleans-Shreveport trade. Went to Confederate registry 1861.

4685 RAPIDES

Stw p wh b. Cincinnati, Oh., 1869. 415 tons. 153.6 x 37.6 x 5.3. Built for Capt. John Haberle, New Orleans. Ran New Orleans-Red River. In 1871 Capt. John Hienn, master, with J.C. Mitchell, clerk. Sank 25 miles below Baton Rouge Feb. 28, 1876, with cargo from Tensas River.

4686 RAPIDS

Stw p wh b. Grand Rapids, Mich., 1905. 134.8 x 28.4 x 4.5. Engines, 12's- 6 ft. One firebox boiler 54" by 20 ft. Built by merchants of Grand Rapids to run to Grand Haven, Mich., to connect with lake steamers for Chicago. They also built the *GRAND* (see) at the same time. Both were bought by merchants of Little Rock, Ark., in 1909, and were brought under their own steam through the Fox River improvement to St. Louis. Ran Memphis-Arkansas River briefly. Capt. Fred McCandless had her in Cairo-Paducah trade 1914, and in 1915, same trade, Capt. Peter Wilton, master, with Lee Rhodes, clerk. Lost in ice at Paducah, Dec. 12, 1917. Machinery went to the *H. G. HILL* (see).

4687 RATTLER

Stw U.S. tinclad wh b. Cincinnati, Oh., 1862. 165 tons. Originally *FLORENCE MILLER* (see) which was sold to the U.S. and became Tinclad #1, named *RATTLER,* Nov. 11, 1862. Participated in the attack on Fort Hindman on the Arkansas River, and Fort Pemberton on the Yazoo, and in the expedition up Black and Ouachita rivers July 1863. Her main claim to fame was that she was almost sold to the enemy by her commanding officer. That estimable gentleman, Acting Master D.W. Glenney, harbored a vague grudge against the Union government and arranged for her sale to the Confederates for $2,000 and 100 bales of cotton. The plot was foiled just in time, and Glenney spent the remainder of the war running from agents of the justifiably irritated Rear Admiral David Dixon Porter. The *RATTLER* was lost off Grand Gulf, Miss., Dec. 30, 1864.

4688 RATTLER

SW p wh b. Wheeling, W. Va., 1863. 33 tons. Ran Wheeling-Sunfish (Clarington) summer 1864 when most other boats were laid up. Snagged and lost at Island 37, Mississippi River, Dec. 13, 1866.

4689 RAVEN

Stw p wh b. McKeesport, Pa., 1852. 96 tons. Off the lists 1859.

4690 RAVEN

Local packet at Evansville in the 1870s commanded by Capt. J.T. Hugo.

4691 REBECCA

SW p wh b. Cincinnati, Oh., 1864. 341 tons. Came out new July 1864 designed for Memphis-De Valls Bluff trade, along with *ROWENA* (see). In early January 1865 made a trip to the upper Ohio and was ice-locked in the mouth of the Muskingum most of January and February. Ran Memphis-De Valls Bluff 1865; and that November made a trip Nashville-Cincinnati. Sold to the Wheeling, Parkersburg & Cincinnati Transportation Co., in March 1867, Charles Muhleman, president. Ran Wheeling-Parkersburg, Capt. Jack Harrison, until she was wrecked at the B&O railroad bridge, Parkersburg, W. Va., Dec. 7, 1869. The towboat *DIAMOND* had sunk two loads of coal there a day or so before, and *REBECCA* hit one of them at Pier 4 of the bridge which was under construction. Four or five deckhands were lost. Some of her machinery went to the side-wheel *COURIER* (see).

4692 REBECCA

SW ferry wh b. Steubenville, Oh., 1868. 32 tons. A double-ender with one stack. Operated at Steubenville along with *JEFFERSON* and *UNION* (both see). Still listed 1876, maybe later.

4693 RED BLUFF

Rig? p wh b. Little Rock, Ark., 1879. 85 tons. Still listed 1882, maybe later.

4694 RED BUCK

SW p wh b. Maysville, Ky. (hull), 1864 and completed at Catlettsburg, Ky., 1865. 29 tons. Built to run up Big Sandy River, owned principally by W.L. Auxier and K.F. Hatcher, both eastern Kentucky merchants. Capt. Alex Smiley was master, with George W. Norris, clerk, in 1867. Hit a well known snag above Peach Orchard on the Big Sandy, downbound with corn and produce, principally dried fruit, Mar. 3, 1868, and was lost.

4695 RED CHIEF

Stw p wh b. Burlington, Oh., 1857. 150 tons. 113 x 30 x 5. Went to New Orleans, Capt. John C. Schute, and ran New Orleans-Shreveport piloted by Jesse Dillon of Lawrence County, Oh., who owned in her. Dillon became sole owner and master, April 1860. Sold Dec. 16, 1861, to Capt. Marion C. Wood, New Orleans, under Confederate registry.

4696 RED CHIEF NO. 2

Stw p wh b. California, Pa., 1859. 86 tons. 109 x 24 x 3.6. Owned by James G. Schute and Jesse Dillon, Lawrence County, Oh. Ran New Orleans-Shreveport. Went to Confederate registry 1861. Owned 1862 by Capt. A.S. Frisilier, St. Mary Parish, La. Was at Mobile May 14, 1865, in U.S. transport service.

4697 RED CLOUD

Stw p wh b. Harmar, Oh., at Knox Yard, 1870. 165 x 27 x 5. Built for Capt. Henry J. Brinker for New Orleans-Red River. Burned on Red River, downbound with 900 bales, June 27, 1871, and was lost.

4698 RED CLOUD

Stw p wh b. Jeffersonville, Ind., by Howard, 1873. 178 x 34.5 x 5.2. Engines, 16½'s- 5½ ft. Three boilers. Owned by Evansville & Tennessee River Packet Co., John Gilbert, president. Crew in May 1876: Capt. Allen J. Duncan, master, with William N. Dunn and Al Maynard, clerks. Sold 1877 to I.G. Baker who had her lengthened at St. Louis to become 228 ft. long, this in winter 1877–1878. Prior to the lengthening Baker had her to Fort Benton three times in 1877. On one of these trips she came up from Bismarck to the Fort in 8 days 17 hours, with arrival July 28, 1877, the all-time record. After the lengthening she brought 215 Mounted Police for Canada, 170 other passengers, plus horses, mules, cattle, and sheep, to the fort on one trip in 1879. Was at Fort Benton in 1881 and brought up 500 tons in 1882. She was snagged and lost at Eight Point, above Fort Peck, July 11, 1882, Capt. John A. Williams. The location later was called Red Cloud Bend. The roof bell was salvaged and I.G. Baker presented it to the Episcopal Church, Bismarck, in 1882. The wreck, long forgotten, was relocated by John Wenner in 1926. As a footnote to all of this, *RED CLOUD* broke her shaft July 1878 upbound for the fort about 80 miles above Bismarck. Her passengers were transferred to *JOSEPHINE,* and her freight to the *GENERAL TERRY.* She was returned to Bismarck, the shaft removed, and shipped by rail to Chicago for welding.

4699 RED RIVER

SW p wh b. Harmar, Oh., at Knox Yard, 1850. 276 tons. 174 x 29 x 6.2. Owned by Capt. Henry V. McCall, New Orleans. Sold December 1852 to Capt. Owen Franks. In November 1851 with Capt. Franks in charge she went to Marietta and loaded out with ploughs from the Marietta Foundry, barrels from Waters's Factory, flour from the Marietta Flour Mill, and potatoes from the valley, destined to New Orleans. She was regularly enrolled at New Orleans thereafter with eight changes in ownership 1852–1856. Ran regularly to Shreveport until 1857 when she was dismantled.

4700 RED RIVER

Stw p wh b. Jeffersonville, Ind., by Howard, 1899. 155 x 28 x 3.5. Owned by Red River Packet Co. Once was sunk from overloading at Alexandria, La., about 1903, Capt. H.M. Carter. She was taken to Cumberland River in 1904 along with *W.T. SCOVELL* and *ELECTRA,* and ran in Cumberland River Packet Co. This venture was short-lived. Finally sank in February 1907.

4701 RED ROVER

SW p wh b. Louisville, Ky., 1857. 625 tons. 256 x 40.9 x 7.5. Engines, 28's- 8 ft. Five boilers. Ran Nashville-New Orleans, and was termed "Fife Major's boat." Teamed up with the *JAMES JOHNSON* and *JAMES WOODS* (both see) in that trade 1860, Capt. W. Strong. She was acquired by the Confederates Nov. 7, 1861, and served at Columbus, Ky., and then Island 10. At the latter place she was hit by a shell and was taken ashore and tied. After the *CARONDELET* ran the batteries and U.S. forces had taken Island 10 the *RED ROVER* was found there, moored to the Tennessee shore. She was taken by the U.S. along with three other steamers. The mechanics from the *MOUND CITY* repaired the *RED ROVER* and she was sent by her own steam to Cairo next day. Then at St. Louis she was made into a hospital boat with bathrooms, laundry, two separate kitchens, a 300-ton ice box, gauze blinds on windows, operating room, an elevator from the main to cabin deck, bedding, furniture, sanitary stores, and medical dispensary. Her first mission was to the relief of the *MOUND CITY* which had been hit by a shell in her boilers at St. Charles, Ark., with many wounded and killed. She took the wounded to Memphis. Sister Angela, the Superior of the Sisters of the Holy Cross Order in the area, kindly offered the services of the sisters aboard the *RED ROVER.* These women became the forerunner of the U.S. Navy Nurse Corps. Wounded were taken to the Mound City hospital, after which the *RED ROVER* was docked at Mound City. Repaired, she went to Vicksburg and got there just in time for the *ARKANSAS* engagement wherein many were wounded on the *CARONDELET.* Later she was at Helena, Ark., and caught fire, but not badly damaged. She then went back to Mound City for the closing in of the decks, etc., for winter operations. While there, Navy took over. Early 1863 she went to Vicksburg and helped support operations for the seige of that place. She was in the area, with a trip to Memphis with wounded, until the surrender. Then went back to Mound City for repairs. The next spring she went to New Orleans distributing medical supplies along the way. Later in the summer did the same job mouth to Donaldsonville, La., and then again to New Orleans. In early 1865 she departed Memphis for Mound City and there spent her remaining days as a U.S. hospital ship. Sold at public auction Nov. 29, 1865, at Mound City to A.M. Carpenter for $4,500. For other U.S. Civil War hospital ships see *CITY OF LOUISIANA* (renamed *R.C. WOOD*), *D.A. JANUARY, IMPERIAL, EMPRESS.* All of these were equipped by the Western Sanitary Commission.

4702 RED ROVER

Recess wheel ferry wh b. Bridgeport, Ind., 1867. 49 tons. Served for a time at Helena, Ark., owned there by J.C. and J.K. Jeffries who bought her May 1871 from Thompson & Quarles. Off the lists 1877.

4703 REDSTONE

SW p wh b. Brownsville, Pa., 1851. 181 tons. Built for the Pittsburgh & Brownsville Packet Co., Capt. I.C. Woodward. Once ran from Pittsburgh to Brownsville in five hours, considered a record on slackwater. Sold to the Cincinnati-Madison trade, Capt. Thomas W. Pate. She had been racing with *HOOSIER STATE* and was backing out from a landing just above Carrollton, Ky., when the boilers exploded, Apr. 2, 1852, with loss of 14 lives. Among the victims was Rev. Henry Scott who had just come aboard. Chief engineer Lewis Berry and second engineer Joe W. Berry, both of Brownsville, lost their lives.

4704 RED STONE

SW p wh b. Cincinnati, Oh., 1854. 173 tons. Snagged and lost, Apr. 12, 1854.

4705 RED WING

SW p wh b. Cincinnati, Oh., 1846. 142 tons. 147 x 24 x 4.5. An Upper Mississippi packet, St. Louis-Galena-St. Peters, Capt. Berger. Burned in the wharf fire at St. Louis, May 17, 1849, along with 22 more.

4706 RED WING

Stw p wh b. Monongahela, Pa., 1856. 150 tons. 139 x 28. An Upper Mississippi packet, out of St. Paul, Capt. Woodburn and Capt. Ward. Snagged and sunk at Smith's Cut Off while in the Memphis-Little Rock trade, May 25, 1860.

4707 RED WING

SW p wh b. Brownsville, Pa. (hull), and completed at Pittsburgh, 1870. 245 x 35 x 6. Engines, 20's- 7 ft. Four boilers, each 38" by 25 ft., two flues. Paddlewheels 28'2" dia. working 11 ft. buckets. Capt. Adam Jacobs superintended construction for Keokuk Northern Line. Ran St. Louis-St. Paul, Capt. W.P. Hight, with P. Flannigan, clerk. Ran until dismantled, c. 1882.

4708 REES LEE

Stw p wh b. Jeffersonville, Ind., by Howard, 1899. 220 x 38 x 5. Owned by the Lee Line, Memphis. The Howard Yard also was building the *BAYLISS LEE* and *ROWENA LEE* when this boat was completed. Sank and lost at Tiptonville, Tenn., June 22, 1906.

4709 REES LEE

Stw p sh b. Ambridge, Pa. (hull), and completed at Pittsburgh, 1906, originally named *S.S. BROWN* (see). Bought by the Lee Line, Memphis, in 1909 and renamed. They ran her Memphis-St. Louis, "the fireproof, elegant flagship of the Line." Sold c. 1919, to Capt. D.W. Wisherd and others who converted her into an excursion boat, renamed *MAJESTIC* (see). A complete story of *S.S. BROWN, REES LEE, MAJESTIC* appears in *S&D Reflector,* June 1972.

4710 REES PRITCHARD

Stw p wh b. Madison, Ind., 1890. 150.3 x 31 x 3.3. Built for the Little Rock Oil Compress Co., Little Rock, Ark., and ran on the Arkansas River, Capt. L. Drake, with S.W. Weaver, clerk. See *S&D Reflector,* Sept. 1978 for account of the career of Capt. Rees Pritchard. Sold to Yazoo River Transportation Co., Vicksburg, Miss. Ultimately burned at Yazoo City, Miss., sometime after 1900.

4711 REGULAR

SW p wh b. Wheeling, W. Va., 1884 using hull and machinery of *SCIOTO* (see). Was entered in the Wheeling-Marietta trade that year, Capt. T.S. Thomas, with T.J. Martin, clerk. The venture was not successful. She was loaded with 2,500 barrels of potatoes and sent off to Cairo, Ill. New owners dismantled her.

4712 REGULATOR

Stw wh b. Shousetown, Pa., 1851. 155 tons. 155 x 24.5 x 4.5. First ran as a low water packet on Upper Ohio, Capt. Woodburn, with G.W. Neare, clerk. Sold to the St. Louis & Keokuk Packet Co., and made trips through to St. Paul. Off the lists 1862.

4713 REGULATOR

SW ferry wh b. McCoy, Oh., 1867. 47 tons. Served as a

ferry at New Cumberland, W. Va. Dismantled and hull used as a barge, 1874.

4714 REINDEER

SW p wh b. New Albany, Ind., 1851. 407 tons. Ran Louisville-New Orleans, and in 1853 came up in 4 days 19 hours 45 minutes, a record to that date. Sold to St. Louis parties and on the delivery trip collapsed a flue at Cannelton, Ind., Mar. 13, 1854, at 10:00 P.M. The *EUROPA* landed her and there was a life loss of 38. Next morning the *MAGNOLIA* towed the wreck to Hawesville where the victims were given a mass burial. A tombstone marks the site, pictured in *S&D Reflector,* September 1966, page 29. The *REINDEER* was rebuilt and served out of St. Louis until snagged and lost Nov. 12, 1857, at Wood River, Ill.

4715 REINDEER

SW p wh b. Marietta, Oh., 1860. 360 tons. Went to Mobile, Ala., and passed to Confederate registry in 1861.

4716 REINDEER

Stw U.S. tinclad wh b. Cincinnati, Oh., 1863, 212 tons. Originally *RACHAEL MILLER,* taken over by the U.S. and renamed *REINDEER,* #35. Visited Pittsburgh in October 1864. Sold to private parties Oct. 5, 1865, who renamed her *MARINER*. Lost at Onawa Bend near Decatur, Neb., on Missouri River, May 9, 1867.

4717 REINDEER

Stw p wh b. Cincinnati, Oh., 1863. 155 tons. She became Tinclad #57, renamed *PERI* in war service. Sold to private owners and renamed *MARIETTA* on Oct. 3, 1865 (see).

4718 REINDEER

SW p wh b. Cincinnati, Oh., 1865. 267 tons. Went to Mobile, Ala. Off the lists 1874.

4719 REINDEER

Rig? p wh b. Terre Haute, Ind., 1878. 103 x 19 x 3. Probably used on Wabash River. Still documented 1886, maybe later. Place of build is taken from U.S. Inspectors Report 1883, although *Lists of Merchant Vessels* use Evansville, Ind.

4720 REINDEER

Stw p wh b. Dubuque, Iowa, 1888. 125 x 23 x 3.3. Engines, 12's- 6½ ft. Dubuque-Clinton, tri-weekly, 1897, Capt. W.M. Moore. She was snagged in Coon Slough summer 1894, believed to have hit wreckage from *LADY FRANKLIN* and *NOMINEE,* raised. Rebuilt in 1901 at Quincy, Ill., to become the *ILLINOIS* of the Illinois Fish Commission (see).

4721 RELIANCE

SW p wh b. Cincinnati, Oh., 1845. 156 tons. 129.3 x 26 x 5. Went to New Orleans owned in part by her master, Capt. William Moore. Sold January 1847 to S.W. Tichenor, Galveston, Tex. Off the lists 1854.

4722 RELIANCE

Stw p wh b. Shousetown, Pa., 1855. 156 tons. In Pittsburgh-Cincinnati trade, Capt. Knight, February 1862. Snagged and lost near Steubenville, Oh., Dec. 1862.

4723 RELIANCE

SW p wh b. Portsmouth, Oh., 1885. 126 x 21.5 x 4.2. A single deck side-wheel packet. She was still listed 1895, maybe later.

4724 RELIEF

SW p wh b. Ironton, Oh., 1848. 68 tons. Snagged and lost at Louisiana, Mo., Nov. 8, 1853.

4725 RELIEF

Stw ferry wh b. Pt. Pleasant, W. Va., 1910. 91 x 23.4 x 3. Owned by the Gardner Docks, Pt. Pleasant, and loaned out to pinch-hit while regular ferryboats were at Gardners for repairs. Later bought by Capt. Gordon C. Greene and used at Maysville, Ky., c. 1925, with L.D. Poor, pilot. Kline O'Neill took her to Augusta, Ky., prior to 1935 for ferry service there. He dismantled her summer 1943 and some of the lumber was used in building the Shamrock Cafe at Augusta. When originally built, parts of *CHAMPION NO. 2* were used.

4726 RENE MCCREADY

SW p wh b. Jeffersonville, Ind., by Howard, 1875. 141 x 28 x 4.8. Ran Memphis-St. Francis River. In April 1882 shuttling between Memphis and Marion, Ark., making connections with the Memphis & Little Rock RR, Capt. O.K. Joplin, with A.L. Penning, clerk. Dismantled 1890 at Memphis. Her oak dining room tables were still stored in the Lee Line wharfboat in 1920.

4727 REPUBLIC

SW p wh b. Brownsville, Pa., 1850. 107 tons. Snagged and lost June 23, 1854, near Dover, Tenn.

4728 REPUBLIC

SW p wh b. Jeffersonville, Ind., 1855. 699 tons. 249 x 40 x 7. Engines, 24's- 9 ft. Built for Louisville-New Orleans trade, Capt. Ed Montgomery. Same trade 1858, Capt. T. Jefferson Stewart. She was considered quite a "floating palace." Sold before start of the war to Capt. A. Baird and others, and last owner under Confederate registry was Eliza Anne Wayne, wife of Alfred Gordon Wayne. The Confederates took her up Yazoo River and were converting her into a ram when Federal forces captured and burned her at Yazoo City, Miss., in May 1863.

4729 RESACA

Stw p wh b. on upper Tennessee River, maybe at Bridgeport, during the Civil War. She was built by U.S. personnel. After hostilities ceased she was owned and operated by Capt. John L. Doss. On one occasion he took her up the Little Tennessee almost to the North Carolina state line. In spring 1870 the Western & Atlantic RR operated her (later the Nashville, Chattanooga & St. Louis RR) and laid her up at Chattanooga in May 1870. Her engines turned up later on the *J. T. WILDER* (see).

4730 RESCUE

Stw p wh b. Shousetown, Pa., 1853. 168 tons. Apparently a wanderer; she made a trip from Pittsburgh to St. Paul 1857 and ran trips to the Falls of St. Anthony. At the present time there is "Rescue Rock" near Derby, Ind., where an old-time steamboat was lost prior to the Civil War, very likely this one. Her demise came Sept. 22, 1857, the location listed in official records as "Derby, Ohio."

4731 RESCUE

Rig? ferry wh b. Metropolis, Ill., 1864. 58 tons. Owned 1874 by the Illinois & St. Louis Railroad & Coal Co. Still listed 1876.

4732 RESCUE

Stw p wh b. St. Louis, Mo., 1884. 121 x 26.8 x 3.4. Owned by Mississippi Navigation Co., Capt. Abe Hutchinson, St. Louis, president. Capt. Robert Farris was first master, and she was put to use towing rafts over the Keokuk rapids, and handling excursion parties. Later owned by Capt. Sol York who ran her in the Peoria-Henry trade, a round trip a day, on Illinois River. By 1895 was running Louisville-Kentucky River, apparently with poor results, inasmuch as she went to a U.S. Marshal sale in November 1897 and was sold to Capt. W.D. Pugh, Vicksburg, for a bid of $1,035.

4733 RESCUE

Stw wh b. Parkersburg, W. Va., 1887. 65 x 15 x 2.1. Possibly a combination towboat and packet. Still listed in the area 1896.

4734 RESERVE

Stw p wh b. Wheeling, W. Va., 1863. 240 tons. Came out with Capt. D.B. Herron, master and W.M. List, clerk, running Pittsburgh-Cincinnati. Same trade spring 1864, Capt. W.M. List. Capt. R.C. Gray made a trip with her Pittsburgh-Nashville, spring 1870. Dismantled later that year.

4735 RESOLUTE

Stw p wh b. Cincinnati, Oh., 1857. 203 tons. Snagged and lost on the Arkansas River between Van Buren and Fort Smith, Apr. 10, 1859. The pilothouse was utilized on a nearby farm and the cabin lumber went to constructing three boat houses.

4736 RETRIEVE

Stw p wh b. Elizabeth, Pa., 1850. 204 tons. Went to Apalachicola, Fla. Off the lists in 1856.

4737 RETURN

Stw p wh b. California, Pa., 1852. 219 tons. 152 x 28 x 5.5. Part owner and first master, Capt. William Stoops, with N. Springer, clerk. Ran upper Ohio trades until sold. Last owner and master, Capt. J.R. Jones. Lost at De Valls Bluff, Ark., July 27, 1859.

4738 REUB WHITE

SW p wh b. Murraysville, Va., 1856. 110 tons. 104 x 27 x 3.8. Principally owned by Capt. John R. Allebaugh, New Orleans. Ran on Red River to Shreveport. Had several changes of ownership. Last owner, August Lahusen of New Orleans. Sank in the Harvey Canal on Feb. 3, 1861.

4739 REVEILLE

SW p wh b. St. Louis, Mo., 1844. 45 tons. She was a regular in the St. Louis-Galena run. Off the lists 1853.

4740 REVEILLE

Stw p wh b. Elizabeth, Pa., 1849. 71 tons. Originally owned by William Colvin, Alexander Goff, and Robert Majors, all of Pittsburgh, and Capt. H.M. Stone, master. Ran Pittsburgh-Allegheny River, Capt. Rees Rees. Sold October 1850 to Ezekiel Day, Pittsburgh, and J.H. Gallagher, McKeesport, Pa., Capt. D.R. Dale. Ran Pittsburgh-Wellsville. Sold 1851 for the Pomeroy-Portsmouth trade, Capt. Brubaker. Was taken to the Upper Mississippi and was a regular out of St. Paul until dismantled 1857.

4741 REVENUE

SW p wh b. Pittsburgh, Pa., 1844. 145 tons. 143 x 22 x 4.9. First master, Capt. A. Bennett, Wheeling, Va. Chief engineer was John Stut Neal. Ran tramp trades to Arkansas River and was up the Wabash in 1845. Engineer J.S. Neal is credited with installing the first steam whistle heard along the Western Waters on this boat, made at the A. Fulton shop in Pittsburgh. Burned on the Illinois River near Peoria, May 24, 1847.

4742 REVENUE

Stw p wh b. Murraysville, W. Va., 1863. 236 tons. Ran Pittsburgh-Cincinnati, Capt. Charles Muhleman, 1864. Same trade 1865, Capt. J.T. Russell, with W.M. List, clerk. Capt. Wash Kerr, clerk, 1866. Snagged and lost near Buena Vista, Oh., Aug. 31, 1866.

4743 REVENUE CUTTER

Stw p wh b. Pittsburgh, Pa., 1844. 127 x 20 x 4.1. 100 tons. First master, Capt. E.C. Hazlip, Pittsburgh. Ran tramp trades on the Ohio, and spring 1845 making trips Cincinnati-Wabash River to Lafayette, Ind. By 1847 was in St. Louis-Galena trade, Capt. McMahon, and later ran Galena-St. Peters. Off the lists 1851.

4744 REVOLUTION

Rig? p wh b. Wheeling, Va., 1848. 210 tons. Ran local trades out of Wheeling, and ran low water Cincinnati-Louisville, August 1848, Capt. R.M. Hill. Burned in 1849.

4745 REX

Stw p wh b. Pittsburgh, Pa., 1891. 194 tons. 126 x 24 x 3. Built for the Des Arc Packet Co., De Valls Bluff, Ark., and ran Des Arc-De Valls Bluff, Capt. William M. Michael. Made a trip from Garland, Ark., to Shreveport, La., 1891. Sank at White Cliffs, 14 miles above Shreveport, Feb. 16, 1901, Capt. Michael listed as owner and master.

4746 RHODA

Stw p wh b. Marietta, Oh., 1870. 90 x 20. Owned by Capt. Dan Sayre and James Stein, the engineer. Capacity of 450 bales of cotton and ran in the headwaters of the St. Francis River "where boats have never run before."

4747 RHODE ISLAND

Stw p wh b. Freedom, Pa., 1844. 85 tons. Hull was built at Smiths Ferry, Pa., 135 x 22 x 4. Owned by Capt. R.D. Dawson and others, and ran local upper Ohio trades, Pittsburgh-Marietta, then Pittsburgh-Wheeling-Sunfish. Off the lists 1849, when machinery was placed on a new hull by Capt. David Green to become the *HAIL COLUMBIA* (see).

4748 RICHARD HENRY LEE

Stw p wh b. Cincinnati, Oh., 1850. 157 tons. Lost in collision with *OCEAN WAVE* near Grafton, Ill., Apr. 23, 1855.

4749 RICHARD ROE

Stw p wh b. Jeffersonville, Ind., by Howard, 1915, originally named *VIM* (see). 125 x 23.2 x 4.3. Engines, 10's- 4½ ft. from *HATTIE BROWN.* Renamed *RICHARD ROE* in August 1919 by Capt. William E. Roe, manager of Louisville & Cincinnati Packet Co., to honor his son. Ran Madison-Kentucky River. Sold to Capt. Lewis Tanner, March 1924, who used her as a towboat. Later went to Green River owned by High View Coal Co., located below Cromwell, Ky., and then sold February 1928 to Billhorn Construction Co., St. Louis, who used her on the Missouri River. Became the towboat *BARBARA HUNT.*

4750 RICHLAND

SW p wh b. New Albany, Ind., 1846. 82 tons. Burned at Pee Dee, Ky., Jan. 17, 1850.

4751 RICHMOND

SW p wh b. Louisville, Ky., 1845. 347 tons. 192.3 x 28.3 x 6.7. Engines, 20's- 8 ft. Three boilers, each 42" by 32 ft. Ran New Orleans-Milliken's Bend that summer, Capt. James McCord. Snagged and lost in Grand Chain, Ohio River, Nov. 13, 1845.

4752 RICHMOND

Stw p wh b. Louisville, Ky., 1866. 359 tons. 142.5 x 34.7 x 4.8. Engines, 16's- 6 ft. Two boilers. First owned by Capt. Andrew R. Harris, New Orleans, who commanded. Ran New Orleans-St. Louis. Sold January 1868 to Capt. W.T. Boardman and others, New Orleans. Ran New Orleans-Shreveport, with C.P. Boardman, clerk. Sank and lost in Red River 12 miles below Shreveport, Dec. 3, 1869.

4753 RICHMOND

SW p wh b. Madison, Ind., 1867. 1,645 tons. 340 x 50 x 9. Engines, 60's- 10 ft. from the *JACOB STRADER* (see). Six boilers, each 63" by 28 ft., and on her wheelhouses for a time in big lettering were the words "35 Pounds Steam" as an inducement to safe travel. Capt. J. Neal commanded and was principal owner. Ran New Orleans-St. Louis-Louisville. Her passenger cabin was 304 ft. long and 13½ ft. high, contained 70 "parlor" staterooms. An unusual feature was a ladies' observation pilothouse built on the skylight roof aft of the texas, access gained by a spiral staircase originating in the main ladies' cabin below. The cost of the boat complete was $240,000. Roustabout term for her was "the Rebel Home," and an oil painting graced the main cabin titled "Richmond on the James." A newspaper was published on board called *The Richmond Headlight.* She came out new with Capt. J. Stut Neal, master, and the following crew: William Winton, chief engineer (late of the *JACOB STRADER*); John S. Woolfolk, first clerk (formerly on *ATLANTIC* and lately on *GREY EAGLE* in the New Orleans-Vicksburg trade); R.P. Lodge, second clerk (lately on the *INDIANA*); Wes Whitlow, mate, and Anderson Lewis, steward. The hull was built at Madison by Vance, Armstrong & Co., and the boat built complete by Alex Temple. Five of her boilers were from *JACOB STRADER* and the sixth one was new, an extra, for auxilliaries. A special steam gauge was mounted in the main cabin for all passengers to see. For all of her magnificence she was not a financial success and in January 1870 was in the hands of a U.S. marshal at Louisville. Capt. Nate Green and others bought her in, and took her to St. Louis for the New Orleans trade. She hit the bank 45 miles below St. Louis Apr. 7, 1870, and cargo had to be jettisoned to keep her from sinking, and had to return to St. Louis for repairs. Regardless, Capt. Nate Green, with B.A. Congar, clerk, turned a profit. By June 1871 Capt. Green was sporting a $1,200 diamond bought from Capt. John W. Carroll and said if the boat blew up he planned to swallow it "but I feel perfectly safe with only 35 pounds of steam." To which a Pittsburgh river reporter retorted in print: "Yes, 35 pounds on the wheelhouses." She was wrecked in the Grand Chain, Ohio River, Dec. 31, 1874. This boat plays a major role in Frances Parkinson Keyes's novel, *Steamboat Gothic.*

4754 RICHMOND

Stw ferry wh b. New Richmond, Oh., 1882. Originally a recess wheel ferry named *G.F. TRUESDELL,* rebuilt 1883 with sternwheel and renamed. 79 x 25 x 3. There was not enough business at New Richmond to support the ferry and she was taken south. Documented at New Orleans 1886, maybe later.

4755 RIDGLEY

SW p wh b. New Albany, Ind., 1847. 97 tons. 123 x 21 x 4. Built for Henry & Cunningham, Van Buren, Ark., John H. Love, and Capt. John Q.A. Smith who commanded, New Albany. Went to New Orleans and ran up Red River. Collapsed a flue at Trinity with many scalded in July 1848. Burned at Recourse Cutoff, La., June 28, 1849.

4756 RIGHT OF WAY

Stw p wh b. Freedom, Pa. (hull), and completed at Wheeling, 1867. 133.9 x 28.2 x 4.1. Built for Capt. Noah Scovell, who commanded, and Josiah W. Warren, both of New Orleans. Ran on upper Red River above Shreveport connecting with the *BART ABLE* for New Orleans. Sold June

1870 to Frank M. Behan, New Orleans, with Capt. Alfred M. Osgood, master. Exploded boilers on Bayou Lafourche July 27, 1870, with loss of nine lives.

4757 RINGGOLD

Stw p wh b. Brownsville, Pa., 1846. 138 tons. Ran Pittsburgh to Wheeling one trip a week, and Pittsburgh to Sunfish (Clarington, Oh.) the other trip, Capt. W.R. Cope. A young man named Lew Kates arrived at Pittsburgh from Philadelphia by stagecoach one day in 1848 and shipped aboard this boat as a deckhand, then became fireman, and then second mate; in later life he owned the *WILL KYLE* (see). Off the lists in 1853.

4758 RINGGOLD

SW p wh b. Louisville, Ky., 1846. 212 tons. The captain on this boat brought the news to Gen. Zachary Taylor that he had been nominated for the U.S. presidency at his Spithead Point plantation. Snagged and lost in the Arkansas River, February 1848.

4759 RIO GRANDE

SW p wh b. Brownsville, Pa., 1846. 162 tons. Tramped from Pittsburgh to St. Louis and elsewhere. Struck a flatboat loaded with rock at Golconda, Ill., in November 1848 and was lost.

4760 RIO GRANDE

SW p wh b. Jeffersonville, Ind., 1846. 166 tons. 149.8 x 24.5 x 4.8. Went to New Orleans owned by Offutt Bros., St. Landry Parish, Capt. John H. Gordon. Sold March 1850 to Capt. Oramel Hinckley, St. Landry Parish, who commanded, and James Johnston, same address. Off the lists 1852.

4761 RIPLEY

SW ferry wh b. Cincinnati, Oh., 1865. 56 tons. Probably served at Ripley, Oh. Off the lists 1873.

4762 RIVER CITY

SW ferry wh b. Portsmouth, Oh., 1874. 88 tons. Ran Portsmouth-Springville, Ky. She appears in a photograph, see *S&D Reflector,* June 1974, page 55.

4763 RIVER QUEEN

Stw p wh b. below Warren, Pa. (hull), and taken to Pittsburgh for completion, 1865. 150 x 30. The hull was built on the Sill farm just below Warren on the upper Allegheny. The principals were "New York parties" represented by William H. Churchill. While being completed at the Monongahela wharf, Pittsburgh, the old towboat *GEORGE ALBREE* caught fire and was destroyed along with the partially completed *RIVER QUEEN,* this on Sept. 10, 1865. The *RIVER QUEEN*'s engineer, William C. Champlain, was arrested in St. Louis and returned on charges of arson. This story is amplified in *S&D Reflector,* September 1968, page 19.

4764 RIVERSIDE

SW ferry wh b. Madison, Ind., 1890. 70 x 20 x 4. Still listed 1896, maybe later.

4765 RIVERSIDE

Stw snagboat wh b. Poplar Bluff, Mo., 1913. 84 x 22 x 3. Used on Black River, Ark., by U.S. Engineers. Still in service, 1925.

4766 ROANOKE

Stw p wh b. California, Pa., 1864. 266 tons. 156 x 32.2 x 5.8. Owned principally by R.W. Harton, Allegheny County, Pa., Capt. Emmett McClure. Ran Pittsburgh-Louisville. Sold in December 1864 to Capt. James Shedden who took her to St. Louis. Lost near Commerce, Mo., Dec. 17, 1865. The *UNDERWRITER,* Capt. R.W. Dugan, took out the wreck.

4767 ROB ROY

Stw p wh b. Madison, Ind., 1861. 148 tons. 153.3 x 22.6 x 5.4. After the war was taken to New Orleans owned jointly by A.L. Mansfield and S.P. Griffin, Capt. James Mahood, master. Sold April 1867 to Capt. John N. Pharr of St. Mary Parish and others. Off the lists in 1870.

4768 ROB ROY

Stw p wh b. Cincinnati, Oh., 1864. 199 tons. 151.6 x 31.5 x 3.4. Engines, 15's- 5 ft. Two tubular boilers. She was at Pittsburgh loading for New Orleans in latter December 1864, Capt. Kenniston, with D.B. Ludwig in the office. Trips up Red River, 1865. In fall of 1866 bringing new oil barrels from Aurora, Ind., to Pittsburgh, Capt. Charles Beers, then loaded out for Cincinnati with T.S. Calhoon in the office. Spring 1868 in Evansville-Owensboro trade, Capt. James L. Magennis with Lew Morris, clerk. Sold to Capt. James M. Kane, St. Louis, who took her to Arkadelphia, Ark., in December 1868. Off the lists 1871.

4769 ROB ROY

SW p wh b. Madison, Ind. (hull and framing), and completed at St. Louis, 1866. 253 x 41 x 6. Engines, 26's- 7 ft. Five boilers, each 46" by 24 ft., four flues. Paddlewheels 28 ft. dia. working 14 ft. buckets. Built for St. Louis-Keokuk trade. On Mar. 27, 1870, she hit the ice breaker while passing through the draw bridge at Quincy, Ill., and lost her port wheel, blacksmith shop, pantry, and lower guard but was safely landed. While departing from St. Louis, Feb. 28, 1871, the head of a mud drum blew out killing a fireman and two camels belonging to Van Amburgh's menagerie. On June 2, 1874, was snagged and sunk near Alton, Ill., downbound. Sank after hitting an obstruction below Louisiana, Mo., Feb. 26, 1880. She was raised and slated for dismantling when the *GOLDEN EAGLE* burned, was brought out of retirement, and late that summer broke a gib on the starboard engine crosshead on the inboard stroke and knocked out the cylinder head, the last running she did.

4770 Rob Roy

Stw p wh b. Lafayette, Ind., on Wabash River, 1878, originally named *SAM BOREE* (see). Rebuilt at St. Louis spring 1882 and renamed, owned by Henry McPherson. Ran on the Missouri River and was snagged six miles below Rocheport, Mo., July 26, 1883, Capt. Sabin E. Phelps. She was swapped around a good bit and in late 1888 her home port was Memphis, and in 1891 went to Cincinnati, thence to Wheeling in 1898 and back to Cincinnati.

4771 Rob Roy

Stw ferry wh b. Commerce, Mo., 1896. 69 x 16.1 x 3.6. Operated between Commerce and Santa Fe, Ill., run by John Daily and his four sons, Willie, Ollie, Alvie, and Eddie. "Uncle" Cline Billings was pilot. Last inspection was at Commerce on Sept. 11, 1902.

4772 Robb

Stw p wh b. Pittsburgh, Pa., 1860, originally named *ALFRED ROBB* (see). She was sold to Henry W. Smith at Mound City, Ill., Aug. 17, 1865, for $9,200 and redocumented *ROBB*. She was dismantled at Ironton, Oh., in late fall of 1873.

4773 Robert B. Carson

Stw p wh b. Evansville, Ind., 1884. 70 x 18 x 3.6. In June 1895 was forced to suspend operations on Salt River, Ky., for low water.

4774 Robert Burns

SW p wh b. Cincinnati, Oh., 1864. 457 tons. 180 x 38 x 6.5. Engines, 22's- 7½ ft. Three boilers. Built for Capt. G.W. Ebert who ran her as an independent in Cincinnati-Memphis trade with Standish Peppard, clerk. He sold control that December to Capt. R.W. Terry. The Memphis & Cincinnati Packet Co., bought her and continued her in the trade, Capt. E. Eugene Bowers, with William Dunlop, clerk. She was laid up in the mouth of the Licking River in 1867 and remained there until May 1868 when she was brought out to handle a picnic excursion. Later in the Memphis trade, Capt. M.L. Virdin, with A.D. Wilson, clerk. Dismantled at Cincinnati, 1872, along with the *ALICE DEAN* and *SILVER MOON* (both see).

4775 Robert Campbell

SW p wh b. Hannibal, Mo., 1849. 268 tons. Burned and lost in a wharf fire at St. Louis, Oct. 13, 1853.

4776 Robert Campbell, Jr.

SW p wh b. Jeffersonville, Ind., by Howard, 1860. 421 tons. 226 x 41 x 6. Ran St. Louis-New Orleans, Capt. John S. Shaw. In the summer of 1863 Capt. Joe LaBarge loaded her out for Fort Benton, Mont., but had to turn back at the Yellowstone River due to low water. Then was sold to a Capt. McCloy and others and was loaded out for Vicksburg. Caught fire in Milliken's Bend on Sept. 28, 1863. Many jumped overboard with life loss set at 22 persons. The *GEN. ANDERSON* rendered aid.

4777 Rob't. E. Lee

SW p wh b. New Albany, Ind., 1866. 1,456.31 tons. 285.5 x 46 x 9. Engines, 40's- 10 ft. Eight boilers, each 42″ by 28 ft. allowed 120 pounds steam. Owned entire by Capt. John W. Cannon, New Orleans. Built at what was known as the "lower yard" at New Albany by DeWitt Hill. She was moved across to the Kentucky shore while the lettering *ROB'T E. LEE* was being applied on the paddleboxes inasmuch as the war was still too fresh; some Hoosiers resented the name of the Rebel leader flaunted at their doorsteps. Captain Cannon chose the name inasmuch as the boat was to operate New Orleans-Vicksburg. The U.S. Steamboat Inspectors Reuben Dawson and John L. Crane of Louisville certificated her and she departed for southern climes Oct. 7, 1866, Capt. Cannon in personal charge, with James F. Smith in the office.

A dispatch from Cairo dated Oct. 10: "The *ROB'T E. LEE* had a slim trip of freight but was full of passengers. She arrived here before midnight and departed before daylight; our citizens had no opportunity of seeing this wonder of marine architecture. There are two notable things connected with her, however, which all the lengthy notices of her in the Louisville papers failed to mention. These are the rich, deep tone of her bell, and the loud noise produced by the escapement of steam from her cylinders. The former is so mellow and musical as to attract, instantaneously, the attention of every hearer; while the latter reverberates on the waters of a cold still night like the old fashioned and almost forgotten 'scape of the first *DIANA,* the *EDWARD SHIPPEN* and the first *LOUISIANA.*"

Not long after the *LEE* was established in her trade, Capt. T.P. Leathers chartered the *BELLE LEE* (see) also for the New Orleans-Vicksburg trade, an understanding having been arrived at between these two principals as to freight rates. Soon a story commenced to trickle into newspapers:

From the New Albany *Commercial,* Nov. 14, 1868: "Capt. John W. Cannon and Capt. Tom Leathers, we are informed, indulged in a knock-down at New Orleans Saturday. The difficulty arose out of the charter of the *BELLE LEE* by Leathers and his subsequent violation of the charter. Capt. Cannon had the best of the fight, so our informant states."

A few days later, from a Cincinnati source:

"In the recent fight . . . we understand very little claret was drawn."

A description of the contenders was written by G.L. Nourse of the New York *Marine Journal* later on:

> ". . . I became well acquainted with both of these prominent men and found there was as much difference in their temperaments as there is between a lion and a lamb. Captain Cannon was a mild-mannered, extremely polite person, approachable at all times and never happier than when exploiting the good qualities of the *LEE,* which was his idol. He held, at that time [1870] no prejudices against his fellow citizens.
>
> "Capt. Thomas P. Leathers, his competitor in the

Vicksburg trade, had one of the most commanding presences possible. He was over six feet tall, a giant in stature, wore a ruffled shirt with a large cluster diamond pin and always dressed in Confederate gray. Woe be to him who referred to the late unpleasantness, as Capt. Leathers did not recognize that the war was over, nor did he ever lose sight of the fact that I was a government official and therefor a carpet bagger. [Note: Captain Nourse was Harbor Master and Supervising Inspector of Steam Vessels at New Orleans 1870–1885.] The decided differences of temperament in these two equally eminent men caused them to have admirers temperamentally constituted as they were, so that Capt. Cannon's friends were largely of those who accepted reconstruction gracefully, while Capt. Leathers had a following that died hard as it were."

Captain Leathers had taken a bad financial mauling during the war, but had recouped by 1869 to let contract at Cincinnati for the construction of a new *NATCHEZ* (see) which soon set for herself a reputation for speed. In June 1870 she ran New Orleans to St. Louis in epic time. A Cincinnati morning newspaper promptly cheered the exploit and made pointed allusion to the *LEE* being so slow that it would appear she was propelled by mules operating a treadmill instead of with steam engines.

The *ROB'T E. LEE* had been advertised New Orleans to Louisville, departing New Orleans on June 30, 1870, at 5:00 P.M., a routine early summer trip at the conclusion of a busy cotton season. The *NATCHEZ* was advertised to St. Louis, same day, same hour. Rumors of an impending race were scotched by Captain Leathers who inserted a notice in New Orleans newspapers: "I take this method of informing the public that the report that the *NATCHEZ,* leaving here next Thursday, 30th inst. intended racing, is not true. All passengers and shippers can rest assured that the *NATCHEZ* will not race with any boat that may leave here on the same day with her. . ."

Denials notwithstanding everybody knew the truth; these two nags had been groomed and prepared, both were headed for St. Louis, and devil get the hindmost. The starting point was abreast the St. Mary's Market; the levee was jammed with sight-seers; invited guests thronged aboard the *GREAT REPUBLIC, GRAND ERA* and *MARY HOUSTON* for grandstand viewing, and excursionists went up the river on the *WM. S. PIKE, HENRY TETE,* and *MAYFLOWER.* The U.S. Inspectors clamped lead seals on the safety valves of both boats to discourage tampering. A cannon was fired from the forecastle of the *LEE* at 1 3/4 minutes before 5, and at 2 minutes past 5 a cannon shot from the *NATCHEZ* announced her departure. So they did not get off to an even start, the *LEE* ahead, a lead she maintained and increased. At no time were the boats side by side, contrary to Currier & Ives's art.

Crew on the *LEE* during the race:

Capt. John W. Cannon, master

Adolph Martin, first clerk

N.W. Calmes, J.H. Mossop and Jack Sullivan were assistant clerks.

Wes Connor, James Pell, George Clayton, Enoch King, and Jesse Jameson, pilots

William Perkins, chief engineer

Tom Berry, second engineer

Steve Jermey, Thomas Yeadon, Joe McClovey, George Brown and John Wiest, assistant engineers.

Robert Singleton, Thomas Hastings, and Mike Peters, mates.

John Buist, carpenter

Frank Smith, steward

Tom Carey, watchman

The official timekeepers were Capt. John Smoker, Capt. John W. Tobin, Capt. John L. Kouns, Governor Warmouth, William McCutcheon, Capt. E.C. Carroll, and Jesse McLean. Some 33 invited guests were aboard, including some wives and children. The *LEE* carried no freight.

An outstanding incident deserves preservation, written later by assistant engineer John Wiest when he was chief steam engineer at the Louisville (Ky.) Water Works:

> Late that first night we sprung a leak in one of our boilers, and it got so bad that it was dousing the fires, and, worse, was putting such a burden on the doctor that water could hardly be supplied fast enough to hold gauge levels.
>
> The immediate question was how to find the leak and how to remedy it. Mr. Perkins, our chief, was too old to tackle such a job, and Mr. Berry, our second, was too stout a man to go crawling in a furnace. I volunteered.
>
> Of course nobody since Shadrach, Meshach and Abednago had crawled into a blazing furnace and come out alive, so the fires were dropped and water hoses played to cool the grate bars and tiling. Meanwhile I pulled on old overalls, tied a big bandana about my head, and pulled on a pair of heavy gloves. I went in there with a hammer, a cold chisel, and a poker. After a good bit of prying around I found that the top flange on the mud drum leg of the fourth boiler from the right hand side was the culprit.
>
> One good glance is all I got for at that moment Capt. Cannon and two other steamboat captains jerked me out of there. They laid me out on the starboard guard and soon as I recovered my speech I told them what I had seen.
>
> The *LEE* had not landed while this was going on, and now that the cause of the leak was known—water from around the flange seam—Mr. Perkins concluded to try the usual remedy for such case, and took hemp packing, cut it into fine bits, and introduced this into the cold water suction valves of the doctor. This dosage was repeated many times until finally the leaking stopped.
>
> Due to this delay the *NATCHEZ* came near overtaking us, and just before daylight I took a look aft and saw the glare from her fire doors, and figured she must be within 400 yards astern.
>
> Back in shape again we began to pull away from her. That next morning Capt. Cannon suggested to Mr.

Perkins that he "tame down" the engines a bit, for the *NATCHEZ* was away behind. Mr Perkins said that the *NATCHEZ* was not bothering him at all; that he was after beating the time of the *PRINCESS* to Natchez. Which we did.

Both boats were burning coal, with a liberal supply of pine knots on hand for tonic. The *LEE* replenished at Natchez, Vicksburg, and Memphis simply by hanging a fuel flat on either side, brought to her by tugs, the roustabouts shoveling the coal aboard under way, and then casting the flats loose for the tugs to catch. At Lake Washington the *FRANK PARGOUD* came alongside the *LEE,* delivered fuel from her deck, both boats working full steam ahead. This performance was hotly debated later on, claims being made that the *LEE* was assisted up the river thereby and so gained unfair advantage. Capt. John L. Kouns later stated that the *LEE* at no time carried excessive steam, remarking that those 40-inch cylinders were drinking all the steam the firemen could produce.

The side-wheel *IDLEWILD* (see) came alongside several miles below Cairo, Capt. Gus Fowler in charge, and transferred some passengers. The *LEE* again fueled from flats on the Missouri shore below Cairo Point, and picked up her St. Louis pilots. The *NATCHEZ* also fueled at Cairo about an hour later. It still was anybody's race with 180 more miles to go. That night the *LEE* was hampered by fog, running on slow bell, but she managed to "break through" by 2:00 A.M., and ran on to St. Louis with no further delay. The *NATCHEZ* had no such luck and was forced to tie at shore twice, losing 4 hours 45 minutes. Thus the victorious *LEE* steamed into the St. Louis harbor on the late morning of July 4, 1870, 3 days, 18 hours and 14 minutes out of New Orleans, the all-time record for a commercial steamboat. The *NATCHEZ* limped in later that evening.

For more details of the celebrated race we would refer the reader to *The Great Steamboat Race* by Roy L. Barkhau, a book issued, 1962, by lithographers Young & Klein, Cincinnati. After the celebrations and banquet at St. Louis, the *LEE* was taken to Mound City, Ill., and hauled on the marine ways July 13, to "screw up her chains." The hogchains had been slackened for the race, a procedure widely accepted, the explanation being that a long wooden hull will pass more easily through the water thereby, when allowed to work freely.

Also the *LEE* acquired double swinging stage planks at this time, an innovation adopted on the rivers but a short time prior, a vast improvement for handling freight and passengers on and off at shore landings. The *NATCHEZ* was similarly provided when built at Cincinnati in 1869, although she unshipped hers and left them on the New Orleans levee prior to the race.

At two o'clock in the morning, Dec. 22, 1870, the *ROB'T. E. LEE* and the side-wheel *POTOMAC* (see) collided opposite Natchez, Miss., with the *LEE* so badly damaged that she was run out on a sandbar where she settled. She was raised and repaired. She brought to New Orleans her record cotton cargo, 5,741 bales, in 1874. She departed New Orleans en route to Portland, Ky., for dismantling in mid-April 1876. Several thousand persons gathered to see her off, the Washington Artillery gave her a 100-gun parting salute, and the *USS CANONICUS* saluted her. All boats and tugs in the harbor blew salutes. She had 60 passengers and a light freight trip. Rivermen at Memphis awaited her arrival there with a big bonfire on the levee, at night, while the tug *N.M. JONES* blew salutes. Upon arrival at Portland her forecastle cannon was twice fired; first shot to honor her birthplace across the river, New Albany, and the second a farewell signal marking the closing of her career. A week or so later she was moved across to New Albany. Following her dismantling the hull was taken to Memphis for use as a wharfboat. Her chandeliers from the cabin were installed in the Presbyterian Church, Port Gibson, Miss., and as these lines are written are still there.

Capt. John W. Cannon lies buried at Frankfort, Ky., long his summer home. Inscribed on the monument: Born June 17, 1820—Died Apr. 18, 1882. His birthplace was the Cannon farm, about two miles above Hawesville, Hancock County, Ky., about opposite the present Cannelton Locks. His parents moved to hilly acres back of Hawesville where the foundations of the brick home were in evidence (1974) and the fallen gravestones lay flat, marked John H. Cannon and wife, who died respectively 1846 and 1842. See *S&D Reflector,* March 1975, page 18. Your scribe in 1953 called on Mrs. John A. Forster at 135 West Bayly Avenue, Louisville, Ky., the former Miss Cordie Cannon, daughter of Capt. John W. Cannon. Through the cooperation of Capts. C.W. Stoll and Roy L. Barkhau, who arranged the visit, we procured a photograph of an excellent oil painting of her illustrious father, which since has been widely reproduced.

4778 ROB'T. E. LEE

SW p wh b. Jeffersonville, Ind. by Howard, 1876. 315 x 48.5 x 10.5. Engines, 40's- 10 ft. Nine boilers, each 42" by 32 ft. Paddlewheels 40 ft. dia. working 17 ft. buckets. Much equipment from the former *ROB'T. E. LEE* went into her construction. Launched Apr. 25, 1876, at 4:00 P.M. She was completed at Portland, Ky., and New Albany, Ind., and was taken to Cairo for finishing touches in mid-summer. She was much more pretentious than her predecessor, designed for the New Orleans-Vicksburg trade. Will S. Hays noted in the Louisville *Courier-Journal* that the first occupants of her lavish bridal chamber were two old maids, "one of whom got the cholera and like to died, and the other never slept a wink. It is sad." She entered her trade Aug. 15, 1876, and ran regularly until Feb. 16, 1877, when she blew a cylinder head, killing one of the crew, and was laid up until March 27 for $3,500 worth of repairs. She then resumed and finished the season July 1, 1878, a total of 43 round trips bringing to New Orleans:

124,084 bales of cotton
416 sacks of cotton
103,029 sacks of cotton seed
11,723 sacks of oil cake
9,841 sacks of cotton seed meal

2,890 barrels of cotton seed oil
490 barrels of flour
513 barrels of apples
3 barrels of whiskey
72 barrels of molasses
95 barrels of potatoes
— plus other miscellaneous cargo.

On various occasions the *LEE* was chosen at Mardi Gras time to act as the Royal Yacht to bring Rex to his Carnival Capital. The first occasion was on Monday, Mar. 4, 1878. In the 1879 festivities Rex again arrived aboard the *LEE,* and his Queen was Miss Courtney Leathers, daughter of Capt. Thomas P. Leathers. In 1880 the *LEE* again was chosen. The South was scourged with yellow fever in the summer of 1878 resulting in depressed business for the packets extending over the next several years. Capt. Cannon retrenched and was forced to cancel insurance on the *LEE.* He died, 62, in the spring of 1882. That fall the boat was renovated, painted, and again entered the trade. She was downbound from Vicksburg at 3:30 A.M., Sept. 30, 1882, at Yucatan Plantation, when fire was discovered. Witnesses said she "went up like gunpowder," with loss of some 30 lives. Ben Stout was the pilot on watch, brother-in-law of the late commander, and in the engineroom was William Perkins. The loss was placed at $118,000. Her roof bell was salvaged several years later by W.J. Pearson and was placed in the belfry of the Methodist Church at Grand Gulf, Miss. When the church was discontinued about 1902, Mr. Pearson presented the bell to Mrs. Callender of Port Gibson, who passed it along to her son B.B. Callender who still had it at Port Gibson in 1947.

4779 ROBERT E. LEE

SW p wh b. Jeffersonville, Ind., by Howard, 1898. 238 x 38 x 5. Owned by the Lee Line of Memphis, Tenn., and not named for the military leader of the Confederacy, but for Capt. Robert E. Lee of Memphis. Ran Memphis-Ashport, Capt. Dennis Conners. Capt. George Carvel was master when she sank opposite Craighead Point, upbound. All passengers and crew were safely removed. The river was rising and she broke up. Capt. Robert E. Lee was son of Capt. James Lee, Jr., and grandson of Capt. James Lee, founder of the Lee Line. His mother was Rowena Bayless Lee. When he died, June 12, 1942, he left a son, Robert E. Lee, Jr. The loss of the boat occurred Dec. 22, 1904.

4780 ROBERT E. LEE

Stw ferry sh b. Jeffersonville, Ind., by Howard, 1925. Originally *CHARLES J. MILLER,* then *GENERAL,* then *WARREN JOHNSON* (all see). Sold to Savannah River in Georgia, fall 1946, and was taken there partly by towing and partly under steam, owned by L.H. Simkins, Augusta, Ga.

4781 ROBERT E. LEE

Stw ferry sh b. Antiquity, Oh., 1939. 100.8 x 36 x 4.2. Engines, 8's- 4 ft. from *VALLEY BELLE.* Built by O.E. Sayre of the Riverside Mill for Fullerton-Portsmouth Ferry Co., Fullerton, Ky. She was damaged in a collision with the diesel towboat *GEORGE T. PRICE* on Feb. 4, 1947, and was retired soon thereafter. Sold to a ferry company at Tell City, Ind., and dismantled. The whistle was taken to Chicago and broadcast on radio by the *Tribune* with much fanfare, claiming it to be the whistle of "the old racing steamer *ROB'T E. LEE*" much to the amusement of some.

ROBERT E. LEE, JR.

See *BOB LEE, JR.,* registered name.

4782 ROBERT EMMETT

Stw p wh b. Cincinnati, Oh., 1846. 147 tons. Went to Mobile, Ala., and snagged and lost May 26, 1847.

4783 ROBERT EMMETT

Stw p wh b. Memphis, Tenn., 1864. 43 tons. In charge of Capt. Keho, snagged on the Missouri River about 20 miles above Hermann, Mo., having on board Col. Poser's Regiment, 350 men, Nov. 3, 1864. The loss happened near midnight during a heavy storm. No life loss. The location has been described as DeWitt, Mo., and also at St. Aubert's Island.

4784 ROBERT EMMETT

SW ferry wh b. Wellsville, Oh., 1890. 75 x 16 x 3.8. Still listed 1895.

4785 ROBERT FULTON

SW p wh b. Pittsburgh, Pa., 1845. 199 tons. Ran on Red River, New Orleans-Alexandria, in 1847, Capt. Len Moore. Noted at St. Paul, July 3, 1851. Snagged and lost at Bainbridge, Mo., Dec. 12, 1851.

4786 ROBERT FULTON

SW p wh b. California, Pa., 1860. 158 tons. 137 x 29 x 4.3. Originally owned in St. Louis by Walter Ransom (5/8) and the balance by Mrs. Margaret Rees, Pittsburgh, and Allen Stockdale, Wellsville, Oh., Capt. James Ransom. She was captured as a Confederate steamer at the mouth of Red River, Oct. 7, 1863, by the U.S. monitor *OSAGE,* together with the *ARGUS.* Both were burned to prevent recapture.

4787 ROBERT HARDY

Rig? ferry wh b. New Albany, Ind., 1870. 84 tons. The Pittsburgh *Gazette* reported, Jan. 7, 1878: "The *ROBERT HARDY,* built for service at Little Rock, Ark., Capt. J.A. Pines, is reported to be a failure, having been badly constructed, with machinery and motive power improperly adapted to the boat."

4788 ROBERT HARRIS

Recess wheel p wh b. Burlington, Iowa, 1872. 11 tons. 88.2 x 14 x 4.5. Ran Winona-Fountain City until 1906. A cute little feller.

4789 ROBERT J. WARD

SW p wh b. New Albany, Ind., 1852. 731 tons. 310 x 36.5 x 8. Engines, 32½'s- 9 ft. Six boilers. Ran Louisville-New

Orleans, named for a prominent Louisville citizen who was once president of the Jockey Club. Capt. Silas Miller commanded, later owner of the Galt House, Louisville. Dismantled at New Orleans in 1860. The machinery was loaded aboard the *MARS,* having been bought by Capt. David White, who planned to use it on a boat he was building at Madison, Ind. The Confederates appropriated it at Memphis, June 1861.

4790 ROBERT M. PATTON

Stw p wh b. McKeesport, Pa., 1851. 185 tons. Went to Tennessee River. Off the lists 1855.

4791 ROBERT M. PATTON NO. 2

Stw p wh b. Louisville, Ky., 1855. 261 tons. Ran Louisville-Tennessee River. Off the lists in 1860.

4792 ROBT. MITCHELL

SW p wh b. Cincinnati, Oh., 1871. 270 x 41 (37 ft. floor) x 8. Engines, 24½'s- 8 ft. from *ALICE V.* Four boilers, each 40" by 28 ft., two flues. First owned by Capt. Henry A. Jones and Thomas Sherlock. Ran Cincinnati-New Orleans, Capt. Richard M. Wade. Sold 1874 to Evansville & New Orleans Packet Co., then ran Louisville-New Orleans, Capt. Gus Fowler, with Gus DuSouchet, clerk. Then sold to Capt. James Paul, entire, who commanded in Cincinnati-New Orleans trade; also Capt. Lew Kates with Frank Stein, clerk. In latter April 1876 she brought to Cincinnati from New Orleans 315 live alligators ranging from six inches to 14 ft. long. Capts. Dan Moore and Frank Stein bought control in August 1877 and continued her in the trade. Capt. John A. Williamson and M.V. Daly also owned in her. Hit an obstruction and sank at Fox Island, Mississippi River, Nov. 3, 1880. The *OUACHITA BELLE* (see) came along soon afterwards and sank within 100 yards of the *MITCHELL.* It was thought that both boats had struck a wheel shaft from the *PENNSYLVANIA* (see) which had exploded boilers there June 13, 1858. At time of loss she was entered in the Southern Transportation Co. Raised, returned to Cincinnati, and dismantled.

4793 ROBERT MOORE

Stw p wh b. Cincinnati, Oh., 1864. 238 tons. Built at John Bruce's yard for Cincinnati-Frankfort, Ky. trade, owned by Lans Moore, Joseph Lattimer, and Joseph Singer. Capt. Jesse Y. Hurd ran her Cincinnati-Big Sandy trade summer 1865 during low water, taking the place of the *TELEGRAPH.* Loading at Pittsburgh for Cincinnati and Louisville, March 1866, Capt. Dan Maratta. In June 1866 she had a martin box slung between her stacks, inhabited, and everywhere she went the martins went along. Sold September 1866 to Capt. Wash Kerr for the Pittsburgh-Portsmouth trade, taking the place of the *REVENUE* (see). Ran there until fall of 1868 when sold to Cincinnati & Nashville Packet Co. She was upbound on the Ohio River in Smithland Island May 17, 1870, at 1:30 A.M., when she hit a snag. The *CAMELIA* was just ahead but had run aground and could not answer the distress call. When she wiggled free she returned to the *MOORE* and rendered aid. This happened at the mouth of the Cumberland River. Jeff Frame, later wharfmaster at Wheeling, was one of the crew.

4794 ROBERT MORRIS

SW p wh b. Elizabethtown, Pa., 1845. 232 tons. Machinery from *VALLEY FORGE.* Capt. Hugh Campbell ran her Pittsburgh-St. Louis. One of the crew was M.W. Beltzhoover, Pittsburgh, later identified with the early Pittsburgh & Cincinnati Packet Line. Dismantled in 1851, and machinery went to *ST. JAMES.*

4795 ROBERT R. ANDERSON

Rig? p wh b. Whitesburg, Ala. (hull), and completed at Nashville, Tenn., 1879. 135.4 x 34.8 x 4. Owned by Capt. S.C. Capehart and ran in the North Alabama trade on the Tennessee. Did not put in many appearances at Chattanooga. In the fall of 1885 was struck by a storm at Fletcher's Ferry, en route from Decatur to Chattanooga, and almost wrecked.

4796 ROBERT RHEA

Stw p wh b. Marietta, Oh., 1908. 149 x 30 x 4.4. Engines, 11 3/8's- 5 ft. Two boilers, each 38" by 18 ft. Built for Cumberland River Steamboat Co., with W.W. Parminter and Thomas G. Ryman, Jr., the principals. Sold to the "new" Ryman Line in 1910, which went bankrupt in September 1916. Bought by Capt. I.T. Rhea at the sale in November 1916 along with *HENRY HARLEY.* The Nashville Trust Co., advertised her for sale in December 1918 as executors to the estate of Capt. I.T. Rhea, deceased. She was bought by the St. Louis & Tennessee River Packet Co., January 1919, who sold her to Irving M. Eanes, Mobile, Ala., in August 1927. She ran there with the *HELEN BURKE,* replacing the *JOHN QUILL.* Originally had no texas but acquired one in her Tennessee River days. May have had a change in machinery, c. 1912, 11 3/4's- 4 ft.

4797 ROBERT ROGERS

SW p wh b. Brownsville, Pa., 1850. 178 tons. Lost in collision with the *REPUBLIC* at Dover, Ky., Apr. 14, 1852.

4798 ROBERT T. GRAHAM

Stw ferry wh b. Madison, Ind., 1918. 64.5 x 22 x 4. Operated at Vevay, Ind., owned by J.L. Graham. Dismantled in 1942.

4799 ROBERT WATSON

Stw p wh b. Elizabeth, Pa., 1858. 138 tons. 129 x 27.9 x 4.1. Acquired by Capt. John Smoker, New Orleans, February 1859, who ran her up Red River. Later went to Shieldsborough, Miss. (now Bay St. Louis), Capt. Albert Pierce under Confederate registry.

4800 ROBERT WIGHTMAN

Stw p wh b. Elizabethtown, Pa., 1848. 62 tons. Ran Pittsburgh-Zanesville, Capt. Perry Kerr, 1850. Went to New Orleans, Capt. George L. Kouns, owned in Lawrence County, Oh., by the Kouns family. Off the lists 1854.

4801 Roberta

Stw p wh b. Jeffersonville, Ind., by Howard, 1903. 138 x 28 x 4.5. A cotton packet owned by Monroe Navigation Co., and ran New Orleans-Ouachita River, Capt. B.F. Tatum. Engines 5 ft. stroke. Lost when she hit the bridge at Grand Encore, La.

4802 Rochester

Stw p wh b. Belle Vernon, Pa., 1855. 197 tons. Was at St. Paul, Minn., 1856. Snagged and lost at Madison, Ind., Dec. 8, 1859.

4803 Rochester

Stw p wh b. Rochester, Pa., 1866. 57 tons. Probably handled produce boats, etc. On July 1, 1868, she was out high and dry on French Island, lower Ohio River, on the Indiana side, 200 feet from the channel. Off the lists in 1869.

4804 Rock Bluff

SW ferry wh b. Shawneetown, Ill., 1859. 27 tons. A dispatch from Evansville, Ind., dated May 2, 1864: "Norris Ranger, the tobacco king, has bought the steamer *ALICE* for $6,500 and the famous *ROCK BLUFF* for the tobacco trade and will command neither, for the present."

4805 Rock City

Stw p wh b. Nashville, Tenn., 1854. 147 tons. Went to Confederate registry 1861.

4806 Rock City

Rig? p wh b. Little Rock, Ark., 1856. 137 tons. 126.3 x 27.3 x 4.3. Open hold, gunnel built. Enrolled at New Orleans October 1859, owned by Francis Moore, Capt. James W. Moore. Went to Confederate registry owned by Capt. William M. Summers, New Orleans.

4807 Rock City

Stw p wh b. Nashville, Tenn., 1897. 110 x 24 x 3.8. Operated by St. Francis River & Helena Packet Co. Sank on St. Francis River six miles from Jeffersonville, Ark., January 1900, and was reported a total loss. Still listed in 1903.

4808 Rock Island

SW ferry wh b. New Albany, Ind., 1857. 172 tons. Operated at Rock Island, Ill. Apparently rebuilt at Rock Island in 1873. Removed from documentation in 1882.

4809 Rock Island

SW p wh b. Madison, Ind., 1870. 200 x 32. Machinery from *CANADA*. Owned by Keokuk Northern Line. Made trips St. Louis-Cincinnati in 1873, Capt. B. Bradbord, with James Gilkeson, clerk. Pilothouse was burned off at Le Claire while tied there for fog, September 1873; she continued to St. Louis without it. Cut down by ice at St. Louis, Dec. 13, 1876.

4810 Rock Island

SW ferry wh b. Clinton, Iowa, 1875, originally named *AUGUSTA*, then *T.J. ROBINSON* (both see). As *ROCK ISLAND* she operated between Davenport and Rock Island teamed up with the *DAVENPORT*. Later went to Helena, Ark., as the ferry there. Beached out and dismantled at Helena. Machinery went to *CAROLYN*, b. Memphis in 1922.

4811 Rockaway

SW p wh b. Elizabeth, Pa., 1846. 221 tons. 155 x 28.7 x 5.7. Originally on the upper Ohio, with trips to New Orleans, Capt. John R. Davis. Other stockholders were Robert Graham, Marshall County, Va., and John Milton Thompson, Pittsburgh. In December 1850 principal owner was Charles Davis, Wheeling. Off the lists 1852.

4812 Rockaway No. 2

SW p wh b. Elizabeth, Pa., 1850. 324 tons. 165 x 30 x 7. Owned entire by Capt. J.R. Davis, New Orleans. Sold June 1852 to William Cooper, Union County, Ky., Capt. John W. Cannon, master. In 1853 Capt. L.J. Moore, Camden, Ark., became part owner and master. Burned at Bayou Sara, La., Apr. 29, 1854 en route from Alexandria, La., to New Orleans with 400 bales of cotton.

4813 Rocket

Stw p wh b. Brownsville, Pa., 1856. 176 tons. Capt. William Dean built her, and she ran Rochester-Wellsville on the upper Ohio. Sold to Capt. John Wolf, Jr., and ran Pittsburgh-Gallipolis, and Pittsburgh-Cincinnati, until the eve of the war. Was sent to Pittsburg Landing, Tenn., with several barges of ammunition in tow and was moored there while the battle was going on. Shells were bursting too close for comfort and Capt. Wolf was backing away when General Rawlins called him back, threatening to shoot every man on the boat if the order wasn't complied with promptly. The *ROCKET* returned with her ammo. Others aboard at the time were Charles B. Hurst, Rochester, Pa., and mate Wash Barr, Pittsburgh. In May 1862 she was loaded with old guns and ammo on the Tennessee River and dispatched to St. Louis. Broke her shaft but delivered the cargo July 28. She was in U.S. service most of the war, taking orders from General Thomas who often rode aboard. He had her at Natchez, and in November 1864 she was repaired at Pittsburgh, Pa., and loaded out for New Orleans and Fort Jackson, carrying a cannon on each deck and outfitted with muskets. She was back in Pittsburgh in mid-September 1865 and was dismantled soon thereafter.

4814 Rockwood

Stw p wh b. Kingston, Tenn., 1882. 130 x 25.6 x 4. Machinery from the *R. C. JACKSON* (see). Operated on the upper Tennessee. Still documented 1896, maybe later.

4815 Rodolph

SW p wh b. Madison, Ind., 1855. 274 tons. 175 x 33 x 5. Engines, 20's- 6½ ft. Four boilers. Built for Capt. William Cecil for Cincinnati-Nashville trade. Made trips to the lower Mississippi and Red River. Sank and lost just below Cairo, Ill., Oct. 17, 1858.

4816 RODOLPH

Stw p wh b. Cincinnati, Oh., 1863. 217 tons. Sold to the U.S.N., Dec. 16, 1863. She was towing salvage equipment near Mobile, Ala., on Apr. 1, 1865, to assist raising operations on the steamer *MILWAUKEE* when she was struck by a torpedo and lost in Blakely River, with loss of four lives.

4817 RODOLPH

Stw p wh b. Cincinnati, Oh., 1864. 249 tons. Snagged and lost 15 miles below Little Rock, Ark., on the Arkansas River, December 1865.

4818 ROEBUCK

SW p wh b. Brownsville, Pa., 1857. 164 tons. 147 x 23 x 5. Went to Greenwood, Miss., owned by Thomas Nelson of that place, with Capt. J.C. Brown, master. In 1860 sold to S.H. Parisot, Yazoo City, Miss., and M.P. Dent, Vicksburg, equal shares, with Capt. M.P. Dent as master. Enrolled at New Orleans November 1860, owned by Andrew Jackson Parmele, with Capt. M. Gwartney, master. Sold April 1861 to William Buchanan, New Orleans, and went to Confederate registry.

4819 ROMEO

SW p wh b. Louisville, Ky., 1850. 140 tons. First home port, Mobile, Ala. Snagged and lost at Campagnolle, Ark., Dec. 31, 1851.

4820 ROMEO

Stw p wh b. Brownsville, Pa., 1862. 175 tons. 154.1 x 31.1 x 4. Engines, 12's- 4 ft. Arrived at Pittsburgh, new, August 1862, built and owned by Capt. John L. Rhoads who had built the *JULIET* just prior (see). Made a trip up Wabash River and a photograph exists of her at Terre Haute with excursionists bound for Clinton, members of the Centenary Baptist Church, Capt. Uriah Shewmaker. Taken over by U.S. and became Tinclad #3 on Oct. 31, 1862. Sold at public auction at Mound City, Ill., on Aug. 17, 1865, for $7,150, bought by Edward Williams. Documents indicate she was changed into a side-wheeler, still *ROMEO,* and ran in trades at Evansville, Ind., Capt. J. Ham Throop, master, with George Throop, clerk. Off the lists 1870.

4821 ROOSEVELT

SW ex wh b. Stillwater, Minn., 1913, originally named *VERNE SWAIN* (see) which was sold March 1927 to D.B.G. Rose, Louisville, Ky., and renamed *ROSE ISLAND* (see). In August 1928 renamed *ROOSEVELT* and came to Pittsburgh May 1929 owned by Capt. Griffith W. Shaw and others. Again sold and during a docking program at Paducah April 1931 was renamed *CITY OF MEMPHIS* (see).

4822 ROSA

SW p wh b. Louisville, Ky., 1851. 265 tons. 115.8 x 27.8 x 6.5. Went to New Orleans in March 1852 owned in part by Capt. William Greig of St. Martinsville, La. Later owned by Capt. Joseph Saliba of New Orleans and ran New Orleans-Red River. Snagged and lost at Lake End, La., June 9, 1856. The remains of the wreck were removed by the snagboat *ALGERINE* the following July.

4823 ROSA BELLE

Rig? p wh b. Shoals, Ind., 1880. 79.9 x 18.2 x 2. Still documented at Evansville in 1886, maybe later.

4824 ROSA BLAND

Stw p wh b. Little Rock, Ark., 1889. 64 tons. 113.2 x 22.8 x 4.4. Sank and lost 22 miles above Shreveport, La., on Red River with 54 bales of cotton and 1,100 sacks of cotton seed, at Douglas Landing, Mar. 15, 1898. The wreck of the *FRIENDLY* (see) was nearby.

4825 ROSA DONNALLY

Stw p wh b. Paducah, Ky., 1865. 218 tons. Off the lists in 1867.

4826 ROSA FRANKS

Stw p wh b. Harmar, Oh., by Knox, 1866. 240 tons. 126 x 28.5 x 4.2. Built for Capt. Henry J. Brinker, New Orleans. Ran out of Shreveport, La. Capt. J.W. Carlton acquired interest in April 1867 and commanded in 1868. Sold August 1869 to Henry F. Vickers, Richland Parish, La., Capt. Charles A. Beard. Burned and lost 15 miles up Red River Mar. 18, 1871. Also documented as *ROSE FRANKS.*

4827 ROSA LEE

SW p wh b. Paducah, Ky., 1887. 225 x 36 x 7. Engines, 32's-7 ft. from *FRANK PARGOUD.* Christened by Jennie Fowler, daughter of Capt. Joe Fowler. Owned by Lee Line of Memphis. Burned at Memphis on Nov. 10, 1892.

4828 ROSA MILLER

Stw p wh b. Pittsburgh, Pa., 1875. 237 tons. She was en route from Pine Bluff, Ark., to Memphis with cotton when snagged and lost, Oct. 21, 1876 at Swan Lake, Arkansas River, just above the wrecks of the *EDINBURG* and *SALLIE.* Capt. Thomas J. Darragh was in charge. The *PINE BLUFF* was sent to rescue 500 bales of cotton.

4829 ROSA TAYLOR

Centerwheel ferry wh b. Madison, Ind., 1863. 132 tons. Went to Quincy, Ill. Removed from documentation in 1879.

4830 ROSADELLA

SW p wh b. New Cumberland, Va., 1862. 28 tons. Off the lists 1869.

4831 ROSALIE

Stw p wh b. Brownsville, Pa., 1854. 158 tons. Ran summer low water Pittsburgh-Wheeling, 1856, Capt. Doyle and later Capt. G.W. Rowley. Same trade summer 1857 and 1858. She made a trip to St. Paul, Minn., in 1857 with Pittsburgh stoves and hardware and sank just below the city. Raised and was at St. Paul again in 1858 and 1859. Sold October 1858 to Capt. J.T. Russell and S.P. Simpson for the Parkersburg-Gallipolis trade replacing the *SILVER STAR* (see). Sank Oct. 10, 1859, below Wheeling. Sold to the St. Louis & Keokuk Line commanded by Capt. Mike Littleton, and was lost in the ice break-up at St. Louis Dec. 16, 1865.

4832 ROSALIE JUDSON

SW p wh b. Jeffersonville, Ind., by Howard, 1857, originally named *DIANA* (see). During the war she was with the USQMD and when sold to private hands was renamed *ROSALIE JUDSON,* Mar. 14, 1866. Off the lists 1867.

4833 ROSALIE M.

Stw p wh b. Vicksburg, Miss., 1906. 66 x 14 x 5. Engines, 10's- 3 ft. One boiler, 60″ by 14 ft. Owned by Capt. Tom Morrissey, short trades out of Vicksburg. In 1907, Capt. Harry Bumgardner, master, with Aubrey D. Haines as pilot. Sank 20 miles above Vicksburg in February 1908 and lost. The *FALLS CITY* (see) was her replacement.

4834 ROSALIE SMOOT

Rig? ferry wh b. Canton, Mo., 1880. 80 x 18.7 x 3.3. Operated at Cape Girardeau, Mo. Still listed 1886, maybe later.

4835 ROSCOE

SW p wh b. Shousetown, Pa., 1846. 225 tons. Ran Pittsburgh-St. Louis, Capt. Javens. Sank and lost three miles below Rising Sun, Ind., while downbound Cincinnati to St. Louis, Mar. 23, 1849.

4836 ROSE

Stw p wh b. Dubuque, Iowa by Iowa Iron Works in 1886. Steel hull 54 x 10. One horizontal boiler 4′4″ long and 2′6″ dia. allowed 170 psi working engines 6″- 18″ stroke. Shipped knockdown to Townsend, Mont., on the Northern Pacific RR where the two sections were put together and launched in the Missouri River. Owned by a ranchman, Nicholas Higler. The original idea was to operate her between Great Falls and the Grand Canyon of the Missouri, several miles from Helena. The plan died aborning due to the building of the Montana Railroad. She then became a sight-seeing boat and in the 17 years she operated carried an estimated 10,000 passengers, one of whom was President Benjamin Harrison. In 1906 the hull was wearing thin and she was hauled out and abandoned. David Higler, son of the builder, removed the brass builder's plate from the wreck and presented it to the Montana Historical Society of which he was secretary and librarian.

4837 ROSE BUD

Stw p wh b. California, Pa., 1877. 177.4 x 31.3 x 4. Engines, 13's- 5 ft. Two boilers. Original owners: S.B. Coulson, William S. Evans, D.S.H. Gilmore, D.W. Maratta, and James C. McVay. Hull built by Eberman & McFall. One of the few boats which made over 50 trips to Fort Benton, Mont. Her first trip up the Missouri terminated at the Yellowstone River in 1877. On four occasions she was the first arrival at Fort Benton in the spring, these in 1880, 1883, 1886, and in 1887, only boat with such a record. On this last occasion she arrived April 26, earliest in the history of Fort Benton steamboating. Bought by the Block P Line about 1884–1885, having been the last of the Coulson fleet. She was equipped with electricity in 1882 and her "illuminators" were the first seen at Fort Benton. Sank below Claggett in the fall of 1882; again below Rocky Point in August 1886. In 1887 Capt. Joe Todd lacked a deck crew by reason of a strike, hired a crew of blanket Indians and arrived at Fort Benton with Gros Ventres, Ree, and Mandan Indians handling the freight. Made trips to Fort Benton in 1888 and 1889 after the railroad had arrived, and then was sold to the Benton Packet Co., and operated on the lower reaches of the Missouri until sunk at the railroad warehouse, Bismarck, S.D., on June 16, 1896. The river was falling rapidly and she settled on some submerged piling.

4838 ROSE CITY

Stw p wh Running Little Rock-Fort Smith on Arkansas River in April 1878, Capt. Rees Pritchard. Dispatch from Cairo, Ill., stated that she was snagged 20 miles above Fulton on Mar. 26, 1880.

ROSE FRANKS

See *ROSA FRANKS.*

4839 ROSE HAMBLETON

SW p wh b. Cincinnati, Oh., 1861. 154 tons. Arrived at Pittsburgh, Pa., June 6, 1866, Capt. Charles Beers, and loaded out for St. Louis, departing next day. Reported sold at Cincinnati to Capt. John Claycomb Nov. 19, 1866, and would load out for Arkansas River with Nip Simonton in the office. Loss was reported Sept. 30, 1869, with no details.

4840 ROSE HITE

Stw p wh b. Louisville, Ky., 1865. 353 tons. Ran Louisville-Henderson, Capt. Anson Ballard, with George Patterson, clerk. Hit a log on Hughes Bar, eight miles below Louisville, and sank in shallow water, Oct. 1873. The ferry *FRANK McHARRY* went to the scene. Off the lists in 1874.

4841 ROSE HITE

Stw p wh b. Jeffersonville, Ind., by Howard, 1895. 155 x 28 x 4. Engines, 13's- 5 ft. Two boilers, each 42″ by 22 ft. Built for the Louisville & Evansville Packet Co., and named for Capt. W.W. Hite's mother. Ran local trades in that area until sold to Pittsburgh in November 1900. New owner was the Mason Line on Monongahela River, headed by Capt. John G. Britton. The Mason Line and the regular line consolidated Feb. 18, 1902, to become the Pittsburgh, Brownsville & Morgantown Packet Co. When Monongahela slackwater was completed from Morgantown to Fairmont the *ROSE HITE* was the first packet to make the trip, May 1904. She was in charge of Capt. Joseph B. Williams, the ex-coal baron for whom the big towboat was named. She didn't get to Fairmont because of the low

B&O bridge one and one-half miles below with but 17 feet clearance. Her stacks were damaged hitting low wires and cables. On Dec. 14, 1905, she collided with the tow of the *JOHN F. KLEIN* in the narrows above Brownsville during a fog, and was sunk with loss of five deckhands. Her master at the time was Capt. John S. Faddis. In latter February 1906, while still sunk, all boats of the line were tied up for debt by the Valley Supply Co., Pittsburgh. Capts. William E. Roe and Martin F. Noll formed the Monongahela & Ohio Packet Co. She ran excursions out of Fairmont in 1906, reentered the trade in January 1907, hampered by three major floods into March, then ran Fairmont excursions until sold August 1907 to Capt. John L. Kerr and others who ran excursions at Pittsburgh with her. Early in 1908 a U.S. marshal attached her for debt at Dravosburg, Pa., where she remained all summer and fall. Capt. J.S. Tyner, Nashville, Tenn., bought her Nov. 10, 1908, and departed south with her. He renamed her *GRACEY CHILDERS* (see). She originally had a full texas with the pilothouse on top of it, but when brought to the Monongahela River she stopped in at Marietta and the pilothouse was placed forward of the texas because of low bridge clearances. She held the unenviable distinction of being in the hands of the U.S. marshal 10 times during the three years she was in Monongahela River.

4842 ROSE ISLAND

SW ex wh b. Stillwater, Minn., 1913, originally named *VERNE SWAIN* (see). She was sold March 1927 to D.B.G. Rose, Louisville, Ky., and renamed. In August 1928 was again renamed *ROOSEVELT* (see).

4843 ROSEDALE

Stw p wh b. Ashland, Ky., 1884, originally *LIZZIE JOHNSON* (see). Operated out of Evansville, Ind. Snagged in Sisters Islands, Ohio River, Oct. 24, 1887, and sank in 10 feet. Again sank four miles below Shawneetown, Ill., loaded with corn, owned by the Hudnuts of Terre Haute, Ind., on Wabash River. This was the second time she had sunk within a year. Happened Aug. 25, 1895.

4844 ROSEMARY

Stw ferry sh b. Pt. Pleasant, W. Va., by Marietta Mfg. Co., 1939. 64.9 x 27 x 4.5. Engines from towboat *CLAIRMONT*, earlier on the packet *HELENE*. (see). Built by Capt. Paul F. Thomas who operated her at 26th Street, Huntington, W. Va. Sold in 1943 to Kline O'Neill, Augusta, Ky., who dieselized her, renamed her *O'NEILL* in October 1944.

4845 ROSEVILLE

Stw p wh b. Sparda, Ark., 1879. 124 tons. Still in the area 1882.

4846 ROSEVILLE

Stw p wh b. Ozark, Ark., 1891. 76 x 24 x 2.2. Still listed 1896, maybe later. Lost on the Arkansas River at Sandy Bayou Crossing, Capt. Sam B. Adams.

4847 ROUGH AND READY

SW p wh b. Cincinnati, Oh., 1846. 80 tons. Off the lists 1849.

4848 ROUGH AND READY

SW p wh b. Elizabethtown, Pa., 1846. 150 tons. Went to war service 1846.

4849 ROUGH AND READY

Stw p wh b. Paducah, Ky., 1856. 126 tons. Lost in collision with *MONONGAHELA* at Napoleon, Ark., 1858.

4850 ROVER

Stw p wh b. Marietta, Oh., 1847. 37 tons. Originally built by Messrs. H. Booth, E.S. Davis and S. Davis, Marietta. Engines from Franks' Foundry, Marietta. Ready to depart for Red River, Nov. 18, 1847. Off the lists in 1849.

4851 ROVER

Stw p wh b. Pittsburgh, Pa., 1847. 39 tons. Enrolled at New Orleans April 1848 owned by Capt. H.F. Heath and others, Minden. 80 x 14.5 x 3.7. Off the lists 1850.

4852 ROWENA

SW p wh b. Elizabethtown, Pa., 1847. 230 tons. Snagged and lost just above St. Charles, Mo., in Penn's Bend, Mar. 12, 1850. Sank to the hurricane roof.

4853 ROWENA

SW p wh b. Elizabeth, Pa., 1858. 435 tons. 225 x 33.5 x 6. Engines, 22's- 6½ ft. Four boilers. Built for Capt. John T. Dozier. Snagged and lost at Devils Island above Cape Girardeau, Mo., Apr. 18, 1863. Another account relates she burned May 13, 1863.

4854 ROWENA

SW p wh b. Cincinnati, Oh., 1864. 341 tons. 180 x 35 x 6. Engines, 22½'s- 7 ft. Three boilers, each 46" by 26 ft. Built by David Gibson, Barker, Hart & Co., and Capt. Frank J. Oakes, all of Cincinnati. Ran Cincinnati-Madison trade, low water, summer 1864. Ran trips Pittsburgh-Cincinnati that winter. In May 1865 running Memphis-De Valls Bluff along with *REBECCA* (see). When she came to Pittsburgh in December 1864 was in charge of Capt. C.A. Dravo with Andy Robinson, Jr., in the office. Snagged and sunk opposite Helena, Ark., on Oct. 27, 1867.

4855 ROWENA

Stw p wh b. Burnside, Ky., 1904. 147.7 x 25.1 x 5. Engines, 10's- 3½ ft. Two boilers each 38" by 18 ft. Owned by Burnside & Burkesville Packet Co. Replaced the *BURNSIDE* which had lately burned at McMillin's Landing (see). Last owned by Cumberland Transportation Co., and ran on the upper Cumberland River. Occasionally ran Ohio River trades during low water seasons. In September 1917 was in Louisville-Evansville trade. Steamboat broker John F. Klein bought her at Burnside and in 1931 attempted to bring her out to Nashville but lost her by sinking at Greasy Creek Shoals about abreast of R. Dunbar's landing.

4856 ROWENA LEE

Stw p wh b. Jeffersonville, Ind., by Howard, 1890. 166.5 x 35 x 4.5. Built for the Lee Line, Memphis. Sank at Mhoon's Landing below Memphis in October 1897 with her head in six feet and the stern in 12 feet. Had 300 bales of cotton and some passengers, removed by the *J.N. HARBIN.* Capt. John J. Darragh was master for some time. Had competition from the *ANNIE LAURIE* operated by Capt. Milt Harry. Carried the whistle from the *RUTH* (b. 1888, see) and it later went to the *JAMES LEE* (2nd) and then to *HARRY LEE* (2nd). Rebuilt at Howards in 1899. Finally sank for keeps at Tyler's, Mo., just above the Arkansas state line. Sid Smith was the pilot on watch, this in 1902.

4857 ROYAL

Rig? ferry wh b. Portsmouth, Oh., 1872. 27 tons. Operated at Portsmouth, Oh., by Capt. John Lauson Mackey. Still documented 1882, maybe later.

4858 ROYAL

Stw p wh b. Hermann, Mo., 1884. 86.6 x 24 x 3. Built by Wohlt Bros., to run opposition to boats of the Hermann Ferry & Packet Co., which lasted the first year. The Heckmanns owned her later, and Capt. Wm. Lewis Heckmann, Sr., once had her up the Gasconade River to Arlington, Mo., the highest a steamboat ever went. Arlington is near Rolla, Mo. The usual trips were to Vienna, Mo., considered the head of navigation.

4859 ROYAL

Stw p wh b. Belle Vernon, Pa., 1890, originally named *T.N. BARNSDALL* (see). She was renamed Dec. 31, 1904, by the Clarington (Ohio) Packet Co., George H. Urpman, secy.-treas. Capt. E.J. Clark was master. Ran in the Wheeling-Clarington trade. Sold Nov. 22, 1909, to Frank Humphrey, entire, Clarington, Oh. On Dec. 11, 1909, boat's name changed to *LIBERTY* (see), and owner became Liberty Packet Co.

4860 ROYAL

Stw p wh b. Evansville, Ind., 1891. 163.6 x 30.6 x 6.6. Engines, 15½'s- 5½ ft. Three boilers, each 40" by 24 ft., allowed 169 psi. Iron cylinder beams, iron rudders, and a staggered paddlewheel. Machinery by Schwitz, Thuman & Co., Evansville. Boilers had five 8-inch flues. Theodore Thompson built the cabin, 17 staterooms, each 6x6 ft. Cabin 12 ft. wide. Drop windows in the forward end of the cabin. Original crew: Capt. J.B. Thompson, master; Frank Thompson, clerk; E.J. Clarke, pilot; Joseph Vandergrift, chief engineer, and Nate Smith, mate. Boat was named for a son of C.G. Perkins who was killed in the *LA MASCOTTE* (see) disaster, Oct. 5, 1886. Trial run made on May 16, 1891. Owners were Capt. J.B. Thompson and C.G. Perkins. The builder was Henry C. Reager, to plans furnished by C.G. Pearce of Kingston, Ontario, a noted ship designer. It is said Mr. Pearce received $1,000 for the hull lines. Ran in the Evansville-Henderson trade until the fall of 1894, then went to Natchez to handle cotton for the winter. Returned and ran Evansville-Henderson, and to Owensboro and Cannelton. This was an exceptional boat of her size; once ran 20 downstream miles in 49 minutes, and came from Henderson to Evansville (13 miles) in 52 minutes, the best time over that stretch. This record was excelled but once by a commercial steamboat when the racer *ROB'T. E. LEE* did it in 49½ minutes taking advantage of high water and going up behind Henderson Towhead saving 3 minutes.

FAST RUNS, HENDERSON TO EVANSVILLE

Boat	Minutes
Rob't. E. Lee (Racer)	49½ minutes
Royal	52
Sunbeam (propeller)	56
Morning Star (old)	56
Eclipse	57
W. W. O'Neil (towboat)	57
Dick Fowler	57
City of Owensboro	58
R.R. Springer	58
Idlewild (SW)	59
Joe Fowler	62½
Big Sandy	64

The *ROYAL* burned tied up for the night about a half mile above the Evansville wharf, Jan. 12, 1896. Her officers at the time: Capt. Moon Miller, master; Walter Brown, pilot, and Jesse Hickman, engineer.

Originally had no texas, and later one was added.

4861 ROYAL

Stw p wh b. Golconda, Ill., 1904. 105 x 19 x 3. Engines, 7"-3 ft. One boiler, 42" by 16 ft. Owned at Golconda by J.M. Anderson. Originally had the pilothouse at the front of the cabin, pool style, later on top of the cabin roof. Came to Louisville-Kentucky River trade about 1915. Struck the wharf at Madison, Ind., and was wrecked, Feb. 12, 1918.

4862 ROYAL ARCH

SW p wh b. West Elizabeth, Pa., 1852. 212 tons. Built for Capt. Adam Poe and others, Georgetown, Pa. Sank in Buffington Island, Ohio River, November 1852, and a few days later the *TUSCARORA* hit the wreck and also sank. Sold to the Galena & Minnesota Packet Co., Capt. E.H. Gleim, 1854, and was entered in the Davenport-Galena-Dubuque trade along with the *GREEK SLAVE* handling reshipping from the Rock Island RR which had just opened business to Rock Island, Ill. Capt. J.J. Smith, master, 1858. Snagged and lost at Nine Mile Island below Dubuque in 1858.

4863 ROYAL GEORGE

Rig? p wh Dispatch in the Pittsburgh *Gazette* dated Dec. 10, 1873: "The New Orleans and Red River steamer *ROYAL GEORGE* exploded a boiler last Friday night at Albany, between Jefferson and Shreveport. The mate and three deckhands were killed; five other persons injured. Capt. Scovell had his jaw fractured, and pilot M.C. Leary was slightly wounded." This information dates the accident Dec. 5, 1873.

4864 ROYAL OAK

SW ferry wh b. Haverhill, Oh., 1866. 27 tons. Haverhill is opposite Greenup, Ky., on the Ohio River. Off the lists 1872.

4865 ROZELLE

Stw p wh b. Charleston, W. Va., 1878. 110 x 19 x 3. When asked about this boat Capt. Jim Rowley, Jr., wrote: "She was kind of a 'home-built' craft and a fast runner; operated daily Charleston and Montgomery. Left Charleston each morning at 9 except Sundays. 'Musty' Snyder was her pilot in 1885."

4866 RUBICON

SW p wh b. Shousetown, Pa. (hull), and completed at Pittsburgh, 1866. 637 tons. 200 x 36 x 6. Engines, 20's- 6½ ft. Three boilers, each 30" by 26 ft., four flues. Built for Capt. William B. Haslett and others designed for St. Louis-Omaha trade. First crew: Capt. Wm. B. Haslett, master; George M. Haslett, first clerk; George Nease, 2nd clerk; John Shoemaker, chief engineer. Downbound on first trip hit the Wheeling bridge, knocked down her stacks, and injured five. Capt. Horace Bixby had her up the Missouri 1866 and had to turn back at Milk River due to low water. She was given cotton guards at St. Louis, fall 1871, and entered the Vicksburg-Greenville trade. Dismantled December 1873 and the hull was used as a barge.

4867 RUBY

SW p wh b. West Elizabeth, Pa., 1851. 103 tons. 116 x 20 x 4.5. Owned by Capt. William Brakefield, Macon County, Miss., and others. Was on Red River 1852. Went to Mobile in 1855 and off the lists 1857.

4868 RUBY

Stw p wh b. New Albany, Ind., 1858. 82 tons. 80.3 x 28.4 x 4.5. Owned 1865 by Charles Roman, New Orleans, with Capt. A. Grevenberg, master. Sank in the Mississippi River, December 1865.

4869 RUBY

SW ferry wh b. Cincinnati, Oh., 1859. 78 tons. Went to Natchez, Miss. Sank in the Mississippi River 1865.

4870 RUBY

Stw p wh b. New Albany, Ind., 1871. 117 tons. From the Pittsburgh *Gazette* dated Aug. 28, 1873: "A dispatch from New Orleans dated 27th says *RUBY* sank below the city at the Cattle Pen. 100 cattle drowned. The cattle stampeded when the larboard rails were let down and those on that side jumped ashore, leaving all the weight on the other side. She keeled and swamped. None of the crew lost, but several injured.

4871 RUBY

SW ferry wh b. De Soto, Wis., 1880. 54 tons. 105 x 23 x 4.2. May have operated at Dubuque. Still listed 1895. *List of Merchant Vessels,* 1895, designates her as a sternwheel vessel, but a photograph shows her side-wheel.

4872 RUBY

Stw p wh b. Rush Point, La., 1899. 118 x 22 x 2.8. Built by Capt. William Maikell who ran her Shreveport-Garland City. In summer 1900 carried excursionists to Ruby Park, five miles above Shreveport. Sold that fall to a Capt. Guss, Trinity, La., who ran her on Black River handling seed for a Baton Rouge oil mill.

4873 RUNAWAY

Stw p wh b. Jeffersonville, Ind., by Howard, 1853. 116 tons. 116 x 24 x 4.5. Owned by Capt. James Crooks and others of Shreveport, La. Ran in upper Red River. Off the lists in 1857.

4874 RUSH

SW ferry wh b. Jeffersonville, Ind., by Howard, 1889. 117 x 36 x 3.2. Owned by Capt. Moses Irwin who operated her New Albany-Portland, the last ferry prior to the building of the K&I bridge. Still listed 1896.

4875 RUSSELL

Stw ferry wh b. Jeffersonville, Ind., 1910, originally named *PEERLESS* (see). Bought by Chesapeake & Ohio RR, and renamed. They ran her Ironton-Russell on the Ohio River until the bridge was built 1922. Bought by Capt. Ernest Suiter, Manchester, Oh., who sold her November 1926 to Pressed Steel Car Co., McKees Rocks, Pa., to replace the *STEEL QUEEN* which had burned. Burned at the foot of Westhall Street, N.S. Pittsburgh, Pa., c. 1930.

4876 RUSSELL HINCKLEY

Recess wheel ferry wh b. Madison, Ind., 1873. 169.8 x 42.6 x 5.6. Went to St. Louis, owned by Illinois & St. Louis Railroad & Coal Co. Came to Evansville, Ind., in July 1889, owned by Louisville, Evansville & St. Louis Railroad Co. The Schoellhorn-Albrecht Machine Co., St. Louis, bought her in March 1896 and tore her up for the machinery.

4877 RUTH

SW p wh b. Jeffersonville, Ind., by Howard, 1862. 702 tons. 270 x 46 x 8. Engines, 27½'s- 9 ft. from *PETER TELLON.* On each wheelhouse a magnificent painting of Ruth, the daughter-in-law of Naomi, gleaning in the harvest field after the reapers of Boaz. Came out new on Jan. 1, 1863. She went in service almost at once as a U.S. transport and burned while downbound on the Mississippi, six miles below Cairo, Ill., Aug. 4, 1863. She was loaded with military stores, had in her safe $2.6 million in greenbacks, and was loaded deep. Thirty lives were lost. The blame for the fire was placed on a Confederate arsonist, confirmed later by Absalom Grimes, a mail runner who wrote a book. Grimes lay the blame on Robert Louden, also a Confederate mail runner.

4878 RUTH

SW p wh b. Jeffersonville, Ind., by Howard, 1865. 1,681 tons. 309 x 48.5 x 9.5. Engines 30's- 10 ft. from the *H. R. W. HILL.* Was in the Atlantic & Mississippi Steamship Co., and ran St. Louis-New Orleans, and also to Louisville. Had several noted masters including Capts. John A. Duble, Ben Taber, and B. Rush Pegram. This boat was a stepper, making the time New Orleans-St. Louis in 4 days 9 hours 54 minutes. In November 1865 while Capt. Ben Taber was master she left New Orleans after the others, passed the *FASHION* at Nine Mile Point, the *MAGENTA* at Philadelphia Point above Donaldsonville; came to Donaldsonville in 4 hours 49 minutes. River was low, channel deep, and current sluggish. Burned at Paw Paw Island, about 30 miles above Vicksburg, Mar. 13, 1869 and everybody got ashore, some 240 persons. About 200 head of livestock were lost. The burning hulk drifted opposite Duckport Landing and lodged.

4879 RUTH

Stw p wh b. Freedom, Pa., 1870. 140 x 35 x 5. Engines, 15's-5 ft. Three boilers. Built for Capts. Tom and John J. Darragh. Owned 1874 by R.P. Burton (5/8) and William Barges, St. Louis. Often took cotton out of White River to New Orleans. Burned in White River in 1879 and was taken to Mobile, Ala., and rebuilt. Burned there Jan. 17, 1890, with two other boats in a cotton shed fire.

4880 RUTH

Stw p wh b. Paducah, Ky., 1888. 160 x 31.5 x 5. Built for Capt. W.P. Hall, Memphis, and ran Vicksburg-Greenville. Crew in March 1900: Capt. Charles Nichols, master; Clarence Nichols and Henry Auter, pilots; Scott Phillips and John Schaffer, clerks; James O'Brien and James Gillespie, mates; Mike O'Keefe and Thomas Wylie, engineers. She also went up the Yazoo River to bring out trips. Still running in May 1900. Her whistle is said to have gone to the *ROWENA LEE, JAMES LEE* (2nd) and *HARRY LEE* (2nd).

4881 RUTH

Stw p wh b. Marietta, Oh., at Knox Yard, 1893. 136.5 x 24.5 x 4.4. Engines, 12's-5 ft. Two boilers, each 44" by 20 ft. Built for the Bay Line, Ironton, Oh., a single-decker. Ran local trades in that area, soon had a cabin added, and ran Pittsburgh-Charleston January through September 1896, Capt. Ira B. Huntington, with Ralph Emerson Gaches, clerk. She entered the Wheeling-Sistersville trade Oct. 21, 1896, Capt. Mike Davis, master-pilot, and Silas Wood, chief engineer. Ran hot competition with *JEWEL* (see) and later *LEROY* (see) and *T.N. BARNSDALL* which was renamed *ROYAL* (see). Capt. J. Mack Gamble became owner entire, May 1, 1906. Sold May 31, 1910, in equal shares to Capts. Fred Hornbrook and Fred Kimpel, and Rose L. Williamson and Harry C. Donnally. They lengthened her at Pt. Pleasant in 1910 to become 153 x 30 x 4.5. Soon after the last *LIBERTY* was built (1912) Capt. Hornbrook took *RUTH* to the Evansville-Paducah trade and added a texas. He brought her to Pittsburgh in 1916 and ran her Pittsburgh-Parkersburg and then Pittsburgh-Charleston. She was lost in ice at Ohio River Dam 13, McMechan, W. Va., in January 1918. While in the Evansville-Paducah trade she used the old *JOE FOWLER* whistle and kept it until the end.

4882 RUTH

Centerwheel ferry sh b. Dubuque, Iowa, by Dubuque Boat & Boiler Works, 1909. 100 x 35.2 x 5. Had a catamaran twin hull. Engines, 10's-4½ ft. One boiler, 96" by 12 ft. Built for Burnside & Donaldsonville Packet Co. Sold later to Capt. W.A. Bisso, New Orleans, who ran her at Napoleon Avenue. Sold 1942 to Mobile City Commission along with *OLLIE K. WILDS* to operate at Pinto Island. She was sold back to Capt. W.A. Bisso in 1946. Dismantled soon thereafter.

4883 RUTH NO. 2

Stw p wh b. Clarington, Oh., 1904. 141 tons. 136.7 x 26.7 x 3.6. Cross compound engines, 10" and 16"-6 ft. One boiler, Built for the Bay Line, Ironton, Oh., and was entered in the Sistersville-Wheeling trade, Capt. Michael B. Davis, master, with Charles Higgs, chief engineer. In the summer of 1906 sold to the Callahan Line and operated on the Apalachicola and Flint rivers between Bainbridge, Ga., and Apalachicola, Fla., 172 miles. A texas was added. In 1913 she was sold to the Columbia (S.C.) Railway & Navigation Co., and was taken to Georgetown, S.C., to serve on the Santee and Congaree rivers. She ran there until wrecked at Columbia, S.C., in 1918. Many details and pictures in *S&D Reflector,* June 1969 issue, pages 5-7.

4884 RUTH ANN

Stw ferry wh b. Levanna, Oh., 1895, originally named *IRONTON* (see). Name was changed Mar. 7, 1924, owned by Bellaire-Benwood & Wheeling Ferry Co. Enroute down the Ohio with ferry *CHARON* in 1928, she wrecked the *CHARON* on the outside lock wall at Lock 23. She tried the Levanna-Dover ferry run, didn't succeed, and sank along shore at Levanna almost at the site of her building.

S

4885 S.B. DUNCAN

Stw p wh b. Jeffersonville, Ind., by Howard, 1898, originally named *CITY OF MEMPHIS* (see). Renamed when bought by Capt. Tom Morrissey for Vicksburg-Greenville trade about 1910. Named for Stephen B. Duncan, cotton planter. Burned at Vicksburg on Jan. 21, 1912 and lost.

4886 S.C. BAKER

Stw p wh b. Industry, Pa., 1860. 97 tons. 133.1 x 32.8 x 3.7. Ran Wheeling-Steubenville and Pittsburgh-Wheeling. Arrived in Pittsburgh June 8, 1862 towing two barges loaded with corn and wheat, plus about 150 excursionists, took aboard a cargo of salt and returned. After 1864 was documented at St. Louis as a towboat owned by Mississippi Ice Co. Still listed 1886.

4887 S.C. DAY

Stw p wh b. 1869. 120 x 24 x 3.5. Moored at Vicksburg in latter September 1870, swells from the *CITY OF ALTON* swamped her and one life was lost. The hull and cabin parted company and capsized. The wreck floated to a sandbar at Point Comfort and lodged. Capt. D. Verden was in charge. After several days Capt. Jack Carter bought the wreck "as-is-where-is."

4888 S.C. POMEROY

Stw ferry wh b. Brownsville, Pa., 1863. 205 tons. Operated at Kansas City, Mo. Sank at Harlem, Mo., across from Kansas City, Mar. 23, 1877.

4889 S.D. BARLOW

SW tr wh b. Madison, Ind., 1888. 249 x 48.6 x 7.2. Built by M.A. Sweeney & Bros., headquartered at Jeffersonville who also operated the Madison yard. Belonged to the Iron Mountain Railway. Burned at the Bird's Point incline, opposite Cairo, Mar. 11, 1898, in charge of Capt. A.J. Gillespie. The superintendent of transfer operations was Capt. W.H. Grapevine.

4890 S.D. BLAIR

Stw p wh b. Grayville, Ill., 1892. 102.6 x 21.6 x 5. Built and operated by Capt. Samuel D. Blair who lived at Grayville on the Wabash River and died there, 90, September 1928. His boat still listed in 1896, maybe longer.

4891 S.F. ARCHER

SW p wh b. New Albany, Ind., 1854. 79 tons. First destination was New Orleans. Off the lists 1858.

4892 S.F.J. TRABUE

SW p wh b. New Albany, Ind., 1854. 577 tons. 280 x 34 x 7.5. Engines, 24's- 7½ ft. Five boilers. Collided with and sank *JAMES McFADDIN* on the Ohio River, Apr. 28, 1854. Ran St. Louis-New Orleans, Capt. James Tucker and owned by Thomas Keeffe, New Orleans. Bought by Capt. James M. White, New Orleans, Nov. 14, 1855. Ran opposition to the *NATCHEZ* in the New Orleans-Vicksburg trade. Trips up Red River in 1856. Burned at Algiers, La., Apr. 10, 1856. The U.S. snagboat *ALGERINE* removed the wreck in 1857.

4893 S.F. VINTON

SW p wh b. Ironton, Oh., 1850. 284 tons. Collided with the *LOWELL* (see) at Captina Island, Ohio River, Mar. 26, 1851, with fifteen persons drowned. Burned at Grand View, La., on Aug. 27, 1851.

4894 S.H. LONG

U.S. snagboat wh Operated on the Missouri and Mississippi in the 1870s. While working above Memphis in the vicinity of Fort Pillow in February 1876, second mate David Griffith picked up a 124-pound solid cannonball on a sand bar, fired from Fort Pillow at Yankee gunboats during the war. Capt. Burch took it home with him to Indianapolis.

4895 S.H. PARISOT

Stw p wh b. Jeffersonville, Ind., by Howard, 1882. 225 x 40.5 x 7.7. Engines, 23's- 7 ft. Four boilers, each 45″ by 28 ft., six flues. Came out with two Brush electric lights. The skylight glasses depicted cotton plants in bloom. Owned by the Parisot Line, Vicksburg. Ran Vicksburg-New Orleans, Capt. John A. Stevenson. Burned six miles above Natchez on Nov. 18, 1883.

4896 S.H. TUCKER

Stw p wh b. Cincinnati, Oh., 1856. 128 tons. 137 x 25 x 4.5. Two boilers. Capt. Rees Pritchard ran her Memphis-White River, and sold her just prior to the war to Capt. Frank Smith for Red River operations. Captured by the U.S. at Columbus, Ky., during the war and was taken to Cairo, Ill.

4897 S.L. ELAM

Stw p wh b. Slidell, La., 1913. 181.9 x 29.8 x 6. Compound non-condensing engines, 12's, 24's- 6 ft. Came out with a patented Kidney boiler which was replaced 1915 with three return-flue boilers. Owned by Carter Bros., New Orleans, and named for Judge Elam of Natchez, Miss. Ran briefly up Red River and then New Orleans-Camden on the Ouachita. Snagged and sank in lower Red River December 1915. Sold to Liberty Transit Co., Wheeling, W. Va., in May 1918 and made one Pittsburgh-Cincinnati trip with original cotton guards and name, then was rebuilt and renamed *GENERAL WOOD* (see).

4898 S.P. WELLS

Stw p wh b. Burning Springs, W. Va., 1875. 23 tons. Still listed 1882, maybe later.

4899 S.R. VAN METRE

Stw p wh b. Murraysville, W. Va. (hull), and completed at Marietta, Oh., 1888. 98 tons. 112 x 18.3 x 3.4. Named for a Marietta merchant, and ran Marietta-Zanesville, Capt. O.J. Stowe the first two years. Damaged by fire at Lowell, Oh., in 1889. Ran Vanceburg-Maysville on the Ohio. Sold 1894 to Capt. D.W. Wisherd who ran her Quincy-Keokuk-Burlington trade and so continued until she burned laid up in Quincy Bay, Mar. 1, 1899.

4900 S.S. BROWN

Stw p sh b. Ambridge, Pa. (hull), and completed at Pittsburgh, 1906. 228 x 44 x 6.6. Compound condensing engines, 15½'s, 30's- 8 ft. Four boilers, each 44″ by 24 ft., three 10″ and three 8″ flues. American Bridge Co. built the hull and she was completed at the James Rees & Sons shop in the Allegheny River, Pittsburgh. Owned by Memphis & Arkansas River Packet Co. Was taken to Memphis, new, November 1906, Capt. Ed Nowland, Jr., with George Ehringer, chief engineer. Entered the Memphis-Vicksburg trade, Chess Wilcox and Charles Nixon, pilots. In May 1907 she made a trip up Arkansas River to Little Rock, Ark. The owning firm failed in May 1908, but the *S.S. BROWN* was brought from retirement to run a special trip from Paducah to New Orleans that July. Later in the year she pinch-hit for the *KATE ADAMS* in the Memphis-Arkansas City trade. Bought by the Lee Line, Memphis, in 1909 and renamed *REES LEE* (see). The story of this steamer with many pictures appears in *S&D Reflector,* issue June 1972, pages 23–32.

4901 S.S. MERRILL

SW p wh b. Cincinnati, Oh., 1870. A large and handsome boat, hull size unavailable, built for the Northwestern Union Packet Co., and named for the general manager of the Milwaukee & St. Paul RR. Her maiden trip was from Cincinnati to Pittsburgh towing two model barges loaded with iron ore, and she then departed Pittsburgh on Apr. 5, 1871, for St. Paul, Capt. A.M. Hutchinson, with J.A. Hauser, clerk. Jim and Joe Witten were the Pittsburgh-Cincinnati pilots. She caught fire in the texas at Warsaw, Ill., and burned on Sept. 18, 1871. She had come up from St. Louis to Keokuk, and then went to Alexandria and Warsaw to load wheat for the return trip. Capt. William Howard was master at the time, and Hunter Ben Jenkins was one of the clerks. Quite a short life; she had made but three trips.

4902 S.S. PRENTISS

SW p wh b. Jeffersonville, Ind., by Howard, 1853. 272 tons. 168 x 30 x 5.8. First went to Vicksburg. Documented at New Orleans Dec. 11, 1854, owned by Shaw & Kuntz, that city. Went to Mobile but was again back at New Orleans, November 1857, owned by Capt. James McQuoid and others. Burned and lost at Algiers, La., Feb. 20, 1858. An iron hull tug of the same name was owned by the Monongahela River Consolidated Coal & Coke Co., later on (see *Towboat Directory*).

4903 S.W. DOWNS

SW p wh b. Louisville, Ky., by D. & J. Howard in 1851. 236 tons. 164.8 x 26.7 x 5.7. Departed Louisville on Feb. 8, 1851, Capt. John W. Cannon, for New Orleans-Ouachita River trade. First documented at New Orleans Mar. 29, 1852, owned by Mrs. L.L. Powell, Hancock County, Ky., Capt. William Swetzer in command. Thence to 1860 the enrollment was altered 18 times, the last owner-master being Capt. John Hanson, Jefferson City (now New Orleans). Off the lists in 1861.

4904 SABINE

Stw p wh b. Pittsburgh, Pa., 1860. 123 tons. Off the lists 1861.

4905 SABINE

Rig? p wh Only clue thus far is an old freight bill dated January 1873 for "Regular New Orleans-New Camden packet, Capt. R. Sinnott, master."

4906 SACCHARINE

Stw p ih b. New Orleans, La., 1883. 145.7 x 33.9 x 4.8. Nice packet with a single tall stack forward of the pilothouse, owned by the Morgan Line who ran her New Orleans-Bayou Teche. The *JENNIE BARBOUR* in 1910 was towing a metal barge named *SACCHARINE* in the same trade, perhaps the hull of this boat.

4907 SACRAMENTO

SW p wh b. Cincinnati, Oh., 1848. 221 tons. 182 x 27.5 x 5.8. Engines, 18's- 6 ft. Two boilers, each 42" by 28 ft. Had 18 staterooms, designed for Cincinnati-St. Louis trade. Snagged at Hardaman's Orchard, six miles above Boonville, Mo., 1849. Removed from documentation in 1855.

4908 SADIE LEE

Stw p wh b. Jeffersonville, Ind., by Howard, 1901. 140 x 26 x 3.5. Built for the Lee Line, Memphis, Tenn. Engines, 12's- 6 ft. Came out in Memphis-Ashport trade, Capt. George Carvell, master; William (Billy) Smithers, first clerk; Frank Watkins, 2nd clerk; Tom Allen and John Seymour, mates; Jack Walsh, steward; George Woodford and Wes Owens, pilots, and Dick Johnson and Joe Riveras, engineers. Later ran Memphis-Vicksburg. Sank at O.K. Landing, Nov. 13, 1910. Hit a snag and sank at Dennis Landing, Miss., Nov. 15, 1912, upbound, Capt. Thomas Staid in command. The *JOHN LEE* was sent down from Memphis and the *KATE ADAMS* picked up some of the passengers. Miss Sadie Ardinger Lee, daughter of the late Capt. and Mrs. James Lee, Jr., died in Memphis, May 16, 1963. She was the last of her generation of Lees for whom boats had been named.

4909 SAILOR

Stw ferry wh b. Memphis, Tenn., 1922. 57 tons. 64.2 x 26.4 x 4.4. Engines, 8"- 3 ft. Sold to R.E. Starkey, Glenwood, W. Va., on Oct. 1, 1924. He ran her Glenwood-Swan Creek. Prior to that, a gas powered side-wheeler, *JOHN B. REED,* owned by Glenwood-based John B. Reed, ran there. By 1929 the owners of the Glenwood ferry had changed to become Swan Creek Steam Ferry Co., still running *SAILOR*.

4910 ST. ANGE

SW p wh b. St. Louis, Mo., 1849. 254 tons. Unique in that she was built on the ways complete, ready to go. Capt. Joseph La Barge made trips St. Louis to Fort Union on the Missouri annually until 1853 for the American Fur Co. In 1850 she made the trip in 28 days, considered a record. In 1851 went up to the mouth of Poplar River, first steamboat there. Named for St. Ange de Bellerive, first French military governor of upper Louisiana. Father De Smet was aboard in 1851 when cholera broke out aboard. A fellow priest died. Lost in ice at St. Louis, Feb. 2, 1854.

4911 ST. ANTHONY

SW p wh b. Belle Vernon, Pa., 1846. 184 tons. 157 x 24 x 5. Engines, 22's- 7 ft. Three boilers. A small boat but highly finished and furnished for the time. The hull was modeled by "Billy" King, noted for his design of the *J.M. WHITE* of 1844. First year ran Galena-St. Peters, Capt. A.G. Montford, and took soldiers to the Mexican War from Alton, Ill. She was back to Pittsburgh 1848 and ran Pittsburgh-

Wheeling briefly, and February 1849 departed for St. Louis. Burned opposite St. Charles, Mo., Mar. 25, 1851, Capt. Jim Gonsaullis.

4912 St. Charles

SW p wh b. Jeffersonville, Ind., by Howard, 1849. 379 tons. 191 x 26.6 x 7.8. Went to Mobile, Ala. Enrolled at New Orleans Apr. 5, 1850, owned by Robert and John Geddes and others. Capt. William A. Chambers bought a share and took command in 1855. Went to Confederate registry in 1861.

4913 St. Charles

SW p wh b. Cincinnati, Oh., 1850. 311 tons. 126 x 30 x 6.3. Built for Capt. Samuel Applegate and others for New Orleans-Red River. She was described in an old-time account as having a beautiful cabin and "great power and the fastest boat of her day," a superlative for so modest a steamboat. She is credited having made the run New Orleans to Shreveport in 2 days 16 hours, which stood until the *R. W. McREA* went up in 2 days 12 hours in 1854. Capt. Applegate sold her 1856 to Capt. William D. Beateman, Cincinnati. In July 1862 again appeared at New Orleans, now documented as a towboat with hull 207 x 32 x 8.9. 379 tons. Owned by Stanton & Co. (3/4) and N.B. Chambers, the latter's share "sequestered by the Government." Sold February 1864 to George W. Moss of New Orleans and was off the lists 1865.

4914 St. Charles

SW p wh b. New Albany, Ind., 1856. 344 tons. First home port, Mobile, Ala. Off the lists in 1875.

4915 St. Charles

Center wheel ferry wh b. St. Louis, Mo., 1862. 205 tons. Bought by the U.S. in April, 1863 and became Tinclad *PAW PAW* (see).

4916 St. Charles

SW p wh b. New Albany, Ind., 1864. 764 tons. 285 x 40 x 6.5. Engines, 24½'s- 8 ft. Seven boilers. Capt. Jesse K. Bell formed the Peoples Line and ran this boat and *WILD WAGONER* in the Louisville-Cincinnati trade in opposition to the U.S. Mail Line. Collided with *MAJOR ANDERSON* Dec. 12, 1865, at Coopers Bar, piloted by Napoleon B. Jenkins. On Aug. 6, 1866, was racing with *GENERAL LYTLE* at Bethlehem, Ind., when the latter exploded (see). The Peoples Line quit, and *ST. CHARLES* was sold at public auction at Cincinnati November 1866 to Thomas Gaylord for $50,000, only bidder. In mid-February 1867, Capt. Hugh Campbell became master and she ran Louisville-New Orleans. Entered Pittsburgh-Cincinnati trade, Capt. Charles A. Dravo, with Andy Robinson, Jr., in the office, March 1868 and ran until latter June when low water stopped her. Resumed in latter September, same master, with George L. Reppart, Henry Chapin, and J.M. Lovett in the office, piloted by Ben Hall and Joe Witten, and with Joe Dodson, steward. Immediately after the *UNITED STATES-AMERICA* collision she was chartered by the U.S. Mail Line Co., for the Louisville-Cincinnati trade and so continued until December 1869. During this term of charter she attempted a race with the *ROB'T. E. LEE,* upbound at Madison, Apr. 4, 1869, and was quickly vanquished. Resumed Pittsburgh-Cincinnati trade December 1869, Capt. Charles A. Dravo, with George L. Reppart, first clerk, and with James Rowley and C.C. Cable, pilots. Sank at Duffs Bar after striking a rock, near Dixmont, Pa., in Neville Island, Feb. 11, 1871, downbound, pilot Ben Hall on watch. She was raised within a week and went to the marine ways at Cincinnati. Resumed and ran until latter April when, upbound, she broke hull timbers in Sisters Islands, the river low, and she couldn't get through Glass House Ripple at Brunots Island, and the *D.T. LANE* brought flats and took her freight to Pittsburgh. Resumed in the fall and got frozen in at Safe Harbor, Pa., in late December. Burned at Cincinnati Mar. 7, 1872, along with the *MAJOR ANDERSON* and others. There is evidence she was shorter than the dimensions given in this account when originally built, and was lengthened at Madison by the Peoples Line, c. 1866.

4917 St. Charles

Stw ferry wh b. Dubuque, Iowa, 1893, originally named *TEAL,* then *POTOSI* (both see). She was bought by the city of St. Charles, Mo., and renamed again when operating there. Sold to a lumber firm in Louisiana and was reported snagged and sunk in 1917.

4918 St. Clair

SW p wh b. West Elizabeth, Pa., 1852. 320 tons. 182 x 31 x 6.5. Built for Capt. Robert D. Cochran and others for the Pittsburgh-St. Louis trade. In March 1853 made the round trip in 17 days, fastest of record. Had 153 through and 107 way passengers leaving St. Louis. Burned at St. Louis July 2, 1856, in a considerable fire which originated aboard this boat and spread to the *PAUL ANDERSON, GRAND TURK, J.M. STOCKWELL, SOUTHERNER,* and *SARANAC* (all see).

4919 St. Clair

Stw p wh b. Belle Vernon, Pa., 1862. 203 tons. 156 x 32.6 x 4.9. Engines, 15½'s- 5 ft. Two boilers, each 38" by 26 ft., four flues. Owned by Capt. Robert D. Cochran and others, built for Pittsburgh-St. Louis trade. Capt. George Cochran went master, with Thomas Shuman in the office. She was bought by the U.S. at St. Louis on the first trip and converted into Tinclad #19. Sold at public sale, Mound City, Ill., Aug. 28, 1865, to John H. Sterrett (or Stearne) of Galveston, Tex. Off the lists in 1869.

4920 St. Cloud

SW p wh b. Wheeling, Va., 1846. 223 tons. Built for Cincinnati-New Orleans trade with a Wheeling crew, Capts. John List, Sam Mason, and William Cecil. Dunning Foster, brother of composer Stephen Collins Foster, wrote Dec. 29, 1848, to report that Capt. Jabez Smith of the *ST.*

CLOUD had died of cholera. Clifford B. Wayne and Thompson Dean, Cincinnati, were associated with the boat later. Off the lists in 1853.

4921 St. Cloud

Stw p wh b. Belle Vernon, Pa., 1859. 291 tons. 176 x 37 x 6. Built for Capt. Charles Dravo and others, Pittsburgh. Ran Pittsburgh-St. Louis principally. She was at Pittsburgh loaded with cargo for the U.S. when sold to Capt. W.W. Fenton and the Gaffs of Aurora, Ind. They sold her at Memphis, March 1864, to others, and she sank at Plum Point on the Mississippi River downbound from Evansville to Memphis, Jan. 24, 1867, Capt. Rusk. Was said to have struck a snag during foggy weather.

4922 St. Cloud

SW p wh b. St. Anthony, Minn., 1861. 25 tons. 89.9 x 13 x 3. Originally ran above St. Anthony Falls, and was skidded around in the summer of 1864 to St. Paul. Owned 1866 by C.R. Muggah, New Orleans, and in 1869 owned at Franklin, La., by the Estate of David R. Muggah, Capt. Alfred Stephens. Off the lists in 1870.

4923 St. Crispin

Stw p wh b. Cincinnati, Oh., 1860. 41 tons. Went to Vicksburg, Miss., and to Confederate registry in 1861.

4924 St. Croix

SW p wh b. St. Louis, Mo., 1844. 158 tons. James Ward, later president of the Northern Line, was one of the builders. Capt. Hiram Bersie commanded, St. Louis-Galena-St. Peters. In collision with *MERMAID* near Quincy, Ill., Apr. 11, 1845, losing her barge. Damaged by fire May 13, 1845. Sometimes ran Cairo-St. Louis during low water. Had a long and successful life, going to the wreckers June 5, 1867, at St. Louis.

4925 St. Croix

Stw p wh b. Maiden Rock, Wis., 1870. 98 tons. Originally a packet on St. Croix River. 115 x 20 x 4. Spent most of her career as a rafter, finally hitting a log while passing the span at the Dubuque bridge, 1894.

4926 St. Elmo

Stw ferry (?) wh b. De Witt, Mo., 1891. 57 x 17.4 x 3. Still listed 1896, maybe later.

4927 St. Francis

Stw p wh b. Brownsville, Pa., 1849. 63 tons. Built for Memphis-St. Francis River trade. Dismantled in 1852.

4928 St. Francis No. 2

SW p wh b. Jeffersonville, Ind., by Howard, 1853. 162 tons. 150 x 28 x 5.5. Replaced former boat of the name in the Memphis-St. Francis River trade. Foundered at Memphis, Sept. 16, 1860.

4929 St. Francis No. 3

SW p wh b. Jeffersonville, Ind., by Howard, 1858. 160 x 29 x 6. Ran Memphis-St. Francis River, Capt. Thomas R. Bowman, with De Witt Abbott, clerk. Burned as a Confederate "cotton-clad" at Little Rock, Ark., Sept. 10, 1863.

4930 St. Francis Belle

SW p wh b. Catlettsburg, Ky., 1875. 127 tons. Ran Louisville-Leavenworth in September 1875 in opposition to *B.H. COOKE.* In April 1878 at New Orleans running from Bienville St. to Westwego in connection with the New Orleans & Texas RR to Donaldsonville.

4931 St. Francis Trader

Rig? p wh b. Madison, Ark., 1874. 47 tons. Primarily a freight carrier. Still documented at Memphis 1876, maybe later.

4932 St. Jacobs Oil

Stw p wh b. Wheeling, W. Va., 1880. 62 x 14 x 2.5. Completed at Middleport, Oh. Built for the owners of a patent medicine of that same name, A. Vogeler & Co., Baltimore, Md. Engines, 7"- 2 ft. One boiler. She toured the rivers touting St. Jacobs Oil and signs were painted on prominent rocks, etc. Sold to the New Orleans *Times-Democrat* and renamed *SUSIE B.* (see). Picture and description in *S&D Reflector,* Sept. 1969 issue, pages 31–32.

4933 St. Helena

SW p wh b. Elizabeth, Pa., 1846. 124 tons. 143 x 22 x 4.1. Documented at New Orleans, June 10, 1847, owned and commanded by Capt. Michael Welsh. Sold Dec. 25, 1848, to Thomas Napoleon Drew, Carroll Parish, La., Capt. John Ross. Foundered Nov. 10, 1849, at Algiers, La.

4934 St. James

SW p wh b. Cincinnati, Oh., 1850. 347 tons. 207.9 x 29.3 x 5.9. Went to New Orleans owned by William H. Wright, of that city. Capt. John E. Hyde, master. She was loaded with an excursion July 5, 1852, at or near Lake Pontchartrain, racing the *CALIFORNIA,* when she exploded killing 30 persons, among them Judge Preston, chief justice of the Supreme Court of Louisiana.

4935 St. James

SW p wh b. New Albany, Ind., 1865. 699 tons. 235 x 35 x 6. Engines, 22's- 7 ft. Three boilers, each 44" by 26 ft. Paddlewheels 28 ft. dia. working 12 ft. buckets, 26" dip. Built for Cincinnati-Pomeroy trade, starting Jan. 3, 1866, Capt. James H. Rice, master; Long Bryson, first clerk; Wes Black and Flor Donnally, clerks; William and Henry Kirker, mates; Zed Williams and William Hawley, engineers; Ambrose Dennis, pilot. That fall went in the newly formed Cincinnati, Big Sandy & Pomeroy Packet Co., Capt. F.J. Oakes. In March 1867 bought for the Wheeling-Cincinnati trade by Capt. J.J. Blagg, running along with the *POTOMAC, EDINBURG, R.R. HUDSON* and *INGOMAR.* This did not continue long, and she again went to the White Collar Line, operating Cincinnati-Portsmouth until the first *BONANZA* was built in 1876.

4936 ST. JAMES

Stw p wh b. Cincinnati, Oh., 1898. 185 x 35 x 6.5. Engines, 17's- 7 ft. Three boilers, each 44" by 26 ft. Built for the Merchants & Planters Packet Co., who ran her tri-weekly New Orleans-Baton Rouge. Later in Mississippi Packet Co., Capt. J.B. Woods, president, semi-weekly, New Orleans-Bayou Sara. Sold to John F. Klein 1914 who ran excursions at St. Louis that season, then brought her to Pittsburgh in 1915 and ran excursions there and along the upper Ohio. Early 1916 departed Pittsburgh on a one-way Mardi Gras trip, and burned soon after arrival at New Orleans. An extensive article and pictures in *S&D Reflector,* June 1978 issue, pages 44–47.

4937 ST. JOHN

Stw p wh b. Madison, Ind., 1869. 464 tons. 175.6 x 34 x 6.1. Owned in part and commanded by Capt. W.R. Greathouse. Ran New Orleans-Upper Coast. James R. Mullens says she had the first swinging stages seen at New Orleans. Returned to the Barmore yard, Jeffersonville, Ind., June 1878, dismantled, and engines went to the new *ST. JOHN* (next listing).

4938 ST. JOHN

Stw p wh b. Jeffersonville, Ind., by Barmore, 1878. 176.6 x 36.2 x 7.1. Engines from prior *ST. JOHN* (see above). Ran New Orleans-Baton Rouge, Capt. J.P. McElroy. Owned at Shieldsboro, Miss., 1892, running New Orleans-Bayou La Fourche along with *ALICE LE BLANC.* Went to U.S. marshal sale February 1895, sold to W.G. Wilmot & Co., New Orleans, for $3,200. Dismantled August 1899 at New Orleans.

4939 ST. JOHNS

Stw p wh b. Murraysville, W. Va. (hull), and completed at Wheeling, 1864. 309 tons. 174 x 36 x 5. Engines, 18's- 6 ft. Construction superintended by Capt. Sam Mason, part owner, along with the Lists of Wheeling. Ran Wheeling-Cincinnati until sold latter February 1865 to St. Louis parties. She loaded at Pittsburgh for St. Louis, Mar. 3, 1865, Capt. S.S. Entriken. In 1875 owned by St. Louis & Illinois Packet Co., and was lost the following year.

4940 ST. JOSEPH

SW p wh b. St. Louis, Mo., 1846. 217 tons. Upbound, New Orleans to St. Louis, on Jan. 12, 1850, racing with the *SOUTH AMERICA,* the larboard boiler exploded killing eight persons. The location is variously described as at the mouth of the Arkansas River, and at Napoleon, Ark. A letter written by J. Lawrence Carter, clerk on the *SOUTH AMERICA,* says the explosion took place at Island 80, above the present-day Ashbrook Cut Off. The *ST. JOSEPH* was destroyed. Her skipper, noticed as a Capt. Baker, handed Capt. Greenlee of the *S.A.* $3,000 for safe-keeping. Greenlee kept $2,700, claiming salvage. Baker had the *S.A.* attached at Memphis pending a hearing, and his money was returned to him.

4941 ST. JOSEPH

SW p wh b. Metropolis, Ill. (hull), and completed at St. Louis, 1865. 502 tons. 194.5 x 35.5. Built for the Hannibal & St. Joe Railroad. Later sold to Memphis & St. Louis Packet Co. Sank above Cairo, Ill., latter July 1871, raised with assistance of *T.F. ECKERT.* Off the lists in 1877.

4942 ST. JOSEPH

Stw p wh b. Madison, Ind., 1893. 170 x 32 x 4.9. Built for the Natchez & Vicksburg Packet Co., J.N. Carpenter, president. She replaced the *CHARLES D. SHAW* (see). Ran under charter New Orleans-Vicksburg summer 1895 in place of the *NATCHEZ.* Capt. Thomas Waldren, master, with A.B. Crittenden and Bob Miller, pilots, 1897. John F. Klein bought her at Natchez early in 1905, brought her to Pittsburgh and renamed her *ISLAND QUEEN* (see). Capt. Waldren died at Natchez November 1911. Her ornate silver water cooler went to the *SENATOR CORDILL.*

4943 ST. LANDRY

SW p wh b. Cincinnati, Oh., 1843. 240 tons. 148 x 29 x 6. Ran New Orleans-Upper Bends. First owned by Wilis Main, New Orleans, and Capt. George W. Haygood, Iberville Parish, who commanded. Sold December 1845 to Capt. J.A. Adams, New Orleans. In June 1846 sold to Capt. A. Dugas and others. She brought the 4th Kentucky Regiment under Major Ward from New Orleans to Louisville, July 1848. Off the lists 1849.

4944 ST. LAWRENCE

Stw p wh b. Brownsville, Pa., 1855. 259 tons. 150 x 34.7 x 5.5. Owned at Pittsburgh by her master Capt. R.D. Cochran, George W. Cochran, Nimick & Co. and John A. Caughey. She "ran on rocks" at Pomeroy, Oh., Mar. 22, 1858, and sank, boat and cargo lost.

4945 ST. LAWRENCE

SW p wh b. Murraysville, W. Va. (hull), and completed at Wheeling, 1879. 266.5 x 41 x 6. Engines from *EXPRESS NO. 2,* also the cabin which was moved over and enlarged. Dan Morton superintended building the hull. Built for Wheeling-Cincinnati trade, and came out in command of Capt. William H. List with C.D. List, clerk. By 1884 her trips had been extended to Pittsburgh. That fall she was sold to the White Collar Line, Cincinnati, following the fire which had destroyed the *MORNING MAIL* and others. She was entered in the Cincinnati-Maysville trade, Capt. E.S. Morgan. In early spring 1866 caught in a heavy wind at Augusta, Ky., and in attempting to turn around was grounded on the upper side of Bracken Creek on the high shore (river was in flood) and could not be released. The water fell and left her with the stern hanging precariously over the creek bottom. She was shored up and remained there until another flood released her. Wind also got this boat into her final difficulty: she was laid up at the foot of Niagara Street, Cincinnati, Sept. 20, 1895, when the wind tripped her spars. She blew inshore over top of an old wrecked boat and sank on it. Her whistle was outstanding; A-flat and C, treble clef, and D-flat and low A-flat, bass clef. The three lower notes were first heard, and after a time high C came in with stunning effect. The instrument was made at Wheeling for *EXPRESS NO. 2,* then transferred to *ST. LAWRENCE* which used it all her days and then it went on the sternwheel *COURIER* for all her days and thence to the *TACOMA* and was destroyed when she burned in 1922. A whistle buff of Portsmouth, Oh., Luther C. Chapman, meanwhile had made successful duplicates used on *GREENLAND* and *CHRIS GREENE* (1st), another for *TOM GREENE,* and at least two others. A widely circulated story is that Chapman, by trade a locomotive engineer with the N&W Railroad, once attached one of these whistles to his engine at Portsmouth, coupled to a drag of empty coal hoppers, and was well into West Virginia tootling it before a superintendent's order caught up with him to desist.

4946 St. Louis

SW ferry wh b. New Albany, Ind., 1847. 210 tons. Exploded boilers at St. Louis Feb. 20, 1851, with loss of 20 lives.

4947 St. Louis

SW p wh b. St. Louis, Mo., 1850. 937 tons. Reputed to measure 307 ft. long, one of the largest of her day. Ran St. Louis-New Orleans and collapsed a boiler flue at Jefferson Barracks, Mo., downbound on her maiden trip, May 23, 1850, at 10:00 P.M. Ten or twelve were killed and 25 others injured. The chief engineer was tried for manslaughter and after a lengthy trial was acquitted. The stigma of this accident turned her into an unprofitable boat. She was dismantled and became a wharfboat in 1856, used at Memphis.

4948 St. Louis

Stw p wh b. West Brownsville, Pa., 1855. 191 tons. Built for Capt. Jesse Dean, and ran Pittsburgh-St. Louis. Her original cost was $15,000 and in December 1863 was sold for like amount due to scarcity of boats as the war got under way. Burned July 18, 1864, on the Cumberland River above Fort Donelson by the Rebels.

4949 St. Louis

U.S. gunboat wh b. St. Louis, Mo., by James B. Eads, 1861. She was the flagship in the engagement at Fort Donelson on the Cumberland River, struck by shot 59 times, her pilot killed and flag officer Foote injured in the pilothouse. Renamed *BARON De KALB* (see).

4950 St. Louis

SW railroad ferry wh b. Freedom, Pa., 1869. 312 tons. 198 x 32.6 x 5.8. Engines, 20½'s- 5½ ft. Four boilers, two on a side. Owned by Iron Mountain RR and ran Belmont, Mo., to Columbus, Ky., also Cairo-Birds Point. She had a compressed air steering rig made by her engineer Fred James to plans designed by Capt. J.J. Gillespie, her skipper. Spent her old days as a wharfboat at Cairo and dismantled at St. Louis in 1912.

4951 Saint Louis

Stw p wh b. Jeffersonville, Ind., by Howard, 1912. 210 x 37 x 6. Owned by St. Louis & Tennessee River Packet Co. A nice roomy boat which was snagged and sunk at Sulphur Springs, Mo., 22 miles south of St. Louis, Sept. 2, 1918.

4952 St. Louis Oak

SW p wh b. St. Louis, Mo., 1842. 108 tons. Ran St. Louis-Galena-Dubuque. Snagged and lost at the head of Howard's Bend, Missouri River, Capt. Dozier in command, 1847.

4953 St. Luke

SW p wh b. St. Louis, Mo., 1868. 648 tons. 210 x 36 x 7. Engines, 22's- 6 ft. Three boilers. Built by Capt. Joe Kinney for St. Louis-Missouri River. Familiarly called the "Yellow Hammer" inasmuch as she was painted yellow. Only packet which succeeded in making two round trips a week, St. Louis-Jefferson City. Owned by Missouri River Packet Co., later, Capt. George Keith. J.S. Hacker recalled that she had "two long spars hanging from her derricks and tremendous blocks carrying 1½" falls, and heavy eye bolts in her harping to hook them to . . . . she was one of the old school of steamboats and was prepared to take care of herself." Hit the bridge at St. Charles, Mo., downbound, May 2, 1875, and sank one-half mile below, total loss. The Missouri was high at the time with a big current. Thomas Townsend was pilot on watch. Four deck passengers and six of the crew lost their lives.

4954 St. Mary

SW p wh b. Cincinnati, Oh., 1844. 183 tons. 153 x 24 x 5.2. Operated out of New Orleans, Capt. David R. Muggah, St. Mary Parish. Off the lists 1849.

4955 St. Mary

SW p wh b. St. Louis, Mo., 1855. 295 tons. 204 x 35 x 4.5. Engines, 14's- 6 ft. Two boilers. Capt. Joe La Barge piloted her up the Missouri River 1855 and that winter had her on the lower Mississippi. Bound up the Missouri, the Sioux City *Eagle* noted on June 4, 1856: "We venture the assertion that the Railroad packet *ST. MARY* left for Omaha Saturday night with the largest passenger list ever before crowded on any steamer on the Western Waters. She had 900 passengers aboard, 735 of whom were Mormons on the lower deck. But very few of the Mormons took cabin passage, probably less than 50, but the decks were one living mass of humanity. What a fearful responsibility rested on the pilot and the engineer! Just think! Nine hundred souls entrusted to their care." In August 1856 she returned to St. Louis with "22,000 buffalo robes, two ponies, two grizzly bears, two buffalo calves, and some strange looking birds." En route from St. Joseph to Omaha she was snagged and sunk at Hemmes Landing, Sept. 4, 1859, broke in two and was lost. Capt. Mot Morrison was master.

4956 St. Mary

SW p wh b. Plaquemine, La., 1862, originally named

ALEXANDRIA (see). Renamed when in Confederate service, and after captured by U.S. and used on patrol duty. Later resumed her original name. As *ST. MARY* she was captured from the Confederates in July 1863 at the same time the *MAGENTA, MAGNOLIA, J.F. PARGOUD, PEYTONA,* and *PRINCE OF WALES* were burned. She was towed up the river by the *NEW NATIONAL* and on Sept. 21, 1863, became a part of the Federal fleet working out of Donaldsonville, La., and had been renamed *YAZOO*. In September 1863 recommendation was made to the Secretary of the Navy that the name be changed to *ALEXANDRIA* inasmuch as there was a steamer named *YAZOO* on the river and confusion was resulting.

4957 St. Mary

Stw p wh b. Jeffersonville, Ind., by Howard, 1871. 146 x 34 x 6. Ran New Orleans-Grand Encore, 1873. Running weekly New Orleans-Opelousas in 1876, Capt. F. Probst, with J.B. Schmidt, clerk. Still documented 1886, maybe later.

4958 St. Marys

SW p wh b. Wheeling, W. Va., 1867. 666 tons. 225 x 36. Engines, 22's- 7 ft. Four boilers, 40″ dia. with two flues. Built for Capt. T.C. Sweeney and others. On May 31, 1867, while moored at New Orleans the "nigger" boiler exploded (an upright auxiliary boiler), went up through the cabin and roof, took off a smokestack, sailed up and out across the stern of the *LEONIDAS* into the ladies' cabin of the *RUTH*, smashing down through and demolished an elaborate chandelier. Four engineers were burned by steam, also a cabin boy and five deckhands, none seriously. In March 1868 she loaded corn up Wabash River and delivered it at Parkersburg. Entered Pittsburgh-Cincinnati trade April 1868, Capt. T.C. Sweeney. That fall she made a trip to New Orleans, and in mid-October was stranded at Flint Island, Ohio River. Entered Pittsburgh-Cincinnati trade on Mar. 30, 1869, Capt. T.C. Sweeney, with Morris Dorsey, clerk. On May 7, 1869, while landing at Cincinnati, she was carried under the suspension bridge knocking down both stacks. In the fall 1869 ran Cincinnati-Portsmouth. Was advertised at New Orleans late January 1870 for Camden, Ark. Loaded at Carondelet, Mo., with 400 tons of iron ore for the Riverside Mill, Wheeling. Capt. John Woodburn bought her at Cincinnati Mar. 27, 1871, and loaded for Arkansas River, then ran Memphis-Pine Bluff, Ark. That summer she was rebuilt at Jeffersonville and Cincinnati. She was snagged and lost at Charlie Morris' Landing, Tenn., on Nov. 13, 1872. The *T.F. ECKERT* removed 100 bales of cotton and other freight, and during the next year the machinery was removed and "there was nothing left."

4959 St. Maurice

SW p wh b. Louisville, Ky., 1858. 462 tons. 172 x 52 x 6. Owned by James S. Hamilton, a British subject, New Orleans. Master was Capt. William Kimball. Ran New Orleans-Bayou Lafourche-Donaldsonville. Off the lists in 1863.

4960 St. Nicholas

SW p wh b. California, Pa., 1853. 666 tons. 264.7 x 35.5 x 7.3. Built for James Wood, P.R. Friend, and P.O. Scully, all of Pittsburgh. First master, Capt. John H. Burk. At time of loss owned entire by Ambrose Reeder, St. Louis with Capt. O.H. McMullen, master. She was at Island 60, Mississippi River, seven miles below the scene of the *PENNSYLVANIA* disaster (see), and nine miles above Helena, Ark., near St. Francis Island, Apr. 24, 1859, when she exploded boilers and burned. Sixty lives were lost including Capt. McMullen. Others of the crew lost included William Few, chief engineer; John Jenkins, 2nd engineer; Edward Stephens, pilot, all of St. Louis. Ben V. Glime, first clerk, was badly scalded and died two days later; his wife of 10 months died. One of the passengers was Gideon J. Pillow, Jr., son of Gen. Pillow, bound from Memphis to his father's plantation in Tennessee near Helena, Ark. He was reported lost. Ben Glime's last words, a quote from "Ingomar,": "Two souls with but a single thought, two hearts that beat as one." He was from Parkersburg, W. Va. The *SUSQUEHANNA* rendered aid, returning 16 persons to Memphis.

4961 St. Nicholas

SW p wh b. New Albany, Ind., 1856. 342 tons. Went to Mobile, Ala. Snagged and lost at Jackson, Ala., Feb. 5, 1866.

4962 St. Nicholas

SW p wh b. New Albany, Ind., 1864. 669 tons. 223.3 x 33.8 x 3.7. Engines, 22's- 7 ft. Seven boilers. Launched June 6, 1864, at the J.B. Ford yard in front of the American Foundry. Owned by Cincinnati-New Orleans Packet Co., with David Gibson a majority owner. Made trips above Cincinnati early 1866, Capt. Enos Moore. Enrolled at New Orleans April 1866 owned by David Gibson (8/12) and her master Capt. Sosthene Heno, and her clerk John Corne Libano. Ran New Orleans-Bayou Sara. In January 1867 owned entire by David Gibson, with Capt. J.C. Dowty, master. Ran New Orleans-Red River. Sank in full view of Natchitoches, La., Dec. 23, 1868, and sat there on the bottom, straight and even all that winter. A flood in May 1869 took off the cabin, texas, and pilothouse. Capt. John C. Dowty chartered the *STONEWALL* (see) to take her place and lost his life when that boat burned Oct. 27, 1869.

4963 St. Patrick

SW p wh b. Cincinnati, Oh., 1862. 414 tons. 246 x 35. Engines, 20's- 7 ft. Four boilers. Built for Capt. Sam Mason, Wheeling, and others and ran Pittsburgh-Cincinnati, and was noticed as quite like the *TELEGRAPH NO. 3* in appearance. She was up the Tennessee River with Grant 1862–1863, and in fall 1863 was back in the Pittsburgh-Cincinnati trade, Capt. Sam Mason with Major Dunlap in the office. Advertised Louisville-Memphis in January 1864, Capt. J.B. Archer. Still there February 1866, Capt. George O. Hart, with B.C. Alvord in the office.

Burned opposite Memphis, Tenn., Apr. 18, 1868. The wreck lay there until August 1871 when it was burned to recover old iron.

4964 ST. PAUL

SW p wh b. St. Louis, Mo., 1847. 358 tons. Engines, 18½'s- 8 ft. Three boilers. This odd sized machinery came from the *JOHN AULL* built by Capt. George B. Cable who also built *ST. PAUL*. Ran St. Louis-New Orleans. Hit a bluff sandbar at Island 21 upbound in August 1848 and sank. New Orleans-St. Louis in September 1851, Capt. Patrick Yore. Snagged and lost near the foot of Mokane Bend, Missouri River, date uncertain. Capt. J.H. Cole was master and part owner, and his owning partner was Martin Burke.

ST. PAUL

See *NEW ST. PAUL,* registered name.

4965 SAINT PAUL

SW p and ex wh b. St. Louis, Mo., 1883. 300 x 37.4 x 6.4. Rebuilt at Dubuque, 1903, to measure 276.6 x 37 x 6.4. Engines, 22's- 7 ft. Originally three boilers, later four. Paddlewheels 26 ft. dia. working 14 ft. buckets. Built by St. Louis & St. Paul Packet Co., and ran that trade under the Diamond Jo banner many years. Ran St. Louis-Vicksburg, chartered to Anchor Line, December 1886, Capt. Charles Zeigler, with W.H. Pritchat and Oscar Moore, clerks. Diamond Jo rebuilt her 1892-1894 and had her on the ways over a year, the work done at the Eagle yard, Dubuque, Capt. John Killeen superintending. Streckfus Line acquired her in 1911, continued her in the St. Paul trade into 1917 and then rebuilt her into an excursion boat for St. Louis service, in charge of Capt. Ben Winters and Capt. Oscar Olson. Capt. Thomas W. Posey became her pilot and was on her until the end. First came to Pittsburgh summer of 1937, Capt. Hilmar Lax. Again ran Ohio River excursions based at Pittsburgh 1938-1939, Capt. Edgar F. Mabrey, with Tom Posey and F. Way, Jr., pilots. In winter of 1939-1940 was rebuilt at Paducah and renamed *SENATOR* (see).

4966 ST. PETERS

SW p wh b. St. Louis, Mo., 1847. 163 tons. Galena-Dubuque. Capt. James Ward was on her from the start and was master 1848-1849. She burned in the wharf fire at St. Louis, May 17, 1849.

4967 STE. GENEVIEVE

SW p wh b. St. Louis, Mo., 1874. 241 x 36 x 6. Machinery from *ADAM JACOBS* (see). Owned by Memphis & St. Louis Packet Co., the early Anchor Line. Dismantled November 1887.

4968 STE. GENEVIEVE

SW tr wh b. Jeffersonville, Ind., by Howard, 1903. 215 x 45 x 7. Engines, 23's- 8 ft. Four boilers (two on a side) each 44" by 26 ft. Owned by Southern Missouri RR and ran between Little Rock Landing, Mo., and Kellogg Incline, Ill. Sank at Kellogg Incline on Mar. 1, 1918.

4969 STE. GENEVIEVE

SW tr sh b. Charleston, W. Va., by Ward Engineering, 1922. 286.3 x 43 x 11. Engines, 22's- 8 ft. Six boilers (three on a side). Could handle 18 railroad cars. On the morning of Apr. 6, 1944, the tow of the *WALTER P. DOLLE* struck her starboard wheel at the Little Rock landing on the Missouri shore. Traffic was rerouted via St. Louis until repairs were made. Dismantled in 1961. Owned by Missouri-Illinois Railroad Co.

4970 SALADIN

SW p wh b. Louisville, Ky., 1846. 346 tons. Thomas C. Coleman and brother John, both Irish born, ran her Louisville-New Orleans. The former's son, Thomas C. Jr., persuaded U.S. President-elect Zachary Taylor to come aboard en route from his Mississippi plantation to Washington, and became widely known as "the Captain who stole the President." Another steamboat, loaded with dignitaries, was supposed to pick Taylor up. Capt. Thomas Fitzgerald also was master. T.C. Sr., ran an iron works in Louisville, Thomas C. Coleman & Co., later the Louisville Rolling Mill Co. He was instrumental in building *TELEGRAPH NO. 1* and *TELEGRAPH NO. 2* (both see). Lost by snagging at Thebes, Ill., Jan. 1, 1851.

4971 SALADO

Stw p wh b. Wheeling, W. Va., 1868. 110 tons. 128.3 x 25.4 x 3.6. Originally run by H.C. Taylor and others, Wheeling, and Dr. L. Robertson, Cincinnati. Sank in Boeuf River upbound from New Orleans, Mar. 16, 1870, Capt. T. Taylor. Sold November 1870 to Capt. W.W. Risher of Trenton, La., and Samuel Lawson of New Orleans, equal shares. Burned Jan. 6, 1876, in upper Red River. She towed barges, but had a half cabin with 12 staterooms also.

4972 SALEM

Stw p wh b. Monongahela, Pa., 1851. 147 tons. Short trades, upper Ohio. Lost in ice at Covington, Ky., Feb. 24, 1856.

4973 SALENA

SW ferry wh b. Louisville, Ky., 1850. 57 tons. Went to the St. Louis area. Off the lists 1852.

4974 SALINE

SW p wh b. New Albany, Ind., 1845. 53 tons. 91 x 20 x 3.2. Enrolled at New Orleans Jan. 1, 1847, owned by Garrett Wall, New Albany, and James M. Backman, New Orleans; Capt. M.A. Wilson, master. Foundered at Carrollton, La., June 5, 1848.

4975 SALINE

Stw p wh b. Louisville, Ky., 1858. 176 tons. 143 x 28 x 4.8. Enrolled at New Orleans Oct. 26, 1859, owned and commanded by Capt. George Miller. George "Old Natural" Miller's wife Mary was issued license as mate Feb. 18, 1884, later won her master's license. Lost by stranding, January 1865 at Clark's Bar (?).

4976 SALINE

Stw p wh b. Louisville, Ky., 1882. 178 tons. This boat and her predecessor (see above) may have handled produce boats south from the Louisville area. Capt. George Miller was associated with both.

4977 SALLIE

Stw p wh b. McKeesport, Pa. (hull), and completed at Pittsburgh, 1868. 184 x 33. 399 tons. Owned in part by her first master, Capt. Thomas S. Calhoon, and Jackman T. Stockdale, and loaded for Missouri River. Then ran St. Louis-Arkansas River. Sank near Cairo, upbound, November 1871. Sank and lost after hitting a snag at Swan Lake, Ark., on the Arkansas River, 1872.

4978 SALLIE ANDERSON

SW p wh b. Louisville, Ky., 1846. 62 tons. Burned at Little Rock, Ark., Sept. 24, 1849.

4979 SALLIE CARNEY

Stw p wh b. Nashville, Tenn., 1876. 115 tons. Said to have been the first steamboat built complete at Nashville. Fletch Bryant was the carpenter, building her for Capt. Lanner Williams. Dick Harmon was engineer. Named for Mrs. Daniel Carney, Hunter's Point, Tenn., at the behest of Capt. W.T. Woolard, first master. She died when the boat was new, and the crew laid off and went to the funeral. Originally had a scow bow, but was given a model bow at Cincinnati in 1879, then owned by Capt. John Watts, Patriot, Ind. In latter 1879 Watts chartered her to take the place of *DELIA* in Vicksburg-Davis Bend trade, and she became a regular, under other owners, there. Still documented 1885, but does not appear in 1886.

4980 SALLIE CARSON

SW p wh b. New Albany, Ind., 1852. 206 tons. Went to Mobile, Ala. Off the lists 1858.

4981 SALLIE FREESE

Rig? p wh b. Ashland, Ky., 1880. 124.5 x 21.3 x 4.3. A Big Sandy packet and ran on the Ohio River in summer. Capt. Freese lived in Louisa, Ky. He also ran the *FANNIE FREESE* (see). Sold to upper Ohio and renamed *LILIAN*, so documented in 1886.

4982 SALLIE J. COOPER

Stw p wh b. Brown's Landing, W. Va. (hull), and completed at Parkersburg, W. Va., 1878. 56 tons. Brown's Landing was opposite Rea's Run, Oh. 92 x 16 x 2. Built by Capt. Ed B. Cooper and ran Parkersburg-Belleville, Oh. Later ran Marietta-Parkersburg, Capt. F.A. Athey, with S.H. Biddle, clerk. Went to the lower Ohio by 1886. See *S&D Reflector*, issue June 1976, page 38 for picture and write-up.

4983 SALLIE LIST

Stw p wh b. Elizabeth, Pa., 1860. 212 tons. Engines, 16's-4½ ft. Three boilers. Sold to Hannibal & St. Joseph Railway who used her on the Missouri River. Snagged five miles above Kickapoo, Kans., May 5, 1863. Was down on Red River spring 1864, and coming back up the Mississippi was fired on in Yellow Bend in early June 1864. Got 10 shots on board, none of the crew hurt, but much damage to boat and machinery. On Jan. 21, 1866, was in a storm at Scrub Grass Bend, lower White River, Capt. Morgan Bateman, and was reported "to have lost her port paddlewheel and was blown ashore about a mile distant." This would raise eyebrows of this historian as to her being a sternwheeler. Sold to Mobile and was snagged and sunk morning of Feb. 21, 1868, at Portland, Ala., about 25 miles below Selma, then owned by Mobile Trade Co.

4984 SALLIE MCKEE

SW ferry wh b. McKeesport, Pa., 1865. 69 tons. She was the ferry there until off the lists in 1871.

4985 SALLIE ROBINSON

SW p wh b. Cincinnati, Oh., 1856. 267 tons. 160 x 33 x 5.5. Owned in part and commanded by Capt. Dyas Power of Aberdeen, Oh. Operated out of Yazoo River and also was known on the Red to Alexandria, La. Capt. Power sold her, April 1861 to Hannah Schille, New Orleans, and boat went to Confederate registry. In 1863 ran New Orleans-Baton Rouge, Capt. Ham, teamed with *IBERVILLE* and *LAUREL HILL* (both see).

4986 SALLIE ROBINSON

Stw p wh b. Cincinnati, Oh., 1876. 165 x 34 x 6. Engines, 16's- 5 ft. Three boilers. Capt. Charles F. Reynolds part owner and master. New Orleans-Alexandria.

4987 SALLIE SPANN

SW p wh b. Jeffersonville, Ind., by Howard, 1852. 190 tons. 180 x 30 x 6. Went to Mobile, Ala., where she burned Oct. 1, 1856.

4988 SALLIE V.

SW p wh b. Wheeling, W. Va. (hull), and completed at St. Marys, W. Va., 1867. 141 tons. Ran Racine-Pomeroy-Gallipolis, Capt. Lang Halliday, with James Patterson, clerk. Sold in July 1868 to run Mt. Vernon-Evansville-Henderson, Capt. M. Wallen, with Lou Coleman, clerk. In March 1871 the Memphis & Little Rock Railroad bought one-half interest. Dismantled at New Orleans 1872.

SALLIE WARD

See *SALLIE WOOD*.

4989 SALLIE WEST

Stw p wh b. Louisville, Ky., 1853. 286 tons. Snagged and lost at Kickapoo, Kans., May 5, 1859.

4990 SALLIE WOOD

Stw p wh b. Paducah, Ky., 1860. 256 tons. 160 x 31. Engines, 14's- 5 ft. Captured by U.S. at Chickasaw, Ala., Feb. 8, 1862. Also known as *SALLIE WARD*. Burned at Island 82, Mississippi River, July 30, 1862. She was built by Capt. George W. Evans.

4991 Salmon

Prop p wh b. Portsmouth, Oh., 1867. 63 tons. Snagged and lost in Mobile Bay, Ala., 1873.

4992 Salt Valley

Stw p wh b. Middleport, Oh., 1874. 347 tons. Ran Pittsburgh-Ironton, Capt. T. Spence Sandford, with Edwin F. Maddy, clerk. Same trade all along, and in 1878 Capt. Sam De Wolf, with clerks Kirker and Buchanan. The following advertisement appeared in the Pittsburgh *Commercial Gazette* dated Dec. 22, 1879: "Owing to a combination made by the so-called Pittsburgh & Cincinnati, the Wheeling & Cincinnati, and Big Sandy Packet companys, preventing the steamer *SALT VALLEY* from carrying freight below Ironton on account of a prohibitory discrimination against her, we would respectfully solicit the patronage of shippers to Ironton and intermediate points where, by the grace of God, and not the monopoly, we are permitted to run. (signed) Sam De Wolf, master; John C. Kirker, clerk." Dismantled and equipment used on towboat *GUS GENIN* in 1881.

4993 Saluda

SW p wh b. St. Louis, Mo., 1846. 223 tons. 179 x 26.7. A double engine, two boiler boat whose hull was built at an Ohio River yard and she was completed at St. Louis, 1846. Ran St. Louis-St. Joseph. In 1850 struck a snag and sank five miles below Rocheport, Mo. The hull was dug off the bar, taken to St. Louis and she was rebuilt. Started for Council Bluffs with Mormon emigrants and upon arrival at Lexington, Mo., Apr. 9, 1852, her boilers exploded, killing 27 and wounding many more. The children of some of the victims were adopted by residents of Lexington and grew up to be respected citizens. Capt. Francis T. Belt was master. Charles S. LaBarge was pilot, and was killed, brother of Capt. Joseph LaBarge. The roof bell went to the Christian Church, Savannah, Mo. The Machapella Cemetery, Lexington, still contains graves of at least 25 victims.

4994 Salvor No. 1

SW wrecking boat wh b. St. Louis, Mo., 1865. 205 tons. Owned by Salvor Wrecking & Transportation Co., and was used to remove freight, machinery and equipment from sunken steamboats. Dismantled 1875.

4995 Salvor No. 2

Centerwheel wrecking boat wh b. Metropolis, Ill. (hull), and completed at St. Louis, 1866. 243 tons. Owned by Salvor Wrecking & Transportation Co., and did similar work to *NO. 1,* listed above. Lost in 1884.

4996 Sam A. Conner

Stw p wh b. Chattanooga, Tenn., 1901. 98.5 x 16 x 2.6. Did packet work out of Chattanooga towing flats, etc. In 1905 owned by Huntington, Ashland & Big Sandy Transportation Co., Russell Black, Kenova, W. Va., agent. Mr. Black soon bought the boat entire. Later owned by Anderson & Tully, Vicksburg. In 1910 they built the towboat *HUNTER* out of her.

4997 Sam Boree

Stw p wh b. Lafayette, Ind., on Wabash River, 1878. A small fry, rebuilt at St. Louis in spring of 1882 and renamed *ROB ROY* (see).

4998 Sam Cloon

SW p wh b. Cincinnati, Oh., 1851. 301 tons. At New Orleans, September 1851, advertised to Cincinnati, Capt. James Siddal. Collided with *HARRY HILL* in Spanish Moss Bend, lower Mississippi, Feb. 14, 1853, and was sunk. Made a trip up the Missouri, 1853, with John P. Keiser, pilot. Wrecked in ice at St. Louis, Feb. 27, 1856, along with *SHENANDOAH.*

4999 Sam Conner

Stw p wh b. Hermann, Mo., 1911, originally named *H.E. MYRTLE* (see). Ran on Tennessee River. In 1921 in Guntersville-Lamb's Ferry trade. In 1929, Chattanooga-Kingston, Capt. C.B. Dobbs, in Tennessee River Navigation Co., which also was running *CAPTAIN LYERLY,* freight only, Chattanooga-Decatur, Capt. Crawford Carter. Later went to the Cumberland River.

5000 Sam Dale

SW p wh b. New Albany, Ind., 1842. 305 tons. 189 x 28 x 6. Built for service out of Mobile, Ala. Back at New Orleans, March 1846, owned largely by Stockley Vinson, Sumner County, Tenn., Capt. Jacob Hunter. In August 1846 sold to Capt. John T. Yoe, New Orleans. In fall of 1848 was in use as a wharfboat at Cairo, Ill. The First Presbyterian Church of Cairo held its first services aboard this boat Feb. 8, 1852 at 3:00 P.M., Rev. Robert Stewart. It still was a wharfboat, and 30 persons attended "much annoyed by the noise of men and boats." T.J. Smith & Co., operated this wharfboat, and also another wharfboat formerly the packet *MAZEPPA* (see).

5001 Sam Dale

SW p wh b. Jeffersonville, Ind., by Howard, 1852. 276 tons. Built for service out of Mobile, Ala. A letter written at New Albany, Ind., Sept. 12, 1852, by Jacob F. Hise has this to say: "Frank Johnson will call his new boat *SAM DALE.* Andy Johnson is in very poor health but Frank looks as well as ever, only a good deal older—he now is 45—it seems but yesterday when we were all on the *JEFFERSON* at Mobile." Burned and lost at Mobile, Feb. 25, 1854. 210 x 30 x 7.5.

5002 Sam Davis

Stw p wh b. Chattanooga, Tenn., 1898. 118 x 21 x 2.5. Engines, 9½'s- 3 ft. One boiler, 42" by 14 ft. Owned by Tennessee River Navigation Co., which operated her out of Chattanooga along with the *N.B. FORREST.* Probably more of a towboat than a packet. Still listed in 1904.

5003 Sam Gaty

SW p wh b. St. Louis, Mo., 1853. 294 tons. 210 x 36.

Engines, 19's- 7 ft. Three boilers. Built for St. Louis & Keokuk Packet Co. Made occasional trips up Missouri River, and was at St. Paul in 1855. Pressed into service during the war she sank at Island 92, Skipworth Landing, Miss., Sept. 30, 1862, upbound from Vicksburg to Memphis with 307 soldiers, 157 horses, 37 wagons, etc. Raised and rebuilt, and again sank at Tower Island, February 1867, Capt. William Brown commanding in the absence of Capt. David Silver. On a trip up Missouri River she took a sheer on the pilot at the point opposite Arrow Rock, Mo., June 27, 1858, struck a bluff bank, dislocated the boilers, and burned. Capt. Frank Dozier was in command, and she was reportedly owned by Capt. John Baldwin.

5004 SAM GRONENDYKE

Prop p wh b. Lafayette, Ind., 1863. 60 tons. Built as a barge, converted to steam in 1866. Probably a freight carrier. Off the lists in 1881.

5005 SAM HALE

Stw p wh b. Cincinnati, Oh., 1856. 103 tons. Engines, 12's- 4 ft. Owned by Charles W. Coles. Went to Confederate registry 1861.

5006 SAM J. HALE

Stw p wh b. Cincinnati, Oh., 1866. 498 tons. Ran in the Dean Line, Cincinnati-Memphis. In 1868 Capt. William P. Walker, with E.C. Miller, clerk. In 1873 same officers. In descending the Louisville Falls Feb. 12, 1871, struck rocks at the head of the chute and again above the bridge and had to be unloaded at Portland, Ky. Pink Varble was piloting and having trouble with a high west wind. In April 1871 burst main steam line and killed six persons, all in the engine room. This was a copper steam line, second-hand from the old *DIAMOND,* and she had 136 psi at the time of the accident, allowed 140. Dismantled at Cincinnati 1875-1877.

5007 SAM J. KEITH

Stw p wh b. Jeffersonville, Ind., by Howard, 1882. 160 x 32 x 5.3. Built for Capt. T.H. Armstrong, Nashville, Tenn., and ran Nashville-Burnside. Named for a Nashville financier. Later bought by St. Louis & Tennessee River Packet Co., who renamed her *CITY OF FLORENCE* (see).

5008 SAM KIRKMAN

Stw p wh b. Paducah, Ky., 1857. 271 tons. 157 x 36.5. Machinery from *HELEN MARR.* Made a trip to St. Paul in 1858. Owned in part by Capt. Josh V. Throop, Evansville, and Capt. Dorsey Smedley, Paducah. Ran Evansville-Paducah-Cairo. She was at Fort Henry, Tennessee River, Feb. 6, 1862 and was burned to prevent her capture by Federal gunboats.

5009 SAM ORR

Stw p wh b. New Albany, Ind., 1861. 179 tons. 150 x 29 x 5. Built for Wabash River, named for an iron merchant of Evansville. She was entered in the Evansville-Paducah trade and was seized by Capt. Wythe Fowler and a group of Paducah citizens, and was taken up Tennessee River. She was burned by the Confederates to prevent her capture. The wreck lay there several years, was retrieved, and she was rebuilt and in 1865 entered the Evansville-Paducah-Johnsonville-Eastport trade, Capt. Allen Duncan, with Vinyard and Breeden, clerks. Sold Aug. 7, 1871, to John Kutch, Tell City, Ind. Upper works were placed on a new hull at Grandview, Ind., in 1875 and she was renamed *ROBERT J. YOUNG,* towing produce. Picture of *SAM ORR* and a detailed write-up in *S&D Reflector,* March 1971, pages 28-30.

5010 SAM P. JONES

Stw p wh b. Jeffersonville, Ind., by Howard, 1881, originally named *L.P. EWALD* (see). Owned by Capt. Tom G. Ryman and W.B. Bowman, Nashville, Tenn. Renamed c. 1886. Under charter in Evansville-Cairo trade, July 1887 hit a snag, upbound, in Diamond Island Chute and sank in eight feet. Pilot James Collins on watch. In the fall of 1887 she loaded with salt at Mason City, W. Va., from the Hope Mfg. & Coal Co., consigned to Ohio River Salt Co.'s orders. Dismantled at Jeffersonville in 1888 and machinery, etc., went to the *I. T. RHEA.*

5011 SAM ROBERTS

SW ferry wh b. Pittsburgh, Pa., 1873. 90 x 25 x 4.5. A drive-through ferry used at Elizabeth, Pa., operated by Capt. J.C. Boyd. In 1888 Frank Billingsley was pilot, and Robert Boyd, Jr., was engineer. Burned in March 1895.

5012 SAM SEAY

SW p wh b. Pittsburgh, Pa., 1844. 190 tons. Ran Cincinnati-Nashville in 1845, Capt. Robert Greenlee. Off the lists 1848.

5013 SAM THE SCARAMOUCH

Stw yacht wh b. Covington, Ky., 1888. 63 x 8.5 x 1.3. A slim-jim affair with one tall stack. Capt. Jesse P. Hughes recalled seeing her moored above the Wheeling wharf in 1894, "a no account pleasure boat." On one occasion she took pilots from Harbor 25, Pittsburgh, on a low water inspection trip. Burned at Bullitt's Bayou, lower Mississippi River, Sept. 25, 1897. Remarked Capt. Hughes: "Too bad."

SAM SNOWDEN

See *SAMUEL SNOWDEN.*

5014 SAM VAIL

Prop freight boat wh b. Portsmouth, Oh., 1866. 70 tons. Operated Dyersburg-Hales Point on the Mississippi. In January 1868 went up the Forked Deer River in Tennessee, going to Eaton in Gibson County. The trip created an immense sensation along that stream, and at Eaton a cannon was fired seven rounds. She brought out a load of cotton. Off the lists 1877.

5015 SAM YOUNG

Stw p wh b. Shousetown, Pa., 1855. 156 x 28 x 3.7. Engines,

18's-4 ft. Three boilers, each 38" by 22 ft., two 14" flues. 154 tons. Owned by her master, Capt. Richard C. Gray, in partnership with William H. Forsythe and Samuel C. Young. Ran tramp trades out of Pittsburgh, and was to St. Paul 1856 and 1857. Had various owners. In 1861 was running above Peoria on the Illinois River. She was reported sold at Cincinnati on Feb. 5, 1865, to Capt. A.R. Irwin for the Memphis-Helena trade. Reported lost July 22, 1865.

5016 SAMPSON

SW diving bell boat wh b. Cape Girardeau, Mo., 1849. 61 tons. Exploded with loss of two lives at Calumet, Wis., May 31, 1855.

5017 SAMUEL B. WIGGINS

Centerwheel ferry wh b. Jeffersonville, Ind., by Howard, 1885. 177.6 x 47.4 x 6.6. 364 tons. One engine, 28½"-6 ft. Three boilers, each 44" by 18 ft. Owned by Wiggins Ferry Co., St. Louis. Operated until about 1913. In 1914 was laid up, out of commission.

5018 SAMUEL C. CHRISTY

Recess wheel ferry wh b. New Albany, Ind., 1862. 410 tons. Owned by Wiggins Ferry Co., St. Louis. Off the lists 1882.

SAMUEL GATY

See *SAM GATY*.

5019 SAMUEL P. HIBBARD

Stw p wh b. Brownsville, Pa., 1856. 178 tons. Ran Pittsburgh-Louisville, a very light boat. On the first trip down, commanded by Capt. R.C. Grace, with Charley Coles in the office, and Sam Dean and George Rowley in the pilothouse. They found 10 inches in Logstown, and 12 inches in the foot of Blennerhassett Island. There was a yoke of oxen pulling a scraper over the bars at Sand Creek. Later operated by Capt. W.C. Harry, father of Capt. Milt Harry. She came in collision with the *CHANCELLOR*, July 26, 1860, on the Louisville Falls, and sank at Point of Rock Bar along the Indiana shore. The wreck went off in high water and lodged at Falling Run, below Portland, Ky. The *GREENBACK* removed it in July 1871.

5020 SAMUEL SNOWDEN

Stw p wh b. McKeesport, Pa., 1853. 194 tons. Capt. W.P. Torrence brought her out in March 1853 and made trips up the Allegheny River with her. Capt. George Smith, Sr., Racine, Oh., later operated her. He became a skiff builder by trade. Off the lists 1862.

5021 SAN ANTONIO

SW p wh b. Freedom, Pa., 1854. 127 tons. Went to Galveston, Tex., and to Confederate registry in 1861.

5022 SAN JUAN

Rig? p wh b. Pittsburgh, Pa., 1871, by Capt. Kennedy for the Rio Grande in Texas. Made trial runs Aug. 31, 1871. Low water prevented her departure until November 16. James Vandergrift (late of the *LORENA*) went down as clerk on her.

5023 SAN NICHOLAS

Stw p wh b. Louisville, Ky., 1865. 74 tons. 86.5 x 19 x 5. Owned and commanded by Capt. N.D. Harvey, New Orleans. Ownership changed October 1867 to Capt. Joseph H. Harvey, entire, who commanded. Rebuilt at New Orleans February 1869 to measure 119.5 x 25 x 5.1. She was put up for sale at New Orleans by a U.S. marshal in December 1873 and was bid in by E.H.J. Blineau for $650. He did not have on hand the required cash and was given ten minutes to go get it. When he returned the marshal started all over again, and this time Blineau bid $600 and took the boat. Off the lists 1876.

5024 SAN FRANCISCO

SW p wh b. Elizabeth, Pa., 1849. 263 tons. Burned and lost at St. Louis, Mo., July 28, 1849.

5025 SANDUSKY

U.S. monitor ih b. Pittsburgh, Pa., 1865, 170 x 50. Built by Tomlinson, Hartupee & Co., single prop. Built too late for war service, and lay in the Allegheny River until Feb. 22, 1866, when she and *MARIETTA*, a similar monitor, were towed to Cairo by the *HAWK*. Name was changed to *MINERVA*, back again to *SANDUSKY* in 1869. Sold away in 1873.

5026 SANDY

Ran Evansville-Cannelton in 1874, Capt. Lafe Elder, with Phil Branham and Sam Elder in the office, in competition with *MARY AMENT*, and lost out. While laid up at Shreveport, La., burned July 21, 1877.

5027 SANDY FASHION

SW p wh b. Catlettsburg, Ky., 1874. 35 tons. A Big Sandy "batwing" with two engines 6" dia. by 12" stroke. One boiler 33" by 8 ft. Owned by R.K. Price and William Smiley. She left Catlettsburg for Big Sandy points Apr. 6, 1878, was called back to receive some late freight, and started again. When abreast of the Sherman House the boiler exploded killing the pilot, Alfonzo Osborn, and one other. The wreck sank. Rebuilt and came out again in June 1878 renamed *L. T. MOORE* (see). The exploded boiler had been built at Pittsburgh in 1866 for the ferry *CONCERT* (see).

5028 SANDY VALLEY

Stw p wh b. Catlettsburg, Ky., 1860. 55 tons. During the war she carried military supplies up Big Sandy River, and one voyage was in charge of James A. Garfield, later U.S. President Garfield. Off the lists 1869.

5029 SANDY VALLEY

SW p wh b. Catlettsburg, Ky., 1888. 110 x 14.7 x 3.1. A Big Sandy "bat wing" bought by Capt. George Bay for low water work. Ran Portsmouth-Proctorville, Gallipolis-Huntington and occasionally to Parkersburg. She made trips to Cincinnati. The Bays sold her to Capt. Lewis Tanner, Ironton, Oh., on Nov. 28, 1900. Sank on Big Sandy in mid-April 1901 and was lost.

5030 SANDY NO. 2

Rig? p wh b. New Albany, Ind., 1873. 266 tons. In 1877 was running New Orleans-Opelousas, Capt. A.P. Trousdale, with J.B. Schmidt as clerk. Struck a log near Baton Rouge downbound at 12:30 A.M., May 15, 1877, floated 12 miles in a sinking condition, hit the bank, and sank a total loss.

5031 SANGAMON

SW p wh b. New Albany, Ind., 1853. 85 tons. On the Upper Mississippi to St. Paul in 1854, Capt. R.M. Spencer. Snagged and lost at St. Charles, Ark., Feb. 12, 1856.

5032 SANTA FE

Stw ferry wh b. Glasgow, Mo., 1919. 65 x 20.5 x 2.9. Owned by W.M. Lessley, Arrow Rock, Mo. In the summer of 1930 she made two inspection trips chartered to the U.S. Engineers, both on the Missouri River. The first was from Lexington to Sioux City and return, and the second was from Lexington to Yankton, S.D., and return. She was wintered at Lexington 1930–1931. On a 1931 trip with the Chief of the U.S. Army Engineers on board, Maj. Gen. Lytle Brown, she was snagged and sunk at Waldron, Mo., 20 miles from Kansas City. As she went down she was beached on a sandbar and didn't go down too far; about three feet.

5033 SANTA LUCIA

Stw p wh b. Pittsburgh, Pa., 1889, originally named *NELLIE HUDSON NO. 2* (see). She was refitted at the James Rees & Sons shop in the Allegheny River, Pittsburgh in 1892, renamed *SANTA LUCIA* and went under her own steam to St. Johns River, Florida.

5034 SANTIAGO

SW p sh b. St. Louis, Mo., 1881. 131 x 26 x 5. This steel hull steamer went to Texas, documented at Galveston in 1882 and at Brownsville through 1896, maybe longer.

5035 SARACEN

SW p wh b. New Albany, Ind., 1856. 241 tons. Went to the Upper Mississippi, Capt. H.B. Stran, with clerk Casey. Was at St. Paul 1857. Off the lists 1859.

5036 SARAH

SW p wh b. Cincinnati, Oh., 1849. 442 tons. Ran St. Louis-New Orleans, Capt. Young. Burned in the steamboat fire at St. Louis, May 17, 1849.

5037 SARAH

SW p wh b. Louisville, Ky., 1850. 138 tons. 137.8 x 22.7 x 4.7. Went to Mobile, Ala. Enrolled at New Orleans Jan. 3, 1854, owned by John S. Crockett, New Orleans, with Capt. N.C. Briggs, master. Briggs bought the boat entire, May 30, 1854. Exploded boilers Feb. 21, 1856, on Trinity River, Tex., with loss of two lives.

5038 SARAH

Prop ship wh b. New Albany, Ind., 1866. 406 tons. Went to Mobile, Ala. Documented at New Orleans (temporary) Apr. 3, 1869, owned by Charles Morgan, New York City, with Capt. A.C. Hutchinson, master. 181 x 37 x 6. She was inspected at New Orleans 1881 and 1882.

5039 SARAH BLADEN

SW p wh b. New Albany, Ind., 1841. 199 tons. 171 x 25 x 5.3. Traded between Florence, Ala., and New Orleans. Enrolled at New Orleans Jan. 24, 1845, owned by Joseph Ahern of New Orleans, James Irvin and Francis Boggs of Florence, Ala., and Edward Bernard, New Albany, Ind. The master was Capt. John B. Boggs. Went to sheriff sale at New Orleans July 3, 1847, and sold entire to Capt. Leonore Gaste, New Orleans. Sold July 14, 1847, to Capt. James E. Newson. Sold Feb. 29, 1848, to Christopher Nicholson, New Orleans, Capt. Joseph H. Short, master. Sold July 1, 1848, to Henry Merritt, New Orleans, Capt. William B. Currie, master. Off the lists in 1850. In 1961 the roof bell from this boat, cast by A. Fulton, Pittsburgh, was hanging in the belfry of the Cumberland Presbyterian Church, Charlotte, Tenn.

5040 SARAH GORDON

SW p wh b. New Albany, Ind., 1850. 150 tons. 135.1 x 22.3 x 5.2. Originally owned by Capt. Oramel Hinckley, New Orleans. Ran New Orleans-Red River. Sold June 1854 to Capt. Benjamin Mason who continued her there. Off the lists 1856.

5041 SARANAK

SW p wh b. Elizabethtown, Pa., 1846. 198 tons. Off the lists 1854.

5042 SARANAK NO. 2

SW p wh b. Brownsville, Pa., 1849. 295 tons. Running New Orleans-St. Louis, Capt. William McIntyre, 1851. Burned and lost at St. Louis, Mo., July 2, 1856. In the old cemetery at Grand Gulf, Miss., is a tombstone marking the grave of a man who died aboard *SARANAK NO. 2* of cholera. We mention the matter inasmuch as debate exists as to the spelling of the boat's name, apparently documented *SARANAC NO. 2.*

5043 SARATOGA

SW p wh b. Louisville, Ky., 1864. 339 tons. 183 x 36.5 x 7. Built at Dan Richards' yard for Louisville-Nashville trade. Ainslee-Cochran engines. Owned (one-half) by David Gibson, Cincinnati, C.R. May of New Orleans, and Morehead & Co., Louisville, Ky. Went to New Orleans September 1864, Capt. A.J. May. Sold September 1865 to A.S. Mansfield, New Orleans, with Capt. Samuel Ayles, master. Ran up Red River to Shreveport. Burned Aug. 9, 1866, at New Orleans.

5044 SATURN

Stw ex wh b. Rock Island, Ill., 1901. 145.5 x 30 x 4. Engines, 16½'s- 5 ft. Three boilers, each 42" by 20 ft. Equipment from rafter *JOHN H. DOUGLASS* used in construction. Owned by Capt. George Winans, then Knapp, Stout & Co., and finally Ledger and Morrissy. Did raft work, and ran excursions at St. Louis and on Missouri River at Omaha, Neb., and elsewhere. Cabin burned off in 1910, rebuilt. Still operating in March 1914.

5045 SAVANNA

SW p wh b. Elizabethtown, Pa., 1848. 337 tons. Snagged and lost at Waterloo, La., Nov. 24, 1849, with loss of one life.

5046 SAVANNA

Stw p wh b. Brownsville, Pa., 1863. 243 tons. Operated originally Pittsburgh-St. Louis, Capt. Isaac M. Mason. 156 x 35 x 5. Owned largely at St. Louis. Was bringing iron ore St. Louis to Pittsburgh in 1871, Capt. M.A. Cox, then owned by George W. Burnett and George Reese of St. Louis, equal shares. She was mauled in an ice gorge at St. Louis Dec. 12, 1876. Was renamed *FLYING EAGLE,* Mar. 28, 1881. Off the lists 1884.

5047 SAWMILL CLIPPER

Rig? saw mill wh b. Wheeling, W. Va., 1880. 111.5 x 25 x 3.4. A second one was built at Haynes Landing, W. Va., on the Ohio River in 1888, named *CLIPPER,* which evolved in 1916 as a packet built at Slidell, La. (see).

5048 SAWYER

Stw p wh b. New Matamoras, Oh., 1884. 93.4 x 19.2 x 2.9. A low water craft which also may have been equipped with a saw mill. Ran low water Wheeling-New Matamoras, David Ewers, master, with L.R. Young, clerk, 1887, connecting with *IDA SMITH* for Marietta. Documented at Louisville 1896.

5049 SAXON

SW p wh b. New Albany, Ind., 1850. 479 tons. 222.2 x 32.1 x 7. Owned in part by Capt. Joseph H. Estes who commanded. Half-owned in Mobile, Ala. Burned and lost at New Orleans, La., Feb. 4, 1854. This same blaze burned the *CHARLES BELCHER, NATCHEZ* (both see).

5050 SCARAB

Stw p wh b. Pierre, S.D., 1906, originally named *W.D. WALDEN* (see). Renamed by Benton Transportation Co., Capt. Joseph Leach. They did not operate her very long inasmuch as she burned expensive "eastern" coal. Sold October 1918 to Flesher Towboat Co., Mt. Vernon, Ind.

5051 SCHUYLER

Stw p wh b. Belle Vernon, Pa., 1863. 241 tons. In March 1864 running St. Louis-Peoria, Capt. DeWitt. Apparently operated in that area until off the lists in 1873. When first delivered to St. Louis, 1863, she brought sick and wounded soldiers to Keokuk, Iowa.

5052 SCHUYLKILL

SW p wh b. Shousetown, Pa., 1846. 271 tons. Ran tramp trades, Pittsburgh-Louisville-St. Louis. First to arrive at scene of loss of *NEW ENGLAND NO. 2* opposite Greenup, Ky., Mar. 17, 1850, and rescued many. Sank after being struck by the *BUCKEYE STATE* at Pittsburgh, Pa., Apr. 5, 1850. One of her owners after August 1848 was Capt. Harrison S. Williams who later on was well known as pilot on *EMMA DUNCAN, DARLING, MOLLIE EBERT,* and others. His partner in ownership was J.T. Fisher, Pittsburgh. Dismantled in 1854.

5053 SCIENCE

Stw p wh b. Wheeling, W. Va., 1869. 94 tons. 150 x 30 x 3. Ran low water, Wheeling-Parkersburg, Capt. Phil Anshutz. She was named for the earlier edition (see below) which had operated Pittsburgh-Wheeling the summer of 1862, Capt. George W. Johnson, and later Capt. Charles Muhleman, taking the place of *MINERVA.* In 1882 her machinery, etc., went to *OLIVETTE.*

5054 SCIENCE NO. 2

Stw p wh b. California, Pa., 1860. 116 tons. 135 x 26.6 x 3.8. Originally owned by Capt. William Reno (one-half), Samuel C. Young, Isaac P. Dunlap, and James R. McClintock, all of Shousetown, Pa., and David Ross, Allegheny City, Pa. Originally operated on the Allegheny River, then Pittsburgh-Gallipolis, Capt. Wm. Reno. Sank at Pomeroy, Oh., February 1862, up to the boiler deck. Burned December 1863 at Portland, Ky., owned by Capt. P. Varble and William P. May, rebuilt, and September 1865 at New Orleans owned by S.P. Griffin, Shreveport, La., Capt. George Alban. Sank and lost at Gretna, La., June 18, 1866.

5055 SCIMITAR II

Stw private pl wh b. Jeffersonville, Ind., by Howard, 1905. 136 x 29 x 4. Engines, 13's- 5 ft. Two boilers, each 40" by 26 ft. Built for A. Hart, St. Louis, who had a mentally-ill son, with the hope that life on the river would be beneficial. Within one year the son's plight was such that he was committed to an institution. The boat then ran briefly Nashville-Burnside in 1906 and was sold to the U.S. Engineers who renamed her *CONTROL* (see *Towboat Directory*).

5056 SCIOTO

SW p wh b. Cincinnati, Oh., 1846. 231 tons. The hull was built at Murraysville, Va., for Capt. James Davis, Portsmouth, Oh., who owned in *SCIOTO VALLEY* prior (see). Off the lists in 1853.

5057 SCIOTO

Stw p wh b. Cincinnati, Oh., 1863. 221 tons. Sold to the U.S., Jan. 23, 1864 and became Tinclad #44, named *METEOR,* Mar. 8, 1864. When sold to private owners she was renamed *DE SOTO,* Oct. 7, 1865.

5058 SCIOTO

Stw p wh b. Portsmouth, Oh., 1863. 54 tons. 110 x 16 x 3. Documented at New Orleans September 1864, owned by James S. Clark and Ed Fulton, both of New Orleans. Had been running New Orleans-Attakapas, 1865, Capt. J.N. Barne. Advertised for sale at New Orleans in 1866, calling her a 450 bale boat. Many changes of ownership at New Orleans, rebuilt 1867 owned by Robert Watson. Sank and lost at Gretna, La., later same year.

5059 SCIOTO

SW p wh b. Ironton, Oh., 1875. 116 tons. Said to have been 122 ft. long. Boilers were set in the hold. Built by the Bay Line for Portsmouth-Huntington trade, originally single-deck, replacing *FASHION* (see). A cabin was added, and she was sold to the Wheeling & Parkersburg Transportation Co. On July 4, 1882, in command of Capt. Thad Thomas, she was upbound with an excursion at Cross Creek, below Mingo Junction, Oh., when she came in collision with the downbound *JOHN LOMAS* (see). The *LOMAS* struck her head-on on the port quarter at the boilers, stoving the hull, and she sank rapidly. The life-loss was around 70 persons, worst on the Upper Ohio. The confusion causing the collision was due to a recent reversal of whistle signals, ordered by the Supervising Inspector General in Washington, D.C., requiring the downbound boat to blow the first signal of intention, thus reversing the time-honored rule. The pilot on watch on the *SCIOTO,* David Kellar, was found guilty on several counts, and was sentenced to a penitentiary and served time. The boat was raised, rebuilt, and renamed *REGULAR* (see). The whistle signals for the Western Waters were put back as they were in the first place, the upbound boat blowing the first signal of intent.

5060 SCIOTO

SW p wh b. Cincinnati, Oh., 1896. 44 x 8 x 3. Small "bat wing" style, for Big Sandy River.

5061 SCIOTO

Stw p wh b. New Albany, Ind., 1898. 94 x 19 x 3.6. Ran Evansville to Hartford, Ky., via Ohio, Green and Rough rivers. Sank near Vicksburg, Miss.

5062 SCIOTO NO. 2

SW p wh b. Cincinnati, Oh., 1851. 265 tons. Ran in the Cincinnati-Portsmouth, Oh., trade, Capt. Keppner. Became a part of the Cincinnati, Maysville & Portsmouth Packet Co., 1855, Capt. Wash Honshell, running Cincinnati-Big Sandy. In the spring of 1858 Jerome D. Duncan and others ran her Louisville-Henderson, Capt. A. Ballard, with J.D. Duncan, clerk. Burned at Shippingport, Ky., June 1, 1860.

5063 SCIOTO NO. 2

Prop p wh b. Portsmouth, Oh., 1865. 59 tons. Off the lists 1867.

5064 SCIOTO BELLE

SW p wh b. Parkersburg, Va., 1842. 95 tons. 118.5 x 18 x 4. She is recalled as the first steamboat up Little Kanawha River to Elizabeth, Va., this in 1842. Documented at New Orleans Dec. 12, 1843, owned by Martin O. Walker, John Fink, and Curran Walker, all of Chicago, Ill., Capt. Philander Reed, Pike County, Ill. Arrived in Galveston, Tex., on May 7, 1844. During a yellow fever epidemic she was utilized as a hospital at Lynchburg, Tex. Off the lists 1845.

5065 SCOTIA

Stw p wh b. Harmar, Oh., at Knox Yard, 1880. 601 tons. 236 x 36 x 5.2. Engines, 20's- 4′8″. Three boilers. Ran Pittsburgh-Cincinnati, and first master was Capt. Martin F. Noll, known as the "boy captain," then 31. His first crew: J.A. Voegtly and Willis Stockdale, clerks; S.R. Lankard and John Oliver, engineers. In 1883 Capt. Frank Maratta, master, with Daniel Moore, clerk. In 1884, Capt. J.M. Kirker, master, with Robert H. Kerr, clerk. In 1885–1888, Capt. George W. Rowley, master, with Robert H. Kerr, clerk. Her last master in the trade was Capt. John Phillips. She ran in the Pittsburgh & Cincinnati Packet Line along with the *KATIE STOCKDALE, BUCKEYE STATE, EMMA GRAHAM,* and others. Artist Emil Bott painted scenes on each stateroom door. Had one of the first electric arc headlights. Broke her shaft near Portsmouth, Oh., in May 1895, was towed back to Cincinnati and sold to Capt. John Barrett, who also bought the *B.S. RHEA* and entered them in the Cincinnati-Louisville trade in opposition to the White Collar Line. Both burned, along with the towboat *SIDNEY DILLON,* at Cincinnati on Nov. 5, 1895.

5066 SCOTLAND

SW p wh b. Jeffersonville, Ind., by Howard, 1855. 567 tons. 225 x 38 x 7.5. Engines, 22's- 8 ft. Four boilers, each 38″ by 28 ft. Built for the Nashville-New Orleans trade, Capt. Desmukes. Enrolled at New Orleans October 1857 owned by C.W. Newton, New Orleans, with Capt. H.G. McComas, master. In September 1861 owned by Capt. A.C. Hopkins, New Orleans. Went to Confederate registry and was burned by the Confederates at Fort Pemberton, Miss., on Mar. 22, 1863, to prevent her capture.

5067 SCOUT

Rig? p wh b. Freedom, Pa., 1875. 55 tons. 85 x 15 x 2. Running during low water fall of 1876, Pittsburgh-Parkersburg, towing a decked flat, operating from Patterson's wharfboat, Pittsburgh. In April 1878 was running above Charleston on Kanawha River, and her master, Capt. Oaks, was killed on the C&O tracks. Still documented at Pittsburgh 1886.

5068 SEA BIRD

SW p wh b. New Albany, Ind., 1844. 261 tons. 174 x 26 x 6. Advertised Pittsburgh to New Orleans, March 1844, Capt. Ballard. Enrolled at New Orleans October 1845 owned by Guilford Griffin, New Orleans, with Capt. William K. English, master. Burned and lost at Cape Girardeau, Mo., Jan. 5, 1848.

5069 SEA GULL

SW p wh b. Jeffersonville, Ind., 1846. 149 tons. 152 x 27 x 5.5. Engines, 17½'s- 7 ft. Boilers each 42″ by 26 ft. Built at

James Murray yard. Engines by John Curry & Co. Ran Louisville-Kentucky River. She carried U.S. President-elect Zachary Taylor and party from Louisville to Frankfort and back to Carrollton in February 1849. Sank on a stump in Grassy Flats above Louisville Aug. 8, 1852. Capt. Isaac L. Hyatt towed coal with her Pittsburgh-Cincinnati starting December 1852. Sold to Henry A. Bausman, Robert McMahan and Capt. James M. Bailey, her master, January 1854, who continued towing coal. Upbound with empties sank at the foot of Newberry Island, Ohio River, April 1854, going down "like a lump of lead."

5069A SEA GULL

SW p wh b. Pikeville, Ky., 1902. 89.8 x 12.1 x 2.7. Exposed wheels, bat-wing type, designed for Big Sandy service. Sold in 1907 to U.G. Hanes and J.A. Plymale, both of Gallipolis, Oh., equal shares.

5070 SEA WING

Stw rafter wh b. Diamond Bluff, Wis., 1888. 110 x 20.8 x 4.5. Engines, 10's-6 ft. Owned by Capt. David N. Wethern of Diamond Bluff who ran a general store there. We are including the boat here inasmuch as she was carrying an excursion on July 13, 1890, and capsized on Lake Pepin drowning some 90 persons including Capt. Wethern's wife. The boat was returned to service. See *Towboat Directory*.

5071 SEARCH

Stw inspection boat wh b. Harmar, Oh., by Knox in 1895, originally named *H.D. MUNSON* (see). Purchased by the Mississippi River Commission in 1895 and renamed. Used in survey and inspection service until 1921 when she was sold to Mexico and her original name was restored.

5072 SELMA

SW p wh b. Cincinnati, Oh., 1845. 227 tons. Went to Mobile, Ala. Lost in collision with the *D.B. MOSBY* at Cahawba, Ala., May 29, 1850.

5073 SELMA

SW p wh b. Covington, Ky., 1853, originally named *N. W. GRAHAM* (see). Renamed Oct. 22, 1856. 174 x 30.5 x 5. Owned by Capt. John J. Kercheval, New Orleans. She had five alterations of ownership in the New Orleans area, and was dismantled in 1860.

5074 SELMA

SW p wh b. Pittsburgh, Pa., 1867. 600 tons. 180 x 37.5 x 7. Engines, 20's- 7 ft. Three boilers, each 48" by 26 ft. Built and owned by Capt. Thomas Rogers, Pittsburgh, who took her to Mobile and ran to Montgomery, Ala. She was back in New Orleans December 1868 having been bought by Capt. William T. Scovell and John Kouns, equal shares. Ran New Orleans-Shreveport. Sold July 1870 to Capt. Charles C. Pickett who ran her New Orleans-Opalousas and Atchafalaya. Sank and dismantled at New Orleans, Jan. 25, 1875.

5075 SEMINOLE

Stw p wh b. Jeffersonville, Ind., 1869. 420 tons. 157.6 x 44 x 5. Engines, 22's- 7 ft. Three boilers. Capt. J.D. Clark, master and part owner (one-half) along with E.R. Perry, New Orleans. Sold December 1869 to White River Packet Co., Moses Greenwood, pres., same master. Was first to scene of *NICK WALL* disaster (see) at Grand Lake in 1870 and took off survivors. In summer and fall 1870 ran New Orleans-Ouachita River, Capt. J.W. Tobin. Ran New Orleans-Shreveport. In April 1878 towed by the *SMOKY CITY* to Jeffersonville for dismantling, and engines went to *LAURA LEE* (see).

5076 SENATE

SW p wh b. Wheeling, Va., 1845. 106 tons. Built by Capt. John McLure and Thomas C. Wilson, both of Wheeling. Ran Wheeling-Cincinnati and made a trip or so up Wabash River. In fall 1845 Henry Clay got on at Maysville and rode to Guyandotte, en route to Washington D.C. Captain McLure notes in his recollections that he and Thomas Wilson sold this boat for more than the original cost. Snagged and lost at Brandenburg, Ky., September 1847.

5077 SENATOR

SW p wh b. Wheeling, Va., 1846. 121 tons. A low water boat, new in June 1846 built by Capt. John McLure. He made a trip to New Orleans with her and brought back to Nashville troops from the Mexican War. He sold her to the Upper Mississippi and she was the first spring arrival at Galena, Apr. 20, 1947, from St. Louis, Capt. E.M. McCoy. Capt. D. Smith Harris ran her Galena-St. Peters in 1848. In 1849–1850 ran Galena-St. Paul, Capt. Orren Smith, in the Galena, Dubuque & Minnesota Packet Co., the second boat they owned (first was *DR. FRANKLIN*, see). Off the lists 1852.

5078 SENATOR

Stw ferry wh b. Yankton, S.D., 1882. 115 x 28 x 4. Engines, 9"- 2 ft. Owned by Yankton Steam Ferry Co. Sunk by ice Feb. 5, 1885. While moored opposite Yankton on Mar. 11, 1887, was carried off in the breaking of the ice to the mouth of Jim River where she was lost.

5079 SENATOR

SW ex wh b. Dubuque, Iowa, 1903, originally *SAINT PAUL* (see). She was rebuilt at Paducah, Ky., winter 1939–1940 and renamed. Owned by Streckfus Steamers, Inc., St. Louis. Operated on the Ohio River based at Pittsburgh seasons of 1940 and 1941. Masters were Capts. Edgar F. Mabrey, Clarence W. Elder and T. Kent Booth. Due to World War II she was retired 1942 to serve at St. Louis as a U.S. Coast Guard training ship. From 1943 on she was used by Streckfus above Eads Bridge as a floating machine shop and warehouse. On Jan. 19, 1953 the tug *SUSIE HAZARD* towed her below St. Louis for abandonment.

5080 SENATOR CORDILL

Stw p wh b. Jeffersonville, Ind., by Howard, 1902. 170 x 33 x 5; lengthened at Pt. Pleasant, W. Va., in 1925 to measure 193 x 36 x 6.9. Engines, 16's- 7 ft.; replaced by compound non-condensing 12's, 24's- 7 ft. Three boilers. Built for Vicksburg & Natchez Packet Co., headed by J.N. Carpenter, Natchez. Ran Vicksburg-Natchez, tri-weekly. Handled U.S. Mail. On Jan. 1, 1910, she was acquired by Capt. George Prince under the corporate title of Royal Route Co. Ltd., and continued her in the trade. In 1912 at Mound City, Ill., he made the change in machinery noted above. On Jan. 27, 1903, the *CORDILL* participated in the parade and celebration when the Yazoo River diversion put Vicksburg back on the river. She had double swinging stages and was a stately looking steamboat. Once sank near Vicksburg in March 1918 and was raised by Capt. George Wilson. In July 1920 she was bought by a group of upper Ohio River produce dealers composed of J. Clarence Sheets, Parkersburg, W. Va.; D. Grover Gill, Gallipolis, Oh.; Art McDade, Millwood, W. Va.; and Ike Matlack, Long Bottom, Oh. She was entered in the Pittsburgh-Charleston trade, and did so well that the owners were persuaded to lengthen the hull as noted in the beginning of this sketch. She was prone to accidents, the most noteworthy:

Sank in Siegrist Riffle; pumped herself out after bulkheading.

Sank in Kanawha River above Lock 7 after hitting a log.

Stranded on Elk Chute Bar, Kanawha River, Mar. 12, 1927, not released until April 2.

Broke her wheel shaft on Kanawha River, June 1927.

Exploded the main throttle valve at Pt. Pleasant, W. Va., Mar. 2, 1928, killing her engineers, George Litman and George McElhose, and a boiler maker, Roy Roe.

Struck a rock and sank below Lock 18, Ohio River, October 1930.

Capt. Melvin O. Irwin, New Matamoras, Oh., was her master for most of her huckster days, and her clerks included Fred Hoyt and Clyde Packard. She was turned over to the Ohio River Transportation Co., in 1929 and ran teamed up with the *QUEEN CITY* in the Pittsburgh-Cincinnati trade at various times until 1933. Capt. Fred Hornbook then ran her under lease in the P&C trade until she hit an improperly lowered wicket at Dam 14, Ohio River, above Clarington and sank, early morning of Feb. 5, 1934. Crew at the time: Capt. Fred Hornbrook, master; Wilson (Wilsie) Miller and Fred Way, Jr., pilots; Fred M. Hoyt, purser; Herbert Swan and Herbert Sidenstricker, clerks; Norwood Chamberlain and Walter Webster, engineers; Wiley C. Hill, mate; Alonzo Sewell, 2nd mate; George Beegle, carpenter. Three deckhands were lost. She was raised by the U.S. Engineers, Huntington District, who towed her to Marietta. Sold to Charles Zubik, Pittsburgh, who had her towed there and dismantled her. In memory of this big lady, let it be said by this scribe (who was master-pilot on her three months in 1931, and pilot in 1932, 1933, and 1934) she was the most comfortable and satisfactory pile of lumber to pilot that I know about. In high wind she was as deliberate as a turtle. She had pretty engineroom bells, a most wonderful whistle—she was one of the very few steamboats I really anticipated coming on watch on, day or night, rain or shine. There is a complete story of the *SENATOR CORDILL* with many photographs in *S&D Reflector,* March 1971 issue, pages 13–25.

5081 '76

SW p wh b. West Wheeling, Oh. (hull), and completed at Wheeling, Va., 1846. 171 x 23.5 x 5.5. Engines, 17's- 7 ft. Three boilers, each 38" by 26 ft. Paddlewheels 21 ft. dia. working 9½ ft. buckets. Hull built at the Dunlevy & McNaughton yard, for Capt. J. Miller of Nashville, Tenn. Engines and boilers by Phillips & Co. Built for the Cincinnati-Nashville trade. (The above notice appeared in the Wheeling *Daily News,* issue Aug. 1, 1846.) Burned in 1848.

5082 SEVENTY-SIX

SW p wh b. Cincinnati, Oh., 1854. 257 tons. Stranded and lost at Alton, Ill., Feb. 6, 1859.

5083 SEVENTY-SIX

Stw p wh b. Pomeroy, Oh., 1863. 20 tons. Off the lists 1864.

5084 76

Rig? ferry wh b. Steubenville, Oh., 1876. 56 tons. 85 x 20 x 4. Still listed 1886.

5085 SEVENTY-SIX NO. 2

Rig? wh b. New Cumberland, W. Va., 1874. 60 x 16 x 3. Probably a ferry. Still listed in 1886.

5086 SEWICKLEY

SW p wh b. Allegheny, Pa., 1864. 25 tons. Reported in the Cincinnati *Commercial,* July 14, 1864: "There was an arrival in Pittsburgh of a non-descript steamer from Sewickley called the *SEWICKLEY.* She is built on a flatboat. She is run by gearing and an endless rope. She leaves this afternoon for Parkersburg. She was taking freight yesterday." There exists a freight bill dated Aug. 29, 1868, showing her handling freight at Sun Fish (Clarington), Oh. Running in the "market trade" in August 1870, Shousetown-Pittsburgh. Report in Pittsburgh *Commercial Gazette,* Apr. 5, 1873: "The steamer *SEWICKLEY* has been purchased by Messrs. G.A. Lashel and Harvey Kendall for the market trade between Sewickley and Pittsburgh." Lost by stranding, July 16, 1873.

5087 SHAMROCK

SW p wh b. Newport, Ky., 1848. 139 tons. 164 x 26 x 4.6. Enrolled at New Orleans Nov. 15, 1850, owned (one-half) by John P. Hart, Mason County, Ky., Capt. George G. Remer. Control (three-fourths) sold to John G. Kendall, New Orleans, Dec. 23, 1850. Was operating Port Caddo-New Orleans. Sold April 1851 to Ebenezer Watson Linn (one-half) of Brookville, Ky., Capt. E.W. Linn. Burned and lost in Lake Bistineau, La., June 29, 1851.

5088 SHAMROCK

Stw p wh b. Cincinnati, Oh., 1863. 217 tons. A dispatch from Cincinnati dated Mar. 31, 1864 indicates that Capt.

Eugene Bowers has purchased the commanding interest from Capt. McDonald and will take charge with W.C. Grubb in the office. Later she is in the Cincinnati-Portsmouth trade, Capt. George W. Cullem, with R.H. Kerr, clerk, connecting with the *EMMA FLOYD* for above. In March 1867 was at Evansville, Ind., Capt. Cullem. A report from Memphis dated Apr. 10, 1873, advises *SHAMROCK* is downbound with 5,000 sacks of corn and 1,000 tons of hay (must have been towing at least two barges) bound for Shreveport, La. She hit the bank 30 miles below Vicksburg and sank in eight feet. Off the lists 1875.

5089 SHANNON

Stw p wh b. Ironton, Oh., 1870. 180 x 36 x 7. Engines, 16's-5½ ft. Three boilers. Built by Capt. Sam Beatty and S. McClure. Engines from *MOLLIE NORTON*. They ran her Cincinnati-New Orleans, selling her to H. King of New Albany, Ind., in 1873. Mr. King was killed that winter in an accident, and the boat was sold to Capt. John DeHart who ran her Cincinnati-Tennessee River, with C.H. Arthurs, clerk. Then they took her to New Orleans and ran to Ouachita River. She burned, laid up with the *COLOSSAL* at St. Louis, Mar. 9, 1878.

5090 SHELBY

SW p wh b. Paducah, Ky., 1850. 225 tons. First home port, Nashville, Tenn. Foundered below Cairo, Ill., Oct. 1, 1852.

5091 SHENANDOAH

SW p wh b. Brownsville, Pa., 1848. 179 tons. Built for Pittsburgh-St. Louis trade, Capt. George Bowman. Capt. C.W. Batchelor made one round on her as master due to illness of Bowman. Knocked down her stacks while passing the draw bridge in the Louisville Canal Oct. 9, 1849. Still in the St. Louis trade 1850. Ran St. Louis-St. Paul, five trips, 1853, and still in that trade 1855. She was at St. Louis when ice destroyed many boats Feb. 27, 1856. She and *SAM CLOON,* moored together, broke loose and lodged against the *CLARA*. One of the local ferryboats hit all three and they were destroyed.

5092 SHENANGO

Stw p wh b. Shousetown, Pa., 1855. 234 tons. 157.2 x 33.5 x 5.2. In June 1864 she arrived in St. Louis having been 10 months at Vicksburg handling supplies for the U.S., and also had been up Red River with the fleet. Owned March 1865 by John Weatherbury, St. Louis, and John P. Knight, Keokuk; Capt. George J. Dodd, master. Off the lists 1867.

5093 SHERLEY

Stw p wh b. Harmar, Oh., at Knox Yard, 1891. 430 tons. 202 x 33 x 5. Engines, 17's- 6 ft. Equipment from *LOUISA. SHERLEY* used in her construction. Built for the White Collar Line of Cincinnati, duplicate of *CONGO* (see). She arrived new at Cincinnati July 28, 1891, and ran low water Cincinnati-Louisville, Capt. Sam Bryant, with Ed Long, clerk. Ran most of her days in the Cincinnati-Pomeroy trade until she sank near Quincy, Ky., in mid-November 1897. Plans to raise her continued into July 1898, and were abandoned.

5094 SHERLEY-BELL

Stw p wh b. Warren, Pa., on Allegheny River, 1878. Owned by Capt. Hiram Sherley, Glade, Pa. Ran Irvineton-Warren. Upbound, Sept. 17, 1878, she exploded her boiler one and one-half miles below Warren. Capt. Sherley was instantly killed. The engineer, Thomas Bell, Warren, Pa., was severely injured, and the fireman Moses Sherley also injured. One passenger, Capt. A. Dingley, Brooklyn, N.Y., was unharmed. The boiler was an old one, having been bought at Tidioute, Pa.

5095 SHERMAN

Stw p wh b. Cincinnati, Oh., 1865. 595 tons. Built for Capt. C.M. Holloway, Cincinnati, who named her for Gen. Wm. Tecumseh Sherman. Sold to George N. and W. Baker, Pittsburgh, and sank near Paducah upbound from New Orleans with cargo. Raised by *UNDERWRITER* which was in the charge of Capt. R.W. Dugan. She discharged cargo at Evansville to go on the marine ways for repairs and burned at the wharf, Feb. 2, 1868.

5096 SHERRARD

SW ferry wh b. Steubenville, Oh., 1886. 73.5 x 18 x 2.9. Operated at Toronto, Oh., or at New Cumberland, W. Va. Still listed 1896.

5097 SHILOH

Stw p wh b. Jeffersonville, Ind., by Howard, 1902. 178 tons. 150 x 28 x 4. Engines, 13's- 5 ft. Two boilers, each 40" by 22 ft. She was built for St. Louis & Tennessee River Packet Co. Came out in Savannah-Danville trade, Capt. Lon Kell, with pilots Charles R. Beard and Ed B. Beard; Sam G. Smith, purser; Tommy Latham, chief engineer; Al Aiken, second engineer; Charles Lewter, second clerk. She was under charter to Delta Navigation Co., Memphis, Capt. Ed Nowland, Jr., and hit the levee while landing at Memphis with a heavy cargo, sank, and was lost, this in December 1913.

5098 SHIPPER

Stw p wh b. Brownsville, Pa., 1849. 78 tons. Ran Pittsburgh-Zanesville, Capt. Parkinson, 1849. Same trade spring 1850, Capt. Henry T. Dexter. Lost by stranding at Harpeth Shoals, Tenn., Oct. 26, 1853.

5099 SHIPPERS' OWN

Stw p wh b. Brownsville, Pa., 1873. 354 tons. Built for Capt. Tom Ryman who took her to Cumberland River. "A very singular but an appropriate name for a steamboat," remarked the Pittsburgh *Gazette*. Came out in late November 1873. Sank in collision with *GRAND TOWER* at Cairo, Ill., night of June 14, 1876. The river was rising rapidly, and carried off the cabin which was caught and moored by tugs. Pilot on watch was H.W. Thompson, the third collision in which he had been involved.

5100 SHORT CUT

SW ferry wh b. Pittsburgh, Pa., 1880. 81 tons. 97 x 25 x 4.5. Engines, 10"- 4 ft. One boiler, 40" by 24 ft. Owned by Capt. John Dippel, Allegheny, Pa., who ran her McKees Rocks-Manchester in the Pittsburgh area. Was damaged by fire 9:00 P.M., Oct. 12, 1893, moored at Allegheny. Sold 1917 to John F. Klein, who promptly sold her to Louisville & Jeffersonville Ferry Co., Nov. 17, 1917. She rode out the big ice that winter at Cincinnati. Was renamed *TRANSIT* (see).

5101 SHREVEPORT

SW p wh b. Louisville, Ky., 1852. 159 tons. 128.8 x 27 x 5. Documented at New Orleans, Aug. 1, 1853, owned by George W. Nichols of Shreveport, La., Capt. Benjamin Turbell, master. Snagged and lost at Black Bayou, La., on Red River, Apr. 20, 1854, with loss of one life. Capt. A.C. Cummings was master, and 800 bales of cotton were recovered.

5102 SHREVEPORT

SW p wh b. Louisville, Ky., 1860. 163 tons. 155.6 x 28.3 x 4.4. Engines, 12's- 4 ft. Two boilers, each 40" by 18 ft. Ran New Orleans-Shreveport, Capt. A.C. Cummings. Served with the U.S. during the war, and was with Porter on Red River. Capt. Joseph S. Nanson, St. Louis, took her to Red River for a cotton speculation scheme in August 1864 which didn't work. Took a cargo of confiscated CSA cotton to Mobile, August 1865, Capt. W.F. Haines. Sold October 1866 to Capt. Warren D. Smith, New Orleans. During her career she made a trip from St. Louis to Fort Benton and return, under charter to Capt. Joseph LaBarge who also had the *EMILIE* under charter. Both boats arrived at the fort June 17, noon, 1862, with Capt. John LaBarge in charge of *SHREVEPORT*. Off the lists in 1871.

5103 SIDNEY

Stw p wh b. Murraysville, W. Va. (hull), and completed at Wheeling, 1880. 221.3 x 35.5 x 5.5. Engines, 17's- 5½ ft. Three boilers. Came out in the Wheeling-Cincinnati trade, Capt. William M. List, with Charles D. List, clerk. Originally painted yellow with colorful trim. She burst a steam line at Goose Island, Ohio River, Mar. 10, 1882; four died and 16 scalded. Sold to the Diamond Jo Line, Upper Mississippi, and ran St. Louis-St. Paul until bought by Streckfus Line to replace the *J.S.* (first) which had burned, and was converted into an excursion boat. She was the first commercial boat to enter the newly-built Keokuk Lock in 1913, and the *G. W. HILL* was right behind her. Capt. Roy Streckfus was in command on this occasion, and 600 St. Mary church people were aboard bound for Burlington, Iowa. She was based at New Orleans in winter months and many musicians who later became big-name got their start on her, bringing the popularity of New Orleans jazz to the northern climes. In 1921 she was completely rebuilt at Mound City, Ill., and renamed *WASHINGTON* (see).

5104 SIGNAL

Stw p wh b. Wheeling, Va., 1862. 190 tons. Sold to U.S. Navy Sept. 22, 1862, and was converted into a tinclad, #8, still named *SIGNAL*. Captured by the Confederates at Dunn's Bayou on Red River, La., May 5, 1864.

5105 SIGNET

SW p wh b. Wheeling, Va., 1862. 33 tons. Off the lists 1864.

5106 SILAS WRIGHT

SW p wh b. Wheeling, Va., 1847. 175 x 21 x 4. Engines, 18's- 7 ft. Three boilers, each 38" by 26 ft. Off the lists 1854.

5107 SILVER BOW

SW p wh b. Pittsburgh, Pa., 1869. 335 tons. 212 x 32 x 5.5. Engines, 18's- 5 ft. Three boilers, each 40" by 26 ft. Left Pittsburgh, new, Feb. 25, 1869. Pilots Tom Morris and John Ferguson took her out. She went to the Missouri River and a photograph exists taken at Fort Leavenworth that summer. Joined in the Carter Line, St. Louis-Shreveport, Capt. Thomas W. Rea. Sank at Price's Landing, Mo., between St. Louis and Cairo, latter September 1871 and was raised by the *T.F. ECKERT*. Sunk by ice at St. Louis, Feb. 26, 1872. Parts were used building *BELLE OF SHREVEPORT* in 1873.

5108 SILVER CITY

Stw p wh b. St. Louis, Mo., 1877, originally named *TYRONE* (see). She was bought from Capt. D.H. Silver early 1878 to replace the lost *LA BELLE* (see) and was renamed. Owned by New Orleans & Red River Transportation Co. Ran New Orleans-Shreveport. The Red River and Coast Line was incorporated July 31, 1882, taking her in. Charles P. Truslow was president, Charles W. Drown, secretary, M.N. Wood, superintendent. They had 21 packets in this "combine" with offices at 46 Camp Street, New Orleans. One time in 1883 the *SILVER CITY* dropped her paddlewheel overboard and was towed to New Orleans by the *JOHN D. SCULLY*, reshipping her freight on the *LAURA LEE*. Still documented 1886.

5109 SILVER CLOUD

Stw p wh b. Brownsville, Pa., 1862. 236 tons. 155 x 33.5 x 5.3. Engines, 16's- 5 ft. Three boilers. Sold by Barker, Hart & Cook at Cairo, Ill., to U.S. Navy to become tinclad #28. Sold at public sale, Mound City, Ill., Aug. 17, 1865, for $11,000 to J.H. Stearne. She was converted to side-wheel, redocumented Oct. 7, 1865, still *SILVER CLOUD*. Snagged and lost at Buffalo Bayou, Tex., Oct. 2, 1866.

5110 SILVER CLOUD

Stw p wh b. Cincinnati, Oh., 1878. 185 x 34 x 5.5. Engines, 16's- 5 ft. from *FLORENCE LEE*. Built for the Evansville & Tennessee River Packet Co., John Gilbert, president, and replaced the *RED CLOUD* which recently had been sold to the Missouri River. Burned at Birmingham, Ky., on the Tennessee River, Oct. 12 or 13, 1887, then owned by H.M. Sweetster and others.

5111 SILVER CLOUD NO. 2

Stw p wh b. Brownsville, Pa., 1863. 287 tons. 156 x 33 x 5.5.

Engines, 15's- 5 ft. Three boilers, each 22 ft. long. Built for Capts. Sam Shuman and John B. Conway. James Rees was a stockholder. Carried U.S. supplies Pittsburgh-St. Louis through September 1864, Capt. J.B. Conway, with Charles Matthews in the office. She was noticed at Cincinnati Mar. 24, 1864, with 350 soldiers of the 5th Virginia Infantry aboard bound for Wheeling. On Monday, May 9, 1864, she hit a rock upbound on Cumberland River, and had to jump 175 head of horses into the river. The *MERCURY,* Capt. James B. Mellon, came along and assisted getting her into shallow water where she sank only 10 inches over the main deck. A lot of government ammunition was damaged. Had her afloat next day at noon. Back in the Pittsburgh-St. Louis trade she showed a gross profit of $43,664.51 in the period October 1864 through July 1865; out of this sum $13,079.40 went toward payment for her construction, and $12,000 as dividends to her owners. Sank in Brown's Island, Ohio River, downbound Pittsburgh to St. Louis in latter April 1866. The *NORA* went down from Pittsburgh to take her freight off. Ran Cincinnati-New Orleans, June-July, 1867. Sank at Bellaire, Oh., going down in deep water, with two feet in the texas, October 1868; fortunately the river was falling rapidly and she was raised. Burned Monday, Jan. 11, 1869, in the afternoon, four miles above Pt. Pleasant, W. Va. One deck passenger was lost. The *ENERGY* came along and rendered aid. Capt. J.B. Conway was on her to the end.

5112 Silver Crescent

Stw p wh b. Clinton, Iowa, 1882. 123.3 x 22.9 x 3.9. 125 tons. Engines, 14's- 4½ ft. Two boilers, each 40" by 22 ft. Engines from towboat *PARK PAINTER.* Originally a raftboat. Capt. Walter Blair bought her 1892 for his Carnival City Packet Co., and ran her Davenport-Burlington with S.R. Dodds, clerk, and Parm Lancaster, mate. She paid a five percent dividend the first season. Replaced in the trade 1895 by the *W.J. YOUNG, JR.,* at which time she went to the Keokuk-Quincy trade, Capt. S.R. Dodds, master-purser. Ran there until 1908 when replaced by *KEOKUK.* Dismantled at Winona, Minn., spring 1909. The *BLACK HAWK* was built using much of her equipment. In the season of 1899 in the Keokuk-Quincy trade she ran until Dec. 16, latest a boat had operated there.

5113 Silver Heels

SW p wh b. Jeffersonville, Ind., by Howard, 1857. 267 tons. 187 x 29 x 6. Engines, 20's- 6½ ft. stroke. Three boilers, each 40" by 26 ft. Built for the St. Louis & St. Joseph Union Line, Missouri River. She ran from St. Louis to Omaha, 678 miles, in 5 days 15 hours on a trip during the first season. In November 1858 sold to New Orleans Coast & Lafourche Transportation Co., Adelard Dugas, pres., Capt. John J. Brown, master. Sold January 1860 to Capt. Charles Cane Pickett and others, Pointe Coupee Parish. Sunk in a storm at Carrollton (New Orleans) on Oct. 2, 1860.

5114 Silver Heels

Stw p wh b. Hooksburg, Oh., on the Muskingum, 1858. 50 tons. Built by Capt. Isaac N. Hook. Made one round trip, Marietta-Zanesville. On Mar. 9, 1860 ascended Little Kanawha River to Palestine, Va., on high water. Capt. Jim Rowley, Jr., described her as "a small towboat" and recalled her demise at the point of rocks below Vanceburg, Ky., on the Ohio. "This was during a violent storm, and the pilot on watch was a small 300 pound chap named Jack Rowland, who generally wore a plug hat and used it to save himself. When I was a kid I often went swimming by that cliff where the water is 50 feet deep. This depth probably accounts for no attempt having been made to raise her." This happened Oct. 14, 1868. She was owned at the time by the Little family, Portsmouth, Oh.

5115 Silver Lake

Stw p wh b. Wellsville, Oh., 1858. 70 tons. Originally documented at Rock Island, Ill. Burned on the Osage River, Mo., Sept. 3, 1862.

5116 Silver Lake

Rig? wh b. Chippewa Falls, Wis., 1877. 31 tons. No record of her service. Inspected at Red Wing, Minn., Aug. 9, 1881.

5117 Silver Lake No. 2

Stw p wh b. Wellsville, Oh., 1861. 129 tons. Sold to the USQMD in 1861. At the conclusion of the war was sold and name changed to *MARION,* Oct. 7, 1865 (see).

5118 Silver Lake No. 3

Stw p wh b. California, Pa., 1862. 212 tons. 157 x 32.5 x 4.5. Engines, 15's- 5 ft. Built for Capt. Henry Willoughby (three-fourths) and Thomas M. Rees, Pittsburgh. Sold to U.S. Navy Nov. 15, 1862. Prior to that she had been in U.S. service transporting ordnance Pittsburgh-St. Louis. Capt. Willoughby added a texas to her at Pittsburgh in July 1862. She served the war as a tinclad #23. Sold at public sale, Mound City, Ill., Aug. 17, 1865, for $9,500 to Capt. James Kenniston, and was renamed *MARY HEIN* Sept. 29, 1865 (see).

5119 Silver Lake No. 4

Stw p wh b. California, Pa., 1863. 224 tons. 155 x 33 x 5.5. Engines, 15's- 5 ft. Three boilers, each 38" by 22 ft. Owned by Capt. Henry Willoughby (three-fourths) and Thomas M. Rees, Pittsburgh. Ran Pittsburgh-St. Louis. Capt. John Todd, Wellsville, Oh., bought interest in March 1865; also W.H. Briggs. Ran Pittsburgh-Cincinnati, with occasional trips to St. Louis, Capt. John Todd, and Feb. 1, 1871, was in Pittsburgh delivering a cargo of sugar and molasses from New Orleans. Went to Missouri River that year operated by Durfee & Peck, Capt. Andy Johnson. Grant Marsh and Joe Todd did the piloting. Joe Todd was wounded by an Indian bullet, mouth of Heart River, 40 miles above Fort Rice, and carried the slug the balance of his life. On Nov. 20, 1871, she was frozen in above Sioux City, Iowa, below Okobogo Island and Fort Sully. Joe Todd, Grant Marsh, Dr. Perry, N. Buison, and L.T. Jones took to shank's mare, wagons, and sleds, and were snowbound several times, getting back to Sioux City. Several feet and ears were frozen. In later years Capt. John Todd made frequent Pittsburgh-New Orleans Mardi Gras trips on the *QUEEN CITY* as a passenger; on the 1910 trip he was 75. Off the lists 1879.

5120 SILVER MOON

SW p wh b. Louisville, Ky., 1857. 171 tons. 124 x 27.5 x 5.5. Enrolled at New Orleans, Oct. 15, 1857, owned by William Vardle of that city, Capt. A. Greenlaw, master. In February 1858 she had returned to New Orleans from a trip to Bayou Plaquemine and was attached for building debt. Was temporarily released, and had cargo aboard when she burned at Bayou Goula, La., Mar. 7, 1858.

5121 SILVER MOON

SW p wh b. Cincinnati, Oh., 1859. 390 tons. Built for Cincinnati & Memphis Packet Co., and was designed to pass through the small locks at the Louisville-Portland Canal. Capt. James Bugher was the superintendent of this early line. Capt. John Bugher commanded, with Frank Stein and J.C. Enyart, clerks. Another of the Bugher family, Capt. A.H., commanded the *GLENDALE* of the line (see). When Sumter was fired on, she was the last boat up from Memphis before traffic closed; had a big reception all along the way, playing "Home. Sweet Home" on the calliope. In April 1862 was at Pittsburgh loading for St. Louis, Capt. John Bugher, her first appearance there. She resumed Cincinnati-Memphis soon as the smoke cleared, Capt. W.G. Voris commanding in 1866, and later that year Capt. Ben M. Merrielees with J.L. Carter, clerk. On Jan. 17, 1866, arrived in Cincinnati with 1,530 bales of Memphis cotton, a record, which later that year was reported to have been surpassed with a 2,200 bale trip. On Jan. 10, 1869, while upbound, she was carried out at the head of the Louisville-Portland Canal and sank in shallow water. Capt. Pink Varble unloaded her freight into two barges. In attempting to run the Falls in May 1869 she grounded and could not be worked free; then a storm with high wind came along and released her. In mid-March 1871 she "stalled" on the Falls upbound due to being heavily laden, her wheels working full ahead, the boat standing still. Capt. Pink Varble was brought to her in a skiff, leaped aboard, and returned her safely to Portland, Ky. Such was the relief of the officers, they presented Varble with "a beautiful pyramid cake." Dismantled 1872. A notorious Negro saloon flourished for many years at the Cincinnati waterfront called the Silver Moon.

5122 SILVER SPRAY

Stw p wh b. West Brownsville, Pa., 1864. 352 tons. Built and commanded by Capt. Sam Shuman, with John A. Dales, clerk. Her first two trips were from Pittsburgh to Cumberland River. On the second of these she intended "running by" Parkersburg downbound but was persuaded to land when U.S. forces sent shots across her bow. Word had gotten about that she had taken aboard at Marietta shipments of salt consigned to Confederate customers along the Cumberland River. Capt. I.N. Hook was involved, relating afterward that he had no idea who the recipients were, but that the salt was confiscated there at Parkersburg. Capt. W.W. Fenton, Cincinnati, bought the boat, and with Ben M. Bush, clerk, ran her Cincinnati-New Orleans. She collided with the U.S. Mail Line's *UNITED STATES* on Christmas Day, 1866 and both on-watch pilots were suspended 30 days, Hiram Cox of the *SILVER SPRAY,* and Louis D. Martin. The responsibility for the collision was settled in rather unusual fashion; the owners of each boat selected an arbitrator and agreed to abide by the decision they may reach. The U.S. Mail Line picked Capt. Dan Collier, and Captain Fenton chose Capt. George W. Neare. These two had a pow-wow and agreed that the *UNITED STATES* was in the wrong and therefore liable for damages sustained to the *SILVER SPRAY.* While en route from New Orleans to Cincinnati with a barge in tow she exploded her boilers Apr. 10, 1870, 30 miles above Memphis at Pacific Place, Tenn., with loss of nine lives. Wash Meredith, engineer at the Federal Building, Cincinnati, used to relate that he was one of the crew when this calamity happened; he died, 94, July 22, 1934. The *CITY OF CAIRO* came along two hours after the explosion and returned to Memphis with the survivors.

5123 SILVER STAR

Stw p wh b. Wheeling, Va., 1856. 150 tons. First ran on the upper Ohio. Parkersburg-Gallipolis, spring 1858, Capt. J.T. Russell, with S.F. Simpson, clerk. Went to the Paducah-Evansville trade, Capt. Gus Fowler, proved too small, and the *DUNBAR* (see) was built to replace her. Burned at Evansville on May 12, 1860, with loss of five lives.

5124 SILVER STAR

SW p wh b. Mason City, W. Va., 1877. 69.7 x 10 x 4. 22 tons. Still documented at Cincinnati in 1896, maybe longer.

5125 SILVERTHORN

Stw p wh b. Jeffersonville, Ind., 1872. She was entered in Evansville-Nashville trade with Capt. Josh V. Throop, master, and George Throop, clerk. Named for Col. Silverthorn, river editor of the Evansville *Journal.* In 1877 owned by Evansville, Cairo & Memphis Steam Packet Co., Capt. George S. Throop, with Sid Humphrey, clerk. Was running Memphis-Hales Point, January 1880. Sold to New Orleans fall of 1883. She was returned to Paducah in the summer of 1883 and was given cotton guards and went back south.

5126 SILVER WAVE

Stw p wh b. Glasgow, Pa. (opposite Georgetown, Pa. on the Ohio), 1854. 245 tons. 159 x 35 x 5. Built for Capt. John S. McMillen who tramped her Pittsburgh-Cincinnati-Louisville, and elsewhere, including the upper Mississippi. On May 9, 1862, she made a rather dramatic appearance in Pittsburgh with the muskets, cartridges, etc., captured from the Confederates after the fall of Island 10, consigned to the Allegheny Arsenal. Capt. McMillen chartered her to the

U.S. and she became the first packet to run the blockade during the siege of Vicksburg in 1863; the first six were gunboats, and then she made it, unprotected. Capt. George O'Neal, Steubenville, Oh., was the pilot on watch. Sank at Columbus, Ky., November 1863, and was with Porter on Red River in 1864. She was retired soon after the war, but was purchased by the U.S. for use in making Upper Mississippi improvements in August 1867.

5127 SILVER WAVE

Stw p wh b. Portsmouth, Oh., 1888. 115 x 21.6 x 4.7. Came out single deck, Capt. George Edgington, and ran local trades out of Maysville, Ky. Sold to Capt. Joe Webb for work around Cincinnati bridges and then was repurchased by the Edgington family and a cabin added. Burned at Portsmouth, Oh., July 21, 1897. The hull was taken to Higginsport, Oh., and used in building the *WM. DUFFEY* (see).

5128 SIMON KENTON

SW p wh b. Cincinnati, Oh., 1844. 198 tons. 180 x 29 x 6. Engines, 23's- 7½ ft. Four boilers, each 38" by 26 ft., two 16" flues. Came out new in the Cincinnati-Maysville trade owned and skippered by Capt. William McLain. Sold to the U.S. Mail Line Co., 1847. Burst a steam line at St. Louis, Aug. 28, 1847. scalding four and a baby was drowned. Capt. Charles Ross was her master for a time. Off the lists in 1851.

5129 SIOUX CITY

SW p wh b. Cincinnati, Oh., 1857. 379 tons. 218 x 33 x 5.8. Engines, 22's- 7 ft. Three boilers, each 44" by 24 ft. First home port, St. Louis. Operated on the Missouri River. She ran trips up Red River in 1860, and was in U.S. transport service 1863-1864. Was lost in the ice break-up at St. Louis, Feb. 26, 1867.

5130 SIOUX CITY

SW p wh b. California, Pa., 1870. 162.5 x 30 x 3.4. Engines, 13's- 4 ft. Two boilers. Original owners were Capt. Edmund B. Cooper, James A. Sawyer, and Andrew M. Haley of Sioux City, Iowa; Capt. E.B. Cooper, master. Made her first trip from Pittsburgh to Fort Randall on the Missouri River. Was back in Pittsburgh in February 1871, the original owners having sold her to the St. Louis & Arkansas River Packet Co. Capt. Edmund B. Cooper later was identified with various upper Ohio packets, and his son Earl Cooper, Parkersburg, W. Va., built and ran several diesel sternwheel towboats, best remembered being the *VICTOR*. Capt. T.P. Johnson took charge of the *SIOUX CITY* for her new owners. She sank in the Arkansas River in October 1871 but was pumped out following emergency repairs. She was given cotton guards at St. Louis in Nov. 1871 but in spring 1882 was sold to J.H. Durfee, Leavenworth, Kan., and others and went to Missouri River. Capt. James McGarry took charge. On Mar. 19, 1873, an ice gorge gave way and crushed her as she lay, about eight miles below Fort Sully. Capt. McGarry and two others rowed a skiff Fort Sully to Yankton, coming down in 3½ days, and reported the wreck swept almost entirely away, and none of the machinery saved. The furniture was on shore under tarpaulins on the Fort Sully side.

5131 SIP BAYES

Stw p wh b. Paintsville, Ky., 1891. 24 tons. 105.5 x 14.3 x 1.9. Built for Big Sandy River by Capt. Green Meek. Still documented in 1896 and maybe later.

5132 SIR WILLIAM WALLACE

Stw p wh b. California, Pa., 1855. 255 tons. 153 x 35 x 5.2. Built for Capt. Hugh Campbell (⅞) and Charles S. Frisbee, Pittsburgh. Ran Pittsburgh-Cincinnati-St. Louis. Was engaged in U.S. troop movements at various times 1860-1862. Sold December 1862 at Portland, Ky., to Capt. G.W. Stewart who planned to load for Memphis. Running Cincinnati-Memphis in 1864. In April 1865 owned by Capt. George H. Alcoke (½) who lived in New York City. She was taken to Mobile, Ala., where she burned, Mar. 27, 1866.

5133 SIREN

Stw U.S. transport wh b. Parkersburg, W. Va., 1862, originally *WHITE ROSE* (see). In U.S. service known as *SIREN*. Sold to private owners 1865 and resumed her original name. At time of sale she was described as 154.6 x 32.2 x 5.1. Engines, 16½'s- 4 ft. She brought $9,050, bought in by E.S. Mills. The sale was at Mound City, Ill., Aug. 17, 1865.

5134 SIREN

Prop p wh b. Peninsula, Oh., 1865. 39 tons. A converted canalboat. Ran McConnelsville-Zanesville, Capt. James R. Martin, and Capt. C.W. Mummey through 1867. Capt. Sextus Scott ran trips Zanesville to New Orleans 1868-1869, taking down refined oil, plows, soap, brooms, candles, clothes horses, etc. In 1870 she was operated by V. Alderman, William Fauts and the Carbon Oil Co., and her freight bills were headed "Muskingum and Ohio River Wholesale Trader." Off the lists 1876.

5135 SKIPPER

Stw p wh b. Freedom, Pa., 1847. 64 tons. Ran Pittsburgh-Freeport on Allegheny River summer 1847 when the Pennsylvania Canal aqueduct burned. That fall ran Pittsburgh-Sun Fish (Clarington, Oh.) and made trips on the Muskingum to Zanesville. Owned by Capt. William Stoops, Stoops Ferry, Pa. She is credited having been the first steamboat to ascend the Youghiogheny River to West Newton, Pa., although the *PLOWMAN* had explored the river previously. Ran Pittsburgh-Parkersburg, Capt. Stoops, 1848. In 1855 she was brought to the Knox Yard, Harmar, Oh., a dilapidated wreck, and was rebuilt by Capt. Jacob Cram and others with an eye to making New Orleans trips. Was at St. Paul, Minn. in 1857. Off the lists in 1858.

5136 SKYLARK

SW p wh b. Brownsville, Pa., 1858. 371 tons. She was in the

flotilla up Tennessee River in spring of 1862 handling U.S. troops and supplies, Capt. William Blake. Burned in Duck River, Tenn., Aug. 9, 1862.

5137 SLIM CHANCE

Rig? p wh Capt. Charles Muhleman and brother of Buckhill Bottom, Oh., had a flat used for moving threshing machines. In 1881 they placed an engine on it, and ran New Matamoras-Marietta from mid-summer until late November during a record low water season, and carried the U.S. Mail. The pilot was Godfrey Muhleman. Jake Suter, Baresville (now Hannibal, Oh.) ran a flat carrying freight, towing it with a team of horses. Connections to Wheeling were made by the *LONE WANDERER*.

5138 SODO

Stw p wh b. about 1854, 108 x 20 x 3.5. One engine. One boiler, 40″ by 20 ft. Ran on upper Red River, La.

5139 SONOMA

Stw p wh b. Harmar, Oh., at Knox Yard, 1881. 115 x 20 x 3. Built for Capt. Edmund B. Cooper who ran her Parkersburg-Belleville on the Ohio. Had one stack. In December 1892 he ran her daily Marietta-Beverly on the Muskingum. Made some trips up Big Sandy River. Capt. E.W. Webster greatly enlarged her at Parkersburg in 1897 to measure 123.5 x 20.5, two stacks. He ran her daily Marietta-Beverly prior to rebuilding (1893–1896) and after, until 1909. Ran Marietta-McConnelsville 1909–1910. Sank, downbound, at Lem Lawrence's landing, between Beverly and Luke's Chute, on Apr. 19, 1910. The *LORENA* took her freight and towboat *DARLING* pumped her out. Ran excursions in 1911 and that October pinch-hit for the *H.K. BEDFORD* in the Pittsburgh-Parkersburg trade. Most noteworthy of her Muskingum days happened May 12, 1905, when she was selected to convey Hon. Theodore E. Burton, chairman of the Congressional Rivers and Harbors Committee, plus ten other members and their friends, up the Muskingum twelve miles from Marietta. They were touring the Ohio River on the *QUEEN CITY*. In 1913 she was in the Madison-Frankfort trade. On May 3rd at 4:30 P.M. she was backing out of a Kentucky River landing one mile above Glen Mary, Henry County, hooked a snag, turned over and sank. Capt. E.W. Webster was master. His sister, Mrs. B.F. Kidwell, was drowned; also baby daughter of Mrs. John Crawford, a passenger.

5140 SONORA

SW p wh b. St. Louis, Mo., 1851. 363 tons. 220 x 32 x 5.5. Engines, 21½'s- 7 ft. Three boilers. Ran St. Louis-Missouri River, Capt. Jos. LaBarge. Made trips up Red River, 1853, Capt. William Terrell. She sank and was lost in ice at Portland, Mo., on Missouri River, Feb. 26, 1856. Machinery and brass were taken out in 1916, and the wreck was still visible during the low water of 1927. In March 1940 the U.S. dredge *KEOKUK* removed the wreck, and her crew reported finding steam pipes joined with hand-wiped lead, and her pumps were faced with leather.

5141 SONORA

Stw p wh b. Wheeling, W. Va., 1865. 229 tons. 139 x 25.9 x 3.3. Built for T.D. Hines, New Orleans, Capt. S.H. Hammond. Snagged and lost in Atchafalaya River, La., Nov. 18, 1865.

5142 SOPHIA

SW p wh b. Louisville, Ky., 1852. 41 tons. Hit bridge pier on Green River, Ky., and lost, Feb. 10, 1854.

5143 SOUTH

SW p wh b. New Albany, Ind., 1856, originally named *ALICE VIVIAN* (see). Renamed when sold by USQMD and redocumented, Jan. 4, 1866. Then described as 546 tons. Hull 196.9 x 33.8 x 7. New owners were Capt. Benjamin L. Blonk (½) and J.R. Bowler, both of New Orleans. Was taken to Mobile, Ala., briefly, then back to New Orleans owned March 1867 by Lee Crandall of that city, Capt. D. DeHaven. She was dismantled May 1867.

5144 SOUTH

Recess wheel ferry wh b. Gretna, La., 1858. 82.2 x 20.2 x 3.5. Owner and master was Capt. Christian Telson, Sr. Sold June 22, 1870, to Levi B. Field, Natchez, Miss. Still listed in 1876.

5145 SOUTH AMERICA

SW p wh b. Elizabethtown, Pa., 1846. 288 tons. Engines, 22's- 8 ft. Four boilers. On Jan. 12, 1850, while racing with the *ST. JOSEPH* at the mouth of the Arkansas River, the latter exploded (see). Burned Dec. 17, 1850, nine miles above New Orleans with loss of 27 lives, including some U.S. soldiers returning from Texas. She was en route from New Orleans to Cincinnati.

5146 SOUTH AMERICA

SW p wh b. McKeesport, Pa., 1854. 284 tons. 170 x 29 x 6.1. Original owner, Andrew Ackley, Pittsburgh, with Capt. A.S. Sheperd, master. Caught in ice in Cypress Bend below Henderson, Ky., on the Ohio River, Feb. 10, 1856, and sank. Capt. Sheperd, of Steubenville, Oh., and mate Jim Fitzgerald got her raised. Came to the aid of the burning *JAMES PARK* and took survivors to St. Louis, May 1856 (see). Collided with and caused the loss of *EAU CLAIRE* at Barnhart, Mo., Mar. 25, 1857. Sold foreign in 1861 and nearly all the crew went over to the *LEXINGTON* (see).

5147 SOUTH BEND

Stw p wh b. Elizabeth, Pa., 1859. 150 tons. Lost in collision with *GOODY FRIENDS* (see) at Fulton, Tenn., Dec. 13, 1860.

5148 SOUTH CAROLINA

SW p wh b. Brownsville, Pa., 1853. 173 tons. Went to Apalachicola, Fla., where she burned Jan. 12, 1860.

5149 SOUTH DAKOTA

Stw p wh b. Running Water, S.D., 1899. 137.5 x 19.4 x 4.5. Engines, 10's- 4 ft. One boiler. Owned by Joseph Leach, Sr. Burned on the Missouri between Running Water and Yankton on May 10, 1902, boat and cargo lost.

5150 SOUTH WESTER

SW p wh b. Jeffersonville, Ind., by Howard, 1857. 418 tons. 217 x 36 x 6.5. Engines, 24½'s- 7 ft. Three boilers, each 44" by 26 ft. Built for the Boonville (Mo.) Steamboat Co., a group of farmers and businessmen. John Howard of the Ship Yard was obliged to travel to Boonville to collect the building costs, which he succeeded in doing. Operated in the St. Louis & St. Joseph Union Line in 1858, Capt. DeHaven. Running New Orleans-St. Louis early 1861, Capt. H.R. Patterson. Badly mauled in ice, moored below St. Louis, January-February 1865, reported "in a quite disjointed condition." Her machinery is said to have been transferred to the *BELLE OF ALTON* (see) in 1868.

5151 SOUTH WESTERN

Stw p wh b. Jeffersonville, Ind., 1870. 411 tons. 180 x 42 x 3. Engines, 18's- 5½ ft. Four boilers, each 33" by 22 ft. Ran New Orleans-Shreveport, Capt. Thornton Jacobs, teamed up with *TEXAS* and *D.L. TALLY,* 1870. Burned at Colfax, La., still in the trade, Mar. 14, 1874, Capt. T.E. Jacobs.

5152 SOUTHERN

Stw p wh b. Wheeling, Va., 1857. 126 tons. 117.7 x 27 x 4.3. Enrolled at Wheeling until she was transferred to New Orleans March 1860, Owned by William Gwartney of that city, and Capt. Samuel Gwartney, master. Sold Mar. 31, 1860 to William W. Logan, St. Tammany Parish, La., and again on Aug. 17, 1860 to Capt. Auguste LeBlanc, New Orleans. Went to Confederate registry in 1861.

5153 SOUTHERN BELLE

SW p wh b. Jeffersonville, Ind., by Howard, 1851. 525 tons. 235.5 x 30.7 x 7.5. Ran in the New Orleans-Vicksburg trade commanded by Capt. J.M. White. Principal stockholders were Elam Bowman, Tensas Parish, and Henry B. and William M. Shaw, Concordia Parish. In 1855 her master was Capt. L.W. Broadwell of New Orleans who, by 1856, became owner entire. Burned Oct. 16, 1857, at Mobile, Ala. She collided with and caused loss of *DANIEL BOONE* at College Point, La., Sept. 10, 1853. Machinery went to the *AUTOCRAT* (see) in 1860.

5154 SOUTHERN BELLE

SW p wh b. Jeffersonville, Ind., at Barmore yard, 1876. 738 tons. 210 x 38 (35 ft. floor) x 7. Machinery from *B.L. HODGE NO. 2,* En route from Bayou Sara to New Orleans, Oct. 11, 1876, she caught fire near Plaquemine, La., and burned. The blaze originated in cotton bales. Four cabin passengers and four of the crew were lost.

5155 SOUTHERN FLORA

Stw trading boat wh b. Wellsville,Oh., 1869. 63 tons. Off the lists in 1861.

5156 SOUTHERNER

SW p wh b. Jeffersonville, Ind., by Howard, 1853. 393 tons. 240 x 34 x 6. Owned by the U.S. Mail Line Co., Cincinnati, and ran in the Louisville-St. Louis trade, Capt. Catterlin. She was "low pressure" similar to *JACOB STRADER*. Primarily a passenger carrier. Sold in April 1861 to Capt. John A. Williamson and others. Sank following a collision at College Point, La., July 21, 1862. The hull was for sale at Cincinnati in December 1862.

5157 SOUTHERNER

Catamaran diving bell boat wh b. New Albany, Ind., 1858. 157 tons. Each hull measured 138 x 14 x 4.6. Owned by Charles Whiting, New Orleans. Originally may have been a ferry. Was altered into a diving bell boat February 1866, owned then by John H. McKee, Asa S. Mansfield and Mary Amanda May, New Orleans, with Capt. C.N. Garvin, master. Owners became the New Orleans Wrecking & Salvage Co., Spencer Field, president. Dismantled in 1870.

5158 SOUTHERNER

SW p wh b. Paducah, Ky., 1860, originally named *AUTOCRAT* (see). 270 x 40 x 7. Engines, 26's- 9 ft. from *SOUTHERN BELLE.* Five boilers, each 44" by 28 ft., five flues. Owned by Richard M. Mason and S.D. Hancock, designed for Memphis-New Orleans trade, and made trips to St. Louis, and to the Ohio River. She was in the hands of a U.S. marshal when she burned at Algiers, La., Apr. 10, 1868 at 3:00 P.M. Her owners had been Clifford G. Wayne and John A. Wayne, and her master Capt. R.M. Mason.

5159 SOUTHLAND

Stw p wh b. Jeffersonville, Ind., by Howard, 1910, originally named *NASHVILLE* (see). The Williams Brothers, Evansville, Ind., rebuilt her at Paducah, Ky., in 1922 and changed the name. Ran Louisville-Stephensport-Evansville and burned laid up at Spottsville, Ky., Dec. 16, 1932. See *TARASCON* (sw) for story of the whistle lost in this blaze.

5160 SOVEREIGN

SW p wh b. Shousetown, Pa., 1855. 337 tons. 228.6 x 37 x 6.4. Engines, 24's- 6½ ft. Was in the St. Louis & St. Joseph Union Line in 1858. Captured as a Confederate steamer, June 5, 1862. Sold at public sale, Mound City, Ill., Nov. 29, 1865, to S. Horner for $2,900.

5161 SPARTAN

SW p wh b. Stouts Run, O. (below Vanceburg, Ky.) 1841. 111 tons. Running Cincinnati-Kanawha River, 1842, Capt. Redden. Made trips up Wabash River. Off the lists 1849.

5162 SPEED

Stw p wh b. Stillwater, Minn., 1886, originally named *VERNE SWAIN* (see). Renamed when bought by the Dixon Bros., Peoria, Ill. 1900. They ran her Peoria-La Salle briefly, then sold her. Lyon Bros., Greenville, Miss., owned her and ran short trades. Sold July 1911 to Capt. E.W. Bewley who brought her to Green River. Once sank at Spottsville, Ky., almost to the roof. Capt. Lewis Tanner swapped the *HAZEL RICE* for her in fall 1919. He took her to the Gallipolis-Huntington trade where she ran about three weeks and gave up, the final boat in that run. Later sold to the Louisiana-Arkansas Barge Service, Monroe, La., who dismantled her about 1932.

5163 SPEEDWELL

Stw p wh b. Middleport, Oh., 1897. 140.7 x 25.5 x 6.5. Engines, 12's-6 ft. Two boilers each 43" by 22 ft. Owned by Carr Milling Co., and ran local trades on Kanawha River. In 1901, Charleston-Gallipolis, Capt. Ralph Emerson Gaches, with John Douglass, clerk. Sold entire to Sam L. Parsons, Pt. Pleasant, W. Va., who changed her name to *HELEN M. GOULD* (see).

5164 SPOTTSVILLE

Stw p wh b. Evansville, Ind., 1900, originally named *HENDERSON* (see). 76.7 x 17 x 3.3. Name changed Feb. 17, 1908. Owned by J.M. Mahan. Paducah-Spottsville in 1912, Capt. W.P. Jaynes. Sank at Evansville, Ind., June 23, 1917.

5165 SPRAY

SW p wh b. New Albany, Ind., 1850. 118 tons. Went to Cedar Keys, Fla. Off the lists 1857.

5166 SPRAY

Stw p wh b. Allegheny City, Pa., 1864. 232 tons. New at Pittsburgh October 1864, Capt. W.B. Donaldson, advertised to St. Louis. Then ran Pittsburgh-Cincinnati. One of the pilots was George E. Smith who took over the operation of the boat, running her Pittsburgh-Portsmouth. Went to U.S. Marshal sale at Cincinnati, Apr. 20, 1868, and was sold to Capt. Vincent Shinkle. Later in Cincinnati-Nashville trade, Capt. Gus Brown, with A.R. Singleton, clerk. Exploded boilers and lost at Evansville, Feb. 17, 1871. Capt. George E. Smith's son George became a builder of yawls at Racine, Oh., and was grandfather of J.W. Weaver, Jr.

5167 SPREAD EAGLE

SW p wh b. Brownsville, Pa., 1857. 389 tons. 210 x 36 x 6. Engines, 22's-7 ft. Three boilers, each 40" by 24 ft. Built by Capt. Ben Johnson who sold her on arrival at St. Louis to Capt. Jos. LaBarge and the American Fur Co. Spent her career in the Missouri River. Sank and lost in Pinckney Bend, three miles above New Haven, Mo., Mar. 20, 1864. The location was known thereafter as Spread Eagle Bend. Capt. William Rodney Massie, who went to the mountains on her in 1861, said years later that her wreck lies buried in sand a mile from the river. Owners at time of loss were reported as Capt. Wharton, Thomas H. Voorhees, Mrs. Saltmarsh, and engineer John Orum.

5168 SPREAD EAGLE

SW p wh b. Madison, Ind., 1873. 180 x 29 x 5. Engines, 18½'s-6 ft. Three boilers, each 38" by 20 ft., five flues. Hull and cabin by J.R. Stewart & Son. Engines came from the *PEMBINA* (see). Came out in Keokuk-Quincy trade, Capt. Henry Leyhe, with G.W. Hill, clerk; Fred Cossett, pilot; Samuel Critchfield, chief engineer, and Buck Bernard, steward. The trade was extended to Hannibal and Louisiana. In spring 1874 ran St. Louis-Alton in opposition to the *DE SMET*. The outcome was that Capt. John A. Bruner sold *DE SMET* to the Eagle Packet Co., and took charge of the *SPREAD EAGLE*. Later he was Eagle Packet's agent at Alton for a year, then again bought *DE SMET* and went back in opposition which wound up in victory for Eagle Packet. *SPREAD EAGLE* came out new with no texas, but one was added; her original engines were replaced with 20's-6'8" from towobat *COMET*. She ran through the season of 1880, then went to Cincinnati and picked up the new *SPREAD EAGLE* (next listing) and towed the uncompleted boat to Paducah where the engines were exchanged. The hull was used as a model barge owned by Cape Girardeau Transportation Co., G.W. Hill, secretary. It was sold October 1888 to Capt. S.S. Brown and James H. Rees, Pittsburgh, who resold it to the Memphis & New Orleans Packet Co.

5169 SPREAD EAGLE

SW p wh b. Cincinnati, Oh., and completed at Paducah, 1881. 224.5 x 33.8 x 5.7. Engines, 20's-6'8" from prior *SPREAD EAGLE* (see above) and maybe boilers as well. Owned by Eagle Packet Co., and ran St. Louis-Alton-Grafton. She had no texas. She was retired in 1897 and replaced by another *SPREAD EAGLE* (next listing).

5170 SPREAD EAGLE

SW p wh b. Jeffersonville, Ind., by Howard, 1892, originally *CITY OF NEW ALBANY*, then *NEW IDLEWILD* (both see). Renamed in 1897 by Eagle Packet Co., when entered in the St. Louis-Alton-Grafton trade. Served the trade until 1910, then renamed *CAPE GIRARDEAU* (see).

5171 SPREAD EAGLE

SW p wh b. Jeffersonville, Ind., by Howard, 1911. 166.8 x 26.7 x 6. She was built "stiff-shaft" with both paddlewheels on a common shaft, a single engine 26"-8 ft. Two boilers. Built for Eagle Packet Co., and ran St. Louis-Alton-Grafton. Lost in ice while laid up for the winter, January 1918, at Paducah, Ky.

5172 SPRINGFIELD

SW U.S. tinclad wh b. Cincinnati, Oh., 1862, originally named *W.A. HEALY* (see). She became Tinclad #22, named *SPRINGFIELD*, Nov. 20, 1862. When sold at public auction, Mound City, Ill., Aug. 17, 1865, she was described as 134.8 x 26.8 x 4.3. Engines, 10's-3½ ft. Went to R.G. Jamison for $4,550. New owners renamed her *JENNIE D.* in 1866.

5173 SPRINGFIELD

SW ferry wh b. New Albany, Ind., 1865. 282 tons. 164 x 46 x

5. Owned by Wiggins Ferry Co., St. Louis. Off the lists 1886.

5174 STACKER LEE

Stw p wh b. Jeffersonville, Ind. by Howard, 1902. 225.5 x 45 x 6.5. Engines, 18's- 8 ft. Three boilers, each 44" by 24 ft. Owned by Lee Line, Memphis. Crew, October 1902: Capt. Shep Lightner; Luther Brashear and Charles B. Ziegler, pilots; William Brannon and Richard Fryer, engineers; John Hermann and Joe Tucker, clerks. Ran St. Louis-Memphis. Capt. Tom Greene once said that name "Stacker Lee" sounded more "south" than any other steamboat's name; which reminds us that Courtney M. Ellis, who was an engineer with the Lee Line for a time, recalled a sign over the crew's table which warned NO STEAMBOATING AT MEALS. The *STACKER LEE* sank four miles above Memphis, downbound, Oct. 21, 1916 at 11:00 P.M. There was water at the back end of the texas. Purser Nick Jokerst gathered up money and papers and with second clerk Walter Jeffords rowed to Memphis in a yawl and got the tug *BART TULLY* to come up for the passengers. On the morning of that same day the *CAPE GIRARDEAU* sank off Fort Gage (see).

5175 STAR GREY EAGLE

SW p wh b. Shousetown, Pa., 1859, officially documented as *GREY EAGLE* (see) but after March 1865 was often called *STAR GREY EAGLE*.

5176 STAR OF THE WEST

An ocean steamship b. New York, N.Y., 1852, 1,172 tons, which wound up her days in a most unlikely place, on the Tallahatchie River in Mississippi, where she was purposely scuttled by the Confederates to block access to Fort Pemberton in March 1863. The wreck lay there until 1895 when U.S. Engineers removed the machinery and iron, and the hulk was still visible during low water in 1951.

5177 STAR OF THE WEST

SW p wh b. McKeesport, Pa., 1855. 435 tons. Ran on Missouri River, St. Louis-St. Joseph, Capt. Dix, 1856. Burned at St. Louis Apr. 22, 1858, along with *KEOKUK* and *OCEAN SPRAY* (see).

5178 STAR OF THE WEST

Rig? p wh b. Cincinnati, Oh., 1874. 27 tons. Owned at New Cumberland, W. Va., and handled fire brick, etc. Ran New Cumberland-Steubenville most of 1878, departing that November for the Yazoo River to handle cotton for the winter.

5179 STAR SPANGLED BANNER

SW p wh b. Cincinnati, Oh., 1845. 275 tons. 183 x 31. Engines, 24's- 9 ft. Four boilers, each 42" by 28 ft. Hull by Litherbury & Lockwood, cabin by Robert Caulfield, and engines by James Goodloe. Had 36 staterooms. Ran Cincinnati-New Orleans, Capt. Dick Phillips, with Elmore Bateman, clerk. Snagged and lost about fifteen miles below Baton Rouge, La., June 29, 1847. Life loss was set at 20, most of them deck passengers.

5180 STAR STATE

SW p wh b. Wheeling, Va., 1851. 264 tons. Built for Galveston, Tex., where she foundered and was lost, June 4, 1853.

5181 STARLIGHT

SW p wh b. Jeffersonville, Ind., 1858. 280 tons. 162 x 31 x 6. Ran New Orleans-Shreveport, Capt. Charles Hayes. Engines, 20's- 7 ft. Rebuilt after the war to measure 166.6 x 33.6 x 6.3. The Hayes family continued to operate her New Orleans-Red River until they sold her in February 1868 to J.B. Simonds, New Orleans who resold her March 1868 to Capt. Daniel J. Crowley, New Orleans. Burned at Algiers, La., Apr. 23, 1868.

5181A STARLIGHT

Stw p wh b. Belle Vernon, Pa., 1862. 214 tons. Capt. T.M. Harton ran her Pittsburgh-Louisville-St. Louis most of the first year. At the time of Morgan's Raid in 1863 she was loaded with flour, etc., at Marietta, Capt. Wood, consigned to the U.S. on the lower river and grounded in the foot of Blennerhassett Island. The Parkersburg ferryboat lightened her off. George Knox, Marietta, was a fireman on her, later engineer on many upper Ohio packets. Burned at Gretna, La., Apr. 25, 1868.

5182 STARLIGHT

Stw p wh b. Nashville, Tenn., 1902. 55 x 14 x 2. Ran on Cumberland River. Owned 1912 by Wabash River Packet Co., Vincennes, Ind., who in March sold her to Grayville, Ill.

5183 STATE OF KANSAS

Stw p wh b. Madison, Ind., 1890. 252 x 52.6 x 6. 1,130 tons. Built for the St. Louis-Kansas City trade which did not pan out. Ran St. Louis-New Orleans, and Cincinnati-New Orleans. The Lee Line, Memphis, chartered her in October 1897 to help move cotton, and the crew of the *ORA LEE* went over on her, and we'll bet they noticed the magnification and magnitude. Burned at New Madrid, Mo., on Dec. 18, 1899, Capt. Don A. Marr, master. The *FERD HEROLD* took off passengers and crew.

5184 STATE OF MISSOURI

Stw p wh b. Madison, Ind., 1890. 252 x 56 x 6.5. Built for the St. Louis-Kansas City trade but never saw the Missouri River inasmuch as a drastic cut in rail freight rates was made during her construction. She was run by the Memphis & Cincinnati Packet Co., in the Cincinnati-New Orleans trade. Sank at Watsons Landing on Feb. 20, 1894, raised. On Jan. 12, 1895, she was downbound from Cincinnati with a big trip, Capt. Joe Conlin, with Jules Wehrman, purser, and Jim Pell, Jr., the pilot on watch. Jim was back on the lazy bench reading a newspaper as she came around Wolf Creek Bend, a steersman at the wheel. The cub turned to

Jim and said, "Mr. Pell, she isn't going to make it." The estimate was correct. She slid in amongst the rocks along the Kentucky shore braodside and went to kindling. Four persons were lost. Jess Singleton told us that her pilothouse was pulled ashore and used as a pig pen. One of the passengers was Mrs. J. Henry (Lottie) Best, Marietta, Oh., who later ran the Marietta wharfboat.

5185 STATESMAN

SW p wh b. Brownsville, Pa., 1851. 247 tons. Ran Pittsburgh-St. Louis, Capt. Gormley. Was noticed at Marietta, Mar. 25, 1852, downbound with "between 400 and 500 passengers destined to St. Joseph, Mo., where they will take the route to California." Off the lists 1859.

5186 STATIE FISHER

Stw ferry wh b. Jeffersonville, Ind., by Howard, 1875. 106 tons. 122 x 28 x 4. Regularly inspected at St. Louis until 1888, perhaps longer. The Howard Ship Yard records list her as *KATE FISHER*.

5187 STEEL CITY

Stw p wh b. Cincinnati, Oh., 1895, originally named *VIRGINIA* (see). Renamed early in 1912 while undergoing repairs at Pt. Pleasant, W. Va., owned by Ohio & Mississippi Navigation Co., John W. Hubbard, president. Her first trip was Pittsburgh-New Orleans and return, advertised as a Mardi Gras cruise. Due to bad river conditions the departure was delayed too late for Mardi Gras but she went anyhow leaving Pittsburgh Feb. 29, Capt. John L. Kerr, master with Billy Sampson, steward, and Arthur Browne, purser. Fought high water all the way home. Entered the Pittsburgh-Cincinnati trade upon her return, Capt. Alfred Pennywitt. Upbound at Vanceburg, Ky., she hit the wharf grade in August, 1912, and was taken across the Ohio to Sandy Springs where she settled in shallow water. Many of the passengers remained aboard until the *QUEEN CITY* took them off several days later. The 1913 Flood delayed her at Ashland, Ky., upbound, Capt. Fred Edgington. In September 1913 she was flagship of a spectacular river parade at Pittsburgh. When the *QUEEN CITY* sank on the Falls, Louisville, Ky., Feb. 17, 1914, she was taken there to receive the *QC's* furniture and apparel, went back up the river and was stopped at Rochester, Pa., for ice. She lay there several months with a sale pending, firmed in May, when she was sold to Chicago, St. Louis & Gulf Transportation Co., and was returned to Pt. Pleasant for dock work. Finally departed Pt. Pleasant in March 1915 for Peoria, Ill., the hull painted cherry red. Capt. E.E. Brown was master in La Salle-New Orleans trade, but U.S. Marshal troubles had her laid up at Cairo in September. Sold to St. Louis & New Orleans Navigation Co., Charles Roger, president, in late 1916, and was renamed *EAST ST. LOUIS* (see).

5188 STEEL QUEEN

Stw ferry wh b. Jeffersonville, Ind., by Howard, 1901. 125 x 28 x 3.5. Engines, 12½'s- 6 ft. Two boilers, each 44" by 28 ft. She was owned by Pressed Steel Car Co., McKees Rocks, Pa., and ferried to Woods Run and Bellevue, handling plant personnel. Built pool style, later had upper deck glass enclosed. Capt. Scott R. Dawson, secretary of Harbor 25, was pilot on her in 1902. Capt. C.R. Ford was master in later years, with Richard Simms, chief engineer. Burned at Woods Run, Pa., Oct. 16, 1926.

5189 STELLA

Stw p wh b. Paducah, Ky., 1886, originally named *CITY OF CLARKSVILLE* (see). She was rebuilt and renamed in 1900. Capt. H.M. Williams ran her Monroe-Camden on Ouachita River. Burned July 24, 1901, at Columbia, La.

5190 STELLA

Stw p wh b. Jeffersonville, Ind., 1904. 101.5 x 25 x 3. Engines, 11's- 4 ft. Two boilers, 44" by 16 ft. Owned by Producers Oil Co. Yazoo City, Miss. Operated 1906 by Yazoo City Packet Co., P Line Steamers, W.D. Pugh, lessee. Montjoy Bros., bought her and changed her name October 1907 to *J.A. TOWNS* (see).

5191 STELLA BLANCHE

SW p wh b. Paducah, Ky., 1853. 202 tons. Off the lists 1855.

5192 STELLA WHIPPLE

Stw p wh b. Eau Claire, Wis., 1862. 90 tons. Built for Chippewa River service, and also was on Minnesota River, Capt. Haycock. Off the lists 1868.

5193 STELLA WILDS

Stw p wh b. Brownsville, Pa., and completed at Wheeling, W. Va., 1886. 289 tons. 156.6 x 30.5 x 4.6. Built for Capt. Tom Prince and others, and named for ten-year-old daughter of a cotton planter. Ran Natchez-Vicksburg. A.J. Sweeney & Son, Wheeling, built her under contract. Carried U.S. Mail and her pilot Sam Pennywitt had a plotted course mapped, and ran her on compass in fog, and was reputed never to have missed a mail delivery. Sank 25 miles below Natchez in December 1897 and passengers were removed by *LULU PRINCE*. Walter Neil was chief engineer and Harry Fitch second in 1898. She burned at Briers, 23 miles below Natchez, January 1900 with 32,000 sacks of cotton seed.

5194 STEPHEN BAYARD

Stw p wh b West Elizabeth, Pa., 1851. 155 tons. Spent a good bit of time in the Wheeling-Sunfish (Clarington, Oh.) trade, Capt. Booth. In the one year period, March 1864–1865, carried 15,921 passengers from Monongahela City, Pa., probably a railroad connection. Ran low water, Wheeling-Parkersburg, fall of 1856. We have seen a freight bill made out in 1857, Capt. C.H. Booth, master; Pancoast, clerk.

5195 STEPHEN DECATUR

SW p wh b. Belle Vernon, Pa., 1857. 308 tons. James Rees, Pittsburgh, owned in part. Ran Pittsburgh-New Orleans and elsewhere. Her master 1861 was Capt. Bart G. Leiper. Hit the Wheeling bridge downbound, knocking down her stacks and damaging the texas, Apr. 25, 1862; had been running to Cumberland River. Worked under charter to the U.S. as a transport during the war, and while so engaged sank at Devil's Island below St. Louis, returning from White River. In 1865 under charter to Parkman & Co., Memphis, bringing Ouachita River cotton up for them, Capt. Seph Goll. Out of service 1866. Machinery went to *HENRY M. SHREVE.*

STERLING PRICE

SW gunboat wh. See *GENERAL PRICE.*

5196 STERLING WHITE

Rig? ferry wh b. New Albany, Ind., 1878. 117 tons. 120 x 30 x 4.5. Inspected at Shreveport, La., in 1881. Still listed 1886, perhaps longer.

5197 STOCKDALE

Stw U.S. tinclad wh b. West Brownsville, Pa. in 1863, originally *J. T. STOCKDALE,* see. She was commissioned Nov. 13, 1863, Tinclad #42. When sold after the war, was renamed *CADDO* (see).

5198 STONE BROTHERS

Stw ferry wh b. Pt. Pleasant, W. Va., 1882. 87 x 26 x 3.5. Still listed 1895.

5199 STONEWALL

SW p wh b. Jeffersonville, Ind. by Howard, 1866. 224 x 42.5 x 6.8. 879 tons. She had been operating out of St. Louis. Capt. John C. Dowty, New Orleans, had lost the *ST. NICHOLAS* and loaded the *STONEWALL* at St. Louis to go south for the New Orleans-Grand Encore trade. She caught fire about 45 miles above Cairo, Ill., at Neelys Landing. Pilot Ed Fulkerson ran her ashore, this on Oct. 27, 1869, just after supper. She beached on a bar instead of getting to the bank, water all around her. Boat was owned by Capt. John Shaw and Dennis Long, Louisville, Ky. Capt. Shaw was not aboard, and Capt. Thomas Scott was master. Chief engineer was George W. Fulton. She had aboard an overload of deck passengers (this came up at the Inspector's hearings later) and in all 209 persons were drowned and lost, including Captain Scott and his first clerk Mr. Albert. The *BELLE MEMPHIS* came along three hours later and rendered assistance. There was much outcry inasmuch as the wrecking boat *SUBMARINE No. 13,* Capt. John T. Washington, passed by the wreck within an hour after the fire and did not stop. The hull was recovered and converted into a wharfboat at St. Louis. In January 1871 the night watchman said the *STONEWALL*'s mate, also lost in the catastrophe, was a frequent ghostly visitor.

5200 STONEWARE

Stw p wh b. Friendly, W. Va., 1892. 100 x 17 x 3. 74 tons. She was operated as a packet in Green River and got into the clutches of the U.S. marshal in April 1895. Bought at Evansville in September 1895 by William Wenzel who used her to tow oak staves out of the Yazoo River to New Orleans. In May 1900 she brought a record of 150,000 staves out of the Yazoo in a single tow.

5201 STORM

SW p wh b. Cincinnati, Oh., 1848. 247 tons. 172 x 28 x 5.7. Engines, 20's- 7 ft. Three boilers. Made trips to the upper Ohio, documented at Louisville. Enrolled at New Orleans June 1852, owned by Robert Moody (two-thirds). Louisville, Ky., and Capt. William Switzer, New Orleans. In October 1853 Capt. Robert Moody owned her entire. She was at Shreveport, La., Capt. S.W. Downs, July 25, 1855. Snagged and lost at Campti, La., Feb. 27, 1857. The snagboat *ALGERINE* took out the wreck in July 1857.

5202 SUBMARINE

Five snagboats were built by the U.S. on the plan developed and patented by Henry M. Shreve officially numbered 1-5. These were sold to James B. Eads, St. Louis, in 1855 and he converted them into wrecking boats numbered and named *SUBMARINE 1-5.* Eads then proceeded building additions to the fleet. At the outbreak of the Civil War he converted *SUBMARINE No. 7* into a U.S. gunboat named *BENTON* (see). The Salvor Wrecking & Transportation Co., St. Louis, owned *SUBMARINE NO. 14* in 1874, the last of the series, and also had others named *SALVOR NO. 1* and *SALVOR NO. 2* (see). The story of these wrecking boats has not been researched by this writer. Only three of the *SUBMARINE* fleet are documented in Lytle-Holdcamper's 1975 edition (*#4, #13,* and *#14*) and we have come upon contemporary evidence of a "bell boat" dismantled at Cairo, Ill., summer of 1848 then six years old, built by Eads and referred to as the *SUBMARINE.* Today there hangs in the R.W. Norton Art Gallery, Shreveport, La., an excellent oil painting by artist Lloyd Hawthorne in which Henry M. Shreve directs the snag removal in Red River (1833-1838) with his ingenious snagboat *ARCHIMEDES* at work. This is reproduced and discussed in *S&D Reflector,* issue June 1970, page 14.

5203 SUCCESS

Sailing ship wh b. Moulmain, India, 1790. 135 x 29. Two masts. Originally a merchantman, England-India. After 1802 it was a convict ship, England-Australia. Sank in Sidney harbor, 1885. Raised and became a tourist attraction, c. 1890. Capt. D.H. Smith bought it 1912 and sailed in it for the U.S., April 10, (same day the *TITANIC* left Southampton on her first and ill-fated voyage) and came to Boston after a 96-day journey. Exhibited at many East Coast ports. Was on the West Coast, 1915, taking in Seattle, Wash., and San Francisco. Toured the Mississippi and Ohio Rivers wintering 1917-1918 in the mouth of Kentucky River where ice broke her loose causing loss of the excursion steamer *PRINCESS* and near-loss of the *ISLAND QUEEN* (see). Showed at Wheeling in summer 1918, wintered below Glenwillard, Pa., and showed in Pittsburgh 1919 moored in the Allegheny River, North Side, below Sixth Street bridge. Went on to tour the Great Lakes and burned and sank at Port Clinton, Oh., July 4, 1946. One of her anchors is in front of the Bayview Yacht Club, Detroit. Her longevity was due to a solid teak hull.

5204 SUCCESS

Stw p wh b. Brownsville, Pa., 1867. 280 tons. Capt. Thomas W. Rea bought her at Cincinnati in March 1868, took her to St. Louis, loaded for Fort Benton, departing March 22, and was the first spring arrival at the fort, May 15. Then back to St. Louis and loaded again for the fort departing June 20. This trip also was completed, a rather unusual stunt. Very few "mountain boats" made two rounds in one season. Lost on the Arkansas River, Dec. 13, 1868.

5205 SUCCESS

Stw p wh b. Harmar, Oh., at Knox Yard, 1882. 119 x 22 x 3.2. Owned by George Strecker who ran a boiler works in Harmar on Gilman Street above Lancaster. Sold to the U.S. Engineers, Mar. 3, 1887, and was taken to the Upper Mississippi.

5206 SUCKER STATE

SW p wh b. McKeesport, Pa., 1860. 394 tons. 230 x 36 x 5.5. Engines, 22's- 7 ft. Construction supervised by Capt. Richard C. Gray for the Northern Line Packet Co. The *HAWKEYE STATE,* almost a duplicate, was built at Shousetown, Pa., that same 1859–1860 winter, both for the St. Louis-St. Paul trade. Capt. T.B. Rhodes took command at St. Louis with Ben A. Congar and J.M. Cousins, clerks, N.T. Hickman, chief engineer, and W.P. Hight and Lud Blakeslee, pilots. Capt. James B. Ward was master 1862–1863. Capt. W.P. Hight commanded 1866–1869. Capt. Ben A. Congar, 1870; Capt. F.S. Lee, 1871. She was first through Lake Pepin to St. Paul in 1866 and 1869. Her fast time St. Louis-St. Paul left St. Louis on June 26, 1867 at 4:06 P.M. arriving St. Paul at 3:34 P.M. June 29; 2 days 23 hours 48 minutes. The *HAWKEYE STATE* (see) trimmed this the next season. Burned in Alton Slough 1872.

5207 SUE SKINNER

A mythical packet initiated in *The River,* issue of Jan. 30, 1892, Abbott Veatch, editor. The inventor was a correspondent who signed himself Buck E.T. Plank. He christened her *SUSAN SKINNER* "expecting that she will be able to make the run from New Orleans to Cincinnati in three days, eighteen hours and two weeks." Later she crept into *The Waterways Journal* as *SUE SKINNER*. Sample: "Laid up at Snagtown, Ark., awaiting green signal oil for the starboard stack light." A similar masterpiece was *HURRONICO,* fathered by Capt. E. Dayton Randolph, Reedsville, Oh., exploited in a book *Pilotin' Comes Natural* by Way. The *ROGER K. DUDLEY* had uncertain origin, probably on Green or Cumberland rivers, often mentioned by Capt. Charles H. Ellsworth, but never got in print. Undoubtedly there were others.

5208 SUGAR LAND

Stw p wh b. Pattersonville, La., 1892. 229 tons. 152 x 34.7 x 4.7. Apparently rebuilt at Patterson in 1900, documented as a new boat same dimensions. Still listed in 1908. Capt. Tom Posey, pilot of the *SAINT PAUL,* used to regale us with tales of *SUGAR LAND* and the *SACCHARINE* (see) operating west of New Orleans in the "sugar trade."

5209 SULLY

SW p wh b. St. Louis, Mo., 1867. 280 tons. Engines, 15½'s- 5 ft. Two boilers. Snagged and lost in Smith's Bend, above Doniphan, Mo., on the Missouri River, Oct. 22, 1869, Capt. C.A. Cunningham, owner and master.

5210 SULTAN

SW p wh b. Cincinnati, Oh., 1845. 125 tons. 124 x 21 x 5. Originally owned by J.F. Bercier & Co., New Orleans, and Joseph Urhan, Opelousas, La. First master, Capt. Paul Queyrouze, later Capt. George W. Haygood. In 1847 sold to Augustin Larose & Co., New Orleans. Snagged and lost in the Atchafalaya River, Oct. 25, 1847.

5211 SULTAN

SW p wh b. McKeesport, Pa., 1854. 349 tons. 185 x 31 x 6.5. Engines, 24's- 8 ft. Three boilers. Advertised in St. Louis, Capt. John McCloy, bi-weekly St. Louis-Omaha, April 1856. Snagged above Amazonia, Mo., on the Missouri River, Capt. McCloy, 1857, the location thereafter called Sultan Bend. Frequently made Cincinnati-St. Louis trips. En route St. Louis to New Orleans she caught fire above Ste. Genevieve, Mo., Apr. 2, 1858. She was rounded to and tied to a fallen tree with the result that the current pulled the tree out, and she burned in midstream with loss of 23 lives. Capt. Phil C. Hannam was in charge.

SULTANA . . . Due to the interest in this ill-fated steamer we will present sketches of her predecessors starting in 1836:

5212 SULTANA

SW p wh b. Cincinnati, Oh., 1836. 385 tons. Ran New Orleans-Vicksburg, Capt. A.W. Tufts. Said to have been the first regular boat in this trade. Also made trips to Louisville in off seasons. Off the lists 1844.

5213 SULTANA

SW p wh b. Jeffersonville, Ind., 1843. 527 tons. 237 x 30.5 x 7.5. Enrolled at New Orleans July 3, 1844, Capt. Horace Pease, master and part owner, his partner being Abijah Fisk, New Orleans Capt. A.W. Tufts took stock in November 1846 and took command. Capt. Pease was son-in-law of Capt. Tufts. Abijah Fisk was quite well-to-do and had high regard for Peace who was killed when the *CONCORDIA* exploded (see). This was the largest steamboat at New Orleans in her day.

5214 SULTANA

SW p wh b. Cincinnati, Oh., 1848. 824 tons. In 1849 came up from New Orleans to Louisville in 5 days 12 hours. Burned at St. Louis, Mo., June 12, 1851 at 1:00 A.M. Capt. George Cable was master, and John Skiles, clerk.

5215 SULTANA

SW p wh b. Paducah, Ky., 1852. 565 tons. Ran Louisville-New Orleans, Capt. Baird. Got in a gale at Mills Point, Lower Mississippi River, and lost her stacks, Jan. 23, 1853. Burned at Hickman, Ky., Mar. 25, 1857. The *A.L. SHOTWELL* had been lost the day prior, above Memphis.

5216 SULTANA

SW p wh b. Cincinnati, Oh., 1863. 660 tons. 260 x 42 (39 ft. floor) x 7. Engines, 25's- 8 ft. Four tubular boilers, quite a fad at the time, each 46" by 18 ft., having twenty-four 5" flues. Paddlewheels 34 ft. dia. working 11 ft. buckets. Built at the John Litherbury yard, and machinery by Moore and Richardson. Launched Jan. 3, 1863, in a double ceremony, the *LUMINARY*, - almost a duplicate, also being launched. Built for Capt. Pres Lodwick, well known on the Upper Mississippi for his *NORTHERN BELLE* and *NORTHERN LIGHT* (both see) and was designed for the New Orleans trade. Due to the uncertainties of war, she was entered in the trade Cincinnati-Wheeling on February 12, which she continued until mid-March. In charge of the office was W.H. Cropper, with Charles Matthews, second clerk. J.W. Keniston was chief engineer. She then loaded for Nashville under U.S. auspices. Joe Curtis looked up the old U.S. Custom files at Memphis for 1864 and she first appears downbound for New Orleans on January 25, Capt. Lodwick. She was sold at St. Louis in early March 1864 to a number of firms and citizens of that place, also her new skipper Capt. J. Cass Mason, and first clerk W.J. Gamboel. They ran her St. Louis-New Orleans. Capt. Mason, about 34, was born in Lynchburg, Va., and was brought to Missouri as a child. He boated on the *A. B. CHAMBERS* and lately had been clerk and master of *ROWENA* in the Memphis trade. First clerk Gamboel lived in Glasgow, Mo., and had been a steamboat agent at Kansas City. The Memphis Custom's entries show that due to the war she was forced to return to St. Louis from that port until along in August when she apparently went on through. On Feb. 9, 1865, Capt. J. Cass Mason, she departed Memphis for New Orleans. She was back at Memphis February 26, and returned to New Orleans from there. On Apr. 26, 1865, she cleared Memphis upbound, Capt. Mason. A notation on the Custom record: "Burned and 1600 persons perished."

The Customs clerk used an approximation. The life-loss afterwards was set at 1,547 lives, at least 1,100 of whom were U.S. soldiers mustered out and returning to Northern homes. A popular and widespread belief was that Confederate spies had secreted dynamite in the coal bunkers, but three of her boilers had exploded without any help from spies. True, she had been having boiler trouble at Vicksburg where the troops came aboard. Nathan Wintringer, chief engineer, later testified that one boiler had been repaired there to his satisfaction. Capt. Speed, U.S.A. ordered 1,886 troops aboard this *SULTANA* which legally was allowed 376 persons, including the crew. It was common talk there at Vicksburg that two other large steamers, *PAULINE CARROLL* and *LADY GAY*, both bid for portions of these troops but were turned down. Landings were made at Helena, Ark. (where a photographer took a picture of her with the soldiers aboard), and another at Memphis. The night leaving Memphis was described as black with a thunderstorm gathering. A few miles above that city, in the crossing at Paddy's Hen and Chickens, the explosion torched a ruddy glare among the cottonwoods of Tennessee and Arkansas and a dull rumble shook the countryside. The storm broke at the same time.

On the downbound trip to New Orleans, the last she made, the *SULTANA* carried the shocking news of the assasination of Abraham Lincoln to towns and hamlets cut off from all communication save what arrived by river. Now as she returned the nation's newspapers were loaded with columns of excitement: J. Wilkes Booth had been located and killed; Lee had surrendered; the President was dead. A country geared to appalling losses took the *SULTANA* disaster with seeming indifference. The explosion happened early morning Apr. 27, 1865.

See *S&D Reflector*, issue June 1965, pages 10-12; also September 1965, page 12.

5217 SUMMER KOON

From the Evansville, Ind., *Journal*, June 10, 1871: "The *SUMMER KOON* took on considerable freight here and left for the Wabash. She moved up the river with fair speed and presented a novel appearance for a steamboat. She is nothing less than a regular flatboat with a wheel at the stern, propelled by a portable engine with adroit gearing." Operating in the Cairo-Memphis area 1872 and was sunk by ice at Memphis Dec. 31, 1872.

5218 SUMMIT

Stw p wh b. Brownsville, Pa., 1850. 128 tons. Foundered at Cincinnati, Oh., June 1, 1853.

5219 SUMMIT

Stw p wh b. Brownsville, Pa., 1855. 180 tons. Burned and lost at New Orleans, Dec. 5, 1855.

5220 SUMTER

SW p wh b. New Albany, Ind., 1860. 212 tons. Went to Mobile, Ala. Captured as a Confederate steamer, June 6, 1862. Sold to private hands, September 16, 1865. Last known document Dec. 9, 1872.

5221 SUN

SW p wh b. Cincinnati, Oh., 1852. 157 tons. 138 x 18 x 5.3. Master and half owner when enrolled at New Orleans Jan. 14, 1853, Capt. John Lewis, New Orleans. His partner was Henry Webb, Cincinnati. Burned on Red River, at Black Bayou, La., Feb. 21, 1853.

5222 SUN

Stw p wh b. Hockingport, Oh., 1898. 121 x 21.2 x 4.3.

Engines, 9½'s- 3 ft. One boiler, 46" by 16 ft. Built by Capt. John Summers for Parkersburg-Creston trade on Little Kanawha. Ran there several seasons in competition with *ONEIDA* and *C.C. MARTIN*, all independently owned, and for a time passengers round tripped Parkersburg-Burning Springs for 25 cents. In November 1899 running Louisville-Kentucky River. In January 1901 running Evansville-Bowling Green, Capt. E.H. Bewley, with Tom W. Sweet, clerk. The Lee Line, Memphis, acquired her for the Memphis-Fulton trade and she burned at the Memphis wharf, Dec. 25, 1901, with loss of four lives. Rebuilt and Lee Line still running her 1905, Capt. Jess P. Irwin. Sold in April 1906 to E.F. Johnson, Milton, Fla. Snagged and sunk in Mobile Bay, Dec. 14, 1906, en route to Pensacola, Fla. Raised, and she went to Flint River after that. On Feb. 2, 1909, lost by stranding at Apalachicola, Fla.

5223 SUN FLOWER

SW p wh b. Louisville, Ky., 1857. 105 tons. 121.5 x 25 x 3.7. Enrolled at New Orleans, February 1858 owned by Frederick Randolph and O. Winn, that city. Sold September 1858 to Capt. William C. Harrison who ran her New Orleans-Alexandria. Sold October 1859 to Capt. Thomas F. Oliver. Sold March 1860 to William W. Ward, New Orleans. Went to Confederate registry, and was wrecked in Galveston Harbor, Tex., Oct. 3, 1867.

5224 SUNBEAM

Stw p wh b. Elizabethtown, Pa., 1846. 153 tons. Built by Capt. John Goff who had previously owned *ALLEGHENY MAIL* (see) for Ohio River trades. Lost in collision with *MOTIVE* near Portsmouth, Oh., Oct. 2, 1847, with loss of eight lives.

5225 SUNBEAM

Stw p wh b. Cincinnati, Oh., 1857. 167 tons. Snagged and lost at Bayou Pierre, La., Feb. 4, 1858.

5226 SUNBEAM

Prop p wh b. Evansville, Ind., 1878. 136 x 23.2 x 6.3. Built by C.Y. Perkins and A.O. Durland as a replacement for *MOLLIE NORTON* (see) in the transfer business to Henderson, Ky., for the Evansville, Henderson & Nashville Railroad. Capt. Jim Rowley, Jr., recalls :"She looked like she had come from Lake Chautauqua, a little lake boat; Sam and Henry Pennywitt had her in the Cincinnati-Maysville trade; she could make 18 to 20 mph, and drew considerable water. She landed only at the wharfboats, viz., New Richmond, Moscow, Foster, Augusta, Higginsport, Ripley, and Maysville. It was not any trouble nor did it require extra effort for this boat to run around the *BOSTONA* or *FLEETWOOD*, and she could come up to Maysville from Cincinnati in 3½ to 4 hours—no freight, just passengers; she left a wharfboat just as suddenly as she appeared."

5227 SUNFLOWER

Rig? p wh b. Jeffersonville, Ind., 1878. 140 tons. Departed Cincinnati October 1878, Capt. S.H. Parisot, for Yazoo River. Still listed 1882, maybe later.

5228 SUNFLOWER BELLE

Rig? p wh Vicksburg-Yazoo River 1875-1878 and was noticed upbound at Memphis early August 1878 for Louisville to be dismantled. "She did not land, but took stores in midstream by means of tugs," concluded the item. A quarantine at Memphis was in effect because of yellow fever.

5229 SUNNY SIDE

SW p wh b. West Brownsville, Pa., 1860. 330 tons. Capt. Frank Maratta loaded her for New Orleans and she sank on the Falls at Louisville, Jan. 26, 1861. She was at Cincinnati in March 1862 loaded and ready to leave for Pittsburgh. The U.S. impressed her, directed she be unloaded forthwith. Maratta sold her right there to Capt. John N. Shunk, and she was reloaded with U.S. goods for Nashville. She burned at Island 16, Mississippi River, Nov. 13, 1863, with 1,130 bales of cotton. Did not get landed and the life loss was "considerable." Capt. Shunk and first clerk McKinney had to swim for it. McKinney in later years ran the Hotel Anderson on Liberty Ave., Pittsburgh.

5230 SUNNY SOUTH

SW p wh b. Wheeling, Va., 1860. 270 tons. 158.7 x 35 x 6.9. Built for Capt. William G. Mitchell, and was taken to Alabama River. She had loaded with cotton at Montgomery and was landed at Portland, Ala., taking wood when she took fire and burned, 45 miles below Selma, Jan. 11, 1867, Capt. Mitchell in command. One life loss.

5231 SUNNY SOUTH

Stw p wh b. Jeffersonville, Ind., by Howard, 1897, originally named *ELECTRA* (see). Renamed in 1914 at Mobile, Ala., owned by the Burke interests. The Burkes sold her to parties in New Orleans and she was taken in tow by the tug *CLAUDE*. Capsized about 25 miles out of Mobile, 6:30 A.M., Apr. 20, 1916. Capt. Matt Jackson was in charge.

5232 SUNRISE

Stw p wh b. Jeffersonville, Ind., by Howard, 1897. 180 x 36 x 5. A cotton packet of the Red River Line, Capt. J.W. Brinker. In 1901 ran New Orleans-Vicksburg in place of *VALLEY QUEEN*, Capt. B.C. Rea, with T.C. Saches, clerk. Burned at New Orleans, Apr. 25, 1902. The *JOHN K. SPEED* (see) burned at the same location May 22, 1902.

5233 SUNSET

Stw p wh b. Pittsburgh, Pa., 1865. 103 tons. Engines, 14's-4 ft. Two boilers. Snagged and lost 40 miles below Sioux City, Iowa, on Missouri River, Capt. A.R. Davenport, July 18, 1869. Austin M. Tate was co-owner.

5234 SUNSHINE

SW p wh b. Elizabeth, Pa., 1860. 354 tons. Ran St. Louis-St. Paul in 1861, Capt. Willard. In September 1861 went to the Missouri River and had some hot times. The Confederates captured her at Glasgow, Mo., and required her to transport their troops across. The 38th Indiana Regiment on *DES MOINES, IATAN, WHITE CLOUD,* and *WAR EAGLE* recovered her. In June 1863 she was fired on near Waverly. Burned at St. Louis, July 13, 1864, along with *GLASGOW, WELCOME,* and others, said to have been a case of arson by the "dreaded Rebel Steamboat Burners."

5235 SUNSHINE

SW ex and ferry wh b. Jeffersonville, Ind., by Howard, 1888. 175 x 37 x 5.8. Engines, 18's- 6 ft. Three boilers, each 42" by 26 ft. Owned by Louisville & Jeffersonville Ferry Co., and a subsidiary Fern Grove Amusement Co. Operated in that area until 1907 when bought by Capt. William McNally who brought her to Pittsburgh, Pa. He made many alterations, narrowing the guards and rebuilding the wheelhouses to fit Monongahela locks; added double swinging stages, and gave her a texas deck in 1918. Triple tragedy struck in 1920 when a son and daughter of Capt. McNally died within a week, then came his death within another week. The boat was sold, going to John W. Hubbard who formed the River Excursion Co., Cincinnati. Name was changed to *PRINCESS* (see) Aug. 21, 1923.

5236 SUNSHINE

Stw p wh b. Brownsville, Pa. (hull and framing), and completed at Wheeling, W. Va., 1892. 200 x 38 x 5. Engines, 16's- 6½ ft. Three boilers. Came out Nov. 12, 1892, Wheeling-Parkersburg with one trip a week to Pittsburgh, Capt. J. Mack Gamble, with J.A. Hyer, clerk. Proved too big for the trade and ran Pittsburgh-Cincinnati. Evidently was making Kanawha River trips also, for in summer 1894 she was aground at Knob Shoals until a rise released her, with Capt. James Wright as watchman. Ran Cincinnati-Coney Island one summer teamed up with *NEW SOUTH.* The Cincinnati, Portsmouth, Big Sandy & Pomeroy Packet Co., bought her, ran her Cincinnati-Pomeroy through 1903 with occasional trips to Memphis. She hit a log near Owensboro and had to be run ashore in May 1898; the towboat *MARINER* pumped her out. On Mar. 10, 1904 she got a hail at Burrows Landing, near Tiptonville, Tenn. She was nearing shore when fire was discovered aft of the boilers. It gained considerable headway, spreading to some oil barrels stowed on deck. They exploded, scattering the flames to other perishable freight. Capt. Sterling McIntyre directed the pilot to beach her on a sandbar, and a head line was made fast to a tree. Everybody got ashore save one. The rope burned and parted, allowing the burning wreck to float along the Tennessee shore where it sank just below Tiptonville. Boat was valued at $30,000 and the cargo at $40,000.

5237 SUPERB

SW p wh b. Cincinnati, Oh., 1844. 536 tons. 217 x 32 x 8. Ran New Orleans-Lake Providence trade, Capt. S.B. Frost, owned in Cincinnati by Morgan Ewing and George McIne, equal shares. She was a cotton carrier of note. A lithograph exists showing her loaded with 3,512 bales. Sold in 1849 to Capt. E.S. Hall of New Orleans who also was master. Off the lists in 1851.

5238 SUPERIOR

SW p wh b. Cincinnati, Oh., 1856. 417 tons. Operated in the U.S. Mail Line Co., principally Cincinnati-Louisville, Capt. David Whitten and others. After the war Capt. Henry T. Dexter brought her to Evansville "terribly riddled with grape and cannister shot and musket balls, cannon balls, and shells; how her officers and crew escaped death is truly astonishing." Capt. Dexter rebuilt her and in 1866 ran her Evansville-Memphis with G.J. Grammar and H.L. Mitchell, clerks. Stranded and lost at Island 35, Mississippi River, Feb. 18, 1869.

5239 SUSAN

Stw ex wh b. Rock Island, Ill., 1896. 128.4 x 34.2 x 5.1. Engines, 15½'s- 4 ft. One boiler. Capt. G.M. Sively owned her when she was snagged and lost at Fort Calhoun, Neb., on the Missouri River, Sept. 17, 1907.

5240 SUSIE B.

Stw press boat wh b. Middleport, Oh., 1880, originally named *ST. JACOBS OIL* (see). Owned in the mid-1880s by the New Orleans *Times-Democrat* who did the renaming. They used her to meet incoming ships, thus procuring news beats. Also they had her up Ouachita River, and bragged a speed record between Camden and Arkadelphia, 5½ hours. In 1888 she was rebuilt at Branforth, Fla., registered as a new boat named *SUWANNEE.* Ran out of Fort Meyers 1900–1920 to Lake Okachobee, and there came to the attention of Thomas A. Edison. He told Henry Ford about her and, rebuilt, she wound up at Greenfield Village, Mich.

5241 SUSIE BROWN

Recess wheel ferry wh b. Murraysville, W. Va., and completed at Portsmouth, Oh., 1882. 95 x 30.5 x 4.9. Operated at Portsmouth until lost there in ice, Feb. 24, 1895.

5242 SUSIE SILVER

SW p wh b. St. Louis, Mo., 1870. 260 x 39 x 6.5. Engines, 22's- 8 ft. Four boilers, each 40" by 26 ft. Owned by Capt. David Silver who incorporated her into his Shreveport, New Orleans & St. Louis Packet Co., 1872–1873. Made frequent trips Louisville-New Orleans, also Cincinnati-New Orleans. Dismantled at Cincinnati summer of 1878 and much equipment went to building *ANNIE P. SILVER* (see).

5243 SUSIE W.

Rig? p wh b. Shreveport, La., 1900. Ran above Shreveport, Capt. C.H. McClelland. In operation May 1903, maybe later.

5244 SUSQUEHANNA

SW p wh b. Pittsburgh, Pa., 1845. 141 tons. Advertised in the Pittsburgh-St. Louis *Express Line* c. 1848. Snagged and lost at Harpeth Shoals, Tenn., Feb. 2, 1852.

5245 SUSQUEHANNA

SW p wh b. Elizabeth, Pa., 1851. 289 tons. Cincinnati-New Orleans, Capt. O.C. Williamson c. 1856. Came to aid of exploded *ST. NICHOLAS* at Island 60, Apr. 24, 1859, taking sixteen survivors to Memphis, four of whom died en route. Off the lists 1860.

5246 SUWANEE

SW p wh b. Paducah, Ky., 1846. 384 tons. First home port, Nashville, Tenn. Sank and lost in Grand Chain, Ohio River, Nov. 19, 1848. According to the Cairo *Delta*, issue of November 23, she had been en route from Nashville to Cairo. The *COMMODORE PERRY* took off some 200 passengers. Owned by Capt. Savage who had bought her just prior for $10,000 and had put $2,000 repairs in her. The wreck was still causing a break in 1873 when the *HENRY PROBASCO* was lost nearby.

5247 SWALLOW

SW p wh b. Louisville, Ky., 1844. 159 tons. 163.5 x 22.5 x 4.5. Documented at New Orleans March 1845, Capt. J.F. Richardson, Louisville, Ky. Sold October 1845 to Capt. John Cochran, New Orleans. Lost by stranding near New Orleans July 15, 1846. There is evidence she ran 1844 St. Louis-Keokuk in opposition to the regular Line.

5248 SWALLOW

SW p wh b. Cincinnati, Oh., 1851. 337 tons. Ran Cincinnati-New Orleans. Capt. Richard M. Wade, long with the U.S. Mail Line, Cincinnati, recalled he did his first piloting on the lower Mississippi on her. Lost in collision with the *E. HOWARD* at Bonnet Carre, La., Jan. 26, 1853. One life lost.

5249 SWALLOW

Stw p wh b. California, Pa., 1854. 198 tons. 153 x 29.5 x 4.7. Built for Albert Culbertson, James Formly, John Anawalt, and others. Capt. G.P. Sloan, first master. In May 1860 Capt. William Parker took one-third interest and was her master. She was at Cairo, Ill., in March 1861 where she was commandeered by U.S. forces to proceed up the Mississippi and apprehend the *C.E. HILLMAN* and *JOHN D. PERRY*, both downbound with shot, lead, and guns for the South. Mission accomplished. Burned October 1862 at Glover, Miss.

5250 SWALLOW

SW p wh b. Cincinnati, Oh., 1862. 359 tons. 180 x 35 x 7. Cincinnati-Nashville, Capt. Parker. Cincinnati-New Orleans after the war, Capt. Richard M. Wade. Capt. Frank Maratta was on her later. Upbound New Orleans to Cincinnati, in a snowstorm about two miles below Cincinnati, came in collision with *CHAMPION No. 6,* Dec. 21, 1869. Had a big cargo. She was sunk and lost.

5251 SWAMP FOX

SW p wh b. Shousetown, Pa., 1851. 280 tons. 162 x 29.8 x 5.8. Enrolled at New Orleans in Nov. 1852 owned (two-thirds) by Charles E. Marshall, Henry County, Ky., Capt. George R. Remer. Owner became Thomas E. Marshall, Henry County, Ky., March 1853. In May 1853 Capt. William Kimball became part owner and master. Snagged and lost at McDade, La., Feb. 4, 1857.

5252 SWAN

SW p wh b. Elizabeth, Pa., 1846. 102 tons. Snagged and lost at or near Marietta, Oh., November 1848.

5253 SWAN

SW p wh b. New Albany, Ind., 1850. 444 tons. Went to Mobile, Ala., and sold foreign 1863.

5254 SWAN

SW p wh b. Jeffersonville, Ind., 1851. 127 tons. 108.7 x 22.3 x 5. Enrolled at New Orleans January 1852 owned by D.G. Hill, with Capt. J.R. Hill, master. Sold in May 1853 to A.H. Donaldson, New Orleans. Sold foreign in 1858.

5255 SWAN

SW p wh b. Louisville, Ky., 1855. 184 tons. 135 x 30 x 5. Enrolled at New Orleans, January 1856, Capt. C. Hayes. Was sold to Galveston, Tex., in August 1858, owned by Capt. William S. Mauck of that place. To Confederate registry 1861.

5256 SWAN

SW p wh b. Wheeling, Va., 1861. 36 tons. Off the lists 1869.

5257 SWAN

Stw p wh b. Mackville, Ky., 1902. 70 x 16.9 x 3.7. One engine, 7″ by 28″. One boiler, 60″ by 7 ft. Owned by R.S. and R.C. Aiken, Aurora, Ind. A single decker, and ran local trades around Vevay, Ind., and Patriot, Ind. *Lists of Merchant Vessels* list place of build at Mackville, probably meaning Maxville, Ky. Still listed 1908, maybe later.

5258 SWATARA

SW p wh b. Brownsville, Pa., 1846. 144 tons. Lost in collision with *YAZOO* at America, Ill., Mar. 11, 1848. The *YAZOO* was upbound, coming around Dog Tooth Bend. Happened at night with all of *SWATARA*'s passengers retired. Broke in two and was lost. No casualties reported.

5259 SWIFTSURE

SW p wh b. Cincinnati, Oh., 1835. 90 tons. Built for the Louisville-Cincinnati trade, Capt. John Blair Summons, owned in part by Jacob Strader. Sold in June 1836 to Grafton Molen and others who ran her Cincinnati-Maysville, the first regular packet in that trade. Off the lists in 1842.

5260 SWIFTSURE

SW p wh b. Cincinnati, Oh., 1840. 116 tons. Came out in August 1840 owned by William and Thomas Higdon, Cincinnati, and James Thomas of Rising Sun, Ind. Capt. D.H. Shaw was master. Cincinnati-Maysville, Capt. Robinson, 1842. She was jumped into the Pittsburgh-Cincinnati trade latter February 1842, Capt. Robinson.

5261 SWIFTSURE NO. 3

SW p wh b. Cincinnati, Oh., 1844. 129 tons. Entered the Pittsburgh-Cincinnati trade in March 1844, Capt. Robinson. In early April went to Galena and Dubuque. In 1845 back in the Pittsburgh-Cincinnati trade, Capt. Robinson, and ran regularly until withdrawn to make a trip to St. Louis spring 1847. Lost below St. Louis on this trip, and a dispatch dated Mar. 27, 1847, from St. Louis says: "We learn from a gentleman who came here yesterday that nearly all the cargo has been removed from the *SWIFTSURE NO. 3,* and the boilers, engines, etc., are now being taken off."

5262 SWIFTSURE NO. 4

SW p wh b. Cincinnati, Oh., 1846. 141 tons. Messrs. U.P. Schenck and Jules P. Schenck, Vevay, Ind., took her to New Orleans with Vevay troops for the Mexican War, 1846. She ran local trades later; Louisville-Madison for a time. Snagged and lost at Utica, Ind., Oct. 21, 1851.

5263 SWISS BOY

SW p wh b. Smithland, Ky., 1847. 167 tons. Made a trip to Pittsburgh, Pa., in summer of 1848. Operated on Cumberland River. Off the lists in 1851.

5264 SWITZERLAND

SW p wh b. Cincinnati, Oh., 1854. 413 tons. 178.4 x 36.8 x 8.1. Built by U.P. and Jules Schenck, Vevay, Ind., who ran her Louisville-New Orleans. Capt. Jules Schenck usually commanded. The boat was named for their native land, both having come from Switzerland. At the commencement of the war she was taken over by USQMD and converted into one of Ellet's rams. After Col. Charles Ellet, Jr., was wounded during the Battle of Memphis he was placed aboard *SWITZERLAND* and taken up to Cairo, but died en route. He was accorded a state funeral in Independence Hall. Ellet's wife went up along on the boat to Cairo, also a young daughter. Mrs. Ellet died shortly after; both she and her husband are buried at Laurel Hill Cemetery, Philadelphia, Pa. Capt. David Force, Pittsburgh, was skipper on this boat for many war doings, including the siege of Vicksburg. She was sold Oct. 21, 1865, to Joseph Leach, New Orleans, Capt. M. Davis. Sold July 1866 to Eclipse Towboat Co., Joseph Leach, secretary, Capt. John C. Norcross. Off the lists 1870.

5265 SYBIL

Stw tinclad wh b. Cincinnati, Oh., 1863, originally named *HARTFORD* (see). She was named *SYBIL* in U.S. service. Described at time of sale, Mound City, Ill., Aug. 17, 1865, as 150.5 x 29.4 x 5.4. Engines, 16's- 6 ft. Purchaser was R.J. Tunstall. Renamed *COMET* (see) Sept. 28, 1865.*

5266 SYBIL

Stw p wh b. Pittsburgh, Pa., 1865. 135 tons. 110 x 24 x 3.8. Went to New Orleans, owned there by M.D. Monserrate, with Capt. H.J. Brinker, master. Sold 1867 to Hugh Derby and O.E. Henry, New Orleans. Off the lists 1875.

5267 SYDONIA

SW p wh b. Cincinnati, Oh., 1851. 235 tons. 162.5 x 28 x 5.5. Enrolled at New Orleans, Jan. 1852, Capt. Joseph Bercier, master and part owner. Had five changes in enrollment into 1857. Last master was Capt. James W. Moore. She ran at times to Shreveport and above on Red River. Lost at Columbia, La., where she burned May 29, 1857.

5268 SYLPH

Stw p wh b. Allegheny, Pa., 1863. 47 tons. 99.2 x 16.5 x 3.1. This small-fry was in the Cincinnati area until May 1866 when she was transferred to New Orleans, owned in part by Capt. George Murphy, Arkadelphia, Ark. Sank and lost on Ouachita River, Feb. 9, 1867.

T

5269 T. C. TWITCHELL

SW p wh b. New Albany, Ind., 1854. 494 tons. In 1858, St. Louis-New Orleans, Capt. H.G. McComas. Louisville-New Orleans, 1859, Capt. McFall. Off the lists 1862.

5270 T. D. DALE

Stw p wh b. Harmar, Oh., at Knox Yard, 1884. 111.6 x 19.7 x 3.2. Engines, 9″- 3½ ft. Short trade upper Ohio River packet named for a Marietta oilfield operator, president of Ohio Transit Co., which owned pipeline from the Mackburg, Oh., fields, and also operated railroad tank cars. He sold his holdings to the National Transit Co., 1885. Made occasional trips Marietta-Zanesville, 1885, Capt. O.J. Stowe. Ran Cincinnati-New Richmond, Capt. Hissom, opposition to *TACOMA*, and was whipped out. Was a local out of Wheeling for a time. Bought by L.A. Carr, Charleston, W. Va., who ran her Charleston-Winfield, latter 1890s, and was sold to Austin Beaver, Racine. Oh., in 1900. He continued her in the trade, and sold to Capt. Gordon C. Greene in 1902, who dismantled her at Parkersburg and put the engines on the *EVERGREEN* built there that year. The hull became a model barge on Big Sandy River used to haul hay and dynamite during the construction of the C&O Railroad from White House to Pikeville in 1904. Machinery later went to the *GREENDALE.*

5271 T. D. HINE

SW p wh b. New Albany, Ind., 1858. 131 tons. 147.7 x 30.1 x 6. Went to Franklin, La., and to Confederate registry in 1861. Taken as a prize and sold by U.S. marshal Aug. 25, 1865, to Mary G. Knors (widow), New Orleans. Had eleven changes of documentation at New Orleans until May 1870, then owned by George B. Cleveland, St. Mary Parish, Capt. Jesse P. Forgey, master.

5272 T. F. ECKERT

Stw salvage boat wh b. Cincinnati, Oh., 1870. 176 x 34.5 x 5. Made her trial trip Jan. 1, 1870, owned by Underwriter Wrecking Co., Capt. Thomas F. Eckert, president, and

John A. Townley, secretary. Her crew when new: Capt. R.W. Dugan, with E.A. Burress, mate, and Caleb Green, engineer. She was well known on the Ohio, Mississippi, and Missouri rivers, sent to wrecked steamboats principally for salvage work. By 1881 Capt. Eckert had passed away, also engineer Green and three succeeding engineers who had been on her, John Crawford, W.J. Hambleton, and Thomas Downard. R.W. Dugan was superintendent in 1881. Capt. Al Burris, a diver, was well known during his association with this boat. Still listed, 1886.

T. H. McRoberts

See *THOMAS McROBERTS,* registered name.

5273 T. J. Emory

Stw p wh b. Cincinnati, Oh., 1863. 45 tons. 101.3 x 16 x 3.5. Documented at New Orleans in June 1865 owned by James T. Tucker of that city, Capt. J.M. White, master. Went to Galveston, Tex., in October 1866, where she was rebuilt to measure 119.4 ft. long; 56 tons. Same owner and Capt. W.D. Wetmore, master. Wrecked and sunk in Bayou Lafourche, La., Sept. 12, 1867.

5274 T. J. Pickett

Stw p wh b. Gallipolis, Oh., 1864. 132 tons. Ran Cincinnati-Zanesville, Capt. George Henderson, 1864; also ran Kanawha River-Cincinnati that summer. In November 1864 a party of New York capitalists went up Kanawha River on her, interested in oil properties. She worked for Union Coal & Oil Co., Cannelton, W. Va., taking crude oil in barrels to Maysville, Ky., along with *MARKET BOY,* into 1867. Ran Zanesville-Parkersburg, 1868, Capt. Henderson. Off the lists 1870.

5275 T. J. Robinson

SW ferry wh b. Clinton, Iowa, 1875, originally named *AUGUSTA* (see). 100 x 29 x 5. She was renamed, c. 1903–1905, then operating at Rock Island, Ill. Engines 14½'s- 4 ft. Two boilers, each 42″ by 18 ft. In 1908 she was extensively repaired, and was reported doing a good business. Later renamed *ROCK ISLAND* (see).

5276 T. L. Brown

Stw p wh b. Chamberlain, Tenn., 1913. 139.5 x 21.6 x 3.4. Engines, 14½'s- 3½ ft. Two boilers, each 36″ by 21 ft. Originally owned by Dykes & Covington; had a full cabin and nine staterooms. Often did towing work. In 1920 was in litigation charged with illegally transporting liquor. Renamed *J. LUTHER TROXELL* in 1920. Owned 1925 by Capt. Paul H. Underwood, Chattanooga, Tenn. Same 1926.

5277 T. L. Crawford

Stw p wh b. Warsaw, Mo., 1858. 155 tons. Snagged and lost at Boonville, Mo., Dec. 12, 1860. Another account locates the wreck six miles above Boonville, at Hardeman's Orchard.

5278 T. L. McGill

SW p wh b. New Albany, Ind., 1857. 598 tons. 238 x 36 (46′ floor) x 7. Engines, 24½'s- 7 ft. Four boilers, each 42″ by 26 ft. Ran in the "Railroad Line" St. Louis-New Orleans, Capt. William Conley, with Lee A. Hall, clerk. Burned at St. Louis in a big wharf fire, Oct. 27, 1862.

5279 T. L. McGill

SW p wh b. New Albany, Ind., 1862. The hull of the former *T.L. McGILL* (see) was used, and new superstructure. She was completed at St. Louis, getting engines from the *W.H. RUSSELL,* 28 ⅜″- 7 ft. Four boilers. She came out named *HOPE* but due to legal difficulties the owners were required to restore *T.L. McGILL* as her name. Ran St. Louis-New Orleans, and also made trips up the Missouri. Owned by Capts. Thomas W. Shields and D.H. Silver. Burned near Memphis at Shoo-Fly Landing, Jan. 16, 1871. The *H.M. YEAGER* rendered aid, and the pilot on the *ST. FRANCIS* saw the light in the night sky and turned back to assist. The life loss was set at 40.

5280 T. M. Bagby

According to F.W. Wooldridge a boat of this name, iron hull, was built at Louisville, Ky., 1868, 508.29 tons. She was taken to Mobile in January 1876, and ultimately was dismantled at Dog Island, off Mobile Bay.

5281 T. M. Bayne

Stw p wh b. Brownsville, Pa., and completed at Wheeling, 1890. 120.5 x 24.4 x 3. Built by A.J. Sweeney & Son for Capt. Dode Berry, Williamstown, W. Va. She entered the Steubenville-Wheeling trade mid-November 1890, Capt. A.F. McCoy. In 1892 entered Zanesville-McConnelsville trade, Capt. Newton Price, and was a regular there through 1897. Went back to the Steubenville-Wheeling trade, Capt. George W. Conant. On Jan. 22, 1904, moored at Steubenville, a field of ice pivoted shoreward on the bridge pier, crushing her. Loss happened at 12:20 A.M. The *NATHANIEL* rendered aid.

5282 T. N. Barnsdall

Stw p wh b. Belle Vernon, Pa., and completed at Marietta, Oh., 1890. 130 x 26 x 3.7. Engines 12's- 5 ft. Two boilers, each 42″ by 20 ft. Capt. Dode Berry, Williamstown, W. Va., owned a large share. Ran Marietta-St. Marys, then Marietta-Raven Rock, W. Va. In April 1892 started Marietta-New Matamoras, Capt. William E. Roe and that fall ran Cincinnati-Chilo under charter. Settled into the Marietta-Sistersville trade, and made occasional trips 1895–1904 in the Marietta-Zanesville trade. By 1899 was owned (three-quarters) by H.L. Ritchie, Portland, Oh., and Henry C. Roe, Williamstown. Henry Roe bought her entire, and continued her Marietta-Sistersville. In the fall of 1901 she was owned briefly by L.D. Davis and John M. Norton, both of Ironton, Oh., but Roe bought her back at Christmas-time. He sold her January 1903 to Admiral J. Merrill of Marietta who shortly took as partners W.R.

Grimes and George W. Horne, both of Marietta. She hit a log one-half mile above Waverly, Oh., June 20, 1904, and sank along the Ohio shore, Capt. George S. Beaver, Antiquity, Oh., in command. The Ohio & West Virginia Transportation Co. was organized at Marietta with an Ohio charter, capitalized at $25,000, in October 1904, the principals being Capts. Martin F. Noll, and William E. Roe. Their associates were W.R. Grimes, George W. Horne, and A.D. Barless. They took over the *T.N. BARNSDALL* but within two weeks swapped her for the *LEROY,* selling her to Clarington Packet Co., owned by E.J. Clarke and others. They entered her in the Wheeling-Clarington trade, and changed her name Dec. 31, 1904 to *ROYAL* (see). T.N. Barnsdall was an oilfield operator of Bradford, Pa., attracted to the Sistersville area when oil was struck near there.

5283 T. N. MILLER

Stw p wh b. Enterprise, Ind., 1872. 72 tons. She was a low water boat built by Capt. T.N. Miller who sold her December 1873 to Capt. Thomas E. Hugo. She then entered the Evansville and Wabash River trade, Capt. J.R. Hugo, with T.E. Hugo, clerk. By 1876 she was documented at Memphis as a ferry, and so served at Fort Smith, Ark., and later at Little Rock in January 1878.

5284 T. P. BENTON

SW p wh b. Onalaska, Wis., 1865. 41 tons. 110.3 x 15.3 x 3.2. In 1867 owned jointly by Capt. Horatio Hinkley, her master, and Daniel E. Johnson, St. Louis. Off the lists 1870. She was classed as a freight boat.

5285 T. P. LEATHERS

SW p wh b. Memphis, Tenn., 1852. 435 tons. 230 x 32.8 x 6.7. Enrolled at Memphis Feb. 6, 1852, owned (5/8) by Capt. Charles Pierce who was master, and James Boro. Took fire near Natchez Jan. 10, 1853. The *JAMES ROBB* came to assist and towed her to New Orleans, whereupon Capt. Carroll of the *ROBB* entered claim and obtained salvage on the cargo in amount $18,000. Enrolled at New Orleans Oct. 8, 1853, owned by Capt. D.R. Carroll, who transferred her the same day to Capt. Caleb P. Bennett. Sold August 1855 to Capt. Grier B. Duncan who transferred her next day to Britton Bennett (2/3) and David Bennett. Off the lists 1856.

5286 T. P. LEATHERS

Stw p wh b. Freedom, Pa. (hull and framing), and completed at Wheeling, W. Va., 1885. This was a large cotton carrier in the Vicksburg-New Orleans trade. Crew in 1888: Capt. Bowling S. Leathers, master, with T. Paul Leathers and Frank Leathers, clerks. Quote from a letter written by John M. Sweeney to F. Way, Jr., dated Mar. 14, 1924: "In the early 1880s I began contracting for completed boats, hull, cabin, and machinery. Before that time our contracts covered machinery only. Bill Spear was operating the Freedom Yard in 1884 but he was about all in, and the last job he did was the hull for the last *ABNER O'NEAL* built for Capt. Nate Wintringer to my designs. After this job Spear quit and the Freedom Yard was idle; it was owned by Capt. Sam Brown who wanted me to take it over but as we had the Belle Vernon Yard with Billy McFall on our hands, I built the *MINNIE BAY, COURIER,* and maybe another there. In 1885 I contracted for the *T.P. LEATHERS,* too big to lock out of the Monongahela River and we did not want to jump her over the dams. I arranged with Capt. Sam Brown to let Tom Dunbar take the Freedom Yard (Tom had just returned from Russia) and we built the *T.P. LEATHERS* and *NETTIE QUILL* at Freedom. Dunbar also built the *HUDSON* for Tom Rees and I think she was the last boat built at Freedom." In another letter Mr. Sweeney notes that Capt. T.P. Leathers visited at Freedom and at Wheeling while the *LEATHERS* was being constructed. In early November 1890, about three miles above Natchez, she sank with a large cargo aboard, loaded down past dry seams with 1700 bales of cotton and 8757 sacks of cotton seed.

5287 T. P. LEATHERS

Stw p wh b. Jeffersonville, Ind., by Howard, 1891. 220 x 40 x 6.5. This cotton carrier had red smokestacks, as did all of the *NATCHEZ* side-wheelers, a custom which continued until August 1898 when this boat's stacks were painted black. Capt. T.P. Leathers died while this boat was running, and the command and management fell to Capt. Bowling Leathers and Capt. W.A. Duke. In June 1900 she was snagged at Bougere's Landing, 40 miles above Natchez, and was lost. Crew at the time: pilots T.C. Sachse, Perkins Boardman, and William Penny; steward James Brady; mates James Duke and Mike Cusick. She had a clock in her cabin which had come down from the *NATCHEZ* (5th) which had been removed for safety when that boat left Yazoo City for Fort Pemberton; it had been entrusted to a private family who returned it to Captain Leathers after the war.

5288 T. R. SELMES

Stw ferry wh b. New Albany, Ind., 1857. 161 tons. Operated in the St. Louis area and later in the Memphis area. Rebuilt in 1871, her size 126 tons. Lost June 5, 1877, place and circumstances unknown.

5289 T. S. CONLEY

SW p wh b. Parkersburg, Va., 1859. 215 tons. 142.3 x 30.6 x 5.6. Ran New Orleans-Red River, Capt. R.B. Roberts. In 1861 Capt. J.C. Shute commanded, owned by Phillip O'Neal and Nathan H. Dumphre. During the war operated by the Kouns Line, still New Orleans-Red River. Dismantled in 1866 and the hull was used as a barge owned by Capt. Newell Tilton, New Orleans.

5290 T. T. HILLMAN

Stw p wh b. Paducah, Ky., 1875. 196 tons. Engines, 10½'s-4 ft. Built for Cumberland River and served in connection with the Ewald Rolling Mill located between Eddyville and Canton. (John W. Zenn and F. Way, Jr., visited the site of this mill in 1941, many traces evident, a brick stack standing, etc.) Later operated Cairo-New Madrid and was sunk by ice at Cairo Jan. 28, 1881. Snagged on a bar in Miami Bend, Mo., Missouri River, Aug. 23, 1882, then owned and commanded by Capt. J.A. Stine.

5291 T.W. ROBERTS

SW p wh b. New Albany, Ind., 1860. 288 tons. 158 x 32 x 6.1. Built for Capt. R.B. Roberts who previously had owned the *T.S. CONLEY* (see) and ran New Orleans-Red River. In 1861 was pinch-hitting for *GRAND ERA* in Red River trade, Capt. Ben B. Kouns. She was purposely destroyed at Shreveport in 1863 to prevent her capture by U.S. forces.

5292 TACOMA

Stw p wh b. New Richmond, Oh., 1883. 180.2 x 30 x 5.1. Engines, 16's- 6 ft. Three boilers, each 40″ by 20 ft. This steamboat holds the record, I think, for the long-living and continuous operation as a packet, never having a name-change nor alteration in appearance. She ran 39 years, always based at Cincinnati. The Ohio River Packet Co. built her for the Cincinnati-Chilo trade. Main cog in this company was David Gibson, a Scotsman who ran many boats, and also owned distilleries at New Richmond, Carntown (old Stepstone), and Moscow, Oh. His fastest and most famed boat was the *TACOMA*. Associated with him in this venture was N.C. Vanderbilt. Her first trip was run on Sept. 28, 1883, with William Cliff, pilot; Asa Reed, chief engineer, and David Cheesman, clerk. About 1890 she was acquired by the Tacoma Transportation Co., Martin L. Hissem, president, and W.T. Hissem, secretary. They continued her in the trade until the Cincinnati, Portsmouth, Big Sandy & Pomeroy Packet Co. (White Collar Line), took her over Apr. 14, 1901. She had been rebuilt and rechained at the Cincinnati Marine Ways in 1897. Capt. Gordon C. Greene and associates purchased the up-river properties of White Collar in 1904 at which time ownership of *TACOMA* was divided between Captain Greene (5/16), Capt. William E. Roe (1/4), Capt. Martin F. Noll (1/4), Junius Greenwood and Capt. Jesse P. Hughes. They put her in the Cincinnati-Pomeroy-Charleston trade where she ran the balance of her days. She was given a new hull and boilers in 1908. Her head clerk for years was Dave Scatterday who was on her in 1896 and in 1915 still was her purser. Capt. Jesse P. Hughes commanded for many years and virtually raised his family on her. As matters turned out Captain Hughes was with the Greene Line longer than any one of the Greene family. He went to work Feb. 28, 1896, on the *H.K. BEDFORD* and retired Dec. 31, 1949, rounding out 53 years. The *TACOMA* was lost by fire at Cincinnati Nov. 4, 1922, in the same blaze which originated on the *MORNING STAR* and also consumed the *ISLAND QUEEN* and *CHRIS GREENE* (all see). Her machinery, rebuilt, went to the *CHRIS GREENE* (2nd).

5293 TACONY

SW p wh b. Paducah, Ky., 1864. 293 tons. Engines, 19½'s-4½ ft. Two boilers. She sank at Fort Peck, Mont., in 1870, then owned by the Lexington Railroad & Transportation Co., Capt. D.C. Riter, master.

5294 TAGLIONI

SW p wh b. Brownsville, Pa., 1847. 253 tons. Ran Pittsburgh-St. Louis, Capt. Marshall. She was lost in the steamboat fire at St. Louis on May 17, 1849, when 22 boats were lost.

5295 TAHLEQUAH

SW p wh b. Brownsville, Pa., 1860. 92 tons. Operated by Capt. W.B. Nowland. Burned by the Rebels at Little Rock, Ark., to prevent her capture, Sept. 10, 1863.

5296 TAHLEQUAH

Stw p wh b. Pittsburgh, Pa., 1866. 338 tons. 149 x 31 x 5. Built for Capt. John Woodburn and others. Control was sold October 1868 to Charles A. Beard, Caldwell Parish, La., and Capt. J.W. Blanks became master, operating at New Orleans. There were two shifts of owners and in August 1869 Capt. G.P. Work became owner and ran her New Orleans-Ouachita River with Capt. F.A. Blanks, master. Off the lists in 1874 and her engines went to the *FLORENCE MEYER* (see).

5297 TALISMAN

SW p wh b. Brownsville, Pa., 1846. 173 tons. Came in collision with *TEMPEST* about one-half mile below Cape Girardeau, Mo., early A.M., Nov. 19, 1847. The impact was forward of her boilers and in ten minutes she had gone down. The *TEMPEST* crew rendered aid. Life loss was set at 51 persons, many of them deck passengers.

5298 TALISMAN

Stw p wh b. Cincinnati, Oh., 1866. 354 tons. This was a rebuilding job. The *VOLUNTEER*, built at Monongahela, Pa., 1862 (see) which had served as a U.S. transport during the war, was classed as a new boat after her Cincinnati rebuilding in 1866. In early March 1871 she was at Smithland, Ky., where a high wind blew down her stacks and demolished her roof back to the skylight. After temporary repairs she proceeded to Nashville. A newspaper editor remarked at the time that she was the sole survivor of all the U.S. boats sold at public sale at Mound City and Cairo after the war. She was last enrolled at Nashville Jan. 5, 1872, although she continued to be carried in *Lists of Merchant Vessels* into 1877–1878.

5299 TALLAHATCHIE

SW p wh b. New Albany, Ind., 1847. 163 tons. Off the lists 1853.

5300 TALLAHATCHIE

Stw U.S. transport wh b. Cincinnati, Oh., 1863, originally *CRICKET No. 4* (see). Bought by the U.S. and renamed *TALLAHATCHIE* Dec. 23, 1863. Sold at public sale and redocumented as *COOSA* (see).

5301 TALLAHATCHIE

Stw p wh Vicksburg and Yazoo River packet. She was alongside the *MARY BELL* at Vicksburg on Feb. 22, 1876, when the *BELL* burned. The tug *JOHN BIGLEY* pulled the *TALLAHATCHIE* to safety.

5302 TALLYRAND

SW p wh b. Cincinnati, Oh., 1842. 324 tons. 229 x 32 x 8. Ran Nashville-New Orleans. She arrived at Nashville on one occasion flaunting a large banner boasting 5 days 23 hours port to port. The *NASHVILLE* soon did better. In 1844 Capt. Jacob Hunter was master. Sank and lost at mouth of Red River, La., Dec. 14, 1846.

5303 TALLYRAND

SW p wh b. (?), 1848. 593 tons. Stranded and lost at Bayou Goula, La., Dec. 20, 1850.

5304 TALMA

SW p wh b. Louisville, Ky., 1843. 306 tons. Engines 19's- 8 ft. Four boilers, each 42″ by 28 ft., with two 16″ flues each. Her stacks were 32 ft. above the roof and fixed to lower for the Louisville-Portland Canal bridge. Her paddlewheels were 26 ft. diameter working 11 ft. buckets. Ran Louisville-New Orleans, Capt. E.T. Sturgeon, and was considered a "crack" boat of her day. Sturgeon later said her fastest time New Orleans to Louisville was 5 days 13 hours. Snagged and lost near New Madrid, Mo., March 1848.

5305 TAMAULIPAS NO. 2

Stw p ih b. Pittsburgh, Pa., 1864. 301 tons. Her hull, entirely of iron, was built by Mason and Snowden within 300 yards of where the *VALLEY FORGE* had been built, and was the second iron hull packet built at Pittsburgh. She departed Pittsburgh in mid-November 1864 destined for Brownsville, Tex. Dismantled in 1880. The *TAMAULIPAS No. 1* was built at Wilmington, Del., 1864, also sternwheel, destined also to Brownsville, Tex.

5306 TAMERLANE

SW p wh b. St. Louis, Mo., 1846. 132 tons. Snagged at the foot of Wakendah Prairie, Missouri River, 1848. Official records state she was snagged finally at St. Louis, Nov. 16, 1849.

5307 TAMPA

SW p wh b. West Brownsville, Pa., 1853. 189 tons. First home port was Apalachicola, Fla. Off the lists in 1856.

5308 TAN BARK

A self-propelled freight boat of some description built at Cincinnati, Oh., 1882. 176.7 x 38.5 x 6.6. 379 tons. Still listed 1886, maybe longer.

5309 TARASCON

SW p wh b. Jeffersonville, Ind., by Howard, 1863. 250 x 38 x 6. Engines, 22's- 7½ ft. Built for the Louisville & Henderson Mail Line and left the shipyard Dec. 5, 1863, and went to Evansville to enter her trade. On December 22 she was at Evansville on her way to Tennessee River where, with other boats, she carried Gen. A.J. Smith's army to New Orleans, and from there she went via the Gulf to Lake Pontchartrain about Feb. 25, 1864. The first attack on Mobile occurred on March 26, and a letter sent to "the folks back home" reported the boat safe in Pontchartrain. Mobile surrendered Apr. 14, 1865, after which the *TARASCON* was taken to Mobile and plied the Alabama River, said to be the largest boat ever to ply that stream. Returned to Evansville in the fall of 1865. In 1866 was in the Louisville-Memphis trade, Capt. J.A. Lusk, with J.M. Pendleton, clerk, but soon dropped back to the Louisville-Evansville trade. In 1870 her master was Capt. William Strong, with H.L. Bonta and A. Jennings, clerks. In 1876 Capt. David Penny was master, with C.V. Jennings and W.W. Huston, Jr., clerks. She once sank two miles below Salt River in shallow water, Sept. 12, 1875. Was retired in the fall of 1877 when the *JAMES GUTHRIE* (see) came out and was dismantled at Jeffersonville summer of 1879.

There is a story about the whistle on the *TARASCON* which may be somewhat gilt-trimmed but which has been repeated so many times it demands inclusion here. The sidewheel *EUGENE* came out in the Louisville-Henderson trade in 1861, Capt. D.F. Sayre commanding and Alf M. Davidson as clerk, taking the place of the *GREY EAGLE* which had entered the Louisville-New Orleans trade. Later she also made New Orleans trips and on one of these, while at New Orleans, a whistle was "appropriated" from an Italian freighter, greatly admired by all who had heard it. Fearing diplomatic complications the whistle was taken safely out of ear's reach before it was installed on the *EUGENE*, but installed it was, and the pilots went tooting up the Mississippi until Plum Point was reached, that notorious graveyard for good steamboats. The *EUGENE* hit the wreck of the *ELIZA* and went to her fresh-water Davy Jones. Ten or twelve lives were lost but the Italian whistle was saved. (Date of the calamity: Nov. 14, 1862). It was brought home to Evansville and put on the *HETTIE GILMORE,* named for the daughter of Capt. A.T. Gilmore, a principal in the Louisville & Henderson Mail Line. It so pleased the sensibilities of the management that the whistle was transferred to the new *TARASCON* when she came out in 1863. Nobody suspected that the *TARASCON* would be involved in war and distant places but soon she was off for New Orleans as chronicled herein. The pilot of the *TARASCON* blew a melodious blast at New Orleans which wafted to the ears of a certain Italian freighter's crew. An uproar ensued. Consuls were called in, debate raged, and the Italians wanted their whistle back. By mutual agreement the case was placed in the lap of the French consul who ruled that the *TARASCON* had acquired the property from a wrecked steamboat (*EUGENE*) and an abandoned wreck at that, and therefore her possession was legal. These events, coupled with the amazing geographical wanderings of the *TARASCON,* made of this whistle a valuable property by the time it got back to Evansville in 1865. It was put over on the *JAMES GUTHRIE* when she came out on the track in 1877, thence to the *TELL CITY,* thence to the *NASHVILLE* and *SOUTHLAND,* all of these boats in the Louisville-Evansville trade. The latter was destroyed by fire in 1932 (see) and that whistle—the voice known there for 70 years while children grew up, and their children, and theirs—was lost. The notes of this whistle chorded high and clear in a soprano tone and, to be properly appreciated, had to be cultivated as a taste, like eating oysters. I say no more for fear of offending the best friend I have in the southland, C.W. Stoll, who thought more of that tooter than the Italians did.

5310 TARASCON

Stw p wh b. Jeffersonville, Ind., by Howard, 1895. 191 x 35 x 5.1. Engines, 15½'s- 6 ft. Three boilers, each 38″ by 20 ft. Built for Louisville & Evansville Packet Co. Came out in March 1896, Capt. David L. Penny. Ran as partner with *TELL CITY* in the Louisville-Evansville trade. The company failed in 1910 and was reorganized as the Louisville & Evansville Transportation Co., F.A. Laidley, president, and T.A. Williams, superintendent. By 1913 she was in sad shape, but was docked in 1914 and given practically a new hull. Capt. J. Edgar Williams, Evansville, was her manager. The Valley Navigation Co., Memphis, headed by R.S. Bryan, president of the Wilson-Ward Cotton Co., chartered her for the Memphis-Caruthersville trade in 1917 and she sank and was lost at Cottonwood Point on the evening of Dec. 26, 1917.

5311 TAWAH

SW ferry wh b. Brownsville, Pa., 1859, originally *EBENEZER* (see). Sold to the U.S. May 9, 1863, and renamed *TAWAH.* Sank and burned at Johnsonville, Tenn., on Tennessee River, Nov. 4, 1864.

5312 TEAL

Stw ferry and p wh b. Dubuque, Iowa, 1893. 85 x 19.6 x 4. Operated at Specht's Ferry on the Mississippi just above Dubuque, operated by Capt. John Specht and his brother Harry. Capt. John Specht died September 1904, and she was sold and renamed *POTOSI* (see).

5313 TECHE

SW p wh Built Cincinnati, Oh., 1860 as the *TOM SUGG.* She was taken over by the Confederates and became a "cotton clad" gunboat. Captured by the Union forces Aug. 14, 1863. Sold to Navy by the Illinois Prize Court Sept. 29, 1863 for $7,000; renamed *TENSAS* and converted into Tinclad #39. 91.5 x 22.4 x 3.6. Engines, 11's- 3 ft. Enrolled as the *TECHE* in October 1865, owned by Capt. E.B. Trinidad, New Iberia, La. Last owned by Atakapas Mail Transportation Co., Tristam Tupper, New Orleans, Pres. Wrecked in Bayou Teche in 1868.

5314 TECHE

Stw p wh b. Jeffersonville, Ind., by Howard, 1886. 190 x 38 x 5.5. Cotton packet owned by Bayou Teche Packet Co., Capt. L.T. Belt. In 1893 Capt. Will T. Jones, master, with George W. Belt, clerk. Ran New Orleans-Jeanerette-Franklin-Pattersonville. Was running New Orleans-Bayou Lafourche, Capt. C.J. Blanchard, April 1896. Is reported to have burned.

5315 TECUMSEH

SW p wh b. Cincinnati, Oh., 1852. 418 tons. 177 x 32 x 7. Engines, 24½'s- 8 ft. Four boilers, each 38″ by 30 ft. Ran Cincinnati-New Orleans, Capt. T.F. Logan. Sank in the Louisville-Portland Canal, Nov. 28, 1860, and blocked traffic for about a week; drowned thirteen trotting horses and pacer John C. Heenan. In 1863 owned by S.O. Noyes, New Orleans, and in charge of Capt. S. Brickell. Burned at West Baton Rouge, La., Dec. 1, 1863. There is a model of her in the Ohio River Museum, presented by Richard C. Brasington, Cincinnati; it was built by an engineer who served on the boat.

5316 TELEGRAM

Stw p wh b. Cincinnati, Oh., 1858. 205 tons. 158 x 31 x 4.5. Went to New Orleans owned by Capt. Joseph P. Chandler and others. Soon was taken over by Capt. Henry Fanning Stewart. She ran in place of the *R. W. McRAE* in the New Orleans-Ouachita River trade, Capt. John W. Tobin, part of 1859. Capt. H.F. Stewart also ran her on the Ouachita. Burned at Algiers, La., May 6, 1861.

5317 TELEGRAM

SW p wh b. Brownsville, Pa., 1876. 147.2 x 25 x 4.4. Engines, 17's- 6 ft. Machinery and other equipment from the *JAMES REES* (see). Built for Capt. Steve Thompson in partnership with James Gatts, Charles Booth, Reuben Thomas, and Thad Thomas. Ran Wheeling-Clarington. In 1885 Capt. John K. Booth bought control and continued her in the trade with E.K. Booth, clerk. F.P. Wiley was clerk 1887–1888, and George H. Urpman succeeded him latter 1888 and 1889. Dismantled 1889 and machinery went to the *LIBERTY* (see) built at Harmar, Oh., that year.

5318 TELEGRAPH

SW p wh b. California, Pa., 1856. 157 x 26 x 4.7. 183 tons. Built for the Pittsburgh & Brownsville Packet Co. Ran regularly in that trade, and when Locks #5 and #6 were completed she extended to New Geneva. Made trips to Morgantown, W. Va., during high water in 1858. Capt. I.C. Woodward was first master. In 1860 he was succeeded by Capt. Z.W. Carmack, and Capt. Doyle Bugher commanded 1863–1865. She carried many a needy soldier for free during the war. When news of Lincoln's death was received the boat was draped in black for her midnight arrival at Brownsville. Mrs. Adam Jacobs was aboard, and some person or group fired a cannon from shore, the ball passing through the skylight glass over Mrs. Jacobs stateroom door. The supposition was that bad feeling against the crew, most of them Democrats, had led to the incident. When this boat was retired a tabulation was made from the records of the Monongahala Navigation Co., to disclose she had carried, 1856–1866, a total of 179,309 passengers, and had paid $28,612.39 in tolls at the locks. She was succeeded by the *FAYETTE* (see).

5319 TELEGRAPH

SW p wh b. Cincinnati, Oh., 1864. 427 tons. 250 x 38 x 5.5. Engines, 22's- 8 ft. Four double flue boilers, each 42" by 28 ft. Paddlewheels 21 ft. diameter working 11 ft. buckets. Cincinnati Marine Ways Co. built the hull; Horsley & Ealer, the cabin; and engines by Niles Iron Works. Raised steam for the first time Mar. 15, 1864, and her first trip was transporting U.S. troops Cincinnati to Louisville. Designed for the Cincinnati-Big Sandy trade, Capt. Wash Honshell. When the Cincinnati, Big Sandy & Pomeroy Packet Co. was organized October 1866 she was included. In 1869 Capt. Wash Honshell, master; George A. Knight, clerk. By 1876 she ran Cincinnati-Pomeroy, Capt. Evan Morgan, with James H. Stratton, clerk. Had twin white collars banded around her stacks same as *ST. JAMES* and *OHIO NO. 4* which also ran that trade. Dismantled 1877.

5320 TELEGRAPH

SW p wh b. Cincinnati, Oh., 1877. 287 x 41.2 x 5.1. Engines, 22's- 8 ft. Three boilers, each 47" by 30 ft., five flues each. She was built on a new hull, and the cabin of the former *TELEGRAPH* was lifted over on it, probably using the old engines. Owned by the Cincinnati, Big Sandy & Pomeroy Packet Co. Capt. James Campbell was master; George Damron, chief engineer. Her fastest time Cincinnati to Pomeroy was 22 hours 26 minutes, run on Jan. 1, 1878. It was a regular business trip making all landings en route, with eight ft. on the Cincinnati marks. In 1887 a blacksmith at Augusta, Ky., James Hafer, made a brass cannon for this boat, about 30" long and 2" bore, the carriage having 30" wheels. His son James Hafer, Jr., later made a similar cannon for the *CITY OF LOUISVILLE.* It later was used on the *GORDON C. GREENE* and today is in the Ohio River Museum, Marietta. This *TELEGRAPH* was taken to Harmar, Oh., and dismantled at the Knox Boat Yard in 1891. The hull was used as the wharfboat at Vevay, Ind.

5321 TELEGRAPH

SW p wh b. Harmar, Oh., at Knox Boat Yard, 1891. 292 x 42.4 x 5.5. Engines, 22½'s- 8 ft. Built for the Cincinnati, Big Sandy & Pomeroy Packet Co. using the machinery from the former boat of the name (see above). Construction was supervised by Capt. Edwin F. Maddy. First crew; Capt. William Kirker, master; D.R. Scatterday, 1st clerk; Carl Crawford, 2nd clerk; Ambrose Dennis and Aaron Williamson, pilots; George Damron, chief engineer with Clarence Hughes, 2nd; Henry Kirker, mate; Theo. Buckles, carpenter; Lloyd P. Gee, steward; Gus Simmons, barkeeper. Dave Scatterday registered the first lady passenger on Dec. 9, 1891—she came aboard at Proctorville, Oh., Miss Lucretia Brewer. In April 1892 she made a "fast run" Cincinnati to Syracuse, Oh., getting to Pomeroy in 19 hours 7 minutes, and to Syracuse in 20 hours 17 minutes. George Damron was chief engineer at the time. She made but one landing, Huntington, and didn't put out a line there—let a man hop off. When the *CITY OF MADISON* was wrecked (see) in 1894 her roof bell, originally on *TELEGRAPH NO. 3*, was transferred to the *TELEGRAPH.* She started running Cincinnati-Louisville. On the night of Nov. 22, 1897, upbound above 12-Mile Island, pilots Charles Williams and Charles Dufour changed watches. They weren't speaking to one another for some obscure cause, and Williams relieved Dufour, whereupon Dufour promptly left the pilothouse before Williams had his "night sight." The boat was headed into the rocky cliff on the Indiana shore, right in her marks for the best water, but before Williams could see the situation she had plowed into the rocks and was wrecked. Both had their licenses revoked as the aftermath of this escapade. The roof bell went to the *CITY OF CINCINNATI* (see).

5322 TELEGRAPH NO. 1

SW p wh b. Louisville, Ky., 1848. 313 tons. 215 x 27 x 5.5. Engines, 24's- 8 ft. Five boilers, each 38" by 27 ft., each having two 12" flues. Built for the Ohio Line Co., a Louisville concern which sold stock at $50 par to several hundred Louisville citizens and firms, headed by Capt. Thomas C. Coleman of that city. Two side-wheelers were built, this one and *TELEGRAPH NO. 2* (next listing) for the Pittsburgh-Louisville trade. No. 1 came out Apr. 11, 1848, Capt. James Perry. That fall Capt. Jacob Hezlep was in charge who stayed until fall of 1849 when succeeded by Capt. Isaac Jones. In all she made 34 round trips and lost $30,000. William Miller was her chief engineer. Dismantled 1850 and machinery built by John Curry, Louisville, went to the *GEORGETOWN* (see).

5323 TELEGRAPH NO. 2

SW p wh b. Louisville, Ky., 1848. 230 x 29 x 6. Owned by the Ohio Line Co., and ran in the Pittsburgh-Louisville trade, Capt. Sam Mason. In all she made 26 trips in the trade through 1849 and broke even. In February 1849 she brought U.S. President-elect Zachary Taylor from Cincinnati to Captina Island where she was stopped by an ice jam. Taylor and party walked to Moundsville, and thence by sleigh to Wheeling and Washington. Today there is a West Virginia state road marker on Route 2 marking the Captina Island debarkation spot. When the Wheeling suspension bridge was built in 1849, Capt. Sam Mason installed a device for lowering the smokestacks on this boat, which was adopted on other boats, and called the "Telegraph plan," or "telegraphing the stacks" which employed an A-frame forward of the stacks, and required that they be hinged at the butts where they arrived through the hurricane roof. This boat ran from Cincinnati to Pittsburgh on one trip in November 1848 in 44 hours 47 minutes racing with *BRILLIANT* all the way, winning by 59 minutes, the record until the *BUCKEYE STATE* came up in 1850 (see). The U.S. Mail Line Co., bought her in 1850 and ran her Louisville-St. Louis. She raced with the *HOOSIER STATE* Jan. 25, 1851, and came from Lawrenceburg, Ind., to Cincinnati in 1 hour 40 minutes. Newspapers of the day referred to her as the "long horned thunderbolt of commercial salvation." Thomas H. Benton came up on her to witness the opening of the Wheeling bridge, November 1849, arrived too late, but had a walk over the new span. Burned at New Albany, Ind., July 12, 1855.

5324 TELEGRAPH NO. 3

SW p wh b. Cincinnati, Oh., 1853. The hull dimensions are not available, but in the Howard Steamboat Museum in 1965 was a half-section model of her hull measuring 74½" long and 4½" wide; the deduction is that she measured 298 x 36. Engines, 30½'s- 10 ft. from *PEYTONA* (see). Owned by the U.S. Mail Line Co. Ran Cincinnati-Louisville teamed up with *JACOB STRADER* (see). Ran her trial trip in the Cincinnati harbor Jan. 20, 1853, during which the jackstaff fell on Capt. Moses Anders and hurt him badly. On Apr. 13, 1853, she ran a speed trial Louisville to Cincinnati and came up in 9 hours 51 minutes, later taken down by *ALLEGHENY* and *CITY OF LOUISVILLE*. Capt. Moses McLellan was master on the fast trip; Capt. Byington, clerk; Samuel Hildrith and Frank Bacon, pilots; Mr. Gough, mate. Sam Hildreth afterwards commanded the boat. Served as a transport during the war and was dismantled

5325 TELEPHONE

Stw p wh b. Ironton, Oh., and completed at Portsmouth, Oh., 1878. 150 x 25. The hull was built high on the shore at Ironton by the Newman Lumber Co. Low water delayed launching, so work went ahead building her cabin. She was floated Apr. 20, 1878, and then was towed to Portsmouth for boilers and machinery. The owners were Capt. Edwin F. Maddy and his brothers, Gallipolis, Oh. The first commercial telephone exchange in the world had opened at New Haven, Conn., five weeks before this boat came out, hence the name. The three Maddy brothers were Capt. Edwin F. (1849–1914), Capt. Will (1850–1900), and Capt. Lewis L. (1853–1884). Ran Pittsburgh-Cincinnati the first season. Was sold that fall to the Kanawha Valley Packet Co., running Wheeling-Charleston, then Gallipolis-Charleston, Capt. J.L. Dudding, master, with George S. Dudding, clerk. She had resumed the Wheeling-Charleston trade when, Jan. 2, 1885, she landed at Hockingport, Oh., and ran afoul of a field of floating ice. No damage was suspected, but about a half-mile below there she sank. The ice finished her.

5326 TELEPHONE

Stw p wh b. Knoxville, Tenn., 1894. 93 x 19 x 2.6. Built by Capt. J.E. Newman, Knoxville. In May 1900 Capts. Fred Hornbrook and Sam Williamson bought her, loaded her with a cargo of Lydia Pinkham's Compound, and brought her to the Upper Ohio. They used her as a low water boat for several seasons, then sold her to A.G. Jackson and C.L. Williams, Parkersburg. She was upbound on the Little Kanawha near the mouth of Hughes River at Big Ripple, when she snagged herself and sank. Capt. M.R. Lowther was in charge, this on Dec. 23, 1902, at 10:00 P.M. In December 1904 Capt. Lewis Tanner, Ashland, Ky., bought half interest and ran her into 1905. Rebuilt at Catlettsburg, Ky., in 1906, renamed *EMMA MARIE*, and ran through September 1908, maybe later, a combination packet-towboat.

5327 TELL CITY

Stw p wh b. Jeffersonville, Ind., by Howard, 1889. 191 x 35 x 5.2. Engines, 17's- 7 ft. Three boilers, each 44" by 26 ft. Built for the Louisville & Evansville Mail Line Co. Originally had double stages, changed to a single stage in Nov. 1898. There was a reorganization in November 1902, and owner became Louisville & Evansville Packet Co. Much of her early story is contained in a booklet named "Oldest Pilothouse," sponsored by Sons and Daughters of Pioneer Rivermen, prepared and written by F. Way, Jr., in 1978, with much assist from Bert Fenn, Tell City, Ind. She was a regular in the Louisville-Evansville trade, teamed up after 1895 with the *TARASCON* (see). In 1901 her master was Capt. Fred Zoll. She was rebuilt and widened at Point Pleasant, W. Va., in 1911 to measure 190 x 38 x 5.2. Financial difficulties beset the owners, and there were changes in management (more on this under *TARASCON*) but she only had one sinking, in the Louisville-Portland Canal, September 1898, pumped out by towboat *TRANSIT*. Capt. Fred Hornbrook and others bought her in the spring of 1916 for the Pittsburgh-Charleston trade, teamed up with *R. DUNBAR* (see) in the Ohio & Kanawha River Transportation Co. She replaced the *KANAWHA* which had overturned below Lock #19, Ohio River. Slightly over one year later the *TELL CITY* met a similar fate at the same location. She was downbound, and had landed at Little Hocking, Oh., Apr. 6, 1917—the same day the U.S. declared war on Germany. Pilot Mike Davis backed her down through the opened beartrap in leaving the landing, she rubbed it, and started taking water. She was forced into shore just below, on the Ohio side, and hit with headway sufficient to knock down her stacks. She settled rapidly. Crew at the time: Capt. Charles H. Ellsworth, master-pilot; Mike Davis and Dan Patchell, pilots; Ed Dunaway, Holly Barr, and Jack Spears, clerks; George Knox, chief engineer; George McElhose, 2nd engr.; Charles Justice, mate; Clark DeWolfe, 2nd mate; and Charles McNichols, steward. The pilothouse was saved by Mr. and Mrs. Clarence Bent, who made of it a summerhouse in the yard of their home overlooking the river at Little Hocking, Oh. One of the many visitors who came to see it was muralist Dean Cornwell who had taken rides on the *TELL CITY* in his youth. One of his early artistic attempts was a watercolor of the boat. The Ohio Historical Society obtained title to the old pilothouse and, after the Bents died, moved it to the premises of the Ohio River Museum, Marietta, Oh., in 1976. The Sons and Daughters of Pioneer Rivermen funded and supervised the restoration in 1977, a project in which many S&D members contributed time and materials.

5328 TEMPEST

SW p wh b. St. Louis, Mo., 1846. 210 tons. 175 x 25 x 5.

Two boilers. Ran St. Louis-Galena-Dubuque-Potosi, Capt. John Smith. She brought news of the outbreak of the Mexican War to Galena on May 15, 1846. Came in collision and sank the *TALISMAN* (see) below Cape Girardeau, Mo., Nov. 19, 1847. Ran St. Louis-Alton in 1849, Capt. Owings. Off the lists in 1854.

5329 TEMPEST

Stw p wh b. Brownsville, Pa., 1849. 48 tons. Built by J.W. Samuel and William H. Clark to handle excursionists between Pittsburgh and Greenwood Gardens, located in the Manchester district. These gentlemen operated a coal mine at Fayette City, Pa., called Tremont Mine, and they utilized this steamboat to bring their loaded barges out from the 4th Pool, Monon River. They built the towboat *CLIPPER* in 1853 and sold *TEMPEST* to Francis A. Dohrman and James K. Logan to tow from the Coal Bluff Mine. Off the lists 1859.

5330 TEMPEST

Stw p wh b. Freedom, Pa., 1856. 63 tons. Lost in ice at Cincinnati, Mar. 28, 1864.

5331 TEMPEST

Stw p wh b. Louisville, Ky., 1857. 144 tons. Snagged and lost Oct. 12, 1860, at Mt. Vernon, Ind.

5332 TEMPEST

Stw p wh b. Louisville, Ky., 1862. 161 tons. 162 x 32.8 x 5.8. Engines, 17's- 5½ ft. She went to U.S. service Feb. 10, 1865, and was sold to private hands Dec. 11, 1865. Saw service on the Missouri River operated by Sims, Silver, and Shields, Capt. James L. Bissell, master. Capt. Grant Marsh relates that he was sent to get her off a sand bar, found the crew and passengers drunk, and had quite a time of it. Burned on the Ouachita River Dec. 27, 1869, at Tattoo Landing. The clerk Mr. Sims lost $1,000 of his own cash. Capt. Silver engaged the *HENRY AMES* as a replacement.

5333 TEMPEST

Stw p wh b. Pittsburgh, Pa., 1863. 364 tons. There is evidence that Capt. Dan G. Parr was associated in building a number of packets named *TEMPEST,* all designed for the Louisville and Cumberland River trade, which may account for the construction of a number of those already enumerated. A listing in the *Missouri Historical Review,* July 1927, notes *TEMPEST* snagged at Upper Bonhomme Island, 28 miles above Yankton, S.D., in 1865, possibly this one.

5334 TEMPEST

SW p wh b. Wheeling, W. Va., 1874. 59 tons. Ran Wheeling-New Martinsville, W. Va., owned by the Davis family. M.B. Davis was her clerk, the same gentleman who later became a pilot and was on watch when the *TELL CITY* was lost (see) at Little Hocking, Oh. Capt. Fred Kimpel ran her Wheeling-New Matamoras, Oh., for some while. She was small fry, square head, side-wheels, and stiff shaft. Had a sawmill boiler and belt-operated wheels. She was laid up in the Muskingum above Lock #1 one winter, got caught out on a falling river, and broke in two.

5335 TENNESSEE

SW p wh b. Louisville, Ky., 1846. 391 tons. Operated Nashville-New Orleans, Capt. Yeatman. Dan Howard, of the Howard Ship Yard, relates that her paddlewheels were too small and he was sent south to enlarge them three ft. in diameter. He did the job with help from five of Yeatman's slaves, which entailed taking down the engines and raising the shafts. This was in the summer of 1846, and Dan went out on her as chief engineer that fall. This *TENNESSEE* conveyed U.S. President-elect Zachary Taylor from Vicksburg to Nashville, on his way to his inauguration, February 1849. She broke her rudder below Memphis and was towed to Cairo by the *MOHICAN* on this occasion. The Cairo citizens watched for her far into the night, saw lights and discharged cannon, but the object of their celebration turned out to be the *ELIZA STEWART* and the Presidential boat didn't appear until 3:00 A.M. Zach refused to get out of bed, so three rounds were fired as she left the wharf "to be sure and waken him up." This celebrated steamboat trip commenced at Baton Rouge where Taylor boarded the *PRINCESS* to his plantation, thence to Vicksburg on *SALADIN,* to Nashville on *TENNESSEE,* thence on *DANIEL BOONE* to Louisville, to Frankfort on *SEA GULL,* on *BEN FRANKLIN* to Cincinnati, and on *TELEGRAPH NO. 2* to Captina Island (all see). Off the lists in 1853.

5336 TENNESSEE

Stw p wh b. Elizabeth, Pa., 1849. 57 tons. Sank and lost at Cincinnati Dec. 2, 1849.

5337 TENNESSEE

Stw p wh b. Belle Vernon, Pa., 1853. 69 tons. First home port, Paducah, Ky. Off the lists 1855.

5338 TENNESSEE

Stw p wh b. Brownsville, Pa., 1862, originally named *EXCHANGE* (see). She became Tinclad #38, still called *EXCHANGE,* Apr. 6, 1863, and was redocumented *TENNESSEE* on Sept. 4, 1865. Was low water boat in Evansville-Cairo trade in July 1868, Capt. Ben Howard, with Marion Wright and Bruce Hunter, clerks. Made a trip up the Missouri River spring 1869, Capt. Joe Wheeler, and was snagged at the head of Louisville Bend, near Decatur, Neb., Apr. 25, 1869. Pilot on watch was E.S. Weaver.

5339 TENNESSEE

Stw p wh b. Jeffersonville, Ind., by Howard, 1897. 170 x 32 x 5.5. Engines, 14's- 5 ft. Two boilers. Built for the St. Louis & Tennessee River Packet Co., and entered the Nashville-Evansville trade in opposition to the Ryman Line, Capt. Shep Green. Crew in May 1901: Capt. S. King Hale, master; Dave Street, purser; George and Joe Smith, pilots; Fay Lyon and Tom Latham, engineers. Was in the boat parade St. Louis to Memphis in 1907 when U.S. President

Theodore Roosevelt went down the Mississippi. In July 1907 was caught in a storm at St. Louis, hit a pier of Eads Bridge, and was considerably damaged. She had been sold to Kansas City-Missouri River Navigation Co., who lost her by snagging at Little Blue Bend, Mo., Sept. 11, 1908. Crew at the time of loss: Capt. W.G. Earp, master; Al and Art Thompson, pilots; L.L. Campbell and George Pash, clerks; Walter Bottom and H.C. Johnson, engineers; Joe Leclaire, steward.

5340 TENNESSEE BELLE

SW p wh b. Paducah, Ky., 1855. 248 tons. Burned and lost above Paducah, Apr. 27, 1860.

5341 TENNESSEE BELLE

Stw p wh b. Paducah, Ky., 1923. 176 x 33 x 6. This was a major rebuilding program, converting the *KENTUCKY* (b. Jeffersonville, Ind., 1904, (see). Owned by St. Louis & Tennessee River Packet Co. Sold to Capt. Dick Dicharry summer of 1927 who took her to the lower Mississippi. She was publicized in Thomas Benton's book *An Artist in America*, published by McBride in 1937, having become the sole remaining steam packet on the lower Mississippi. Sank Feb. 3, 1936, between Lake Providence and Vicksburg. Burned at Natchez Island, three miles below Natchez, early November 1942. Capt. Charles G. Barker was master at the time.

5342 TENSAS

SW p wh b. Cincinnati, Oh., 1860. 62 tons. Originally named *TOM SUGG* (see), a Confederate cotton-clad captured by U.S. forces Aug. 14, 1863, and renamed *TENSAS* on Sept. 29, that year in U.S. service. 91.5 x 22.5 x 3.6. Engines, 11's- 3 ft. Navy sold her to E.B. Trinidad on Aug. 17, 1865, and she was renamed *TECHE* on Oct. 13, 1865 (which see).

5343 TENSAS

Stw p wh b. Jeffersonville, Ind., 1875. 333 tons. Went to New Orleans and in 1877 was running New Orleans-Bayou Macon-Tensas trade, Capt. W.W. Cooley, master, with L.V. Cooley, clerk. Same trade in 1885, Capt. L.V. Cooley, master, with Thomas Knee, clerk. She had between her stacks a large circular saw with the number ten cut into it.

5344 TERREBONNE

Stw p wh b. Madisonville, La., 1908. 132 x 21 x 2.3. Engines, 10's- 5 ft. One boiler. Owned by Bradford Transportation Co., who ran her New Orleans-Bayou Teche and in later years New Orleans-Baton Rouge. Sank near Donaldsonville, La., August 1926, losing a large cargo of rice.

5345 TEXANA

SW p wh b. Covington, Ky., 1853. 348 tons. Originally named *FRANKLIN PIERCE,* renamed in February 1855. 179 x 32 x 6.1. Owned by Capt. W.W. Withenburg, Cincinnati, and L.T. Murdock, New Orleans, equal shares. Upon initial arrival in New Orleans they took her on down to Pointe-a-la-Hache and loaded her with emigrants from a ship and started north. Many of them died en route. Then they entered the Yazoo River trade in competition to the regular line, and on the second trip out to Vicksburg cotton caught fire in the hold. The crew got ashore and watched the boat smoulder in midstream as Capt. W.H. Daniel scuttled her. As she filled with water she tipped the cotton off one guard, rolled hard the other way and tipped the cotton off the other guard, and went over on her side. This happened on Apr. 18, 1855. The hull was raised and used as a barge. There was much talk at the time that the blaze was set by an Irishman in the employ of the established line.

5346 TEXARKANA

Stw p wh b. Jeffersonville, Ind., by Howard, 1869. 343 tons. 136 x 35.5 x 6. Built for Capt. Noah Scovell who ran her New Orleans-Shreveport, with G.C. Hamilton, clerk. She sank Aug. 31, 1870, and was recovered. Still in the trade until 1872.

5347 TEXAS

SW p wh b. New Albany, Ind., 1849. 148 tons. 137 x 22.9 x 5. Documented at New Orleans on Nov. 22, 1850, owned by a large group of shareholders including $500 contributions from Red River County, Tex., and Bowie County, Tex. Her master was Capt. Joseph Claiborne of New Orleans. She was badly damaged in a fire at New Orleans on Feb. 15, 1853, and was sold about a month later to Simon B. Allen, Lamar County, Tex., Capt. Henry D. Woodsworth, master. Three months later Capt. Woodsworth became the sole owner. Off the lists 1860.

5348 TEXAS

SW p wh b. Cincinnati, Oh., 1859. 170 tons. 138 x 30 x 4.5. Owned by Capt. Charles W. Stinde, New Orleans, who ran her New Orleans-Red River to Shreveport and above. She survived the war and was still in her trade, same owner, until she was snagged and lost at Barbin's Landing, La., Mar. 8, 1867 with loss of two lives. Capt. G.W. Rea was in command.

5349 TEXAS

Stw p wh b. Jeffersonville, Ind., by Howard, 1869. 135.5 x 35 x 6.2. Built for Capt. Charles W. Stinde, although boat's title was documented as Mary J. Stinde, owner. Ran New Orleans-Shreveport. In 1870 was teamed up with *SOUTHWESTERN* and *D.L. TALLY.* She was taken to Madison, Ind., summer of 1871 and her length was increased 33 feet. Capt. George W. Rea commanded. Handled U.S. Mail and was still in Red River trade April 1878, Capt. Rea commanding with H.C. Boazman, clerk.

5350 TEXAS RANGER

SW p wh b. New Albany, Ind., 1851. 159 tons. 136.5 x 22.3 x 5.5. Capt. William Stockman was master and part owner. Sold to the USQMD in 1853, then transferred Nov. 30, 1858, to William E. Starke, New Orleans. Had several owners and went to Confederate registry 1861.

5351 The New Era

Stw ferry wh b. Clarington, Oh., 1918, originally ferry *TRANSIT* (see), a side-wheeler. Was converted to sternwheel at Clarington, Oh., in 1922, owned by Wellsburg (W. Va.)-Brilliant Bridge & Ferry Co. Sold to Lee Van Tilburg, Steubenville, Oh., and sank and lost at Brilliant, Oh., Jan. 30, 1948.

5352 The New Idea

Stw ferry wh b. Jeffersonville, Ind., by Howard, 1889. 125 x 26 x 4. Engines, 14's- 5 ft. Two boilers, each 40" by 24 ft. Went to New Orleans area. Sometime after 1895 sold to Cairo, Ill., and renamed *KATHERINE* (see).*

5353 The Purchase

Stw p wh b. Pittsburgh, Pa., 1869, originally named *MOUNTAIN BELLE* (see). 140 x 27 x 4.4. Renamed when operating at St. Paul owned by William McCraney and commanded by Capt. Roy Wethern. Condemned and dismantled at Wabasha, Minn., 1917.

5354 The 7 Wonders

Stw ferry wh b. Augusta, Ky., 1917. 64.5 x 20 x 3.5. Operated at Augusta, Ky., owned by Capt. Kline O'Neal. The seven wonders were his seven children. Rivermen had another version, counting them off on fingers: (1)-where the money came from to build the boat; (2)-how it keeps running now he's got it built; (3)-why he built it in the first place, etc.

5355 Thealka

SW batwing p wh b. Paintsville, Ky., 1899. 116 x 19.2 x 3.2. Engines, 6 ¾'s- 1 ft. One boiler, 36" by 11½ ft. Machinery from the *BEULAH BROWN* (see). Built by Capt. Green Meek for Catlettsburg-Big Sandy River trade. Named for the Captain's daughter Alka Meek who married John C.C. Mayo and resided at Paintsville and Ashland, Ky. By some misadventure the lettering artist ran together the two words *THE ALKA* and forevermore the boat was the *THEALKA*. There is a town with a post office in Kentucky named Thealka (Zip 41259) for this boat. Capt. Jesse P. Hughes observed that this batwing "was the last of the species on Big Sandy." Ran 1900 in Big Sandy Navigation Co., along with *H.M. STAFFORD, MAXIE YOST,* and *ARGAND* (all see). Still running 1902.

5356 Thirteenth Era

Stw p wh b. Pittsburgh, Pa., 1870. 150 x 33 x 4.4. Owned by Isaac H. Kouns, New Orleans, and R. Ranshottom of Lawrence County, Oh. Her first master at New Orleans, Capt. C.P. Truslow. Dismantled and machinery went to *DAWN,* b. Madison, Ind., 1875.

5357 35th Parallel

SW p wh b. Cincinnati, Oh., 1859. 419 tons. Ran New Orleans-Arkansas River, Capt. Levi Chapman, through to Fort Smith. At the outbreak of the war converted into a Confederate "cottonclad" and was burned to avoid capture on the Tallahatchie River, Miss., Mar. 13, 1863. Associated with Capt. Chapman in the building of this boat was Capt. Philip Pennywitt, then at an advanced age, originally from the Cincinnati area, who pioneered on the Arkansas and White Rivers in 1828 on the *FACILITY,* and had been on *WAVERLY* to Batesville January 1831.

5358 Thistle

Stw p wh b. Belle Vernon, Pa., 1863. 210 tons. Operated in tramp trades, Pittsburgh-Cincinnati-Louisville-St. Louis by Capt. C.L. Brennan. Snagged and lost at Big Hurricane Island, Ohio River, July 31, 1864. The wreck was noted in the Milnor Roberts Report dated Oct. 31, 1866, and said "to be dangerous."

5359 Thistle

Stw p wh b. La Crosse, Wis., 1889. 150.1 x 28.4 x 4.7. Although regularly a rafter, she operated for the Carnival City Packet Co., in the St. Paul-La Crosse trade in 1894 along with *LIZZIE GARDNER*. In the fall of 1900 she was taken to Higginsport, Oh., for dismantling, and her engines went to the towboat *HERMANN PAEPCKE* being built there at the time.

5360 Thos. B. Florence

U.S. snagboat stw ih b. South St. Louis, Mo., 1875. 96 x 20 x 4. Long operated in the Vicksburg District for Ouachita River service. One stack behind the pilothouse. Was there in 1918. Gone by 1925. In 1915 on Red River.

Thomas Conner

See #5367

5361 Thomas D. Fite

Stw p wh b. Jeffersonville, Ind., by Howard, 1880. 149 x 29 x 4.3. Went to Cumberland River. Later renamed *PHIL ARMOUR* (see).

5362 Thomas E. Tutt

SW p wh b. Cincinnati, Oh., 1855. 351 tons. 200 x 35 x 5.5. Engines, 22's- 7 ft. Four boilers. Ran St. Louis-Brunswick, weekly trips, Capt. P.M. Dozier, 1856. She was in U.S. service Dec. 9, 1864, upbound on the Cumberland River with 6,000 sacks of government oats when captured at Cumberland City, just below Nashville, by the command of C.S.A. General Lyons. They used her as a ferry to transfer Confederate troops across and then burned her. The ferry *BEN SOUTH* suffered the same fate (see).

5363 Thomas H. Allen

Boat of the name in Memphis-White River trade, May 1871.

5364 Thomas H. Benton

Stw ferry wh b. Madison, Ind., 1889, originally named *PEOPLE'S FERRY* (see). Renamed September 1906 when sold to Missouri River Packet Co., Hugh F. Koch, president. Operating at Vidalia, La., in 1918 and burned soon after.

5365 THOMAS H. LARKIN

SW p wh b. St. Louis, Mo., 1855. 1,096 tons. Ran St. Louis-New Orleans, Capt. William B. Miller. One of the largest and most elegant of her day. Burned five miles below Chester, Ill., July 21, 1856, valued at $100,000.

5366 THOMAS J. PATTEN

Stw p wh b. Bellaire, Oh., 1860. 118 tons. Ran Pittsburgh-Wheeling competing with *MINERVA* in November 1862. Reported sold to Capt. Albert Brown, Marietta, Oh., Dec. 24, 1862. Working for the U.S. during the siege of Vicksburg, Capt. Willaim R. Smith. Pittsburgh-Zanesville trade, Capt. Harvey Darlington, 1862–1863. Burned in Walker's Bend below Memphis, Jan. 25, 1864.

5367 THOMAS CONNER

SW ferry wh b. Madison, Ind. 1865. 175 tons. Plied between Portland, Ky., and New Albany, Ind. Capt. Thomas Conner was associated with this ferry operation many years, and was father of Capt. James Wesley (Wes) Conner who was a pilot on the *ROBT. E. LEE* during the race with *NATCHEZ* in 1870. Dismantled 1887. This ferry was 108 x 41 x 4, and was teamed with the *EXCELSIOR* and *BEN SOUTH* (both see). The last ferry built for the service before the bridge was built was the *RUSH* (also see).

5368 THOMAS P. RAY

Stw p wh b. Brownsville, Pa., 1852. 66 tons. Off the lists 1857.

5369 THOMAS JEFFERSON

SW p wh b. Cincinnati, Oh., 1846. 279 tons. Owned by Clifford B. Wayne and others, and ran Cincinnati-New Orleans, Capt. C.B. Sedam. Sank and lost at Waterloo, La., Nov. 8, 1849.

5370 THOMAS McROBERTS

Stw ferry wh b. New Albany, Ind., 1865. 108 tons. Operated at La Crosse, Wis., under the ownership of her namesake, Thomas McRoberts, who had been running the La Crosse ferry since 1856. His first ferry was the *HONEY EYE* (or *HONAEYE*) built at Pittsburgh in 1856 and which was cut down by ice at La Crosse in 1857. He then chartered the *GEORGE GALE* until the *THOMAS McROBERTS* was ready. She was dismantled in 1880 and the machinery was on shore at the La Crescent landing, La Crosse, and the old boat was on the bottom nearby. The *WARSAW* replaced her.

5371 THOMAS PARKER

Stw p wh b. St. Louis, Mo., 1894. 100 x 18.1 x 4.5. Engines, 10's- 6 ft. One boiler, 46" by 20 ft. Owned by R.L. Wescott. For a time she was in the Nashville-Burnside trade on Cumberland River, owned by W.T. Carroll, Alex Kendall and W.W. Parmenter. Towed ties out of Tennessee River, 1902, owned by R.T. Williams and others. Capt. Alex Kendall died on board passing Kuttawa, Ky., that July. She burned below the wharf at Owensboro, Ky., in December 1908. Machinery went to the *GOLDEN GIRL*.

5372 THOMAS PICKLES

Catamaran center-wheel ferry sh b. Jeffersonville, Ind., by Howard, 1892. 125 x 53 x 7. Engines, 17's- 6 ft. Two boilers, each 42" by 22 ft. Owned by Union Ferry Co., New Orleans, then Algiers Public Service Co., and finally by Jackson Ave.-Gretna Ferry, Inc. Handled 50 cars and 250 passengers, and burned fuel oil in her latter days. Lost Sept. 9, 1965, during Hurricane Betsy, approx. 100 miles above the head of the Passes, Mississippi River.

5373 THOMAS POWELL

Rig? p wh b. Covington, Ky., 1865. 109 tons. 101.4 x 20.2 x 3.8. Ran New Orleans-Donaldsonville-Lafourche twice weekly, Capt. Joseph Dalferes. Sold June 1867 to Capt. Joseph A. Ruiz and in December that year to Capt. Theophile Dinvant. Went to Vicksburg in February 1869 owned by Capt. Joshua Wiley and John King. Sold by U.S. marshal at Vicksburg in May 1871 to Miss C.J. Edwards for $700.

5374 THOMAS SCOTT

Stw p wh b. Elizabeth, Pa., 1849. 50 tons. Came out that spring owned in part by James Irwin, Elizabeth, Pa., and Joseph, B.B. and George Vandergrift, Pittsburgh. Ran excursions to Greenwood Gardens (in Manchester) going down in 7 minutes, and 10 minutes return. Her place was taken by *TEMPEST* (see) that July 1849. Was in Pittsburgh-Kittanning trade on Allegheny River until early 1852. Then went to the Steubenville-Wheeling trade. Off the lists 1856.

5375 THOMAS SCOTT

Stw p wh b. Freedom, Pa., 1856. 149 tons. Operated in local trades around Wheeling, and Capt. Michael Davis of Fish Creek, Va., was master. Was making trips up the Wabash River spring of 1863. Wrecked above Warsaw, Ky., July 13, 1863. The wreck was still visible in low water, October 1871 with the wrecked sidewheel *AMERICA* nearby. She ran before the war in the Paducah-Cairo trade for a time.

5376 THOMAS SHERLOCK

SW p wh b. Cincinnati, Oh., 1873. 1,353 tons. 290 x 46 x 8. Engines, 24's- 8 ft. Five boilers, each 38" by 28 ft., two flues each. Machinery from *ALICE DEAN* (2nd). Built for Capt. Henry U. Hart, Henry A. Jones, Thomas Sherlock, James Mack, and Charles G. Pearce. Ran Cincinnati-New Orleans, Capt. Henry U. Hart, with M.L. Virden, clerk. Capt. M.L. Virden later commanded, born in Camden, Del., Feb. 2, 1811. He worked as a boy with Knox, McKee & Co., Wheeling, and went on the river aboard *TROUBADOUR*, Capt. John Staley. He was twice married, to sisters named Dulty of Wheeling whose father once was mayor there. Capt. Henry U. Hart later owned in the *R.R. SPRINGER* (see). James Mack ran the boat yard where she was built. Capt. Charles G. Pearce was identified with the U.S. Mail Line Co., and served as president, having superintended building the *JACOB STRADER*, and was president when the *UNITED STATES* and *AMERICA* collided. He died at Cincinnati in 1880. Thomas Sherlock, Esq., was a Cincinnati attorney, and was associated with the U.S. Mail Line and also in boat-building operations. Capt. Lew Kates was master in 1878. Col. Will S. Hays came aboard at Louisville one day and reported: "Capt. Lew Kate's famed mockingbird Dick is with him on the *THOMAS SHERLOCK* but he has grown old and feeble now and his once cheerful voice, so full of melody, is now reduced to a faint refrain, sad to listen to. Poor old Dick! Age and time have dealt kindly with him but the Terrible Reaper will soon call him to sing no more on earth, but to enter the kingdom of that beautiful bird heaven where his melodies will make his kindred jealous of his musical voice." In 1880 the *SHERLOCK* was bought by Capt. James Nichols who then commanded, and later was in the White Collar Line. She was loaded out at Cincinnati and departed for New Orleans shortly before 7:00 P.M., on Feb. 16, 1891. While rounding to (always a precarious adventure for heavily-laden steamboats because of bridge piers) she collided with a pier of the C. & O. bridge and was wrecked. Crew at the time: Capt. Sterling McIntyre, master; M.M. McIntyre, purser; Pres Ellison and William C. Lepper, Jr., clerks; George Trunnel, pilot; J. Lee and J. Dupee, mates; John Streffer, steward; Will Jones, watchman, and Eugene McClain, chief engineer. An excellent first-hand description of this fatality appears in *Down Memory Lane,* a privately published booklet authored by Capt. Billy Lepper.

5377 THOMAS SHRIVER

SW p wh b. McKeesport, Pa., 1850. 153 tons. When the Youghiogheny River locks and dams were completed she ran briefly McKeesport-West Newton, Capt. Hendrickson. In 1856 was in Marietta-Cincinnati trade. An ice gorge at Cincinnati on Feb. 7, 1857 shoved the *YORKTOWN* into her, squeezing her fatally against the *CAMBRIDGE.* Owned then by Capts. Coulter, Terry and Guthrie.

5378 THOMAS SWANN

SW p wh b. Wheeling, Va., 1853. 651 tons. 300 x 34 x 6.5. Built for the Wheeling-Louisville trade coinciding with the completion of the Baltimore & Ohio Railroad from Baltimore to Wheeling. Launched Friday, Dec. 24, 1852, same day the tracks were joined at Rossby's Rock to complete the railroad at 6:05 P.M. that day. Named for the president of the B&O, and a handsome oil portrait of Thomas Swann, Esq., adorned her cabin, the work of Zanesville artist James Pierce Barton, who did the work in Baltimore in 1853. Made her trial trip to Grave Creek and back to Wheeling on Feb. 18, 1853. By then the new railroad was running, the first train having arrived at Wheeling at 1:55 A.M., Jan. 12, 1853. Grave Creek, Va., was officially renamed Moundsville the day this boat came out. Original crew: Capt. John McLure, Jr., master; J. DeCamp, first clerk; Thomas Campbell, Jr., 2nd clerk; Thomas Witten and Thomas Kinsey, pilots; Dan Dunbar, 1st engineer; Nathan Wintringer, 2nd engineer; John Raipe, steward; Augustus Simmons, 2nd steward; Andrew Johnson, mate, and John Morrison, carpenter. The tableware was marked "Wheeling & Louisville Union Line," the queensware imported from Staffordshire, England. Silverware from Messrs. Filley & Mead, Philadelphia, with the boat's name on each piece. Cutlery from New York and all glassware from T. Sweeney & Son, Wheeling. The cabin was outfitted with walnut chairs having scarlet velvet cushions. Each bed had a damask spread with *THOS. SWANN* woven in. The cabin was white and gold, with six suspended chandeliers. The ladies cabin section of the main cabin was separated by sliding doors. The Wheeling Union Line had a boat scheduled each day from either port, Wheeling and Louisville. Capt. John McLure, Jr., was master until he built *CITY OF WHEELING* (see) in 1853, was succeeded by Capt. Henry Conant until Mar. 30, 1854, then Capt. Nelson Crooks, and lastly Capt. W.B. Boies. Came in collision with *FANNY FERN* at Little Grave Creek Mar. 3, 1854 (see) and the resulting litigation cost the stockholders dearly. When the new Wheeling suspension bridge was demolished in a windstorm May 18, 1854, the *THOMAS SWANN* cleared away the cables, etc., obstructing the channel. Unusual low water and ice conditions hampered her operation, and on Jan. 24, 1854, a rapidly falling river caught her high and dry on shore at Wheeling where she remained four days. Sold at public sale June 12, 1856, to Hugh Nicols, Wheeling, for $15,500, and he resold her next day to the Alton & St. Louis Packet Co. Dismantled 1857.

5379 THOMPSON DEAN

SW p wh b. Cincinnati, Oh., 1868. 1,512 tons. 290 x 55 x 10. Engines, 30's- 10 ft. Seven boilers. Made her trial trip at Cincinnati on Aug. 1, 1868, going down to Sedamsville where she was moored for finishing touches. Capt. James H. Pepper in command. This was the largest carrier on the rivers, owned jointly by Thompson Dean, Capt. Pepper, and Stillwell, Powell & Co. of St. Louis. Capt. Pink Varble took her over the Falls Aug. 10, 1868, at 1:00 P.M., on very low water. Ran St. Louis-New Orleans. A newspaper was published on board said to rival that of the *RICHMOND* (see). She never set a spar, was proverbially lucky in operation, and was said to have made her owners $110,000 from her first trip until she burned. During the *LEE-NATCHEZ* contest in 1870 a huge crowd at Memphis awaiting the *LEE* saw a boat approaching in the night, set off fireworks and cannon, only to discover it was the *THOMPSON DEAN.* Burned at New Orleans Jan. 1, 1871, in a great fire which also claimed the *MAGENTA, GRAND ERA, JULIA A. RUDOLPH,* and *JOHN HOWARD* (all see).

5380 THOMPSON DEAN

SW p wh b. Cincinnati, Oh., 1872. 1,564 tons. 306 x 46 x 9. Engines, 30's- 10 ft. Seven boilers, each 37″ by 30 ft. Machinery from first of the name (see above). Built and operated by Thompson Dean and Capt. James H. Pepper. Ran Cincinnati-New Orleans-St. Louis. When Captain Pepper retired (quite wealthy they say), Capt. William B.

Miller took charge. The boat then was plying Memphis-New Orleans in the winter cotton season. Captain Miller grew up in Austinburg, Oh., near Lake Erie, and after attending Grand River Institute (from which he was expelled for a minor infraction of rules) he set out for the Atlantic Coast via the Beaver River Canal. At Rochester, Pa., he saw the *HIBERNIA NO. 2* approaching to land, changed his mind, and took passage on her to Cincinnati. A river career followed, and he married a daughter of Capt. A.P. Howell, Miss Emily Howell. Some years back Percy K. Smith, Painesville, Oh., grand-nephew of Captain Miller, presented to Sons and Daughters of Pioneer Rivermen some of the Miller keepsakes, one of which was a letter written by Captain Miller to his children. We present it here for the double reason of its timeliness and with a comfortable prediction that it is a classic worthy of high regard anywhere in American literature.

Upward bound, Dec. 6, 1875

My Dear Children:

I am a bad correspondent these days, as I suppose you already know. This is the busiest winter I have ever had. I seem to find no time to write letters except occasionally on my upward trips and then the boat shakes so that it is almost impossible to use a pen. I am reduced to the necessity of a pencil and even then it is difficult business. I wish for your company a great deal this winter. There is much that would interest you in the course of a trip, the chief of which is the change from winter to summer and again from summer to winter which I undergo every trip.

I wear winter underclothing and overcoat in Memphis one week and next in New Orleans I put on my lightest underwear and go in my shirt sleeves for comfort and down there the leaves are green on the trees and the gardens full of roses as they are with you in summer. On my table as I write you tonight are three large bouquets given me at Baton Rouge and Bayou Sara as I came up. They contain the choicest roses and camelias and, although they have been four days in my room they are almost as fresh as when cut and new buds open every day. One of the bouquets contains 26 roses and camelias besides smaller flowers that I don't know the names of.

We leave Memphis always on Wednesday night, every alternate week, and the weather there is usually chilly, although not as cold as with you. We generally start with one or two thousand bales of cotton and fifty or sixty passengers. The first night out we land at Bennets, and Mhoons, and O.K., and Trotters landings, where we usually add three or four hundred bales to our cargo and arrive at Helena (90 miles) at daylight. Here we generally spend three or four hours, and sometimes longer. Last trip I was there all day and took aboard 1,700 bales. Leaving Helena we stop during Thursday and Thursday night at Delta, Friar's Point, Sunflower, Australia, Laconia, Carsons, Waxhaw, White River, Terrene, Floryville, Riverton, Napoleon, Prentiss, Nibletts, Storms, Bolivar, Kentucky, and Chicora, adding 30, 50, or 100 bales of cotton and hundreds of sacks of cottonseed at each place, and passengers are getting on and off at every landing.

The cotton bales, as you know, are about five feet long, two feet thick, and three feet wide, and weigh about 500 pounds each. The seed is in sacks nearly the size of a wheat sack and weighs about 120 pounds per sack.

Friday morning we usually reach Chicot City, and by that time business has commenced in earnest with us. Leaving there we make the crossing of Choctaw Bar, where the *INDIANA* lies sunk, and rounding to at the head of Choctaw Bend we land at Eutaw, Stops, Mound Place, Glencoe, Welcome, and Wilkinsons, the landings being so near together that we back down from one to the other the whole length of the bend about six miles. This is a wealthy bend and the plantations are yet white with unpicked cotton, although the pickers have been three months at work.

The darkies come running from the fields in droves to see "de big *DEAN*" and our brass band has an appreciative audience. In this bend we add several hundred bales and sacks and then go on down the river stopping at Arkansas City, Port Anderson, Greenwood, Utopia, Gaines Landing, Point Comfort, Shady Side, Lewellyn, Linwood, Luna, Point Chicot, Argyle, and Greenville adding freight and passengers everywhere. By this time it is Saturday night and we begin to notice that we are entering a different country and climate.

From Memphis to White River is an almost unbroken wilderness except at the little landings I have mentioned, but the past 24 hours we have been in a better country and the weather is growing warmer. Leaving Greenville on Saturday night we are nearly loaded but we still take on board a few hundred bales and sacks from those who ship by us regularly at Leland, Sunnyside, Refuge, Eggs Point, Auburn, Longwood, Bernards, Leota, Maryland, Carolina, Pilchers Point, Duncans, Skipworths, Wilson Point, Homochitta, Ben Lomond, and Lake Providence.

By this time it is Sunday morning and we are looked for by every darky and colored child along the shore for the next 100 miles. Sunday is their holiday, the day of their best clothes, and our band plays for them as we take on a few thousand sacks at Tallula, Wilton, Melbourne, Goodrich, Belle, Duvall, Chotard, Henderson, Villa Vista, Ditchley, Omega, and Millikin's Bend. The antics of these darkies—old, middle aged and young—as they cut up on a Sunday under the influence of a brass band is more than I can hope to convey even a faint idea of; a circus wouldn't hold a candle to it.

We are now loaded, 5,000 bales and 10,000 sacks, and the cotton is twelve tiers high on our guards. If our passengers get a peep of daylight they have to go on the hurricane deck or in the pilothouse. Our guards are dragging the water and our mates and our 100 men on deck are worn out with four days constant work day and night. We are now at Vicksburg, 400 miles from Memphis and halfway to New Orleans. We take on 2,000 bushels of coal here and swing out into the stream at 10 P.M. and stretch off to Natchez (107 miles) without a landing. We are there at daylight on Monday morning, and the flowers begin to come on board, sent by the friendly hands of those who are connected with us in a business way.

After this we are in a different country and probably stop only at Bayou Sara, and Baton Rouge. The cotton plantations have disappeared and far as we can see is sugar cane, looking very much as cornfields do in summer with you. The steam from the sugar mills is seen in all directions. Liveoak and orange, and china trees dot the landscape, and there are elegant mansions along the "coast" so close to one another as to make an almost continuous village, and over all the fleecy clouds and the bright sunshine of a continuous summer.

Sometimes during Tuesday afternoon the church steeples of New Orleans come into view and we are over an hour making the circuit of the crescent on which the city is built. We pass Carrollton Gardens and the coal fleets and make our way for miles among the shipping, steamers, and ships from all parts of the world. About 4 P.M. we move into our dock at the foot of Canal Street where a thousand or two of Negroes, French, Italian, Mexicans, etc., speaking almost every language under the sun, await our arrival. After the last line is secure I leave the deck with a feeling of relief that another trip is ended.

New Orleans is a queer old city, unlike any other in this country; it has a foreign look throughout, and the mansions and the customs of its people differ from those of the North. I suppose the climate does it; we are more influenced by our climatic surroundings than we realize sometimes. Here we put out our cargo and receive on board hundreds of hogsheads and barrels of sugar and molasses, boxes and barrels of oranges and cocoanuts, bunches of bananas, etc., and on Thursday evening we drop out into the stream and commence our upward journey.

Going up we make the same landings we made coming down but our stops are shorter, merely putting off small lots of plantation supplies that were ordered as we went down. Our brass band plays at the principal points during the day and in the evenings our very excellent string band amuses the passengers in the cabin and our old French darky quartette sings "Silver Threads Among the Gold" in a way that always brings down the house. So we go, and amid it all, I have little time for play, or letter writing, or anything else but attending to the thousand demands upon my time that are necessary to keep the machine moving.

Tuesday morning we reach Memphis and then begin precisely the same programme over again. I write you tonight about 100 miles below Memphis and the weather is growing rapidly cold and flurries of snow are in the air. I suppose it is winter with you tonight. Write me oftener, can't you? I don't get many letters from you, and the few that I do get indicate that you are both in need of a little practice in that line, and, do you know, I find misspelled words in them. So you must brush up a little, both of you, and write me oftener. My best love to you all. Affectionately, Papa.

Capt. W.B. Miller left the *THOMPSON DEAN* to build and command the *GUIDING STAR* (see) in 1878. Command then fell to Capt. Dan Moore with Frank Stein as clerk, this team having just lost the *ROBERT MITCHELL* by sinking. In 1882 she was towed to Freedom, Pa. by the *TOM REES NO. 2* and the cabin lifted over to a new hull, and so emerged the side-wheel *WILL S. HAYS* (see).

5381 THREE BROTHERS

Prop p wh b. ?, date ? In the Gallipolis-Syracuse trade, replacing the *HUMMING BIRD* which had just been sold. She was new, owned by Brown Bros.

5382 THREE BROTHERS

Stw p wh b. South Carrollton, Ky., 1895. 100 x 20 x 4. Owned and operated by three Wolcott brothers; James F., George A., and C. E., all of South Carrollton. They ran her as a packet handling wholesale groceries for the Bement-Sietz Grocery Co., Evansville, Ind. Ran opposition to the regular Green River line and were quite successful. The boat started out as a floating sawmill before going into this grocery venture. Wolcott Bros. sold her in February 1903 to the White Oak Handle Factory.

5383 THREE STATES

Stw ferry wh b. Jeffersonville, Ind., by Howard, 1873. 150 tons. 148 x 35 x 4. Operated at Cairo, Ill. Still there in 1896, maybe later.

5384 THREE STATES

Stw ferry wh b. Jeffersonville, Ind., by Howard, 1904. 150 x 32 x 4.8. Burned at Cairo, Ill., May 30, 1913.

5385 THREE STATES

Stw ferry wh b. Jeffersonville, Ind., by Howard, 1914. 118 x 26 x 4. Owned by Cairo City Ferry Co. Still there 1929, maybe later.

5386 TIBER

SW p wh b. Marietta, Oh., 1851. 184 tons. 155 x 25 x 5. Built by William Knox for Capt. Wash Kerr and others. Ran Pittsburgh-St. Louis and elsewhere. Went to the Arkansas River owned largely by Henry Roberts, Desha County, Ark. Enrolled at New Orleans, March 1857, at which time Henry Roberts had died, and his seven-eighths share was administered by James T. Roberts. Capt. George Wairing was in command. Off the lists 1858.

5387 TIDAL WAVE

Stw p wh b. Brownsville, Pa., 1870. 160 x 36 x 5. Engines, 14's- 6 ft. Three boilers, each 38" by 22 ft. Had a 60-foot texas. First owners were John Kouns, W. T. Scovell, W.C. Newton, H.H. Bailey, and James Newton, the latter three of Gallipolis, Oh. Originally ran New Orleans-Red River, Capt. W.T. Scovell. Diamond Jo Reynolds bought her

1872 and took her to the Upper Mississippi. Sold to the Davidson Line in 1877.

5388 TIDAL WAVE

Stw p wh b. La Crosse, Wis., 1878. 300 x 45 x 6.5. Work was done at the Keokuk Northern Line yard. Renamed *GRAND PACIFIC* (see) in October 1878.

5389 TIDIOUTE

Stw p wh b. Tidioute, Pa. (hull), and completed at Pittsburgh, 1865. 63 tons. Owned by Capt. Amos Dingley, Warren County, Pa. Had engines brought from Erie, Pa. Very light draft. In June 1866 the *IDA REES* was stopped by low water 30 miles below Oil City and the *TIDIOUTE* took her freight and passengers and delivered them. Sold in 1867 to the U.S. Coast Survey who renamed her *MAJOR SAUNDERS* (see).

5390 TIGER

Prop p wh b. Sauk City, Wis., 1849. 83 tons. Machinery from *OTTER*. Capt. Maxwell ran her to St. Paul, 1850, and then in the Minnesota River. Very slow. Off the lists in 1852.

5391 TIGER

SW p wh b. Cincinnati, Oh., 1858. 333 tons. Went to Mobile, Ala., Capt. M. Cook. Was returned to New Orleans and ran up Red River Snagged and lost at Alexandria, La., Mar. 2, 1860.

5392 TIGER

Rig? freight boat wh b. Sioux City, Iowa, 1876. 120 x 25 x 5. Documented at Memphis in 1886, maybe later. 94.65 tons.

5393 TIGRESS

SW p wh b. Cincinnati, Oh., 1858. 321 tons. 178 x 32 x 6. Built for Capt. Alfred B. Hopkins, Marion County, Va. (now W. Va.), who commanded, and William Hopkins, same place, and Jonathan Aumiller, Meigs County, Oh. Engines, 18's- 6½ ft. Three boilers. Ran New Orleans-Ouachita River in cotton season, and tramped north in summer. Took survivors from the wrecked *EUGENE* (see) at Osceola, Ark., November 1862. She was Grant's dispatch boat between the Cherry mansion, Savannah, Tenn., and Pittsburg Landing (seven miles) during the trouble on the Tennessee. On the night of Apr. 22, 1863, a number of U.S. transports ran the Vicksburg batteries. The *TIGRESS* was in the lead, and following her were *ANGLO-SAXON*, *J. W. CHEESMAN*, *EMPIRE CITY*, *HORIZON*, and *MODERATOR*. The Rebel batteries were opened up on them. A barge had been lashed to the port side of *TIGRESS* to protect her, but it tended to pull her to port and hence was cut loose, exposing her to the punishment. She was riddled. Just as she passed the lower battery she got a shot in the stern that opened a four foot hole in the hull. She was beached on the Louisiana side, and was lost. The *J. W. CHEESMAN* stopped in and took off the crew, and not a man was lost. The other transports got by safely. Capt. George W. Graham of the Graham, Halliday & Co., wharfboat, Cairo, stopped at the wreck soon after this event and procured the boat's flagpole and flag. As late as 1953 this flagpole was in the park at Cairo where Walnut Street and Holbrook Avenue converge.

5394 TILDA-CLARA

Stw ferry wh b. New Haven, Mo., in 1880s. Operated by four horses on treadmills, and had pilothouse control—a brake to slow or stop the steeds. Owned by Capt. Frank L. Blaske and Henry Strutman, and named for the eldest daughters of the two partners; Clara Blaske and Tilda Strutman.

5395 TILLIE

Stw p wh b. Harmar, Oh., 1881, originally named *M.G. KNOX* (see). Renamed 1885 and ran daylight trade on the Monongahela, Elizabeth-McKeesport. Then was used in local towing on Monon River. Turned over in a windstorm at foot of Page Street, North Side, Pittsburgh, and lost, Aug. 18, 1895.

5396 TIME

SW p wh b. Elizabeth, Pa., 1860. 263 tons. First home port, Apalachicola, Fla. Burned at Duck Creek, Tenn., Feb. 9, 1862.

5397 TIME AND TIDE

SW p wh b. Louisville, Ky., 1847. 161 tons. Ran St. Louis-Galena-St. Peters, Capt. E.W. Gould. Ran St. Louis-Naples in 1848 connecting with a new railroad, owned by Capt. E.W. Gould and C.S. Rodgers. Stranded and lost at St. Louis, Mar. 21, 1853.

5398 TIME AND TIDE

Stw p wh b. Freedom, Pa., 1853. 130 tons. 128 x 26.7 x 4.1. Owned in part by Capt. E.W. Gould, St. Louis, along with other St. Louis stockholders. Replaced former boat of the name. In 1855-1856 was at St. Paul, Capt. Lewis Robert. In Minnesota River, same master, 1857-1858. Capt. Robert Nelson, same trade, 1859. Went to New Orleans November 1861, owned by Mary Hiern of that city. Sold December 1861 to owners in Terrebonne and Jefferson Parishes, Capt. James Taylor. Rebuilt August 1862, now 143.5 x 27 x 4.8, owned by William Taylor, New Orleans. In December 1862 sold to Isaac Russell, New York City. Burned at New Orleans, May 28, 1864.

5399 TIMMIE BAKER

Stw p wh b. Jeffersonville, Ind., by Howard, 1875. 78 tons. 100 x 21 x 3. In 1877 on the Ouachita River, going up Bayou Bartholomew, connecting with *JOHN H. HANNA*. Inspected at Refuge, La., 1881. Still listed 1882, maybe longer.

5400 TIMOLEON

Stw p, wh b. Griggsville, Ill., 1847. 132 tons. Operated on the Illinois River, built by Capt. Samuel Rider, native of Cape Cod, Mass. Off the lists 1851.

5401 TIMOUR

SW p wh b. St. Louis, Mo., 1849. 232 tons. Made trips up Missouri River, Capt. Miller. Badly damaged in the great steamboat fire at St. Louis, May 17, 1849. Rebuilt at St. Louis in 1851, and then had engines 19's- 7 ft., and three boilers. Collided with and wrecked the *FLORA* (see) at Tunica, Miss., January 1852. She ran aground at Smith's Bar on the Missouri River and was out high-and-dry all that summer. Exploded boilers at a wood yard three miles below Jefferson City, Mo., Aug. 20, 1854 killing nineteen persons including the master, pilot, and clerk. The office safe landed atop of the bluff where many of the passengers were ashore picking wild flowers. Owned at the time by Capt. Edmund F. Dix, Charles F. Eckler, and others. The wreck was exposed in 1927 during low water.

5402 TINSIE MOORE

Stw p wh b. Brownsville, Pa., 1890. 165.6 x 35 x 5. Completed at Wheeling where she got cabin and machinery. Went to the Alabama River. Brought 1,804 bales to Mobile one trip in October 1895.

5403 TIOGA

SW p wh b. Wheeling, Va., 1840. 170 tons. Ran Pittsburgh-Cincinnati, Capt. H. Mason. In 1841 made a Missouri River trip, Capt. David Blashford, to site of Kansas City, and took up a party of Wyandotte Indians. Capt. C.W. Batchelor, Pittsburgh, made the trip and recalled a white girl with the Indians who so greatly attracted his attention that he considered leaving the boat at Kansas City and marrying her, but didn't. Was at Pittsburgh the day of the Big Fire, April 1845, and took first news of the blaze to Wheeling. Capt. L.T. Belt started his boating career on *TIOGA* and recalled it when he was associated with the "big" *TECHE* (see) at New Orleans in 1886. Dismantled 1849.

5404 TIPPAH

SW p wh b. Memphis, Tenn., 1851. 107 tons. 1103 x 24.1 x 4.8. Owned by Capt. Hudson Butler and others of Lafayette County, Miss., and ran to New Orleans from Tallahatchie River. Burned, downbound, at Pt. Pleasant, La., about 25 miles above Vicksburg, Jan. 13, 1852. The second engineer was drowned.

5405 TISHOMINGO

SW p wh b. New Albany, Ind., 1852. 188 tons. Named for the Indian prince of the Choctaw tribe featured in the novel *Tap Roots* by author James Street, Dial Press, N.Y., 1942. Ran Louisville-Memphis, and also Louisville-Henderson. Went to the Upper Mississippi and ran opposition to Minnesota Packet Co., to St. Paul but was sold for debt at Galena winter of 1856. St. Louis-St. Paul, 1857. Off the lists 1860.

5406 TITANIA

Stw pl wh b. Pittsburgh, Pa., 1856. 14 tons. She was bought by Maj. John D. Adams to handle U.S. Mail on White River, Ark. Was said to have towed the first coal down the Arkansas, from a mine at Short Mountain Creek, 75 miles below Van Buren to Little Rock. Exploded and lost Oct. 13, 1858, with loss of one life at Crystal Hill Crossing above Little Rock.

5407 TOBACCO PLANT

SW p wh b. Pittsburgh, Pa., 1843. 207 tons. Hull was built at the Samuel Walker yard, Elizabeth, Pa. Ran Cairo-St. Louis. She was in Pittsburgh in March 1848 loading for St. Louis and took with her 6,000 bushels of coal (on barges no doubt) for a St. Louis gas works. Lost by stranding at Chester, Ill., Mar. 7, 1853.

5408 TOBE HURT

Rig? p wh b. Evansville, Ind., c. 1870. Capt. John H. Maratta took her to the Sabine River in fall of 1871. She was reported burned at Orange, Tex., on Apr. 24, 1873, with boat and cargo a total loss. All well and good for a final disposition save that we have seen a freight bill dated July 7, 1874, when she was running Evansville-Cumberland River, Capt. W.H. Thompson, master, with John W. Enders, clerk. More research indicated.

5409 TOLEDO

SW ferry wh b. Keokuk, Iowa, 1865. 69 tons. 104 x 25 x 4. Owned 1866 by John Van Dyke, A. Hine, and Capt. R.N. Martin who commanded. Operated at Keokuk. Still there spring 1868.

5410 TOLULU

Rig? ferry wh b. Andalusia, Ill., 1868. 17 tons. Operated Andalusia-Buffalo, Iowa. Was inspected at Andalusia Oct. 8, 1881.

5411 TOM C. POWELL

Stw p wh b. Paducah, Ky., 1915. 137 x 28 x 3.7. Built for St. Louis & Tennessee River Packet Co., to replace *CITY OF FLORENCE* (see) in Danville-Lamb's Ferry trade. Was chartered on various occasions to run Louisville-Stephensport. She had several sinkings, one of them coming up over the pass at Dam 44 when a wicket speared her; this on a 4th of July with many passengers and a big freight trip. Pilot on watch was Jesse Singleton. Another time she hit something below Smithland, Ky., Capt. Fred McCandless had the towboat *MARCIA RICHARDSON* tied up at Hamlettsburg, Ill., on Jan. 31, 1924, when he got word that the *POWELL* was sunk at Brick House Light, about five miles below. He got steam and when he got there he found eighteen persons marooned in the *POWELL*'s pilothouse, about all that showed above water. After getting them off, he got two more at Catfish Point and three others at Kinkaid Ldg. Light. Heavy ice was running and had cut into her hull. Five lives were lost.

5412 TOM BRIERLY

SW ferry wh b. Elizabeth, Pa., 1856. Apparently operated on the Missouri River. Lost there in 1868.

5413 TOM BROWN

Stw p wh b. Louisville, Ky., 1848. 47 tons. Lost by stranding at Bolivar Point, Tex., June 25, 1851.

5414 TOM CORWIN

SW p wh b. Elizabethtown, Pa., 1846. 194 tons. Built for Cincinnati-New Orleans trade, owned in part by Clifford B. Wayne, with Capt. James Bugher, master. Snagged and lost at Plum Point, Tenn., on the Mississippi, Oct. 9, 1846.

5415 TOM GREENE

Stw p sh b. Pt. Pleasant, W. Va., by Marietta Mfg. Co., 1923. 200 x 38 x 6. Engines, 22's- 7 ft. Four boilers. Owned by Greene Line Steamers, Cincinnati. Built for Cincinnati-Huntington trade, Capt. Gordon C. Greene. After his death in 1927 his son Capt. Tom R. Greene (for whom the boat was named) took command and ran her Cincinnati-Pomeroy-Charleston with *CHRIS GREENE* (see) as partner. Won two celebrated races with *BETSY ANN* at Cincinnati in 1929 and 1930. Docked at Madison, Ind., in November 1930. Entered Cincinnati-Louisville trade in May 1931 and continued there until the trade was discontinued by Greene Line in February 1947. Her passenger cabin was removed under way October 1936 to make space for carrying new automobiles. Taken to Dravo Marine Ways, Neville Island, Pa., in March 1939 for extensive hull work, and Jesse P. Hughes and F. Way piloted her up in 51 hours, Cincinnati to the Ways. Sold to Commercial Barge Line, Evansville, Ind., Nov. 1, 1950, who had plans to convert her into a triple-deck auto carrier but never did. She was bought by Walker Boat Yard, Paducah, Ky., and made into a landing boat with offices.

5416 TOM HACKNEY

Stw p wh b. Catlettsburg, Ky., 1871. She was built for the Big Sandy River trade, Capt. O.C. Bowles. Often ran short trades on the Ohio and Kanawha rivers. The Point Pleasant, W. Va., banker Capt. C.C. Bowyer, used to tell that the only watch he ever stood was on this steamboat downbound on Kanawha River. The head clerk handed Bowyer the key to the cash drawer and hopped off saying "You've got 'er," and Bowyer took care of the balance of the trip. Capt. B.L. Miles had her in 1876 and was running Gallipolis-Millersport with C.T. Latham, pilot, and Clark Coffman, engineer. Sold to Capt. Price, Catlettsburg, March 1878 for the Big Sandy.

5417 TOM JASPER

SW p wh b. Madison, Ind., 1867. 677 tons. 265 x 41 x 6.5. She had seven small boilers taken from the *ECLIPSE of 1852* (see). They proved insufficient to make steam for her 27" cylinders and as consequence she was the slowest of the large Upper Mississippi packets. Built for the Quincy & St. Paul Packet Co. Once ran St Louis-Keokuk but didn't make it. Finally sold to the Davidson Line, La Crosse. In April 1875 was loaded with iron ore at St. Louis and delivered it to Wheeling, W. Va. A new and longer hull was built for her in 1876, and she emerged renamed *CENTENNIAL* (see).

5418 TOM KIRKMAN

SW p wh b. Louisville, Ky., 1846. 120 tons. Off the lists in 1851.

5419 TOM METCALF

SW p wh b. Louisville, Ky., 1844. 131 tons. Built for the Louisville-Frankfort trade, along with *LITTLE MAIL* and *BOB LETCHER*, owned by Lexington & Louisville Transportation Line, operated by William R. McKee and Philip Swigert. Capt. John A. Holton was master 1845. Sank and lost at Aurora, Ind., Feb. 23, 1847, with loss of two lives.

5420 TOM MORGAN

Stw p wh b. Hobbs Mills on Missouri River, 1866. 97 tons. Engines, 8"- 16". One boiler. Owned by Morgan, Baker and Hall. Sank near Leavenworth, Kansas, Feb. 15, 1866, Capt. William Gould, pilot. Exploded her boiler at head of Scrubgrass Bend, seventeen miles above mouth of White River, Nov. 10, 1877. One death was reported. Another account states she was built at Rocheport, Mo., and measured 106 x 18 x 3.5.

5421 TOM PARKER

Rig? p wh b. Madison, Ind., 1875. 84 tons. Ran New Orleans-Boeuf and Black rivers, Capt. L.P. Delanhoussaya, 1877. At other times ran local on Boeuf River connecting with the *JOHN H. HANNA*. Transferred to Galveston, Tex., area and was there in 1882.

5422 TOM RODGERS

Stw ferry wh b. Grand River, Mo., c.1870. 67 tons. One engine, 12"- 3 ft. One boiler. Owned 1874 by T.A. Kennedy. Burned laid up for the night at Arrow Rock, Mo., on the Missouri River, May 5, 1887, owned by J.M. Green and others.

5423 TOM ROSS

Prop yacht wh b. Buffalo, N.Y., 1878. 10 tons. Owned by Capt. T.W. Disken and Capt. T.J. Meek, their first joint venture. Later they built the towboat *REBA REEVES*. Listed at Cincinnati, Oh., 1882, maybe later.

5424 TOM SPURLOCK

SW batwing p wh b. Ashland, Ky., 1883. 114 x 18.6 x 3. Ran Catlettsburg-Big Sandy River. Still listed 1886, maybe later.

5425 TOM STALLINGS

Stw snagboat sh b. Charleston, W. Va., 1929. 127 x 30 x 4.1. Engines, 10's- 4'2", non-condensing. Two boilers. Built at the Ward Engineering Co., plant. Owned by U.S. Engineers, Memphis, Tenn. Sold at public sale, December 1952 to Patton-Tully Transportation Co., Memphis.

5426 TOM STEVENS

Stw p wh b. St. Louis, Mo., 1866. 170 tons. Noted in river lore for her excursion from Fort Benton, Mont., to Great Falls, Mont., on the Missouri River. Capt. John H. Burk was master, and the pilots were Frank A. Murray and Thomas H. Bigger. Among the guests were Capt. H.H. Symmes, I.G. Baker, Sam DeBow, Lieut. Townsend, Major Wright and a Mr. Roosevelt who was associated with

Wells, Fargo & Co. Arrival was made July 15, 1868. Actually she ascended to the foot of the first falls, about twelve river miles below and five miles by land. The point of arrival is marked on a rock in which pilot Murray cut his name, still visible, called "Murray's Rock." The place was called "Burk's Return" to honor the captain. The boat was 134 x 28 x 3.5. Engines, 12's- 4 ft. Two boilers, each 36" by 18 ft. Prior attempts had been made: *PETER BALEN* on June 16, 1866, had been up to the mouth of Belt River, said to be thirty miles, and in 1867 the *GALLATIN* achieved High Wood Creek, said to be 45 miles. On another occasion the *TOM STEVENS* went up the Osage River, the city of Fort Scott, Kans., having offered $1,000 to any captain who could get his boat there. The timber was so thick she didn't quite make it, but was said to have been in sight of the town. Was sunk by ice in Osage Chute at the mouth of Osage River on Feb. 5, 1873, raised. In winter months she was loaded out at St. Louis for White River of Arkansas. She was dismantled in 1878 and the hull was used as a barge.

5427 TOM SUGG

SW p wh b. Cincinnati, Oh., 1860. 62 tons. Captured as a Confederate "cottonclad" Aug. 14, 1863, and entered U.S. service as *TENSAS* one month later. Redocumented *TECHE* Oct. 13, 1865.

5428 TOUNALEUKA

SW p wh b. Elizabeth, Pa., 1846. 169 tons. Noted in newspapers as stranded at Beaver Shoals, Ohio River, summer 1846 due to low water. Off the lists 1848.

5429 TOURIST

Stw ferry wh b. Harmar, Oh. at Knox Yard, 1889, originally *ELIZA H.,* then *ELOISE,* then *WENONA,* then *PETERSON-MILLER BOX CO.* This takes her to 1925, and after that she was renamed *TOURIST,* operated as a ferry at Cairo, Ill., owned by H. Weber. By 1932 her guards had been removed and she was a towboat.

5430 TRADE PALACE

Prop ferry and trade boat wh b. Jeffersonville, Ind., 1868 by Howard. 295 tons. 154 x 29.5 x 5. Originally owned by Jeremiah Wilson of New Orleans, Capt. B.J. Butler, master. Had a store on deck. Sold November 1869 to Capt. John H. Bright, New Orleans. One month later sold to C.W. Norton, Montgomery, Ala., and went to Mobile. Was returned to New Orleans 1871 and operated as a stock transfer boat and ferry. Still functioning December 1878.

5431 TRADER

SW p wh b. Louisville, Ky., 1851. 40 tons. When this smallfry appeared in Red River, La., in 1855 a newspaper remarked "she can carry more freight on less water than any." Off the lists 1855.

5432 TRADER

SW p wh b. Evansville, Ind., 1858. 40 tons. Off the lists 1860.

5433 TRADER

Stw p wh b. Pocahontas, Ark., 1870. 81 x 21. Locomotive boiler. Owned by Fred Inman.

5434 TRADER

Stw p wh b. Pittsburgh, Pa., 1870. Engines, 9"- 3 ft. Two boilers, each 34" by 14 ft. Owned by Capt. John S. Reno and others. Ran Pittsburgh-Wheeling in August and September of 1870 in place of the *W.F. CURTIS* during low water. Documented at Memphis 1876. A small boat of this name burned at Memphis on Oct. 26, 1880.

5435 TRADER

Rig? p wh b. Terre Haute, Ind., 1873. 37 tons. Documented at Evansville 1876, mayber later.

5436 TRANSFER

SW p wh b. Marietta, Oh., 1862. 84 tons. She first ran Syracuse-Chesire on the upper Ohio, three round trips a day, one way fare five cents. Sold to USQMD in 1863. Docked at Cincinnati in December 1864 and then proceeded to Louisville. Sold and renamed *HELEN* (see) Dec. 15, 1865.

5437 TRANSFER

Stw ferry wh b. Ironton, Oh., 1880. 90 x 26.5 x 3.6. Operated at Huntington, W. Va., first owned by Honshell and Crawford, then J.M. Noble, and lastly by Richard M. Eaton. She replaced the old *NEW CASTLE NO. 2* between 7th Street and Frampton's Landing, Oh. Still documented 1896.

5438 TRANSFER NO. 2

SW tr wh b. Wheeling, W. Va., 1866, originally named *MINNESOTA* (see). Was renamed Aug. 23, 1881, at St. Louis, and was at New Orleans in 1882. Registered at New York, N.Y., 1886.

5439 TRANSIT

SW ferry wh b. Murraysville, W. Va. and completed at Wheeling, 1878. 80 x 18 x 4. Operated in the Wheeling area, and by 1895 was at Sistersville, W. Va.

5440 TRANSIT

SW ferry wh b. Pittsburgh, Pa., 1880, originally ferry *SHORT CUT* (see). Name changed in 1918, documented at Louisville, Ky.

5441 TRANSPORT

Stw p wh b. Paducah, Ky., 1848. 91 tons. First home port, St. Louis. Snagged and sunk at foot of Cumberland Island, Ohio River, October 1848 with loss of cargo, Sank at Donaldsonville, La., May 6, 1849, lost.

5442 TRAVELER

Stw ferry wh b. Middletown, Pa., 1864. 69 tons. Originally owned by William and John Pedder and Ernest Succop. In 1868 owned by Capt. Thomas O'Reilly and others. She was the ferry on the Monongahela River between South 22nd

Street and Glenwood for many years. Dismantled in 1883. Machinery, 13's- 5 ft., went to *TWILIGHT* (towboat).

5443 TRAVIS WRIGHT

Stw p wh b. Madison, Ind., 1869. 202 tons. 129 x 31.7 x 4.6. Owned by Capt. J.T. Feeder of New Orleans and others. In 1870 running New Orleans-Jefferson on Red River, Capt. E.D.C. Smith, with W.T. Rapley, clerk. She went to the wreck of the *R. T. BRYARLY* (see) and salvaged 173 bales of cotton and en route to New Orleans with this salvage she sank at Pecan Point, Oct. 7, 1876, and was lost.

5444 TRENTON

SW p wh b. Brownsville, Pa., 1847. 207 tons. Burned at Maysville, Ky., Feb. 27, 1848.

5445 TRENTON

SW p wh b. Monongahela, Pa., 1851. 144 tons. 122.3 x 24 x 5.3. Originally owned (⅔) by G.L. and John Kouns along with the Pittsburgh firm of Scaife, Atkinson & Oakley, Sold outright to this Pittsburgh firm, Apr. 1, 1853. The principals were William B. Scaife, James Atkinson, and John M. Oakley. Ran New Orleans-Ouachita River. She was lengthened in summer 1854 to 172.3 ft., then owned by John James Kercheval, New Orleans. Briefly owned 1855 by Wilson W. Jenkins, St. Mary Parish, La., and after October 19 by Capt. Varnum Sheldon, New Orleans. Off the lists 1857.

5446 TRENTON

Stw p wh b. Jeffersonville, Ind., by Howard, 1869. 260 tons. 130 x 32.2 x 4.2. Built for Capt. J.W. Carleton, New Orleans, who commanded. Connected at Camden, Ark., with the *GOV. ALLEN* (see) for Arkadelphia, Ark. Sold, Apr. 23, 1870, to Capt. John W. Tobin, entire, of New Orleans. In January 1876 running New Orleans-Opelousas.

5447 TRES HERMADOS

Stw p sh b. Pittsburgh, Pa., by James Rees & Sons Co., for foreign destination. One stack. No date.

5448 TRIBUNE

SW p wh b. New Albany, Ind., 1849. 251 tons. Burned Nov. 2, 1849, at Bayou Goula, La.

5449 TRIBUTARY

SW p wh b. Pittsburgh, Pa., 1845. 148 tons. Came out in Pittsburgh-Cincinnati trade, Capt. J. Klinefelter. Sold to St. Louis and thence to New Orleans, owned there December 1846 by Joseph McIntyre, St. Louis. Several ownership changes at New Orleans in 1848 and was sold at U.S. marshal sale at Louisville, Ky., in November 1848 to James W. Denny and others who were considering the Wabash River trade. She burned at foot of 5th Street, Louisville, Dec. 29, 1848. There was a high river at the time, and she was set free, and floated against the *ARKANSAS MAIL* (see) and both were lost.

5450 TRIBUTARY

Rig? p wh b. Madison, Ind., 1880. 83 x 18.6 x 3. Went to Vicksburg for Yazoo River trade. Still there 1886, maybe longer.

5451 TRIMBLE

SW ferry wh b. Madison, Ind., 1895. 110 x 30 x 3.5. Served Madison-Milton, Ky. There were many owners over the years; C.L. Melcher, J.D. Taylor, Clarence Hisle, Capt. John W. Hughes, D.T. Voiers, Harry Voiers, John Niehouse. In 1921 Capt. George W. Monroe became sole owner. Finally dismantled and much haberdashery went to building the sternwheel gas boat *MARGARET J.* The opening of the bridge in 1929 ended the service.

5452 TRINITY

Stw p wh b. Jeffersonville, Ind., by Howard, 1851. 238 tons. 175 x 28 x 6.5. Went to the Galveston, Tex., area. Lost by stranding at Last Island, La., Nov. 26, 1851.

5453 TRIO

Stw p wh b. Louisville, Ky., 1858. 150 tons. Made trips to upper Red River, La. Louisville-Madison, Capt. John A. Dickenson, spring 1862 and ran low water, Louisville-St. Louis, Capt. W.B. Russell, summer 1862. Was taken to Cumberland River and was burned by the Rebels at Harpeth Shoals, Jan. 14, 1863. The machinery was removed and shipped to Louisville that summer.

5454 TRIUMPH

Stw p wh b. Pittsburgh, Pa., 1845. 121 tons. Operated on the Kanawha River by Capt. B.J. Caffrey, his first venture. He sold her south and Dec. 3, 1849, she hit the bank ten miles below Cincinnati bound for the Arkansas River with a full cargo and was wrecked. The pilot on watch was a youngster—happened after dark.

5455 TROPIC

SW p wh b. Brownsville, Pa., 1853. 242 tons. 225 x 23. Snagged and lost on the Missouri River one-half mile below and opposite Waverly, Mo., Oct. 14, 1857. Life loss was estimated at twelve to fifteen.

5456 TROUBADOUR

Prop yacht sh b. Pittsburgh, Pa., 1893. 74 x 10 x 4. Compound condensing, single prop. Built for Capt. Samuel S. Brown, Pittsburgh, and named for a racehorse. Ten staterooms and quite swank. Made several trips to Memphis and New Orleans. After Brown's death the executors of his estate, Union Trust Co., and his brother W. Harry Brown, sold the yacht to Capt. William B. Rodgers, Pittsburgh, May 17, 1906 for one dollar and other considerations. Rodgers visited Clarington, Oh., aboard this boat, his hometown. When he died in 1925 the boat was kept in the Rodgers Sand Co. fleet in the Manchester section of Pittsburgh until sold in 1930 to Capt. Robert J. Hasley, August 1930. In 1935 the Snapp Foundry Co., Fairmont, W. Va., acquired her, and she towed sand and gravel for May Bros., there, Capt. A.C. Lyons in charge. She was returned to Pittsburgh and lay in the Allegheny River near the 6th Street Bridge where she was caught out on shore on a falling river. Officially abandoned in fall of 1936.

5457 TROUT

Stw p wh b. Manchester, Oh., 1874. 83 tons. Built for the Cincinnati-Moscow, Oh., trade, Capt. Henry W. Pennywitt. In 1876 ran Cincinnati-Ripley, Oh., operated by Jim Frost who also ran the Ripley wharfboat, and in ten weeks carried 1,000 hogsheads of tobacco down. She went to Evansville, Ind., in February 1878 and then to Red River, La., Capt. George L. White. She burned at Shreveport, La., Mar. 29, 1880, with 132 bales of cotton aboard.

5458 TROY

Stw p wh b. Louisville, Ky., 1846. 92 tons. Named for Troy, Ind., and was built for Capt. Dobbins of that place. He sold her to the U.S. in 1846 for use on the Rio Grande River during the Mexican War. Capt. W.H. Daniel, Troy, Ind., was her pilot. Sold private August 1849, and off the lists 1851.

5459 TROY

SW p wh b. Brownsville, Pa., 1852. 97 tons. Off the lists 1858.

5460 TROY

Stw freighter wh b. Jonesville, La., 1907. 74.8 x 24 x 3.5. Sank on Ouachita River near Poplar Grove, September 1909, raised. In 1918 she was registered at Kansas City, Mo.

5461 TRUSTEE

SW p wh b. Cincinnati, Oh., 1849. 146 tons. Snagged and lost at Van Buren, Ark., on Arkansas River, Feb. 18, 1852.

5462 TRY US

Stw p wh b. Parkersburg, Va., 1862. 32 tons. Burned and lost at Evansville, Ind., June 30, 1875.

5463 TURTLE

Rig? ferry wh b. Wabasha, Minn., 1863. 25 tons. Rebuilt at Winona, Minn., 1871. Off the lists 1877.

5464 TUSCARORA

Stw p wh b. Glasgow, Pa., 1848. 138 tons. Came in collision with *ROYAL ARCH* in Buffington Island, Ohio River, November 1852 and sank, later raised. Off the lists 1855.

5465 TUSCARORAS

Confederate gunboat wh In 1870 her wreck was visible thirteen miles above Helena, Ark., at Harbeth's Landing where she exploded on her way to Columbus, Ky., in the winter of 1861. She was a handsome little craft carrying guns. In 1870 she lay about 30 yards from the Mississippi shore in the upstream channel.

5466 TUSCUMBIA

SW p wh b. New Albany, Ind., 1846. 281 tons. 172 x 26.2 x 6.5. Enrolled at New Orleans in July 1847 owned by Samuel Hutchins and Nahum B. Baldwin Story of that city, and William Jones, New Albany, Ind., Capt. Jamerson Eager, master. Sold December 1848 to Capt. Alfred Morgan, Louisville, Ky. Sold Jan. 4, 1851, to Frederick A. Sherman, New Orleans, with Capt. Edward S. Johnson, master. Sold June 19, 1852, to Capt. Isaac Chauncey Cable, St. Louis. She was reported snagged and lost at Memphis on Oct. 10, 1852. An odd sequel to this story is that in the annals of St. Louis there appears record of the first steam railroad locomotive having arrived there, Nov. 12, 1852, brought up on the *TUSCUMBIA* from New Orleans. It was consigned to the Pacific Railroad of Missouri, having been built at Stanton, Mass., and sent by sea to New Orleans. At St. Louis it was hauled up the levee by mules, set on rails, and fired up. ". . . And so commenced a new era for the west." An account of this event appears in *The Waterways Journal* with picture, issue Dec. 30, 1939.

5467 TUSCUMBIA

US gunboat wh b. New Albany, Ind., 1862. 565 tons. 175 x 72.5 x 8.1. This side-wheel gunboat also had props. Engines, 30's- 6 ft. Six boilers, each 40" by 26 ft., five flues each. Sold at U.S. sale at Mound City, Ill., Nov. 29, 1865, to W.H. Adams for $3,000. She was stripped of iron plating, etc., and was beached near the mouth of the Cache River there, where she lay until October 1870 when the woodwork was burned to get her out of the way.

5468 TUSCUMBIA

Rig? p wh b. Ashland, Ky., 1881. 86.4 x 14.6 x 2.8. A boat of this name was running on the Osage River in 1881. Documented at New Orleans 1886, maybe later.

5469 TUSKALOOSA

SW p wh b. Cincinnati, Oh., 1844. 320 tons. Exploded and lost at Mobile, Ala., Jan. 29, 1847, with loss of twelve lives.

5470 TWELFTH ERA

Stw p wh b. Madison, Ind., 1869. 136.4 x 29 x 4.5. Built for Capt. I.H. Kouns, New Orleans. Went to Galveston, Tex., in 1871, Capt. W.N. Gillen. Was lost in Galveston Bay in mid-October 1871 during a storm. Gillen had a contract for handling shells and had recently lost two barges en route from New Orleans to Galveston.

5471 TWILIGHT

SW p wh b. Jeffersonville, Ind., by Howard, 1857. 335 tons. 215 x 33 x 6. Ran briefly Louisville-Henderson, then went to St. Louis and was part of the St. Joseph Union Line, Capt. J. Shaw. By 1861 was at New Orleans owned there by William C. Buffington, with Capt. Thomas W. Scott, master. Was in the upper Red River during the war. Sold Aug. 21, 1865, by U.S. marshal at New Orleans to Moses W. Wetmore, with Capt. Henry Nelson, master. Scrapped.

5472 TWILIGHT

SW p wh b. St. Louis, Mo., 1865. 230 tons. 180 x 32. Engines, 16's- 4½ ft. Two boilers. Owned by John P. Keiser, J. Henry, C.M. Sombart, H.W. McPherson.

Capt. William Massie, master. She was snagged and lost opposite the mouth of Fire Creek, one-half mile above Napoleon, Mo., on the Missouri River, Sept. 10, 1865. She was upbound and heavily loaded. The cargo contained a generous shipment of whiskey, a fact which persuaded various expeditions to make recovery later on. During one such effort a cofferdam was built around the wreck, and one barrel of whiskey was located. The workers celebrated, a rising river flooded the coffer, and the project ended.

5473 TWIN CITY

Stw p wh b. California, Pa., 1852. 209 tons. 154 x 28.1 x 5.1. Built for Capt. Hugh McKelvey, first master, and others of Allegheny County, Pa. Ran Pittsburgh-St. Louis. Last owner was Benjamin F. Easley, St. Louis, with Capt. S.J. Ball, master. She had been to St. Paul in 1855 and burned Dec. 7 that year at St. Louis along with *PRAIRIE CITY* (see) and another.

5474 TWIN CITY

Rig? ferry wh b. Port Byron, Ill., 1865. 33 tons. Still documented 1876.

5475 TWIN CITY

Stw p wh b. Diamond Bluff, Wis., 1900. 134 x 26 x 4. Sold to Cumberland River and renamed *WARRENN* (see).

5476 TWO BROTHERS

SW p wh b. California, Pa., 1854. 193 tons. 120 x 30 x 6. Built for Capt. Martin Broderick, New Orleans, who commanded. Later sold to George Sanford, that city. Off the lists in 1860.

5477 TWO SISTERS

SW p wh b. Algiers, La., 1850. 117 tons. 97 x 10.4 x 5.9. Owned by Capt. Martin Broderick, New Orleans. Off the lists 1855.

5478 TWO SISTERS

Rig? ferry wh Operated Marietta-Harmar, Oh. across the Muskingum, 1857, Capt. William H. Gurley. Capt. Charles Atha also is named as a master of her in Muskingum service.

5479 TWO STATES

Stw p wh b. Evansville, Ind., 1877, originally named *H.M. SWEETSTER* (see). Bought by Capt. John Adams and renamed. Ran Evansville-Owensboro. Later renamed *EDNA ADAMS* (see).

5480 TYCOON

SW p wh b. Brownsville, Pa., 1860. 332 tons. Built for Capt. I.C. Woodward and others of Brownsville. He went master, and ran Pittsburgh-Cincinnati spring 1861, and made a trip to Red River, La. Ran Louisville-Cumberland River early 1862 and was bought Mar. 16, 1862 by Thompson Dean and Capt. J.H. Pepper. They took her to Pittsburgh, Pa., and loaded out with soldiers for the South, Capt. Pepper commanding. She was on the Tennessee that May in use as a temporary hospital ship along with the *GLENDALE*. Following the war she was loaded with cotton at New Orleans, 1,595 bales, and started north with cotton piled clear around the pilothouse. Caught fire and burned at Tiptonville, Tenn., en route, Oct. 9, 1865.

5481 TYLER

SW U.S. gunboat wh b. Cincinnati, Oh., 1857, originally *A.O. TYLER* (see). 180 x 45.3 x 7.7. Sold to the U.S. early June 1861 and rebuilt into a gunboat, renamed *TYLER*. At the conclusion of the war was sold Aug. 17, 1865, at Mound City, Ill., to Capt. David White for $6,000.

5482 TYRONE

Stw p wh b. Louisville, Ky., 1864. 177 tons. 155 x 32.5 x 4.5. Engines, 15's- 5 ft. Two boilers. Owned by Capt. W.T. Harman who commanded, with Alex and J. Hard, clerks. Ran Nashville-Cairo. Said a Cairo editor in January 1865: "...the *TYRONE* is, we believe, now the only living representative of a Nashville craft owned and commanded by a gentleman of the olden time marine persuasion." She sank in the Cumberland River 75 miles above Smithland, Ky., May 15, 1870, raised. By 1874 was in the St. Louis & Illinois Packet Co. Off the lists in 1876.

5483 TYRONE

Stw p wh b. St. Louis, Mo., 1877. 138 tons. 190 x 32 x 5. Engines, 15's- 5 ft. Two boilers. Replaced former boat of the name (see above). Owned by Capt. David H. Silver and others. Also made Missouri River trips. Sold 1878 to New Orleans & Red River Packet Co., who renamed her *SILVER CITY* (see).

U

5484 U. K. RIGGS

Stw p wh b. Harmar, Oh., 1883, originally the *GENERAL DAWES* (see). Renamed when owned by Huling Bros., contractors, c. 1892, to honor the lockmaster at Davis Island Dam (No. 1) on the Ohio River. U. Kidd Riggs was born at Wade, Oh., and lived in Bellevue, Pa., while he was lockmaster; died, 78, December 1943. His father James Riggs also had served at Davis Island Dam. The *U.K. RIGGS* was sold to Arkansas River where she served as a packet last enrolled at Memphis Oct. 4, 1894. Dismantled soon thereafter.

5485 U. P. SCHENCK

Stw p wh b. Cincinnati, Oh., 1876. 1,086.72 tons. 251 x 42 x 6.5. Originally had engines from *JAMES HALE,* and later had 22½'s- 7 ft. from *PAT ROGERS*. Ran Cincinnati-New Orleans owned by the Schenck family at Vevay, Ind. In summer 1878 a full length cabin was built on her at Cincinnati. Capt. J. Lawrence Carter was master, with R.C. (Dick) Burns, clerk. Sometime after 1888 she was lengthened and renamed *LONGFELLOW* (see).

5486 U. S. Aid

Stw p wh b. Zanesville, Oh., 1852. 125 tons. Capt. Thomas Vaughn, master. Ran low water, Wheeling-Cincinnati, summer 1852, Capt. Vaughn in command. Made a trip up Wabash River January 1853, hit the Covington bridge taking away the stacks, pilothouse, and part of the cabin, and the boat's carpenter was killed. Off the lists 1856.

5487 U.S. Mail

SW p wh b. Elizabeth, Pa., 1852. 196 tons. 181 x 27 x 6. Engines, 18's- 5 ft. Three boilers, each 42" by 22 ft. Entered the St. Louis-Louisville, Ky., trade, Capt. T. Haslep. Rammed by the *BEN COURSIN* at the Louisville wharf, Sept. 12, 1853, and sunk. Ran St. Louis-Missouri River, Capt. M.E. Lucas, and was snagged and lost at Atchison, Kansas, June 1857.

5488 U & I

Stw p wh b. Jeffersonville, Ind., by Howard, 1898. 132 x 22 x 3. Engines from *BESSIE SILER*. Capt. H.M. Carter operated her on the upper Red River. Burned at Coushatta Chute, La., Feb. 23, 1899.

5489 Uchee

SW p wh b. Elizabeth, Pa., 1860. 174 tons. Went to Apalachicola, Fla., and to Confederate registry 1861.

5490 Umpire

Stw p wh b. Shousetown, Pa., 1847. 87 tons. Ran Pittsburgh-Hockingport, Oh., in 1848, Capt. Samuel C. Young. Snagged and lost in Aransas Pass, Tex., 1852.

5491 Umpire

Stw p wh b. Nashville, Tenn., 1854. 124 tons. Engines, 13½'s- 3½ ft. Two boilers. Burned June 12, 1860, in Osage River, Mo. Her master was Capt. Lewis Baldwin.

5492 Umpire

Stw p wh b. Paducah, Ky., 1868. 255 tons. In 1872 advertised as a regular Evansville-Cairo-Memphis-New Orleans packet, Capt. G.J. Grammar, master, with N.S. Pennington, clerk. In September 1873 the wrecking boat *CHARLIE HILL* was working at Shawneetown Bar, Ohio River, and she was to proceed from there to the wreck of the *UMPIRE*.

5493 Umpire No. 2

Stw p wh b. Shousetown, Pa., 1850. 101 tons. Snagged and lost above Little Rock, Ark., Aug. 1, 1854.

5494 Umpire No. 3

SW p wh b. Newport, Ky., 1852. 110 tons. Off the lists in 1860.

5495 Una

SW p wh b. Portland, Ky., 1863. 121 tons. Perhaps built as a barge. First documented at New Orleans in 1865, 160.56 tons. 131.9 x 23.2 x 4.3. Built under the direction of Capt. Homer Kellogg, who owned part interest. Ran New Orleans-Upper Coast-Bayou Lafourche. In December 1865 principal owner became John C. Dowty, with Capt. T.J. Dowty, master. In October 1866 owned by Robert Roberts, New Orleans, with Capt. W.C. Neal, master. She ran then to Red River. Sold February 1867 to H. Samuel, New Orleans, Capt. William A. Gibson. Sank and lost in Atchafalaya River, Aug. 12, 1867.

5496 Uncle Oliver

Stw p wh b. Jeffersonville, Ind., by Howard, 1906, originally named *CONCORDIA* (see). Capt. George Prince bought her for the Royal Route Co., Vicksburg, in 1914. Renamed to honor Hon. Oliver Wilds, father of Capt. Ollie K. Wilds. Ran Vicksburg-Greenville. Was rebuilt at Slidell, La., in 1925 by Capts. Oliver Bradford and Dick Dicharry. Burned at Vicksburg, and Capt. Dicharry bought the *TENNESSEE BELLE* (see).

5497 Uncle Sam

SW p wh b. Louisville, Ky., 1845. 432 tons. The first steam whistle appeared on *REVENUE* in 1844, and this steamer also carried one, and startled the natives along the Ohio. Off the lists in 1850.

5498 Uncle Sam

SW p wh b. Louisville, Ky., 1848. 741 tons. 285 x 38 x 6. Engines, 26's- 10 ft. Five boilers, each 42" by 31 ft. Hull by James Murray; machinery by Lent, South & Shipman; cabin by Thomas & Beeler. Primarily a freight carrier. Ran Louisville-New Orleans. She was at Cairo, Ill., in March 1849 downbound with 1,450 tons, part of which was 15,000 sacks of corn. Dismantled in 1859. In December 1855 she rammed and sank the *SWITZERLAND* opposite Natchez, Miss.

5499 Uncle Sam

Rig? ferry wh b. Valley Creek, Iowa, 1878. 23.74 tons. Inspected at Cordova, Ill., Apr. 20, 1881. Cordova is about five miles above Le Claire, with Princeton, Iowa, opposite.

5500 Uncle Sam

Stw p wh b. Sterling Island, Ill., 1898, originally excursion steamer *JACOB RICHTMAN* (see). Prior to 1904 bought by Clat Adams and his brother, Quincy, Ill., and burned in Quincy Bay, 1904, having been renamed. Rebuilt and by 1910 was owned by the Missouri River Excursion Co., Capt. E.H. Mattheus, master. While backing away from the landing at Kansas City, Mo., on May 18, 1910, she collided with a sand barge and sank after having been run ashore. There were 95 passengers on board but no life loss due largely to John J. Pryor, one of the owners who, although he could not swim, stood by and saw all safely ashore.

5501 Uncle Toby

SW p wh b. Pittsburgh, Pa., 1844. 109 tons. At St. Peters from St. Louis, Capt. George B. Cole, 1845. St Galena from St. Louis, Apr. 9, 1846, same master. Regular St. Louis-

Galena-Dubuque season 1847, Capt. Henry R. Day. Regular St. Louis-St. Peters, 1851. Arrived at Port Douglass, Minn., Nov. 20, 1851, and due to ice teamed her freight to St. Paul, then returned to St. Louis. Off the lists 1853.

5502 UNDERWRITER

SW salvage boat wh b. Cincinnati, Oh., 1865. 559 tons. Operated by Capt. R.W. Dugan and did a thriving business salvaging wrecked steamboats. Burned at Cairo, Ill., along with *LOUISIANA,* July 6, 1869. Contract was let for a new boat to replace her, built at Cincinnati in 1870, named *T.F. ECKERT* (see).

5503 UNDINE

SW p wh b. Cincinnati, Oh., 1845. 197 tons. 138 x 23.5 x 6.5. Built for Nicholas Henry Wyse, New Orleans, with Capt. Warren A. Grice, master. Sold, Oct. 15, 1845, to Gershom Kurscheedt, New Orleans, same master. Sold Feb. 21, 1846, to James McMaster, New Orleans, Capt. A. Carlisle, master. Went to U.S. war service.

5504 UNDINE

SW p wh b. Brownsville, Pa., 1859. 158 tons. Ran Pittsburgh-Gallipolis, Capt. M.A. Cox, January 1862. Capt. Woodburn took command, with M.A. Cox, clerk. They sold her July 1862 to Capt. Conway and others, Madison, Ind., who ran her Louisville-Madison. Sank in ice at New London, Ind. (near Payne Hollow, Ky.), in January 1864. The cabin came off and went over the Falls at Louisville.

5505 UNDINE

Stw tinclad wh b. Cincinnati, Oh., 1863, originally named *BEN GAYLORD* (see). Acquired by U.S. Navy and renamed, Mar. 7, 1864. Bore the number #55. She was convoying the *VENUS* down the Tennessee River when attacked from shore and captured by the Confederates in October 1864 and was burned at Johnsonville, Tenn., Nov. 3, 1864.

5506 UNDINE

SW ferry wh b. Wellsville, Oh., 1868. 76 tons. 115 x 30 x 4. Went to the Missouri River, owned in 1874 by Lexington Ferry, Coal & Railroad Transportation Co. Still documented at Bismarck, Dak., 1886, and reported lost that year.*

5507 UNICORN

SW p wh b. Brownsville, Pa., 1853. 188 tons. Carried a calliope. Burned at Natchez, Miss., Dec. 11, 1855.

5508 UNION

SW p wh b. Wellsville, Oh., 1845. 240 tons. Ran Pittsburgh-New Orleans. Engines, 28's- 7½ ft. Two boilers, each 42" by 30 ft. Built to pass through the Louisville-Portland Canal. She burned 20 cords of cottonwood, or 17 cords of hard wood daily. Lost by stranding at Cape Girardeau, Mo., Jan. 11, 1850.

5509 UNION

SW p wh b. Marion, Ala., 1845. 168 tons. 125 x 24 x 6.5. Built in Perry County, Ala., and documented at Mobile until transferred June 7, 1850, to New Orleans, owned there by James Davis, Capt. John H. Browne, master. Davis sold her to Capt. Browne and others. Sold Apr. 15, 1852, to Capt. Thomas G. Mackey and others, New Orleans. One year later she was owned by Capt. Henry G. Abbott, New Orleans. Off the lists 1855.

5510 UNION

SW p wh b. Wellsville, Oh., 1846. 30 tons. Off the lists 1855.

5511 UNION

Stw p wh b. Elizabeth, Pa., 1850. 65 tons. First home port, Paducah, Ky. A boat of this name was on the upper Tennessee prior to the war, Capt. C.C. Spiller. There also is mention of *UNION* bought by Gen. James Gamble who hauled copper ore with her from the Ducktown mines to Charleston, upper Tennessee. Off the lists 1852.

5512 UNION

SW p wh b. Cincinnati, Oh., 1852. 209 tons. First home port, Apalachicola, Fla. Lost in collision with *CUSSETA* in the Apalachicola River, Fla., Feb. 5, 1856.

5513 UNION

SW p wh b. Brownsville, Pa., 1853. 143 tons. 125 x 28 x 4.5. Went to New Orleans owned by Capt. John Kellar. Sold Mar. 3, 1856, to Nathaniel Moore, Shreveport, La., Capt. J.G. McWilliams, Shreveport, master. On Sept. 2, 1857, sold to Wilson, Pomroy & Co., New Orleans, and transferred several days later to Capt. Hugh H. Beard of that city. Off the lists in 1859.

5514 UNION

SW p wh b. Louisville, Ky., 1857. 139 tons. Snagged and lost at Clinton, Ind., Apr. 2, 1861.

5515 UNION

Stw ferry wh b. Mason City, Va., 1860. 17 tons. Off the lists 1862.

5516 UNION

SW ferry wh b. Madison, Ind., 1860. 116 tons. There was a ferry plying Natchez-Vidalia in 1866, D.G. Renner & Co., possibly this one. Off the lists 1869.

5517 UNION

SW ferry wh b. Steubenville, Oh., 1861. 44 tons. Operated at Steubenville along with the *JEFFERSON* and *REBECCA* (both see). Off the lists 1868.

5518 UNION

Centerwheel f wh b. Brunswick, Mo., 1861. 99 x 27 x 4. 100 tons. Engine 16's- 4 ft. stroke. See Addendum for full details on this boat.

5519 UNIQUE

Prop yacht sh b. Charleston, W. Va., 1901 by Charles

Ward. 90 x 14 x 4.3. Triple compound condensing engine, 7″ - 10½ - 16″ by 10″ stroke with one water tube boiler. Sold in 1904 to U.S. Engineers, Memphis. Sold to Walter S. Dickey, Kansas City, Mo. Converted to diesel, and had a Wolverine 100 hp. Renamed *ETTA J.* and in 1929 operated by Northwestern Terminals Co., Evansville, Ind. Fred Smith, president of Dixie Greyhound Bus Lines, Memphis, had her by 1933, and she was converted to towing at Paducah. Delta Transportation Co., Memphis, hauled beer between Evansville and Memphis until 1935. Erlbacher Bros., Cape Girardeau, Mo., were the last owners, and she sank in 1942.

5520 UNITED STATES

SW p wh b. Cincinnati, Oh., 1847. 332 tons. Bought c. 1853 by Capt. Clifford B. Wayne and others for Cincinnati-Memphis trade. Dismantled in 1854 and machinery went to *GLENDALE* (see).

5521 UNITED STATES

SW p wh b. Cincinnati, Oh., 1865. 1,106 tons. 294 x 40 (38 ft. floor) x 6.5. Engines, 26's- 10 ft. Five tubular boilers, each 42″ by 22 ft., equipped with 5″ flues. Valued at $240,000 and carried $105,000 insurance. Owned by the U.S. Mail Line Co., and ran Cincinnati-Louisville teamed up with the *GENERAL LYTLE* and after April 1867 with the *AMERICA*. She was involved in several collisions: On Christmas night 1866 she and *SILVER SPRAY* collided (see) at North Bend, and on another occasion she collided with a towboat. On the night of Dec. 4, 1868, about 11:00 P.M., she collided with her sister packet *AMERICA* above Warsaw, Ky., at Rayl's Landing, Ind., about 300 yards above Bryants Creek.

AMERICA was upbound, Capt. David Whitten in command, and Napoleon B. Jenkins pilot on watch.

UNITED STATES was downbound, Capt. Richard M. Wade in command, and Jacob Remlein pilot on watch.

Night was clear.

River stage about 16 ft.

Cause: Misunderstanding of passing signals.

Speed: *UNITED STATES* was making 18 to 20 mph downbound; *AMERICA* making about 10 mph upbound.

Rivermen agree that the underlying cause of the accident was the unfamiliarity of Napoleon B. Jenkins with a custom. He was pinch-hitting for the regular pilot Charles Dufour. The two partner boats often met in this vicinity and the upbound boat kept to the Kentucky side. Jenkins elected to do it the other way and blew two whistles. Remlein testified that he heard but one whistle, and only expected one whistle. As consequence he answered so promptly that he drowned out the second blast. This set the stage for the worst catastrophe in that territory.

The *UNITED STATES* continued down the Indiana side and into the path of the *AMERICA* which was crossing to that side. The result was that the upbound *AMERICA* rammed the *STATES* about amidships on her port side with great headway and inflicted mortal damage. The *STATES* rounded to and was landed along the Indiana shore where she was found to be on fire. The *AMERICA* drifted back and then was driven ashore immediately below the burning *STATES*. Disabled, burning, and unmoored, the *STATES* left the shore and the current took her down against the *AMERICA*. Soon both boats were ablaze. Many persons jumped to the shoreward boat. The *STATES* sank alongside of the *AMERICA*. Charles Dittman sprang to the pilotwheel of the *AMERICA* and backed her down the river, and landed her about 200 yards below, but the flames were beyond control and she burned and sank.

Toll of life:

AMERICA 4 cabin passengers

UNITED STATES 31 cabin passengers

5 deck passengers

23 officers and crew

The hull of the *STATES* was salvaged and towed to Cincinnati by the *UNDERWRITER* (see) and towboat *COAL HILL*. It was auctioned off to the U.S. Mail Line Co., who rebuilt it into the second *UNITED STATES* (next listing.)

Crew of *UNITED STATES* at the time of the loss: Capt. Richard M. Wade, master; Robert Riley, first clerk; Andy Harrington, 2nd clerk; James Jones, 3rd clerk; Oliver Noble, mate; Henry---, 2nd mate; A. Marshall, 1st engineer; Charles Marshall, 2nd engineer; John Hamilton and J. Remlein, pilots; James Fennell, barkeeper; John Fennell, steward; Mary Perkins, head chambermaid.

This collision receives detailed treatment in the *S&D Reflector,* issue December 1968, pages 18–22, with photographs and drawings.

5522 UNITED STATES

SW p wh b. Cincinnati, Oh., 1869. 1,083 tons. Hull from former boat of the name, lengthened six feet, making her full 300 ft. long. Engines from prior boat. Seven new boilers, each 38″ by 26 ft., two flues each. Owned by U.S. Mail Line Co. The earlier boat, like her partner *AMERICA,* was double cabin. This *UNITED STATES* was single cabin. Capt. Richard M. Wade came out master of her. The *ANDY BAUM* (see) came in collision with her two miles below Aurora, Ind., on Dec. 19, 1877, knocking the starboard wheelhouse off the *STATES*. In making repairs Captain Wade took sick and died at his Covington, Ky., home, Feb. 19, 1878, aged 62, closing an interesting career. He was a Virginian by birth, flatboated on the Kanawha as a boy, became a pilot, then master of the *CINCINNATUS* (see) and *QUEEN OF THE WEST*. During the war he was one of the more noted U.S. gunboat pilots, running the Island 10 batteries with the *CARONDELET*. The command of the *STATES* went to Capt. Charles O. David who had with him clerks Will Taylor, Dan Neal, and James Dillon. Capt. Ben Merrielees also commanded at times. Dismantled at Madison, Ind., February 1884.

5523 UNITED WE STAND

SW ferry wh b. Wellsville, Oh., 1861. 48 tons. Off the lists 1868.

5524 UNIVERSE

SW p wh b. Cincinnati, Oh., 1857. 399 tons. 180 x 35 x 7. Engines, 22's- 7 ft. Three boilers. Ran Cincinnati-New Orleans, Capt. Watts, and later Capt. Albert Stein. She was serving as a transport for the U.S. in the war on the Tennessee, and was with Porter on Red River. Snagged and lost at Plum Point on the Mississippi, Oct. 30, 1864, with loss of seventeen lives.

5525 UPPER FERRY

Catamaran ferry wh b. St. Louis, Mo., 1861. 215 tons. Off the lists 1863.

5526 URANIA

Stw p wh b. Harmar, Oh., by Knox Yard, 1896. 160.4 x 29 x 5.3. Engines, 18's- 5 ft. Owned by the Bay Line, Ironton, Oh. Ran Pittsburgh-Charleston, Capt. Howard Donnally, with George Hunter, clerk. In spring of 1899 ran Cincinnati-Gallipolis, Capt. Dave Scatterday, master, with George Hamilton, pilot. She and the *QUEEN CITY,* Capt. Robert Agnew, were on the same upbound schedule out of Cincinnati and staged various races, one all the way to Gallipolis (which the *QC* won by an hour). The first one was from Proctorville to Gallipolis, Apr. 12, 1899, in which the *URANIA* landed at Crown City briefly, then caught up to and passed the *QC,* landing at Gallipolis a mile ahead. Spring of 1901 was in Cincinnati-Ironton trade, three trips a week, Capt. T.T. Johnson, with L.E. McLaughlin, clerk. Capt. Walter Blair bought her at Cincinnati midsummer 1901, and took her to Burlington, Iowa, and she went in her Upper Mississippi trade next day. She caught fire and burned off the cabin, texas, and pilothouse at Muscatine, Iowa, Sept. 5, 1901 (President McKinley was shot afternoon of the next day). Rebuilt at Kahlke's Yard, Rock Island, Ill., and renamed *HELEN BLAIR* (see).

5527 URCIE BOYCE

SW p wh b. Jeffersonville, Ind., by Howard, 1900, originally named *COL. A. MACKENZIE* (see) then renamed *DAVID TIPTON.* Sold at public sale to Meyer Katz, St. Louis, and John F. Klein, Pittsburgh. Sold late 1923 to two Memphis railroad men, Messrs. Peel and Bachelor, who renamed her *URSIE BOYCE.* She was placed in the Memphis-White River trade and after a few trips was withdrawn due to lack of business. Later became *CITY OF CAIRO* (see).

5528 URILDA

SW p wh b. Pittsburgh, Pa., 1842. 77 tons. Off the lists 1848.

5529 URILDA

Stw p wh b. Monongahela, Pa., 1863. 168 tons. Came out in December 1863 owned by William S. Evans (one-half) along with D.S.H. Gilmore and S.B. Coulson. Capt. Thomas W. Laughrey was master in Pittsburgh-Oil City trade on the Allegheny River. Ran Ohio River trades summer 1864 and then back into the Allegheny. On Sept. 19, 1865, departed Pittsburgh for Pithole with freight and passengers, and *IDA REES* left same day for Tionesta. The U.S. Inspectors Report, 1867, states she was built at Tidioute on the Allegheny; perhaps a rebuilding there at the time. Left Pittsburgh for Fort Benton, Mont., Apr. 9, 1868, Capt. G.J. Hazlett, owned in part by William J. Kountz. That winter she was caught at Farm Island and Captain Hazlett came on to Omaha leaving a crew aboard to protect her from Indians. She was snagged and lost in Kate Swinney Bend, Missouri River, Apr. 23, 1869, John C. Ball, pilot.

5530 UTAH

SW p wh b. Cincinnati, Oh., 1851. 89 tons. First home port, St. Louis. Off the lists in 1853.

5531 UTAH

Rig? p wh b. Metropolis, Ill., 1869. 428 tons. 185 x 37 x 5. Engines, 16½'s- 5 ft. Three boilers. Machinery from *HERO.* The St. Louis, Arkansas & White River Packet Co. sent her from St. Louis to Fort Smith, Ark., in mid-March 1870 with 600 tons of freight, said to have been the heaviest cargo sent there to that date. Ran St. Louis-Vicksburg for the Anchor Line during low water in August 1871. She was at Pittsburgh, Pa., advertised to Winona, Minn., departing Apr. 2, 1875, Capt. Thomas K. Voorhees, with G.W. Briggs, clerk. Owned at this time by Benjamin F. Beasley and Voorhees. On Arkansas River, spring 1876, and went to U.S. marshal sale at St. Louis that August, sold to P.B. Marrion. Two months later on Yazoo River, Miss., Capt. J.N. Smith. Burned at an island opposite Vicksburg, Miss., March 1877.

V

5532 V. OWEN

Stw ferry wh b. Paducah, Ky., 1876. 114 tons. 125 x 35 x 4. Was the ferry at Paducah until replaced in 1891 by the *CARRIE OWEN* (see).

5533 VALERIA

Stw pl wh b. Clinton, Iowa, 1904. 130 x 25 x 4. Owned by Mrs. Dwight Lamb, Clinton, Iowa. First voyage was from Clinton to the St. Louis Fair, September 1904. Engines, 12's- 6 ft. Sold to Interstate Materials Co., Davenport, Iowa, and renamed *ALICE,* a towboat, and eventually burned at Arkansas City, Dec. 24, 1924.

5534 VALLEY BELLE

Stw p wh b. Harmar, Oh., 1883. 127 tons. 127 x 22.4 x 3.4. Engines, 8's- 4 ft. Two boilers, each 36'' by 26 ft. Built at the Knox Yard. Machinery by J.H. McConnell. Built for Marietta-Beverly trade, Muskingum River, Capt. Thomas Clark, with Robert Bunch, engineer. On board for the first trip were Harry D. Knox, Frank L. Sibley, and her pilot was Aaron McLaughlin. She was floated over top of Devols

Dam "but did not sink as many thought she would." This small steamboat deserves special handling here—she ran 60 years. She entered the Ravenswood-Middleport trade in 1884, Capt. J.C. Edwards, with W.W. Hayman, clerk. In 1885 J.H. Roedel was clerk, this team continuing until 1890 when Will Chapman went clerk. She made occasional Marietta-Zanesville trips 1895–1898, Capt. Robert Edwards. By 1897 her master was Capt. W.W. Hayman, with Harry Donnally, clerk, running Marietta-Middleport. Ralph Emerson Gaches was clerk 1898–1899. In 1900 ran Marietta-Gallipolis with Hayman, master, with J.H. Williamson, clerk. In 1901, C.B. Crow was clerk. By 1903 back in Marietta-Middleport trade, Capt. H.L. Ritchie, with Charles F. Ritchie, clerk. By 1907 Capt. T.D. Wilkinson, with P.L. Wolf, clerk, same trade. This trade played out about 1911 although the *DAISY* tried it in 1912, then the *W.J. ROBERTS.* The *CALVERT* took a whack at it and lastly the *GREENDALE* in 1914 running Marietta-Gallipolis but only made a few trips and quit. She then went to the upper Kanawha owned by Capt. John Lane and ran Charleston-Montgomery teamed up with *HELEN LANE* but due to high price of coal and scarcity of labor she was sold March 1917 to E.P. Matthews, Pt. Pleasant, W. Va., who did job towing. Billy Bryant, of showboat fame, got her March 1919 and towed his showboat with her until he got the *NEW LOTUS,* then sold her to Ben Raike, Kanauga, Oh., who took off the original engines and put on the machinery from the *LIBERTY* (see). He did job towing with her until she sank at Kanauga in 1943 and was dismantled. So, to sum up, she ran as a packet for 34 years and can't claim laurels there (the *TACOMA* ran 37 years), then she was a towboat 26 years. But for a wooden hull steamboat operating almost continuously, without change of name, she has no peer.

5535 VALLEY GEM

Stw p wh b. Harmar, Oh., by Knox Yard, 1897. 125.2 x 26.4 x 4.2. Engines, 13's- 5 ft. Two boilers, each 40" by 18 ft. Built for McConnelsville-Zanesville trade on the Muskingum River, Capt. Newton Price, master and part owner. Other stockholders in 1898: C.F. Siler, McConnelsville; J.H. Shipps and Charles F. Hearing, Zanesville; H.S. Shaner, Durant, Oh., and Lee Humphrey, Malta, Oh. She ran this trade 1898–1917, round trip a day. Capt. J. Orville Noll bought her spring of 1917 for the Pittsburgh-Fairmont trade on the Monongahela River. She was destroyed by ice at Morgantown, W. Va., about Feb. 1, 1918. She was the last packet in the Fairmont trade, although *LEROY* (see) later ran to Morgantown.

5536 VALLEY QUEEN

Stw p wh b. Jeffersonville, Ind., by Howard, 1889. 192 x 35.8 x 5.6. Engines, 16's- 5 ft. Two boilers, each 46" by 28 ft. This cotton-style packet was built for Capt. George W. Rea and others and ran New Orleans-Red River to Shreveport. Charles P. Truslow was president of the owning line, and Charles W. Drown was traffic manager. Clerk was H.C. Boazman. In early January 1896 brought 2,888 bales of cotton, 643 bundles of hides and an assortment of cargo into New Orleans on a single trip. Operating in Chalmette Packet Co., March 1900; crew: Capt. Ben Rea, master; Walter Shinkle and Frank Cooper, pilots; Theodore Jobin, Will Carlton, and H.W. Gribble, clerks; Dan O'Neill, mate, and Al Brill, steward. In 1902 running with *CHALMETTE,* New Orleans-Vicksburg, Capt. Isaac Brooks, with J.C. Bergeron, clerk. Burned March 1903 near Hardscrabble Landing, a short distance below St. Joseph, La., with a big trip of cotton and seed. Another account says she was at Bruinsburg Landing, Tensas Parish, La.

5537 VALLEY QUEEN

Stw p and ex wh b. Jeffersonville, Ind., by Howard, 1913, originally *JO HORTON FALL* (see). Capt. Peters Lee, Memphis, and others bought her, c. 1926, ran her in short trades to Caruthersville, Mo., and elsewhere, renamed *VALLEY QUEEN,* and fitted out for excursions. She made a Missouri River trip and was sunk and lost at Omaha, Neb., May 17, 1934.

5538 VAN BUREN

Stw p wh b. Pittsburgh, Pa., 1866. 229 tons. 135 x 31 x 3.5. Engines, 10's- 3½ ft. Two boilers, each 34" by 18 ft. Hull was built at McKeesport, Pa., by Crissinger & Co. Very light draft, and built for Capt. W.B. Nowland who ran her Little Rock-Fort Smith on the Arkansas River. Snagged and lost above Pine Bluff, Ark., Oct. 30, 1869.

5539 VAN BUREN

Stw p wh b. Van Buren, Ark., 1893. 73 x 18 x 4. Still listed 1896, maybe later.

5540 VAN GORDER

Rig? ferry wh b. Winona, Minn., 1877. 64 tons. Operated at Winona, and inspected there May 20, 1881.

5541 VENANGO

Stw p wh b. California, Pa., 1858. 120 tons. Trial trip was run Pittsburgh to Sewickley and return, Jan. 23, 1858, Capt. Thomas H. Reynolds. Original owners: John H. Reynolds, John Heath, and M. Reynolds, all of Allegheny City, Pa., and James P. Hoover, Franklin, Pa. Designed for Pittsburgh-Franklin trade on the Allegheny. When the oil excitement started in the Allegheny River regions, she brought down 55 barrels of crude from the William Phillips well and 20 from the Graff well, all consigned to Samuel M. Kier, Pittsburgh, one of the first packet shipments. Left Pittsburgh Jan. 18, 1861, with seventeen steam engines and boilers for the oil fields. That fall she ran Kittanning, Pa., to the oil fields, connecting with the Allegheny Valley Railroad. Capt. Rees Rees owned her in 1862 and sold her in the fall to Capt. Carner, Cincinnati, who raised her main deck eighteen inches and ran her in low water trades on the Ohio. She sank at Scuffletown Bar loaded for Cumberland River, August 1862. Sold to Capt. Victor F. Wilson,

Vicksburg, Miss., on Feb. 17, 1864, and burned at Pilcher Point, La., on Dec. 31, 1864.

5542 VENZUELA

SW p wh b. Elizabeth, Pa., 1848. 328 tons. 152 x 29 x 8. Built for Oronoco Steam Navigation Co., headquartered in New York City.

5543 VENICE

Recess wheel ferry wh b. Jeffersonville, Ind., by Howard, 1871, originally *JAMES WATHEN* (see). Went to the St. Louis area and was renamed. Came to Evansville, Ind., July 5, 1889 owned by Louisville, Evansville & St. Louis Railroad Co.

5544 VENICE

Stw p wh b. Pittsburgh, Pa., 1884. 89.6 x 16.2 x 2.8. A single deck packet owned by Capt. William S. Reno, with Capt. John Richey, master. Ran short trades on the Monongahela and upper Ohio. Captain Reno died 1894 and Capt. Isaac L. Reno had her in the Charleroi-Brownsville trade summer 1895. Also ran between Pittsburgh and Chartiers Creek teamed with *VENUS* and *LENI LEOTI* (both see). Sold October 1896 to William F. James, Braddock, Pa., and thence to Capt. John O. Watson of Washington County, Pa., and Capt. George C. Demain of Fayette County, Pa. She sank and was lost near the middle pier of the 7th Street Bridge, Allegheny River, Pittsburgh, in July 1901, then owned by Capt. J.H. Schneider, Rochester, Pa.

5545 VENTURE

SW p wh b. Franklin, La., 1851. 61 tons. 102 x 20 x 3.2. Capt. James Crooks, Caddo Parish, master, 1852, and owned in the Teche District. Sold January 1853 to Samuel Applegate, New Orleans. Ran on Red River. Capt. A.S. Kottwitz became owner May 21, 1853.

5546 VENTURE

Stw p wh b. Elizabeth, Pa., 1851. 125 tons. Ran Pittsburgh-Beaver, Pa., connecting with canalboats up Beaver River, Capt. Gordon. She went to the Pomeroy-Portsmouth trade. Capt. Donnally, and capsized during a severe storm at Gallipolis, Oh., while rounding to, to land at the wharfboat. Went down within three feet of the roof. About 20 passengers were aboard, and six lives were lost. This happened about 2:00 P.M., Mar. 12, 1858. The cabin floated off several days later. The wreck was still there Oct. 31, 1866.

5547 VENUS

Stw p wh b. Carondelet, Mo., 1863. 235 tons. Burned at Fort Hindman, Tenn., Nov. 4, 1864. Life loss was set at seventeen. The pilot got to Louisville, Ky., some days after the event and gave an account: "We were downbound below Johnsonville on the Tennessee River with three empty barges in tow when the Rebs fired on us. Capt. John Allen was wounded, and most of the crew were killed; four men on deck were literally split in two. There were 18 soldiers on board belonging in Paducah and of these fifteen were killed. Capt. Allen's wife was aboard, also the mate's wife, Mrs. William Allen, and the chambermaid. Also two families consisting of two women and ten children." The pilot who showed up in Louisville was Joseph A. Enghauser. After the boat was run ashore he jumped in the river and swam across, and walked to Fort Donelson, some 30 miles. The *J. W. CHEESMAN* came down a half hour behind the *VENUS* and also tried to run the gantlet (see).

5548 VENUS

Stw p wh b. Pittsburgh, Pa., 1885. 90 x 18 x 3.6. A single deck daylight packet owned by Capt. Isaac L. Reno, Pittsburgh. Ran to McKees Rocks, Pa., along with *VENICE* and *LENI LEOTI* (both see) until the West End Electric Street Railway was opened in 1893. She then went up the Monongahela, and sank at Rice's Landing, Pa., summer 1895. Later ran occasionally in the Muskingum to Zanesville, and was in the Marietta-Sistersville trade. Sank in the mouth of the Muskingum in January 1898. Was renamed *M. G. GOBLE* (see).

5549 VERA VITA

SW p wh b. Harmar, Oh., 1885. 26 tons. 101 x 16 x 2.5. Was in the Memphis area 1895 and 1896, maybe later.

5550 VERMONT

SW p wh b. West Elizabeth, Pa., 1848. 161 tons. She was noticed at Cairo, Ill., fall of 1848, described as a handsomely furnished boat, runs well, and only 22 inches draft. "We believe she is intended for the Pittsburgh and St. Louis trade," said the editor. Burned Feb. 5, 1856, at Carrollton, Ky.

5551 VERNE SWAIN

Stw p wh b. Stillwater, Minn., 1886. 122 x 22.6 x 5. Engines, 12" and 24"- 6 ft. cross-compound. Locomotive boiler and fan blower. Built by D.M. Swain who entered her in the Clinton-Davenport trade. Capt. John Streckfus bought her in 1889 and retained her there. Zack Suiter was her pilot, then Fuller Smith. The *JO LONG* came into opposition in 1896, at which time Capt. William Knaach was master of the *SWAIN,* and Frank Black, clerk. This rivalry went on several seasons until the *LONG* withdrew. In 1898 Capt. A.M. Lovett was master, then Capt. Frank Black in 1899 and 1900. In late 1900 sold to Dixon Brothers, Peoria, Ill., and name changed to *SPEED* (see). She was rebuilt 1893 and had engines 12's- 6½ ft., and two new regular boilers, 40" by 20 ft. Much about all of these Swain boats in *S&D Reflector,* issue June 1971, pages 15-30.

5552 VERNE SWAIN

Stw p wh b. Stillwater, Minn., 1904. 131.2 x 28.5 x 4.4. Compound condensing engines, 10's, 20's- 6 ft. Two boilers, each 42" by 16 ft. Built to handle excursionists from Peoria to the St. Louis World's Fair by D.M. Swain. Sold soon thereafter to Capt. George Prince and others, Natchez, Miss., and then to Lyons Bros., Greenville, Miss., and then to Valley Line Steamers, Memphis. They ran her Memphis-Rosedale with a U.S. Mail contract which was terminated in August 1924, one of the last river mail contracts. Sank and lost at Dismal Point in Arkansas, August 1929.

5553 VERNE SWAIN

SW p wh b. Stillwater, Minn., 1913. 186.4 x 31 x 4.9. Compound condensing engines, 10's- 20's- 6 ft. Two boilers, fan blowers. Built by Capt. David M. Swain. Primarily an excursion boat with full length dance floor. Operated on the Illinois River until sold in the spring of 1918 to Capt. Fred Hornbrook who put her in the Pittsburgh-Wheeling packet trade. Capt. David Swain made the trip to Pittsburgh, became ill, and died in the West Penn Hospital there, July 3, 1918. Capt. J. Orville Noll ran excursions with her until March 1927 when he sold her to D.B.G. Rose, Louisville, Ky. She was renamed *ROSE ISLAND,* then came back to Pittsburgh in 1928 and was renamed *ROOSEVELT* in 1929, and lastly was renamed *CITY OF MEMPHIS* (all see).

5554 VERNON JR.

Prop yacht wh b. Manitowoc, Wis., 1902. 78 x 14.5 x 7. Triple compound condensing engine, 8"- 10"- 16" by 10" stroke. One water tube boiler. Owned by Vernon Deering and based at Peoria, Ill. Was there in 1905, maybe later.

5555 VESPER

Stw p wh b. Harmar, Oh., at Knox Yard, 1891. 110.5 x 20.8 x 4. Engines, 9½'s- 3 ft. One boiler, 43" by 20 ft. Single deck packet in upper Ohio short trades. Ran Marietta-Parkersburg summer of 1892 in place of *T.M. BAYNE* and in June 1895 ran Gallipolis-Huntington with zero on the Gallipolis marks. Rebuilt at Pt. Pleasant, W. Va., in 1897 and renamed *KLONDIKE* (see).

5556 VESTA

SW p wh b. New Albany, Ind., 1845. 92 tons. 117 x 21 x 4. Owned at Louisville by James D. Todd who sold her September 1846 to Capt. James C. Scott, New Orleans. Sold Mar. 6, 1848, to David E. Muggah, St. Mary Parish, La., Capt. George W. Jackson, master. Off the lists in 1850.

5557 VETERAN

SW p wh b. Beverly, Oh., 1864. 37 tons. Off the lists 1869.

5558 VICE PRESIDENT

SW tr wh b. Madison, Ind., 1872. 197 tons. 164 x 34 x 5. Engines, 18's- 5½ ft. Four boilers (two on a side). Went to the Missouri River. Inspected at Nebraska City, Neb., Sept. 20, 1880. While descending the river near Aspinwall, Neb., on May 23, 1889, she hit a wire cable taking off pilothouse and stacks. John Gunsaullis, pilot, fell to the main deck and died several hours later. Capt. Overton Butt was master at the time. She was used at Cape Girardeau, Mo., and burned there on Feb. 14, 1892.

5559 VICKSBURG

SW p wh b. New Albany, Ind., 1857. 635 tons. 244.5 x 36 x 7.5. Engines, 24's- 7 ft. Five boilers, Built for Capt. John W. Cannon and originally owned in equal shares by Jane Stout of Frankfort, Ky., and C.B. Lindsey, New Orleans. She came up from New Orleans to Portland, Ky., Capt. St. Clair Thommason, in 5 days 1 hour 25 minutes, having lost 7 hours making landings en route, 41 in all, arriving at Portland on June 6, 1858. Downbound on this trip Capt. John W. Cannon got into a fracus on the Paducah wharfboat with pilot Allen Pell. Pell stabbed Cannon in the groin, an injury which required Cannon's removal on a litter to a hotel. Ownership in *VICKSBURG* was changed Apr. 21, 1859, to Henry Streck and Capt. T.P. Leathers, both of New Orleans, with Capt. J.M. White, master. She ran in the New Orleans, Vicksburg, and Skipworth's Landing trade. At the outbreak of the war she became a Confederate transport. The *QUEEN OF THE WEST* ran the Vicksburg batteries Feb. 2, 1863, with orders to ram the *VICKSBURG* en route, which she did, and left her in near-sinking condition. The Confederates managed to get the engines, etc., removed before they lost her.

5560 VICKSBURG

SW p wh b. New Albany, Ind., 1861, originally named *LOUISVILLE* (see). The *LOUISVILLE* became the U.S. gunboat *OUACHITA* and when sold to private owners 1865 was renamed *VICKSBURG.* Owned April 1866 by Daniel T. Head, New Orleans, Capt. John W. Tobin, master. She was the "summer boat" New Orleans-Ouachita River, and in cotton season ran New Orleans-Vicksburg, Capt. J.M. White. Sold February 1868 to George P. Work, New Orleans, Capt. F.A. Blanks, master. Burned at Cairo, Ill., along with *UNDERWRITER* in July 1869.

5561 VICKSBURG

Stw p wh b. Jeffersonville, Ind., by Howard, 1890, originally named *OUACHITA,* then *FRED A. BLANKS* (both see) and lastly bought by Capt. E.W.B. Nowland for the Memphis-Vicksburg trade and he renamed her *VICKSBURG.* He didn't have her long, and in June 1903 she was laid up at South Memphis below Trainor Ave., and sank during the night, taking a list of 45 degrees and was lost.*

5562 VICKSBURG

Stw ferry wh b. Jeffersonville, Ind., by Howard, originally named *CITY OF CAIRO* (see). Owned by C.J. Miller, Vicksburg, renamed, in 1925. Owned 1929 by Mississippi River Ferry Co., Vicksburg.

5563 VICTOR

Stw p wh b. Ironton, Oh., 1858. 41 tons. Ran Gallipolis-Charleston, Capt. A.W. Carner, with Thomas Winters, clerk. In 1860 same trade, Capt. S. Christy, master, with W.T. Thayer, clerk. She was attached by a deputy U.S. marshal in April 1862 for running up the Kanawha River without a U.S. license. Lost in ice at Green River, Ky., Jan. 28, 1864.

5564 VICTOR NO. 2

Stw p wh b. Ironton, Oh., 1860. 67 tons. Ran Gallipolis-

Charleston on Kanawha River. She had one brief encounter during the war when a man hailed her on a downbound trip and when Capt. Fred Ford went in to get him, he proved to be a decoy for a considerable Confederate force. Ford ordered the boat backed away, and came off with injury to the boat no worse than a good riddling with shot, and nobody hurt. Snagged and lost 20 miles above Memphis, Oct. 27, 1868.

5565 VICTOR NO. 3

Stw p wh b. Cincinnati, Oh., 1862. 100 tons. Ran Gallipolis-Charleston, and during the war was active in U.S. transport service. Sold in March 1865 to Capt. W.L. Maddy, Gallipolis, who with R.W. Goodwin, clerk, continued her in the trade. She was running low water in the Portsmouth-Big Sandy trade when she hit an obstruction below Sciotoville and sank, July 23, 1867. The *TELEGRAPH* took her passengers to Portsmouth. Off the lists 1869.

5566 VICTOR NO. 4

Stw p wh b. Cincinnati, Oh., 1866. 286 tons. Ran Portsmouth-Huntington, Capt. Uriah B. Scott. 171 x 25.5 x 4.5. In 1869 running Portsmouth-Pomeroy, tri weekly, Capt. J.T. Campbell, with C.P. Sheplar, clerk. Owned in 1870 by Dennis H. Clark, Ironton, Oh. Sold to James Rees & Sons Co., Pittsburgh, who took her there, removed the machinery, and sold her to Messrs. Howard and Love who were building the Connellsville Railroad, and they used her for a boarding house. Note: There is possibility *VICTOR NO. 4* was built from the wrecked U.S. tinclad *UNDINE* (see) which had been burned at Johnsonville, Tenn., in 1864. Also Capt. Uriah B. Scott is said to have been identified with all four in this *VICTOR* series.

5567 VICTORIA

SW p wh b. Louisville, Ky., 1855. 161 tons. 133 x 29.5 x 4.5. Owned Feb. 1856 by Robert N. Jones, Doaksville, Ark., Capt. Edmond Burke listed as master. First home port, Galveston, Tex. Ran on Red River 1857-1858. Off the lists 1858.

5568 VICTORIA

SW p wh b. Elizabeth, Pa., 1858. 405 tons. 233 x 33 x 6. Ran in the Lightning Line on Missouri River, Jefferson City-St. Joseph, Capt. Louis A. Welton. Capt. Ben V. Glime also commanded. Captured as a Confederate steamer on June 6, 1862. Was used as a wharfboat by the USQMD during the war, and afterwards was sold to become *LEXINGTON* (see).

5569 VICTORY

SW p wh b. Cincinnati, Oh., 1863. 160 tons. 157 x 30.2 x 4.1. Engines, 13's- 4½ ft. She was to have been named *BUNKER* but was sold before documentation to the U.S. for war service after which she was sold to private hands and renamed *LIZZIE TATE* Oct. 7, 1865 (see).

5570 VICTORY

Stw p wh b. Metropolis, Ill., and completed at St. Louis, 1864. 278 tons. 172 x 34 x 5. Was making trips New Orleans-Shreveport, 1866. Memphis-Napoleon, c. 1869. Served as a towboat later, owned 1874 by Keokuk Northern Line Packet Co. In 1873 she came to Pittsburgh and took coal in barges to Galena and Dubuque, after which she got in a storm which carried away pilothouse, stacks, etc., and she was rebuilt at La Crosse. Off the lists 1883.

5571 VICTRESS

SW p wh b. Cincinnati, Oh., 1841. 190 tons. 155 x 25 x 5.2. Ran Cincinnati-New Orleans. Sold December 1844 to Capt. George M. Kendall, New Orleans, mortgaged for $2,700 payable to Thurston Chance, Thomas Eckert and James Montgomery. Sold February 1845 to Capt. Berthilde Landreaux. Sold July 1846 to Henry Legendre, New Orleans. Sold March 1847 to W.W. Hill, Lafayette, La., Capt. S.J. Bickerstaff. Off the lists 1849.

5572 VICTRESS

Stw p wh b. Cincinnati, Oh., 1862. 106 tons. Engines, 12's- 4 ft. Two boilers, each 38" by 20 ft. Ran Gallipolis-Charleston, 1863. In 1867 running Gallipolis-Pomeroy-Syracuse daily with Capt. E. Barringer, master, and R.S. Lallance, clerk. Also there in May 1868. By spring 1870 was running Pittsburgh-Wheeling, Capt. W.T. Dausen, with James W. Dausen, clerk. Owned 1871 by Rhoads, Bidell & Co., Capt. David Cunningham. On Jan. 28, 1871, a field of ice at East Liverpool, Oh., dislodged *VICTRESS*, the wharfboat, and small craft and sent them free-astray down the river. Off the lists 1871.

5573 VIENNA

Stw p wh b. Monongahela, Pa., 1853. 169 tons. Owned and operated by Charles A. and George B. Hay, brothers, of Haysville, Pa. Went to the St. Louis-St. Paul trade 1855-1856 and lost in ice on the Illinois River, Feb. 7, 1857.

5574 VIENNA

Stw p wh b. Plattsmouth, Neb., 1879, originally named *CITY OF PLATTSMOUTH* (see). 73 tons. 89.6 x 24 x 2.3. Engines, 8's- 14". One boiler. Snagged and lost one-half mile below New Haven, Mo., Dec. 10, 1889, owned at the time by E. Schleff and others. Henry Zeiblin was the pilot. Part of the cargo was salvaged.

5575 VIGO

SW p wh b. Brownsville, Pa., 1859. 144 tons. 130 x 26 x 4.6. Engines, 18's- 5½ ft. Three boilers. Went to New Orleans owned by Capt. E.D. Abrams of that place. Sold April 1860 to Capt. R.W. Doyle, New Orleans. Went to Mobile and worked for Mobile & Montgomery Railroad. Back in New Orleans May 1861 when sold to R.N. Doyle, that city, Capt. R.H. Martin. Ran on Red River, and was taken to Louisville, Ky., in 1868 for dismantling. Engines went to *LEO*.

5576 VIGO

Rig? p wh b. Terre Haute, Ind., 1870. 87½ tons. 100 x 18 x 3. On Feb. 5, 1871, burned at Terre Haute with a cargo of walnut lumber on board, owned by a Mr. Carter, and loss set at $6,000. Sold to Capt. T.P. Agnew, rebuilt. Still in that area 1876. Documented at Cincinnati 1881, inspected at Wheeling 1882 and still listed 1886, maybe later.

5577 VIGOR

Prop p wh b. La Crosse, Wis., 1873. 24 tons. 52 x 9 x 4. Single deck, one stack, one boiler set in the hold. Ran Brownsville-La Crosse for years owned by G.W. Winslow. Was still documented 1886, maybe longer. Said to have burned, and was rebuilt to become the *WHITE BEAVER*.

5578 VIM

Stw p wh b. Jeffersonville, Ind., by Howard, 1915. 125 x 23.2 x 4.3. Machinery from the *HATTIE BROWN* (see). Owned by Louisville & Cincinnati Packet Co., and ran Madison-Warsaw. In 1919 a cabin was added upstairs, and she then ran Madison-Kentucky River, renamed *RICHARD ROE* (see).

5579 VINDICATOR

SW U.S. ram wh b. New Albany, Ind., 1863. 750 tons. 210 x 41.5 x 9.5. Engines, 28's- 6 ft. She was sold to the U.S. before documentation and became the ram *VINDICATOR* May 24, 1864. Sold at Mound City, Ill., Nov. 29, 1865, to William Hambleton for $5,000. Renamed *NEW ORLEANS* on Feb. 27, 1866 (see).

5580 VINT SHINKLE

Stw p wh b. Cincinnati, Oh., 1874. 620 tons. In the fall of 1875 in the Louisville-Evansville trade, Capt. James Kenniston, with W.F. McIntyre and Amos Day, clerks, two round trips a week. Captain Kenniston was master for many years, popularly known as "Old Tubular," and was referred to by Will S. Hays as "Old Tub'lar." Spent her career in the Memphis & Ohio River Packet Co. On Aug. 22, 1878, upbound Memphis to Cincinnati broke her shaft near Golconda, Ill., and threw her wheel overboard. The *CHAMPION NO. 8* went down to tow her in. In 1879 Capt. Sterling C. McIntyre was master, with J.A. Lindsay, clerk. Burned at Belmont, Mo., Christmas Day, 1884.*

5581 VINT STILLINGS

Stw p (?) wh b. Metropolis, Ill., 1881, originally named *WILLIE CADE* (see). She was renamed on the Missouri River and was based at Omaha, Neb., 1896 named *VINT STILLINGS*. We have seen no reference to this boat under either name, and cannot say whether she was a packet, towboat or otherwise.

5582 VIOLA

SW p wh b. Louisville, Ky., 1846. 199 tons. 161 x 22.1 x 5.5. Enrolled at New Orleans Nov. 25, 1847, owned by Ferdinand M. Streck and Justinien Laroque Turgeau of Ascension Parish, La., the latter being master. In February 1848, owned entire by Streck, with William C. Wilson as master, of Lafourche Interior (now Terrebonne and Lafourche Parishes.) Lost in collision with the *AMERICA* at Donaldsonville, La., on Oct. 27, 1849.

5583 VIOLA

Stw p wh b. Cincinnati, Oh., 1863. 86 tons. Shows up briefly in the Pittsburgh-Wheeling trade, Capt. Henderson, February-March, 1866. Ran Big Sandy-Portsmouth in 1869 competing with *JONAS POWELL*. Was owned by Lexington & Big Sandy Railroad in 1870, and they sold her to W.W. Little & Co., Portsmouth, Oh., that February for $4,000. Made herself heard at Portsmouth on the night of Apr. 17, 1871, when her whistle got stuck open and blew until her steam was spent. Crowds congregated. Lost in ice Jan. 29, 1872.

5584 VIOLA

SW p wh b. Maquoketa, Iowa, 1865. 39 tons. Probably assisted rafts, etc., but ran as a packet between Prescott and St. Croix in 1873, but proved too slow. She was backing out of Richland Slough between La Crosse and Winona on May 9, 1876, hit a snag and sank. Machinery was recovered and the balance abandoned.

5585 VIOLA BELLE

SW p wh b. Pearl Landing, Ill., 1866. 345 tons. 200 x 30 x 5. Engines, 17's- 6 ft. Three boilers, each 36" by 22 ft. Pearl Landing is on the Illinois River. During her career made five trips to Fort Benton, Mont. She was lengthened 25 feet at Daggett's Docks, St. Louis, March 1868 and got a new bow. Was in the Northwestern Transportation Co. Twice snagged, first in 1870 and again Aug. 21, 1871, which proved fatal. She was upbound, sank in six feet, the sand washed out from under the hull, and she broke in two—this at Smith's Bar, Doniphan Bend, Missouri River. Owned at the time by Augustus C. Erfort and others.

5586 VIOLETT

Stw p wh b. Brownsville, Pa., 1856. 89 tons. 123 x 22 x 3.5. Burned and lost at Van Buren, Ark., on Arkansas River, Dec. 27, 1862.

5587 VIRGIE LEE

Rig? p wh b. Madison, Ind., 1876. 183 x 35 x 5. Built for Capt. J.V. Reynolds and others and ran Kanawha River-Cincinnati replacing *JULIA NO. 2* (see). In 1878 ran Cincinnati-Madison, Capt. W.H. Kirby, with A.J. Harrigan, clerk. Documented at Wheeling in 1886, and is said to have sunk at Augusta, Ky., later on, whereupon Dr. S.L. Wait built a houseboat using the cabin, and called it *VIRGIE LEE*. Her roof bell wound up in a church at Henderson, W. Va.

5588 VIRGIE RATLIFF

SW batwing p wh b. Catlettsburg, Ky., 1887. 113 x 16 x 4.3. The hull was built on the river bank at Guyandotte, W. Va. Built by Capt. John Hopkins and others for Big Sandy

River. He also ran *ANDY HATCHER,* both rivals of the *FRANK PRESTON.* During low water in September 1896 she ran Pittsburgh-Parkersburg, Capt. Lee Anshutz, under charter.

5589 VIRGINIA

SW p wh b. Elizabethtown, Pa., 1848. 60 tons. Came out May 1848 owned by George Ledlie, Pittsburgh, Capt. William T. Dawson. Was in Wheeling-Steubenville trade when she exploded her boiler at Rush Run, Mar. 31, 1849, with loss of ten lives. The *MOUNT VERNON* rendered aid. In 1851 running Pittsburgh-Bradys Bend-Catfish trade on the Allegheny River, Capt. Martin Millinger. Sold July 1851 to Capt. Robert Galloway and made one Pittsburgh-Zanesville trip. Dismantled soon after.

5590 VIRGINIA

SW p wh b. West Elizabeth, Pa., 1853. 642 tons. 277 x 34 x 7. Built for the Wheeling-Louisville trade. The two major shareholders were Capt. Charles V. Wells, Sistersville, Va., who commanded, and Wm. B. Scaife & Co., Pittsburgh. Wheeling shareholders included W.W. Shriver, Charles W. Russell, Edward H. Fitzhugh, John Eoff, John W. Gill, and Yallent & Dilliplain. J.C. Russell, Sistersville, also had a share. She was entered in the Wheeling Union Line operating a boat a day from either terminal. Unusual low water and ice ended this operation after a brief attempt, and she went to the St. Louis-New Orleans trade. Captain Wells later built *PLANTER* at Wheeling (see) and then removed to a farm on the Osage River, Mo., where he died February 1880.

5591 VIRGINIA

Rig? p wh b. Parkersburg, W. Va., 1863. 228 tons. 122.1 x 22.7 x 4.4. Owned 1865 by H.W. Taylor, New Orleans, Capt. A. Grant, master. Burned on the Tombigbee River, Ala., Mar. 1, 1868. Listed in Lytle-Holdcamper as *VIRGINIA NO. 2*

5592 VIRGINIA

SW p wh b. Jeffersonville, Ind., by Howard, 1865. 890 tons. 226 x 42 x 6.8. Ran Louisville-New Orleans, Capt. John W. Carroll. By 1870 commanded by Capt. Charles G. Schultze, with Len S. Miller, clerk. She was fatally snagged at Osceola, Ark., Oct. 7, 1871. The hull was ripped from the stem to the hatches. The *T.F. ECKERT* did the salvage work. She was downbound at the time, and the *HENRY M. SHREVE,* Capt. Boyd, stood by.

5593 VIRGINIA

Stw p wh b. Cincinnati, Oh., 1895. 235 x 40 x 7. Compound condensing engines, 15's, 33's- 7 ft. Four boilers, each 42″ by 20 ft., six flues each. Built by Cincinnati Marine Railway Co. Machinery by Griffith & Wedge, Zanesville, Oh. Built for the Pittsburgh & Cincinnati Packet Line, construction superintended by Capt. J. Frank Ellison. Came out new on New Year's Day 1896; crew: Capt. Thomas Calhoon, master; Robert H. Kerr, purser; Harry Ollom and Spence Sandford, pilots; Johnson and Owens, engineers; John Sweeney and Hod Knowles the mates, and Irwin Johnson, steward. She was noticed as being exceptionally quiet in operation, and we have heard Capt. William D. Kimble remark that those in the office did not know whether she was in motion until they looked out the window. Had 50 staterooms in the cabin and 10 more in the texas. Her cabin was done in white with elegant panels of a material known as Lincrusta Walton. Also she was one of the first on the Upper Ohio to have a carbon arc searchlight contained in a glassfronted case with a reflector, called a White Squadron light imported from the Atlantic seaboard. Paddlewheel 23½ ft. diameter working 30 ft., buckets, staggered. Had distinctive arch hogchains, an innovation later used on the *QUEEN CITY, KANAWHA,* and others. She had good water all 1896 and is said to have paid for herself that first season.

Capt. Alf Pennywitt became master, c. 1902. She struck a submerged bridge pier at Steubenville, Oh., on March 3, 1904, rupturing the hull, but prompt assistance from the local fire department and from towboats *RAYMOND HORNER* and *IRONSIDES* prevented her sinking. She was the first packet to pass under the completed Wabash Railroad bridge, Pittsburgh, 1904. Her original fancy-topped stacks were replaced with plain "towboat" stacks prior to April 1909 when she sank at the lower landing, Wellsville, Oh., on the 13th of that month. The towboat *RIVAL* was sent down from Pittsburgh to assist but arrived too late.

The celebrated event of this boat's career came when she quit the river on the night of Mar. 6, 1910, and was turned into a cornfield decoration. Capt. Charles W. Knox was master, and Billy Anderson was pilot on watch. The river was in flood, and a landing was made at Willow Grove, W. Va., below Ravenswood to put off a passenger. In departing, she sidled down over Williamson's submerged field and stuck. In another week she was the Ark on Ararat, high and dry, the river a half mile away. Steamboat excursions were run from St. Marys, Marietta, and Gallipolis with sightseers, and the B. & O. Railroad ran excursions to accommodate the curious. The Pittsburgh contracting firm, John Eichleay Jr. Co., was called in to move her back to the river, which was done, but she could not be launched because of the sandy riverbank soil. A fortunate rise came in the Ohio River and lifted the boat back to its bosom. The story of this epic is recounted with many photographs in the *S&D Reflector,* issue March 1966. Another feature story on *VIRGINIA* appears in the same publication's March 1973 issue, copiously illustrated. She struck an overhead cable at the construction site of Dam 26, Ohio River, Dec. 18, 1911, upbound, and knocked down her stacks and tore up the pilothouse. After temporary repairs she continued to Pittsburgh and then returned to Pt. Pleasant, W. Va., for repairs. At this time she was renamed *STEEL CITY* (see).

Capt. Jesse P. Hughes once told this scribe that he sat up late the night of Feb. 27, 1896 to watch the new *VIRGINIA* pass Grape Island "lighted up wonderfully," and then went next day to Marietta and got a job with Capt. Gordon C. Greene. "That compound machinery gave them lots of trouble," he recalled. "I think she cut a hole in the Maysville wharfboat, her first mishap; later she did the same at Portsmouth."

5594 VIRGINIA

SW ex wh b. Brownsville, Pa., 1898, originally named *I. C. WOODWARD* (see). The *WOODWARD* was built into an excursion steamer in 1914 and renamed. She went to U.S. marshal sale at Evansville, Ind., in August 1915 and was bid in by Capt. Fred Hornbrook for $2,775. He never raised steam on her, and traded her in as part payment for the *TELL CITY* in early 1916 (see). Operated at Louisville and vicinity in 1917 and in 1918 was a ferry between Charleston and Nitro, W. Va., during the construction of a munitions plant. In August 1919 again was in the hands of a U.S. marshal at Pt. Pleasant, W. Va., and after the sale became the *CITY OF CHARLESTON* (see).

5595 VIRGINIA BARTON

SW p wh b. Brownsville, Pa., 1864. 219 tons. Sold to USQMD Nov. 23, 1864. She was completed at the Rees shop, Pittsburgh, and the Rees family had interest in her. Sale price was said to have been $36,000. After the war she was sold to private hands and renamed *NORTH ALABAMA*, Jan. 27, 1866 (see).

5596 VIRGINIA BELLE

Stw p wh b. St. Louis, Mo., 1846. 132 tons. Off the lists in 1850.

5597 VIRGINIA BELLE

Stw p wh b. Allegheny, Pa., 1856. 70 tons. Engines, 12's-3½ ft. Capt. James G. Saint was master in 1856, with W.P. Cobb, clerk. Dismantled, and her engines went to the *CONWAY* (see) b. Lewisburgh, Ark., 1859.

5598 VIRGINIA FARMER

Stw ferry wh b. West Wheeling, Oh., 1850. 33 tons. Off the lists in 1857.

5599 VIRGINIA HOME

Stw p wh b. Gallipolis, Oh., 1858. 70 tons. Her hull was built up Raccoon Greek, Oh., by John Viney, 100 feet long. Capt. W.F. Gregory bought it, lengthened it out to 140 feet, 26 ft. floor, 28 ft. beam, and 4 ft. depth. Engines, 12's- 4 ft. She was designed for Kanawha River trades and named to honor Richmond, Va., Capt. Gregory's homeplace. During the first season's operation she was taken to Kanawha Falls, head of the river, and was the first boat there. Wrote Capt. Gregory later: "Col. Stockton offered $500 for the first boat to go to the Falls but he never paid me the reward; instead he gave me 2 barrels of flour, 1 bu. of meal, some venison hams and one ham of bear meat. His daughter gave me 6 chickens and a whole lot of preserves. During the war a good many boats went to the Falls, that being 1863 and 1864, during high water." Capt. Wm. F. Gregory married a sister of John F. Rust, and through him Capt. Rust took to the river. Ran Gallipolis-Charleston, 1859, Capt. J.B. Coffman, with Charles Regnier, clerk. That fall ran Cincinnati-New Richmond-Neville with Capt. Gurley in command, owned by William N. Orr & Co., Neville, Oh. Turned over in a storm at Crawfish Bar, four miles above Cincinnati, May 21, 1860.

5600 VIRGINIAN

SW p wh b. Cincinnati, Oh., 1841. 107 tons. Running Cincinnati-Kanawha River, Capt. Cable, January 1842. 145 x 20 x 5.3. Enrolled at New Orleans, Feb. 8, 1844, owned and commanded by Capt. Silas Ruffner, Kanawha, Va. Off the lists in 1848.

5601 VIROQUA

Stw p wh b. Monongahela, Pa., 1849. 92 tons. Ran Marietta-Zanesville on the Muskingum in 1850, Capt. Robert Galloway; again in 1851, Capt. John Henderson. Then went to the Wheeling-Steubenville trade, Capt. O'Neal. She was at Sunfish, Oh. (Clarington) during the April 1852 Flood (43.3 ft. at Marietta April 20) and goods were transferred from William F. Booth's warehouse and placed on the *VIROQUA* and *TOM SCOTT*. This same flood took away the big warehouse owned by William Cecil at Moundsville; also the warehouse there owned by Alexander & Anshutz. There was an earthquake at Marietta April 29, ringing many doorbells. Ran Wheeling-Sunfish 1856, Capt. Jack Harrison, with Jacob Cramer, pilot; James Venon, engineer; J.W. Cochran, clerk, and Jeremiah Steenrod, mate. Ran there about two years. Off the lists 1859.

5602 VISITOR

SW p wh b. Elizabethtown, Pa., 1848. 141 tons. Owned by Capt. William Stewart and others, and made frequent trips up Wabash River when the stage permitted, and on the Ohio River otherwise. Collided with *HIRAM POWERS* at Terre Haute, Ind., May 30, 1851, and was lost.

5603 VIVIAN GRAY

Rig? yacht wh b. La Crosse, Wis., 1886. 33 x 6.3 x 2.9. Still documented 1896, maybe later.

5604 VIXEN

Stw p wh b. Brownsville, Pa., 1856. 232 tons. Often made trips Pittsburgh-St. Paul and return. Burned at Louisville, Ky., Dec. 25, 1859.

5605 VIXEN

Prop yacht wh b. North Bend, Oh., 1899. 50.5 x 9.5 x 3.7. Originally named *J.P. TARVIN*. Renamed prior to 1902.

5606 VOLANT

SW p wh b. New Albany, Ind., 1852. 136 tons. Burned and lost on the Yazoo River at Cardiff, Miss., Nov. 4, 1853. One life was lost, a drunken passenger.

5607 VOLANT

Stw pl wh b. Roanoke, Ind., 1862. 12 tons. Exploded her boiler and was lost leaving Henderson, Ky., on Dec. 20, 1868. The engineer, David Cooper, of Grave Creek, W. Va., was killed. Owned by a Mr. Morris who was on board at the time and was slightly injured. First home port was Wheeling.

5608 VOLUNTEER

Stw p wh b. Monongahela, Pa., 1862. 210 tons. 125.1 x 33 x 4.5. Engines, 15's- 5 ft. Hull by William Latta, cabin by Bunton, Miller & Co., Pittsburgh, machinery by Rees. Built for Capt. Lewis F.L. Vandergrift and others. Her first trip, December 1862, was Pittsburgh to Cincinnati and return, Thomas Shuman, clerk. Then loaded for Gallipolis, Oh., and returned to Cincinnati where she was chartered to the U.S. at $150 a day. Operated in the vicinity of Natchez, Miss. She was seized by the *FORT HINDMAN* near Natchez Island, Nov. 25, 1863, engaged in loading illegal cotton, then in the possession of army troops. She was condemned a prize of war. Sold by the U.S. at Mound City, Ill., Nov. 29, 1865, purchased by B.F. Goodwin for $9,100. Renamed *TALISMAN* (see) and operated later out of Nashville, Tenn.

5609 VOLUNTEER

Stw p wh b. Cincinnati, Oh., 1863. 106 tons. Lost on the Cumberland River, July 1865.

5610 VOLUNTEER

Prop p wh b. Mason City, W. Va., 1887. 91.3 x 12.6 x 2.3. Engine single 14″ x 14″ stroke, 125 psi. single boiler, single prop. She was fast, 14 mph against a four mile current. Built by the Bay brothers for Ironton-Proctorville trade. *GEORGIA* (2319) was built to replace her. Sold 1892 and went to Tampa, Fla., rebuilt with wider hull and renamed *CITY OF TAMPA*. Still there in 1896, and maybe longer.

5611 VOLUNTEER

Stw p wh b. Le Claire, Iowa, 1891. 137.8 x 24.3 x 4.3. Engines, 13's- 4½ ft. Owned by Le Claire Navigation Co., and primarily was a raftboat. Capt. S.R. Vansant ran her in the Davenport-Burlington trade 1899. She ran through herself that July and lost a pitman overboard. Burned at the Kahlke Yard, Rock Island, Ill., April 1900 along with *SATURN* and *MASCOT*.

W

5612 W.A. ANDREW

SW p wh b. Madison, Ind., 1857. 229 tons. 132 x 30 x 5.5. Owned by Capt. Robert Moody, New Orleans, La. In 1858 ran New Orleans-Grand Encore, Capt. C.J. Barstow in place of *RAPIDES*. Sold 1860 to Robert Means, New Orleans, who transferred her next day to Capt. Joseph T. Landry, Donaldsonville, La. Went to Confederate registry owned by Capt. J.A. Tarrier, New Orleans, Mar. 29, 1862.

5613 W.A. CALDWELL

Stw p wh b. Pittsburgh, Pa., 1866. 297 tons. Owned by Capt. John Woodburn and others, and ran Pittsburgh-Arkansas River, and also made trips New Orleans-Arkansas River. Capt. Woodburn came to be called "the Arkansas Traveler." He sold his interest in the boat to the Memphis & Arkansas River Packet Co., in mid-May 1868. Snagged and lost in what came to be called Caldwell's Bend in the cut-off between White and Arkansas rivers, Dec. 6, 1870.

5614 W.A. EAVES

SW p wh b. Brownsville, Pa., 1854. 145 tons. Ran Louisville-Henderson, Capt. S. Sullivan. Sold 1857 to Capt. Jerome D. Duncan and others of Cloverport, Ky. They traded her off in the spring of 1858 for *SCIOTO NO. 2* (see). Off the lists in 1860.

5615 W.A. EDDY

SW p wh b. Cold Spring, N.Y., 1870. 41 x 10. 10 hp. engine. One boiler. Paddlewheels 2′ dia. with 10″ dip. Arrived at the Allegheny wharf, Pittsburgh, Apr. 16, 1870, "the smallest side-wheeler afloat." According to the Pittsburgh *Commercial* she "will carry 14 tons of freight or 50 passengers; has one deck with the engines amidships and with cabins fore and aft; cost $2500 and will make 10 mph. To ply between Parkers Landing and Foxburg on the Allegheny." Be this so, she already had covered a good bit of territory, Cold Spring being on the Hudson River.

5616 W.A. HEALY

SW p wh b. Cincinnati, Oh., 1862. 146 tons. Bought by the U.S. and became Tinclad #22, renamed *SPRINGFIELD*, Nov. 20, 1862. Sold at public sale and renamed *JENNIE D.*, Apr. 1, 1866 (see).

5617 W.A. HILTON

Stw p wh b. Elizabeth, W. Va., 1890. 104 x 21.5 x 3.5. Engines, 11's- 4 ft. Two boilers, each 42″ by 16 ft. Ran on Little Kanawha River, Capt. A.B. Hilton. Sold to Pittsburgh and renamed *KATHRYN* (see).

5618 W.A. JOHNSON

Stw p wh b. Evansville, Ind., 1878. 150 x 29 x 4. Ran Paducah-Florence, also Evansville-Florence on Tennessee River. Capt. James Till, master, 1887. Still operating 1890.

5619 W.A. MOFFITT

SW p wh b. Metropolis, Ill., 1865. 553 tons. Burned at St. Louis, Mo., Nov. 17, 1865.

5620 W.A. VIOLETT

SW p wh b. Elizabeth, Pa., 1848. 162 tons. 120 x 23.3 x 5.2. Documented at New Orleans, Jan. 13, 1849, as *WILLIAM A. VIOLETT* owned by R.L. Gillett, New Orleans, Capt. Joseph Claiborne, master. Sold June 1849 to Capt. William Kay, Lafayette (now New Orleans) La. Sold November 1849 to A.S. Brown, Samuel W. Land, and Robert R.

Kendell, all of New Orleans, Capt. Samuel Gwartney master. Burned at Torras, La., Jan. 24, 1853.

5621 W.B. CLIFTON

SW p wh b. Jeffersonville, Ind., by Howard, 1851. 341 tons. 225 x 33 x 6.5. Ran Louisville-New Orleans. Master in January 1854 was Capt. Shearer who lately had been head clerk on *ECLIPSE.* Collided with *CHICKASAW* in French Island, Ohio River, Apr. 26, 1852, resulting in loss of the latter (see). Collided with the *OHIO* at Columbus, Ky., on Apr. 1, 1854, and went down in 22 feet drowning seven deck passengers.

W.B. DANCE

See *WALTER B. DANCE,* registered name.

5622 W.B. DUNCAN

SW tr wh b. Jeffersonville, Ind., by Howard, 1881. 201 x 45 x 7.4. Engines, 23's- 7 ft. Four boilers, each 44″ by 28 ft., two on a side. Named for W. Butler Duncan, and owned many years by Illinois Central Railroad. Original cost was $50,000, and her value for insurance purposes increased over the years until by 1913 she was carried at $70,000. She was docked every couple of years and was kept tip-top. Served many points, Metropolis, Vicksburg, Helena. Retired in 1931.

5623 W.B. TERRY

Stw p wh b. Belle Vernon, Pa., 1856. 175 tons. Ran Paducah-Eastport on Tennessee River prior to the war. Seized at Paducah on Aug. 21, 1861, by U.S. gunboat *LEXINGTON* for engaging in traffic with the enemy and for flying the Confederate flag, and was towed to Cairo. Burned at Duck River, Tenn., Sept. 3, 1862.

5624 W.C. GRAY

SW ferry wh b. Pittsburgh, Pa., 1865. 50 tons. A double-ender ferry. Served in the Pittsburgh area until removed from documentation in 1879.

5625 W.C. HITE

SW ferry wh b. Jeffersonville, Ind., by Howard, 1882. 155 x 36 x 6.3. Engines, 20's- 6 ft. Two boilers, each 44″ by 18 ft. Owned by Louisville & Jeffersonville Ferry Co. Named for Capt. W.C. Hite, Louisville. His life story and pictures of the boat appear in *S&D Reflector,* issue March 1969, pages 29–31. Rebuilt into an excursion boat 1914 and renamed *CORONA* (see).

5626 W.C. MANN

Stw p wh b. Cincinnati, Oh., 1863. 192 tons. Capt. John M. Shunk, Cincinnati, sold her to the U.S. for $35,000 in latter February 1864 and she became Tinclad #52, renamed *ELFIN.* Sunk and burned at Johnsonville, Tenn., to prevent her capture, Nov. 4, 1864.

5627 W.C. PUSEY

SW ferry wh b. New Martinsville, W. Va., 1889. 85.7 x 18 x 3.2. Operated at Sistersville, W. Va. during the oil boom 1894–1896, maybe longer. She was converted into a passenger and freight barge March 1900 owned by William Terry, Sistersville, W. Va.

5628 W.D. WALDEN

Stw ferry wh b. Pierre, S.D., 1906. 101 x 31 x 3.7. Built for the Chicago & North Western Railroad and carried passengers and freight across the Missouri at Pierre before the bridge was opened Oct. 4, 1907. After that she lay around a good bit, and by 1914 had been sold and renamed *SCARAB* (see).

5629 W.F. CURTIS

Stw p wh b. Parkersburg, W. Va., 1864. 211 tons. Named for a Marietta citizen who dealt extensively in real estate. Entered the Pittsburgh-Gallipolis trade, Capt. Thornily in early September 1864. Burned at the Marietta wharf, June 27, 1867. Rebuilt at Marietta by Capt. Albert Brown and others, using the original engines and parts from the *EAGLE* (see) which was wrecked in ice winter 1866–67. She ran Louisville-Cairo low water in fall 1868 in place of *JOHN KILGOUR.* Was sent south with produce in winter months. In February 1870 was in New Orleans-Attakapas trade. Rebuilt at the Knox Yard, Marietta, 1871, and may have been lengthened. Sold to the Upper Mississippi and in October 1873 was loading produce at Muscatine, Iowa, for New Orleans, Capt. Cooley. He planned to run her that winter New Orleans-Tensas. Dismantled 1876.

5630 W.F. NISBET

Stw p wh b. Jeffersonville, Ind., by Howard, 1883. 200 x 35 x 6.1. Owned by Evansville & Tennessee River Packet Co. They sold her October 1895 to the White Collar Line, Cincinnati, Oh., Fred A. Laidley, manager. Ran in trades above Cincinnati most of the time until she sank and was lost at Wellsburg, Ky., about five miles below Augusta, Ky., Jan. 1, 1900.

5631 W.G. CAMPBELL

SW p wh b. Louisville, Ky., 1847. 168 tons. Ran Cincinnati-Tennessee River, Capt. Jesse K. Bell. Sank on the Falls, Louisville, Ky., downbound, May 25, 1850. Out of service in 1856.

5632 W.G. LITTLE

SW p wh b. California, Pa., 1878. 140 x 25 x 3.5. Originally named *NIOBARA* (see). She was renamed when operated out of Mobile, Ala., May 16, 1885. Lost in 1888.

5633 W.G. WOODSIDE

Stw p wh b. Moundsville, Va., 1855. 197 tons. Made a trip to St. Paul, Minn., in 1856. Running Pittsburgh-Cincinnati, Feb. 1861, Capt. Booth. Off the lists 1862.

5634 W.H. CHERRY

Stw p wh b. Jeffersonville, Ind., by Howard, 1882. 169 x 32 x 5.2. Built for the Ryman Line, Nashville, Tenn. who ran her Nashville-Paducah-Cairo. According to advertisements she was the "most refined" boat in the line. Later operated by St. Louis & Tennessee River Packet Co. Taken to New Orleans, c. 1892, and was made into a convict transport, renamed *COL. T.G. SPARKS.* The wreck of this boat was going to pieces at St. Gabriel, La., June 1898.

5635 W.H. DENNY

Stw p wh b. California, Pa., 1855. 276 tons. 150 x 34.2 x 5. Originally owned by Capt. Thomas Lyons, Beaver, Pa., who was master. Was in the St. Louis-St. Paul trade 1857, Capt. Lyons. Burned at Quincy, Ill., Sept. 16, 1858.

5636 W.H. GRAPEVINE

Stw p wh b. Mound City, Ill., 1898. 142.5 x 30 x 3.5. Engines, 10's- 4 ft. Had the machinery and part of the upper works of the *J.A. WOODSON* (see). Owned by Iron Mountain Railroad, named for Capt. William H. Grapevine, superintendent of Missouri-Pacific's transfer boats. Designed for White River, Ark., to connect with their trains. After brief service there she went to the Missouri River and ran St. Louis-Rocheport, Capt. W.L. Heckmann with pilots E.M. Baldwin, Roy Coulter, Bill Thompson, Tom La Barge, and W.L. Heckmann, Sr. Her engineers included Sam Clifford, Bert Coulter, Fred J. Heckmann, Frank Blaske, and Bill Kay. Ran excursions at Kansas City in 1900 under charter to A.F. Baughman. In spring of 1903 sold to Capt. Doss Davis, Ironton, Oh., who ran her briefly Cincinnati-Ironton. On Christmas Day 1903 she broke loose in ice at Cincinnati, hit the C.&O. Railroad bridge, and sank. The machinery went to a Big Sandy boat named *ECLIPSE.*

5637 W.H. LANGLEY

Stw p wh b. Fraziers Landing, Oh., 1856. 128 x 23 x 4, 110 tons. Taken over by Confederates in spring of 1861. See Addendum for full details on this boat.

5638 W.H. OSBORN

SW p wh b. Pittsburgh, Pa., 1865. 1,156 tons. Named for the president of the Illinois Central Railroad, built by William J. Kountz and others for St. Louis-New Orleans trade. Her master was Capt. Thomas Rogers, and J.M. Hare was clerk. She was moored at the foot of Customhouse Street, New Orleans, where she caught fire about 3:00 A.M., aft of the port wheelhouse, Dec. 24, 1866. Her cargo had been discharged, and she was preparing to take a trip to Louisville. Captain Rogers and crew escaped with only the clothes they wore. The *STARLIGHT* was alongside, but was cut loose and drifted several miles downriver unharmed. The hull was not severely damaged; she did not sink, and was towed over to Algiers. She was changed into a barge November 1867.

5639 W.H. OSBORN

SW railroad ferry wh b. Jeffersonville, Ind., by Howard, 1884. 819 tons. 285 x 45 x 7.6. Owned by Illinois Central Railroad, and used at Cairo, Ill. They also used her later at other places, including New Orleans. Sometime after 1903 she was renamed *LOUISIANA*, and under that name was brought north with a load of lumber and converted into a wharfboat for the Lee Line, Memphis, 1909.

W.H. RUSSELL

See *WILLIAM H. RUSSELL,* registered name.

5640 W.H. WHITEMAN

Stw ferry wh b. Newport, Ky., 1892. 32 tons. 71.5 x 23 x 3.2. Engines, 8"-3 ft. One boiler, 40" by 13 ft. Named for a tobacco dealer of Cincinnati. Long operated at Manchester, Oh., owned by Capt. Ernie Anshutz, and later by Capt. E.B. Suiter who incorporated as Manchester Ferry Co. Burned January 1936.

5641 W.I. MACLAY

Stw p wh b. Brownsville, Pa., 1856. 245 tons. 159 x 33 x 5.5. Engines, 17's- 5 ft. Three boilers, each 38" by 22 ft. Pittsburgh-St. Louis, Capt. F.Y. Batchelor, 1856. Ran same trade, often terminating at Cincinnati, same master Sank and lost below St. Louis, Oct. 19, 1861.

5642 W.J. BEHAN

Stw p wh b. Jeffersonville, Ind., 1873. 165 x 33 x 4. Engines, 15's- 5½ ft. Two boilers. Ran New Orleans-Shreveport, and carried a cotton bale between her stacks. Operated in the New Orleans & Red River Transportation Co., in 1876, Capt. George Wilkinson. Joseph A. Aiken was president of the line. Sold to the Fort Benton Transportation Co., 1878, and was lost in ice at Bismarck, N.D., Mar. 28, 1884. The *BLACK HILLS* was lost in the same ice (see).

5643 W.J. QUINLAN

Stw ferry wh b. Rock Island, Ill., 1904, originally named *DAVENPORT.* Renamed in the latter 1920s. Owned by Rock Island-Davenport Ferry Co. Capacity 528 passengers. Out of service in 1946, laid up at the Kahlke Yard, Rock Island, Ill. Burned there in 1965.

5644 W.J. ROBERTS

Stw p wh b. Frankfort, Ky., 1908. 75 x 16 x 3.5. Combination packet and towboat. Bought by Capt. David Boyles and Charles N. Buckley, Parkersburg, W. Va., in June 1910. Ran in the Marietta-Middleport trade, 1912. Sold January 1913 to J.C. McCain, St. Marys, W. Va., and Elmer and Charles Beaver, New Matamoras, Oh., and in 1914 sold to Capt. John L. Howder and Charles T. Campbell who rebuilt her into a full-time towboat at Dravosburg, Pa., and renamed her *W.C. McCUNE.*

5645 W.J. YOUNG, JR.

Stw p wh b. Dubuque, Iowa, 1882. 146 x 32 x 5.5. Engines, 14's- 6 ft. Two boilers, each 30" by 30 ft. She was a raft boat on the Upper Mississippi until 1895 when bought by Carnival City Packet Co. They extended her cabin, built a half-texas behind the pilothouse, added a swinging stage, and ran her Davenport-Burlington, Capt. Walter Blair, master. Bernard Suiter was clerk, and Spence and Andy Burtnett, engineers. Never broke down in the whole nine years she ran in that trade. In 1903 was sold to the K&I Bridge & Terminal Co., Louisville, Ky., who renamed her *HIAWATHA* (see).

5646 W.K. PHILLIPS

Stw p wh b. Jeffersonville, Ind., by Howard, 1892. 165 x 30 x 4. Came out as an independent packet in Nashville-Paducah trade precipitating a ruinous rate war with the established Ryman Line, continuing at intervals into 1896. Ran Paducah-Cairo in place of the *DICK FOWLER* fall of 1897 with Capt. J.A. Crouch, master; Jolly P. Hard, purser; John Freedle, 2nd clerk; James Hart and C.P. Yarbrough, pilots; Joe Vandergrift and Jack Smoke, engineers, and Gus Weitzel, steward. Bought by the Ryman Line, and burned at Dover Island, just above Dover, Tenn., Dec. 13, 1897. Pilot on watch was Shep Green.

5647 W.L. HECKMANN

Stw f wh b. Hermann, Mo., 1904. 95 x 20.3 x 3. Owned by Capt. W.L. Heckmann, Sr. of Hermann, Mo. She was a ferry at Hermann, also handled wheat on the Osage and Missouri Rivers. Burned at Canton, Mo. June, 1913. Rebuilt and renamed *ILLMO,* so documented 1918.

5648 W.L. NORTON

Stw p wh b. Lenoir, Tenn., 1888. 67.5 x 12 x 3. Burned at Evansville, Ind., along with the *ALEX PERRY* (see) on Apr. 18, 1896.

5649 W.M. LEANE

SW p wh b. Louisville, Ky., 1852. 130 tons. Off the lists in 1854.

5650 W.M. PORTER

Stw p wh b. Shreveport, La., 1906. 119.9 x 21 x 4.3. A rather primitive craft with full second deck and cabin, Capt. Jonathan Hamilton. Still there in 1909, maybe later.

5651 W.N. CHANCELLOR

Stw p wh b. Parkersburg, W. Va., 1879. 175 x 30 x 3.8. Came out new Pittsburgh-Parkersburg, Capt. E.P. Chancellor, with clerks Ira Huntington and John Brookhart. Ran Pittsburgh-Cincinnati 1880, same crew. Ran Kanawha River-Cincinnati, 1881, same crew, with Elmer Ellsworth Stone, 2nd clerk. In 1882 entered the Pittsburgh-Charleston trade, the first regular boat in that run, one which proved so lucrative that boats ran there until the end of the packet days (see *LIBERTY*). She was the first boat to the scene of the *SCIOTO-JOHN LOMAS* disaster, July 4, 1882 (see). Ira B. Huntington left the boat 1887 and Clarke Barringer took his place One of her pilots was William H. Clarke, later U.S. Hull Inspector at Point Pleasant, W. Va. Jeff Frame, Wheeling, was the mate, and named his son James Chancellor Frame in honor of the owner-captain. Carried a black orchestra, and Ben Coleman played bass viol whistling and singing "Listen to the Mocking Bird." Wore out of old age and was taken to Hartford City, W. Va., dismantled, and much equipment went to building the towboat *GEORGE W. MOREDOCK,* 1892. The fancy nameboard from her cabin today is in the River Museum, Marietta, Oh. Capt. E.P. Chancellor (1833-1927) lived at Parkersburg, W. Va. and had been associated with the *W.P. THOMPSON, CHESAPEAKE, KATYDID, CLARA SCOTT, EMMA GRAHAM* and others, and your scribe has heard him relate of hearing a cannon fired at Belpre, Oh., whereupon he looked across the river to see the side-wheel *BUCKEYE STATE* upbound, and later learned the shot celebrated her "24 hour mark" out of Cincinnati (see), this in 1850. Capt. Chancellor was an uncle of C.C. Bowyer, the Pt. Pleasant, W. Va., banker, and the boat was named for his brother.

5652 W.N. DAY

Stw p wh b. Louisville, Ky., 1846. 57 tons. Off the lists 1854.

W.N. SHERMAN

See *WILLIAM N. SHERMAN,* registered name.

5653 W.O. HUGHART

Stw ferry wh b. Conway, Mich., 1894. 73.4 x 16.8 x 4.3. Came from Crooked Lake, Mich., via Chicago and the Illinois River dismantled of pilothouse and stack. She was used at Cincinnati as a private excursion boat, and then was bought by W.L. Thomas (father of Paul F. Thomas) who used her as a ferry at Augusta, Ky. Sold to Pickens Ferry Co., of which John J. Dower, Graham Station, W. Va., was managing owner, May 27, 1902, and served as the wharfboat at Racine, Oh., until it sank in September 1914.

5654 W.P. HALLIDAY

SW p wh b. Jeffersonville, Ind., at Barmore Yard, 1878. 285 x 41 x 9.2. Engines, 24's- 10 ft. Built for Capt. E.W. Gould and others for St. Louis-New Orleans trade. Later sold to the Anchor Line, Capt. Jos. W. Bryant, master. Burned at 4:00 A.M., Feb. 12, 1884, at the cotton compress, foot of Barton Street, St. Louis. W.P. Halliday was a prominent figure at Cairo, Ill., owning interest in the City National Bank of Cairo, the Halliday & Phillips wharfboat, Cairo City Coal Co., Cairo City Gas Co., Cairo City Electric Light & Power Co., and the Halliday Hotel. He died, 72, in the Lexington Hotel, Chicago, September 1899. The roof bell of his namesake went to the *DICK FOWLER*, and later was on the St. Louis & Tennessee River Packet Co., packets *KENTUCKY* and *SAINT LOUIS,* and finally was presented to the First Christian Church, Paducah, where it was still serving in 1953.

5655 W.P. SWINNEY

SW p wh b. Jeffersonville, Ind., by Howard, 1852. 199 tons. 170 x 39 x 6. Originally owned at Vicksburg, Miss. Bought May 1855 by Capt. John W. Boles who ran her New Orleans-Alexandria, La., on Red River. Off the lists in 1857.

5656 W.P. THOMPSON

Stw p wh b. Harmar, Oh. at Knox Yard, 1876. First owned by J.N. Camden & Co., oil producers, Parkersburg, W.

Va., and named for one of the directors. One of her first missions was to run Pittsburgh-Cincinnati in spring of 1877 in place of the *EMMA GRAHAM* while the "new" *EMMA GRAHAM* was being built, Capt. E.B. Cooper, with Nat Earhart, clerk. Capt. J.N. Williamson owned a part of her. She then ran Cincinnati-Charleston, Capt. John Thornburg. In the fall of 1878, ran Pittsburgh–Cincinnati, and was there again in the fall of 1879, Capt. Hod Knowles, with Nat Earhart, clerk, at that time owned by Parkersburg & Ohio River Transportation Co., Capt. E.P. Chancellor, president, and J.N. Williamson, superintendent. Capt. Ellis Mace recalls that she once ran Cincinnati-Vanceburg, Ky. In fall 1883 went south to handle cotton out of Yazoo River. In the winter went south with John Robinson's circus and came in collision Dec. 7, 1884, 60 miles below Vicksburg and was lost. Dispatches said the other boat was *CAPTAIN MILLER*.

5657 W.Q. Srodes

Stw ferry wh b. Guy's Ferry on Monongahela River, 1867. 15 tons. Ran Belle Vernon-Brownsville, Capt. Brooks, replacing earlier *MINNIE HARRIS*. Succeeded by *ATHLETIC*. Also spelled *W.Q. SHRODES*.

5658 W.R. Arthur

SW p wh b. Shousetown, Pa. (hull), and completed at Louisville, Ky., 1864. 763 tons. 260 x 42 (38½ ft. floor) x 8.5. Engines, 30's- 8 ft. Five boilers, each 46" by 24 ft., twenty-one 5" flues. E. & N. Porter built the hull under supervision of Capt. C.W. Batchelor for Capt. Dan Able and others, St. Louis. Operated St. Louis–New Orleans, Capt. Hugh Campbell, with Stanton J. Batchelor, clerk. She was hauled on the Carondelet Marine Ways January–February 1868 and the hull was enlarged to measure 296 x 53 (floor 50) x 8. She also got new engines, 30's- 10 ft., working side-wheels 33′8″ diameter with 14′8″ buckets. In the winter 1869–70 got new boilers, six in all, 46" by 28 ft., five flues each. Was in the Atlantic & Mississippi Steam Ship Co., until that firm failed May 1869 and then had other owners. Hit a log near Grand Tower, Ill., and sank in latter December, 1869. Exploded boilers upbound abreast of Island 40 on Jan. 28, 1871. She had on board 1000 tons molasses and sugar and 1066 bales of cotton; had 75 cabin passengers and 20 on deck. Capt. Harry W. Brolaski was her master. George Ritchie, pilot on watch, was blown to the hurricane roof, jumped overboard, and clung to a cotton bale until rescued. The burning boat floated to Redman's Point where she sank with the bow under water and the stern high in the air. Death toll was set at 45. A repercussion many years later happened when a loaded barge in tow of the *J.D. AYRES* struck something and sank, September 1929, believed to have been part of the *ARTHUR* wreck. Later investigation showed that five of the six boilers exploded; one was found badly twisted, gouged, but otherwise intact. The Memphis U.S. Inspectors revoked the license of George Reed, chief engineer, and suspended for 60 days the license of Hugh Reed (brother), 2nd engineer.

5659 W.R. Carter

SW p wh b. Louisville, Ky., 1864. 563 tons. Built for Capt. Linas Logan, and named for a citizen and merchant of St. Louis, formerly of Louisville. Exploded boilers at Island 98, about 35 miles above Vicksburg, Feb. 9, 1866. The life loss was set at 125 persons. She had "tubular" boilers something on the style of the original set placed on the *W.R. ARTHUR* (see last listing). These tubulars had won wide acceptance due to fuel economy, but a series of disasters resulted. The *MISSOURI*'s tubulars had exploded several days prior to the *CARTER* tragedy; the *SULTANA* tragedy was another such case. The U.S. Inspectors outlawed tubular boilers soon after the *CARTER* exploded, and many packets were promptly taken out of service until reboilered with proven Western style boilers. Capt. Jacob S. Hurd was master of the *CARTER*, brother of Capt. Jesse Y. Hurd of the *MISSOURI*. The *EVENING STAR* brought some survivors to Vicksburg, and *LUNA* took others to Memphis. The *EMERALD* also picked up a few.

5660 W.R. Douglas

SW p wh b. Louisville, Ky., 1856. 167 tons. 126 x 28 x 4.5. Enrolled at New Orleans Dec. 28, 1857, owned by Thornton Jacobs, Shreveport, La., Capt. B. Tarbell. Sold December 1858 to William Gwathney, New Orleans, Capt. Michael Gwathney. Burned and lost at Holcomb, Miss., Feb. 28, 1859.

5661 W.S. Johnston

SW p wh b. Louisville, Ky., 1859. 116 tons. First home port, Galveston, Tex. 126 x 25 x 4. Owned in 1861 by Sam W. Hammond, New Orleans. Sold 1862 to Thomas Moore, Covington, La., and John Y. Snead, Lamesa, Tex. Went to Confederate registry.

5662 W.S. McChesney, Jr.

SW ferry sh b. Jeffersonville, Ind., by Howard, 1912. 169 x 50 x 7. Built for Wiggins Ferry Co., St. Louis. Later bought by Falls City Ferry & Transportation Co., and served Louisville–Jeffersonville, partner to *HENRY WATTERSON*. Converted to diesel-electric drive for her side-wheels in spring of 1925 and was renamed *FROMAN M. COOTS*. (see).

W.S. Nelson

See *WILLIAM S. NELSON*, registered name.

5663 W.S. Pike

SW p wh b. Jeffersonville, Ind., 1869. 616 tons. 200 x 33 x 6. Four boilers. Owned and commanded by Capt. John J. Brown, New Orleans. Ownership transferred Dec. 13, 1869, to W.J. Hodgson, New Orleans, same master. Made trips Cincinnati-New Orleans. Ran on Red River 1873. New Orleans-Bayou Sara later. Burned while laid up at New Orleans, Dec. 17, 1875.

5664 W.T. Scovell

Stw p wh b. Jeffersonville, Ind., by Howard, 1895. 160 x 31

x 4. Ran in the Red River Line, New Orleans-Shreveport, Capt. F.E. Scovell, with R.W. Adams, clerk. President of the line was Charles P. Truslow, and Charles W. Drown was manager. Sank 20 miles below Shreveport at Devil's Elbow, September 1903. Crew at the time: Capt. H.J. Brinker, Jr., with A.A. Roland and William Gulon, clerks; Sam Readman and George Barren, pilots; Charles Moore, mate. Went to Nashville, Tenn., and ran in the Cumberland River Packet Co., along with *RED RIVER* and *ELECTRA* in 1905. Went back to the south country, Capt. John Quackenbush, with Wade Quackenbush, and Joseph Smith, clerks. She exploded her boiler Dec. 20, 1906, with loss of ten lives including the three aforementioned. She had one large patented boiler, 44" by 28 ft. Engines 12's- 3½ ft. Accident happened at Gold Dust Landing, La.

5665 W.T. WHELESS

Stw p wh b. Belle Vernon, Pa., 1880. 168 x 29 x 4.5. Engines, 16's- 7 ft. Three boilers, each 42" by 22 ft., ten 6" flues. Hull by William McFall and machinery by James Rees & Sons Co.

W.V. GILLUM

See *WILLIAM V. GILLUM,* registered name.

5666 W.W.

Stw ex wh b. Dubuque, Iowa, 1882 originally named *CITY OF WINONA* (see). Rebuilt spring 1905 by Capt. John Streckfus and renamed. The initials honored Capt. Walter Wisherd, an associate. She and the *J.S.* (see) were popular Upper Mississippi excursion boats in their day. Capt. Frank T. Rounds, Owensboro, Ky., bought her April 1917 to replace the *GOLDEN GIRL* (see) and ran excursions; he had her at Nashville, Tenn., summer 1918. Boat broker John F. Klein had her in 1920 towing barges loaded with pipe from the upper Ohio to the lower Mississippi. Capt. Ralph Emerson Gaches bought her spring 1921 after he lost the *CONTROL* and towed his showboat with her. While touring the upper Kanawha River the natives of Crown Hill, W. Va., boycotted the show because of the towboat's name which they figured stood for Woodrow Wilson. Gaches spread the word that Western Waters was the correct answer, and the show went on. She was caught broadside in high swells at the head of Brush Creek Island, Ohio River, spring 1922, and sank.

5667 W.W. BIERCE

Prop p wh b. Peninsula, Oh., 1863. 38 tons. 75.4 x 14 x 4.2. Small trading boat built on the lines of a canalboat, documented at Cincinnati 1864. Enrolled at New Orleans May 30, 1868, owned by John W. McCracken and William J. Davis, both of that place. They sold her that October to Capt. Adolphe E. Hotard, New Orleans. Removed from documentation in 1876.

5668 W.W. CRAWFORD

SW p wh b. Cincinnati, Oh., 1861. 123 tons. Ran Louisville-Carrollton, Capt. Parr, January 1862. Handling U.S. supplies Louisville-Nashville, March 1862. Off the lists 1868.

5669 W.W. FARMER

SW p wh b. Louisville, Ky., 1854. 207 tons. 140 x 32 x 5.1. Ran New Orleans-Ouachita River, Capt. John W. Cannon who owned 5/8 interest in the name of Louisa Cannon. Other owners were Capt. William Cooper and N.A. Delerno, both of New Orleans. Capt. Cooper bought control in Nov. 1855 and Cannon dropped out. Capt. John Glenn was master 1857 and owned her entire 1858. Capt. W.W. Risher, Catahoula Parish, ran her December 1858 through Feb. 25, 1860. Control went to John Freeze, Wheeling, W. Va. (7/10) March 1860, Capt. B.F. Goodwin. Went to Confederate registry in 1861.

W.W. FRY

See *WILLIAM W. FRY,* registered name.

W. BURTON

See *WILLIAM BURTON,* registered name.

5670 W. HARLOCK

Prop ferry wh b. Lyons, Iowa, 1905. 65 x 12.8 x 3.8. Documented at Rock Island, Ill., 1908. At Des Moines, Iowa, 1918.

5671 WABASH

Stw p wh b. Evansville, Ind., 1868. 123 x 29 x 4.5. Built at the Cavender Yard for Capt. Henry Scott. At the launching Capt. Andy Hutchinson paid tribute to Capt. Scott who, since residing in Evansville, had paid to shipbuilders and carpenters $120,000 for building boats at that place.

5672 WABASH VALLEY

SW p wh b. Pittsburgh, Pa., 1844. 99 tons. Ran Cincinnati-Wabash River, Capt. Larimer, running high as Lafayette, Ind. Other boats same trade 1845 in a "Line" were *REVENUE CUTTER* and *ADELAIDE.* Ran cotton trades in the south also. Was sunk in collision with *YORKTOWN* at Jefferson College, La., en route White River to New Orleans with 160 bales, Mar. 23, 1846. Off the lists 1848.

5673 WABASH VALLEY

SW p wh b. Louisville, Ky., 1853. 136 tons. Ran New Orleans-Shreveport, La., Capt. M.N. Wood. Off the lists 1855.

5674 WABASHA

Stw ferry wh b. Wabasha, Minn., 1894. 80 x 22 x 2.9. Still listed in 1908, maybe longer.

5675 WADE ALLEN

SW p wh b. Louisville, Ky., by Howard, 1850. 175 x 24 x 6. Went to Mobile, Ala. Burned there July 30, 1855. One life lost.

5676 WADE HAMPTON

SW p wh b. Jeffersonville, Ind., 1870. 217.6 x 38 x 7.8.

Engines, 28's- 7 ft. Six boilers, each 38" by 28 ft. Ran New Orleans-Ouachita River owned by Capts. John W. Tobin and G.P. Work. Also in 1870 ran New Orleans-Fort Adams, Capt. John C. Libano. Sold Mar. 21, 1871, to Capt. A.C. Goddin to replace the *WILD WAGONER,* Natchez-New Orleans. In July 1871 Capt. Goddin was standing in the boat's office when a bullet creased his brain, fired by a New Orleans citizen. Goddin recovered. In November 1871 sank opposite Donaldsonville, La., and slid clear out of sight. Wreck was abandoned.

5677 WAGONER

Stw ferry wh b. St. Louis, Mo., 1842. 107 tons. Off the lists 1849. Catamaran.

5678 WAGONER

Stw p wh b. Louisville, Ky., 1846. 43 tons. Lost in 1847.

5679 WAKENDAH

SW p wh b. Elizabethtown, Pa., 1846. 193 tons. 160 x 27. Sent to Missouri River, owned in part and commanded by Capt. J.M. Convers. Owned by Convers, Tompkins, Kennett, and White. Sank at mouth of Fishing River on the Missouri, Apr. 2, 1846. Off the lists 1848.

5680 WAKEROBIN

Stw lighthouse tender sh b. Neville Island, Pa., by Dravo, 1926. 182 x 43 x 5.3. Condensing high pressure engines, 18's- 7½ ft. Built for U.S. Lighthouse Service, Dept. of Commerce, and later in U.S. Coast Guard. She operated after 1950 under lease to the U.S. Engineers, Memphis, and shortly after they took title in 1955 she was sold at public sale to Comet River Co., Cincinnati. In 1945 she was given two B&W three-pass water tube boilers, and fuel oil burners. At Cincinnati she became a landing boat, with little appreciable change in architecture, and so continued until sold to Capt. Dennis Trone. He took her to Chattanooga, Tenn., where, winter 1975-1976, changes were made to use her as a harbor landing boat. Towed to Illinois River 1978 and Capt. Trone still has her in 1980.

5681 WALK IN THE WATER

SW ferry wh b. New Albany, Ind., 1850. 118 tons. Out of service 1855.

5682 WALL CITY

Stw p wh b. Ironton, Oh., 1874. 99 tons. Ran daily Ravenswood-Middleport on the Ohio River, Capt. Alf. Day. Had several clerks, including W.T. Cox, H.W. Resener, and J.F. Cromley. In the 1880s still there with Capt. J.C. Edwards, master, and C.H. Crow and J.E. Wilkinson, clerks. Capt. Edwards owned a large Newfoundland dog which regularly rode the boat and had been instructed in various deck duties—could pull lines ashore, etc. Her engines went to the towboat *MARLEN RIGGS.* She was succeeded in the trade by *VALLEY BELLE* (see).

5683 WALNUT HILLS

SW p wh b. Cincinnati, Oh., 1841. 190 tons. Off the lists 1846.

5684 WALTER B. DANCE

SW p wh b. Paducah, Ky., 1866. 571 tons. 200.3 x 34.2 x 5.7. Four boilers. Ran on the Missouri River first season or so, then went to New Orleans-Shreveport trade. Registered at New Orleans Jan. 4, 1868, Capt. George W. Boyd, owned by the firm of Baylan & Gettys, St. Louis. Dismantled 1871 and the hull was used as a cargo barge, towed by the *CHAS. B. CHURCH* and others.

5685 WAMADEE

Stw p wh b. Green Bay, Wis., 1864. 46 tons. 89.2 x 17.2 x 2.2. Running Evansville-Henderson daily trade, May 1864. In June 1866 was at New Orleans, Capt. James L. Kendall, owned in one-third shares by Nathan J. Crocker, Crittenden County, Ky.; James L. Morton, Evansville, Ind.; and Jasper C. Hazel, Union County, Ky. Off the lists in 1870. Also spelled *WANADIE.*

5686 WANDERER

Stw pl wh b. Clinton, Iowa, 1897. 100 x 21 x 3.6. Owned by C. Lamb & Son, Clinton. Towed the family houseboat *IDLER.* In fall 1898 the Lambs and guests toured to New Orleans and back. In 1906 she was replaced with a larger boat (see next listing) and was sold to the Florida East Coast Railroad which then was extending its line to Key West. She sank in Jew Fish Creek, near Miami, Capt. F.L. Moody, Oct. 14, 1906. She was lost Mar. 24, 1909, in the Keys, Capt. Edward A. Graham. Crew removed by *COLUMBIA.*

5687 WANDERER II

Stw pl wh b. Clinton, Iowa, 1906. 115 x 24 x 4.5. Built by Lafayette Lamb, Clinton. Towed the family houseboat *IDLER,* 120 x 20 x 4.4, b. Clinton, 1898. *WANDERER II* was sold October 1915 to Standard Oil of Louisiana. Crew, July 1926: Capt. D.W. Gourner, with Oscar T. Aucoin, pilot; William Geisler, chief engineer, C.M. Bondurant, 2nd engineer. Officially abandoned, Nov. 10, 1933.

5688 WAPELLO

SW p wh b. Pittsburgh, Pa., 1844. 248 tons. First home port, St. Louis. Off the lists in 1846.

5689 WAPSIE

Rig? ferry wh b. Princeton, Iowa, 1867. 31 tons. Documented at Galena, Ill., 1876, maybe later.

5690 WAR EAGLE

SW p wh b. Cincinnati, Oh., 1845. 155 tons. 152 x 24 x 4.5. Built at Best & Co., yard for Capt. Daniel Smith Harris, who commanded, and brother Scribe Harris, engineer. They ran her Galena-St. Peters through the 1847 season, then St. Louis-St. Peters in 1848. Ran Louisville-St. Louis fall of 1848. Was at Cairo, Ill., in June 1849 and was noticed by a newspaper editor as "the swiftest boat of her size on the western waters, and during the principal part of her existence has been running on the upper Mississippi." Dismantled and hull used as a barge in 1851.

5691 WAR EAGLE

SW p wh b. Fulton (Cincinnati), Oh., 1854. 296 tons. 225 x 27. Three boilers. Built for Minnesota Packet Co., Capt. Orrin Smith, president. Ran Galena-St. Paul 1854–1856, Capt. Daniel Smith Harris. In 1857 ran Dunleith-St. Paul, Capt. Kingman; same 1858 with Capt. W.H. Gabbert. In 1859 in the La Crosse Line, Capt. J.B. Davis. In 1861, Dunleith-St. Paul, Capt. A. Mitchell, later Capt. Charles L. Stephenson. In March 1862 made a trip to Tennessee River for the U.S., and got a shot in one of her stacks. That summer ran Dunleith-St. Paul, Capt. N.F. Webb. Burned at La Crosse, Wis., with loss of six lives and property damage of $215,000, May 15, 1870.

5692 WAR EAGLE

SW p wh b. Cincinnati, Oh., 1858. 446 tons. First home port, St. Louis. Built by H.L. White and others. 223 x 35 x 6. Engines, 22½'s- 7 ft. Three boilers, each 36" by 28 ft. Designed for Missouri River, and had several ownership changes. Was sent up to Boonville, Mo., August 1861, with troops commanded by Col. W.H. Worthington of the 5th Iowa Volunteers. Got there on the 26th and seized Confederate goods, took prisoners, and returned to St. Louis with 11 skiffs and the steam ferryboat. Capt. Epstein is mentioned as master at the time. A dispatch from St. Louis dated Apr. 2, 1867: "Thornburg sold the *WAR EAGLE* to Joseph and John B. LaBarge for $20,000; she was built by H.L. White in 1858 and cost $48,000. Burned at St. Louis, Aug. 24, 1869.

5693 WAR EAGLE

SW p wh b. St. Louis, Mo., 1876. 279.2 x 42 x 6.1. 941 tons. Engines, 26's- 8 ft. Four boilers, each 45" by 28 ft., five flues. Owned by Keokuk Northern Line Packet Co., and ran St. Louis-Keokuk, Capt. T.L. Davidson. Later owned by St. Louis & St. Paul Packet Co. She hit the Keokuk bridge, downbound, at 9:30 P.M. on Nov. 4, 1881, and sank. Capt. Hiram E. (Hi) Beedle was pilot on watch. Crew at the time: Capt. Jerry Wood, master; William R. Tibbals, pilot off watch; F. McCord, chief engineer; C.R. Gregg, 1st clerk; Thomas Conners, mate; William (Billy) Blank, steward. She was raised and taken to Madison, Ind., for rebuilding. In October 1891 Capt. H.W. Brolaski and son Harry formed Mississippi River Excursion Co., and bought *WAR EAGLE* for the St. Louis-Riverside Park trade, the boiler deck glass enclosed forward. In March 1893 Capt. Milt R. Harry put her in the Cairo-Memphis trade. Went to U.S. marshal sale at Cairo, Dec. 30, 1893, and was dismantled the following year.

5694 WAR EAGLE

SW p wh b. Madison, Ind., 1899. 250 x 38 x 6. Engines, 22's- 6'8". Four boilers, each 42" by 20 ft. Built for Eagle Packet Co., St. Louis. Capt. Buck Leyhe came out master of her, St. Louis-Cape Girardeau-Commerce. She partially burned at the St. Louis wharf and was rebuilt at the Carondelet, Mo., marine ways in April 1901, renamed *CAPE GIRARDEAU* (see).

5695 WARREN

SW p wh b. Aurora, Ind., 1846. 109 tons. 109.6 x 20.4 x 5.2. Enrolled at New Orleans, Jan. 21, 1846, owned by Samuel Montgomery, New Albany, Ind.; Irastus Bassett, Dearborn County, Ind. Master, Capt. Andrew Worley, Gretna, La. Sold June 27, 1846, to Capt. Daniel B. Mosby, who commanded, and William H. Lillard, both of New Orleans. Off the lists in 1848.

5696 WARREN

SW p wh b. New Albany, Ind., 1851. 72 tons. Off the lists 1857.

5697 WARREN

Stw p wh b. Cincinnati, Oh., 1882. 184 x 37.6 x 6.5. Running New Orleans, Atchafalaya River and Washington trade, 1885, Capt. Max Kenison, with J.C. Bergeron, clerk. Same trade and master, 1889, with Eugene Quatrevous as clerk. A cotton carrier, capacity 2,800 bales. Owned 1896 by New Orleans & Washington Packet Co. Replaced *CITY OF SAVANNAH* in the Memphis-Vicksburg trade, March 1898.

5698 WARREN BELLE

SW p wh b. Jeffersonville, Ind., 1865. 242 tons. 144 x 25 x 5.4. Built for Green River, owned by W.F. Van Miler, E. Claypool, and S.A. Barton, Bowling Green, Ky. Capt. E.S. Butler, Vicksburg, Miss., bought one-half interest that fall. Sold Dec. 29, 1866, to Edmund M. Richeson, New Orleans, with Capt. L.H. Patterson, master. Sold Dec. 23, 1867, to Attakapas Mail Transportation Co., Tristram Tapper, president. Capt. E.B. Trinidad, master. Sank in Bayou Teche Feb. 5, 1870, raised. Was dismantled at Louisville, Ky., 1871.

5699 WARREN JOHNSON

Stw ferry sh b. Jeffersonville, Ind., by Howard, 1925, originally named *CHARLES J. MILLER*, then *GENERAL* (both see). The Todd-Johnson Dry Dock Co., New Orleans, renamed her in 1944 and used her in ferry service. She handled 754 passengers at a loading. Sold to Savannah River, fall 1946, owned there by L.H. Simkins.

5700 WARRENN

Stw p wh b. Diamond Bluff, Wis., 1900, originally named *TWIN CITY* (see). By 1903 she had been renamed and was at Vicksburg, Miss. Documented at Louisville, Ky., 1905, and was on upper Cumberland River. She was beached and dismantled at Burnside, Ky., Oct. 9, 1907. Her boilers were still alongside the Burnside ferry landing in 1941.

5701 WARRIOR

SW p wh b. Cincinnati, Oh., 1844. 204 tons. First home port, Mobile, Ala. 170 x 25 x 5.5. Went to Mobile but was returned to New Orleans owned Dec. 10, 1846, by J. & R. Geddes and others, Capt. Robert Geddes. Sold Dec. 14, 1846, to Capt. Franklin Keeling, New Orleans. Several days later bought by James A. Stevens, Yazoo City, Miss., and Sidney Flower, Concordia Parish, La., Capt. James H. Woods. Sold Feb. 2, 1850, to Joseph Dyer, New Orleans, with Capt. Alfred Bruner, master. Exploded and lost on the Meramec River, Mo., Feb. 20, 1852, with loss of two lives.

5702 WARSAW

Stw p wh b. Madison, Ind., 1858. 457 tons. Owned by Keokuk Packet Co., operating St. Louis-Keokuk. Capt. J.W. Malin, with H.W. Browlaski, clerk, in 1865. Sunk and lost in ice above Miller Street, St. Louis, Mo., Jan. 12, 1866.

5703 WARSAW

Center wheel ferry wh b. Madison, Ind., 1871. 123 x 36 x 5. Operated at La Crosse, Wis. Replaced the *THOMAS McROBERTS* in the service. Caught fire in midstream Mar. 23, 1880, and was beached on an island where all safely got ashore. The *SILVER LAKE* and a barge pinch-hit while repairs were made at the P.S. Davidson Yard, La Crosse. In 50 days *WARSAW* was back in service, Capt. Day. Still listed 1886, maybe later.

5704 WARSAW

Stw ferry sh b. Keokuk, Iowa, 1914. 64.3 x 22 x 4. Owned in 1920s by Quincy Steamboat Co., Quincy, Ill. Sold to Valley Line Steamers, Memphis, Tenn., who used her in short trades. Sold January 1936 to Wolf River Transportation Co., Memphis, ending operations of the Lee Line.

5705 WASH OBENCHAIN

Stw tb wh b. Logansport, Ind., 1874. 66 tons. 81 x 14 x 3. Engines, 9″- 3 ft. One 5-flue boiler, 44″ by 16 ft. Built by Capt. Bruce Obenchain to tow produce boats out of Wabash River. She came to the Muskingum River and operated Marietta-Zanesville, Capt. A.B. Wiley, usually towing, this in 1881-1882. In 1883 still on the Muskingum, Capt. C.F. Siler who used her engines 1884 in building the *BESSIE SILER* (see).

5706 WASHBURN

Stw p wh b. Bismarck, N.D., 1901. 98.7 x 24.8 x 3.1. She became one of Benton Packet Co.'s fleet organized 1904 by Capt. Isaac P. Baker, Bismarck. In 1909 the fleet composed of the *EXPANSION, WASHBURN, BISMARCK, WESTON,* and *IMELDA*. Lost in ice at Crockett's Bluff, Ark., on Jan. 12, 1918.

5707 WASHINGTON

SW p wh b. Cincinnati, Oh., 1847. 74 tons. Lost in ice at Covington, Ky., Feb. 1867. Our educated guess is that she was a ferry in that area.

5708 WASHINGTON

Stw p wh b. West Elizabeth, Pa., 1848. 102 tons. First home port, Galveston, Tex. Off the lists 1854.

5709 WASHINGTON

Stw p wh b. West Elizabeth, Pa., 1850. 154 tons. Lost in ice at Rock Island, below Louisville, Ky., Jan. 31, 1852.

5710 WASHINGTON

SW ferry wh b. Wellsville, Oh., 1867. 53 tons. 90 x 19. One cylinder (stiff shaft), 12″- 3½ ft. One boiler, 40″ by 20 ft. The hull was built at Freedom, Pa. Built for Capt. John Patton and spent a career on the Missouri River. Ferried at Hermann, Mo., and long operated by August Wohlt of that place. A.S. Bryan and others had owned her in the 1870s. Burned at Hermann, Mo., Apr. 10, 1880.

5711 WASHINGTON

Stw ex wh b. Wheeling, W. Va., 1880, originally named *SIDNEY* (see). Rebuilt at Mound City, Ill., in 1921 and renamed. Owned by Streckfus Steamers, Inc., St. Louis, Mo. 221.3 x 35.5 x 5.5. Engines, 18's- 7 ft. Four boilers from *GREATER NEW ORLEANS*. Operated on the Ohio River managed by Capt. D. Walter Wisherd based at Cincinnati, then Pittsburgh. Captains included Coburn Pratt, Edgar F. Mabrey, C.W. Elder; pilots: Lee Willis, Grover Litten, Homer Litten, Charles H. Ellsworth, William I. Weldon, Phil C. Elsey, William S. Pollock, and F. Way, Jr. The latter two (Gold Dust Twins) served 1934-1937. Damaged her bow when she struck the lower lock gate at Dam #8, Ohio River, Aug. 16, 1936, with no injury to passengers. In 1937 operated part of the season. Dismantled at St. Louis in 1938.

5712 WASHINGTON

Stw ferry wh b. Osage City, Mo., 1901. 100 x 22 x 3.4. Documented at New Orleans in 1908.

5713 WASHINGTON CITY

SW p wh b. Freedom, Pa., 1852. 282 tons. 181 x 29 x 6.5. Engines, 18 ¾'s- 6½ ft. Three boilers, each 40″ by 26 ft. Capt. George W. Ebert, Georgetown, Pa., was master 1855. Ran Pittsburgh-St. Louis. Off the lists in 1859.

5714 WATER LILY

Stw p wh b. Rockwood Landing, Tenn. (hull), and completed at Knoxville, Tenn., 1880. 112 x 21 x 3. Owned by A.R. Love, Knoxville. Still listed 1886, maybe later.

5715 WATER MAIDEN

Stw p wh b. Zanesville, Oh., 1890. 69 x 12 x 2.6. Said Capt. Jesse P. Hughes: "Was an odd little passenger boat and ran around Sistersville and New Matamoras in 1895—don't know what became of her—one stack, sternwheel, steel pitmans."

5716 WATER WITCH

Rig? p wh b. Cincinnati, Oh., 1875. 3.31 tons. Ran Cincinnati-Dayton, Ky., in 1876 with *J.M. McARTHUR* and *MARY KENNER*.

5717 WATKINS

Stw p wh b. Peoria, Ill., 1902. 95 x 18.8 x 3. Built by Capt. George Watkins. Once was owned by Chicago Sanitary

District. Ran in Memphis-St. Francis River trade in 1911.

5718 WATOSSA

Stw p wh b. Brownsville, Pa., 1857. 127 tons. Engines, 15½'s- 4 ft. Three boilers. First home port, Kansas City, Mo. While bound from Council Bluffs to St. Joseph on Sept. 26, 1858, she sank on a snag in 15 feet, 12 miles above St. Joseph, Mo., and was lost.

5719 WAUHATCHIE

SW p wh b. by U.S. forces during the Civil War on upper Tennessee River. Quite picturesque and small. After hostilities she became a wharfboat.

5720 WAUKESHA

Stw p wh b. Carolina Bluff, La., 1898. 106 x 24.4 x 3. Built by Capt. W.H. McWhorter who ran her Shreveport-Fulton, Ark. Fulton is 468.6 miles up Red River, 156.8 miles above Shreveport. Named for Waukesha, Wis., home of Capt. McWhorter. He was up in years and color-blind, and was forced to sell the boat in 1900 to A.P. Seaman who lost her by sinking at Crewshaws Bar, 26 miles above Fulton, October 1900. A rising river carried away the cabin. No insurance.

5721 WAUNETA

Prop yacht sh b. Pittsburgh, Pa., 1901. 82 x 7.8 x 3.8. Came out with two 11″ by 11″ cylinders and a Roberts boiler. Built at the Charles Rogers Machine Co., 72 Water Street, Pittsburgh, for George E. Painter and Charles A. Painter. About 1906 she was given a Seabury triple-expansion engine, 350 hp. at 950 rpm., working a 28x44 prop. Later she got a Mosher boiler of the flash type. The Painters were always changing this yacht hoping to get 40 mph. with her, which they never did. Herman B. Mertz was engineer on her for the Painters. Once on a test run she made one mile in one minute 52 seconds. Rush and Harry Burnside tried her in the Carrollton-Louisville trade fall of 1911. They sold her that December to George E. Berry and Charles E. Bailey, who summer 1912 ran her daily round trips on Kanawha River, Pt. Pleasant-Charleston. The St. Louis & Tennessee River Packet Co. tried her in the Johnsonville-Savannah trade in May 1913 but she didn't make the required time. Was at Memphis in 1916. See *S&D Reflector,* issue March 1972, pages 20–22; also June 1972 issue, page 8.

5722 WAUNITA

Stw p wh b. Brownsville, Pa., 1864. 318 tons. Ran Pittsburgh-St. Louis, Capt. Sam Shuman, with H.H. Devinney, clerk. Capt. Rees Rees commanded briefly in 1868, his last boating. Lost in ice at Cincinnati, Feb. 14, 1872.

5723 WAVE

SW p wh b. New Albany, Ind., 1844. 231 tons. 166 x 27 x 5.7. In 1845 owned by her master, Capt. John F. Harris, Paducah, Ky., and William A. Violett, New Orleans, equal shares. Off the lists in 1851.

5724 WAVE

SW p wh b. Louisville, Ky., 1844. 78 tons. 114.1 x 22.2 x 3.3. Owned at New Orleans in 1845 by Jacques Larose, with Capt. John C. Northup, master. Had three ownership changes at New Orleans into January 1849. Stranded and lost at St. James, La., Mar. 7, 1849.

5725 WAVE

SW p wh b. Green Landing, Oh., 1844. 93 tons. Off the lists 1854. This may be the boat that ran on Kaskaskia River to St. Louis, 1851, and in spring 1852 went to the Sangamon and ascended to Petersburg, Ill.

5726 WAVE

Stw tinclad wh b. Monongahela, Pa., 1863, originally named *ARGOSY NO. 2*. She was purchased by the U.S. and became tinclad #45, renamed *WAVE* on Nov. 14, 1863. Captured by the Confederates at Calcasieu, La., May 6, 1864.

5727 WAVE NO. 2

Stw p wh b. Elizabeth, Pa., 1848. 101 tons. Single deck, built for Allegheny River service and often went to Warren, Pa., Capt. William H. Gordon. The "No. 2" was added inasmuch as a prior boat on the Allegheny was *WAVE,* a towboat. Sold to the Kanawha River, fall 1850. Off the lists 1855.

5728 WAVERLY

SW p wh b. Metropolis, Ill., and completed at St. Louis, 1866. 452 tons. 200 x 34 x 5.5. Engines, 17's- 5 ft. Two boilers. On June 17, 1867, arrived at St. Louis from Fort Benton with 508 bales of buffalo robes, 43 wolf skins, 37 bundles of elk skins, 10 packages of deer skins, and 5 packages of antelope skins, having come down in 13 days 2 hours. On Nov. 24, 1867, downbound Omaha to St. Louis, she was snagged and lost in Bowling Green Bend, Glasgow, Mo. Owned at the time by John P. Keiser, Thomas Raigin and Capt. Thomas W. Rhea who also was master. The machinery was salvaged and went to the *SILVER BOW* (see). This packet cost $50,000, and she was said to have paid for herself on the first round trip to Fort Benton.

5729 WEBB CITY

Rig? wh b. Jeffersonville, Ind., 1883. 130 x 26 x 3.8. Within a few years was renamed *POPLAR BLUFF,* documented at New Orleans.

5730 WEBSTER

SW p wh b. Cincinnati, Oh., 1848. 324 tons. 182 x 27 x 8. Engines, 24's- 8 ft. Four boilers, each 42″ by 30 ft. Built to pass through the canal locks at Louisville. Burned in the head of Island 86, Mississippi River, about 4:00 P.M., May 2, 1851. Life loss was set at 40 persons, including her master, Capt. Sam Reno, whose body was located almost 100 miles below some days later. The large life loss was attributed to the burning boat having left the shore, floating out into midstream, after having been landed. The wreck was raised and returned to Cincinnati along in June, but was scrapped, including machinery.

5731 WELCOME

SW p wh b. Shousetown, Pa., 1863. 449 tons. 214 x 36.2 x 6. Advertised at St. Louis for Fort Benton, Mont., in March 1864, Capt. Thomas Townsend, with Moses Hillard, clerk. Burned at St. Louis during a major steamboat fire, July 15, 1864. The wreck was towed to the Illinois shore and there sold in August 1864 by the Underwriters. Rebuilt. Owned in 1868 by David W. Chandler, Camden, Ark., and J.W. Terril, St. Louis, with Capt. A.S. McLaughlin, master. Sold at New Orleans Feb. 12, 1871, to Capt. Matt H. Wheat for New Orleans-White River. She burned at New Orleans that August.

5732 WELCOME

SW ferry wh b. Cincinnati, Oh., 1874, originally named *DR. GEORGE MACKEY* (see). Renamed prior to 1886. 66.4 x 18 x 3.3. Still documented at Cincinnati in 1896.

5733 WELCOME

Stw p wh b. Wheeling, W. Va., 1879. Ran short trades on the Ohio River. Capt. Jim Rowley recalled her in the Cincinnati-Portsmouth trade handling U.S. Mail. Reported sunk on upper Red River above Shreveport and raised Mar. 6, 1883.

5734 WELCOME

Stw p wh Running Greenville-Sunnyside trade in March 1900 owned by the Lyons of Greenville who also operated *LUELLA BROWN* (see).

5735 WELLSVILLE

Stw p wh b. Industry, Pa., 1847. 143 tons. Ran Pittsburgh-Sunfish (Clarington, Oh.) in 1848, Capt. Barnes. Running Pittsburgh-Wheeling in 1850. Off the lists in 1852.

5736 WENONA

SW p wh b. St. Louis, Mo., 1852. 247 tons. Engines, 20's-6½ ft. Two boilers. Ran on Missouri River. She was twice snagged in 1854 and recovered. Again snagged in 1855 near Claysville, Mo., recovered. Owned by Robert Barclay, John McClurg, and W.D. Murphy. Off the lists in 1857.

5737 WENONA

SW p wh b. Hokah, Minn., 1859. 74 tons. 100 x 20.2 x 4.2. Sold to New Orleans, September 1865, Capt. C.E. Richter. Had various owners at New Orleans and was off the lists October 1869.

5738 WENONA

Stw p wh b. Harmar, Oh., 1889, originally towboat *ELIZA H.*, converted into a packet and renamed *ELOISE* (see) by Capt. William E. Roe and others. Sold October 1907 to Capt. Walter Blair who renamed her *WENONA* and entered her in the Burlington-Keokuk trade. One cold October night in 1910 she hit something and sank at Pontoosac but was easily raised. Blair sold her in 1911 to Caruthersville, Mo., and she became a towboat named *WM. HEIL*, then *PETE LANGAN*, then *PETERSON-MILLER BOX CO.*, and wound up as a ferry at Cairo, Ill., named *TOURIST* (see).

5739 WENONA

Stw ferry wh b. Cincinnati, Oh., 1893. 96.4 x 26 x 4. Engines, 10's- 4 ft. One boiler, 48" by 16 ft. Long operated at Ashland, Ky., owned by Ashland & Ironton Ferry Co., later by C. & O. Railroad. Lost in ice at Ashland on Jan. 29, 1918. Had a recess wheel.

5740 WENONAH

Prop yacht sh b. Pittsburgh, Pa., 1894. 65 x 8 x 5. Owned by Charles A. Painter, Pittsburgh, and was quite speedy. Sold to the U.S. Engineers, Pittsburgh about 1908. She collided with tow of the *JAMES MOREN* just below Davis Island Dam, West Bellevue, Pa., at 11:30 A.M., Oct. 18, 1911, turned over and drowned her engineer, J.W. Dickey. Later sold to Capt. Henry Murnane of the Memphis Dry Dock Co., who converted her for towing in February 1913.

5741 WEST END

SW ferry wh b. Brownsville, Pa., 1890. 80.5 x 20.5 x 4. Operated at Wellsville, Oh., and was sold August 1902 to Brilliant (Ohio) Bridge & Ferry Co., Capt. Charles I. Waddle. Ferried there to Wellsburg, W. Va. Associate owner was Oliver M. Waddle, Pittsburgh. Sold entire October 1911 to Thomas M. Axton, West Brownsville, Pa.

5742 WEST NEWTON

SW p wh b. Elizabeth, Pa., 1849. 163 tons. Ran Galena-St. Paul, operated by Capts. D.S. and R.S. Harris along with *DR. FRANKLIN NO. 2* (see). Snagged and lost at Alma, Wis., Oct. 13, 1853. Location was afterwards called West Newton Chute, just below Alma.

5743 WEST POINT

SW p wh b. Pittsburgh, Pa., 1841. 124 tons. Operated by Capt. Redmund J. Grace from Pittsburgh to Nashville and St. Louis. Off the lists in 1846.

5744 WEST VIRGINIA

Stw p wh b. Parkersburg, W. Va., 1863. 104 tons. Renamed *VIRGINIA* on Jan. 26, 1864 (see), and lost 120 miles above Cairo, 1871.

5745 WEST VIRGINIA

Stw p wh b. Brownsville, Pa., 1871. 111 tons. Built for the Pittsburgh-Morgantown trade on the Monongahela River, Capt. Peter Donaldson. Lay at Charleston, W. Va., winter 1875-1876, then entered Gallipolis-Charleston trade, Capt. Martin. Capt. J.B. Dudding later ran her same trade. He sold her to the upper Ohio in December 1878 and bought the *TELEPHONE* (see) from the Maddy Bros., to replace her.

5746 WEST VIRGINIA STAR

SW ferry wh b. Industry, Pa., 1867. 51 tons. Operated

Wellsville, Oh., to Congo, W. Va., into early 1870s. Off the lists 1872.

5747 WEST WHEELING

Stw ferry wh Capt. Jesse P. Hughes recalls seeing her in the ferry trade based at the Belmont Mill Landing, Wheeling, owned by a Capt. Wolf, this prior to 1895.

5748 WEST WIND

SW p wh b. Cincinnati, Oh., 1842. 208 tons. Cincinnati-St. Louis-New Orleans in 1842, Capt. Dick Phillips. On or about May 31, 1842, a steam explosion shortly after leaving Louisville, upbound St. Louis to Cincinnati, resulted in the drowning of Dr. Valentine Barger (see *S&D Reflector,* December 1979). Off the lists 1848.

5749 WEST WIND

SW p wh b. Elizabeth, Pa., 1859. 350 tons. 215 x 33 x 5.7. Engines, 18's- 7 ft. Three boilers. Built for Capt. Samuel Lewis for the Missouri River. In the fall of 1864 she was in U.S. service. Brought troops down and landed them at Glasgow, Mo. The town was attacked and captured by Gen. John B. Clark and Gen. Joe G. Selby while the boat lay there and she burned the following night, Oct. 16, 1864.

5750 WEST WIND

Running Cincinnati-Madison in 1870, tri-weekly, Capt. James B. Troy, with Frank Morten, clerk. A dispatch from Memphis dated Jan. 6, 1873, states that Capt. W.G. Clark's *WEST WIND* lies sunk at Memphis and the wreck has just changed hands for $2,000.

5751 WESTERN

SW p wh b. Wheeling, Va., 1845. 116 tons. Struck and caused loss of *MONEDO* on the Cumberland River in 1847. Snagged and lost in Wabash River at "the horseshoe" in January 1849 loaded with flour, whiskey, pork, and bacon.

5752 WESTERN

Stw p wh b. Pittsburgh, Pa., 1872. 475 tons. 212 x 34. Engines, 16's- 5 ft. Three boilers. Left Pittsburgh Apr. 6, 1872, for Fort Benton, Mont., Capt. S.B. Coulson, with J. Todd, clerk. In all she made nine trips to Fort Benton, the last one in 1878. Cut down by ice during the great gorge at Yankton, S.D., on Mar. 27, 1881. After she sank the pressure of the ice flattened her port boilers.

5753 WESTERN BELLE

SW p wh b. New Albany, Ind., 1841. 137 tons. Advertised Cincinnati-New Orleans, January 1842, Capt. W. Young. Off the lists 1849.

5754 WESTERN WAVE

Yacht wh b. Cincinnati, Oh., 1874. 4.25 tons. Inspected in the Cincinnati area through 1882.

5755 WESTERN WORLD

SW p wh b. Elizabethtown, Pa., 1848. 338 tons. 180 x 35 x 7.8. Engines, 25½'s- 8 ft. Four boilers, each 40" by 28 ft., two 15" flues. Built for Capt. Alex Norton, Steubenville, Oh., who commanded. Ran Pittsburgh-New Orleans. Came in collision with *H. W. R. HILL* (see) just above Princeton, Miss., Dec. 14, 1852. The *WESTERN WORLD* turned turtle with loss of 12 lives. Part of the wreck floated 15 miles. A lengthy lawsuit resulted, and Capt. Norton eventually collected $30,000 damages. It is said she had been lengthened at Cincinnati several years before her loss. Norton operated a boat store and commission business at New Orleans after the war.

5756 WESTERNER

SW p wh b. St. Louis, Mo., 1853. 461 tons. Owned by St. Louis & Keokuk Packet Co., Capt. John G. Prather. Lost in ice at Commerce, Mo., Jan. 3, 1855.

5757 WESTMORELAND

SW p wh b. Brownsville, Pa., 1861. 184 tons. Capt. Ed Evans long commanded her in the Cincinnati-New Orleans trade. Following the fall of Fort Sumter one passenger was killed when this boat was fired upon. Capt. Evans lived on a farm near Perrysville, Pa. The *WESTMORELAND* was burned in the Cincinnati steamboat fire, May 12, 1869. Evans was in New Orleans when Gen. Robert E. Lee died in 1870 and he refused to half-mast the flag on the *KATE PUTNAM* he then commanded.

5758 WESTON

Stw p wh b. Running Water, S.D., 1901. 89 tons. 110 x 30 x 4.5. Engines, 10's- 4 ft. One boiler. Originally named *LITTLE MAUD* (see). Owned by Benton Packet Co. While she was bound from Bismarck to Fort Yates, N.D., was snagged Sept. 7, 1909, lost.

5759 WESTWOOD

SW p wh b. Nashville, Tenn., 1843. 249 tons. 163.5 x 20.6 x 7. Collided with and sank the *GULNARE* 20 miles above Helena, Ark., Sept. 8, 1844. Owned July 1846 by Malby & Goodrich, New Orleans, Capt. H.L. Goodrich, master. In October 1845 owned by J.R. Brogstede & Co., New Orleans, composed of George W. Cable and John R. Brogstede. In February 1847 owned by Capt. Joseph Hugh Short, New Orleans, who was master, and Oscar Maureau, New Orleans. Exploded boilers and lost, Dec. 19, 1847. Twelve lives were lost.

5760 WETUMPKA

Stw p wh b. Cincinnati, Oh., 1852. 313 tons. Went to Mobile, Ala., and was lost in collision with *MAGNOLIA* on the Alabama River, Feb. 12, 1854, with loss of five lives.

5761 WHEEL OF FORTUNE

SW p wh b. Louisville, Ky., 1845. 165 tons. Ran Louisville-New Orleans in 1845, Capt. Jas. Murphy. Burned at Enterprise, Ind., 1847.

5762 WHIRLWIND

SW p wh b. Elizabeth, Pa., 1846. 226 tons. Part owner and master was Capt. Wallace Dodge, Marietta, Oh., who took the boat to St. Louis and made Missouri River trips which proved "unprosperous." Dodge later became inspector of hulls, stationed at Carondelet, Mo., and died there July 14, 1858. *WHIRLWIND* was off the lists in 1853.

5763 WHISPER

Stw p wh b. Jeffersonville, Ind., at Barmore yard, 1878. 180 x 36 x 6.5. Engines, 17's- 5½ ft. Departed from Louisville on maiden trip south, July 1878, Capt. J.A. Comstock, with George M. Woods, clerk. Ran New Orleans and Upper Coast. In 1890, New Orleans-Bayou Goula, Capt. J.J. Dodd, three trips weekly. Later was in Mississippi Packet Co. Her original engines, said to have come from Kentucky River packet *BLUE WING,* were removed July 1900 and she was given compound engines. Running November 1901 under charter to Comeaux-LeBlanc Packet Co., with Capt. E.R. Comeaux, master. Laid up for repairs "until she rotted away" in 1903.

5764 WHISPER

Stw ferry wh b. Ashland, Ky., 1881. 75 x 20 x 4.3. Served Proctorville-Guyandotte, Capt. George Smith. Also Augusta, Ky.-Boudes Ferry, Oh., and at Athalia, Oh., where she was dismantled in 1924, and parts were used building the ferry *ALCO* (see).

5765 WHISPER

Stw p wh b. Luxora, Ark., 1907. 86.4 x 22.5 x 4.3. Engines, 8″- 3 ft. One boiler, 42″ by 16 ft. Lengthened to become 105.5 ft. Ran short trades out of Memphis. Capt. James E. Wolf was master in 1921.

5766 WHITE BEAVER

Prop p wh b. La Crosse, Wis., 1885. 27 tons. 65.4 x 10.5 x 3. Said to have been built from the *VIGOR,* b. 1873 (see). Ran La Crosse and Brownsville trade. Still listed 1896.

5767 WHITE CLIFF

SW p wh b. Little River, Ark., 1856. 142 tons. 137 x 27 x 4.5. Owned by Capt. John Graham, Shreveport, La., and others. Off the lists in 1858.

5768 WHITE CLOUD

SW p wh b. Pittsburgh, Pa., 1843. 261 tons. 166 x 26 x 6.7. Three boilers. Running Cincinnati-St. Louis, Capt. Newman Robirds, 1845. St. Louis-New Orleans, Capt. Adams. Caught fire on the night of May 17, 1849, at the St. Louis wharf and the resulting conflagration destroyed 23 steamboats.

5769 WHITE CLOUD

SW p wh b. McKeesport, Pa., 1857. 345 tons. 200 x 35 x 5.5. Four boilers. Had double rudders. Reputation for speed. Ran St. Louis-St. Paul, Capt. Alford, 1857. In 1858 was running up the Missouri River from St. Louis, Capt. James O'Neal, in the Great Mail and Transportation Co. Served as a transport during the war; handled the 7th Iowa Volunteers after Fort Donelson, taking them up the Tennessee to Pittsburg Landing; they lived aboard until the eve of the battle there. Was with Porter on Red River in 1864. Sank in ice at St. Louis Feb. 12, 1867; a gorge shoved her on top of the wrecked *BELLE MEMPHIS.*

5770 WHITE CLOUD

Rig? ferry wh b. Wellsville, Oh., 1868. 57 tons. 101 x 23 x 3. Probably side-wheel. She served on the Missouri at White Cloud, Kans., until removed from the lists. Still documented 1886.

5771 WHITE CLOUD NO. 2

SW p wh b. Paducah, Ky., 1863. 545 tons. Ran St. Louis-New Orleans, Capt. A.C. Hopkins with Joseph Fay, clerk. Said to have been the first steamboat arrival at Mobile following Federal occupation in late April or early May 1865. Hopkins and Fay were on her at the time. Snagged and lost at St. Louis, Feb. 13, 1867.

5772 WHITE EAGLE

Stw p wh b. La Crosse, Wis., 1877. 238 x 29 x 3.8. Originally named *ANNIE* (see). St. Louis & St. Paul Packet Co. Capt. Robert Roehring was master for a time. Still documented 1886.

5773 WHITE RIVER

Stw p wh b. Cincinnati, Oh., 1852. 71 tons. Snagged and lost on Barren River, Ky., Jan. 21, 1854.

5774 WHITE ROSE

SW p wh b. Cincinnati, Oh., 1847. 194 tons. 179 x 26.5 x 4.2. First master and part owner was Capt. E.B. Slow, St. Louis, and his partner was Capt. John Broughton, Alton, Ill. Sold, February 1848, to Capt. Hiram Goodrich, New Orleans. In summer of 1848 was in Louisville-Cairo trade. Burned at Cairo, Ill., July 24, 1848, alongside the Mazeppa wharfboat (see *MAZEPPA*). Had 200 tons aboard at the time. The wreck was cut loose and drifted across the Ohio River and lodged; later the boilers and machinery were removed.

5775 WHITE ROSE

Stw p wh b. Parkersburg, Va., 1862. 232 tons. 155.9 x 33 x 5.3. Engines, 16½'s- 4 ft. Loaded out, new, at Pittsburgh for St. Louis, October 1862, Capt. Dickerson, with Mr. Whittaker in the office. Sold February 1864 to Capt. Shinkle, late of the *CITIZEN,* who made a trip to Pittsburgh with her, and then sold her to the U.S. Renamed *SIREN* in U.S. service, Aug. 30, 1864. When sold Oct. 3, 1865, she resumed her name of *WHITE ROSE,* Capt. E.S. Mills, master, of Cincinnati. Was taken to Apalachicola, Fla., in April 1867 and was dismantled soon thereafter.

5776 WHY NOT

Stw ferry wh b. Franklin, La., 1893. 73 x 16.5 x 3.2. Operated at Abbeville, La. Was documented at Brashear, La., 1908.

5777 WICHITA

Stw snagboat wh b. Little Rock, Ark., 1881. 134 x 29 x 3.

Used on the Arkansas River. When she was new, she was purported to have made a trip to Wichita, Kans. This event was verified by Capt. Henry A. Mayer who was aboard as clerk, and later commanded the snagboat *ARKANSAS.* He died, 93, at Cairo, Ill., March 1946. The U.S. Engineers still had her on the Arkansas in 1896, maybe later.

5778 WIDE AWAKE

SW p wh b. Wellsville, Oh., 1855. 49 tons. Off the lists 1858.

5779 WIGGINS FERRY

Recess wheel ferry wh b. Cincinnati, Oh., 1852. 232 tons. 146 x 41 x 5.9. Operated by Wiggins Ferry Co., St. Louis until 1865 when sold to H.W. Hills, New Orleans, Capt. Thomas Fisher. In January 1870 sold to Baton Rouge Brick Co., Baton Rouge, La. Off the lists in 1875.

5780 WILCOX

SW p wh b. Cincinnati, Oh., 1851. 260 tons. Went to Mobile, Ala. Off the lists 1858.

5781 WILCOX'S ADVERTISER

Rig? wh b. New Albany, Ind., 1876. 5.90 tons.

5782 WILCOX ADVERTISER NO. 2

Rig? wh b. New Albany, Ind., 1877. 28 tons. Inspected in New Orleans District 1881; in Memphis District 1882.

5783 WILD BOY

Rig? p wh b. Cincinnati, Oh., 1871. 120 tons. A boat of this name once ran on Big Sandy River, perhaps this one. Documented at Memphis in 1876.

5784 WILD BOY

Rig? p wh b. Poplar Bluff, Mo., 1881. 77 x 18 x 3.5. Documented at Memphis in 1886.

5785 WILD DEER

Rig? p wh Running Evansville-Wabash River in 1874-1875, Capt. Sam D. Blair. Capt. Blair died, 90, in 1928, Grayville, Ill.

5786 WILD DUCK

SW ferry wh b. Brownsville, Pa., 1858. 37 tons. First home port, St. Louis. Off the lists in 1862.

5787 WILD GAZELLE

Prop p wh b. near Buffalo, N.Y., c. 1876. John and Sam Hamilton brought her to Marietta, Oh., by the canal route, drawing about five feet, and ran her in Ohio River short trades. John Hamilton was a coal dealer at Maysville, Ky., and Sam Hamilton later was on the *BONANZA.* In 1878 they had her in the New Orleans-Upper Coast trade, John Hamilton, master, with C.E. Holmes, clerk. Yellow fever ended that. In August 1878 they sold out.

5788 WILD GOOSE

Stw p wh b. Charleston, W. Va., 1878. 70 tons. Built by James Laidley, brother to Commodore Fred A. Laidley, for the Brownstown-St. Albans trade on Kanawha River. Was inspected in the Wheeling District 1882.

5789 WILD WAGONER

SW p wh b. Cincinnati, Oh., 1864. 477 tons. 180 x 39 x 5.5. Engines, 25 ½'s-8 ft. Three boilers. Paddlewheels 20 ft. dia. working 12 ft. buckets. Built at the Leatherbury Yard for Capt. Henry H. Drown, David Gibson, and Alfred Hoff (who was her engineer). Came out new with tubular boilers, each having twenty-one 6″ flues. Named for Thomas Buchanan Read's poem "Wagoner of the Alleghenies." Came out in the Wheeling-Cincinnati trade, Capt. H.H. Drown, with Chris Best and Charles Knox, clerks; Ellis Mace and Brose Dennis, pilots; Alfred Hoff (or Nuff), engineer; James Dodson, steward. Sold in 1865 to the Peoples' Line headed by Capt. Jesse K. Bell organized to run competition with the U.S. Mail Line between Cincinnati and Louisville. She and *ST. CHARLES* ended up in the hands of a U.S. marshal by November 1866. Capt. Charles Muhleman ran her briefly Wheeling-Cincinnati and in February 1867 she had been sold to the New Orleans & Bayou Sara Mail Line, Capt. A.C. Goddin. She ran there until dismantled in 1873. Her "wild cat" whistle in October 1873 was sold to Capt. William Thorwegan who placed it on his *GREAT REPUBLIC.* The original tubular boilers were replaced with standard 2-flue river boilers while she was in the Bayou Sara trade.

5790 WILDWOOD

Prop p wh b. Hockingport, Oh., 1869. 25 tons. Ran local trades and probably handled produce boats. Ran briefly in Muskingum River, 1874, Parkersburg-Zanesville, Capt. A. Sprague. Sold at U.S. marshal sale in April 1878 near Middleport, Oh., for $180.

5791 WILDWOOD

SW p wh b. Madison, Ind., 1871. 401 tons. Ran Maysville-Portsmouth. Lengthened 30 feet at Madison, Ind., in fall of 1876, extending her aft of the wheelhouses, which gave her an awkward look. Then ran Maysville-Cincinnati, Capt. James C. Power, with John Henderson, pilot. Capt. James Rowley, Jr., did his first "cubbing" on her. Sank and was dismantled at Augusta, Ky., about 1880, and the *MORNING MAIL* (see) was built to replace her.

5792 WILL J. CUMMINS

Stw p wh b. Jeffersonville, Ind., by Howard, 1895. 160 x 30 x 4. Ran in the Cumberland River, Capt. Tim Armstrong, making trips to the headwaters at Burnside, Ky., in opposition to the Ryman Line and once raced the *R. DUNBAR* (see). Bought by Capt. J. Mack Gamble in April 1897 who entered her in Wheeling-Cincinnati trade on June 13. Low water tied her up a week or so later. Ran low water that fall in Louisville-Cincinnati trade with *H.K. BEDFORD* for partner. Back to Wheeling-Cincinnati run, but ice laid her up in the Muskingum. Ran Pittsburgh-Cincinnati in 1898. Sold March 1899 to Louisville & Nashville Railroad Co., who took her to Tennessee River with Capt. James Till, master, and William Hunter, first mate. St. Louis & Tennessee River Packet Co. were running her when she was snagged and lost at Beech Creek, below Clifton, Tenn., on the Tennessee River, April 1901.

5793 WILL KYLE

Stw p wh b. Cincinnati, Oh., 1879. 260.5 x 45.7 (floor 43.7) x 6.3. Engines, 22's- 7 ft. Four boilers, each 42″ by 30 ft., two flues. Paddlewheel shaft 40 ft. long, 12″ in journal. Wheel 24 ft. dia. working 30 ft. buckets, each 28″ dip. Had a goose stern (no skegs). Built for the Cincinnati-New Orleans trade. First crew: Capt. Lew Kates, master; James Alexander, first clerk; Gus Young, 2nd clerk; John Jackman, 1st engineer; Dan Barr, mate; Wes Conner and Ike Gough, pilots; Henry Alvord, steward; Susan Tinsley, stewardess; Mike Shields, barkeep. Named for the late Capt. Will Kyle who died, 33, on Oct. 4, 1879, at San Antonio, Tex., native of Burlington, Oh. He and brother John Kyle had built the *ASHLAND* (see) and then went to Texas. Capt. Lew Kates was a New Jersey native who had spent three years at sea, then came by stage from Philadelphia to Pittsburgh in 1848 and went to steamboating. The forward cabin of the *WILL KYLE* was graced with a fine oil painting of a Texas scene, the Verde River emptying into the Guadaloupe, location of a stock ranch Will Kyle had planned before his untimely death. A portrait of Capt. Will Kyle also was hung in the forward cabin. She once sank at Slim Island, Ohio River, upbound, Nov. 7, 1881, and was successfully raised. Struck a log at Australia, Miss., and was lost, Nov. 15, 1883.

5794 WILL S. HAYS

Stw p wh b. New Albany, Ind., 1865. 151.5 x 30.8 x 4.5, 340 tons. Engines 14's- 4 ft. Two Western boilers, 48 in. diameter by 24 ft. long. Built by Capt. J.B. Ford for the Louisville-New Orleans trade. Sold in July, 1866 to St. Louis parties. She was laid up a long time at Peoria, Ill.; still there in October, 1868. Dan Rice, the showman, loaded his circus aboard in 1869 and toured from St. Paul to New Orleans, repeated for several years. Reported Jan. 29, 1873 as having sunk when caught on a log by a falling river, seven miles below Arkadelphia, Arkansas on the upper Ouachita River.

5795 WILL S. HAYS

SW p wh b. Freedom, Pa. (hull), and the cabin of the *THOMPSON DEAN* was moved over, also the engines. 1882. 305 x 44 x 9. Engines, 28's- 10 ft. Six boilers, each 50″ by 28 ft., seven flues. Paddlewheels 30 ft. dia. working 15 ft. buckets, 28″ dip. Cabin was 246 ft. long, 18 ft. wide. This and the prior *WILL S. HAYS* were named for Col. Will S. Hays, Louisville, Ky., song writer and news reporter. Was electrically lighted, 60 "illuminators" in all. Ran Cincinnati-New Orleans, Capt. John J. Darragh, and once came up in 6 days 11 hours making 51 landings. Capt. W.C. Tichenor became master with Wash Floyd as purser and Hi Beedle as chief engineer. The *HAYS* became called the "Wild Bill" and whipped many of the fast nags of the day; came near taking down the *J.M. WHITE* time to Baton Rouge. The Anchor Line owned her in her latter days, running her in the St. Louis-New Orleans trade. She was cut down by ice at the foot of Lesperance Street, St. Louis, Jan. 31, 1888.

Col. Will S. Hays wrote the song "Mollie Darling" which sold two million copies; another popular favorite was "Keep In de Middle ob de Road." He once was thrown in jail in New Orleans by orders of General Butler, said to have resulted from his song, "My Sunny Southern Home." He died, 70, at Louisville on July 23, 1907, having suffered apoplexy in the Iroquois Theatre fire in Chicago Dec. 30, 1903.

5796 WILLARD V. KING

SW tr sh b. Dubuque, Iowa, 1910, originally named *B.F. YOAKUM* (see). Renamed by New Orleans, Texas & Mexico Railroad Co., prior to 1925. The Missouri-Pacific brought her to St. Louis in 1927 and she continued there until January 1940 at which time the transfer business was discontinued, the trains having been rerouted over the Municipal bridge at that time. Dismantled at New Orleans.

5797 WILLIAM ARMSTRONG

Stw p wh b. Wheeling, Va., 1846. 89 tons. Snagged and lost at Little Rock, Ark., November 1849.

5798 WILLIAM BAGALEY

SW p wh b. Belle Vernon, Pa., 1854. 396 tons. Captured by the U.S. as a Confederate steamer, July 18, 1863. Saw service in the USQMD.

5799 WILLIAM BAIRD

Stw p wh b. Elizabeth, Pa., 1855. 286 tons. While upbound on Missouri River, en route St. Louis to Sioux City with 160 passengers and cargo, lost by snagging opposite Waverly, Mo., Apr. 19, 1858. No life loss.

5800 WILLIAM BURTON

SW p wh b. New Albany, Ind., 1857. 253 tons. 151 x 29 x 5.5. Running New Orleans-Opelousas-Atchafalaya in 1860, Capt. G.E. Louaillier. Had many ownership changes in the New Orleans area. Ran New Orleans-Shreveport, Capt. F.A. Boissat, 1861, then Capt. Edward Schiller, under Confederate registry. Captured by the U.S. Apr. 28, 1862, and placed in USQMD.

5801 WILLIAM BUTLER

Stw p wh b. Cincinnati, Oh., 1864. 205 tons. 157 x 30 x 4. Owned by Capt. William Knight and Charles G. Pearce, Cincinnati. Ran in the Marietta-Cincinnati trade, September 1864. Went to New Orleans February 1866 and ran New Orleans-Ouachita River, Capt. A. Lewis, with C.R. Hopkins, clerk. Rebuilt in 1867 to measure 158.7 x 31.2 x 4.4. The original owners had her back on the upper Ohio 1868. Caught fire at Wheeling mid-October 1868, and the cabin burned off. Decision was reached not to rebuild her.

5802 WILLIAM C. ROBINSON

Stw p wh b. McKeesport, Pa., 1857. 87 tons. Off the lists 1862.

5803 WILLIAM C. YOUNG

SW p wh b. Louisville, Ky., 1854. 199 tons. 140 x 28 x 5.5. Went to Texas, Capt. John S. Curd owned by stockholders in Lamar County and elsewhere. Sold to New Orleans owners in November 1855. Owned by Capt. William C. Harrison of New Orleans, 1858. Last owned by J.J. Miller, New Orleans, Capt. John Heinn. Foundered and lost at Ship Island, Miss., Aug. 15, 1860, with loss of seven lives.

5804 WILLIAM CAMPBELL

SW p wh b. St. Louis, Mo., 1856. 322 tons. Ran St. Louis-Weston on Missouri River, Capt. William Edds, 1856. Burned at New Orleans, May 27, 1860.

5805 WM. D. ELLIS

Stw p wh b. Harmar, Oh., 1883, originally named *O.M. LOVELL* (see). Prior to 1866 sold to Col. W.D. Ellis for Chattahoochee River and renamed. Later owned in the south by the Plant System of railroads, then by Capt. George L. Lapham. Retired in 1892 and towed to Woolfolk's Bend where she was sunk as a jetty.

5806 WILLIAM DIXON

Stw p wh b. New Albany, Ind., 1855. 179 tons. Went to Confederate registry 1861.

5807 WM. DRUHE

Stw p wh b. Fort Smith, Ark., 1885. Operated on upper Arkansas River.

5808 WM. DRUHE NO. 2

Stw p wh b. Fort Smith, Ark., 1890. 126 x 24.3 x 4.8. Operated on upper Arkansas River. Documented at Memphis 1896, maybe later.

5809 WM. DUFFEY

Stw p wh b. Higginsport, Oh., 1897. 126 x 21.2. Hull and other equipment from the *SILVER WAVE* which had burned at Portsmouth, Oh., on July 21, 1897 (see). Owned by A.P. Duffey, Marietta, Oh. In 1898 ran Marietta-Waverly, four round trips a day.

5810 WILLIAM FAGAN

Stw p wh b. Jeffersonville, Ind., by Howard, 1879. 166 x 34.6 x 4.9. Ran New Orleans, Donaldsonville and Bayou Lafourche, Capt. L.P. Delahoussaye, with Gus Hodge, clerk. Burned at New Orleans Jan. 5, 1881, destroying all of the upper works. Rebuilt and named *ALTO* (see).

5811 WM. FOX

Stw p wh Ran Marietta-Zanesville, Capt. Wm. Edgill, 1868. Occasional trips on the Muskingum, Capt. Thomas McCormick, 1869. Running Zanesville-McConnelsville-Roxbury, Capt. A. Morrison, 1871.

5812 WM. GARIG

Stw p wh b. Jeffersonville, Ind., by Howard, 1904. 175 x 35 x 5.2. Engines, 14's- 6 ft. Two boilers, each 44" by 28 ft. Machinery and boilers from *JULIAN POYDRAS* (see). Built for Baton Rouge & Bayou Sara Packet Co. Owned after 1908 by Carter Bros., New Orleans. Her last running in the south was New Orleans-Camden, on Ouachita River, Capt. Sam Cotton, this in 1917. Sold to Eagle Packet Co., St. Louis, March 1918 who rebuilt her to become the *GOLDEN EAGLE* (see).

5813 WM. GARVIN

SW p wh b. Louisville, Ky., 1853. 299 tons. Ran Louisville-Evansville, Capt. Sam Sullivan, replacing *FAWN* (see). Made trips to New Orleans. Ran St. Louis-Chester, Ill., Capt. Alex Zeigler, 1857-1859. Burned at St. Louis in November 1859 apparently having been laid up after a sinking at Carroll's Island, Mississippi River, Sept. 10, 1859.

5814 WM. H. DUNLEVY

SW ferry wh b. Wheeling, Va., 1858. 78 tons. Off the lists in 1868.

5815 WM. H. RUSSELL

SW p wh b. Madison, Ind., 1856. 405 tons. 204 x 34 x 5.5. Engines, 24½'s- 7 ft. Four boilers, each 38" by 28 ft. Ran St. Louis and Missouri River, Capt. Joseph Kinney. Named for a founder of the "Pony Express" out of St. Joseph, Mo. Burned at St. Louis in a large steamboat fire, Oct. 27, 1862. Machinery went to the *T.L. McGILL* (see).

5816 WILLIAM H. WEBB

SW ocean liner wh b. New York, N.Y., 1856. 655 tons. Low pressure, walking beam type, about 200 feet long. She was used as an ice breaker in the East, and was sold in 1861 to New Orleans merchants, arriving there from Havana May 15. Two days later she was commissioned as a Confederate privateer and seized three vessels carrying oil. She was sent to Shreveport when the Federals occupied New Orleans. Took part in capturing the *INDIANOLA,* Feb. 24, 1863. Was in the Battle of Grand Lake where the *QUEEN OF THE WEST* was lost. Went back to Shreveport and was there until April 1865 and made a mad dash out to New Orleans, arriving noon, Apr. 24, 1865. At 4:00 P.M., same day met the *USS RICHMOND* and the Confederates beached and fired the *WEBB* to prevent her capture. This happened 23 miles below New Orleans. Known in Confederate service as *WEBB.*

5817 WM. J. LEWIS

SW p wh b. Metropolis, Ill., 1866. 503 tons. A fair sized boat with engines 22's- 6 ft. and three boilers. She left St. Louis for Fort Benton at 4:30 P.M., Mar. 27, 1866, and had cleared $60,000 by the time she returned on Sunday June 17—83 days out. Capt. E.T. Herndon was master; C.J. Atkins, pilot (at $800 per month); Henry Smith and Bob Clark, clerks; Bob Ferguson and Oliver Catterel, engineers; Tom Hill, mate; W.F. Whitney and George W. Vaughan, assistant pilots. She carried 260 tons of freight drawing 3½ ft. According to "Steamboat Bill" Heckmann she once made two round trips to Fort Benton from St. Louis in one season. Wrecked on Apr. 3, 1873, at Grand Tower, Ill., below St. Louis. She was bound for Red River with a heavy cargo at time of loss.

5818 WM. J. LEWIS

Stw p wh b. Jeffersonville, Ind., 1873. It was reported that much equipment from the former boat of the name (above) was used in construction. Snagged in Brickhouse Bend, Missouri River, Sept. 14, 1874, raised. While en route from St. Louis to New Orleans, burned at Chester, Ill., Capt. J. Cartwright, Mar. 16, 1875.

5819 WILLIAM KNOX

Stw p wh b. Harmar, Oh., at Knox Yard, 1852. 208 tons. 160 x 26 x 5. Owned by Harlow Chapin and Col. D. Barber, Harmar, and William F. Curtis, Marietta. Capt. I.N. Cook, Harmar, was first master. Designed for the Pittsburgh-Gallipolis trade. Carried Marietta residents to Wheeling to witness the arrival of the first B. & O. train from the East, Jan. 11, 1853. Took fire on the roof while passing Flint Island, Ohio River, late April 1855 and burned, Capt. William Yard. The *CRYSTAL PALACE* took her passengers, and the crew returned to Louisville on the *STATESMAN*.

5820 WILLIAM L. EWING

SW p wh b. New Albany, Ind., 1856. 335 tons. 181 x 32 x 5.5. Engines, 21's- 6½ ft. Three boilers. Ran St. Louis-St. Paul. In the Northwestern Line, Capt. Green, 1858–1859. In the Northern Line, Capt. J.H. Rhodes, 1860–1861. Served as a U.S. transport during the war. Stranded at Hardscrabble Bar, below St. Louis, Nov. 25, 1864, and broke in two. The machinery went to *DES ARC* (see).

5821 WILLIAM M. LEVY

SW p wh b. New Albany, Ind., 1860. 140 tons. 125 x 27.5 x 4.5. Went to New Orleans owned by Capt. L.G.C. Prickette. Sold October 1861 to Capt. Marcus Radovich, Confederate registry.

5822 WM. M. MORRISON

SW p wh b. Cincinnati, Oh., 1856. 662 tons. Ran in the St. Louis-New Orleans trade, Capt. John Bofinger. At the outbreak of the war she was laid up opposite Memphis and fell into the hands of the Confeds. She had been one of the "Railroad Line" and Mark Twain is said to have been pilot on her briefly. Governor Cameron of Virginia was once her clerk. Capt. Patrick Yore commanded in 1857 with Ben Taber, clerk. River historians seem to agree that the Confederates burned her at New Orleans to prevent her capture. Even so, she was renamed *ALICE V.* (see) as of Jan. 2, 1867.

5823 WM. MCBEAN, SR.

Rig? ferry wh b. Metropolis, Ill., 1874. 35 tons. Inspected in the Evansville, Ind., area through 1882, maybe longer.

5824 WILLIAM N. SHERMAN

SW p wh b. New Albany, Ind., 1855. 194 tons. 130 x 30 x 5.5. Went to New Orleans, Capt. Michael Gwartney. Ran New Orleans-Shreveport. In May 1857 Capt. Hugh C. Funk took command and was part owner. Burned and lost at Algiers, La., Feb. 20, 1858.

5825 WM. NOBLE

SW p wh b. Cincinnati, Oh., 1848. 289 tons. Ran Cincinnati-New Orleans, Capt. J.M. Newcomb. Named for former master of *PARAGON*. Off the lists 1858.

5826 WILLIAM OSBORN

SW ferry wh b. Pittsburgh, Pa., 1866. 162 tons. 126 x 32 x 4. Long served at Savanna, Ill. Off the lists 1892.

5827 WM. P. FISKE

Stw freight boat sh b. Nashville, Tenn., by Nashville Bridge Co., 1922. 120.5 x 22.5 x 4. Owned by Nashville Builders Supply Co., and named for Capt. Wm. P. Fiske, U.S. Inspector at Nashville 1918–1948. This was the first steel hull steamboat built by Nashville Bridge although they had built the steel hull for the U.S. snagboat *KENTUCKY* the year prior. She sank at Wooddale Grove, 10 miles from Nashville, May 18, 1925, and drowned four persons, one of whom was pilot Ed Bell. Owned in 1933 by H.E. Richardson, Nashville, who planned to make of her a pile driver and derrickboat.

5828 WM. P. HALLIDAY

SW p wh b. Louisville, Ky., 1878. See *W.P. HALLIDAY*, registered name.

5829 WILLIAM PENN

SW p wh b. West Wheeling, Oh., 1847. 113 tons. Ran low water in Wheeling trades, Capt. Sam Mason and Capt. William Cecil. They sold her to the Cincinnati-Rising Sun, Ind., trade. Snagged and lost in Red River, La., May 12, 1854.

5830 WILLIAM PHILLIPS

Stw p wh b. Elizabeth, Pa., 1849. 62 tons. Came out new in February 1849, Capt. John McPhail. Made a trip up the Allegheny River and then ran Pittsburgh-Beaver, Pa., that summer and fall. Sold Nov. 30, 1849, to Capt. Newton for Gallipolis-Kanawha River. Off the lists 1858.

5831 WILLIAM PORTER

Stw p wh b. Jeffersonville, Ind., by Howard, 1886. 150 x 25.5 x 5. Ran out of Nashville on Cumberland River, Capt. T.H. Armstrong. Burned below the mouth of Salt River below Louisville, Ky., Jan. 2, 1888.

5832 WM. PRESTON DIXON

Stw snagboat wh b. Jeffersonville, Ind., at M.A. Sweeney & Bro. yard, winter 1889–1890. 123.5 x 32 x 5. Operated on Green and Barren rivers. Was taken to the Howard Yard, Jeffersonville, Ind., in 1909 and much equipment used in building snagboat *MAMMOTH CAVE*.

5833 WILLIAM R. JONES

Stw p wh b. Pittsburgh, Pa., 1880. 100 x 20 x 3. Engines, 13's- 5 ft. Ran short trades on Monongahela River. In June 1883 was up the Youghiogheny with the troupe of showboat *THE NEW SENSATION* aboard, Capt. Packer, showing at Greenock, Alpsville, and other places. Went to U.S. marshal sale August 1885 and was bought by James Rees & Sons Co., Pittsburgh, for $1,025. Dismantled, and machinery went to *NELLIE HUDSON,* b. 1886 (see).

5834 WILLIAM R. KING

SW p wh b. Louisville, Ky., 1846. 233 tons. Went to Mobile, Ala. Lost in collision with *WINONA* on Tombigbee River, Feb. 5, 1847. Two lives were lost.

5835 WM. R. MCKEE

SW p wh b. Cincinnati, Oh., 1845. 165 tons. 154 x 26 x 5. Engines, 17's- 7 ft. Hull by Gordon and Temple. Ran Cincinnati-Kentucky River along with *ISAAC SHELBY* (see). McKee was active in the transportation business on the Kentucky in this period. Off the lists in 1848.

5836 WM. RUPRECHT

Stw ferry wh b. Jeffersonville, Ind., 1913. 87 x 23 x 3.5. Documented at St. Louis 1918.

5837 WILLIAM S. BARRY

SW p wh b. New Albany, Ind., 1859. 275 tons. Went to Mobile, Ala. Renamed *ADMIRAL,* July 5, 1865. Off the lists 1872.

5838 WILLIAM S. NELSON

Stw p wh b. Paducah, Ky., 1856. 324 tons. Ran on the Upper Mississippi to St. Paul. Burned at Carrollton, La., November 1859.

5839 WM. S. PIKE

SW p wh b. Jeffersonville, Ind., 1869. See *W.S. PIKE,* registered name.

5840 WILLIAM THAW

SW ferry wh b. Pittsburgh, Pa., 1876. 230 tons. 138 x 55 x 5. Owned by Capt. William J. Kountz and operated across the Ohio River from the Manchester district, North Side, Pittsburgh, to West End. Billy Abrams long was the pilot. Still listed in 1896.

5841 WILLIAM V. GILLUM

Stw p wh b. New Albany, Ind., 1855. 70 tons. Ran Evansville-Green River, summer 1858, Capt. J.W. McCarty. She was loaded with lumber at New Orleans and started for Matamoras, Tex., but was wrecked in the Gulf enroute, Sept. 1, 1864. Officers and crew survived on a raft and were picked up days later by the Mexican schooner *CORCY.*

5842 WILLIAM W. FRY

SW p ih b. Jeffersonville, Ind., 1849. 303 tons. Went to Mobile, Ala. Off the lists in 1858.

5843 WILLIAM WHITE

Stw p wh b. Cannelton, Ind., and completed at Evansville, Ind., 1865. 140 tons. Owned by Capt. Al Drinkwater, with Tom Suttlemire, pilot. Exploded boiler in Green River in latter January 1867 killing Capt. Drinkwater and the engineer. The blast was heard at Owensboro. She was rebuilt and was running Evansville-Green River, fall of 1867, Capt. E.D. Rust, with H.C. Lancaster, clerk. By 1869 was in the Paducah-Cairo trade, Capt. Northern, with Jimmy Beverly, clerk. Later was used as a towboat on the Upper Mississippi, and was removed from documentation in 1886.

5844 WILLIE AUSTIN

Stw p wh b. Clarington, Oh., 1878. 109 x 20 x 3. Engines, 10"- 3 ft. One boiler, 42" by 22 ft., each with five flues. Built by John Mallory and named for Will and Austin Mallory. Ran low water, Gallipolis-Marietta, summer of 1878 in place of *KATYDID.* Ran Beverly-Zanesville, Capt. James R. Martin, summer 1879. Was rebuilt into a small towboat, renamed *DUQUESNE,* operated out of Pittsburgh.

5845 WILLIE CADE

Stw p wh b. Metropolis, Ill., 1881. 131 x 31 x 4. Went to the Missouri River based at Leavenworth, Kans. Later renamed *VINT STILLINGS* (see).

5846 WILLIE GAMAGE

SW p wh b. Cincinnati, Oh., 1864. 187 tons. 148.2 x 30 x 4.5. Engines, 14's- 5 ft. Sold to U.S. Navy on Dec. 22, 1864, and was known as *GAMAGE* in service. Sold to private hands and renamed *SOUTHERN BELLE* Oct. 4, 1865. Off the lists in 1869.

5847 WILLIE J.

A small packet which ran low water in the Wheeling-Clarington trade, Ohio River, in the latter 1860s, Capt. John Mallory. Also ran on Big Sandy River.

5848 WILLOW

SW Lighthouse tender sh b. Dubuque, Iowa, by Dubuque Boat & Boiler Works, 1927. 200 x 65 x 8. Engines, 27's- 7 ft. Six return flue boilers, each 40" by 28 ft. in two batteries. Burned fuel oil. Operated on the Mississippi River, notoriously slow. Carried the whistle formerly on *OLEANDER,* said to have originated on side-wheel *MINNEAPOLIS.* Dismantled at the U.S. Engineer yard, West Memphis, Ark., spring of 1945. Used as a quarterboat by the U.S. Engineers thereafter, and by construction and oil firms along the Louisiana coast. In November 1970 the hull was repaired at the Hunt Shipyard in the Harvey Canal preparing to send her to British Honduras, which didn't come about. In 1973 Paul W. Jennings had her at Panama City, Fla., where she beached during a hurricane. In 1979 was taken to Pensacola, Fla., owned by Bob Snow, with plans to make of her a restaurant.

5849 WILLSBURG

SW p wh b. Louisville, Ky., 1860. 71 tons. First home port,

Memphis. Went to Confederate registry 1861.

5850 WILMINGTON

Stw p wh b. Pittsburgh, Pa., 1844. 77 tons. Built for service on Allegheny River, Capt. Hugh Dennison. During low water 1845 ran Pittsburgh-Zanesville. Was a local out of East Liverpool and Steubenville into 1847. Off the lists 1849.

5851 WINCHESTER

SW p wh b. Freedom, Pa., 1851. 180 tons. Ran Pittsburgh-Wheeling, Capt. George D. Moore teamed up with *DIURNAL* (see). There is some evidence she went to St. Louis & Keokuk Packet Co., later on. She fell into Confederate hands and they sank her purposely to block the Mississippi River at Island 10 on Apr. 7, 1862.

5852 WINCHESTER

SW p wh b. McKeesport, Pa. (hull), and completed at Pittsburgh, 1866. 560 tons. 214 x 31.2 x 6.4. Engines, 22's- 7 ft., formerly on *BAYARD*. Four boilers, each 40" by 24 ft., two flues. Owned by Capt. Dan Moore, James Hamilton, John Ackley, and Capt. George D. Moore, all of Pittsburgh, and S. Sheets and M. Sheets, both of Washington County, Oh. Came out in the Pittsburgh-Parkersburg trade and burned downbound on her first trip at Babbs Island, Ohio River, above East Liverpool, Oh., at 4:00 A.M. She was run ashore on the West Virginia side, hit a gravel bar and didn't get completely landed. Crew at the time: Capt. Asa Shepherd, master; Dan Moore and Oliver C. Bunting, clerks; William J. Abrams, pilot. Loss happened Feb. 23, 1866. Five lives were lost.

5853 WINDSOR

SW p wh b. Fulton, Oh. (now Cincinnati), 1854. 199 tons. Off the lists in 1866.

5854 WINFIELD SCOTT

SW p wh b. Wheeling, Va., 1849. 280 tons. Hull was built at the Knox Yard, Harmar, Oh., engines, etc., placed at Wheeling, and outfitted at Pittsburgh. 182 x 34 (27 ft. floor) x 8. Engines, 22's- 7 ft. Three boilers, each 42" by 26 ft. Built by Capt. Alex Devenny for Pittsburgh-New Orleans trade. Came up to Louisville from New Orleans May 16, 1849, reporting 28 or 29 deaths from cholera; one child was buried in the mud on the wharf at Cairo, Ill., without benefit of a coffin. Sank and lost at Corn Creek, Ky., on the Ohio River above Bethlehem, Ind., Jan. 6, 1855.

5855 WING AND WING

SW p wh b. Pittsburgh, Pa., 1843. 227 tons. 164 x 24 x 6. Built for Capt. Duncan Campbell of Brownsville, Pa. Other stockholders were Aaron Bugher, Cookstown, Pa., and John Hough, Pittsburgh. Ran Pittsburgh-Cincinnati-St. Louis. Capt. A. Bugher often commanded. Off the lists 1850.

5856 WINNIFRED

Prop yacht wh b. Pittsburgh, Pa., 1892. 58 x 9.5 x 3.9. Sank and lost while laid up on the Monon River above Brownsville, Pa., in a flood, Mar. 13, 1907, owned by Samuel M. Green, Pittsburgh, Pa.

5857 WINONA

SW p wh b. New Albany, Ind., 1845. 135 tons. Went to Mobile, Ala. Snagged and lost on the Warrior River, Ala., May 7, 1847.

5858 WINONA

Stw p wh b. Belle Vernon, Pa., 1855. 170 tons. Ran on the Upper Mississippi out of St. Paul. On Minnesota River, Capt. L. Brown. Also on St. Croix River. In the Davidson Line, La Crosse-St. Paul, 1861. Off the lists 1864.

5859 WINONA

Stw p wh b. Charleston, W. Va., 1881. 102.7 x 27.5 x 3.7. There is evidence the hull was built at Chambersburg, Oh., 1879. Operated by Capt. Josiah Cornwell in the Gallipolis-Crown City, Oh., trade. Off the lists after 1886.

5860 WIOTA

SW p wh b. Elizabethtown, Pa., 1845. 219 tons. 180 x 24 x 5. Engines, 18's- 7 ft. Three boilers. Ran St. Louis-Galena, Capt. R.A. Reilly who also owned in part, along with Corwith Bros., and William Hempstead of Galena. Off the lists in 1847.

5861 WIRT

Stw p wh b. Burning Springs, W. Va., 1872. 35 tons. 97 x 16 x 3. Still listed 1885.

5862 WISCONSIN

SW p wh b. Pittsburgh, Pa., 1845. 192 tons. 172 x 24 x 4.9. Ran Pittsburgh-Cincinnati, Capt. Redmund J. Grace. Owned in Pittsburgh by James Holmes, David Holmes, Wm. Eichbaum, Wm. Frampton. Three stockholders lived in Beaver, Pa., H. Clarke, F.J. Clarke, and G.M. Horton. Occasionally made trips through to New Orleans. Sold to Madison, Ind., in December 1847. Capt. T.T. Wright then ran her Cincinnati-Madison, with Charles David, pilot. Off the lists 1849.

5863 WISCONSIN

SW p wh b. Rock Island, Ill., 1849. 139 tons. Snagged and lost at Grafton, Ill., Oct. 31, 1857.

5864 WISCONSIN NO. 2

SW p wh b. Cincinnati, Oh., 1849. 297 tons. 200 x 28 x 6. Engines, 22½'s- 8 ft. Five boilers. Ran Louisville-Madison, Capt. T.T. Wright. Came up Feb. 12, 1853, in 3 hours 53 minutes. Captain Wright lived in a colonial style home on the Indiana hillside about five miles below Vevay. His wife was aunt of Edward Eggleston. She was a Craig, and her brother DeKalb Craig was clerk on the *WISCONSIN NO. 2* and others. This boat also ran Cincinnati-Madison. In April 1855 she was sent to Pittsburgh and brought down a coal tow to Madison, 26,000 bushels. Off the lists in 1862.

5865 WOODFORD

SW p wh b. Louisville, Ky., 1856. 487 tons. 221 x 34 x 6.1. Ran Louisville-New Orleans, Capt. James Mather. In 1860 Capt. Moses Irwin was master and she was owned largely at Louisville, her stockholders including W.C. Hite, E.T. Sturgeon, D.T. Benedict, and others. She made trips Louisville-Evansville in early 1862. Laid up at New Albany she was taken over by the U.S. in December 1862 and was used as a hospital ship. Sank on the falls at Alexandria, La., Red River, 1864.

5866 WOODSMAN

SW p wh b. Marietta, Oh., 1848. 80 tons. 100 x 19.5 x 4.5. Owned 1849 by Owen Frank, Marietta, Capt. Ankrin, master. Ran in the south. Collapsed a flue leaving Bayou Sara bound for Red River on Mar. 2, 1849, killing three and wounding others. John Ankrin was master until the boat was sold September 1851 to Capt. William O. Western, New Orleans. Sold September 1852 to Capt. William Randolph, Algiers, La. Off the lists 1854.

5867 WREN

SW p wh b. Louisville, Ky., 1862. 189 tons. Built by the Howard Yard. 150 x 30 x 5.5. Owned by John Watson & Co., Frankfort, Ky., and served on Kentucky River.

5868 WREN

SW p wh b. Cincinnati, Oh., 1866. 43 tons. Dispatch dated July 16, 1866: "There is to be found at Livesay's saw mill in the Licking River a miniature side-wheel steamer called the *WREN,* built at Cleveland, Oh., at a cost of $3,000. Her captain assures us she will make two miles an hour upstream." Off the lists in 1868.

5869 WYACONDA

SW p wh b. La Grange, Mo., 1864. 239 tons. Burned and lost at Ste. Genevieve, Mo., July 14, 1865, with loss of one life.

5870 WYANDOT

Stw p wh b. Johnsonville, Tenn., 1891. 91 x 18.4 x 3. Owned and operated by Capt. Henry E. Warren. Sank and lost in White Horse Bend, Duck River, about 1895. The *LULA E. WARREN* was built to replace her (see).

5871 WYANDOTTE

SW p wh b. Cincinnati, Oh., 1847. 314 tons. She landed on Paw Paw Island, above Vicksburg, Miss., to unload quarreling deck passengers, hit a snag, and went down, Nov. 21, 1848. The life loss was set at 30 persons.

5872 WYNNTON

SW p wh b. Shousetown, Pa., 1849. 137 tons. Off the lists in 1851.

5873 WYETH CITY

Stw p wh b. Chattanooga, Tenn., 1888. 120 x 21.5 x 4.8. Built from the former *CHATTANOOGA* (see). Employed for some time as a ferry at Knoxville, Tenn., when the L. & N. Railroad bridge was being built there. Still listed 1896.

5874 WYOMING

SW p wh b. Jacksonville, Pa., 1846. 198 tons. Capt. William J. Kountz bought her with others in 1847. Later was on the Upper Mississippi and burned at Pekin, Ill., on Dec. 16, 1853.

5875 WYOMING

Stw p wh b. Sewickley, Pa. (hull), and completed at Pittsburgh, 1879. 257 x 45 x 6. 1,034 tons. Engines, 18's- 7 ft. Four boilers, each 42" by 26 ft., two flues. Paddlewheel 22 ½ ft. dia. working 29 ft. buckets. Ran Pittsburgh-St. Louis, Capt. W.W. Coulson. Made a trip to Fort Benton, Mont., in 1882, arriving June 25. On the return she took aboard 316 head of cattle for Asa Samples, the largest stock shipment by river from Fort Benton. S.S. Coulson was clerk. She ran trips Cincinnati-New Orleans in 1883 for the Southern Transportation Co., Capt. Frank Stein, with Dan Moore, clerk. In later years she was rebuilt into a railroad transfer steamer renamed *GEORGE W. PARKER* (see).

Y

5876 YALOBUSHA

SW p wh b. Harmar, Oh., 1844. 115 x 24 x 5. 116 tons. Engines, 16's- 5 ft. Two boilers, each 40" by 20 ft. Owned by stockholders from Marietta, Oh., Capt. John Ankrin, master, and Hugh Hill, John B. Burlingame, and Thomas Gilchrist; also John A. Outway, New Orleans. Ran Cincinnati-New Orleans. Owned 1847 by H. Kendall Carter & Co., New Orleans, same master. Last owned by James Scott and Andrew J. Armstrong, Ouachita County, Ark. Burned and lost opposite Donaldsonville, La., Jan. 18, 1848, with loss of 35 lives.

5877 YANKEE

Stw p wh b. Glasgow, Pa., 1847. 97 tons. First work was transferring freight and passengers when the Allegheny River aqueduct for the Pennsylvania Canal burned at Freeport, Pa., on May 13, 1847. Ran Pittsburgh-Zanesville 1849–1850, Capt. Adam McKee. On Aug. 1, 1850, went up the Minnesota River exploring the navigation possibilities, Capt. M.K. Harris, with J.S. Armstrong, pilot; G.R. Girdon, clerk; and G.W. Scott and G.L. Sargent, engineers. Operating at St. Paul, 1851, Capt. Orren Smith. Off the lists in 1852.

5878 YAZONIA

Stw p wh b. Yazoo City, Miss., 1894. 62 tons. 95 x 19.8 x 3.5. Belonged to the "P" Line run by the Parisot family. Burned and lost June 23, 1898, at Brown's Landing on the Tallahatchie River.

5879 YAZOO

SW p wh b. Cincinnati, Oh., 1842. 304 tons. 151 x 28 x 6.8. Operated Yazoo River to New Orleans, Capt. James C.

Cockrell, originally owned by William M. Porter, Cincinnati, and C.C. Cockrell, Lexington, Ky. In 1844 Capt. Charles C. Brenham became master and part owner. J.H. Morrison & Co., New Orleans, bought the boat outright Feb. 1, 1845, Capt. Isaac Wright, master. In May 1847 sold to Capt. James H. Culver. Snagged and lost at Carrollton, La., Apr. 3, 1848. She took part in Mexican War activities, bringing troops from Natchitoches to New Orleans, six trips, in 1845; later returning troops.

5880 YAZOO

SW p wh b. Jeffersonville, Ind., 1860. 371 tons. Went to the Yazoo River, Miss. Enrolled as a Confederate steamer, and was sunk by U.S. troops at Island 10, Mississippi River, Apr. 7, 1862.

5881 YAZOO

Stw p wh b. Jeffersonville, Ind., 1873. She loaded out at Cincinnati, September 1877 en route to Vicksburg, Miss., to serve in the Parisot Line. Inspected regularly through 1882, maybe later.

5882 YAZOO BELLE

SW p wh b. New Albany, Ind., 1843. 122 tons. 113 x 25 x 4.8. Originally owned at Louisville, Ky. Sold September 1846 to Capt. Joshia Wiley, master, and Alexander O'Neal, New Albany, Ind. Off the lists in 1848.

5883 YAZOO BELLE

SW p wh b. Jeffersonville, Ind., 1855. 138 tons. 134 x 28 x 4. Owned at Louisville until sold January 1857 to Capt. John C. Rieves, Carroll County, Miss. Transferred several weeks later to Capt. Joseph M. Keys, Jr., same place. In 1859 running New Orleans-Red River, Capt. C.W. Ewing. Snagged and lost above the raft in Red River, June 23, 1860.

5884 YAZOO CITY

SW p wh b. Cincinnati, Oh., 1843. 299 tons. 146 x 28 x 6. Owned in November 1844 by Robert C. Young and William Moore, New Orleans. Sold in January 1847 to Geo. S. Kausler & Co., New Orleans, Capt. John Sylvester, master. Sold in July 1848 to Capt. Robert Abbott, master, and William Kennedy, New Orleans. Snagged and lost at Commerce, Miss., Sept. 3, 1848.

5885 YAZOO VALLEY

Stw p wh b. Jeffersonville, Ind., by Howard, 1876. 180 x 36 x 5. Engines, 16's- 5½ ft. Two boilers. Owned by S.H. Parisot & Co., Vicksburg, Miss. In 1877 ran New Orleans-Vicksburg-Yazoo River, Capt. S.H. Parisot, with Frank Beck, Jr., clerk. Sold in 1883 and ran New Orleans-Red River in the Red River and Coast Line headed by Charles P. Truslow, with M.N. Wood, superintendent. Sank Mar. 4, 1883, some 35 miles above New Orleans; again at Tessier's Landing below Grand Encore in 1886, and on Mar. 8, 1887, burned and lost above Grand Encore with loss of three lives.

5886 YELLOWSTONE

SW p wh b. Cincinnati, Oh., 1864. 378 tons. 206 x 30 x 5.5. Engines, 16's- 5½ ft. Two boilers. Operated on Missouri River. While laid up at St. Louis, July 11, 1867, she and the *G. W. GRAHAM* (see) burned. Owned at the time of loss by her master, Capt. McDonald, and Capts. Bart Able and D.N. Greenleaf.

5887 YELLOWSTONE

Stw p wh b. Jeffersonville, Ind., 1876. 167 tons. 150 x 30 x 5. Engines, 14's- 4½ ft. Two boilers. Very light draft. Owned by Dr. Achilles Lamme, Bozeman, Mont. She made three trips to Fort Benton, Mont., in three successive years, 1876–1878. Lost at Buffalo Rapids on the Yellowstone River in latter May 1879.

5888 YORK

Prop yacht wh b. Manitowoc, Wis., 1902. 38 tons. 86.4 x 14.4 x 6. One compound engine, 8", 17"- 10" stroke. One boiler. Owned by W.F. York, Peoria, Ill. Inspected at Peoria through 1908.

5889 YORK STATE

SW p wh b. Brownsville, Pa., 1852. 247 tons. Built for the St. Louis & Keokuk Packet Co. Ran St. Louis-St. Paul, Capt. Griffith, 1855. Capt. James Ward in command in 1856. Snagged and lost at Madison Landing, Ill., head of the Chain of Rocks, Sept. 1, 1859. The wreck lay there until November 1871 when it was removed by crew of the wrecking steamer *AID*.

5890 YORKTOWN

SW p wh b. Cincinnati, Oh., 1844. 336 tons. 182 x 31 x 8. Engines, 24's- 9 ft. Four boilers, each 42" by 30 ft. Ran Cincinnati-New Orleans. Collided with and sank *WABASH VALLEY* at Jefferson College, La., Mar. 23, 1846 (see). Brought news of the Mexican War from Louisville to Cincinnati in April 1846, having received the bulletins from the *PEYTONA* fresh in from New Orleans. The *CAMBRIA* took the news on up the Ohio to Wheeling and Pittsburgh. She had a texas, one of the first.

5891 YORKTOWN

Stw p wh b. Pittsburgh, Pa., 1853. 143 tons. Ran Pittsburgh-Cincinnati-Louisville, owned by Capt. Jacob Poe and Capt. Ebert of Georgetown, Pa. Was wrecked in ice at Cincinnati in the winter 1856–1857 along with others.

5892 YORKTOWN

SW p wh b. Freedom, Pa., 1864. 253 tons. Capt. Jacob Poe brought her out in October 1864, Pittsburgh-Louisville, with J.W. Clark, clerk. In January 1865 Capt. George W. Ebert bought control, with Standish Peppard in the office. Ran Pittsburgh-Cincinnati, with occasional trips to Nashville "and the Cumberland oil regions." Sank at Proctor, W. Va., Oct. 12, 1866, raised. Ran Pittsburgh-St. Louis in 1867 and made a trip to Fort Benton, Mont., Capt. G.W. Ebert, leaving there June 14. Much delay because of scarcity of cordwood, and had to cut her own. She was advertised at Pittsburgh in March 1868 "for the mountains," Capt. Ebert, with Standish Peppard in the office. Off the lists 1869.

5893 YORKTOWN NO. 2

SW p wh b. Cincinnati, Oh., 1848. 298 tons. 182 ft. long, built "canal size" to get through the Louisville & Portland Canal. Engines, 24's- 9 ft. Four boilers, each 42" by 30 ft. Owned by T.J. Haldeman, Kellogg, and Kennett. Ran Cincinnati-New Orleans, Capt. T.J. Haldeman. Sank at Cincinnati, having been stove by ice, February 1857, partially loaded for New Orleans and was en route to Mobile where she had been sold.

5894 YOUGHIOGHENY

Stw p wh b. Marsh Landing, Pa., 1850. 65 tons. After a brief career in the McKeesport, Pa., area, sold to upper White River in Arkansas, owned at Batesville. Snagged and lost on White River, Dec. 25, 1853.

5895 YOUNG AMERICA

Stw p wh b. Monongahela, Pa., 1853. 127 tons. Snagged and lost at Bath, Ill., June 13, 1855.

5896 YOUNG EAGLE

SW p wh b. Warsaw, Ill., 1861. 28 tons. Came out October 1861 in Keokuk-Warsaw-Alexandria (Mo.) trade, Capt. J.H. Brandom. 80 x 14 x 2.5. Engine 8"- 16" stroke. Locomotive boiler, 36" by 10 ft. with twenty-three 1½" flues. Brandom previously had run *EAGLE* and *MENOMINEE* in the same trade (see). In 1862 owned jointly by Brandom and Henry Leyhe. A new stock company was formed that year composed of Henry Leyhe, William Leyhe, Albert Wempner, J.W. Bishop, and G.R. Smith. Brandom, having sold out, competed briefly with *MENOMINEE* and soon dropped out of the trade. This proved the start of the Eagle Packet Co. Off the lists in 1872.

5897 YUBA

SW p wh b. Murraysville, Va., 1852. 348 tons. Built for Capt. R. Hill. Lost by stranding at Wood River, Ill., Dec. 27, 1856.

5898 YUCATAN

SW p wh b. Cincinnati, Oh., 1843. 141 tons. Operated in the Cincinnati-Kanawha River trade in 1846. Off the lists 1848.

Z

5899 Z. BIDDLE

Rig? ferry wh b. Griggsville Landing, Ill., 1878. 60 x 16 x 2. Inspected at Valley City, Ill., in 1881. Still listed in 1886, maybe longer.

5900 Z.M. SHERLEY

SW ferry wh b. Jeffersonville, Ind., by Howard, 1873. 154 x 34 x 4. Ran Louisville-Jeffersonville ferry trade. Still listed 1886, maybe longer.

5901 ZACHARY TAYLOR

SW p wh b. Brownsville, Pa., 1848. 174 tons. Owned by Capt. M.E. Lucas, Steubenville, Oh., who ran her Pittsburgh-Wheeling. Was sold to run Cincinnati-Lawrenceburg, Ind. Collapsed a boiler flue Dec. 21, 1853, above Lawrenceburg, having two barges of hogs in tow, resulting in loss of five lives, loss of the boat, and hogs were scattered over the countryside.

5902 ZANESVILLE

Stw p wh b. Zanesville, Oh., 1846. 70 tons. 100 x 19 x 4. In all, she spent seven years in Muskingum River service, commanded by Capts. Emlen Cadwalder, J.T. Hahn, and John Henderson. Ran Marietta-Zanesville through 1849, then Zanesville-Dresden, through 1852.

5903 ZANESVILLE PACKET

Stw p wh b. Zanesville, Oh., 1844. 88 tons. Came out in Pittsburgh-Zanesville trade 1844, Capt. Wm. Scales. Lengthened in 1845. Capt. Scales was up in years, and he and Jane McMillan ran the boat, familiarly known as "Old Jane" and she had a hand in every department. This continued through 1846. In 1847 the boat was sold to W.W. Graham, Zanesville, and Capt. Charles Gallagher commanded in the Zanesville-Cincinnati trade. Off the lists in 1847.

5904 ZANETTA

SW p wh b. Harmar, Oh., 1898, at Knox Yard. 149 x 23.8 x 5.6. Engines, 15's- 6 ft. Two boilers. Built for Zanesville-McConnelsville trade. Capt. William Richardson was master, and she was operated by Muskingum & Ohio River Transportation Co., the stockholders being Capt. Dana Scott, Charles Beckwith, W.W. Richardson, George Wallace, and John Rice. She had hot competition with the *VALLEY GEM* (see) into 1903 when *ZANETTA* was withdrawn and sold to Capt. Gordon C. Greene who dismantled her at Harmar and used the engines, etc., in building the *GREENLAND* (see). The hull was sold to Kanawha River to become the *J. Q. DICKINSON* (see).

5905 ZEPHYR

Stw p wh b. Brownsville, Pa., 1864. 158 tons. 140 x 29 x 3.8. Engines, 11's- 4½ ft. Two boilers, each 36" by 20 ft. Capt. Albert Williams was the first master, with W.A. Devenny, clerk. Left Pittsburgh on initial trip to St. Louis, Sept. 26, 1864. Operated out of Memphis for Arkansas River, Capt. Ben Johnson. She went up the Missouri and was loaded out with railroad ties for Arkansas delivery, and sank on rocks near Sibley, Mo., July 20, 1870, and was lost.

5906 ZERAH, JR.

Stw ferry wh b. Helena, Ark., 1901. 106 x 29 x 4.8. Owned

by Zerah Oldham, and was the ferry at Helena. Sank July 16, 1914, at Trotters Landing, Miss.

5907 ZOUAVE

Prop p wh b. Boston, Oh., 1863. 40 tons. First home port, Memphis. Boston is on the Ohio and Erie Canal, Summit County, Ohio where boatyards operated by Edward McLaughlin and William Fairweather were located (circa 1886). The canal connected with the Muskingum River at Dresden and the Ohio River at Portsmouth, Ohio. Canal locks were 90 ft. x 15 ft. which limited the boats to 75′ x 14′. Off the list 1866.

5908 ZOUAVE

Stw p wh b. Port Andrew, Wis. 1863. 55 tons. First home port was Quincy, Ill. Built for Capt. Thomas Andrews whose wife was Charlotte Caumbe. This was a rather odd looking little boat with a low pilothouse on the cabin roof at the forward edge and twin stacks on each side (photo, *S&D Reflector* March, 1987). On May 2, 1864 a St. Louis report says she was downbound from Quincy, Ill. to enter the Osage River trade. Off the list in 1865.

Addendum

0044A ACACIA

Stw p wh Built Fraziers Landing, Oh., 1856 as the *W.H. LANGLEY.* 128 x 23 x 4, 110 tons. Taken over by the Confederates in 1861 and renamed. Captured by Union forces at Memphis 1862, then valued at $2,750. Following repair, operated in the Memphis-Helena trade. Downbound about 25 miles above Helena on August 21, 1862 she was snagged with a reported loss of about 40 lives. Survivors were rescued from the wreckage by the *CONWAY* (1302) and the towboat *WILLIAM H. BROWN* (T664). It was suspected that the *ACACIA* was involved in moving contraband cotton for the benefit of a few Union officers at the time of her loss.

0057 ADA V.

This boat is reported as operating as a packet in her early years but later she was a towboat. A photograph in the Bert Fenn collection shows her as a decrepit looking little boat, pilothouse on the boiler deck with a small cabin behind, alongside a coal flat at a coal yard.

0246A AMERICAN QUEEN

Stw tourist boat sh b. Amelia, La., 1994. 375 x 89 x 8.5. Engines Nordberg compound 15's, 30's- 8 ft. from the U.S. dredge *KENNEDY* driving the sternwheel which can be augmented by twin diesel-props. Built at McDermott Shipyard for the Delta Queen Steamboat Co., New Orleans. Staterooms for 420 passengers with all the cruise boat amenities including swimming pool, elevators, theater, etc. In size, the *AMERICAN QUEEN* surpasses the fabled *ECLIPSE* (1688), the largest of the packets at 365 x 40 x 9 and built in 1852. She will join the *MISSISSIPPI QUEEN,* built 1976, and the *DELTA QUEEN,* built 1926, in the tourist trades. To be in service spring 1995.

0248A AMITY

Rig? f wh b. McKeesport, Pa., 1871. 64 tons. Inspected in Pittsburgh District 1873.

0311 ARABIA

The remains of *ARABIA* were finally unearthed in 1988. The wreck was located in Wyandotte County, Kansas about one half mile from the present river channel and under some 40 feet of cornfield by a group known as River Salvage, Inc. The hull and much of the machinery of the *ARABIA* was found intact and the hull proved to hold a wealth of cargo. The Arabia Steamboat Museum housing the artifacts recovered from the site of the wreck opened in downtown Kansas City, Missouri in 1990.

0439 BALTIMORE

The bell became the property of Capt. L.E. Patton, Memphis after the *FRED A. BLANKS,* renamed *VICKSBURG,* sank in 1903; bought by Capt. William B. Rodgers, Sr. and donated to Greenstone Methodist Church, 939 California Ave., Bellevue, Pa.

0715A BRILLIANT

Stw p wh 1862–1865 b. Brownsville, Pa., 154.7 x 33.5 x 4.9, 226 tons. Engines 16 ⅜'s- 4½ ft. stroke. Three boilers. Built for Albert G. Mason, Joshua Michem and William Cook, all of Brownsville, Pa. Came down to Pittsburgh in latter July, 1862, Capt. A.G. Mason, to load for St. Louis. Upon arrival in St. Louis, bought by the U.S. for $19,750 on August 13, 1862. Converted into Tinclad #18. Sold at auction at Mound City, Ill. on August 17, 1865 to John H. Duffer for $8,000. Renamed *JOHN S. McCUNE* on October 11, 1865.

1114A CITY OF OWENSBORO

Rig? f wh b. Pittsburgh, Pa., 1879. 64 tons. Inspected in the Evansville District October 5, 1882.

1364A CREOLE

Rig? f wh b. Helena, Ark., 1875. 34 tons. Inspected in Memphis District 1878.

1456A DAUNTLESS

Stw f. wh b. Tuscumbia, Mo., 1898. 59.3 x 11.9 x 3.1. 26 tons. A neat little ferry with a single stack. She operated at New Haven, Mo., on the Missouri River until 1905 and afterwards was documented at Memphis. Disappears from the lists after 1910; disposition unknown.

2023A FAVORITE

Prop f wh b. Joliet, Ill., 1866. 93 tons. This was a canalboat that was converted to steam in 1867. Inspected in New Orleans District 1876. Off the list 1884.

2032 FAWN

William Kratz (1857–1916) was a brother of George Kratz who built calliopes at Evansville, both sons of Christian Kratz.

2040A FERRY

Rig? f wh b. Paducah, Ky., 1869. 127 tons. Inspected in the Nashville District 1873. This is a fair sized boat and we know not whether the name was official or possibly the inspector's notation.

2117A FRANCIS H. MILLER

Rig? f wh b. Bridgeport, In., 1877. 34 tons. Inspected in Louisville District 1878.

2166A FRUITLAND

Rig? f wh b. 1872 Cottleville, Mo. 28 tons. Inspected in the St. Louis District 1877.

2178A G. H. WILCOX, JR.

Rig? f wh b. Baytown, Minn., 1877. 33 tons. Inspected in the Galena District 1877.

2200A GAMAGE

SW p wh 1864–1865. Built Cincinnati, Oh., 1864 as *WILLIE GAMAGE,* 148.5 x 30.3 x 4.5. Went into U.S. service Dec. 22, 1864 and name shortened to *GAMAGE.* Converted into Tinclad #60. Sold Oct. 4, 1865 to J.R. Griffith et al. for $11,000 and renamed *SOUTHERN BELLE.*

2267A GENERAL PILLOW

SW f(?) wh 1862–1865 b. ? This boat was captured by the gunboat *PITTSBURG* near Ft. Pillow as the *B.M. MOORE* in June, 1862, 81.4 x 17.1 x 3.7. Engines 10's- 3½ ft. Single boiler. Converted into Tinclad #20 at Cairo. Sold Nov. 25, 1865 to Wetzel & Hallerberg for $2,000. *B.M. MOORE* not in Lytle List; probably built in Confederacy.

2426A GRAND REPUBLIC

SW p wh 1886–1898. Built Pittsburgh Pa. in 1878 as the *J.B.M. KEHLOR* which had been rebuilt and renamed *HELENA* in 1881. 260 x 50 x 8.5. Engine single, compound connected to a stiff shaft when built and we have no indication that she was re-engined later. Running New Orleans-Bayou Sara trade in 1890. She was an excursion boat at St. Louis in 1896, then licensed for 3,500 passengers, Capt. Jule Douglass. Believed owned in the excursion trade by Columbia Excursion Co. who also owned the *CITY OF PROVIDENCE* and *CITY OF VICKSBURG.* Burned in March, 1898 just below the mouth of the River Des Peres, a short distance above Jefferson Barracks, Missouri.

2510A H. W. MURRAY

Rig? f wh b. Chattanooga, Tenn., 1873. 23 tons. Inspected in the Nashville District 1873.

2588 HENRY C. YAEGER

This boat appears to have been primarily a freighter, an odd design with the twin stacks located far aft where the boilers were just ahead of the engine room. *S&D Reflector* carried photos June, 1985; June, 1993; centerspread drawing September, 1993.

2896A J. W. STONE

Rig? f wh b. Middleport, Oh., 1872. 28 tons. Inspected in Gallipolis District 1878.

2986A JENNIE D.

SW p wh 1866–1875 b. Cincinnati, Oh., 1862 as the *W. A. HEALY* and had been *SPRINGFIELD* then Tinclad #22 during the Civil War. 134.8 x 26.8 x 4.3. Engines 10's- 3½ ft. stroke. Sold at Mound City, Ill. on Aug. 17, 1865 to R.G. Jamison for $4,550. Renamed in 1866. Trades or other adventures of this boat are unknown. Off documentation 1875.

3072 JOHN HECKMAN

The machinery and boilers came from the twin dredge tenders *U.S. ENGINEER NO. 6* and *U.S. ENGINEER NO. 7* which were dismantled at St. Louis in 1919.

3266A KENTUCKY

Rig? f wh b. Thebes, Ill., date unknown. 24 tons. Inspected in the Evansville District 1873; not listed as inspected 1877.

3363A LANSING

Rig? f wh b. Dubuque, Ia., 1868. 123 tons. Inspected in Galena District 1873; not listed as inspected 1876.

3677A MADISON

Rig? f wh b. Madison, In., 1877. 53 tons. Inspected in Louisville District 1878.

3789A MARY BELL

Centerwheel f wh b. Laynesville, Mo., 1876. 70 x 12 x 2.5, 50 tons. Engine, single, 12 in. by 6 in. Single boiler 30 in. diameter by 80 in., allowed 90 psi. Owned by W.B. Milam and William Sturgis. Sunk by a snag at Scotts Island, Near DeWitt, Carroll County, Mo. in 1878.

3943A MINNA

Stw p wh b. Logansport, La., 1897. 111 x 26.6 x 4.4, 104 tons. Built for the Austro American Stave & Lumber Co., Ltd. and hauled oak staves from the upper Sabine River to Orange, Texas. The *MINNA* was taken to Red River and in 1900 was bought by Red River Lines at Shreveport, La.; operated on the upper Red River and as a low water boat. Last documented at New Orleans in 1900; disposition unknown.

4228A NORTH BEND

Rig? f wh b. North Bend, Neb., 1876. 20 tons. Inspected in the St. Louis District 1877. A small boat, possibly a passenger ferry only.

4308A OMAHA CITY

Rig? f wh b. Brownsville, Pa., 1857. 133 tons. Inspected in the New Orleans District as a ferry in 1873. It is possible that this boat is a rebuild of 4308, which information is from the *Lytle List.*

4466 PETREL

This vessel, Tinclad #5, is shown as *PETREL 2ND* in the Lytle List.

4509A PINK

Rig? f wh b. Roseville, Ark., 1880. 46 tons. Inspected in the Memphis District September 25, 1882.

4544A POLOWONOK

Rig? f wh b. Ft. Madison, Ia., 1880. 74 tons. Inspected May 10, 1882 at Ft. Madison.

4551A PORTER

Prop f wh b. Philadelphia, Pa., 1864. 280 tons. Built for *USQMD* and first documented July 6, 1866. Inspected in

New Orleans District 1878. Last documentation April 1, 1884.

4607A QUEEN

Rig? f wh b. Van Buren, Ark., 1873. 36 tons. Inspected in the Memphis District 1876.

4676A RAMONA

Stw yacht wh b. Higginsport, Oh., 1902 for Albert Bettinger, Cincinnati. 60 x 12 x 3. She started out with steam power but was converted to gasoline about 1905. Capt. Ed Maurer did his first paid piloting after getting his license when he took the *RAMONA* from Cincinnati to Louisville for Albert Bettinger. This boat was the first through Lock 37 at Fernbank, below Cincinnati, when it was opened July 22, 1911. Mr. Bettinger died in 1922 and the *RAMONA* was dismantled.

4707A RED WING

Stw rafter-pkt wh 1906?–1926. Originally the rafter *JUNIATA* built in 1889 at Winona, Minn., 134 x 22.5 x 4.2. Engines 12's- 6 ft. stroke. Was renamed *RED WING* about 1906–07. Capt. M.H. Newcomb of Pepin, Wis. ran her in the Wabasha-St. Paul packet trade and after 1916 towed the excursion barge *MANITOU* with her. Capt. Newcomb one time took her up Chippewa River to Durand, Wis. and back along with the excursion barge *MANITOU*, this in 1912, first boats seen there in 26 years. Capt. Ralph Emerson Gaches bought both the *RED WING* and *MANITOU* and brought them to Pittsburgh, running excursions at Morgantown, W. Va. and elsewhere on the Monongahela River and up the Allegheny. The *RED WING* burned, laid up at the Eichleay yard, Hays, Pa., December 24, 1926. The *MANITOU* stayed around Pittsburgh until April, 1932 when Howard Morris sold her to J.S. Slyfield of McGregor, Ia. and Lyman Howe of Prairie du Chien, Wis.

4856A ROY

Rig? f wh b. Bridgeport, Ind., 1879. 50 tons. Inspected in the Louisville District October 6, 1882.

4886A S. C. CLUBB

SW f wh b. Metropolis, Il., 1872. 85 x 18 x 6, 53 tons. Inspected in the St. Louis District 1877 and still on the lists in 1895.

4925A ST. ELMO

Rig? f wh b. Mobile, Ala., 1869. 389 tons. Inspected in the New Orleans District 1873.

5099A SHOO FLY

Rig? f wh b. Bedford, Il., 1869. 30 tons. In 1874 owned by Seth G. Thompson (½) and J.W. Seaman (½). Inspected in the St. Louis District 1877.

5122A SILVER SPRING

Rig? f wh b. Searcy's Spring, Ind., 1873. 29 tons. Inspected in the Nashville District 1873.

5142A SOPHIE

Rig? f wh b. Grafton, Ill., 1871. 51 tons. Inspected in the New Orleans District in 1873 and 1876.

5153A SOUTHERN BELLE

SW p wh 1865–1869. Built Cincinnati, Oh., in 1864 as *WILLIE GAMAGE*, 148.4 x 30.3 x 4.4. Sold Dec. 14, 1864 to U.S. and became Tinclad #60, *GAMAGE*. Sold to J.R. Griffith et al. Aug. 17, 1865 and renamed *SOUTHERN BELLE*. Off the list 1869.

5265 SYBIL

As the *COMET*, she was converted into a towboat (T0480). See *Way's Steam Towboat Directory* for this boat's later adventures.

5282A T. N. CLIGG

Rig? f wh b. Pine Bluff, Ark., 1877. 24 tons. Inspected in Memphis District 1878.

5352 THE NEW IDEA

This boat was built for Eugene Robinson at the same time as the Eugene Robinson Museum and Theatre boats at Howard; towed the outfit until the show folded in 1893.

5438A TRANSIT

Stw f wh b. Evansville, Ind., 1868. 90.5 tons. Inspected in Louisville District 1878. Lost 1881; cause not given in Lytle List.

5476A TWO MACS

Rig? f wh b. Le Claire, Ia., 1870. 65 tons. Inspected in the St. Louis District 1877.

5506 UNDINE

One report indicates that this boat sank in the ice just above the Bismarck Bridge April 13, 1868, owned by Capt. Wm. Braithwaite. Called a total loss but evidently salvaged.

5506A UNDINE

Centerwheel f wh b. Mound City, Il., 1873. 112 x 30 x 2, 73 tons. Single engine 4″ x 17″ stroke. Two boilers, 36 in. by 14 ft., allowed 110 psi. Owned by Lexington Ferry, Coal and Railroad Transportation Co., Capt. T.J. Anderson, master. While lying at Lexington, Mo., Sept. 5, 1889, the boat filled and sank due to the oakum having worked out of the seams. Total loss.

5518 UNION

Centerwheel f wh b. Brunswick, Mo., 1861. 99 x 27 x 4. Shown in Lytle List as 100 tons but also reported as being 72 tons; not documented until February 11, 1868 which may have followed a rebuilding. Engine 16's- 4 ft. stroke. Single boiler 42 in. diameter by 16 ft. allowed 110 psi. Sept. 25, 1873: "The little steamer *UNION* has been purchased at a cost of $3,500 to take the place of the *MOUNTAINEER* between St. Joseph and Peru on the Missouri River." Reported March 25, 1874 as en route to Bismarck, Dakota Territory as a transfer boat for the Northern Pacific RR.

Owned by McClane, McNeider & Cameron, Capt. Jimmy Emmords master when sunk by a snag opposite Ft. Lincoln, Dakota Territory in 1879.

5561 VICKSBURG

The bell became the property of Capt. L.E. Patton, Memphis after the *VICKSBURG* sank in 1903; bought by Capt. William B. Rodgers, Sr. and donated to Greenstone Methodist Church, 939 California Ave., Bellevue, Pa.

5580 VINT SHINKLE

Capt. Vint Shinkle died of a stroke on board the *GOLDEN CROWN* at Cairo, Ill. in November, 1885, age 64.

5618A W. A. KING

Rig? f wh b. Van Buren, Ark., 1877. 64 tons. Inspected in the Memphis District 1878.

5637 W. H. LANGLEY

Stw p wh b. Fraziers Landing, Oh., 1856. 128 x 23 x 4, 110 tons. She was built by Aaron Frazier who owned a farm at Hanging Rock, Ohio, a short distance below Ironton. Owner was Capt. Augustus Donnally, Gallipolis, Ohio; operated in the Gallipolis-Cincinnati trade. W.H. Langley was a prominent merchant and miller of Gallipolis, age 46 in 1856. Sold in 1858 to Capt. John T. Sherley of Memphis to operate in the Memphis-Napoleon-White River trade. This Capt. Sherley was a son of Z.M. Sherley, president of the U.S. Mail Line, Cincinnati. Sold Feb. 12, 1859 to J.C. and William Williams of Memphis who continued her in the White River trade. She was at Memphis on Mar. 23, 1860 when the *PERSIA* burned nearby but was not injured. Sold again in October, 1860 to Lawrence Henry, Memphis. Taken over by the Confederates in the spring of 1861 for use as a transport, renamed *ACACIA* (see) and later captured by the Union forces at Memphis June 6, 1862.

5669A W. W. WALKER

SW transfer ferry wh b. Industry, Pa., 1869. 175 ft. long, 237 tons. Industry, Pa. is 33 miles below Pittsburgh; probably, the hull was built here and the boat was completed at Wellsville, Ohio, cost $30,000, capacity five railroad cars. Engines 20's- 6½ ft. Four boilers 38 in. by 20 ft. allowed 121 psi. Owners were J.I. Blair, Capt. Joseph Loomis and others operating as the Sioux City & Pacific Transfer Co. Snagged near Plattsmouth, Neb., Nov. 14, 1874 and a total loss.

5855A WINNECONNA

Rig? f wh b. Winneconna, Il., 1875. 42 tons. Inspected in Galena District 1878.

5877A YANKTON

Centerwheel f wh b. St. Louis, Mo., 1866. 32 tons. Single engine 12″ x 3½′ stroke. Single boiler 38 in. by 10 ft., allowed 95 psi. She was owned by Bramble, Miner and Foster. Capt. Jacob Branch, pilot. Snagged at Yankton, SD in 1870 and became a total loss. Machinery salvaged and reported placed on the *KATIE,* a boat for which we find no definitive information.

5877B YANKTON

Rig? f wh b. St. Louis, Mo., 1872. 33 tons. Inspected in St. Louis District 1873.

Compound Name Index

Beach, General
Bealer, C.
Bealle, Jennie
Bean, Cecil N.
Beauregard, General
Beauty, Little
Beaver, White
Bedford, H. K.
Bee, Borough
Bee Line, Dixie
Behan, W. J.
Behm, Capt. A. O.
Behrman, Martin
Beirne, Oliver
Belcher, Charles
Bell, Alice
Bell, Cora
Bell, Fanny
Bell, J. H.
Bell, Jesse K.
Bell, John
Bell, Joseph H.
Bell, Laura
Bell, Lucy
Bell, Mary
Bell, Mattie
Bell, Ollie
Bell, Sherley
Belle, Alabama
Belle, Allegheny
Belle, Appleton
Belle, Arkansas
Belle, Bayou
Belle, Braddock
Belle, Buckeye
Belle, Caddo
Belle, Cairo
Belle, Carmi
Belle, Chautauqua
Belle, Cincinnati
Belle, City
Belle, Coosa
Belle, Dayton
Belle, Florence
Belle, Hamilton
Belle, Illinois
Belle, Island
Belle, Kanawha
Belle, La
Belle, Louisiana
Belle, Madison
Belle, Maggie
Belle, May
Belle, Minnesota
Belle, Monongahela
Belle, Mountain
Belle, Newport
Belle, Niota
Belle, Nora
Belle, Northern
Belle, Ohio
Belle, Okaw
Belle, Osceola
Belle, Ouachita
Belle, Ozark
Belle, Peoria
Belle, Rosa
Belle, St. Francis
Belle, Scioto
Belle, Southern
Belle, Sunflower
Belle, Tennessee
Belle, Valley
Belle, Viola
Belle, Virginia
Belle, Warren
Belle, Western
Belle, Yazoo
Bellevue, Belle of
Bem, General
Ben, Little
Bend, South
Bends, Belle of the
Benedict, Col.
Benner, H. H.
Bennett, Andrew S.
Bennett, B. F.
Bennett, Elisha
Bennett, Mary E.
Bent, Governor
Benton, T. P.
Benton, Thomas H.
Berger, Jessie
Bertram, John
Bertram, Lucy
Bess, Mary
Best, J. H.
Bett, Emma
Betty, Little
Bicknell, E. M.
Biddle, Z.
Bierce, W. W.
Bird, Blue
Bird, Early
Bird, Mocking
Bird, Prairie
Bird, Sea
Bishop, R. M.
Bissell, Belinda H.
Bisso, Edwin M.
Bisso, Leo B.
Bisso, Joseph
Blackford, J. G.
Bladen, Sarah
Blair, Alice
Blair, Helen
Blair, S. D.
Blaine, James G.
Blanche, Stelle
Blanco, El
Bland, Rosa
Blanks, Bob
Blanks, Fred A.
Blanks, H. Hanna
Blees, Mary S.
Bliss, Hattie
Blue, Bonnets O'
Bluff, Pine
Bluff, Poplar
Bluff, Red
Bluff, Rock
Bluffs, Council
Blunk, D. H.
Bly, Nellie
Bob S.
Bodman, Charles
Boeuf, Bayou
Bofinger, Effie
Bogey, Lewis V.
Bolt, Ben
Bolton, G. W.
Bon Accord, New
Bonham, Ike
Boon, Little
Boone, Daniel
Boone, Lady
Boone, Little
Borden, Lucile
Boree, Sam
Boston, New
Bouford, P. E.
Bow, Silver
Bowman, Isaac
Bowell, J. M.
Bowen, Charley
Bowyer, C. C.
Boy, Market
Boy, Mill
Boy, Mountain
Boy, News
Boy, Plough
Boy, Plow
Boy, Post
Boy, Swiss
Boy, Wild
Boyce, Ursie
Boyd, Emma
Boyd, Linn

—C—

—D—

—E—

—F—

Fairchild, E. H.
Faison, Addie E.
Fall, Jo Horton
Falls, Chippewa
Falls City, New
Farmer, Virginia
Farmer, W. W.
Farragut, Admiral
Farrar, Fanny
Fashion, Sandy
Fe, Santa
Fearn, Fannie
Fellow, Odd
Fellows, Mollie
Fenton, Laura
Ferguson, J. L.
Ferguson, John L.
Fern, Fanny
Ferry, L. C.
Ferry, People's
Ferry, Upper
Ferry, Wiggins
Filson, Laura
Fisher, Clara
Fisher, Francis
Fisher, John A.
Fisher, Statie
Fisk, Clinton B.
Fish, James Jr.
Fiske, Wm. P.
Fite, Thomas D.
Fitzhugh, Henry
Fleece, Golden
Fleet, Circus
Fleming, Kate
Fleta, Little
Fletcher, John G.
Fletcher, Judge
Flora, Southern
Flore, La
Florence, City of
Florence, Thomas B.
Flower, May
Flower, Sun
Floyd, Emma
Foley, Mary
Folsom, Frankie
Foot, Big
Ford, E. I.
Ford, J. B.
Fork, Caney
Forrest, Frank
Forrest, G. W.
Forrest, N. B.
Forsyth, Mary E.
Fortune, Wheel of
Foster, Ed
Fouche, C. M.
Fountain, Belle of
Fowler, Charles
Fowler, Dick
Fowler, Gus
Fowler, Joe
Fowler, John
Fox, Swamp
Fox, Wm.
Francis, St.
Francis No. 2, St.
Francis No. 3, St.
Francisco, San
Frank, A.
Frank, Henry
Frankfort, City of
Franklin, Ben
Franklin, Dr.
Franklin, Jane
Franklin, Lady
Franks, Rosa
Freese, Fannie
Freese, Sallie
Fremont, Col.
Fremont, John C.
French, Kate
Friends, Goody
Frisbee, Kate
Fry, C. D.
Fry, W. W.
Fry, William W.
Fuller, E. W.
Fulton, Andrew
Fulton, Andy
Fulton, Ida
Fulton, Robert
Fuselier, A.

—G—

Gaff, James W.
Gage, Col. D. S.
Gage, J. P.
Gales, Jo
Gallagher, A.
Garden, Castle
Gardner, J. G.
Gaines, Fort
Gaines, General
Gamage, Willie
Garig, William
Garland, Governor
Garvin, Wm.
Gastrell, Lucy E.
Gate, Golden
Gates, Belle
Gaty, Sam
Gaty, Samuel
Gault, John
Gay, Edward J.
Gay, Lady
Gaylord, Ben
Gazelle, Wild
Geisse, P. F.
Gem, Masonic
Gem, Valley
Genevieve, Ste.
George, Jennie
George, Royal
Gibson, David
Gibson, Fort
Gilbert, Bettie
Gilbert, Fannie
Gilbert, Fanny
Gilbert, John
Gill, Lizzie
Gillum, W. V.
Gillum, William V.
Gilmer, Jim
Gilmore, Hettie
Gilmore, James R.
Girardeau, Cape
Girl, Golden
Girl, Mountain
Given, D. A.
Givens, India
Glaze, Alice W.
Glover, Allen
Goble, M. G.
Goddin, A. C.
Goebel, F. A.
Golconda, City of
Goldberg, A. L.
Golden, Mary F.
Golding, Belle
Goldman, Carneal
Go 'Long, John
Goodin, D. A.
Goose, Wild
Gorder, Van
Gordon John B.
Gordon, Sarah
Gould, Belle
Gould, Helen M.
Grace, John D.
Grace, Lady
Grace, M. A.
Gracey, Frank P.
Gracey, Julien
Gracey, Matt F.
Graff, Henry
Graham, Emma
Graham, G. W.
Graham, J. L.
Graham, N. W.

—H—

—I—

—J—

—K—

—V—

—W—

—Y—

—Z—

Index